HISTORY OF INDIAN PHILOSOPHY

Routledge's *History of Indian Philosophy* is a comprehensive and authoritative examination of the movements and thinkers that have shaped Indian philosophy over the last three thousand years. An outstanding team of international contributors provide fifty-eight accessible chapters, organised into three clear parts:

- knowledge, context, concepts
- philosophical traditions
- engaging and encounters: modern and postmodern.

This outstanding collection is essential reading for students of Indian philosophy. It will also be of interest to those seeking to explore the lasting significance of this rich and complex philosophical tradition, and to philosophers who wish to learn about Indian philosophy through a comparative lens.

Purushottama Bilimoria is Honorary Professor of Philosophy and Comparative Studies at Deakin University and Senior Fellow with the University of Melbourne, Australia. He is also Visiting Professor at the University of California, Berkeley, where he has been Chancellor's Scholar. He has been a Fellow at Harvard and Oxford (All Souls and OCHS). He serves as Distinguished Teaching Fellow and Doctoral Faculty at the Center for Dharma Studies in the Graduate Theological Union, Berkeley, as well as Editor-in-Chief of two journals, *Sophia* and the *International Journal of Dharma Studies*. His research and publications are on classical Indian philosophy, emotions, aesthetics, comparative ethics, continental philosophy, comparative philosophy of religion, diaspora, bioethics, secularity and customary law.

J. N. Mohanty is an Emeritus Professor of Philosophy at Temple University in Philadelphia, USA. Professor Mohanty earned his PhD from the University of Göttingen. He has taught at the University of Burdwan, the University of Calcutta, the New School for Social Research, the University of Oklahoma and Temple University. His area of expertise includes both European and Indian philosophy. He has written widely on different areas of philosophy and founded the journal *Husserl Studies*. Professor Mohanty has been a past President of the Indian Philosophical Congress and the Society for Asian and Comparative Philosophy. In 2013, he received an honorary DLitt degree from the University of Calcutta.

Amy Rayner completed a joint degree in Philosophy, Literature and Creative Arts at the University of Melbourne, Australia. She has served as editorial secretary of *Sophia* and is an editorial assistant for Sophia Studies in Cross-Cultural Philosophy of Traditions and Cultures (Springer). She has served as Assistant Editor and Project Secretary for publications including *Globalization, Transnationalism, Gender and*

Ecological Engagements (2015), *Postcolonial Philosophy of Religion* (2009) and *Indian Ethics*, vol. 1 (2007/2017). She has contributed an article on dying from the Hindu and Buddhist perspective to *Ageing and Spirituality across Faiths and Cultures* (2010) and presently is co-editing *Indian Ethics*, vol. 2 (forthcoming 2018).

John Powers is a former Professor of Asian Studies in the College of Asia and the Pacific, Australian National University, Canberra, Australia. Currently, Dr Powers is Research Professor at the Alfred Deakin Institute in Deakin University, Geelong, Australia. His PhD is from the University of Virginia, USA. He is author of several books on Buddhist philosophy, with a focus on the Yogācāra school and internal debates within the Madhyamaka and Abhidharma schools, drawing from Tibetan, Chinese and Sanskrit textual sources. He has contributed a chapter to this volume.

Stephen Phillips is Professor of Philosophy and Asian Studies at the University of Texas at Austin and has been Visiting Professor of Philosophy at the University of Hawai'i, Manoa, and Jadavpur University, Kolkata. He is the author of seven books, including *Yoga, Karma, and Rebirth* (2009) and *Epistemology in Classical India* (2011). Phillips is perhaps best known for his first-time translations of late classical Sanskrit philosophic texts, including the fourteenth-century *Tattva-cintā-maṇi*. He has contributed a chapter to this volume.

Richard King is Professor of Buddhist and Asian Studies and Head of the Department of Religious Studies, University of Kent, UK. His work examines classical Indian (Hindu and Buddhist) philosophy and its ongoing representation through the category of 'religion' in the modern period. Dr King's current research work explores comparative approaches to apophatic discourse (Buddhist, Vedantic and Christian) and the philosophical and ethical questions arising from the transformation of what has come to be called 'mindfulness meditation' from its roots as a Buddhist monastic practice to its current deployment as a modern 'secularised' therapy.

Christopher Key Chapple is Doshi Professor of Indic and Comparative Theology and founding director of the Master of Arts in Yoga Studies at Loyola Marymount University, Los Angeles, USA. He has published *Karma and Creativity* (1986), *Nonviolence to Animals, Earth, and Self in Asian Traditions* (1993), *Reconciling Yogas* (2003), *Yoga and the Luminous* (2008) and several edited volumes on religion and ecology. He serves on the advisory boards for the Forum on Religion and Ecology (Yale), the Ahimsa Center (Pomona) and the Jaina Studies Centre (London). He edits the journal *Worldviews: Global Religions, Culture, and Ecology*. He has contributed a chapter to this volume.

Routledge History of World Philosophies

For a full list of titles in this series, please visit: www.routledge.com/Routledge-History-of-World-Philosophies/book-series/SE0243

Other titles in the series:

Routledge History of Indian Philosophy
Edited by Purushottama Bilimoria

Routledge History of Chinese Philosophy
Edited by Bo Mou

Routledge History of Jewish Philosophy
Edited by Daniel H. Frank and Oliver Leaman

Routledge History of Islamic Philosophy
Edited by Seyyed Hossein Nasr and Oliver Leaman

ROUTLEDGE HISTORY OF WORLD PHILOSOPHIES

HISTORY OF INDIAN PHILOSOPHY

Editor-in-Chief: Purushottama Bilimoria
Associate Editors: J. N. Mohanty, Amy Rayner, John Powers, Stephen Phillips, Richard King, and Christopher Key Chapple

Routledge
Taylor & Francis Group
LONDON AND NEW YORK

First published 2018
by Routledge
2 Park Square, Milton Park, Abingdon, Oxon OX14 4RN

and by Routledge
52 Vanderbilt Avenue, New York, NY 10017

First issued in paperback 2020

Routledge is an imprint of the Taylor & Francis Group, an informa business

British Library Cataloguing-in-Publication Data
A catalogue record for this book is available from the British Library

Library of Congress Cataloging-in-Publication Data
Names: Bilimoria, Purushottama, editor.
Title: The Routledge history of Indian philosophy / [edited by] Purushottama Bilimoria.
Description: 1 [edition]. | New York : Routledge, 2017. |
Series: Routledge history of world philosophies | Includes bibliographical references and index.
Identifiers: LCCN 2017023453 (print) | LCCN 2017033543 (ebook) | ISBN 9781315666792 (E-book) |
ISBN 9780415309769 (hardback : alk. paper)
Subjects: LCSH: Philosophy, Indic–History. | Philosophy–India–History.
Classification: LCC B131 (ebook) | LCC B131 .R67 2017 (print) | DDC 181/.4–dc23
LC record available at https://lccn.loc.gov/2017023453

ISBN 13: 978-0-367-57256-3 (pbk)
ISBN 13: 978-0-415-30976-9 (hbk)

Typeset in Goudy Old Style
By Out of House Publishing

This volume is dedicated in memory of:

Bimal K. Matilal, Kyabje Choden Rinpoche, Wilhelm Halbfass, Daya Krishna, K.T. Pandurangi, R. Balasubramanian, Unebe Toshiya, Nathmal Tatia, Pamela Sue Anderson, Peter Kakol, Sibajiban Bhattacharyyya, and Venerable Thubten Kunsang (Henri Lopez)

CONTENTS

Notes on contributors xiii
Preface xxiv

I Knowledge, context, concepts 1

1 Interpretations or interventions? Indian philosophy in the global cosmopolis 3
Christian Coseru

2 Methodology in Indian philosophy 15
Nirmalya N. Chakraborty

3 *Pramāṇa* epistemology: origins and developments 27
Purushottama Bilimoria

4 Buddhist hermeneutics 40
John Powers

5 Process philosophy and phenomenology of time in Buddhism 49
Hari Shankar Prasad

6 Philosophy and religion in India 59
Jessica Frazier

7 Indian skepticism 71
Raghunath Ghosh

8 Self in Indian philosophy: questions, answers, issues 81
Michael P. Levine

9 Contents of consciousness: perception 91
Monima Chadha

10 Indian materialism 99
Raghunath Ghosh

IIa Philosophical traditions 111

11 Philosophy of the Brāhmaṇas 113
Herman Tull

12 Upaniṣads 122
Brian Black

13 Sāṃkhya 131
Mikel Burley

14 The diverse traditions of Sāṃkhya 141
Knut A. Jacobsen

15 Mīmāṃsā 148
Elisa Freschi

16 The categories in Vaiśeṣika: known and named 157
ShashiPrabha Kumar

17 Nyāya 175
Stephen Phillips

18 The Nyāya on inference and fallacies 184
J. L. Shaw

19 Embodied connectionism: Nyāya philosophy of mind 195
Douglas L. Berger

20 A phenomenological reading of the Nyāya critique of the no-self view: Udayana and the phenomenal separateness of self 204
Chakravarthi Ram-Prasad

21 Udayana's theory of extrinsic validity in his theistic monograph 214
Taisei Shida

22 Early Vedānta 223
Andrew J. Nicholson

23 Advaita Vedānta of Śaṅkara 233
Thomas A. Forsthoefel

24 Avidyā: the hard problem in Advaita Vedānta 242
Stephen Kaplan

25 Viśiṣṭādvaita Vedānta 251
Christopher Bartley

26 An overview of classical Yoga philosophy as a philosophy of embodied self-awareness 263
Ana Laura Funes Maderey

27 A reassessment of classical Yoga philosophy 271
Ian Whicher

IIb Philosophical traditions 281

28 Indian Yogācāra Buddhism: a historical perspective 283
William S. Waldron

29 Early Mahāyāna 293
Peter Gilks

30 *Abhidharma* 302
Joseph Walser

31 Nāgārjuna 311
Jay L. Garfield

32 Nāgārjuna's early Madhyamaka: "deconstruction" and moderation 321
Douglas L. Berger

33 A spectrum of metaphysical positions concerning the existence or non-existence of a self: Nyāya, Śaiva Siddhānta, Mīmāṃsā, Jainism and Buddhism 331
Alex Watson

34 Svātantrika Madhyamaka metaphysics: Bhāvaviveka's conception of reality 343
Sonam Thakchoe

35 The two truths in Madhyamaka: Jñānagarbha 351
Sonam Thakchoe

36 Vajrayāna Buddhism 360
Joseph Loizzo, edited by Amy Rayner

IIc Philosophical traditions 371

37 Hermeneutics: Hindu, Buddhist, and Jaina 373
Arthur Dudney

38 Basic Jaina epistemology 381
Jayandra Soni

39 Anekāntavāda, Nayavāda, and Syādvāda: the history and significance of the Jaina doctrines of relativity 390
Jeffery D. Long

40 Jaina ethics and moral philosophy 399
Christopher Key Chapple

41 Tantra and Kashmiri Śaivism 408
David Peter Lawrence

42 Looking beyond the Darśanas: Tantric knowledge systems and Indian philosophy 418
Jason Schwartz

43 The epistemology of classical Hindu Law 428
Donald R. Davis, Jr.

44 Abhinavagupta 437
Loriliai Biernacki

45 Cognition and language: Buddhist criticism of Bhartṛhari's thesis 446
Toshiya Unebe

46 Alaṃkārkaśāstra as a philosophical discipline 456
David Mellins

47 Indian philosophy of music 467
William J. Jackson

III Engaging and encounters: modern and postmodern 477

48 Islamic modernism in India 479
Muhammad Kamal

49 Gur-Sikh *dharam* 487
Balbinder Singh Bhogal

50 Buddhist ethics 496
Damien Keown

51 Process Buddhism: ethics and social engagement 506
Peter Paul Kakol, edited by Amy Rayner

52 Indian and European philosophy 516
Thomas B. Ellis

53 Modern philosophy in India 526
A. Raghuramaraju

54 Gandhi's truth: debating Bilgrami 536
Bindu Puri

55 Understanding Indian philosophical traditions 545
Anna-Pya Sjödin

56 G. R. Malkani 554
Sharad Deshpande

57 Postmodern approaches 561
Carl Olson

58 Philosophy in an age of postcolonialism 569
Joseph Prabhu

Glossary of sanskrit terms 580
Index 600

CONTRIBUTORS

Christopher Bartley teaches philosophy at the University of Liverpool. His publications include *An Introduction to Indian Philosophy: Hindu and Buddhist Thought* (2013); "Hinduism," in *Death and Dying* (2013); and the entry on Radhakrishnan in *Encyclopedia of Hinduism* (2013).

Douglas L. Berger is an Associate Professor of Indian and Chinese Philosophical Traditions and Cross-Cultural Hermeneutics at Southern Illinois University, Carbondale. He is chief editor of the University of Hawai'i book series Dimensions of Asian Spirituality and former president of the Society of Asian and Comparative Philosophy. He is the author of numerous articles as well as two books, *The Veil of Māyā: Schopenhauer's System and Early Indian Thought* (2004) and *Encounters of Mind: Luminosity and Personhood in Indian and Chinese Thought* (2015).

Purushottama Bilimoria is Honorary Professor of Philosophy and Comparative Studies at Deakin University and Senior Fellow with the University of Melbourne, Australia. He is also Visiting Professor at the University of California, Berkeley, where he has been Chancellor's Scholar. He has been a Fellow at Harvard and Oxford (All Souls and OCHS). He serves as Distinguished Teaching Fellow and Doctoral Faculty at the Center for Dharma Studies in the Graduate Theological Union, Berkeley, as well as Editor- in- Chief of two journals, *Sophia* and the *International Journal of Dharma Studies*. His research and publications are on classical Indian philosophy, emotions, aesthetics, comparative ethics, continental philosophy, comparative philosophy of religion, diaspora, bioethics, secularity and customary law.

Balbinder Singh Bhogal joined Hofstra University in 2007, and currently holds the Sardarni Kuljit Kaur Bindra Chair in Sikh Studies. Previously, he has been a professor at the University of Derby, UK, James Madison University, Virginia, and York University, Toronto. His Ph.D. was titled "Nonduality and Skilful Means in the Hymns of Guru Nanak: Hermeneutics of the Word" (School of Oriental and African Studies, University of London, 2001). His primary research interests are South Asian religions and cultures, specializing in the Sikh tradition, particularly the Guru Granth Sahib, its philosophy and exegesis.

Loriliai Biernacki is Associate Professor at the University of Colorado at Boulder. Her research interests include Hinduism, ethics, gender, and the interface between religion and science. Her first book, *Renowned Goddess of Desire* (2007), won the Kayden Award in 2008. She is co-editor of *God's Body: Panentheism across World Religious Traditions* (2013), and is currently working on a study on Abhinavagupta, wonder, and ideas of the body.

Brian Black is Lecturer in Religious Studies in the Department of Politics, Philosophy and Religion at Lancaster University, UK. He is the author of *The Character of the Self in Ancient India: Priests, Kings, and Women in the Early Upaniṣads* (2007); co-editor (with Simon Brodbeck) of *Gender and Narrative in the* Mahābhārata (2007); and co-editor (with Laurie Patton) of the book series Dialogues in South Asian Traditions: Religion, Philosophy, Literature and History.

Mikel Burley is Associate Professor of Religion and Philosophy at the University of Leeds, UK. His books include *Rebirth and the Stream of Life: A Philosophical Study of Reincarnation, Karma and Ethics* (2016); *Contemplating Religious Forms of Life: Wittgenstein and D. Z. Phillips* (2012); *Classical Sāṃkhya and Yoga: An Indian Metaphysics of Experience* (2007); and *Haṭha-Yoga: Its Context, Theory and Practice* (2000). He compiled the annotated bibliography on "Sāṃkhya and Philosophical Yoga" for *Oxford Bibliographies Online* (2013) and is co-editor of *Language, Ethics and Animal Life: Wittgenstein and Beyond* (2012).

Monima Chadha is a Senior Lecturer in Philosophy at Monash University, Australia. In 2013 she was awarded the Contemplative Studies Fellowship by the Mind and Life Institute and Templeton Foundation, USA. Her principal research area is the cross-cultural philosophy of mind, specifically the classical Indian and contemporary Western philosophy of mind.

Nirmalya N. Chakraborty is Associate Professor in Philosophy at Rabindra Bharati University, Kolkata. He was a Commonwealth Fellow at the University of Glasgow and served as the Member Secretary of the Indian Council of Philosophical Research, New Delhi. Chakraborty is the author of *Pursuit of Meaning* (2004) and *In Defense of Intrinsic Value of Nature* (2004). He has edited *Empiricism and Two Dogmas* (2006) and *Perspectives on Radhakrishnan* (2011).

Christopher Key Chapple is Doshi Professor of Indic and Comparative Theology and founding director of the Master of Arts in Yoga Studies at Loyola Marymount University, Los Angeles. His published books include *Karma and Creativity* (1986), *Nonviolence to Animals, Earth, and Self in Asian Traditions* (1993), *Reconciling Yogas* (2003), *Yoga and the Luminous* (2008), and several edited volumes on religion and ecology. He serves on the advisory boards for the Forum on Religion and Ecology (Yale), the Ahimsa Center (Pomona), and the Jaina Studies Centre (London). He edits the journal *Worldviews: Global Religions, Culture, and Ecology*.

Christian Coseru is an Associate Professor of Philosophy in the Department of Philosophy at the College of Charleston, working in the fields of philosophy of mind, phenomenology, and cross-cultural philosophy, especially Indian and Buddhist philosophy in dialogue with Western philosophy and cognitive science. He is the author of *Perceiving Reality: Consciousness, Intentionality, and Cognition in Buddhist Philosophy* (2012) and is currently working on a book manuscript on the intersections between perceptual and affective consciousness, tentatively entitled *Sense, Self-Awareness, and Sensibility*. Previously Christian taught in the Centre for Asian Societies and Histories at the Australian National University.

Donald R. Davis, Jr. is Associate Professor of Sanskrit and Indic Religions in the Department of Asian Studies at the University of Texas at Austin. He has published *The Boundaries of Hindu Law: Tradition, Custom, and Politics in Medieval Kerala* (2004) and *The Spirit of Hindu Law* (2010).

Sharad Deshpande is former Professor of Philosophy at University of Pune. Currently a Tagore Fellow at the Indian Institute of Advanced Study, Shimla. His publications include *The Philosophy of G. R. Malkani* (ed.), *200 Years of Kant* (ed.), and *Theories and Forms in Indian Aesthetic Tradition* (co-ed.). He has been a visiting fellow at various universities in India and the UK.

Arthur Dudney is currently a Leverhulme Early Career Fellow at the University of Cambridge. His research considers philological discourse (literary criticism and associated disciplines) in Persia during the Mughal period, with a particular interest in how Persian philology shaped Urdu and Hindi. He was formerly a Mellon Postdoctoral Fellow at Oxford University. He received his Ph.D. from Columbia University's Department of Middle Eastern, South Asian, and African Studies (MESAAS) in 2013, and an AB in Classics from Princeton University in 2005.

Thomas B. Ellis (Ph.D., University of Pennsylvania) is an Associate Professor in the Department of Philosophy and Religion at Appalachian State University, North Carolina, USA. He is the author of *On the Death of the Pilgrim: The Postcolonial Hermeneutics of Jarava Lal Mehta*. Ellis has also published articles in the journals *International Journal of Hindu Studies*, *Journal of Vaishnava Studies*, *Method and Theory in the Study of Religion*, and the *Journal of the American Academy of Religion*.

Thomas A. Forsthoefel, Ph.D., is a Professor of Religious Studies at Mercyhurst University, USA, specializing in Indian philosophy and religion. He has written, edited, or co-edited four books: *Knowing beyond Knowledge*, a study of the cognitive dimension of religious experience in Hindu non-dualism; *Gurus in America*, an edited volume which considers the social and philosophical negotiations of late twentieth-century Hindu spiritual leadership in America; *Soulsong: Seeking Holiness, Coming Home*, a cross-cultural exploration of holiness and human flourishing; and *The Dalai Lama: Essential Writings*.

Jessica Frazier is Lecturer in Religious Studies at the University of Kent, UK, managing editor of the *Journal of Hindu Studies*, and a Fellow of the Oxford Centre for Hindu Studies. She is the author of *The Continuum Companion to Hindu Studies*; *Reality, Religion and Passion: Indian and Western Approaches in Hans-Georg Gadamer* *and Rūpa Gosvāmi*; numerous chapters on Hindu philosophies and arts; and is editor of *Thinking Inside the Box: The Concept of Categories in Indian Philosophy*.

Elisa Freschi has published on Mīmāṃsā and on its interactions with other systems. After her *Duty, Language and Exegesis in Prābhākara Mīmāṃsā* (2012), she co-authored *Rule-Extension Strategies in Ancient India: Śrautasūtra, Mīmāṃsā and Grammar* (2013) and edited *The Re-Use of Texts in Indian Philosophy* (2014).

Jay L. Garfield is Kwan Im Thong Hood Cho Professor of Humanities and Head of Studies in Philosophy at Yale-NUS College, Professor of Philosophy at the National University of Singapore, Recurrent Visiting Professor of Philosophy at Yale University, Doris Silbert Professor in the Humanities and Professor of Philosophy at Smith College, Professor of Philosophy at Melbourne University, and Adjunct Professor of Philosophy at the Central University of Tibetan Studies. He earned his Ph.D. in Philosophy at the University of Pittsburgh. Professor Garfield teaches and pursues research in the philosophy of mind, foundations of cognitive science, logic, philosophy of language, Buddhist philosophy, cross-cultural hermeneutics, theoretical and applied ethics, and epistemology.

Raghunath Ghosh is Professor of Philosophy at the University of North Bengal. He has published fourteen books. Ghosh is a widely travelled lecturer and researcher. He was a recipient of Best Book Award and a National Visiting Professorship from the Indian Council of Philosophical Research, New Delhi.

Peter Gilks completed his Ph.D. in Buddhist Studies at the Australian National University in 2011. He now is an Assistant Professor in the Entertainment Management Department at I-Shou University in Taiwan, where he teaches among other things Asian popular culture, creative thinking, and the social impact of science and technology. His research interests include popular culture, narratology, Buddhism, and the Chinese language.

William J. Jackson is Professor Emeritus at Indiana University-Purdue University at Indianapolis. He has published books about South Indian religious culture, including *Tyagaraja: Life and Lyrics* (1992), *Songs of Three Great South Indian Saints* (1998), and *Vijayanagara Visions* (2007). He has also written *Tyagaraja and the Renewal of Tradition* (1994) and *Vijayanagara Voices* (2005). He is the author of *Heaven's Fractal Net: Retrieving Lost Visions in the Humanities* (2004) and *The Wisdom of Generosity* (2008).

Knut A. Jacobsen is Professor in the Study of Religions at the University of Bergen, Norway. His most recent publications include: *Modern Indian Culture and Society* (2009), *Sikhs in Europe: Migration, Identities and Representations* (2011, with Kristina Myrvold), and *Sikhs across Borders: Transnational Practices among European Sikhs* (2012, with Kristina Myrvold), and *Yoga Powers: Extraordinary Capacities Attained through*

Meditation and Concentration (2012). Jacobsen is the founding editor-in-chief of the six-volume *Brill's Encyclopaedia of Hinduism* (2009–2014).

Peter Paul Kakol lived in the Australian state of Victoria. Raised a Catholic, he began early to question his faith, leading to an interest in philosophy and world religions. Christianity and Buddhism fascinated him the most. But the only religion in which he could truly believe was one of his own creation. Hence he began to develop a blend of Process philosophy and Buddhism. This culminated in his doctoral dissertation at Deakin University in Geelong, Australia. A year before his death from cancer, Peter Kakol completed his Ph.D. He passed away in 2002, aged 34. His thesis was turned into a book by his brother Richard Kakol and mentor Purushottama Bilimoria, and published as *Emptiness and Becoming: Integrating Mādhyamika Buddhism and Process Philosophy* (2009), with a Foreword by Robert Neville.

Muhammad Kamal is currently a Senior Lecturer at the University of Melbourne, Australia. He has written extensively on topics in Western and Muslim philosophy. He is the author of *Mulla Sadra's Transecendent Philosophy* (2006) and *From Essence to Being: The Philosophy of Mulla Sadra and Martin Heidegger* (2010), and translator into Kurdish of a number of philosophical text including Aristotle's *Metaphysics*, Heidegger's *Being and Time*, and Sartre's *Being and Nothingness*.

Stephen Kaplan is Professor of Religious Studies at Manhattan College, New York, USA. Many of his publications, which include two books and numerous articles, have been comparative in nature, engaging the neurosciences and employing holography as a heuristic tool. He is currently working on a new book entitled *Advaita Vedānta and the Neurosciences: Reductionism, Not Yet or No Longer*.

Damien Keown is Emeritus Professor of Buddhist Ethics at Goldsmiths College, University of London. His main research interests are theoretical and applied aspects of Buddhist ethics. He is the author of *The Nature of Buddhist Ethics* (2001), *Buddhism and Bioethics* (2001), *Buddhism: A Very Short Introduction* (2000), *Buddhist Ethics: A Very Short Introduction* (2006), and the *Oxford Dictionary of Buddhism* (2003). In 1994 he founded the *Journal of Buddhist Ethics* with Charles S. Prebish, with whom he also co-founded the Routledge Critical Studies in Buddhism series.

ShashiPrabha Kumar is currently the Vice-Chancellor of Sanchi University of Buddhist-Indic Studies, Bhopal, India. Her major publications are: *Sanskrit Studies*, vol. 3 (2014), *Classical Vaiśeṣika in Indian Philosophy: On Knowing and What Is to Be Known* (2013), and *Vaiśeṣika Darśana mein Padārtha Nirūpaṇa*, 2nd ed. (2013).

David Peter Lawrence is a Professor in the Department of Philosophy and Religion at the University of North Dakota. He specializes in nondual Kashmiri Śaivism and related areas of Hindu and Buddhist philosophy and religion. His publications include

Rediscovering God with Transcendental Argument: A Contemporary Interpretation of Nondual Kashmiri Śaiva Philosophy (1999) and *The Teachings of the Odd-Eyed One: A Study and Translation of the Virūpākṣapañcāśikā with the Commentary of Vidyācakravartin* (2008).

Michael P. Levine is Professor of Philosophy at the University of Western Australia. He has taught at the University of Pennsylvania, Swarthmore College, the University of Virginia, and in Moscow as a Fulbright Fellow. His publications include *Prospects for an Ethics of Architecture* (co-authored with Bill Taylor), *Thinking through Film* (with Damian Cox), *Politics Most Unusual* (with Damian Cox and Saul Newman), *Integrity and the Fragile Self* (with Damian Cox and Marguerite La Caze), *Engineering and War: Ethics, Institutions, Alternatives* (with Ethan Blue and Dean Nieusma), and *The Analytic Freud: Philosophy and Psychoanalysis* (ed.). He is currently a Senior Fellow at Durham University's Institute of Advanced Study, writing a book with Bill Taylor on catastrophe and the built environment

Joseph (Joe) Loizzo, M.D., Ph.D., is a psychiatrist and Buddhist scholar with over thirty years' experience studying the beneficial effects of meditation on healing and learning. He is Assistant Professor of Clinical Psychiatry in Integrative Medicine at Weill Cornell Medical College and an adjunct Assistant Professor of Religion at the Columbia Center for Buddhist Studies at Columbia University. Dr. Loizzo has published numerous scientific articles and scholarly chapters on Indo-Tibetan mind and health science and mind–body methods in medicine and psychiatry. These include: five articles on meditation in the *Annals of the New York Academy of Sciences*; his translation study, *Nagarjuna's Reason Sixty with Candrakirti's Commentary*; his book *Sustainable Happiness: The Mind Science of Well-Being, Altruism, and Inspiration* published by Routledge; and an edited volume of essays, *Advances in Contemplative Psychotherapy: Accelerating Transformation*, forthcoming from Routledge.

Jeffery D. Long is Professor of Religion and Asian Studies at Elizabethtown College in Elizabethtown, Pennsylvania, where he has taught since receiving his Ph.D. from the University of Chicago Divinity School (2000). He is the author of *A Vision for Hinduism: Beyond Hindu Nationalism* (2007), *Jainism: An Introduction* (2009), the *Historical Dictionary of Hinduism* (2011), and the forthcoming *Indian Philosophy: An Introduction* and *Indian Philosophy: The Essential Readings.*

Ana Laura Funes Maderey is an assistant professor in philosophy at Eastern Connecticut University, USA, and she taught for Master of Arts Yoga Studies at Loyola Marymount University. Her PhD in Comparative Philosophy is from the University of Hawai'i: 'The Subtle Layers of Bodily Awareness: An Approach from Indian Philosophy'. She is editing and contributor to *Thinking with the Yoga-Sūtra of Patañjali, translation and interpretation.* NY: Lexington Books, 2018 (forthcoming).

David Mellins is a scholar of Sanskrit poetics, poetry, and classical Indian semantic philosophies. He received his Ph.D. from Columbia University and has taught at Columbia, Rutgers, and Yale universities. His research topics include Jayadeva's *Candrāloka*, Mammaṭa's *Kāvyaprakāśa*, the *Nyāyasūtra* and its associated commentaries, Sanskrit benedictory verses, and the deification of speech in South Asia.

Andrew J. Nicholson is Associate Professor at Stony Brook University. His first book, *Unifying Hinduism: Philosophy and Identity in Indian Intellectual History*, received the award for Best First Book in the History of Religions from the American Academy of Religion in 2011. His second book, *Lord Śiva's Song: The Īśvara Gītā*, was published in 2014. Professor Nicholson's research interests include the Vedānta, Sāṃkhya, Pātañjala, and Pāśupata philosophical traditions, the history of yoga, and the reception history of Asian philosophy in nineteenth- and twentieth-century Europe.

Carl Olson teaches at Allegheny College, USA. Besides numerous essays in journals, books, and encyclopedias, he has published seventeen books on subjects such as Hinduism, Buddhism, comparative philosophy, and method and theory in the study of religion. His most recent books include *The Allure of Decadent Thinking: Religious Studies and the Challenge of Postmodernism* and *Indian Asceticism: Power, Violence, and Play*, both published by Oxford University Press. Professor Olson has been appointed to the following positions: holder of the National Endowment for the Humanities Chair, 1991–1994; Holder of the Teacher-Scholar Chair in the Humanities, 2000–2003; Visiting Fellowship at Clare Hall, University of Cambridge, 2002; and elected Life Member of Clare Hall, University of Cambridge, 2002.

Stephen Phillips is Professor of Philosophy and Asian Studies at the University of Texas at Austin and has been Visiting Professor of Philosophy at the University of Hawai'i, Manoa, and Jadavpur University, Kolkata. He is the author of seven books, including *Yoga, Karma, and Rebirth* and *Classical Indian Epistemology*. Phillips is perhaps best known for his first-time translations of late classical Sanskrit philosophic texts, including the fourteenth-century *Tattva-cintā-maṇi* ("Jewel of Reflection on the Truth about Epistemology").

John Powers is a Research Professor in the Alfred Deakin Institute for Citizenship and Globalisation at Deakin University and a Fellow of the Australian Academy of Humanities. He is the author of sixteen books, including *The Buddha Party: How the People's Republic of China Works to Define and Control Tibetan Buddhism* (2017), *Dignāga's Investigation of the Percept: A Philosophical Legacy in India and Tibet* (with Douglas Duckworth, David Eckel, Jay Garfield, Sonam Thakchoe, and Yeshes Thabkhas; 2017), and *A Bull of a Man: Images of Masculinity, Sex, and the Body in Indian Buddhism* (2009).

Joseph Prabhu is Professor of Philosophy and Religion at California State University, Los Angeles. He is both a scholar and a peace activist. He has edited *The Intercultural Challenge of Raimon Panikkar* (1996) and co-edited the two-volume *Indian Ethics: Classical Traditions and Contemporary Challenges* (Ashgate, 2007; Springer and Oxford University Press, India, 2016). He has authored *Raimon Panikkar as a Modern Spiritual Master* (2016). He served on the Board of Trustees and the Executive Committee of the Council of a Parliament of the World's Religions from 2005 to 2011. He also serves on a panel of experts advising the UN High Commission for Human Rights and the International Security Forum based in Geneva. He has lectured and taught at more than seventy universities around the world. In 2015 Joseph was a Visiting Fellow at the Oxford Centre for Hindu Studies and a Visiting Professor at the University of Oxford. In 2016, California State University, Los Angeles, honored him with an annual endowed lecture series in his name, called the Joseph Prabhu Fund for Interfaith Peace and Justice.

Hari Shankar Prasad is Professor of Philosophy, University of Delhi. He is presently working on the project: "Consciousness and Time in Buddhism: A Phenomenological Perspective." His major independent book is *The Centrality of Ethics in Buddhism* (2007). His edited books include: *Essays on Time in Buddhism* (1992) and *Time in Indian Philosophy* (1992).

Bindu Puri teaches in the Department of Philosophy, University of Delhi. She is interested in political philosophy, moral philosophy, and modern Indian philosophy. Bindu is the author of *Gandhi and the Moral Life*, has edited *Mahatma Gandhi and his Contemporaries*, co-edited *Reason, Morality and Beauty: Essays on the Philosophy of Immanuel Kant* and *Terror, Peace and Universalism: Essays on the Philosophy of Immanuel Kant*. Her most recent publication is "Finding Reasons for Being Reasonable: Interrogating Rawls" (*Sophia*, 2014).

A. Raghuramaraju teaches philosophy at the University of Hyderabad. He is series editor of *Porugununchi Teluguloki: Charcha Kosam, Vimarsha Kosam*. This series published by Emesco, Vijayawada, is meant to translate 100 books from other languages into Telugu. His publications include: *Philosophy and India: Ancestors, Outsiders and Predecessors* (2013), *Ramchandra Gandhi: The Man and his Philosophy* (ed., 2013), *Modernity in Indian Social Theory* (2011), *Enduring Colonialism: Classical Presences and Modern Absences in Indian Philosophy* (2009), *Debating Gandhi: A Reader* (ed., 2006), and *Debates in Indian Philosophy: Classical, Colonial and Contemporary* (2006).

Chakravarthi Ram-Prasad is Professor of Comparative Religion and Philosophy at Lancaster University, UK. He is the author of over fifty papers. His books include *Knowledge and Liberation in Classical Indian Thought* (2000), *Advaita Epistemology and Metaphysics* (2001), *Eastern Philosophy* (2005), *Indian Philosophy and the Consequences of Knowledge* (2007), and *Divine Self, Human Self: The Philosophy of Being in Two Gītā Commentaries* (2013).

Jason Schwartz is a Ph.D. candidate at the University of California, Santa Barbara. His dissertation research examines the juridical, institutional, and social structures of the Tantric knowledge systems of the medieval period, demonstrating how these structures were deliberately challenged and dismantled under the direction of the polymath ritualist-legalist Hemādrisūri, resulting in the invention of a new paradigm religious-juridical praxis that effectively defined early modern north Indian religion. His work has been published in the *Journal of Hindu Studies* and the *International Journal of Hindu Studies* (forthcoming, 2017). He is a post-doctoral fellow at Stanford University.

J. L. (Jaysankar Lal) Shaw, Department of Philosophy, Victoria University of Wellington, New Zealand, studied at Calcutta University and received his Ph.D. at Rice University, Houston. He has taught at Jadavpur University, the University of Alabama, and the University of Hawai'i. His work includes some ninety papers and eleven books, including *Meaning and Identity: An Interdisciplinary Perspective*; *Human Beings and Freedom: An Interdisciplinary Perspective*; *Knowledge, Belief and Doubt: Some Contemporary Problems and their Solutions from the Nyāya Perspective*; *Causality: Sāṃkhya, Bauddha and Nyāya*; *Some Logical Problems Concerning Existence*; and *Analytical Philosophy in Comparative Perspective*. He is the first New Zealand-based philosopher to be honored with his own Festschrift: *Contemporary Philosophy and J. L. Shaw*, a book of essays honoring his philosophy.

Taisei Shida is an Assistant Professor at the Hakubi Center for Advanced Research, Kyoto University, and a visiting scholar at the Harvard–Yenching Institute. He received his M.A. and Ph.D. from the University of Tokyo. His main research interest is in philosophical texts, such as arguments over the proof for the existence of God, ways to justify cognition, and the authorization of scripture, especially in the treatises of Nyāya and Mīmāṃsā. His current research focuses on the philosophy on the nature of sound, language, and scripture in classical India.

Anna-Pya Sjödin is a Senior Lecturer in the Study of Religions at Mid-Sweden University. She completed her Ph.D. in Indology at Uppsala University and was a research fellow at Södertörn University, Sweden. Anna-Pya's areas of study include Indian philosophical debates about knowledge and cognition, how the idea of philosophy has shaped the way Indian philosophy is viewed within Western academia, and conceptualizations of the human being (*ātman*) within the Vaiśeṣika school of philosophy.

Jayandra Soni retired in May 2012 from the Department of Indology and Tibetology, University of Marburg, Germany, having taught Indian languages and philosophy from 1991. He now regularly lectures in the Philosophy Department, University of Innsbruck. He edited *Jaina Studies: Proceedings of the DOT 2010 Panel in Marburg, Germany*. He is the main editor of *Buddhist and Jaina Studies: Proceedings of the Conference in Lumbini, February 2013*.

Sonam Thakchoe is a Senior Lecturer in Philosophy at the University of Tasmania. His specialization is in Indo-Tibetan philosophy, with a particular focus on Madhyamaka philosophy. He obtained his Ph.D. in 2003 from the University of Tasmania, and a Master's in 1997 in Indo-Tibetan philosophy from the Central University of Tibetan Studies. His publications include *Moonshadows: Conventional Truth in Buddhist Philosophy* (2011), co-authored with The Cowherds, and *The Two Truths Debate: Tsongkhapa and Gorampa on the Middle Way* (2007).

Herman Tull (Ph.D., Northwestern University) has been a faculty member at Princeton University, Rutgers University, and Lafayette College, where he taught courses in the history of religions, the study of India, and the Sanskrit language. Dr. Tull is the author of *The Vedic Origins of Karma* (1989) and of a number of published essays that range broadly in the field of Indian studies. Among his recent projects is a study of the history of Sanskrit pedagogy in the West.

Toshiya Unebe until his premature passing in November 2016 was Associate Professor in the Department of Indian Studies at Nagoya University, Japan. He gained his M.A. from Nagaya University (1993, Indian Philosophy) and his Ph.D. from Otani University (2001, Buddhist Studies). He was special researcher at Otani University (1996–1998); JSPS Research Fellow (2001–2003); and Associate at Harvard University (2002–2003). He is the author of *Illuminating the Life of the Buddha: An Illustrated Chanting Book from Eighteenth-Century Siam* (with Naomi Appleton and Sarah Shaw; 2013).

William S. Waldron teaches courses on Buddhism, Hinduism, and the Study of Religion at Middlebury College, Middlebury, Vermont. He received his Ph.D. in Buddhist Studies from the University of Wisconsin. His research focuses on Indian Buddhism in general and the Yogācāra school in particular. He has published a monograph on the Yogācāra notion of 'store-house consciousness' (*ālaya-vijñāna*) (*The Buddhist Unconscious*, 2003) and numerous articles comparing Buddhist and modern theories of mind from evolutionary biology, cognitive psychology, and neuroscience perspectives.

Joseph Walser is Associate Professor of Religion at Tufts University. He is the author of *Nagarjuna in Context* (2005) and is finishing a book on the origins of Mahayana Buddhism (*A Social History of Emptiness*) and a book on the political origins of yoga.

Alex Watson has been Preceptor in Sanskrit at Harvard University since 2012. He is currently Professor of Indian Philosophy and Sanskrit at Ashoka University. He is the author of *The Self's Awareness of Itself* (2006) and, with Dominic Goodall and Anjaneya Sarma, *An Enquiry into the Nature of Liberation* (2013). After completing his D.Phil. at the University of Oxford, he held research fellowships at Wolfson College, Oxford, the EFEO, Pondicherry, and Kyushu University, and was Guest Lecturer at the University of Vienna.

Ian Whicher earned his Ph.D. from the University of Cambridge. A long-time Yoga practitioner, Dr. Whicher is a Professor and Head of the Department of Religion at the University of Manitoba in Winnipeg, Canada. He specializes in approaches to spiritual liberation in India and the Yoga tradition and is the author of several books and articles, including *The Integrity of the Yoga Darśana* (1998), and co-editor of *Yoga: The Indian Tradition* (2003). Dr. Whicher is currently writing a book on *The Yoga of Intelligence*.

PREFACE

This much-awaited volume – which began in a conversation with the late Professor Bimal K. Matilal and continued at the early planning stages with Professor Jitendra N. Mohanty, the late Ninian Smart, the late Daya Krishna and the late Bhibuti Yadav – has been a long time in the making; or as Bob Dylan would say, 'a long time a-comin''. The year this volume was conceived and contracted, I as Editor-in-Chief suffered a tragic loss; it has taken me several years to fully come out of the seemingly unending state of shock and grief. But for the help of colleagues, friends, contributing editors and authors (whose names appear in the pages that follow), family members and well-wishers across three continents, this volume would not have seen the light of day.[1] I have many, many people, gods and animals to thank for their relentless support. And most of all Amy Katherine Rayner, who never gave up hope and worked tirelessly to bring the project together, communicate with the authors, organize the manuscript and edit all of the chapters. Likewise, Stephen Phillips and John Powers (who assiduously took charge of the Buddhist section), Christopher Chapple (who took charge of the Jaina section) and Richard King cannot be thanked enough for their esteemed support. Christian Coseru graciously agreed to write the introductory chapter, which provides, to even a keen novice or beginner in Indian philosophy, a concise overview of the volume, elucidating in a comparative frame certain key philosophical problems that have concerned and continue to engage Indian thinkers. There are others whose collegiate support helped as the volume progressed and reached completion; to name a just a few: Guy Peterson, David Zmood, Sara Kerr (during the Melbourne phase), Colette Walker (in Berkeley) and Laura Dunn (at GTU); last but not least, Tony Bruce, Adam Johnston and Rebecca Shillabeer, along with the editorial and production team – Gabrielle Coakeley, and Liz Davey and Christopher Feeney – from the Routledge end are to be acknowledged for their patience and immense support.

Our associate editors helped structure the volume into three parts; each is self-explanatory and marks in the most general terms not so much the chronology but rather the heterogeneous developments that could be classed as clusters of schools or systems of thought (Brāhmaṇic, Buddhist, Jaina, Sikh, etc.). Even then there are overlaps and odd alignments as various themes are taken up under conceptual problems, with a tinge of time-frame added towards the third division when the analytics move onto the postcolonial discourse (only just marking a most recent era). But even in retrospect a periodization is not intended as it is not a concern any longer within contemporary Indian philosophical (as, perhaps, distinct from indological) circles.

It may appear that the volume is thin on the concerns of ethics or moral philosophy, particularly in the Hindu Dharma tradition. This is partly due to constraints of space and partly because the current editors with a number of the contributors have been involved in a two-volume distinctive project on Indian ethics.[2] Nonetheless, we have covered Jaina and Buddhist ethics, deontic strands in the Vedas, Brāhmaṇas and the Mīmāṃsa, and Hindu law in the context of the discourse of Dharma.

In terms of the intellectual backgrounds, this volume from its inception has been intended to be a very differently crafted account of the *history* of Indian philosophy from what is available in the field. It interweaves historical narrative based on thematic investigation rather than as said above a petrifying chronology; and it presents this with a flow and continuity of the foundational, conceptual, developmental and critical terrains from the ancient inspirational insights, medieval forays, classical analyses, to current rethinking going on in certain quarters of Indian philosophy. We cannot avoid broad periods for the more distinctive historiographical narratives that link together problems, ideas, controversies, traditions and evolving systems of thought. But the discursive scheme here provides an alternative to the restricted methodology and chronological approach of earlier orientalist and comparativist accounts. We wanted to avoid the currently fashionable ahistorical grand narrative that certain disciplinary discourses within South Asian studies wish to promote in all areas of Indian cultural and intellectual achievements. That just would not work.

Our concern then has been to bring out the historical development of philosophical ideas within particular schools or against other critical systems, but also in their interaction with broader cultural, social and paradigm shifts within Indian civilization that may have influenced or thwarted the optimal achievement in the area. This point is crucially important to the expected innovative and creative approach taken in this volume, as it is intended for specialists but also for a wider audience of philosophers, graduates, students and scholars who may have no real background in Indian philosophy. So this has been the challenge on our hands, and we pray the volume does justice to that aim.

Purushottama Bilimoria
Berkeley (USA) and Venus Bay (Australia)

Notes

1 *Vide:* www.pbilimo.com; Bilimoria 2012.
2 Bilimoria *et al.* 2017 and forthcoming.

References

Bilimoria, P., 2012. 'Of Grief and Mourning, Thinking a Feeling'. In Kathleen Higgins and David Sherman (eds), *Passion, Death and Spirituality: The Philosophy of Robert C. Solomon.* Sophia Studies in Cross-Cultural Philosophy of Traditions and Cultures 1, 149–174. Dordrecht and New York: Springer.

Bilimoria, P., Joseph Prabhu, Renuka Sharma and Amy Rayner (eds), 2017. *Indian Ethics: Classical and Contemporary Challenges*, vol. 1. London: Routledge; Delhi: Oxford University Press (2008).

Bilimoria, P., Joseph Prabhu, Renuka Sharma and Amy Rayner (eds), forthcoming. *Indian Ethics: Gender, Justice and Ecology*, vol. 2. Dordrecht: Springer; Delhi: Oxford University Press.

I

KNOWLEDGE, CONTEXT, CONCEPTS

Chapter 1
INTERPRETATIONS OR INTERVENTIONS? INDIAN PHILOSOPHY IN THE GLOBAL COSMOPOLIS

Christian Coseru

If the history of philosophy could be told without gaps, where and how would Indian philosophy fit in? And, when all is said and done, what are some of the arguments and positions that could be recruited to advance contemporary debates in metaphysics, epistemology, philosophy of mind, logic, philosophy of language, ethics, metaethics, moral psychology, political philosophy, aesthetics, and philosophy of religion? Introductions to Indian philosophy seldom engage these questions. Instead, they proceed to offer prospective readers an appreciation of the richness and real depth of the Indian philosophical tradition in its own terms, and of the intellectual rewards that stand to be gained by delving into it. In this sense, introductions to Indian philosophy differ from introductions to Western philosophy in one significant way: the latter typically lack such incentives, given the widespread assumption (some might say, prejudice) that Western philosophers have shaped not only the way people in the West think about the world today but, in the wake of colonialism, people across the planet. If the study of Indian philosophy, then, is to have scope beyond the confines of intellectual history, questions about its own claims and aspirations to truth cannot be ignored. Indeed, such questions concern the ongoing relevance of its rich repertoire of methods, views, and arguments, and not simply their preservation value.

The chapters of this volume make their own case for how particular figures and texts articulate and seek to answer fundamental questions about the nature of reality and the self, the sources and methods of knowledge, and the norms of moral, social, political, religious, and aesthetic conduct relative to specific goals. They map the conceptual terrain of a primarily, but by no means exclusively, Sanskritic philosophical culture of similar ancestry and equal breadth and depth to that of China, Greece, and the Latin West. The present introduction concerns the place that this vast body of literature should occupy in the history of philosophy, and the challenge of championing pre-modern modes of inquiry in an era when philosophy, at least in the anglophone world and its satellites, has in large measure become a highly specialized and technical discipline conceived on the model of the sciences. This challenge is particularly acute when philosophical figures and texts that are historically and culturally distant from us are engaged not only exegetically but also with a view to recruiting their topics and arguments for contemporary philosophical debates.

Canon, style, and the question of method

One way to address the questions raised here is to consider the current standard philosophy curriculum. When students in Kolkata, Hong Kong, and Tokyo are introduced to philosophy in philosophy programs, for the most part they end up reading some of the same figures and works that students in Oxford, Berlin, and New York do: Plato, Aristotle, Descartes, Kant, John Stuart Mill, and their influential twentieth- and twenty-first-century descendants. But in Kolkata a student might also get exposure to the works of Vātsyāyana, Gaṅgeśa, and Ragunātha Śiromaṇi, and wonder how their contributions to, say, epistemic norms or category theory fit in with contemporary debates in epistemology and philosophy of language. Likewise, students in Tokyo and Hong Kong might get to read Dōgen and Mozi, and ponder the historical roots of paraconsistent logic and rule consequentialism. On the whole, whether it is read in Oxford or in Kolkata, philosophy's Western bias holds sway, which explains why calls for expanding the canon to accommodate important sources of philosophical skill from other cultures have been largely unsuccessful. Cultural chauvinism and a devaluation of indigenous knowledge sources are partly to blame. But what looms large in the imagination of the great majority of philosophers trained on a predominantly Western curriculum, whether in Kolkata or Oxford, is the issue of incommensurability.

When we see the history of philosophy as a series of dialogues among philosophers pursuing unresolved problems by building on the achievements of their acknowledged forbears we can understand why voices that are not part of the received canon are hard to fit in. Philosophy –the story goes –is constrained by its own genealogy. Consider the student who learns in an epistemology seminar that Gaṅgeśa, a fourteenth-century philosopher from Mithilā and founder of the so-called 'new reason' (Navya-Nyāya) school, is the author of an influential non-semantic theory of truth. By making truth statements dependent on the actual occurrence of cognitive events, Gaṅgeśa is able to block such paradoxical statements as the antinomy of the liar (e.g., Epimenides' paradox) that would be commonplace on, say, a Tarski-inspired, semantic conception of truth.[1] But to account for Gaṅgeśa's philosophical contribution our student would have to get acquainted with *pramāṇa*-theory – that is, the theory of the means or sources of knowledge – and with a centuries-old debate about whether truth is apprehended intrinsically (*svataḥ*) or dependent on extraneous conditions (*parataḥ*), and the implications of these positions (and their variants) for self-knowledge, testimony, and the grounds of certainty.

Making sense of Gaṅgeśa's theory of truth by gaining a measure of familiarity with his own Nyāya, Mīmāṃsā, and Buddhist interlocutors, then, is a necessary step. But it is by no means sufficient. One must also become acquainted with the distinctive features of the Indian philosophical genre. There are four categories of writing that stand out: (i) terse formulaic *assertions* (*sūtra*), of an aphorism-like quality, (ii) basic *commentary* (*bhāṣya*), aimed at unpacking the elusive assertions, (iii) main *subcommentary* (*vārttika*), extending the scope of various positions within the commentary usually by way of revision, and further (iv) *subcommentarial* additions (*nibandha*), which continue the process of interrogation and revision until all interpretive and argumentative possibilities have been exhausted. Some subcommentaries are limited in scope either to clarifying the syntax of the text and providing more clear alternatives (the *vṛtti* and *vivaraṇa*) or to elucidating obscure terms (the *ṭīkā*).

Furthermore, the commentarial genre comprises a distinct set of nested statements that begins with 'the topic' (*viṣaya*) of discussion, followed by the expression 'of a doubt' (*saṃśaya*), the citing 'of an opponent's position' (*pūrvapakṣa*), an affirmation 'of the decided view' (*siddhānta*), and ending with a statement 'of purpose' (*prayojana*). Lastly, there are several types of relations that obtain among the sections of a given commentarial text, all of which aim to ensure some form of dialogical unity. A successive section should either serve as a corollary (*prasaṅga*) or as a prerequisite (*upodghāta*) to a prior section, either exhibit causal dependence (*hetutva*) on the former or eliminate some potential obstacle (*avasara*), and either share a common goal (*nirvāhakaikya*) or act as the causal condition (*kāryaikya*) of a common outcome. Beyond these structural features there are conceptual rules to ensure that proper channels of belief acquisition are followed, and that beliefs are produced in the right way. And last, but not least, it is paramount that fallacies (*hetvābhāsa*) of reasoning are carefully identified and avoided.

This cursory acquaintance with the discursive strategies of the commentarial genre may signal analytic rigor or a pedantic scholasticism. Either way, it would seem obvious that engaging Indian philosophy without sharing some of its own presuppositions and concerns about the nature of evidence, the proper place of reason, and the aims of inquiry, is a remote possibility at best.[2] Most important, the contemporary reader looking for the Indian equivalent of a Descartes, Hume, or Kant (or, closer to the present age, of a Husserl, Sartre, or Quine) would need to suspend belief about style and method and proceed with caution so as not to let assumptions about the 'natural' order of events get in the way. In India, concerns with the justification of true belief occupied thinkers long before it became fashionable in twentieth-century analytic philosophy with Gettier. And debates about consciousness, intentionality, and self-knowledge flourished during the exact same period – the second half of the first millennium – when philosophy in the West went into progressive decline after the closing of Plato's Academy in 529 CE.

Shifting attitudes toward doctrine

The new spirit of rational and scientific inquiry that we associate in the West with Descartes and the British empiricists may be absent in India prior to the advent of British colonial rule in the nineteenth century.[3] But methodical reasoning of an unprecedented degree of sophistications and technicality, as the Navya Nyāya literature attests, is part of the course. While for the most part still motivated by the need to explain and justify scholastic positions, a new attitude of *critical deference* to (if not yet *distance* from) authority, heralds the arrival of a proto-modernity. This new attitude is born of the progressive recognition, first, that beliefs justified without any extra-textual evidence – as traditions of thought indebted to the Mīmāṃsā had considered – could be fallible and, second, that causal explanation often trumps appeals to textual coherence and doctrinal consistency.

The roots of this new attitude reach deep into the latter part of first millennium. Indeed, from Dharmottara (eighth century) and Ratnakīrti (eleventh century) to Gaṅgeśa (fourteenth century) and Raghunātha (sixteenth century), Indian philosophers engaged in lengthy debates about such epistemic notions as 'defect' (*doṣa*) and 'excellence' (*guṇa*). While recognizing the potential fallibility of belief they also noted that veridical cognitions could not be based solely on beliefs one held intrinsically. However, not all traditions of thought embraced this attitude of *critical* deference. But those that did – primarily the 'new reason' thinkers following in the footsteps of Gaṅgeśa – ended up scrutinizing more carefully the nature and sources of belief formation. Rather than placing the burden of epistemic responsibility on the belief itself (and how it is held), these 'new reason' thinkers gradually shifted the focus to its sources: to how we come to form beliefs in the first place. For instance, they reasoned that if it could be understood that mirrors function the way that they do because of their reflective properties, then the belief that mirrors possess the object reflected, however mysterious these properties might turn out to be, could no longer be justified. If epistemic reliability is a factor of descriptive accuracy, then the view that there are such things as brute common-sense facts becomes untenable.

It is hard to assess how widespread this new attitude toward the scope and aims of philosophical inquiry became in pre-colonial India, and several chapters in this volume seek to tackle this question. What is certain is that a great deal of Indian philosophy, even when directly concerned with the justification of textual, testimonial, or experiential issues, is still permeated by tradition-specific doctrinal assumptions (some of which hinge on the precise number and nature of reliable sources of belief formation (*pramāṇa*), while others on whether constructive philosophical debate requires any such doxastic practices at all). Most emblematic of this hermeneutical approach are Mīmāṃsaka thinkers such as Kumārila and Prabhākara (seventh to eighth century), whose primary concern is the interpretation of the Vedas and the justification for the observance of Vedic ritual. Kumārila in particular is best known for granting that language has an inexhaustible and unmatched capacity for expression, and for defending a view of the Vedas as repositories of epistemically warranted statements. To claim that cognitions formed on the basis of such statements are inherently justified, argues Kumārila, is to say that they are the bearers of language's own self-expressive and self-revealing power.

Doctrinal assumptions are also at the heart of more robustly metaphysical systems of thought concerned with the nature of ultimate reality and the self. When Rāmānuja – an influential twelfth-century philosopher of religion and founder of a qualified nondualist school of thought – claims that Advaita (e.g., 'nondual' or lacking in any attributes) conceptions of Brahman are logically incoherent, he appeals to the intuitions of the Sanskrit grammarians about the category of 'being' or 'existence' (*sattva*). For the grammarians, *sattva* serves by definition as the locus of generic properties, qualities, and actions. Likewise, when Utpaladeva and Abhinavagupta (tenth to eleventh century) – proponents of a nondualist, but theist, metaphysical system within the Kashmir Śaiva tradition – put forward a quasi-Sartrean conception of the self as the pure and unhindered freedom (*svātantrya*) of consciousness, they are responding to Buddhist epistemological efforts, championed by Dharmakīrti (seventh century) and his followers, to reconcile a conception of consciousness as inherently self-revealing with the cardinal Buddhist doctrines of momentariness and no-self.

Confronting the metaphilosophical question

As it should be obvious by now, Indian philosophy has its own genealogy and its own rich repertoire of intramural debates. The responsible approach, at least according to the historian of philosophy, would be to chart its course without constant reference to periods and categories in Western philosophy or, worse, outmoded (although still popular) Orientalist conceptions of Indian thought as dominated by religious and spiritual concerns, and, hence, as not really philosophy by the standards of contemporary anglophone philosophy. But the historical approach ignores pragmatic considerations about what, in the absence of cultural affinities, should motivate the study of Indian philosophy outside its traditional sphere of influence, that is, outside the *gurukula* system and India's modern secular universities. After all, acknowledging the presence of important sources of philosophical insight in the Indian tradition is not enough to motivate contemporary philosophers to engage it, let alone take up the study of Sanskrit.

Whether we are dealing with claims about language, reality, and the self, or with principles of reason and empirical grounding, pragmatic exigencies demand that Indian philosophical views face the same sort of scrutiny as all other presuppositions of the genre. Indeed, from a metaphilosophical standpoint – that is, from the standpoint of inquiry into the nature of philosophy – the question "Is the Indian philosophical genre *philosophy*?" is a perfectly legitimate way to seek clarity about what should count as philosophy.[4] But the metaphilosophical question cannot be countenanced, if sufficient care to avoid any one conception of its nature and scope from defining the genre as a whole has not been taken. Philosophy may well be emblematic of the human quest to "understand how things in the broadest possible sense of the term hang together in the broadest possible sense of the term."[5] But that understanding has already been shaped by a long history of such enduring attempts. And yet, answering the metaphilosophical question requires that we bracket historical considerations altogether and eschew their normative challenges. Are the moral and metaphysical lessons of the *Upaniṣads*, the *Yoga-sūtras*, and the *Bhagavad-Gītā philosophy*, in the critical sense in which that practice has been retrospectively interpreted and adopted in both fourteenth-century India and eighteenth-century Europe? Maybe that is the wrong question. Perhaps we should reconsider, with Ludwig Wittgenstein, Pierre Hadot, and Martha Nussbaum, whether it would not be more appropriate to ask what specific *forms of life* these texts promote, rather than how *philosophical* the seemingly insoluble problems they give rise to are.[6]

Indigenism, comparison, and the cosmopolitan ideal

In so far as philosophy in English or the Anglophone culture at large defines itself against the backdrop of a distinct community of inquiry – nowadays constituted largely of professional philosophers – the question whether the Indian philosophical genre qualifies as philosophy cannot be answered without engaging in the type of intellectual exercise known as 'comparative philosophy'. As Bimal Krishna Matilal observed some time ago, anyone who seeks "to explain and translate systematically from Indian philosophical writings into a European language will, knowingly or unknowingly, be using the method of 'comparative philosophy'."[7] Not only explicit attempts to bring Indian and Western philosophers in dialogue, but even text-critical approaches to the genre fall under this category. Doing Indian philosophy in English also means operating with a conceptual vocabulary shaped by the Greek culture of first millennium BCE, the scholasticism of the Latin Middle Ages, and the predominantly French, English, and German intellectual movements of early modern Europe. Thus, one cannot do Indian philosophy without at the same time doing Western philosophy, which means that questions about whether the tenets of one tradition can sustain statement in the other become paramount. Practitioners of the genre 'comparative philosophy' are no strangers to expressing misgivings about comparisons that merely tag theories bearing certain resemblances. And skeptics who champion various forms of indigenism have gone as far as to argue that the adoption of English as a medium for doing Indian philosophy has been profoundly alienating, despite invaluable contributions from such influential early modern Indian philosophers as Krishna Chandra Bhattacharya, Surendranath Dasgupta, Mysore Hiriyana, and Anukul Chandra Mukherji.[8]

Reflecting on this practice as a philosopher trained in both the Indian and the Western, primarily phenomenological, tradition, Jitendranath Mohanty singled out the mutually enhancing value of thinking across cultural boundaries, and the promise that such enterprise might one day usher a new kind of philosophy that is global in scope and outlook.[9] While we are still a long way from fulfilling that promise, a sort of open-ended and non-committal thinking across traditions has taken root among practitioners of what some now call 'fusion philosophy,' others 'cross-cultural philosophy,' but what might be best described as 'cosmopolitan philosophy.'[10] This idea is neither new nor particularly revolutionary. When Dignāga (*c.* fifth to sixth century) embarks on his synthesis of the prevalent epistemological, grammatical, and psychological theories of his day and Vācaspati Miśra (tenth century) authors his empathetic and influential commentaries on Advaita Vedānta, Nyāya, and Sāṃkhya-Yoga texts, they do so as members of a Sanskrit cosmopolis.[11] That cosmopolis endures today among traditionally trained scholars in India and the Indian diaspora. But it functions within, and relative to, an all-encompassing and universalizing cosmopolis that we now call the global West. Doing Indian philosophy today means operating within a larger horizon whose cardinal points of reference are no longer geographical but for the most part conceptual and institutional. Academic philosophy in the global West is a cosmopolitan phenomenon that mirrors the progress of the sciences in its open-ended practice of asking questions and pursuing knowledge.[12]

If one cannot do Indian philosophy in English without doing comparative philosophy, the question naturally arises: is comparative philosophy *philosophy*? The cosmopolitan approach is partly motivated by a deep skepticism about the possibility of doing philosophy comparatively. If comparative religion is not religion and comparative politics is not politics, how is comparative philosophy *philosophy*? Answers to this question run the gamut from outright rejection of the possibility of meaningful comparisons, because of the incommensurability of Indian and Western traditions, to the view that the content of these traditions, save for minor stylistic differences, is practically the same. Skeptics point out that while doctrinal and spiritual concerns are not uncommon for Western figures like Augustine, Aquinas, and Kierkegaard, they are not representative of the dominant ideals of discursive rationality and argumentation that Western philosophy has inherited from the Greeks. Brushing aside such superficial dismissals, defenders argue that the most influential Indian philosophers (e.g., Nāgārjuna, Dharmakīrti, Kumārila, Śrīharṣa, and Gaṅgeśa, among others) show as much penchant for rational deliberation and argumentative rigor as Descartes, Hume, Kant, and Wittgenstein.

Philosophical interventions at the confluence of cultures

So, then: how is comparative philosophy *philosophy*? Pursuing a similar line of inquiry, Arindam Chakrabarti and Ralph Weber give an example of the sort of interventions in solving long-standing philosophical debates in both India and the West that only comparative philosophy is equipped to handle.[13] Take reflexivism – the thesis that consciousness consists in conscious mental states being implicitly self-aware. In India a group of mainly Buddhist philosophers beginning with Dignāga and Dharmakīrti have defended versions of this thesis against Naiyāyikas, who claimed instead that the self-awareness which accompanies each instance of cognition is inferred from the effects of that cognition. Where the reflexivist thinks that I can know something only to the extent that each instance of cognition is inherently self-revealing or self-illuminating, his opponent counters that such cognitive acts as 'seeing something' are transparent with regard to their own operations. If knowing is an act, we are only aware of it indirectly, when reflection turns within and toward its own operations. We see the tree outside the window, not the seeing of that tree. But we can infer that seeing has occurred for someone from the tree that is now seen. And yet, to postulate a basis for self-knowledge outside the structure of experience, or to locate it solely in the conceptual realm, is to problematically assume that experience is an emergent property of something that is not itself experiential.

Readers familiar with contemporary debates in phenomenology and philosophy of mind would immediately recognize these positions as versions of conceptualism versus non-conceptualism with regard to perceptual content, and of the Higher-Order versus First-Order theories of consciousness. Such recognition opens the possibility of intervention, either from the direction of Indian philosophy or, in this particular case, from that of contemporary philosophy of mind, in solving long-standing debates in each tradition. Examples of such interventions abound in the comparative and cross-cultural philosophical literature, often yielding novel ways of tackling long-standing problems. Sometimes they also provide effective platforms from which to interrogate Western hegemonic forms of language, thought, and morality, and take to task those influential philosophers – with Nietzsche as the prototypical example – most responsible for perpetrating a sort of 'neglect by appropriation' approach to Indian philosophy.[14] On this 'interventionist' model comparative philosophy is *philosophy* – in the sense of an open-ended concern with asking questions and pursuing knowledge. But is it the sort of philosophy that showcases, if not the unique features, at least the unique trajectory of Indian philosophy?

One worry is that such interventions end up treating Indian philosophy as a sort of standing reserve to be mined for interesting or even original statements, with utter disregard for their historical context and significance. We only need look at such "manuals of reason" as Mokṣākaragupta's *Tarkabhāṣā* (twelfth century) and Annambhaṭṭa's *Tarkasaṃgraha* (seventeenth century) to realize that these worries are misplaced. What is distinctive about these indigenous interventions is precisely their systematic effort to identify, analyze, and evaluate the basic tenets of each school, often disregarding context or attribution, with the aid of various epistemological, methodological, and logical techniques.

An altogether different sort of worry is that many such interventions are anachronistic. Take the example of cutting across historical and cultural boundaries to make the case that, say, the twelfth-century Advaitin Śrīharṣa rather than Gettier should be credited with the Gettier Problem. But a history of philosophy without gaps will have to look beyond linear narratives and realize that such juxtapositions are inevitable if we are to do justice to the progression of thought. If Śrīharṣa is the first to frame and illustrate the (Gettier) problem, and the first to venture interesting solutions, then he addresses not only the concerns of his twelve-century Naiyāyika opponents, but also those of late twentieth-century analytic epistemology.

I have already hinted that chronologies are relative to a given philosophical culture and epoch. If 'classical' is an apt term for much of the early period of Indian philosophy, 'mediaeval' is not. There is no break with the past in India similar to the onset of the European Middle Ages. Foundational *sūtras* for the Sāṃkhya, Yoga,

Buddhist, Jaina, Cārvāka, Nyāya, Vaiśeṣika, Mīmāṃsā, and Vedanta traditions are continuously composed over several centuries beginning around 500 BCE, and the commentarial tradition continues well into the middle of the second millennium of the Common Era.[15]

Apart from these worries there is also the objection that this sort of cosmopolitan intervention either ignores or glosses over issues of cultural difference and conceptual incommensurability. Indian philosophy is host to conceptual, argumentative, and experiential strategies that do not map neatly onto Western categories and practices. Render classical Indian logic in Western terms, and the *anumāna* system of inference ends up being indistinguishable from the Aristotelian syllogism. Retain the original format with its distinctive steps and characteristics, and the Indian tradition of debate can seem alien and contrived. One response to this objection is predictably straightforward: whether one thinks inside or outside the categorical framework of a particular philosophical tradition or culture,[16] one need not endorse its conceptual schema. Mādhyamika philosophers make good use of the sophisticated categorical frameworks of Abhidharma, Nyāya, and the Sanskrit grammarians, and yet treat them as 'worldly conventions' (*lokasaṃvṛiti*) that do not capture the way things are ultimately. For Mādhyamikas, just as for many contemporary global antirealists, seeking to capture the intrinsic order of reality through a categorical framework (be it that of Vaiśeṣika or Aristotle) has to contend with the very notion of an 'essence' or 'intrinsic order' of things. Effective as they may be, such categories are subject to revision. And, if it should turn out that there are better ways of knowing and being, it is hard to see how pursuing them would not be preferable to the status quo.

Sometimes the best way to make progress is not to start anew, by breaking with the past, but to consider an alternative course, specifically one that philosophy might have taken had it been shaped by a different cultural geography. In the West philosophy begins in wonder about the natural world and the reach of reason; in India, by contrast, it begins in speculations about the origins, nature, and function of language as a vehicle of philosophical insight. While the Pre-Socratics wonder about the ultimate principle of things (*arche*) using the vocabulary of nature, Indian philosophers beginning with Jaimini (fourth century BCE), Gautama (second century CE), and Nāgārjuna (*fl.* second century CE) are concerned with finding out what the relation between words and their referents is ultimately like. Is it a primordial (*autpattika*) relation, as Jaimini claims? Does it depend on a certain capacity to generate knowledge that awareness-episodes (*pramā*) have, as Gautama stipulates? Or is this relation simply the result of an illegitimate metaphysical use of language prone to reification, as Nāgārjuna would have it? As should be obvious to all readers of *Cratylus*, such concerns are by no means unique to the Indian philosophical tradition. But in India they contribute to the articulation of a sophisticated philosophy of language that does not become the norm in the West until the middle of the eighteenth century.

If the study of Indian philosophy is to resist retreat into the familiar terrain of tradition and its scholastic proclivities, perhaps a confluence of perspectives rather than their comparison is more methodologically apt. Such confluence is not without historical precedent. Contact between India and the Greek world following Alexander the

Great's military campaigns set the stage for a work of Buddhist apologetics (the *Milinda Pañha*), and allowed such attitudes as 'freedom from emotion' (*apatheia*) and 'contentedness' (*eukolia*) – which Pyrrho is said to have witnessed among the so-called 'naked wise men' (*gymnosophists*) of India – to inform Hellenistic skepticism. The cosmopolitan oasis towns of Bukhara, Samarkand, Kashgar, Khotan, and Kucha served as a land bridge between Indian Buddhists and Chinese intellectuals drawn to the philosophy of emptiness. Their encounter resulted in a practice of matching Buddhist and Daoist concepts (*ko-i fo-chiao*) that, by the fourth century CE, would render core Mahāyāna Buddhist ideas indistinguishable from the teachings of *Daodejing* and *Zhuangzi*. And, the more tolerant sixteenth- and seventeenth-century Mughal rules of Akbar and Shah Jahan made possible Dārā Shukoh's momentous translation project of the Upaniṣads, exposing Persian and Arabic intelligentsia to the same Sanskrit philosophical lore that a century and a half later would end up, via translations from Persian to Latin, on Schopenhauer's desk.

Significant as these confluences are we must not forget that they tell as much of a story of admiration as of appropriation, assimilation, and refutation. For the anonymous compilers of *Milinda Pañha* ('Questions of Milinda'), the Greek philosopher-king Milinda (Menander I) is simply a foil for Nāgasena's compelling defense of the Buddhist no-self view. Pyrrho, to the extent that we can reconstruct his views, mainly engages with Democritus, Plato, and the Eleatics. And Schopenhauer's main interlocutor is Kant rather than Yājñavalkya, despite his high regard for the Upaniṣads.

As we look to the future of philosophy in the twenty-first century we can only hope that a better knowledge of Indian philosophy would result in many and more fruitful conversations about knowledge, being, and what there is, and about the proper place of reason in the midst of it all.

Notes

1 See Mohanty (1966), Matilal (1985), and Phillips (2012: 87–91) for detailed treatments of Gaṅgeśa's theories of truth that also engage contemporary issues in epistemology.

2 As I have argued elsewhere (Coseru 2012: 279), the most important aspect of this intercultural philosophical engagement is not the recognition that there are different approaches to philosophy, but the promise that such recognition holds for enhancing, refining, and expanding the range of argument and possibilities that are available to us.

3 Ganeri (2012: 6) argues otherwise, but see Garfield (2014) and Phillips (2016) for more skeptical views about whether the outlook of 'new reason' Naiyāyika like Raghunātha is of a piece with that of early modern thinkers in Europe.

4 Perrett (2016: 3), rightly in my view, notes that as exasperating as this question can be for Indologists and historians of Indian philosophy, is it perfectly legitimate if we are to distinguish between 'descriptive' and 'evaluative' (or 'normative') uses of the term 'philosophy'. By the same token one could ask the question: "Is this creative form *art*?" or "Is this writing *literature*?" and conclude that while something does descriptively fall under the category 'art' or 'literature,' it may still not belong to the class of *good* art or literature.

5 Sellars (1962: 1).

6 See Wittgenstein (2001: 192), Hadot (2001: ch. 1), and Nussbaum (1994: 14).

7 Matilal (1971: 13).
8 Daya Krishna went so far as to claim that "anyone who is writing in English is not an Indian philosopher" and thus is doing neither philosophy nor Indian philosophy (in Bhushan and Garfield 2011: xiii–xiv).
9 Mohanty (1992: 401).
10 Siderits (2015) canvases the 'fusion philosophy' model, while Garfield (2002) and Ganeri (2012) champion the 'cross-cultural' and 'cosmopolitan' approaches, respectively.
11 Pollock (2006: 12) argues that in exercising its transregional cultural power, Sanskrit did engender a conceptual and methodological universalism. But the Sanskrit cosmopolis "never objectified, let alone, enforced its universalism" (Pollock 2006: 12).
12 Halbfass (1988: 273) thinks that this is precisely the reason why Western philosophy has undergone such dramatic changes in modern history.
13 Chakrabarti and Weber (2016: 15ff.).
14 Bilimoria (2008: 375) finds in Nietzsche's ambivalent encounter with Asian perspectives the resources of an 'instrumentalist' approach to Asian thought, one whose lingering effects comparative philosophy has been struggling to counter for nearly a century.
15 New attempts at the periodization of Indian philosophy that reflect its own evolution rather than how that evolution maps onto periods and movements in Western philosophy are found in Franco (2013) and contributions therein.
16 See Frazier (2014: 7) for a plea for thinking with, rather than against, Indian categories inherited from the Naiyāyikas and their followers, and thus "inside the box" rather than outside of it.

Bibliography

Bhushan, Nalini and Garfield, Jay L. 2011. Eds. *Indian Philosophy in English: From Renaissance to Independence*. New York: Oxford University Press.

Bilimoria, Purushottama. 2008. "Nietzsche as 'Europe's Buddha' and 'Asia's Superman'." *Sophia* 47: 359–376.

Chakrabarti, Arindam and Ralph Weber. 2016. "Introduction." In *Comparative Philosophy without Borders*, ed. Arindam Chakrabarti and Ralph Weber, 2–33. London: Bloomsbury.

Coseru, Christian. 2012. *Perceiving Reality: Consciousness, Intentionality, and Cognition in Buddhist Philosophy*. New York: Oxford University Press.

Franco, Eli. 2013. Ed. *Periodization and Historiography of Indian Philosophy*. Vienna: De Nobili Research Library.

Frazier, Jessica. 2014. "Introduction." In *Categorization in Indian Philosophy: Thinking Inside the Box*, ed. J. Frazier. London: Routledge.

Ganeri, Jonardon. 2012. *The Lost Age of Reason: Philosophy in Early Modern India: 1450–1700*. Oxford: Oxford University Press.

Garfield, Jay L. 2002. *Empty Words: Buddhist Philosophy and Cross-Cultural Interpretation*. New York: Oxford University Press.

Garfield, Jay L. 2014. "Review of Jonardon Ganeri, *The Lost Age of Reason: Philosophy in Early Modern India 1450–1700*." *Philosophical Quarterly* 64(255): 343–346.

Hadot, Pierre. 2001. *Exercices spirituels et philosophie antique*. 2nd ed. Paris: Albin Michel.

Halbfass, Wilhelm. 1988. *India and Europe: An Essay in Philosophical Understanding*. Albany: State University of New York Press.

Matilal, Bimal K. 1971. *Epistemology, Logic and Grammar in Indian Philosophical Analysis*. The Hague: Mouton.

Matilal, Bimal K. 1985. *Logic, Language, and Reality: Indian Philosophy and Contemporary Issues*. 2nd ed. Delhi: Motilal Banarsidass, 1990.

Mohanty, J. N. 1966. *Gaṅgeśa's Theory of Truth, Containing the Text of Gaṅgeśa' Prāmāṇya(jñapti)vāda*. 2nd rev. ed. Delhi: Motilal Banarsidass, 1989.

Mohanty, J. N. 1992. "On Matilal's Understanding of Indian Philosophy." *Philosophy East and West* 42(2): 397–406.

Mohanty, J. N. 1997. "Introduction: Bimal Matilal, the Man and the Philosopher." In *Relativism, Suffering, and Beyond: Essays in Memory of Bimal K. Matilal*, ed. P. Bilimoria and J. N. Mohanty, 1–15. New Delhi: Oxford University Press.

Nussbaum, Martha. 1994. *The Therapy of Desire: Theory and Practice in Hellenistic Ethics*. Princeton: Princeton University Press.

Perrett, Roy. 2016. *An Introduction to Indian Philosophy*. Cambridge: Cambridge University Press.

Phillips, Stephen. 2012. *Epistemology in Classical India: The Knowledge Sources of the Nyāya School*. London: Routledge.

Phillips, Stephen. 2016. "Creative Commentary." *Philosophy East and West* 66(3): 1020–1026.

Pollock, Sheldon. 2006. *The Language of Gods in the World of Men: Sanskrit, Culture, and Power in Premodern India*. Berkeley: University of California Press.

Sellars, Wilfred. 1962. "Philosophy and the Scientific Image of Man." In *Frontiers of Science and Philosophy*, ed. Robert Colodny, 35–78. Pittsburgh, PA: University of Pittsburgh Press.

Siderits, Mark. 2015. *Personal Identity and Buddhist Philosophy*. 2nd ed. Farnham: Ashgate.

Wittgenstein, Ludwig. 2001. *Philosophical Investigation*. 3rd ed. Trans. G. E. M. Anscombe. Oxford: Blackwell.

Chapter 2
METHODOLOGY IN INDIAN PHILOSOPHY[1]

Nirmalya N. Chakraborty

Classical Indian philosophy has been marked by the presence of intuitive knowledge since the time of the *Upaniṣads*. The Vedic people found language inadequate to express some of their feelings. The grandeur and the vastness of natural powers (conceived as deities by the Vedic thinkers) overwhelmed them. This ineffable nature of reality became more evident in the *Upaniṣads*. Any positive description of reality was found inadequate. Reality falls under description and also outside it, because reality is omnipresent. This led the Upaniṣadic thinkers to describe reality in two ways. First, reality is often described negatively (*neti neti*). Reality is described as inconceivable, unchangeable, untouched, inaudible, invisible indestructible, etc. Second, reality is also described as possessing contrary attributes like 'greater than the greatest,' 'subtler than the subtlest,' etc. The intellect works within categories such as space, time and causality, but reality is beyond all these. However, the *Upaniṣads* assert that man has the faculty of intuition by which the unheard becomes heard, the unperceived becomes perceived, and the unknown becomes known. This knowledge is a direct insight into the nature of reality. Though it is a kind of knowledge, it is different from ordinary kinds of knowledge in that this knowledge is not verifiable or communicable. It is not amenable to formal exposition. Later, when systematic schools of philosophy developed in India, they incorporated this idea of intuitive knowledge in their own metaphysical and epistemological systems. We have *yogaja pratyakṣa* in Nyāya, *prajñā* in Buddhism, and *aparokṣānubhūti* in Advaita Vedānta.

It has become common to use the term '*darśana*' as the equivalent of the English term 'philosophy.' However, the term '*darśana*' is narrower in its connotation than the Western term 'philosophy.' Philosophy nowadays primarily refers to a discussion of certain fundamental problems of the subject concerned, like 'philosophy of law,' 'philosophy of science,' etc. '*Darśana*' in the Indian context primarily refers to a discipline that helps in gaining knowledge of various kinds. The word '*darśana*' is conveniently vague, for it might mean simply perception (sensuous or non-sensuous), or it might also mean conceptual seeing and logical inquiry. S. N. Dasgupta (1992, 68) tells us that the earliest use of the word '*darśana*' in the sense of philosophical knowledge is found in *Vaiśeṣika Sūtras*. Haribhadra, Ratnakīrti, and Mādhava use the word '*darśana*' in the sense of philosophical systems. Vedic literature has provided the background by setting the parameters of reasoning—the horizon against which questions were asked and solutions were proposed, evaluated, and criticized. Even the etymological meaning of the term 'philosophy' (love of wisdom') has very little to do with the modern sense of the term, at least as it is used by professional philosophers. This has led some philosophers to take the meaning of the term '*ānvīkṣikī*' as coming close to what we nowadays mean by philosophy (Matilal 2002, 358). '*Ānvīkṣikī*' is normally defined as a rational investigation of what is obtained through perception and what is stated in scriptures, carried out with the help of accepted means of knowledge (*pramāṇas*). What is perhaps unique in the Indian philosophical context is that *ānvīkṣikī* (in the sense of philosophy) is concerned with demonstrating the possibility of an ideal existence. *Ānvīkṣikī*, by itself, is not causally efficacious to bring about the state of ideal existence. The task of *ānvīkṣikī* is to convince oneself of the truth of what has been heard and to remove all doubts.

One of the earliest *Upaniṣads* (*Bṛhadāraṇyaka Upaniṣad* 2.4.5) claims that the self is to be heard, argued about, and meditated upon (*śrotavyo mantavyo nidhidhyāsitavyaḥ*). This involves three processes: *śravaṇa* is the hearing of the truths contained in the *Upaniṣads*, *manana* consists of rational defense of these truths against actual or imagined opposition, and *nididhyāsana* stands for meditation on these truths. *Manana*, the second step in acquiring the knowledge of the self, is responsible for the appearance of different philosophical schools (*darśana*) in India. Both the Vedic systems and their opponents emerge out of defending or opposing the tenets of the Vedic thinking. The Vedas form the background for much of the Indian philosophical system, either in the form of defending or opposing the Vedic doctrines. Needless to say, significant differences exist even among the defenders of the Vedic tenets with regard to their epistemological, metaphysical, and logical doctrines. Radhakrishnan's comment "Philosophy in India is essentially spiritual" needs a careful and nuanced understanding (Radhakrishnan 1977, 24). This statement is true in the sense that Indian philosophical literature is inclined to intellectually demonstrate the feasibility of an idea of perfect existence viz., *mokṣa*. This does not mean that Indian philosophy is itself spiritual in the sense that it does not care for logical exploration, banking on only some experience that defies any reasoning. The vast amount of literature that has developed in each of the systems of Indian philosophy bears testimony to the fact that *manana* has flourished unhindered, resulting in lively philosophical debates among the adherents of different theories.

One must add a word of caution here. Falling back on the threefold distinction of *śravaṇa-manana-nididhyāsana*, it would be proper to situate this intuitive knowledge in the realm of *nididhyāsana*. There is ample evidence in many classical Indian texts on the basis of which it is safe to suggest that *nididhyāsana* must be preceded by *manana*. Unless one is cognitively certain of the goal to be achieved, one cannot sincerely adopt the path of meditating on that goal. But according to those who admit the authority of the *Veda*-s, *manana* has a restriction and limit.

Manana must function within the ambit of the Vedic world-view. *Manana* that goes against the Vedic insights is actually not *manana* proper. After *manana*, when one possesses the cognitive certitude of the conclusion, then one can enter into the realm of *nididhyāsana*. *Śravaṇa* by itself won't lead anywhere. It must be followed by *manana*. After a successful *manana*, *nididhyāsana* steps in. The systems like Cārvāka, Buddhist, and Jaina, which are known as *nāstika*, do not admit the authoritativeness of the *Veda*-s. The Cārvāka-s, to the best of our knowledge, did not have any scripture of their own. The Buddhist and Jaina schools, however, admit as authoritative the words of Buddha and Mahāvīra, respectively; and in their case, *śravaṇa* would consist in acquaintance with such scriptures.

Thus we see that all these stages are important, and also that they have their limitations. Philosophy, as we understand it today, falls under *manana*. Looked at in this way, *manana* only shows intellectually the possibility of an ideal existence. If one wants to proceed further, than one can take the help of *nididhyāsana*, but in that case, one goes beyond philosophy. *Manana* does not causally bring intuitive truth into existence, it demonstrates the possibility of the knowledge of such truth.

One of the most important aspects of Indian philosophical methodology is the procedure to be followed in an argument or debate between followers of different *darśanas* or between any particular group of philosophical opponents. Thus, one finds records of sustained arguments and debates in early works like *Bṛhadāraṇyaka Upaniṣad*, *Kathāvatthu*, and *Milinda-pañha*. Even though all the schools in the Indian philosophical tradition have a long, chequered history of debate, the most systematic exposition of the varieties of arguments and their function can be found in Nyāya philosophy. After listening to the knowledge of self, *manana* requires arguing about that knowledge. Exposition of this inferential knowledge of the self is known as *anvīkṣā* and the science where this is discussed is called *ānvīkṣikī*. This is also known as *nyāya*. Reference to this Nyāya philosophy can be found in ancient works like *Chāndogyopaniṣad*, *Mahābhārata*, *Manusmṛti*, *Bhāgavatapurāṇa*, *Viṣṇupurāṇa*, *Arthaśāstra*, etc. It must be noted here that according to the adherents of the *āstika* schools (i.e. those who admit the *Veda*-s as authoritative), the chief motive of *ānvīkṣikī* is to defend the Vedic world-view with the help of inferences. So the Nyāya presentation of the nature and function of different kinds of arguments is not independent of the Vedic conclusions, rather it is aimed at supporting the Vedic stance. The idea is that once the Vedic doctrines are defended by arguments, people will not be likely to doubt them. Since the five-membered argument is one of the sources of knowledge; Vedic views, once supported by some such inference, will also be accepted by all.

Naturally, the question arises: what does motivate one to enter into an argument? We do not enter into an argument about something that is completely unknown to us. Nor do we entertain any argument about something that is fully known to us. The idea is that we enter into argument to acquire knowledge; and so, we won't be motivated to know something that is entirely unheard of, or which we know in every detail. We can argue about something that we know in a very general way, but at the same time, want to know in detail. When we want to know about something in a specific manner, we think about two features of the said thing. For example, even after we know that there is something called soul, we want to know further whether it is eternal or non-eternal. The specific feature of the soul is what we would like to know. Even though there are arguments in support of the eternal nature of the soul, there may be doubt in our mind confirming the non-eternity of the soul. Even the arguments in support of eternity of soul won't be able to do anything because of this persistent doubt. This is where we need *tarka*. Those who admit the bondage and freedom of soul argue that it is only if soul is eternal, that we can talk about bondage and freedom of soul. Freedom and bondage of soul won't make any sense once soul is regarded as non-eternal. So, the soul is eternal and cannot be non-eternal – this bit of knowledge is obtained through *tarka*, which is a *reductio* type of argument, where the thesis of the opponent is refuted by assuming it for the sake of argument, and then drawing undesirable consequences from that thesis. This *tarka* removes the doubt about the nature of soul, and convinces one of the validity of the arguments in support of the eternal nature of soul. Thus *tarka* helps in establishing the validity of a particular argument, even though it is not itself of the nature of valid argument. Notice also that this *tarka* is different from both doubtful knowledge and certain knowledge. Where we have doubt, we have awareness like 'Is it this or that?' Where we have certain knowledge, we have knowledge like 'This is so and so.' *Tarka* does not have either of these forms. The form of *tarka* is 'This should be like this, and not otherwise.' *Tarka* is the demonstration of an epistemic possibility that strengthens the original argument. It is thus subsidiary to the original argument.

With the help of *pramāṇa*-s, we arrive at certain knowledge (*nirṇaya*). *Nirṇaya* can be achieved through perception, inference, etc. But *nirṇaya* can also be achieved by the mediator (*madhyastha*) after listening to the defender (*vādī*) and the counter-defender (*prativādī*) participating in a debate. When the defender and the counter-defender argue about two opposing views regarding the same object, a doubt arises in the mind of the mediator (*madhyastha*) who acts as an arbitrator in the debate, since two contrary properties cannot be present simultaneously in the same locus. When the mediator listens to the defender establishing his own thesis and the counter-defender refuting the former, he has to decide which of the arguments are admissible; and on the basis of that, he has to declare the final result of the debate. When the mediator finds the arguments in favor of one of the theses maintained by one of the parties to be admissible, he supports that party, and the other party has to accept defeat. Where this defending and countering of the respective theses are done in accordance with the rules of debate, one party must win and the other must lose. The defender and the counter-defender, being certain about their own positions, advance arguments in support of their respective theses. They do not have any doubt. It is only the mediator who entertains doubt, and it is he who arrives at *nirṇaya*. Since neither of the parties involved in the debate is willing to give up his own position, no *nirṇaya* can be arrived at without the mediator, if the debate is such that one must identify the party that has been defeated. (If, however, the debate takes place purely for the sake of arriving at truth, then the question of someone being the winner and someone being defeated does not arise; and in such cases, the presence of a mediator is not mandatory.) This *nirṇaya* can be arrived at only through the knowledge of Nyāya, and process through which one arrives at *nirṇaya* is initiated by the doubt that arises in the mind of the mediator.

Not all forms of argumentation are equally valid. The type of debate (*kathā*) between the two parties may be of three kinds, depending upon the different purposes of the undertaking of the debate. These three types of debate are known as *vāda*, *jalpa*, and *vitaṇḍā*. Where the argument and counter-argument are taken up to gain proper knowledge of some entity, this debate is called *vāda*. When a student enters into an argument with his teacher, the student aims at gaining knowledge. There is neither the necessity of the presence of any mediator, nor any question of getting the better of the adversary. *Vāda* involves honest search for truth. Of course the parties involved in *vāda* could point out the fallacies that might be present in their respective arguments, for this is absolutely necessary for the proper knowledge of the object under dispute.

When the parties enter into arguments and counter-arguments for the sake of winning in the debate, it is more like an intellectual sport that is known as *jalpa*, where defeating the other party is the aim. In *jalpa*, the arguments and counter-arguments proceed like this. First, the defender puts forward his thesis, and defends this with the help of some inference; and then shows how this inference is supposed to be free from all fallacies. Second, the counter-arguer explains the defender's thesis and then shows fallacies in it. Third, the defender again explains the counter-arguer's thesis and then attempts to show that his own thesis is free from the alleged fallacies. Thus the debate proceeds, and when one of the contending parties fails to show that his thesis is free from the fallacies alleged by the opponent, or fails to refute the thesis of the opponent, he is declared by the mediator as the defeated party.

In *vitaṇḍā*, one party refutes the thesis of the other party, but never defends any thesis of its own. One could of course argue that it is not true that the participant in a *vitaṇḍā* does not have any thesis of his own, for if one does not have any thesis to defend, then there is no need for entering into a debate. It may be the case, however, that the performer of *vitaṇḍā* does not defend his thesis explicitly. Perhaps he tends to think that once he is able to refute the thesis of the other party, it would automatically amount to his victory and the defeat of his opponent. So, while the participant in a *vitaṇḍā* may very well have a thesis of his own, he may not choose to defend his thesis in an explicit manner.

A dishonest contestant may also employ verbal tricks in such a debate to defeat his opponent. These are known as *chala* in Nyāya terminology. If the counter-arguer uses a term used by the defender in a sense different from the defender's sense, and then shows some fallacy in the defender's argument, then such a verbal trick is obviously being employed for gaining victory, and such a practice is patently unfair. Such verbal tricks may be of three different kinds. Suppose the defender says 'This boy is rich because he has *nava* blankets (*navakambala*)' ('*nava*' in Sanskrit might mean either new or nine), and the defender uses the word '*nava*' to mean some new and costly blanket (*kambala*). But the counter-arguer might, in order to malign his opponent, take the word '*nava*' to mean nine; and then argue that the probans (*hetu*) of the proposed argument is inadmissible, since the boy does not have nine blankets. This sort of quibbling is called *vākchala*.

Of course, such quibbling does not vitiate the defender's argument. Again when the defender of a thesis uses a particular word, the defender of the counter-thesis might deliberately take that word in a wider sense that is not intended by his opponent, and then find fault with the thesis. This sort of quibbling is called *sāmānyachala*. The application of *sāmānyachala* is dependent on the presence of a universal or common property in the object under dispute. Suppose a person says about a Brahmin: 'This Brahmin possesses *vidyācaraṇa*' ('knowledge of *Veda*-s and good conduct'), with the purpose of praising that Brahmin. Suppose thereupon someone says 'it is indeed possible for a Brahmin to possess these qualities.' Now, a third person might point out that the second statement is unjustified, since these features (viz. knowledge of *Veda*-s and good conduct) are not present in all the Brahmins. A child Brahmin, or a fallen Brahmin who has deviated from his duties, is bereft of these features. Such a person takes the universal Brahminhood to be the means of establishing *vidyācaraṇa*, and then argues that if that be the case, then even a fallen Brahmin would possess *vidyācaraṇa*. But surely this is not true. Here, the property '*vidyācaraṇa*' is taken by this third person to reside in all Brahmins by virtue of the universal Brahminhood residing in them, irrespective of whether they have observed the requisite rituals or acquired the necessary learning.

Another kind of *chala* is known as *upacārachala*. *Upacāra* means the use of a word in its secondary meaning. When, for example, one says 'The whole podium is crying,' one means that the people on the podium are crying, and not the podium itself. But if the counter-arguer employs the rejoinder that it is not possible for the podium to cry, since the podium is a material object, then he takes recourse to *upcārachala*. *Jāti* is another kind of debate where the counter-arguer finds fault in the arguer's argument not on the basis of some universal concomitance (*vyāpti*) relation that should obtain between the probans (*hetu*) and probandum (*sādhya*), but merely on the basis of some similar features (*sādharmya*) or dissimilar features (*vaidharmya*) of the things concerned. Suppose someone employs the argument "Sound is non-eternal, since it is an effect, e.g. a pot." If his adversary employs the counter-argument "In that case, let sound also be visible, since it is an effect, e.g. the pot," then this would be a case of *jāti*. It must be noted, however, that such counter-arguments are not admissible.

In a debate, the parties involved might have false awareness or ignorance regarding the things that are the objects of debate or regarding the rules of argumentation. Once detected by the opponent or the mediator, this would certainly ensure the defeat (*nigraha*) of the party that possesses this false awareness. This is known as *vipratipatti*. When the counter-arguer defends his own position, or finds faults in the arguer's argument, the arguer must criticize that position or refute the alleged fallacies. If the arguer fails to do that, then he fails to do what should have been done. And this is due to his ignorance. This is called *apratipatti*. This also ensures the defeat of the arguer.

Using examples (*dṛṣṭānta*-s) in a debate is a well-known practice. In a debate only that can be used as an example about which both the arguer and the counter-arguer are in agreement. If the example itself is not unanimously admitted, then that cannot be treated as an example in the debate. In other words, the example must be established by some accepted means of knowledge (*pramāṇa*) that is acknowledged by both the contending parties.

In a debate, when we arrive at the conclusion, the nature of the object concerned under debate has been proven. The conclusion is the end of this proof (*siddha anta*). The *pramāṇa*-s are the means of establishing the exact nature of the object under dispute. In the conclusion, we arrive at the knowledge of the form 'This is like this and not like that.' This *siddhānta* could be of four kinds: (1) When there is a conclusion that is not contrary to the doctrines admitted by any of the systems, and is accepted by at least one of the systems, it is called *sarvatantrasiddhānta*; (2) There may be a conclusion that is not accepted by all the systems, though it is accepted in only a specific system, and this is called *pratitantrasiddhānta*; (3) When proving one conclusion requires the proving some other, the original conclusion is the basis of the proof of those other conclusions, and this original conclusion is called *adhikaraṇasiddhānta*; (4) When in a debate one provisionally accepts the conclusion of the other party and then argues about the features of that conclusion, then that conclusion is called *abhyupagamasiddhānta*.

The subjective counterpart of *siddhānta* is known as *nirṇaya*. *Nirṇaya* is the debater's acquisition of knowledge of reality through *tarka*. *Nirṇaya* is the result of *tarka* that one adopts on the basis of the *prāmaṇa*-s. So one cannot be said to have *nirṇaya* unless one takes the help of *pramāṇa* and *tarka*. *Tarka* is the thus one of necessary prerequisites of *nirṇaya*. *Vāda thus starts with doubt* (*saṃśaya*), *and ends with ascertainment* (*nirṇaya*). *Nirṇaya* is important for continuance of our everyday life, depending on which one could accept what is to be accepted and reject what is to be rejected. Nyāya philosophy also contains a detailed discussion of the 'defects of probans' (*hetvābhāsa*-s) that might vitiate an inference. The parties involved in a debate must have a thorough knowledge of these defects so that by avoiding such defects, they can employ valid inferences. A detailed presentation of these defects would take us beyond the scope of the present chapter.

Another aspect of Indian philosophical methodology is the hermeneutic task concerning meaning and interpretation. The Pūrva Mīmāṃsā school of Indian philosophy, which was particularly concerned with ascertaining the meaning of the Vedic statements, has provided us with a detailed discussion of the ways of deciphering the meaning of different kinds of sentences. A sentence has been defined as a collection of words having semantic competence (*yogyatā*), syntactic expectancy (*ākāṅkṣā*), import (*tātparya*), and contiguity (*āsatti*); all of which expresses a specific meaning. A sentence expresses a unified meaning, but when it is divided into parts, the parts expect each other in order to express the unified meaning expressed by the sentence as a whole. When a sentence is such that there is no anomaly in grasping the relation between the meanings of the words constituting the sentence, or between the sense initially expressed by a sentence and the context in which it is uttered, we determine the meaning of the sentence following the general rules of grammar. Such normal cases do not always draw the attention of Pūrva Mīmāṃsakas, who are more interested in deviant sentences that may be of five kinds: (1) where we have some doubt regarding the meaning of the sentence (*sandigdhārthapratipādaka*); (2) where there is some obstacle in determining the meaning of the sentence (*vyāhatārthabodhaka*); (3) where some meaning that is apparently contrary to the meaning of another sentence is expressed (*viruddhārthapratipādaka*); (4) where the meaning expressed by a sentence is already known through another source of knowledge (*anuvādaka*); and (5) where something that is apparently nonsensical is conveyed by a sentence (*āpātata anarthaka*).

Let us explain some of these cases with the help of examples. Since Mīmāṃsakas are interested in explaining the significance of problematic Vedic sentences, the sentences that they discuss are usually taken from the Vedic corpus. But the Pūrva Mīmāṃsaka explanation of such sentences can very well be extended to ordinary sentences as well. Take the Vedic sentence '*agnirvai brāhmaṇaḥ*' (the Brahmin is indeed fire). Apparently, the Brahmin (the person belonging to a particular caste) and fire are two completely different things, and there cannot be any identity between the two. Here, in order to understand the meaning of this sentence, we have to fall back on the secondary meanings of these two words. What is being meant here is that the same thing is the origin of Brāhmin and fire. In Vedic literature, it has been said that Brāhmin and fire originated from the mouth of Prajāpati, the creator. This Vedic sentence is expressive of praise, i.e. it conveys the thought that both Brahmin and fire are sacred and occupy the central place in the history of creation, because both had their origin in the mouth of the creator. Of course, there are many other reasons why we take the secondary meaning to explain the significance of a sentence. The most important of them is the fact that we take resort to the secondary meaning of a word, when the primary meaning of the same is incompatible with the import of that sentence.

Some sentences do not contain a verb, and therefore, their meaning cannot be grasped. Hence, they fail to prescribe or prohibit any action. In these cases, we complete the meaning of such sentences following methods called *anuṣaṅga* and *adhyāhāra*. *Anuṣaṅga* is a method of inserting a word for completing the sentence; the word being such that it has been used in some earlier sentence expressing a complete meaning. Thus the word carries its meaning from one sentence to another sentence lacking a verb, helping the latter sentence to express a complete meaning. *Adhyāhāra* is a method of imagining a word in the sentential context where the relevant word is absent. We come across Vedic sentences where there is more than one subordinate clause, but only one 'remainder of sentence' (*vākyaśeṣa*) with a verb. Here, in order to complete the meaning of the subordinate clauses, we have to insert in each of the subordinate clauses the verb that occurs in the remainder of the sentence. If this verb is not applicable due to any grammatical rule (e.g. the number and person of the verb should agree with that of the subject), then we have to imagine the correct verb by *adhyāhāra*.

Some of the Vedic sentences are called *arthavāda*. This kind of sentence either praises some action that has been enjoined, or denigrates some action that has been prohibited. Though these sentences do not directly give any direction to perform an action or refrain from it, they motivate the interested person either to perform or to refrain from the said action. In many cases, the literal meaning of such sentences cannot be admitted. In order to get the intended meaning of such an *arthavāda* sentence, we need to connect them with positive injunctions (*vidhi*) or prohibitory sentences (*niṣedha*). A *niṣedha* sentence like '*varhiṣi rajataṃ na deyam*' (one should not offer silver as a fee to the priests officiating in a sacrifice) is followed by the *arthavāda* sentence '*so'rodīt yadarodīt tadrudrasya rudratvam, tasya yadaśru śīryantu*' (Rudra is so known because he cried, and his tears became silver). Here, Rudra's tears are called 'silver.' The literal meaning of this sentence does not seem to be something that can be true. But if we take the *niṣedha* sentence and the *arthavāda* sentence together, then one can grasp the significance of the *arthavāda* sentence, which is that if one offers silver as fee to the priests officiating in the sacrifice, then one's family will experience such a turmoil within a year, that the members of that family will go on crying. This is why offering silver as fee to the priests officiating in a sacrifice is not sanctioned.

The principles established by schools such as Nyāya and Pūrva Mīmāṃsā were of great significance to the development of Indian philosophical tradition, and they continue to play an important role in determining the nature of Indian philosophical investigation and debate.

1

In Indian intellectual tradition, it is a common convention that at the beginning of any technical treatise, it is customary for the author to state (or at least to indicate) four factors known as *anubhandha*-s, the knowledge of which is supposed to motivate an intelligent and interested person to study that text. Such factors do not directly form the core of the subject(s) to be dealt with in that text, but they provide some idea about the subject-matter of that text, and also the purpose that may be served by such a study. These four factors are as follows:

1 *adhikārī* (i.e. the eligibility of the person who is entitled to read the text);
2 *viṣaya* (i.e. the subject-matter of the text);
3 *sambandha* (i.e. the relation between the text and its subject-matter);
4 *prayojaṇa* (i.e. the purpose to be served by the study of the text).

The knowledge of these factors is supposed to motivate the potential reader for the following reasons.

A sensible person embarks on a course of action only when he is certain that the action to be undertaken by him is such that (i) it can be accomplished by his own endeavor, (ii) it leads to the attainment of something that is desirable, (iii) it does not lead to the attainment of something that is extremely undesirable. In philosophical jargon, the cognitions of these three facts are known as (i) *kṛtisādhyatājñāna*, (ii) *iṣṭ asādhanatājñāna*, and (iii) *balavadaniṣṭāsādhanatājñāna*, respectively. When a person comes to know that he is eligible for reading a particular text, he thereby knows that he is capable of studying that text, and this serves here as the requisite *kṛtisādhyatājñāna*. If that person is interested in achieving the purpose that is supposed to be served by the study of that text, and if he also feels that the trouble of studying the text is more than compensated by the benefits to be yielded by that study, then he would also have *iṣṭa sādhanatājñāna* and *balavadaniṣṭāsadhanatājñāna* as well. Thereupon, the person concerned would proceed to study that text. The necessity of indicating these *anubandha*-s has been pointed out by Kumārila Bhaṭṭa in his *Ślokavārttika* (*Jijñāsāsūtra*, verses 12–17). Sometimes, these *anubandha*-s are also pointed out by the commentator(s), in case they have not been mentioned in the book commented on.

2

A large number of texts pertaining to Indian philosophy are in the form of commentaries. There are extensive commentaries on the *Tripiṭaka*-s of the Buddhists, the *Āgama*-s of the Jainas, and the *Upaniṣad*-s. Most of the philosophical schools have some aphorisms (*sutra*-s) as their starting point (e.g. *Nyāyasūtra*-s of Gautama, *Vaiśeṣikasūtra*-s of Kaṇāda, *Yogasūtra*-s of Patañjali, *Mīmāṃsāsūtra*-s of Jaimini, and *Brahmasūtra*-s of Bādārayaṇa), on which a large number of commentaries and subcommentaries were written. These commentaries not only explained the texts that were being commented on – they also answered the objections that could be raised (or were actually raised) against some doctrine expounded in the text concerned, and in some cases, either supplemented the text or even proposed alterations to the views or doctrines that seemed to be erroneous or defective to the commentators. Depending on their size and the purpose served by them, such commentaries were classified into various types, e.g. (i) *bhāṣya*, (ii) *vārttika*, (iii) *ṭīkā*, (iv) *pañjikā*, (v) *vṛtti*, and so on. The *bhāṣya* on an aphorism should explain the latter by words that closely follow the wordings of that aphorism, and it may also make short statements and then expand them. A *vārttika* type of commentary has three tasks to perform – (i) explaining what has been said in the text commented upon, (ii) stating what should have been stated, but has not been stated in that text, and (iii) pointing out improper statements in that text, and then suggesting corrections to them. A *ṭīkā* type of commentary is supposed to give just sufficient hints for understanding the text commented on. A *vṛtti* type of commentary is usually brief, and its purpose is to make the text commented upon intelligible to beginners. For example, we have *Nyāyabhāṣya* by Vātsyāyana on the *Nyāyasūtra*-s, *Nyāyavārttika* of Uddyotakara on *Nyāyabhāṣya*, *Nyāyavārttikatātparyaṭīkā* by Vācaspati Miśra on *Nyāyavārttika*, and also *Vṛtti* by Viśvanātha on the *Nyāyasūtra*-s. An ideal or full-fledged commentary should perform the following tasks:

1 *padaccheda* (splitting up euphonic combination and identifying the individual words of the text commented on);
2 *padārthokti* (stating the meanings of the isolated terms identified by the first step);
3 *vigraha* (expounding the *samāsa*, i.e. nominal compound that may be involved in a word);
4 *vākyayojanā* (determining the meaning of the entire sentence from word meanings);
5 *ākṣepa* (raising possible questions or objections);
6 *samādhāna* (providing answers to such anticipated questions or objections).

The best example of such a commentary is *Mahābhāṣya* of Patañjali on the *Aṣṭādhyāyi* of Pānini that contains the rules of word formation in Sanskrit.

A well-written book should contain chapters which have some intimate connection with the book as a whole; and there should also be some connections that relate each chapter to the chapters preceding it and succeeding it. In the absence of such intimate connections, the different portions of the book will look like a disjointed collection, without having any unity. Such interconnections, that are known as *saṅgati*-s, may be of six kinds: (1) *prasaṅga*, (2) *upodghāta*, (3) *hetutā*, (4) *avasara*, (5) *nirvāhakaikya*, and (6) *kāryaikya*. The commentators of *Tattvacintāmaṇi*, a text of the new school of Nyāya, have discussed in detail the nature of such interconnections or relevance, and they have also shown how the different sections of *Tattvacintāmaṇi* are related to each other through such *saṅgati*-s.

Another classification of *saṅgati*-s can be found in the commentaries and sub-commentaries of *Mīmāṃsā-sūtra*-s and *Brahma-sūtra*-s, both of which aim at determining the meaning of Vedic sentences. Each of these books consists of some chapters (*adhyāya*-s), that have sections (*pāda*-s), which again consist of sub-sections (*adhikaraṇa*-s), which contain some aphorisms (*sutra*-s) that are supposed to deal with some Vedic utterances (*śruti*-s). Now, the commentators have shown how each of these aphorisms bears some relevance to the discipline (*śāstra*) of Pūrva-Mīmāṃsā or Vedānta taken as a whole, then they determine how it is also connected with the relevant section and sub-section in which it occurs, and how it is also connected with some specific Vedic statement. These are known as *śāstrasaṅgati*, *adhyāyasaṅgati*, *pādasaṅgati*, *adhikaraṇasaṅgati*, and *śrutisaṅgati*, respectively. A detailed discussion of this topic with proper examples is beyond the scope of this chapter.

3

The two systems of Pūrva-Mīmāṃsa and Vedānta (which is also known as Uttara-Mīmāṃsā) are concerned with explaining Vedic sentences and determining their meaning as well as their significance or import (*tātparya*). While Pūrva-Mīmāṃsa deals with sentences that mostly pertain to rituals, the rules devised by them for explaining deviant or problematic sentences may be applied to other types of sentence as well, and this has actually been done by the adherents of Vedānta for explaining problematic or disputed sentences in the *Upaniṣad*-s, and also for determining the significance or import of such sentences. One way of determining the import of a sentence is to consider the context in which the sentence is being uttered, and this procedure often helps us in determining the import of a sentence in which some ambiguous word has been used. The Sanskrit word '*saindhava*' may mean either a horse born in the Sindhu province, or it may also mean rock salt. Now, if a person utters the sentence "bring *saindhava*" when he is having his meals, then he is obviously asking for salt; whereas if he utters this sentence on the eve of a journey, then he is obviously asking someone to bring a horse. But sometimes, the import of a sentence may have to be determined by a more complex process. In order to do this, one has, first of all, to consider what has been said at the beginning (*upakrama*) and also at the end (*upasaṃhāra*) of the passage in which the disputed sentence occurs. Next, one has to consider the statement that is being repeatedly stated. Such repetition is known as *abhyāsa*. Scripture usually reveals what is not known through other sources. Thus, in determining the import of some scriptural passage, one should see which of the sentences is expressing something that has not been known previously from other sources. This element of novelty is known as *apūrvatā*. Another means of finding import is to notice the sentences that declare something as a desired result (*phala*). Thereafter, one has to note what is being praised in some way or other. Such laudatory sentences are known as *arthavāda*. Finally, one has to note what is being sought to be supported by some reasoning (*upapatti*). In *Vedāntasāra*, a preliminary book of Advaita Vedānta, it has been decided with the help of such criteria that the import of the sentence "*tattvamasi*" that occurs in *Chāndogya Upaniṣad* is the identity between *jīva* (i.e. the individual self) and *Brahman* (i.e. the ultimate reality).

Note

1 I am grateful to Professor Prabal Kumar Sen for his suggestions for improving an earlier version of the chapter.

References

Bhattacharya, Gopinath. 1989. *Essays in Analytical Philosophy*. Calcutta: Sanskrit Pustak Bhandar.

Bhattacharya, Lakshmi Narayan. 2005. *PūrvaMīmāṃsar dṛṣṭite vākya mahāvākya tātparya nirupaṇer upāya samīkṣā*. Calcutta: Sanskrit Book Depot.

Bhutnath, Saptatirtha. (Ed.). 1938. *Mīmāṃādarśanam*. Calcutta: Basumati Sahitya Mandir.

Dasgupta. S. N. 1992. *History of Indian Philosophy*, vol. 1. Delhi: Motilal Banarasidass.

Matilal, Bimal Krishna. 1998. *The Character of Logic in India*. Ed. Jonardon Ganeri and Heeraman Tiwari. New Delhi: Oxford University Press.

———. 2002. 'On the Concept of Philosophy in India.' In his *Mind, Language and World*. Ed. Jonardon Ganeri. New Delhi: Oxford University Press.

Mohanty, J. N. 2001. *Explorations in Philosophy: Indian Philosophy*. New Delhi: Oxford University Press.

Radhakrishnan, S. 1977. *Indian Philosophy*, vol. 1. London: George Allen & Unwin; New York: Humanities Press.

Tarkasāṃkhyavedāntatīrtha, Jogendranath. 1958. *Bhāratīya Darśansāstrer Samanvaya*. Calcutta: University of Calcutta.

Tarkavāgīśa, Phaṇibhūsan. (Ed.). 1917 [1324 (Beng.)]. *Nyāyadarśana*, vol. 1. Calcutta: Bangiya Sahitya Parisad.

Chapter 3
PRAMĀṆA EPISTEMOLOGY: ORIGINS AND DEVELOPMENTS[1]

Purushottama Bilimoria

While the Vaiśeṣika system began with an inquiry into metaphysics and ontological categories (*prameya*), and moved gradually towards strengthening its treatment of epistemology, the Nyāya school began with a specialization in epistemology and the methodology of investigation. The *Nyāya-sūtra* commences with the very expression *pramāṇa* 'means of cognition' and ends with a sūtra on *hetvābhāsa* 'fallacious reasoning', and *pramāṇabhāsa* 'pseudo-pramāṇa (Thakur 1967, *NS*: 1, 18). Of the sixteen categories (*padārtha*-s) to be treated in the Nyāya system, fifteen are concerned with the *pramāṇa*-s; the remaining one is designated as *prameya* 'objects to be correctly cognized [for gaining the highest good, *niḥśreya*] by means of the right deployment of *pramāṇa*-s' (*NB*: 32, 183). In Nyāya, interestingly, these categories cannot be known without reference to the proper epistemic methodology: hence the supervenience on the *pramāṇa*-s. That is why the Nyāya has come famously to be known as *pramāṇaśāstram*, the science of correct cognition.

Where does the idea of *pramāṇa* come from, what are its origins, and is there treatment of this investigative methodology that pre-dates the Nyāya?

The first appearance of *pramāṇa* theory is arguably in medical literature, particularly in *Caraka-saṃhitā* and, to a lesser extent, *Suśrata-saṃhitā*. In the former, dated to around the first to second century CE, is to be found the theory of *pramāṇa*, i.e. the instruments or means by which knowledge is acquired. In *Suśrata* (dated around third century CE), the term *pramāṇa* seems to denote 'measurement' or size. Caraka was keen to suggest a form of inquiry that requires the practitioner to investigate the cause of the disease of discomfort as per the symptoms presented, the means by which the ailment could be alleviated, and the prognosis, or predictability of the healing and survival prospects of the patient. It is the first part of the inquiry – the search for the unobserved and perhaps unobservable cause of the disease – that calls for perception, induction, abduction, analogy, and a conclusion: in other words systematic reasoning. The *Arthaśāstra* of Kauṭilya added *naya* as calculative logic (in multivariate forms we get *nyāya*) to be part of the larger artful practice of *ānvīkṣikī* (inquiry, wisdom, investigation). Caraka offers a rigorous, detailed description of the components of 'debate' (*vāda*), that includes, among other methodological devices, a full discussion of the parts of formal inference, the *pramāṇa*-s, distinguishing sound from unsound arguments, and the value and protocols of argument (Lusthaus 2013, 151, 157).

Various schools proposed different *pramāṇa*-s as viable means of acquiring certain knowledge. Virtually all agreed that perception and logical inference were *pramāṇa*-s (with the Cārvākas or materialists rejecting inference, and some Buddhists rejecting perception). Other Hindu schools included in the list *śabdapramāṇa* or reliable testimony (see below), as a viable source of knowledge (which too the Buddhist rejected); additional *pramāṇa*-s proposed by others included 'comparison', 'analogy', and also 'absence' (either as stand-alone valid cognitions or subordinated to perception and inference, as for the Buddhist and the Vaiśeṣika). Caraka in his *Caraka-saṃhitā* (CS) describes perception (*pratyakṣa*) as contact between the self and what is present; inference, on the other hand, is explained as a cognition based on having previously perceived or learned something. There are three types of inferences, corresponding to inferences about the past, present, and future. 'Fire is inferred from smoke, and sexual intercourse from pregnancy' (present and past, respectively), and a future fruit can be inferred from a seed, based on having previously observed, i.e. perceived, that process (CS: 209 [ch. 11, passages 21–22]). Caraka also adds an intriguingly new *pramāṇa* not found anywhere else, namely, synthetic inductive reasoning (*yukta-pramāṇa*, or just *yukta*), which he explains with the help of examples, thus:

> Growth of crops from the combination of irrigation, ploughed land, seed and seasons; formation of embryo from the combination of six *dhātus* (five *mahābhūta*-s and *Ātman*); Production of fire from the combination of the lower-fire-drill, upper fire-drill, and the act of drilling; cure of diseases by fourfold efficient therapeutic measures.
>
> (CS, 11: 23–24; Lusthaus 2013, 160)

Lusthaus (ibid.) explains *yukta* here to mean something like: the coordination of multiple factors converging into a trajectory in which something is changed or transformed. It is a method of taking into account the coordination of multiple causes, a process with contributive factors that might affect the outcome, as in crops or medical treatments. There is no one-to-one cause–effect relation between a seed and the fruit; there are multiple contributing and additional factors that mediate it. So *yukta* (from *yukti*, to tie) carries out the task of connecting together or grouping *x* number of factors to produce a result; it later comes to be one of the numerous terms for 'reasoning' or 'logic'. As can be seen, diagnosis is inductive, not purely deductive. Unlike *yukta*, inference or *anumāna* is treated as inferring from a specific condition or cause to a specific effect, i.e. a fruit from a seed. Caraka also insists that inference requires previous perception (*pratyakṣa-pūrva*). One recognizes the relation between the fruit and seed on the basis of prior observations of this process, and so one can predict a future fruit is likely from a present planted seed.

We shall now leave the discussion of the origins of *pramāṇa* theory and move to its robust development in classical Indian philosophy, mostly during the medieval period.

So let us take it that as far as the theory goes, *pramāṇa* deals with the question of the possibility and grounds for means of knowledge, and issues relating to the justification of the knowledge so obtained, or the criteria for discerning correct knowledge from ignorance and false understanding. For valid knowledge (*pramā*) to be produced, the instrument (*karaṇa*) must be reliably valid also (*pramākaraṇaṃ pramāṇam* (*VP* 1971, #3). In other words, correct knowledge can be attained only through the instrumental efficiency (*karaṇa*) of a valid and reliable means of knowing. And there are distinct forms of *pramāṇa* for each kind of objective (and trans-objective) knowledge, beginning as we saw earlier with the more or less uniformly accepted *pramāṇa* of perception.

Mysore Hiriyanna (1973, 178), who was amongst the first modern Indian philosophers to attempt to make the discourse of *pramāṇa* intelligible to a non-Indian audience, explicated *pramāṇa* in terms of three basic functions: first, knowledge; second, a means of scrutinizing, criticizing, evaluating through ratiocination the understanding or knowledge-claim derived through the source; third, as *prāmāṇya*, the 'measurement' in terms of the criteria for 'truth' or 'falsity', which is characterized as the problem of validity. Together these constitute the grounds for the possibility of knowing.

In the rest of the chapter we shall delineate three major areas within *pramāṇa-śāstra* which have engaged modern minds, and describe the ways in which these have been interpreted and their ramifications explored or extended in the light of contemporary critical reflections. These comprise *jñāna* or 'awareness-episode' – and related to that *pramā* or 'knowledge' as *true* awareness – *prāmāṇya* or the notion of validity or 'truth', and, by way of illustration, very briefly, the *pramāṇa*-s of perception and *śabda* or linguistic statements as reliable testimony.

Jñāna

One of the concepts central to the *pramāṇa* theories is *jñāna*, which at a general level is cognate with the Western term 'cognition': only after much further qualification could it be rendered as 'knowledge'. Not all schools, however, were agreed on the exact epistemic status of *jñāna*. It was ambiguously used for experience which is neutral as to its truth or falsity and for cognition with truth-value. Thus there could be *jñāna* that is neither true nor false, and there could be *jñāna* that could be true, as there could be *jñāna* that could be false or in error.

Recent authors have discussed this issue at length in the attempt to arrive at some consensus. The rendering of *jñāna* as 'knowledge' has, by and large, been rejected, since the term *pramā* seems better suited for this. Very simply, *jñāna* may be taken to be a mental or psychical act or 'episode', and in this respect may denote 'ideation', 'remembering', 'doubting', 'wondering', guessing', 'dreaming', 'inferring', 'understanding', and so on, as modes of experience (*anubhava*) (Bilimoria 1985). More fundamentally, however, *jñāna* has the nuance of 'cognition' or, more correctly, 'awareness'. Potter (1984) argued that *jñāna* should be rendered as 'an act of awareness' in the sense of cognitive or mental episode or occurrent, rather than as a disposition, which, say, 'belief' implies. In short, *jñāna* is an awareness, and only after such *jñāna* would amount to knowledge (*pramā*) as would yield truth. *Jñāna* as awareness, then, is the starting point in *pramāṇa* theory, for it provides the 'subjective' or phenomenological basis of 'objective' knowledge that is the supposed goal of epistemology (Matilal 1986, 23; 105–107).

But, again, a theory may circumscribe its conditions and requirements in such a way that *jñāna* may be identified with *pramā*, *ceteris paribus*.

At the outset two things should be said about *jñāna*: first, that it is direct and immediate (*vyavasāya*, *aparokṣānubūti*, at least in the case of sensory awareness); and, second, that it has a content (or 'contentness', *viṣayatā*), that is to say, an awareness is intentional for it is *of* or *about* or *directed* towards an 'object' (either externally or internally) (Matilal 1986). Matilal links this observation with Peter Strawson's notion of a pre-theoretic scheme or view of the world reflected in, and presupposed by, all our mature perceptual judgments (1986, 11). *Jñāna* has a relational-qualificative structure, which may be stated in terms of the two following stages: (1) whenever an object *x* features or 'floats' in my awareness, it presents itself there as something, 'this', 'it', i.e. under some guise or mode, distinguished in some way or other (this distinguishing element is called *viśeṣaṇa*); (2) the guise of mode (*prakāra*) under which the object is presented is the purported property or qualifier of the object *x*, the qualificand. This qualifier–qualified structure is regarded as implicit in the content of any cognitive episode that has a claim to be regarded as cognition: *F(a)* or *a* as qualified by or distinguished by *F-ness*. Using a different formulation, the oblique object I notice on the table would be like this:

Q (this, cupness).

In the next moment when tea is being poured into this vestibular object, I have this more complete qualificative experience (*viśiṣta*) in which the substratum is qualified by the property of object (*tadvidviśeṣyakam*):

Q (cup, tea-ness).

Although there is a causal element involved, this by no means amounts necessarily to a representational theory of cognition, though in some realist epistemologies it does (Matilal 1986, 374ff.). In other words, according to the Nyāya, the object of cognition, the sense-contact with the object and the contact with the qualified object of the form *a* is *F* are the appropriate causal conditions of a true perceptual cognition (Shaw 2007,14).

A further observation is made that the structure of a qualificative awareness-episode can – but need not necessarily – be represented linguistically. The qualification is meant to restrict the stronger view supported by some Indian philosophers, such as Bhartṛhari (*c.*400–500 CE), that all knowledge is, as it were, shot through with language, i.e. that the phenomenological datum is itself essentially linguistic or conceptual. Some earlier Nyāya commentators seemed also to have maintained that the penetration of conceptual and verbal elements is necessary for an immediate but unformed experience to be presented as a well-formed judgment to consciousness. For most others, cognition and language are two distinct events (Sibajiban Bhattacharyya 1977; Bilimoria 2008b).

Prāmāṇya

Prāmāṇya is the other important category that we have chosen to discuss. *Prāmāṇya* has been rendered as 'truth' by Mohanty (1966, 77), and hence *prāmāṇya* has to do with a theory of truth and criteria for evaluation of truth and falsity of *jñāna*. But the theory is complicated by the fact that there are two wide divisions within Indian epistemology on the notion of 'truth', and how truth is constituted. The two divisions fall roughly into what are called the *svataḥ* ('intrinsic') and *parataḥ* ('extrinsic') theories or theses of truth. Either the conditions that generate the cognition also generate its truth (i.e. a *jñāna* is self-validating or is self-evidentially true), or the two conditions are different such that the 'truth' of the cognition requires certain supplemental factors or conditions *ab extra*. *Prima facie*, the *svataḥ* thesis seems to analytically rule out the possibility of error, for if the conditions that generate a cognition are those that yield its truth then no cognition would arise without its truth tagged on to it, so to speak. The *parataḥ* thesis would seem to be more in keeping with common-sense recognition of the possibility of error in every instance of awareness-episode. Mohanty (1966, 70–80), like a few other modern thinkers, tried to wrestle with the chasm between the two views, and came to the opinion that perhaps these views were responding to rather different sets of problems in the interests of quite different definitions and theories of truth. They might even be incommensurable (ibid., 1–2).

Karl Potter has tried to accommodate or reconcile the opposition between the two views by urging a radically different way of conceiving the relation between *jñāna* and its content. This relation is characterized by Potter (1984) in terms of purposive fulfillment, or satisfaction, taken as a mark of 'fit' for the content so 'measured out' by the awareness-episode in question. Potter construes the classical Sanskrit term that characterizes the relation of 'fit', namely, *yathārtha*, to mean "in accordance with the purpose that motivated J [*jñāna*]" (ibid., 312). The play obviously is on the troublesome term '*artha*', which could mean 'object', 'purpose', 'goal', 'system of ends', and so on. The question, however, is whether any of these senses of *artha* are epistemically weighted as it appears to be in *prāmāṇya* discourse. Potter juxtaposes the thus-derived 'purposive' structure on the more familiar classical *prāmāṇya* theories, viz.: There is *prāmāṇya* where the qualificandum (i.e. the subject term) of a *jñāna* (1) possesses a certain property (*viśeṣaṇa*) which property is the chief qualifier (predicate term) of the *jñāna* (J). Potter argues that the notion of 'right' awareness, implied in later Navya-nyāya definitions, as in certain Buddhist accounts, invariably relates itself to "previously identified purpose or purposive object" (1984, 313). But Potter has overstepped the strictures that the concept *prāmāṇya* is normally goaded with, and interpolates this in terms of another, albeit connected concept, namely, *sāmarthya* (or *saṃyaktva*), which has to do with satisfaction or purpose or desired goal. This enables Potter to argue, against the usual reading of *prāmāṇya* as 'truth', for a more or less pragmatic or 'workability' criterion in terms of the capacity of *jñāna* to effect satisfaction in action. If a 'correspondence to reality' is entailed in such a theory, for Potter this is to be interpreted in terms of the 'fit', or the 'frustration', of satisfaction that results from *jñāna*. Thus, 'correspondence' or *yathārthya* (literally, 'such-as it actually is') is subsumed under the satisfaction or *sāmarthya* principle (which might encompass ethical, normative, and aesthetic descriptions). In short, Potter opts for a reworking of the *prāmāṇya* concept towards a 'workability' theory of truth, wherein the chasm between 'fact' and 'value' is virtually collapsed (in the interest also of a noncognitivist approach to value theory).

A number of scholars have taken up Potter's challenge indifferent ways, but virtually all are agreed that Potter's proposal does not seem to square easily with the spirit of the classical theories. Mohanty, whose earlier ascription of a Justified True Belief theory of knowledge to the Indian philosophers was called into question by Potter, shifts his strategy and questions in turn the viability of the 'workability' interpretation of *prāmāṇya*. Mohanty (1984) first clarifies the two distinct understandings of *prāmāṇya* in the two opposing (Indian) theories of truth, in the following terms. It is true that the *svataḥ* theorists identify *prāmāṇya* with *jñānatva* (the property of 'knowingness') in such a way that the generating conditions of the two coincide. This *a fortiori* rules out error, which is opposed to *pramā* (true judgment), but by this definition *jñāna* is also opposed to error, considering also that *jñāna* reveals its object as having had no unknown existence prior to being apprehended while error does not. Thus, to have *a jñāna* (in the stronger sense) is to know something to be true. Either *apramā* or error and falsified judgments are not regarded as species of *jñāna* (excepting mistaken instances); or, alternatively, one might say with the Prābhākaras that all *jñāna* are *pramā*, there being no such thing as erroneous awareness or *apramā*. The Advaita Vedānta school opts for the former, while Nyāya maintains that even error or *apramā* is a species of *jñāna*, so that the generating conditions of truth (and falsity) do not coincide entirely with those of *jñāna*. Thus, to know (in the weaker sense) is tantamount to a 'belief' or simply a judgment that awaits confirmation or falsification. That is not to say, according to the Nyāya writers, that the truth of the cognition cannot arise simultaneously with the cognition; Nyāya says that their generating conditions are different. Hence, the judgment that it is raining outside might arise confirmed or with due certainty (*niścaya*) and without any doubt as to its truth. If a doubt subsequently arises, one might have to examine the special feature or 'mark of excellence' (*guṇa*) that gave the judgment its particular truth-value. There might have been a defect (*doṣa*) or a vitiating condition that gave rise to the error in the judgment, in which case the *jñāna* has to be rejected as being false or an instance of *apramā*.

As to the suggestion of *prāmāṇya* as 'workability', Mohanty and others have taken issue with Potter, arguing that:

(a) it is based on a rather stretched interpolation of *artha* as purposive 'object-value' or *satisfaction*;
(b) it involves testing in a practical action, when in fact *jñāna* need not as such entail in any action;
(c) it equivocates on the dicta: *p* works because *p* is true, *p* is true because *p* works; and
(d) practical outcome may well be significant for corroboration of the 'truth-claim', but is not essential to the determination of truth, which, according to the *svataḥ* thesis at least, is taken to be self-evidentially given ('I *know* that *a* is *F*; it works, so I am quite sure that *a* is *F*').

Thus, if falsification comes about as a result of doubt and subsequent tests or scrutiny, then the *a* is *F* is repudiated as being a conjecture and indeed its very claim to being a reliable *jñāna* is thereby undermined. Advaita would argue therefore that a *jñāna* is not a piece of knowledge which is not 'true' knowledge, and that 'false' knowledge is no knowledge at all: it is rather the opposite of knowledge, however mistaken one might have been about its truth-value. Clearly, an epistemological requirement is built into the Advaita definition of *jñāna*, and which therefore, under these circumstances, is quite appropriately translated as 'knowledge' (Mohanty 1984, 332).

Perception

There are several theories of perception in the Indian tradition, and the age-old controversies between idealism–realism–phenomenalism surface here as much as elsewhere. While the variety of phenomenalism, and consequent anti-realism represented largely by the Buddhists (e.g. Dignāga, fourth century), has been expounded in earlier works (see relevant chapters in this volume), the overt realism in Indian theories of perception, represented largely by Nyāya-Vaiśeṣika, has been contrasted with the 'realisms' of Anglo-American variety. On this Matilal has perhaps made the most advancement, and the ensuing discussion will draw on his *Perception* (1986) (see also Bilimoria 1980; Vaidya and Bilimoria 2015; Phillips and Chadha, both in this volume).

Bearing in mind the analysis in the foregoing sections, especially as regards the episodic ('event-based') interpretation of cognitive awareness, the general observation is made that all perceptual experiences, including those that we call illusory, imaginary, erroneous, even hallucinatory, have objects which they grasp, and that a causal explanation, in principle, is possible for each object grasped in perceptual experience. However, the precise ontological status of the perceptual object and the kind of causality involved are matters of intense dispute among the rival theories. While for the Buddhist, illusion is a 'revelation of the non-existent', for the Nyāya the principal object in illusion is a material object which, however, may not be present in the locus of perception but rather presented by memory, recollection, or sensory stimulation, albeit wrongly connected with the experience, resulting in an experience overall of, but not a totally, non-existent object. Still, the question arises: what is it that one 'sees' first which triggers off this event? The answer to this has implications for the further analysis of non-illusory perceptual experience.

It might be argued that in the case of perceptual illusion, nothing is 'seen', that there is really no *perceiving* going on, only a belief or an inclination to believe that we are *immediately* perceiving something (Armstrong, in Matilal 1986, 218). The occurrence is said to be 'perceptual' in a rather loose sense of the term. But the Nyāya view, as explicated by Matilal, is that one does have a strong visual, tactical, etc. experience in such an illusion, and in this respect it is perceptual and so calls for explanation.

Alternatively, a sense-data theorist might say that what is immediately presented is a raw baggage of sense-data (even *unsensed* sense-data), which is mind-dependent, and that it is this that is causally responsible for our 'mediate' cognition of objects. She might further state that in the case of illusion a false inference is made of the existence of an actual object where none is present. Of course, much hinges on the coherence of the assumption, typified in most representationalist views, that our perception is based upon a causal inference from what is presented through the senses. Could it not be possible, as the phenomenalist maintains, that what we perceive is, in the final analysis, *constructed* out of what is presented through the senses? Let us say that for both the representationalist and phenomenalist views the *immediate* object of awareness is sense-impression, or a *sense-data*, or a sensible quality (thus the given in our sensory experience). The difference is in the way each links the sense-impressions to the external objects, regressively or progressively.

The Nyāya brings several objections to these two major positions, as well as against a variation of the phenomenalist view which considers the sense-data or percepts ('sensibilia') not to be mind-dependent but to be as *real* as the perception itself or the very object by which the awareness is also designated. Basically, it is argued that these views make a great deal of the distinction between immediate/direct and mediate/indirect, and that they posit entities (mental or physical) which are presented 'up front' as the properties or constituent parts and from which the perceptual object is (causally) derived or constructed piecemeal.

For one, the part–whole distinction seems to be spurious (Matilal 1986, 273) There are no parts without a whole: to speak of parts is to assume a whole of which they are said to be parts, even if they are now scattered apart. Do I see a 'part' of a chair (even if do not see its rear legs), or do I see the whole chair, and possibly the parts in virtue of seeing the whole chair? Do I see a tomato in virtue of the red patch that appears in front of me – for if I did, would I not be seeing two things, albeit in sequence, viz. the red patch and the tomato? Do we ever see properties, as it were, hanging in mid-air, independent of the substance which they qualify? Even those Buddhists who dismissed the existence of substantive entities were moved to grant nominal existence to the composite entity made up of the qualias of color, shape, tactical feel, etc., which in themselves might be imperceptible or 'unsensed' (ibid., 246).

Second, although it is true that our normal perceptual judgment 'goes beyond' the sensory experience which give rise to them, the 'gap' need not be as large as it has often been assumed; and while in many instances we do make inferences from what is immediately presented, a theory of perception need not devolve around these factors and these factors alone. Again, the Nyāya argument in favor of its own more radical theory of what Matilal has christened 'naïve' or 'direct realism' dwells on the inappropriateness of the part–whole distinction underlying most 'indirect' theories of perception (whether realist or idealist). Nyāya gets round the obviously common-sense assumption that the relation between parts and whole (e.g. branch and tree) is contingent by suggesting that the relation that obtains is in fact one of inherence (*samavāya*), such that one could say that the tree is as much in the branch as the branch is in the tree! Thus when I see a tree and someone asks me later, "Did you see that drooping branch?" I might well reply, "I can't quite recall ... but I did notice the tree being uneven." I may have to go back and take a second look to 'see' the branch (a part) apart from the tree (the whole). Thus Nyāya argues in favor of whole–part distinction at the ontological level; while talking about perception Nyāya claims that we see the *whole* first in virtue of its having parts.

Arguing in such a manner, Matilal takes the Nyāya theory a stage further in contending that the traditional distinction between mediate and immediate objects of perception does not quite hold (1986, 267). And this provides grounds for casting serious doubts on the representationalist theory of perception, in respect of both its long-suspected assumption of sense-data and its formidable view of the causal relation between the sense-data and the object – apart from being locked into the Lockean dualism of secondary and primary qualities, one of which is imperceptible and therefore has to be inferred on the basis of the other (presumably perceptible).

To be sure, the troublesome term is not 'causal', for Nyāya has its own way of making the part 'causally responsible' for the perception of the body–whole. The following quotation from Matilal clarifies this point:

> Nyāya direct realism eliminates the third entity, sense-datum, entirely from the discussion of perception. By giving a different *causal* explanation of perceptual illusion and hallucination Nyāya aims at characterizing the causal factors in a naive or non-specialist conception of perception. Obviously, then, the consideration for the so-called causal relation between sense-datum and the material object (which has been the cornerstone of modern representationalist and causal theorists) is conspicuous by its absence in Nyāya. It is not contended here that a person claims to have a perception of a familiar body in virtue of the occurrence of some sense-impression.
>
> (1986, 268)

On the contrary, Matilal goes on to argue, using the earlier example of the tomato (and switching to substance–property–language), that the visual perception is to be regarded as the material substance (tomato) not the property, or that the *thing* tomato is the substratum of a particular instance of the property red, which in its turn, instantiates the property-universal *red*. In short, one sees the tomato *not because* one sees the red color patch (appearance) one first encounters, but that one sees the tomato because, among other things, it is colored, and one sees the red color because the color-particular resides (inheres) in a composite substance and it has a specific nature (Matilal 1986, 283).

Putting the view advanced in another way, the 'in virtue of' relation is moved from the 'sense-data' representationalist account, after denuding it of the sense-datum assumption, and placed differently. This is succinctly expressed in the following remarks, which may well be regarded as the veritable motto of Nyāya-Vaiśeṣika (direct) realism: "One does not see the tomato *in virtue* of seeing a coloured shape. Rather one sees the tomato *in virtue of* its having a coloured shape" (Matilal 1986, 285).

Śabdapramāṇa: 'testimony as knowledge'

The other *pramāṇa* or means of knowing in Indian epistemology that has begun to receive considerable attention is *śabdapramāṇa* or knowledge derived from linguistic utterance or testimony (Bilimoria 2008b). Its origins go back to the traditional protagonists who made the intriguing claim that the Vedas (canonical Brāhmaṇical texts) are an inviolable resource of authority on all manner of things. The classical material on this is extensive and varied; initially concerned with providing grounds for accepting the wisdom of *Śruti* or 'the heard word', i.e. the canonical scriptures. What we present will only be the gist of the thinking. The Buddhists saw no need for taking *śabda* as an independent *pramāṇa*, arguing that any utterance (including the Buddha's) that has not been tested in one's own experience cannot be relied upon; and in any case, the operation can be accounted for in terms of inference and perception. The Nyāya, following the Mīmaṃsā, developed sophisticated analyses and a spirited defence of testimony for its viability, reliability and autonomy as a mode of knowing.

A key defining feature of any *pramāṇa*, as we saw in the foregoing section, is the distinctive instrument among the aggregate of conditions that has the unique function of presenting the 'object' (of cognition) to the (cognizing) subject. While in perception it is generally said to be direct contact via the senses (*indriya*-s) with the particular object of cognition, in the case of *śabdapramāṇa* it is non-trivially words themselves. This response underscores a swift and remarkable recognition of the deep connection between word and knowledge, beyond the usual preoccupations with words and objects, names and things, and even knowing words. It does not take much argument to point out that a vast body of our knowledge and beliefs are derived from resources other than perception and inference, namely, by relying upon words of others, notably through hearing in direct conversation, hearsay, rumour, listening-media, or from reading words written in books, newspapers, documents, lexicons, inscriptions, etc., not to mention the role of testimony under oath ('nothing but the truth') submitted as justifying 'evidence' in legal proceedings and courts of law. It is to be noted also that the account, thus far, is not committed to suggesting that words exhaust or constitute the sole set of conditions that deliver the knowledge, or that the delivery is unproblematic in every instance. A number of factors are involved, and words arguably happen to be the primary causal antecedent without which the entire operation would flounder.

The basic element of *śabdapramāṇa* is said to be *śābdabodha* or linguistic understanding; and the distinctive 'instrument' or *karaṇa* for *śābdabodha* is said to be the 'word' or *śabda*, but not just any string of words, rather more specifically a *vākya* or sentence utterance. *Śābdabodha*, like any cognition, has a relational-qualificative structure, constitutive of 'meanings' or *arthas*, their relations (*saṃsarga*), and the intentionality relevant to the particular speech-act or utterance.

There are, however, other, perhaps even more challenging problems with the doctrine of *śabdapramāṇa* that we are not able to pursue in this short compass. For example, is all verbal knowledge of the relational, qualificative, kind? What of the 'identity' statements that Vedānta is seen to champion, such as 'You are That', 'I am Brahman'? And, in what sense is a linguistic understanding a grasping of the relational ontological structure (or of a properly qualified individual)? Suppose the same object or state of affairs is perceived by one person and heard of or about by another person, do both their respective awarenesses share the same structure of propositions, or is one more directly related to the 'objective' reality than the other, or might one be more 'linguistic' than the other, and would they be interchangeable without compromising the significance and truth-claim of one against the other (i.e. is there verisimilitude)? If there is difference, is it in respect of the intentionality of each, or is it fundamentally in the way each is phenomenologically constituted and related to its 'objective reference'? Further, what are the ramifications of this doctrine for a hermeneutics of the *text*, particularly of scriptures, and moreover, of that class of scriptures thought of, in the Hindu philosophic tradition, as embodying 'authorless revelation'? These and other questions, only partly attended to in current research, stand in need of more thorough investigation. For more forays into this area see Bilimoria (1989, 2000).

Note

1 This chapter draws generously from previously published articles: Bilimoria 1993, 1998, 2008a; the introductory discussion is owed largely to Dan Lusthaus (2013); and the Advaita Extended Mind thesis portion to Anand Vaidya (from Vaidya and Bilimoria 2015).

References

Bhattacharyya, Sibajiban.1977. "Some Principles and Concepts of Navya-Nyāya Logic and Ontology." *Our Heritage* (Calcutta) 24 and 25.

Bilimoria, P. 1980. "Perception (*pratyakṣa*) in Advaita Vedānta." *Philosophy East and West* 30. 1: 35–44.

———. 1985. "*Jñāna* and *Pramā* – the Logic of Knowing, a Critical Appraisal." *Journal of Indian Philosophy* 13(1): 73–113.

———. 1989. "The Idea of Authorless Revelation (*Apauruṣeya*)." In *Indian Philosophy of Religion*, ed. Roy W. Perrett. Dordrecht: Martinus Nijhoff/Kluwer Academic Publishers, pp. 143–166.

———. 1993. "Pramāṇa Epistemology: Some Recent Developments." In *Contemporary Philosophy: A New Survey*, vol. 7: *Asian Philosophy*, ed. Guttorm Fløistad. Dordrecht: Kluwer Academic, pp. 137–154.

———. 1998. "Testimony (in Indian Philosophy)." In *Routledge Encyclopaedia of Philosophy*, ed. Edward Craig. London: Taylor & Francis, vol. 7, pp. 315–319.

———. 2000. "J. N. Mohanty's Critique of Word as a Means of Knowing and 'Authorless Tradition'." In *The Empirical and the Transcendental: A Fusion of Horizons*, ed. Bina Gupta. New York: Rowman & Littlefield, pp. 199–218.

———. 2008a. *Śabdapramāṇa: Word and Knowledge, Testimony in Indian Philosophy*. New Delhi: DK Printworld Ltd. (with new prologues added to 1998 edition, Dordrecht: Reidel/Kluwer Academic Publishers) = Vaidya and Bilimoria (and Shaw), 2015; Vaidya, and Bilimoria, and Shaw, 2016.

———. 2008b. "Bimal Matilal's Navya-Realism, Buddhist 'Lingo-Phobia' and Mental Things." In *Language and Mind, vol. 2: The Classical Indian Perspective*, ed. K. S. Prasad. New Delhi: Decent Books, pp. 17–34.

———. 2016. "Negation (*Abhāva*), Non-existents, and a Distincitve *pramāṇa* in the Nyāya-Mīmāṃsā." In *Comparative Philosophy and J. L. Shaw*, ed. P. Bilimoria and M. Hemmingsen. Sophia Series in Cross-Cultural Philosophy of Traditions and Cultures. Dordrecht/London: Springer Nature, pp. 183–202.

Chadha, M. 2010. "Perceptual Experience and Concepts in Classical Indian Philosophy." In *The Stanford Encyclopedia of Philosophy* (Winter 2010 Edition), ed. Edward N. Zalta, http://plato.stanford.edu/archives/win2010/entries/perception-india/.

CS = *Caraka-saṃhitā*, 1976. *Agniveśa's Caraka saṃhitā: Text with English Translation*, vol. 1, Rama Karana Sharma and Bhagwan Dash. Varanai: Chowkhamba Sanskrit Series Office.

EIP = *Encyclopedia of Indian Philosophies* (Karl H. Potter, General Editor). 1977, *Nyaya-Vaiśesika: Indian Metaphysics and Epistemology, The Tradition of Nyāya-Vaiśeṣika up to Gaṅgeśa* (part 1); 1978, *Advaita Vedānta up to Śaṅkara and His Pupils* (part 1). Princeton: Princeton University Press; Delhi: Motilal Banarsidass, vols. 1 and 2, respectively.

Hayes, Richard. 1988. *Digñāga on the Interpretation of Signs*. Dordrecht: Reidel/Kluwer.

Hiriyanna, Mysore. 1973. *Outlines of Indian Philosophy*. Bombay: George Allen and Unwin.

Lusthaus, Dan. 2013. "Philosophy, Medicine, Science, and Boundaries." In *After Appropriation: Explorations in Intercultural Philosophy and Religion*, ed. Morny Joy. Calgary: Calgary University Press, pp. 139–172.

Matilal, Bimal K. 1971 *Epistemology. Logic and Grammar in Indian Philosophical Analysis*. The Hague and Paris: Mouton.

———. 1986. *Perception: An Essay on Classical Indian Theories of Knowledge*. Oxford: Oxford University Press.

———. 1990. *The Word and the World India's Contribution to the Study of Language*. Oxford: Oxford University Press.

Matilal, Bimal K. and Chakrabarti, A. (eds.). 1994. *Knowing from Words: Western and Indian Philosophical Analysis of Understanding and Testimony*. Dordrecht: Kluwer Academic Publishers.

Matilal, Bimal K. and Shaw, J. L. (eds.). 1985. *Analytical Philosophy in Comparative Perspective: Exploratory Essays in Current Theories and Classical Indian Theories of Meaning and Reference*. Dordrecht: D. Reidel.

Mohanty, J. N. 1966. *Gaṅgeśa's Theory of Truth*. Visvabharati, Santiniketan: Centre of Advanced Study in Philosophy. (Revised ed. 1989. Delhi: Motilal Banarsidass.)

———. 1970. "Nyāya Theory of Doubt." In his *Phenomenology and Ontology*. The Hague: Martinus Nijhoff.

———. 1980. "Indian Theories of Truth: Thoughts on their Framework." *Philosophy East and West* 30(4): 439–451.

———. 1984. "Prāmāṇya and Workability: Response to Potter." *Journal of Indian Philosophy* 12(4): 329–338.

———. 1992. *Reason and Tradition in Indian Thought: An Essay on the Nature of Indian Philosophical Thinking*. Oxford: Clarendon Press.

———. 1993/1995. *Essays in Indian Philosophy Traditional and Modern*. Edited with Introduction by P. Bilimoria. New Delhi and New York: Oxford University Press.

Potter, Karl H. 1978. "Towards a Conceptual Scheme for Indian Epistemologies." In *Self, Knowledge and Freedom: Essays for Kalidas Bhattacharyya*, ed. S. P. Banerjee and J. N. Mohanty. Calcutta: The World Press, pp. 17–30.

———. 1984. "Does Indian Epistemology Concern Justified True Belief?" *Journal of Indian Philosophy* 12(4): 307–382.

Shaw, J. L. 2007. "Knowledge, Belief and Doubt: Some Contemporary Problems and Their Solutions in the Nyāya Perspective." Asian Studies Institute (paper), Victoria University of Wellington.

Siderits, Mark. 1991. *Indian Philosophy of Language: Studies in Selected Issues*. Dordrecht: Kluwer Academic Publishers.

Strawson, P. F. 1976. "Knowledge and Truth." *Indian Philosophical Quarterly* 3(3): 273–282.

Thakur, Anantalal (ed.). 1967. *Nyāyadarśana, Nyāya-sūtras (NS) with Bhāṣya of Vātsyāyana (NB), Vārtikka of Uddyotkara*. Mithila: Mithila Institute Series, no. 20.

Vaidya, A. and Bilimoria, P. 2015. "Extended Mind Hypothesis and Advaita Vedānta." *Journal of Consciousness Studies* 22(7–8): 201–225.

Vaidya, A., Bilimoria, P., and Shaw, J. L. 2016. "Absence: An Indo-Analytic Inquiry." *Sophia* 55(4): article no. 5. July 20. doi:10.1007/s11841-016-0547-8.

VP 1971 = *Vedānta-Paribhāṣā* of Dharmarāja Adhvarindra. Trans. Swami Madhavananda. Belur Kolkata: Math Ramakrishna Mission Sarada Pitha.

Chapter 4
BUDDHIST HERMENEUTICS

John Powers

Introduction

The term hermeneutics is derived from the name of the Greek god Hermes, the messenger of the gods. His position required that he translate the gods' wishes to humans and report their responses to his divine colleagues. Gods and humans spoke different languages and had profoundly divergent worldviews, and so Hermes had to translate from one idiom into another. Interpretation was a central factor in his mission, and this is true of contemporary understandings of hermeneutics. Most actions involve some sort of interpretation, as do thoughts and beliefs, but hermeneutics is generally not simply conceived as interpretation *per se*, but rather is connected with *theories of* interpretation, the principles that allow conceptual understanding to emerge from sensory experience and cognitive activity.

The first usage of the term hermeneutics in Western literature was related to principles of scriptural interpretation. Scriptures are allusive, open to multiple readings, and contested between groups of exegetes and belief communities. Biblical hermeneutics attempts to provide rules and standards for exegesis. In recent times hermeneutics has been expanded in scope, and is commonly viewed as foundational to all the humanities and social sciences and as an aspect of all human thought and experience.

There is no exactly equivalent term in Buddhism, nor has Buddhist interpretation theory been extended to the present range of Western versions of hermeneutics. Buddhist exegetes are primarily concerned with scriptural interpretation, much like the medieval Christians who first developed systems for understanding the Bible and other sacred writings. Buddhist hermeneutical treatises commonly focus on the intention (*abhipraya*) behind scriptural statements, particularly in instances of conflict between texts or doctrines. One concern of Buddhist thinkers in India was distinguishing the authentic "word of the Buddha" (*buddha-vacana*) from spurious texts attributed to him. According to Buddhist tradition, shortly after the founder died some of his followers became concerned that new apocryphal works would begin to appear, and they wished both to forestall this and to develop a canon resistant to expansion.

Hermeneutics in the Pāli canon

A "first council" was convened at Rājagṛha, headed by the great monk Mahākāśyapa and attended by 500 *arhats* (monks who had overcome all mental afflictions and whose memories and perceptions were untainted by bias or sectarianism), who recounted from memory oral discourses delivered by the Buddha during his forty-year ministry. His personal attendant Ānanda recited the sermons (Pāli: *sutta*; Sanskrit: *sūtra*) and Upāli recited the discourses relating to monastic discipline (*vinaya*). Later traditions claimed that Anuruddha recounted the higher doctrine (*abhidharma*), a collection of scholastic treatises that categorize and systematize doctrines of the first two collections and that were purportedly spoken by the Buddha to his mother during a three-month sojourn in the heaven of Trāyastriṃśa. Following the recital of each text, the assembled arhats agreed with it or made corrections, and at the conclusion of the council the canon was declared closed. No further texts would be admitted as the "word of the Buddha." This canon was passed on orally from generation to generation for several centuries and then written down. It used a language called Pāli, and so is generally referred to as the "Pāli canon." It is divided into three "baskets" (*piṭaka*): discourses, monastic discipline, and higher doctrine.

Despite the canonizing aspirations of these monks, new texts appeared in India, and as the religion spread to other countries new apocryphal "sūtras" were composed. Some of these made their way back to India, and along with indigenous apocrypha created exegetical issues for Buddhist thinkers. For the Theravāda tradition (the dominant Buddhist school in Southeast Asia), the central concern was distinguishing what the Buddha actually said from spurious compositions attributed to him. Theravāda prides itself on being the most conservative Buddhist tradition and restricts its scriptures to the Pāli canon. All other texts attributed to the Buddha are regarded as inauthentic.

The Pāli canon contains some statements by the Buddha that provide guidelines for exegetes. In the *Great Instruction Discourse* (*Mahāpadesa-sutta*, traditionally attributed to the Buddha but probably composed after his death), he advises his followers to compare new teachings with those they heard previously; if the contents agree with the doctrine and monastic discipline they already know, then they can be regarded as authentic. In this formulation, a restrictive hermeneutic is proposed: new material should be evaluated in light of the established canon, and deviant notions should be rejected. It is important to qualify this, however: there is no suggestion that Buddhists who lack a thorough knowledge of the Buddha's teachings will be able to conduct such enquiries, and the text assumes that only learned senior monks will do so. Ordinary Buddhists will presumably rely on such authorities.

The other guideline was given to Ānanda, who expressed concern about future proliferation of new teachings attributed to the Buddha. In response, he was told that "whatever is well spoken is the word of the Buddha" (*Aṅguttara-nikāya* IV.163). As interpreted by the commentators, this implies that if a teaching contributes to the goals of Buddhist soteriology – mainly diminution of suffering, promotion of happiness, undermining of ignorance and mental affliction, and liberation from cyclic existence (*saṃsāra*) – then it can be viewed as Buddhist, regardless of who initially propounded it. This expansive principle potentially leaves the door open for future additions to the canon, but Theravāda commentators have maintained a closed canon down to the present day. New texts may be read and studied, but only those traditionally contained in the three baskets are the word of the Buddha.

A third noteworthy directive regarding competing claims to authority is found in the Pāli *Discourse to the Kālamas* (*Kālama-sutta*), in which the Buddha is approached by a group of people who express confusion with respect to the many claims by religious teachers of the day. Each propounds a particular system and dismisses those of all rivals, and each is well regarded by a particular group of disciples, but they all appear diminished by their unseemly sectarian rhetoric. Rather than simply asserting that his teachings are superior to theirs and denouncing his competitors, the Buddha advised the Kālamas to examine truth claims for themselves: those that accord with empirical evidence are most likely to be valid. Moreover, if one puts them into practice and derives positive results, this confirms their validity.

This passage is often cited by contemporary Buddhists as evidence that the Buddha propounded an empirical and pragmatic approach to scriptural interpretation and wanted his followers to decide such matters for themselves through reasoning, each arriving at a personal realization based on individual examination. But they only mention the first section and ignore what follows. It goes on to advise the Kālamas to discern whether or not a particular teaching is accepted by "the wise" and to base their final decisions on this. There is an implicit appeal to authority: "the wise" are obviously not those who disagree with the Buddha or propound divergent doctrines and practices. Ultimately the directive of this passage resonates with those of the previous two, because validity is correlated to congruence with already canonized teachings and subjected to the judgments of authoritative figures.

Mahāyāna hermeneutics

While the Theravāda tradition has been conservative with regard to the canon, new texts continued to appear in India, and other schools accepted them as authentic. The most important wave of new scriptures is generally referred to as "Mahāyāna" (Greater Vehicle). This originated sometime around the first century CE, and during successive centuries many new sūtras were composed, claiming to have been spoken by the historical Buddha, even though he had been dead for centuries. The chronological discrepancy was explained away by asserting that these texts were only given to the most advanced disciples and were hidden in the undersea realm of *nāgas* until the proper time for their wider dissemination. This required the appearance of human sages with the requisite insight to interpret these higher teachings, the most important of whom was Nāgārjuna (*c.* late second century CE).

The Mahāyāna sūtras accepted the discourses of the Pāli canon as authentic teachings of the Buddha, but relegated them to a secondary and inferior status. They are characterized as introductory instructions for people of limited capacity, and those who followed them were adherents of the "Inferior Vehicle" (Hīnayāna). Mahāyāna teachings, by contrast, were delivered to the most advanced practitioners. Some Mahāyāna sūtras portray the Buddha as a skilled physician who prescribed the correct remedy for every spiritual affliction. Just as a competent doctor does not provide the same medicine to every patient, but expertly diagnoses his or her specific affliction and applies the most effective antidote, so the Buddha delivered different teachings to people of varying capacities, adapting his message to what they needed to hear and what would be most beneficial in each circumstance.

This approach makes sense as soteriology, but creates significant problems for exegetes. If each discourse attributed to the Buddha was aimed at a specific person at a particular level of attainment, how do we determine his final thought? What is the bottom line for a practitioner, and what guidelines are available to make such a determination? Mahāyāna sūtras contain a variety of tropes to establish their superiority over other texts, the most pervasive of which are direct statements that a particular teaching contains the "definitive meaning" (*nītārtha*) while others are of "interpretable meaning" (*neyārtha*).

In some cases previous discourses are mentioned and dismissed as provisional, and the present one is declared to be the Buddha's final thought, but the Tibetan scholar Tsong Khapa (1357–1419) states that mere scriptural testimony provides insufficient grounds for making such determinations. There are numerous claims of definitive status in Buddhist scriptures, and in some cases a particular teaching is declared to be definitive in one text and then relegated to inferior status in another. Thus, Tsong Khapa contends, Buddhists must examine doctrinal statements for themselves in order to ascertain what the Buddha's true intention was.

He advocates the use of "stainless reasoning" as the only viable tool for sorting out the Buddha's thought. He compares the process to the way a goldsmith cuts, rubs, and physically examines gold in order to determine its quality. Similarly, Buddhist exegetes should carefully consider teachings attributed to the Buddha with reasoning based on sound principles of analysis. Like the "Discourse to the Kālamas," however, he adds that one should rely on authorities of greater wisdom, particularly the "openers of the chariot ways" (*shing rta*) Nāgārjuna and Asaṅga. The former is traditionally regarded as the founder of the Middle Way School (Madhyamaka), and the latter is the main figure in the inception of the Yogic Practice School (Yogācāra). These are the two great philosophical traditions of Indian Buddhism. Thus reasoning is never truly independent or individual, but should always conform to traditional norms and follow established exegetical parameters.

In his treatise *Essence of the Good Explanations* (*Legs bshad snying po*), Tsong Khapa highlights hermeneutical schemes in two Indian Mahāyāna texts and contends that they represent the respective approaches to scriptural interpretation of the Middle

Way School and the Yogic Practice School. The former tradition emphasizes logic and dialectical debate and takes the Perfection of Wisdom (Prajñā-pāramitā) discourses as its main scriptural basis. Its primary emphasis is on the doctrine of emptiness (*śūnyatā*), according to which all phenomena lack any substantial essence (*svabhāva*); they are merely collections of parts brought into being by causes and conditions that change from moment to moment. Thus they are "dependently arisen" (*pratītya-samutpāda*). There is no enduring self, soul, or essential nature for anything, either persons or phenomena. This logic is extended to doctrines and philosophical notions, and even the Buddha's teachings are declared to be words spoken for heuristic reasons, but ultimately empty of inherent existence.

Madhyamaka philosophers developed a powerful critique of rival philosophical systems. They examined non-Buddhist traditions as well as rival Buddhist schools, subjecting them to a *reductio ad absurdum* analysis that demonstrated the conceptual limitations of their systems while refusing to propound an alternative view that would in turn become reified as "truth." Instead, the Mādhyamikas took seriously the implications of the doctrine of emptiness and declared that all philosophical views rest on unsupportable assumptions and are subject to internal contradictions. This, they declared, is the Buddha's final thought, and all of his teachings are intended to lead his followers to a direct, non-conceptual realization of this insight.

Madhyamaka hermeneutics relies primarily on the *Discourse Spoken by Akṣayamati* (*Akṣayamati-nirdeśa-sūtra*), which considers the problem of determining the Buddha's final thought from among the plethora of competing doctrines and the vast number of canonical texts. The solution it proposes is apparently simple: the definitive teachings are those that relate to emptiness, which is the final nature of all phenomena. When the Buddha discusses emptiness, he only does so with his most advanced disciples, and he reveals his ultimate message to them. If the primary subject is emptiness, one can be certain that this is the Buddha's authoritative word on the matter. The problem with this approach is that discussions of emptiness are not all compatible in Indian Mahāyāna literature, and the Buddha takes a number of divergent philosophical paths in discussions of emptiness. In practice, then, exegetes generally rely on a particular text or group of texts that are regarded as definitive within their respective traditions, generally in conjunction with commentaries the tradition has authorized as normative. For Mādhyamikas, the most important scriptures are the Perfection of Wisdom sūtras, and the philosophical texts of Nāgārjuna and Candrakīrti (*c.* seventh century) are the most respected commentaries.

The other hermeneutical approach identified by Tsong Khapa is found in the *Discourse Explaining the Thought* (*Saṃdhinirmocana-sūtra*), the main scriptural source of the Yogic Practice School, which was probably composed around the third century CE. It provides a novel approach to discerning the Buddha's final thought: in it the Buddha reflects on his previous teachings and declares that they can be divided into three "wheels of doctrine," each of which represents a cycle of related discourses given to a particular type of practitioner. The core doctrines associated with the Pāli canon, such as the four noble truths (suffering, its origin, its cessation, and the path to eliminating it) and dependent arising, are the primary focus of the first wheel. They were taught to beginners – practitioners with limited cognitive capacities – and these people tended to reify the teachings and assign them a special truth status. Such disciples held to the literal reading of his words. Because they only understood the letter of the discourses and not their deeper meaning, they remained at a superficial level of comprehension.

In order to counteract this tendency, the Buddha subsequently taught a "second wheel" that emphasized the doctrine of emptiness. The established categories of the scholastic philosophers were subjected to a thoroughgoing analysis that showed them to be ultimately empty – mere words and concepts lacking ultimate validity. They were spoken for heuristic purposes, but are not the Buddha's final thought. The main texts of the second wheel are the Perfection of Wisdom discourses, some of which contain radical critiques of Buddhist doctrine and declare that the Buddha's true intention can never be captured in words: it is only understood through spontaneous apprehension of the final nature of reality.

The third wheel contains the Buddha's definitive instructions. The *Discourse Explaining the Thought* declares that when the Buddha delivered first-wheel teachings he knew that because of their limited capacities his audiences would reify his words and hold to the literal level of interpretation. For those of greater intelligence, he undermined this implicit tendency with second-wheel teachings, which weaned some advanced followers from their dogmatic complacency and caused them to recognize the ultimate emptiness even of the Buddha's words. This wheel also had inherent problems, however, and some disciples tended to move toward an extreme of nihilism that rejected existence *in toto*, and not merely inherent existence. In order to settle all the conceptual difficulties that arose from previous teachings, he delivered the third wheel – represented by the *Discourse Explaining the Thought* – which contains the final word of the Buddha.

From the context it is clear that not all Buddhist teachings fall into the three-wheels schema. For example, instructions regarding monastic comportment, such as how to wear one's robes or when to eat, cannot convincingly be assigned to any of the three wheels. Only certain contested doctrines are part of the three-wheels schema, and the sūtra provides a paradigm for deciding which texts and teachings are included, and where they should be placed within its hierarchy. It also indicates a way to regard all of the multifarious texts attributed to the Buddha as having some value: each has a place within the hierarchy, and each was intended for a particular species of practitioner, providing the best possible instruction for each.

Robert Thurman's perspective is that the three-wheels paradigm is based on a chronology of when particular teachings were delivered during the Buddha's life. Yet an interpretation such as this was anticipated and rejected by Tsong Khapa and is, in any event, at variance with how this is presented in the *Sūtra Explaining the Thought* (Thurman 1978, 19–21). Rather, each wheel is a *cycle* of teaching. The articulation of one requires the prior explication of its predecessor, but biographies of the Buddha indicate that he spoke to various types of practitioners throughout his life and adapted his message to each. There is no indication that he only taught first-wheel doctrines for the first part of his ministry, then switched to the second wheel, and later exclusively taught the third. The first wheel is appropriate to those for whom it was delivered, and the same is true of the others. According to the *Discourse Explaining the Thought* and Tsong Khapa, all three were part of his repertoire during his entire life.

The Buddhist hermeneutic enterprise

When Indian Buddhism traveled to East Asia, interpreters faced similar problems to those of Indian exegetes. The Chinese canon contains a vast literature imported from India, and many of these texts claim to contain the Buddha's final word. Like their Indian counterparts, East Asian Buddhists generally took a particular Indic text as the standard for the Buddha's definitive thought and ranked other texts and doctrines in accordance with how closely they agreed with the primary scripture. Several schools created classification schemes (判教 *panjiao*), which generally held one text to be the norm and ranked others hierarchically. One of the most important of these was devised by Zhiyi (智顗, 538–597), who based his system on the *Lotus Scripture of the True Doctrine* (*Saddharma-puṇḍarīka-sūtra*) and arranged other texts and doctrines below it.

In India and East Asia, Buddhist exegetes were mainly involved in what Hans-Georg Gadamer has labeled the "Romantic Endeavor," an attempt to discern the intention of the purported author of their scriptures. For those who accept the voluminous literature credited to the Buddha as his actual words, the task of sorting through it to ascertain what he really meant is a monumental one. Few scholars ever attempted to read all of them, and most belonged to interpretive communities that valorized a particular work as definitive, and so their standard was ready-made. Someone in a Yogācāra lineage, for example, would learn that the *Discourse Explaining the Thought* is the final word of the Buddha and the norm for valid interpretation, and its schema would be applied in categorizing and reading other works (in conjunction with philosophical texts written by luminaries of the tradition). Throughout Buddhist history it has been assumed that competent exegetes are capable of correctly discerning the Buddha's thought and reproducing it. This should ideally be based on a combination of academic study, instruction from authority figures, and personal realization based on meditative experience. Underlying the enterprise is a conviction that ultimately the plethora of texts and doctrines attributed to the Buddha are part of a coherent whole that is internally consistent and the product of a perfected consciousness. As such, it is free from contradiction, and any apparent inconsistencies are reflections of the limitations of an individual interpreter. The Buddha speaks only the truth and makes no mistakes, and so his followers must find ways to reconcile any apparent difficulties in the teachings attributed to him.

Contemporary scholars of a historical bent dismiss the claims of Buddhist tradition that all of the vast collections of texts believed to have been spoken by the Buddha by traditional Buddhists could have actually originated with him and conclude that they were composed by many different individuals with a range of sectarian intentions and redacted and augmented over the course of millennia.

For faith communities that accepted as authentic the works of the Pāli canon, the hundreds of Mahāyāna scriptures contained in various canons, the *Vinaya* literature, the texts of the higher doctrine, and various other works contained in Indic scriptural collections, the sheer volume of this literature makes it virtually impossible to postulate convincing internal consistency. The obvious solution, one that was adopted by most thinkers, was to relegate most of it to the status of interpretable meaning and reserve definitive status for one text or a related corpus of works. The option of discarding texts regarded by their respective traditions as authoritative did not occur to any Buddhist thinker of whom I am aware; instead, all had to be taken seriously as the word of the Buddha and a place created for them. The Theravāda tradition rejected Mahāyāna works, and so only had to interpret the Pāli canon, but even this presented significant conceptual and doctrinal problems. For Mahāyāna philosophers, the task was significantly more difficult in light of the vast literature they inherited, containing thousands of texts claiming to have originated with the founder of the tradition, and which they believed had been taught with a particular purpose and that constituted a part of the canon that could not simply be dismissed.

Underlying all Buddhist hermeneutics is a conviction that these texts all make sense and are products of an awakened consciousness. The Buddha provided each audience with those teachings that would have the greatest soteriological benefit. Later interpreters were forced to try to make sense of these texts in terms of this assumption. Their efforts should ideally be guided by personal realization because the Buddhist path is not merely a conceptual abstraction, but rather a system of belief and practice designed to result in individual re-enactment of the Buddha's experience of awakening.

Ultimately hermeneutics is for those still on the path: in one famous analogy, the Buddha compares his teachings to a raft that is built in order to cross a river. When one has reached the other shore, it would be foolish to carry the raft on one's back, because it has served its purpose. Similarly, a trainee on the path should rely on the guidance of more advanced practitioners and follow their instructions regarding which texts to view as normative and which practices to adopt. A buddha has no need for hermeneutical principles, because he or she can understand the definitive meaning of any scriptural statement. Advanced trainees are also credited with the ability to sort out merely interpretable statements and perceive the Buddha's often hidden intention in delivering them. In the final analysis, interpretation may be guided by the principles of a particular philosophical system or faith community, but it is an initial stage of the path to awakening. At the level of buddhahood, all apparent contradictions vanish and intuitive understanding dawns. Thus hermeneutics is at best an approximation or adumbration of the perspective of a buddha.

References

Bond, George. 1982. *The Word of the Buddha: The Tipiṭaka and Its Interpretation in Theravāda Buddhism.* Colombo: Gunasena.

Lopez, Donald S., Jr. (ed.). 1988. *Buddhist Hermeneutics*. Honolulu: University of Hawai'i Press.

Powers, John. 1993. *Hermeneutics and Tradition in the Saṃdhinirmocana-sūtra*. Leiden: E. J. Brill.

———. 1995. *Wisdom of Buddha: The Saṃdhinirmocana-sūtra*. Berkeley: Dharma Publishing.

Thurman, Robert. 1978. "Buddhist Hermeneutics." *Journal of the American Academy of Religion* 46(1): 19–39.

Chapter 5
PROCESS PHILOSOPHY AND PHENOMENOLOGY OF TIME IN BUDDHISM

Hari Shankar Prasad

Buddhism: a process philosophy

The birth of Buddhism lies in the Buddha's awakening consisting in the intuitive realization of the universal principle of dependent co-arising (*paṭiccasamuppāda*), which defines a process view of reality, both physical and mental. According to it, a thing is not a static but a dynamic entity, which means it is a process of temporally ordered occurrences of events. It is a self-organized system of coordinated causal relations between these events. It sets becoming against invariable being, and event ontology against substance ontology. In process philosophy, time is temporality, which is intrinsic to the successive occurrences and characterizes the passage of time as asymmetric and transitive. Process philosophy can provide an adequate account of a wide range of issues within Buddhism concerning ontology, epistemology, ethics, and philosophy of mind. Both systems also have a phenomenologically informed perspective. The present chapter develops itself within this framework. Note that here Buddhism is primarily interested in the analysis of the first-person singular experience; knowledge of the dynamic conscious phenomena; and the basic factors of mind and its cognitive, conative, and affective functioning within the paradigm of the process of moral action and its result. This makes Buddhism a unique process philosophy and phenomenology, which in its approach is empirical, practical, and exclusively concerned with human interest. In the present chapter, we will work out a Buddhist view of time through the analysis of the dynamic conscious phenomena.

Temporal view of life and the Buddhist path

Buddhism recognizes the central position of an individual in the society and the world in which he or she is born and lives. A person can transform their destiny through their own transformation in terms of awakening and virtuous ethical conduct, which can be equated with nirvāṇa, i.e. freedom from perpetual suffering. Also, their intentional ethical behaviour bears qualitatively corresponding fruits with the passage of time, not only for themselves, but also for the society and the world in which they are living. All this involves temporal stages. In essence, human life is a temporal life. So the Buddhist project of human transformation is a temporal enterprise; it is a temporal journey from suffering to nirvāṇa. In this scheme, a human's present life, although determined by past karmas, also has a scope for freedom and interest to regulate their own moral conduct, which in turn is projected towards future and makes the agent responsible for ethical action. Actually, this is a temporal journey of the dynamic consciousness or mind, which is fuelled and perpetuated by the intentional ethical karmas. Thus ethics becomes the first philosophy for Buddhism.

Temporality and temporal indexicals

The compatibility of the experience of the passage of time in a process philosophy, which is founded on the fact of continuous change governed by the law of causality, is very obvious and undeniable, To understand the issue of the passage of time, it is desirable to take into consideration the following temporal indexicals, which we find in Indian and Buddhist philosophical discourse on time (*kāla*):

1 past (*atīta, bhūtam*), present (*pratyutpanna, bhavat*), and future (*anāgata, bhavyam*); three time epochs (*adhvan, traikālya*);
2 earlier (*aparatva*), later (*paratva*), simultaneous with (*yaugapadya*); succession (*ayaugapadya*); quickness (*kṣipratva*);
3 now (*adhunā*);
4 moment (*kṣaṇa*);
5 opportune time for occurrence (*samaya*);
6 substantial time (*dravyakāla*);
7 temporality (*khaṇḍakāla*); atemporal (*akālika*), etc.

(In addition, periods of time like day, night, hour, minute, second, etc. are also used for counting the objective time.)

These temporal indexicals, which are parts of our usage in our linguistic behaviour (e.g. thinking, speaking, and writing), are not only effective in philosophical deliberations, but also a rich source of metaphysical doctrines. The Indian languages belong to the Indo-European language family whose grammatical structures are highly tense based and of subject–predicate form, which are most suitable for process philosophy.

Dependent co-arising: the principle of continuity and time

Before we come to the complex debate on the issues of consciousness, time, and their synchronized continuity among the various schools of Buddhism, it is necessary that we discuss in brief the principle of dependent co-arising, which captures and explains the way of the thing, whether material or mental. It is also called the principle of interrelations or mutual dependence. Its various interpretations give rise to the notions of impermanence, perpetual change, momentariness, atomism, non-substantialism, no-self, and ultimately an event-worldview, which go against not only counterintuitive experiences, but also against metaphysical absolutism (= *ekam sat*, *advaita*) of the Vedas and the Upaniṣads and also common-sense pluralistic realism. In its original form, this principle means that things, the way they appear to us, are not spatio-temporally invariable, but dynamic and processional. The allied principle of general conditionality (*idappaccayatā*), which defines the conditioned and conditioning characters of each temporal factor (*dharma*), which as an event, if taken in an ontological sense, is not a single spatio-temporal point-instant, but a complex combination of other compatible factors, which also has a conditioning role to give rise to another such factor. The entire process can be explained by using the analogy of the stream of a river.

Atomistic view of consciousness and time

The atomistic view of consciousness and time, which is the result of the interpretation of the basic Buddhist doctrine of impermanence, if taken in a strict sense, gives rise to the discrete moments of consciousness and time devoid of any unity and continuity. Buddhists are aware of this danger. Their primary conceptual paradigm is formed by the two principles of causality: dependent arising (*pratītyasamutpāda*) and conditionality (*idappaccayatā*). These together offer an integrated system of multiple causal factors, each member of which is conditioned, i.e. causally connected to the past, and in turn has the conditioning capacity to condition and thus to connect the next factor, i.e. future, in the series. This mechanism maintains the continuity of the series and the *extended time* along with it.

Intentional and temporal acts of consciousness

In Buddhism, the priority is to understand the intentional and temporal acts of consciousness, which is by nature not only self-structuring and self-transcending, but also cognitive, conative, and affective. So the focus is on understanding the dynamic temporal character of consciousness. As a common person, when we see a successively flowing river, which is a temporal object, our experience of it presents itself as unified across the flow. The most difficult problem here is how to explain and reconcile, within the framework of process philosophy, (i) the synchronic unity of the simultaneously functioning multiple causal factors on both sides, i.e. within the consciousness itself and the empirically observable sensibilia (e.g. form, sound, odour, taste, and touch, each one of which is a separate series) separately in the mode of our perception, and (ii) the relation between the two sides. The Buddhist answer will be: first, it is the natural characteristic of the sensibilia to be causally efficient and thus to effect stimuli to the consciousness, whose natural characteristic is to open itself to them; and second, within the Buddhist paradigm of karmic formation, an act of consciousness in the present moment of 'now' is connected to both its preceding moment (i.e. past) and its succeeding moment (i.e. future).

Husserl on internal time-consciousness

Here a comparison with Husserl's phenomenology will be very helpful in understanding the Buddhist position on the issue under consideration. The temporal structure of consciousness in the Husserlian phenomenological sense explains the intentional-cum-temporal structure of consciousness and internal time-consciousness, which is regarded by Husserl not only as the most significant, but also the most difficult of all phenomenological problems. Regarding their relation, it can be said that since both sides have the atomistic temporal character, their each moment is at the same time scale, and so are mutually compatible. This account will be authenticated by the Buddhist textual sources below. In the meantime, let us see what the Husserlian position on this issue is, as explained by Gallagher (2007, 690):

> If we imagine a momentary phase of consciousness, abstracting it from the flowing continuum of consciousness, it appears to be structured by three functions:
>
> 1 *primal impression*, which allows for the consciousness of an object (a musical note, for example) that is simultaneous with the current phase of consciousness;
> 2 *retention*, which retains the previous phase of consciousness and its intentional content (the just-past note of the melody); and
> 3 *protention*, which anticipates experience that is just about to happen.
>
> Since retention retains the entire just-past, which also includes retention of the previous phase, then there is a retentional continuum that stretches back over prior experience, maintaining the sense of the past moments in the present.

In what follows, we will explore the discussions of the three issues of consciousness, time, and their continuity in various strands of Buddhist literature within their respective conceptual frameworks.

Time in the *Sutta* literature

The *Sutta* literature, a repository of the Buddha's discourses (*dhamma*), is more empirical, psychological, and practical than scholastic and ontological in approach. This is evident from its indifference toward the critical analysis of the concepts of past, present, and future. Nevertheless, the Buddha's discourses are loaded with profound meanings and a radical worldview. In a nutshell, their main focus is to differentiate between 'what appears to be' and 'what actually is' so that we make effort to cleanse our deluded mind and devise a mechanism to execute this programme. Throughout, the *Sutta* literature recognizes the primacy and creativity of mind or consciousness, which is expressed in such statements as "mind has primacy over other *dharmic* factors; it is the controller of these factors; everything is mental in character" (*Dhammapada*, 1–2); "mind leads the world" (*Saṃyuttanikāya*, 1.39), etc. In its outlook, it is very much phenomenologically informed as it deals with cognitive awareness, predispositions, habits, and cultural factors, but it avoids analysing intentional and temporal structure of consciousness. However, it does talk of the three divisions of time (i.e. past, present, and future), but in the sense of the human cycle of birth–death–rebirth (*saṃsāra*) within the karmic framework as we see in the twelvefold formula (*dvādasanidāna*), which is divided into three temporal segments (past, present, and future).

This formula describes in temporal sequence the constitution, nature, and worldly journey of suffering across multiple lives of a person, as a result of unwholesome karmic action, for which the person themselves is responsible. It also has the possibility of reversing it by the same person without the help of any external divine agency, if they follow the Buddha's path. We can interpret each chain of this formula phenomenologically, i.e. in terms of the conscious phenomenal experiences. It depicts various forms of temporality in respect of the analysis of the *existential temporal life*, which comes to an end only when the process comes to an end, which is the atemporal state of being, freedom from suffering, and a blissful life. It also tells about *atomic temporality*, *extended temporality*, and *transcendental atemporality*.

Time in the Theravāda literature

Among the later developments, the Theravāda canonical literature comprising its Pali Abhidhamma texts is the closest to the original *dhamma*, which are considered by their followers on par with the *Sutta* literature on their core doctrines of dependent co-arising, the three characteristics of reality (impermanence, non-substantiality, and suffering), and ethical principles. However, this is not the case with its post-canonical literature, which includes commentarial and sub-commentarial literature. But in its later phase, under the Sarvāstivāda and Sautrāntika influence, it joins the debates on such issues as momentariness, intentional and temporal structure of consciousness, continuity of dynamic consciousness across three temporal aspects of life within present as well as across multiple lives, and the detailed taxonomy of the *dharmas*. For the later Theravādins, time *per se* is a mere concept (*paññato kālo*) and conventional (*vohāra-mattako*), whereas temporality (= past, present, and future) is considered to be the three aspects of a *dharma*, i.e. an evanescent event. But they attribute the status of present-cum-existence only to 'present,' whereas 'past' and 'future' are considered to be deposited in the predispositions (*saṃkhāra*).

Further, like Sarvāstivādins and the Sautrāntikas, the Theravādins also subscribe to the atomistic view of time, which seems to propound discrete moments and deny the possibility of their continuity, but they differ radically in their interpretations of it. Theravāda looks for an account of continuity of dynamic consciousness within the 'present' itself, which provides sufficient ground for establishing the intentional and temporal structure of consciousness. Its invention of the notion of *bhavaṅga-citta*, meaning inactive states of mind during the break of two awarenesses or transition between a person's two forms of life, such as past and present, or between present and future, explains the synchronic (between momentary awarenesses) and diachronic (over a period of extended time) unties and continuity.

Within the paradigm of process philosophy, the *Dhammasaṅgaṇī*, a Theravāda canonical text, uses a highly meaningful word for time, i.e. *samaya*, which is identified with an act of consciousness or mind (*citta*) and said to limit and determine the latter. This shows that time is the principle of evanescent change and so the essential aspect of mind or a conditioned *dhamma*. In other words, one can aver that the acts of consciousness cannot be understood without reference to time. On the relation between a *dhamma* and time, Ronkin (2005, 84, n. 142) quotes Steven Collins's translation of a *Sutta* passage:

> [T]his division into past (present and future), is (a division) of *dhamma*-s, not of time; in relation to *dhamma*-s which are divided into past, etc., time does not exist in ultimate truth, and therefore here "past", etc., are only spoken of by conventional usage.

Buddhism in general is not interested in metaphysics of time *per se*. It is singularly focused on universalizable ethics and soteriology. In this respect, in the *Sutta* and early Abhidhamma literature, both Pali and Sanskrit, the discussion of time is non-contemporary, i.e. not rigorously intellectualized; rather it is based on the day-to-day experience (of phenomena like impermanence, temporal continuity of life, and three divisions of time, etc.) and the very unusual philosophical usage of time, which is technically called *samaya*, in the sense of a crucial moment (*khaṇa*), which is assigned various temporal meanings by the *Aṭṭhasālinī*, a commentary on the *Dhammasaṅgaṇī*. Each one of these meanings is meant to alert every follower of the Noble Path and advise him to realize its specific significance within the paradigm of awakening, ethical development, and nirvāṇa, which together connect to the Buddha's way of living. For examples, the use of the adverbial sub-clause "At a time when (*yasmin samaye*) ...," while describing various past events related to the Buddha's awakening, sermons, and movements shows (i) the special significance of that very moment, which demands an immediate response; and (ii) the concurrence of necessary and sufficient conditions (*samavāya*), which marks a special opportune time for action. In the same vein, the *Sumaṅgalavilāsinī*, the commentary on the *Dīghanikāya*, gives nine meanings, which cannot be discussed here due to constraints on space. We can note that Buddhism is very empirical, practical, and value-oriented. However, all these are the phenomenological referents of time as they are mental phenomena. Needless to say, missing an opportune time has unfavourable consequences of various types. Thus, time-sensitivity is indispensable, more so in respect of self-promotion in the course of the Buddhist Noble Path. But in later Abhidharmic scholasticism, the discussion of time takes the course of analytical argumentation and endless debates.

Time in the Sarvāstivāda literature

Sarvāstivāda is a prominent Buddhist school of thought. It derives its name from its ontological doctrine of the conditioned *dharma*-s, which are mind-independent, substantial, endowed with self-nature, and dynamic. Also, they continue to retain their existential identities throughout their temporal transition from future to present to past. In other words, their *dharmic* thesis is that all *dharma*-s exist (*sarvam asti*) and always exist in all the three modes (*sarvadā asti*). This is the most radical and controversial thesis, which contradicts the very foundation of Buddhism expressed in the doctrines of impermanence and non-substantiality, and it is for this reason that the Sarvāstivādins have been vehemently criticized by their fellow Buddhists of all denominations. Since they hold atomistic view of *dharma*-s and time, i.e. momentariness, according to which, every moment is discrete in nature, it becomes impossible for them to present an account of causal continuity within the crucial two kinds of process: (i) process of cognitive awareness, which involves the arising of one momentary awareness (= *dharma*), (ii) after the destruction of its preceding awareness, for example. In a fit of desperation to explain the required continuity, they assume four phases (arising, enduring, degenerating, and disappearing), thus accommodating an element of duration within a moment (= *saṃskṛta-dharma*) before its destruction. These four are called by them the four characteristics (*saṃskṛtalakṣaṇa*, the secondary characteristics) of the primary moment. They are considered to be the external factors, which make the basic *dharma* capable of causally relating itself to its preceding and succeeding moments. In a non-Buddhistic way, they declared them to be independent substantial realities.

In causal continuity, every *dharma* with its twin characteristics of conditioned and conditioning can be said to exist, although in different senses, during its temporal journey. Four Sarvāstivādins – Dharmatrāta, Ghoṣaka, Vasumitra, and Buddhadeva – offer different explanations of this process. The first two are criticized for being substantialist Sāṃkhya and the fourth is rejected as being relativist, despite being philosophically admissible. The third, i.e. Vasumitra's innovative efficiency (*kāritra*) theory, is accepted by its fellow Sarvāstivādins. Their opponent Sautrāntikas also accept this concept, but modify it drastically. We will discuss it in the next section. Now, within the *kāritra* paradigm of Sarvāstivāda, the three times can be defined as follows. A *dharma* is present when it discharges its efficiency (*kāritra*) and exists in its present mode, which combines both existence and presence; it exists as past when it loses its status of presence after discharging its efficiency and slips into memory; and it exists as future when it is yet to acquire its status of presence by discharging its efficiency. In this manner, a *dharma* maintains its dynamic temporal continuity.

Phenomenologically, if Sarvāstivāda sets its ontological commitment aside, these three modes can be called three types of intentional objects having different phenomenological senses and referents. As discussed above, they can also be termed as primal impression (= now), retention (= past), and protention (= future), which together constitute the intentional and temporal structure of dynamic consciousness containing synchronic and diachronic unities within it.

Time in the Sautrāntika and Yogācāra literature

Within the Abhidharma system, the Sautrāntika also holds the atomistic view of time, but defines the moment as extremely irreducible entity and so without various temporal phases within it. Only the present moment has presence and existence, that too, without duration within it. In this situation, only the present mode of moment is genuinely real and it disappears as soon as it appears. It comes into existence after having been non-existent and destroys itself completely. The other two modes, past and future, are unreal. This analysis seems to present a more chaotic scene, while avoiding the mess created by the Sarvāstivādin. But the ingenuity of the Sautrāntika in this conceptual crisis is remarkable. He simplifies the procedure and the multi-layered independent substantial *dharma*-s. To maintain temporal continuity of dynamic consciousness, he introduces two explanatory principles using the imageries of botanical seed (*bīja*) and chemical perfume (*vāsanā*). He argues: just as a seed is sown in the soil, transforms itself amidst various factors, grows as a plant, and bears fruit with the passage of time by spreading itself throughout this process, in the same manner, a wholesome or unwholesome intentional thought (*dharma*, a root-factor) gets absorbed in the mind, matures in it, and produces a karmic results without maintaining its separate identity. The same idea gave rise to the notion of *ālayavijñāna* in the Yogācāra system of Asaṅga, Maitreya, and the later Vasubandhu. The Yogācārin Asaṅga defines time against the backdrop of the continuing mental cause–effect process. In this way, time is just a conceptual designation having no independent ontological status (*hetup halaprabandhapravṛttau kāla iti prajñaptiḥ*: *Abhidharmasamuccaya* of Asaṅga).

The Mādhyamika Nāgārjuna on deconstruction of time

Nāgārjuna in his *Mūlamadhyamaka-kārikā* presents a critique of the various views of time and temporality. He himself claims to be the holder of 'no-view philosophy' within the paradigm of the emptiness of hypostatizing mental proliferation (*prapañca-śūnyatā*), independent substantial self-nature (*niḥsvabhāvatā*), and all philosophic views (*sarvadṛṣṭi-śūnyatā*) by subjecting them to rigorous dialectical analysis. This is a thorough negative approach, but then he is exclusively guided by the Buddha's programme of universal compassion, execution of which is possible only by emptying the mind of all conceptual and linguistic constructs. In order to stop developing emptiness into a metaphysical doctrine, he also pronounced the emptiness of emptiness. He is well aware of the dangerous consequences of the various kinds of conflicting identities – metaphysical, religious, and ideological for examples. In chapters II and XIX (also elsewhere throughout the text in sporadic manner) of the above text, he takes upon the Theravāda, Sarvāstivāda, and Sautrāntika views of reality, causality, and the three divisions of time, which are propounded within the framework of process philosophy but with conflicting approaches. In the analysis of every view, he resorts to the two identical principles of dependent co-arising and conditionality, which rules out any autonomous factor (*dharma*). He applies them to conceptual networking and shows emptiness of their claims. Thus he breaks the nexus between meaning and reference without denying the existence of the external world, which is also governed by these principles.

The *Jātaka* view of time

Collins (2010, 36) presents a Buddhist *Jātaka* view of time, and its commentarial elaboration:

> Time (*kāla*) eats all beings, along with itself,
> But the one who eats time cooks the cooker of beings.

> 'Time' refers to such things as the morning and mid-day meals. 'Beings' here means living beings; time does not (actually) consume beings by tearing off their skin and flesh, but it is said to 'eat' and 'consume' them by wasting away their life, beauty and strength, crushing their youth, and destroying their health .... It leaves nothing, but eats everything, not only being but also itself; (that is to say) the time of the morning meal does not reach the time of the mid-day meal, and likewise with the time of the mid-day meal (and what follows). 'The one who eats time' is a name for the Enlightened person, for he wastes away and eats the time of rebirth in the future by the Noble Path .... 'Cooks the cooker of beings' (means): he has cooked the craving which cooks being in hell, burnt it and reduced it to ashes.

This passage clearly paints the image of the inexorable temporal destiny of an unenlightened human being whose unwholesome karmas are responsible for their miseries here and hereafter. But the great hope is that they can reverse it by following the Buddhist path, which is a path of mental purity from such defilements as craving and bad ethical conduct. This process ultimately ends in the dissolution of a person's temporality itself. This means noble persons can destroy their suffering by destroying their craving, which is the real monster.

From the preceding discussion and exploration of process philosophy, we can safely say that although time *per se* is denied in Buddhism, temporality is accepted as the essential mode of human life, society, and the physical world.

Bibliography

Primary sources

Abhidharmakoṣa-bhāṣya of Vasubandhu; *Abhidharmasamuccaya* of Asaṅga; *Aṭṭhasālinī*; *Dhammapada*; *Dhammasaṅgaṇī*; *Mūlamadhyamaka-kārikā* of Nāgārjuna; *Saṃyuttanikāya*; and *Sumaṅgalavilāsinī* on *Dīghanikāya*.

Secondary sources

Collins, Steven. 2010. *Nirvāṇa: Concept, Imagery, Narrative*. Cambridge: Cambridge University Press.
Cox, Collett. 1995. *Disputed Dharmas: Early Buddhist Theories on Existence*. Tokyo: The International Institute for Buddhist Studies.
Gallagher, Shaun. 2007. "Phenomenological Approaches to Consciousness." In Max Velmans and Susan Schneider (eds.), *The Blackwell Companion to Consciousness*. Malden, MA: Blackwell Publishing, 686–696.
Ronkin, Noa. 2005. *Early Buddhist Metaphysics: The Making of a Philosophical Tradition*. London: RoutledgeCurzon.
Waldron, William S. 2003. *The Buddhist Unconscious: The Ālayavijñāna in the Context of Indian Buddhist Thought*. London: RoutledgeCurzon.
Willemen, Charles, Dessein, Bart, and Cox, Collett. 1998. *Sarvāstivāda Buddhist Scholasticism*. Leiden: E. J. Brill.

Chapter 6
PHILOSOPHY AND RELIGION IN INDIA

Jessica Frazier

> Discoursers on God say: "What is the cause? God? Why were we born? Whereby do we live? And on what are we established? Time, or inherent nature, or necessity, or chance?"

For the last two and a half thousand years or more of Indian history, the marriage of religion and philosophy has essentially been a happy one. While it is wrong to see Indian cultures as intrinsically religious – for sciences, scepticism, and purely utilitarian reasoning all flourished – nevertheless the West's perceived division between mystical and rational goals, or theology and science, misses an important axis of Indian thought. Philosophy and religion joined together in the sphere of important concerns that they both shared. We will see that reason in India could serve as a spiritual practice and philosophers were often portrayed as heroes of self-discipline. The highest reality was generally identified by its metaphysical roots, and the protagonists of literary narrative frequently paused to indulge in detailed philosophical discussion. The very fact that epistemological and metaphysical insights formed the engine of early Buddhist and Hindu Vedāntic religious doctrines, respectively, indicates that it is the categories of 'religion' and 'philosophy' that need to be redefined for the Indian context.

Cultures of reason in the broadest sense – that is, the rendering comprehensible and coherent of one's beliefs – and cultures of religious worship and transformation were closely intertwined in Indian history for a number of important reasons:

1 **Shared cosmological concerns:** some of the earliest texts in India, as in Greece, addressed themselves to cosmological concerns that span both religion and philosophy. As we will see, sources such as the hymns of Book 10 of the *Ṛg Veda* and the speculative cosmologies contained in the Upaniṣads, as well as the later texts that drew on them, all evince a central concern with identifying the nature of the cosmos and the human person.

2 **Reasoning as a religious practice:** much as Pierre Hadot (1995) has observed of classical Greek culture, philosophical reflection of different kinds served as an important form of spiritual exercise in many Indian schools of thought. The discipline of self-control that yogis sought began not with the body, but with the reasoned manipulation of one's own mind.
3 **The spread of rational methodology**: the methods of accurate reasoning came to pervade texts across the spectrum of religious and secular sciences. In due course arguments became subject to formal conventions for valid debate; the Nyāya school set out templates for logical analysis, and the interpretation of Hindu source texts became similarly controlled by Mīmāṃsā standards of good hermeneutic conduct. Rigour became a consistent theme of much Indian religious life.
4 **The scholastic way of life:** the explicitly philosophical genres of literature that developed (such as the *sūtras* and their *bhaṣyas*) gave voice to an emerging professional culture in which clarity of expression, in both written form and oral debate, was an essential skill. The pedagogical traditions of Brahmin culture, the debating structures of Buddhist intellectual life, and the external patronage given to particular schools by India's many kingdoms, together provided a social space in which scholastic life could flourish.
5 **The narrativisation of philosophy:** some of the earliest philosophical discussions are found in stories that would normally be considered literary or theological. The result was a style of *narrative philosophy* that was woven throughout literatures of every period and region. A common trope developed in which two characters are depicted having an extended discussion together, with one often interrogating the other, or taking an opposing viewpoint, until the issue is finally resolved. Examples include discussions between Brahmins, pupils, kings, and courtiers, and one of the most important forms of such dialogues is that in which a deity, a seer or a Buddha instructs someone seeking knowledge; the *Bhagavad Gītā* is one of the most influential examples of this form. This has meant that philosophy was richly woven into religious narratives. Philosophically minded priests, kings, monks, yogis, teachers, saints, ascetics, and gods could all become popular heroes in the Indian way of looking at life.

Thanks to formative conceptual and historical factors such as these, Indian religious culture can be seen as incorporating rationality at its core. Indeed, Frauwallner suggested that the trajectory of Indian intellectual history can be contrasted with the way in which Greek philosophy 'is related to religion dialectically and develops itself out of contrast to it', whereas Indian speculation 'has never departed from the soil or field of religion'. The relation between religion and philosophy in India is not merely incidental, but constitutive, reminding us that the culture of 'speculation' has 'reformed and developed the structure of religion from the inside' (Frauwallner 1973, xiii). This development of both rational and religious reflection within a broader context of inquiry created what Dasgupta terms a 'concrete unity of many-sided developments in art, architecture, literature, religion, morals and science so far as it was understood in those days' (Dasgupta 1922, vii). In many respects the relationship between religion and philosophy is one that holds strong at the level of what Peter Berger has called world-building or 'nomization' – the process by which Indian thinkers have sought to build viable models of the universe that lead us toward meaningful ends (Berger 1967, 22).

The realist impulse: the origins of philosophical religion in India

Many of the texts that stand at the root of intellectual traditions in India grounded their thinking in speculation about the nature of the cosmos. Such texts implied that natural law carries epistemological force as something 'basic' which reveals the normative conditions of truth in the cosmos. Thus cosmology served as a foundation for metaphysical, religious, and ethical insights in texts ranging from the Upaniṣads to the Dharma Śāstras, the Buddhist Tripiṭaka and Sūtras, as well as the various Purāṇas and Tantras which begin with cosmogonic accounts of the creation of the universe designed to add authority to the teachings that follow, and to frame them within a 'dharmic' sense of the Good. One of the earliest examples of this is in the *Ṛg Veda Saṃhitā* (*c.* 1800–1000 BCE), which contains a large number of hymns dedicated to personal deities, but also various cosmological speculation in which the seeds of philosophical reasoning can be found. The *Nāsadīya*, for instance, is concerned specifically with the origins of the universe and ponders whether there was anything or maybe nothing at all in the beginning (Bilimoria 2012). But unlike Vedic creation myths such as the *Puruṣa Sūkta*, which tells us about the genesis of the universe from the body of a primal cosmic person, the *Nāsadīya Sūkta* starts by questioning basic presuppositions about the nature of the universe itself:

> Then [at the time of creation], there was not [what is], non-existent nor [what is] existent: there was no realm of air, no sky beyond it …
>
> … Who really knows and who here can say it, whence it was born and whence flows this creation? The Gods are later than this world's production. Who knows then whence it first came into being?
>
> (*Ṛg Veda* 10:129)

This initial questioning continued in late Vedic texts such as the Upaniṣads, which had a higher proportion of philosophical content. Not one, but many different kinds of philosophical reflection can be found here. The *Chāndogya Upaniṣad*, for instance, includes a dialogue in which a father teaches his son doctrines about the nature of reality, of the self and ways of reasoning. He teaches these doctrines in a way that explicitly highlights their grounding in inference from empirical data, and their avoidance of incoherent or ill-grounded ideas. The notion of a divine ground of all Being is given an explanatory backing against the critiques that would have been levelled at it by the sceptical schools of the time:

> "In the beginning," my dear, "there was only that which is, one only, without a second. Others say, in the beginning there was that only which is not, one only, without a second; and from that which is not, that which is was born."
>
> "But how could it be thus, my dear?" the father continued. "How could that which is, be born of that which is not?"
>
> (*Chāndogya Upaniṣad* 6.1–2)

This short rejection of the coherence of an *ex nihilo* conception of the origin of Being is typical of the casual 'natural theology' that is scattered through the late Vedic texts. The *Chāndogya Upaniṣad* also includes a scene depicting the enthusiastic 'discovery' of the importance of induction. The same father notes that once one has identified a universal feature of one thing, the ability to identify it in new contexts yields an almost prophetic ability – the inductive knowledge of things that are as yet unknown:

> ... you must have surely asked about that rule of substitution by which one hears what has not been heard of before, thinks of what has not been thought of before, and perceives what has not been perceived before? ... By means of just one lump of clay one would perceive everything made of clay ... now no one will be able to spring something upon us that we have not heard of or thought of or understood before.
>
> (*Chāndogya Upaniṣad* 6.1.3–4, 6.4.5, trans. Olivelle 1996, 148)

Patil has shown how essential the process of inference would come to be in Hindu arguments for the existence of an origin, ground and designer of the universe, and how meticulous would be the Buddhist critiques arguing against it (Patil 2009).

These proto-philosophical discourses set the explanatory tone of revelation in subsequent religious literature. The *Bhagavad Gītā* takes the form of a teaching by the highest deity (Krishna, in this case), on the nature of reality and the self. The symbiosis of religion and philosophy is striking here; in contrast to the discourses of, for instance, Jesus to his followers in texts such as the Gospel of Matthew, the deity Krishna's discourse to his human friend Arjuna is prompted by questions rooted in uncertainty and doubt, and continues in an interrogatory dialogue in which Arjuna probes the deity. One of the main goals of the text is to ground ethics and lifestyle in correct understanding of the nature of world and self.

In many respects such discourses reflect an Indian inclination to ground religious doctrine in metaphysical or epistemological truths (as much as in historical events, and sometimes in preference to them). This is best understood as a strongly 'realist' impulse in Indian religions (see Frazier 2009). They are 'realistic' in the sense that they seek not only to describe what is the case (a project that Ram-Prasad terms 'descriptive metaphysics') (Ram-Prasad 2002, 28), but also to make their theologies take their cue from the fundamental metaphysical facts of the world. Ram-Prasad points out that this yields interesting results in some cases, as in Advaita ('non-dualism'), where the eighth-century CE theologian Śaṃkara's positioning of his account of the divine, in relation to careful reflection on the conditions of knowledge, result in the development of ingenious 'transcendental' arguments (Ram-Prasad 2002). But throughout Indian history religious thinkers have returned again and again to the idea that it is recognition of the true state of things that 'saves'.

Philosophy as a spiritual practice

Words signifying reflection (*citta, manīṣā*), knowledge (*jñāna*), insight (*dhyāna*), intentional focus (*saṅkalpa*), discriminative discernment (*vijñāna*) (see, for instance, *Aitareya Upaniṣad* 3.1–4), and other forms of refined thought feature prominently in core texts of Buddhism and Hinduism, often taking altered cognition to be a central method of self-improvement. The controlled and aptly directed mind is contrasted with that which is fragmented in its attention, limited in its scope, and fickle in its intentions. The *Dhammapada* describes the typical Indian religio-rational hero in its depiction of the man who 'sees in a clear vision the coming and going of inner events' (25.374), who reflects on the nature of the everyday phenomena of 'name and form' (25.367), and 'whose mind is well trained in the ways that lead to light' (6.89). In the Vedāntic tradition, specific rational mechanisms such as inference provided a way in which reasoning offered a special generalised philosophical knowledge that could allow one to become 'the eye of the world', as texts such as the *Aitareya Upaniṣad* 3.1.4 put it (see Frazier 2017, 99–119). Linked to this was the idea that a comprehension of reality would directly impact on the mind of the person achieving that realisation. Thus, for instance, the realisation of 'immortal' truths is depicted in the Upaniṣads as producing a commensurate change in the self. The *Kaṭha Upaniṣad* (4.1–3) describes self-reflection as something through which its audience will better understand the central aspect of self that is not 'unstable' in the way that empirical sensations typically are:

> A certain wise man in search of immortality,
> Turned his sight inward and saw the self within …
> the wise know what constitutes th'immortal
> And in unstable things here do not seek the stable.
> Touches and sexual acts –
> That by which one experiences these,
> By the same one understands.

Reason here leads not to a 'soul', defined as a vague immortal entity, but rather to a cognitive centre of 'witnessing' awareness that is as much of interest to the philosopher as the religious practitioner. Throughout periods and schools of thought, the idea of the 'self consisting of knowledge' (*Aitareya Upaniṣad* 3.4) remained one of the common ideal figures of Indian religious life.

This spiritualisation of reasoning is linked to a 'phenomenological' tendency that some scholars have identified in Indian thought. Early sources, from the Buddhist Tripiṭaka to the *Upaniṣads*, the discussions in the 'Mokṣadharma' section of the *Mahābhārata* and the sciences of the Yoga Sūtras, all advocate a careful attention to the contents of one's awareness. Indeed, a distinctive Indian form of stoicism motivated many texts, advocating the mental control of one's own thought. This explicitly focused on the mind's ability to direct attention to particular ideas and use one's rational agency to manipulate the form that those ideas give to the mind. Thus consciousness provided a shared arena of activity for work on both *truth* and the *self*.

Systematic reasoning and scholastic theology

While the reflection found in texts such as the Upaniṣads, *Bhagavad Gītā*, and *Dhammapada* are often fairly loose in their argumentation, frequently taking the form of speeches or dialogues, over time the conventions of formal debate became increasingly standardised across different schools and regions. Epistemologically speaking, the spread of a formal culture of good reasoning seems to have been prompted in part by the empirical sciences of medical observation (as in the *Caraka Saṃhitā*), and in part by a widespread classical debate about what Bronkhorst (2011: 3–4) calls the 'correspondence principle', a metaphysical connection purported to link words and ideas to their intentional objects. Thus *Sāṃkhya Karikā* 6–8 defines inference as the principle by which a sign indicates a signified by reference to empirical precedent, and the *Nyāya Sūtras* 1.1.5–6 applies this to the practical process of comparison (*upamāna*) by which inference can be used to derive knowledge about new data. Ultimately inference was taken up in the broader formalisation of instructions for reliably good reasoning. It stood alongside the regularisation of key logical mechanisms such as the principle of non-contradiction, *modus ponens* and *tollens*, and *reductio ad absurdum* – a technique of refuting arguments that became very popular in the lively public debates that flourished across Indian traditions from classical India well into the early modern period. One popular model of good argument advocated five steps: the proposition (*pratijñā*), its reason (*hetu*), the example on which that is based (*dṛṣṭānta*), the application of the reason (*upanaya*), and the conclusion (*nigamana*) (see for instance *Nyāya Sūtra* 1.1.32 as well as Ganeri's (2009) account of the discovery of basic mechanisms of reasoning in the Nyāya tradition, and Brendan Gillon's (2010) short survey of early forms of Indian logic). Variations developed, but the basic idea of a template for good reasoning, which could be applied to a wide range of different claims for knowledge, was put to use in texts, religious and otherwise.

Many Indian religious literatures were peppered with dramatisation of the proper methodological form of good reasoning. One sees this is countless stories of discussion in epics, hagiography, and other literatures. Thus, for instance, the female ascetic Sulabhā is a character who turns up in the *Mahābhārata*, where she is belittled by a king but asserts her own independent authority on the basis of her training in the qualities of valid argumentation. her parity is established on the level playing ground of reason:

> Sulabhā said, O king, speech ought always to be free from the nine verbal faults and the nine faults of judgment .... The words I utter will be fraught with sense, free from ambiguity (in consequence of each of them not being symbols of many things), logical, free from pleonasm or tautology ... not elliptical or imperfect, destitute of harshness or difficulty of comprehension, characterised by due order, not far-fetched in respect of sense, corrected with one another as cause and effect and each having a specific object.
>
> (*Mahābhārata* 12.321, trans. Ganguli 1983–1996, Book 12: 64)

Sulabhā's boast about her good arguments is a way of establishing her equal value as a subject, independently of her social or physical identity. Philosophy, then, had become not only a method, but also a medium of reason as a public practice and a universal source of authority. Similarly, as Buddhism began to proselytise, it too drew on philosophy to appeal to the masses and establish an equality that transcended gender or social status. In the first-century BCE Buddhist text, the *Milinda-pañha*, the newly converted king named Milinda initiates a philosophical dialogue with the sage Nāgasena, in order to ensure that the Buddha's own words are sufficiently clear and consistent for the purposes of further conversion of the masses. The Buddha's authority alone will not do – only good arguments will succeed. Possibly the text marks the point at which the early Buddhist community felt it needed to bring its more informal revelations into line with the wider culture of coherent argumentation and logical analysis. Religion was expected to be able to convince the 'everyman'.

In the world of 'professional' philosophy associated with brahmanical families and monastic community, new genres arose. The terse doctrinal genres of Sūtra, Kārikā and Śāstra gave rise to new derivative genres of philosophical literature, such as commentaries (*bhāṣya*), clarifications (*dīpikā*), adornments (*alaṃkāra*), surveys (*saṃgraha*), critical annotations (*vārttika*), proofs (*siddhi*), and other works of explanation. Teachers engaged in the didactic exegesis of revealed texts to generate a rich culture of philosophical exposition. But sectarian dispute was crucial for constantly raising the bar of quality. During the eighth and ninth centuries educational institutions such as the Buddhist university at Vikramaśīla hosted disputes, while many teachers would cross verbal swords with any other theologian he encountered on his travels. In a culture that has rarely seen compulsion in religion, debate became the medium of religious battle, and sound argument became the weapon. Many of the classic 'scholastic' treatises are effectively summaries of their authors' debates, addressing the critiques and counter-arguments that had been put to them by counter-locutors (*pūrva-pakṣas*) and which had helped the author to refine his own arguments.

In the Vedāntic tradition of reflection on the nature of reality sophisticated arguments were developed to square the sole, infinite, changeless, and undivided divine reality of Brahman with the existence of the limited, changing and pluriform world. The Bhedābheda school of thought drew on philosophical debates about the status of transformation to argue that contingent changes of form are non-essential and non-compromising of identity, relative to the constancy of substance. The famous monist theologian Śaṃkara came, through participation in philosophical debate, to 'utilize a coherent logic that consequently led to the establishment of 'seeing' as the only reality' (Timalsina 2009, 4), and, under the Buddhistic influence of his predecessor Gauḍapāda, he further augmented this ontological insight with the epistemological observation that a change may be only in the eye of the beholder, 'super-imposing' contingent identities onto the 'real' identity of Brahman. Rāmānuja explored notions of agency and the nascent reality of future possible actions, to suggest that the world is the medium (body) of divine action, itself changing, while the divine agent remains the same. Another early modern theologian, Vallabha, went further in hinting that the changes that take place in a thing whose essential nature is to change, are not really changes at all. In all of these and other cases, theology became a kind of 'metaphysical generator' for ontological insights (see Frazier 2014, 36). In the medieval period popular religious poetry, drama and myth became the new clothing for philosophical ideas. Yet even within these more popular forms of discourse, the realist impulse remained intact, cloaked in metaphor and poetic evocation.

Religion and the limits of reason

Yet even the established scholastic thinkers of Hindu tradition had strong, principled reservations about the ultimate authority of reason. The nature of reality was sometimes argued to be unsusceptible to basic structures of rationality, such as differentiation, reification, and reduction to a single cognisable form. At the heart of many early Buddhist texts, for instance, there lies an observation about the reifying or 'aggregating' influence of our reasoning on the raw empirical data of phenomenal reality. Cognition was seen as fundamentally distorting. Thus early Buddhist soteriology relies upon realisation of the consequent falsity of our most basic ontological assumptions. Jaina thinkers also linked soteriology to the mind's ability to realise the non-one-sidedness (*anekānta-tva*) of truth, and the conditioned (*syād*) or partial (*naya*) character of our understanding. The notion that the ultimate character of reality might be '*acintya*' or 'inconceivable', as one early modern school of Vedāntic thought held, similarly has a long history even in Hindu schools that believed reality to be possessed either of no properties, or of too many for the mind to encompass. In some cases, special forms of reasoning were necessary. Śaṃkara's didactic strategies, intended to teach the true nature of a reality he considered unamenable to rational comprehension, included dialectical questions and provocations, analogies, best-fit descriptions, negative theological statements, and other means of teaching that go beyond the style of direct assertion and exposition that we think of as being characteristic of philosophy. As Hirst puts it, Śaṃkara's 'knotty problem is to make known to human beings the ultimate reality that transcends words', and thus his philosophical theology 'may be seen to work as much by laying down fruitful methods for gaining such an understanding, as by trying to describe that which is, by definition, indescribable' (Hirst 2005, 1).

By contrast, in the philosophies associated with devotional religion, reason's difficulty was that it lacked affective value; the early modern devotional and aesthetic texts of Rūpa Gosvāmī in his *Laghu Bhāgavatāmṛta* (1.1.7–9) are critical of 'dry' logicians as lacking sensitivity to realities perceived through our *emotional* experience. Interestingly, the practical reality of debate had also revealed its susceptibility to rhetoric and subjective differences. The *Brahma Sūtra* notes that reasoning on certain matters fails to ground doctrines such that they cannot be 'established [from] reasoning' (*tarka-apratiṣṭhānāt*) (*Brahma Sūtra* 2.1.11). Śaṃkara takes this up in his commentary on that text, arguing that conjecture 'has no limits' and 'lacks conclusiveness' so that adept arguments from one camp will always be susceptible to falsification from another (*Brahma Sūtra Bhāṣya*, commentary on 2.1.11). He asks:

> How can any knowledge derived from reasoning, be correct, when its content has no fixity of form? ... [I]t is not also possible to assemble all the logicians of past, present, and future at the same place and time, whereby to arrive at a single idea, having the same form and content, so as to be the right knowledge.
>
> (Gambhirananda 1965, 322–3)

So even reason could produce relative truths. Indeed, Ram-Prasad argues that the Indian tradition as a whole has tended towards what he calls a 'multiplist metaphysics' that tries 'to make sense of competing claims by searching for some level of explanation at which they cease to be incompatible' – a view that is reminiscent of Hans-George Gadamer's epistemological views (Ram-Prasad 2007, 18). Buddhism exemplified the complex relationship between religion and scepticism; once one has realised the truth about the flaws to which human cognition is susceptible, the only rational step – and for early Buddhism the one which 'saves' – is to abandon (or mitigate) the truth of conventional perception. Philosophy, then, could not always produce a clear and univocal picture of reality – although on closer inspection this often turned out to be for philosophically well-grounded reasons.

Religion and the goals of philosophy

What, finally, of philosophy's attitude to religion? The accumulation of *sūtras*, *śāstras*, *saṃhitās*, and other theoretical genres addressing nominally secular topics such as political acumen, aesthetics and dramaturgy, alchemy and metallurgy, medicine, sculpture and architecture, contributed to the development of a discourse of secular reason. These have formed the basis of an important reclamation by thinkers such as Dominik Wujastyk, Jonardon Ganeri, Sheldon Pollock, and Amartya

Sen of India's secular and scientific heritage; they remind us that India deserves to be accorded her own 'lost age of reason', full of 'argumentative' (rather than dogmatic) Indians.

But it is helpful to keep in mind that even many strictly philosophical and scientific texts maintained a declared set of overarching goals that included religious and moral concerns. The *Kāma Sūtra*'s nominally secular instructions for pleasure nevertheless begin with a praise of *mokṣa* or liberation. The *Caraka Saṃhitā* is a manual of medicine, yet it starts by telling us that its source is the teachings sent down by the gods in order to ensure that illness did not prevent humans from religious pursuits. The *Nātya Śāstra*'s analysis of the dramatic arts begins with the author's own 'bow' to the gods, and an account of how they devised drama as a diversion from less exalted pleasures. Nīti Sāstra texts on political ethics, such as the *Pañcatantra* and *Hitopadeśa* which are sometimes hailed as Machiavellian manuals of political pragmatism, actually advise on pragmatic decision-making in pursuit of all sorts of goals, including religious ones. The Nyāya school of logic itself was devoted to belief in a personal god and argued copiously with the Buddhists on the matter.

Thus philosophy was considered a great tool, equal to a king's might or a god's magic spell – but it was rarely a goal in itself. Ganeri has argued that classical Indian intellectual culture was suspicious of 'goalless, capricious, ungrounded' thought, but saw intellectual discourses as best framed within valid goals – whether of compassion (*karuṇā*) or ethical action (*dharma*), pleasure or happiness (*kāma*), success (*artha*), or liberation (*mokṣa*, *kaivalya*, *nirvāṇa*, etc.) (Ganeri 2009, 8). This Indian tendency to position philosophical texts within the broader *telos* of religious and other goals is crucial. It prompts us to question the dichotomy not only between philosophy and religion, but between content and motivation. Within Indian texts, one can often identify multiple discursive 'moments' of analysis and proof, metaphysical and cosmological speculation, epistemological self-reflection, mythic narrative, theological reflection, commentary and exegesis, aesthetic expression, and consideration of practical and ethical applications. These are interwoven or captured within a 'Russian doll' of speeches framed within dialogues within treatises within mythological narratives, etc. While this can make such texts seem eclectic, it highlights the fact that thinking was done outside of strong disciplinary boundaries, as a way of guiding life itself – life in all its interwoven and many-faceted complexity.

In this light the very notion that philosophy and reason are two separate disciplines seems suspect, suggesting that we find other ways of remapping those two territories. Here we have suggested that important tropes for thinking about life combined religion and philosophy into seamless unities in certain spheres. We see *spiritual reasoning* in traditions that employed rational speculation to transform the mind for religious purposes. We find a *metaphysical ultimacy* celebrated in key religious texts that teach about the ontological foundations. We also see a kind of *narrative philosophy* pervading the cultural *imaginaire* of literary India through the ages, positioning philosophers as religious exemplars.

Echoing Said's orientalist critiques, Matilal noted that the West repeatedly finds itself tempted to force India into a dichotomy between Indian philosophy (that is, Schopenhauer's India) and Indian 'mysticism' (that is, the India that Madame Blavatsky loved, and Hegel hated) (see Matilal 2002). King has supported this concern by suggesting that scholars reorient their categories, and no longer cast India in the role of a 'shadow' of the Occident, forced to mirror the West's own discomfort about reason and revelation (King 1999). As Hadot has noted of Greece, so too in India the realist impulse toward truth and the discipline of self-transformation through reasoning, have served as a 'way of life' accorded innate value for human life.

Bibliography

Berger, Peter. 1967. *The Sacred Canopy*. New York: Anchor Books.

Bilimoria, P. 2012. "Why Is There Nothing Rather than Something? An Essay in the Comparative Metaphysic of Nonbeing." *Sophia* 51(4), 509–530.

Bronkhorst, Johannes. 2011. *Language and Reality: On an Episode in Indian Thought*. Leiden: E. J. Brill.

Dasgupta, Surendranath. 1922. *A History of Indian Philosophy*, vol. 1. Delhi: Motilal Banarsidass.

Frauwallner, Erich. 1973. *History of Indian Philosophy*. Delhi: Motilal Banarsidass.

Frazier, Jessica. 2009. *Reality, Religion and Passion: Truth and Ethics in Hans-Georg Gadamer and Rūpa Gosvāmī*. Lanham, MA: Lexington Books.

Frazier, Jessica. 2014. "On Vedānta: Metaphors for the Category of Existence." In *Categorisation in Indian Philosophy: Thinking inside the Box*. London: Routledge.

Frazier, Jessica. 2017. *Hindu Worldviews: Theories of Self, Ritual and Reality*. London: Bloomsbury.

Gambhirananda, Swami. 1965. *Brahma Sūtra Bhāṣya of Shankarācārya*. Calcutta: Advaita Ashrama.

Ganeri, Jonardon. 2009. *Philosophy in Classical India: The Proper Work of Reason*. New Delhi: Motilal Banarsidass.

Ganeri, Jonardon. 2010. *The Concealed Art of the Soul: Theories of the Self and Practices of Truth in Indian Epistemology*. Oxford: Oxford University Press.

Ganeri, Jonardon. 2011. *The Lost Age of Reason: Philosophy in Early Modern India 1450–1700*. Oxford: Oxford University Press.

Ganeri, Jonardon. 2012. *Identity as Reasoned Choice: A South Asian Perspective on the Reach and Resources of Public and Practical Reason in Shaping Individual Identities*. London: Continuum.

Ganguli, K. M. 1983–1996. *The Mahabharata of Krishna Vaipayana Vyasa*. New Delhi: Munshiram Manoharlal.

Gillon, Brendan. 2010. "Logic in Early Classical India: An Overview." In *Logic in Early Classical India*. Delhi: Motilal Banarsidass.

Hadot, Pierre. 1995. *Philosophy as a Way of Life* (Michael Chase, trans.). Oxford: Blackwell.

Hirst, Jacqueline. 2005. *Śaṃkara's Advaita Vedānta: A Way of Teaching*. London: Routledge.

King, Richard. 1999. *Orientalism and Religion: Postcolonial Theory, India, and the 'Mystic East'*. London: Routledge.

Matilal, Bimal K. 2002. *Philosophy, Culture and Religion: The Collected Essays of Bimal Krishna Matilal*, vol. 1. New Delhi: Oxford University Press India.

Nicholson, Andrew. 2010. *Unifying Hinduism: Philosophy and Identity in Indian Intellectual History*. New York: Columbia University Press.

Olivelle, Patrick (trans.). 1996. *The Early Upaniṣads*. New York: Oxford University Press.

Patil, Parimal. 2009. *Against a Hindu God: Buddhist Philosophy of Religion in India*. New York: Columbia University Press.

Ram-Prasad, Chakravarthi. 2002. *Advaita Epistemology and Metaphysics: An Outline of Indian Non-Realism*. London: Routledge.

Ram-Prasad, Chakravarthi. 2007. *Indian Philosophy and the Consequences of Knowledge: Themes in Ethics, Metaphysics, and Soteriology*. Aldershot: Ashgate.

Rangacharya, M. and Aiyangar, M. B. Varadaraja. 1988. *The Vedānta Sūtras with the Śrībhāṣya of Rāmānujācārya*. New Delhi: Munshiram Manoharlal.

Timalsina, Sthaneshwar. 2009. *Consciousness in Indian Philosophy: The Advaita Doctrine of 'Awareness Only'*. London: Routledge.

Chapter 7
INDIAN SKEPTICISM[1]

Raghunath Ghosh

I

The theory of skepticism in Indian philosophy is called *saṃśayavāda* and it has conceptual if not historical connections with Pyrrhonian skepticism (though arguably Indian skeptical tradition preceded the Greek *epistemé*). Although the concept of 'doubt' or '*saṃśaya*' of a general nature has been accepted by most schools of Indian philosophy, there are certain thinkers who have been and remain absolute, hard-core skeptics. Among these thinkers, Jayarāśi and Śrīharṣa (1970, 70–71) fall into that category; Jayarāśi, for his part, has challenged the vast array of epistemological and metaphysical tenets and presupposition of classical Indian philosophy, and he set out to refute them all (Jayarāśi 2010, 73–74). To his way of thinking, no feature of 'certitude' (*niścaya*) can be maintained with regard to the epistemological and metaphysical standpoints of the philosophers. He evolves a hair-splitting analytical apparatus in order to refute the definitions of 'valid cognition' (*pramā*) and 'means of valid cognition' (*pramāṇa*), particularly by the Nyāya, in segment of *TUS*. He himself denies providing any valid definition and a theoretical account of the world in response to the views of the opponents. Jayarāśi neither justifies the faultlessness of any instrument of cognition nor puts forward any thesis of his own. His main objective is to show inconsistencies and lack of clarity in others' positions. He introduced the concept of *sallakṣaṇa* ('real defining characteristic') as the determinant of the faultlessness of the *pramāṇa*-s (*sallakṣaṇanivandhanaṃ māna-vyavasthānam*) (Jayarāśi 1940, 1, 68).

The term *sallakṣaṇa* of *pramāṇa* means 'its capacity of being devoid of doubt and error' (*saṃśaya-viparyaya-rāhitya*). To Jayarāśi the valid cognition has been defined by the cognitivists as 'non-erroneous' (*avyabhicārī*). But how can the non-erroneous character be known? It may be said that a piece of cognition may be taken as non-erroneous if it is produced by a set of causal factors which are non-defective in nature, if it is not sublated, and if it is conducive to successful inclination (ibid., 2). Jayarāśi has shown that the term *avyabhicārī* ('non-erroneous') cannot be used in the above-mentioned three senses. The first alternative cannot be taken into account because the non-defective nature of sense-organs—the cause of perception—does not depend on a sense-organ. The non-defective character of sense-organs is not capable of being known definitely due to the super-sensuous nature (*atīndriya*) of sense-organs as envisaged by the Naiyāyikas. The same cannot be confirmed with the help of inference, because the function of inference depends on perceptual cognition. Cognition may be taken as non-erroneous if it is originated through non-defective causes; at the same time, if an object becomes meaningful due to its origination from a non-defective cause, it can give rise to a non-erroneous cognition leading to the defect of 'mutual dependence' (*anyonyāśraya*). Hence non-erroneous cognition is not possible at all. Second, the absence of falsification is not to be taken as the meaning of the term *avyabhicārī*, because the term 'absence of falsification' (*bādhārahitatva*) may mean 'the adequacy of cause' in respect to the origination of cognition. If it so, there are many cases where there are an adequacy of causes, but no effect is produced. Hence the term *avyabhicārī* does not necessarily mean 'the absence of sublation'. If the term 'non-erroneous' means 'conduciveness to successful inclination' (*pravṛtti-sāmarthya*), a question may be raised whether the conduciveness to successful inclination is known or unknown. If it is known, then how can one be aware that the known object is identical with its knowledge? If the real nature of successful inclination is not known, how can it be known that non-erroneousness indicates the property of successful inclination? In this way, Jayarāśi has come to the conclusion that the phenomenon of non-erroneous awareness is not possible at all, leading to the non-acceptance of perception as a source of knowing (*pramāṇa*). Jayarāśi has taken pains in refuting the use of other terms like *vyavasāyātmaka* ('certain'), *avyapadeśya* ('non-verbal'), *indriyārtha-sannikarṣa* ('the contact of sense-organ with object'), *artha* ('perceptible object'), etc., which are incorporated in the definition of perception (Gautama 1967; 2003, I.i.4). To him nothing in this world can be known in a non-dubious way due to the non-availability of non-defective way of knowing (*pramāṇa*). For this reason the objects in this world remain unproven due to the absence of proper or non-defective proof or *pramāṇa*. All objects have been used by people without any critical assessment and hence they seem to be beautiful. In such case the proof (*pramāṇa*) is taken as defective, due to which the provable entities (*prameya*-s) are also defective. Jayarāśi himself is not free from contradiction. On the one hand, he has taken recourse to *pramāṇa* to justify public usages; on the other hand, after refuting *pramāṇa* as an entity, he supports the prohibition of public usage (*tadevam upaplutesvevatattvesu avicāritaramaṇīyāḥ sarve vyvahārāḥ ghaṭanta iti*) 'When, in this way, the principles are entirely destroyed, all everyday practices are made delightful, because they are not deliberated'[2]. To him both the children and scholars are of the same kind in respect to the normative usage of language, and thus this usage alone should always be imitated for practical purposes (Jayarāśi 1940, 125). Hence the doctrine of *Tattvopaplavasiṃha* is equivalent to absolute skepticism in respect of non-normative beliefs and claims. In other words, all principles are annihilated; actions bear no result, such as heaven, etc. The worldly path should be followed (*tattvopaplavasiṃha eṣa viṣamo nūnaṃ mayā … nāsti tatphalaṃ vā svargāditi satyaṃ. … laukiko mārgo'nusarttavyaḥ*) (ibid., 1). The title suggests that it is a lion that demolishes all philosophies or philosophical views as such. It implies a demolition of the Cārvāka view too. The texts open with a rejection of the materialist principle; hence Jayarāśi was not a materialist but a radical skeptic (Franco 1994, xii).

To sum up, Jayarāśi's whole thesis critically examines some of the definitions of the means of knowledge, such as perception and inference. Afterwards he makes a general observation that it is not possible for us to attain knowledge in the required sense (Matilal 2002, 79).

II

The Naiyāyikas have enumerated 'doubt' or *saṃśaya* as one of the forms of *apramā* (improper cognition), the definition of which is given by Viśvanātha as cognition characterized by the contrary properties of positivity and negativity of a single object (*ekadharmika viruddha bhava-abhāvaprakārakaṃ jñānaṃ saṃśayaḥ; Siddhāntamuktāvalī* [2012, #129]). The knowledge of the common properties between in two objects becomes the cause of doubt. The common height between the trunk of a tree and person, for instance, gives rise to a dubious cognition in the form: 'whether this is a trunk of a tree or otherwise (i.e., a human person)'. The common cognition of both trunk of a tree and a person is the cause of doubt. In the same manner, after apprehending the property of soundness (*śabdatva*) in a sound, which is different from eternity or non-eternity, one can have doubt about 'whether sound is eternal or non-eternal'. Even though a word being uttered can give rise to a cognition touching two alternatives (*koṭidvaya*), yet doubt has to be taken as a mental phenomenon (*kintu tatra śabdena koṭi-dvayaṃ janyate, saṃśayastu mānasa eva iti*). Again, in the same manner it can be said that in the event of the doubt of validity (*prāmāṇya-saṃśaya*) of cognition, there arises the doubt of the object, and the doubt of the pervaded (*vyāpya-saṃśaya*) generates the doubt of the pervader (*vyāpaka-saṃśaya*). Moreover, it has been admitted by the Naiyāyikas that the cognition of the possessor of the properties (*dharmi-jñāna*) and the contact of the sense-organ with the possessor of property (*dharmi-indriya-sannikarṣa*) are the causes of doubt. Even though it is through the word that something is known dubiously, words do not have the capacity of generating doubt. And though two alternatives come to our mind through the instrumentality of a word, doubt is said to be a distinctively mental phenomenon (2012, 129).

Gautama, the earliest known systematizer of the Nyāya canon, has defined doubt as follows. Doubt is nothing but a conflicting judgment regarding the precise character of an object. It originates from the recognition of properties common to many objects or of properties uncommon to any of the objects, from the conflicting testimony, and from irregularity of perception and non-perception. From this definition it can be presumed that there are five kinds of doubt arising from different causes. First, it may arise from the recognition of common properties (*samāna-dharma-upapatti*). Seeing an object in dim light, it is not possible for us to ascertain whether it is a person or the trunk of a tree on account of the fact that common properties like tallness, etc., belong to both the objects. Second, the recognition of properties not common (*aneka-dharma-upapatti*) may sometimes be cause for doubt. For example, after hearing a sound one cannot ascertain whether it is eternal or non-eternal, because the property of soundness belongs neither to human beings, beasts, etc., that are non-eternal nor atoms, etc., that are eternal. Third, conflicting testimony sometimes may give rise to doubt. For example, it is very difficult to ascertain whether the self exists or not depending on some textual references alone. As we have ample references in favor of both the alternatives, it is not always possible to ascertain the status of the self. Fourth, an irregularity of perception is sometimes the cause of doubt. For example, we may have some perceptual awareness about water, but it is difficult to ascertain whether we are seeing real water or the appearance of water in a mirage. A question always remains in one's mind whether water is perceived in a place where water really exists or even when it does not exist (*upalabdhi-avyavasthātaḥ*). Lastly, an irregularity of non-perception (*anupalabdhi-avyavathātaḥ*) may become the cause of doubt in some cases. We do not find water, for example, where it really exists and also in the dry land where it does not exist. The situation leads us to a confusion. A question arises whether water is not perceived only when it does not exist and also when it does exist (*Nyāyasūtra* I.i.23).

As J. N. Mohanty (Bilimoria 2002, 101) observes, following the Nyāya tradition, all philosophical enterprises presuppose some sort of doubt. We are eager to understand the reasons for its preoccupation with doubt. For an enquiry (or as the *Nyāyabhāṣya* says, *pramāṇair arthaparīkṣaṇam*, i.e., the attempt to determine the nature of the object with the help of the various sources of true knowledge) presupposes the prior existence of doubt.

III

Now an effort is made to deal with the arguments given by Nāgārjuna in denying doubt or *saṃśaya* as a category (*padārtha*) in his famously attributed text *Vaidalyaprakaraṇa*, which is available in the Tibetan version (1995). In this small but philosophically significant text Nagarjuna has refuted all the sixteen categories accepted by the Naiyāyikas with special reference to their treatment by Vātsyāyana. Now an attempt will be made to highlight the arguments given by Nāgārjuna in refuting *saṃśaya*, which is a very significant moment in Indian philosophical analysis. In this connection there is a tendency to defend the Nyāya-position, which is in favor of accepting *saṃśaya* as a category for some solid reasons or for some presuppositions accepted in their philosophical system. In this connection Bimal Matilal's observation is worth pondering. According to him, the development of Indian skeptical writings of three different philosophers have to be consulted (Matilal 2002, 74). They are: Nāgārjuna, Jayarāśi, and Śrīharṣa, representing three different philosophical traditions of India. Nāgārjuna is a Mādhyamika Buddhist, Jayarāśi was either a materialist or an agnostic, and Śrīharṣa was an Advaita Vedāntin. In spite of their differences they shaped a common attitude towards the discovery of truth. Their philosophical method was critical, skeptical, refutational, and destructive. An opponent is not to be taken as a skeptic. The function of an opponent is to refute a rival position and at the same time to retain his own position. If an opponent does not want to substantiate his own position nor any position of his own, and is only interested in refuting the other's position, he becomes a skeptic or a follower of the skeptical methodology.

In the treatise *Vaidalyaprakaraṇa*, Nāgārjuna opines that the Naiyāyikas have introduced a new category called *saṃśaya* or doubt in order to prove the existence of *pramāṇa* and *prameya*. If someone thinks whether something is *pramāṇa* or *prameya*, a doubt arises regarding this (Nāgārjuna 1995, verses xxi–xxiii; 100–114). The phenomenon of doubt allows someone to infer the existence of *pramāṇa* and *prameya*. By virtue of being a *padārtha*, doubt cannot refer to an unreal object (see also Nāgārjuna 1978).

Nāgārjuna has encountered this position of the Naiyāyikas and refuted their position with some convincing arguments. Nāgārjuna has emphatically established the impossibility of doubt as a category, because doubt is not related to something which is perceived and to something which is not perceived. The importance of such a statement is grounded in the fact that the perceived object is an existent object while the non-perceived object refers to a non-existent one.

Nāgārjuna, however, assumes a third alternative, which may be taken as an object of doubt. To him there may remain an object which *seems to be perceived* apart from the two alternatives—a pure perceptible and a pure imperceptible. Even this third alternative cannot justify doubt, because there does not exist an entity, *which seems to be perceived*. Hence, the three probable alternatives cannot justify doubt as an entity (Nāgārjuna 1995, verse xxi).

IV

If the above-mentioned logical stance of Nāgārjuna is analyzed, the following clarifications can be offered. When an object is seen, a mere mental representation of that particular object is manifested. If an entity is known as 'as a person or a trunk of a tree' (*sthāṇurvā puruṣovā*), the corresponding image in the form of either person or a trunk of a tree is produced in the mind. If the object is a person and it is perceived as such, there is a valid cognition. On the other hand, if the object is a trunk of a tree but it is perceived as a person or vice versa, there is an illusory or invalid cognition, which is nothing but the lack of valid cognition. Perception, as Nāgārjuna suggests, provides us the data of the perceived object, and hence our expression, which is dependent on these data, cannot provide us the cognition of the object as otherwise, which can generate doubt. If a person is perceived, the mere representation of a person bears no elements which can generate doubt in the form: 'I am seeing a person or a trunk of a tree,' or can lead one to think that what is known as a person is not an actual person. If, on the other hand, there is the mere absence of the perception of an object, it will lead to the cognition of its non-existence, but it does not bear any element which can provoke doubt.

Apart from the above-mentioned two alternatives, there may be a third one. An object may be related to something that *seems to be perceived*. When a rope is perceived as a serpent, a rope is related to serpent, which *seems to be perceived* as accepted by the Naiyāyikas. In such cases, Nāgārjuna argues, there is only the false representation of a serpent in the place of rope – this false representation of a serpent is nothing but the lack of representation of rope generated through the mere absence of its perception. Hence there are no elements that can give rise to doubt (Nāgārjuna 1995, verse xxiii).

The Naiyāyikas may come up with the following justification. To them doubt does not arise at all if there is no reference (*ltos pa, apekṣā*) to particular attributes or peculiarities (*khyad par, viśeṣa*). First, the Naiyāyikas give a description of an instance of doubt. After seeing an object from a distance there arises an uncertain cognition or a wavering judgment (*vimarśa*), which provides an uncertain cognition in the form: 'It is a person or a trunk of a tree'. In this case some common features between person and a trunk of a tree are perceived. It is justified by the definition; *tadanavadhāraṇaṃ jñānaṃ saṃśayaḥ*. Second, Vātsyāyana explains how the doubt is resolved. To him, when the specific characters or differentiating features of a person or trunks of a tree are known, the doubt ceases due to having certainty in the mind in the form: 'It is a person or a trunk of a tree'. Lastly, Vātsyāyana has added a novel feature of doubt. The perceived object can be or cannot be a person or a trunk of a tree, as the qualities common to the both are seen. This uncertainty of mind can generate a tendency to search (*ltos pa, apekṣā*) for specific qualities, which can distinguish an object from the other (*khyad pa, viśeṣa*). As soon as these are available, doubt is resolved. As these differentiating factors or 'some features different from that' (*de lasgzan du na*) are searched for, it leads to the presupposition that doubt persists in our minds. The 'looking for' or the search of (*Itos pa, apekṣā*) 'this desire to know' (*bubhutsā*) the specific feature of the thing is the new element in the Vātsyāyana's definition of doubt (*viśeṣāpekṣo vimarśaḥ saṃśayaḥ*). Overall we get three stages: (a) perception in a correct cognition or erroneous cognition; (b) the perception of special features, which generate the correct cognition and rectify the wrong one; (c) and the third moment is when a knower's mind wavers due to the non-ascertainment of the thing perceived, which leads her to look for the specific character. The third stage generates doubt in her mind (ibid., #xxii).

Nāgārjuna in his *sūtra* xxiii has refuted the above-mentioned view and proved that doubt does not exist. As the doubt is nothing but a fiction to him, there is no room for the relation between doubt and peculiarities. In the stock example—whether it is a person or a trunk of a tree—if the characteristic features distinguishing them are perceived, there is no doubt at that particular moment, as it gives rise to certain cognition presenting things as such (*yan dag pa jiltababzin du, yathābhūta*), i.e., a person as a person or a trunk of a tree as a trunk of a tree. On the other hand, if the characteristics perceived are not adequate to give a correct cognition, there is no doubt due to having 'a lack of cognition' (*mi ses pa, ajñāna*). In other words, if the peculiarities of ascertaining an object exist, there is knowledge. If these do not exist, or are not perceived, there is the lack of knowledge. The third alternative, which asserts the existence and non-existence of peculiarities at the same time, is denied by Nāgārjuna. Hence doubt does not at all exist. Considering the above, D. P. Chattopadhyaya (1997, 51) concludes: "What is worse, an apparent air of paradoxicality seems to have taken away all the deemed force of Nāgārjuna's critique of *pramā* and *pramāṇas*." (For a response, see Sidertis 1997, 75.)

V

When Nāgārjuna considers the third alternative (i.e. rope is considered as serpent due to the lack of presentation of rope (*ajñāna*)) it reminds one of the Mīmāṃsā theory of error, technically called *akhyātivāda*. It explains error (e.g., snake in the place of rope) as the absence of the knowledge of discrimination between snake and rope (*yatra yadadhyāsastad vivekāgrahanivandhano bhramaḥ*) (Śaṅkara 1964, 12–13; Bādarayaṇa 1962, 10–11). Nāgārjuna takes the same position when he says that the understanding of snake as rope is due to the absence of the cognition of rope.

The Naiyāyika could say that doubt arises when there is a cognition touching both the alternatives (*ubhayakoṭika jñāna*). When an object is known as either a person or a trunk of a tree, it is true that there is some lack of cognition. It can be interpreted that when there is cognition of a man, it is due to the lack of cognition of a trunk of a tree. When there arises the cognition of a trunk of a tree, it is due to the lack of the cognition of a man. Whatever may be the case, we must admit that there is certainly a cognition the sometimes takes a person as its content and sometimes takes a trunk of a tree as its content. An individual's mind wavers between two cognitions successively, but not simultaneously. That is why such wavering cognition arises from the mental state metaphorized as the movement of the cradle (*dolācalacittavṛtti*). The cognition of a person may be caused by the absence of the cognition of a trunk of a tree or otherwise, but the existence of the cognition of a person for one moment and the cognition of a trunk of a tree for the next moment must be accepted. In this case the existence and non-existence of the peculiarities in a person are known in the successive moment, but not simultaneously as accepted by Nāgārjuna. Herein lies the difference between two schools – the Buddhist and the Nyāya.

When the determinants are not available in determining the nature of an object, doubt arises. The absence of determining proof of an entity, which is the object of knowledge, is the cause of doubt. Doubt plays a positive role in generating critical thinking after removing blind faith. In other words, doubt is the revealer of the windows of our critical and open-minded thinking. Considering this aspect, Gautama has enumerated it as one of the sixteen categories, the right cognitions of which lead us to the heights of success – mundane and transcendental (*nihśr eyasādhigamaḥ*). To Vātsyāyana's thinking, doubt has been given a due emphasis in Nyāya on account of the fact that logic alone can be applied to the object in doubt, but not to an object which is purely known or unknown (*tatra nānupalabdhe na nirṇīte'rthe nyāyaḥ pravarttate / kiṃ tarhi? saṃśayite'rthe*) (*Nyāyabhāṣya* I.i.1.). From this statement it is proven that Nāgārjuna's thesis that something is either known or unknown is not entirely correct. If it is known, he says, it is a kind of valid cognition. If it is unknown, it is to be taken as illusion. Vātsyāyana is of the opinion that this is the ideal case where we can have doubt. For him, doubt is a kind of intellectual activity arising out of the confrontation by two different philosophical positions called thesis (*pakṣa*) and anti-thesis (*pratipakṣa*) at the same time (*vimṛśya pakṣa-pratipakṣābhyāṃ arthāvadharaṇaṃ nirṇayaḥ*) (*Nyāyasūtra* 1.i.41). To think an entity as both known and unknown does not lead us to admit its fictitious character; rather, it is a kind of doubt. This view of the Naiyāyikas will find support in Vācaspati Miśra's *Bhāmatī* where he accepts the dubious character of an object as a criterion of an enquiry about it (*atha yadasandigdham aprayojanam, ca na tatprekṣavat pratipitsā-gocaraḥ*) (Vācaspati Miśra 1973, 3).

We may recall Udayana in this connection. To him if there is mistrust among family members, social beings, etc., our empirical doubt will not be possible. If, on the other hand, there is no doubt, there does not arise any philosophical enquiry (*śamkā ced anumāstyeva na cecchankā tatastarām/vyāghātavadhirāśankā tarkah śamkāvadhirmatah*) (*Nyāyakusumāñjali* 3/7; 341–342). If there is doubt, there is inferential cognition or an inferential procedure to be resorted to with a view to resolving doubt. If not, inference is established easily. Such doubt is permissible so long as there does not arise self-contradiction (*vyāghāta*). Sometimes the method of *tarka* (*reductio ad absurdum*) is taken into account. From this it is proven that doubt has a positive role in philosophical methodology if it is taken as a category.

The Buddhists in general and Dignāga and Dharmakīrti in particular cannot accept perceptibility and imperceptibility simultaneously due to various presuppositions in their minds. To them a perceptual entity remains only for a moment as per the theory of momentariness, and hence it is of *svalakṣaṇa* nature. An imperceptible entity does not come under its purview due to its vitiation by mental constructions (*kalpanā*), and hence it bears the character of *sāmānyalakṣaṇa* (general features). On account of such ontological commitments the Buddhists cannot behold the existence of contradictory properties in an entity. For this reason Nāgārjuna does not accept the existence and non-existence of the peculiarities of an object at the same time, thus leading him to the non-acceptance of doubt as an existent object. For this reason Nagarjuna 'cannot accept' to 'later developments within Abhidharma and Yogācara traditions, could not countenance the dubious character of an object which is *svalakṣaṇa* (unique particular) in nature. The skeptics have a different maxim. They do not extrapolate if there is any possibility of error. As the human being is a finite being, there is always a possibility of error and so the skeptics' maxim implies that it is never rational to extrapolate (Ganeri 2009, 28).

Note

1 With significant input and reworking of submitted draft by Purushottama Bilimoria.

2 Translation provided by Ethan Mills, with other helpful review comments.

References

Primary (textual)

Bādarayaṇa. 1962. *Brahmasūtras*. Trans. Swami Vireswarananada. Calcutta: Advaita Ashrama.

Gautama (Aksapāda). 1967. *Nyāyasūtras: Nyāyadarśana*, text with Vātsyāyana's *Bhāṣya*. Ed. Anantalal Thakur. Mithila Institute Series. Darbhanga: Mithila Institute of Research in Sanskrit Learning.

———. 2003. *The Nyāyasūtra of Gotama*. Trans. Satish Chandra Vidyabhushana, re-edited by Raghunath Ghosh. Delhi: New Bharatiya Book Corporation.

Jayarāśi Bhaṭṭa. 1940. *Tattvopaplavasiṃha (The Lion of Upsetting All Principles)*. Ed. Sukhlalji Sanghavi and Rasikalāla Choṭālāla Parīkha. Gaekwad Oriental Series 87. Baroda: Oriental Institute.

———. *Tattvopaplavasiṃha*. 2010. Ed. Shuchita Mehta; trans. Esther Solomon. Delhi: Parimal Publications.

Nāgārjuna. 1995/2004. *Vaidalyaprakaraṇa* (Tibetan with English trans.). Ed. Fernando Tola and Carmen Dragonetti. Buddhist Tradition Series 24. Delhi: Motilal Banarsidass.

———. 1978. *Vigrahavyāvartanī (The End of Disputes)*. Translated as *The Dialectical Method of Nāgārjuna* by Kamaleswar Bhattacharya. Delhi: Motilal Banarsidass.

Śaṅkara. 1964. *Brahmasūtra-Śaṅkarabhāṣya (Adhyāsabhāṣya)*. Varanasi: Chowkhamba Vidya Bhawan.

Śrīharṣa. 1970. *Khaṇḍana-Khaṇḍa-khādy [Amassed Morsels of Refutation]*. Ed. Navikanta Jha. Kashi Sanskrit Series 197. Varanasi: Chaukhamba Sanskrit Series Office.

———. 1936/1948. *Khaṇḍanakhaṇḍakhādya*. With Five Commentaries. Ed. Sūrya Nārāyaṇa Śukla. Benares: Chowkhamba Sanskrit Series Office.

Udayana. 1970. *Brahmasūtrabhāṣya with Bhāmatī*. Ed. Kṣemarāja Śrīkṛṣnadāsa Śreṣṭhī. Mysore: Mysore Estate Publications.

———. 1973. *Nyāyakusumāñjali*. Ed. Durgadhara Jha. Granthamala Series. Varanasi: Research Institute, Sampurnanand Sanskrit Vishvavidyalaya.

———. 1996. *Nyāyakusumāñjali*. Trans. N. S. Dravid. Delhi: Indian Council of Philosophical Research.

Vācaspati Miśra. 1973. *Bhāmatī on Adhyāsābhāṣya*. Bengali trans. Srimohun Bhattacharya. Calcutta: Sanskri Pustak Bhandar.

Viśvanātha Nyāyapañcānana. 2004. *Bhāṣāparichheda with Siddhāntamuktāvalī*. Trans. Swami Madhavananda. Calcutta: Advaita Ashrama.

———. 2012. *Siddhāntamuktāvalī Kārikāvalī with Dinakarī and Rāmarudrī*. Ed. Atmaram Narayana Jere. Varanasi: Chowkhamba Krishnadas Academy.

Secondary (further reading)

Bhattacharya, Sibjiban. 1992. "Meaning and Scepticism: Some Indian Themes and Theory." In *Philosophy, Grammar, and Indology: Essays in Honour of Professor Gustav Roth*, Gustav Roth and H. S. Prasad (eds.). Delhi: Sri Satguru Publication, pp. 20–31.

Bhattacharya Chakrabarti, Bhaswati. 1987. *Absolute Skepticism, Eastern and Western*. Calcutta: Prajna.

———. 2006. "Indian Scepticism and its Refutation." In *Philosophical Concepts Relevant to Sciences in Indian Tradition*, vol. 3.iv, Pranab Kumar Sen and Prabal Kumar Sen (eds.). Delhi: Centre for Studies in Civilizations, pp. 257–262.

Bhattacharya, Ramkrishna. 2015. *Tattvopaplavāda of Jayarāśi and its Alleged Relation to Cārvāka/Lokāyata. Cārvāka 4 india. Defending Secularism and Rational Inquiry*. January 28. http://www.carvaka4india.com/2015/01/tattvopaplavavada-of-jayarasi-and-its.html. accessed 10/07/2017.

Bilimoria, P. and Mohanty, J. N. (eds). 1997. *Relativism, Suffering and Beyond: Essays in Memory of Bimal Krishna Matilal*. Delhi: Oxford University Press (paperback 2005).

Chattopadhyaya, D. P. 1997. "Scepticism Revisited: Nāgārjuna and Nyāya via Matilal." In Bilimoria and Mohanty, pp. 50–68.

Deutsch, Eliot and van Buitenan, J. A. B. (eds.). 1971. *A Source Book of Advaita Vedānta*. Honolulu: University Press of Hawai'i.

Franco, Eli. 1994. *Perception, Knowledge and Disbelief: A Study of Jayarāśi's Scepticism*. Delhi: Motilal Banarasidass.

Ganeri, Jonardon. 2009. *Philosophy of Classical India*. Delhi: Motilal Banarasidass.

Matilal, Bimal K. 2002. *Mind, Language and World: The Collected Essays of Bimal Krishna Matilal*. Ed. Jonardon Ganeri. New Delhi: Oxford University Press.

——— 1982. 'Scepticism'. In Bimal K. Matilal. *Logical and Ethcial Issues of Religious Beliefs*, pp. 42–66. Calcutta: University of Calcutta.

Mills, Ethan. 2015. "Jayarāśi's Delightful Destruction of Epistemology." *Philosophy East and West* 65(2): 498–541.
Mohanta, D.K. 1998. *Tattvopaplavasiṃha: Jayarāśibhaṭṭer Saṃśayavāda*. Kolkata: Sanskrita Sahitya Bhandar.
Mohanty, J. N. 2002. "Nyāya Theory of Doubt." In *Essays on Indian Philosophy by J. N. Mohanty*, Purushottama Bilimoria (ed.). Delhi: Oxford India Paperbacks, pp. 101–121.
Siderits, Mark. 1997. "Matilal on Nāgārjuna." In Bilimoria and Mohanty, pp. 69–92.

Chapter 8
SELF IN INDIAN PHILOSOPHY: QUESTIONS, ANSWERS, ISSUES

Michael P. Levine

What is the real nature of the self? How and why does this differ from what we ordinarily perceive, think, and treat the self to be? What role does the self, and/or knowledge about the nature of the self, play both before death and after death in relation to the enlightenment, salvation, annihilation, or more generally, to the purpose, or goal (*telos*) of oneself or of life? One can try to answer each of these questions separately, but no matter which of the questions one begins with, the remaining will soon be a relevant ingredient in any developed response. As to be expected, in Indian philosophy, as in Western philosophy, these questions are all intimately and inseparably connected to each other and with philosophical accounts about the nature of reality.

A great deal, though by no means all, of Indian philosophy can be explored by examining just these questions and the myriad answers that have been given by the different schools (*darśanas*) of philosophy. These religious and philosophical systems are seemingly constructed and developed to answer just these questions as well as to give practical guidance in achieving the goal—a goal that is the same for all persons or selves. Not only do the many different schools of thought often give conflicting or incompatible answers to one or more of the central questions, but in each of the schools themselves there are often conflicting interpretations of key doctrines and ideas. Going to the source may help in answering these questions; it should be remembered that the different schools and commentators worked from many of the same sources and yet interpreted them differently. The source material itself—the Vedas, Upaniṣads, Mahābhārata, and Buddhist Pāli canon and scripture, etc.—is often the origin and focus of the disputes.

The Rig Veda is the oldest and largest of the four groupings of "poems, prayers, lyrics, and magical charms" called the Vedas (Organ 1964, 24). It contains early reflections about the nature of the self that are developed in the later Upaniṣads. These were originally oral commentaries on the Vedas, mostly the Rig Veda, and were not redacted until several centuries later. The six traditionally classified *nāstika* (orthodox) philosophical schools (*darśanas*), later there were many more, accept the Upaniṣads as "authoritative" and supreme, even though they have different interpretations of the doctrines and develop them very differently.[1] The *nāstika* (heterodox) philosophical schools, Cārvāka (empiricist/materialist), Jaina and Buddhist, rejected the Upaniṣads as "authoritative" and took some of the central Upaniṣadic views, particularly with regard to the self, to be profoundly and importantly mistaken.

To take one example of a central dispute: historically and in terms of contemporary Buddhist thought, there have long been and continue to be dramatically different interpretations as to how the fundamental Buddhist doctrine of "no-self" or no abiding self (*anātman*) is to be understood. What does it mean, and what are its implications? Does it for instance entail the self's or rather the "no-self's" absolute annihilation, and if so what does *this* mean or amount to? And if the no-self is not annihilated then in what sense does the no-self endure? Who or what is it, if anything, that experiences *nirvāṇa* (enlightenment or liberation)—literally "blowing out" or extinguishing craving, greed, delusion, and along with it the illusion of any permanent self? What sense can be made of *nirvāṇa* apart from a self—a non-transitory locus of consciousness—in some sense experiencing it?[2] Perhaps this is at least partly why Buddhism, particularly Theravāda, emphasises a *via negativa* with regard to *nirvāṇa*—emphasising what it is not rather than conceptualising or describing what it *may* regard as essentially indescribable. On this account concepts belong and are applicable only to the conditioned world whereas *nirvāṇa* is "unconditioned" and described as such.

In the Vedic traditions *Brahman* too is regarded as indescribable. *Brahman* is what underlies all experience and as such cannot itself be experienced. It is described as "*neti, neti*" ("not this, not that"). "Unconditioned" *Brahman*, Brahman without qualities, is both the first cause and final goal. It constitutes the only Real or fully Real thing and is nothing other than the self (*ātman*) (see Organ 1964, ch. 3).

What is the "self" (orthodox schools)?

Śaṅkara's philosophical system of *Advaita Vedānta*[3] presents what has come to be widely accepted as the quintessential Vedic account of the true nature of the self as it relates to reality and liberation from the cycle of rebirth. Whether it is true to the *Vedas* is contested and there are many other influential interpretations as well. *Advaita* means non-dual and according to Śaṅkara's absolute non-dualism (or monism), Reality is "one." Knowledge that *atman* is *Brahman* ("*tat tvam asi*," "thou art that" in the "great sayings" (*mahavākyas*) of the Upaniṣads) is the key to liberation (*mokṣa*) from the cycle of rebirth (*samsara*) and its world of illusion (*māyā*). *Mokṣa* constitutes a form of immortality—perhaps best described as a kind of impersonal immortality. The required knowledge is not wholly discursive but experiential as well. What one needs to come to know is that the true nature of the self (*atman*) is identical with *Brahman* ("one without a second"), and to know this mediative self-knowledge is necessary. Ignorance of the true nature of things is what binds oneself (the illusion of a self as separate from *Brahman*) to rebirth throughout endless cosmic cycles of creation and destruction (*kalpas*). It also binds one to the phenomenal world—a world that is ultimately illusory—and results in actions that produce *karma* which connects one's past lives to one's current life. This release constitutes the state of enlightenment (*mokṣa*).

The Cārvāka school (sixth and fifth centuries BCE) rejected virtually all of the central Vedic views on the self and reality accepted in one form or another by the other Vedic schools. This school was radically empiricist, claiming that sense perception alone tells us what exists, and sceptical of any alleged knowledge not based on sense perception. The Cārvāka school was materialist, hedonistic (pleasure alone is worth pursuing) and naturalistic. It thus denied the existence of any soul or *atman* and so the identification of *ātman* with *Brahman*. It also denied rebirth, afterlife, and along with it the doctrine of *karma*. Human beings are simply made up of the four elements—earth, water, fire, and air (see Harrison 2013, chs. 1, 3; Organ 1964, 40ff.).

Atman as that which is one's true self, ultimately real and identical with *Brahman* (the only "One" genuine Reality as such) is distinguished from *jīva*. A *jīva* is a "conventional" or "empirical," though not material, self. It is the self in the physical world determined by the body it inhabits and its sense organs and mind. It is, however, still not what we ordinarily mean by an embodied self. A *jīva* is a living entity or rather that essential part of a living entity that survives death. Unlike *atman*, a *jīva* is subject to *karma* and is reborn, re-embodied in accordance with its *karma*.

The connection and continuity between various embodiments of the *jīva* is karmic. Thus, spatio-temporally separate embodiments can have the same *jīva*, though the *jīva* is physically/temporally and generally psychologically (but not karmically) separated from and discontinuous with its various bodies. They may be some psychological continuity insofar as an embodied self may be capable of knowing one's—that is, the *jīva*'s—past embodiments and lives. On Śaṅkara's account the *jīva* is "conventionally" but not ultimately real and not one's true self; this despite its being described in the *Bhagavad Gītā* and other scriptures as eternal, immutable, and indestructible. The idea of a *jīva* solves what may at first seem a serious problem. It would make little sense to suppose that *atman*, as identical to *Brahman*, could be subject to *karma* and reincarnation (*saṃsāra*). Therefore there is a need for something (the *jīva*) that does.[4]

The difficulties with *karma* are notorious and arguably insuperable. How would this non-physical form of moral causation operate across time and even lives? Does *karma* contravene the laws of nature (see Reichenbach 1988; Griffiths 1982)? Leaving aside possible difficulties with the laws of nature, supposing *karma* does operate. Morally speaking the consequences seem problematic at best. Are those apparent innocents who suffer terribly (those killed in concentrations camps or born with terrible defects) responsible for their own horrible fate due to past misdeeds? To describe or talk about *karma* in terms of naturalistic psychological states that "good" and "bad" intentions are identical with, rather than in terms of laws of nature, does not appear to address the morally problematic nature of *karma*.

More generally, *karma* seems to promise a kind of moral meritocracy where one gets, one deserves, and deserves what one gets. It may seem that such a meritocracy is, by its nature, inherently fair, just, and even desirable. Nevertheless, while it may be true that at times we want others to get what they deserve, morally speaking, we want something else for ourselves—compassion (perhaps) and an ability to learn rather than to pay for one's moral misdeeds. In ethics as in life the notion of a meritocracy is something few would actually wish for or like. Does anyone really want what he or she deserves?

It is difficult to imagine any philosophical system that places a greater emphasis on self-knowledge and its importance than these Vedic schools of thought—though the roles self-knowledge plays in Plato's, Aristotle's, Spinoza's, and Hegel's systems are in their own ways and contexts not only as important, but also significantly similar.

Mokṣa is conceived of as enlightenment and pure joy, yet giving a coherent account of what such a state could be without an identity of one's own, a personal subject experiencing it, is problematic. In fact—and much the same is true of Western monistic mystical traditions—although the state is described in various ways as a loss or merging or absorbing of self into ultimate reality (or God) as such; it is also depicted as a state the individual not only attains through hard-won self-knowledge across countless rebirths, but also as a state that the enlightened person experiences and enjoys. This is certainly the case with enlightenment (*mokṣa, nirvāṇa*) achieved when alive. What happens after death is a somewhat different story, although essentially the same troublesome questions arise. These questions are more philosophically than religiously or personally bothersome.

If enlightenment is not annihilation of the self and yet the self (a personal identifiable sense of self) as such does not survive, then who is experiencing enlightenment and why should it matter (to oneself)? If enlightenment does constitute annihilation of the self then why is this a good thing and why should one care about or desire achieving one's annihilation? For those who think that "religions say the same thing" it is worth considering the opposition between Vedic and Buddhist traditions (no personal immortality) and Western traditions that hope for "personal immortality." The notion of personal immorality is an anathema to Buddhism—a terrible thing—and it is antithetical to the Vedic traditions as well. *Mokṣa* is not a form of personal immortality.

If life is not *too* painful or "unsatisfactory" (*dukkha*), contrary to the first noble truth of Buddhism (all life or existence is suffering), then why not remain shackled, for as long as possible in the illusory phenomenal world where one at least has the illusion of identity and a life? The desirability of either *mokṣa* (*Advaita Vedānta*, Hinduism) or *nirvāṇa* (Buddhism) rests on suppositions about the character and quality of lived experience and about the role a "self" would have to play in any post-mortem state of enlightenment. These are suppositions that many not only do not share, but that philosophically speaking may appear barely, if at all, intelligible.

The issue here is not about the possibility of a disembodied existence or existence in some other body—for example, a "resurrection body." Nor, more generally, is it about the possibility of personal survival after death or immortality. These are all apparently coherent questions raised in the context of considering the nature and possibility of life after death in Western theistic (and nontheistic) thought. What is at issue here is not the value of something like eternal "life" in an enlightened state or of what a desirable form of eternal life might be. Rather, here the principal question is whether such enlightened states even make sense apart from some conventional notion of a self as an enduring centre of awareness and consciousness existing through time/space and united by memory.

Buddhism: *anātman* (no-self, or not-self, or "no abiding self")

There are those who claim the no-self theory entails that the self or rather what we mistakenly take to be a self (the *skandhas*—five ever-changing aggregates of physical and non-physical aspects) literally ceases to exist upon enlightenment. Buddhism, however, (the texts) is generally seen as explicitly denying both that the enlightened "self" ever exists (let alone persists after death), or that any real—that is, continuously existing permanent, substantial self that is the subject of experience—is ever annihilated. How could it be if no such self ever existed? Given that enlightenment appears to rely on some robust personal sense of self, it might seem that this two-fold denial about the self would forestall the kinds of concerns regarding the cogency of enlightenment raised above. Nevertheless, it is far from clear that it does.

Given that whatever Buddhism does or does not mean to deny with its theory of no-self, the personal sense of self (one's personal identity) at least seemingly necessary to a coherent account of enlightenment *is denied*. Indeed its denial is fundamental to Buddhist doctrine, since the illusion of such a self, ignorance of its true nature, along with the impermanence of everything, is alleged to be the principal source of desire and craving that leads to suffering or "unsatisfactoriness" (*dukkha*). The world, including (especially) our psycho-physical constitution, is impermanent. Such impermanence allegedly makes permanent peace of mind impossible, and so living with the illusion of a permanent self cannot be a genuine source of happiness or peace but its opposite.

This suffering or "unsatisfactoriness" is essential to "dependent co-arising"—also called or theorised as "the wheel of dependent origination or dependent arising" because, while operative, there is no proper beginning or end to it. This is the set of mutually sustaining causal relations that generates the cycle of rebirth and keeps it going. The craving that results from ignorance binds a person (the aggregate of ever-changing processes) to the cycle of Dependent Arising for countless rebirths. The mere intellectual recognition of the truth won't suffice for enlightenment unless the cravings (greed, etc.) cease; thus, Buddhism's emphasis on meditation, the practical and Noble Eight Fold Path. One who achieves *nirvāṇa* (the *arahant*) is characteristically wise, compassionate, and generous—the antithesis of one who is ignorant, greedy, and craves.

The idea that ignorance of the true nature of things, most importantly the true nature of the self as impermanent, is what underlies suffering is central to Buddhism and its worldview. This view is expounded in the Four Noble Truths, the Noble Eightfold Path as the way to the cessation of suffering, the theories of dependent origination and no-self, and the doctrines of karma and rebirth. Within that worldview it is virtually impossible to challenge either the premise that impermanence is a source of suffering or that life generally is "unsatisfactory" in the relevant sense. Nevertheless, neither of these premises appears remotely obvious. With exceptions, they are rejected not only by those who do not have such a worldview, but also by those who regard themselves as fundamentally unhappy. Neither impermanence nor the related illusory sense of self appears to be convincing as the sources of the suffering we endure. Nor of course is the first Noble Truth (translated as "life is suffering") obvious without significant qualification. It seems unacceptable even when it is explained that what is meant is not that *all* life is *always* suffering (or unsatisfactory), but rather that suffering is essential or constitutive of life as impermanent.

Furthermore, to one who does not share the Buddhist worldview, the explanations of or arguments in favour of the Noble Truths exacerbate rather than resolve their most problematic aspects. An elaboration of the Second Noble Truth, that the cause of suffering is craving, explains that delusion, greed, and aversion are symptomatic of a failure to understand the impermanent nature of things. Given that the nature of things in the world is impermanent, by craving them and greedily desiring them, one will never find in them lasting satisfaction. Suffering will therefore continue on indefinitely. But one who is disinclined to see such craving as the cause of suffering in the first place is not likely to accept this explanation in defence of the Second Noble Truth either. Undue and unmeasured "craving" and desire can certainly be a source of dissatisfaction and unhappiness, but so can many other things. In any case, why link the suffering caused by greed and inordinate desire to the impermanent nature of things? Is the fact that my delicious meal will soon be gone really a source of dissatisfaction—let alone unhappiness and suffering? Isn't the more natural view the one that sees appropriate desire as a great—a very great—and wonderful source of (at times) meaningful pleasures and satisfaction?

Buddhism does not regard the truth of the Four Noble Truths as subject to dispute. They are taken to be non-speculative and empirically verifiable. It is supposed that anyone who carefully and seriously attends to their own experience will affirm them once their content is understood, and so argument on their behalf is not needed. With regard to the claim that Buddhist doctrine is empirical it should be noted that the Buddha also claimed that the doctrine of reincarnation could be empirically proven and that he remembered (or saw) his past lives. He claimed reincarnation could be shown to be the case by means of the senses, though on his account there were more than the five senses ordinarily recognised.[5] It was an additional (sixth) sense that allegedly allowed Gautama Buddha to "empirically" verify reincarnation.

What happens to the *arahant*, one who achieves enlightenment (*nirvāṇa*), is a question that the Buddha notoriously refused to discuss. He also refused to answer in any direct way the question of whether or not there is a self. This may appear surprising given the centrality of the "no-self" (*anatta*) doctrine to Buddhism. One might think that this is because he regarded it as something that could not be meaningfully discussed because it was beyond conceptualisation. This is not Bhikkhu's (1996) view. He says the Buddha "said that to hold either that there is a self or that there is no self is to fall into extreme forms of wrong view that make the path of Buddhist practice impossible. Thus the question should be put aside" (see Bhikkhu 1996, para. 1). The suggestion here is not that there is no answer but that looking for an answer is somehow necessarily counterproductive to the goal of enlightenment; that is to the "end of suffering and stress" (see Bhikkhu 1996, para. 2). And yet the questions "why is it counterproductive? How could it be? And, why can't it be answered with a yes or no, along with an explanation?" remain. Why can't these intelligible questions about "self' get—in Bhikkhu's terms—a "categorical" (yes or no) answer, or an analytical ("defining and qualifying the terms of the question") answer? Why do they not "deserve a counter-question, putting the ball back in the questioner's court" (see Bhikkhu 1996, para. 2)? The only explanation Bhikkhu gives is that such questions belong to "The last class of question [that] consists of those that don't lead to the end of suffering and stress" (see Bhikkhu 1996, para. 2).

According to Bhikkhu (1996, para. 6) "the *anatta* teaching is not a doctrine of no-self, but a not-self strategy for shedding suffering by letting go of its cause, leading to the highest, undying happiness. At that point, questions of self, no-self, and not-self fall aside. Once there's the experience of such total freedom, where would there be any concern about what's experiencing it, or whether or not it's a self?" But the fact that once one achieves enlightenment, any concern for a self, along with questions about its nature, is otiose is hardly the point. Rather it is beside the point of asking whether a self exists and if so what it is.

The best answer to the question about whether there is a self and if so what it might be, is to give the kinds of answers that philosophical interpreters have long given. That is, there is no underlying substantial "Self" or personal identity and existence through time but merely the illusion of one. The "self" is made up of the five ever-changing *skandhas* or aggregates and these are what, in a sense, constitute the "self" and give rise to the illusion of an enduring self. Bhikkhu (1996, para. 4) says "instead of answering 'no' to the question of whether or not there is a self—interconnected or separate, eternal or not—the Buddha felt that the question was misguided to begin with. Why? No matter how you define the line between 'self' and 'other', the notion of self involves an element of self-identification and clinging, and thus suffering and stress". But this is perfectly compatible with the explanation of the "no-self" that the Buddha himself gives in terms of the *skandhas*.

Bhikkhu sees his account as coming straight from the Pāli canon, which are the earliest extant teachings of the Buddha. But so too have other interpretations of the Buddha's "refusal to answer." Some for example say that he did not want to speculate, that is to move away from what could be "empirically" ascertained. The Pāli canon contains a great deal of philosophy but it is not simply (or just) a philosophical treatise and its content is certainly not self-explanatory. Interpreting Buddhist teachings (scripture) or for that matter philosophical texts generally, is hardly ever a matter of reading what is written and taking it literally.[6]

Contemporary analytic philosophy and Buddhism

In the relatively recent and unprecedented engagement of analytic contemporary philosophy of mind and consciousness with Indian, especially Buddhist philosophy, the emphasis has been on extracting or separating the naturalistic elements or genuine philosophical insights from the religious ones. The general view is that once one gets rid of the "hocus-pocus" (Flanagan 2011) in Buddhism, there remains an "empirically responsible" and materially grounded philosophy that is useful or could be useful, in helping to explain subjective consciousness and the first-person stance; the sense of self we have.[7] One question about this approach is whether Buddhism naturalised is Buddhism at all. It is a question that does not seem to concern those like Flanagan whose interest in Buddhism is focused on a specific set of analytic and philosophical issues related to consciousness. Some deny that Buddhism is fundamentally a religion at all. Whatever the merits of this approach turn out to be, it's worth considering whether, philosophically speaking, there is not more of value, and a different kind of value, in these traditions than appears to be supposed by those like Flanagan who emphasise a naturalistic (if not scientistic) stance.

This is not to suggest that such insight is usually or even often to be found in the superstitious or magical elements—though there are sound intellectual reasons why one should not dismiss myth, any more than fiction, as useless or harmful, or as lacking insight and even truth. Rather, it is to point out that there is wisdom and value in some of the views, doctrines, and associated practices that constitute the practical or religious side of the quest for self-knowledge and enlightenment—Vedic or Buddhist. It is not enough to merely acknowledge this or suggest it is assumed. Articulating such insights may require as much if not more skill than that of the analytic philosopher who decontextualises and mines Indian philosophy for views helpful and congenial to their own. In any case, approaches like those of Flanagan, Ganeri, Siderits, and others, whether they mean to or not, do not rule out such Indian and Eastern philosophical systems being insightful and useful in these other, more traditional ways.[8]

Notes

1 (1) *Sāṃkhya*: atheistic and dualist; (2) Yoga: aligned with Sāṃkhya, focuses on meditation and techniques leading to liberation (*mokṣa*); (3) *Nyāya* (*Nyāya Sūtras*): explores logic and sources of knowledge; (4) *Vaiśeṣika*: empiricist and atomistic; (5) *Mīmāṃsā*: emphasised practice over asceticism in accordance with strict adherence to the Vedas; (6) Vedanta: literally the end of the Vedas (last part of the Vedas) split into different schools including Advaita, Viśiṣṭādvaita, and Dvaita and came to dominate Hindu thought.

2 There is no shortage of fine introductory, intermediate, and advanced texts that philosophically, historically, and from religious and religious studies perspectives discuss the nature of self and associated issues in Indian thought. (See, for example, Organ's (1964) historical introduction.) The introductions generally explain and endorse various established interpretations with more advanced texts presenting arguments for theories of the self in relation to accounts of reality, *karma*, rebirth, and *mokṣa* (or *nirvāṇa*) as these are all intrinsic to accounts of the nature of self. Recent advanced texts, drawing on Eastern as well as Western philosophical sources, focus mainly on Buddhist philosophy and they do so in ways unprecedented in Western analytic philosophy and phenomenology. These overlap and

synthesise with contemporary work in the philosophy of mind and consciousness. See, for example, Ganeri 2012; and Siderits *et al.* 2011.

3 See the *Māṇḍūkya* Upaniṣad, and his commentary on the *Vedānta Sūtra*. Also see Deutsch (1969).

4 See Harrison (2013, 87–88). She says (88): "Śaṅkara claims that each *jīva* is the expression of a confused *ātman* that has lost sight of its genuine nature."

5 In Buddhism there are six internal–external (organ–object) pairs of sense bases (*Āyatana*). Mental activity (mind and mental objects pairing) is a sixth sense. Hamilton (2001, 53) says: "six senses, including one relating to non-sensory mental activity, are recognised in Buddhism and other Indian schools of thought." Cf. Thanissaro Bhikkhu (www.accesstoinsight.org).

6 Bhikkhu continues with what is patently his own didactic interpretation. It may be right, but it is an extrapolation from and not literally in the Pāli texts. He says, "This holds as much for an interconnected self, which recognises no 'other,' as it does for a separate self. If one identifies with all of nature, one is pained by every felled tree. It also holds for an entirely 'other' universe, in which the sense of alienation and futility would become so debilitating as to make the quest for happiness—one's own or that of others—impossible. For these reasons, the Buddha advised paying no attention to such questions as "Do I exist?" or "Don't I exist?" for however you answer them, they lead to suffering and stress" (Bhikkhu 1996, para. 4). Why would identifying with all of nature suggest that one would be "pained by every felled tree"?

7 Also see Ganeri (2012). Logicians say that one man's *modus ponens* ("If P, then Q. P. Therefore, Q.") is another man's *modus tollens* ("If P, then Q. Not Q. Therefore, not P."). Without denying the reality of either hocus or pocus it can also be said that one man's hocus-pocus may be another's reasoned demonstration. In any case, and perhaps beside the point, one would have to be myopic (in the grip of *māyā*) to deny that analytic philosophy has its share of magicians.

8 My thanks to the Indian Council for Cultural Relations (Fellowship) (ICCR); University of Delhi; Institute for Advanced Studies, Shimla; The Institute for Advanced Studies, Durham University, Senior Fellowship.

Bibliography

Bahm, A. 1968. "Is There a Soul or No Soul? The Buddha Refused to Answer. Why?" In P. T. Raju and A. Castell (eds.) *East–West Studies on the Problem of the Self*, 133–141. The Hague: Martinus Nijhoff.

Bhikkhu, T. 1996. *No-self or Not-self?* Available from: www.accesstoinsight.org/lib/authors/thanissaro/notself2.html, accessed 13 December 2013.

Bhikkhu, T. 1999. *Mind like Fire Unbound: An Image in the Early Buddhist Discourse*, 4th edn. Available at: www.accesstoinsight.org/lib/authors/thanissaro/likefire/, accessed 13 December 2013.

Billington, R. 1997. *Understanding Eastern Philosophy*. London: Routledge.

Black, B. 2007. *The Character of the Self in Ancient India: Priests, Kings, and Women in the Early Upanisads*. Albany: State University of New York Press.

Chakrabarti, Kisor K. 1999. *Classical Indian Philosophy of Mind: The Nyāya Dualist Tradition*. Albany: State University of New York Press.

Collins, S. 1982. *Selfless Persons: Imagery and Thought in Theravāda Buddhism*. Cambridge: Cambridge University Press.

Deutsch, E. 1969. *Advaita Vedānta: A Philosophical Reconstruction*. Honolulu: East–West Center Press.

Duerlinger, J. 1993. "Reductionist and Nonreductionist Theories of Persons in Indian Buddhist Philosophy." *Journal of Indian Philosophy* 21(1): 79–101.

Flanagan, O. 2011. *The Bodhisattva's Brain: Buddhism Naturalized*. Cambridge, MA: MIT Press.

Flood, G. 1996. *An Introduction to Hinduism*. Cambridge: Cambridge University Press.

Ganeri, J. 2012. *The Self: Naturalism, Consciousness, and the First-Person Stance*. Oxford: Oxford University Press.

Gethin, R. 1998. *The Foundations of Buddhism*. Oxford: Oxford University Press.

Giles, J. 1993. "The No-Self Theory: Hume, Buddhism and Personal Identity." *Philosophy East and West* 43(2): 175–200.

Griffiths, P. J. 1982. "Notes Towards a Critique of Buddhist Karmic Theory." *Religious Studies* 18(3): 277–291.

Griffiths, P. J. 1994. *On Being Buddha: The Classical Doctrine of Buddhahood*. Albany: State University of New York Press.

Hamilton, S. 2001. *Indian Philosophy: A Very Short Introduction*. Oxford: Oxford University Press.

Harrison, V. S. 2013. *Eastern Philosophy: The Basics*. London and New York: Routledge.

Harvey, P. 1995. *The Selfless Mind: Personality, Consciousness and Nirvāṇa in Early Buddhism*. Richmond: Curzon Press.

Horner, I. B. 1936. *The Early Buddhist Theory of Man Perfected: A Study of the Arahan Concept and of the Implications of the Aim to Perfection in Religious Life*. London: Routledge & Kegan Paul.

King, R. 1999. *Indian Philosophy: An Introduction to Hindu and Buddhist Thought*. Edinburgh: Edinburgh University Press.

Laumakis, S. J. 2008. *An Introduction to Buddhist Philosophy*. Cambridge: Cambridge University Press.

Levine, M. P. 2016. "Does Comparative Philosophy Have a Fusion Future?" *Confluence* 4: 209–237.

Olivelle, P. 1998. *The Early Upaniṣads: Annotated Text and Translation*. New York: Oxford University Press.

Organ, T. 1964. *The Self in Indian Philosophy*. The Hague: Mouton and Co.

Ovens, M. (ed.). 2013. *What is Comparative Philosophy?* Cambridge: Cambridge Scholars Press.

Potter, K. (ed.). 1983. *Encyclopedia of Indian Philosophies*. Delhi: Motilal Banarsidass.

Radhakrishnan, S. and Moore, C. A. (eds.). 1989. *A Sourcebook in Indian Philosophy*. Princeton: Princeton University Press.

Reichenbach, B. 1988. "The Law of *Karma* and the Principle of Causation." *Philosophy East/West* 38(4): 399–410.

Siderits, M. 2003. *Personal Identity and Buddhist Philosophy: Empty Persons*. Aldershot: Ashgate.

Siderits, M., Thompson, E., and Zahavi, D. 2011. *Self, No Self?* Oxford: Oxford University Press.

Chapter 9
CONTENTS OF CONSCIOUSNESS: PERCEPTION[1]

Monima Chadha

All the classical schools of Indian philosophy accept perception (*pratyakṣa*) as a source of knowledge (*pramāṇa*) par excellence, although there is much disagreement about its nature, kinds, and objects. The problems of perception are generally discussed in the Indian context with reference to three main theories: direct realism, representationalism, and phenomenalism. The Nyāya, Sāṃkhya and Mīmāṃsā, and the early Buddhists (Vaibhāsikas) are representatives of the direct realist stance; the Buddhist Abhidharma schools advocate the latter two theories, among them the Sautrāntikas adopt representationalism and the later Yogācāra argue for a full-blown phenomenalism. The debates among these schools centered on questions familiar to Western epistemologists, for example, does all perception involve a sensory connection with an object that is responsible for providing its content or intentionality (*nirākāra-vāda*, Nyāya), or is the content of perception internal to itself (*sākāra-vāda*, Yogācāra)? Is the content restricted to individuals or are universals and relations also perceived? Is the sensory core *all* there is to the content of a perceptual experience? Is the *content* of a perceptual experience restricted to being unconceptualized (*nirvikalpaka*), or can any part of it be conceptualized (*savikalpaka*) as well? How do we differentiate veridical perception from illusions and hallucinations? How are illusions to be explained?

This list is not exhaustive; there are other issues that exercised the mind of classical Indian philosophers.[2] However, we cannot discuss all the issues that exercised the mind of ancient Indian epistemologists. I will begin by listing the definitions of perception given by the classical Indian schools representing the three main theories mentioned of direct realism, representationalism, and phenomenalism. This will be followed by a discussion of the controversial classical Indian epistemology issue—whether perception is conceptualized or not? Finally, I will give the reader a flavor of the analytic techniques at work in classical and contemporary debate in Indian philosophy.

1 Definitions of perception

The most comprehensive definition of perception representing the direct realist view in classical Indian philosophy is offered in Gautama's *Nyāya-sūtra* 1.1.4:

> Perception is a cognition which arises from the contact of the sense organ and object and is not impregnated by words, is unerring, and well-ascertained.

Expectedly, each part of this definition has raised controversy and criticism. If perception is a cognition (and non-erroneous), then it is a state of knowledge, rather than a means to knowing. How does that constitute a primary means of knowledge? Some Naiyāyika commentators, Vācaspati Miśra (*c*. 900–980 CE) and Jayanta Bhaṭṭa (*c*. ninth century CE) among them, suggest that the *sūtra* is to be understood by adding to it the term 'from which (*yataḥ*),' since the preceding *sūtras* indicate that Gautama's formulation of this *sūtra* was intended to define the instrument of a valid perceptual cognition. Another issue has been the interpretation of the word 'contact'. In what sense are the eye and the ear, the sense organs for vision and auditory perception, respectively, in contact with their objects? Here a careful look at the term '*sannikarṣa*,' generally translated as contact, helps resolve the issue *Sannikarṣa* literally means 'drawing near,' and can be interpreted as being in *close* connection with or in the *vicinity of*. Thus perception is that which arises out of a close connection between the sense organ and its object.

More substantial debates on the nature of perception focus on the adjectives in the latter part of the *sūtra*: non-verbal (*avyapadeśyam*), non-erroneous or non-deviating (*avyabhichāri*), and well-ascertained or free from doubt (*vyavasāyātmaka*). There is some disagreement among the Naiyāyika commentators about the interpretations of the adjectives *non-verbal* and *well-ascertained*. Vātsyāyana, in his commentary on the *Nyāya-sūtra*, argues that the adjectives non-verbal and well-ascertained are really part of the definition; non-verbal to point out that perceptual knowledge is not associated with words (Bhartṛhari, the famous Grammarian, on the other hand, holds that awareness is necessarily constituted by words and apprehended through them) and well-ascertained to affirm that perceptual knowledge is only of a definite particular and specifically excludes situations in which the perceiver may be in doubt whether a perceived object 'a' is an *F* or a G. Vācaspati Miśra argues that the adjective well-ascertained need not be used to exclude the so-called perception in the form of doubt, as doubtful knowledge, being invalid, is already excluded by the adjective non-erroneous. Rather, the term *vyavasāyātmaka* stands for determinate perceptual judgment. Thus understood, the adjectives *non-verbal* and *determinate* seem to be complementary; a piece of *non-verbal* perceptual knowledge cannot be said to be, at the same time, *determinate*. Vācaspati Miśra posits that these two adjectives indicate two different forms of perceptual cognition and are not to be regarded as its defining characteristics. According to him, Gautama included these adjectives to identify two *kinds* of perceptual knowledge: *avyapadeśyam* indicates non-conceptual or non-verbal perception and *vyavasāyātmaka* indicates conceptual or determinate perceptions. He contends that by the term non-verbal, Gautama refutes the Grammarian view and includes non-conceptual perception and, by the term well-ascertained, he refutes the Buddhist view and includes conceptual or judgmental perceptions as valid.

The Sautrāntika definition of perception which embodies the representationalist view in the Buddhist tradition is crystallized in the definition given by Vasubandhu (fourth century CE), "Perception is a cognition [that arises] from that object [which is represented therein]" (Frauwallner 1957, 120). The Sautrāntika representationalism follows directly from the doctrine of momentariness together with the belief that a cause necessarily precedes its effect. Perceptual consciousness arises in the second moment as an effect, when the cause (the object of cognition) has become the past and is no longer in existence. The Sautrāntika philosophers regard sensory perception as a successive process. For example, in the case of visual perception the visual object exists in the first moment, conditioning the arising of the visual consciousness of that object in the second moment, which in turn conditions the mental consciousness of the very same object in the third moment. This definition and the account of the perceptual process has been criticized on the grounds that, contrary to their own definition, consciousness can arise without an object. Vasubandhu claims that even though the object of cognition does not exist at the present moment of mental consciousness, its recollection is possible because "from the [previous] *citta* [that object-field], another thought of recollection [now] arises through the process of a [progressive] transformation of the serial continuity" (Dhammajoti 2007, 160). But then it appears that the perceptual process is clearly a case of retrospection. So, why call it a perception? The Sautrāntika claims that it qualifies as a perception because there is exact correspondence between what is known in the third moment when mental consciousness arises and the sensory object-field in the first moment. The cognitive object (*ālambana*) in the present retrospection is an exact mental representation, that is, has the same appearance (*ākāra*) as the former object field.

The direct realist and the representationalist views are criticized by the later Yogācāra philosophers on the grounds that the object of perceptual consciousness is an agglomerated collection of atoms, and since the agglomerated form has only a conceptual existence, it is unreal, it cannot serve as the basis or a condition of sensory consciousness. According to the Yogācāra, although the external object does not exist in the present moment in which the sensory consciousness arises, it exists as the cause (*ālambana pratyaya*) of the mental activity in the succeeding moment. So, the object of perceptual consciousness is an internal form (*ākāra*) which resembles the external object and serves as the object of cognition.

The later Yogācāra philosopher Diṅnāga (*c.* 480–540 CE) defines perception simply as a cognition "devoid of conceptual construction (*kalpanāpodhaṃ*)". There are two important implications of this definition. First, perception is non-conceptual in nature; no seeing is seeing-as, because that necessarily involves intervention of conceptual constructs, which contaminate the pristine given. Perception is mere awareness of real particulars without any identification or association with words for, according to Diṅnāga, such association always results in falsification of the object. Referents of the words are universals which, for the Buddhist, are not real features of the world. Second, Diṅnāga's definition only indicates a phenomenological feature of perception; it says nothing about its origin and does not imply that it arises from the contact of a sense faculty with the object. Therefore, for the Yogācāra phenomenalist, the object that appears in perceptual cognition need not be an external physical object, but a form that arises within consciousness itself. Dharmakīrti adds a further qualification to Diṅnāga's definition; perception is that which is free from conceptual construction and errors.

2 The Nyāya–Buddhist controversy: is perception conceptual or purely non-conceptual?

The distinction between non-conceptual and conceptual was first drawn by Diṅnāga, who, as explained above, contended that all perception is non-conceptual because what constitutes seeing things as they really *are* must be free from any conceptual construction. The claim is that a verbal report of proper perception is strictly impossible, for such a report requires conceptualization, which is not perceptual in character. The object of perception, 'the given', in its intrinsic nature is inexpressible. The objects of perception, the real particulars (*svalakṣaṇas*), do not, as Quine would say, wear their names on their sleeves, they come to be associated with names as we superimpose categories and concepts on the given. Furthermore, the sense faculty cannot grasp a concept or a name; if I have never tasted absinthe before I first encounter it, I cannot taste it *as absinthe*, though I can taste IT; a gustatory awareness can only grasp a taste present in the gustatory field, it cannot grasp its name. The Buddhists argue that a perceiver apprehends only the real particulars, *arbitrarily* imposes concepts/words on them, and believes, mistakenly, that these are *really there* in the objects. The conceptual awareness conceals its own imaginative quality and, because it results directly from experience, the perceiver takes it to be a perceptual experience. The perceiver fails to notice that imagination is involved and mistakenly thinks that he really perceives the constructed world. From the Buddhist standpoint, therefore, a perceiver can only perceive real particulars, so that any perceptual experience is always and only at the non-conceptual level.

The Nyāya view on this particular issue evolves in response to the Buddhist account of perception. The Nyāya regard perception as a cognitive episode triggered by causal interaction between a sense faculty and an object. This interaction first results in a sensory impression, nothing more than mere physiological change. This sensory impression is a necessary first step in the process of perception and is invariably followed by a structured awareness leading to conceptually loaded perception. A cognition that is independent of preliminary sensory awareness cannot result in a perceptual judgment. The first awareness does not destroy the perceptual character of the second; rather, it facilitates this subsequent awareness. Non-conceptual perception is an indispensable causal factor for generation of conceptual perception, although memory, concepts, and collateral information may also be required. It is important to note that the Nyāya notion of *vikalpa* (in their distinction of *nir-vikalpa* and *sa-vikalpa*) is different from that of the Buddhists. Unlike the latter, the Naiyāyikas do not think of *vikalpa*-s as mental creations or imaginative constructions but as objectively real properties and features of objects. *Vikalpa* in this sense indicates the operation of judging and synthesizing rather than imagining or constructing. Thus conceptual perceptions *truly* represent the structure of reality. Of the five types of concepts (*vikalpa*-s) recognized by the Buddhists: *nāma* (word), *jāti* (universal), *guṇa* (quality), *kriyā* (action), and *dravya* (substance), the Naiyāyikas regard all but the first *vikalpa* as categories of reality (Mondal 1982, 364). Unlike the Grammarians, the Nyāya schools do not accept the objective reality of words; words are not inherent to the object presented in perception. Rather, the Naiyāyikas hold that the relation between word and object is created by convention in a linguistic community. Although a concept is associated with a word (*nāma-vikalpa*) by means of a convention, it is not merely a fabrication. For example, when someone brings a garlic clove near my nose and teaches me by pointing to it that it is called garlic, then subsequently confronted with the garlicky odor and a similar clove, I can see it and smell it *as garlic*. Thus perceptual awareness includes knowledge of words but, insofar as it is perceptual awareness, it is brought about by sensory contact with the object and its properties which exist independently of words.

The Buddhists reject this argument on the basis that the conventional meaning of a word relates the word with the concept or the universal. Universals or concepts cannot be objects of our perception; they cannot be sensed. Universals, attributes, and concepts are theoretical constructs for the Buddhists; what is sensed is the actual object, the real particular, the ultimate existent. The Buddhists offer two arguments in favor of the claim that only particulars are real. First, knowledge by means of words or verbal testimony is very different from perceptual knowledge, for what we are aware of when we hear the words "garlic is pungent" is very different from what we are phenomenologically aware of when we smell garlic; words do not denote or stand in for actual objects and can be uttered in the absence of any objects, but perception cannot arise in the absence of objects. Second, the particulars are real or existent because they have causal efficacy (*arthakriyāsāmarthya*). Only particular real garlic can flavor one's food or ruin it, but the universal garlichood cannot do any of these; in this sense, only the particulars are real for they fulfill the purposes (*artha*) of humans.

The foregoing discussion shows that the epistemological debate between the Buddhists and the Naiyāyikas regarding the nature of perception rests on, and brings to the fore, their metaphysical disagreement about the nature of universals (Chadha 2015). The Naiyāyikas are realists about universals; universals are objective features of the world that impress themselves upon minds; they are not mere figments of our imagination. The Naiyāyikas hold that particulars are qualified propertied wholes and we directly perceive them *as they are*, without any kind of manipulation or imposition; we do not impose universals on property-less real particulars, rather we find stable, durable, relational wholes in reality that do not require any imposition or manipulation. They argue that there is no evidence of a world of bare particulars, as claimed by the Buddhists. Therefore conceptual or determinate perception does not involve distortion of reality; rather it presents things as they really are. To see a piece of sandalwood as it *really* is, we do not need to see the sandalwood as a colorless, odorless pure particular; indeed, since the piece of sandalwood is *really* brown and *really* fragrant, to see it as a propertied whole is to see it as it *really is*.

The idea that the world consists of propertied particulars seems to put pressure on the notion of non-conceptual perception. If there are no indeterminate particulars, what is the object of indeterminate perception? Indeed some Navya-Nyāya thinkers hold that the raw data of perception ('real particulars' in the Buddhists sense) is too inchoate and elusive to count as objects of knowledge. Recently, Arindam Chakrabarti (2000), a prominent contemporary Navya-Nyāya thinker, offered seven reasons for altogether eliminating nonconceptual or immaculate perceptions, as he calls them, from Nyāya epistemology in an attempt to understand the "deeper relation between direct realism and concept-enriched perception." Chakrabarti's skepticism about non-conceptual perception as a cognitive state stems from the fact that we cannot assign an intentional role to the object of indeterminate perception because the object of non-conceptual perception is incapable of being apperceived or directly intuited in any fashion. Chakrabarti's gauntlet has been picked by several Nyāya enthusiasts (Phillips 2001 and 2004; Chadha 2001, 2004 and 2006) and defenders of Buddhist doctrine (Siderits 2004). This debate brings to the fore an important feature of non-conceptual perception first highlighted by Gaṅgeśa, suggesting that while there is no direct, apperceptive evidence for non-conceptual perception, it is posited as the best explanation for the availability of the qualifier (property, feature), since the cognizing subject is not immediately aware of the object of non-conceptual perception. Phillips (2001,105) presents Gaṅgeśa's argument for the inclusion of non-conceptual perception as an essential part of Nyāya epistemology:

> [I]t [*nirvikalpa pratyakṣa*] is posited by the force of the following inference as the first step of a two step argument. "The perceptual cognition 'A cow' (for example) is generated by a cognition of the qualifier, since it is a cognition of an entity as qualified (by that qualifier appearing) like an inference". The second step takes a person's first perception of an individual (Bessie, let us say) as a cow (i.e., as having some such property) as the perceptual cognition figuring as the inference's subject (*pakṣa*) such that the cognizer's memory not informed by previous cow experience could not possibly provide the qualifier cowhood. The qualifier has to be available, and the best candidate seems to be its perception in the raw, a qualifier (cowhood), that is to say, not (as some are wont to misinterpret the point) as divorced from its *qualificandum* (Bessie) but rather as neither divorced nor joined, and, furthermore, not as qualified by another qualifier (such as being-a-heifer) but rather just the plain, unadorned entity. In the particular example, the entity is the universal, cowhood, or being-a-cow, although, again, it would not be grasped as a universal. Or as anything except itself.

The Navya-Nyāya notion of non-conceptual perception differs from that of the Buddhists in many respects, two of which are very important. First, according to Navya-Naiyāyikas, there is no apperceptive evidence for non-conceptual perception, unlike the Buddhists, who contend that conception-free awareness is necessarily self-aware. The Navya-Naiyāyikas, as is obvious from the quotation above, emphasize that the evidence for a non-conceptual sensory grasp of universals comes in the form of an inference. Second, according to Navya-Nyāya, the object of non-conceptual perception is a qualifier (concept), although not given as that in the first instance, but not a bare particular as the Buddhists hypothesize. It is, as the above quotation explains, posited by the force of an inference; the 'bare object' of non-conceptual perception *becomes* the qualifier in a resultant determinate perception. While this does not satisfactorily address Chakrabarti's concern that lack of apperceptive evidence implies that the subject cannot assign an intentional role to the object of non-conceptual perception, Chadha (2006) argues that the subject's not being in a position to assign an intentional role to the object of non-conceptual perception is no hindrance to the intentionality of non-conceptual perception itself. Non-conceptual perception is awareness *of* a "non-particular individual" (Chakrabarti 1995) and can be assigned the intentional role of a qualifier in virtue of the recognitional abilities acquired by the subject on the basis of the perceptual episode. The subject *sees* a non-particular individual but, since there is no apperceptive or conscious awareness, the subject does not see it *as* an instance of a universal or a qualifier. Chadha explicates Gaṅgeśa's insight that a qualifier is given as a non-particular individual, neither divorced from nor joined to the *qualificandum* and, therefore, it is wrong to suggest that lack of apperceptive evidence implies that non-conceptual perception is not an intentional perceptual state.

Notes

1 Portions of this chapter are taken from the author's "Perceptual Experience and Concepts in Classical Indian Philosophy," *The Stanford Encyclopedia of Philosophy (Winter 2010 Edition)*, Edward N. Zalta (ed.), http://plato.stanford.edu/archives/win2010/entries/perception-india/.

2 For a thorough treatment see Matilal (1986).

Bibliography

Texts in English translation

Akṣapāda Gautama, *Nyāya-Sūtra*, with Vātsyāyana's *Nyāyabhāṣya*, Uddyotakara's *Nyāyavaarttika*, and Udayana's *Pariśuddhi*, A. Thakur (ed. and trans.), vol. 1. Darbangha: Mithila Institute, 1967.

Bhartrhari, *Vākyapadīya*, K. V. Abhyankar and V. P. Limaye (eds.). Poona University, 1965.

Gaṅgeśa, *Tattvacintāmaṇi*, in *Epistemology of Perception: Gaṅgeśa's Tattvacintāmaṇi, Jewel of Reflection on the Truth (About Epistemology): The Perception Chapter (Pratyakṣa-khaṇḍa)*, transliterated text, translation, and philosophical commentary by Stephen H. Phillips and N. S. Ramanuja Tatacharya. Treasury of the Indic Sciences. New York: American Institute of Buddhist Studies, 2004.

Kumārila Bhaṭṭa, "The 'Determination of Perception' Chapter of Ślokavārttika." In *A Hindu Critique of Buddhist Epistemology: The 'Determination of Perception' Chapter of Kumārila Bhaṭṭa's Ślokavārttika*, commentary by J. Taber (trans.). RoutledgeCurzon Hindu Studies Series. New York: RoutledgeCurzon, 2005.

Uddyotakara, *Nyāya-Vārtika*, in *The Nyāya-Sūtras of Gauṭama: With the Nyāya-sūtra-Bhāṣya of Vātsyāyana and the Nyāya-Vārtika of Uddyotakara*, Gangānāṭha Jhā (trans.). Delhi: Motilal Banarsidass, 1984.

Uddyotakara, *Nyāya-Sūtra-Bhāṣya*, translations from the introductory commentary on *Nyāya-Sūtra-Bhāṣya*, Arindam Chakrabarti (trans.), published as an appendix to A. Chakrabarti, "The Nyāya Proofs for the Existence of the Soul," *Journal of Indian Philosophy* 10(1982): 211–238.

Vācaspati Miśra, *Nyāyavārttikatātparyaṭīkā*, Anantlal Thaur (ed.). New Delhi: Indian Council of Philosophical Research, 1996.

Vasubandhu, *Viṃśatikā-Vṛtti, Triṃśatika, and Tri-Svabhāva-Nirdeśa*, Thomas Kochumuttom (trans.), in *A Buddhist Doctrine of Experience: A New Translation and Interpretation of the Works of Vasubandhu the Yogācārin*. Delhi: Motilal Banarsidass, 1982.

General works

Appelbaum, D. 1982. "A Note on Pratyakṣa in Advaita Vedānta." *Philosophy East and West* 32(2): 201–205.

Bhatt, Govardhan P. 1989. *The Basic Ways of Knowing*. Delhi: Motilal Banarsidass.

Bilimoria, P. 1980. "Perception (*Pratyakṣa*) in Advaita Vedānta." *Philosophy East and West* 30(1): 35–44.

Chadha, M. 2001. "Perceptual Cognition: A Nyāya-Kantian Approach." *Philosophy East and West* 51(2): 197–209.

Chadha, M. 2004. "Perceiving Particulars-as-Such Is Incoherent: A Reply to Mark Siderits." *Philosophy East and West* 54(3): 382–389.

Chadha, M. 2006. "Yet Another Attempt to Salvage Pristine Perceptions!" *Philosophy East and West* 56(2): 333–342.

Chadha, M. 2015. "On Knowing Universals: The Nyāya Way." *Philosophy East and West* 65(2): 287–302.

Chakrabarti, A. 1995. "Non-Particular Individuals." In P. K. Sen and R. R. Verma (eds.), *The Philosophy of P. F. Strawson*. New Delhi: Indian Council of Philosophical Research, pp. 124–144.

Chakrabarti, A. 2000. "Against Immaculate Perception: Seven Reasons for Eliminating Nirvikalpaka Perceptions from Nyāya." *Philosophy East and West* 50(1): 1–8.

Chakrabarti, A. 2001. "Reply to Stephen Phillips." *Philosophy East and West* 51(1): 114–115.

Chakrabarti, A. 2004. "Seeing without Recognizing? More on Denuding Perceptual Content." *Philosophy East and West* 54(3): 365–367.

Dhammajoti, B., KL. 2007. *Abhidharma Doctrines and Controversies on Perception*. Hong Kong: Centre of Buddhist Studies.

Dreyfus, G. B. J. 1997. *Recognizing Reality: Dharmakīrti's Philosophy and Its Tibetan Interpretations*. New York: State University of New York Press.

Feldman, J. 2005. "Vasubandhu's Illusion Argument and the Parasitism of Illusion upon Veridical Experience." *Philosophy East and West* 55(4): 529–541.

Gupta, B. 1991. *Perceiving in Advaita Vedanta: Epistemological Analysis and Interpretation*. London: Associated University Presses.

Matilal, B. K. 1986. *Perception: An Essay on Classical Indian Theories of Knowledge*. Oxford: Clarendon Press.

Mohanty, J. N. 2000. *Classical Indian Philosophy*. Lanham, MD: Rowman & Littlefield.

Mondal, P. K. 1982. "Some Aspects of Perception in Old Nyāya." *Journal of Indian Philosophy* 10(4): 357–376.

Phillips, S. H. 2001. "There's Nothing Wrong with Raw Perception: A Response to Chakrabarti's Attack on Nyāya's 'Nirvikalpaka Pratyakṣa'." *Philosophy East and West* 51(1): 104–113.

Phillips, S. H. 2004. "Perceiving Particulars Blindly: Remarks on a Nyāya-Buddhist Controversy." *Philosophy East and West* 54(3): 389–403.

Siderits, M. 2004. "Perceiving Particulars: A Buddhist Defense." *Philosophy East and West* 54(3): 367–382.

Thrasher, A. W. 1993. *The Advaita Vedanta of Brahma-Siddhi*. Delhi: Motilal Banarsidas.

Wezler, A. and Motegi, S. (eds.). 1998. *Yuktidīpikā: The Most Significant Commentary on the Sāṃkhyakārikā*, vol. 1. Alt und Neu-Indische Studien 41. Stuttgart: Franz Steiner Verlag.

Chapter 10
INDIAN MATERIALISM[1]

Raghunath Ghosh

Cārvāka/Lokāyata

In Indian philosophy we find the seeds of materialism in a stray manner from the Vedic period to the modern age, and hence materialism is not neglected in Indian philosophy (Bilimoria 1998). There is a common complaint that Indian philosophy has placed undue emphasis on spiritualism, while all but marginalizing materialism.[2] In this chapter it will be demonstrated that the material and worldly side of life is not at all neglected in the Indian intellectual tradition. In other words, a naturalist worldview is not anathema to traditional thinking; in fact, such a worldview is developed quite consciously in Śruti, particularly the Upaniṣads also (Riepe 1961, 32).

Though the seeds of materialism are to be found in many places in different systems of thought and critiques, a more robust form of materialism is developed and systematized by the reconstructive Cārvāka school taking up various established views that had inclinations towards a naturalized universe. (There may have been more than one school of Cārvāka, but this is a scholastic debate that need not detain us here.) The Cārvākas however left behind no texts of their own, and thus much of the foundational thinking underpinning their distinctive system is reconstructed from fragments, mostly referenced in adversarial texts addressing arguments of the materialists. One such compilation is the chapter titled *Cārvakādarśana* in the celebrated 'compendium of all philosophies,' *Sarvadarśanasaṃgraha* (SDS, cited here by paragraph number), by one Mādhavācarya, who lived around the fourteenth century CE (Mādhavācarya 1961, 1905, 1924/1978). The author presents a rather modest view without any attempt to defend or decisively refute the Cārvāka *epistemé*.

Etymologically speaking, the derivative meaning of the term '*cārvāka*' is nuanced in different ways. First, the term or trope comes from two words – '*cāru*' (sweet) and '*vāk*' (word). Those who favor what is called sweet words to the common people due to their palatability are called Cārvākas. Second, the term '*cārvāka*' is derived from the verb – '*carv/carvā*' (meaning 'to chew', 'chewing'). Those who *chew* and spit out (i.e. absolutely refute) the theories in respect of scriptural authority, merit, demerit, the transcendental realities such as gods, God, liberation, etc. are called Cārvākas. In this context, the term 'chewing' signifies and underscores destroying or smashing—i.e. dissimulating or deconstructing—with the help of logic. Third, some are of the opinion that the appellation Cārvāka comes from the name of a great teacher called Cārvī. Whatever may be its derivative meaning, Cārvāka is well known as a pure materialistic school of thought in the Indian context. The populist term 'Lokāyata', which designates something akin to people's philosophical appetite, began to be used interchangeably with 'Cārvāka' around the sixth century CE to underscore the school's firm commitment to 'this-worldly worlding', or in more derogatory tone, the undergirding hedonism implicit in the amoral folly of materialism (Gokhale 2015; Bhattacharya 2012; 2016; 2017).

In Indian philosophy the term '*bhūta*' may be taken as a Sanskrit rendering of the term 'matter' from which the term 'materialism' comes into being. The Cārvākas are of the opinion that there are only four matters (*bhūtacatuṣṭaya*), namely, earth (*kṣiti*), water (*ap*), light (*tejas*), and air (*marut*), excluding *ākāśa* or space, because it is not realizable through perception (*tatra pṛthivyādīni bhūtāni catvāri tattvāni* (SDS #7)) (Mādhavācarya 1961, 2; 1924, 2, line 23[3]). Everything in the material world is constituted out of the four matters or elemental materials, and hence there is the non-existence of self that is otherwise conceived and conceptualized by most of the orthodox schools. Apart from the combination of the four matters, there is nothing that we call the self, and hence the self, if it is anything, is constituted of the four matters described. Just as the color red comes into being through the combination of factors like nut, lime, pigments, etc., and just as a kind of liquid substance called *mada* comes from a particular tree, the existence of the self may also be thought of as being nothing other than the four matters and their combination. Had there been a substance called the self, it would have been known through perception; hence there is no existence of the self apart from body and the awareness thereof (*bhūtacaitanya*). The resemblance to the Buddhist critique and Humean skepticism is palpable here; one could say that a skeptical naturalist anti-ontology of the self is anticipated in Cārvākan elementalism (Frauwallner 1984).

The Cārvākas do not believe in the existence of something which is not perceived, i.e. in imperceptible entities or forces (*adṛṣṭārtha*). To them perception alone is the source of valid cognition (*pramāṇa*). If perception is taken as sole *pramāṇa*, objects which are not perceptible in nature cannot be taken as existents. That is why the Cārvākas do not acquiesce in the existence of God, the self, other worlds, liberation, etc. To them the self is nothing but the body associated with consciousness, and liberation is nothing but the destruction of the body (*dehasya nāśo muktiḥ*) (Mādhavācarya 1924, 7, line 59). This leads them also to reject the doctrine of *karma*, particularly in the supposed transmigratory process, which itself seems to have been a postulate motivated by the supposition of unrequited *karma* in one lifetime.

From the above-mentioned presupposition it is also admitted by the Cārvākas that inference (*anumāna*), verbal testimony (*śabdapramāṇa*), inclusive of *śruti* (Vedic 'revelation'), cannot be the reliable sources of truth-making cognition. The Cārvākas have provided some independent arguments in favor of not admitting inference, etc. as sources of valid cognition. The arguments may be summarized in the following manner.

The Cārvākas are opposed to the common theory that physical enjoyment is not a human pursuit, because it is always mixed with misery. To them foolish persons consider the physical enjoyment arising out of an enjoyable object to be forsaken, because it cannot provide happiness unmixed with suffering (*tyajyaṃ sukhaṃ viṣayasaṅgamajanma puṃsāṃ, duḥkhopasṛṣṭamiti mūrkhavicāraṇaiṣā*) (SDS #10; Mādhavācarya 1961, 3; 1924, 4, lines 39–40). Because each and every human pursuit though mixed with misery is always desired by an individual. It is found in society that an individual desiring his or her own well-being does not forsake the paddy, endowed with hidden fresh white rice, due to being afraid of its external cover, the husk (*tuṣa*) mixed in it (*vrīhīñjihāsati sitottamataṇḍulāḍhyān, ko nāma bhostūṣakaṇopahitanhitārthī*) (ibid., lines 41–42). Not only this, there are certain problems in everything if we want to proceed for its enjoyment. If we want to take fish, there are bones; if we want to take coconut, there is the hard outer cover; if we wish to take ice-cream, there is the sugar in it. Bankim Chandra Chatterjee (1942/1973, 133) has rightly pointed out that there is some non-desirable property or element behind or in every entity that is desirable to us. He says that in flowers there are insects; in smell there is poison, and so on (*kusume kīṭ āche gandheviṣ ācche*). Hence, there is no pleasure unmixed with misery; even so, no one refrains from enjoyment. That is why we should abide by the principle *sāram tato grāhyamapāsya phalgu*: it is always advisable to accept the substantial thing after removing the undesirable or unsubstantial ones.

It has already been stated that the Cārvākas have not admitted the Vedas as authority because there is no perceptual evidence in them. Notwithstanding this disavowal of Vedic authority, they do not bear any dogmatic ideas about the Vedas, because they have made a study of the Vedic literature that had led them to draw certain conclusions against the Vedas. To them, the Vedas are written by a section of what could best be described as non-sophisticated persons who are clever, hypocritical, and malevolent (*trayo vedasya karttāro bhaṇḍadhūrtaniśācarāḥ* (SDS #21; Mādhavācarya 1961, 10; 1924, 14, line 129)). They have identified certain reasons behind arriving at such conclusions. First, the Cārvāka claim, the Vedic writing is vitiated by obscene statements, such as: the king's wife (queen) has taken semen from a buffalo. Moreover, the Vedic writers seem to be obsessed with using grammatically incorrect words like *jurbharī, turpharī*, etc., only to misguide others (1924, 14, line 129). The Vedic authors prefer to prescribe those injunctions through which they become the beneficiary after the accomplishment of sacrifice, which goes to prove their cunning and selfish nature. They are non-sophisticated in another sense in that the authors accuse each other – or the other – of being corrupt and uttering false (*anṛta*), contradictory (*vyāghāta*), and repetitive (*punarukta*) words (SDS #2; Mādhavācarya 1961, 2–4; 1924, 4, line 45). When the Vedic authors say, "O herbal plant, relieve him" (*oṣadhe, trāyasva enam*), "O solid (rock), do not harm me" (*śṛṇota grāvāṇaḥ*) (Mādhavācarya 1924, 4–5, commentary), these are taken as false words, because no sensible person can address an unconscious object. The Vedic authors have made many contradictory statements, such as "Rudra is One indeed; for him there is no second; others say Rudra is thousand-fold like the thousand pillars of the world" (*eka eva rudro na dvitīyāya tasthe* and *sahasrāṇi sahasrśo ye rudrā adhibhūmyām*), "one performs sacrifice at the time of sunrise" (*udite juhoti*) and "one performs sacrifice at the time of sunset" (*anudite juhoti*) in the same context, "He is far away" (*tad dūre*) and "He is nearer" (*tad antike*), etc. (1924, 5, commentary). The performance of Agnihotra sacrifice, three Vedas, the mendicant's three staves, smearing oneself with ashes., etc. according to Bṛhaspati are the means of maintaining the livelihood of the persons who have no intellect and exercise no effort (*agnihotraṃ trayo vedāstridaṇḍaṃ bhasmaguṇṭanam / buddhipauruṣahīnānāṃ jīvikā iti Bṛhaspatiḥ*) (SDS #3; 1961, 5; 1924, 5, lines 50–51).

Hell is to be taken as metaphorical in the sense that suffering arising out of the prickle of thorns, etc. is called hell as per the view of the Cārvākas. The king who protects the honest and destroys the wicked or offenders is looked upon as God, while in fact, there is no separate existence of God as such. As there is no evidence to support of the existence of God, hell, liberation, the self, and so forth, for all these are products of misguided thinking of deranged persons.

One may raise the question, if there is no self at all, how are verbal usages such as 'My body' etc. possible? In reply, the Cārvākas argue that all these usages are again metaphorical. 'My body' means 'self as identical with body' – the genitive case-ending here is figurative as we use 'The head of Rāhu' (*rāhoḥ śiraḥ*) where genitive case-ending is of no use in the sense that the head itself is Rāhu (SDS #3; 1961, 5; 1924, 6, line 55).

To the Cārvākas nothing is connected causally with anything, which means anything may be connected with anything else without the linkage of causality. The relation is one of mere regulatory association in the subjective experiences of people. Hence, no objective causal relation can be established between two objects; this gives birth to the theory called *yādṛacchikavāda* or *ākasmikatāvāda* (accidentalism). If something follows really from something, it is to be taken as accidental, as is seen in the case of jewel, *mantra*, and medicine (*maṇimantrauṣadhādivad yādṛacchikaḥ*) (SDS # 9; 1961, 9; 1924, 12, line 103). A jewel, if taken, cannot provide fortune to the bearer logically. If she comes by some fortune, it is a mere accidental. Such is the case with *mantra* and medicine also. Taking on the celebrated Nyāya reliance on *vyāpti*, the supposed invariable commitment relation said to obtain between two causally related entities or events – such as fire and smoke, as in the kitchen stove – the Cārvāka critic dismisses such causal presumption as something that is accountable purely on grounds of association based on prior perception or habit as not a relation that is either of the form of inherence or of an intrinsic (natural) kind. In other words, this is a purely accidental property that the Nyāya is desperate to elevate to a formal property to give weight to the *hetu*, reasoning power, in its syllogistic argumentation, which is untenable. This error leads to the collapse of the much-touted *pramāṇa* of inference (*dhūmādjijñānānantara magnyādijñāne pravṛttiḥ pratykṣamūltayā bhrāntya vā yujate. Kvacitphalapratilambahastu maṇimantrauṣadhādivad yādṛcchikaḥ*) (ibid.).

Now the Cārvākas raise some problems for the priests who believe in the authority of the Vedas. If a performer of a *jyotiṣṭoma* sacrifice thinks that an animal that is killed in the sacrifice actually goes to heaven, why does the performer not kill his own father in the same sacrifice? (*svapitā yajamanānena tatra kasmānna hiṃsyate*). Second, if the performance of the funeral ceremony (*śrāddha*) becomes the cause of the satisfaction of the dead animals, why do they not provide oil to enhance the flame of the lamp which is already extinguished? Third, if somebody staying in heaven receives satisfaction through a gift from earthlings, why are the rich treasures stored up in the palace not given as gifts? The horse-sacrifice that involves rather poly-perverse rites demanded of the queen are nothing but self-indulgent pastimes invented by knaves who are encouraged by dark-wandering demons to devour animal flesh (*aśvayatra hi śiśnaṃ tu patnīgrahyaṃ prakkīrtitaṃ … māṃsānāṃ khādanaṃ tadvanniścācarasamīritaṃ iti*, ibid., 15, verse 22). These questions lead to the earlier presupposition that the authors of the Vedas are clever, hypocritical, and of malicious intent.

The theory of *puruṣārtha* (human pursuits) arguably consisting of four 'kingdoms of ends' – *dharma* (righteous acts), *artha* (economic well-being and effort), *kāma* (desire), and *mokṣa* (liberation) – is rejected for its excesses by the Cārvākas, who admit only two from the list, namely, *artha* and *kāma*. Of course, it is a matter of some contention whether Cārvākas were the only ones to reject *mokṣa*, liberative end, if not *dharma* also, for there has been a long-standing debate from ancient times in India over the number of life-goals of humanity (the *arthas* within *puruṣārtha*); indeed, some have argued in more recent times that the *puruṣārtha*-s began with two, moving to three, and the fourth – *mokṣa*– was added rather later, and that there was no hierarchy or 'pecking order' assumed among these. In other words, the ends were somewhat scrambled, depending on which perspective one came from or what one's cultural agenda was, whether simple earthly gains, other-worldly proclivity, or imperial goals (Daya Krishna 2007/2008). In this connection, it is to be noted that economic value and desire as such are not neglected in the tradition after considering their mundane importance. The *Arthaśāstra* of Kauṭilya and *Kāmasūtra* of Vātsyāyana point to the truth that mundane needs are not negligible but rather inevitable and should therefore be fulfilled. That sexuality is a kind of desirable pursuit in the world (*loke*) is evidenced from the celebration of the god of love called *mādana-mahotsava* (Chattopadhyaya 2006, 18 and 50). A question may be raised to the Cārvākas whether they have any specific reasons for admitting only the two above-mentioned human pursuits (*puruṣārtha*-s)? If there is no solid reason for admitting these two only (rather than all four), the proposition made by them becomes 'unfoundational', which has been described by the Buddhists as a 'headless statement' (*aśiraska-vacana*), and hence it will fall flat to the ground (*ekākinī pratijñā hi pratijñātaṃ na sādhayet*) (Mādhavācarya 1961, 6; 1924, 18, line 29). If, on the other hand, the Cārvākas advance some reasons in favor of admitting *artha* (livelihood) and *kāma* (desire) as the preeminent human pursuits, the reasoning may be taken as justificatory and interpreted as moral or value-based reasoning. This moral or value-based reasoning may be considered as having the status of regulative principle by which the choice is made of only two as distinct from the traditional four (or more) as the basic human pursuits or what could also be called capabilities (*puruṣārtha*).

To the Cārvākas, political policies and religious purity cannot go together; hence there arises a conflict between *artha* and *dharma* (not unlike the argument for separation of state or polity and church), according to the treatises of Yājñavalkya and Nārada. Among the masters of political science there were some who refused to acknowledge any kind of authority from *dharma*, and instead declared that in the world of human beings (*loka*), God, gods and priests should not interfere – as is known from the statement: *trayīsaṃvaraṇamātram*. In this way, *artha* is separated from *dharma* and ultimately it goes against it (*dharma*). A historical account shows that there were two *artha* schools: the orthodox one remaining under the authority of *dharma* and hence included under the domain of *Dharmaśāstras*, while the other following its heretical principles asserted *artha* and *kāma* to be the principal and prized human pursuits (*arthakāmau eva puruṣārthau*) (Mādhavācarya 1961, 2; 1924, 2, lines 19–20). They do not consider *dharma* as being separate or different from *kāma*. Foolish people are influenced by the statements of deceitful persons who leave aside or belittle the pleasures of the ordinary world while hankering after absurd things, such as heaven and so on. Apparently Bṛhaspati in his *sūtra* (11.5 and 11.6), according to Chattopadhyaya who cites another authority, H. P. Sastri, has mentioned that one should follow the principles followed by the ordinary earthly people (*lokāyatika*) while desiring to earn money and uplifting the economy of the people (*sarvathālokāyatikam eva śāstramarthasādhanakāle*). At the same time the person is advised to follow the principles laid down by the Kāpālika sect (an ascetic Śāivite order that engages in erotic praxis) wherein enjoyment of sexual pleasure is rendered as a desirable and salubrious end (*kāpālikameva kāmasādhane*) (Chattopadhyaya 2006, 16–17 and 51–53).

It has also been observed by Debiprasad Chattopadhyaya that the Cārvāka–Lokāyata hedonism – if one may call it that – prevailed in a very popular manner, which is evidenced from the following fact. Due to the influence of such hedonistic attitudes everywhere in India there was a tendency towards fulfilling sexual pleasure leading to the deluge of sexual art and esoteric practices, such as certain forms of (so-called left-hand) tantra and the famous temple of Khajuraho. All persons from various walks of life, starting from Brahmin to *Caṇḍāla*, king to beggar, appeared to have been drawn to if not physically engaged in the festival of sex (*mādana mahotsava*). During this occasion 'festival' was taken to mean 'the festival of sexual pleasure' or the celebration of the pleasure principle, which ultimately is known as *dolotsava* (festival of color) by the Vaiṣṇava sect of Bengal (Chattopadhyaya 2006, 18)

Some of the Buddhist sects with laxity in sexual morals also became affiliated to the *Lokāyata* school. One of these sects is the Kāpālika sect that engages in the consumption of wine, offering flesh sacrifices, and sexual acts between couples. As *kāma*, i.e. sexual or sensual enjoyment, was the goal of this sect, it also became affiliated to *nāstika* or ultra-heterodox form of the Lokāyata school, according to which the *summum bonum* of human life is the enjoyment of gross sensual pleasure; further, the virility of a male person lies in attaining pleasure in the embrace of a female (*aṅganāliṅganājjanyasukhameva pumarthatā*) (Mādhavācarya 1924, 6, line 56). The nature of everything depends on the attitude developed towards an object. The Sahajiyas believe that there remains only pleasure, nothing else. The pleasure described by them as happiness arises out of the union of male and female (Chattopadhyaya 2006, 16–18).

In order to enquire the cause of the polemical attitude towards *dharma* by the Cārvākas, their interpretation of Maitrī Upaniṣad may be referred to. It is said in the Maitrī Upaniṣad that among the accepted *puruṣārtha*-s by others, *dharma* has to be taken as an impediment to the enjoyment of worldly pleasure. Bṛhaspati, in the disguise of Śukra, created ignorance in this world for the security of Indra and the destruction of demons. Due to the effect of such ignorance, the demons consider good as evil and evil as good. Their desire is to create deliberate misunderstanding about the efficacy of *dharma*. Let people consider *dharma* as the destroyer of scriptures like Vedas, etc. For this reason the pious thinkers must not discuss *dharma* at all. It is improper, fruitless, and non-conducive to the most desirable end: worldly pleasure (Chattopadhyaya and Gangopadhyaya 1990, 6–8).

Haribhadrasurī in his *Ṣaḍdarśana-samuccaya* (1986, 82) has expressed his opinion that for the sake of enjoyment one should drink and eat. To him that which is past does not belong to an individual, because the past does not come back. Hence it is very much essential to engage an individual in enjoyment through the consumption of liquor. In this context the term 'drink' has two meanings: the consumption of liquor and kissing the beloved. The term 'eat' means 'enjoyment of the objects of pleasure'. In short, an individual is asked to crown his youth with success.

The Cārvākas also believe that there is no gift or gain to be made in charity, nor in sacrifice and any offerings. There is no fruit and ripening of good and bad actions. In this world there are no ascetics or the Brāhmaṇas who claim to have gone along the right path of conduct and follow right conduct. A human being is, as said earlier, constituted of four elements. When a person dies, earth goes into the mass of earth (cf. "Then shall the dust return to the earth as it was" (Ecclesiastes 12:7)), the water into the mass of water, the fire into the mass of fire, breath into the mass of air, etc. Fools and wise men are destroyed and disappear when the body falls into pieces (Chattopadhyaya 2006, 50–52). They are no more after death. There is diversity in our life which is experienced in a situation when we feel sometimes joy and sometimes grief. It is due to the good and bad actions which are under the rigorous law of *karma*. It has been admitted by the Cārvākas that joy and grief are nothing but accidental events as the bubbles of water. They also assert that natural feelings and experiences are ascribed to the life-forces, and this entails the denial of a persistent self. When a person says "I am lean", "I am fat", the 'I' refers to the body but not some elusive self. As each and every event is accidental (*yādṛacchikaḥ*), i.e. without having causal relationship, there can never be any law of action leading to the eradication of future life or after-life or after-effect of an action performed. That is why there does not arise any question of vice and virtue. These factors have propelled the Cārvāka to take to enjoying something as soon as the possibility arises without waiting for another day or occasion (Frauwallner 1984, 215–226).

Let us try to see the justification of the Cārvāka-view with the help of following arguments. If, by murdering a person, someone attains some worldly gains, such as money or wish-fulfillment, the act of violence would not be considered wrong, because an action leading to one's own benefit cannot really be turned into an offence. If so, it (the action) can never be taken as unjust by the performer who is deriving some benefit from it. Other people may consider such an act as an instance of violence, and hence a person is considered guilty on account of the fact that his or her action is harmful to society or to others. The Cārvākas would not think them as being true judges.

The Cārvākas would agree with the political parties or nations if they obtain benefit from deceptive statements, such as "The policy would benefit all human beings" etc. This is due to the fact that each and every person has a right to do everything in their means to achieve his or her own benefit, very much in the libertarian spirit. If someone attains happiness even after adopting falsity, it is taken to be a desirable position (*satyājjyāyo'nṛtaṃ vācaḥ*). If some political party or intelligent persons achieve their own benefit by trumping out false statements, they will be supported by the Cārvākas. The criteria of justness or unjustness remain in terms of an action's efficacy toward the attainment of pleasure and avoidance of suffering. If something generates pleasure in a person, it is fair from his perspective, while something generating suffering in him is quite unjust to him (Chattopadhyaya 2006, 19–20). Hence, to the Cārvākas there is no uniform policy in determining justness or unjustness.

From the above discussions it is to be noted that the Cārvākas do not believe in the *traditional morality* where the well-being of the society and other human beings is taken into account without regard first to the interests and preferences of the individual *qua* individual. The greatest good for the smallest number is not a problem from their materialist point of view.

If so, such moral value informing the choice of *puruṣārtha*-s is not to be admitted as a guiding principle behind pursuing money and desire. This moral value is nothing but *dharma* which has been abandoned by them as a human pursuit. The term '*dharma*' has various connotations, such as 'rites', 'rituals', 'nature of an object', 'rule', 'law', and 'morality'. It is common knowledge that the *Mahābhārata* and *Manusaṃhitā* interpreted *dharma* in the sense of morality. It is said in the *Mahābhārata* (1974) that to adopt a non-malicious attitude to all beings is *dharma* as per the view of honest persons (*adroheṇaiva bhūtānāṃ yo dharmaḥ sa satām mataḥ*). An individual possessing thirteen moral virtues, such as awareness of Brahman, devotion to gods and forefathers, sobriety, having sympathy in others' pain, non-jealousy, softness in temperament, non-harshness, friendliness, habituated in speaking lovely words, sense of gratitude, giving refuge to others, compassion, and mental calmness is called *dhārmika* (*tadāha hārītaḥ brahmaṇytā devapitṛbhaktatā saumyatā aparopatāpitā ansūyatā mṛdutā apāruṣyaṃ maitratā priyavāditvaṃ kṛtajñatā śaraṇyatā kāruṇyam praśāntiśceti trayodaśavidhaṃ śīlam*) (Kullukabhaṭṭa in Bandyopadhyaya 2013, 254; see also Raghunath Ghosh 1994, 41–43). But the term '*dharma*' is to be taken in the sense of the nature of something, e.g. the nature (*dharma*) of water is to flow downwards and to quench thirst. The Cārvākas would, I believe, admit such a notion of *dharma*, because they accept the attainment of pleasure (*sukha-prāptiḥ*) by an open act, by defiance, or by stealth. They believe in *svabhāvavāda* or *yadṛchhā* instead of *kārya-kāraṇa-vāda* as admitted in other schools. *Yadṛchhā* is defined as *ākasmika-prāptiḥ* or coincidence by Śaṅkara. The terms *svabhāva* and *yadṛchhā* have been taken as identical, as the causal principle is wholly rejected by them. When a jar is produced from clay (but not from thread), the Cārvāka will emphasize that it is due to the nature of the thing which is unchangeable as per the theory of *svabhāvavāda*. To them *svabhāva* is of two kinds – *nisarga* and *svabhāva*-proper. The former is explained as habit and the latter as nature. Habit is said to originate from the impression sedimented through habitual repeated effort in the past; while nature is spontaneous and has no extrinsic source of origin at all. When an individual makes an effort to achieve happiness by any means, it may be called *svabhāva* in the sense of *nisarga*, i.e. due to undertaking repeated effort for its achievement. So far as my understanding goes, *svabhāva* in the sense of *nisarga*, if matured or attained habitual status (*abhyāsa-daśā*), attains the level of *svabhāva*. Under these circumstances, the *svabhāva* remaining between the attainment of happiness and enjoyable objects can be interpreted as *dharma* in the sense of nature or *svabhāva*, which may also be admitted as human pursuit (*puruṣārtha*). In other words, it is the nature or *svabhāva* (*dharma*) of an object to provide happiness. In fact, there are no other alternatives than to admit naturalness between happiness and the object providing it, owing to the denial of any causal relationship between them.

Considering the material needs of the ordinary people, Gautama, in his *Nyāyasūtra* as endorsed by Vātsyāyana also, has drawn our attention towards two types of *summum bonum* or highest good (*niḥśreyasa*), namely, this-worldly – which is seen (*dṛṣṭa*) – and other-worldly – which is unseen (*adṛṣṭa*). The right cognition (*tattvajñāna*) of the categories like *pramāṇa* (means of knowing), *saṃśaya* (doubt), *hetvābhāsa* (pseudo-problems), *tarka* (hypothetical argument), etc. lead one to the attainment of this-worldly well-being (*dṛṣṭaniḥ śreyam*), while the right cognition of the knowable entities, i.e. *prameya*-s, leads an individual to the attainment of the other-worldly or unseen well-being (*adṛṣṭaniḥ śreyasaḥ*). So far as the former is concerned, the right cognition of the categories such as *pramāṇavāda*, *jalpa*, *chala*, *hetvābhāsa* can help an individual to defeat the arguments or viewpoints of others and to defend her own position. If she is well conversant with the categories and their application, she can easily understand the points of defeat (*nigraha-sthāna*), quibble (*chala*), and 'pseudo reason' (*hetvābhāsa*) in another's argument, which can lead her to the world of victory in the field of philosophical debate. In the same way, the right cognition of the self, one of the *prameya*-s, can conjoin to us the transcendental well-being (*adṛṣṭa-niḥśreyasa*), i.e. the attainment of liberation. In this way, the Naiyāyikas have shown the method of achieving both spiritual and mundane well-being, in a more balanced way, without undue emphasis on one or the other side of the paradox of spiritual vis-à-vis material naturalism – as Professor Bimal Matilal was fond of saying (Matilal 2002). Hence it is that the materialism is an integral part while not being an exclusive proclivity of Indian philosophy.

Notes

1 I am grateful to Purushottama Bilimoria for sincerely commenting on this chapter and editing it with substantial additions and alterations, in his own elegantly eloquent style.

2 Bimal K. Matilal, who held the Spalding Chair in Eastern Religion and Ethics at All Souls College, Oxford, had himself championed this complaint and tended to be something of an apologist for the spiritual divergence or interlude in the long history of Indian philosophy. See discussion in Bilimoria 2009, 22, 27. For another critique of Indian philosophy's alleged mystical proclivity, see Krishna 1991. Chapters (especially 33) in Part III of this volume also deal with this contentious claim in modern (European and Indian) representations and Daya Krishna's rebuttal. See also Jessica Frazier's chapter for a counter-counter exposition.

3 This 1924 edition by Vāsudeva Śāstrī Abhyankara is confusing in its pagination; there are some 158 pages of introductory material, by the editor, and preface matter (*arpaṇapatrikā*, *prāstāvikaṃ nivedanam*,

prastāvanā), which surprisingly appear on pages stamped in Arabic/Western numerals; the SDS text proper starts thereafter with page 1 again (in Sanskrit numerals) and has the editor's own *Darśānakura* (an insightful gloss) from line 12 onwards.

References

Bandyopadhyaya, Manabendu. 2013. See under Kullukabhaṭṭa.

Bhattacharya, Ramkrishna. 2009. *Studies on the Cārvāka/Lokāyata*. Florence: Società Editrice Fiorentina.

———. 2010a. "Commentators on the Cārvākasūtra: A Critical Survey." *Journal of Indian Philosophy* 38: 419–430.

———. 2010b. "Lokāyata Darśana and a Comparative Study with Greek Materialism." In P. Ghose (ed.), *Materialism and Immaterialism in India and the West: Varying Vistas*. New Delhi: Centre for the Studies on Civilizations, pp. 21–34.

———. 2010c. "Lokāyata Materialism: Classification of Source Materials." In S. Charan Goswami (ed.), *Lokāyata Philosophy: A Fresh Appraisal*. Kolkata: The Asiatic Society, pp. 37–42.

———. 2010d. "What the Cārvākas Originally Meant: More on the Commentators of the Cārvākasūtra." *Journal of Indian Philosophy* 38: 529–542.

———. 2012. "Svabhāvavāda and the Cārvāka/Lokāyata: A Historical Overview." *Journal of Indian Philosophy* 40: 593–614.

———. 2013. "Development of Materialism in India: The Pre-Cārvākas and the Cārvākas." *Esercizi Filosofici* 8: 1–12.

——— 2016. 'Significance of the *Kaṭha Upaniṣad* in the Philosophical Development (of Materialism) in India'. *Antiquorum Philosophia* no. 10 (doi: 10.29272/2016302201008): 153–173.

——— 2107. 'Who are the *lokāyatika brāhmaṇas*?' *Annali di'Ca Foscari*. *Serie Orientale*. Vol 53 Guigno: 185–204.

Bilimoria, P. 1988. "Kauṭilya." In Edward Craig (ed.), *Routledge Encyclopaedia of Philosophy*. London and New York: Routledge, vol. 5, pp. 220–222.

Bilimoria, P. 2009. "What is the 'Subaltern' of the Philosophy of Religion?" In P. Bilimoria and Andrew Irvine (eds.), *Postcolonial Philosophy of Religion*. Dordrecht and New York: Springer, pp. 9–33.

Chatterjee (Chattopadhyay), Bankim Chandra. 1942/1973. *Kamalākānter Daptar in Bankim Racana Samagra* [in Bengali], vol. 1. Kolkata: Paschim Banga Niraksharta Drudikaraṇa Samiti (original composition 1875).

Chattopadhyaya, Debiprasad. 1989. *In Defence of Materialism in Ancient India*. New Delhi: People's Publishing House.

———. 1990. Ed. *Cārvāka/Lokāyata: An Anthology of Source Materials and Some Recent Studies*. New Delhi: Indian Council of Philosophical Research.

———. 2006. *Lokāyata: A Study in Ancient Indian Materialism*. Delhi: People's Publishing House, 8th ed.

Chattopadhyaya, Debiprasad and Gangopadhyaya, MrinalKanti (eds.). 1990. *Cārvāka/Lokāyata*. New Delhi: Indian Council of Philosophical Research.

Frauwallner, Erich. 1984. *History of Indian Philosophy*, vol. 2. Delhi: Motilal Banarsidass.

Ghosh, Raghunath. 1994. *Sura, Man and Society: Philosophy of Harmony in Indian Tradition*. Calcutta: Academic Enterprise.

Gokhale, Pradeep. 2015. *Lokāyata/Cārvāka: A Philosophical Inquiry*. New Delhi: Oxford University Press.

Haribhadrasurī. 1986. *Ṣaḍdarśanasamuccaya*. Trans. K. Satchidananda Murty. Delhi: Eastern Book Linkers, 2nd ed.

Krishna, Daya. 1991. *Indian Philosophy: A Counter Perspective*. Delhi: Oxford University Press.

———. 2008/2007. "The Myth of the Ethics of Puruṣārtha or Humanity's Life-Goals." In P. Bilimoria, J. Prabhu, and R. Sharma (eds.), *Indian Ethics*, vol. 1: *Classical and Contemporary Challenges*. Aldershot: Ashgate; New Delhi: Oxford University Press, pp. 103–115 (paperback ed. London: Routledge, 2017).

Kullukabhaṭṭa. 2013. *Manvarthamuktāvalī on Manusaṃhitā*, 2/6. Ed. Manabendu Bandyopadhyaya. Kolkata: Samskrit Pustak Bhandar, 3rd ed.

Mādhavācārya. 1905. *Sarvadarśanasaṃgraha*, Cārvāka-darśana. Ed. Udaya Narain Sinh. Sanskrit with Hindi translation. Bombay: Khemarāja Śrīkṛṣṇadāsśreṣṭin.

———. 1924. *Sāyaṇa-Mādhava, Sarvadarśanasaṅgraha*. Ed. with original commentary by Vāsudeva Śāstri Abhyankara. Prachya Vidya Samshodhana Mandir, Nirnaya Sagar. 3rd ed., 1978, Pune: Bhandarkar Oriental Institute.

———. 1961. *Sarvadarśanasaṃgraha*, Cārvāka-darśana. English trans. and elucidation by E. B. Cowell and A. E. Gough. Varanasi: Chowkhamba Sanskrit Series Office, 6th ed.

Mahābhārata, The (Critical Edition). 1974. Ed. V. S. Sukthankar and S. K. Belvalkar. *Mahābhārata*, vol. 3, *Śāntiparva*, 21/10. Pune: Bhandhakar Oriental Research Institute (BORI) (1st ed., 1933–1966).

Matila, Bimal K. 2002. *Ethics and epics: the collected essays of Bimal Krishna Matilal, Volume 2* Jonardon Ganeri (ed). New Delhi: Oxford University Press.

Mittal, Kewal Krishan. 1974. *Materialism in Indian Thought*. New Delhi: Munsihiram Manoharlal Publishers Pvt. Ltd.

Radhakrishnan, Sarvepall. 1957. *A Sourcebook in Indian Philosophy*, ed. Charles A. Moore. Princeton: Princeton University Press.

Riepe, Dale M. 1961. *The Naturalistic Tradition in Indian Thought*. Seattle: University of Washington Press.

Smart, Ninian. 1964. *Doctrine and Argument in Indian Philosophy*. London: Allen and Unwin; rev. ed., via Purushottama Bilimoria, 1992, Leiden: E. J. Brill.

Turner-Lauck Wernicki, Abigail. n.d. "Lokayata/Carvaka: Indian Materialism," in *The Internet Encyclopedia of Philosophy* www.iep.utm.edu/indmat accessed November 11, 2015.

IIa

PHILOSOPHICAL TRADITIONS

Chapter 11
PHILOSOPHY OF THE BRĀHMAṆAS

Herman Tull

The Brāhmaṇas

The Brāhmaṇas are a class of Vedic texts generally considered to have been composed in north India sometime between 1000 and 500 BCE. The precise derivation of the term "Brāhmaṇa" is unclear; it may refer to the ritualist-authors of the texts (from *brahman*, "priest"), or it may refer to the texts as a collection of sacred knowledge (from *brahman*, "sacred utterance") (Winternitz 1981 [1909], 174). There are ten extant Brāhmaṇas; in modern, printed Sanskrit editions, they range in size from a few hundred to a few thousand pages. Each Brāhmaṇa is attached to one of the four Vedic Saṃhitās or "collections": the *Ṛgveda*, the *Sāmaveda*, the *Yajurveda*, and the *Atharvaveda*.[1] However, between the Saṃhitās and the Brāhmaṇas there are marked differences in language and in style; the language of the Saṃhitās, which is in verse, is more archaic than that of the prose Brāhmaṇas, suggesting a significant gap in years between these texts (Keith 1925, 19). The historic relationship between the Saṃhitās and the Brāhmaṇas is further complicated by the apparent existence of earlier, non-extant Brāhmaṇa-type texts that were closely aligned with the Saṃhitās (Witzel 1997a, 298). This layer of "lost" texts may well account for the mass of shared material in the extant Brāhmaṇas, seen in the repetition of certain stock phrases; in the emphasis on a few key mythological episodes; and, in the common epistemological and ontological foundation that underlies much of the Brāhmaṇic discourse (see, further, Witzel 1997a, 288; 297–299).[2]

The *raison d'être* of the Brāhmaṇas—and, so, too, the point around which their authors' discussions begin and end—are the great Vedic rites of sacrifice. These sacrificial rituals hark back to the oldest layers of Vedic culture and are glimpsed—though not fully described—throughout the Saṃhitās. A chief characteristic of the Brāhmaṇas is their two-leveled discussion of the rites: as performance (*vidhi*, literally "injunction") and as explication (*arthavāda*) (Winternitz 1981, 187; Gonda 1975, 340–341). Whereas the *vidhi* or "how-to" portion of the text tends to be somewhat muted (the authors apparently presumed that their audience knew how to perform the rites), the explanations can be expansive, as the authors delve into the "higher" and "mysterious" meanings of the Vedic rites (cf. Malamoud 1998, 29–30). Thus, a rather simple direction (*vidhi*), such as, "Entering the vow, he stands between the *āhavanīya* and the *gārhapatya* fires, turning eastward, he touches water" (*ŚB* 1.1.1.1), leads to a discussion of the mystic import that connects the vow to the god Agni, and then to the (*arthavāda*) declaration of the "higher" meaning of the ritual object, namely, the water used in the rite, which connects it to "all this": "He brings forward water because all this (the cosmos) is filled up by water; so by this first act, he acquires all this" (*ŚB* 1.1.1.14).

Although the history of the Brāhmaṇas' composition cannot be recovered, a number of significant developmental elements can be discerned beneath the surface of these texts. Thus, occasional references to one ritualist contradicting another, or to certain obsolete or "incorrect" practices or interpretations (often said to be regionally based), almost certainly reflect the expansion of Vedic culture during the first millennium BCE (Witzel 1997a, 301ff.). With expansion, new schools were founded (evidenced in the compilation of new Brāhmaṇas), providing an opportunity for fresh interpretations of the ritual forms. Coordinate with this expansion was the rise of a large class of ritualists whose charge was to ensure that the rites were performed with the utmost accuracy but who also served to explicate the ceremonies. These ritualists were subdivided into groups of specialized functionaries, each charged with undertaking a specific element of the rite (see Müller 1859, 450; 469ff.). Among these functionaries was the *brahman* who performed the rite mentally as a means of averting possible errors in performance (Müller 1859, 450). This ritualist was said to be "all-knowing"; that is, to encompass within his own mind the rite in its entirety (Gonda 1975, 271). Although there is no certain evidence connecting the mental performance of the rite to the emergence of Brāhmaṇic speculation, this element of the ritual resonates deeply with what has been broadly identified as the "internalization" of the sacrifice, "in which physiological functions take the place of libations and ritual objects," a notion which stands as a foundational element in ancient Indian philosophy (Eliade 1969, 111–114).

European Indologists and the Brāhmaṇas

Throughout the nineteenth century, European (in particular, German) Indologists evinced an intense interest in the Vedic literature, producing critical Sanskrit editions and translations into European languages of these texts, a project that included several major Brāhmaṇas. However, as modern Indology changed direction from what was in fact a misguided focus on the Veda, the study of the Brāhmaṇas became peripheral. As a result, several Brāhmaṇas remain untranslated, and thus are inaccessible to Western scholars. Along with this early textual work, Western scholars produced a handful of important studies of the sacrificial ritual in the Brāhmaṇas (see, e.g., Lévi 1898; Oldenberg 1919; Bodewitz 1973; Heesterman 1985; 1993; and Smith 1989), and a few other studies that focus on Brāhmaṇic mythologies (see, e.g., Weber 1850, 1885; Hopkins 1909; and Doniger 1985). A. B. Keith, who translated several Brāhmaṇas, devoted considerable portions of his monumental work, *The Religion and Philosophy of the Veda and Upanishads* (1925), to discussing (albeit often dismissively) the nature of Brāhmaṇic thought. Recently, Michael Witzel has produced a number of studies that draw deeply on the Brāhmaṇas, examining aspects of their thought (1979, 1996; cf. Oldenberg 1919) as well as exploring them for what they reveal of their socio-political milieu (1997a; 1997b; 1987; cf. Rau 1957).

The first generation of European Indologists to study the Brāhmaṇas almost universally disparaged them (the one notable exception being Lévi 1898). In what may be the most oft-repeated description of these texts, F. Max Müller notoriously declared that the Brāhmaṇas were "twaddle, and what is worse theological twaddle" (1867, 1, 113), likening their thought to the "raving of madmen" (1859, 389). These same sentiments occur in nearly every nineteenth- and early twentieth-century scholarly work that examines the Brāhmaṇas (for a conspectus, see Doniger 1985, 5; Tull 1989, 19, 16ff.; Tull 1991, 39; Smith 1989, 32–33). In addition to being deeply troubled by the nature of Brāhmaṇic reasoning (see Oldenberg 1919; cf. 1991, 12; Keith 1925, 440; Eggeling 1882, ix), these scholars took a dim view of the ritualistic atmosphere of the Brāhmanas. With their post-enlightenment protestant view of "priestcraft," these scholars were repulsed by the Vedic ritualists' description of themselves as "gods among men" (*ŚB* 2.2.2.6) and found abhorrent the priests' demands for a heavy recompense for their ritual work (see, e.g., *ŚB* 2.2.2.2-5) (Tull 1989, 17, 129 n.24).

The Brāhmaṇas as philosophy

As indicated in the foregoing, the Brāhmaṇas were composed with a singular focus on the Vedic sacrificial rites. Accordingly, areas that in modern usage broadly fall under the scope of philosophy, but that are related to everyday social existence—such as ethics, the nature of justice, political power, and so forth—have virtually no place in Brāhmaṇic discourse. On the other hand, however, the Brāhmaṇic thinkers were deeply engaged by metaphysical inquiry. Here, conditioned by the performance of the Vedic rituals, which entail a carefully orchestrated series of acts that are themselves divorced from ordinary reality, the Brāhmaṇic thinkers developed a systematic method of inquiry that provided them access to meaning where no obvious everyday meaning existed (see Keith 1925, 482). As noted above, this system of thought is built on the notion that any number of identities can be found between entities, a system that is, as Sylvain Lévi (1898, 9) noted long ago, "net, logique, harmonieux" ("neat, logical, and harmonious").[3] Of course, that the system is neat and logical does not preclude the possibility that nothing of substance arises from it. The critical question in approaching the Brāhmaṇa texts as "philosophy" then becomes whether this system of identification is merely a form of hollow symbolism, as nineteenth-century Indologists tended to see it, or if it holds within it substantial insights into the nature of being (ontology) and the nature of knowledge (epistemology).

A fundamental question of philosophy is, "How is a thing known?" The Brāhmaṇas contain innumerable declarative statements identifying one entity with another, in effect, creating a series of equations that define things by what they are akin to. Often the entities being identified with one another are linked through quasi-syllogistic reasoning; that is, if A = B, and B = C, then A = C. Here, in seeking out the underlying meaning of the rites, even the thinnest connections might be exploited. Thus, a typical example drawn from the *Śatapatha Brāhmaṇa* shows the author citing a numerical resemblance to connect the twelve verses in a particular prayer to the meter of the hymn (which has twelve syllables), then to the earth (since the name of the meter [*jagatī*] approximates a word used for the earth [*jagat*]), to the god Agni (since the earth is the locus of the fire altar, also referred to as *agni*), and ultimately to the cosmos itself (since Agni, the god, is related to the creator god, Prajāpati) (*ŚB* 6.2.1.28–30). In addition to seeking all sorts of numerical correspondences, the ritualists also looked to language as an important means of establishing identity; here, words with common derivations (or supposed common derivations, for the etymologies given are often "false" ones), as well as words that possessed homonymous qualities, are seen as expressing fundamental truths. For example, the authors of the *Śatapatha Brāhmaṇa* draw on the etymological connection between Agni (the fire god) and the priest known as the Agnīdh to establish that an essential identity exists between them (*ŚB* 5.5.1.8) and to the homonymous quality of the two words *agni* (the fire god) and *agre* ("in front") to establish an identification between the sacrificer (when he is positioned in front of the sacrifice) and the fire god (*ŚB* 2.2.4.2). Augmenting these linguistic identifications was a vast body of archaic mythology that could be used to create identifications between any number of seemingly disparate entities (see Witzel 1979, 1996); thus, for example, Agni's ancient identification as a bird (*ṚV* 1.164.46) becomes the basis for his identification with the bird-shaped altar used in one particular ritual (the *agnicayana*) (see, e.g., *ŚB* 6.1.2.36). The Brāhmaṇic thinkers were keenly aware that these identifications were not empirically verifiable; accordingly, an oft-repeated phrase in declaring such identifications is that, "the gods love the unseen" (*parokṣa*, literally, that which lies "beyond the eye," but which also expresses the sense of the "mysterious" [*ŚB* 14.1.1.14; 6.1.1.2; 6.7.1.23; 7.4.1.10.]). However, here again the question of meaning intrudes; for, given these interminable equations, and the numerous means of establishing them, it may be asserted that the Brāhmaṇic thinkers created a system in which, as one scholar observed, "anything can result from anything; everything is all" (Thite 1975, 5); that is, a system so overburdened by equivalence that the possibility of real meaning is denied.

However, it is important to point out here that the Brāhmaṇic principle of identity is built not merely on ideas of similitude but draws on the foundational concept of "connection" (*bandhu*), a notion often seen as the hallmark, if not the underlying principle, of Brāhmaṇic thought (for discussion and citations to relevant sources, see Smith 1989, 31). In general use, *bandhu* designates any association, but also indicates the particular type of connection that is established through family ties, thus suggesting an element of shared being.[4] In the context of the Brāhmaṇas, *bandhu* has the particular sense of connecting ritual objects to the ritual performers (in particular, to the figure of the sacrificer, who may not actually perform the sacrifice, but who benefits from it) on the one side, and to the ritual act itself on the other (see Gonda 1965). Here, connectedness goes beyond mere identification to assert a state of shared being so that actions that affect one element also affect identically the element, or elements, to which it is connected. From this point, the ideology of identification that pervades the Brāhmaṇas as a means of knowing becomes effectively a means of becoming; that is, in Brāhmaṇic thought, the means to knowledge (epistemology), which is the knowledge of identity, builds upon and reaffirms particular states of being (ontology). Thus, the ritualists state, "The one that knows this, he is indeed [firmly] placed and connected (*bandhumān*)" (*PB* 10.1.2ff.). This connectedness, which is to say this theory of being, however, is not a meaningless connectedness of everything to everything, but a connectedness specifically to the defined space of the ritual arena and through it to the cosmos as a *created* and *ordered* place.

Underlying the Brāhmaṇic ritual form is the act of sacrifice; that is, a violent act that uses the death and destruction of a victim to create life anew. The quintessential expression of this ideology is found in the famed Ṛgvedic hymn of the sacrifice of Puruṣa, the (cosmic) Man (*ṚV* 10.90). According to this hymn, before the ordered cosmos arose, there existed the primeval Puruṣa. The gods (whose origins are not here accounted for) use the Puruṣa as the oblation in a great first sacrifice, an act that is at once destructive *and* creative, as a series of hierarchically ranked beings and elements that, taken together, form the ordered cosmos—the beasts of air, forest, and village; the hymns, chants, and sacrificial formulae; horses, cattle, goats, and sheep; men of each of the four castes; the moon, the sun, and the three spheres of heaven, earth, and atmosphere—arise from the Puruṣa's dismembered body (these entities are related hierarchically to the order of that body: the head above, the shoulder below, etc.). In Vedic thought, the hymn's underlying ideology of creation through the sacrifice of a man can be seen in several fundamental ideologies regarding the ritual of sacrifice: (1) the Brāhmaṇic sacrificial ritual replicates the creative event of "world" creation—that is, establishing a place or foundation for the sacrificer (see Gonda 1967); (2) the sacrificial victim should be a man, like Puruṣa (which simply means "man"), and therefore the man who seeks new life through the sacrifice must take the onus of death and destruction upon himself (see Heesterman 1987, 91). This ideology is clearly understood by the authors of the *Śatapatha Brāhmaṇa*, as they declare, "The sacrifice is a man" (*ŚB* 3.5.3.1) and also tell us that the sacrificial fires "think about the sacrificer, they desire the sacrificer" (*ŚB* 11.7.1.2). However, unlike the god Puruṣa who, by definition, cannot die, the mortal sacrificer (Vedic thought distinguishes men and gods by the dichotomy of mortality/immortality) cannot be the victim of the sacrifice; for, if the sacrificer were to be the victim of the sacrifice, then the ritual would end not in a creative act but in self-defeating death (see Heesterman 1987, 105).

To avoid his own death in the sacrifice, the sacrificer employed any of a number of "substitute" victims, from the four domestic animals that arose from Puruṣa's sacrifice (horse, cow, sheep, and goat) to offerings of milk, grains, and even an effigy (in the famed *agnicayana* ritual, a gold man is employed for this purpose [*ŚB* 7.4.1.15]). Additionally, the sacrificer "distanced" himself from the death and destruction implicit in the Vedic sacrifice by employing ritual specialists who actually performed the sacrifice on his behalf. The need to avoid his own death in the sacrifice, and the sacrificial theory that demanded that the sacrificer should be the victim, becomes a central tension in the ritual performance; thus the authors of the Śatapatha Brāhmaṇa equivocate on whether or not the sacrificer should hold the victim (that is, his own substitute, and in some sense, identical to him) and finally conclude that to establish a firm connection to the victim, the sacrificer must hold the victim, but he should do so in a "mysterious" (*paro'kṣa*) way (*ŚB* 3.8.1.10).

At this point we must return to the Brāhmaṇic way of thinking that seeks identity (in knowledge) and correspondences (in being) as a means of establishing the relationship between the sacrificer, who *ought* to be the victim of the sacrifice, and the victim who gives up his life in the enactment of the sacrificial rite. Although the Brāhmaṇic thinkers' ceaseless identifications may give the appearance that "anything can result from anything; everything is all," in fact, the identifications that are made in the ritual world come to rest within the locus of the sacrificer's own being. Thus, the entire sacrificial arena, the offering spoons, and in particular the sacrificial stake (to which the victim is tied) is made to the proportions of the sacrificer's own body (*ŚB* 1.2.5.14; 10.2.1.2; *TS* 5.2.5.1; see Eggeling 1882, 78); the victim is equated with the sacrificer himself (see Heesterman 1987, 105; Smith and Doniger 1989, 199–205); and the individual elements of the sacrifice are themselves identified with the sacrificer's own body ("the *āhavanīya* altar is his mouth … the priest's tent, his belly … the two fires behind, his feet …" *ŚB* 3.5.3.1ff.). This is both the purpose and the great achievement of the philosophy of the Brāhmaṇas, to see the identities (often invisible, or "mysterious") between the entities that inhabit the ritual world (the sacrificer, sacrificial arena, victim, and priests), and through this knowledge, to create a connection from the world of men to the sacrifice and through it to the cosmos itself, that which ultimately defines the very being of man, the sacrificer.

Beyond the Brāhmaṇas: connections to the Upaniṣads

The Brāhmaṇas end with the Upaniṣads. However, the demarcation between these classes of texts is not a precise one, but rather one of a gradual merging. Although scholars tended to denigrate the former and celebrate the latter—thus, Oldenberg contrasted "the cold, stale rigidity, of the Brāhmaṇa tradition" with the "electrifying vivacity" of the Upaniṣads (1991, 36)—the fact is that Upaniṣadic thought is wholly built on the foundation of the Brāhmaṇas. In particular, the Upaniṣadic thinkers continued to seek connections between entities and build their philosophy around assertions of identity, such as the famous equation between *ātman* and *Brahman*, and to emphasize the unseen or "mysterious" nature of these connections. Where the Upaniṣadic authors diverge from their predecessors, however, is in their gradual movement away from the Vedic ritual performances *per se* (after all, they did not need to explore the rites beyond what the authors of the Brāhmaṇas had already exhaustively provided for them) to look more broadly at the human person (Olivelle 1998, 24), and such "real-world" concerns as birth and death (see, *BĀU* 4.1ff.; 3.2.11–13). Yet, the connection to Brāhmaṇic thought remains vivid as the symbolism of the sacrifice endures as a cornerstone in the Upaniṣadic thinkers' approach to understanding the nature of man. Thus, the famed Upaniṣadic description of what becomes of a man after death, that "his speech disappears into the fire, his breath into the wind, his sight into the sun, his mind into the moon ..." (*BĀU* 3.2.13), replicates precisely the ideology of Puruṣa's cosmogonic sacrifice, or the Upaniṣadic notion that a man's life is a sacrifice ("his first twenty-four years are the morning pressing ... his next forty-four, the midday pressing ..." [*CU* 3.16.1–3]), which recalls the deeply etched bond between man and the ritual of sacrifice as it was established in Brāhmaṇic thought. Although the Upaniṣads mark the end of the Brāhmaṇas, it is through the Upaniṣads that the Brāhmaṇic thinkers continued to be heard in the Indian philosophical tradition.

Abbreviations

BĀU *Bṛhad-Āraṇyaka-Upaniṣad*
CU *Chāndogya Upaniṣad*
PB *Pañcaviṃśa Brāhmaṇa*
ṚV *Ṛgveda Saṃhitā*
ŚB *Śatapatha Brāhmaṇa*
TS *Taittirīya Brāhmaṇa*

Notes

1 The extant Brāhmaṇas are the *Aitareya* and the *Kauṣītaki* (*Ṛgveda* tradition); the *Tāṇḍya Mahābrāhmaṇa* (also known as the *Pañcaviṃśa*), *Ṣaḍviṃśa*, and *Jaiminīya* (*Sāmaveda* tradition); the *Taittirīya* and the *Śatapatha* (*Yajurveda* tradition); and the *Gopatha* (*Atharvaveda* tradition). For references to critical editions and translations of the Brāhmaṇas, see Santucci 1976, 272–278.

2 The term "Brāhmaṇic" is used throughout this chapter to indicate the milieu of the Brāhmaṇa texts, and not the priestly caste generically referred to as the Brahmins.

3 Even Keith (1925, 455), who frequently denigrated Brāhmaṇic thought, noted, "it is impossible to deny the name of philosophy to an ordered view of the universe, fully thought out, and within its fundamental limitations logical and complete." See also Mylius (1976), though his study is limited to the *Kauṣītaki-Brāhmaṇa*.

4 The term *nidāna* is also used frequently in the Brāhmaṇas to suggest connectedness. The oldest meaning of the term is that of "rope" or "halter"—that is, something that physically binds objects together; in later usage, it has the sense of a first or primary cause. See, further, Knipe 1975, 42–43.

Bibliography

Bodewitz, H. W. 1973. *Jaiminīya Brāhmaṇa 1–65: Translation and Commentary*. Leiden: E. J. Brill.

Doniger, Wendy. 1985. *Tales of Sex and Violence: Folklore, Sacrifice, and Danger in the Jaiminīya Brāhmaṇna*. Chicago: University of Chicago Press.

Eggeling, Julius. 1882. *The Śatapatha Brāhmaṇa according to the Text of the Mādhyandina School*. Part I. Oxford: The Clarendon Press.

Eliade, Mircea. 1969. *Yoga: Immortality and Freedom*. Trans. Willard Trask. Princeton: Princeton University Press.

Gonda, Jan. 1965. *Bandhu* in the Brāhmaṇas. *Adyar Library Bulletin* 29: 1–29.

Gonda, Jan. 1967. *Loka: World and Heaven in the Veda*. Verhandelingen der Koninklijke Nederlandse Akademie van Wetenschappen, Afd. Letterkunde 73. Amsterdam: N. V. Noord-Hollandsche Uitgevers Maatschaapij.

Gonda, Jan. 1975. *Vedic Literature: Saṃhitās and Brāhmaṇas*. Wiesbaden: Harrassowitz.

Heesterman, J. C. 1985. *The Inner Conflict of Tradition*. Chicago: University of Chicago Press.

Heesterman, J. C. 1987. Self Sacrifice in Vedic Ritual. In *Gilgul: Essays on Transformation, Revolution, and Permanence in the History of Religions*, ed. S. Shaked, 91–106. Leiden: E. J. Brill.

Heesterman, J. C. 1993. *The Broken World of Sacrifice*. Chicago: University of Chicago Press.

Hopkins, E. W. 1909. Gods and Saints of the Great Brāhmaṇa. *Transactions of the Connecticut Academy of Arts and Science* 15: 23–69.

Keith, A. B. 1925. *The Religion and Philosophy of the Veda and Upanishads*. Harvard Oriental Series, 31–32. Cambridge, MA: Harvard University Press.

Knipe, David. 1975. *In the Image of Fire*. Delhi: Motilal Banarsidass.

Lévi, Sylvain. 1898. *La Doctrine du sacrifice dans les Brāhmaṇas*. Paris: Ernest Leroux.

Malamoud, Charles. 1998. *Cooking the World: Ritual and Thought in Ancient India*. Trans. David White. Delhi: Oxford University Press.

Müller, F. Max. 1859. *A History of Sanskrit Literature as far as it Illustrates the Primitive Religion of the Brahmans*. London: Williams and Nordgate.

Müller, F. Max. 1867. *Chips from a German Workshop*. London: Longmans Green and Co.

Mylius, Klaus. 1976. Die vedischen Identifikationen am Beispiel des Kauṣītaki-Brāhmaṇa. *Klio* 58(1): 145–166.

Oldenberg, Hermann. 1919. *Vorwissenschaftliche Wissenschaft. Die Weltanschauung der Brâhmana-Texte*. Göttingen: Vandenhoek und Rupprecht.

Oldenberg, Hermann. 1991. *The Doctrine of the Upanishads and the Early Buddhism*. Trans. Shridhar Shrotri. Delhi: Motilal Banarsidass.

Olivelle, Patrick. 1998. *The Early Upaniṣads: Annotated Text and Translation*. New York: Oxford University Press.

Rau, Wilhelm. 1957. *Staat und Gesellschaft in Alten Indien nach den Brāhmana-Texten Dargestellt*. Wiesbaden: Harrassowitz.

Santucci, James. 1976. *An Outline of Vedic Literature*. Missoula: Scholars Press.

Smith, Brian K. 1989. *Reflections on Resemblance, Ritual, and Religion*. Oxford: Oxford University Press.

Smith, Brian K. and Wendy Doniger. 1989. Sacrifice and Substitution. *Numen* 36: 189–223.

Thite, G. U. 1975. *Sacrifice in the Brāhmaṇa-Texts*. Poona: University of Poona.

Tull, Herman W. 1989. *The Vedic Origins of Karma: Cosmos as Man in Ancient Indian Myth and Ritual*. Albany: SUNY Press.

Tull, Herman W. 1991. F. Max Müller and A. B. Keith: "Twaddle", the "Stupid" Myth, and the Disease of Indology. *Numen* 38(1): 27–58.

Weber, Albrecht. 1850. Zwei Sagen aus dem Satapatha-Brahmana über Einwanderung und Verbreitung der Arier in Indien, nebst einer geographisch-geschichtlichen Skizze aus dem weissen Yajus. *Indische Studien* 1: 161–232.

Weber, Albrecht. 1885. Eine Legende des Śatapatha Brāhmaṇa über die Strafende Vergeltung nach dem Tode. *Zeitschrift der Deutschen Morgenländischen Gesellschaft* 9: 237–243.

Winternitz, Maurice. 1981 (1909). *A History of Indian Literature*, I. Trans. V. Srinivas Sarma. Delhi: Motilal Banarsidass.

Witzel, Michael. 1979. On Magical Thought in the Veda. Inaugural Lecture. Leiden: Universitaire Pers.

Witzel, Michael. 1987. On the Localisation of Vedic Texts and Schools. In *India and the Ancient World. History, Trade and Culture before A.D. 650. P. H. L. Eggermont Jubilee Volume*, ed. G. Pollet, 173–213. Leuven: Departement Oriëntalistiek.

Witzel, Michael. 1996. How to Enter the Vedic Mind? Strategies in Translating a Brahmana text. In *Translating, Translations, Translators from India to the West*, ed. Enrica Garzilli, 163–176. Harvard Oriental Series, Opera Minora 1. Cambridge, MA: Harvard University Press.

Witzel, Michael. 1997a. The Development of the Vedic Canon and its Schools: The Social and Political Milieu (Materials on Vedic Sakhas 8). In *Inside the Texts, Beyond the Texts. New Approaches to the Study of the Vedas*, ed. Michael Witzel, 257–345. Harvard Oriental Series, Opera Minora 2. Cambridge, MA: Harvard University Press.

Witzel, Michael. 1997b. Early Sanskritization: Origins and development of the Kuru State. In *Recht, Staat und Verwaltung im klassischen Indien*, ed. B. Kölver, 27–52. Munich: R. Oldenbourg.

Chapter 12
UPANIṢADS

Brian Black

Introduction

The Upaniṣads are often considered the beginning of Indian philosophy. Yet despite containing some of the first detailed discussions about philosophical topics such as the self and the nature of existence, there has been considerable disagreement about whether the Upaniṣads themselves constitute philosophy and about their status within the later philosophical tradition in India. This chapter examines some of the main ideas put forth by the texts, as well as some of their most significant influences on subsequent developments in Indian philosophy, while also briefly considering the question of whether the Upaniṣads themselves are philosophy, or merely the pre-philosophical basis for later traditions.

The Upaniṣads and the Vedas

The Upaniṣads are the fourth and final section of a larger group of texts called the Vedas. There are four different collections of Vedic texts, the *Ṛgveda*, *Yajurveda*, *Sāmaveda*, and *Atharvaveda*, with each of these collections containing four different layers of textual material: the Saṃhitās, Brāhmaṇas, Āraṇyakas, and Upaniṣads. In addition to those attached to the Vedas, there are literally hundreds of other texts bearing the name *Upaniṣad*. Because the Vedic ones have been the most influential in Indian philosophy and beyond, this discussion will focus exclusively on them.

From ritual to philosophy

Due to their connection with previous Vedic material, the Upaniṣads generally assume a ritual context, containing many passages that explain the significance of ritual actions or interpret *mantras* (sacred verses) spoken during the ritual. One of the most prevalent tendencies to continue from the ritual texts is an attempt to identify the underlying connections (*bandhus*) that exist among different orders of reality. Often these connections were made among three spheres: the cosmos, the body of the sponsor of the ritual (*yajamāna*), and the ritual grounds – in other words, between the macrocosm, the microcosm, and the ritual.

The Upaniṣads, particularly the earlier ones, extend such Vedic modes of thinking beyond the ritual context. In its earliest textual contexts the word *upaniṣad* takes on a meaning similar to *bandhu*, describing a connection between things, often presented in a hierarchical relationship. In these contexts *upaniṣad* designates equivalences between components of different realms of reality that were not considered to be observable by the senses, but remained concealed and obscured, and required special knowledge or understanding. On several occasions, *upaniṣad* means 'secret teaching' (i.e. CU 1.1.10; 1.13.4; 8.8.4; BU 2.1.20; 4.2.1; 5.5.3–4), a notion that is reinforced by the use of other formulations such as *guhyā ādeśā* ('hidden instruction'; BU 3.5.2) and *para guhya* ('supreme secret'; KaU 3.17; SU 6.22).

Another important idea that emerges out of a ritual context is karma (*karman*), which literally means 'action'. In earlier Vedic material karma refers to any ritual action, which, if performed correctly, yields beneficial results, but, if performed incorrectly, brings about negative consequences. The Upaniṣads do not offer any explicit theory of karma, but do contain a number of teachings that seem to extend the notion of karma beyond the ritual context to a more general understanding of moral retribution. Yājñavalkya, for example, when asked by Ārtabhāga about what happens to a person after death, responds that a person becomes good by good action and bad by bad action (BU 3.2.13).

Similarly, in the *Chāndogya Upaniṣad* (5.4–10) King Pravāhaṇa Jaivali links karma to the process of rebirth when he discloses to the brahmin Uddālaka Āruṇi the knowledge of the five fires (*pañcāgnividyā*). Pravāhaṇa's instruction, which also appears in the *Bṛhadāraṇyaka Upaniṣad* (6.2.9–16) but without the explicit connection to karma, describes human life as part of a cycle of regeneration, whereby the essence of life takes on different forms as it passes through different levels of existence. In both the *Chāndogya* and *Bṛhadāraṇyaka Upaniṣads*, Pravāhaṇa combines his teaching of the five fires with the discourse of the two paths of the dead – a discourse which also appears in slightly different variations in other Upaniṣads: e.g. *Muṇḍaka* (1.2.10–11), *Kaṭha* (1.3), *Praśna* (1.9–10). According to Pravāhaṇa, those who know the teaching of the five fires follow the path of the gods and enter the world of *brahman*, but those who do not know this teaching will follow the path of the ancestors and continue to be reborn.

In the *Chāndogya Upaniṣad* (5.10.7–8), Pravāhaṇa elaborates further, stating that one's actions in this lifetime affect one's birth status in the next. Although the *Bṛhadāraṇyaka* version of this teaching does not contain this explicit link between *karma* and rebirth, in both accounts Pravāhaṇa teaches that knowledge of the teaching of the five fires will affect the conditions of one's future births. In the *Bṛhadāraṇyaka* (6.2.16) he warns that those who do not know will become worms, insects, or snakes, while in the *Chāndogya* (5.10.10) he suggests that knowledge can lead one to be free of karmic consequences.

Such discussions linking actions in one lifetime to consequences in a future one would become widely accepted in subsequent philosophical discourse – not only among Hindus, but also by Buddhists and Jainas, and, to a certain extent, by the Ājīvikas. A related term, *saṃsāra*, which refers to the cycle of birth, life, death, and rebirth, begins to be used in the comparatively late *Kaṭha* (3.7) and *Śvetāśvatara* (6.16) *Upaniṣads*. Closely related to *saṃsāra* is *mokṣa*, the concept that one can escape or be released from the endless cycle of repeated births. Similar to *saṃsāra*, the Upaniṣads to not contain an explicit theory about *mokṣa*, with the term only assuming its connotations of spiritual liberation in the later texts (i.e. SU 6.16). The Hindu *darśanas* would subsequently consider *mokṣa* to be a fundamental teaching of all the Upaniṣads, but the texts themselves, particularly the early ones, focus much more attention on securing wealth, status, and power in this lifetime than on describing existence as an endless cycle. They also tend to present life as desirable, and not as a condition from which people need release or escape. One of the most common soteriological goals is immortality, *amṛta*, which literally means 'not dying'. The Upaniṣads describe immortality in a number of different ways, including having a long life span, surviving death in the heavenly world, becoming one with the essential being of the universe, and being preserved in the social memory.

The self in the Upaniṣads

One of the most widely discussed topics throughout both the early and late Upaniṣads is the self (*ātman*). In its earliest textual appearances, *ātman* is used as a reflexive pronoun, much like 'self' in English, but by the time of the late Brāhmaṇas and early Upaniṣads, the word was associated with a wide range of meanings, sometimes referring to the material body, but often designating something like an essence, a life-force, consciousness, or even ultimate reality.

Although *ātman* does not have one consistent meaning across all of its textual appearances, there is considerable consistency as to its meaning according to any particular teacher. Indeed, it is perhaps more fruitful to consider the Upaniṣads as collections of teachings from different teachers, than it is to consider them as unified texts. Not only do different Upaniṣads often have discernibly different philosophical agendas, but different teachers offer distinct teachings that are often in contradistinction to each other, as teachers compete to recruit students, to secure patronage, and to win public debating competitions.

One of the best-known teachings of the self appears in the *Chāndogya Upaniṣad* (6.1–16), as the instruction of Uddālaka Āruṇi to his son Śvetaketu. Uddālaka begins by explaining that one can know the universal of a material substance from a particular object made of that substance: by means of something made of clay, one can know clay; by means of an ornament made of copper, one can know copper; by means of a nail cutter made of iron, one can know iron. Uddālaka uses these examples to explain that objects are not created from nothing, but rather that creation is a process of transformation from an original being (*sat*) which emerges into the multiplicity that characterizes our everyday experiences. Uddālaka's explanation of creation is often assumed to have influenced the *satkāryavāda* theory – the theory that the effect exists within the cause – which was accepted by the Sāṃkhya, Yoga, and Vedānta *darśanas*.

Later in his teaching, Uddālaka makes a series of inferences from comparisons with empirically observable natural phenomena to explain that the self is a non-material essence present in all living beings. He first uses the example of nectar, collected by bees from different sources, but when gathered together becomes an undifferentiated whole. Similarly, water flowing from different rivers merges together without distinction when reaching the ocean. Uddālaka uses these examples to illustrate that the self will eventually merge into the original being (*sat*). After each of these descriptions Uddālaka brings attention back to Śvetaketu, as he repeats the words 'you are that' (*tat tvam asi*), emphasizing that the self operates the same way in him as it does in all living beings (CU 6.8.7).

Yājñavalkya, the most prominent teacher in the *Bṛhadāraṇyaka Upaniṣad*, characterizes *ātman* more in terms of consciousness than as a life-force. In a debate that pits him against Uddālaka – his senior colleague and, by some accounts, his former teacher (BU 6.3.7; 6.5.3) – Yājñavalkya explains that the self is the inner controller, present within all sensing and cognizing, yet at the same time distinct: 'He is the seer that cannot be seen, the hearer that cannot be heard, the thinker that cannot be thought, the knower that cannot be known' (BU 3.7.23). Here, Yājñavalkya explains that we know the existence of the self through actions of the self, through what the self does, not through our senses – that the self, as consciousness, cannot be an object of consciousness. As Yājñavalkya rhetorically asks his wife Maitreyī later in the *Bṛhadāraṇyaka Upaniṣad*: 'By what means can one know him, by means of whom one knows this whole world?' (4.5.15).

Prajāpati, the creator god of Vedic ritual texts, is recast in the *Chāndogya Upaniṣad* as another prominent teacher of the self. Similar to Yājñavalkya, Prajāpati conceptualizes the self in terms of consciousness, describing *ātman* as the agent responsible for sensing and cognizing: *ātman* is 'the one who is aware' (CU 8.12.4–5). However, despite some similarities with Yājñavalkya's teaching, Prajāpati rejects a description of *ātman* in terms of dreamless sleep, a teaching of the self that Yājñavalkya describes as the 'highest goal' and 'the highest bliss' in his instruction to King Janaka (BU 4.3.32).

Perhaps the most famous teachings of the self, the identification of *ātman* and *brahman*, is delivered by Śāṇḍilya in the *Chāndogya Upaniṣad*. Similar to the term *ātman*, *brahman* has a number of different, yet related, connotations in Vedic literature. The oldest usages of the word are closely connected with the power of speech, with *brahman* meaning a truthful utterance or powerful statement. In the Upaniṣads *brahman* retains this connection with speech, but also comes to refer to ultimate reality.

Śāṇḍilya begins his teaching by stating that *brahman* is the entire world. He then explains what happens to people at the time of death as in accordance with their resolve in this world. After describing *ātman* in various ways, Śāṇḍilya equates *ātman* with *brahman*: 'This self (*ātman*) of mine within the heart is *brahman*. On departing from here, I will enter into him' (CU 3.14.4). This teaching clearly implies that if one understands *brahman* as the entire world, and one understands that the self is *brahman*, then one becomes the entire world at the time of death.

Although Śāṇḍilya's teaching of *ātman* and *brahman* is often considered the central doctrine of the Upaniṣads, it is important to remember that this is not the only characterization either of the self or of ultimate reality. While some teachers, such as

Yājñavalkya, also equate *ātman* with *brahman* (BU 4.4.5), others, such as Uddālaka Āruṇi, do not make this identification. Indeed, Uddālaka, whose famous phrase *tat tvam asi* is later taken by Śaṅkara to be a statement of the identity of *ātman* and *brahman*, never uses the term the *brahman* – neither in his instruction to his son Śvetaketu, nor on any other of his many appearances in the Upaniṣads. Moreover, it is often unclear, even in Śāṇḍilya's teaching, whether linking *ātman* with *brahman* refers to the complete identity of the self and ultimate reality, or if *ātman* is considered an aspect or quality of *brahman*. Such debates about how to interpret the teachings of the Upaniṣads have continued throughout the Indian philosophical tradition, and are particularly characteristic of the Vedānta *darśana*.

Furthermore, while most teachings about *brahman* assume that the world emerged from one undifferentiated abstract cosmic principle, there are a number of passages explaining creation in terms of a more materialist point of view, describing the world as coming forth from an initial natural element, such as water or air. The *Bṛhadāraṇyaka Upaniṣad* (5.1), for example, contains a teaching attributed to the son of Kauravyāyanī, depicting *brahman* as space. This same section of the *Bṛhadāraṇyaka Upaniṣad* (5.5.1) includes a passage describing the world as beginning from water. Similarly, in the *Chāndogya Upaniṣad* (4.3.1–2), Raikva traces the beginnings of the world to wind in the cosmic sphere, and breath in the microcosm.

Returning to the self, despite the differences among various teachers' conceptions of *ātman*, there are some general tendencies. Most of the philosophers in the Upaniṣads assume that *ātman* dwells within the body when it is alive, that *ātman*, in one way or another, is responsible for the body being alive, and that *ātman* does not die when the body dies, but rather finds a dwelling place in another body. Such depictions of *ātman* seem to have been a catalyst for or to have developed alongside early Buddhist conceptions of selfhood. The Buddhists explicitly rejected any notion of an indivisible and unchanging self, not only introducing the term not-self (*anātman* in Sanskrit; *anattā* in Pāli) to describe the lack of any fixed essence, but also explaining karmic continuity from one lifetime to the next in terms of the five *skandhas* – a theory maintaining that what Upanishadic thinkers take to be a unified self is really made of five components, all of which are subject to change.

The Upaniṣads as represented in the Hindu *darśanas* before Vedānta

Five of the six so-called 'Hindu' *darśanas* officially recognize the Upaniṣads as a source of philosophy in so far as they recognize *śabda* as a valid means for attaining knowledge. *Śabda* literally means 'word', but in philosophical discourse refers to verbal testimony or reliable authority, and is sometimes taken to refer specifically to *śruti*. Despite the nominal acceptance of *śabda* as a *pramāṇa*, however, the Upaniṣads are only cited occasionally in the surviving texts, and rarely as a source to validate fundamental arguments, before the emergence of the Vedānta school in the seventh century.

Rather, in the extant sources from the early period of the systematized philosophical schools, the influence of the Upaniṣads is more oblique than explicit, with few direct references, yet with many of the dominant terms and concepts seemingly inherited from them. Perhaps most notably, the Upanishadic notion of self – as a spiritual essence separate from the physical body – is generally accepted by the classical Hindu philosophical schools. The Nyāya and Mīmāṃsā *darśanas*, for example, which do not cite the Upaniṣads to prove its existence, nevertheless describe the self as an immaterial substance that resides in and acts through the body. In addition to conceptual similarities with certain passages from the Upaniṣads, both schools seem to consider the Upaniṣads as texts that specialize in the self. The Nyāya philosopher Vātsyāyana (*c.* 350–450 CE), for instance, characterizes the Upaniṣads as dealing with the self.

Similarly, the early texts of the Sāṃkhya and Yoga *darśanas* do not reference the Upaniṣads when making their fundamental arguments, but do seem to inherit much of their terminology, as well as some of their views, from them. At the beginning of Uddālaka Āruṇi's instruction to Śvetaketu in the *Chāndogya Upaniṣad* (6.2–5), for instance, he describes existence (*sat*) as consisting of three forms (*rūpas*): fire (red), water (white), and food (black) – a scheme that closely resembles the later Sāṃkhya doctrine of *prakṛti* and the three *guṇas*. The *Śvetāśvatara Upaniṣad* (4.5), the oldest extant text in Indian literature to use the word *sāṃkhya* (5.2), seems to build on Uddālaka's threefold scheme when describing the unborn as red, white, and black. Also, a number of core terms in Sāṃkhya philosophy first appear in the Upaniṣads, such as *ahaṃkāra* (CU 7.25.1) and the *tattvas* (BU 4.5.12), while some passages contain groups of terms appearing together in ways that are similar to how they appear in later Sāṃkhya texts: the *Kaṭha Upaniṣad* (3.10–11), for example, lists a hierarchy of principles including consciousness (*puruṣa*), discernment (*buddhi*), mind (*manas*), and the sense capacities (*indriyas*).

A number of details about the practice of yoga, which would become more systematized by the Yoga *darśana*, are also first found in the Upaniṣads. The *Kaṭha* (3.3–13; 6.7–11) and *Śvetāśvatara* (2.8–11) *Upaniṣads* both contain some of the first descriptions of exercises for controlling the senses, breathing techniques, and bodily postures, with the *Śvetāśvatara Upaniṣad* (e.g. 2.15–17) making explicit connections between yogic practice and union with a personal god – a connection that would be of central importance in the Yoga *darśana*. The *Maitrī Upaniṣad* (6–7) has the most extensive and systematic discussion of yoga in the Upaniṣads, containing a number of parallels with the *Yoga Sūtra*.

In addition to employing terms and concepts from the Upaniṣads, there are occasions when classical Indian philosophers cite the Upaniṣads directly. Vātsyāyana, of the Nyāya school, quotes passages from the *Bṛhadāraṇyaka* and *Chāndogya Upaniṣads* when discussing *mokṣa*, the means of attaining it, and the stages of life. Additionally, the grammarian Patañjali (*c.* 150 BCE) argues that the study of grammar is useful for a correct understanding of passages from the Upaniṣads, and thus for attaining *mokṣa*.

Such examples indicate that the philosophers of classical Hindu philosophy knew the Upaniṣads quite well and would dip into the texts from time to time to provide an analogy or, occasionally, to support one of their arguments. However, the early surviving texts of the Nyāya, Vaiśeṣika, Mīmāṃsā, Sāṃkhya, and Yoga schools do not tend to use the Upaniṣads to validate their core positions. The *Vaiśeṣika Sūtra* (3.2.8), for example, agrees that the self is discussed in the Upaniṣads, but then argues that proof of the existence of the self should not be established exclusively by means of *śruti*, but also can be determined through inference. Additionally, none of the early schools produced a commentary on the Upaniṣads, nor did any of them aim to offer an interpretation on the Upaniṣads as a whole. As such, the Upaniṣads provided a general philosophical framework, as well as served as a repository for terms and analogies, but none of the early schools claimed the texts for themselves.

An interesting illustration of this point is that competing schools would sometimes recognize that their rival's positions were also to be found in the Upaniṣads. The Nyāya philosopher Jayanta Bhaṭṭa even finds the positions of the heterodox Lokāyata *darśana*, or Materialist school, in the Upaniṣads. In the context of criticizing the validity of *śabda* as a *pramāṇa*, Bhaṭṭa argues that if *śabda* were a valid means for establishing knowledge, then even the doctrines of the Lokāyatas must be true, because their doctrines can be found in the Upaniṣads. Due to lack of sources from the Lokāyata school, we do not know if they ever referred to the Upaniṣads in their own texts, but Bhaṭṭa's argument is illustrative of a general reluctance of most of the early schools to put too much stake in *śruti* as a means of knowledge. His comments also reflect an acknowledgement that the Upaniṣads contain a variety of viewpoints.

The Upaniṣads and Vedānta

The oldest surviving systematic interpretation of the Upaniṣads is the *Brahma Sūtra* (200 BCE–200 CE), attributed to Bādarāyaṇa. Although not technically a commentary (i.e. it is a *sūtra* rather than a *bhāṣya*), the *Brahma Sūtra* is an explanation of the philosophy of the Upaniṣads, treating the texts as the source for knowledge about *brahman*. Despite being considered a Vedānta text, the *Brahma Sūtra* (aka *Vedānta Sūtra*) was composed centuries before the establishment of Vedānta as a philosophical school.

The Vedānta *darśana* was the first philosophical school to attempt to present the Upaniṣads as holding a unified philosophical position. Vedānta means 'end of the Vedas' and is often used to refer specifically to the Upaniṣads. The school of Vedānta divides the Vedas into two sections: *karmakānda*, the section of spiritual exegesis (consisting of the Saṃhitās and the Brāhmaṇas); and *jñānakānda*, the section of knowledge (consisting of the Upaniṣads and, to a certain extent, the Āraṇyakas). According to the Vedānta school, the ritual section contains detailed instructions on how to perform the rituals, whereas the Upaniṣads contain transcendent knowledge for the sake of achieving *mokṣa*. There are three main branches of the Vedānta school: Advaita Vedānta, Viśiṣtādvaita Vedānta, and Dvaita Vedānta. Although these branches of Vedānta would put forth distinct philosophical positions from each other, they all took *śabda* as the exclusive means to knowledge about its central doctrines and considered the Upaniṣads, the *Brahma Sūtra*, and *Bhagavad Gītā* as its core texts (*prasthānatraya*). Despite disagreeing with each other, all three of the best-known philosophers of the Vedānta school – Śaṅkara, Rāmānuja, and Madhva – wrote commentaries on the Upaniṣads, presenting them as having a single, consistent philosophical position.

The best-known philosopher of the Vedānta school was Śaṅkara (*c.* 700 CE), whose interpretations of the Upaniṣads made a major impact on the Indian philosophical tradition in the centuries after his lifetime and continued to dominate readings of the texts throughout the nineteenth and early twentieth centuries. Śaṅkara was the main proponent of Advaita Vedānta, which put forth a position of non-dualism. According to Śaṅkara the fundamental teaching of the Upaniṣads is that *ātman* and *brahman* are one and the same.

Despite the significance of Śaṅkara's philosophy, it is important to note that his interpretation of the Upaniṣads was not the only one accepted by philosophers of the Vedānta school. Rāmānuja (*c.* 1000 CE), the main proponent of a form of Vedānta known as Viśiṣṭādvaita, or qualified non-dualism, used the Upaniṣads to argue that *ātman* is not identical with *brahman*, but an aspect of *brahman*. Rāmānuja also found in the Upaniṣads a source for *bhakti*, as he identified the Upaniṣadic *brahman* with God. Two centuries later, Madhva (*c.* 1200 CE) used the Upaniṣads as a source for a dualist branch of the school, known as Dvaita Vedānta. Madhva interpreted *brahman* as an infinite and independent God, with the self as finite and dependent. As such, *ātman* is dependent upon *brahman*, but they are not exactly the same.

It is well known that the Vedānta school became extremely influential in shaping subsequent philosophical debates, and we may conjecture that the tendency for various Vedānta philosophers to use the Upaniṣads in support of their own positions, as well as in their criticisms of rival schools, prompted other schools to engage the Upaniṣads more closely. This is illustrated by the fact that schools such as Nyāya and Sāṃkhya, which previously seem to have relied very little on the Upaniṣads, began invoking them to counter the claims of Advaita Vedānta.

The Upaniṣads as philosophy

Despite their undeniable contribution to subsequent Indian philosophical traditions, there has been disagreement about whether or not the Upaniṣads themselves constitute philosophy. Much of this debate depends, of course, on how one defines philosophy.

A recurring argument as to why the Upaniṣads might not be considered philosophy is that they do not contain a unified or systematic position. This, however, largely reflects the composite and fragmented nature of the texts. Moreover, the teachers portrayed in the Upaniṣads do not seem to make linear arguments that start with premises and build to larger conclusions, but rather tend to make points through analogies and metaphors, with many core ideas presented as truths or insights known to particular teachers, not as logical propositions that can be independently verified.

Nonetheless, in a number of sections of the texts there appear to be implicit philosophical methods in place. We have already noted that Yājñavalkya's discussion of the self is based on a reflective introspection. The early Upaniṣads do not contain passages explicitly articulating method, but with the development of *yoga* and meditation in the later texts, introspection begins to be formalized as a philosophical mode of enquiry. Also, many of Uddālaka Āruṇi's descriptions of *ātman* are derived from his observations of the natural world. Moreover, some dialogues contain an implicit dialectic, where opposing views lead towards a unified position. Indeed, the Upaniṣads appear to have been influential in the development of debate, which would become one of the central social practices associated with Indian philosophy. Although the texts do not discuss debate reflectively, a number of the most important teachings are articulated within the context of discussions between teachers and students, and verbal disputes among rival brahmins. In this way, debate is another way by which the Upaniṣads extend ideas first articulated in the context of the Vedic ritual into a more philosophical discourse.

Bibliography

Black, Brian. 2007. *The Character of the Self in Ancient India: Priests, Kings, and Women in the Early Upaniṣads*. Albany: State University of New York Press.

Black, Brian. 2011a. "Ambaṭṭha and Śvetaketu: Literary Connections between the Upaniṣads and Early Buddhist Narratives." *Journal of the American Academy of Religion* 79(1): 136–161.

Black, Brian. 2011b. "The Rhetoric of Secrecy in the Upaniṣads." In *Essays in Honor of Patrick Olivelle*, ed. Steven Lindquist. Florence: Florence University Press, pp. 101–125.

Black, Brian. 2015. "Dialogue and Difference: Encountering the Other in Indian Religious and Philosophical Sources." In *Dialogue in Early South Asian Religions: Hindu, Buddhist, and Jain Traditions*, ed. Brian Black and Laurie Patton. Farnham: Ashgate, pp. 243–257.

Brereton, Joel. 1990. "The Upanishads." In *Approaches to the Asian Classics*, ed. Wm. T. de Bary and I. Bloom. New York: Columbia University Press, pp. 115–135.

Cohen, Signe. 2008. *Text and Authority in the Older Upaniṣads*. Leiden: Brill.

Ganeri, Jonardon. 2007. *The Concealed Art of the Soul: Theories of Self and Practices of Truth in Indian Ethics and Epistemology*. Oxford: Oxford University Press.

Killingley, Dermot. 1997. "The Paths of the Dead and the Five Fires." In *Indian Insights: Buddhism, Brahmanism and Bhakti: Papers from the Annual Spalding Symposium on Indian Religions*, ed. Peter Connolly and Sue Hamilton. London: Luzac Oriental, pp. 1–20.

Lindquist, Steven. 2008. "Gender at Janaka's Court: Women in the *Bṛhadāraṇyaka Upaniṣad* Reconsidered." *Journal of Indian Philosophy* 36(3): 405–426.

Lindquist, Steven. 2011. "Literary Lives and a Literal Death: Yājñavalkya, Śākalya, and an Upaniṣadic Death Sentence." *Journal of the American Academy of Religion* 79(1): 33–57.

Olivelle, Patrick. (Trans.). 1998. *The Early Upaniṣads: Annotated Text and Translation*. New York: Oxford University Press.

Olivelle, Patrick. 1999. "Young Śvetaketu: A Literary Study of an Upaniṣadic Story." *Journal of the American Oriental Society* 119(1): 46–70.

Patton, Laurie. 2004. "Veda and Upaniṣad." In *The Hindu World*, ed. Sushil Mittal and Gene Thursby. London: Routledge, pp. 37–51.

Roebuck, Valerie. (Trans.). 2004. *The Upaniṣads*. Harmondsworth: Penguin.

Thapar, Romila. 1993. "Sacrifice, Surplus, and the Soul." *History of Religions* 33(4): 305–324.

Witzel, Michael. 2003. "Vedas and Upaniṣads." In *The Blackwell Companion to Hinduism*, ed. Gavin Flood. Oxford: Blackwell Publishing, pp. 68–98.

Chapter 13
SĀṂKHYA

Mikel Burley

Introduction

Sāṃkhya is widely regarded as the oldest, or one of the oldest, systems of Indian philosophy (Mainkar 1972, 1). Its influence is pervasive throughout traditional Indic mythology and religion as well as philosophy. The Sāṃkhya system is held by its adherents to comprise the infallible teachings of Kapila, who has a mythic status and is lauded as the 'prime seer' (*paramarṣi*). The earliest extant comprehensive presentation of Sāṃkhya philosophy is the *Sāṃkhyakārikā* (*SK*) of Īśvarakṛṣṇa (c. 350–450 CE). It is this text that has long been identified as the classical source, and much of the available Sāṃkhya literature consists of commentaries upon it.

Sāṃkhya is typically counted as one of the six 'orthodox viewpoints' (*āstika darśanas*) of classical Indian philosophy, and is closely allied with Yoga. Indeed, the classical Yoga of Patañjali is itself traditionally classed as an 'exposition of Sāṃkhya' (Dasgupta 1930, 2). Although this should not be taken to indicate that Patañjali's Yoga and classical Sāṃkhya are identical, it is highly likely that they developed out of the same pool of philosophical ideas.

In common with much Indian philosophical thought, Sāṃkhya's guiding motivation is soteriological. The system offers a means by which dissatisfaction or distress (*duḥkha*) can be alleviated and finally eradicated, and the 'self' (*puruṣa*) can achieve a state of liberation or 'aloneness' (*kaivalya*). Most distinctive of Sāṃkhya is its doctrine of 'creative emergence' (*SK* 21), according to which the beginningless conjunction of two primordial principles, namely *puruṣa* and the 'creative source' (*prakṛti*, *pradhāna*), generates a series of twenty-three further principles. The main task in any exegesis of Sāṃkhya is to interpret what this ostensibly metaphysical schema represents.

Sāṃkhya-related themes in early sources

The understanding of Sāṃkhya's origins within the tradition itself is that in some unspecified epoch a great seer named Kapila communicated the Sāṃkhya teachings to a disciple named Āsuri out of compassion for suffering humanity; Āsuri in turn transmitted them to Pañcaśikha, and by Pañcaśikha they were 'widely disseminated' (*SK*

70). Īśvarakṛṣṇa endorses this account and claims to be faithfully expounding in verse form the doctrines derived from Kapila (*SK* 71). Modern scholars, by contrast, have for the most part regarded the system presented in the *Sāṃkhyakārikā* as the product of a gradual evolution of ideas, fragments of which are scattered throughout many earlier works of Indian thought.

The oldest sources of motifs distinctive of Sāṃkhya are the early prose Upaniṣads, notably the *Chāndogya*, *Bṛhadāraṇyaka*, *Aitareya* and *Kauṣītaki*. The doctrine that *prakṛti*, out of which all phenomena emerge, comprises three complementary 'strands' (*guṇas*) is prefigured in *Chāndogya Upaniṣad* 6.4.1–7, where fire, sun, moon and lightning are each said to be constituted by three 'forms' (*rūpas*). These forms are fire, water and soil, and are associated with the colours red, white and black, respectively. They correspond to *rajas* (energy), *sattva* (purity) and *tamas* (opacity) in classical Sāṃkhya.

The *Chāndogya Upaniṣad* also contains the earliest known occurrence of the term *ahaṃkāra*. Literally 'I-maker', this can be understood as the self-individuating principle – the thought of oneself *as a self*. *Chāndogya Upaniṣad* 7.25.1 elaborates this as the thought that 'I am, indeed, all this'; in other words, I am the whole empirical world. This and similar passages can be interpreted to mean that the affirmation of one's individuality is what instigates the world's coming into manifestation (Van Buitenen 1957, 19–21), an idea that foreshadows *Sāṃkhyakārikā* 24–25. In the latter verses, *ahaṃkāra* is described as the source of both the full range of sensory capacities and the five modes of sensory content, which in turn engender material elements.

A common way of distinguishing between variant streams of Sāṃkhya is in terms of the attitude adopted towards a deity (*deva*) or 'lord' (*īśvara*). Versions of Sāṃkhya that explicitly revere a divine being are designated *seśvara* ('with lord') and those that do not are designated *nirīśvara* ('without lord') (Gopal 2000, 301–317). The *seśvara* stream is exemplified by the *Śvetāśvatara Upaniṣad*, whereas the *Sāṃkhyakārikā* is generally regarded as *nirīśvara*. Although this is a legitimate distinction to make, it can easily be misrepresented when expressed in terms of 'theistic' versus 'atheistic' Sāṃkhya. Examination of some of the ways in which the divine being is described in the *Śvetāśvatara Upaniṣad* reveals them to resemble descriptions of the self (*puruṣa*) in so-called *nirīśvara* texts. *Śvetāśvatara Upaniṣad* 6.11, for example, declares that the one deity 'dwells in all beings' as 'witness, consciousness, alone, and without *guṇas*'.[1] This pre-echoes *Sāṃkhyakārikā* 19, where *puruṣa* is characterized in terms of 'witnessing, aloneness, equanimity, awareness and inactivity'. Caution is thus advisable before assuming there to be a clear theological divergence between versions of Sāṃkhya that appear to affirm, and those that appear to reject or ignore, the existence of a divine being.

Classical Sāṃkhya's metaphysical analysis, which can plausibly be understood as an analysis of the constitutive features of possible experience, is anticipated in several Upaniṣads. *Kaṭha Upaniṣad* 1.3.10–11, for example, presents an ascending order of capacities for sensation and mentation, beyond all of which lies the self (*puruṣa*). Similarly, *Praśna Upaniṣad* 4.8–9 offers an extensive list of capacities that are required for worldly engagement along with the intentional objects of those capacities, followed by the proclamation that *puruṣa* is 'the highest, undecaying self' (*pare'kṣara ātmani*). A relatively late Upaniṣad, the *Maitrāyaṇīya*, identifies *puruṣa* with consciousness (*cetas*) and describes *prakṛti*, comprising 'three strands' (*triguṇa*), as acting for the sake of *puruṣa*'s enjoyment (see Radhakrishnan 1978, 823–825). All of these are prevalent notions in classical Sāṃkhya and Yoga.

Sāṃkhya doctrines and concepts also occur in treatises on Āyurvedic medicine, ethical and legal compendia such as the *Mānava Dharmaśāstra*, an early account of the life of the Buddha by Aśvaghoṣa (*c*. 80–150 CE), and in India's vast epic and mythological literature, including several Purāṇas and sections of the *Mahābhārata* (notably the *Mokṣadharma* and *Bhagavadgītā*). This wealth of material strongly suggests the existence of systematic Sāṃkhya treatises prior to the *Sāṃkhyakārikā*, though none have survived.

Classical Sāṃkhya

The term 'classical Sāṃkhya' is used by scholars to denote the philosophical system expounded primarily in Īśvarakṛṣṇa's *Sāṃkhyakārikā* and secondarily in traditional commentaries thereon, eight of which are extant. The *Sāṃkhyakārikā* comprises seventy-two (or sometimes seventy-three) two-line verses, each expressing one or more pithy propositions. Argumentative support for the propositions is not fully explicated within the text but is occasionally implied, and the text as a whole constitutes a comprehensive philosophical vision.

Little biographical information is known about Īśvarakṛṣṇa. From an early Chinese translation of the *Sāṃkhyakārikā* we learn that he belonged to a Brahmin family named Kauśika, and a commentary called the *Yuktidīpikā* (*c*. 680–720 CE) places him within the lineage of a Sāṃkhya teacher named Vārṣagaṇya, but corroborating evidence within the *Sāṃkhyakārikā* itself is lacking. Since we know that the Chinese translation was made by the Buddhist sage Paramārtha between 557 and 569 CE, the *Sāṃkhyakārikā* must have been composed earlier than 569. Moreover, to have acquired a status warranting translation into Chinese by this date, it would need to have been composed considerably earlier. Thus the *Sāṃkhyakārikā* is normally dated to between 350 and 450 CE.

It appears that, prior to the *Sāṃkhyakārikā*'s composition, theoretical disputes occurred both within the Sāṃkhya school and between proponents of Sāṃkhya and those of rival systems such as Buddhism, Jainism, Nyāya and Vaiśeṣika (Larson and Bhattacharya 1987, 315). From at least as early as the eighth century, however, both polemical critics of Sāṃkhya and compilers of doxographical compendia typically regarded the *Sāṃkhyakārikā* as Sāṃkhya's exemplary treatise. Sāṃkhya's importance as a philosophical system is attested to by its having attracted critical attention from prominent figures such as the Buddhists Śāntarakṣita and Kamalaśīla, and the Advaita Vedāntin Śaṅkara.

Although there is not space here to enter into critical discussion of Sāṃkhya philosophy, the principal doctrines put forward in the *Sāṃkhyakārikā* will be summarized below.

Dualism

The most characteristic feature of Sāṃkhya philosophy is its ontological dualism, the two co-ultimate principles being *puruṣa* and *prakṛti* (or *pradhāna*). *Prakṛti* is constituted by three 'strands' (*guṇas*), whose natural state is passive and equanimous; when this state obtains *prakṛti* is unmanifest (*avyakta*). The natural state is disrupted, however, by the 'proximity' of *puruṣa* (*Tattvakaumudī* 20); and the conjunction of *puruṣa* and *prakṛti* results in a process of creative emergence, which is *prakṛti*'s becoming manifest (*vyakta*).

Prakṛti's 'three-stranded' (*traiguṇya*) constitution comprises *sattva* (purity, existence, the quality of being able to manifest); *rajas* (energy, radiance, the quality of motility and expansion); *tamas* (opacity, inertia, the quality of restriction and stability). Anything appearing to consciousness must instantiate these qualities, though not necessarily in equal proportions. The qualities work together 'like [the parts of] a lamp' in order to liberate the selves (*SK* 13).

In some places the 'self' (*puruṣa*) of Sāṃkhya is talked about as though it were a singular transcendental subject, whereas in other places the existence of a plurality of empirical subjects is admitted. The latter are differentiated by means of their respective character traits and temporal life-spans (*SK* 18). The doctrine implied in the *Sāṃkhyakārikā* is that, in the case of each self, its essence is pure consciousness yet it becomes involved with a complex entity known as a *liṅga*. Literally 'mark' or 'sign', *liṅga* is the collective term for all of *prakṛti*'s twenty-three manifest principles except the five 'elements' (*bhūtas*) (*SK* 40). The *liṅga* may be regarded as a kind of soul which undergoes rebirth from one lifetime to another; it is the locus of psychological dispositions which engender the 'dance' of worldly experience enjoyed by each *puruṣa* (*SK* 42).

The doctrine of a plurality of selves serves an important theoretical role for Sāṃkhya and Yoga, as it enables these systems to explain how the liberation of one individual need not precipitate the liberation of all other sentient beings (cf. *Yogabhāṣya* 2.22).

Creative emergence

The *Sāṃkhyakārikā* presents two complementary taxonomies of emergent principles, one of which is the 'emergence of representations' (*pratyaya-sarga*) and the other of which is the 'creative emergence' (*krtaḥ sargaḥ*). The latter concerns the series of twenty-three principles whose manifestation is initiated by the conjunction of *puruṣa* and *prakṛti* (see *SK* 21–38). Though often portrayed by commentators as a cosmogony, it can also be understood as the product of an analysis of the constitutive features of any possible experience. This interpretation makes sense both of the obviously psychological nature of the majority of the emergent principles and of the taxonomy's relevance to meditative practice, which is central to the soteriological orientation of Sāṃkhya and Yoga. When viewed in this light, the schema of twenty-three manifest principles can be regarded as a 'map' delineating the items from which *puruṣa*

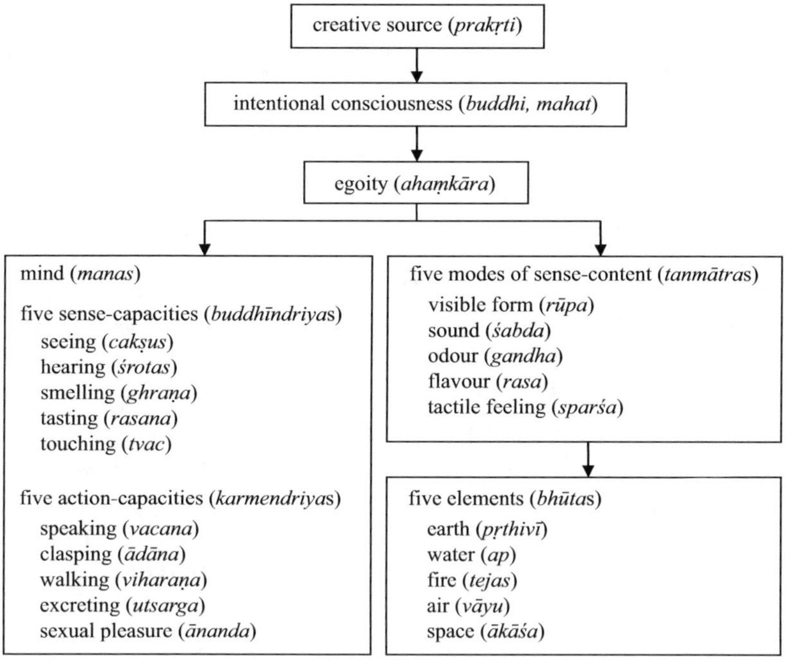

***Figure 13.1* Prakṛti plus the twenty-three principles of the creative emergence**

is to be distinguished. The schema of principles is represented diagrammatically in Figure 13.1.

In *Sāṃkhyakārikā* 63 *prakṛti* is said to 'bind herself' by means of seven 'forms' (*rūpas*) and to liberate herself by means of one form.[2] Though commonly identified as seven of the eight dispositions of *buddhi*, which are mentioned in *Sāṃkhyakārikā* 23 (Larson 1979, 274), the seven binding forms might alternatively be interpreted as the seven main categories into which the manifest principles are divided, namely: (1) *buddhi*, (2) *ahaṃkāra*, (3) *manas*, (4) *buddhīndriyas*, (5) *karmendriyas*, (6) *tanmātras* and (7) *bhūtas*. This would leave *prakṛti* herself, in her unmanifest aspect, as the one 'form' by means of which she is liberated. Since her liberation is 'for the sake of each *puruṣa*' (*SK* 63), there is a sense in which *puruṣa*'s liberation depends on that of *prakṛti*. This doctrine emphasizes the fact that *prakṛti* is the active partner in the dualist ontology, even though her activity is ultimately not for her own sake.

Taking each of the seven main categories of manifest principles in reverse order, the following points can be noted. With regard to the five *bhūtas*, traditional commentators concur that these are the four classical elements plus 'space' (*ākāśa*). They can be interpreted as states or qualities of matter, such that 'earth' (*pṛthivī*) stands for solidity or hardness, 'water' (*ap*) for liquidity, 'fire' (*tejas*) for light or heat, 'air' (*vāyu*) for gaseousness and *ākāśa* for the three-dimensional space which is necessary for each of the other elements to manifest (Burley 2007, 124).

The *tanmātras* (literally 'measures of that') are the five modes of sensory content, with the *buddhīndriyas* being the 'doors' through which these contentful modes enter conscious experience (*SK* 35). The *karmendriyas*, though literally 'action-capacities', are probably best understood as capacities for bodily awareness in the form of proprioception, kinaesthesia and sexual pleasure. Together, the *buddhīndriyas* and *karmendriyas* constitute the ten 'capacities' (*indriyas*); the role of *manas* is to synthesize these into an experiential whole.

Ahaṃkāra, the principle of 'egoity' or 'self-consciousness', facilitates the attribution of inner and outer experience to oneself, and *buddhi* (also called 'the great', *mahat*) is intentional consciousness – the discernment of any experiential content whatsoever. *Buddhi* has two aspects, one lucid (*sāttvika*) and the other dull (*tāmasa*). The former of these comprises the qualities of virtue (*dharma*), knowledge, non-attachment and masterfulness, whereas the latter comprises the opposite qualities (*SK* 23).

Thus the series of twenty-three emergent principles, divided into seven categories, forms a comprehensive schema, which appears to be based on a combination of phenomenological analysis and reflection upon the necessary conditions of possible experience. A 'metaphysics of experience' may therefore be a more apt term for it than a cosmogony or cosmic ontology.

Exposition of character traits

In addition to the 'creative emergence', the *Sāṃkhyakārikā* outlines a secondary emergent series, the 'emergence of representations' (*pratyaya-sarga*), comprising fifty personal dispositions or character traits (*bhāvas*). The functions of these traits and that of the *liṅga* are said to be mutually dependent, thus suggesting that experience and character formation go hand in hand. The traits are categorized as follows:

five kinds of delusion (*viparyaya*),

subdivided into eight kinds of dullness, eight kinds of perplexity, ten kinds of severe perplexity, eighteen kinds of depression and eighteen kinds of intense depression (*SK* 48);

twenty-eight kinds of incapacity (*aśakti*),

comprising eleven kinds of sensory impairment (that is, impairments to one or other of the ten *indriyas* plus *manas*) and seventeen kinds of impairment to *buddhi* (*SK* 49);

nine kinds of contentment (*tuṣṭi*),

comprising four 'internal' kinds, concerning, respectively, natural constitution, acquisition, time and fortune;[3] and five 'external' kinds, each consisting in non-attachment to one or other of the five modes of sensory stimulation (*SK* 50);

eight kinds of excellence (*siddhi*),

distinguishable by virtue of their respective means of attainment, namely: reasoning, verbal instruction, study, eradication of the threefold distress, friendliness, generosity and the transcendence of each of the previous three categories (that is, delusion, incapacity and contentment) (*SK* 51). Of these excellences, the commentator Vācaspatimiśra singles out eradication of the 'threefold distress' (*duḥkha-traya*) as the principal attainment, the others being primarily means to that end (*Tattvakaumudī* 51). This contention gains plausibility from the fact that such eradication is presented in *Sāṃkhyakārikā* 1 as the motivation for the whole Sāṃkhya system.

Hierarchy of beings

According to Sāṃkhya there are three main realms of existence 'from Brahmā down to a blade of grass' (*SK* 54). These are: the 'upper' (*ūrdhva*), populated by eight varieties of divine beings and in which luminosity (*sattva*) predominates; the 'middle' (*madhya*), populated by human beings alone and in which energy or activity (*rajas*) predominates; and the 'basal' (*mūlata*) realm, populated by five varieties of beings 'of animal origin' (*tairyagyona*) and in which darkness (*tamas*) predominates. This hierarchy of a total of fourteen levels of beings represents the various forms of life that any *puruṣa* may undergo, enduring repeated bouts of decay and death until its final liberation (*SK* 55).

Doctrine of pre-existent effect

Sāṃkhyakārikā 9 tersely propounds what is commonly referred to as the 'doctrine of pre-existent effect' (*satkāryavāda*). This is normally interpreted as the view that anything which is an effect pre-exists in its cause, and hence that novelty is entirely absent from the universe (see, e.g., Sastri 1948, 23–24). When interpreted in this way, the terms 'cause' and 'effect' are assumed to refer specifically to processes of *material* causality. Thus, in both the traditional and more recent commentarial literature, the doctrine is illustrated by means of analogies such as that of threads being the cause of a piece of cloth or a lump of clay being the cause of a clay jar that is made from it (*Tatvakaumudī* 9).

The intended purpose of analogies such as those just mentioned is to elucidate the relation between unmanifest *prakṛti* and the manifest principles that constitute the creative emergence. The underlying thought is that the emergence is not literally creative, but is rather the appearing of something, or of a series of things, which existed *in potentia* all along. Thus, with reference to the analogy of the clay jar, it would be inappropriate to think of unmanifest *prakṛti* as an amorphous lump that is somehow made into a formal entity by means of an efficient agent analogous to a potter. Rather, the jar is to be thought of as the phenomenal appearance of something which, in itself, has no phenomenal qualities. By analogy, *buddhi* and the other constituents of possible experience are the appearance that *prakṛti* assumes when she is in the presence of *puruṣa*. In this light, the doctrine can be read as implying a kind of subject-dependence concerning the constitution of the empirical world: although that out of which experience is formed has an unmanifest existence independently of consciousness, it acquires phenomenal characteristics only by virtue of its being an object for a conscious subject.

Soteriology

According to Sāṃkhya the manifestation of *prakṛti* occurs not for its own sake but exclusively for the purpose of *puruṣa*. This purpose is said to be twofold, involving both the perceiving of *pradhāna* (= *prakṛti*) and the attainment of 'aloneness' (*kaivalya*) (*SK* 21; *Yogasūtra* 2.18). Although this suggests that perceptual experience is itself of benefit to *puruṣa*, it would seem that it is beneficial only insofar as it leads to the ultimate goal of transcendence. *Prakṛti*'s primary imperative is to expedite *puruṣa*'s recognition of his non-identity with her, which recognition itself precipitates the dissolution of all manifest phenomena into their source, namely unmanifest *prakṛti*.

Sāṃkhya's guiding philosophical impulse is soteriological, its goal being to put an end to the 'threefold distress' (*SK* 1), which is typically explicated as the distress caused by (a) mental and physical disturbance; (b) the influence of other people, animals and things; and (c) supernatural forces (*Tattvakaumudī* 1). The prescribed method for achieving this goal is termed *tattva-abhyāsa*, literally 'the [assiduous] practice of that-ness' (*SK* 64), which involves sustained attentiveness to the constitutive features of experience and a progressively refined discernment of the ontological difference between manifest phenomena (*vyakta*), their unmanifest ground (*avyakta*) and the knower itself (*jña*, *puruṣa*) (*SK* 2).

The systematic dissociation of the knower or conscious subject from everything that is other than itself engenders a state in which the subject persists in an embodied form only due to the 'momentum of impressions' (*saṃskāravaśāt*), these being psychologically ingrained habit patterns that have built up over multiple lifetimes (*SK* 67). Once these patterns have burnt themselves out, embodied existence ceases and the liberated *puruṣa* abides in solitary aloneness (*kaivalya*), 'which is both singular and conclusive' (*SK* 68).

Sāṃkhya after the Sāṃkhyakārikā

The esteemed position of the *Sāṃkhyakārikā* within the Sāṃkhya tradition is evinced by the fact that the majority of subsequent Sāṃkhya texts are commentaries upon it. Of the eight surviving commentaries, the two most important are the *Yuktidīpikā* and the *Tattvakaumudī*. Since its rediscovery in the 1930s, the *Yuktidīpikā*, whose authorship is unknown, has provided a rich source of information pertaining to Sāṃkhya's pedagogical lineage. Much of its commentary takes the form of dialectical exchanges between a proponent and an opponent of Sāṃkhya, thereby shedding light on the kinds of debates that would historically have surrounded Sāṃkhya doctrines. The *Tattvakaumudī* is reliably ascribed to Vācaspatimiśra (ninth or tenth century CE) and is 'by far the best-known text of Sāṃkhya all over India' (Larson and Bhattacharya 1987, 302). It provides informative exegetical elaborations of each verse of the *Sāṃkhyakārikā* in turn.

Subsequent to the period in which the *Sāṃkhyakārikā* and its commentaries prevailed, two further Sāṃkhya texts appeared, composed in concise *sūtras* rather than verses and named, respectively, the *Tattvasamāsasūtra* and the *Sāṃkhyasūtra* (or *Sāṃkhyapravacanasūtra*). Both of these have been apocryphally attributed to Kapila, and have attracted commentarial treatments. The *Tattvasamāsasūtra* is a schematic work comprising a mere twenty-five short *sūtras*, the last of which was probably added by the unknown author of a commentary entitled *Kramadīpikā*. This commentary dates from the late fourteenth century CE, and the *Tattvasamāsasūtra* is likely to be only a little older, though it contains phrases that are prefigured in much earlier works (Larson and Bhattacharya 1987, 318–319). Neither the text nor its commentaries adds to previous Sāṃkhya philosophy but serves instead to summarize the system's salient doctrines.

A commentary by Aniruddha on the *Sāṃkhyasūtra* first appeared in the late fifteenth century, and it is thought likely that the *Sāṃkhyasūtra* itself was composed a little earlier in that century. A second commentary, by Vijñānabhikṣu, was composed during the second half of the sixteenth century, and two further commentaries exist from the late seventeenth and early eighteenth centuries, respectively. The text itself comprises 527 *sūtras*, divided into six chapters. The contents of the first three chapters closely resemble that of the *Sāṃkhyakārikā*; the fourth chapter comprises a series of references to proverbs or parables designed to illustrate themes from Sāṃkhya philosophy; the fifth chapter contains objections to the views of opponents, some of these objections being based on reasoned argument and others being based on appeal to Vedic authority (*śruti*); and the sixth chapter contains reiterations of key Sāṃkhya doctrines along with additional reasons for upholding them. Overall, the work is of considerable philosophical importance, though it has failed to supersede the *Sāṃkhyakārikā* as the foremost encapsulation of Sāṃkhya teachings.

Notes

1 My translation. For the Sanskrit text, see Radhakrishnan 1978, 746.
2 *Puruṣa* and *prakṛti* are characterized as masculine and feminine, respectively.
3 Contentment of 'time' and 'fortune' are probably equivalent to the virtues of patience and forbearance, respectively.

References

Burley, Mikel. 2007. *Classical Sāṃkhya and Yoga: An Indian Metaphysics of Experience*. London: Routledge.

Dasgupta, Surendranath. 1930. *Yoga Philosophy in Relation to Other Systems of Indian Thought*. Calcutta: Calcutta University Press.

Gopal, Lallanji. 2000. *Retrieving Sāṁkhya History: An Ascent from Dawn to Meridian*. New Delhi: DK Printworld.

Larson, Gerald J. 1979. *Classical Sāṃkhya: An Interpretation of Its History and Meaning*, 2nd ed. Delhi: Motilal Banarsidass.

Larson, Gerald J. and Ram Shankar Bhattacharya (eds.). 1987. *Sāṃkhya: A Dualist Tradition in Indian Philosophy*. Delhi: Motilal Banarsidass.

Mainkar, T. G. (trans.). 1972. *Sāṁkhyakārikā of Īśvarakṛṣṇa, with the Commentary of Gauḍapāda*, 2nd ed. Poona: Oriental Book Agency.

Radhakrishnan, Sarvepalli (trans.). 1978. *The Principal Upaniṣads*. London: George Allen & Unwin.
Sāṃkhyakārikā of Īśvarakṛṣṇa. In Burley 2007, 163–179.
Sāṃkhyasūtra (attributed to Kapila). J. R. Ballantyne (trans.). 1885. *The Sánkhya Aphorisms of Kapila*, ed. F. E. Hall, 3rd ed. London: Trübner & Co.
Sastri, S. S. Suryanarayana (trans.). 1948. *The Sāṅkhyakārikā of Īśvara Kṛṣṇa*, 3rd ed. Chennai: University of Madras.
Tattvakaumudī of Vācaspatimiśra. Gangânâtha Jhâ (trans.). 1896. *Tattva-Kaumudî (Sânkhya) of Vâchaspati Miśra*. Bombay: Tookaram Tatya.
Van Buitenen, J. A. B. 1957. 'Studies in Sāṃkhya (II)', *Journal of the American Oriental Society* 77(1): 15–25.
Yogabhāṣya of Vyāsa. James Haughton Woods (trans.). 1914. *The Yoga-System of Patañjali*. Cambridge, MA: Harvard University Press.
Yogasūtra of Patañjali. See Woods 1914 above.

Chapter 14
THE DIVERSE TRADITIONS OF SĀṂKHYA

Knut A. Jacobsen

Openness to the greatest possible plurality of traditions seems to be a good approach for understanding the history of Sāṃkhya. It has been argued that before the Sāṃkhya system of philosophy developed, there were probably many Sāṃkhya centers where more or less parallel doctrines developed, and that in the analysis of this development, we should allow for the greatest diversity of doctrine (van Buitenen 1957, 101–102; Larson 1979, 95). An illustration of this plurality is to be found in the many versions of Sāṃkhya in the *Mahābhārata* that is associated with different enumerations of the *tattvas*. However, plurality characterizes the later history of Sāṃkhya, and the contemporary situation as well (Jacobsen 2005, 2008, 2011a, 2011b). In addition to the identifiable schools of Sāṃkhya, nondifferentiated Sāṃkhya, which mostly was theistic and probably preceded the systems (Gupta 1982, 1986), continued to flourish after the arising of the philosophical systems. There continued to be several traditions of Sāṃkhya with more or less parallel doctrines, and nondifferentiated Sāṃkhya as well continued to be an important trend of thought in large parts of the Hindu mythological and theological traditions.

The plurality of Sāṃkhya traditions is much larger than what is often presented as Sāṃkhya in academic literature on Indian philosophy. This is especially the case in general overviews of the systems or when making comparisons to Sāṃkhya when the main focus is on presenting other differing systems such as Vedānta, Nyāya, etc. In this literature, the term "*sāṃkhya*" most often refers to the Sāṃkhya tradition of the *Sāṃkhyakārikā* and the tradition of philosophical commentaries on that text. However, the Yoga school of philosophy began as an interpretation of Sāṃkhya philosophy, although practices identified as yoga are described in texts that are older than the *Yogasūtra*. The *Yogaśāstra* of Patañjali, the *Pātañjalayogaśāstra* which is constitued by a *sūtra* text and a *bhāṣya* text, the *Yogasūtra* and the *Yogabhāṣya*/*Vyāsabhāṣya* (Maas 2013), is therefore also a school of Sāṃkhya philosophy. The promotion of the Sāṃkhya philosophy of the *Pātañjalayogaśāstra* (the text was perhaps written by Vindhyavāsin, *c*. 350–400 CE) might have prompted Īśvarakṛṣṇa to compose the *Sāṃkhyakārikā* (*c*. 350–400 CE) (Larson and Bhattacharya 2008), which represented a different school of Sāṃkhya, going back to Vārṣagaṇya (*c*. 100–200 CE) and which emphasized different aspects of Sāṃkhya. The fundamental difference between these two Sāṃkhya systems is that Sāṃkhya of the *Sāṃkhyakārikā* represents a "discernment (*adhyavasāya*, *vijñāna*) philosophy", while Pātañjala Sāṃkhya of the *Pātañjalayogaśāstra* represents a "cessation (*nirodhasamādhi*) philosophy" (Larson and Bhattacharya 2008). These represent different methods, and it is not historically correct therefore, as some do, to call *Sāṃkhya* the theory part and Yoga the practice part of one system.

These two different approaches are crystalized in the two texts where they discuss the way to realize the principle of consciousness, which occurs with the attainment of *vyaktāvyaktajñavijñāna* ("knowledge of the manifest, unmanifest, and the knower") according to *Sāṃkhyakārikā* 2, and the attainment of *cittavṛttinirodha* (cessation of the changes of the awareness) according to *Yogasūtra* 1.2. This distinction certainly shows that these two Sāṃkhya systems are different; but they are nevertheless both Sāṃkhya systems. On the relationship between Sāṃkhya and Yoga, Gerald Larson writes:

> Yoga appears to represent … an updating of the old Sāṃkhya, an attempt to bring the old Sāṃkhya philosophy into conversation with many of the issues that were developing in the more technical traditions of Indian philosophizing occurring in the fourth and fifth centuries (300–500 CE). One is tempted to use the expression "neo-Sāṃkhya" because of its close association with the work of Vindhyavāsin. Also, it is clearly an explanation of Sāṃkhya.
>
> (Larson and Bhattacharya 2008, 45)

Larson emphasizes, correctly, especially the strong influence of Buddhist philosophy on Yoga, and argues that Yoga philosophy is "an updated and revised Sāṃkhya", a Sāṃkhya philosophy that was "revised as a result of polemical interaction with Abhidharma" (Larson and Bhattacharya 2008, 67). Because these days the concept and practice of yoga are associated with a variety of traditions (which most often, unlike Sāṃkhya, focus on union between soul and a supreme divine power, or refer to body exercises [*āsanas* and *prāṇāyāma*]), this identity of Yoga philosophy as a school of Sāṃkhya tends to get forgotten, and scholars of Hinduism and South Asian religions with only basic knowledge of Sāṃkhya are often not aware of this Sāṃkhya identity of Yoga.

Nondifferentiated Sāṃkhya

The enumeration of the basic principles (*tattvas*) in Sāṃkhya and Yoga starts with the causes of the gross material world, the *mahābhūtas*, the earth element, *pṛthivī*, being the first *tattva*, and ends, in classical Sāṃkhya philosophy, with the ultimate principles of *prakṛti* (the material principle) as the twenty-fourth principle and *puruṣa* (the consciousness principle) as the twenty-fifth and final principle. *Prakṛti* and *puruṣa* are not the first principles in the enumeration, but the last. This enumeration shows that the purpose is the attainment of salvific liberation. That the principles are listed in the order in which they are realized by the seeker of salvific knowledge, and not in the order in which they would have become manifest if mapping a cosmogony had been the intention, shows that the main purpose of the enumeration in Sāṃkhya originally was to instruct in the attainment of salvific knowledge and not to explain the origin of the world. Cosmogony most probably was unrelated to Sāṃkhya (Brockington 1999, 477), which originally was primarily a salvific way of knowing.

Nondifferentiated Sāṃkhya, which was found in the Upaniṣads as well as in the *Mahābhārata*, seems to have continued to flourish, unrestrained by the *Sāṃkhyakārikā* and the *Pātañjalayogaśāstra* traditions (Bronkhorst 2006). This Sāṃkhya can be defined as a way of thinking about the world by means of certain concepts for the sake of salvific liberation and seems not to be a system of philosophy. In nondifferentiated Sāṃkhya the highest principles are sometimes considered to be *brahman*, *ātman*, *kṣetrajña*, *puruṣa*, Īśvara, Nārāyaṇa, or Kṛṣṇa. Nondifferentiated Sāṃkhya continued to flourish from the period of the theistic Upaniṣads, the *Kaṭha Upaniṣad* and *Śvetāśvatara Upaniṣad*, and the *Mahābhārata* up to the present. One important textual tradition of Sāṃkhya different from the Sāṃkhya systems of the *Sāṃkhyakārikā* and the *Pātañjalayogaśāstra*, emerging perhaps from this undifferentiated Sāṃkhya, is found in the Sāṃkhya chapters of *Bhāgavatapurāṇa* called the *Kapilagītā* or *Kapilopadeśa* (*Bhāgavatapurāṇa* 3.25–3.33). This Sāṃkhya is, as is the Sāṃkhya *darśana*, promoted by a sage by name Kapila. In this text Kapila starts the teaching of the *tattvas* by stating that by knowing (*jñāna*) the *tattvas*, the *puruṣa* is freed from the *guṇas* of *prakṛti* (*Bhāgavatapurāṇa* 3.26.1–2; *Kapilagītā* 2.1–2). In the first volume of *A History of Indian Philosophy*, Surendranath Dasgupta has correctly given the chapter dealing with Sāṃkhya systems (in plural) the title "The Kapila and the Pātañjala Sāṃkhya (Yoga)" (Dasgupta [1922] 1975, 208–273), signaling that both the Sāṃkhya and Yoga *darśanas* are Sāṃkhya philosophies, one associated with Kapila and the other with Patañjali. In the fourth volume of the same history of Indian philosophy (in the chapter "Kapila's Philosophy in the *Bhāgavata Purāṇa*"), Dasgupta treated in addition in depth a third variant of Sāṃkhya philosophy, the one found in the *Kapilagītā*. It is often emphasized as the distinguishing mark of the Sāṃkhya philosophy of the *Kapilagītā* when compared to other Sāṃkhya systems that it is theistic. But a similar distinguishing mark of Kapila's philosophy of the *Bhāgavatapurāṇa* is that it argues that above the *prakṛti* (the twenty-fourth) principle, there is a twenty-fifth principle, which is not the *puruṣa* principle as in Sāṃkhya of the *Sāṃkhyakārikā*, but time, *kāla*, on which, according to this text, the activities of *prakṛti* depends. *Puruṣa* is here the twenty-sixth principle.

Different views of time in the Sāṃkhya systems

The view of time differs markedly in the Sāṃkhya systems and makes an interesting subject for comparison. In the *Kapilagītā*, *kāla* is the power that makes the activities of *prakṛti* possible. Time seems here to be thought of as an instrumental cause of change.

It is *kāla* that transforms beings into different forms. The will of the supreme divinity is the creative power, and time a presupposition for the creative process to get started. Time (*kāla*) is in the *Kapilāgitā* the twenty-fifth *tattva* (*kālaḥ pañcaviṃśakaḥ*; *Bhāgavatapurāṇa* 3.26.15; *Kapilagītā* 2.15). "Time exists in God as His transcendent power and effort" (Gupta 1986, 125), and he uses *kāla* to disturb the original equilibrium of the *guṇas*.

However, according to the *Sāṃkhyakārikā* and the *Pātañjalayogaśāstra*, change is a function of *prakṛti*, not time. From the point of view of realization of salvific knowledge, that is the effort to dissolve the less subtle principles into the more subtle principles, based on the concept of *satkārya*, it is difficult to see how time can be a substratum of *prakṛti*. Time seems rather to be involved in trying to understand origination of the world rather than salvation of the self, and especially when attempting to connect a supreme divine being to the function of creator. In *Kapilagītā* Viṣṇu initiates the movement of *prakṛti* and thus disturbs the equilibrium of the *guṇas* (*Bhāgavatapurāṇa* 3.26.17; *Kapilagītā* 2.17) by means of the principle of *kāla*. The *Kapilagītā* states that Viṣṇu pervades everything inside as the *puruṣa* and outside as time (*antaḥ puruṣarūpeṇa kālarūpeṇa yo bahiḥ, samanvety eṣa sattvānāṃ bhagavān ātmamāyayā*; *Bhāgavatapurāṇa* 3.26.18; *Kapilagītā* 2.18).

Both *kāla* and *Viṣṇu* thus take over some of the functions of *prakṛti*. According to the *Bhāgavatapurāṇa kāla* gives rise to the fear of death of all those who identify themselves with *prakṛti* and its transformations. Time gives rise to fear of Viṣṇu as well. Punishments in hell are described in connection with the presentation of the principle of time and function to propagate the power of Viṣṇu and the need for his grace. The *Kapilagītā* is a theistic text with focus on Viṣṇu/Kṛṣṇa, of whom Kapila here is presented as an *avatāra*. Several researchers (Dasgupta 1922 [1975]; Gupta 1986) have believed that the views of the *Kapilagītā* constituted the teaching of the "original" Kapila but there is no evidence to support such a view.

The *kāla* principle of *Bhāgavatapurāṇa* is similar to *prakṛti* in the sense that it is what one should be separated from. But according to *Sāṃkhyakārikā prakṛti* saves *puruṣa* since salvific knowledge (*jñāna*) is part of *prakṛti* (*jñāna* is one of the *bhāvas* of the *buddhi*). *Kāla* has no such function. In the Sāṃkhya schools of *Sāṃkhyakārikā* and *Pātañjalayogaśāstra*, *kāla* is not a separate principle in addition to the twenty-five *tattvas*. These systems reject the theory of absolute time, and view the concept of beginningless and endless time as a fiction (*vikalpa*) (Sen 1968, 411). In the *Sāṃkhyakārikā* tradition, time "is only a construction of the imagination (*buddhinirmāṇa*) … and a word which has nothing corresponding to it in reality" (Sen 1968, 411). Change is the transformation (*pariṇāma*) of *prakṛti*. Activity (*kriyā*) is real, but time is "nothing apart from actions or events that are revealed in experience" (Sen 1968, 412). In Sāṃkhya "a separate entity distinct from actions (*kriyā*) is rejected, the use of all temporal expressions being accounted for by events or actions" (Sen 1968, 413). Change is real, but time is not. The present is a material manifestation of something already pre-existing in the material cause. Change is a material transformation and time is not a substantive reality but only a mental concept, just a *vikalpa*, appearing in the mind as verbal knowledge. Also, *kāla* seems foreign to the Sāṃkhya practice because the evolutes of *prakṛti* are mental material principles, and they are able to be dissolved in *prakṛti* as part of a practice of the individual of discernment or cessation. *Buddhi* then dissolves in *prakṛti*, but who is the agent that would dissolve *prakṛti* in *kāla*?

The *Pātañjalayogaśāstra* includes one more element in its view on the reality of time. The smallest moment of time, the moment (*kṣaṇa*), is real, according to the commentary on the *Yogsūtra* 3.52. But there is no aggregation of time as succession of moments. The present is a single moment, and earlier or later moments do not exist. In the one "present moment the whole universe is experiencing a change as all those characteristics—past, present and future—exist in that one present moment" (*Vyāsabhāṣya* on *Yogsūtra* 3.52). Hariharānanda Āraṇya in his commentary on *Yogsūtra* 3.52 explains:

> [T]here is no such thing as time, because it will give rise to the question: "Wherein does time exist?" That which is absent is either past or future. Absent means non-existent, Therefore, past or future is non-existent.
> (Āraṇya 2000, 337)

Āraṇya defines time as "flow of moments collected together in thought, i.e. built up in imagination" (Āraṇya 2000, 338). Time has no substratum and therefore time cannot be conceived without the help of words. Interestingly, in Yoga, "time is nowhere explicitly identified with change" (Sen 1968, 418). The sequence of moments is transformations of *prakṛti*, the material substratum, and not time. In the *Yogasūtra* and *Vyāsabhāṣya* 4.12 it is said that the past and the future are present in their fundamental form (*svarūpa*), they are in existence in a subtle form in the causes of which they are effects.

In later Sāṃkhya of the *Sāṃkhyasūtra*, time is referred to as a manifestation of *ākāśa* (*sūtra* 2.12, *dikkālāv ākāśādibhyaḥ*), which means that the principles preceding *ākāśa* are outside of time and that time does not apply to the *tattvas* (principles) (Sen 1968, 414). In this *sūtra* of the *Sāṃkhyasūtra* the reality of time is not denied, but since time cannot be part of the twenty-fourth principle, *prakṛti*, its origin has to be postulated in one of the other *tattvas*. Perhaps a perceived similarity between empty space and the idea of time suggested *ākāśa* as a possible substratum of time.

The view of god also differs in these systems and may relate to the view of time. In the *Sāṃkhyakārikā* the only gods mentioned are those that are part of the material process (part of the world of rebirth) such as the god Brahmā. In the *Yogasūtra*, however, an additional divine being is described, Īśvara, who is a particular *puruṣa* (*puruṣaviśeṣa*) who has never been bound and who is an object of *bhakti*. Both the idea of time as the reality of the moment (*kṣana*) only, and of the divine teacher (*īśvara*) who desires to save human beings (*bhūtānugraha*) and out of compassion (*karuṇā*) for living beings assumed a created mind (*nirmāṇacitta*) to instruct them (*Yogasūtra* and *Vyāsabhāṣya* 1.25), but who is not creator or in other ways connected to the world, seem to be related to Śramaṇa ideas. The Īśvara is perhaps modelled on the *buddhas* and *tīrthaṅkaras*, but which he supersedes because *īśvara*, unlike the *buddhas and tīrthaṅkaras*, was never bound. Īśvara is outside of time, since *puruṣa* is unchangeable.

According to Sāṃkhya and Yoga, changes are manifestations ultimately of the three *guṇas* of *prakṛti* which is the substratum of all change, but *prakṛti* and *puruṣa* are outside of time. There is in reality therefore no such thing as time. There are actions (*kriyā*) but time is nothing but these changes, and therefore nothing in addition to the changes. The inclusion of time as a principle in the Vaiṣṇava Sāṃkhya of the *Kapilagītā* is probably due to its promotion of a divine supreme principle and *bhakti* as the means to attain this divinity's grace. The *Kapilagītā* tradition is theistic, and cosmogony is an important feature of this tradition of Sāṃkhya. As is often the case in the Purāṇas, the Sāṃkhya categories are utilized to explain the creation of the world, which in the Purāṇas was considered an important function of the supreme god. With a theistic soteriology, Sāṃkhya was turned upside down. The text seems to be an attempt to systematize theistic and Vaiṣṇava nondifferentiated Sāṃkhya, perhaps, with the view that this was the original and real Sāṃkhya teaching of Kapila.

The diverse understandings of time (*kāla*) in these three Sāṃkhya schools illustrate the variety of views of the Sāṃkhya systems. The view on time of three Sāṃkhya systems briefly discussed here presents Sāṃkhya in association with three different religious cultures: the Śramaṇa movement (*Pātañjalayogaśāstra*), the Purāṇic world (*Sāṃkhyakārikā* and *Kapilagītā*), and the Vaiṣṇava theism (*Kapilagītā*), and illustrates that Sāṃkhya is much more than just one *darśana*. As a *darśana*, Sāṃkhya is a name of one of the Hindu systems of religious thought, but this limited use tends to hide the fact that there is a plurality of Sāṃkhya traditions. Sāṃkhya terminology is found in contexts that are theistic, monistic, polytheistic, and so on, from their earliest manifestations to contemporary Hinduism.

References

Āraṇya, Hariharānanda. 2000. *Yoga Philosophy of Patañjali with Bhāsvatī*. Calcutta: University of Calcutta.

Bhāgavata Purāṇa. *The Bhāgavata-Purāṇa*. 1989–1994. Trans. and annotated by Ganesh Vasudeo Tagare, 5 vols. Delhi: Motilal Banarsidass. Sanskrit text: *Srimad Bhagavata*. 1980. Trans. Swami Tapashyananda, 4 vols. Madras: Sri Ramakrishna Math.

Brockington, John. 1999. "Epic Sāṃkhya: Texts, Teachers, Terminology." AS/ÉA 53(3): 473–490.

Bronkhorst, Johannes. 2006. "Systematic Philosophy between the Empires: Some Determining Features." In P. Olivelle (ed.), *Between the Empires: Society in India between 300 BCE to 400 CE*, 286–313. Oxford: Oxford University Press.

Buitenen, J. A. B. van. 1957. "Studies in Sāṃkhya (III)." *Journal of the American Oriental Society* 77: 88–107.

Dasgupta, Surendranath. 1922 [1975]. *A History of Indian Philosophy*, vol. 1. Repr. Delhi: Motilal Banarsidass.

Edgerton, Franklin. 1924. "The Meaning of Sānkhya and Yoga." *American Journal of Philology* 45(1): 1–46.

Gupta, Anima Sen. 1982. *Classical Sāṃkhya: A Critical Study*. New Delhi: Munshiram Manoharlal.

Gupta, Anima Sen. 1986. *The Evolution of the Sāṃkhya School of Thought*. 2nd ed. New Delhi: Munshiram Manoharlal.

Jacobsen, Knut A. 2005. "In Kapila's Cave: A Sāṃkhya-Yoga Renaissance in Bengal." In Knut A. Jacobsen (ed.), *Theory and Practice of Yoga: Essays in Honour of Gerald James Larson*, 333–350. Leiden: Brill.

Jacobsen, Knut A. 2008. *Kapila: Founder of Sāṃkhya and Avatāra of Viṣṇu*. New Delhi: Munshiram Manoharlal.

Jacobsen, Knut A. 2011a. "Sāṃkhya." In Knut A. Jacobsen, Helene Basu, Angelika Malinar, and Vasudha Narayanan (eds.), *Brill's Encyclopedia of Hinduism*, vol. 3, 685–698. Leiden: Brill.

Jacobsen, Knut A. 2011b. "Pātañjala Yoga." In Knut A. Jacobsen, Helene Basu, Angelika Malinar, and Vasudha Narayanan (eds.), *Brill's Encyclopedia of Hinduism*, vol. 3, 745–759. Leiden: Brill.

Kapilopadesha. 1990. Text in Devanagari with running translation in English and an Introduction. Trans. Swami Tapasyananda. Calcutta: Advaita Ashrama.

Larson, Gerald J. 1979. *Classical Sāṃkhya: An Interpretation of Its History and Meaning*. Delhi: Motilal Banarsidass.

Larson, Gerald James and Ram Shankar Bhattacharya (eds.). 1987. *Sāṃkhya: A Dualist Tradition in Indian Philosophy*. *Encyclopedia of Indian Philosophies*, vol. 4. Delhi: Motilal Banarsidass.

Larson, Gerald James and Ram Shankar Bhattacharya (eds.). 2008. *Yoga: India's Philosophy of Meditation*. *Encyclopedia of Indian Philosophies*, vol. 12. Delhi: Motilal Banarsidass.

Maas, Phillip A. 2013. "A Concise Historiography of Classical Yoga Philosophy." In Eli Franco (ed.), *Periodization and Historiography of Indian Philosophy*. De Nobili Series. Vienna: Institute für Südasien-, Tibet- und Buddhismuskunde der Universität Wien, 53–90.

Sāṃkhyakārikā. Sanskrit and English. In Gerald J. Larson. 1979. *Classical Sāṃkhya: An Interpretation of Its History and Meaning*, 235–277. Delhi: Motilal Banarsidass.

Sen, Sanat Kumar. 1968. "Time in Sānkhya-Yoga." *International Philosophical Quarterly* 8: 406–426.

Vyāsabhāṣya. Sanskrit and English. In Hariharānanda Āraṇya. 2000. *Yoga Philosophy of Patañjali with Bhāsvati*. Trans. P. N. Mukerji. Calcutta: University of Calcutta.

Yogasūtra. Sanskrit and English. In Hariharānanda Āraṇya. 2000. *Yoga Philosophy of Patañjali with Bhāsvatī*. Trans. P. N. Mukerji. Calcutta: University of Calcutta.

Chapter 15
MĪMĀṂSĀ

Elisa Freschi

Mīmāṃsā ("inquiry" or "reflection"), also called Pūrva Mīmāṃsā, was an influential school of classical Indian philosophy. Originating from an ancient tradition of scriptural exegesis, the primary focus of the school is on the Veda. The school's foundational text (called *Mīmāṃsā Sūtra*, henceforth MS) is mainly concerned with rules for systematically interpreting Vedic passages. These hermeneutic efforts led later Mīmāṃsā authors to investigate linguistic, epistemological, exegetical, and deontic issues. The MS opens with a chapter on general theoretical issues: the nature of *dharma*, the means of knowledge, and language. The remaining chapters and books deal primarily with hermeneutic issues.

Historical development

The bulk of the Mīmāṃsā system is based (as is common in India) on a collection of aphorisms (*sūtra*), the MS. This collection is traditionally attributed to Jaimini, who is also mentioned in the Vedic exegetical literature, as well as, among eleven other authors, in the *Vedāntasūtra* and in the MS itself (Parpola 1981). Similarly, Bādarāyaṇa, who is traditionally believed to have been the author of the *Vedāntasūtra*, is often mentioned in both the MS and the *Vedāntasūtra*.

The Vedānta system is also known as Uttara Mīmāṃsā. These two names, Pūrva Mīmāṃsā and Uttara Mīmāṃsā, can be interpreted as referring to the object of the two systems. Accordingly, Pūrva Mīmāṃsā means "investigation of the (logically) preceding part of the Vedas (the Brāhmaṇas)" and Uttara Mīmāṃsā, "investigation of the (logically) subsequent part of the Veda (the Upaniṣads)." In line with this, the final form of the *Vedāntasūtra* was possibly modelled on the MS. But as is maintained by Parpola, it is also possible that the names "Pūrva Mīmāṃsā" and "Uttara Mīmāṃsā" originally referred to the two parts of the MS, with the first part (*Pūrva*-MS) being attributed to the author Jaimini, and the later part (*Uttara*-MS), to the author Bādarāyaṇa. In the former interpretation (exemplified in Bronkhorst 2007), Vedānta modelled itself along the lines of Mīmāṃsā, whereas in the latter interpretation (that of Parpola), they originated from a single tradition. Whatever the case, both systems are based on Vedic exegesis and share the same hermeneutical rules. They differ insofar as they focus respectively on the Brāhmana and the Upaniṣad portions of the Veda, thus on orthopraxy and achieving insight into the ultimate reality.

The oldest preserved commentary on the MS, Śabara Svāmin's *Bhāṣya* 'Commentary' (henceforth *ŚBh*) is composed in a fluent and clear Sanskrit style, and touches on all the themes which were later to become prominent during the "golden" age of Mīmāṃsā philosophy (from Kumārila and Prabhākara to their subcommentators). While Śabara attacks Buddhist and Grammarian opponents, his attacks are too general to use as support for attempts at dating him precisely. He quotes from Patañjali's *Mahābhāṣya* and Vedic literature, but does not cite any later author other than a few Mīmāṃsā predecessors whose works are now lost. Thus, Śabara's usual dating to the third to fifth century CE is only tentative.

Around the seventh century CE, Kumārila Bhaṭṭa and Prabhākara Miśra wrote commentaries on the ŚBh. The chronological relationship between the two authors is still unsettled, although they are generally believed to have been more or less contemporary, with Kumārila being probably a bit older (see Yoshimizu 1997, Introduction). It is traditionally believed that they founded Mīmāṃsā's two sub-schools, the Bhāṭṭa and the Prābhākara.

Maṇḍana Miśra, who flourished one generation later, wrote both Mīmāṃsā and Vedānta works. While he acknowledged most Bhāṭṭa tenets, he also elaborated on Kumārila's doctrines of error and prescription in three independent treatises that deeply influenced most subsequent Indian philosophers. These three works are also of formal interest because they are among the earliest monographs (i.e., treatises dedicated to a single topic and not commenting on a previous text) in Indian philosophical literature.

Śālikanātha Miśra (eighth to ninth century), wrote two independent treatises as well as a subcommentary on Prābhākara's commentary. Since Prabhākara's style is often terse and dense, most classical authors preferred (as contemporary scholars still do today) to quote the works of Śālikanātha. Of his two treatises, the *Prakaraṇa Pañcikā* resembles a modern work in its thematic exposition of the Prābhākara system. A systematic reply to Śālikanātha's exposition of the Prābhākara system was undertaken by Kumārila's commentator Pārthasārathi Miśra (eleventh century).

Uṃveka Bhaṭṭa (eighth century) and Sucarita Miśra (tenth century) wrote commentaries on Kumārila's *Ślokavārttika* (henceforth *ŚV*, a commentary on the first theoretical chapter of the *MS* and the *ŚBh* thereon). Commentaries were also written on Kumārila's *Tantravārttika* (a commentary on the *MS* from the second chapter of the first book through the third book and on the *ŚBh* thereon, dealing mainly with deontic and exegetical principles) by Bhāvadeva (eleventh century), Paritoṣa Miśra (twelfth century), and Someśvara Bhaṭṭa (thirteenth century).

The two sub-schools of Mīmāṃsā, the Bhāṭṭa and the Prābhākara, were to influence all sub-schools of Vedānta, which borrowed many Mīmāṃsā principles (on the links between Mīmāṃsā and Viśiṣṭādvaita Vedānta, see Freschi forthcoming). Of the two, however, the Bhāṭṭa system enjoyed greater success.

Most Mīmāṃsā treatises after the thirteenth century specialize in ritual. Today Mīmāṃsā tends to be studied as a sacrificial discipline, preliminary to the study of

Vedānta (see Clooney 1990, 255–258). For more details see Verpoorten 1987, the Introduction in Ramaswami Śāstrī 1936, and, on the adoption of the Nāvya Nyāya style, McCrea 2002. The contribution of Mīmāṃsā to the methods of interpretation in law, or jurisprudence, is treated in Chapter 43 of this volume (and see in that chapter the reference to Bilimoria 2011).

Mīmāṃsā as exegesis

The Mīmāṃsā differs from mere exegesis of difficult Vedic passages insofar as it aims at providing general rules of interpretation. Such rules create a coherent edifice out of a mass of sacrificial prescriptions, and they have thus been adopted since ancient times in Indian ritual and juridical literature. In fact, the Veda as understood by Mīmāṃsakas shares two important features with the systems of law as understood in most modern legal theories: it is independent of any author (laws are to be interpreted independently of the intentions of law-makers), and it is concerned with what should and should not be done.

The exegetical rules developed by the Mīmāṃsakas presuppose that all Vedic passages ultimately make sense. This theme is directly addressed in MS 1.2, immediately after the opening chapter on epistemology and linguistics. In response to objections that the Veda is either meaningless, false (where it contradicts direct experience), or futile (where it states, e.g., "fire is hot"), Jaimini and Śabara explain how the only portions of the Veda that are direct means of knowledge are prescriptions (*vidhi*). In contrast, explanatory passages (*arthavāda*, such as "Vāyu is the fastest Deity") have only an ancillary role. They do not yield knowledge directly. They are rather to be interpreted figuratively as eulogizing the deity to whom a sacrifice is offered, the result to be obtained through a sacrifice, or the various substances employed and procedures followed in a sacrifice. In this way, Mīmāṃsakas are able to interpret Upaniṣad statements such as "The self is to be seen, to be heard, to be thought about, to be meditated on" as consistent with ritual duty as the ultimate purport of the Veda.[1] This strategy of depriving descriptive statements of any independent epistemic status makes any literalist and fundamentalist reading of the Veda by Mīmāṃsakas very unlikely.

Epistemological issues

From its inception the Mīmāṃsā has been intent on portraying the Veda as the unquestioned source of knowledge regarding *dharma*. However, the Veda is employed as an instrument of knowledge (*pramāṇa*) only with regard to *dharma*, which is defined as "what has to be done" and as leading one to one's best (the Mīmāṃsā definition of *dharma* is strikingly minimal if compared with the emphasis on *dharma* as a religious and moral norm, as is common to much Indian literature). Thus, the Veda enjoys an absolute authority, which is however strictly deontic. A member of one of the three upper classes of Hindu society, to whom the Veda is addressed, must perform sacrifices and rituals as prescribed in the Veda, and this deontic authority extends over them regardless of their commitments or beliefs. The Mīmāṃsā does not require adherence to a fixed system of beliefs; it only requires correct conduct.

In this way, the Mīmāṃsā is a tenacious defender of the Veda's authority but also an empiricist system. The Veda is the only instrument that can yield knowledge about what one must do. For knowledge about everything else, one can rely solely on one's faculties. As soon as it veers away from *dharma*, the Mīmāṃsā is crudely anti-metaphysical and sceptical. Mīmāṃsakas (e.g. Kumārila, *ŚV codanā* 139) laugh at "blind believers"; they boast that they repudiate extraordinary powers, superhuman beings, etc., and in general, they avoid any unnecessary assumptions. Kumārila professes himself an empiricist: "By the Mīmāṃsakas ... now, as always, nothing is accepted except what is directly perceivable" (*ŚV codanā* 98d–99ab).

The means of knowledge accepted by all Mīmāṃsakas are sense perception (*pratyakṣa*, which is limited to the sense faculties, as opposed to any kind of intellectual intuition), inference, linguistic communication, analogy, and exclusion. Bhāṭṭas accept human communication alongside the Veda as an autonomous instrument of knowledge, whereas the Prābhākaras argue that since, unlike the Veda, humans are fallible, in their case the natural ability of language to communicate meanings is suspended and one rather needs to infer the intention of the speaker out of the words she utters. Hence, according to this school, human communication is a case of inference. Bhāṭṭas also introduce absence as an instrument of knowledge. This is the means consisting in the non-arousal of other means of knowledge through which one grasps the absence of something. Through sense perception we can grasp that a table is standing in front of us, but it is only through absence as an instrument of knowledge that we can grasp the absence of our glasses on it. Prābhākaras, on the other hand, like Buddhists and Naiyāyikas, claim that one infers absences on the basis of the non-perception of what would have been perceived, had it been present.

The main characteristic of the Mīmāṃsaka epistemology is the theory of self-validity, which serves as the ultimate foundation for direct realism, which all Mīmāṃsakas defended in opposition to Buddhist idealism. The essence of the self-validity theory appears already in the *ŚBh* and was later fully developed by Kumārila. At its core, it credits every cognition, as soon as it arises, with full validity. Thus, every cognition from the moment it arises presents itself as valid, unless or until it is later falsified by a succeeding cognition. The opposite opinion (held by Naiyāyikas and Buddhist Epistemologists) that only those cognitions which have been confirmed are valid, leads, according to Mīmāṃsakas, to a *regressus ad infinitum*. If every cognition must be tested, then also the testing cognition must be tested, and even the cognition testing the testing cognition must be tested, and so on. If instead one proposes that there are certain cognitions that can test other cognitions without needing any further test, then—as Kumārila writes— since one must stop at a certain point, why not stop at the first step?

In regard to the Veda, the self-validity theory amounts to saying that the Veda is valid in and of itself unless or until it is proven to be false. But since its sphere of application is *dharma*, and since *dharma* cannot be known by human beings because it is not accessible to human means of knowledge, the Veda can never be falsified. Hence, it is fully valid. Some Western scholars, like Sheldon Pollock and John Taber, have argued that in this way the Veda stands uncontradicted merely by default. A Mīmāṃsaka would reply by saying that since intellectual intuition, yogic perception, etc. are sheer fantasies, either one accepts the Veda as an instrument for knowing *dharma*, or one is stuck in agnosticism. Moreover, the Veda is not just one among many possible authorities on *dharma*. It is not like the Buddhist Sacred Texts, which would need to be validated on the basis of their origin, the Buddha. Buddhist Sacred Texts are not to be trusted, because they are supposed to have issued from a human being whose extraordinary compassion and omniscience cannot be proven and run against our common experience. By contrast, the Veda is already the commonly accepted authority regarding *dharma* and nothing impugns its authority. All else being equal, we should continue to rely on it as our guide in knowing what we should and should not do.

Both of the main sub-schools of Mīmāṃsā offer an original account of erroneous cognition. Their common point of departure is the doctrine of the self-validity of cognitions. The Bhāṭṭa view of error resembles that of the Naiyāyikas in holding that perceptual error chiefly consists in grasping something according to the aspect of something else. Following the standard example of such an error, one believes one is apprehending silver instead of the mother-of-pearl one actually has in front of one's eyes. The erroneously apprehended silver, explain the Bhāṭṭas, has been seen elsewhere and is now remembered. Thus, error is by no means creative and imagination plays no role in it. Prābhākaras are even more radical in maintaining that there is no error at all and what appears to be an error is instead an incomplete cognition. One cognizes rightly but incompletely, e.g., the mother-of-pearl as something bright and lustrous, and one remembers rightly the silver, but fails to grasp its memory-character. One only fails to distinguish between the lustrous and indefinite object one has before one's eyes and the lustrous silver one remembers.

Linguistic issues

As in its analysis of Vedic ritual, Mīmāṃsā did not only explain single instances of linguistic use, but rather attempted a systematic study of linguistic phenomena as a whole. In this field, Mīmāṃsā and Vyākaraṇa appear to have been closely connected since their prehistory. Pāṇini's terminology is for instance frequently informed by a ritual background and the first statement of Kātyāyana's commentary on Pāṇini's *Grammar* very closely resembles MS 1.1.5. This *sūtra* depicts the relation between word and meaning:

> The relation of word and meaning, on the other hand, is natural. Knowledge of [*dharma*] is the instruction (*śāstra*) [of Sacred Texts], and it is infallible in regard to an unperceived entity. This is an instrument of knowledge [of *dharma*], according to Bādarāyaṇa, because it is independent.[2]

The second part of the *sūtra* refers to the exclusive relation between *dharma* as an epistemic content and the Veda as an instrument of knowledge. The interpretation of the first part of the statement, however, is more challenging. *Autpattika*, which I translated above as 'natural', is a derivative of *utpatti*, 'origin' and thus could also mean 'originated'. But all commentators, starting from Śabara and the Vṛttikāra (whose commentary, now lost, is extensively quoted by Śabara) interpret it rather as *apauruṣeya*, 'non-human', not dependant on a human author (according to the Vṛttikāra) or as *nitya*, 'fixed' (according to Śabara). This evokes the above-mentioned gloss of Kātyāyana stating that "The relation between word and meaning is established (*siddha*)," for *siddha* is explained in Patañjali's commentary thereon as *nitya*. Thus, the relation between word and meaning escapes any possible human agency. As with their general attitude, Mīmāṃsakas do not propose a historical account. Rather, they underline, with their typical commitment to the world as it is observed now, that language is not something humans can influence. Although it is spoken by humans, it has not been invented nor can it even be really altered by them. It is always there ready to be used; it logically pre-exists any possible author. The Vṛttikāra elaborates further by explaining (against Naiyāyika and Buddhist conventionalists) how a creator of linguistic conventions is simply unthinkable. In order to establish a convention, one would indeed need words to say, e.g., "*x* means this", "*y* means that". Words would also be needed in order to transmit such a convention to other people. Thus, the public nature of language is evidence of its independence of any human author.

Against Bhartṛhari's (fifth century CE) *sphoṭavāda* (see Chakrabarti 1989), which holds that word-meanings are only postulated *ex post* out of the unitary sentence meaning, Mīmāṃsakas argue that it would be cumbersome for every sentence to have a unique, unanalyzable meaning. One would have to postulate a completely different meaning of a sentence whenever a word is added. The sentences "Bring [the] cow," "Tie [the] cow," "Bring [the] horse," "Tie [the] horse" (in brackets are the words not needed in Sanskrit) would all have to be learned separately according to the Sphoṭavādins, whereas Mīmāṃsakas maintain that by learning the meanings of "bring," "tie," "cow," and "horse" it is possible to understand all sentences composed of those words.

According to the Bhāṭṭa theory of sentence meaning, the so-called "connection of what has been expressed" theory (*abhihitānvayavāda*), words initially convey their meanings, and then those word-meanings combine to form a unitary sentence meaning. According to the Prābhākara "expression through what has been connected" theory (*anvitābhidhānavāda*), words instead express their meanings only insofar as they are already connected with the meanings of all other words of a sentence.

Bhāṭṭas accuse the Prābhākaras of not accounting for our intuition that we understand the meaning of a sentence through the meanings of its individual words. Prābhākaras are in the difficult position of having to fight both the Bhāṭṭas and the Sphoṭavādins. Against the former, they maintain that our intuition is that the sentence meaning is conveyed through words. Thus, to postulate an intermediate stage of an awareness of unconnected word-meanings is an unnecessary assumption. Words express instead an already related meaning, that is, they express a meaning which is ready to be linked to the other words in the sentence. This means that "cow" has a slightly different meaning in "bring the cow" and "tie the cow," as it is linked with a different word in each case. In one case it conveys as meaning "cow+<bringing>" and in the other "cow+<tying>". The same applies to "bring!" and so on.

In order to justify this view, the Prābhākara recurs to the requisite of saturation (*ākāṅkṣā*) as necessary for identifying a sentence meaning. Thus, in "bring the cow!", "bring!" is non-saturated and this non-saturation "evokes" the word's counterpart, "cow." Already in the *ŚBh* (ad 1.2.17) an objector proposes the following retort: Suppose one hears "Bring the cloth!" In one's mind, the first word conveys the meaning "bring+<cloth>," and the second "cloth+<bring>," But what if the sentence goes further, say "bring the cloth, [the] white [one]"? One cannot claim that "white" is expected, since "bring" had been already saturated by "cloth." Mīmāṃsakas have no answer apart from the appeal to actual cases. So, in "bring the cloth, [the] white [one]!", "bring" and "cloth" are still unsaturated just because there is an extra word in the sentence.

The Bhāṭṭa and the Prābhākara accounts further differ regarding the import of a sentence in worldly language. Prābhākaras state that it is something to be done, as in the Veda, whereas Bhāṭṭas claim that this is the case only within Vedic language, whereas as for worldly language they subscribe to the view of all other Indian and Western linguistic systems, namely that a sentence conveys (i.e., describes) something that is already established.

Deontic issues

"Deontic" indicates the field of philosophy dealing with prescriptive language, its logic and the epistemological issues it raises. Mīmāṃsā's very commitment to the Veda made it reflect on prescriptive statements long before this field of logic had been developed in Europe.

Kumārila, Prabhākara, and Maṇḍana Miśra described the action of prescriptive language on human beings in different ways. Śabara (*ŚBh* ad *MS* 2.1.1-4) explained it by saying that verbal endings are endowed with a power of bringing about, called *bhāvanā* ('the causing to be') consisting in the undertaking of an action by human beings. The verbal root constitutes, according to this analysis, the instrument (*karaṇa*), and the textual passages minutely describing a ritual constitute the procedure (*itikartavyatā*). The result, e.g., heaven, is embedded in the formula enjoining the ritual, e.g., "The one who desires heaven should sacrifice with the new- and full-moon sacrifice," which, in this way, becomes in Śabara's paraphrase, "Heaven (result) is caused to be (*bhāvanā*) through a sacrifice (instrument) with such-and-such ritual actions (procedure)." But this account neglects the specificity of prescriptive forms. Thus, Kumārila added to the *bhāvanā* conveyed by all verbal endings and indicating human effort another *bhāvanā* that is specifically conveyed by prescriptive endings and that enjoins such effort. This "linguistic *bhāvanā*" has human effort, that is, the first *bhāvanā*, as its result, and the awareness that the action enjoined will lead to something desired as its instrument.

In contrast, Maṇḍana Miśra states that the effect of prescriptive language on human beings can only be explained by assuming that prescriptions directly convey the idea that the action being enjoined will lead to something desired. This theory is countered by Bhāṭṭas and Prābhākaras alike, on the grounds that being prescribed is not tantamount to being a means to a desired end.

Unlike the Bhāṭṭas, Prābhākaras maintain that prescriptive endings convey the idea that the action being enjoined is to be done, i.e., that it is one's duty (*kārya*). Since something to be done cannot exist abstractly, such a duty must be supported by an action, which is hence secondarily signified by the same prescriptive endings. In common usage, sentences often refer just to the action, but this happens only through secondary signification (*lakṣaṇā*). Through the Veda a duty can rather be known in its non-preceded (*apūrva*) nature, that is, as something which cannot be known through any other instrument of knowledge.

Mīmāṃsā and God

As a system, the Mīmāṃsā is atheist. It states that the belief in God is internally untenable and that it consists in unnecessarily postulating something unseen (Bilimoria 2001). After the eleventh century, however, almost all Mīmāṃsakas seem to be theist. They open and often close their works by dedicating them to God (usually a form of Viṣṇu) and some of them further develop on the relationship between a sacrificial action if performed according to all prescriptions and an uninterested action performed in order to obey God. This contradiction can be solved because the God negated by the Mīmāṃsā system is an ontological support to sustain weak metaphysical theories rather than an object of devotion. Devotion is not negated, but any endeavour to develop a rational theology and theodicy is keenly rejected.

Notes

1 Accordingly, the above statements would mean "One should know the agent of the sacrifice."

2 *autpattikas tu śabdasyārthena sambandhas tasya jñānam upadeśo 'vyatirekaś cārthe 'nupalabdhe. tat pramāṇaṃ bādarāyaṇasyānapekṣatvāt.*

References

Bilimoria, P. 2001. "Hindu Doubts about God: Towards a Mīmāṃsā Deconstruction." In Roy W. Perrett (ed.) *Indian Philosophy: A Collection of Readings*, pp. 87–106. New York and London: Garland Publishing.

Bronkhorst, Johannes (ed.). 2007. *Mīmāṃsā and Vedānta: Interaction and Continuity*. Delhi: Motilal Banarsidass.

Chakrabarti, Arindam. 1989. "Sentence-Holism, Context-Principle and Connected-Designation *anvitābhidhāna*: Three Doctrines or One?" *Journal of Indian Philosophy* 17: 37–41.

Clooney, Francis X. 1990 *Thinking Ritual: Rediscovering the Pūrva Mīmāṃsā of Jaimini*. Vienna: De Nobili Research Library.

Dwivedi, R. C. (ed.). 1994. *Studies in Mīmāṃsā: Dr Mandan Mishra Felicitation Volume*. Delhi: Motilal Banarsidass and L.B.S. Rashtriya Sanskrit Vidyapitha.

Freschi, Elisa. 2012. *Duty, Language and Exegesis in Prābhākara Mīmāṃsā*. Leiden: Brill.

Freschi, Elisa. Forthcoming. "Śrīvaiṣṇavism: The Making of a Theology". In Archana Venkatesan (ed.) *Many Vaiṣṇavisms: Histories of the Worship of Viṣṇu*. Oxford: Oxford University Press.

Jhā, Gaṅgānātha. 1942. *Pūrva Mīmāṃsā in Its Sources*. Benaras: Benares Hindu University (2nd ed., 1964).

Kataoka, Kei. 2011. *Kumārila on Truth, Omniscience, and Killing*. Part 1. An annotated translation of *Mīmāṃsā-Ślokavārttika* ad 1.1.2 (Codanāsūtra). Vienna: VÖAW.

McCrea, Lawrence. 2000. "The Hierarchical Organization of Language in Mīmāṃsā Interpretive Theory." *Journal of Indian Philosophy* 28(5–6): 429–459.

McCrea, Lawrence. 2002. "Novelty of Form and Novelty of Substance in Seventeenth-Century Mimamsa." *Journal of Indian Philosophy* 30(5): 481–494.

Pandurangi, K. T. 2004. *Prakaraṇapañcikā of Śālikanātha with an Exposition in English*. New Delhi: Indian Council of Philosophical Research.

Parpola, Asko. 1981. "On the Formation of the Mīmāṃsā and the Problems Concerning Jaimini with Particular Reference to the Teacher Quotations and the Vedic Schools I." *Wiener Zeitschrift für die Kunde Südasiens* 25: 145–177.

Ramaswami Śāstrī, V. A. 1936. *Tattvabindu by Vācaspatimiśra*. Annamalainagar: Annamalai University.

Taber, John A. 2005. *A Hindu Critique of Buddhist Epistemology: Kumārila on Perception. The* "Determination of Perception" *Chapter of Kumārila Bhaṭṭa's* Ślokavārttika. London: RoutledgeCurzon.

Verpoorten, Jean-Marie. 1987. *Mīmāṃsā Literature*. Wiesbaden: Harrassowitz.

Yoshimizu, Kiyotaka. 1997. *Der "Organismus" des urheberlosen Veda: eine Studie der Niyoga-Lehre Prabhākaras mit ausgewählten Übersetzungen der Bṛhatī*. Vienna: De Nobili Research Library.

Chapter 16
THE CATEGORIES IN VAIŚEṢIKA: KNOWN AND NAMED[1]

ShashiPrabha Kumar

The Vaiśeṣika system is of the view that a complete knowledge of seven categories (*padārtha*-s), which it believes to be essential to the world, namely (*padārtha*-s), substance (*dravya*), attribute (*guṇa*), activity (*karma*), universal (*sāmānya*), particularity (*viśeṣa*) [and] inherence (*samavāya*), and '*abhāva*' (negation), is capable of leading one towards the attainment of the highest good (*summum bonum*), *niḥśreyasa*. These seven categories are therefore the real objects of knowledge; and these are divided into either the substrata (*dharmins*) or the attributes (*dharmas*) of all there is, and what there is not (i.e. *abhāva*, 'absences'), as in the very last category. It is important to emphasize that both of the *dharmin*-s and *dharma*-s are held to be two separate, independent entities in the Vaiśeṣika, although related through a peculiar relation of inherence (*samavāya*). The enumerations and permutations can proliferate into many more nameable and knowable objects or properties thereof, as we shall see.

In view of the above, anything which exists and can be given a name and thus is said to belong to the class or subclass of '*padārtha*', In other words, designation depends on knowability; therefore that which has the capacity to be the object of knowledge is *padārtha*.

We shall now explain the categories as delineated in classical Vaiśeṣika philosophy in some detail.

Substance (*dravya*)

Substance denotes the self-existence of reals, which may also be characterized as 'being-in-itself'. Kaṇāda defines substance as that to which the attributes are ascribed and which is an inherent cause. In simple terms, '*dravya*' is the substratum or '*dharmin*', while activity and attributes are its '*dharma*-s', This essential dichotomy of *dharmin* and its *dharma*-s is at the crux of Vaiśeṣika realism, which has been strongly opposed by the Buddhist non-realists. Vyomaśiva has quoted the opponents' view:

> There is nothing like *dravya* which is different from and beyond the attributes, since our cognitions are confined to the attributes only. Our sense-organs, like eye and skin, can only grasp the colour and touch, respectively. We do not perceive anything else which may be held to be independent of these. It is only our mental construct which presents things in a conglomerated manner, otherwise there is nothing beyond these attributes.

The Vaiśeṣika response to the above objection is mainly based on the argument of 'co-relation' (*pratisandhāna.*) It means that seeing and touching are two different cognitions which point towards something else to which these two attributes pertain. For example, one can 'see' a pot and also 'touch' it, both these properties of colour and touch cannot be cognized unless and until there is a self-sustaining single substratum, which in turn is not just a conglomerate of attributes but an independent whole in itself, that precisely is a substance (*dravya*).

Therefore, conception of substance as an independent entity in itself and also a substratum of its attributes is, in fact, foundational to the Vaiśeṣika theory of reals: it is not only supported by the common-sense experience but also logically justified. Accordingly, the self-dependence of substance is proved by its independent understanding. In other words, activity and attribute cannot be comprehended without being associated with a substance while a substance does not need any other substratum for its comprehension.

Natural kinds of substance (dravyas)

According to the Vaiśeṣika scheme of categories, substances are nine in their natural kind:

- *earth (pṛthvī);*
- *water (jala);*
- *fire (tejas);*
- *air (vāyu);*
- *time (kāla);*
- *ether (ākāśa);*
- *direction (dik);*
- *self (ātman);*
- *mind (manas).*

The nine substances (*dravyas*) are again classified into various groups depending on the similarities or dissimilarities amongst them.

Earth (pṛthvī)

Earth is defined in the Vaiśeṣika as the substratum of the property of odour. Although there are fourteen attributes assigned to earth, odour or 'smell' is its specific attribute, in the sense that both of these are inherently related while other properties residing in earth are related to it through conjunction. Besides odour, the other thirteen properties attributed to earth are:

- *colour (rūpa);*
- *taste (rasa);*
- *touch (sparśa);*
- *number (saṅkhyā);*
- *magnitude (parimāṇa);*
- *severalty (pṛthaktva);*
- *conjunction (saṃyoga);*
- *disjunction (vibhāga);*
- *priority (paratva);*
- *posteriority (aparatva);*
- *weight (gurutva);*
- *instrumental liquidity (naimittika dravatva);*
- *elasticity (sthitisthāpaka saṃskāra).*

Earth is classified as eternal (*nityā*) and non-eternal (*anityā*): it is eternal in the form of ultimate causes or atoms and non-eternal in the form of produced effects, which are again stated to be of three types:

- body (*śarīra*);
- sense organ (*indriya*);
- object (*viṣaya*).

Water (jala)

Kaṇāda defines water (*jala*) as the liquid substance possessing colour, taste, viscidity and touch. The revised definition of water (*jala*) would be that it contains wateriness as its generic attribute and cold touch as its specific attribute. Water as a substance possess fourteen properties in all:

- *colour (rūpa);*
- *taste (rasa);*
- *touch (sparśa);*
- *natural liquidity (sāṃsiddhika dravatva);*
- *viscidity (sneha);*
- *number (saṅkhyā);*
- *magnitude (parimāṇa);*
- *severalty (pṛthaktva);*
- *conjunction (saṃyoga);*
- *disjunction (vibhāga);*
- *posteriority (paratva);*
- *proximity (aparatva);*
- *weight (gurutva);*
- *velocity (vega saṃskāra).*

The colour of water is non-luminous white or clear (*abhāsvara śukla*). Water is held to be unchanging even with the application of heat (*apākaja*); it just takes on different forms, such as vapour, mist, clouds and so on. Sweet taste is the natural attribute of water. Viscidity (*sneha*) is another property which is specifically attributed to water only. Likewise, natural liquidity (*sāmsiddhika dravatva*) is also to be found in water only Water is also initially divided into two types: eternal and non-eternal. Watery atoms are the eternal form of water, while watery products are the non-eternal ones and are accordingly classified into three types:

- watery body (*jalīya śarīra*);
- sense organ (*jalīya indriya*);
- object (*jalīya viṣaya*).

Fire (tejas)

Fire (*tejas*) possesses two specific attributes:

- luminous white colour (*bhāsvara śukla rūpa*);
- hot touch (*uṣṇa sparśa*).

Besides these two, fire has nine more properties:

- *number (saṅkhyā);*
- *magnitude (parimāṇa);*
- *severalty (pṛthaktva);*
- *conjunction (saṃyoga);*
- *disjunction (vibhāga);*
- *proximity (aparatva);*
- *remoteness (paratva);*
- *instrumental liquidity (naimittika dravatva);*
- *velocity (vega saṃskāra).*

Fire is also divided into two groups: eternal and non-eternal. The fiery atoms are held to be eternal and fiery products are said to be non-eternal; these are classified under three headings:

- fiery body (*taijasa śarīra*);
- fiery sense-organ (*taijasa indriya*);
- fiery object (*taijasa viṣaya*).

Air (vāyu)

The fourth categorical substance is air, which is defined as possessing airness (*vāyutva*), the substratum of natural moderate touch and devoid of colour. Air has been stated to possess nine attributes:

- *touch (sparśa);*
- *number (saṅkhyā);*
- *magnitude (parimāṇa);*
- *severalty (pṛthaktva);*
- *conjunction (saṃyoga);*
- *disjunction (vibhāga);*
- *proximity (aparatva);*
- *remoteness (paratva);*
- *velocity (vega saṃskāra).*

Air cannot be perceived visually, so its existence is proven through inference in the Vaiśeṣika tradition. Like the previous three substances, air has also been classified into two types – eternal and non-eternal. Eternal air is in the form of atoms while non-eternal air is divided into four types:

- airy body (*vāyavya śarīra*);
- airy sense organ (*vāyavya indriya*);
- airy objects (*vāyavya viṣaya*);
- vital air (*prāṇa vāyu*).

Ether (ākāśa)

Ether is the fifth substance in the Vaiśeṣika enumerology, and is held to be the substratum of sound, one, pervasive and eternal. Unlike the first four material substances, it cannot be classified as eternal and non-eternal because it has no parts and is indivisible.

Ether cannot be visually perceived because even though it has gross magnitude, it does not have colour. Therefore, the existence of ether as a substantial basis for the property called sound (*śabda*) has to be proved by inference only. Kaṇāda and Praśastapāda have through the process of elimination shown that the attribute of sound cannot inhere in any of the other eight substances. The have argued that ether has to be accepted as the inherent cause of sound. The Mīmāṃsakas (and the Grammarians) have objected to this view, asserting instead that sound itself is a substance and not a property of ether. However, the Vaiśeṣikas have rejected their theory and have propounded that since no substance can inhere in a partless substance, sound cannot be held to be a substance; it is a specific property which is externally perceptible through a particular sense organ, and is inherent in an eternal, partless, pervasive substance which is none other than ether. In this way, sound (*śabda*) is the sign that leads us to the acceptance of ether. Sound being its specific property, ether has five more general properties:

- number (*saṅkhyā*);
- magnitude (*parimāṇa*);
- severalty (*pṛthaktva*);
- conjunction (*saṃyoga*);
- disjunction (*vibhāga*).

Time (kāla)

Time is the sixth in the Vaiśeṣika scheme of substances and has been stated to be a necessary precondition for all sorts of action. It is held to be a substance, because it possesses certain common properties:

- number (*saṅkhyā*);
- magnitude (*parimāṇa*);
- severalty (*pṛthaktva*);
- conjunction (*saṃyoga*);
- disjunction (*vibhāga*).

The existence of time is proved on the basis of cognitions regarding proximity, remoteness, simultaneity, early and late. All of these types of understanding are actually dependent upon the notion of time. Therefore, the commonsensical experience of all such types as past, present and future, etc. is rooted in the acceptance of time. The notions of proximity and remoteness are explained on the basis of solar movements; one who has observed more solar movements in her life is held to be senior in age, while the other one who has seen fewer solar movements is known as comparatively junior in age. In other words, remoteness and proximity are based on the concept of time, which is experienced daily by each one of us in the form of solar movements.

Here a question naturally arises as to the relation between these solar movements and the person being characterized as older or younger. The Vaiśeṣikas have answered this question and proposed that neither of the relations, conjunction or inherence, is exclusively possible in this case; it has to be a special kind of relation which is termed as '*saṃyuktasaṃyuktasamavāya*'. It means that the person being proposed as elder (*para*), is conjoined (*saṃyukta*) with some substance (*saṃyukta*), which is in turn in contact with the sun, wherein the solar movement is inherent (*samavāya*). In short, there has to be a substance which is conjoined with the sun and this substance is time. Obviously, the first four substances cannot serve this purpose because they are of a limited magnitude and so cannot be related with all the available objects. The fifth substance, ether, cannot connect these properties with a substance which is already conjoined with the object in question. Therefore, we are left with no choice but to accept time as an additional and independent substance which is responsible for explaining these cognitions.

Moreover, the visible changes in the phenomenal world also point to the notion of time; the obvious difference between the bodies of a young and an elderly person can only be explained on the basis of temporal difference, so the existence of time is proved beyond doubt. Interestingly, another argument has also been adduced by a Vaiśeṣika scholar in this regard: the mere presence of various objects denotes the existence of time, but this 'presence' is different from 'isness' because the latter merely connotes their individual existence, while the former signifies their temporal relation. Besides, isness is excluded in the case of each object, while presence is inclusive of all that is present.

Direction (dik)

The seventh substance in the Vaiśeṣika list is direction, which is not just the ordinarily understood space or locus; rather it is the basis for our cognitions such as 'from here' or east, west, far, near, etc. Since direction cannot be directly perceived its existence is proven through inference, i.e. proximity and remoteness are the signs of direction. The very fact that we use words like remote and near is evidence that there is a substance which makes such usage possible.

Five attributes are ascribed to the substance termed direction:

- number (*saṅkhyā*);
- magnitude (*parimāṇa*);
- severalty (*pṛthaktva*);
- conjunction (*saṃyoga*);
- disjunction (*vibhāga*).

As regards the difference between ether and direction, Vaiśeṣika texts state that the temporal proximity or remoteness between two objects remains unchanged, while the spatial proximity and remoteness are changeable. For example, the father of 'A' will always be elder (temporally remote) to him, he can never become younger; but anybody who is spatially remote from 'A' can be spatially near him at another point of time. Moreover, time can only refer to solar movement or activity, while direction relates the solar direction with worldly objects.

Self (ātman)

The next and the most important substance in the Vaiśeṣika list is the self, which is held to be the substratum of knowing: its existence is proven by the process of inference since it, like the mind, is not directly perceived. Twelve reasons have been advanced by Kaṇāda himself in this regard; these have been explained by Praśastapāda and elaborated by his commentators, who are also inclined to believe that the self is directly cognized through mental perception. A close examination of all these arguments reveals that although the self (*ātman*) cannot be perceived by external sense-organs due to its being a subtle substance, at the same time none can deny the self-experience of one's own self. In fact, Kaṇāda has categorically stated that the yogins can perceive their own self.

It is noteworthy that in the Vaiśeṣika view, self is not accepted as conscious by nature, rather it is held to be the inherent cause of consciousness or knowledge. Since according to the Vaiśeṣika the cause and effect as well as substance and qualities are two independent entities, knowledge is accepted as an adventitious attribute of the self.

In all, fourteen attributes have been ascribed to the self according to the Vaiśeṣika; of these knowledge is the first and foremost:

- *knowledge (buddhi)*;
- *pleasure (sukha)*;
- *pain (duḥkha)*;
- *desire (icchā)*;
- *aversion (dveṣa)*;
- *effort (prayatna)*;
- *merit (dharma)*;
- *demerit (adharma)*;
- *impression (saṃskāra)*;
- *number (saṅkhyā)*;
- *magnitude (parimāṇa)*;
- *severalty (pṛthaktva)*;
- *conjunction (saṃyoga)*;
- *disjunction (vibhāga)*.

Another important assertion of the Vaiśeṣika in this regard is the plural number of the self which is based on the argument of the law of individual retribution, i.e. *vyavasthā*. The same has also been explained as a rule for regulating pleasure and pain, etc. The dimension of the self has been propounded as the pervasive one, i.e. *paramamahat* or *vibhu* in terms of the Vaiśeṣika, because if it is accepted to be of medium size (*madhyamaparimāṇa*), as held by the Jaina philosophers, then it cannot be eternal, as theorized by Vaiśeṣika scholars.

Existence of the self has been discussed in detail by several Vaiśeṣika scholars who have argued that the physical body cannot be the substratum of knowledge, because it is produced out of material substances and all material products are obviously unconscious. Moreover the dead body does not have consciousness, which itself is evidence to prove that there is something beyond the physical body in which consciousness inheres.

Knowledge or consciousness cannot be an attribute of sense-organs either, because these being only the instruments of cognitive activity are themselves unconscious and therefore cannot be accepted to be the substrata of knowledge. Besides, the possibility of memory cannot be explained reasonably if the sense-organs are held to be the substrata of knowledge, because even when a particular sense-organ is not working, one can remember the objects perceived by the same. This means that there is some substratum of knowledge other than the sense-organs. Likewise, the mind also cannot be held to be the substratum of knowledge or conscious because it is the instrument of knowing and not the agent. Moreover, it would pose the problem of several simultaneous cognitions, which is not the case in our daily experience. One of the later Vaiśeṣika scholars has argued that mind being a minute substance cannot be held to be the substratum of knowledge because in that case, all the attributes such as desire, pain, etc. ascribed to the self will cease to be perceptible because gross magnitude is a precondition of perceptibility.

Mind (manas)

Last but not least is the ninth substance, the 'mind', which is held to be the internal organ and an instrument for knowing. Existence of the mind is proven through inference and the argument given in this regard is as follows: even though the self, sense-organs and the objects are in contact, sometimes cognition occurs and at another time it does not occur; this proves that there is something more than these three which is instrumental in the occurrence of cognition, and that is the reason for acceptance of mind as an instrument of knowing. Mind has no specific attribute but is stated to be a substratum for the five generic attributes besides three others:

- number (*saṅkhyā*);
- magnitude (*parimāṇa*);
- severalty (*pṛthaktva*);
- conjunction (*saṃyoga*);
- disjunction (*vibhāga*);
- remoteness (*paratva*);
- proximity (*aparatva*);
- velocity (*vega*).

Accordingly, in terms of numbers, mind is stated to be innumerable, for each body is associated with an independent mind. The magnitude of mind is accepted to be minute. Gautama, the author of *Nyāyasūtras*, gave an important argument for proving the minuteness of mind, suggesting that all our cognitions are successive and not simultaneous. It is therefore quite logical to accept a minute object like the mind, which acts as a medium between the external sense organs and the self, that is eternal and pervasive. Otherwise, each one of us should have simultaneous cognition of all objects at all times. Moreover, the mind and the self both being pervasive (*vibhu*), their conjunction cannot take place because two pervasive substances cannot conjoin according to the Vaiśeṣika view. So the process of cognition will become impossible if we do not accept mind as being minute. Severalty is another attribute of the mind besides conjunction, disjunction, remoteness, proximity and velocity. Being minute and corporeal, mind is also a substratum of activity, because activity is ascribed to corporeal substances only.

This concludes the enumeration of substances, the first category that we have examined. We shall now move to examine the remainder of the *padārtha*-s, beginning with the category of '*guṇa*' or 'attribute' as 'property'.

Attribute (*guṇa*)

The second category or the object of knowing is attribute, which is defined by Kaṇāda as that which inheres in a substance, is not the substratum of attribute and is not the cause of conjunction or disjunction independently. Praśastapāda has elaborated the nature of attribute by describing four similarities (*sādharmya*-s) among all the attributes enumerated by him: association with attributeness (*guṇatvābhisambandha*), being inherent in any of the nine substances (*dravyāśritatvam*), being devoid of attributes (*nirguṇatvam*) and activities (*niṣkriyatvam*). In fact, these are the common characteristics of all attributes. What follows from the above is that the attributes (*guṇa*-s) are inhered in by the class character (*jāti*) of attributeness (*guṇatva*); are themselves inherent in the substances, and are never inhered in by the attributes and the activities.

An earlier list of attributes given by Kaṇāda mentions only seventeen:

- *colour (rūpa)*;
- *taste (rasa)*;
- *odour (gandha)*;
- *touch (sparśa)*;
- *number (saṅkhyā)*;
- *magnitude (parimāṇa)*;
- *severalty (pṛthaktva)*;
- *conjunction (saṃyoga)*;
- *disjunction (vibhāga)*;
- *proximity (aparatva)*;
- *remoteness (paratva)*;
- *intellect (buddhi)*;
- *pleasure (sukha)*;
- *pain (duḥkha)*;
- *desire (icchā)*;
- *aversion (dveṣa)*;
- *effort (prayatna)*.

Later, seven more were added to the list by Praśastapāda:

- *weight (gurutva)*;
- *liquidity (dravatva)*;
- *viscidity (sneha)*;
- *impression (saṃskāra)*;
- *merit (dharma)*;
- *demerit (adharma)*;
- *sound (śabda)*.

In this way, a total of twenty-four attributes were accepted in the Vaiśeṣika tradition. Questions have been raised regarding the lesser or greater number of attributes, but the list of twenty-four attributes has been prevalent and acceptable after Praśastapāda,

As regards the knowability of these twenty-four attributes (*guṇa*-s), Praśastapāda has clearly mentioned that only four out of these twenty-four attributes – namely, weight, merit, demerit and mental faculty – are imperceptible and so are to be known through inference, while the others are perceived either by one or more than one sense organs; the remaining six specific attributes pertaining to the self, cognition, pleasure, pain, aversion, desire and effort, are to be known through mental perception.

Activity (*karma*)

The third category in the Vaiśeṣika view is held to be activity which is in fact the principle of motion or movement pertaining to corporeal substances. It has been defined as inhering in one substance (*ekadravyam*), being devoid of attributes (*aguṇam*) and being an independent cause of conjunction and disjunction (*saṃyogavibhāgeṣvakāraṇam*)

The Vaiśeṣika view of activity maintains that at a given time, one single activity can stay in one object only. Accordingly, the first epithet in the definition of activity signifies that one particular activity pertains to one substance at one point in time, otherwise when one object starts moving, or stops moving, all other objects should be affected. In cases of simultaneous movement of various objects, there are a number of different activities operating in different objects, so the definition given by Kaṇāda is clear in its intent.

Moreover, it is the peculiar nature of activity that although it is caused through anyone of the four attributes – namely, weight, fluidity, effort and conjunction – and is also the non-inherent cause of attributes like conjunction or contact, disjunction and velocity, yet it is not inherently related to attributes as such and so, not being inhered in by any of the attributes (*aguṇatva*), is a common characteristic of all the activities.

In the Vaiśeṣika view activity is also held to be an independent cause of conjunction or contact and disjunction; this particular aspect of activity clearly distinguishes it from attributes.

Besides the above-mentioned three defining features, there are other characteristics of activity which have been suggested in Vaiśeṣika texts:

- Activity is destroyed by its own effect, i.e. the subsequent conjunction (*uttara-saṃyoga*) which is produced in the fourth moment of activity.
- Activity is invariably the non-inherent cause of movement according to Vaiśeṣika, because only a substance can be the inherent cause (*samavāyikāraṇa*) of an effect, while attribute can be both the non-inherent cause (*asamavāyi kāraṇa*) as well as the instrumental cause (*nimitta kārana*).
- Activity can never generate another activity, just as a substance can cause another substance and attribute can cause another attribute.
- Activity also cannot be a cause of substances, because a substance is produced only after the activity is over and no decaying activity can cause a substance.

- Activity is transitory by nature, because it cannot last more than four or five moments. In other words, activity is the transient feature of substance (*dravya*), while attribute (*guṇa*) is the intransient one.
- Activity cannot pertain to pervasive substances, so it is ascribed to corporeal substances only.

The existence of activity is proved by perception itself, since 'it moves' it is directly perceived by each and every person.

As far as the types of activity are concerned, the Vaiśeṣikas have classified them into five types:

- throwing upwards (*utkṣepaṇa*);
- throwing downwards (*avakṣepaṇa*);
- contraction (*ākuñcana*);
- expansion (*prasāraṇa*);
- going or moving in general (*gamana*).

Obviously, these five types are described as being due to the particular direction in which the movement takes place. All of these five types of activity are manifested through their respective movements, which are also expressed by the prefixes used in each of the titles.

There is one more interesting aspect of activity which needs to be outlined here; Praśastapāda has elaborated this aspect which was originally hinted by Kaṇāda himself. It pertains to the causal relationship of several attributes with activity and provides a ground for the eight factors responsible for generating of various types. The above-mentioned eight factors are listed and elaborated by B. N. Seal as follows:

- pressure (*nodana*);
- impact (*abhighāta*);
- velocity (*vega saṃskāra*);
- elasticity (*sthitisthāpakatā*);
- weight (*gurutva*);
- liquidity (*dravatva*);
- effort (*prayatna*);
- unseen force (*adṛṣṭa*).

Universal (*sāmānya*)

Universal inheres in all of the three categories mentioned above. It signifies the natural class characters pertaining to substances, attributes and activities in general. It is defined as that which is the ground of universal being experienced in all the individual members of a particular class. In other words, the one eternal principle which inheres in many is termed as universal (*sāmānya*).

Significantly, three features of universal are explicitly mentioned in the definition quoted above:

- Universal is eternal: this aspect of the definition is important: otherwise the definition of universal would become too broad and entities like conjunction (which are inherent in more than one) would fall into its ambit.
- Universal inheres in many: if this part of the definition of universal is removed, then again the fallacy of over-wideness will crop up, since the magnitude of ether is also eternal and one.
- Universal inheres (in its particulars). This part of the definition, i.e. 'inhering in' is also unavoidable, otherwise it will apply to absolute negation as well, which is eternal and is available in many; but since non-being cannot be related to anything through inherence, it is excluded.

It is also noteworthy that in the earlier phase of Vaiśeṣika, this category was termed as universal (*sāmānya*), but later another term, '*jāti*', came to be used as its equivalent. Some scholars have noted that since the Grammarians have also used these two terms, there may be some interrelation.

The acceptance of universal is widely discussed in the various texts of Vaiśeṣika and several arguments have been advanced in this regard, the most important being the commonsensical experience based on the law of causation. Buddhists have vehemently criticized the concept of '*jāti*' propounded by the Nyāya-Vaiśeṣika and have instead advocated the concept of '*apoha*'; long debates have taken place between these two camps. It would be out of place here to go into detail (see the discussion of Buddhist philosophy in this volume), suffice to say that Vaiśeṣika scholars have refuted almost all the objections raised by the opponents and that they are joined by the Bhāṭṭa Mīmāṃsakas in this case.

Universal has been broadly classified in two types:

- wide (*para*);
- narrow or limited (*apara*).

Out of these the widest class character (*para sāmānya*) or being (*bhāva*) is the ground for experiencing the inclusive notion only, while the concept of universal usually performs both the functions, inclusion as well as exclusion. Kaṇāda has proclaimed earlier that both these categories of universal and particularity are actually dependent on the understanding (of the knower). However, in the very next statement he clarifies that the widest form of universal (*para*) is that which can never be understood as the basis of differentiation. Those types of universal which also act as particularity are in fact the limited class character (*apara sāmānya*) and are said to be three in number: substancehood (*dravyatva*), attributeness (*guṇatva*) and activityhood (*karmatva*). These are only broadly counted as three, because there may be many more narrower forms of these three also, such as earthiness (*pṛthvītva*), wateriness (*jalatva*) and fieriness (*tejastva*), etc.

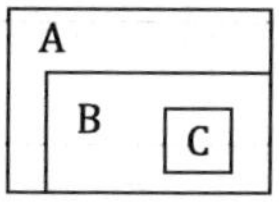

A = *para*

B = *parāpara*

C = *apara*

Figure 16.1 **Three types of universal**

In this way the classification of universal (*sāmānya*) into two types (*para* and *apara*) is only meant to explain the principle of inclusion and exclusion. Of these two kinds of universal, the former is the more inclusive because it incorporates all of the three possible categories in its ambit and does not exclude any one of these at any level.

The other type of universal, i.e. the limited universal, is a relative one; when it is comprehended in relation to the wider form of universal, it will be termed as narrow; but when it is compared with the narrower forms of universal, it will be stated to be wide.

In view of the above, some of the later Vaiśeṣika scholars have divided universals into three types: the widest (*para*), the medium (*parāpara*) and the narrowest (*apara*). Figure 16.1 shows how all these three types of universal can be illustrated:

Of these three types, the most inclusive form of universal is expressed through another technical term used in Vaiśeṣika texts, '*sattā*' (existence). Kaṇāda has himself explained the concept of supreme universal (*sattā*) in clear terms: the widest universal is that due to which all the first three categories, namely substance, attribute and activity, are understood to be existent. It must be clarified that the supreme universal (*sattā*) here should not be taken in its literal sense of 'existence' since it is different from isness (*astitva*), which is the common characteristic of all the six categories, barring the seventh (*abhāva*), so the term *sattā* is used in a restricted sense in Vaiśeṣika sources. It is aptly explained as that which subsists in the first three categories, namely substance, attribute and activity.

In the Vaiśeṣika view universal is held to be perceptible, since the same sense-organ which grasps an object also perceives the class character pertaining to that object. Although it is the individual that comes in direct contact with the sense-organ, at the same time the class character inherent in a particular object is also perceived by the same sense-organ.

Particularity (*viśeṣa*)

The fifth category, particularity, is the basis for nomenclature of the Vaiśeṣika because it is the innovative idea of this school. Kaṇāda suggested a significant aspect of particularity by using the term 'ultimate particularity' (*antya-viśeṣa*), distinguishing it from particularity in general.

Particularity is known as ultimate particularity because it subsists in the ultimate atoms and eternal substances and distinguishes its substrata from other entities.

The number of particularity is said to be countless because it inheres in each of the innumerable atoms, selves and minds. Now a question might arise as to when each of the eternal substances is associated with separate particularities and a single particularity is not accepted to inhere in many substances (*dravyas*) simultaneously, why is particularityness (*viśeṣatva*) a class character, since it is not needed for inhering in all the countless particularities. In this regard, the response provided by the Vaiśeṣika is interesting, i.e. if '*viśeṣatva*' is accepted as a universal, then the very purpose of propounding particularity will be defeated and the nature of particularity will also be contradicted; so it is logical to hold that there is no need to accept another distinguishing factor for each of the countless particularities, because they are accepted to be self-differentiating (*svatovyāṛtta*) by nature. Although particularity is held to be a distinguishing factor among eternal substances, none of the particularities is related to universal as such (*sāmānya*) or (*jāti*). In other words, particularities perform double roles: on the one hand, they distinguish their respective substrata from each one of its kind and, on the other hand, they distinguish themselves from their own counterparts, i.e. the particularities.

Regarding the knowability of particularity, it has been said in several Vaiśeṣika texts that particularity cannot be directly perceived by ordinary mortals, for whom it is a matter of inference only. However, the yogins can and do perceive particularity (*viśeṣa*) through their extraordinary faculties. Particularity is said to be cognizable by inference, since all its substrata, i.e. the eternal substances, are themselves to be inferred. They are, however, directly perceived by the yogins through extraordinary perception. So the multiple number of particularities are also said to be directly perceptible for the yogins in Vaiśeṣika, although the claim has been questioned by none other than Raghunātha Śiromaṇi, one of the later stalwarts of the Navya-Nyāya-Vaiśesika school. It is worth mentioning here that the concept of particularity as an independent category has not only been refuted by both the schools of Mimāṃsā, but also the Buddhists and Advaita Vedānta.

The necessity for postulating an independent category in the name of particularity has been argued as follows: all the gross objects of the visible world can be differentiated from each other due to their form, parts, properties or activity. But the question remains as to how the subtle but numerous substances of similar or of dissimilar kind can be distinguished from others. The category of particularity is envisaged for differentiating amongst the atoms, souls and minds, which are held to be distinctly numerous. In fact, particularity is the principle of atoms, selves and minds. It is due to particularity that each atom is different from other atoms of its own class or of another class. To put it more precisely, particularity is the factor which separates each of the eternal substances from one another. More importantly, particularities are held to be self-differentiating, so there is no need to accept another principle for differentiating amongst multiple particularities. If another particularity be accepted for differentiating one particularity from another, there will be the fallacy of infinite regress (*anavasthā*).

Particularities are stated to inhere only in the eternal substances, so it follows that the non-eternal substances and the remaining categories do not have any particularity.

In other words, the products of the first four substances, attributes or properties, activity, universal and particularities themselves do not require any further particularity, nor do the remaining two categories, inherence (*samavāya*) and negation (*abhāva*).

According to the Vaiśeṣika view, the category of particularity is related to the respective individual entities through the relation of inherence.

Inherence (*samavāya*)

Samavāya is of the nature of inherence, which is defined as an eternal relation between the cause and the effect; it is stated to subsist in the following five pairs of relata:

- parts and the whole (*avayava-avayavī*);
- properties and the substance (*guṇa-guṇī*);
- activity and the substance (*kriyā-kriyāvān*);
- universal and the individual (*jātī-vyakti*);
- particularity and the eternal substances (*viśeṣa-nityadravya*).

In the Vaiśeṣika worldview, there are three types of objects in the universe: the substances, the attributes and the relation between them. All of these are independent and real objects, but are of course related in an inseparable manner through a relation conceived in the name of inherence. Obviously, the first two are in the form of relata while the last is a relation which binds them both.

Inherence is the foundation for causation theory propounded by the Vaiśeṣika school. Accordingly, the effect is stated to be non-existent in its cause before production; it is held to be a new product (*asatkāryavāda* or *ārambhavāda*). This does not mean that there is no rule as such and anything can be produced out of anything because it is observed by everyone that a particular effect is produced out of a particular cause only. In other words, the cause and the effect are inseparably related through inherence. It is therefore not wrong to surmise that the Vaiśeṣika school must have propounded inherence as an independent category to explain the essential distinction between the cause and the effect accepted by them.

Accordingly, inherence (*samavāya*) is held to be a relating principle between:

1 substances and properties;
2 substances and activity;
3 substance and universal;
4 eternal substances and particularity.

But there is no inherence for relating inherence to its relata, and no inherence for relating negation to anything else. In other words, inherence operates amongst the first five categories only. Besides, the Vaiśeṣika holds the view that inherence is only one in number. Kaṇāda has explicitly mentioned that the singularity of inherence is explained by the oneness of being (*sattā sāmānya*), but this view has also been refuted by various scholars from within the Vaiśeṣika tradition.

The knowing of inherence is stated to be by inference because it is not perceptible according to Vaiśeṣika, while the Naiyāyikas hold that inherence can be perceived through adjectival contact of the sense-organ with its object. Without going into detail, it can be said that since the Vaiśeṣika scholars have offered several arguments to prove the existence of inherence, hence it is clear that they do not accept its perceptibility.

Negation (*abhāva*)

The seventh category, negation (*abhāva*), is the last one in the Vaiśeṣika scheme. According to the Vaiśeṣika view, reality has two aspects, positive and negative. The six categories enunciated above are covered under positive while the seventh category, '*abhāva*', represents the negative.

It has been argued by Vaiśeṣika scholars that reality does not consist of positive entities only, it also points towards a negative aspect of being. Therefore, an additional category has to be accepted as the foundation for explaining such experiences. It is termed as '*abhāva*' and has been differently interpreted as negation, non-existence or absence by various scholars.

It is noteworthy here that the term negation is confined only to the field of language, while the *abhāva* of Vaiśeṣika is a metaphysical entity. In other words, negation deals with form but non-being is an essential category.

Interestingly, Kaṇāda has not listed *abhāva* as an independent category. In his aphorisms, he has used the term *abhāva* in more than one aphorism and has also delineated the four types of *abhāva*. Praśastapāda has also not described *abhāva* as an independent category, but discussed it under the means of knowing and said that *abhāva* is not an independent means of knowing, it is a form of inference only. This clearly proves that *abhāva* was not actually accepted as an independent category until the time of Praśastapāda, because since the time *abhāva* was accepted as a category, it was also established that it is directly perceived. In other words, *abhāva* was meant to be a negation of something and in that form it was taken to be an object of inference. It means that until the time of Praśastapāda logical acceptance of *abhāva* (as negation) was in the Vaiśeṣika tradition, but its metaphysical existence was yet to be proved. Śrīdhara has clarified the position of Praśastapāda in the following manner: he has not mentioned non-being (*abhāva*) as a separate category, because its existence depends upon being and not because he does not accept non-being (*abhāva*).

As stated above, Kaṇāda has not explicitly mentioned *abhāva* as an independent category, but he has referred to all the four types of it accepted in the later period by his followers from Śivāditya and Udayanācārya onwards. Accordingly the Vaiśeṣika school has classified *abhāva* into four types:

- antecedent negation (*prāgabhāva*);
- consequent negation (*pradhvaṃsābhāva*);
- absolute negation (*atyantābhāva*);
- reciprocal negation (*anyonyābhāva*).

The first of these four is explained as the non-existence of the effect in its cause; the second occurs when the effect is destroyed; the third is a type of non-existence which is forever; and the fourth is atemporal in the sense that it is the absence of mutual identity in various objects of the world.

As far as the knowledge of *abhāva* is concerned, the Vaiśeṣika (along with the Nyāya) school holds that it is directly perceived. Kaṇāda has also accepted that all the four types of *abhāva* are perceptible, just as the positive categories are.

Surprisingly, Praśastapāda does not accept perceptibility of non-being and includes it under inference.

However, his commentator Śrīdharācārya has questioned him on the point and enquired as to when the vacant ground is directly perceived without an object, i.e. a pot, then how can we not accept that non-being is directly perceived? It is noteworthy here that the Bhāṭṭa Mīmāṃsakas do not accept perceptibility of non-being (although they accept an objective reality like non-being and four of its types), rather they have posited an additional means for cognizing non-being, i.e. non-mental apprehension (which is also called *abhāva*, or later with Prabhākara, *anupalabdhi*) (see Bilimoria 2016). But Śrīdhara has refuted the Bhāṭṭa position and propounded that *abhāva* is perceptible through a specific kind of contact between the sense-organ and the locus of *abhāva*.

Other schools of Indian philosophy, such as the Buddhists, Sāṃkhyas, Vedāntins and Prābhākaras, are not ready to accept *abhāva* as an independent category of reals, rather they have criticized and rejected the Vaiśeṣika view in this regard. However, later Vaiśeṣika scholars, after arguing against all such objections, have re-established that it is more logical to accept *abhāva* as an independent, additional category.

On the basis of the above delineation, it may be said that the Vaiśeṣika view of the world is a comprehensive one and it encompasses all that is to be known, i.e. the sevenfold objects of knowing. There is a logical ground for enunciation of the seven categories in sequential order. Accordingly, the substances are the basic substrata, attributes and activity are the qualifying properties which express different aspects of the same. Just as the system of Kaṇāda propounded a category called universal (*sāmānya*) to explain the similarities found in several classes of objects, similarly they went on to posit a category called particularity (*viśeṣa*) so that the distinctness of each of the ultimate invisible objects could be accounted for. At one end of our knowledge stands the notion of being, i.e. '*sattā*', and at the other end of human understanding is this concept of particularity (*viśeṣa*), which is the ultimate idea of particularity, i.e. *antyaviśeṣa*. Besides the above five categories, inherence (*samavāya*) was also accepted as an independent category to relate all of those entities mentioned above. However, the process of knowing the reals is incomplete until we include the negative aspect of reality. Finally, the category *abhāva* was added to the list of Vaiśeṣika categories and was claimed to cover all the objects worth knowing in its exposition.

Note

1 This chapter has been adapted from ShashiPrabha Kumar, 'Objects of knowing', in *Classical Vaiśeṣika in Indian Philosophy: On Knowing and What Is to Be Known*. Routledge Hindu Studies Series. London: Routledge, 2013, pp. 14–37.

References

Primary sources

Bhāṣāparichheda with a commentary by Viśvanātha Panchanana. 1850. Ed. and English trans. E. Roer. Calcutta: Asiatic Society.

Nyāyakandalī of Śrīdhara Bhaṭṭa. 1997. Ed. Sri Durgadhara Jha Sharma. 2nd ed. Varanasi: Sampurnananda Sanskrit University.

Nyāyakoṣa or Dictionary of Technical Terms of Indian Philosophy. 1996. Bhīmācārya Jhalkīkar, Vāsudeva Śāstrī Abhyankar (rev. ed.). Repr. Pune: Bhandarkar Oriental Research Institute.

Nyāyasiddhāntamuktavalī (Commentary on *Bhāṣāparichheda*) of Viśvanātha. 2005. Ed. Hariram Sukla Śāstri. Repr. Varanasi: Kashi Sanskrit Series.

Praśastapādabhāṣyam (*Padārthadharmasaṅgrahākhyam*) of Praśastapādācārya. 1997. Ed. Sri Durgadhara Jha Sharma. 2nd ed. Varanasi: Sampurnananda Sanskrit University.

Tarka-saṃgraha of Annambhaṭṭa with the author's *Dīpikā* and Govardhana's *Nyāya Bodhinī* (*Tarkadīpikā*). 1974. Ed. Y. V. Athalye; English trans. M. R. Bodas. 2nd ed., 3rd impression. Poona: Bhandarkar Oriental Research Institute.

The Vaiśeṣika Aphorisms of Kaṇāda, with comments from the *Opaskāra* of Śaṅkara Miśra and *Vṛtti* of Jayanārāyaṇa Tarkapañcānana. 1975. English trans. A. E. Gough. 2nd Indian ed. Delhi: Oriental Books Reprint Corporation.

Vyomavatī of Vyomaśivacārya. 1930. Ed. Gopinath Kaviraj and Dhundhirāja Shastri. Benaras: Chowkhanba.

Sources in English

Bhaduri, S. 1975. *Studies in Nyāya-Vaiśeṣika Metaphysics*. Poona: Bhandarkar Oriental Research Institute.

Bilimoria, Purushottama. 2016. 'Negation (*Abhāva*), Non-existents, and a distinctive *pramāṇa* in the Nyāya-Mīmāṃsā', in *Comparative Philosophy and J. L. Shaw*, ed. P. Bilimoria and Michael Hemmingsen, pp. 183–202. Sophia Studies in Cross-Cultural Traditions and Cultures 13. Dordrecht and New York: SpringerNature.

———. 2017. 'Thinking Negation and Nothingness in early Hinduism & classical Indian philosophy', *Logica Universalis*. 11 (1): 13–33; DOI 10.1007/s11787-017-0161-8.

Bodas, M. R. 1974. 'A historical survey of Indian logic', in *Introduction to Tarka-Saṃgraha*, ed. Y. V. Athalye, English trans. M. R. Bodas. Poona: Bhandarkar Oriental Research Institute, 2nd ed., 3rd impression.

Halbfass, W. 1993. *On Being and What There Is: Classical Vaiśeṣika and the History of Indian Ontology*. Delhi: Indian Books Center. 1st Indian ed.

Kumar, ShashiPrabha. 1999. 'Matter, mind and motion in Vaiśeṣika pluralism', in *Facets of Indian Philosophical Thought*, 110–111. Delhi: Vidyanidhi.

———. 2014. 'Early *Vaiśeṣika*: The concept of categories in Vaiśeṣika philosophy', in *Categorisation in Indian Philosophy: Thinking Inside the Box*, ed. Jessica Frazier, 89–100. Farnham: Ashgate.

Matilal, Bimal K. 1977. *Nyāya-Vaiśeṣika*. History of Indian Literature Series. Wiesbaden: Otto Harrassowitz.

Sankaranarayan S. 2003. *Vaiśeṣika-Catuḥsūtrī. A Historical Perspective*. Chennai: The Adyar Library and Research Center.

Thakur, A. 2003. *Origin and Development of Vaiśeṣika System*. New Delhi: Centre for Studies in Civilization.

Chapter 17
NYĀYA

Stephen Phillips

Nyāya, commonly rendered as 'Logic,' is a school of classical philosophy whose texts span almost two thousand years. Nyāya philosophers include some of the greatest minds of classical India, with positions as wide-ranging as those of any classical system. Nyāya's primary focus is knowledge, the means thereto, and right procedures in debate and critical inquiry, but the school also largely accepts the ontology of a sister school, Vaiśeṣika, 'Atomism.' Vaiśeṣika posits seven fundamental categories (*padārtha*, 'type of things to which words refer'), all used by Nyāya authors. The later philosophers in particular devote much effort to defending the Vaiśeṣika system, or, in a few instances, revising it. Nyāya philosophers also make outstanding contributions to rational theology and philosophy of language as well as to theories of karma and rebirth which are coupled with advocacy of yoga. Most importantly, they develop an extensive arsenal of metaphysical arguments employed against adversaries, Buddhists and Mīmāṃsakas mainly. Much of the history of classical Indian thought lies in the exchanges, the arguments and counterarguments, among rival schools.

Nyāya takes its name from the Sanskrit *nyāya*, 'logical or investigative procedure,' a word that within the system means, more specifically, 'procedures for removing doubts and resolving disputes.' Nyāya's root text is the *Nyāya-sūtra* (= *NS*), *c.* 200 CE, attributed to Gautama, a legendary figure. Some of the *sūtra*-s, or 'aphorisms,' of the text probably originated before the edition we have was written, and were passed from generation to generation by memorization. We know that Nyāya as a *darśana* or 'world view' has origins earlier than the Buddhist philosopher Nāgārjuna who lived in the second century of the Common Era. For Nyāya views are among those targeted by the Buddhist dialectician. On the other hand, some *sūtra*-s seem later, as they target Nāgārjuna. Nyāya is one of the few schools whose literature extends to the very end of the classical period and indeed continues in our day among some Sanskrit-speaking pundits.

The *NS* spells out both debate strategies and veritable (proto)scientific methodologies, and scholars have claimed to identify a manual of debate and informal logic as a subset of the whole. Since the text as we have it includes much more than logic—metaphysics, ontology, and philosophy of language, and ethics as well—the *NS* could be regarded as the product of centuries of development, with the logical portions the oldest. On the other hand, one can also discern a unity indicative of a single author. The five chapters, each comprising two 'daily lessons' of varying length, formulate a multi-dimensional philosophy which is progressively refined and expanded by *NS* commentators and by later authors writing non-commentarial works. From about 900 CE to the present, there is increasing output, especially in the late classical age. In the expansion of the school's later years, particularly in the period of what is called 'New Logic,' Navya Nyāya, from approximately the eleventh century, Nyāya reasoning becomes intricately technical and analytically refined. Sensitivity to subtleties of argument and what makes considerations carry the day become extraordinary by any measure. New techniques of logical and linguistic analysis emerge, along with new arguments. However, the basic positions of Nyāya undergo very little change.

At the center of the world view is a commitment to realism, that is, to the metaphysical thesis that things are what they are independently of our knowings and perceivings. At the center of Nyāya epistemology is a causal theory, an externalist approach that centers on knowledge sources, processes that generate knowledge. Nevertheless, Nyāya's views on justification include much internalism, confirmation of veridicality through examination of beliefs when called for by reasonable doubt. That is to say, the central Nyāya contention in epistemology is that perception, inference, analogical vocabulary acquisition, and authoritative testimony are reliable sources of information. Being justified in a belief is in the first instance a matter of the belief's 'source' being a knowledge-generator, *pramāṇa*, and in the second instance a matter of checking, in the face of reasonable doubt, that there are no abnormalities, *doṣa*, in its operation.

At the center of Nyāya's religious perspective is a rational theology: an omniscient Creator is established by argument. There is also yoga advocacy, and endorsement of mainstream views about karma and rebirth.

At the center of Nyāya's ontology is a view of individual things as particular substances that bear different types of properties and relations to other things. The ontology is developed, in the earlier centuries, within the Vaiśeṣika school. Nyāya and Vaiśeṣika are sister schools in the early period, but from about 1000 CE on become a single system.

The history of Nyāya is the history of its authors. After Gautama, the '*sūtra*-maker,' we have Vātsyāyana (*c.* 400 CE), to whom is attributed the oldest *NS* commentary. Since Vātsyāyana mentions other interpretations of particular *sūtra*-s, probably there were earlier commentators whose work is lost. Uddyotakara (*c.* 600 CE) is the next Nyāya author whose work has survived. Uddyotakara wrote an 'elucidation' on Vātsyāyana's *NS* commentary. Others before Uddyotakara wrote commentaries on Vātsyāyana and the *NS*, but their work is lost. Uddyotakara is concerned to defend Nyāya positions principally against competing Buddhist views both in epistemology and ontology, particularly concerning generality.

These three—Gautama with the *NS*, Vātsyāyana with his *Bhāṣya*, and Uddyotakara with his *Vārttika*—form the core of early Nyāya. No *NS* commentary after Uddyotakara's is extant until that of Vācaspati Miśra, who flourished in the latter part of the tenth century. Vācaspati, a prolific writer who wore more than one philosophic hat, wrote notes on Uddyotakara's work, advancing in several respects the Nyāya cause. There are, however, two non-commentarial, independent treatises composed before Vācaspati that are extant, by Jayanta Bhaṭṭa (*c.* 875 CE) and Bhāsarvajña (*c.* 950 CE). Both authors advance criticism of Buddhism and defenses against Buddhist attacks.

Udayana (*c.* 1000 CE) explicitly merges the Nyāya and Vaiśeṣika schools. He writes commentaries on texts in both systems as well as non-commentarial treatises that draw on both traditions. From his time on, the combined school is known simply as Nyāya. Udayana is also most innovative. He is responsible for several advances in Nyāya theory, but is best known for his refutations of Buddhist positions and for rational theology. Some count Udayana as the originator of Navya Nyāya, 'New Logic,' since he pioneers techniques of analysis as well as arguments that become solidified in the Navya ('New') movement. However, that judgment is counter to the preeminence afforded within the later tradition to the fourteenth-century *Tattva-cintā-maṇi* ('Wish-fulfilling Jewel of Reflection on the Truth about Epistemology') by Gaṅgeśa, which becomes the premier Nyāya text.

Gaṅgeśa's son Vardhamāna (*c.* 1350) heads a list of post-Gaṅgeśa Navya Nyāya authors too extensive to enumerate here. The greatest names of the later tradition are Raghunātha (*c.* 1500), who revises the system of categories, and the seventeenth-century authors, Jagadīśa, Mathurānātha, and Gadādhara, who make further ontological and logical refinements.

Let us turn to Nyāya's theory of knowledge and cognition. Nyāya reflection on what we know and how we know it, including, especially, procedures for resolving doubts and disputes, is organized around the topic of *pramāṇa*, 'source of knowledge,' also (in some contexts) 'justifier.' This is complemented by reflection on 'cognition,' *jñāna*, in general. A *pramāṇa* gives rise to a cognition that is veridical. In other words, a *pramāṇa*-caused cognition is a bit of knowledge in that it reflects a fact, indicates it, presents a thing as having a certain property that in fact it has.

Ontologically, cognitions are short-lived, episodic attributes or qualities of an individual self, and, in the case of sensory cognitions, are causally continuous with physical realities as the result of sense organ–object connection. A cognition is a mental event, but it is a product or state rather than an act. Comprehending what someone says, doubting, inferring, remembering, perceiving, and apperceiving are important examples.

In all periods four *pramāṇa*-s are identified, each related to perception. Nyāya philosophers are empiricists in the precise sense of viewing perception as our principal cognitive link with the world. The three additional knowledge sources—inference, expert testimony, and analogy—are all related to perception in specific ways.

There are two senses of the word in Sanskrit that I am translating 'perception,' *pratyakṣa*. First, there is perception as veridical cognition, characterized at *NS* 1.1.4 as (1) a cognition (2) that arises out of the operative relation between an object and a sense faculty, (3) that is not intrinsically conceptual or verbal (although it is verbalizable), (4) that accurately presents the world, and (5) that is sufficiently specific not to give rise to doubts. The second sense is perception as a *pramāṇa*, 'knowledge source,' that gives rise to perceptions as the results of its operation.

Perception in the sense of the resulting veridical cognition becomes viewed differently in the later period. Partly under pressure from Buddhists, a distinction between determinate and indeterminate perceptions is introduced into the system. Only determinate perceptions are verbalizable. Indeterminate perceptions are a first stage of the perceptual process, where, so to say, perceptual data is gathered but is not structured in the way that permits verbalization.

Concerning inference, sustained progress occurs, particularly with the New school. But inference is never, it seems, throughout the long history of Nyāya, abstracted out of the context of the *pramāṇa* theory. That is to say, inference is taken up only as a tool for knowledge of the world. Thus a good inference must have premises that are themselves justified. Nyāya philosophers do not distinguish between a formally 'valid' deductive argument (which may or may not contain premises known to be false) and deductive arguments that are 'cogent' (with no unjustified premises and no errors in the logic). Though the Nyāya theory abstracts from all actual employment, it holds that any good inference must have a conclusion about the real world.

The stock example:

1 There is fire on yonder hill. (The conclusion to be proved.)
2 There is smoke rising from it. (The reason.)
3 Wherever there's smoke, there's fire. (The pervasion or general rule backed up by positive correlations, such as smoke and fire in kitchens, and negative correlations.)
4 This smoke-possessing-hill is an example of the 'wherever' of the general rule, 'Wherever ...' (The application.) (Therefore:)
5 There is fire on yonder hill. (The conclusion now proved.)

New information can affect the warrant of believing the general premise—i.e., the premise expressing invariable concomitance, or (literally) 'pervasion,' *vyāpti*, between two things *x* and *y*—in the example above, line 3. Reasoning based on an assumption of *vyāpti* can be defeated. Nyāya philosophers here as elsewhere are fallibilists. Pervasions are only fallibly known.

Inference-grounding pervasions, *vyāpti*, are of different sorts, but they obtain in nature, such as that between smoke and fire. The question of how these natural connections that ground inferences are themselves known comes more and more to occupy great Nyāya minds. For Udayana, causal relations—which, as a kind of *vyāpti*, underpin inferences—are relations among universals. We can know that a particular *x* is invariably present where any particular *y* is present by knowing that *x*-ness and *y*-ness are suitably connected, Udayana says. Gaṅgeśa—indeed all Navya Nyāya—is also much occupied with pervasions, their nature, and how they are known, although many eschew Udayana's (excessive) reliance on an ontology of universals. There can be pervasions among other types of property.

Expert testimony is defended by Nyāya philosophers as irreducible to perception and inference. An example would be that when someone tells you something you did not know before, you know it through the person's testimony insofar as he or she is an *āpta*, an 'authority' on the subject, and intends to tell you the truth. What in general makes a person trustworthy is, first, knowing, and, second, having no intention to lie or mislead. But unlike Western theories of the epistemic value of testimony, in Nyāya one does not have *to have evidence* that the testifier is trustworthy. Trust is the normal, default position, possibly undermined but not normally needing to be reinforced by information about the testifier. We 'give the benefit of the doubt,' so to say.

New vocabulary can be acquired through 'analogy,' *upamāna*. Told that a water buffalo is *like* a cow except in certain respects, one, previously ignorant, acquires the term 'water buffalo.' This is proved by the ability to use the term correctly in identifying a water buffalo even for the first time. According to most Nyāya philosophers (though not all), knowledge of the meaning has as its source a *pramāṇa* irreducible to the other three.

Nyāya philosophers also take up the question of whether epistemology—i.e., the view of *pramāṇa* presented—is legitimate. The Buddhist Nāgārjuna challenges the project by asking, 'What justifies the justifiers?' The first line of Nyāya reply: that depends on what you are worried about. Consider what you would do were you worried about the correctness of a scale used to weigh gold, Vātsyāyana says in commenting on *NS* 2.1.16, 'As a scale can be an object of knowledge as well.' According to him, you would take a piece of gold to another scale, determine its weight, and bring it back to calibrate the scale in question. What was formerly an instrument in determining the weight of gold—thus a justifier in the sense that the scale is what is consulted for the weight of the gold—becomes what is justified, *prameya*, in this special instance. Similarly, the piece of gold, which was the object of knowledge, becomes an instrument of knowledge. There is no rule that a specific instance of a source of knowledge—whether perception, inference, analogical vocabulary acquisition, or testimony—may not itself become the object of inquiry. In that case, some other instrument or justifier would be employed.

'Then you are faced with an infinite regress, since the question would arise of what would justify that new instrument, *ad infinitum*.' The Nyāya response to this criticism is fourfold: (a) to draw upon a theory of doubt, (b) to embrace fallibilism, (c) to reveal a confusion about the charge of an infinite regress, and (d) to point to pervasion (*vyāpti*) between success in action and the cognition guiding action having a reliable source.

Doubt is meaningful only in certain circumstances. Doubt provokes inquiry and attention to putative sources, but the cognitive default is 'doubt-free.' Normally, we do not need to wonder about justification. Meaningful doubt itself has grounds; all-encompassing doubt is self-defeating.

Moreover, the process of questioning and providing justification normally ends somewhere. We make our best determination; that best supported by the evidence available. The determination may turn out to be wrong; there seems to be nothing in principle about which we might not be in error. Cognition guides action. When circumstances lead to doubt, we find out enough to guide our behavior—which might involve giving up some of our former opinions—and go on with our lives.

There is nothing *per se* wrong with an infinite series. Consider causal infinite series, as with a seed, a sprout, a seed, and so on. If you want us to answer what stands at the end of the series, your demand seems ill-formed: infinite series have no ends.

If the question is, however, what justifies the entire *pramāṇa* program, the answer is inference based on generalization from the success of action guided by knowledge. To point to the natural, causal process whereby a bit of knowledge arises is to justify the proposition. The process is reliable, i.e., cognitively hooks one up with the world such that action can be successful. Thus we can infer from the success of a course of action that the cognition guiding it was veridical.

The *NS* lays out a procedure of inquiry with a degree of sophistication extraordinary for its early date, a procedure that is open and undogmatic. The basic principle is that when there is reasonable disagreement, throwing a topic into question and arousing doubt on all sides, investigation in accordance with proven sources of knowledge is to be undertaken. In this way, the *pramāṇa* epistemology connects with the debate theory and theory of inquiry. But over the centuries, indeed in the *sūtra*-s of the *NS* itself, some of the results of such investigations apparently became official Nyāya doctrine, and were little debated as still other issues emerged.

Beyond Nyāya's paradigm of inference, types of reasoning are discussed in the context of debate. One wins by identifying fallacies in the arguments of an adversary. Also, there are the ways of dialectical reasoning, *tarka*, that help people make the right inferences, and, especially, give up wrong views. Thus dialectical reasoning is seen as part of the method of discussion aimed at ascertaining the truth. In dialectical reasoning, unwanted consequences of views that compete with Nyāya doctrine are flushed out. But no truly warranted view can be supported by dialectical reasoning alone, for dialectical reasoning is not—Vātsyāyana declares, seconded by the later tradition—an independent knowledge source.

Udayana provides what appears to be the first classification of varieties of dialectical reasoning, which he also employs in his writings. He brings out that dialectical reasoning is counterfactual: by considering what would follow *were* the opponent's thesis true, we are supposing what is false—as is shown by the falsity, or impossibility, of one or another consequence. The five types identified: (a) self-dependence, (b) mutual dependence, (c) circularity, (d) infinite regress, and (e) undesired ramification. The fifth variety appears to be a catch-all in that all dialectical reasoning involves showing an undesired ramification of an alternative hypothesis. Later philosophers explain, expand, and modify the list, with the fifth item tending to be replaced from early in the period of Navya Nyāya by (f) contradiction.

Concerning ontology, we would misrepresent Nyāya were we to ignore this sometimes very large dimension of concern. In the early centuries of the system, Nyāya does in large part borrow and presuppose the ontology of its sister Vaiśeṣika school. But especially on the topic of universals, Nyāya philosophers of all periods advance and refine a theory of universals as real-world underpinnings of the meaning of general terms as well as causes of consecutive character in our experience. For example, the universal 'cowhood' is designated when we say 'Bessie is a cow,' and this same cowhood is the content and cause of our experience of Bessie and Flossie and all the other cows that we have perceived as cows. We can rightly say, 'A cow, another (cow), another (cow), and another cow'—a proposition in part made true by cowhood inhering in each of the cows.

Nature exhibits repeatable features and recurrent kinds, and we both directly experience them and designate them in using general terms (such as 'cow'). Now Udayana and Navya-Nyāya philosophers come to realize that although all universals recur (ontologically speaking), neither experience of recurrence nor the truth of a statement employing a general term is in itself sufficient to establish a universal. There are conditions that 'block' or rule out the presence of a real universal. Udayana identifies six blocking conditions.

Udayana also presents a new causal argument. Causal relations are lawful, and, though causal relations hold among particulars, they do so only in that particulars fall into types, that is to say, exhibit universals, as Devadatta would be said, in being a human being, to exhibit the universal 'humanity.' Indeed, particulars are identified by the general features they exhibit. Devadatta cannot be known except through general features he exhibits, such as being human, being male, etc.—features that regularly give rise to our experience of him. Universals stand as indirect causes of bits of perceptual content through inhering, for example, in the case of potness, in an individual pot in relation to a sensory faculty. In this way, the 'experience of recurrent character' argument is understood in causal terms: we classify a new instance of a type X as an X because of the causal relation between that thing and our perception. A cow is classified as a cow because our perception of it is caused by the kind of thing it is.

Preceding conditions that are regulative (*niyāmaka*) are the causes that Gaṅgeśa identifies in explaining varieties of perception. That is, a cause is for him a factor F that is necessary to the arising of an effect G. And its being necessary amounts to no G arising without being preceded by an F so long as the F cannot be counted 'irrelevant' (*anyathā-siddha*). The stock example of precedence that is irrelevant is an ass that just happens always to be used to bring the clay out of which a particular kind of pot is made. The ass is not regulative. A modern example would be a barometric change that invariably precedes a storm.

The theory of causality also has ties with other parts of the philosophy. The presence of an effect logically entails the prior occurrence of all its true (non-irrelevant) causal factors. The presence of one such cause, however, does not entail the occurrence of the effect. Other factors may well be necessary, too, and typically are. For example, the presence of smoke entails the occurrence of fire, a necessary factor. But fires can be smokeless, for instance, the fire in molten metal. So fire does not entail smoke. A cause is a necessary factor; sufficient causality is a distinct concept, namely, a set of necessary conditions, *sāmagrī*, whose being in place unfailingly brings about an effect of a particular type.

Such necessary factors are considered *instrumental* causes, which are distinguished from two other types, *inherent* and *emergent*. An inherent cause is a substratum of a superstratum related to it by inherence. For example, in the case of a blue pot, the pot is the inherent cause of the blue color. A cow is an inherent cause of cowhood. The inherent cause of a cloth are the threads in which it is nested. And so on. Note that substances are not the only inherent causes, since universals inhere in qualities and in motions as well as substances. Thus, a cognition, itself a quality whose inherent cause is an individual self, is an inherent cause of the universal, cognitionhood, which has multiple inherent causes, all the cognitions in the universe. An emergent cause, in contrast, is always a quality or a motion. A whole is said to inhere in its parts. A quality that inheres in the inherent causes of something *x*, a whole, can emerge as, or 'cause' (in this sense) a quality of *x* itself, and is thus said to be its emergent cause. For example, the blue color of the threads of a blue piece of cloth is the emergent cause of the blue of the cloth.

An important metaphysical topic with Udayana is rational theology. The later tradition is unequivocally theistic. But whether the *NS* itself is theistic is disputed by modern interpreters. Clearly, theism is not prominent, for the word *īśvara*, 'God,' occurs only once, at *NS* 4.1.19. However, *NS* 4.1.19–21 can be read as theistic. Interestingly, this passage concerns in part the question of the moral order of the universe, and of moral payback insured for those whose *karman* (or 'action') deserves it. Does God ensure this justice? The *NS* seems to say yes, but the passage is ambiguous.

Udayana argues cosmologically in support of a Creator: 'The earth, etc., being effects, presuppose a conscious agent in the bundle of causes that produces them.' As from an awareness of a pot as an effect, we can infer the existence of its instrumental cause, the potter, so from our experience of the world as an effect, we can infer the existence of God. This is the most prominent argument but several others are advanced as well.

Later Nyāya theists have much in common with Vedāntic theists. The two groups come to be loosely allied, although it is a comparatively limited deity that Udayana and most other Logicians endorse. But whereas theistic Vedāntins take the authority of the Upaniṣads as preeminent in philosophy, Nyāya philosophers take argument.

Finally, Nyāya objectivism and realism fit nicely with its theism. God has the perfect bird's-eye view. Everything is knowable though not everything is by human beings known. Human beings have limited cognitive capacities; many knowables remain unknown to us. But not to God. God knows everything as it is.

References

Chakrabarti, Kisor. 1999. *Classical Indian Philosophy of Mind*. Albany, NY: SUNY Press.

Chemparathy, George. 1972. *An Indian Rational Theology*. Vienna: De Nobili.

Jha, Ganganatha. (Trans). 1984. *The Nyāya-sūtra of Gautama* (= *NS*, with the commentaries of Vātsyāyana and Uddyotakara). 4 vols. 1912–1919. Delhi: Motilal Banarsidass.

Matilal, Bimal K. 1977. *Nyāya-Vaiśeṣika*. Wiesbaden: Otto Harrassowitz.

Matilal, Bimal K. 1986. *Perception: An Essay on Classical Indian Theories of Knowledge*. Oxford: Oxford University Press.

Phillips, Stephen H. 1996. *Classical Indian Metaphysics*. Chicago: Open Court, 1995. Indian ed.: Delhi: Motilal Banarsidass.

Phillips, Stephen H. 2012. *Epistemology in Classical India: The 'Knowledge Sources' of the Nyāya School*. New York and London: Routledge.
Potter, Karl H. (Ed.). 1977. *Encyclopedia of Indian Philosophies*, vol. 2: *Nyāya-Vaiśeṣika*. Delhi: Motilal Banarsidass.
Potter, Karl H. and Sibajiban Bhattacharyya. (Eds.). 1993. *Encyclopedia of Indian Philosophies*, vol. 6: *Nyāya-Vaiśeṣika from Gaṅgeśa to Raghunātha Śiromaṇi*. Delhi: Motilal Banarsidass.

Chapter 18
THE NYĀYA ON INFERENCE AND FALLACIES

J. L. Shaw

I

The nature of an inference for others may be expressed in the following way:

Thesis (*pratijñā*): *a* is G.
Reason (*hetu*): Because of *F*.
Example (*udāharaṇa*): Wherever there is *F*, there is G, as in *b*, etc.; and wherever there is absence of G, there is absence of *F*, as in *c*, etc.
Application (*upanaya*): *a* has *F* which is pervaded by G; or *a* has *F* which is the counterpositive (i.e. negatum) of the absence which pervades the absence of G.
Conclusion (*nigamana*): Hence *a* is G, or G is present in *a*,

where *a* is the locus of the inference (*pakṣa*), *F* is the probans, G is the probandum, *b* is the locus where G is known to be present (*sapakṣa*), and *c* is the locus where the absence of G is known to be present (*vipakṣa*).
Example:

The hill has a fire.
Because of smoke.
Wherever there is smoke, there is fire, such as a kitchen, etc.; and wherever there is absence of fire, there is absence of smoke, such as a lake, etc.
The hill has smoke which is pervaded by fire; or the hill has smoke which is the negatum of the absence which pervades the absence of fire.
Therefore, the hill has a fire, or a fire is on the hill.

An inference involves three terms, viz., *sādhya*, *pakṣa* (locus of inference), and *hetu*. These terms may be simple or complex, empty or non-empty. The term '*sādhya*' refers to what is to be inferred. In other words, it refers to the predicate of the inferential cognition, which corresponds to the conclusion of an inference. The term '*pakṣa*' refers to the locus of an inference where there is some doubt about the presence of the *sādhya*. Since the *pakṣa* has *pakṣatā*, the term '*pakṣatā*' signifies some doubt about the presence of the *sādhya* in the locus of inference. The term '*hetu*' (or '*liṅga*') refers to the reason by means of which the *sādhya* is inferred in the *pakṣa*. The validity of an inference depends on certain characteristics of the hetu. Since the terms '*sādhya*' and '*hetu*' are usually translated as 'probandum' and 'probans', respectively, I shall follow this convention.

Causal conditions of an inferential cognition

An inference is a cognition, which results from certain other cognitions. Hence it may be defined in terms of its causal conditions. Since an inferential cognition is a quality of the cognizer, it inheres in the self of the cognizer. Hence the cognizer is the inherent cause (*samavāyī-kāraṇa*) of an inferential cognition. Since in the Nyāya system cognition is due to the contact of the mental sense-organ (*manas*) with the self, the contact is the similar-to-inherent cause (*asamavāyī-kāraṇa*) of an inferential cognition.

In addition to these two types of causal conditions, an inferential cognition has certain instrumental causal conditions (*nimitta-kāraṇas*) such as *parāmarśa* (operation), *vyāptijñāna* (the cognition of invariable concomitance of the probans with the probandum), and *pakṣatā* (a special relational property of the locus). An inferential cognition is usually defined in terms of *parāmarśa* (operation) and *pakṣatā* (a special relational property of the locus).

Parāmarśa (operation) is defined as the cognition of the presence of the probans pervaded by the probandum in the locus of the inference. It has the form: *a* has *F* which is pervaded by G, where *a* is the locus of inference, *F* is the probans and G is the probandum. Hence it presupposes the cognition of the invariable concomitance of the probans with the probandum. The observation of the presence of the probans and the probandum in some loci and the non-observance of the presence of the probans and the absence of the probandum in some other loci are required for the cognition of the rule of invariable concomitance between the probans and the probandum. The rule takes the form of a universal sentence which can be stated as:

(x) (if $F x$, then $G x$).

Pakṣatā refers to certain epistemic attitude of the cognizer towards the probandum. The ancient Nyāya defines *pakṣatā* as doubt about the presence of the probandum (*sādhyasaṁsaya*) in the locus of inference (*pakṣa*). But this definition is not acceptable to the Navya-Nyāya philosophers, as the desire to infer leads to inferential cognition even if there is no doubt about the presence of the probandum in the locus. Hence the Navya-Nyāya philosophers define it as the absence of certainty about the probandum in the locus qualified by the absence of desire to infer (*siṣādhayiṣāvirahaviśiṣta-siddhyabhāva pakṣtā*). This definition may be explained in terms of the following disjunction:

There is absence of certainty about the probandum in the locus or there is desire to infer the probandum in the locus. Hence this definition rules out the possibility of inferential cognition in a cognizer in the presence of *parāmarśa* (operation) if the cognizer is certain about the presence of the probandum in the locus and there is no desire to infer the probandum in the locus.

From the above discussion of *pakṣatā* it follows that a dubious mental state or a desire to infer, or simply absence of certainty is related to *pakṣa* (the locus of inference). Therefore, when we say that *pakṣa* has *pakṣatā* what we mean is that an attitude of doubt or a desire to infer is directed towards the *pakṣa*.

Types of inference for others

The Nyāya philosophers have classified inferences into three types depending upon the nature of the invariable concomitance (*vyāpti*) of the probans with the probandum (see Wada 2016, 205–213). Again the probantia (*hetus*) have been divided into three types depending upon the nature of the invariable concomitance. If the rule of invariable concomitance used in an inference takes the form of agreement in presence of the probans with the probandum, then the inference is called '*anvayī*' ('agreement in presence'). If this rule takes the form of agreement in absence, then the inference is called '*vyatirekī*' ('agreement in absence'). And if the rule takes both the forms, then the inference is called '*anvaya-vyatirekī*' ('agreement in presence and absence').

Valid and invalid inferences

Now I would like to discuss the Nyāya distinction between valid and invalid inferences. Each of the sentences in an inference for others is an answer to a question and each of them except the last one will give rise to a question. Moreover, each of them is used to generate cognition in the hearer. Since a self-contradictory sentence such as '*a* is both G and not G' cannot generate a cognition, it cannot be used either as a premise or conclusion of an inference. If the inference (not the inferential cognition) is valid (*nyāya*), then all the sentences must be true and the conclusion will follow from the premise or the premises. In other words, there is no true preventer cognition. Hence the application (*upanaya-vākya*), which represents the operation (*vyāpāra*) of an inferential cognition (*anumiti*), will entail the conclusion.

Invalid inferences (*nyāyābhāsas*) are divided into two types. One type of invalid inference contains a false premise or premises, but the other type does not contain any false premise. Hence the former may be called 'logically invalid' and the latter 'epistemically invalid'. Hence the truth of the premises and the conclusion is not sufficient to define the validity of an inference. But any inference, valid or invalid, must satisfy the relevance condition. This point also is very important for understanding the difference between the Western and the Indian concept of inference.

In an inference for others, all the five sentences are needed, because each of them is an answer to a different question and gives some new information. But in an inference for oneself all of them are not required and there is no need to use a sentence. What is required is the operation (*parāmarśa*), which corresponds to the application in our above example and the cognitions that will give rise to this operation.

In our above example, the thesis (*pratijñā-vākya*) is an answer to the question what is to be established in a *pakṣa*. The reason (*hetu-vākya*) is an answer to the question what signifies the probandum. Hence it states that the probans signifies the probandum. The signifier–significate (*jñāpya-jñāpaka*) relation holds between the objects of two cognitions. The reason does not state that the locus a (*pakṣa*) is characterized by the probans.

Now it may be asked, why should we consider the probans as the signifier? The answer is given by stating a rule (*vyāpti*) along with some examples which give rise to the cognition of the invariable concomitance of the probans with the probandum (*vyāpti-jñāna*). For this reason the third step is called 'example'.

The application (*upanaya-vākya*) is an answer to the question whether *a* (i.e. *pakṣa*) is characterized by this type of *F*. Since the reason does not state that *a* is characterized by *F*, the application gives us some new information about *a*. The reason simply states that *F* is the signifier of G. The conclusion (*nigamana-vākya*) is an answer to the question whether the probandum which is the significate of that type of probans is in *a*. Hence it is an answer to the question whether G, which is the significate of *F* which is pervaded by G, is present in *a*.

The difference between the thesis and the conclusion lies in the fact that the thesis simply states what is to be established in the locus, but the conclusion states how it is to be established in the locus. Since each of the members in an inference is related by the relation of relevance, an inference, valid or invalid, is considered a large sentence (*mahāvākya*).

Now let us discuss the nature of the probans in a valid inference. If the valid inference is of the agreement in presence and agreement in absence type, then its probans has the following five characteristics:

(1) It is present in the locus of the inference (*pakṣa*). Hence it has the property of being present in the locus (*pakṣa-sattva*).
(2) It is also present in some of the loci which are known to be characterized by the probandum. Hence it has the property of being present in similar loci (*sapakṣa-sattva*).
(3) It is not present in those loci which are known to be characterized by the absence of the probandum. Hence it has the property of being absent from dissimilar loci (*vipaksāsattva*).
(4) It has no counter-probans (*prati-hetu*) which will demonstrate the absence of the probandum in the locus of the inference. A counter-probans is different from the probans in question and it is pervaded by the absence of the probandum. Hence it has the property of not having a counter-probans (*asatpratipakṣattva*).
(5) It is different from the probans which can be used to establish the probandum in the locus which is characterized by the absence of the probandum. Hence it has the property of being different from this type of probans (*abādhitattva*).

Fallacies

An inference, according to the Nyāya, will be fallacious if the probans lacks one of these characteristics. In other words, if the probantia of the inferences of the agreement in presence and absence type do not have all the five characteristics, and the probantia of the other types of inferences do not have the remaining four characteristics, then they are fallacious. It is to be noted that there are two types of fallacies. One of them would render some of the sentences false and hence the cognitions expressed by those sentences would not correspond to facts. Another type of fallacy would simply prevent the occurrence of doubt-free cognitions expressed by the sentences of an inference.

Since a probans is used to infer the probandum, the fallacy of an inference has been ascribed to the probans. Hence a fallacious inference is called '*hetvābhāsa*' ('defective probans').

A fallacy or *hetvābhāsa* has been defined in the following way:

x is a *hetvābhāsa* if the true cognition of *x* prevents the occurrence of an inferential cognition (*anumiti*) or the operation (*parāmarśa*) which is the *vyāpāra* of an inferential cognition, where *x* is a qualified object of cognition.

Let us consider a fallacious inference, for example, this lake has fire because of smoke. In this case the inferential cognition this lake has fire is false. From the above definition of fallacy it follows that if the person had known that this lake has no fire, then the inferential cognition would have been prevented. The absence of fire in the lake which is the object of cognition is the defect of the probans. Since smoke is the probans in this inference, it is infected with this defect. Now the question is, how can smoke be qualified by this defect?

The Nyāya philosophers explain the relation between them in terms of the relation of a cognition to its object, which is called '*viṣayatā*', and the limitor of the property of being the probans (*hetutāvacchedaka*). In other words, it is explained in terms of a conjunctive cognition such that one of them is the defect and the other one is the probans. In our above example, one of the objects of this conjunctive cognition would be the lake qualified by the absence of fire and the other one would be smoke.

If we would have known this property of smoke, then we would not have inferred the presence of fire in the lake. Since smoke was used to make this inference, and since this function of smoke will be restricted by our cognition of smoke qualified by the absence of fire in the lake, smoke as a probans is considered defective. In other words, it will fail to perform its function as probans for the above inference.

II

In this section I shall discuss the fallacies which are due to the defects of the probantia. There are five types of fallacies, viz., (1) *asiddha* (unestablished), (2) *vyabhicāra* (deviation), (3) *viruddha* (opposed), (4) *satpratipakṣa* (existence of a counter-thesis), and (5) *bādha* (absence of the probandum in the locus).

(1) *asiddha* (unestablished): If the probans cannot be established, it is called '*asiddha*'. This type of fallacy can occur in five ways:

(a) The locus of the inference (*pakṣa*) is not real. For example, the golden mountain has fire, because of smoke. Here the golden mountain is the locus (*pakṣa*), smoke is the probans, and fire is the probandum. Since the locus is unreal or unexemplified (*aprasiddha*), the probans cannot reside in it. Since the locus cannot be established, this fallacy is called '*āśrayāsiddha*' ('unestablished locus').

Here the defect is the absence of gold in the mountain. The cognition of this defect is opposed to the cognition of the presence of the probans in the locus (*pakṣadharmatā-jñāna*) and the inferential cognition (*anumiti*). Here the probans lacks the property of being present in the locus (*pakṣa-sattva*).

(b) The probans does not reside in the locus of the inference, although the locus is real and the probans is real. For example, sound is non-eternal, because of visibility. Here both sound and visibility are real entities, but visibility does not qualify sound. Since the probans cannot qualify the locus of the inference, this type of fallacy is called '*svarūpāsiddha*' ('unestablished in the locus').

This type of fallacy is opposed to the cognition of the presence of the probans in the locus (*pakṣadharmatā-jñāna*). Here also the probans lacks the property of being present in the locus (*pakṣasattva*). The defect (*doṣa*) is the absence of visibility in the sound.

(c) The probans is unreal or unexemplified, although the locus is real. For example, the mountain has fire, because of golden smoke. In this case the golden smoke which is the probans is itself unreal. Since the probans is unreal, this type of fallacy is called '*hetvasiddha*' ('unestablished probans').

This type of fallacy is opposed to the cognition of the presence of the probans in the locus of inference and the cognition of the rule of invariable concomitance between the probans and the probandum. Since the probans is unexemplified, it cannot have any property of a genuine probans.

(d) Another type of *asiddha* (unestablished) fallacy will occur if the probans of an unexemplified probandum is not present in the locus of an inference. For example, the mountain has golden fire, because of smoke. In this case, smoke is present on the mountain, but not as the probans of the golden fire. Hence this type of fallacy is called '*sādhyāsiddha*' ('unestablished probandum'). Here the probans lacks both *sapakṣasattva* (the property of being present in similar cases) and *vipakṣāsattva* (the property of being absent from dissimilar cases).

Here the defect is the absence of gold in fire. The cognition of this defect is opposed to both the operation and the inferential cognition.

(e) There is another type of *asiddha* fallacy known as *vyāpyatvāsiddha* (unestablished property of being the pervaded). In this case the locus is real, the probans is real and the probans is present in the locus but the probans is not qualified by the property of being the pervaded which is limited by a property.

The mode under which the probans has been cognized becomes the limitor of the property of being the pervaded (*vyāpyatāvacchedaka*). This type of fallacy will occur when the mode under which the probans has been cognized does not limit the property of being the pervaded which resides in the probans. For example, the mountain has fire, because of blue smoke.

If blue smoke is the probans, then the rule of invariable concomitance would be between blue smoke and fire. The property of being the pervaded residing in blue smoke will be limited by blue smokeness. But this rule of invariable concomitance cannot substantiate the rule of invariable concomitance between smoke and fire.

Since there is no property of being the pervaded which is limited by blue smokeness and resides in blue smoke, the type of fallacy present in the above inference is called '*vyāpyatvāsiddha*'. Here the defect will be the absence of the property of being the pervaded which is limited by blue smokeness and which resides in blue smoke. The cognition of this defect would prevent the cognition of the invariable concomitance between blue smoke and fire, and thereby the cognition of the operation.

(2) *vyabhicāra* (deviation).

There are three types of fallacy of deviation. In all the three cases the cognition of the defect would prevent the cognition of the rule of invariable concomitance between the probans and the probandum.

(a) *sādhāraṇa-vyabhicāra* (common deviation).

If the probans is present in *pakṣa* (locus of the inference), *sapakṣa* (locus known to be characterized by the probandum), and *vipakṣa* (locus known to be characterized by the absence of the probandum), then this type of fallacy would occur, and the probans is called '*sādhāraṇa-vyabhicārī-hetu*' ('common deviating probans'). For example, the mountain has fire, because of knowability.

Since the probans is present in the locus of the absence of the probandum, the cognition of deviation (*vyabhicāra*) is opposed to the cognition of the invariable concomitance between the probans and the probandum. If we take a lake as *vipakṣa*, then fire is absent from it, but knowability is present in it. Hence there cannot be a cognition of the invariable concomitance between knowability and fire. Moreover, since there is deviation, the rule of invariable concomitance will not hold good between the probans and the probandum. In this case, the defect (*doṣa*) is the absence of fire in a lake which has knowability. Hence the cognition of this defect will prevent the cognition of the invariable concomitance between knowability and fire, and thereby the cognition of the operation. In this fallacy the probans lacks the property of not being present in *vipakṣa*.

(b) *asādhāraṇa-vyabhicāra* (uncommon deviation).

If the probans is present in the locus of the inference (*pakṣa*) only, then it is called '*asādharaṇa-vyabhicārī-hetu*' ('uncommon deviating probans'). In other words, the probans is not present in *sapakṣa* (the locus of the probandum) and in *vipakṣa* (the locus of the absence of the probandum), but is present in *pakṣa* (the locus of the inference). For example, sound is non-eternal, because of soundness.

In this case, sound is *pakṣa*, a non-eternal object such as a pot is *sapakṣa* and an eternal object such as space is *vipakṣa*. Since soundness is not present in a pot, it lacks the property of being present in *sapakṣa*. Since soundness cannot be perceived in non-eternal objects, there cannot be cognition of the agreement in presence type of invariable concomitance between the probans and the probandum. But the probans is absent from the eternal objects. Since the agreement in absence between the probans and the probandum can be observed, the agreement in absence type of invariable concomitance (*vyatireka-vyāpti*) can be cognized.

In this example, the defect is the absence of soundness in a non-eternal object such as a pot, and the probans lacks the property of being present in *sapakṣa*. The cognition of this defect would prevent the cognition of the agreement in presence type of invariable concomitance (*anvaya-vyāpti*). But it will not prevent the cognition of the agreement in absence type of invariable concomitance (*vyatireka-vyāpti*). Since there are two types of invariable concomitance, there would be two types of operation. The agreement in presence type of operation will be prevented by this type of defect. Hence the cognition of this type of defect does not prevent the cognition of all types of invariable concomitance or operation. For this reason it may be treated as an epistemic fallacy as opposed to a logical one (where some of the sentences or cognitions are false). In the example above, the sentences would not be false, but we fail to cognize the agreement in presence type of invariable concomitance and thereby the agreement in presence type of operation.

Moreover, this type of epistemic defect can also be removed. In our example, this defect can be removed if there is certainty about the presence of the probandum in some sounds such as the sound of a music. If it were so, then the locus would not be sound in general as it is in the above example, but some specific sounds such as the one which follows lightning. Since this defect can be removed, it is called '*anitya*' ('impermanent').

(c) *anupasaṃhārī-vyabhicāra* (unsupported deviation).

If everything becomes *pakṣa* and thereby the probans does not have either *sapakṣa* or *vipakṣa*, then the fallacy of *anupasaṃhārī-vyabhicāra* will occur. Let us consider the following two examples.

(i) Everything is non-eternal, because of knowability.
(ii) Everything is nameable, because of knowability.

In both (i) and (ii) everything is the locus of inference. There is doubt about the presence of non-eternality in (i) and nameability in (ii). Since everything is *pakṣa*, there is no *sapakṣa* or *vipakṣa*. Since the co-presence of the probans and the probandum cannot be observed, the agreement in presence type of invariable concomitance cannot be cognized. Similarly, since the co-absence of the probans and the probandum cannot be observed, the agreement in absence type of invariable concomitance cannot be cognized. Since neither type of invariable concomitance is cognized, neither type of operation will occur. Since there is neither *sapkṣa* nor *vipakṣa*, the probans lacks both the property of being present in *sapakṣa* and the property of being absent from *vipakṣa*.

As regards the nature of this fallacy, it is not logical, but epistemological. If a person does not have doubt about the presence of the probandum in everything, then this epistemic defect can be removed.

(3) *viruddha* (opposed).

If the probans is pervaded by the absence of the probandum, the probans is called '*viruddha-hetu*' ('opposed probans'). Hence the invariable concomitance would be between the probans and the absence of the probandum, not between the probans and the probandum. In other words, wherever the probans is present, the probandum is absent. For example, sound is eternal, because of the property of being an effect. Since an effect is non-eternal, the probans, far from establishing the probandum, establishes the absence of the probandum.

In the case of *viruddha* fallacy, the probans lacks the property of being present in *sapakṣa* and the property of being absent from *vipakṣa*. Hence the agreement in presence (*anvaya-sahacāra*) and agreement in absence (*vyatireka-sahacāra*) cannot be observed. From this it follows that neither the invariable concomitance in presence nor the invariable concomitance in absence can be cognized. Moreover, since both the types of invariable concomitance are false, the defect would be the falsity of the invariable concomitances. Hence the cognition of this defect will be opposed to the cognition of both the types of invariable concomitance and thereby both the types of operation. It is also opposed to the inferential cognition. Since it is a permanent defect, it may be called 'logical fallacy'.

(4) *satpratipakṣa* (existence of counter-thesis).

The word '*satpratipakṣa*' has two meanings. It may mean either the thesis of the opponent or a type of defect (*doṣa*) which will prevent an inferential cognition. Hence as a fallacy it refers to a defect. Consider the following operations:

(a) The lake has smoke which is pervaded by fire.
(b) The lake has water which is pervaded by the absence of fire.

The operation (b) will prevent the occurrence of the inferential cognition 'The lake has fire' which is due to the operation (a).

The object of the operation (b) is the defect, and the probans of the operation (a) is infected with this defect.

Since there is a counter-probans which is pervaded by the absence of fire, the probans of (a) lacks the property *asatpratipakṣattva* (the property of not having a counter-probans which is pervaded by the absence of the probandum).

(5) *bādha* (absence of the probandum characterizing the locus).

The fallacy of *bādha* occurs when a probans is used to establish a probandum in a locus which is characterized by the absence of the probandum. For example, fire is cold, because of substancehood, as in water.

In the case of a *bādha* fallacy the inferential cognition is directly prevented by the cognition of the absence of the probandum in the locus. In the above example, the operation is the cognition 'Fire has substancehood which is pervaded by coldness'. This operation will yield the cognition 'Fire is cold'. But the cognition 'Fire has absence of coldness' will prevent the occurrence of the inferential cognition. Since the preventer cognition is true, its object is the defect (*doṣa*). Hence the cognition of *bādha* fallacy is directly opposed to the inferential cognition.

From the Nyāya discussion of different types of fallacies it follows that the Nyāya philosophers are dealing not only with the falsity of the premise(s) or the conclusion of a fallacious inference but also with the different ways the operation or the inferential cognition of an inference can be prevented.

From the above discussion it follows that the Nyāya philosophers have emphasized the relevance condition for any inference, valid or invalid. Hence the inference does not have the form:

P, Therefore, *Q*, where '*P*' and '*Q*' range over sentences or cognitions.

Hence the following valid inference of Western logic is not treated as an inference in the Nyāya logic:

P and not *P*,
Therefore, *Q*.

This is due to the fact that it violates the relevance condition as well as certain epistemic conditions for understanding the meaning of a sentence. As a result, we cannot derive 2 + 2 = 4 from it is raining and not raining, which is valid in classical symbolic logic. Since the Nyāya logic has emphasized the relevance condition, it might throw some light on contemporary discussion on relevant logic. Since it deals with the preventer–prevented relation at epistemic level and the ways a cognition can be prevented, it will throw some light on epistemic logic as well.

References and further reading

Bhattacharya, Gopinath. 1976. *Tarkasaṁgraha-Dīpikā on Tarkasaṁgraha by Annṁbhaṭṭa*. Calcutta: Progressive Publishers.

Bhattacharyy, Sibajiban. 1987. *Doubt, Belief and Knowledge*. New Delhi: Indian Council of Philosophical Research.

———. 1990. *Gadādhara's Theory of Objectivity*. New Delhi: Indian Council of Philosophical Research.

Bilimoria, P. and Hemmingsen, M. (Eds.). 2017. *Comparative Philosophy and J. L. Shaw*. Sophia Studies in Cross-Cultural Philosophy of Traditions and Cultures 13. Dordrecht and New York: SpringerNature.

Madhavananda. (Trans.). 1977. *Bhāṣāpariccheda with Siddhānta-Muktāvalī*. Calcutta: Advaita Ashrama.

Matilal, Bimal K. 1985. *Logic, Language and Reality*. Delhi: Motilal Banarsidass Publishers.

Mohanty, J. N. 1992. *Reason and Tradition in Indian Thought*. Oxford: Clarendon Press.

Shaw, J. L. 1996a. 'Cognition of Cognition', Part I. *Journal of Indian Philosophy* 24(2): 165–207.

———. 1996b. 'Cognition of Cognition', Part II. *Journal of Indian Philosophy* 24(3): 231–264.

———. 2005. *Causality and Its Application: Sāṁkhya, Bauddha and Nyāya*. Calcutta: Punthi Pustak.

Vidyabhusana, S. C. 1971. *A History of Indian Logic*. Delhi: Motilal Banarsidass Publishers.

Wada, Toshihiro. 2016. 'The Logical Structure of the Third and Fifth Definitions in the Vyāptipañcaka Section of Gaṅgeśa's Tattvacintāmaṇi.' In Bilimoria and Hemmingsen, pp. 203–216.

Chapter 19
EMBODIED CONNECTIONISM: NYĀYA PHILOSOPHY OF MIND

Douglas L. Berger

Classical Nyāya philosophers represented their view of consciousness as a corrective to major alternative scholastic depictions, namely those of Sāṃkhya, Cārvāka, and Buddhism. In Sāṃkhya thought, the elements of which were powerfully formative of Yoga and Vedānta models, consciousness was the luminous essence (*svayaṃprakāśatva*) of the transcendent self (*puruṣa, ātman*) which, when reflected through unconscious bodily organs, makes the world manifest. In the thoroughgoing materialism of Cārvāka, consciousness is produced through strictly bodily processes, belongs solely to the empirical individual and is eliminated with death. For the Buddhists, consciousness is causally co-produced (*pratītyasamutpanna*) from one moment to the next through the dynamic interaction of psychophysical tendencies and worldly phenomena, but is not the property of any kind of stable self-consciousness, either spiritual or bodily. Proponents of Nyāya fiercely criticized each of these influential systems, insisting that Sāṃkhya conflated the roles of the spiritual and the physical in the production of conscious experience, that Cārvāka wrongly reduced consciousness to physical processes with which it could never be identified, and that Buddhists did not take the experiential continuity of self-consciousness seriously enough. In other words, the preceptors of the School of Logic were concerned to accurately assess the relation of consciousness to the body on the one hand and on the other to insist that an intimate, albeit contingent, connection be made between consciousness and self-consciousness. These dual goals were thought by the Logicians necessary in order to give an adequate account of the causal roles of consciousness in the world as well as of our experience of the world and ourselves. In this effort, the Naiyāyikas committed themselves to understanding consciousness both as an object (*prameya*), in its causally conditioned mediation between the self, body and world, as a contingent property (*guṇa*) of the embodied self, as well as the subjective apprehension (*upalabdhi*) and subjective knowledge (*pramathā*) that constitute first-person experience. This methodological willingness to examine consciousness both objectively and subjectively, resisting explanations that render consciousness only a physical or a spiritual process, is what enabled the Brāhmaṇical Logicians to extrapolate a truly robust philosophy of mind. This robustness has defied contemporary attempts to characterize Nyāya according to Western categories such as dualism, physicalism, or emergentism, all born of the philosophically provincial Cartesian problematic. It is also by virtue of this very robustness that Nyāya can continue to contribute to philosophical reflections on consciousness.

In one of the earliest aphorisms of the *Nyāyasūtra* (= *NS*), Gautama (second century CE) identifies all of the relevant items pertaining to the philosophy of consciousness, the self (*ātman*), body (*śārīra*), objects of sensation (*indriyārtha*), awareness (*buddhi*), and inner sense (*manas*) as objects of knowledge (*prameya*) (*NS* 1.i.9). Cognitions (*jñāna*) directed outwardly (*vāhya*) at worldly objects are the result of contact (*saṃyoga, sannikarṣa*) between the self (*ātman*), the inner sense (*manas*), a sense organ (*indrīya*), and its object (*artha*).[1] Cognitions that are internal (*āntara*), such as doubt (*saṃśaya*), conviction (*niścāya*), desire (*prāthanā*), the awareness of pleasure and pain (*sukhadukha*), and memory (*smṛti*) result from the connection of the inner sense (*manas*) with the self.[2] This means that any given cognition is a temporal event, what Matilal styled a 'mental episode' that can only happen within the limits (*avaccheda*) of the body (*Nyāyasūtrabhāṣya* [= *NSB*] 3.ii.27). Since for instance external perceptions require that distinct substances (*dravya*), at least one of which must be physical like the sense organs, and the self to be in a previously non-occurrent contact (*aprāptayoṃ prāptiḥ*), such contact is enjoined and removed temporally. Perhaps most dramatically, the organ of inner sense (*manas*), which is necessary in order to explain private experiences such as inattention, pain, pleasure and desire, is thought to be an atomic (*anutva*) organ that moves throughout the body at an incredible speed, picking up sensations as it goes, and this guarantees that no two awareness events will occur simultaneously, but rather in a distinctly analyzable, if not always distinctly perceptible, sequence.[3] In addition, any cognition, even internal sensations and inferences, are effects (*kārya*) brought about by preceding physical and cognitive events all belonging to an objectively trackable, contingent (*āgantuka*) causal continuum (Matilal 1986, 124). A causal process that accounts for any given event of awareness then is going to require bodily sensation, be it external or internal, as one variety of instrumental cause (*nimittakāraṇa*), namely a specific cause (*asādhāraṇakāraṇa*), that triggers the cognition.[4] The full commitment of the Logicians to the temporal and causal dependence of the self's consciousness on embodiment is witnessed by their argument, quite peculiar in the Brāhmiṇical tradition, that any given *ātman* finally liberated from rebirth and bodily existence loses consciousness entirely.

These Nyāya representations of consciousness stood in stark contrast to depictions of other schools that associated consciousness with the self-luminosity (*svayaṃprakāśatva*) of the eternal soul (*puruṣa, ātman*). The main target of the Logicians' critiques of such a view was Sāṃkhya, whose ontology had such indelible influences on Yoga and the various sects of Vedānta. The Sāṃkhya school also attests to the notion of an inner sense (*antaḥkaraṇa*), constituted by awareness (*buddhi*), ego-construction (*ahaṃkāra*), and mental synthesis (*manas*), whose predominance in *sattva* or transparent brilliance permits it to permeate the heavy (*tamas*) bodies of worldly objects.[5] The *darśana* also argues for the physicality of these cognitive mechanisms, as they are the primordial evolutes of dynamic, energetic matter (*prakṛti*), and so are related to all the embodied individual's psychic, affective, and physical states (*Sāṃkhyakārikā* 29; 32). However, all these cognitive processes, of their own accord, are claimed to be entirely unconscious in virtue of their exclusively material nature, and require luminous personhood or spirit (*puruṣa*) to be the witness (*śākṣin*) to all their external and internal modifications (*vṛtti*) (*Sāṃkhyakārikā* 37). Such a relation between conscious spirit and unconscious matter places consciousness effectively on the side of spirit, for while consciousness is reflected through the cognitive instruments of the physical body during the process of rebirth, consciousness is the exclusive essence of the self, and persists in an unlimited and eternal state after release from transmigration.

The early Naiyāyikas focused furiously critical attention on the Sāṃkhya model, for it hopelessly conflates in their estimation the roles of self and body in the very attempt to spiritualize consciousness. Cognitions, on the Sāṃkhya view, are modifications of the *buddhi* in its capacity of discerning the object (*adhyavaśaya*) and taking on the object's form (*sākāra*), and the functions of recognizing it through *manas* and associating it with the ego through *ahaṃkāra* are also material. But even though *puruṣa*'s eternal luminosity is borrowed by the inner sense in revealing objects, *puruṣa* does not own that cognition and is not affected by it. This presents a number of problems according to the Naiyāyika. First, since, for Sāṃkhya, cognition, recognition, and association of objects with the ego are all activities of the intellect and not spirit, cognitions would appear to be properties of the unconscious body and not properties of what the Sāṃkhyan overtly associates with consciousness, namely *puruṣa* (Vātsyāyana, *NSB* 3.ii.3). Second, the fact that the inner sense is a primordial evolute of matter and thus endures as long as an individuated spirit is embodied would seem to suggest that the intellect is a permanent repository of all the latter's awarenesses that holds all the causal conditions for their apprehension within itself, and that *puruṣa*, in any given moment, illuminates them all. But such an implication militates openly against the fact that, due to their temporality and causal production, cognitions are not eternal, since we know that cognitions, and especially all of them at once, are not simultaneously apprehended, but rather succeed and replace one another in accordance with causal factors (Vātsyāyana, *NSB* 3.ii.4–8, 20–25). In sum, a dualism of matter and consciousness such as that presented in Sāṃkhya-Yoga-Vedānta ends up conflating the parts played by the body and self-consciousness in the production of conscious awareness. The essential problem with Sāṃkhya's philosophy of consciousness, in other words, is that, though it aims to attribute consciousness to spirit only, it cannot talk about cognitions without invoking physical processes, and this should alert us to the more plausible view that consciousness is not the essence of spirit, but is a feature of the self resulting from its causal interaction with the physical world.

An equally decisive mistake, in the Nyāya view, is made by classical Indian materialism (Cārvāka), which holds that consciousness is brought about by the physical body alone. The *Sarvadarśanasaṃgrah* attributes to the Cārvākas the belief that consciousness emerges in the body through the combination, or literally chemical fermentation (*kiṇva*), of its ingredients, perishing when it does, and since no perceptual evidence confirms the existence of a non-bodily soul, we are safe in assuming such a soul does not exist. The Naiyāyikas consider and reject several important arguments for the body being the substrate of consciousness.[6] The first set of arguments is epistemological. We can know that certain qualities are bodily qualities in two ways, through external perception which attests to a body's visible qualities or through inference, which attests to a body's invisible properties, like weight. Knowledge that one is having a cognition is not known like color is, through external perception, but neither is it known through inference, as body weight is inferred from the measure of a scale. Instead, knowledge and awareness are internally perceived by the inner sense (Vātsyāyana, *NSB* 3.ii.57). That is to say, I do not know that I am having cognitions by simply observing my body. Rather I already know that I am having cognitions because I perceive them internally as events of my own conscious life, and only then might I be prompted to look for and understand their physical, causal correlates through various means and thus analyze them, as above, objectively. This means that our investigations into the physiology involved in our awareness is parasitic on our already knowing, through the inner sense, what kinds of awareness events we have and want to understand further. The locus of cognitions, on the basis of this argument, cannot be the body, for we know about the features properly belonging to the body through epistemic means entirely different from how we primarily know we are having cognitions.[7]

Apart from these epistemological considerations, there are ontological reasons why cognitions cannot be features of the body or one of its organs. In the Nyāya architectonic, since the recognized substances of earth, water, fire, air, *ākāśa* (the medium of sound), space, and time obviously do not serve as causal supports of cognition, the only two remaining candidates are the inner sense (*manas*) and the self (*ātman*). However, the Logicians also consider the possibility that cognitions could belong to external sense organs such as the eyes. Each sense organ, claims Nyāya, is restricted to the sensation of objects that are made out of the same element as each of them are; the nose is made from the earth element, and so can sense earthy smells, the eye is made of the light element, and so can sense light, the ear is made of *ākāśa* and so can sense sound (*NSB* 1.i.12–14). Since the external sense organs are restricted to the sensation of their corresponding element, they are not susceptible to the sensations of the other sense organs, even when in contact with the same object; the eyes sense the color of a jar but not its texture, the touch senses the texture of a jar but not its color (*NSB* 3.i.1). Since the individual sense organs do not synthesize the sensations of the other organs in such a way as to produce cognitions like 'I saw a jar and now I hold it,' 'those oranges must be sweet,' 'those letters I read in succession form the following word,' then neither do the aggregation (*saṃghāta*) of those external organs do so. Such synthetic cognitions that apprehend (*upalabdhi*) and remember sensations of many different kinds and fuse them must be explained as having an agent other than the sense organs themselves (*NSB* 3.i.1–3; 3.i.14). As for the inner sense, as we saw above, it is required to explain both internal perceptions of pleasure, pain, desire, and aversion as well as mental phenomena such as inattention and focused concentration, so, should it not be considered the locus of cognitions? It is a serious candidate for this role, especially since it is not restricted to the sensation of only one kind of object (*aniyata viśāyaka*), but, being successively in contact with eyes, ears, skin, and internal states, it can sense all.[8] However, Vātsyāyana rejects the *manas* as the locus of consciousness, largely because doing so would make it both the instrument (*kāraṇa*) of knowing and the agent (*kārtṛ*) of knowledge, and since the *manas* is a sense organ, even though it is not restricted to one type of sensation, it is, like the other sense organs, only an instrument and not an agent of sensations. We say of the eye, for example, that it is an instrument for sensing colors, and not, for reasons just mentioned, that the eye is the agent of cognition, and the same applies, according to Vātsyāyana, to the inner sense. This is so because, were we to deny that the sensation of internal states like pain, pleasure, desire, and aversion required an instrument, we would obviate the need for postulating a *manas* in the first place, and so the very arguments that justify the existence of an organ of inner sense attest to the fact that it is an instrument for the sensation of such internal states, and not the agent of their knowledge (*NSB* 3.i.17–18; 3.ii.41–42). Instruments require a controller (*vaśī*), for there are no instruments that consciously control themselves, and therefore the *manas* must be controlled by another agent that uses it to cognize, and this must be the self (*ātman*).[9]

Vātsyāyana offers one additional metaphysical reason why the *manas* cannot be considered the substrate of cognitions and must be considered only their instrument, namely that it is an atomic (*anutva*) organ which, because it is partless and thus has no internal structure, cannot serve as the locus of more than one sensation at once (*NSB* 3.ii.41–42). This detail permits us to examine briefly the Nyāya depiction of the physiology of consciousness, and how that physiology incorporates the notions of an atomic internal sense and a non-material but nevertheless extended self. The external sense organs (*indrīya*), as mentioned, are eyes, ears, nose, tongue, and skin, and because they are physically constituted to be sensitive to elements of uniquely specified sorts, they have their own objects. As for the self (*ātman*), it is certainly immaterial, in that, unlike material objects, it does not obstruct other objects from occupying the same space as it does. But even so, the self, like all other substances, does have extension (*parimāna*) in space, and so it is in contact (*saṃyogitva*) with the body, in fact, it pervades the entire body during life. Now, if the sense organs continually retrieve sensations corresponding to their elements and if the self pervades the body and is said to be the locus of knowledge, why would the self need any additional inner instrument in order to cognize? If sensations were merely a matter of the self's simultaneous contact with all the body's sense organs, two contrary-to-fact consequences would ensue. First, the self would in this circumstance be inundated not only with many different sensory stimuli at any given moment, but with memories that occur simultaneously with them and with one another. But we know from experience that such cognitions, sensory stimuli and memories, occur in succession (*NSB* 3.ii.35). Furthermore, were the self directly inundated by the sense organs at every given moment, there would be no distinct apprehension of any given object, only a flood of successive sensations, but since we do experience distinct apprehension of, say, a lamp and not just successive streams of light, apprehension must be accounted for (*NS* 3.ii.49). From this, we may surmise that an internal sensory organ serves as an instrument for mediating both outward and inner sensations to the self in succession, leaving the contingencies of apprehension and unequal attention to the self's agency (*NS* 3:ii.22). We may also surmise of this inner instrument of sensation that it is atomic in size, for as Vātsyāyana points out, were it to have more magnitude, it would have parts and touch more than one sensory organ at once, again giving us the simultaneous sensations that have already been ruled out by other arguments (*NSB* 3.ii.63). Since both the bodily organs and the inner sense are mere instruments of cognition, they are, like all other instruments judged to be unconscious, and so consciousness cannot be a feature of the physical body alone. By exclusion, then, only the embodied self can be the substrate and possessor of consciousness.

Given their obvious concerns to proffer a robust theory of consciousness and accurately assess the relationship of consciousness to the body and self-consciousness, the temptation is natural enough to compare Nyāya's theory of mind to modern and contemporary Western theories. A major and thoroughgoing attempt at such a comparison was Kisor Kumar Chakrabarti's (1999) *Classical Indian Philosophy of Mind: The Nyāya Dualist Tradition*. In this extensive study, which culminates in an annotated translation of Udayana's *Ātmatattvaviveka*, Chakrabarti argues that the Brāhmaṇical Logicians construct a fully defensible and appealing form of dualism. He is careful to make important distinctions between Nyāya and Cartesian dualism. For one thing, since Naiyāyikas believed that the immaterial self was an extended substance pervading the body, they could give a description of the causal interaction between the self and body in cognitive states, while Descartes' strict distinction between intentional consciousness and extensional physical substance left him with no compelling way to describe how these two substances interact (Chakrabarti 1999, 24–26). It is also noted that Nyāya can offer a better causal account of conscious life because, for them, consciousness is a contingent feature of all embodied selves, even in animal forms, whereas for Descartes, the soul is a thinking substance and material bodies are not, a position which hands over an advantage to materialists when they can show that animals, which Descartes considered to be automatons, are conscious (Chakrabarti 1999, 27–28). Furthermore, while Cartesian dualism seems to commit one to rationalism, essentialism, and necessitarianism, Nyāya dualism embraces empiricism, fallibilism, and probabilism (Chakrabarti 1999, 28). Despite these distinctions, Chakrabarti still believes that Nyāya's philosophy of mind can only be characterized as a form of dualism because of its unwavering insistence that conscious awareness, when it occurs, is always a property of the immaterial self and never of the body. This is a form of dualism much 'weaker' than that of the Cartesian variety, but one that spells out a process of causal interaction between soul and body as two distinct substances nonetheless (Chakrabarti 1999, 28).

In recent articles and book chapters, Chakravarthi Ram-Prasad (2007; and see his Chapter 20 in this volume), has argued that Nyāya might be better understood, at least heuristically in comparative discussions, as holding a sort of non-reductive physicalism (Ram-Prasad 2007, 93). It is of course the case, he concedes, that the Logicians defended the existence of an immaterial self and made consciousness a contingent property of it and not the body. This fact would prevent anyone from aligning Nyāya with eliminative physicalism lest they do major reinterpretive violence to that system. What should impress us however, in Ram-Prasad's characterization, is that consciousness requires embodiment. The self cannot be conscious at all if it is not in contact with *manas*, which is a bodily sensory organ, and upon death and release, the Naiyāyikas consistently assert that the self loses consciousness (Ram-Prasad 2007, 91–93). Consciousness as a *guṇa* or 'a functionality (*kriyātva*)' of the self witnesses to its distinctness from the self as such, and this confines analyses of consciousness in Nyāya to inquiries into the bodily and causal conditions for the arising of conscious states (Ram-Prasad 2007, 92). However, despite these comparative speculations, Ram-Prasad is quite careful to insist that the contributions Nyāya can make to our understanding of consciousness lie more in what it says about the 'processes, conditions for occurrence and types of functions' consciousness involves. It is best not to get too caught up in the hermeneutic confusion that would result in drawing Nyāya into contentions about what consciousness 'is made up of,' which is the focus of the dualism–emergentism–physicalism debate in the West and was not the framework over which the classical Indian schools were at odds (Ram-Prasad 2007, 93).[10]

It would hardly be right to say, as Ram-Prasad forthrightly acknowledges, that Naiyāyikas were not concerned to articulate the relation between consciousness and the body. They were on the contrary quite keen to do this because of their ultimately soteriological determination to quell the sufferings of embodied selves so that they could work toward their release from rebirth (Ram-Prasad 2007, 94).[11] Still, it seems clear that Ram-Prasad's hermeneutic suspicion that Brāhminical Logic does not comport with modern constitutive debates in the West is well founded. Various forms of dualism in the West, whether they are substance dualism or property dualism, and even Davidson's 'anomalous monism,' are all based on an anti-reductionist belief that qualitative states of consciousness are irreducible to physical states of the brain. Ironically, in Jaegwon Kim's non-reductive physicalism too, while most cognitions can be functionally and hence physically reduced, some qualitative states cannot be reduced, and these latter we must consider causally impotent. Naiyāyikas would probably have found the same fault with non-reductive physicalism as they would with dualism, for there is no such thing on the Logicians' view as a human cognition that, when treated as a *prameya*, in principle resists causal analysis. Obviously, this does not make Nyāya amenable to some form of reductive materialism either, for Nyāya's notion that the immaterial *ātman* is not only a necessary condition of conscious states, but their owner and possessor, would be rejected by materialists, even were the latter aware of the fact that in Nyāya, the body-pervading self has extension. Emergentism would be out too, since the Logicians do not argue that the body produces consciousness, but rather that the body is an instrumental cause of particular cognitions. If one were to insist on giving the Nyāya depiction of the constitution of consciousness a classification, it may be more fruitful to look at possible Saṃskrta neologisms. In terms of an objective analysis of cognitions, one may be tempted to label the Naiyāyika position *Sannikarṣa-vāda* or 'Connectionism,' since the causal description of any cognition must involve some connection between the sense organs (in the case only of outward-directed perceptions), the inner sense, and the self, and this framework would therefore make room for Nyāya's pluralist and not dualist ontology. In terms of a subjective analysis, on the other hand, Nyāya does argue, contra the Indian Materialists as seen above, that our primary awareness that we are having cognitions is the result of the inward perception of the self of its own conscious states. Such subjective introspection we could label *Ātmapratyakṣa-vāda* or 'Self-Sensation,' which would do justice to the Nyāya arguments that apperception and self-awareness are required in order for us to consciously attend to our mental states. Indeed, it is precisely these Naiyāyika arguments that consciousness can be analyzed both objectively and subjectively, and that such empirical and introspective considerations of our conscious, embodied lives can and should be mutually supporting and informative, that may be the Brāhmaṇical Logicians' most valuable legacy for anyone who takes the philosophy of mind seriously.

Notes

1 This axiom is found in *Vaiśeṣika Sūtra* 3.ii.1, and is defended by the Naiyāyikas in their definition of perception in *NS* 1.i. 4.

2 This is ascertainable through inference, according to Vātsyāyana, because such internal states are not objects of the outward-directed senses, and so must be properties of the self perceived by the instrument of the inner sense; see *NSB* 3.i.17.

3 *NS* 1.i.14; *NSB* 3.ii.62–63.

4 See Uddyotakara's *Nyāyavārtika* 1.i.9.

5 *Sāṃkhyakārikā* 22–24.

6 The Logicians spend some time constructing other arguments than the ones considered here against Cārvākas that are, unhappily, completely spurious. These arguments point out in various ways that consciousness cannot be identical with the body because the body undergoes states, the most important one being death, where consciousness is not present (see *NSB* 3.ii.46–49). These arguments completely miss the point that Cārvākas argued that only living bodies could produce consciousness in the first place, and so these particular Nyāya rebuttals entirely beg the question at hand.

7 Uddyotakara supplements this argument by making the point that physical properties lend themselves to perception by both oneself and others (*ātmaparātma pratyakṣa*), so since a person's conscious states are not visible to two or more separate observers, they cannot be known as *guṇa* of the body.

8 *NSB* 3.i.16. Arindam Chakrabarti attributes to the *manas* the capacity of 'cross-modal comparison' between different sensations, such that we can think about sensing the same object with more than one sense and desire such experiences as well.

9 Vātsyāyana gives this argument in *NSB* 3.i.17 and Uddyotakara clarifies it by denying the implication that selves are never controlled by others, but finds it justifiable by invoking *vyāpti* between a thing's being an instrument and its unconsciousness.

10 This latter point is one Chakravarthi Ram-Prasad has more emphatically underlined in recent conference interactions and personal correspondence with the author.

11 See also Vātsyāyana's discussion in *NSB* 3.ii.70–78.

References

Berger, D. L. 2001. "'The Social Meaning of the Middle Way': B. S. Yadav and the Mādhyamika Critique of Indian Ontologies of Identity and Difference." *Journal of Dharma* 26(3), 282–310.

———. 2007. "Deconstruction, *Aporia* and Justice in Nāgārjuna's Empty Ethics." In Youru Wang (ed.) *Deconstruction and the Ethical in Asian Thought*, 40–59. London and New York: Routledge.

Chakrabarti, Arindam. 2011. "The Connecting Manas; Inner Sense, Common Sense, or the Organ of Imagination." In Morrey Joy (ed.) *After Appropriation: Explorations in Intercultural Philosophy and Religion*, 57–75. Calgary: University of Calgary Press.

Chakrabarti, Kisor Kumar. 1999. *Classical Indian Philosophy of Mind: The Nyāya Dualist Tradition*. Albany: SUNY Press.

Chakravarthi, Ram-Prasad. 2007. *Indian Philosophy and the Consequences of Knowledge: Themes in Ethics, Metaphysics and Soteriology*. Farnham: Ashgate.

Matilal, Bimal K. 1986. *Perception: An Essay on Classical Indian Theories of Knowledge*. Oxford: Oxford University Press.

Thakur, A. L. (ed.). 1967. *Nyāyasūtra with Bhāṣya of Vātsyāyana, Nyāyavārtika of Uddyotakara, Nyāyavārt ikatātparyatikā of Vācaspati Miśra and Parisuddhi of Udayana*. Darbangha: Mithila Institute.

Chapter 20
A PHENOMENOLOGICAL READING OF THE NYĀYA CRITIQUE OF THE NO-SELF VIEW: UDAYANA AND THE PHENOMENAL SEPARATENESS OF SELF

Chakravarthi Ram-Prasad

The long history of Buddhist arguments for various conceptions of no-self (*anātman*) and the brāhmaṇical/Hindu (and Jaina) arguments for an even more varied range of conceptions of self (*ātman*) has generated a rich contemporary literature, and offers the potential for illuminating comparative study with Western philosophy. The Nyāya system had a long history in the effort to explore a range of arguments in support of its particular theory of *ātman*, some of them from Uddyotakara being laid out in Arindam Chakrabarti's seminal essay (Chakrabarti 1982).

The particular concern in this chapter is Udayana's argument in the *Ātmatattvaviveka* (= *AV*) that, without a unitary locus of consciousness capable of reflexively using the first-personal 'I' diachronically across states of consciousness, the undeniable distinction between subjects that is available in experience would be inexplicable.

Self and person: what is at issue in this debate?

Recent work on various Buddhist thinkers has opened up the question of precisely what *anātmavāda* means. One tendency that has to be resisted is to think that the debate on *an/ātman* between Buddhists and Brahmins was one about personal identity. This is clearly the case with Udayana, as his concern is to defend a much more abstract sense of self than of a person. Regardless of precisely what Buddhists took to be at stake in the debate, Udayana is not concerned directly with personal identity.

It must be noted that the unity for which Udayana argues does not directly pertain to personal identity; it is something more minimal, a persistence of phenomenological continuity in which even elements of what is remembered or recognized may be mistaken. Udayana is not arguing with his Buddhist opponent over whether there are persons. Buddhists generally maintain that persons have some sort of status in ordinary human experience, physically, psychologically, and socially speaking. In short, they have conventional reality; only a deeper metaphysical analysis reveals that persons are constructs, and that there are no irreducible, psychologically individuated entities who/that own a series of states of consciousness.[1] Nyāya agrees with much of what is said by them about personal identity. This is because Nyāya too holds that personal identity is erroneous (*mithyā*) in the sense of being misleading; but misleading only when taken to be an irreducible metaphysical entity.[2] Udayana is concerned with a deeper argument, turning on his understanding of self as *ātman*.

Phenomenologically, the *ātman* defended by Udayana is a unitary subject of consciousness: what is experienced diachronically and synchronically together has the same subject. Ontologically, the Nyāya *ātman* is an elemental being (*dravya*) that is qualified – i.e., essentially charactered – by consciousness (*cit*). But this subject is singular in a formal and abstract way, in that while there is a plurality of such diachronically persistent and synchronically unitary subjects, they cannot be distinguished one from the other. Anything that permits individuating differentiation between subjects requires more extended, physical, psychological, and social characterization; in short, the *ātman* does not have personal identity. Personal identity is given by an *ātman* having specifiable psychophysical states. The Nyāya *ātman* provides no personal identity but provides the condition through which a formal consciousness unifies the psychophysical complex that makes the person. Personal identity is given by – and refers to – the psychophysical complex, so that it can never be peeled away from that embodied being. This formal self is not a bare locus of awareness (cf. Johnston 1987, 59–83) for it is not encountered in experience (phenomenologically, there is nothing it is like to be such a locus; Nyāya would say nothing is 'illuminated' thus, meaning that there is no cognition of this bare self). This self, Udayana maintains like all his Nyāya predecessors, is evident in the use of the 'I'. 'The 'I' notion is established in simply all living beings'.[3] He also talks of the I-cognition (*ahaṃ pratyaya*) (e.g., AV, 360).

The modern Western conception of this formal self was primarily made in response to the older Western notion of a soul – a non-physical being with personality. The modern response, going back to Kant, locates all capacity for personal characteristics in the embodied experience of humans, while what is left is a minimal self that provides the condition for the possibility of experience (and therefore of personhood) but is itself not so individuatable.

> We have an impersonal or transpersonal representation of self which is expressed in our use of the expression 'I' to refer to ourselves. When each of

> us refers to him- or herself by means of the expression 'I,' each of us refers to him- or herself in a way that could, in principle, apply to any one of us. This is the basic, minimal, idea that Kant tries to express with his notion of transcendental self-consciousness.
>
> (Keller 1998, 2–3)

In the Western phenomenological tradition, a rather different line of thinking also generated a distinction between self and person. Dan Zahavi has explored (Zahavi 2009) this distinction in both Husserl and Heidegger. In Husserl, there is the peculiar mineness (*Meinheit*), which is inherently individuated but only with a 'formal kind of individuation', which characterizes every possible subject and requires no contrasting with others; and there is what Husserl calls 'personality', formed only in relations and which Zahavi points out is actually personhood. Heidegger makes a slightly different distinction, but one that perhaps is even more strikingly similar (*mutatis mutandis*) to Udayana's view that personhood is erroneous and misleading. For Heidegger, while mineness is always found in the subject (the being-there, the *Dasein*), the everyday *Dasein* is a 'what', a rich notion that is also somehow inauthentic; whereas *Dasein* can also appropriate itself in an authentic manner, in a core phenomenological mineness that addresses the question of 'who'. Setting aside the more detailed ways in which this distinction is developed in each case, it is possible to see Nyāya's *ātman* as always being about this core and minimal notion. It is individuated formally in the sense that there is a plurality of selves, but the content of individuation is always given through psychophysical states, which Udayana warns against taking as *ātman*.

Udayana's core self is in fact some sort of elemental being, a class of entities within ontology; phenomenologists, on the other hand, deny that there is any such entity to which the quality of consciousness belongs. I have made above a distinction between a phenomenological and an ontological description of the Nyāya theory of *ātman* – but it is not one Udayana himself makes. As far as he is concerned, every argument he offers ultimately leads to the establishment of his ontological theory. But the interesting thing is that almost all the arguments in this section of the book, directed at what he holds to be the Buddhist doctrine that there is no self because none is cognized,[4] turn out to be phenomenological ones. In other words, Udayana argues that there is an *ātman* from the facts of experience. This is because he takes the basic reason for the Buddhist rejection of *ātman* to lie in the claim that no such *ātman* is found – i.e., cognized. He must therefore argue that cognition is such that *ātman* alone explains it; and that therefore one must infer that it exists.

Keeping this is mind, I will take his argument to be about a subject (or subject-self), a self that is experiential, or has consciousness. But it should be remembered that, in fact, Udayana ultimately wants to establish the existence of a self that has the quality of consciousness is a subject in embodied life, but is ontologically distinct from it.

It is this metaphysical theory of self that leads Udayana to oppose his Buddhist interlocutors, for the latter are taken to maintain that there is no such *ātman* to ground the person composed by the elements of the psychophysical complex; in that sense, his Buddhist opponents abide by some or other version of a no-ownership or non-egological theory, the sense of self being an illusion; for them, personhood is fictitious because there is no unity underlying it at all, no core, diachronically continuous phenomenological being.

The critical target in Udayana's *Ātmatattvaviveka* as a whole is the momentarist thesis that there are only point-instants, each a complex of consciousness and object, the contiguity and sequence of which generate the illusion of a synchronic and diachronic subject-self. Udayana's strategy in the *Anupalambha* section is generally to take it that his Buddhist *anātmavāda* opponent seeks to reduce away all claims to a diachronically unitary subject, leaving only streams of consciousness with causal interconnections but no further unifying principle. Udayana argues back that the features of ordinary experience cannot be explained without such a unitary subject. It can be said that in the *Ātmatattvaviveka*, we do not see an alternative no-self account that is then critically analyzed; rather, we have a series of arguments about how such ordinary features of experience as recognition, and the phenomenological distinction between subjects, cannot be explained without assuming that there are persistent and unitary subject-selves.

The Nyāya argument that there needs to be a diachronically unitary subject of cognitions

Udayana criticizes the view that there is no diachronically unitary subject. The denial of *ātman* amounts to the denial of an entity whose presupposition can explain why states of consciousness in a phenomenal stream (*saṃtāna*) are such that each stream is unitary and one stream is distinct from another. The subject whose persistence across a temporal flow of states of consciousness renders those states the states of the same subject is, for Udayana, the self or *ātman*. He seeks to demonstrate that it is not possible to explain the undeniable sense of diachronic unity without appeal to a persistent subject.

Udayana's critique is an analysis of what he takes to be efforts by his Buddhist opponent to allow contingent causal connections between states of consciousness, and the structure of individual states of consciousness themselves, to perform the task of explaining (away) the apparent unity of phenomenal life, without recourse to any notion of a unitary consciousness. The view Udayana criticizes bears a resemblance to the views of Husserl as described by Barry Dainton. Dainton argues that Husserl held the view that, in a stream of consciousness there are only pulses that partially connect through similarities (Dainton 2000, ch. 6; Dainton 2003). Anyone who rejects a unitary subject must still explain why there is phenomenal unity; it is undeniable that there appears to be, in a sequence of experiences, a sense that those experiences belong to a subject. That is how the ordinary distinction is made between those experiences that 'I' undergo and those experiences of 'yours' and 'others', which do not happen to 'me'.

Udayana agrees with the Buddhist view that the first view of ego concerns precisely the person, and should be discarded. Common to both classical Indian schools is the gnoseological project of being rid of the ego, understood as the 'I-maker' (*ahaṃkāra*). Udayana calls this is the 'conditioned' (*sopādhi*) self; it is that which is given by the senses, etc. (*indriyādi*) and as such, the body (*śarīra*). As that which is the cause of suffering (*duḥkhahetuḥ*), it is to be discarded (*heya*) as being the self (AV, 377).

Udayana takes the Buddhist position as one in which there is nothing to the unity of experience above and beyond their interdependent connections. In that sense the second view of ego in the early Husserl can plausibly be compared to the Buddhist view that Udayana is set against. For him, as with all Naiyāyikas, there is indeed more than the interconnections between experiences.

Udayana adheres to the view that diachronic phenomenal unity – the experience of individual states of consciousness cohering across time – is possible only because (and therefore intimately related to) the unity of the subject. Diachronic experience, as in recognition (*pratisaṃdhāna* or *pratyabhijñā*), is taken by Udayana to be inferential proof (*nyāya*) for a self (AV, 348–349). He clarifies what recognition means: it is just the strictly determined sequencing of cause and effect.[5] By this he rules out any accidental conjunction of two states of consciousness. But, in itself, this is insufficient, and he recognizes that his opponent could allow of such sequences as occur in recognition ('Now, at t2, I see the jar that I saw at t1') precisely without a unitary subject. In order to clarify this, Udayana refines his definition of recognition: it is the definite ascertainment of earlier and later cognitions being that of a single agent.[6] It is by way of the agency involved in acts of recognition that the mineness of cognition is delivered, one which allows (a) the recognition of sequence and (b) the differentiation between one's own sequence and those of others (e.g., 'I, at t2, recognize the jar that I saw at t1; did you too see the jar at t1?').

There are therefore three elements to Udayana's position: (i) there is phenomenal unity, in that there are causal connections between states of consciousness (i.e., cognitions) across time, as in recognition. This is granted even by his opponent: the very debate about self arises out of the co-consciousness of states, that is, their appearing to belong together for a subject. But this, Udayana argues, requires (ii) a unitary subject; where (iii) the unity of this subject is its being the single agent of the different cognitions. Therefore, diachronic – but not personal – unity is essential for selfhood, and this requires a phenomenological appeal to the structural nature of cognition, without drawing on personal identity. Furthermore, accounts of unity that are 'non-egological' are problematic.

Agency: how to distinguish between diachronically unitary streams in a way no-self theories cannot

Let us now turn to Udayana's claim that the phenomenological given of what appear to be distinct, unitary streams cannot be explained through the diachronically reductionist strategies of his opponent. The basic objection to no-self theories is clear: given that, as an undeniable fact, experience is not of phenomenal streams flowing in and out of different unities, no factor that avoids the principle of a single subject-self in each phenomenal stream can actually deliver an explanation for such experience.

Udayana offers two strategies by which his opponent might distinguish between phenomenal streams without recourse to unitary subjects, a distinction that would provide a criterion for the mineness unique to each stream. Whatever the way of distinguishing between streams of consciousness, such a criterion should allow us to explain the phenomenological distinction evident in the idiosyncratic 'I'-usage with regard to 'my' stream.

The first option is 'heterogeneity' (*vaijātya*) (*AV*, 355). In other words, we might think that there are two distinct subject-selves, each with its own phenomenal stream, only because there is some generic distinguishing property (*jātikṛtaṃ viśeṣaṃ*) whose origin is common to states within one stream but different from that of the states of another stream. This origin has to be generic, i.e., sufficiently and exactly general for the purpose of individuating each phenomenal stream. Any explanation pertaining to the causal origin of a particular state might, if highly enough detailed, explain its link to a succeeding one, but it would not be sufficiently general, for what we are looking for is something that can explain the links within and between the states of a whole stream. On the other hand, the links have to be particular enough to explain the links between the states of a stream and that stream alone; so it cannot be too general. Udayana claims that there is no such factor indicating the causal origin of one set of connected states that does not implicitly refer to a prior subject-unity. 'We surely do not observe any generic particularity at all that distinguishes between [the cognition stream of] the teacher's and [the cognition stream of] the pupil's cognition of [e.g.,] blue.'

Udayana then offers his no-self opponent another option for securing a distinction between two phenomenal streams that does not go back to causal origin: He considers whether it might be that the apparent unity of each stream is provided by the governing condition of being co-operating states (*sahakāribhedāt niyamaḥ*) (*AV*, 357). That is to say, functional connections between states could constrain the relationship between them and thereby provide unity within a stream, with the absence of such connections rendering other states extraneous to that stream. In this way, a quite general criterion for what makes one set of states those of one stream and not another, is available. The relevant candidate for linking precisely one set of states and distinguishing that set from another must be such as to explain how the states of one set (or stream) act on one another, constraining and being constrained through what they do to and with each other.

Udayana immediately (*AV*, 357) says: 'Indeed; and that [condition] is that of being a single (*ekaḥ*) agent (*kartṛ*).' He shows his hand: the relevant linking candidate is the agency of a subject. Those states that are constrained by or constrain through one locus of agency are different from those with another locus. In effect, this is the criterion for determining why some states are part of one stream and others are not.

This initial suggestion, however, is not enough. Udayana recognizes that while it may be the case that agency is the function that operates across one set of states (thereby binding them as one stream) and not another, it might still be argued that such agency itself need not be unitary. If agency were generated by the co-operation within one set of states, then contingently, that set would phenomenally delineate one apparent subject from another. That is to say, the no-self theorist could admit that agency was the relevant link but nevertheless claim that that did not point to a unitary agent.

> It could be asked, 'What special ground would determine that this so-called agent was unitary and not a series of states [merely] co-operating in this manner?' The special ground is this: being the states of a unitary agent are excluded from those that are states of multiple [other] agents, but the states of a series are not so excluded.[7]

Udayana poses this question to himself and then goes on to answer that a no-self agency, one that was not unitary but only gave the illusion of being so, is insufficient for the job. Agency is intrinsically diachronic: unity of past experiences and the expectation of future experiences is integral to agency. So where it functions, agency is preserved across phenomenal time. States of consciousness that are not within the scope of a subject's agency do not belong to that subject. This distinction is not available when states of consciousness are seen as merely a series and not that of a unitary subject, as the diachronic unity of agency will not be found in a mere series. More specifically, a no-ownership theory cannot explain the origin of the sense of doership towards states of consciousness that is provided by a theory in which there is an agentive subject of those states. In effect, then, an agent is a unitary subject, which can be distinguished from other loci of agency, namely, other unitary subjects.

Udayana then states his opponent's question: 'Could something do that [i.e., provide a special characteristic to permit a distinction between one series and another without recourse to a unitary agentive subject]?'[8] In response to this, he considers different ways in which a state of consciousness might be thought to have such a function as links it to other states in a stream or series but only to them (and not those of another).

His first option on behalf of his opponent is this: (i) It could be something that is intrinsic (*svabhāvatva*) to each state. But that explains nothing, as what is required is something intrinsic to the relationship between states in a series, something that would link them together. If the defining feature were intrinsic only to each state, then it would not be able to unify different states.

An alternative non-self explanation could be that (ii) there is a generic feature (*jātīyatva*) for all states, such that they were prone to unifying with others; perhaps he had the Buddhist notion of interdependent causation in mind. But that will not do the job either. What is required is a feature that marks some states – making them those of one stream, but not others (i.e., those of other streams). So it must be a feature that marks the states of one unified stream, with another feature marking the states of another stream. Causal origin might be one way of distinguishing them, saying that each stream has a distinct causal origin, so the generic feature of causal origin permitted the distinction between different streams. But as Udayana has already noted, that will not take us far without referring back to subjects themselves, for distinctness of causal origins ultimately can only go back to the distinctness of subject-selves.

Finally, (iii) it could be what characterizes the co-functioning of particular states (*tādṛk sahakāritva*), but as he has already pointed out, that will not determine the difference between streams, as it only relates to how, in general any two states function in relation to one another. What is required is something that characterizes the co-function of one set or stream of states, and that alone.

The only viable possibility, then, is the one he has already suggested: (iv) the functioning of the unitary (*ekaḥ*) agent (*kartṛ*) of cognition. If the special characteristic is an agentive self with regard to states of consciousness, then the distinction between streams is rendered possible. The reason why some states are 'mine' (belong to one stream) is that with regard to them I am the agent, in being able to act on and with them (in recalling, feeling, seeing, etc.). Those states with regard to which I cannot so act are those of other streams (see Ram-Prasad (2011).

Conclusion: a note on the tension between the phenomenological and ontological conceptions of self in Nyāya

It is well known that Naiyāyikas are committed to an ontological theory of *ātman*, for which they have to prove that a plurality of *ātmans* exist as basic constituents of reality, each qualified by consciousness. As such, cognitions are distinct from the cognizer, an action is distinct from the agent. At the same time, other Nyāya commitments guide their arguments against Buddhists in a phenomenological direction. The self that is conscious is conscious only in embodied existence, and in such existence, is accessible only as the conscious self. So Nyāya has a double task. First, it must look at the phenomenological evidence – the way 'I' is used in experience, the manner in which recognition occurs – in order to establish that experience requires a persistent, unitary subject, i.e., a conscious self within all conscious life. But it seeks also, secondly, to prove that such a subject (a conscious self) is an elemental being distinct from consciousness, the latter merely being its quality. The latter, ontological claim turns in Udayana on a rather weak argument against an idealist conflation of cognitions and their objects: just as the blue is distinct from the cognition of blue (assuming that the realist argument against the denial of external objects has worked), so too the self is distinct from self-cognition, which is the 'I'-consciousness (*AV*, 347). But this is not very effective, since even if the attempted refutation of the denial of external objects is successful, that the self is an object in the first place is not established. The contrast is clear: cognition presents objects as if they were distinct, and the Yogācāra Buddhist denies that they are so distinct. It is then up to the Naiyāyika to refute that denial. But cognition does not present an object called the self as distinct (which the Buddhist opponent then denies is so distinct); rather, the question is whether the phenomenology of self-consciousness can be explained only with a subject-self. Yet Udayana offers nothing more than this argument for the ontological claim for the Nyāya *ātman* as a self that is distinct from its quality of consciousness.

What remains much more effective is the phenomenological argument for a persistent, non-momentary subject of consciousness. The notion of the subject as a recessed agent of conscious states across time goes quite some way towards explaining the diachronic unity, where a persistent 'I' owns those states agentively but not those of another unitary subject. The further commitment to that agent being distinct from its states is not so well established, if at all. Perhaps this is because Nyāya is oriented to a realist ontology that requires third-personal accounts of all reality, including selves. But the essentially phenomenological analysis – oriented to the first-personal sense of self given by the 'I'-cognition – that Udayana provides in response to what he takes to be the Buddhist argument that there is no self because none is experienced, could work quite effectively to explain the persistence of the subject-self across time through acts of recognition, recollection and the like.

Consequently I have explored the subtle and elegant phenomenological argument provided by Udayana for a subject-self; but I have not tried to defend the ontological claim for a self distinct from its subjectivity. That itself seems a remarkable achievement on Udayana's part.

Notes

1 For two different accounts of this position, see: Deurlinger: 2003 and Siderits 2003, chs. 2–3.
2 See Chakravarthi 2001, ch. 2.
3 *ahamiti vikalpasya prāṇabṛnmātrasiddhatvāt*; AV, 344.
4 *nairatmyamanupalabdheḥ*; AV, 343.
5 *kāryakāraṇayorevasaṃtānapratiniyamaḥ*; AV, 348.
6 *pūrvāparadhiyāmekakartṛtayā viniścayaḥ*; AV, 349.
7 *athaika eva kartā na tu tādṛk sahakāriparampareti kuto viśeṣaditi cet? tatkartṛkatvaṃ bhinnakartṛkebhyo vyāvartate na tu tādṛk sahakāritvamityato viśeṣāt*; AV, 357.
8 *kutaścidevamapi syāditi cet?* ibid.

References

Chakrabarti, A. 1982. 'Nyāya Proofs for the Existence of the Soul.' *Journal of Indian Philosophy* 10(3): 211–238.

Dainton, B. 2000. *Stream of Consciousness*. London: Routledge.

———. 2003. 'Time in Experience: Reply to Gallagher.' *Psyche* 2003. Retrieved May 1, 2011, http://psyche.cs.monash.edu.au/symposia/dainton/index.html.

———. 2008. 'Review of Dan Zahavi's *Selfhood and Subjectivity* (MIT).' *Mind* 117(465): 241–245.

Deurlinger, J. 2003. *Indian Buddhist Theories of Persons: Vasubandhu's 'Refutation of the Theory of Self'*. London: RoutledgeCurzon.

Johnston, M. 1987. 'Human Beings.' *Journal of Philosophy* 84(February): 59–83.

Keller, P. 1998. *Kant and the Demands of Self-Consciousness*. Cambridge: Cambridge University Press.

Lowe, E. J. 1989. *Kinds of Being: A Study of Individuation, Identity and the Logic of Sortal Terms*. Oxford: Blackwell.

Parift, D. 1984. *Reasons and Person*. Oxford: Oxford University Press.

Ram-Prasad, Chakravarthi. 2001. *Knowledge and Liberation in Classical Indian Thought*. Basingstoke: Palgrave Macmillan.

———. 2007. *Indian Philosophy and the Consequences of Knowledge*. Aldershot: Ashgate.

———. 2011. 'The Phenomenal Separateness of Self: Udayana on Body and Agency.' *Asian Philosophy* 21(3): 323–340.

———. 2012. 'Self and Memory: Personal Identity and Unitary Consciousness in Comparative Perspective.' In Jonardon Ganeri, Irina Kuznetsova, and Ram-Prasad (eds.) *Self: Hindu and Buddhist Perspectives in Dialogue*. Aldershot: Ashgate.

Siderits, M. 2003. *Personal Identity and Buddhist Philosophy: Empty Persons*. Aldershot: Ashgate.

Sorabji, R. 2006. *Self. Ancient and Modern Insights about Individuality, Life, and Death*. Oxford: Clarendon Press.

Strawson, G. 2009. *Selves*. Oxford: Clarendon Press.

Strawson, P. F. 1970. 'Persons.' Repr. in T. Buford (ed.) *Essays on Other Minds*. Chicago: University of Illinois Press.

Udayana. 1986. *Ātmatattvaviveka (= AV), with the Commentaries of Śaṅkara Miśra, Bhagīratha Thakkura, and Raghunātha Tārkikaśiromaṇi*. Mahamohopadhyaya Vindhyesvariprasada Dvivedin and Pandit Lakshmana Sastri Dravida (eds.). Calcutta: The Asiatic Society. (First published 1907–1939.)

———. 1995. *Ātmatattvaviveka*. N. S. Dravid (ed., trans.). Shimla: Indian Institute of Advanced Study.

Wollheim, R. 1984. *The Thread of Life*. Cambridge: Cambridge University Press.

Zahavi, D. 2005. *Subjectivity and Selfhood: Investigating the First-Person Perspective*. Cambridge, MA: MIT Press.

———. 2009. 'Is the Self a Social Construct?' *Inquiry* 52(6): 551–573.

Chapter 21
UDAYANA'S THEORY OF EXTRINSIC VALIDITY IN HIS THEISTIC MONOGRAPH

Taisei Shida

Nyāya has played a dominant role in the history of Indian philosophy as one of the orthodox Brāhmaṇical schools. Nyāya asserts the authority of both the Vedic scriptures and omniscient God as their composer. Nyāya has originally specialized in logic and argumentation, but its theistic tendencies have gradually become more pronounced. A leading Nyāya polemicist, Udayana (*c.* eleventh century CE), is famous for his contribution to the rational proof for the existence of God.

In this chapter, I will consider a crucial component of Udayana's proof of the existence of God that appears in his theistic monograph, the *Nyāyakusumāñjali*. In particular, I will focus on the topic of *prāmāṇyavāda*, or the theory of validity, from the standpoint of the historical development of this argument.

In his analysis of the crucial topic of *prāmāṇyavāda*, Udayana argues how we justify our cognition and undertake actions. Udayana's discussion was informed by previous Nyāya polemicists who had argued this topic in order to justify the Vedic scriptures and to encourage people to perform Vedic rituals. Previous treatment has not contextualized Udyayana's argument within the broader theological debates. Nonetheless, Udayana implicitly weaves his argument for *prāmāṇyavāda* together with his theological theory. The task of this chapter is to elucidate Udayana's argument for *prāmāṇyavāda* and to isolate the implicit linkage between the *prāmāṇyavāda* and the assumption of an omniscient being.

Introductory remarks

Classical Indian thought, comprising a number of systems of thought, is figuratively characterized as 'an integrated combination of philosophy and religion.' Brāhmaṇism, Buddhism, Jainism, and so on, are basically scholastic and conservative traditions of thought, their arguments developed and conceptual problems addressed by creating new commentaries on the authoritative texts of the received tradition. While defending their religio-philosophical dogmas, scholars from these diverse traditions have debated across sectarian and religious boundaries, and through dialogical writings on various topics including: the path of liberation, the authority of scripture, and the existence of God (*īśvara*). This body of commentarial works generally evinces two attitudes: one is an apologetic attitude, that is, an attempt to defend and consolidate traditional doctrine, while the other is a logical or naturalistic attitude, namely, an attempt to make each doctrine accessible in discussion with rival schools. It is at the intersection of these two aspects that many religious and philosophical aporias arise, which in turn become the threshold of the next development of thought.

The curricula of each of these schools are constituted by basic texts known as *sūtra*, or 'collection of succinct teachings.' Over hundreds of years, polemicists have developed innovative interpretations by producing new commentaries on each type of *sūtra*. Thus, in principle, the contents and structure of these commentaries correlate to their *sūtra* text. On the other hand, in later periods, monographs (*prakaraṇa*) focusing on individual topics, including God, self (*ātman*), and Brahman, gradually began to appear. The structure of these monographs is distinct from the traditional works falling under the commentarial genres.

For example, a leading Nyāya polemicist, Udayana, composed both traditional commentaries, as well as two seminal monographs: the *Nyāyakusumāñjali* (*NKus*) and the *Ātmatattvaviveka* (*ATV*). These two monographs respectively prove the existence of God and of the self. One novel aspect of these works worthy of special note is that Udayana collated and re-organized philosophical topics that in previous eras had been argued in separate venues.

Rational theology

Although the concept of God as the principal object of belief or veneration has pervaded Hindu culture since ancient times, it is well known that there were some schools both inside and outside of Brāhmaṇism that did not accept the existence of an omniscient God. In the philosophical debate, the theists did not always hold the advantage. This trend is exemplified within the debates between atheistic schools such as Buddhist schools, as well as Mīmāṃsā and the theistic traditions of orthodox Brāhmaṇism (Chemparathy 1972, 28–29; Bilimoria 2001).

Chemparathy (1972, 7) has developed a bipartite classification of theistic traditions within Indian thought: the first type is primarily based upon the sacred scriptures, and the second type is based upon logical reasoning. For example, the Vedānta school, which corresponds to the former type of theistic tradition, emphasizes devotional faith (*bhakti*) in God; since most Vedānta theologians have considered the absoluteness of God to be self-evident, they generally have held a negative opinion of the project of attempting to prove the authority of God and scripture through logical argumentation (Ishitobi 2002). On the other hand, the Nyāya school, which corresponds to the latter type of theistic tradition, appeals to rational inference to form the foundation for the proof of the authority of God as well as the Vedic scriptures (Bilimoria 2011). Within the Nyāya school, Udayana is regarded as the foremost contributor to the rational proof of the existence of God. His achievements in theological argumentation, especially those innovative arguments appearing in his theistic monograph *NKus*, have been greatly admired even by other rival schools (Thakur 1974, 405; Joshi 2002, 15).

Nyāyakusumāñjali

The *NKus* consists of 73 verses divided into five chapters (*stavaka*) and there also exists prose commentary by Udayana himself. As pointed out by previous studies,[1] the rich philosophical contents of each verse are so compressed that it is impossible to unpack their contents without the auto-commentary. The verse-part is called *Nyāyakusumāñjalikārikā*, or sometimes simply *Nyāyakusumāñjali*, and the entire text, consisting of both verses and auto-commentary, is called *Nyāyakusumāñjaliprakaraṇa*.[2] In this chapter I will designate the former as *Nyāyakusumāñjalikārikā*[3] and the latter as *Nyāyakusumāñjali* (*NKus*).

In the first four chapters of the text, Udayana focuses on the refutation of atheistic views. In the fifth chapter, he presents a number of logical formulations that prove the existence of God. Each argument on epistemology and linguistics seems more or less in line with traditional discussions, but it is notable that Udayana rearranges the structure of the received arguments and implicitly shows their relationships to his theory of theology.

In order to analyze a crucial component of Udayana's rational theology in the *NKus*, I will focus on a topic called *prāmāṇyavāda*, or the theory of validity, on which Udayana elaborates in detail at the beginning of the second chapter. Before the time of Udayana, this topic was pursued in isolation from the theistic context. However, in the *NKus*, Udayana elaborates on the concept of *prāmāṇyavāda* in order to prove the existence of God. Nevertheless, even in his auto-commentary, Udayana does not explicitly state the logical connection between *prāmāṇyavāda* and the argument for theism. Addressing this problem, I will first present some characteristics of Udayana's *prāmāṇyavāda* by comparing it with the prior Nyāya theory. I will then consider the possibility of how and why the *prāmāṇyavāda* can serve to prove the existence of God.

Prāmāṇyavāda

The extrinsic theory of validity as foundationalism

Each school regarded its own method of obtaining valid cognition (*pramāṇa*) as indispensable for fulfilling human goals. In the earlier period, thinkers revealed their methods of obtaining valid cognition by focusing on the trans-empirical and religious 'Truth' revealed in the scriptures. As time went on, the arguments became more generalized in targeting the validity of everyday mundane cognition.

The problem of how we should justify our cognition has been a crucial topic of discussion since the time of Kumārila (*c.* sixth to seventh century CE), and various theories of justification have been elaborated by each school. The debates between the Mīmāṃsā and the Nyāya concerning this problem are very famous; it is generally stated that the Mīmāṃsā asserts intrinsic validity (*svataḥ-prāmāṇya*), and that the Nyāya asserts extrinsic validity (*parataḥ-prāmāṇya*). This argument gradually came to constitute a critical component of a larger body of epistemic concepts called *prāmāṇyavāda*, or the theory of validity/truth.

The *prāmāṇyavāda* is the cardinal subject of analysis from the points of view of whether the validity and invalidity are intrinsic or extrinsic (see Chapter 3 on *pramāṇa* epistemology in this volume). In this chapter, I will treat only the aspect of justification/apprehension (*jñapti*), which focuses on how one apprehends the validity of a cognition.

The theory of the extrinsic apprehension of validity (henceforth, simply 'the extrinsic theory of validity,' or more simply 'the extrinsic theory') may be stated as follows: in order to justify a cognition, another cognition is needed. This theory has been characterized as 'Foundationalism' by Taber (1992) and Tanizawa (2000), and connotes the problem of infinite regress. This difficulty of extrinsic theory is relentlessly pointed out by the leading Mīmāṃsā philosopher, Kumārila (*ŚVc* v. 75).

After Kumārila challenged the extrinsic theory, both Bhaṭṭa Jayanta (*c.* ninth century CE) and Vācaspati Miśra (*c.* tenth century CE) were at pains to defend the extrinsic theory by eliminating the problem of regress. Their analyses followed two directions: the first was to postulate certain self-justified cognitions, which are valid on a priori grounds. The second was to admit a type of undertaking of action, caused by an unjustified cognition. Another important point is that these extrinsic theories are aimed at proving the authority of Vedic scripture. According to their explanations, since this theory is able to justify a particular type of cognition before undertaking an action, including the performance of Vedic rituals, it can prompt people to perform Vedic rituals even though these rituals require much money and effort.

Thereupon, Udayana seems to support Vācaspati's theory in his commentary. However, when Udayana discusses the theory of *prāmāṇyavāda* in his theistic monograph, the *NKus*, the presentation of this theory is different.

The extrinsic theory in the Nyāyakusumāñjali

In the second chapter of the *NKus*, the *prāmāṇyavāda* is referred to in the first verse as follows:

> **Since valid cognition is extrinsic**, [and] since both the creation and destruction [of the world] are possible, [and] since there is no confidence in anyone other than Him (= God), **there is no other possibility remaining [than to postulate the existence of such an omniscient being]**.
>
> (*NKus* II. v. 1, 210)

At the first and last quarters of this verse, the *prāmāṇyavāda* is intimately related to the assumption of the existence of a supreme being, because of the ablative case ending. As far as the contents of this verse are concerned, it is difficult to determine any explicit logical connection between the two. When we take a look at Udayana's autocommentary on the first quarter, the extrinsic theory of validity is explained in detail. Nevertheless, we cannot find any single instance of the word '*īśvara*' or any expression correlating to the assumption of an omniscient being (*sarvajña*) and creator of the world. Rather, it seems as if the extrinsic theory is argued as an epistemic topic. Even though the extrinsic theory is intimately connected to the assumption that God exists, it is stated in a highly implicit way.

In order to analyze his theory under these circumstances, I will first show the characteristic features of the extrinsic theory in the *NKus*, and compare it to the theories previously posed by Jayanta and Vācaspati. The content corresponding to previous arguments is condensed into short dialogues in the *NKus*. While both Jayanta and Vācaspati focus on the justification of Vedic scripture, Udayana does not mention any justification of concrete scripture or cognition, but argues in more general terms.

On the other hand, the *NKus* contains arguments on topics that had not been argued previously. First, regarding the apprehension of validity, Udayana pursues the issue of to what degree justification is certain. In his discussion of this issue, Udayana uses expressions such as 'more certain grasp of validity' and 'undertaking of more action [from such justification]' (*NKus*, 229). As Udayana argues, justification is probably not the dichotomy of apprehending validity or invalidity. For Udayana, the apprehension of validity and the undertaking of an action based on it both entail a spectrum of degrees.

Second, Udayana argues for justification from a more skeptical point of view. Jayanta and Vācaspati, in order to avoid the regress problem, constructed their theories based upon an inference that apprehends the validity of relevant cognition. Vācaspati, insisting that this particular type of inference is infallible, laid the foundation for the process of justification. However, his opponent in the *NKus* skeptically reexamines the reliability of justifying inferences. Udayana does not make his own view explicit on this issue; he merely adduces a so-called 'retaliative argument.'[4] Here, he formulates the intrinsic theory as 'apprehension of a cognition implies the apprehension of the validity of that very cognition' and argues as follows:

[Opponent:] Even in the case [that the justifying inference can apprehend the validity of relevant cognition preceding to undertaking an action], if there is a fallacious cognition of that inferential mark, what will ensue?

[Udayana:] If the fact (= that a cognition is apprehended) which is not yet explicable [and is supposed to imply the validity of the cognition in your intrinsic theory] is fallacious, what will ensue? In this way, there would be same fault [in both theories].

[Opponent:] That [fact which may be fallacious] also principally implies the validity. And it will be [exceptionally] negated by a falsifying factor in some cases.

[Udayana:] It would be same in the case of inferential mark [in the extrinsic theory]. Therefore, [the soundness of justification is] same [in both theories].

[Opponent:] Then, in the case of the inference of validity as well, the doubt [about the validity] falls into the same situation as that [of possibly fallacious cognition]. Therefore, the effort [of resorting to the extrinsic theory] would be fruitless.

[Udayana:] [In the case of the implication of the validity in the intrinsic theory,] it would be in such a manner.

[Opponent:] There would be some kind of inexplicable fact which would never be fallacious even in dream. Therefore, there is no doubt [about the validity apprehended by implication].

[Udayana:] This is also in same manner in case of inferential mark [of validity], therefore the answer would be the same.

(*NKus*, 231.8–232.5)

In this way, Udayana does not explicitly reveal his own extrinsic theory, and it is very difficult to determine his exact intentions on this issue. Nevertheless, as explained in Vardhamāna's commentary (*NKusPra* ad *NKus*, 233.6–9), it is possible to explain Udayana's intentions as follows: Even though infallible justification is very difficult, it is possible to make a 'more certain justification' and to 'undertake more vigorous action' by means of rational inference, and thus, it can encourage people to perform Vedic rituals and to expect results, even though such rituals cost much in terms of money and effort.

As a denouement to his discussion (*NKus*, 232.5–233.2), Udayana adds a discussion over whether a criterion exists which completely removes the possibility of error. Udayana emphasizes there that such a criterion *does* exist because there must be a distinction between truth (*tattva*) and falsity (*atattva*), though he does not clarify whether these ultimate criteria are always accessible, nor to whom and in which case it is accessible.

Ultimate criterion for infallible justification

Above, I sketched out the characteristic features of Udayana's extrinsic theory. I will now present what can be surmised from these features.

In comparison to previous Nyāya philosophers, Udayana is very skeptical and critical of the infallible justification of cognition. He maintains the position of the extrinsic theory by assuming a spectrum of degrees to the extent validity is apprehended. A later commentary explains that this extrinsic justification is not necessarily infallible, but that it is certain enough to encourage people to undertake actions such as costly Vedic rituals.

If the goal of this argument is to construct a pragmatic theory that enables people to undertake actions such as Vedic rituals, then the argument so far is sufficient. In addition to his dominant concern for encouraging observance of Vedic rituals, Udayana also argues for the existence of the criterion which can ultimately evaluate truth or falsity. He does not concretely discuss what this criterion is, nor whether or not it is possible for us to establish such an ultimate justification.

Furthermore, if, as foreshadowed in his cryptic verse, Udayana's assumption of the existence of an omniscient being directly bears upon his extrinsic theory of validity, then this crucial component of the ultimate justification would have important consequences for Udyayana's extrinsic theory. Namely, there may exist what we cannot ascertain as being true or not within the scope of empirical justification, nevertheless, the distinction between truth and falsity certainly exists on the ontological level, and the ultimate criterion for it must exist. Udayana holds that the faculty of judging truth and falsity is incorruptible after having known the ultimate criterion, even if there remains something unknown besides it (*NKus*, 233.2–3). Therefore, this faculty is not limited to a 'truly omniscient being' but is also accessible to an 'adequately knowledgeable being' who can obtain this ultimate criterion of justification.

Udayana generally argues for the extrinsic theory in order to leave room for the application of this theory to the case of our everyday cognition and to the undertaking of actions. However, he also intended that the existence of 'the truly omniscient being,' God, would fall within the range of this argument. For, otherwise, the logical relationship between the extrinsic theory and the assumption of the omniscient being, which is alluded to in the opening verse of the section, would not be apposite.

Concluding remarks

In the opening verse of the second chapter of the *NKus*, Udayana alludes to the logical relationship between the extrinsic theory of validity and the assumption of an omniscient being; however at first sight, the logic is unclear. Udayana's autocommentary thereupon argues to the epistemic topic within an empirical framework, as it had been argued by the previous philosophers within the tradition. Udayana, however, engages new issues: namely, (a) the spectrum of degrees of the certainty of cognition and of the undertaking of action, and (b) the existence of ultimate criteria for infallible justification.

If the task of Udayana's theory is to justify Vedic scriptures and to encourage the performance of Vedic rituals, then (a) is sufficient. By introducing the spectrum of degree regarding the certainty of cognition and confidence in the undertaking of action, we can obtain justification with sufficient probability before undertaking an action, even if the action costs much money and effort. So this solves the regress problem on a pragmatic level. On the other hand, when considering why Udayana argues over (b), I believe that his intention was to guarantee the existence of the ultimate criterion for extrinsic justification: If an adequately knowledgeable being accesses that criterion at some point, he can accomplish and terminate the process of justification, thus resolving the regress problem even on the epistemic level.

According to Udayana's theory, the incorrigible justification is accomplished in the case that all the necessary factors for justification are apprehended. This means that he does not necessarily presuppose the 'truly omniscient being' to accomplish the process of extrinsic justification on the epistemic level, but he argues from the viewpoint of empiricism: If we were adequately knowledgeable, we could incorrigibly justify a cognition based on empirical process. Nevertheless, from this general observation, it is unclear whom the adequately knowledgeable being is in each case of cognition. Put differently, is it possible for us, as finite being, to access all of the necessary factors to guarantee incorrigible justification? At this point, we may see Udayana's argument (b) with the understanding that this alludes to the existence of the truly omniscient being, God.

This logical relationship between the extrinsic theory and the assumption of the existence of the omniscient being can be characterized as a relationship of abduction. The point is that the antecedent of the logic is the observed fact (i.e., the extrinsic theory) and the consequent is the hypothesis (i.e., the assumption of the existence of the omniscient being) which entails that fact.[5] In the *NKus*, in contradistinction to the fourth chapter where Udayana explains the idea of omniscient God and its cognition in detail, each argument situated in the second chapter is firmly located within the framework of empirical epistemology. Udayana, while standing upon purely empirical grounds, finally alludes to this consequence. Based on the considerations above, it is possible to interpret Udayana's logic and allusion to God in the cryptic opening verse of the second chapter.

Notes

1 See Chemparathy 1972, 37–38; Sinha 1999, xiii.
2 See Kaviraj 1923,159; Mishra 1966, 173–174; Joshi 2002, 9–10; S. Ishitobi and M. Ishitobi 1989, 3.
3 Abbreviation for a particular verse, for example, the first verse of the second chapter, will be expressed as '*NKus* II.v.1.'
4 This is one of Udayana's characteristic styles of argumentation, which Chemparathy (1972, 40, n. 69) calls *retorqueo argumentum*: In the dialogue with the opponent, when the opponent argues that the Udayana's reasoning contains a fallacy, the author replies that the opponent's argument is also not free from the same fault. This argumentation is confirmed in the whole part of the auto-commentary, as well as his other works.
5 See Shida 2011, 515–517, for the details of this logic.

References

Primary sources (with abbreviation)

ATV *Ātmatattvaviveka* of Udayana. 1940. Dhundhirâja Shâstri (ed.). ChSS 84. Varanasi: Chowkhamba Sanskrit Series Office.

NKus *Nyāyakusumāñjali* of Udayanācārya with Four Commentaries. 1957. Pt. Śrī Padmaprasāda Upādhyāya and Pt. Śrī Dhuṇḍhirāja Śāstri (eds.). Kashi Sanskrit Series 30. Varanasi: Chowkhamba Sanskrit Series Office.

NKusPra *Prakāśa* of Vardhamānopādhyāya, see *NKus*.

NM *Nyāyamañjarī* of Bhaṭṭa Jayanta. 1969/1983. Vidvan K. S. Varadacharya (ed.), 2 vols. Mysore: Oriental Research Institute.

ŚVc *Ślokavārttika* of Kumārila Bhaṭṭa (Codanā section) with a Commentary *Nyāyaratnākara* of Pārthasārathi. 1898–1899. Rāmaśāstri Tailanga (ed.). Varanasi: Chowkhamba Sanskrit Series Office.

Other sources

Bilimoria, P. 2001. 'Hindu Doubts about God: Towards a Mīmāṃsā Deconstruction.' In *Indian Philosophy: A Collection of Readings*. Roy W. Perrett (ed.). 87–106. New York and London: Garland Publishing.

———. 2011. 'Nyāya and Navya-Nyāya.' In *Brill's Encyclopedia of Hinduism*. K. A. Jacobsen (ed.). Vol. 3, 657–671. Leiden: E. J. Brill.

Chemparathy, G. 1972. *An Indian Rational Theology: An Introduction to Udayana's Nyāyakusumāñjali*. Vienna: Publications of the De Nobili Research Library.

Ishitobi, S. 2002. (石飛貞典) 'Vedānta Deśika to Shusaishin no Suiron', ヴェーダーンタ・デーシカと主宰神の推論 [Vedāntadeśika and īśvarānumāna]. *Indo-Tetsugaku Bukkyōgaku* 印度哲学仏教学 [*Hokkaido Journal of Indological and Buddhist Studies*] 17: 179–190.

Ishitobi, S. and Ishitobi, M. 1989. (石飛貞典・石飛道子) 'Chūsei Indo no Shusaishin Ronshō', 中世印度の主宰神論証 [The Argument for the Existence of God (*īśvara*) in Medieval School of Indian Logic: A Japanese Translation of *Nyāyakusumāñjali* of Udayana]. Komazawa Daigaku Hokkaido Kyōyōbu Ronshū 駒沢大学北海道教養部論集 [*Hokkaido General Education Review of Komazawa University*] 4: 1–12.

Joshi, Hem Chandra. 2002. *Nyāyakusumāñjali of Udayanācārya (A Critical Study)*. Delhi: Vidyanidhi Prakashan.

Kaviraj, G. 1923. *Nyāya Kusumāñjali* (English trans.). 159–191. The Princess of Wales Sarasvati Bhavana Studies II. Benares: Government Sanskrit Library.

Mishra, U. 1966. *History of Indian Philosophy*. Allahabad: Tirabhukti Publications.

Shida, T. 2006. (志田泰盛) 'On the Causal Factor for Validity at the Origination of Cognition: What Are the *guṇa* and the General Cause of Cognition in Naiyāyikas' *parataḥprāmāṇyavāda*?' *Journal of Indological Studies* 18: 115–136.

———. 2011. 'Hypothesis-Generating Logic in Udayana's Rational Theology.' *Journal of Indian Philosophy* 39: 503–520.

Sinha, Bh. 1999. *Nyāyakusumāñjali Hindu Rational Enquiry into the Existence of God: Interpretative Exposition of Udayanācārya's Auto-Commentary with Translation of kārikās*. New Delhi: Aryan Books International.

Taber, J. 1992. 'What Did Kumārila Bhaṭṭa Mean by Svataḥ Prāmāṇya?' *Journal of the American Oriental Society* 112(2): 204–221.

Tanizawa, J. 2000. (谷沢淳三), 'Indo-Tetsugaku ni okeru *prāmāṇya* no 'Mizukara-setsu to Takara-setsu', 'インド哲学における*prāmāṇya*の<自ら>説と<他から>説' [Indian Svataḥ Theory and Parataḥ Theory of Prāmāṇya from the Point of View of Modern Philosophy]. Jinbun-Kagaku Ronshū: Ningen-Jōhō-Gakka-hen 人文科学論集 人間情報学科編 [*Studies in Humanities <Human Sciences>*] 34: 1–14.

Thakur, A. 1974. 'Udayanācārya and His Contribution.' In *Charudeva Shastri Felicitation Volume*. C. D. Shastri Felicitation Committee (eds.). 400–406. Delhi: Charu Deva Shastri Felicitation Committee.

Chapter 22
EARLY VEDĀNTA

Andrew J. Nicholson

Introduction

Vedānta is perhaps the most widely known and celebrated of all Indian philosophical traditions, yet its early history is obscured by half-truths and misconceptions. The word 'Vedānta' itself means 'the end (*anta*) of the Veda.' This Sanskrit epithet commonly refers to the Upaniṣads, the part of the Vedic corpus in which philosophical speculation becomes most prominent. Vedānta takes its name from this part of the Vedas because its central focus is the systematic interpretation of the Upaniṣads. Most Vedāntins understand the Vedas to be the most important source of knowledge about the origin of the world, its structure, and the relation between the individual self (*jīvātman*) and the ultimate reality (*brahman*).

Other common names for Vedānta are Brahma-Mīmāṃsā ('The Exegesis of Brahman') and Uttara-Mīmāṃsā ('Later Exegesis'). These names indicate the close relationship between Vedānta and the Pūrva-Mīmāṃsā ('Prior Exegesis') tradition of Vedic interpretation. Vedānta shares many exegetical principles in common with the Pūrva-Mīmāṃsā, including the notion that the entire Veda comprises a single extended sentence. Any Vedāntic interpretation must treat the Vedas as a single whole, explaining and harmonizing all apparent contradictions between texts that historians now believe were composed at different times and places. Pre-modern Vedāntins and Mīmāṃsakas both considered the Vedas to be eternal and beyond human authorship. The central difference between Vedānta and Pūrva-Mīmāṃsā is that Vedānta concerns itself with the part of the Veda that imparts knowledge of ultimate reality (*jñāna-kāṇḍa*), while Pūrva-Mīmāṃsā focuses its exegetical efforts on the part of the Veda concerned with correct performance of ritual action (*karma-kāṇḍa*).

Some introductory books list the three major schools of Vedānta as the Advaita Vedānta of Śaṅkara (eighth century CE), the Viśiṣṭādvaita Vedānta of Rāmānuja (eleventh to twelfth century CE), and the Dvaita Vedānta of Madhva (thirteenth to fourteenth century CE). In fact, there are many more schools of Vedānta than these three. The seeds of this great diversity of schools already existed among the early Vedāntins, those thinkers prior to Śaṅkara who composed texts concerned with exegesis of the Upaniṣads and inquiry into the nature of Brahman. 'Early Vedānta' is obviously a relative, retrospective category, reflecting the dominance of Śaṅkara and his Advaita school in later eras.[1] Medieval Advaitins, Dvaitins, and Viśiṣṭādvaitins have tended to read their own doctrines back into the works of pre-Śaṅkara Vedāntins, as well as back into the Upaniṣads themselves. While these later commentators are invaluable to historians of early Vedānta for the clues they provide to the meaning of pre-Śaṅkara Vedānta, their interpretations are frequently biased by their own philosophical commitments.

This chapter has four sections, each dealing with a significant early Vedānta thinker, focusing primarily on ontology and theories of causation. The first section will outline the teachings of the *Brahma-sūtra* of Bādarāyaṇa, the most influential and commented-upon work of the early Vedāntic period. The second section will present Bhartṛprapañca, an early Vedāntin whose works are only available in secondhand or fragmentary form, but who is important for understanding mainstream interpretations of the *Brahma-sūtra* in the sixth century. In the third section, I will present the Vedāntic aspects of the thought of Bhartṛhari, the late fifth-century philosopher-grammarian whose specific contributions to Indian philosophy of language are treated at greater length elsewhere in this volume. After this, I will introduce the *Māṇḍūkya-kārikā* of Gauḍapāda (late seventh century), a work that is remarkable both for its conceptual borrowing from Mahāyāna Buddhism and for its direct influence on the Advaita Vedānta doctrines of Śaṅkara. Although brief discussions of these four thinkers cannot take the place of comprehensive analysis of the many early Vedāntic thinkers and their teachings, it can at least give an indication of the range of viewpoints in this period and suggest links between early Vedānta and later, more familiar schools of Vedānta.

The *Brahma-Sūtra*

Vedāntins have considered the *Brahma-sūtra* one text in the trilogy of Vedāntic sources known as the *prasthānatraya*, along with the Upaniṣads and *Bhagavad-gītā*. The *Brahma-sūtra* has been a central concern for almost all Vedāntic schools. The *Brahma-sūtra* is a collection of terse aphorisms (*sūtras*, or literally 'threads'), traditionally attributed to an author named Bādarāyaṇa. From a historical perspective the *Brahma-sūtra* is best understood as group of *sūtras* composed by multiple authors over the course of hundreds of years, most likely compiled in its current form between 400 and 450 BCE.[2] The earliest stratum of *sūtras* in the *Brahma-sūtra* is concerned with the interpretation of the Upaniṣads. In later periods the *Brahma-sūtra* was revised and expanded, and new *sūtras* were added to refute the doctrines of rival philosophical schools. The majority of these attacks are directed against the Sāṃkhya school, although Vaiśeṣika, Buddhist, Jaina, Pāśupata, and Bhāgavata teachings are also subject to critique.

The aphorisms of the *Brahma-sūtra* are quite terse, making them almost unintelligible without reference to a commentary (*bhāṣya*). The cryptic quality of the aphorisms would have assured that those without the proper qualifications, perhaps including *śūdras* and outcastes, would have had little access to the philosophical content of the *Brahma-sūtras* (*BS*).[3] It is this same quality that led to the proliferation of competing schools in later Vedānta, as there were very few textual restraints on later commentators to keep them from reading into the *Brahma-sūtras* later ideas, such as the concept of *bhakti*, that were beyond the purview of the *Brahma-sūtra*'s fifth-century compiler. In spite of the text's challenges, it is possible for the historian of ideas to reconstruct probable meanings of the original sūtras by careful comparison of the different extant commentaries and by paying close attention to the terminology of the *sūtras* themselves. This project should not be understood as a disproof of later developments in Vedānta. In fact, it can lead modern readers to a new appreciation of the ingenuity of later Vedāntins, who often show a level of philosophical sophistication in their commentaries that goes beyond the *Brahma-sūtra*'s text.

All early commentators, following *Brahma-sūtra* 1.1.2, agree that Brahman is cause of the world. But the precise nature of this causality has been a source of contention among Vedāntins. Medieval Vedāntins distinguished two basic positions. One theory, Pariṇāma-vāda, states that the world is a real transformation (*pariṇāma*) of Brahman. Just as clay is transformed into the multiple forms of pots, saucers, cups, and so forth, Brahman is the material cause, transforming itself into the many real entities visible in the world. The alternative to this model is Vivarta-vāda, the theory that the world is merely an unreal manifestation (*vivarta*) of Brahman. Vivarta-vāda states that although Brahman appears to undergo a transformation, in fact no real change takes place. The myriad of beings are essentially unreal, as the only real being is Brahman, that ultimate reality which is unborn, unchanging, and entirely without parts. The most visible advocates of Vivarta-vāda are the Advaitins, the followers of Śaṅkara who went on to establish a powerfully influential network of monastic schools across India. In the Pariṇāma-vāda camp we find the majority of other schools of Vedānta, who see the phenomenal world as real. Among commentators on the *Brahma-sūtra*, two prominent realists are Bhāskara, the ninth-century advocate of Bhedābheda (Difference and Non-Difference) Vedānta, and Rāmānuja, the eleventh/twelfth-century philosopher of Qualified Non-Dualist (Viśiṣtādvaita) Vedānta.

The *Brahma-sūtra* itself espouses the realist Pariṇāma-vāda position, which is the most common view among early Vedāntins.[4] Of all of the extant *Brahma-sūtra* commentaries available to us, the one that comes closest to preserving the Bhedābheda-vāda of the *Brahma-sūtra* and its early Vedānta commentaries belongs to Bhāskara, the Difference and Non-Difference Vedāntin who lived slightly after the time of Śaṅkara. For the *Brahma-sūtra* as for Bhāskara, the world is a real transformation of Brahman from one state to another. Brahman is the material cause of the world (*BS* 1.4.23; 2.1.18–20). This causal process should be seen as analogous to the process by which milk turns into curds (*BS* 2.1.24), transforming itself without any outside agent or the existence of some type of lower Brahman that engages in creative activity while the higher Brahman remains unchanged.

Brahma-sūtra 2.3.43 defines the individual self as being both different and non-different from Brahman. This is because it is a part (*aṃśa*) of Brahman: "[the individual self is] a part [of Brahman], on account of the declaration of difference [between the two] and also the opposite."[5] This passage has been seen as problematic since in another sūtra, *BS* 2.1.26, Brahman is described as 'partless' (*niravayava*). The latter supports the monistic position of Śaṅkara and other Advaitins, who mention that Brahman is absolutely without parts, and that each individual self exists in a relation of identity with Brahman. So, when confronted with the definition of the individual self as being a part at *BS* 2.3.43, Śaṅkara chooses to explain this passage away using a figurative interpretation: "'Part' means 'like a part' (*aṃśa iva*), since a thing that is free from parts (*niravayava*) cannot literally have parts (*aṃśa*)."[6] By contrast, both Bhāskara and Rāmānuja read this sūtra literally. Although apparently contradictory, the terminological difference in the two passages allows some interpretive leeway for commentators who wish to uphold the relation part and whole between individual self and Brahman. Although Brahman is free from one type of part (*avayava*), it is nonetheless correct to say that it possesses another kind of part (*aṃśa*). Nor, according to the *Brahma-sūtra*, is the individual self completely dissolved into Brahman at the time of its liberation. Although *BS* 4.2.16 describes the liberated self as 'non-separate' (*avibhāga*) and indistinguishable from Brahman, there remains a trace of individuality. Unlike a person in a state of deep sleep or unconsciousness, the liberated self retains volition and discriminative awareness (*BS* 4.4.8; 4.4.16). The *Brahma-sūtra*'s basic understanding of individual self and Brahman as part and whole influenced many early Vedāntins, including the Bhedābheda Vedāntin Bhartṛprapañca.

Bhartṛprapañca

One of the challenges of reconstructing the intellectual world of the early Vedāntins is that the works of many important figures such as Bhartṛprapañca (sixth century) are only available secondhand. Bhartṛprapañca follows the general outlook of the *Brahma-sūtra*, upholding Pariṇāma-vāda and his own distinctive version of Bhedābheda (Difference and Non-Difference) Vedānta. But his extant works illustrate how even at this early stage, Vedānta commentators elaborated on and expanded the meanings they found in the *Brahma-sūtra* and Upaniṣads, claiming the authority of tradition while transforming tradition through creative reinterpretation of authoritative texts. It is only thanks to Bhartṛprapañca's later philosophical opponents, the Advaitins Śaṅkara, Sureśvara, and Ānandagiri, that his views are available to us at all. Śaṅkara's commentary on the *Bṛhadāraṇyaka-upaniṣad* repeatedly attacks Bhartṛprapañca's interpretations, and Śaṅkara's followers Sureśvara and Ānandagiri flesh out these disagreements, sometimes repeating direct quotations from Bhartṛprapañca's commentary on the same Upaniṣad. These attacks indicate the major split between the Advaitins and the Bhedābheda interpreters that came before them.

According to Bhartṛprapañca, Brahman is that "whose nature is dual and non-dual."[7] He claims that both duality and non-duality are absolutely real, and that it is not appropriate to subordinate one to the other. He cites the example of a turbulent ocean: both the water and the waves are real, and it is not appropriate to claim that waves are somehow less real than water. Bhartṛprapañca shares this view with the later Vedāntins Yādavaprakāśa (eleventh century) and Nimbārka (thirteenth century). But not all Bhedābheda Vedāntins embrace his position that ultimate reality is in its nature both dual and non-dual (Svābhāvika Bhedābheda). The majority position in later times was the view of Bhāskara (ninth century), who held that Brahman in itself is non-dual, and duality in the world is only due to limiting conditions (*upādhis*) that are extrinsic to Brahman's absolute nature. While Bhāskara still maintains that the world of duality is real, his theory suggests that there are different grades of reality, proceeding from the ultimate reality of non-dual Brahman to the mundane reality of the phenomenal world. Bhāskara's 'Aupādhika Bhedābheda' view is much closer to Advaita than is Bhartṛprapañca's uncompromising insistence that duality and non-duality are equally real.[8]

Bhartṛprapañca's acceptance of the world's absolute reality creates an opportunity for increased reliance on rational inference (*anumāna*) in understanding Brahman. Indian logicians typically maintained that rational inference (*anumāna*) depends on perception (*pratyakṣa*) for its data, as the five-step logical syllogism developed by the Nyāya school requires a real-world example (*udāharaṇa*). So, in the common Naiyāyika example, after seeing smoke somewhere we can only infer that there is fire if we have seen smoke accompanied by fire in other places. Rational inference is therefore not independent of worldly experiences. If Brahman is transcendent, completely other than the world of lived experience, it follows that the types of reasoning useful in worldly interactions will not be helpful in understanding Brahman. This explains the tendency among Advaita Vedāntins to criticize perception, which provides us with a dualistic understanding of the world, and rational inference, which takes this erroneous dualism as its basis.

Bhartṛprapañca teaches us that our senses do not deceive. There really are many things in the world, not just in a conventional sense but in an ultimate sense—the pots, cloths, and cows of our everyday experiences have the same ontological status as Brahman. Accepting this, new possibilities open up in the application of *a posteriori* reason. Since we see Brahman's effects firsthand, we can investigate the nature of these effects in order to understand the nature of their cause. No longer are we solely dependent on Vedic authority for knowledge of Brahman. According to Bhartṛprapañca, the universal proposition we abstract from all of our experiences in the world is this: "All things are in their nature both different and non-different" (*bhedābhedātmakaṃ sarvaṃ vastu*).[9] For Bhartṛprapañca, there are four categories of difference and non-difference relations.

1 Cause (*kāraṇa*) and effect (*kārya*), such as clay and pot.
2 Whole (*bhāgin*) and its parts (*bhāga*), such as a chariot and its hub.
3 The subject of a state (*avasthāvat*) and the state itself (*avasthā*), such as sea water and foam.
4 Universal (*sāmānya*) and particular (*viśeṣa*), such as a cow and its dewlap.[10]

Bhartṛprapañca's general interest in rational inference as well as his concern with the relation of universal and particular shows a similarity to the concerns of the Nyāya school of logic. The Naiyāyikas' stock example of the universal–particular relation is the cow. On Bhartṛprapañca's interpretation, an individual cow possesses the universal property of 'cowness.' Without this property, we would not be able to understand her as a member of a species of animals. Yet she also possesses particular characteristics that belong to her alone, a certain pattern of markings, a slight tilt to one of her horns, and so forth, that allow us to distinguish her from the other members of her class. Both aspects of the cow are real and necessary, and neither aspect can be subordinated to the other. We look around and find that everything possesses this dual aspect, both different (as particular) and non-different (as universal). Bhartṛprapañca maintains that every entity, including Brahman, is in some sense a 'thing.' It therefore follows that Brahman, like the cow, has a nature that is both dual (*dvaita*) and non-dual (*advaita*). In this way Bhartṛprapañca applies *a posteriori* reasoning, examining the phenomenal world to make conclusions about Brahman, the ultimate cause.

Bhartṛhari

The linguistic philosopher Bhartṛhari lived in the late fifth century CE. In Bhartṛhari's well-known *Vākyapadīya* ('On Sentences and Words') he integrates the Indian grammatical tradition of Pāṇini and Patañjali with the *Brahma-sūtra*'s tradition of inquiry into Brahman. This combined orientation is evident in the first verse of the *Vākyapadīya*, where Bhartṛhari describes Brahman as the cause of the universe and as 'having Word as its essence.' Bhartṛhari's philosophy draws from earlier Vedic notions of Word (*śabda*) that depict it as an eternal creative principle beyond all human agency. Language did not begin with human beings. Rather, Word shapes all of phenomenal reality according to its own structure. An anthropocentric approach to language makes it impossible to comprehend the role of Word in Brahman's process of world-creation.

Although their names may sound similar, there are marked differences between the grammarian-philosopher Bhartṛhari and the Svābhāvika Bhedābhedavādin Bhartṛprapañca. First, Bhartṛhari denies that Brahman is in its nature both one and many. For Bhartṛhari, Brahman is just the One (*Vākyapadīya* = *VP* 1.2, 1.4). It appears as different due to the many powers it possesses. The terms we use to describe it are limiting conditions (*upādhis*) conforming to everyday usage (*vyavahāra*), and any attempt to express Brahman in terms of difference or non-difference, being or non-being, fail to capture its essence (*VP* 3.3.59). For Bhartṛhari, Brahman is transcendent and beyond worldly categories. He avoids Bhartṛprapañca's tendency to treat Brahman as yet another thing (*vastu*) like a cow or a pot, just a cause that possesses the same worldly characteristics as its effects. For Bhartṛhari, it is futile to use human reason to try to understand Brahman by looking at its creation in the world around us. Like most Vedāntins, Bhartṛhari is insistent on the weakness of rational inference based on perception and emphasizes the necessity of relying on the Vedas and on the insights of the ancient sages (*VP* 1.30–43). Given the fragility of human reason, we must rely on the eternal, impersonal authority of the Veda as the ultimate guide.

This emphasis on Brahman's transcendence may suggest that unlike the Vedāntins discussed so far, Bhartṛhari is an exponent of Vivarta-vāda. Numerous readers of the *Vākyapadīya*, often influenced by the nondualist commentaries of Puṇyarāja and Helārāja, have interpreted the text this way.[11] Bhartṛhari himself uses the verbs *vivartate* (*VP* 1.1) or *vartate* (*VP* 1.2) to describe Brahman's creative process. However, at other times he uses the word *pariṇāma* for this activity, and in one verse he employs both *pariṇāma* and *vivartate* (*VP* 1.120). This may be puzzling until we remember that these categories are somewhat anachronistic—he wrote at a time before *pariṇāma* and *vivarta* had been assigned technical meanings corresponding to two different philosophical views about the world's creation. Other passages from the *Vākyapadīya* imply that Bhartṛhari teaches something closer to what was later called Pariṇāma-vāda.

We can shed more light on the question of the reality or unreality of the world by returning to Bhartṛhari's conception of Word (*śabda*), the essence of Brahman, and its intimate involvement with the process of creation. Word is the energy (*kratu*) that exists within Brahman, just as the yolk exists within the peacock's egg. In its latent state, Word is undifferentiated, just as the yolk is a uniform color (*VP* 1.51). Yet the yolk contains within itself all of the variegated colors of the peacock, just as Word contains within itself all sentences and words. For Bhartṛhari, as for other grammarians concerned with Vedic exegesis, words and their meanings are eternal (*VP* 1.23). The relations between words and their meanings are also eternal, not arbitrary and variable as taught by Saussurean linguistics (as well as Buddhist linguistic philosophy). According to Bhartṛhari's ontology of Word, Word in its absolute state is the ground of all words, meanings, and indeed all knowledge: "There is no cognition in the world in which Word does not figure. All knowledge is, as it were, intertwined with Word" (*VP* 1.123).[12]

Word is originally one, yet unfolds itself as many. Bhartṛhari distinguishes three aspects of Word: the manifest (*vaikharī*), the middle (*madhyamā*), and the seeing (*paśyantī*) (*VP* 1.142). These three aspects exist in a hierarchy. The most concrete aspect of Word is the manifest. This refers to an actual physical effect—the sounds that arise through the activity of the vocal apparatus. For Bhartṛhari as for almost all Indian linguistic philosophers, speech is the central modality, not reading and writing. The 'middle' Word refers to the mental aspect of language, words as they exist before they are exteriorized. The 'seeing' aspect of Word is the highest of the three. It is Word in its form before differentiation. It is the 'seeing' aspect that makes the other two possible. These three levels of Word illustrate Bhartṛhari's hierarchy of being, in which the most subtle and unified forms are the most real, and the grosser, more differentiated forms of Word (and of Brahman) are successively less real.[13]

If this understanding of the *Vākyapadīya* as teaching a hierarchy of being is correct, then it nuances the attempt to categorize Bhartṛhari in terms of two later philosophical viewpoints, Pariṇāma-vāda and Vivarta-vāda. For Bhartṛhari, the world of diversified names and forms is not completely unreal, like a hare's horns or a sky-lotus. But it is also not completely real, as compared to Brahman in its ultimately non-dual form. This phenomenal world of differentiated forms plays a key role in Bhartṛhari's soteriology. According to him, it is by means of the lower, differentiated forms of Word that human beings have the possibility to know Brahman. The best of all sciences is grammar, because it is the shortest route to the 'supreme essence of speech' (*VP* 1.12). For this reason, grammar is the door to liberation (*VP* 1.14).[14] Grammar allows us to ascend back through the hierarchy of being, to purify language beginning in its grossest forms, moving to its subtler forms, until we are able to understand the nature of Word in its absolute unity (*VP* 1.131). Unlike his Vedāntic counterparts, who generally prescribe Vedic study and meditation on Brahman for achieving liberation, for Bhartṛhari the path to liberation is the path of language itself.

Gauḍapāda

The *Māṇḍūkya-kārikā*, a commentary and elaboration on the *Māṇḍūkya Upaniṣad*, is ascribed to the Vedāntin Gauḍapāda (seventh century CE). Advaitins revere Gauḍapāda, who is recorded as having been the teacher of Śaṅkara's teacher Govinda. There are numerous Advaita commentaries on the *Māṇḍūkya-kārikā*, including one that may have been written by Śaṅkara himself. Of all of the extant texts of the early Vedānta period, sections two through four of *Māṇḍūkya-kārikā* most clearly express what was later termed Vivarta-vāda, the view that the world is an unreal manifestation of Brahman. Each of the *Māṇḍūkya-kārikā*'s four sections builds on the previous, but the substantial differences in terminology and worldview are different enough to indicate that the text had multiple authors.[15] The fourth section of the text contains obvious influences from Madhyamaka and Yogācāra Buddhism, which has led some historians to suggest that Gauḍapāda was himself a Buddhist, or writing for a Buddhist audience. However, Gauḍapāda's basic Vedāntic orientation—his belief in an unborn, unchanging ultimate reality called Brahman—is far from the views of the Mādhyamikas and Yogacārins.

The first section of the *Māṇḍūkya-kārikā* hews fairly close to the *Māṇḍūkya Upaniṣad*, analyzing the four modes of being taught in that text: the 'universal' (*viśva*), associated with waking consciousness; the 'shining' (*taijasa*), which is the state of dreaming sleep; the 'conscious' (*prājña*), which is dreamless sleep, pure subjectivity free from any objects of knowledge; and the 'fourth' (*turīya*) state beyond all mundane states of consciousness. The second section, known as the 'Section on Falsity,' advocates an illusionistic doctrine not explicitly taught in the first section.[16] It argues that objects perceived in both dreaming and waking states are false, and that wise people know that the two states are actually one (MK 2.1–5). This dream-like universe comes about due to the illusory power (*māyā*) of the self (*ātman*), who imagines individual selves, and external and internal things. The mistaken notion that all of these different things exist is due to conceptual construction. The third and fourth sections of the *Māṇḍūkya-kārikā* elaborate upon the theory of the falsity of the phenomenal world taught in section two. These final two sections develop the doctrine of non-origination, Ajāti-vāda. The text derives this doctrine from arguments featured in Nāgārjuna's *Mūlamadhyamakakārikā* (Foundational Verses on the Middle Way). There, Mādhyamika Buddhist philosopher Nāgārjuna attempts to show that causality, and specifically the arising of beings, is impossible. This leads Nāgārjuna to conclude that all things are empty (*śūnya*), that is, devoid of essence (*svabhāva*). If a thing has an essence, then it cannot arise, since in Nāgārjuna's understanding essences exist from themselves (*sva-bhāva*), and do not originate from any other cause. Origination is only a conventional truth, and at the level of ultimate reality origination is unreal.

Gauḍapāda repeats Nāgārjuna's claim that nothing that exists essentially can have an origin outside of itself. Not only do the Upaniṣads deny the Buddhist message of absolute dependence, they teach that Brahman, the highest self, exists essentially.[17] While everything in the world of *saṃsāra* is part of the chain of causation, caused by something else, Brahman stands apart. Since Brahman is ultimate reality, it must be uncaused, free from the cycle of *saṃsāra*. But Vedāntins speak of Brahman as the material cause of the world, and it appears to transform itself into many different things. These different things that make up the phenomenal world cannot exist essentially, since it is taught that they have their origin in something else, namely Brahman. This view, that the phenomenal world is an unreal manifestation of the absolutely real Brahman, became known in later times as Vivarta-vāda.

Conclusion

Our understanding of the early origins of Vedānta philosophy is still provisional. This is especially the case with thinkers such as Bhartṛprapañca, whose works have been handed down to us indirectly by his philosophical opponents. Much evidence points to the possibility that the mainstream position of Vedāntins from the *Brahma-sūtra* up until the eighth century CE was Bhedābhedavāda (the doctrine of difference and non-difference). Even within this Bhedābheda tradition there were various interpretations, some emphasizing the essential difference and non-difference of Brahman itself, others subordinating difference to non-difference and arguing that the non-dual Brahman exists at a higher level of reality than the variegated world of forms. By the seventh century, the notion of world as dream or illusion, so influential in earlier Mahāyāna Buddhism, was developed by some Vedāntins as an alternative to the theory of the real transformation of Brahman (*pariṇāma*). While Gauḍapāda was not the only source for this anti-realist view, his *Māṇḍūkya-kārikā* clearly had a profound effect on the later Advaita Vedānta promulgated by Śaṅkara and his followers.

Notes

1 In this periodization I follow Hajime Nakamura, who defined the chronological span of 'early Vedānta' to be the time between the composition of the Upaniṣads and the works of Śaṅkara (Nakamura 1989, 9).

2 Nakamura (1989, 432–436).

3 *BS* 1.3.34–39 argues that only twice-borns are allowed to study Vedānta.

4 Dasgupta (1922, 42), Nakamura (1989, 489–490).
5 See Nakamura's analysis of Śaṅkara (Nakamura 1989, 450).
6 For more on the relation of part (*amśa*) and whole (*aṃśin*) in Vedānta, see Nicholson (2010, 50–56).
7 Nakamura (2004, 137).
8 On Aupādhika and Svābhāvika Bhedābheda, see Nicholson (2010, 24–38).
9 Nakamura (2004, 137).
10 Nakamura (2004, 139), taken from Ānandagiri's summary of Bhartṛprapañca.
11 Nakamura (2004, 415–417).
12 Bhartṛhari (1965, 110).
13 Isayeva and Biardeau have likened this to Neo-Platonism (Isayeva 1995, 85–96).
14 By 'grammar' Bhartṛhari means Sanskrit grammar. All other languages are corrupted forms of Sanskrit, and these corrupted languages are only able to convey meaning indirectly, by means of Sanskrit (*VP* 1.147–155).
15 See King (1995, 45–49), Nakamura (2004, 287–304).
16 Nakamura (2004, 323–339).
17 See Richard King on similarities between Madhyamaka and Ajāti-vāda (King 1995, 119–140).

References

Bhartṛhari. 1965. *The Vākyapadīya (= VP) of Bhartṛhari with the Vṛtti*, ch. 1. K. A. Subramania Iyer (trans.). Poona: Deccan College.

Bhāskara. 1903. *Brahmasūtrabhāṣyam*. Pandit Vindhyeshvari Prasada Dvivedin (ed.). Benares: Chowkhamba Sanskrit Book Depot.

Dasgupta, Surendranath. 1922. *A History of Indian Philosophy*, vol. 2. Delhi: Motilal Banarsidass.

Isayeva, Natalia. 1995. *From Early Vedānta to Kashmir Shaivism: Gauḍapāda, Bhartrhari, and Abhinavagupta*. Albany: State University of New York Press.

King, Richard. 1995. *Early Advaita Vedānta and Buddhism: The Mahayana Context of the Gauḍapādīya-kārikā*. Albany: State University of New York Press.

Nakamura, Hajime. 1989. *A History of Early Vedānta Philosophy*, Part 1. Delhi: Motilal Banarsidass.

———. 2004. *A History of Early Vedānta Philosophy*, Part 2. Delhi: Motilal Banarsidass.

Nicholson, Andrew J. 2010. *Unifying Hinduism: Philosophy and Identity in Indian Intellectual History*. New York: Columbia University Press.

Chapter 23
ADVAITA VEDĀNTA OF ŚAṄKARA

Thomas A. Forsthoefel

Introduction

Perhaps the most famous school of Indian philosophy owing to its transcendent mysticism, Advaita ('Non-dual') Vedānta constitutes one of the six traditional schools of Indian philosophy. While these school differ considerably, especially in metaphysics and philosophical anthropology, they all share an ambition to explore the nature of reality in its most complete context, the importance of knowledge and the mechanisms that produce valid knowledge, and the conviction that the human person is more than merely the body; a 'soul', however understood, is the animating feature of the human person. On this view, consciousness is not an emergent characteristic, as the Materialists held, or merely a changing mental flux that, conditioned by karma, triggers repeated rebirths, as the Buddhists held; instead, consciousness is a spiritual substance both foundational and essential to one's identity. Thinkers of these schools would then unpack and argue for their particular position and dispute those contrary to it. All schools shared certain methodological approaches: engaging rigorous, systematic reflection and argumentation; appealing to a foundational text (*sūtra*) encapsulating in pithy aphorisms the content of their position; and using particular pedagogical devices, commentaries and sub-commentaries, to interpret their foundational texts.

At the same time, these schools are often paired with another, sharing an even greater affinity in terms of philosophical content or methodology. In the case of Vedānta, a close relationship obtains with the Mīmāṃsā school on the basis of their shared value of and approach to scripture. All Indian philosophical schools consider the Vedas as authoritative and are therefore considered 'orthodox' (*āstika*), even if, in practice, some rely far more on systematic reflection than Vedic revelation. Mīmāṃsā and Vedānta, on the other hand, begin with scripture and base their philosophical analyses on it. They are, therefore, primarily exegetical schools. In fact, a traditional qualifier of the two schools bears this out: Pūrva Mīmāṃsā (Early Inquiry) and Uttara Mīmāṃsā (Later Inquiry). Owing to its own set of priorities and assumptions, the Pūrva Mīmāṃsā focuses on the 'early' portions of Vedic texts, the so-called '*karma kaṇḍa*', the 'action portion' of scripture, namely, scriptural texts concerning the sacrifice, the religious program *par excellence* in ancient Hinduism. The Uttara Mīmāṃsā focuses on the later Vedic texts, the '*jñāna kaṇḍa*', the 'knowledge portion' of scripture. The Vedic texts which engage sacred knowledge, particularly concerning the deepest meaning of sacrificial ritual, are the Upaniṣads. Since the Upaniṣads represent the last or final genre in the Vedic canon, the school of thought which trains its analyses on them is called Vedānta, literally 'end of the Vedas.' A standard trope of this school considers the term 'end' in a rhetorical fashion, as well. Vedānta, from this perspective, is the 'last word' on Vedic thought, the peak or pinnacle of Vedic revelation.

As this volume illustrates, the Vedānta school itself is not homogenous, with at least three schools rendering their accounts of Vedic revelation in substantially different ways. Here, we address the rigorous non-dualistic Vedānta of Śaṅkara (*c.* eighth century CE), whose work is a signal contribution to the intellectual heritage of humankind, on par with classical Greek thinkers, Thomas Aquinas in the Christian world, and Muslim philosophers such as Al-Ghazzali. While many texts are ascribed to Śaṅkara, some, particularly the so-called hymns of Śaṅkara, are considered spurious. However, scholars, by detailed textual-critical analyses, accept the commentaries on the principal Upaniṣads, the *Bhagavad Gītā*, and the *Brahma Sūtra*, as legitimate texts of Śaṅkara (Malkovsky 2001; Nakamura 1983; Hacker 1995). An independent treatise, the *Upadeśasāhasrī* has also been convincingly attributed to Śaṅkara (Mayeda 1992). Another treatise, *Vivekacūdāmaṇi*, has been traditionally attributed to Śaṅkara. While not accepted as such by scholars, the text represents a strong non-dualism in keeping with Śaṅkara's views, if not written by Śaṅkara himself. Moreover, in terms of accessibility, it is an excellent stand-alone text that makes for a good entrée into the thought of Advaita for the student new to the philosophy.

Philosophical context

Śaṅkara wrote in perhaps the eighth century of the Common Era, a time in India which had already seen many centuries of reflection on the deepest investigations into the nature of reality and the nature of the self. These reflections began in incipient fashion in the earliest Vedas themselves, at least a thousand years earlier. We see the early origins of philosophical reflection in the cosmogonic hymns of the Ṛg Veda, particularly the *Puruṣa Sūkta* and the remarkably skeptical *Nāsadīya Sūkta*. Both attempt to engage fundamental points of reflection, namely, to consider the source or origin of the universe.

While the *Nāsadīya* reveals an honest skepticism about the ability to know such things, the *Puruṣa Sūkta* is much less ambiguous, indicating that the phenomenal universe began from a primordial sacrifice, the sacrifice of the holy one or the primordial 'man' (*puruṣa*). This cosmogonic hymn implies a key train of thought developed in the Upaniṣads and by later non-dualists, namely, the idea that the plurality of the world emerges from the One. This, in turn, implies divine immanence in the phenomenal world. This early attempt to discover the source of the universe in a primordial sacrifice carried deep liturgical, social, and, ultimately, philosophical implications that shape incipient non-dualist thought later systematized by Śaṅkara.

By the sixth century BCE two schools of thought developed with respect to Vedic revelation. On the one hand, taking its cue from the *Puruṣa Sūkta*, one group of Brahmins—ritualists—developed a theology of sacrifice that emphasized both a macrocosmic and microcosmic benefit. The sacrificer, the one who endowed the ritual, would ostensibly gain certain material benefits in virtue of that endowment. On the other hand, the sacrifice itself, abstracted from personal gain, became a ritual representation of the primordial sacrifice, in effect 're-creating' the universe. For this school of thought, later systematized by Jaimini and the Mīmāṃsā school, the primary Vedic obligation was sacrifice, for sacrifice was the central mechanism for maintaining the fluid movement of the universe and therefore germane to universal welfare and harmony. At the same time, personal benefits were presumed to accrue to the sacrificer—wealth, prosperity, health, longevity, etc.

However, another school of thought—represented by sages and mystics—called this into question on the basis of the transitory nature of external rewards, the existential problem of suffering, and a developing theory of karma and rebirth. The persistence and ubiquity of suffering eventually led to intense reflection, particularly in the Upaniṣads, on what constituted ultimate satisfaction, some experience of joy or bliss that does not fade or erode in time. At the same time, a second train of thought developed from early speculation on the potential immanence of the divine and the supposed unity within the plurality. These two trains of thought dovetailed together in early versions of non-dualism.

The sages or mystics held that a repeated program of sacrificial action motivated by material benefits provided no lasting reward. The Mīmāṃsā dictum—'the one who desires heaven must sacrifice' (*svarga kāmo yajeta*)—was fundamentally problematic on this view. The sacrifice, fueled by desire, produced its natural 'fruit' or consequence. Unfortunately, on this view, the fruit itself is not eternal; once consumed, one dies again, repeating the cycle and therefore enmeshed in a futile search for lasting contentment found in external rewards. Since action therefore is fundamentally problematic, non-dualists turned their scrutiny to the knowledge portion of scripture, the Upaniṣads. Much goes on in these complicated texts, among which is the aim to access a transcendent, saving knowledge, one approach to which was to determine the ultimate meaning of the sacrifice. To this end, they looked to the power that made the sacrifice efficacious. That power was Brahman, the supreme, the generative and spiritual force behind the sacrifice and, indeed, behind the universe. Through numerous illustrations, parables, and anecdotes, the authors of the Upaniṣads articulate a profoundly unitive, interior, and mystical relationship to ultimate reality. For example, as salt, however invisible and imperceptible to the eyes, pervades the entire cup of water, so Brahman, invisible and imperceptible to the senses, pervades the universe. The sages then apply this 'pervasion' to anthropological reflection. If Brahman pervades the universe, and we are part of the universe, then Brahman pervades us. While the Upaniṣads can be read with a variety of philosophical nuance (and not necessarily even non-dualistic), there is no question that non-dualism is one of those nuances. Indeed, several of the 'great sayings' (*mahāvākyas*) of the Upaniṣads indicate an ultimate identification between one's true self (*ātman*) and the supreme self (Brahman), perhaps the most famous being '*tat tvam asi*' (that you are). This saying represents a conclusion of the ultimate identification of the 'true self' with the supreme self, which, when internalized, was assumed to issue in liberation. Following a classic dialogue in which a father elucidates to his son the unitive and pervasive presence of Brahman in the world, the father concludes with an ultimate identification, namely 'That (supreme Brahman) you (in your 'essence') are.' In other words, one's truest identity—not ego, not body, not temporary attributions, etc.—is non-different from the supreme Brahman, which, while formally indescribable (because it is infinite) is nonetheless 'asymptotically' described as being, consciousness, and bliss (*sat, cit, ānanda*). If the supreme Brahman, unconditioned by time or space and therefore suffering no erosion or diminution, is our true identity, it then behooves the wise to realize it. Metaphysics, therefore, leads to soteriology.

For the sages and yogis, an inward, introspective turn was required to discover the true self, this ultimate identification between Ātman-Brahman. While there are substantial differences between the yoga school and the non-dualist school, they are similar in key assumptions, namely, that fundamentally misconstruing identity produces suffering. Misidentifications, localized by temporary circumstances, will inevitably produce suffering because they are conditioned and fleeting. When they are 'insulted', as it were, by age, sickness, poverty, loss, or when the supposed identity is threatened, one suffers anguish. The mind, clouded by a roiling mix of congenital misperceptions about self, world, and others, is deluded about personal identity. Not realizing the truth of the divine self, and therefore suffering the traumas which misidentification causes, is akin to the distress over losing a bejeweled necklace, absent-mindedly unaware that the treasure is draped around one's neck. The treasure is innate, unlosable, infinite. The prescription? As the twentieth-century non-dualist Ramana Maharshi urged, "Enter the heart diving with questioning mind or through breath control, and be established in the Self" (Maharshi 1988: 1).

Meditation or the introspective turn allows the cloudy obscurations of the mind to settle. When the mind is clear, on this view, it is transparent to the transcendent, and the sage realizes the true self. From the perspective of non-dualism, the mystic 'sees' the supreme Brahman, the one true real, one's deepest, truest identity. This sacred knowledge is of maximal value and importance for the sages and for Vedāntins. Hence, the first *sūtra* of *Brahma Sūtra* is '*athāto Brahma jijñāsa*': now the enquiry into Brahman. Unlike the Mīmāṃsakas, whose premiere inquiry examined dharma or ritual action (*athāto dharma jijñāsa*), Śaṅkara, commenting on Brahma Sūtra, itself composed by the earlier Vedāntin Bādārayaṇa, expounds in his prologue the key dynamic of non-dualism.

Śaṅkara's prologue

In this famous passage, we see a standard representation of the cardinal existential flaw represented by earlier non-dualists, yogis, and sages. Humanity mistakes the real for the unreal and the unreal for the real. The 'real' in Śaṅkara has a particular—and some might say idiosyncratic—definition, namely that which endures or is not 'sublated' (or negated or contradicted or, finally, does not suffer change or loss) in the three phases of time—past, present, and future (*trikālābhādita*). Assuming the truth of Brahman, on this view there is only one true real, namely Brahman itself. All else, by definition, is unreal, for what makes up phenomenal reality are changing, finite events or existents. In fact, the nature of phenomenal reality is change itself. In analyses that compares well with Buddhism, according to which the source of suffering lies in clinging to changing phenomena as if they are changeless, and this fundamentally pertains to misguided notions of self. These 'misconstruals' are typically ego-based or based on mistaken perception that the so-called 'mind–body complex' constitutes in a decisive way our very self. In the view of Śaṅkara, this fundamental ignorance is the source of suffering and the cause of the enmeshment of the soul in the cycle of birth, death, and rebirth (*saṃsāra*). The antidote to this crisis: liberating knowledge.

Śaṅkara conveys a relentless non-dualism in his writings, and to do this systematically he must engage not only metaphysics but epistemology. On the one hand, given his assumptions concerning the One Real—that which perdures in the three phases of time—he must articulate a view that accounts for the 'seemingly real' as well as the plurality of phenomenal reality. In terms of metaphysics, he does this by appealing to the so-called two standpoints, the relative standpoint (*vyāvahārika avasthā*) and the ultimate standpoint (*paramārthika avasthā*). From the relative standpoint, its radical non-dualism notwithstanding, Advaita is decidedly realistic and pluralistic, admitting any number of metaphysical, epistemological, and ethical distinctions—for example, subject, object, categories, whole–part relations, means of producing knowledge, merit, demerit, duty, etc. Despite its non-dualism, Advaita requires the *vyāvahārika avasthā*; without it, it would be fundamentally incoherent, for the tactile, perceptible world consistently confounds any purported mystical oneness. The *vyāvahārika* is a necessary plank in the Advaita platform for a number of reasons, not the least of which is that it allows Advaita to meet on the philosophical playing field with other schools to argue and defend its position. Some might hold that the appeal to an axiomatic 'ultimate' point of view assumes what is to be proven. In any case, the two standpoints are necessary. Without the *vyāvahārika*, the Advaita cannot utter a word. With the *vyāvahārika*, the Advaitin has a device to engage in debate, persuade, or evoke a commitment to a non-dualist metaphysic. Some thinkers, however, may be dissatisfied with the trump card of the 'ultimate standpoint', for in this case no discourse is possible (because discourse involves plurality of subject–object). The *paramārthika* (or *mokṣa* or Brahman or Ātman) is by definition transpersonal, trans-phenomenal, absolute. It has nothing to do with any common intercourse with the world. The *vyāvahārika* is like a dream or an illusion into which are senses are inevitably keyed. Indeed, Śaṅkara writes that imperishable real (*akṣaraṃ satyam*) is "entirely beyond the scope of perception (*atyantāparoṣtvat*)" (Forsthoefel 2002, 43). The knowledge which saves or is salvation, according to Śaṅkara, is not constricted by time or space. The knowledge that saves, however, cannot be understood on terms typically associated with knowledge, for knowledge involves knower, object of knowledge, and process of knowing, and these are plural phenomena. The knowledge that saves must be understood to be a 'transcendent genius' to borrow Robert Thurman's description of *prajña* in Mahāyāna Buddhism, or, as I have argued elsewhere, a 'knowing beyond knowledge,' a state or awareness that is not limited or conditioned by traditional subject–object dichotomies (Forsthoefel 2002). Attaining this state cannot properly be called an 'experience', because experience itself implies subject–object dualism. On the other hand, Śaṅkara places a premium on experience, *anubhava*, as a self-certifying, self-guaranteeing event in the economy of liberation. But his use of 'experience' must be read as un-moored from the philosophical implications layered into its common linguistic use (though with careful analysis one can attempt to 'read' a unity of being in the plural world of experience, which Śaṅkara and other non-dualists have done). In the end, *anubhava* is a specific kind of 'religious' experience, namely, a realization of the true self. It can not be properly captured in the locution '*x* experiences *y*', which indicates subject–object dichotomy and therefore dualism. *Anubhava* is an 'experience' beyond duality.

So, what are the existential situation and the economy of salvation? In the prologue to his commentary on the *Brahma Sūtra*, Śaṅkara elucidates the fundamental crisis, the confusion or 'mutual superimposition' of Self and Not-Self, whose fundamental differences, according to Śaṅkara, are as opposed as the light and the dark. Śaṅkara defines superimposition as the apparent presentation to consciousness of something previously observed elsewhere. Perhaps his most famous illustration is the rope/snake. At night, one might see a coiled rope and mistake it for a snake. The error lies in wrongly superimposing the features and qualities of a snake onto a rope. The rope in this case is the basis or substrate of the superimposition. Similarly, Brahman is the substrate or basis for profound metaphysical misconstruals, such as pluralism and dualism. The rope/snake error indicates not only a cognitive malfunction, but the manner in which emotion may be stimulated by it as well. The person who mistakes the unreal snake for the real rope experiences a flush of emotions—fear, anxiety, distress. For Śaṅkara, as well as for other thinkers and saints in the Advaita tradition and in other religious systems, the economy of liberation involves a kind of cognitive and emotional therapy. When one 'sees' rightly, one is free from the grasp of afflictive emotions. One is calm, free, unthreatened.

In Śaṅkara's analysis, we typically confuse identity by superimposing limiting attributes of non-self upon the Self. This identification is marked by predicate nominatives or predicate adjectives: I am a man; I am tall; I am stout; I am happy; I am sad, and so on. These identifications wrongly confuse the infinite, transcendent Self—'constituted' by being, consciousness, bliss— and not-Self. At the same time, we also confuse the qualities of the limited self as characteristic of the true self. The true self is the transcendent Real, unconditioned by time or space. The fundamental misperceptions here involve reducing, as it were, the Supreme Self by identifying it with limiting adjuncts or conditions. At the same time, the process overly 'inflates', as it were, the value of these limited identities. The ego, the limited 'I', 'steals', so to speak, consciousness, thereby generating a putative identity in these limited constructions. But these identities are, with everything else in the phenomenal world, fundamentally unreal and illusory. They do not last. Our misguided attachment to these limited identities—'I am handsome, beautiful, smart, wealthy, successful'—will be the source of our suffering when these identities will be threatened, as they will be inevitably, by the passage of time, aging, sickness, and competition with others. The prescription? Discrimination between the real and unreal. In Śaṅkara's emphasis on knowledge as the premier vehicle for liberation, there is an affinity with the Sāṃkhya school, which also places premium on discriminating knowledge as the supreme mechanism for liberation.

There is a confidence in Śaṅkara's thought that suggests that insight into reality decisively nullifies the profound misconstruals that generate so much affliction and discord. The example of the rope/snake is again illustrative. When we see the rope as it is—as a rope, and not a snake—we are freed from the distress that obtains by misconstruing it as a dangerous snake. While phenomenal reality may have a dream-like sensibility, even dreams can be frightening and disturbing—until we recognize the dream as a dream, having no purchase on 'real' life. However, this confidence in knowledge as a decisive vehicle for salvation may appear overly optimistic, perhaps flying in the face of empirical reality. Śaṅkara's later disputant, Rāmānuja, holds that merely repeating, 'I am Brahman' is ineffective; he of course will hold that devotion, as a particularly intense, collected meditative concentration is the supreme path of liberation. Indeed, he quite rightly registers that devotion itself is a particular kind of knowledge. That is to say, there is a knowledge one gains through devotion, for love 'cathects' to an object, allowing for a range of conative and affective energies which impact cognitive awareness. Through a loving attentiveness one comprehends, gains depth of knowledge and insight. This may be easily illustrated by significant relationships—or even professional vocations—where love for a person or field of study creates an intensity to know its subject ever more deeply.

The yoga school also held that 'mere knowledge' was insufficient without practice. The reason for this was clear: a longstanding pattern of 'wrong identification' would issue in a particularly insidious nexus of cause and effect. The wrong 'mental' premise eventually issues in misguided ego-centered actions; these in turn not only have karmic consequences but also leave residues or latent tendencies that subtly reinforce the original misconception. This is turn results in repeated misguided actions, karma, tendencies, etc. The result is enmeshment in the cycle of suffering, which has its origins in a habituated mental cycle. Yoga philosophy, as with that of Rāmānuja, holds that this mental habituation is so strong that it requires considerable mental training to erode it or to re-wire the circuitry, as it were. While it is reductive and unfair to Śaṅkara to suggest that saving knowledge is by any means facile, he nonetheless appears confident about the liberating power of transcendent knowledge.

Despite this confidence, Śaṅkara is very clear about the salutary benefits of particular culture of liberation. And, given his Brahmin origins—his non-dualism notwithstanding—Śaṅkara concedes much to culture and ethics, creating a soteriological program which includes powerful socially established doxastic (belief-forming) practices. These include, first and foremost, the Veda, particularly the sacred knowledge transmitted in the *mahāvākyas*, but also spiritual eligibility (*adhikāra*), the guru, and a host of other ethical and spiritual practices. One sees a tension between a profoundly 'internalist' program of liberation—profoundly interior, self-evident, and immediate—and another that is profoundly dependent on an 'externalist' program, a set of socially established mechanisms which promotes a 're-wiring' of consciousness, or, to put it in Śaṅkara's terms, removes ignorance. The adept taps into an 'external circuity'—Veda, guru, ethics, etc.—which facilitates realization. However, in terms truer to the non-dualist spirit, no transformation of consciousness actually obtains; to borrow from Anantanand Rambachan, the process of 'transformation' becomes one of 'accomplishing the accomplished' (Rambachan 1991). 'Accomplishing' wrongly implies gaining what one does not have, suggesting in turn the possibility of losing what one gains; both processes imply change and dualism, which Śaṅkara categorically rejects. The true self does not change, being always complete and self-established (*svataḥ siddhaḥ*). The economy of liberation, in the end, is not about 'gaining' or becoming something one is not, but about realizing one's truest identity, that is, discovering the internal treasure, always present however obscured by ignorance. Realizing this treasure spells the end of suffering, for one is no longer buffeted by praise or blame or success or loss or death or life. One's true identity is beyond these limited configurations. One already has—or, more correctly, *is*—infinite being, consciousness, bliss. The innately endowed treasure is internal. Realization, therefore, becomes a process of destroying ignorance in the form of wrong ego-identifications and the afflictive habits which they generate.

There are social and philosophical implications in approaches that favor externalist or internalist epistemologies of religious experience. If the 'external' circuity of Advaita is absolutely necessary, then such externalism decisively indexes its soteriology to local culture. If, however, internalism is dominant, then that circuitry is relativized, opening up space for Advaita as a trans-cultural, universalist program. In the non-dualism of Śaṅkara, an electric engagement obtains between the two poles of internalism and externalism. While internalism may be truer to the spirit of non-dualism and, to a considerable extent, to Śaṅkara himself, that cannot and ought not be overstated. Śaṅkara is quite clear about the formative contexts of text, tradition, and teacher, the socially established practices in the economy of liberation. Still, beginning especially with the Bengali mystic Ramakrishna in the nineteenth century and extending to twentieth-century Indian non-dualists, such as Jiddu Krishnamurti and Ramana Maharshi, we can see an increasing emphasis on an inward turn that, true to Advaitin premises, naturally relativizes the value and importance of social context. This in the end 'liberates' Advaita from its localized forms, rendering it genuinely trans-cultural and universalist, in keeping with its fundamental metaphysic.

References

Bader, J. 1990. *Meditation in Śaṅkara's Vedānta.* Delhi: Motilal Banarsidass.

Forsthoefel, T. 2002. *Knowing beyond Knowledge: Epistemologies of Religious Experience in Classical and Modern Advaita.* Farnham: Ashgate.

———. 2014. Śaṅkara. In K. A. Jacobsen (ed.) *Brill's Encyclopedia of Hinduism*, vol. 5. Leiden: Brill.

Grimes, J. 2004. *Vivekacūdāmaṇi.* Farnham: Ashgate.

Hacker, P. 1995. Śaṅkarācārya and Śaṅkarabhagavatpāda: Preliminary Remarks Concerning the Authorship Problem. In W. Halbfass (ed.) *Philology and Confrontation: Paul Hacker on Traditional and Modern Vedānta*. Albany: State University of New York Press.

Maharshi, R. 1988. *Eka Sloki*. C. Sudarsan (trans.). Bangalore: Ramana Maharshi Centre for Learning.

Malkovsky, B. 2001. *The Role of Divine Grace in the Soteriology of Śaṁkarācārya*. Leiden: Brill.

Mayeda, S. 1992. *A Thousand Teachings: The Upadeṣasāhasrī of Śaṇkara*. Albany: State University of New York Press.

Nakamura, H. 1983. *A History of Early Vedanta Philosophy*. Delhi: Motilal Banarsidass.

Potter, K. 1981. *Encyclopedia of Indian Philosophies*, vol. 3. Delhi: Motilal Banarsidass.

Rambachan, A. 1991. *Accomplishing the Accomplished: The Vedas as Source of Knowledge in Śaṅkara*. Honolulu: University of Hawai'i Press.

———. 2006. *The Advaita Worldview*. Albany: State University of New York Press.

Śaṅkara. 1990. *Brahmasūtra with Śaṅkarabhāṣya*. Delhi: Motilal Banarsidass.

Chapter 24
AVIDYĀ: THE HARD PROBLEM IN ADVAITA VEDĀNTA

Stephen Kaplan

Avidyā, *ajñāna* (ignorance, nescience) is one of the first terms one confronts when studying Indian philosophy. *Avidyā* is declared to be the source of rebirth, the root of *saṃsāric* existence. From such Upanishadic declarations (*KaU* 2.5; *MuU* 1.2.8) that 'the blind are led by the blind from birth to birth because of their ignorance' to the Buddhist twelvefold chain of dependent origination (*pratītyasamutpāda*), which regularly places *avidyā* in the first position, ignorance is understood to be the root problem of human existence and suffering. Here the fundamental existential problem is understood not to be a moral problem, not a problem of good and evil, but a problem of knowledge (*vidyā*) or rather lack of knowledge, *avidyā*. *Avidyā* is lack of knowledge of *ātman*/Brahman; it is the imposition of duality on the non-dual *ātman*/Brahman. Like many things whose nature at first appears straightforward and simple, upon closer inspection the notion of ignorance becomes complicated and diverse. A scan of different schools of Indian philosophy would yield a detailed lattice of ideas on *avidyā* distinguishing an array of positions. In this chapter, we will survey the Advaita school in an attempt to illuminate a truly crucial aspect of that school.

The hard problem

Avidyā is the hard problem for Advaita Vedānta. As one scholar has put it: 'It is impossible for us to explain in any intelligible way the relation between Brahman-Ātman and *avidyā*' (Balasubramannian 1988, xxxv). And, we find '[i]f the concept of *avidyā* is logically analyzed, it would lead the Vedānta philosophy toward dualism or nihilism and uproot its fundamental position' (Mayeda 1992, 82). And, Śaṅkara's student Sureśvara tells us: 'He who desires to see *avidyā* through the knowledge generated by a *prāmaṇa* [valid means of knowledge] could as well certainly see the darkness in the interior of a cave by means of a lamp' (*TUBhV* II:177). In Western philosophy of mind, consciousness is the 'hard problem' (Chalmers 1995). How can a universe that was without conscious, subjective, first-person experience, without qualia, develop such experience? For Western theologians, theodicy is the hard problem. How can an all-powerful, loving God create a world in which evil runs amok? In Sāṃkhya, which encounters the problem of *avidyā*, the hard problem is how a detached self-illuminating self, *puruṣa*, and a non-conscious material world, *prakṛti*, become entangled. For Advaita there is no ontological dualism between *puruṣa* and *prakṛti* and hence no explanation is needed to unravel how these two ontological natures become entangled. For Advaita, from the highest perspective (*paramārtha*), there is no creation, no origination (*ajātivāda*), hence there is no all-powerful God, *īśvara*, who creates a world with or without evil. For Advaita, there is *ātman*, Brahman, the one non-dual Being, one without a second, which is *cit* (consciousness). As such, Advaita need not ponder how consciousness can arise from a world billions of years old that had been devoid of consciousness. Rather, Advaita must contemplate how ignorance appears if all is the non-dual, self-illuminating (*svaprakāśa*) consciousness?

We must first acknowledge that '*the* hard problem' is really '*a* hard problem.' There is no single hard problem; each philosophical/theological system has '*a* hard problem' concomitant with its presuppositions and its worldview. Second, *avidyā*, as a hard problem and the hard problem for Advaita, must be understood within the Advaita Vedānta landscape of ideas.

Advaita Vedānta declares that that which appears as empirical truth (*samvṛtti satya*), as a world of subjects and objects, as a world of duality, is, from the perspective of *paramārtha satya* (the highest truth), false (*vaitathya*). The highest truth is *advaya*, non-dual. It is *ātman*/Brahman the one, undivided Being (*sat*), the one existence which is without beginning, middle, or end, without measure and without end to measure, without birth or death, without parts, without change, without subjects and objects. This Being is the true Self (*ātman*), self-illuminating (*svaprakāśa*), consciousness (*cit*, *caitanya*), the witness consciousness (*sākṣin*) that is without form (*nirākāra*), without qualities (*nirviṣaya*). This unqualified, uncompromising non-dualism presents Advaita with its hard problem. If *ātman*/Brahman is this self-illuminating, partless, unchanging, non-dual, Being and Consciousness, how does duality with its parts and changes appear? *Avidyā* declares the Advaitin.

Avidyā: an overview

Śaṅkara, the most famous Advaitin, opens the *BSBh*, the text by which all other Śaṅkara texts are measured, with a definition of *avidyā* in order to elucidate how we experience duality when all is the non-dual, unchanging Brahman. The *BSBh* declares that *avidyā* is *adhyāsa*, imposition. Ignorance is the imposing of the qualities of the object upon the subject and the subject upon the object. Imposing on a current situation knowledge of a past experience is ignorance. Or, more generally, it is the imposing of qualities of one thing onto another thing. Specifically, it is the imposition of an embodied person upon the true self. For without the notion of an embodied subject one cannot locate a knowing agent who perceives and acts within the world. Śaṅkara tells us:

> This superimposition ... is considered by the learned to be *avidyā*, nescience... whenever there is a superimposition of one thing on another, the locus is not affected in any way either by the merits or demerits of the thing superimposed. All forms of worldly and Vedic behavior that are connected with valid means of knowledge and objects of knowledge start by taking for granted this mutual superimposition of the Self and non-Self, known as nescience; and so do all the scriptures dealing with injunction, prohibition, or emancipation.
>
> (*BSBh* 1.1)

All distinctions without exception arise from these impositions; but these impositions have no effect upon their object, Brahman. Furthermore, one cannot locate the cause of *avidyā* since the location of a cause assumes such distinctions. Such logical enigmas illustrate exactly how hard a problem *avidyā* is for the Advaitin.

Avidyā and *māyā* are frequently linked terms. The earliest extant Advaita text, the Agamaśāstra of Gauḍapāda [*MK*] by Gauḍapāda, often uses the term *māyā*, but not *avidyā*, yet Śaṅkara in his commentary on the *MK* (1:16) glosses *māyā* with *avidyā*. (See also *BSBh* 1.4.3.) On the one hand, each of these terms has a number of parallel meanings—an epistemological connotation involving cognitive error, a phenomenological connotation involving illusory appearances such as the falsely appearing snake of the rope–snake analogy, and a more cosmological/ontological connotation indicating the power or material cause from which appearances arise. On the other hand, a general sense often leads us to assume that *avidyā* has more of an epistemological quality and *māyā* has more of a cosmological quality. Vidyāraṇa (*PD* 3:37), for example, associates ignorance with the *jīva* and *māyā* with *īśvara* (lord). Examining the particular usage of each term (Solomon 1969 and Hacker 1995) by particular Advaita thinkers is essential in uncovering the complexity of these issues.

The perplexing questions

Expanding our understanding of *avidyā* will require (1) presenting a series of questions (Kaplan 2007) which further expose *avidyā* to be the hard problem for Advaita, (2) presenting the divide between two Advaita schools that illustrate the philosophical battles that have been fought, and (3) delineating a series of categories by which *avidyā* is understood. First, some questions: if Brahman is both everywhere and self-illuminating consciousness, from where does ignorance arise and where does it exist? Does it exist as a part of Brahman? But, how can that be, if Brahman is partless? If Brahman is partless, does *avidyā* permeate all of Brahman? But, how can ignorance pervade the Self (*ātman*), if the latter is always *svaprakāśa* (self-illuminating)? Does it exist apart from *ātman*/Brahman? But, how can that be, if Brahman is all and without anything other than it? If Brahman is the one real, then is *avidyā* unreal and if it is unreal, can it have any effect? If it has no effect, how do we experience it? Ultimately, each of these questions leads us to the hard problem for Advaita—namely, how can *vidyā* and *avidyā* be simultaneous and co-terminus? If each existed in different locations or at different times there would be no problem, but each 'exists' at the same time and in the same place. How can Advaita explain this apparent contradictory nature?

This apparent contradictory nature between *vidyā* and *avidyā* has been the source of much criticism by opponents of Advaita. For example, Śāntarakṣīta's Buddhist critique of Advaita questions how bondage due to ignorance and liberation due to knowledge can simultaneously exist in the always pure Brahman (*TS* 7:333). Rāmānuja and the Viśiṣṭādvaita Vedānta tradition do not maintain that Brahman is without qualities and without distinctions. Brahman for them is without defiling qualities and the individual self is not Brahman, but only a part or aspect of Brahman. Therefore, they do not have to confront the Advaita hard problem of how a non-dual, self-illuminating, pure consciousness/being can appear with distinctions. Viśiṣṭādvaita aims its polemical discourse at the Advaita notion of ignorance, enumerating seven reasons to dismiss this Advaita doctrine (Grimes 1990). Among these reasons are the contradictory nature of *avidyā* and *vidyā* and the problem of discerning how ignorance can conceal the self-illuminating consciousness that is Brahman (*RSBh* 1.1.1:12–24).

Advaitins, like Śaṅkara and Sureśvara, deny that any contradictory nature exists even though they admit that it certainly appears to exist, just as the rope appears as a snake, which does not exist (*NS* II.50). Others dismiss this problem of the alleged contradictory nature of these two terms by informing us that *viveka* (discernment) or *jñāna* (knowledge) is the opposite of *avidyā* rather than *cit* (Fort 2000; Mohanty 2001). Nonetheless, we find Śaṅkara telling us that only knowledge of Brahman will remove ignorance. *BSBh* 1.1 states 'the ascertainment of the nature of the real entity by separating the superimposed thing from it is called *vidyā* (illumination).' The *US* 1.1.6 tells us that *vidyā* is the cause of the destruction of ignorance (*vidyaivājñānahanāya*). Sureśvara declares: 'This ignorance is without any support. It is opposed to any logic. It cannot endure inquiry in the same way as darkness cannot endure the sun' (*NS* 3.66). Whether contradictory or not, ignorance, removed by *vidyā*, is the Advaita hard problem.

Compounding the hard problem according to a number of leading scholars including Hacker (1995), Ingalls (1953), and Mayeda (1992) is the fact that Śaṅkara left some questions unanswered because he was more concerned with

> what he considers the heart of the matter, the teaching that is necessary for the attainment of *mokṣa*. This teaching is that *avidyā*, whatever its modality, is never truly connected with the self. Here, as in other differences that may be noticed between Śaṃkara and his disciples, one may say that Śaṃkara's approach to truth is psychological and religious.
>
> (Ingalls 1953, 72)

From this perspective, Śaṅkara was unconcerned with whether *avidyā* resides in Brahman or in the *jīva*, the individual self? Routinely cited to support this understanding of Śaṅkara is his commentary on the *Bhagavad Gītā* (13: 2. 6) and his *BSBh* (4.1.3).

There, in response to the opponent's inquiry 'whose ignorance?', Śaṅkara declares that this question is without sense (*praśna nirarthakaḥ*). His response did not resolve this issue for later Advaitins who wanted to ascertain where ignorance resided. How can it reside in Brahman? But equally enigmatic is how ignorance could reside in the *jīva* if the *jīva* is the product of ignorance?

Two Advaita schools

Wrestling with these questions Advaita has divided into two schools—the Bhāmatī and Vivaraṇa. This internal Advaita debate can be traced to two of Śaṅkara's contemporaries and students—Maṇḍana Miśra and Sureśvara. The former in the *Brahmasiddhi* maintains that ignorance belongs to each *jīva*. Following this line of thought, Vācaspati Miśra articulates the ideas that form the Bhāmatī school, which contends that the *jīva* is the locus (*aśraya*) of ignorance. In other words, ignorance resides in the individual self because *ātman* is pure, self-illuminating consciousness and could not be the locus of ignorance. This notion leads them to contend that *avidyā* is plural since it is specific to each individual; and furthermore, since the liberation of one *jīva* does not entail the liberation of all *jīvas*, ignorance must be as multiple as the *jīvas* whose individual ignorance keeps them in bondage.

The Vivaraṇa school is associated with Padmapāda, Vidyāraṇa, Sarvajñātman, and Prakāśātman. (There is some debate over the exact relation between Sureśvara, the Vivaraṇa school and the aforenamed Advaitins, but for purposes of the issues raised here, Sureśvara is included with the Vivaraṇa school.) Taking its name from the *Pañcapādikā-Vivaraṇa* of Prakāśātman, for this school the *jīva* cannot be the locus of ignorance; *ātman* must be its locus; and, as such, there is only one *avidyā*, not multiple *avidyās*. This one *avidyā* has different capacities to entrap each *jıva*. Sureśvara articulates a series of reasons why the *jīva* cannot be the locus of ignorance.

> [T]he not-Self cannot be the locus of ignorance, because ignorance is its very nature; and what is of the nature of ignorance cannot, indeed, be the locus of ignorance .... The non-Self does not have the possibility of attaining knowledge; should there be this possibility, it could be said that ignorance which is by nature the negation of knowledge is located in it. Further, since the not-Self is a product of ignorance, [it cannot be the locus]. Indeed, what exists earlier cannot be located in that which itself comes into being from that [earlier] thing. There is also the reason that the not-Self has no nature of its own independently of ignorance. Owing to these very reasons it should be known that ignorance is not about the not-Self.
>
> (*NS* 3.1)

Sureśvara's attack on the notion that the *jīva* can be the locus of ignorance, an attack on the ideas associated with the Bhāmatī school, is strong; essentially, how can the individual self which is an effect of ignorance be the locus of ignorance? But in fairness to the Bhāmatī school, one need only return to one of Rāmānuja's criticisms—how does the presence of ignorance in that which is a 'uniform self-illuminating nature' not destroy that nature (*RSBh* 1.1.1: 60)? This balance of strong criticisms of each side leaves us with the hard problem facing Advaita.

The Bhāmatī school, the Vivaraṇa school, and Śaṅkara all agree that the object (*viṣaya*) of ignorance is Brahman. The object of ignorance refers to that upon which ignorance is projected and that which is concealed by that projection. In the rope–snake analogy, the object of ignorance is the rope upon which the snake is projected and this projection conceals the true object, the rope. Utilizing the analogy of the dreamer and the dream (*BSBh* 2.1.28), Śaṅkara informs us that just as a single dreamer can experience a multitude of dream objects without becoming other than a single dreamer, so also can the one, unchanging Brahman be the object of the multitude of diverse appearances without ever changing its nature.

Explanatory categories and analogies

A number of categories, analogies, and other methods of clarification are used in the Advaita attempt to elucidate *avidyā*. While each of these issues has particular proponents within Advaita, space permits only a cursory overview. First, *avidyā* is associated with two powers— the power of concealing (*āvaraṇaśakti*) and the power of projecting (*vikṣepaśakti*). With Brahman concealed or obscured, the multitude of things can be projected. These powers can operate together, but each can operate separately. For example, Brahman is concealed in deep sleep without the multitude of appearances projected. And, to the lord, *parameśvara*, a multitude of appearances can be projected without the concealment of Brahman (*SS* 2:183). The notion that *avidyā* has two powers returns us to another perplexing problem—is *avidyā* and its powers real and if so, is it a second reality to Brahman? Advaitins tackle this problem by declaring that ignorance is *anirvacanīya*, that which cannot be spoken about, indescribable. *Ātman*/Brahman is the one true Being, the one Real, and in contrast, imaginary notions such as the 'barren woman's son' or the 'footprints of birds in the sky' are unreal, *asat*. The latter are never experienced. *Avidyā* is experienced, but it is neither real nor unreal; therefore, it is indescribable. As experienced, it is said to be something positive (*bhāvarūpa*). Just as the word *amitra*, literally 'no friend,' does not mean the absence of a person who is a friend, but rather means 'enemy,' the presence of someone who is not to be trusted, so also does *avidyā* imply the presence of something experienced (*TUBhV* 2.179).

Advaitins have utilized three theories to illustrate how ignorance can be related to the appearance of a multiplicity of individual things without affecting Brahman. *Avacchedavāda* (limitation theory) utilizes the analogy of space and the space of a pot. The pots merely seem to divide space, but in reality space is not affected by the pots. Likewise, ignorance seems to affect Brahman, but in reality Brahman remains unaffected. Second, *pratibimbavāda* (reflection theory) utilizes the analogy of a mirror and a face. The mirror reflects the face and allows for two faces to appear when in fact there is only one face. So also, multiplicity appears in the world, but there is only Brahman. Finally, there is the *ābhāsavāda* (appearance theory). A single moon appears as many moons in the waves of the ocean, but there is only one moon just as there is only one Brahman.

The use of analogies in Advaita is ubiquitous. In addition to the analogies briefly mentioned above, other analogies such as the eye disease causing multiple images are also invoked. Each of these analogies is trying to tackle the hard problem of Advaita—trying to illustrate how an unchanging, undivided, self-illuminating Brahman can appear to be changing, divided and lack awareness of *cit*. Each analogy addresses a different aspect of this problem and presents a different challenge to the Advaitin. For example, in the dreamer–dream analogy Advaitins secure the notion that there is only one dreamer, only Brahman, yet are challenged by the fact that the dreamer/Brahman is changing as the dreamer dreams. The rope–snake analogy illustrates how an illusory snake can appear when in fact there is only an unchanging rope. As such, this analogy does not suffer the same limitations as the previous example. However, it introduces, like a number of other Advaita analogies, a new element—someone who experiences the rope as snake. If the rope is *ātman*/Brahman and the snake is the world of appearances, which are superimposed on the rope, who experiences the snake, who is the knower of these appearances (Potter 1963, 172)?

Recognizing each analogy suffers limitations, two options can be explored. First, in turning from one analogy to the next as Advaita texts frequently do, one should not get stuck on the problematic points, but instead relish the insights of each analogy. This perspective on analogy follows Padmapāda's contention that the success of the analogies is their ability to remove doubt and to assist the *pramāṇas*, not to prove their point (Potter 1981, 576).

Second, one can develop a new analogy that overcomes the aforementioned limitations. Holography, the technique by which three-dimensional optical artifacts are produced from a two-dimensional space, is one such possible candidate (Kaplan 2007). The two-dimensional space, the holographic film, is without subjects and objects; it is without images; it is without any discrete parts that can be distinguished from any other part. Adding to its uniqueness, each piece of this space can reproduce the entire holographic, three-dimensional image and yet the entire two-dimensional film only reproduces one such image. In other words, tear the holographic film in tenths and each tenth will reproduce the entire image, but put the ten pieces back together and only one image is produced. Each piece contains the whole yet the whole is without the distinctions of subject and object, self and other. This phenomenon provides us with an analogy of how there is only one *ātman*/Brahman, which is without subjects and objects, discrete entities. In addition, just as different holographic images can be projected from the film (with a light source) without affecting the holographic film, one can envision that the projection of different objects would not affect Brahman if the self-illuminating nature of Brahman were the analog to the light source. This would allow us to ask: could the self-illuminating nature of an infinite holographic space be the analog to the self-illuminating, Being, Consciousness of *ātman*/Brahman? Such possibilities and questions lead us beyond our limits here, but offer a new way to approach the hard problem of Advaita Vedānta.

Postscript

In addition to the references cited above, P. Bilimoria's *Encyclopedia of Religion* entry (2005) offers a valuable overview of this topic. The two Advaita Vedānta volumes, 3 and 11, in the *Encyclopedia of Indian Philosophies* series, edited by Karl H. Potter, are very rich resources for the study of Advaita. Among contemporary interpreters of Advaita, K. C. Bhattacharyya offers an extraordinarily profound analysis that harkens back to Śaṅkara, filtered through continental philosophy.

> The individuality is understood as me, i.e. as the illusory objectivity of the subject and not merely illusory identity with the object taken as real .... The idea of the object, in fact, as distinct from the subject is derived from the idea of the embodiment, which itself is born in the consciousness of the individual self as false in respect of its individuality.
>
> (Bhattacharyya 1956, 114)

Compare Bhattacharyya to Śaṅkara:

> Since a man without self-identification with the body, mind, senses, etc., cannot become a cognizer ... since nobody engages in any activity with a body that has not the idea of the Self superimposed on it ... therefore it follows that the means of knowledge, such as direct perception as well as the scriptures, must have a man as their locus who is subject to nescience.
>
> (BSBh 1.1.1)

Another contemporary interpreter, Swami Satchidānandendra Saraswati, argues that Padmapāda and the subsequent Advaita tradition misinterpreted the notion of *avidyā* as put forth by Gauḍapāda and Śaṅkara. Only Sureśvara proffered the correct interpretation of the founders' position (Doherty 1999).

Abbreviations

BSBh	*Brahma Sūtra Bhāṣya*
KaU	*Kaṭha Upaniṣad*
MK	*Māṇḍūkya Kārikā*
MuU	*Muṇḍaka Upaniṣad*
NS	*The Naiṣkarmyasiddhi*
PD	*Pañcadaśī*
RSBh	*Śrībhāṣya of Rāmānuja*
SS	*Saṃkṣepaśārīraka*
TS	*The Tattvasaṅgraha*
TUBhV	*The Taittirīyopaniṣad Bhāṣya-Vārtika*
US	*Upadeśasāhasrī*

References

Bhattacharyya, Krishnachandra (K. C.). 1956. 'The Advaita and its Spiritual Significance.' In *Studies in Philosophy*, vol. 1. Gopinath Bhattacharyya (ed.). Calcutta: Progressive Publishers.

Bilimoria, Purushottama. 2005. 'Avidyā.' In *Encyclopedia of Religion*, 2nd ed. Lindsey Jones (ed.). Detroit: Thomson Gale.

Chalmers, David. 1995. 'Facing Up to the Problem of Consciousness.' *Journal of Consciousness Studies* 3: 200–219.

Doherty, Martha J. 1999. 'A Contemporary Debate in Advaita Vedānta: Avidyā and the views of Swami Satchidānandenra Saraswati.' Ph.D. Dissertation, Harvard University. Ann Arbor: UMI.

Fort, Andrew O. 2000. 'Reflections on Reflection: Kūṭastha, Cidābhāṣā and Vṛtti in the Pañcadaśī.' *Journal of Indian Philosophy* 28: 497–510.

Gauḍapāda. 1989. *The Agamaśāstra of Gauḍapāda* [MK]. Vidhushekara Bhattacharya (ed., trans.). Delhi: Motilal Barnarsidass.

Grimes, John. 1990. *The Seven Great Untenables*. Delhi: Motilal Banarsidass.

Hacker, Paul. 1995. 'Distinctive Features of the Doctrine and Terminology of Śaṅkara: Avidyā, Nāmarūpa, Māyā, Īśvara.' In *Philology and Confrontation*. Wilhelm Halbfass (ed.). Albany: State University of New York Press.

Ingalls, Daniel H. H. 1953. 'Saṃkara on the Question: Whose is *avidyā*.' *Philosophy East and West* 3: 69–72.

Kaplan, Stephen. 2007. '*Vidyā* and *Avidyā*: Simultaneous and Co-terminus? A Holographic Model to Illuminate the Advaita Debate.' *Philosophy East and West* 27: 178–203.

Mohanty, J. N. 2001. *Explorations in Philosophy: Essays by J. N. Mohanty*. Bina Gupta (ed.). New Delhi: Oxford University Press.

Potter, Karl H. 1963. *Presuppositions of Indian Philosophies*. Westport, CT: Greenwood Press.

———. (ed.). 1981. *Encyclopedia of Indian Philosophies*, vol. 3. Delhi: Motilal Banarsidass.

———. (ed.). 2006. *Encyclopedia of Indian Philosophies*, vol. 11. Delhi: Motilal Banarsidass.

Radhakrishnan, S. 1969. *The Principal Upaniṣads*, ed. trans., with Introduction. London: George Allen and Unwin.

Rāmānuja. 1959. *Śrībhāṣya of Rāmānuja* [RSBh], Part I. R. D. Karmarkar (ed.). Poona: University of Poona.

Sadānanda. 1974. *Vedāntasāra or The Essence of Vedānta of Sadānda Yogındra*. Swami Nikhilananda (trans.). Calcutta: Advaita Ashrama.

Śaṅkara. n.d. *Bhagavad Gītā Bhāṣya of Sri Saṃkarācārya*. A. G. Krishna Warrier (trans.). Madras: Sri Ramakrishna Math.

———. 1965. *Brahma-Sūtra-Bhāṣya of Śaṅkarācārya* [BSBh]. Swami Gambhirananda (trans.). Calcutta: Advaita Ashrama.

———. 1992. A *Thousand Teachings: The Upadeśasāhasrī of Śaṅkara* [US]. Sengaku Mayeda (ed., trans.). Albany: State University of New York Press.

Sarvajñātman. 1985. *The Saṁkṣepaśārīraka of Sarvajñātman* [SS]. N. Veezhinathan (ed., trans.). Madras: Radhakrishnan Institute.

Śāntarakṣita. 1986. *The Tattvasaṅgraha of Śāntarakṣita with the commentary of Kamalaśīla* [TS], vols. 1 and 2. Ganganatha Jha (trans.). Delhi: Motilal Banarsidass.

Solomon, E. A. 1969. *Avidyā: A Problem of Truth and Reality*. Ahmedabad: Gujarat University.

Sureśvara. 1988. *The Naikarmyasiddhi of Sureśvara* [NS]. R. Balasubramanian (ed., trans.). Madras: University of Madras.

———. 1984. *The Taittirīyopaniṣad Bhāṣya-Vārtika of Sureśvara* [TUBhV]. R. Balasubramanian (ed., trans.). Madras: Radhakrishnan Institute for Advanced Study in Philosophy.

Vidyāraṇya. 1965. *Pañcadaśī* [PD]. Hari Prasad Shastri (ed., trans.). London: Shanti Sadan.

Chapter 25
VIŚIṢṬĀDVAITA VEDĀNTA

Christopher Bartley

Viśiṣṭādvaita Vedānta is the doctrinal articulation of the theistic Śrī Vaiṣṇava religious tradition that still flourishes in Tamil Nadu. Its philosophical stance is pluralistic and realistic: the complex universe of individual spiritual and material substances is a real occurrence depending essentially upon the godhead, whose delight is the reason for its being. The term 'Viśiṣṭādvaita', frequently mistranslated as 'qualified non-dualism', is held by the tradition to mean 'the integral unity of complex reality'. Vedānta is the systematic hermeneutic of the Upaniṣads, the brief summaries of the teachings of the latter in the *Brahma-sūtras*, as well as the *Bhagavad Gītā*. The principal concern of Viśiṣṭādvaitin thinkers is to show that their tradition is the authentic expression of those scriptures.

The Śrī Vaiṣṇava tradition absorbed elements from the enthusiastic devotion (*bhakti*) towards a personal deity found in the hymns of the Tamil Ālvārs, the temple and domestic rituals and theology of the Tantric (i.e. non-Vedic) Pāñcarātra *Āgamas*, and a lineage of learned Vaiṣṇava teachers (*ācārya*) specialising in Upaniṣadic exegesis and adept in sophisticated śāstric traditions. They were mainstream orthodox (*smārta*) Brahmins who had adopted Viṣṇu as their patron deity (*iṣṭa-devatā*). The Viśiṣṭādvaitin *ācāryas* Nāthamuni (980–1050 CE), Yāmuna (*c.* 1050–1125 CE) and Rāmānuja (*c.* 1100–1170 CE) and their successors belong to that tradition. Rāmānuja was a creative genius who, following Yāmuna and an earlier commentator on the *Brahma-sūtras* Bodhāyana, synthesised ideas current in the tradition into a realistic and pluralistic philosophical and theology. Other major Viśiṣṭādvaitins and their works include:

Nāthamuni (980–1050): *Nyāyatattva* (known only from quotations).
Yāmuna (1050–1125): *Ātmasiddhi*, *Īśvarasiddhi*, *Saṃvitsiddhi*; *Āgamaprāmāṇyam* (on the validity of the Pañcarātra).
Rāmānuja (1100–1170): *Śrī Bhāṣya* (commentary on the *Brahma-sūtras*), *Vedārthasaṃgraha* (précis of the former); *Bhagavadgītā-bhāṣya*.
Paraśara Bhaṭṭa (1170–1240): *Tattvaratnākara* (quotations from Vedānta Deśika).

Varada (1200–1270): *Prameyamālā*.
Ātreya Rāmānuja (1220–1300): teacher of Vedānta Deśika.
Vedavyāsa (Sudarśanasuri) (1120–1300): *Śrutaprakāśikā* (commentary on *Śrī Bhāṣya*).
Vedānta Deśika (Venkaṭanātha) (1270–1350): *Tattvamuktākalāpa*, *Sarvārthasiddhi*, *Nyāyapariśuddhi*, *Nyāyasiddhāñjana*, *Tātparyacandrikā* (commentary on Rāmānuja's *Gītābhāṣya*), Tattvaṭīkā (commentary on *Śrī Bhāṣya*), *Pāñcarātrarakṣā*.
Śrīnivāsadāsa (1600–1650): *Yatīndramatadīpikā*.

Where the formation of the Śrī Vaiṣṇava tradition is concerned we have to reckon with a confluence of various trends and factors. There is the intense ecstatic devotional cult of the Tamil Ālvār poets, who thought of all devotees equally as servants of God. They model the soul's relationship with God upon that between human lovers and sing of the agony of separation and the bliss of reunion. The theologians, at least in the prose works where they were concerned to demonstrate the concordance of their beliefs and practices with the normative *varṇāśramadharma*, tended to suppress the ecstatic emotionalism and potential social inclusivism of the Ālvār tradition. Nevertheless, they belonged to a monotheistic devotional milieu in which one is encouraged to delight in the awareness that one exists to be a servant of the divinity named Nārāyaṇa. This godhead is a person, a being with will, agency and purposes, upon whom one is radically dependent and in whom one may take refuge. The deity is a compassionate personal being who invites praise and love. This entirely self-sufficient divinity creates and sustains the cosmos for no purpose other than his own delight (*līlā*). He is immanent both as the inner moral guide (*antaryāmin*), and as present in the consecrated temple icon. This is reflected in the soteriologies of Yāmuna and Rāmānuja: performance of the duties appropriate to one's caste and stage of life informed by understanding of the natures of the individual and highest selves combined with ritual worship and devotion invites the grace of the supreme person.[1]

The liturgy in Śrī Vaiṣṇava temples in informed by the non-Vedic Pañcarātra system of theology and ritual. That tradition is probably as old as the Christian era, but it is unlikely that any of the surviving texts were composed before *c*. 850 CE.[2] It sees the world as a real creation by a personally conceived divinity. It emphasises divine immanence and accessibility in the temple icon. It understands people as individual souls. In his *Āgama Prāmāṇyam*, Yāmuna defends against attacks from *Smārtas* the orthodoxy of *Bhāgavata Brahmins* or *Sātvatas* who perform Pāñcarātra temple rituals. Some of these who belong to the *Vājasaneyaśākhā* of the white *Yajur Veda* are of unimpeachable Brahmin status. There are others, who claim adherence to the *Ekāyanaśākhā* and identify the Pāñcarātra *tantras* as the fifth Veda, but Yāmuna sees their activities as on a par with those of *Smārtas*. Suffice it to say here that Rāmānuja accepts the authority (*prāmāṇya*) of the Pāñcarātra-Bhāgavata teaching, rejecting the claim that it is opposed to *śruti* in that that those *tantras* teach that the individual self has a beginning. He denies that the system teaches this. Rāmānuja interprets the Pauṣkara Saṃhitā as teaching that the Supreme Brahman, called Vāsudeva, out of kindness to his devotees continuously chooses to exist in four modes so as to make himself accessible to those resorting to him. The Pāñcarātra teaching was composed by God and conforms to that of the Vedas, understanding of which it facilitates. The system teaches the nature of Nārāyaṇa and the proper way of worshipping him.[3]

Viśiṣṭādvaita Vedānta represents a renewal of an ancient tradition of realistic exegesis of the Upaniṣads. Rāmānuja's sophisticated theological formulation of the *bhakti* religion in opposition to the world-renunciatory Advaitic gnostic tradition was not new. He cites a list of teachers belonging to the Vedāntic tradition of Upaniṣadic exegesis who taught that *bhakti* alone, expressed in action and involving profound understanding, is the path to God.[4]

But Advaitic monism had flourished after the seminal works of Maṇḍana Miśra and Śaṅkara (*fl. c.* 700 CE). They hold that ordinary experience articulating a plurality of individual conscious and non-conscious entities is a beginningless global misconception (*anādi-avidyā*) superimposed upon an inactive and undifferentiated *brahman* whose nature is consciousness, pure and simple. They say that the soul's liberation from rebirth is simply the cessation of ignorance about the true nature of reality, subsequent to the intuitive realisations that one's true identity (*ātman*) is simple awareness (*jñapti-mātra*) and that one is not an individual agent subject to ritual duties and transmigration. This outlook is at odds with what is probably an older tradition of Upaniṣadic exegesis, which sees the real cosmos (*prapañca-sadbhāva*) as an emanation (*pariṇāma*) of the Absolute, as the real self-differentiation of the Supreme Soul – the material cause of all existents.[5] The Viśiṣṭādvaitin teaching that the actual, non-illusory world of conscious and unconscious entities is an organic complex that is both essentially dependent upon God and intrinsically distinct from him belongs to this realistic tradition of thought.

Like all Vedāntins, Rāmānuja assumes that the truth about God can only be known from the timeless Vedic scriptures, primarily the Upaniṣads, the knowledge-portion (*jñāna-kāṇḍa*) of the Vedas. Although only scriptural language, not perception and inferences based upon it, can reveal the truth about the transcendent, Rāmānuja does indicate that we have natural knowledge of God as that which possesses unsurpassable greatness. This is the meaning of the verbal root *bṛh* from which the term Brahman is derived. Unsurpassable greatness includes powers such as omniscience and omnipotence that are properties of that which is both the material and efficient causes of the cosmos. Further content may be added to this concept by texts such as *Taittirīya Upaniṣad* 2.1.1. 'Brahman is reality, consciousness, infinite'.[6]

Only scripture (*śruti*) can tell us about the nature and existence of God. Rāmānuja uses philosophical argument to show that argument cannot prove the existence of God. He adduces a number of considerations against the standard inferences for the existence of God, all of which rely on the general principle (*vyāpti*) that products require an intelligent maker with the appropriate capabilities. For example, although we can infer a producer from human artefacts, we have no knowledge of the origination of natural features. Can we treat the cosmos as a whole as a single product? The complex world consists of many different types of effects and as such cannot license the inference of a single maker. In our experience agents, however capable, are finite and embodied. Brahman is different in kind from everything else. Thus we cannot infer that it is an agent in the sense in which we understand agency.[7]

The Advaitic concepts of the simple Absolute as impersonal, static, consciousness, and of the non-individual soul (identical with that Absolute principle) as utterly transcendental and detached from personal experiences are the fruits of the mystic renouncer's contemplative experience in whose light the everyday world appears as less than fully real. But these basic insights are problematic when it comes to explaining the genesis of the finite universe and its relation to an authentic reality that has nothing in common with the world. The developed Advaitin attributes the plural universe and our diversified experiences to the operation of a positive force (*bhāva-rūpa*) called *avidyā* (non-knowing). This *avidyā* is the substrative cause of the cosmos, and as such is not to be equated with our everyday notions of ignorance and misconception. Avidyā is said to project diversity and conceal the state of undifferentiated being that is termed *brahman*. When it is obscured by *avidyā*, the one spiritual reality appears (*vivartate*) as the world.[8] *Avidyā* explains why we unenlightened beings mistakenly but inevitably believe that there are any individual entities that are really distinct from one another. Causative *avidyā*, and its product, the cosmos, are indeterminable or inexpressible (*anirvacanīya*) as either real or unreal. The Viśiṣṭādvaita tradition rejects the latter claim as incoherent: if something is not real, it is unreal. If it is not unreal, it is real. If it is neither real nor unreal, it is both real and unreal. If *avidyā* is a real force that is different from the *brahman*, then monism is compromised. If *avidyā* belongs to the *brahman*, then it exists absolutely or never. They insist that ignorance cannot be a subsistent entity with causal efficacy. It is just the absence of knowledge. Moreover, the putative causal ignorance must have a substrate. It cannot be *brahman*, which is pure knowledge. Nor can it be individual selves since they are said by Advaitins to be products of ignorance. There is also the consequence that the capacity of the scriptures to convey the truth is undermined because they belong to the differentiated world that is the sphere of *avidyā*.[9]

The Advaitic proposition that reality is unitary and undifferentiated quickly attracted the objection that there is no means of establishing its truth (*pramāṇa*). The successful operation of means of knowledge on their objects presupposes a duality of act and its object. Rāmānuja is elaborate in his argumentation that there is no rational means of proving that reality is undifferentiated pure consciousness (*nirviśeṣa-cinmātra*).[10] Rāmānuja is an epistemological direct realist, holding that all cognitions are intrinsically valid just in virtue of their occurrence. Apprehension is always of the real (*sat-khyāti*). All perceptual cognition, even when misleading (*bhrama*), is in accordance with what is the case independently of our thoughts (*yathārtha*). Direct realism involves minimising or explaining away what are ordinarily viewed as perceptual errors and hallucinations. For example, when mother-of-pearl is mistaken for silver, we are actually detecting traces of silver in the mother-of-pearl.[11] Cognitions are intrinsically formless (*nirākāra*) and assume the forms of their objects. The lack of subjective contribution eliminates perceptual distortion. An extra-mental environment, consisting of stable objects that endure through space and time, is responsible for the variety of experiences. Truth is correspondence, understood as structural isomorphism, between cognition and the world. The subject–object structure of cognition is self-evident and embodied in normal language. Every cognition belongs to a subject to which it is manifest. All cognitions are about objects outside the mind.[12]

Implicit in Rāmānuja's critique of the notion that authentic reality (the *brahman*) is simple consciousness is an appeal to a principle upheld by the Indian realist traditions: whatever is, is knowable and nameable. All the means of knowledge grasp entities having properties. Thought and language are possible only with respect to entities identifiable by their specific characteristics. The language of scripture (*śabda-pramāṇa*), like all language, is composite and relational, and its complexity reflects that of its objects.[13] Sensory perception (*pratyakṣa*), whether non-conceptual (*nirvikalpaka*) or conceptual (*savikalpaka*), cannot establish the existence of a non-differentiated reality. Thinkers of the Nyāya-Vaiśeṣika and Mīmāṃsaka traditions tried to distinguish the two types of perception in various ways. The problem is difficult: to what extent can non-conceptual perception lack specificity while still referring to something? Is it possible to apprehend a 'bare particular' devoid of specific and generic features? Advaitin thinkers appeal to the example of non-conceptual perception in arguing that there can be apprehension of simple being or a featureless reality.[14] The Viśiṣṭādvaitins reject the mainstream view upheld by Naiyāyikas and Mīmāṃsakas that *nirvikalpaka* perception grasps the bare particular (*vastu-mātra*) without reference to features such as names, quality, substance and generic property.[15] Rāmānuja says that the object of *savikalpaka-pratyakṣa* (conceptual perception) is differentiated since it refers to that which is characterised by several categorial features (*padārtha*) including generic property, qualities and substance. The non-classificatory perception (*nirvikalpa*) must be differentiated too since it provides the information that enables the comparison and classification of entities in conceptual perception. Rāmānuja says that non-conceptual perception is the apprehension of an entity as lacking some differentia, but not of every differentiating feature, since apprehension of the latter kind is never encountered and is in any case impossible. Every cognition arises in virtue of some differentia and is specifically verbalised in the form, 'this is such and such a kind of thing'. The difference lies in the fact that in *nirvikalpa-pratyakṣa* a complex entity, analysable in terms of the categories of substance, specific and generic properties, is cognised, but what is missing is knowledge of the recurrence (*anuvṛtti*) of those features in other entities of the same kind. In *nirvikalpa-pratyakṣa* we cognise an individual and its concrete generic structure (*jāti*, construed as *ākṛti* or *saṃsthāna*) as distinct. But since the structure has been seen in but one individual we cannot generalise and form a concept. The key point is that since non-classificatory perception is complex and since there is a structural isomorphism between knowing and the known, it cannot yield knowledge of an undifferentiated reality. Finally, inference (*anumāna*) relies upon perceptual data and is thus incapable of revealing featureless reality.[16]

The Advaitins think that one's true identity (*ātman*) is a state of tranquil, impersonal consciousness. Devotional theism requires that the soul is an individual entity, capable of responding to God. Viśiṣṭādvaita maintains that we are such beings, enduring substantial entities that are really distinct from our bodies. We are subjects of experiences, without being reducible to streams of experiences. Each eternal soul has its own ineffable identity that is known only to itself. Agency, which requires some form of embodiment, is always a contingency whether the soul is bound or released.[17] The Viśiṣṭādvaitin philosophers propound defences of common-sense realism about selves as persisting centres of reflexive awareness oriented towards mind-independent realities. Embodiment is crucial in that it enables agency and the sorts of experience that exhaust the accumulated *karma* of souls in bondage to rebirth. (The tradition does not understand *karma* as an automatic mechanism. Rather it is an expression of the will of God. It operation is a perfectly just mechanism, rewarding and punishing souls for their actions.) It is *karma* (not ignorance *per se*) that contracts the soul's intrinsically unlimited consciousness. This means that we misidentify ourselves with the particular embodied status that is its product.[18]

The Viśiṣṭādvaitins say that consciousness is self-luminous, intentional and active. It is unique in that it does not require anything else to establish its existence (*svataḥ siddha*). Consciousness is an essential property of a soul, which is its agent and substrate.[19] The soul is incorrigibly revealed as 'I' in every conscious state.[20] We are immediately aware (*ātma-sākṣika*) of ourselves as persisting identities whose essential property is consciousness. Consciousness is a property of the soul that is its agent. It is directed towards objects. It is disposed to illuminate objects to its substrate.[21] Thoughts are properties that require a thinking subject. All conscious states are intentional: they are acts on the part of a subject directed towards some object or fact.[22] They are also self-illuminating or intrinsically reflexive (*svayaṃ prakāśa*). This means that when a subject cognises something, simultaneously and in virtue of the same act he is aware of himself as cognising that reality. More broadly, the quality of each and every experience of the external world is informed by the mood of its subject. The Viśiṣṭadvaitins rule out the possibility of contentless awareness (*nirviśeṣa-cinmātra*). Awareness is always complex and always of something. Moreover, consciousness is in a state of flux. Were it identical with the self, it would be impossible to recognise something seen today as the same thing seen the previous day.[23] The self is not a bundle of fleeting experiences. It is the persisting subject that has the experiences – a principle of continuity with a witness' perspective upon the states that it co-ordinates. It is the agent of mental acts and its permanence as such and the momentary nature of those acts are both directly perceived. Consciousness is both substance (*dravya*) and quality-particular (*guṇa*) and its nature is to render entities susceptible of thought speech and action. As the essential property (*svarūpa-nirūpaṇa-dharma*) of the soul, it exists substantially, but as discrete mental acts possessed by the self, it exists attributively.[24]

The Advaitic tradition says that one's everyday feeling of personal identity, the sense of oneself as an individual agent subject to religious and social duties and confronting a world of objects, is a mask concealing the identity of one's consciousness with the impersonal, inactive Absolute beyond differentiation. The illusion occurs when the light of consciousness is confused with the activity of the material intellect (*buddhi*). Rāmānuja's tradition denies that our everyday feeling of continuous personal identity is an illusion or a case of mistaken identity. It is integral to theistic *bhakti* that the self that understands itself as a servant and lover of God should be the authentic self. The 'I' that thinks, intends and acts is the real self. The pronoun 'I' ultimately stands for the inner self that is itself ensouled by God, its inner guide and sustainer.[25]

As Nāthamuni puts it in the *Nyāya-tattva*:

> If 'I' did not refer to the true self, there would be no interiority of the soul. The interior is distinguished from the exterior by the concept 'I'. The aspiration, 'May I, having abandoned all suffering, participate freely in infinite bliss', actuates a person whose goal is liberation to study scripture etc. Were it thought that liberation involved the destruction of the individual, he would run away as soon as the subject of liberation was suggested .... The 'I', the knowing subject, is the inner self.[26]

Rāmānuja's ontology is structured as a hierarchy of three really distinct categories: the personal God Nārāyaṇa who is the first cause and sovereign of the cosmos, and also immanent in the individual souls; individual souls that are the subjects of experience; physical bodies occupying the material environment that are the objects of experience.[27] Rāmānuja's basic conception, derived from *śrutis* such as *Bṛhadāraṇyaka Upaniṣad* 3.7.ff. and *Subāla Upaniṣad* 7, is that the cosmos of souls and matter is the body of God (*śarīra-śarīri-bhāva*).[28] This is not intended as merely one possible interpretation amongst others, one provisional model, a useful way of thinking about God and the world. It is thoroughly Vedically based. It is what the Upaniṣads, the sole source of Vedāntic theology, teach.

The relationship between God and the world is parallel to that between an individual self and its body. The key features are essential dependence and difference. He defines a body as any substance (*dravya*) can control and support entirely for its own purposes and whose *raison d'être* is to be an ancillary (*śeṣa*) to that entity. All conscious (*cit*) and non-conscious (*acit*) entities are the body of the Supreme Person since they are controlled and supported by him exclusively for his own purposes and their *raison d'être* is to be his ancillaries. The relation between soul and body is that between ontic ground (*ādhāra*) and dependent entity (*ādheya*) that cannot exist separately, between controller and thing controlled, between master and servant. The 'body' term is a dependent mode (*prakāra*) incapable of existing separately (*apṛthak-siddhi*; *pṛthak-sthiti-pravṛtti-anarha*). Souls and matter may exist potentially (Brahman's causal state) or actually (Brahman's effected state). In either case they are ensouled by God and cannot exist independently of him because they are internally controlled by God and constitute his body. By being present in the individual selves, God is present in matter. It is only because souls and material objects are ensouled by God that they are entities. Just as a parcel of matter only becomes a body when animated by a soul, so the souls are entities only by virtue of the divine presence in turn. Ontic dependence means that entities exist only as sustained by God.

Rāmānuja accepts the *satkāryavāda* theory of causation according to which an effect exists potentially in its causal substrate prior to its actualisation as an entity with determinate name and form. An effect is a different state of the material cause (*upādāna-kāraṇa*) of which it is a transformation (*pariṇāma*). It is not a completely different substance. Brahman is held to be the material and efficient cause of the cosmos, which is accordingly a single, organic and intelligible process. There is an *analogia entis*, a commonality of being, between God and the world. Rāmānuja interprets the Upaniṣadic principle that 'by knowledge of the one, there is knowledge of the whole' as meaning that by understanding the nature of a substrative cause one understands the nature of its effects. Understanding the scriptural statements about Brahman is the key to understanding the world.

God, 'one without a second', is the material or substrative cause (*upādāna-kāraṇa*) of the cosmos and not an independent principle such as the *pradhāna* of the Sāṃkhyas or the real *māyā* of the Śaiva Siddhāntins. God is both cause and effect: cause when *cit* and *acit* entities are in their latent condition, and effect when they have evolved and acquired names and forms. Cause and effect are ontically continuous. The manifest cosmos is a real transformation (*pariṇāma*) in which the three categories maintain their discrete identities.

'Since everything forms the body of the Supreme Person, he is directly signified by every word.' Rāmānuja has a semantic principle that the signification of essentially dependent modal entities (such as bodies) extends to the mode possessor. Whenever something is *essentially* in an attributive relation to something else (this includes the relations between qualities (*guṇas*), generic properties (*sāmānya, ākṛti*) and the individual substances (*dravya*) to which they belong as well as that between souls and bodies), the terms for the attributes may also refer to the possessor. God has created the denotative force of words together with the entities for which they stand. Any self is a mode of Brahman since it is included in Brahman's body. Types such as human bodies are modes of their souls. Words for bodies signify in their primary senses both the conscious entities ensouling them and God *qua* the inner controller and guide (*antaryāmin*) of the self. Thus God's immanence as the soul of each soul is the basis of the literal reference of scriptural language to Him.

Thinkers of the Bhedābhedavāda tradition such as Bhāskara and Yādava Prakāśa (1050–1125: originally an Advaitin, then Rāmānuja's teacher) formulated versions of pantheism according to which the cosmos of souls and matter emanates from God.[29] This was repugnant to Rāmānuja's tradition. According to the Bhedābhedavāda, Brahman is the all-encompassing category of being of which all entities are instances – the emanations are actually instances of God. Their Absolute is originally undifferentiated being, void of qualities, actions, kinds and individualities, but becomes threefold as subjects of experience, objects and the controller. This self-limitation is a form of conditioning. The cosmos is just a different form of its material cause. Effects are not really different from their material causes and the world is non-different from Brahman. The individual self is but Brahman affected by ignorance (*avidyā*), *karma* and appetite (*kāma*). Rāmānuja's objection is that this view converts the Unconditioned into finite reality, subject to transmigration, imperfection and suffering. One reason for developing the 'three-level ontology' in which Brahman, souls and matter are essentially distinct is to avoid the undesirable consequence that the Absolute is implicated in the vicissitudes of finite existence. Thus he replaced the *Brahma-pariṇāma* theory with the idea that real transformation occurs only in the sphere of the entities that constitute Brahman's body. Brahman is essentially distinct from its dependent modes: its proper form abides intact.

It is in the field of scriptural exegesis that the soul–body model comes into its own. The interpretation of co-referential (*samānādhikaraṇa*) statements such as '*Tat tvam asi*' ('That thou art', expressing a relation between the self and Brahman) and '*Satyaṃ jñānam anantaṃ Brahma*' ('Brahman is reality, consciousness, infinite': *Taittirīya Upaniṣad* 2.1.1) is central to Vedāntic theology. *Samānādhikaraṇa* means the co-occurrence of two or more items (e.g. an individual substance and its properties) in the same locus or substrate. In grammatical usage, it is the reference to one object by several terms having different grounds for their application. The words are in apposition. Such constructions appear in scriptures expressing the relationship between God and the world, God and the self or, in the case of '*Satyaṃ jñānam anantaṃ Brahma*', as saying something about the divine nature.

Vedāntins believe that the language of revealed *śruti* is our only means of knowledge (*pramāṇa*) about transcendent reality. We have no cognitive access to God independently of the infallible and authorless scriptural authorities. Rāmānuja is a realist holding that there is an isomorphism between knowledge and the known. There is also a structural isomorphism between scriptural statements and the reality of which they speak. It is not just the meanings of words that are informative. Grammatical constructions reflect the nature of reality. There is a sense in which the theory of meaning determines metaphysics. Advaitins emphasise the singularity of reference and construe co-referential constructions as identity-statements conveying an impartite essence void of properties (*akhaṇḍārtha*). This involves attributing non-literal senses (*lakṣaṇā-artha*) to the co-ordinated words, and this is seen as an exegetical failing. Advaitins think that the different grounds for the application of the terms are subjective modes of presentation, on the level of human understanding rather than that of objective being. Rāmānuja's tradition maintains that the grounds for the application are objective differences proper to the referent. *Sāmānādhikaraṇya* (co-referentiality) is thus the reference to a complex reality by words expressing its different features. 'I am fat' is a typical co-referential statement, where the body is spoken of in co-ordination with the self. Rāmānuja says that co-referentiality expresses a single entity characterised by its essentially dependent modes. He interprets co-referential statements about God and features of creation as expressive of the soul–body relation. Advaitins attribute a specialised sense to each term: 'that' stands for the impersonal Absolute, and 'thou', purged of its everyday connotations of finitude and individuality, stands for the true inner self, immutable pure consciousness. The statement expresses the identity of the two. But according to the Viśiṣṭādvaita exegesis, the 'that' stands for the creator God, the inner guide of the soul. 'Thou' stands for an individual self, an essentially dependent mode of God. '*Tat*' denotes the Highest Self, which is the cause of the universe, whose purposes are ever-actualised (*satya-saṃkalpa*), who possesses every exalted quality and who is devoid of every trace of imperfection. '*Tvam*' denotes the same Brahman embodied by the individual self, along with the body of the latter. The grammatical co-ordination conveys the unity (not identity) of the two. The co-referential terms apply in their primary senses.

The principles that words for modes also refer to mode possessors and that co-referential constructions express dependent modality enable Rāmānuja to interpret many scriptural statements that had been treated as favourable to Advaitic monism in a theistic manner.[30] His work invigorated the intellectual articulation and defence of the devotionalism that has always been at the heart of Indian religious life.

Abbreviations

GBh: Gītābhāṣyam = Buitenen (1953)
SBh: Śrībhāṣyam = Abhyankar (1914)
ST: Siddhitrayam = Ramanujachari and Srinivasacharya (1972)
Veds: Vedārthasaṃgraha = Buitenen (1956)
YID: Yatīndramatadīpikā = Svāmī Ādidevānanda (1949)

Notes

1 Veds §3. Cf. Yāmuna's *Gītārthasaṃgraha* 1 (in GBh): Nārāyaṇa, the Supreme Brahman, is only accessible by devotion (*bhakti*) accomplishable by the observance of one's social and religious duty, informed by knowledge and dispassion.For the important notion of *antaryāmin* (deriving from *Bṛhadāraṇyaka Upaniṣad* 3.7.1ff. and Pāñcarātra), see Oberhammer (1998).
2 Schrader (1973); Gupta (2000); Oberhammer and Rastelli (2002, 2007); and Sanderson (2001) for dating. and the argument that the received forms of two of the best known, the *Lakṣmī Tantra* and *Ahirbudhnya Saṃhitā*, exhibit signs of Śaiva (Pratyabhijñā) philosophical influences and probably belong to the twelfth century.
3 Van Buitenen (1971); Neevel (1977). SBh 2.2.40–43.
4 Veds §§92–93.
5 Danielson 1980 (Ādiśeṣa's *Paramārthasāra*). Sanderson (2006) establishes that the Kashmiri Śaiva Siddhāntin Sadyojyotis (c. 650–700) refers to realistic theism and emanationism (*pariṇāma-vāda*) in his *Nareśvaraparīkṣā*. The views appear to be those of Bhartṛprapañca (c. 550 CE), expressed in his commentary on the *Bṛhadāraṇyaka Upaniṣad*, q.v. Hiriyanna (1972).
6 SBh 1.1.2. See Bartley (2002, ch. 5) for exegeses of the *Taittirīya* definition.
7 SBh 1.1.3. See Yāmuna's *Īśvarasiddhi* for a Nyāya-style inferential proof of a creator God.
8 For exposition of the Advaitic position and identifications of Rāmānuja's actual opponents see Bartley (2002, ch. 1 *et passim*) and Mesquita (1984).
9 GBh 2.12; SBh 1.1.1, pp. 83ff.; Veds §§36, 40, 44, 46–52.
10 SBh 1.1.1, p. 28.
11 YID ch.1, §§ 23–24 for a synopsis.
12 SBh 1.1.1, p. 39; See Lipner (1986, ch. 4).
13 SBh 1.1.1, p. 28.
14 Bartley (2002, 34ff.) for sources.
15 YID p. 20.
16 SBh 1.1.1, pp. 29ff.; Veds §30.
17 Veds §5.

18 SBh 1.1.1, p. 45.
19 SBh 2.3.19.
20 SBh 1.1.1, p. 39. ST p. 5.
21 SBh 1.1.1, pp. 34, 39–39. ST p. 30.
22 Veds §28.
23 SBh 1.1.1, p. 39; ST p. 25.
24 YID ch. 7. Lipner (1986, ch. 3).
25 SBh 1.1.1, p. 41. Bartley (2002, pp. 58ff.). Lipner (1986, pp. 51–52).
26 SBh 1.1.1, pp. 40–41.
27 SBh 1.1.1, p. 116.; Veds §65.
28 For a succinct account: GBh 13,1–2. For detailed exposition see Bartley (2002) Ch. 3; Lipner (1986) Ch. 7; Carman (1974).
29 For the former see Veds §§54–57. For the latter, Veds §§58–64; Bartley (2002, pp. 80f.); Oberhammer (1997) for Yādava.
30 For the synthesis see Veds §§84–85.

References

Primary sources

Abhyankar, V. S. 1914. *Śrībhāṣya by Rāmānujācārya*. Bombay: Government Central Press.

Buitenen, J. A. B. van. 1953. *Rāmānuja on the Bhagavadgītā*. The Hague: H. L. Smits.

———. 1956. *Rāmānuja's Vedārthasaṃgraha*. Poona: Deccan College.

———. 1971. *Yāmuna's Āgama Prāmāṇyam or Treatise of the Validity of Pāñcarātra*. Madras: Adyar Library.

Danielson, Henry. 1980. *Ādiśeṣa: The Essence of Supreme Truth (Paramārthasāra)*. Leiden: E. J. Brill.

Olivelle, P. 1998. *The Early Upaniṣads*. New York and Oxford: Oxford University Press.

Ramanujachari, R. and Srinivasacharya, K. 1972. *Sri Yamunacharya's Siddhi Trayam*. Madras: Ubhaya Vedanta Granthamala.

Svāmī Ādidevānanda. 1949. *Yatīndramatadīpikā*. Madras: Sri Ramakrishna Math.

Other sources

Bartley, C. J. 2002. *The Theology of Rāmānuja*. London: RoutledgeCurzon.

Carman, J. B. 1974. *The Theology of Rāmānuja*. New Haven, CT: Yale University Press.

Gupta, Sanjukta. 2000. *Lakṣmī Tantra: A Pāñcarātra Text*. Delhi, Motilal Banarsidass.

Hardy, Friedhelm. 1983. *Viraha-Bhakti: The Early History of Kṛṣṇa Devotion in South India*. Delhi: Oxford University Press.

Hiriyanna, M. 1972. 'Fragments of Bhartṛprapañca.' In *Indian Philosophical Studies*, vol. 2. Mysore: Kavyalaya Publishers.

Lipner, Julius. 1986. *The Face of Truth*. Basingstoke: Macmillan.

Mesquita, R. 1984. 'Rāmānuja's Quellen im Mahāpūrvapakṣa und Mahāsiddhānta des Śrībhāṣya.' *Wiener Zeitschrift für die Kunde Südasiens* 28: 179–222.

Neevel, W. G. 1977. *Yāmuna's Vedānta and Pāñcarātra: Integrating the Classical and the Popular*. Montana: Scholars Press.

Oberhammer, G. 1997. *Yādavaprakāśa, der Vergessene Lehrer Rāmānujas*. Vienna: Verlag der Österreichischen Akademie der Wissenschaften.

———. 1998. *Der 'Innere Lenker' (Antaryāmī): Geschichte eines Theologems*. Vienna: Verlag der Österreichischen Akademie der Wissenschaften.

Oberhammer, G. and Rastelli, M. 2002. *Studies in Hinduism III: Pāñcarātra and Viśiṣṭādvaitavedānta*. Vienna: Verlag der Österreichischen Akademie der Wissenschaften.

———. 2007. *Studies in Hinduism IV: On the Mutual Influences and Relationship of Viśiṣṭādvaitavedānta and Pāñcarātra*. Vienna: Verlag der Österreichischen Akademie der Wissenschaften.
Sanderson, A. 2001. 'History through Textual Criticism.' In Grimal, F. (ed.) *Les Sources et le temps. Sources and Time*. Pondicherry: Institut Français de Pondichéry.
———. 2006. 'The Date of Sadyojyotis and Bṛhaspati.' *Cracow Indological Studies* 8: 39–91.
Schrader, F. O. 1973. *Introduction to the Pāñcarātra and the Ahirbudhnya Saṃhitā*. Madras: Adyar Library.

Chapter 26
AN OVERVIEW OF CLASSICAL YOGA PHILOSOPHY AS A PHILOSOPHY OF EMBODIED SELF-AWARENESS

Ana Laura Funes Maderey

Introduction

In the wider sense of the term, yoga refers to a method or a set of different physical and mental disciplines that were practiced throughout South Asia to attain human liberation even before it became a philosophical orthodox system approximately in the second or fourth century CE with the appearance of the *Yogasūtra* of Patañjali. Not only what we now call Hindu, but also Buddhist and Jaina, traditions incorporated the practice of yoga as a means to realizing an enlightened state of being. We could say that it was due to the different ways in which these groups related to the practice of yoga that their varied philosophical traditions developed. The influence of a self-discipline is of such importance to the formation of Indian philosophies that some scholars like Stephen Phillips refer to most of the classical philosophical schools of India as 'Yoga philosophy' (Phillips 2009, 31). This idea finds its precedent in Mircea Eliade's *Patañjali and Yoga* where he states that: 'No one knows of a single Indian spiritual movement that is not dependent on one of the numerous forms of yoga' (Eliade 1969, 5).

With some exceptions, like the materialist heterodox school of the Cārvākas and the Mīmāṁsā orthodoxy, a common element in classical Indian philosophies is the acceptance of a 'yogic perception', that is, a special type of *pramāṇa* (means of knowledge) distinguished from the one provided by the senses, reasoning, analogy, or testimony. Yogic perception can be defined as the immediate presentation to awareness of an object or truth through meditation, i.e., through a practice of concentration and contemplation (*samādhi*) that is not mediated by the senses or thoughts. Indeed, the debate on the veracity of this type of perception is relevant for the history of Indian epistemology. However, the purpose of this chapter is to demonstrate the development of a non-reductionist conception of embodiment and a multilayered process of self-awareness implicit in the possibility of such 'yogic perception', especially as these developments were articulated during the initial stages of orthodox Yoga philosophy and up to its classical formulation in Patañjali's *Yogasūtra*.

The anatomy of a chariot

The practice of yogic meditation probably first developed within the context of ritual and world-affirming values like those present in Vedic culture. The elaboration of Vedic rituals in ancient India involved many elements that we would recognize as precursors of Yoga doctrines and practices, such as the recitation of mantras, purificatory practices and austerities in preparation for the ritual, rigorous breathing and concentration techniques, precise movements of the body and hands in connection with the instruments used for the sacrifice (*yajña*), and devotional invocations to obtain the blessing of a god. The term '*yoga*' appears in the Rig Veda where it is used with its etymological meaning derived from the root '*yuj*', to yoke, join, fasten, or harness (White 2012, 3). Initially, 'yoking' emerged in the context of harnessing warhorses to a chariot or yoking oxen to a plow, both of which required a certain degree of skill and mastery. It was during a later stage of the Vedic scriptures, in the Upaniṣads, when the former image became a clearer metaphor for the embodied self, used to convey a 'yoking' of the senses and mental processes in order to experience mastery of the self over the body–mind complex.

We can first see a concise articulation of yogic ideas on embodiment and self-awareness in the *Kaṭha Upaniṣad*. A young brahman, Naciketas, asks Yama, the Lord of Death, about the destiny of a person when she dies. Yama refuses to answer the question, and tries to distract Naciketas by offering him worldly pleasures, but Naciketas remains undisturbed by them. Yama is pleased with Naciketas' level of detachment and determination demonstrated and reveals to him the truth about death that lies beyond the senses and immediate gratification of desires. Then the metaphor of the chariot is introduced as an injunction to: 'Know the self as the one who possesses and rides the chariot; the body as the chariot itself. Know the intellect as the charioteer; and the mind as the reins' (*Kaṭha Upaniṣad*, 3.3–6 in Olivelle 1998, 389). The senses are the horses which, if not trained, follow the path of desire and ignorance. Only someone with a disciplined mind can govern the senses. With these under control, then one is able to look within and become aware of the layers of one's own being. Only then can the truth be known and immortality achieved (ibid., 3.10–16.).

The ultimate goal for cultivating an extrasensory insight of oneself is to liberate the Self from its attachment to the chariot, that is, from the body (*śarīra*), which, in the full sense of the term, includes the organs of perception and action (*indriya*-s) as well as the intellect (*buddhi*) and mind (*manas*), and thus gain mastery over it. Those who accept the possibility of a yogic perception do it on the grounds that verbal statements are not enough to know those objects that are beyond the range of senses (such as the true nature of the self; the identity between the individual self and Brahman; the law of cause and effect of actions, or spiritual liberation). Yogic philosophies consider that if a statement is true, then we should be able to experience those truths directly through adequate means.

Yogic perception, self, and embodied awareness

Mīmāmsaka philosophers argued that yogic perception cannot be a means of knowing the truths transmitted by tradition, because, even if possible, it would be useless. People who are not yogis would not be able to distinguish whether someone is a yogi or not (McCrea 2009, 56). In other words, it would be impossible to determine whether someone knows what they claim to know unless we knew it ourselves, in which case, we would not need the teacher or the tradition. But we do need them, so yogic perception seems to be useless after all. Those who claim their traditions to be founded on yogic perception or meditative insight face the problem of explaining why their founder's vision is so different and contrary to the vision of another. They end up, according to this objection, arbitrarily validating a private perception as universal.

Certainly, the traditions arising from the Upaniṣads, the Buddha, and the Jaina are seen as being founded on a yogic meditative experience; and true enough, at least as far as their metaphysical views go, they diverge considerably. For example, the image of the chariot is used in *Milindapañha* (II.1.25), a Buddhist dialogue between King Milinda and Nāgasena, to show, contrary to the Upaniṣads, that there is no self that commands the chariot. Nāgasena argues that, if the human being is analogous to a chariot, then there is nothing in the chariot that would correspond to a 'self', for what we call 'self' is but a convenient designation of the ephemeral parts, their organization and functions, and the chariot itself is nothing beyond that. Within the Buddhist context, yogic perception is the capacity by which we directly experience the impermanence of all things and the non-existence of the self; the only experience that is able to bring liberation according to Buddhist philosophy.

Rich and heated philosophical debates regarding the content of yogic perceptions developed within orthodox Indian philosophies and Buddhism reaching no formal agreement. For the Mīmāṃsākas, the only way to avoid the arbitrariness of personal yogic insights was to postulate an authorless, non-human source for the tradition and deny any meaningful epistemological validity to yogic perception, for knowledge of the tradition is available to everyone in their normal capacities, and not just for those with yogic capacities (McCrea 2009, 57). Even though it is true that the content of yogic perception or, perhaps better said, the interpretation of the experience given by yogic insight, might diverge from one tradition to another, all Yoga philosophies admit the following: that there is an extrasensory insight available to anyone who undergoes a process of self-awareness, whatever the ultimate sense of 'self' may be. Although personal, a process of self-awareness is not private, for it is not a mere mental process, but a practice that engages the body–mind system as a whole in a methodical way, and it is this which gives the yogic experience its intersubjectivity. The specificities of the method may depend on the tradition, but it is presupposed by all Yoga philosophy that such method is needed for the simple reason that to know one's self (or non-self) is something that cannot be done just by the senses, reason, or speech, but by direct, unmediated self-perception, in other words, through meditation (*Manduka Upaniṣad*, 3.8, in Olivelle 1998, 451)

Meditation, embodiment, and self-awareness in classical Yoga philosophy

Yoga is defined as 'a state of meditative contemplation or absorption (*samādhi*)' by Vyāsa (*yogah samādhih*, *YBh* I.1), the earliest known commentator of the *Yogasūtra* of Patañjali (*YS*). Later commentators called this work the *Sāṁkhyapravacanabhāṣya* (A Commentary on an Interpretation of the Sāṁkhya) because, philosophically, it was always understood within the metaphysical framework of the Sāṁkhyan system and, historically, because it seems to have been originated as a creative elaboration on the old Sāṁkhya philosophy (see Larson and Bhattacharya 2008; Frauwallner 2008).

Sāṁkhya philosophy had argued for the need of knowing one's self (*puruṣa*)—pure consciousness, infinite and immutable—as metaphysically distinct to matter (*prakṛti*)—mutable and insentient—in order to eradicate suffering from its root. Without discriminating self from matter, the individual undergoes a process of misidentification where there is no knowledge of one's own nature as pure consciousness, and thus the person is subjected to and affected by the changes and limiting conditions of matter. Both principles, although ontologically distinct, are always co-present and all-pervasive, and it is precisely this conjunction (*samyoga*) which creates the evolutionary process (*Sāṁkhya Kārika* [*SK*] 21). The self, by its very nature, cannot help but to observe the changes and transformations of the material principle which, without an observer, would not have any purpose at all (*SK* 17). One of the very first combinations of the qualitative substances (*guṇa*-s) that constitute the material principle gives origin to the intellect (*buddhi*), from which egoity or the I-sense (*ahaṁkara*) emerges (*SK* 22). From egoity matter reconfigures itself in five subtle elements (*tanmātra*-s)—sound, touch, smell, form, and taste— which will then constitute the gross elements (*bhuta*-s)— ether or space, air, earth, fire, and water—on the objective side of the process. On the subjective side, egoity gives rise to the mind (*manas*), the five sense capacities (vision, smell, taste, hearing, touch) and the five action capacities (speech, grasping, walking, excreting, reproducing). Although Yoga does not take the functions of the intellect, egoity, and the mind to be separate ontological elements, but rather aspects of the same mental capacity or *citta*, it agrees with Sāṁkhya in that twenty four material elements or *tattvas* constitute the whole realm of experience (physical and phenomenal), and thus, the embodiment with which sentient beings experience such realm.

With few variations, Yoga philosophy assumed the same evolutionary process as described by the classical Sāṁkhya school. However, in working out the distinction between *puruṣa* and *prakṛti*—the seer and the seen— the *YS* does not start with a metaphysical point of view that focuses on the dualistic relationship between these principles. (See Whicher 1998 and his chapter in this volume.) The distinction is found instead through an embodied approach to self-awareness (*svarūpadarśana*). The knowledge of one's self as distinct from that which is constantly changing is the result of an effort that involves becoming aware of all aspects of the body, clearly outlined by Patañjali in the eight parts of Yoga (*YS* II.28–29).

Samādhi is the culmination of a process that starts with the purification of the body and its actions, both in the physical and moral sense (with the *yama*-s and *niyama*-s, *YS* II.30–32); followed by a practice of physical stillness and steady posture that allows for the mental faculties to rest and focus despite distractions posed by opposite sensations (*YS* II.46–48). The yoga posture (*āsana*) is understood as a position of the body that creates the conditions for meditation. Keeping the physical body still and steady is an embodied way to become aware of the more subtle internal transformations that normally go unnoticed, like the constant movement of our breath. The aim is to achieve a moment of stillness within the movements of inhalation and exhalation (*prāṇāyāma*) so that even subtler movements of matter become noticeable (*YS* II.49–52). Then sensations may come to the forefront, but the tendency of the sense organs to go after them is also to be withdrawn (*pratyāhāra*) so that an internal and even more refined awareness can emerge (*YS* II.54). Having withdrawn the faculties of sensory perception, the movements of the mind —*cittavṛtti*, i.e., perceptions, thoughts (correct and incorrect), images, dreams, memories—become more evident. At this point, the process of self-awareness follows the same structure as before: one must observe the objective mutations taking place within oneself and detach from them until a point of arrest is achieved.

The self reaches an awareness of the movements of the mind because the mind has a natural capacity for fixation. Every time the mind perceives, thinks or remembers something, it becomes fixated on a particular object. A distracted mind switches its point of focus continuously. However, when focus is maintained and a similar flow of ideas and attention is given to one object, then the mind enters in a meditative state (*dhyānam*). The continuous and steady practice of meditation gives rise to *samādhi*, or the yogic state of contemplation. To place the mind in a point of focus or *dhāraṇā* (*YS* III.1); to maintain a constant flow of attention towards an object or *dhyānam* (*YS* III.2); and *samādhi*, to let the object shine forth in the mind as if it was empty of its own form, constitute the three final most internalized processes of the practice of classical yoga, in which complete integration (*saṁyama*) of the cognitive faculties is meant to occur.

It is through meditation and the awareness of one's subjectivity that our body–mind system ('the chariot') is 'yoked' to the will (Bhattacharya 1956, 221–222). The sensory and mental faculties are not permitted to function as they would normally do: when affected by the object, they cannot help but chase it when moved by desire (*rāga*) or to avoid it when moved by aversion (*dveṣa*), thus creating the illusion that it is the self who enjoys and suffers. Yogic practice brings this normal tendency to a point of arrest (*nirodha*). It is by exercising the power of not being automatically affected by the object that we have experience of our will. The power of detachment (*vairāgya*) is experienced throughout the different levels of awareness arising in the eightfold yogic process just described, and becomes more refined during the stages (*samāpatti*-s) that constitute the structure of yogic meditative absorption (*YS* I.17): absorption in the awareness concerning the empirical objects (*vitarka*); absorption in the rational awareness concerning the subtle elements (*vicāra*); absorption in bliss or awareness concerning the faculties of sensing (*ānanda*); and absorption in the sense of I-ness or awareness concerning the faculty of self-knowledge (*asmitārūpa*). The specific content of these levels of awareness varies within commentaries, but what is relevant in all of them is the process that takes place in *samādhi*. The object appears directly in the mind and is liberated from the 'grasping' of the cognitive faculties, especially when concentration on the object is done without verbal or conceptual construction. Through meditative absorption, the subjective function is gradually arrested, letting the object be in its own form (be it a physical object, a thought, an emotion, a sensation, or the mere sense of being oneself) at the same time that the self is liberated from the willingness to act towards it.

A deeper form of absorption called *asamprajñāta samādhi* arises when the meditative mind has no object as its content (*YS* I.18). At this level, even the sense of I-ness that accompanies every act of fixation and concentration is surrendered. With the subjective and cognitive apparatus arrested, one would suppose that any sense of awareness would completely black out. However, the state that remains is one of 'arrested-experience', an experience characterized by surrendering the will to know or act on an object. In the absence of mutation or a changing object to observe, even the arresting-experiences vanish, leaving the self in a state of pure awareness where it realizes itself in its own form, unmediated by the senses, thoughts, or words, distinguishing itself (*vivekhyāti*) from the intellect and the rest of the cognitive and sense capacities. *Asamprajñāta samādhi* is thus the ultimate liberating state of self-knowledge (*svapuruṣadarśana*) even though, paradoxically, there is no knowledge beyond the discerning point for even this is arrested at the end of the process (*YS* IV.25). The self, then, rests alone in self-aware freedom (*kaivalya*) (*YS* IV.34).

The Lord of the Adamantine Chariot

In the third book of the *YS* entitled 'on Power (*vibhūti pāda*)', Patañjali says that when the distinction between the self and the intellect is realized, one attains supremacy over all beings, becomes omniscient and free from affliction (*YS* III.49). Omnipotence and omniscience are clear attributes of God. Yoga considers that the only thing that distinguishes God from us is that God was never deluded about its own self, thus, never afflicted (*YS* I.24). The role of God or *īśvara*—better translated as Lord or Master (White 2014, 177)—in Yoga philosophy is rather limited without the function of being creator of the universe. God is, instead, the first teacher, the first source of insight for the realization of one's true nature (*YS* I.25). The inclusion of the Lord in the Yoga system of Patañjali has traditionally been taken to be one of the main differences between Yoga and Sāṁkhya philosophies. But the role of the Lord in Yoga philosophy seems to go beyond the mere possibility of providing a 'theistic yogic concentration'. The inclusion of *īśvara* as a possibility for directing our minds in contemplation brings to the practice an emphasis in discernment (*viveka*). Without surrendering the mind to something or someone higher than oneself, the yogic discipline would turn into a product of egoistic effort. Like mental contents, actions are also to be purified, detached from the idea that it is the ego or the 'I' who acts. By meditating on God, the mind is pulled to acknowledge a power that is not coming from one's own faculties alone.

A theistic yogic concentration includes God as the object of contemplation and devotion (*īśvarapraṇidhāna*) in the form of reciting the sacred sound OM, which is the name that traditionally embodies the Lord (*YS* I.27). The sustained effort of the mind that is focused in the sacred mantra will eventually subside until the appearance of the object alone remains. When the vision of God is established, Vyāsa explains, the yogi acquires the vision of his or her own self (*YBh* I.29) as similar to God's: pure, clear, and free from afflictions. In the end, the vision and realization brought about by *asamprajñāta samādhi* and theistic contemplation is, according to Yoga, the same: self-aware embodied freedom, detached even from the knowledge of its own omniscience and omnipotence.

The injunction to detach from the highest yogic knowledge occurs in the same chapter that lists more than twenty powers that can be attained by yogic knowledge and perception. The third chapter is replete with different objects towards which yogic concentration can be directed and describes the results that can be achieved from each. Famous yogic powers (reading minds, becoming invisible, etc.) are considered to be a natural consequence of the yogic process. The most important philosophical aspect of this chapter lies in that what is usually taken as an 'eccentric' dualist system can actually be read as advocating for the complete integration of mind, body, and reality. The basic assumption behind the possibility of yogic 'supernatural' attainments is that by transforming the mind, there is also an immediate transformation of reality, for the world that we normally perceive is based on a limited perception mediated by the senses. We see in this section of the *YS*, more than in any of the other chapters, a philosophy of the body that does not reduce it to the mechanical and biological body, and which will be elaborated later in other types of Yoga systems like Tantra and Haṭha Yoga.

The body (*kāya*) on which the meditations of the third book focus includes the physical body (*YS* III.24, 29–31), the body image (*YS* III.21), the willful body (*YS* III.38), the visualized subtle body (*YS* III.32, 34, 39–40), and the cosmic body (*YS* III.26–27). In this section, Patañjali mentions that one of the results of practicing yoga is the perfection of the body (*kāyasampat*) which consists of beauty, charm, strength, and adamantine hardness (*YS* III.46). In the previous *sūtra*, Vyāsa explains that yogis who have achieved a perfected body attain powers such as mastery over the natural elements—the ability to control the appearance and disappearance of those elements— but also, paradoxically, the stronger power of not using them. The perfect adamantine body is, thus, the body freed from its own will to know and act in the same way that the discerning self is freed from its own omnipotence and omniscience.

Only within the body–mind unit can the experience of self-awareness be liberating, for it is within this that the self experiences the spontaneous exercise of its will and, at the same time, the supreme power to withdraw it. This is the supreme yogic insight (*prajñā*) and the attainment of the supreme mastery (*vaśikara*) over one's embodiment, the 'lordship' (*aiśvarya*) of the chariot (*YS* I.40). Through the phenomenological analysis of embodiment implicit in the yogic process of self-awareness, we find a conceptually rich notion of the body that transcends the dualist–materialist categories. In the multilayered process of yogic perception, the highest attainment that results from it is not only the absolute freedom of the self, but also the liberation from a reduced and limited conception of one's own embodiment (body–mind unit).

References

Āraṇya, Hariharānanda. 1983. *Yoga Philosophy of Patañjali*. Albany, NY: SUNY Press.

Bhattacharyya, K. C. 1956. *Studies in Philosophy*, vol. 1. Calcutta: Progressive Publishers.

Eliade, Mircea. 1969. *Patañjali and Yoga*. New York: Funk & Wagnalls.

Frauwallner, Erich. 2008. *History of Indian Philosophy*, vol. 1. Delhi: Motilal Banarsidass.

Īśvarakṛṣṇa. 1930. *Sāṁkhya Kārika*. Suryanarayana Sastri (trans.). Madras: University of Madras.

Jacobson, Knut A. (ed.). 2012. *Yoga Powers. Extraordinary Capacities Attained through Meditation and Concentration*. Leiden and Boston: Brill.

Larson, Gerald and Bhattacharya, Ram Shankar. 2008. *Yoga: India's Philosophy of Meditation*. *Encyclopedia of Indian Philosophy*, vol. 12. Editor in-Chief Karl Potter. Delhi: Motilal Banarsidass Publishers.

McCrea, Larry. 2009. '"Just Like Us, Just Like Now": The Tactical Implications of the Mīmāṃsā Rejection of Yogic Perception.' In Eli Franco (ed.) *Yogic Perception, Meditation and Altered States of Consciousness*, 55–70. Vienna: Österreichische Akademie der Wissenschaften.

Maas, P. A. 2009. 'The So-called Yoga of Suppression in the Pātañjala Yogaśāstra.' In Eli Franco (ed.) *Yogic Perception, Meditation and Altered States of Consciousness*, 263–282. Vienna: Österreichische Akademie der Wissenschaften.

Milindapañha. 1890. V. Trenckner (trans.). Oxford: Clarendon Press.

Olivelle, Patrick. 1998. *The Early Upaniṣads. Annotated Text and Translation*. New York: Oxford University Press.

Phillips, Stephen. 2009. *Yoga, Karma, and Rebirth: A Brief History and Philosophy*. New York: Columbia University Press.

Raveh, Daniel. 2012. *Exploring the Yogasūtra. Philosophy and Translation*. New York: Continuum.

Tattva-Kaumudī of Vāchaspati Miśra. 1896. Gangānātha Jhā (trans.). Bombay: Tookaram Tatya.

Whicher, Ian. 1998. *The Integrity of Yoga Darśana: A Reconsideration of Classical Yoga*. Albany, NY: SUNY Press.

White, David G. 2012. 'Yoga, Brief History of an Idea.' In D. G. White (ed.) *Yoga in Practice*, 1–23. Princeton, NJ: Princeton University Press.

White, David. G. 2014. *The 'Yoga Sutra of Patañjali': A Biography*. Princeton, NJ: Princeton University Press.

Chapter 27
A REASSESSMENT OF CLASSICAL YOGA PHILOSOPHY

Ian Whicher

Introduction

This essay centers on the thought of Patañjali (*c.* second century CE), the great exponent of the authoritative classical Yoga school (*darśana*) and reputed author of the *Yoga-Sūtra*. I argue that Patañjali's philosophical perspective has been looked upon as excessively 'spiritual' or isolationistic to the point of being a world-denying philosophy, neglecting the world of nature and culture and overlooking the highest potentials for human reality, vitality, creativity, and service. Contrary to arguments presented by scholars which associate Patañjali's Yoga exclusively with extreme asceticism, mortification, denial, and the renunciation and abandonment of 'material existence' (*prakṛti*) in favor of an elevated and isolated 'spiritual state' (*puruṣa*) or disembodied state of spiritual liberation, I suggest that Patañjali's Yoga can be seen as a responsible engagement, in various ways, of 'spirit' and 'matter' resulting in a highly developed, transformed, and participatory human nature and identity, an integrated and embodied state of liberated, yet engaged selfhood (*jīvanmukti*). The interpretation of Patañjali's Yoga *Darśana* I present suggests an open-ended, epistemologically and morally oriented hermeneutics which, I maintain, is more appropriate for arriving at a genuine assessment of Patañjali's system.

Cessation (*nirodha*) and the 'return to the source' (*pratiprasava*): transformation or elimination/negation of the mind?

Patañjali defines yoga as 'the cessation (*nirodha*) of [the misidentification with] the functioning/fluctuations (*vṛtti*) of the ordinary mind (*citta*)' (YS I.2). What *kind* of 'cessation' is Patañjali actually referring to? What does the process of cessation actually entail for the yogī: ethically, epistemologically, ontologically, and psychologically? I have suggested (Whicher 1998) that *nirodha* denotes an epistemological emphasis and refers to the transformation of self-understanding through the purification and illumination of consciousness. *Nirodha* is not the ontological cessation of *prakṛti* (in this case, the mind and *vṛttis*). *Nirodha* is not an inward movement that annihilates or suppresses *vṛttis*, thoughts, intentions, or ideas (*pratyaya*), nor is it the nonexistence or absence of *vṛtti*. Rather, *nirodha* involves a progressive unfoldment of perception (*yogi-pratyakṣa*) that eventually reveals our authentic identity as being rooted in *puruṣa*. It is the state of affliction (*kleśa*) evidenced *in* the mind and not the mind *itself* that is at issue. Spiritual ignorance gives rise to a profound dysfunction or misalignment of *vṛtti* with consciousness that in Yoga can be remedied thereby allowing for a proper alignment or 'right' functioning of *vṛtti* (Whicher 1998). It is the *cittavṛtti* as our confused and mistaken identity, not our *vṛttis*, that must be brought to a state of definitive cessation. Ordinary awareness consists of our mental patterns that are governed by spiritual ignorance and define our normal sense of self or identity. Patañjali clearly wanted to distinguish that mode of self from pure consciousness (*puruṣa*). Yoga thus purifies and liberates the *cittavṛtti* from ignorance and enables one, I suggest, to get beyond afflicted identity. This is significant to beneficial world engagement because when one engages the world through the lens of an afflicted and deluded identity, the resulting actions and reactions will be similarly afflicted and disordered.

To be sure, there is a suspension and transcendence of all the mental processes as well as any identification with an object. However, it would be misleading to conclude that higher union or *samādhi* results in a permanent cessation of the *vṛttis*, thereby predisposing the yogī who has attained purity of mind to exist in an incapacitated, isolated, or mindless state and therefore of being incapable of living a balanced, useful, and productive life.

The three *guṇas* of *prakṛti* are purity/light/virtue, dynamic activity, and dullness/inertia/delusion, or *sattva*, *rajas*, and *tamas*, respectively. The purpose of the *guṇas* as outlined in YS II.18 and 21 is to provide experience (*bhoga*) and liberation (*apavarga*) for the unliberated practitioner. They have ultimately a soteriological role. From the perspective of the discerning yogī, human identity contained within the domain of the three *guṇas* amounts to sorrow and dissatisfaction (*duḥkha*) (YS II.15). The declared goal of classical Yoga, as with Sāṃkhya and Buddhism, is to overcome all dissatisfaction (YS II.16) by bringing about an inverse movement or counter-flow (*pratiprasava* YS II.10; IV.34) understood as a 'return to the origin' (Chapple and Kelly 1990, 60) or 'process-of-involution' (Feuerstein 1979, 65) of the *guṇas*, a kind of reabsorption into the transcendent purity of being itself. What does this 'return to the origin' actually mean? Is it a definitive ending to the perceived world of the yogī composed of change and transformation, forms and phenomena? Ontologically conceived, *prasava* signifies the 'flowing forth' of the primary constituents or qualities of *prakṛti* into the multiple forms of the universe in all its dimensions. *Pratiprasava* on the other hand denotes the process of 'dissolution into the source' of those forms relative to the personal, microcosmic level of the yogī who is about to attain freedom (*apavarga*). Thus, *pratiprasava* refers to the involution, on the personal level, of the essential attributes of *prakṛti* which form nature, materiality, physicality, and cognitivity, both on the cosmic and individual levels.

Does a 'return to the origin,' *pratiprasava*, culminate in a state of freedom in which one is stripped of all human identity and void of any association with the world including one's practical livelihood? The ontological emphasis usually given to the meaning of *pratiprasava*, implying for the yogī a literal dissolution *of prakṛti*'s manifestation, would seem to support this view. Is this the kind of spiritually emancipated state that Patañjali had in mind? In *YS* II.3–17 Patañjali describes *prakṛti*, the 'seeable' (including our personhood), in the context of the various afflictions (*kleśas*) that give rise to an afflicted and mistaken identity of self. Afflicted identity is constructed out of and held captive by the root affliction of ignorance (*avidyā*). Despite the clear association of *prakṛti* with the bondage of ignorance (*avidyā*), there are no real grounds for purporting that *prakṛti* herself is to be equated with or subsumed under the afflictions. To equate *prakṛti* with affliction implies that *prakṛti*, along with the afflictions, is a reality that the yogī should ultimately abandon or discard completely.

Patañjali leaves much room for understanding 'dissolution' or 'return to the source' with an epistemological emphasis, allowing the system of the Yoga *Darśana* to be interpreted along more open-ended lines. In other words, what actually 'dissolves' is the yogī's misidentification with *prakṛti*, a mistaken identity of self that, contrary to authentic identity (*puruṣa*), can be nothing more than a product of the three *guṇas* under the influence of spiritual ignorance. Understood as such, *pratiprasava* need not denote the definitive ontological dissolution of manifest *prakṛti*, but rather refers to the process of 'subtilization' or sattvification of consciousness necessary for the uprooting of misidentification – the incapacity of the yogi to 'see' our authentic identity as *puruṣa*.

The discerning yogī sees (YS II.15) that this guṇic world is in itself dissatisfaction (*duḥkha*). But we must ask, what exactly is the problem being addressed in Yoga? Is our ontological status as a human being involved in day to day existence in need of being negated in order for authentic identity (*puruṣa*) to dawn? Having overcome all ignorance, is it then possible for a human being to live in the world and no longer be in conflict with oneself and the world? Can the *guṇas* cease to function in a state of ignorance and conflict in the mind? Can spiritual ignorance be replaced by an aware, conscious, nonafflicted identity that transcends the conflict and confusion of ordinary, saṃsāric life? Can we live, according to Patañjali's Yoga, an embodied state of freedom?

'Aloneness' (*kaivalya*): implications for an embodied freedom

In the classical traditions of Sāṃkhya and Yoga, *kaivalya* (from *kevala*), meaning 'aloneness,' is generally understood to be the state of the unconditional existence of *puruṣa*. 'Aloneness' is often misconstrued as a disconnection from others and severance from world engagement. However *kaivalya* can refer more precisely to the 'aloneness of seeing' or 'oneness of life' which, as Patañjali states, follows from the disappearance of ignorance and its creation of confusion of identity (*saṃyoga YS* II.17). 'Aloneness' thus can be construed as *puruṣa*'s innate capacity for pure, unbroken, non-attached seeing/perceiving or 'knowing' of the content of the mind (*citta*) (*YS* II.20; IV.18). The *sūtra* (*YS* IV.34) also classifies *kaivalya* as the establishment in one's own form/nature (*svarūpa*) the power of higher awareness (*citiśakti*). Although the seer's (*draṣṭṛ*/

puruṣa) capacity for seeing is an unchanging yet dynamic power of consciousness that should not be truncated in any way, our karmically distorted perceptions vitiate against the natural fullness of seeing. Patañjali defines spiritual ignorance as: 'seeing the non-eternal as eternal, the impure as pure, dissatisfaction as happiness, and the non-self as self' (*YS* II.5). Having removed the failure-to-see the soteriological purpose of the *guṇas* is fulfilled. The mind is relieved of its former role of being a vehicle for *avidyā*, the locus of egoity and misidentification, and then the realization of pure seeing takes place.

We are told as well that *kaivalya* is established when the *sattva* of consciousness has reached a state of purity analogous to that of the *puruṣa* (*YS* III.550). Through the process of subtilization or return to the origin (*pratiprasava*) in the *sattva*, the transformation (*pariṇāma*) of the mind (*citta*) takes place at the deepest level, bringing about a radical change in perspective. The former impure, fabricated states are dissolved resulting in the complete purification of mind. Through knowledge (in *saṃprajnāta-samādhi*) and its transcendence (in *asaṃprajnāta-samādhi*), self-identity overcomes its lack of intrinsic grounding. The yogī is no longer dependent on liberating knowledge (mind-*sattva*) (*YB* III.55) and is no longer attached to the constant fluctuations of thought processes (*vṛtti*) as a basis for self-identity.

Cessation does not mark a definitive disappearance of *the guṇas* from *puruṣa*'s view and the yogī's experience (Āraṇya 1963, 123). For the liberated yogī, the *guṇas* cease to exist in the form of *avidyā* and its mental impressions (*saṃskāras*), *vṛttis*, and false or fixed ideas (*pratyaya*) of selfhood that formerly veiled true identity. The changing modes of nature cannot alter the yogī's now purified and firmly established consciousness. The mind and *puruṣa* attain to a sameness of purity (*YS* III.55), of harmony, balance and evenness: the mind appearing in the nature of *puruṣa* (*YB* I.41).

The crucial (ontological) point to be made here is that in the aloneness of *kaivalya*, *prakṛti* ceases to perform an obstructing role. *Prakṛti* herself has become purified, illuminated, and liberated from *avidyā*'s grip including the misconceptions, misappropriations, and misguided relations implicit within a world of afflicted identity. There being no power of misidentification remaining in *nirbīja-samādhi* (*YS* I.51; III.8), the mind ceases to operate within the context of the afflictions, karmic accumulations, and consequent cycles of *saṃsāra* implying a mistaken identity of selfhood subject to birth and death.

The severence of *puruṣa* from *prakṛti*

The *Yoga-Sūtra* has often been regarded as calling for the severance of *puruṣa* from *prakṛti*; concepts such as cessation, detachment/dispassion, and so forth have been interpreted in an explicitly negative light. Max Müller, citing Bhoja Rāja's commentary (eleventh century CE), refers to Yoga as 'separation' (*viyoga*) (*RM* I.1, 1; Müller 1899, 309). More recently, numerous other scholars[1] have endorsed the interpretation of the absolute separateness of *puruṣa* and *prakṛti*. In doing this, scholars and non-scholars alike have tended to disregard the possibility for other hermeneutical options. This separation has proved detrimental to a fuller understanding of the Yoga *Darśana* by continuing a tradition based on an isolationistic, one-sided reading (or perhaps misreading) of the *Yoga-Sūtra* and Vyāsa's commentary. Accordingly, the absolute separation of *puruṣa* and *prakṛti* can only be interpreted as a disembodied and non-relational state implying death to the physical body. To dislodge the yogī from bodily existence is to undermine the integrity of the pedagogical context that lends so much credibility or 'weight' to the Yoga system. It need not be assumed that, in Yoga, liberation coincides with physical death.[2] This would only allow for a soteriological end state of disembodied liberation (*videhamukti*). What is involved in Yoga is the death of the atomistic, individualistic identity and the dissolution of the karmic web of *saṃsāra*.

The reason for challenging such an isolationistic understanding of Patañjali's system is as follows: Not being content with mere theoretical knowledge, Yoga is committed to a practical way of life. To this end, Patañjali included in his presentation of Yoga an outline of the 'eight-limbed' path (*aṣṭāṅga-yoga*) (*YS* II.29) dealing with the physical, moral, psychological, and spiritual dimensions of the yogin, an integral path that emphasizes organic continuity, balance, and integration.

Far from being misconceived exclusively as an introverted path, classical Yoga acknowledges the intrinsic value of support and sustenance and the interdependence of all living (embodied) entities, thus upholding organic continuity, balance, and integration within the natural and social world. Having achieved that level of insight (*prajnā*) that is truth-bearing (*ṛtaṃbharā*) (*YS* I.48), the yogin perceives the natural order (*ṛta*) of cosmic existence, and unites with and embodies that order. To fail to see clearly (*adarśana*) is to fall into disorder, disharmony, and conflict with oneself and the world. Through Yoga one gains proper access to the world and is therefore established in right relationship to the world. Far from being denied or renounced, the world, for the yogī, has become transformed, properly engaged.

In the last chapter of the *Yoga-Sūtra* aloneness (*kaivalya*) is said to ensue upon the attainment of *dharmamegha-samādhi*, the cloud of dharma *samādhi*. At this level of practice, the yogin has abandoned any attachment to profit from his or her meditational practice; a non-acquisitive attitude (*akusīda*) must take place at the highest level of yogic discipline (*YS* IV.29). Vyāsa emphasizes that the identity of *puruṣa* is not something to be acquired (*upādeya*) or discarded (*heya*) (*YB* II.15). The perspective referred to as '*Pātañjala Yoga Darśana*' culminates in a permanent state of clear 'seeing' brought about through the discipline of Yoga. Yoga thus incorporates both an end state and a process.

Dharmamegha-samādhi presupposes that the yogī has cultivated higher dispassion (*para-vairāgya*). Thus, *dharmamegha-samādhi* is more or less a synonym of *asaṃprajnāta-samādhi* and can even be understood as the consummate phase of the awakening disclosed in enstasy, the final step on the long and arduous yogic journey to authentic identity and aloneness.[3] Now free from any dependence on or subordination to *vṛtti*, and detached from the world of misidentification, the yogī yet retains the purified guṇic powers of virtue including:

(i) illuminating 'knowledge of all' (due to purified *sattva*) (*YS* III.49; III.54);
(ii) nonafflicted activity (due to purified *rajas*) (*YS* IV.7; cf. *YS* IV.30);
(iii) a stable body-form (due to purified *tamas*).

YS IV.30 declares: 'From that [*dharmamegha-samādhi*] there is the cessation of afflicted action.' Hence the binding influence of the *guṇas* in the form of the afflictions is overcome; what remains is a 'cloud of dharma' which includes an eternality of knowledge free from all impure covering (*āvaraṇa-mala*, YS IV.31) where 'little (remains) to be known' (YS IV.31).

Culmination: *jīvanmukta* (the living enlightened)

The culmination of the Yoga system is found when, following from *dharmamegha-samādhi*, the mind and actions are freed from misidentification and affliction and one is no longer deluded with regard to one's true form (*svarūpa*) or intrinsic identity. This clarity about identity is highly significant to selfless action in the world. At this stage of practice the yogī is disconnected (*viyoga*) from all patterns of action motivated by egoity. According to both Vyāsa (*YB* IV.30) and the sixteenth-century commentator Vijnāna Bhikṣu (*YV* IV.30), one in whom this high state of purification takes place is designated as a *jīvanmukta*: one who is liberated while still alive (i.e., embodied or living liberation). Engagement by such individuals occurs without selfishness, greed, insecurity, narcissism, false perception, delusion, or wrong motivation.

Relinquishing selfish concern with the results of activity, the yogī remains detached from the egoic fruits of action.[4] This does not imply that the yogī loses all orientation for action. It is only attachment, not action itself, that sets in motion the law of moral causation (karma). The yogī is said to be non-attached to either virtue or non-virtue, and is no longer oriented within the ego-logical patterns of thought. This does not mean, as some scholars have concluded, that the spiritual adept or yogī is free to commit immoral acts,[5] or that the yogī is motivated by selfish concerns.[6] Actions must be executed in the spirit of unselfishness and be ethically sound, reasonable, and justifiable. The yogī's commitment to the sattvification of consciousness includes the cultivation of moral virtues such as compassion (*karuṇā*) (*YS* I.33) and nonviolence (*ahiṃsā*) (*YS* II.35). It is not an expression of indifference or an uncaring attitude to others. Moral disciplines are engaged as a natural outgrowth of intelligent, (*sattvic*) self-understanding.

Having defined the goal of Yoga as aloneness (*kaivalya*), the question must now be asked: What kind of aloneness was Patañjali talking about? Aloneness is not the isolation of the seer (*draṣṭṛ*, *puruṣa*) separate from the seeable (*dṛśya*, *prakṛti*), as is often maintained as the goal of Yoga. Rather, it refers to the aloneness of the power of seeing (*YS* II.20, 25) in its innate purity and clarity without any epistemological distortion and moral defilement. Aloneness refers to an absolute oneness of life which reveals itself through the power of seeing, a full vision which includes both consciousness and manifest or unmanifest existence. The cultivation of *nirodha* uproots the compulsive tendency to reify the world and oneself with an awareness that reveals the transcendent, yet immanent seer (*puruṣa*).

Through clear seeing the purpose of Yoga is fulfilled, and the yogī, free from all misidentification and impure karmic residue, gains full, immediate access to the world. By accessing the world in such an open and direct manner, in effect uniting epistemologically with the world, the yogī ceases to be encumbered by egoism which, enmeshed in confusion, misappropriates the world. The sacrifice of afflicted identity for the purpose of identifying as *puruṣa* is precisely what renders *prakṛti* sacred and ultimately reveals her intrinsic significance and value. Yoga can be recognized as a highly developed and integrated state that extends and enhances our self-identity. The yogī can dwell in a state of balance and fulfillment serving others while feeling at home in the world; the yogī's entire way of being is embodied within the lived world itself.

Yoga can be seen to unfold states of epistemic oneness that reveal the non-separation of knower, knowing, and the known (*YS* I.41). *Kaivalya* implies a power of seeing in which the dualisms rooted in our egocentric patterns of attachment, aversion, fear, and so forth have been transformed into unselfish ways of being with others (*YS* I.33).

The psychological, ethical, and social implications of this kind of identity transformation are immense. Yoga does not anesthetize our feelings thereby encouraging indifference toward others. On the contrary, the process of cessation (*nirodha*) steadies one for a life of compassion, discernment, and service informed by a seeing that is able to understand and is in touch with the needs of others.

Yoga presupposes the integration of contemplation and activity; there can be no scission between *theoria* and *praxis*. The *Yoga-Sūtra* is a philosophical text where *praxis* is deemed to be essential. Without actual practice the theory that informs Yoga would have no authentic meaning. In an original, and penetrating style, Patañjali bridges metaphysics and ethics, transcendence and immanence, and contributes a form of philosophical investigation that, to borrow J. Taber's descriptive phrase for another context following Heidegger's ideal of the authentic actualization of Dasein, can properly be called a 'transformative philosophy.' It is a philosophical perspective which 'does not stand as an edifice isolated from experience; it exists only insofar as it is realized in experience' (Taber 1983, 26).

Conclusion

To conclude, it can be said that *puruṣa* indeed has some precedence over *prakṛti* in Patañjali's system, for *puruṣa* is what is ordinarily concealed in human life and is ultimately the state of consciousness one must awaken to in Yoga. The liberated state of aloneness (*kaivalya*) need not denote either an ontological superiority of *puruṣa* or an exclusion of *prakṛti*. *Kaivalya* can be positively construed as an integration of both principles. The integration or 'absolute oneness of life' is what is most important for Yoga. I have proposed that the *Yoga-Sūtra* does not uphold a path of liberation that ultimately renders *puruṣa* and *prakṛti* incapable of co-operating together. Rather, the *Yoga-Sūtra* seeks to unite these two principles without the presence of any defiled understanding, to bring them together, properly aligning them in both being and action. Isolationism may not be and indeed does not seem to be the experience of those who have undertaken these practices at a deeper and mature level.

The purified mind that has been transformed through yogic discipline is certainly no ordinary worldly awareness nor is it eliminated for the sake of pure consciousness. To confuse the underlining purificatory processes involved in the cessation of ignorance as being the same thing as a radical elimination of our psychophysical being is, I suggest, to misunderstand the intent of the *Yoga-Sūtra* itself. There are strong grounds for arguing that through 'cessation' *prakṛti* herself (in the form of the *guṇas* that constitute the makeup of the yogī's body–mind) is liberated from the grip of ignorance rooted in afflicted identity. Vyāsa explicitly states (*YB* II.18) that emancipation happens in the mind and does not literally apply to *puruṣa*. The liberated one realizes and thereby experiences, this freedom.

Both morality and perception are essential channels through which human consciousness, is transformed and illuminated. Yoga combines discerning knowledge of self and reality with an emotional, affective, and moral sensibility allowing for a participatory epistemology that incorporates a moral plenitude for empathic identification with others and the world. The enhanced perception gained through Yoga must be interwoven with Yoga's rich affective and moral dimensions to form a spirituality that retains the integrity and vitality to transform our lives and the lives of others in an effective manner. In Yoga proper there can be no support, ethically or pedagogically, for the misappropriation or abuse of *prakrti* for the sake of freedom *or purusa*-realization. By upholding an integration of the moral and the mystical, Yoga supports a reconciliation of the prevalent tension within Hinduism between (1) spiritual engagement and self-identity within the world (*pravṛtti*) and (2) spiritual disengagement from worldliness and self-identity that transcends the world (*nivṛtti*). Yoga discerns and teaches a balance between these two apparently conflicting orientations. While Patañjali can be understood as having adopted a provisional, practical, dualistic metaphysics, there is no proof that his system either ends in duality or eliminates the possibility for an ongoing cooperative duality. Yoga is not simply '*purusa*-realization'; it equally implies 'getting it right with *prakṛti*'.

To be sure, the yogic path must be transcended. One must step outside of the vehicle of *prakṛti* and dwell as the consciousness of *puruṣa* in true form (*svarūpa*). Yet I want to suggest that transcendence need not be taken to mean a 'static finality': abiding in nonafflicted, disengaged, formless bliss. Rather Patañjali may well have set the stage for an inclusive awakening allowing for a convergence and engagement in life, a growing up in life with integrity and fullness that perhaps knows no bounds. Now that is a matured Yoga, the possibility of which we must not overlook or close the door on.

Abbreviations

RM Rāja-Mārtaṇḍa of Bhoja Rāja (*c.* eleventh century CE).
YB Yoga- Bhāṣya of Vyāsa (*c.* fifth–sixth century CE).
YS Yoga-Sūtra of Patañjali (*c.* second–third century CE).
YSS Yoga-Sāra-Saṃgraha of Vijñāna Bhikṣu (*c.* sixteenth century CE).
YV Yoga-Vārttika of Vijñāna Bhikṣu.

Notes

1 See, for example, Eliade (1969), Koelman (1970), Feuerstein (1979), and Larson (1987).
2 See Chapple (1983, 103–119).
3 See Feuerstein (1980, 98).
4 This is said to be the essence of Śri Kṛṣṇa's teaching on *karmayoga* in the *Bhagavadgītā*.
5 See Zaehner (1974, 97–98).
6 See Scharfstein (1974, 131–132).

References

Āraṇya, Swāmi Hariharānanda. 1963. *Yoga Philosophy of Patañjali*. P. N. Mukerji (trans.). Calcutta: University of Calcutta.

Arya, U. 1986. *Yoga-Sūtras of Patañjali with the Exposition of Vyāsa: A Translation and Commentary*, vol. 1: *Samādhi-Pāda*. Honesdale, PA: Himalayan International Institute.

Chapple, Christopher K. 1983. 'Citta-vṛtti and Reality in the Yoga Sūtra.' In *Sāṃkhya-Yoga: Proceedings of the IASWR Conference, 1981*. Christopher K. Chapple (ed.). Stony Brook, NY: The Institute for Advanced Studies of World Religions.

Chapple, Christopher K. and Yogi Ananda Viraj (Eugene P. Kelly, Jr.). 1990. *The Yoga Sūtras of Patañjali: An Analysis of the Sanskrit with Accompanying English Translation*. Delhi: Sri Satguru Publications.

Eliade, Mircea. 1969. *Yoga: Immortality and Freedom*. Willard R. Trask (trans.). Bollingen Series 56, 2nd ed. Princeton: Princeton University Press.

Feuerstein, Georg.1979. *The Yoga-Sūtra of Patañjali: A New Translation and Commentary*. Folkstone: Wm. Dawson and Sons, Ltd.

Feuerstein, Georg. 1980. *The Philosophy of Classical Yoga*. Manchester: Manchester University Press.

Jha, G. (Ed., Trans.). 1894. *Yogasāra-Saṃgraha of Vijñāna Bhikṣu*. Bombay: Tattva-Vivechaka Press.

Koelman, Gaspar M. 1970. *Pàtañjala Yoga: From Related Ego to Absolute Self*. Poona: Papal Anthenaeum.

Larson, Gerald J. and Bhattacharya, Ram S. (Eds.). 1987. *Sāṃkhya: A Dualist Tradition in Indian Philosophy. The Encyclopedia of Indian Philosophies*, vol. 4. Princeton, NJ: Princeton University Press.

Larson, Gerald J. and Bhattacharya, Ram S. (Eds.). 2008. *Yoga: India's Philosophy of Meditation. The Encyclopedia of Indian Philosophies*, vol. 12. Delhi: Motilal Banarsidass.

Müller, Max. 1899. *The Six Systems of Indian Philosophy*. London: Longmans, Green and Co.

Pātañjalayogadarśana, with the *Vyāsa-Bhāṣya* of Vyāsa, the *Tattva-Vaiśāradī* of Vācaspati Miśra, and the *Rāja-Mārtaṇḍa* of Bhoja Rāja. 1904. Kāṣīnātha Śāstrī Āgāśe (ed.). Poona: Ānandāśrama Sanskrit Series 47.

Rukmani, T. S. (Trans.). 1981–1989. *Yogavārttika of Vijñānabhikṣu: Text along with English Translation and Critical Notes along with the Text and English Translation of the Pātañjala Yogasūtras and Vyāsabhāṣya*. 4 vols. New Delhi: Munshiram Manoharlal.

Scharfstein, B.-A. 1974. *Mystical Experience*. Baltimore, MD: Penguin Books.

Taber, John. 1983. *Transformative Philosophy. A Study of Śaṇkara, Fichte and Heidegger*. Honolulu: University of Hawai'i Press.

Whicher, Ian R. 1998. *The Integrity of the Yoga Darśana*. Albany: State University of New York Press.

Whicher, Ian and David Carpenter. (Eds.). 2003. *Yoga: The Indian Tradition*. London and New York: RoutledgeCurzon.

Zaehner, R. C. 1974. *Our Savage God*. London: Collins.

IIb

PHILOSOPHICAL TRADITIONS

Chapter 28
INDIAN YOGĀCĀRA BUDDHISM: A HISTORICAL PERSPECTIVE

William S. Waldron

Yogācāra Buddhism developed in India during the third to fifth centuries CE and is one of two main schools of Indian Mahāyāna Buddhist philosophy. One way or another it influenced most later forms of Buddhism in India, Tibet, and East Asia. This influence was due both to the encyclopaedic scope of its concerns—developing nearly every dimension of contemporaneous Buddhism—and the distinctiveness of its doctrines—such as the 'store-house' consciousness (*ālaya-vijñāna*), Cognition Only (*vijñapti-mātra*), and the Three Natures (*trisvabhāva*).

As its name 'Practitioners of Yoga' suggests, the school was primarily concerned with the role of consciousness in *saṃsāric* life and its transformation on the path to liberation. But what exactly 'consciousness' or 'mind' means was, and is, hotly debated. Some modern scholars take a more historically contextualized approach, such as my approach here, and interpret Yogācāra in terms of the traditions preceding it, stressing its continuity with the doctrinal formulations and cognitive models of early Buddhism. This contrasts with the 'received tradition' advocated by most classical Hindu and Buddhist scholars and their contemporary proponents, who take a more doxographical approach, interpreting Yogācāra in terms of the sectarian categories developed by subsequent generations. They typically interpret Yogācāra as a thoroughgoing idealism, which posits mind as a substantial reality, contradicting the Buddha's Middle Way. Our account seeks to explain both these perspectives.

Early Buddhist background: dependent arising

In many respects the trajectory of Indian Buddhist thought represents ever deepening attempts to draw out the implications of the distinctive Buddhist theory of dependent arising: that all phenomenon arise, persist, and cease in dependence on causes and conditions. This was the Buddha's liberating insight under the Bodhi tree in the fifth century CE, which freed him from the mis-knowledge (*avidyā*) that any phenomenon, particularly a Self (*ātman*), is either unitary or exists independently of its conditions. Accordingly, analysis of experience in terms of dependent arising is thought to reveal how things 'truly are' (*yathā-bhūtam*), liberating us from our ingrained ignorance and attachments.

This is especially crucial in analysing cognitive awareness (*vijñāna*)—so central that Yogācārins were also called *Vijñāna-vādins*, the 'Consciousness School.' In the early teachings *vijñāna* was analysed in terms of the five senses and mind: dependent upon the eye and visible form (*rūpa*), etc., visual cognitive awareness, etc. arises.

Several implications follow from this simple mode of analysis. First, cognitive awareness is neither an agent that acts, nor a subject that cognizes. It results from conditions. Second, it occurs when appropriate stimuli impinge on its respective faculty. *Vijñāna* is a function of these two coming together, a process called contact (*sparśa*). Third, what counts as an 'object' is determined by the structure of its respective faculty, by what it responds to, e.g. what is vis*ible*, aud*ible*, etc. Fourth, stimuli are only experienced as discrete 'objects' when accompanied by constructive cognitive processes such as recognition (*saṃjñā*) and sensation (*vedanā*). Hence, *vijñāna* is neither purely objective nor solely subjective. It provides neither an exact reflection of things 'as they are,' since 'objects' are determined by our faculties and constructive cognitive processes; nor is it a unilateral projection of cognitive categories onto the world, since our faculties only operate in relation to specific stimuli. In short, the dependent arising of cognition involves constructive, interactional processes, not independent, substantive objects *or subjects*.

Such analyses are also inescapably experiential, i.e. they analyse our cognitive and affective processes, not what exists outside such processes which, strictly speaking, is unknowable. The 'world' (*loka*) then refers to the world we engage. As the Buddha declared: 'In this fathom-long body, with its perceptions and thoughts, I proclaim the world (*loka*) to be, likewise the origin … the destruction … the method leading to the destruction of the world' (Waldron 2003, 162f.). While most scholars of early Buddhism concur with this constructivist interpretation of cognition, scholars of later Buddhism often overlook these implications and their deep continuity with Yogācāra.

The 'origin of the world' comes about, moreover, from our fundamental ignorance (*avidyā*) and its ensuing actions (*karma*). We (falsely) imagine we are an unchanging Self (*ātman*) which cognizes pre-existing objects outside ourselves. We act as if self and object were *in*dependent entities, not aspects of *inter*actional processes. This crucially occurs in relation to mental cognitive awareness (*mano-vijñāna*), which arises in dependence on (1) previous moments of sensory cognitive awareness, a reflexive awareness *that* we have seen or heard something, as well as on (2) its own 'objects': concepts, thoughts and language. The most pernicious of these is the notion 'I am' (*asmīti*), considered a verbal or conceptual designation superimposed onto our mental and physiological processes. Self-consciousness is therefore not an independent *precondition for* perceptual awareness, but the dependent *result of* cognitive processes. Mental *vijñāna* is not 'mind seeing itself,' but an awareness which only occurs under complex conditions. If we treat consciousness as an entity or agent rather than an event or process, we miss this most distinctive feature of Indian Buddhist thought: its radically depersonalized model of experience.

Actions (*karma*) refer, instead, to our affective and behavioural responses informed by these misapprehensions. Our attempts to attain pleasure and security by grasping onto imaginary unchanging selves or independent objects not only lead to frustration, they also reinforce our tendencies (*anuśaya*) toward ignorance, desire, aggression and other afflictions (*kleśa*). The most deeply entrenched of these tendencies, the notion 'I am' (*asmīti*) and the 'view of self-existence' (*satkāyadṛṣṭi*), persist until the last stages of liberation. The persistence of these actions and tendencies simply *are* the origin and continuation of the 'world,' of the compulsive behavioural patterns called *saṃsāra*, the 'going around' from one lifetime to the next.

And crucially for Yogācārins, the medium of this continuity is also *vijñāna*, the only process said to persist throughout one's *saṃsāric* existences. *Vijñāna* 'descends' into the womb at conception, continuously arises throughout one's lifetime, and 'departs' the body at death for the next life. As long as it is perpetuated by karmic activities, this stream of mind continues uninterruptedly and is only stopped or transformed upon realizing *nirvāṇa*. Although most Pāli scholars recognize these two distinct dimensions of *vijñāna*, the cognitive and *saṃsāric*, only Yogācārins explicitly integrated them.

In sum, early Buddhist thought analysed our 'world' of experience in terms of dependent arising, seeing cognitive awareness (*vijñāna*) as a result of interactive processes which arise in dependence upon our faculties and their respective objects, but which are typically reified as a substantive self cognizing independent objects. Since these reifications tend to evoke the afflicted actions that perpetuate our compulsive behavioural patterns, they are the very illusions that must be overcome in the path toward liberation, at which point, the tradition claims, one sees reality 'as it is,' i.e. without fixed and unchanging substances.

Abhidharmic context

Developing from 200 BCE on, Abhidharma traditions systematized the Buddha's diverse teachings, focusing on the central concept of *dharma*—discrete factors into which all experiential processes could be analysed. Although their ontological and epistemological status was continuously disputed, the aim of *dharmic* analysis was not. The classical Abhidharmist and Yogācārin, Vasubandhu, states that 'the world (*loka*) in its variety arises from actions (*karma*), [which] accumulate through the power of the latent afflictions (*anuśaya*).' Moreover, he declares, 'there is no means of extinguishing the afflictions than through the discernment of *dharmas*' (*Abhidharma-kośa*, *ad* V 1, I 3; Pruden 1988, 767, 57).

To this end, Abhidharmists developed a 'phenomenological psychology' which systematically dissects the momentary arising of cognitive and affective processes into their *discernible* factors—*dharmas* which 'carry their own mark' (*svalakṣaṇa-dhāraṇa*). Although they disagreed about the definitions of specific *dharmas*, most schools agreed that only such momentary *dharmas* are ultimately real (*paramārtha*) and causally effective. Entities composed of such *dharmas* are merely conventional. This distinction between ultimate, momentary *dharmic* discourse and conventional language was central to Abhidharmic analysis.

In conjunction with meditation, *dharmic* analysis proved a powerful tool for discerning one's current cognitive processes and constraining one's afflictive actions (*kleśa*). But its very success underscored its limitations. An analysis of mind in terms of *discernible momentary events* cannot explain, in *dharmically* 'real' terms, the very thing it aims to eliminate: the persistence of latent afflictions throughout multifarious states of mind over multiple lifetimes. Latent afflictions are axiomatically indiscernible until they manifest, as is our accumulated karmic potential (*karmopacaya*) from past actions for results to ripen in the future. Although both of these were thought to persist until far along the path, they remained opaque to *dharmic* analysis. Abhidharmists addressed these serious lacuna, not by disputing the widely accepted *fact* of such continuities, but by rethinking how *dharmic* discourse, wherein only the immediately present is real, might best describe them.

Vasubandhu's *Abhidharmakośa* records three such responses. First, the latent afflictions persist as *vāsanā*, impressions or predispositions representing a 'special power' (*sāmarthya-viśeṣa*) for the afflictions to arise. Second, seeds (*bīja*) metaphorically represent the potential for previous karmic actions to come to fruition. Last, a subtle form of mind (*sūkṣma vijñāna*) describes how the mental stream persists even during meditative practices when all overt mental processes stop. However, until Yogācārins brought them together, these concepts remained *ad hoc*, addressing problems in a piecemeal and unsystematic fashion. Moreover, Vasubandhu considered *vāsanā* and *bīja* mere nominal entities (*prajñapti-sat*), not real *dharmas*, tacitly admitting the limitations of *dharmic* analysis.

Mahāyāna critiques

There were other responses to these limitations. Some *Mahāyāna* and *Tathāgata-garbha sūtras* rejected Abhidharma altogether, advocating instead a path of faith. The two main Indian Mahāyāna schools, however, sought to preserve the aspects of *dharmic* analysis while skirting its limitations by reconceiving the status of *dharmas*, either ontologically, like the Madhyamaka school of Nāgārjuna (first century CE) and his followers, or epistemologically, like the Yogācāra school of Asaṅga and Vasubandhu (fourth to fifth centuries CE). These different approaches largely explain their differing interpretations of Yogācāra.

Nāgārjuna critiqued the very conception of *dharmas*, reframing the entire discussion. Whatever is dependently arisen cannot possess its own-nature or mark (*svabhāva*; *svalakṣaṇa*), he argues, because that implies an unchanging and ultimately real essence, which Buddhists reject. Dependently arisen phenomena are 'empty' (*śūnya*) of such essences and, in this limited sense, are 'unreal' (*asat*). Though rejecting an ultimate essence, this 'unreality' of *dharmas* actually affirms their conventionality, their dependently arisen character. Emptiness, though, has been widely misunderstood, leading countless critics, ancient and modern, to consider it nihilistic. Nāgārjuna, though, is simply reformulating the Two Truths: a *dharma*'s ultimate nature is its lack of essence (*nairātmya*), its emptiness (*śūnyatā*), and Abhidharmic doctrine, indeed all doctrines, are just conventional designations (*prajñapti-sat*), useful for pragmatic purposes. For Mahāyānists, selflessness is thus extended from persons to phenomenon (*dharma-nairātmya*). Accordingly, they see the reification of *dharmas*, imputing essences where there are none, as the fundamental cognitive fault perpetuating *saṃsāric* existence.

Though reification and imputation are clearly cognitive functions, Mādhyamikan deconstruction typically focuses on *dharmas*' *mode of existence*, their ontology, as if one could speak of *dharmas*' 'existence' independently of the cognitive processes apprehending them. This evoked a second, explicitly epistemological, reframing.

The *Samdhinirmocana Sūtra* (third century CE), considered a 'Yogācāra' *sūtra*, argues that the earlier *Prajñā-paramitā Sūtras* which Nāgārjuna elucidated had taught emptiness without, however, explicating (*nirmocana*) its implicit intent (*samdhi*): to teach the non-dual nature of reality. In its famous trope, the 'Three Turnings of the Wheel of Doctrine,' it argues that the Second Turning, i.e. the *Prajñā–pāramitā Sūtras*, requires interpretation (*neyārtha*) since it is only addressed to our tendencies toward reification, while its own teaching, the Third Turning, is definitive (*nitārtha*) since it explicitly elucidates the non-dual nature of reality. Accordingly, it redefines emptiness as the non-duality of grasper (*grāhaka*) and grasped (*grāhya*), of subject and object. This reformulation emphasizes the interdependence the two as well as their karmic significance.

Yogācāra

Resuscitating Abhidharma

The central question then becomes: why do we reify subject and object and how can we rectify these tendencies? To answer this, Yogācārins returned to cognitive analysis, developing a '*śūnyatized*' Abhidharmic system. They also developed an explicit depth psychology based on the keystone *dharma*, *ālaya-vijñāna*, the 'base' or 'store' consciousness, articulating a robust constructivist cognitive theory that explains the construction of reified appearances.

First prominent in the *Saṃdhinirmocana Sūtra* and later elaborated in treatises associated with Asaṅga (*Yogācārabhūmi*, *Abhidharma-samuccaya*, *Mahāyāna-saṃgraha*), this '*ālaya*' *vijñāna* addresses problems created by a *dharmic* discourse limited to conscious cognitive factors. Like the '*saṃsāric*' dimension of *vijñāna* in early Buddhism, *ālaya-vijñāna* is a stream of mind-moments that persists uninterruptedly over multiple lifetimes, even during meditative cessation, while also 'storing' the metaphorical impressions (*vāsanā*) and seeds (*bīja*) of past karma. All this is articulated in synchronic, *dharmic* discourse.

It is the non-conscious, subtle (*sūkṣma*) cognitive processes of *ālaya-vijñāna*, however, that are crucial to its constructivist theory. As a dependently arisen form of *vijñāna*, *ālaya-vijñāna* arises depending on internal and external conditions: our physiological structures and psychological schemas (*saṃskārāḥ*), such as the sense-faculties and predispositions (*vāsanā*) toward images, names and concepts, as well as a continuous, albeit indistinct shared world (*bhājana-loka*). Moreover, this subtle *ālaya* awareness, informed by these conditions, simultaneously supports the six traditional forms of manifest cognitive awareness (*pravṛtti-vijñāna*), informing the way objects consciously appear (*ākāra*). All these factors, schemas, seeds and predispositions are *constitutive* conditions for any ordinary cognition to occur. Apparent 'objects' are thus not the causes, but the *products*, of complex cognitive processes. Unfortunately, in many treatments of Yogācāra this deeply constructivist theory is either wholly neglected or effectively eclipsed by focusing on the *metaphors* of seeds and storage, inverting the traditional priority of *dharmic* analyses over conventional discourses.

This model also articulates how constructive processes, like habits, develop through repeated actions. Afflictive actions made in response to these constructed objects 'plant seeds' and 'infuse impressions' into *ālaya-vijñāna*, which then influences how subsequent objects appear, evoking similar afflictive responses, etc. This feedback process between sub- and supra-liminal forms of awareness occurs both from moment-to-moment and accumulatively over extended periods of time, progressing from a theory of learning to what is effectively a karmic theory of evolution.

The 'origin of the world' also explicitly includes the intersubjective influences of language and culture. *Ālaya-vijñāna* arises depending on the predispositions of images, names and concepts, which unconsciously shape how disparate stimuli coalesce into apparently discrete objects. Manifest forms of *vijñāna*, one Yogācāra text explains, arise in regard to expressions of selves, *dharmas* and actions due to the 'special power' (*śakti-viśeṣa*) of 'the impressions of speech' (*abhilāpa-vāsanā*) (Waldron 2003, 158f.) The very way cognitive objects appear (*ākāra*) is thus informed by our deep-seated, mostly unconscious categories, whereby reified conceptions of selves and *dharmas* inform our everyday perceptions.

Since language is shared, these predispositions constitute the 'shared aspect' (*sādhāraṇa*) of our subliminal awareness (*ālaya-vijñāna*), which arises depending on its correlative object, an indistinct 'shared world' (*bhājana-loka*). We humans inhabit a shared, species-specific 'world' because our past similar karma leads to similar cognitive capacities, which are similarly reinforced as our perceptions and actions arise shaped by shared, largely implicit, categories of language and culture. Yogācāra cognitive theory thus describes the long-term, collective unconscious construction of our species-specific world.

This discussion differs from most scholarly accounts which treat *bhājana-loka* as an objective reality existing independently of our engagement with it. But this implicit realism overlooks the traditional interdependence of subject and object and the role of karmic action in appropriating our 'world.' Yogācārins have arguably deepened, rather than departed from, these implications of dependent arising.

The final component of Yogācāra's depth psychology emphasizes how karmic actions are influenced by subliminal self-grasping (*kliṣṭa-manas*). Our self-centered dispositions toward self-view (*satkāyadṛṣṭi*), the conceit 'I am,' self-love and ignorance, occur uninterruptedly and simultaneously with all cognitive processes until far along the path, yet remain *karmically neutral* until acted upon. But as long as this deep-seated, unconscious self-centeredness remains, the *Yogācārabhūmi* states, no moments of mental *vijñāna* will be entirely free from seeing phenomena in terms of self and other, entailing endless self-centered activities. The object of this self-view is *ālaya-vijñāna*—closely associated with our embodied existence, our persisting dispositions and karmic histories, and exhibiting the most consistency of all our cognitive processes.

The basic insight behind the *ālaya-vijñāna* model is that only a multi-layered constructivist view of mind could adequately explain the continuities that all Indian Buddhist schools accepted: of karmic potential, latent afflictions and the mental stream itself. It additionally provides robust explanations for the processes of reification and appropriation which concerned all Buddhist schools. Building on this constructivist theory, Vasubandhu examines the (ir)reality of external objects, labelling them 'mere cognitions' the second signature concept of Yogācāra thought.

Vijñapti-mātra: *on the (ir)reality of external objects*

Does Yogācāra teach a form of idealism, wherein mind is the only substantial reality? Most traditional Indian and Tibetan scholars answer affirmatively, based on doxographical systems developed centuries later. How one answers this typically depends on whether one thinks Yogācārins are answering ontological questions about 'what exists,' or epistemological ones about 'how we know.' This then largely determines how one interprets statements like 'the three worlds are just cognitions' (*traidhātukaṃ vijñapti-mātraṃ*). Is this mainstream Buddhism, restating that the 'world' we experience is correlative with our cognitive processes and accumulated actions, which we cannot see as it 'really is' without the Buddha's wisdom (*prajñā*)? Or is this positing a truly existent subject that alone is real? Vasubandhu examines these questions in his *Twenty Verses* (*Viṃśatikā*; Anacker 1984), where he critiques the view that *dharmas* exist independently of our engagement with them, as a way to articulate the 'selflessness of *dharmas*' (*dharma-nairātmya*) in specifically Yogācāric terms.

Vasubandhu contrasts a realist position, that we perceive truly independently existing objects, with his own Mahāyāna position, that objects *as perceived* crucially depend on our own cognitive processes. He targets the term '*artha*,' which means not just 'object' but 'aim, meaning or purpose.' *Artha* is thus never simply neutral, but something we are necessarily engaged with. He argues that the four criteria realists cite for distinguishing truly 'external' objects from merely 'subjective' ones—they occur only at specific times and specific places, exhibit causal efficacy, and are experienced by multiple beings—also apply to situations where external objects are patently absent. Objects in dreams only occur when and where one is sleeping as well as exhibit causal efficacy (e.g. in a wet dream); while hell-beings collectively experience the tortures of hell-guardians who cannot, he argues, logically exist. We need not posit external objects *wholly* independent of our cognitive processes, he concludes, when we can adequately explain the appearance of cognitive objects as specific transformations of mind (*pariṇāma-viśeṣa*) resulting from the fruition of karmic seeds. Likewise, the maturation of seeds from similar past deeds explains our similar, shared experiences: we inhabit a shared human world. Taken out of their larger context, as if the metaphors of 'seeds' 'stored' 'in' *ālaya-vijñāna* referred to *in*dependent entities rather than *inter*-dependent processes, these passages indeed seem to argue that mind alone generates objects and 'worlds.'

Thus, Vasubandhu asks rhetorically, are these 'internal' conditions enough? There must be some 'external' stimuli that causes experience; they can't occur from absolutely nothing. Vasubandhu retorts that he is not denying the existence of *dharmas* altogether only, somewhat tautologically—that *dharmas* (i.e. objects) *as we experience them* are ultimately inseparable from our own cognitive processes. It is their imagined (*kalpita*) independent existence he refutes, not their ineffable nature (*anabhilāpya*) known only by the buddhas. In this sense, like Nāgārjuna before him, Vasubandhu calls *dharmas* 'unreal.' One would have to assume the realist position most Mahāyānists reject in order to object to his critique of *dharmas* as substantially and independently 'real.'

Instead, what we experience are 'only cognitions' (*vijñapti-mātra*). This realization is just one stage in progressively eliminating our reifying tendencies; it is an appropriate antidote, not an alternative ontology. Yogācāra texts repeatedly argue that after we stop mistaking objects as truly existing and see them as 'only cognitions' then we also stop taking mind (*citta*) as an independently existing entity, since there is no mind without an object. One then realizes the non-duality of grasping subject (*grāhaka*) and grasped object (*grāhya*), the realization of emptiness in Yogācāra.

Ordinarily subject and object seem separate, but that appearance of duality is now treated in texts attributed to the future Buddha, Maitreya (*Madhyānta-vibhāga*, *Dharma-dharmatā-vibhāga*, *Ratna-gotra-vibhāga*) as a result of a singular process. For underlying all states of mind, according to many Mahāyānists, is an intrinsically pure awakened mind (*tathāgata-garbha*), which bifurcates into a 'seeing-part' (*darśana-bhāga*) and a 'seen-part' (*nimitta-bhāga*), i.e. apparent subjects and objects. This marks a significant shift in Mahāyāna thought. For what now needs to be explained is not the sequential process of overcoming karma and ignorance in order to realize non-duality, but how to understand and reverse the appearance of duality that *arises from non-dual awareness in the first place*. This shift, to a singular awareness experienced either dualistically or non-dualistically, underlies the last key Yogācāra teaching, the Three Natures.

The Three Natures and soteriological transformation

The basic purpose of the Three Natures seems clear enough. We are ordinarily fooled by conceptually constructed appearances we imagine are true (*parikalpita-svabhāva*; imagined nature); though false, these appearances arise dependent on constructive cognitive processes (*paratantra-svabhāva*; dependent nature) and, in this limited sense, are 'real,' i.e. effective. When we see them as they 'truly are' (*pariniṣpannā-svabhāva*; perfected nature), we are freed from bondage to appearances. For example, mirages look like water; these appearances do occur, we all see them, and they have discernible causes and conditions. Rightly understood, though, we can recognize them for what they 'truly are.' The mirages remain, but we are no longer fooled by their appearances.

The apparent clarity, though, stops there. That appearances dependently arise due to false imagination seems patently epistemological, particularly in light of Buddhist cognitive theory; the 'perfected nature' seems to express the perfect symmetry between insight and reality, between correct epistemology and ontology, the classical ideal of realization; and that false imagination 'exists' seems tautological, simply acknowledging the problem of illusion. And since it 'exists,' imagination is 'not empty' in the conventional sense of 'not absent,' it has discernable deleterious effects.

Such shifting semantic frames understandably evoked controversy. Though the term '*svabhāva*' often means 'definition,' it seems overtly ontological to Mādhyamikans, who reject any inherent nature whatsoever, even linguistic ones. This return to conventional senses of 'empty' and 'exist,' similarly convinced Mādhyamikans that Yogācārins had misunderstood emptiness and were positing truly existent minds. As in many disputes, they talked past each other.

The Three Natures nevertheless epitomize central themes in both Yogācāra epistemology and soteriology: a consciousness purified of its cognitive obscurations can nevertheless skilfully communicate with beings beleaguered by dualistic consciousness; buddhas see *through* the multiple 'mirages' that entrance others. This was true for the cognitive models above, and here is true in Yogācāra soteriology as well.

During liberation, our cognitive processes are transformed or 'revolved' at their base (*āśraya-paravṛtti*), so that consciousness now operates non-dualistically (*jñāna*) instead of dualistically (*vi-jñāna*). The subliminal processes (*ālaya-vijñāna*) that comprise the totality of karmic potentialities and distorting cognitive schemas are emptied out and transformed into Mirror-Like Wisdom (*mahādarśana-jñāna*), which accurately reflects things as they are. Subliminal self-centeredness (*kliṣṭa-manas*) is transformed into the Wisdom of Perfect Equality (*samatā-jñāna*) between self and other. Based on these, mental *vijñāna* now functions as the Discerning Wisdom (*pratyavekṣaṇā-jñāna*) that accurately differentiates phenomena without obstruction or bias, facilitating awakened activity by our purified sensory consciousnesses, which then implement All-Accomplishing Wisdom (*kṛtya-anuṣṭhāna-jñāna*). In short, an ultimate non-discriminative wisdom (*nirvikalpa-jñāna*) supports and informs the pragmatic, subsequently attained wisdoms (*pṛṣṭhalabdha-jñāna*).

The ultimate and conventional are not only combined cognitively. Awakened Beings dwell in non-abiding liberation (*apratiṣṭhita-nirvāṇa*), remaining neither in nirvanic bliss nor bound to *saṃsāric* phenomena. Their Buddha-Bodies—idealized forms of awakened qualities—straddle the unconditioned, undifferentiated realm of the ultimate Dharma-body (*dharmakāya*) and the conventional Appearance and Visionary bodies (*nirmāṇa-kāya, saṃbhoga-kāya*) of the buddhas and bodhisattvas in Mahāyāna traditions. *Nirvāṇa* is now an ultimate awareness underlying all phenomena, to be experienced in its original purity once our adventitious obscurations are removed. In this sense Yogācāra does seem idealistic: for the ultimate reality of *dharmakāya* is nothing but undifferentiated, non-dual awareness itself. But this hardly distinguishes Yogācāra from other Mahāyāna schools, nor even from many other forms of Indian religion.

References

Anacker, S. 1984. *Seven Works of Vasubandhu*. New Delhi: Motilal Banarsidass.

Gold, J. 2014. *Paving the Great Way: Vasubandhu's Unifying Buddhist Philosophy*. New York: Columbia University Press.

Pruden, L. 1988. *Abhidharmakośa-bhāṣya*. Berkeley: Asian Humanities Press.

Waldron. W. 2003. *The Buddhist Unconscious: The Ālaya-vijñāna in the Context of Indian Buddhist Thought*. New York: RoutledgeCurzon.

———. 2010. *Yogācāra: A Select Annotated Bibliography*. Oxford Online Bibliography. www.oxfordbibliographiesonline.com.

Chapter 29
EARLY MAHĀYĀNA

Peter Gilks

Introduction

Scholarly understanding of early Mahāyāna has undergone substantial change over the last three decades, with many once-influential theories having been re-examined, revised, and in some cases abandoned. Prior to the 1980s, common beliefs about the rise of Mahāyāna included the ideas that it had originated as a reaction to the selfishness of the early Buddhist goal of liberation for oneself alone (La Vallée Poussin 1910) (Przyluski 1934), that its popularity was due to accommodating the needs of the laypeople (Dayal 1932) (Lamotte 1958), that it was a movement initiated by the laity (Hirakawa 1963), or that it grew out of, or split away from, the Mahāsāṃghika sect (Conze 1951) (Warder 1970).

More often than not, these theories were based on preconceived notions about the nature of schisms and selective readings of relatively late Sanskrit sources. Nevertheless, they still managed to gain wide currency, and this was especially true when they seemed consistent with Mahāyāna's own rhetoric vis-à-vis its ideological counterpart, the so-called Hīnayāna (lit. "inferior vehicle"), hereafter called Mainstream Buddhism.

When scholars began to shift the focus of their research to early Chinese translations of Mahāyāna *sūtras* and compared their findings with archaeological and epigraphic evidence from India, a somewhat different picture began to emerge. Scholars now generally hold the view that, despite its enormous literary output, for the first 500 years or so of its existence Mahāyāna was a minority movement within, or at the fringes of, various Mainstream monastic institutions. These conclusions raise several interesting questions. How could Mahāyāna have slipped beneath the epigraphic radar for so long? Why did early Mahāyāna struggle to gain acceptance among the majority of Buddhists? And for the minority who did accept it, what factors caused them to do so?

Conditions

Before turning to these questions, two conditions that played an important role in the rise of Mahāyāna warrant a brief mention. The first is the popularity among pre-Mahāyāna Buddhists of tales about the Buddha's former lives when he was known as the

Bodhisattva, i.e., "one destined for awakening". The underlying theme running through these tales, known as *Jātakas*, is that the Buddha attained his awakening as a result of the great merit he had accumulated over many lifetimes of self-sacrificial deeds. The significance of these tales as far as Mahāyāna is concerned is that they provided a basic model of religious practice in which Buddhahood was the goal and merit was the key driver of progress on the path. The existence of friezes at the site of the Bharhut *stūpa* depicting events from the *Jātakas* suggests that knowledge of the Buddha's earlier career as a bodhisattva was already well established by the second century BCE.

Basham (1981) accounts for the popularity of the *Jātakas* by pointing out that although the Buddhist monastic code of discipline (*vinaya*) prohibited monks from entering villages to participate in storytelling, this ban could have been evaded by telling stories that were attributed to the master himself. The Buddha, like many other Indian mystics of his time, was believed to be able to remember his past lives, and in due course many popular legends and fables eventually came to be recast as stories about those past lives and attributed to him. On the one hand then, the *Jātakas* can be seen as stories to edify and entertain the common lay-folk, while on the other hand, they also functioned to legitimize the practice of storytelling, which was important for gaining and maintaining their support.

The second important condition that allowed for the advent of Mahāyāna was the idea that Śākyamuni Buddha was not unique. Rather, he was but one of many buddhas who appear in the world, albeit rarely. We know from an inscription that records the enlargement of a *stūpa* dedicated to the former Buddha Koṇāgamana that belief in the existence earlier buddhas had been established by the third century BCE. It is not unreasonable given that inclusivism is a common feature of Indian religions, to hypothesize that the acceptance of buddhas other than Śākyamuni may have had something to do with a strategy of spreading Buddhism through recognizing past teachers of other traditions as awakened and adopting them as buddhas. There is evidence from around the same time for belief in the existence of future buddhas too, with the *Sūtra on Lion's Roar of a Wheel-turning Monarch* (*Cakkavatti-sīhanāda sutta*) containing the first known mention of the future Buddha Maitreya. This *sūtra*, which is preserved in the Pāli canon, has been dated by Basham (1981) to around the time of Aśoka's reign.

These two factors—widespread knowledge of how Śākyamuni had attained awakening through accumulating merit over many lifetimes as a bodhisattva and a belief that he was not unique—are not *causes* of Mahāyāna, but they were important conditions that made its existence possible. They also offer clues about when the initial rise of Mahāyāna may have occurred, though scholars generally agree that it is impossible to say with any historical accuracy when, or indeed where, Mahāyāna began. That said, *conceptually*, its inception can be defined as the time when the career of the bodhisattva began to gain acceptance as a soteriological option among certain communities of Indian Buddhists.

Social aspects

After it emerged as a topic of Western academic interest in the late nineteenth century, the study of Mahāyāna tended to focus on its doctrines—especially those of its later, more developed forms—while much less attention was given to Mahāyāna as a social phenomenon. Against this trend, the argument that scholars should study the practices, customs, and popular beliefs of a religion as much as they do its doctrines has been convincingly made by Schopen (1991). The attempt to find the essence of a religion in its scriptures, he says, is a throwback to "a sixteenth-century Protestant polemical conception of where 'true' religion is located" (p. 22). In the case of Mahāyāna, a strong textual orientation among earlier generations of scholars seems to have led to interpretations that tended to reflect Western history and values rather than how Mahāyāna was actually understood and lived by the majority of Indian Buddhists, most of whom, it should be remembered, were probably not literate.

Schopen's earlier research had already turned up an interesting conundrum. When he analysed the many Buddhist donative inscriptions known to have been written during the first centuries of the Common Era, all he found were the names of Mainstream sects and references to the aspirations commonly associated with them. Yet this was a period when Mahāyāna was supposed to have been flourishing as a refreshing new breakaway tradition. Strangely though, neither the name 'Mahāyāna' nor any mention of the aspiration to attain the fully awakening state of a buddha become common among the available epigraphic evidence until the fifth century CE (Schopen 1979).

These unexpected findings forced scholars to reconsider whether Mahāyāna was the schismatic popular reaction to narrow conservatism that they had imagined it to be. It also meant that if they wanted to know what life was like for the first Mahāyānists, there were virtually no sources of information other than the *sūtras*. But the *sūtras* are, of course, not documents that were created for the purpose of recording history; first and foremost, they are normative texts whose purpose was to guide people's beliefs and actions.

In an insightful article, Harrison (2003) explains how having no other sources besides the *sūtras* is not the problem—it is in fact the solution. Bringing together Gombrich's (1990) theory that Mahāyāna owed its survival to the early adoption of writing, Ong's (1988) idea that writing can transform human consciousness, and Ray's (1994) "forest hypothesis", which states the that the earliest Mahāyānists were communities of forest-dwelling ascetics, Harrison argues that the *sūtras* were the literary "residue" of those ascetics' visionary meditative experiences. In other words, since early Mahāyāna was a tradition in which revelation through meditation was an important feature, it is only natural that it should have produced so many texts. Moreover, if they were produced in communities that were isolated from towns and villages, it would explain why there are no donative inscriptions from the early period that refer to Mahāyāna.

While Harrison's explanation certainly has much merit in terms of accounting for Schopen's unexpected findings, three related points bear mentioning. First, as Rawlinson (1983) convincingly argues, and as Harrison himself would agree, Mahāyāna shows too much diversity to be anything other than multi-origin in nature. Thus, while communities of forest ascetics may have authored some *sūtras*, others may well have been produced within traditional monastic settings. Rawlinson opines that the reason why these *sūtras* cannot be identified with any Mainstream sect is because early Mahāyāna was a Pentecostal-like tradition for which institutional distinctions were irrelevant. Second, Harrison's theory is consistent with an interesting though somewhat problematic proposition set forth by Schopen (1975), who argued that some early Mahāyāna cultic groups lived in isolated communities centred on book shrines that functioned as Mahāyāna's "institutional bases". Third, although the length and structural complexity of some Mahāyāna *sūtras* suggests they may have started life as written texts, this does not preclude the existence of concurrent or earlier oral Mahāyāna traditions to which the written texts were a response.

Harrison has not articulated in any great detail his methodology for analysing the early Mahāyāna *sūtras*, but it clearly starts from the recognition that they contain much more than just doctrines. Like all texts, there is implicit within them a certain kind of audience. By identifying their implied audiences and assuming that they existed in actuality, Harrison and others have been able to learn much about what early Mahāyāna looked like on the ground. For example, in addition to his conclusion that some early *sūtras* were composed by communities of ascetics for other ascetics, Harrison has also found that the early Mahāyānists identified themselves as bodhisattvas, that they counted women among their number, and that they generally did not worship so-called "celestial" bodhisattvas (Harrison 1995). Nattier's (2003) analysis of the *Inquiry of Ugra Sūtra* (*Ugraparipṛcchā-sūtra*) reveals that although bodhisattvas included both monks and laypeople, these two groups did not engage in the same practices. She also found that some bodhisattva monks lived in monasteries together with non-bodhisattvas and that some tension existed between the two groups. And a study of the *Inquiry of Rāṣṭrapāla Sūtra* (*Rāṣṭrapālaparipṛccha-sūtra*) by Boucher (2008) suggested that many early bodhisattvas rejected the soft life of the monastery and engaged in rigorous ascetic practices (*dhutaguṇa*), thereby lending some support to Harrison's findings. Perhaps the most important early Mahāyāna *sūtra*, the *Perfection of Wisdom in Eight Thousand Lines* (*Aṣṭasāhasrikā-prajñāpāramitā-sūtra*; hereafter: the *Eight Thousand*), presupposes that its audiences had a deep familiarity with the scholastic systems of Abhidharma. This fact not only points to the important role that monks played in the rise of Mahāyāna, it is also seen as evidence by at least one researcher that the influential Perfection of Wisdom (*prajñāpāramitā*) tradition probably originated in Gandhara (Bronkhorst 2012).

Early Mahāyāna's low profile

If Mahāyāna had a relatively low profile in Indian Buddhist society for the first few centuries of its existence, what obstacles could have stood in the way of its wider acceptance? First, from a Mainstream perspective, the career of the bodhisattva may have held little attraction because it was seen as extremely long and difficult. We see in the *Eight Thousand*, for example, Māra the devil appearing before a bodhisattva and conjuring up an image of thousands of bodhisattvas who have led virtuous lives for countless eons but have not yet achieved full awakening. At the same time Māra conjures another image of monks who have abandoned the bodhisattva path and achieved release from cyclic existence as arhats. Of course, the *sūtra* teaches that a true bodhisattva is not tricked by Māra into forsaking his quest. But by imagining the audience for whom this passage was intended, one can detect the tension that must have existed between early Mahāyānists and Mainstream Buddhists, for whom arhatship was not just the ultimate spiritual goal, but something that could theoretically be achieved in a single lifetime.

A second reason why the path of the bodhisattva would have held little attraction was that a large section of the Mainstream did not see the awakening of the Buddha as significantly different from that of an arhat. Prior to the advent of Mahāyāna, there was only one path and only one goal—nirvana. Although it was recognized that the Buddha knew things that arhats did not—thereby implying a higher level of realization—their awakening was the same in the sense of gaining final release from cyclic existence. The main difference was that, due to his great merit and perseverance, the Buddha had done it on his own without a teacher.

A more serious obstacle to acceptance would have been the fact that the Mahāyāna *sūtras* were viewed by the Mainstream as spurious fabrications and not the genuine word of the Buddha. For evidence, we need look no further than the passage in the *Eight Thousand* that describes how Māra appears in disguise before a bodhisattva and urges him to abandon the Mahāyāna teachings, for they are not the word of the Buddha. Again, by imagining the audience for whom passages like this were intended, one can gain some appreciation of how the authenticity of the Mahāyāna *sūtras* must have been contested.

The appeal of the bodhisattva path

Despite these obstacles to acceptance, early Mahāyāna nevertheless managed to gather new converts. Doubtlessly, several factors were influential in enabling this to happen, but perhaps the most significant was the fact that the goal at the end of the bodhisattva path was presented as far superior to the spiritual goal of Mainstream Buddhists, namely, mere release from cyclic existence. Like some sub-branches of the Mainstream Mahāsāṃghika sect, Mahāyānists viewed the Buddha as a transcendent, supramundane being who continued to exist and continued to be accessible; he was not simply someone who had disappeared into nirvana. His earthly deeds, such as achieving awakening while sitting under the Bodhi tree, were viewed as merely the display of someone who had already achieved awakening eons ago. Moreover, some *sūtras* equated Buddhahood with a state of omniscience (*sarvajñatā*), which was a mystical state of knowing the nature of all phenomena—or to put it more general Indian philosophical terms, a knowledge of absolute truth. However it was understood, it was definitely believed to be superior to the knowledge of an arhat.

By clearly differentiating the transcendent state of Buddhahood from the eternal peace of nirvana, the goal of the bodhisattva would certainly have great appeal to some Buddhists of the time. It is important to note, however, that later Mahāyāna's standard teaching that a Buddha is superior to an arhat because of his power to liberate all beings from suffering is not something that is given much emphasis in the earliest Chinese translation of the *Eight Thousand*. Significantly, the vow to liberate all beings is not mentioned at all in its chapter on the characteristics of an ideal bodhisattva.

The bodhisattva path may have been extremely long and difficult, but there was a way in which it could have been made to seem less so. A well-known story describes how in a former life Śākyamuni received a prediction of his future awakening by a Buddha named Dīpaṃkara, from which point onward he was deemed an "irreversible" bodhisattva and assured of attaining full awakening. References to irreversible bodhisattvas turn out to be quite common in the early *sūtras*, with a large part of one chapter in the *Eight Thousand* devoted to describing the various signs that indicate to bodhisattvas that they must have already received a prediction of full awakening in a former lifetime. For those fortunate ones who manifested such signs, the problem of the great length of the bodhisattva path could have been attenuated since they were irreversible and their awakening was guaranteed.

Legitimizing the texts

Although the Mahāyāna *sūtras* are presented in the style of the earlier *sūtras* insofar as they purport to record the words of Śākyamuni or his authorized disciples, they are, as MacQueen (1982) observes, very poor imitations, differing not only in length and style but in some cases even going so far as to proclaim themselves as new revelations. How was it possible, then, for the adherents of early Mahāyāna to accept them as the word of the Buddha (*buddhavacana*)? Part of the answer lies in recognizing the role of "dharma preachers" (*dharmabhāṇaka*), whom MacQueen (1982) hypothesizes were inspired through a special mental clarity and receptivity to speak (*pratibhā*). In a sense, these dharma-preachers were channelling the Buddha, or more precisely, his liberating wisdom. When their teachings (which may be likened to the "residue" of visionary experiences hypothesized by Harrison) were written down in *sūtra* format, it required only a small leap of faith to recognize them as the word of the Buddha or at least a valid equivalent.

In effect, the Mahāyānists justified the authority of the new *sūtras* to themselves and others through the creation of a new episteme in which the Buddha's wisdom became invested with a transcendent timelessness that was accessible to anyone with the right training. Even the verbal expression of that wisdom was timeless; as the *Eight Thousand* states:

> In these very words, by monks called Subhūti, etc. has this very perfection of wisdom been expounded, just this very chapter of the perfection of wisdom. Maitreya also, the bodhisattva, the great being, will after he has won supreme awakening, at this very spot of earth teach this very same perfection of wisdom.

Like the Vedas, which have no historical referentiality and therefore must be true, Mahāyāna *sūtras* also appear to have gained their legitimacy from embodying a truth that exists independent of any human agency.

Key doctrinal points

Since Mahāyāna appears to have grown out of a number of Mainstream sects, it is not surprising to find a high degree of doctrinal diversity across the early *sūtras*. Some texts such as the *Lotus Sūtra* (*Saddharmapuṇḍarīka-sūtra*) or the *Inquiry of Ugra Sūtra*, for example, pay little attention to the notion of non-essentialism, or "no own-being" (*asvabhāva*), which is a central concern of the *Eight Thousand*. Yet, since the ontological doctrines presented in this important *sūtra* were later debated and variously interpreted by Mahāyāna's main philosophical schools, a brief summary of their expression in the *Eight Thousand* is given here.

The *Eight Thousand* is not a philosophical tract, and it does not present any logical arguments. Rather, its standard approach is to make assertions about the unreality of the elements of existence (*dharma*) and repeat them over and again using different examples. The choice of the term *dharma* here to describe these basic elements of existence is significant. At its root it means "to bear", for it was believed by earlier Abhidharma scholars that these elements were ultimately real due to bearing their own intrinsic nature, or "own being" (*svabhāva*). In contrast, the *Eight Thousand* asserts that in the final analysis nothing is capable of bearing its own nature—the revolutionary entailment of which was that nothing is ultimately real.

The *sūtra* goes on to expound the various ramifications of this position. One of them is the claim that since phenomena never truly exist, their production is equally unreal. This non-production of dharmas turns out to be another one of the central themes of the *Perfection of Wisdom sūtras*, where it is repeatedly said that dharmas are unproduced (*anutpāda*), do not cease (*anirodha*), and that this mode of being (which is also, in a sense, their non-being) is called their "suchness" (*tathatā*). The realization of this truth is often described as very frightening, and to overcome this fear, great importance is placed on developing the "certitude that dharmas are not produced" (*anutpattikadhar maksānti*). A bodhisattva who gains this realization is said to have entered the state of irreversibility.

Although there is a great deal of literature in later Mahāyāna that articulates the path of the bodhisattva and differentiates it from that of the "hearer" (*śrāvaka*), the early Mahāyāna *sūtras* do not clearly delineate any distinct path for bodhisattvas. Of course, accumulating merit through virtuous deeds was seen as one very important aspect of the bodhisattva path, but in order to gain release, bodhisattvas still had to undertake all the traditional practices of Mainstream Buddhism, such as the four stations of mindfulness, (*smṛty-upasthāna*), the thirty-seven wings of awakening (*bodhi-pākṣika*), and the eightfold noble path (*ārya-aṣṭāṅga-mārga*).

This presented a soteriological problem, for the natural result of such practices was not Buddhahood but the state of arhatship—something a bodhisattva was supposed to avoid. Here, the concept of "skill-in-means" (*upāya-kauśalya*) became important, but not in the better-known sense of the Buddha's use of skilful techniques for leading disciples, as seen in the *Lotus Sūtra*. Rather, in the *Eight Thousand* it usually refers to a kind of practical application of the doctrine of no own-being. In one passage, it is taught that a bodhisattva's skill-in-means is the practice of "not treating anything as a sign". To appreciate the significance of this definition, one needs to understand that in traditional Abhidharma philosophy a "sign" (*nimitta*) is an object of perception, and meditators were instructed to cultivate a state in which they refrained from seizing upon objects of the senses, or "signs". For the authors of the *Eight Thousand*, however, to treat the data of sensory experience as signs meant to treat them as if they pointed to actually existing objects, so bodhisattvas were taught *not* to view their experiences in such a manner. Through skill-in-means a bodhisattva could thus undertake all the practices that cut the bonds to cyclic existence without entering nirvana or accidentally attaining the lesser goal of arhatship.

The end of early Mahāyāna

While the beginning of the early phase of Mahāyāna is easy to define conceptually (if not chronologically or geographically) positing a division between its early and middle period is somewhat harder. Harrison (1993) observes that by the time the first Mahayana *sūtras* were translated into Chinese in the second century CE, Mahāyāna was already in the full bloom of the Early Middle period. This is a conclusion based on evidence in the early *sūtras* that considerable doctrinal development and cross-pollination had already occurred by the time these early versions were written down. For example, the *Sūtra on the Samādhi of Direct Encounter with the Buddhas of the Present* (*Pratyutpanna-Buddha-saṃmukhāvasthitasamādhi-sūtra*) combines the *Perfection of Wisdom* tenets on the unreality of the elements of existence with a tradition of devotion to the Buddha Amitābha (Harrison 1978).

The transition from early to middle can thus be thought of as a time when the doctrines in various Mahāyāna *sūtras* gradually coalesced into a more coherent worldview with the bodhisattva path at its centre. It was also a time when new *sūtras* that showed an awareness of this systematized worldview began to be produced. The *Sūtra on the Ten Grounds* (*Daśabhūmika-sūtra*), for example, is based on a methodical and coherent scheme for a bodhisattva's spiritual progress whereas the *Eight Thousand* shows little evidence of composition in accordance with any plan.

Not all scholars see the transition from early to middle in terms of doctrinal development. Some such as Deleanu (2005), for example, see the early phase as extending up to the fifth century CE, for this was a the time when epigraphic evidence Mahāyāna becomes relatively common and the movement seems to gain greater awareness of itself as a distinct institution. While the notion of the institutionalization of Mahāyāna is a useful one, it is difficult, if not impossible, to identify a point in time when Mahāyāna became an institution. Conceptually, however, we may think of it as a time when the bodhisattva ideal began to recede—when bodhisattvahood became equated with the state of being an *ārya* and was no longer open to anyone who simply underwent a conversion experience. There is a sense, then, in which the end of early Mahāyāna may also be thought of as the beginning Mahāyāna, for it marks the time when, instead of seeing themselves a bodhisattvas, its adherents may have for the first time begun to think of themselves primarily as Mahāyānists.

References

Basham, A. L. 1981. 'The evolution of the concept of the bodhisattva.' In Kawamura, L. S. ed. *The Bodhisattva Doctrine in Buddhism*. Waterloo: Wilfrid Laurier University Press, for the Canadian Corporation for Studies in Religion, 19–59.

Boucher, D. 2008. *Bodhisattvas of the Forest and the Formation of the Mahāyāna: A Study and Translation of the Rāṣṭrapālaparipṛcchā-sūtra*. Honolulu: University of Hawai'i Press.

Bronkhorst, J. 2012. 'Reflections on the origin of Mahāyāna.' In Güell, J. M. and Quevedo, A. J. eds. *Séptimo Centenario de los Estudios Orientales en Salamanca*. Salamanca: Ediciones Universidad de Salamanca, 489–502.

Conze, E. 1951. *Buddhism: Its Essence and Development*. Oxford: Bruno Cassirer.

Dayal, H. 1932. *The Bodhisattva Doctrine in Buddhist Sanskrit Literature*. London: Routledge & Kegan Paul.

Deleanu, F. 2005. 'A preliminary study on meditation and the beginnings of Mahayana Buddhism.' In Williams, P. ed. *Buddhism: Critical Concepts in Religious Studies*, vol. 3. London: Routledge, 26–73.

Gombrich, R. 1990. 'How the Mahāyāna began.' In Skorupski, T. ed. *The Buddhist Forum*. London: School of Oriental and African Studies, 21–30.

Harrison, P. 1978. 'Buddhānusmṛti in the *Pratyutpanna-buddha-saṃmukhāvasthitasamādhi-sūtra*.' *Journal of Indian Philosophy* 6: 35–57.

Harrison, P. 1993. 'The earliest Chinese translations of Mahāyāna Buddhist sūtras: Some notes on the works of Lokakṣema.' *Buddhist Studies Review* 10(2): 135–177.

Harrison, P. 1995. 'Searching for the origins of the Mahāyāna: What are we looking for?' *Eastern Buddhist* 28(1): 48–69.

Harrison, P. 2003. 'Mediums and messages: Reflections on the production of Mahāyāna sūtras.' *Eastern Buddhist* 35(1&2): 115–151.

Hirakawa, A. 1963. 'The rise of Mahāyāna Buddhism and its relationship to the worship of stupas.' *Memoirs of the Research Department of the Toyo Bunko* 22: 57–106.

La Vallée Poussin, L. de. 1910. 'Mahāyāna'. In Hastings, J. ed. *Encyclopaedia of Ethics and Religion*. Edinburgh: T.&T. Clark, 330–336.

Lamotte, É. 1958. *Histoire du Bouddhisme indien: Des origines à l'ère Śaka*. Louvain: Institut Orientaliste.

MacQueen, G. 1982. 'Inspired speech in early Mahāyāna Buddhism II.' *Religion* 12: 49–65.

Nattier, J. 2003. *A Few Good Men: The Bodhisattva Path According to the Inquiry of Ugra*. Honolulu: University of Hawai'i Press.

Ong, W. J. 1988. *Orality and Literacy: The Technologizing of the Word*. London: Routledge.

Przyluski, J. 1934. 'Origin and development of Buddhism.' *Journal of Theological Studies* 35: 337–351.

Rawlinson, A. 1983. 'The problem of the origin of the Mahāyāna.' In Slater, P. and Wiebe, D. eds. *Traditions in Contact and Change*. Waterloo: Wilfred Laurier University, 163–170; 693–699.

Ray, R. 1994. *Buddhist Saints in India*. New York and Oxford: Oxford University Press.

Schopen, G. 1975. 'The phrase '*sa pṛthivīpradeśaś caityabhūto bhavet*' in the *Vajracchedikā*: Notes on the cult of the book in Mahāyāna.' *Indo-Iranian Journal* 17: 147–181.

Schopen, G. 1979. 'Mahāyāna in Indian inscriptions.' *Indo-Iranian Journal* 21: 1–19.

Schopen, G. 1991. 'Archaeology and Protestant presuppositions in the study of Indian Buddhism.' *History of Religions* 31(1): 1–23.

Warder, A. K. 1970. *Indian Buddhism*. Delhi: Motilal Banarsidass.

Chapter 30
ABHIDHARMA

Joseph Walser

Overview

Abhidharma is a designation of Buddhist literature in which the core teachings from the Buddha's sermons are systematized, interpreted, and defended. Ideally, *abhidharma* texts form the third "Basket" (*piṭaka*) of the Buddhist "Three Baskets" (*Tripiṭaka*) or canon, but many *sūtra* texts (discourses attributed to the Buddha) and post-canonical texts share important features with the texts comprising the *Abhidharmapiṭaka*. It will be useful, then to make a distinction between canonical *abhidharma* texts (i.e., those texts comprising the *Abhidharmapiṭaka*) and those texts not included in the *piṭaka*, but sharing important features with and developing the ideas of canonical *abhidharma* texts. The latter may usefully be referred to as *abhidharma* as well, even though it is technically not part of the *Abhidharmapiṭaka*. *Abhidharma* texts comprising this category display considerable variation as to genre. The texts range from simple commentaries on, or indexes to, the Buddha's sermons (e.g., the *Dharmaskandha*, *Mahāniddesa*), to sectarian debate manuals (e.g., *Kathāvatthu*, *Vijñānakāya*), to treatises meant to be comprehensive of all Buddhist doctrine (e.g., *Abhidharmakośa*, *Abhidhammathasaṅgaha*), to shorter treatises on specific topics (e.g., *Lokaprajñāpti*, *Puggalapaññati*). The lasting significance of *abhidharma* as a genre lies in its innovations to and systemizations of the basic Buddhist doctrines found in the *Sūtrapiṭaka*. As such, *abhidharma* texts became a critical component in the formation of early Buddhist sectarian identity.

After a brief discussion of the meaning of the term "*abhidharma*," I will discuss the chronology of the *abhidharma* collections of the different Buddhist sects. Against this backdrop, I will then trace the development of *Abhidharma* ontology.

The meaning of the term

The meaning of the term "*abhidharma*" has been subjected to considerable discussion in *abhidharma* literature itself (see, e.g., *Abhidharma Mahāvibhāṣā Śāstra* (AM), T. 1545, pp. 1a8–3b22). On the most fundamental level, *abhidharma* consists of the word "*dharma*" (notoriously difficult word to define, but one that seems to span the English words "teaching," "truth," and "real thing") to which the prefix *abhi-* has been attached. It is the prefix that has caused the most problems in defining *abhidharma*. According to Monier-Williams, the prefix *abhi-* when attached to a noun not derived from a verb means it "expresses something like superiority or intensity" (Monier-Williams 1982, *s.v.*). Scholars seem to be divided between translating it as "concerning the dharma," and "the higher dharma." For our purposes, it will be most useful to think of *dharma* as the teaching of the Buddha contained in the *Sūtrapiṭaka* and *Vinayapiṭaka* and *abhidharma* as a kind of "meta-*dharma*" or the distilled essence of that *dharma*. Here we can find a nice parallel between the *Abhidharmapiṭaka* which extracts the topical lists (*mātṛkā*) from the *Sūtrapiṭaka* and the term *abhivinaya*, used in the various *vinayas* in reference to the list of *Prātimokṣa* rules extracted from the *Vinayavibhaṅga* (see La Vallée Poussin 1988, vol. 1, xxx–xxxiv; Walser 2005, 128–129).

Chronology

Scholars are generally agreed on a relative chronology for *abhidharma* texts, even if assigning absolute dates to any of the texts is fraught with difficulties. In brief, the composition of *abhidharma* texts falls into four periods (see Willemen *et al.* 1998, 173–174). The first period consists of those texts that are closely tied to specific *sūtras* (indeed, some, like the *Saṅgīti Sutta* of the *Dīgha Nikāya* are actually included in the *Sūtrapiṭaka* itself), culling lists of doctrines from those *sūtras* with minimal commentary. These texts may or may not be written in *sūtra* format themselves. The second period texts consist of lists of the same doctrines or topics (*mātṛka*) that are no longer explicitly referenced to specific *sūtras*. During this period lists are cross-referenced against other lists, the combinatorics of which account for the bulk of many of the works belonging to this period. As *abhidharma* texts become more established as an independent genre, we find *abhidharma* texts introducing new technical terms and new articulations of practice. Concomitant with doctrinal innovations, there arose doctrinal disagreements. It is in *abhidharma* literature of this period that we find the beginnings of sectarian consciousness. The third period comprises texts displaying full-blown sectarianism. Important texts of this period attempt to encompass the *abhidharma* teachings of the second period while defending their innovations against challenges raised by other sects. Finally, the fourth period consists of post-canonical digests of or commentaries on third-period texts, often with heightened sectarian rhetoric.

Though there are presumably many *abhidharma* texts that are no longer extant, there is evidence that the following sects had at least one freestanding *abhidharma* or *abhidharma*-like text if not an entire collection: Theravāda, Sarvāstivāda, Dharmagupta, Haimavata, Mahāsaṅghika, Saṃmitīya, Vatsīputrīya and Bāhuśrūtīya, and Gokulika/Kukkutika. Turning to the archaeological record, *abhidharma* manuscripts seem to predominate in Kuṣaṇa Era find-spots on the Silk Route (Sander 1991, 147–148). Since these sites are either Sarvāstivādin or Dharmagupta, we can surmise that the use of *abhidharma* materials was an important part of the everyday curriculum for those sects in that area.

The status of *abhidharma*

As *abhidharma* literature developed into a genre distinct from the *sūtra* genre, its status became a matter of some debate. By the second period mentioned above, some sects of Indian Buddhism formed *abhidharma* collections distinct from the *sūtra* and *vinaya* collections. It also appears that some were not comfortable with the innovations introduced in *abhidharma* texts. By the time of the *Abhidharmakośa* (fourth or fifth century), there were some among the Sarvāstivādins who were designated as "Sautrāntikas" or "those who only follow the *sūtra*." (For some of the modern debates over the significance of this term, see Cox 1995, 38–39.) Similar tendencies can be found in Skandhila's *Abhidharmāvatāra*, where the author explicitly renounces the "method of questions and answers" i.e., the catechetical style characteristic of *abhidharma* treatises (Willemen *et al.* 1998, 284–285). For these Sautrāntikas, the word "*abhidharma*" simply referred to certain kinds of texts within the *Sūtrapiṭaka* itself and was not an independent collection of texts (we find the same thing in the *Mahāsaṃghika Vinaya* [Walser 2005, 128–129). At the other extreme were the Gokūlikas or Kukkutika, who, according to Paramārtha, went so far as to declare that the *Tripiṭaka* denotes the *Abhidharmapiṭaka* alone, and not the *Sūtrapiṭaka* or the *Vinayapiṭaka* (Bareau 1955, 79).

Abhidharma collections

Despite the relatively high number of schools reported to have had *abhidharma* collections, there are only two complete *Abhidharmapiṭakas* extant and only a handful of *abhidharma*-style texts belonging to other sects. In addition, there are fragments of *abhidharma* manuscripts that have been found that have no known corresponding text in any existing collection. The two complete collections are those of the Theravādins, who predominate in Sri Lanka and Southeast Asia, and the Sarvāstivādins who were prevalent in Northern India and on the Silk Route.

Theravāda abhidhamma

The Theravāda *Abhidharmapiṭaka* consists of seven main texts. The ideas of these texts are clarified and expanded in important ways by later commentaries, i.e., the *aṭṭhakathā*, and the *mūla-* and *anuṭīkā* commentaries and a handful of "extra-canonical" or "paracanonical" works. The seven texts of the *Abhidhammapiṭaka* are: the *Dhammasaṅgaṇi*, *Vibhaṅga*, *Dhātukathā*, *Puggalapaññatti*, *Kathāvatthu*, *Yamaka*, and *Paṭṭhāna*. As to the relative dates of these texts, Robert Buswell and Padmanabh Jaini place the *Puggalapaññatti* and parts of the *Dhammasaṅgaṇi* and the *Vibhaṅga* in the earliest stage, the *Dhātukathā* and *Katthāvatthu* in the second period, and the put the *Yamaka* and *Paṭṭhāna* toward the end of the composition of the canonical seven texts (Buswell and Jaini 1996: 90–91).

Later post-canonical treatises include the *Peṭakopadesa* (parts of which are preserved in Chinese; see Zacchetti 2002), *Nettippakaraṇa*, *Paṭisaṃbhidhāmagga*, and

Abhidhammatthasaṅgaha. Though not considered *abhidharma* texts per se, Upatissa's *Vimuttimagga* and Buddhaghosa's *Visuddhimagga* develop many of the themes of early canonical *abhidharma* texts and hence are relevant to any discussion of *abhidharma*. There is some controversy regarding the former of these two, since many scholars have assigned the *Vimuttimagga* (preserved in Chinese with fragments in Tibetan) to the Abhayagiri *vihāra* Theravādins, a renegade branch that became extinct in the twelfth century. This attribution has been roundly criticized (Crosby 1999).

Sarvāstivāda

The Sarvāstivādins also claimed seven texts to be authoritative: the *Jñānaprasthāna* (alt. *Aṣṭhagrantha*), *Prakaraṇapāda*, *Vijñānakāya*, *Dharmaskandha*, *Prajñaptibhāṣya*, *Dhātukāya*, *Saṅgītiparyāya*. Though the traditional ordering of the core seven texts places the *Jñānaprasthāna* first, modern scholars place it last, dividing the development of the tradition into three phases as well. Ryogon Fukuhara places the *Saṅgītiparyāya* and *Dharmaskandha* in the earliest group, the *Prajñaptibhāṣya*, *Dhātukāya*, and *Vijñānakāya*, and *Prakaraṇapāda* in the second group, and finally the *Jñānaprasthāna* in the third group (Buswell and Jaini 1996, 102).

While generally treatises of the fourth period come later than these core seven, there are two exceptions. Erich Frauwallner (1995, 152) and Bart Dessein (1996, 647) have both made a case for the *Abhidharmāmṛta* (aka *Abhidharmasāra*) by Dharmaśrī and the anonymous *Pañcaskandhaka* to pre-date the *Jñānaprasthāna*.

At the time of the composition of the *Jñānaprasthāna* and *Aṣṭhagrantha*, a regional division arose from within the Sarvāstivāda sect and this division is reflected in the post-canonical *abhidharma* literature of the school. While there is no indication that there was actually a schism within Sarvāstivāda at this time, there was definitely some tension on a number of doctrinal points. These tensions appear to have fallen along a regional divide. Representing the masters of Kaśmīr is the *Mahā-Vibhāṣa* (*The Great Commentary* [on the *Jñānaprasthāna*]). Kaśmīri Sarvāstivādins are subsequently known as "Vaibhāṣikas" or "those who follow the *Vibhāṣa*." There are three such *Vibhāṣa* extant in Chinese translation, with many others reputed to have existed (for a summary discussion of the work that has been done on the different versions, see Willemen *et al.* 1998, 233–237). According to a legend contained in the *Vibhāṣa* commentary itself, the *Vibhāṣa* was compiled at a council convened by the Kuṣāna king Kaniṣka, c. second century—although by the testimony of one of the extant versions, Kaniṣka was already dead at the composition of the *Mahāvibhāṣa* (see Willemen *et al.* 1998, 116–119; 232). In addition to the *Vibhāṣa* commentaries, there exist two shorter texts from this time period reflecting Vaibhāṣika predilections, namely: the *Ārya Vasumitra Bodhisattva Saṅgīti Śāstra* (AM, T. 1549) and the *Pañca Vastuka Vibhāṣā Śāstra* (AM, T. 1555 and 1557).

The other side of the divide was represented by masters from Gandhāra, whose representative texts were Dharmaśreṣṭhin's (alt. Dharmaśrī's) *Abhidharmahṛdāya*, the *Saṃyuktābhidharmahṛdaya*, and the *Abhidharmahṛdayaśāstra* by Dharmatrāta. In the fourth or the fifth century, Vasubandhu championed the cause and wrote a sharp criticism of Vaibhāṣika tenets entitled the *Abhidharmakośabhāṣya*. The latter was in turn attacked by a Vaibhāṣika named Saṅghabhadra in his *Nyāyānusāra* and *Abhidharmasamayapradīpikā*, and by the anonymously penned (also Vaibhāṣika) *Abhidharmadīpa*. Other texts of "western masters" include the *Abhidharmāmṛtarasa* by Ghoṣaka, the *Abhidharmāvatāra* by Skandhila, the *Abhidharmakośasphuṭārtha* by Yaśomitra and the *Tattvārtha* of Sthiramati. The last two of these are commentaries on Vasubandhu's *Abhidharmakośabhāṣya*. There does not appear to be any one issue that divided the two camps but rather a host of smaller technical points. If one were to attempt to summarize the disagreement from Vasubandhu's writings it would be that the Western Masters thought that the Vaibhāṣikas had taken too many liberties in postulating *dharmas* not explicitly mentioned in the sermons of the Buddha.

Abhidharma ontological innovations

It is in the second period of development that we find the beginnings of *abhidharma* contributions to Buddhist thought. *Abhidharma* writers were responsible for important developments in Buddhist taxonomy, ontology, and soteriology. To give the reader a sense of these innovations I will focus on innovations ontology.

The major ontological innovations of *abhidharma* literature revolve around the concept and status of *dharmas*. In early Buddhism, *dharmas* probably were considered to be "distinct, but not unrelated to one another; they represent causally significant points within the complex web of experienced activities, but points that can only be determined relationally and that can only be defined dynamically" (Cox 2004: 555). By the time of later works like the *Viṃśatikākārikāvṛtti* of Vasubandhu, or the *Kṣaṇabhaṅgasiddhiḥ Vyātirekātmika* of Ratnakīrti, *dharmas* are treated as temporally and substantially discrete entities. These later texts treat *dharmas* as existing essentially (*svabhāvatas*), substantially (*dravyatas*), and momentarily (*kṣaṇika*). For later Buddhists, *dharmas* coming into existence and passing out of existence are ontologically distinct from one another and yet form a continuous stream (*saṃtāna*) that makes up each personality. This view of *dharmas* as temporally and substantively discrete took a long time to develop and was probably never the univocal position of any Buddhist school.

There are two ways scholars trace the development of the individuation of *dharmas*, and both lead us back to the Brāhmaṇical Vaiśeṣika theorists. One approach traces the idea of discrete *dharmas* back to the Vaiśeṣika idea of atoms. The *Sūtrapiṭaka* refers often to the "great elements" of earth, air, fire, and water. While these are associated with qualities, such as cohesion, motion, heat, etc., nowhere in the *Sūtrapiṭaka* is there any mention that these elements are atoms (*aṇu*). The first hint of atomism in Sarvāstivāda *abhidharma* occurs in Dharmaśrī's *Abhidharmasāra*. In this work, Dharmaśrī includes a discussion of the elements existing as groups of four atoms, thereby at least making material *dharmas* into discrete existents (Ronkin 2005, 56). Thereafter, discussions of the theory of atoms become a staple in Sarvāstivāda *abhidharma*, finding a place in the *Mahāvibhāṣa* and the *Abhidharmakośabhāṣya* among others. Noa Ronkin finds that the Theravāda tradition comes to the theory of atoms much later: the first work to explicitly mention the theory is the *Abhidhammāvatāra* of Buddhadatta (*c.* 450 CE). Later commentarial literature and the *Visuddhimagga* discuss atoms as existing in "packages" (*kalāpa*), perhaps in response to the Vaiśeṣika notion of groups of atoms, but it is "only in the period of the sub-commentaries and the medieval manuals did *kalāpa* become the standard term for the collective atom" (see Ronkin 2005, 58).

Collett Cox takes another approach, arguing that the notion of *dharmas* as discretely existing things was a consequence of the adoption of the *Pañcavastuka* taxonomy. One of the early uses of lists of *dharmas* was for the practice of *dharmapravicaya*, or distinguishing of *dharmas*. This practice can be seen in such exercises as the mindfulness of *dharmas* in the *Satipaṭṭhāna Sutta*. An important part of disambiguating and distinguishing mental components was to determine the category into which a particular factor should be included. Categorical inclusion led Buddhists to shift from talking about the *dharma* (singular) of form to talking about which *dharmas* (plural) are to be included in the category of form. Cox notes that the *Śāriputrābhidharma* was the first *abhidharma* text to discuss the categorization of *dharmas* (plural). At this point, however, there was no problem maintaining an understanding of *dharmas* as fluid, interrelated categories while still holding no ontological commitment to their ultimate existence. According to Cox, when the categories of formations dissociated from consciousness (*cittaviprayuktasaṃskāra*) and the unconditioned (*asaṃskṛta*) were brought into Buddhist taxonomy by way of the *Pañcavastuka*, the emphasis shifted from *dharma analysis* as an experiential practice toward *dharma categorization* aimed at theoretical comprehensiveness. The move away from practice to theory was a function of the fact that the *cittaviprayuktasaṃskāra* and *asaṃskṛta* categories comprised items that, by definition, could not be directly experienced. The change in theoretical use of the concept of *dharmas* ended up leading to a shift in the very concept of what a *dharma* was.

While noting that there are no definitions of a *dharma* per se in Sarvāstivādin literature until Upaśānta's and Dharmatrāta's commentaries on the *Abhidharmahṛdaya*, Cox shows that it is in the *Mahāvibhāṣa*'s discussions of unconditioned *dharmas* that categorization based on substance (*dravya*) and nature (*svabhāva*) become standard for the school (Cox 2004, 558). One needs to be exceedingly careful, however, in the interpretation of the latter terms. While it is tempting to always read the term "*svabhāva*" through a Mahāyāna (or more specifically a *Perfection of Wisdom*) lens as an indication of reified or concrete existence, Cox argues that the terms *svabhāva*, *bhāva*, *dravya*, and *svalakṣaṇa* were originally used epistemologically as indicators of class inclusion and took on ontological significance in the *Mahāvibhāṣa* only by a kind of logical extension (Cox 2004, 562–563).

For example, it is the essential nature of fire to combust. Stated more broadly, in any possible world (past, present, future, Mars, Narnia, etc.) if something is fire, it will burn something. Hence, combustion will always and in every case be included in the category of fire. This makes the category eternal insofar as its class inclusion is an atemporal fact. The necessity of class inclusion leads the Sarvāstivādins in the direction of (one of the first?) properly ontological statements about *dharmas*. The *Vijñānakāya* opens with the doctrine from which the Sarvāstivādin school derives its name, namely: that past, present, and future exist. Here, the argument requires more than a mere categorical existence of past, present, and future entities since the argument rests on the assumption that any cognition requires an existent object (*ālambana*). For instance, desire exists and must have an object that is desired. Yet, objects of desire can be in the past or in the future (see AM, T. 1539, pp. 531a27ff.). Under the *Vijñānakāya*'s argument, the cause of those desires must be real. While the *Vijñānakāya* does not discuss the ontological *dharmas* qua *dharmas*, the *Mahāvibhāṣa* discussion of this doctrine explicitly refers to the status of "all *dharmas*." The *Mahāvibhāṣa* presents four different interpretations of the three times doctrine. All agree that the term "existence" pertains to *dharmas* in the past, present, and future; they only differ in what they ascribe modification to. The four interpretations ascribe the modification to a change in: (1) mode (*bhāva*); (2) characteristic (*lakṣaṇa*); (3) position (*avasthā*); and (4) relative difference *vis* past and future (*anyathā*). In each case, Vasubandhu repeats what appears to be a stock phrase from the *Mahāvibhāṣa* itself: "There is a modification of the (*bhava*, *lakṣaṇa*, *avasthā*, and *anyathā*, respectively), there is no modification of the substrate (*dravya*)" (cf. Pradhan 1975, 296; AM, T. 1545, p. 396a21). The accepted position of the school glosses the *dravya* of the earlier passage with "nature" (*svabhāva*) and states that the nature of a *dharma* exists in the past, present and future, while its function (*kāritra*) is discharged only in the present (AM, T. 1545, pp. 396b22–23).

The idea that *dharmas* exist in the future, pop up in the present, and disappear into the past highlights the theory that there is a stream of *dharmas* coming from the future to the present and then from the present to the past. The term "stream" (*saṃtāna*) is subsequently used to refer to the flow of *dharmas* that make up an individual person. Once a future and past string of *dharmas* is posited, two new entities (both included in the *cittaviprayuktasaṃskāra*) needed to be postulated to describe how one could acquire or be cut off from something that always exists: acquisition and non-acquisition (*prāpti* and *aprāpti*). The use of these terms appears in early Sarvāstivāda texts such as the *Dharmaskandha* and the *Prakaraṇapāda*, although its full application does not become set until the *Mahāvibhāṣa* (Cox 1995, 79).

There is another context in which *dharmas* are treated as existing substantially. In the *Mahāvibhāṣa*, the distinction is often made between something existing substantially (*dravyatas*) and nominally (*prajñaptitas*). While the word *dravya* itself can, like *svabhāva*, simply be an indicator of class inclusion, we can safely assume it refers to substance properly understood when it is contrasted with nominal existence.

Theravāda *abhidharma*, for its part, seems to have tended farther away from a commitment to the substantiality of *dharmas*. Noa Ronkin argues (2005, 98–99) that while the *Peṭakopadesa* refers to Skr. *sabhāva* as the cause (*hetu*) of a *dharma*, it is only in the commentarial literature that we find statements such as "a *dharma* is the bearer of its *sabhāva*." Even there, Ronkin argues that this reflects more of a process-oriented metaphysics than a substance metaphysics. For the Theravādins, the move toward substance metaphysics (if they ever do, in fact, arrive there—for a counter argument see Gethin 2005) is tied closely with the theory of momentariness. Nevertheless, we find *dharmas* to be increasingly individuated as the history of Theravādin *abhidharma* progresses, even if what is being so individuated are events rather than things. The *Kathāvatthu*, for instance, argues that only mental *dharmas* are momentary, whereas material *dharmas* persist for varying durations. Further, it is stated only in the commentarial literature that a material *dharma* lasts for sixteen or seventeen thought moments (Ronkin 2005, 62–63). Indeed, Theravādins seem to have been more interested in thought moments than the Sarvāstivādins. One of the unique doctrinal developments in Theravādin *abhidharma* literature is the "consciousness series" (*citta-vīthi*) which first appears in the *Paṭṭhāna* (Cousins 1981). The consciousness series is defined as a series of moments of thought (*citta*) and mental concomitants (*cetasika*) that arise from an "intermediate," (*bhavaṅga*) contentless consciousness.

Abhidharma literature takes Buddhist thought from its basic presentation in the *Sūtrapiṭaka* to new levels of sophistication and complexity in later *abhidharma* treatises. Its arguments regarding the nature and classification of reals and the soul (or more precisely its absence) clearly articulated the Buddhist philosophical position which could then be defended against the doctrines of competing Buddhist and non-Buddhist philosophical schools.

References

The Abhidharma Mahāvibhāṣā Śāstra (c. 150 BCE). 2007. B. K. L. Dhammajoti (ed.), As *Śravāstivāda Abhidharma*. Hong Kong: Center for Buddhist Studies.

Bareau, André. 1955. *Les sectes bouddhiques du petit véhicule*. Paris: École française d'Extrême-Orient.

Buswell, Robert and Padmanabh Jaini. 1996. "The Development of Abhidharma Philosophy." In Karl Potter (ed.). *Encyclopedia of Indian Philosophies*, vol 2: *Abhidharma Buddhism to 150 AD*, 73–120. Delhi: Motilal Banarsidass.

Cousins, Lance. 1981. "The *Paṭṭhāna* and the development of the Theravādin Abhidhamma." *Journal of the Pali Text Society* 9: 22–46.

Cox, Collett. 1995. *Disputed Dharmas: Early Buddhist Theories on Existence*. Tokyo: The International Institute for Buddhist Studies.

———. 2004. "From Category to Ontology: The Changing Role of *Dharma* in Sarvāstivāda Abhidharma." *Journal of Indian Philosophy* 32: 543–597.

Crosby, Kate. 1999. "History versus Modern Myth: The *Abhayagirivihāra*, the *Vimuttimagga* and *Yogāvacara* Meditation." *Journal of Indian Philosophy* 27: 503–550.

Dessein, Bart. 1996. "*Dharmas* Associated with Awarenesses and the Dating of the Sarvāstivāda Abhidharma Works." *Asiatische Studien* 50: 623–652.

Frauwallner, Erich. 1995. *Buddhist Philosophical Systems*. Sophie Kidd and Ernst Steinkellner (trans.). Albany, NY: State University of New York Press.

Gethin, Rupert. 2005. "On the Nature of *Dhammas*: A Review Article." *Buddhist Studies Review* 22: 175–194.

Jaini, Padmanabh. 1977. *Abhidharmadīpa with Vibhāṣāprabhāvṛtti*. Patna: Jayaswal Research Institute.

La Vallée Poussin, Louis de. 1988–1990. *Abhidharmakośabhāṣyam*, 4 vols. Leo Pruden (trans.). Berkeley: Asian Humanities Press.

Monier-Williams, Monier. 1982. *Sanskrit–English Dictionary*. Repr. Delhi: Motilal Banarsidass.

Pradhāna, P. (ed.). 1975. *Abhidharmakośabhāṣyam*. Patna: K. P. Jayaswal Research Institute.

Ronkin, Noa. 2005. *Early Buddhist Metaphysics: The Making of a Philosophical Tradition*. London: Routledge.

Sander, Lore. 1991. "The Earliest Manuscripts from Central Asia and the Sarvāstivāda Mission." In Ronald Emmerick and Dieter Weber (eds.). *Corolla Iranica: Papers in Honour of Prof. Dr. David*

Neil MacKenzie on the Occasion of his 65th Birthday on April 8th, 1991, 133–150. Frankfurt am Main: Peter Lang.

Walser, Joseph. 2005. *Nāgārjuna in Context*. New York: Columbia University Press.

Willemen, Charles, Bart Dessein and Collett Cox. 1998. *Sarvāstivāda Buddhist Scholasticism*. Leiden: E. J. Brill.

Zacchetti, Stefano. 2002. "An Early Chinese Translation Corresponding to Chapter 6 of the *Peṭakopadesa*, An Shigao's *Yin chi ru jing* T. 603 and its Indian Original: A Preliminary Survey." *Bulletin of the School of Oriental and African Studies* 65(1): 74–98.

Chapter 31
NĀGĀRJUNA

Jay L. Garfield

Nāgārjuna's life, times and corpus

Not a great deal is known of the life of Nāgārjuna with certainty. The canonical biographies are entirely hagiographic. The best evidence suggests that he lived in the second half of the second century CE in the lower Krishna River valley in what is now Andhra Pradesh (Walser 2005). He appears to have been an influential Mahāyāna monk scholar residing in a mixed Mahāyāna-Śrāvakayāna monastery, and was apparently an advisor to at least one king, to whom several of his texts are addressed.

Several sets of texts are ascribed to Nāgārjuna by some or all of his principal Indian commentators (Buddhapālita, Bhāviveka, Candrakīrti and Avalokitavrata), later Indian Buddhist scholars, Tibetan and Chinese philosophers and doxographers. These include a set of systematic philosophical texts, including *Mūlamadhyamakakārikā* (*Fundamental Verses on the Middle Way*), *Sūnyatāsaptati* (*Seventy Verses on Emptiness*), *Yuktiṣaṣṭika* (*Sixty Verses of Reasoning*), *Vigrahavyāvartanī* (*Replies to Objections*), *Vaidalyaprakaraṇa* (*Devastating Discourse*), *Pratītyasamutpādahṛdayakārikā* (*Verses on the Heart of Dependent Origination*), *Ratnāvalī* and *Suhṛllekha* (*Letter to a Friend*). All of these texts are widely attributed to Nāgārjuna by canonical sources; stylistic and content considerations suggest that they are written by a common author. A commentary on *Mūlamadhyamakakārikā*, *Akutobhayā*, is attributed by some to Nāgārjuna, but there are good reasons to doubt this attribution. The style of the text is very different from those of the other two prose commentaries by Nāgārjuna (those to *Vigrahavyāvartanī* and to *Śūnyatāsaptati*); the text cites Nāgārjuna's student Āryadeva; and Nāgārjuna's most erudite Indian commentator, Candrakīrti, rejects the attribution.

Nāgārjuna may have composed two other texts of some philosophical interest. *Sūtrasammucaya* (*Collection of sūtras*) is probably Nāgārjuna's. His authorship of *Bodhicittavivaraṇa* (*Explanation of Bodhicitta*) is much less certain. The former is of interest because of its collection of early Mahāyāna texts, demonstrating the texts taken as authoritative by Mahāyāna scholars at this early stage; the latter because it would provide evidence of the development of a sustained theory of *bodhicitta* as early as the second century CE.

The second set of texts attributed to Nāgārjuna comprises devotional hymns (*stotras* or *stavas*). Four hymns (the *Catuḥstava*) are regarded as Nāgārjuna's by Candrakīrti and by Prajñākaramati, as well as by many Tibetan commentators. Those are *Lokātītastava* (*Hymn to the Supramundane*), *Niraupamyastava* (*Hymn to the Incomparable Lord*), *Acintyastava* (*Hymn to the Inconceivable One*) and *Paramārthastava* (*Hymn on the Ultimate*). There is little ground for doubt about the attribution of these hymns (see Lindtner 1982, 1986).

Dozens of other hymns are attributed to Nāgārjuna, but with less certainty. Most interesting among these, and of contested attribution is *Dharmadhātustava* (*Hymn on the Domain of Reality*). This text is stylistically consistent with Nāgārjuna's work, but doctrinally it appears at odds with the core philosophical texts. Bhāviveka attributes it to Nāgārjuna and it is represented as among his corpus in the Tibetan canon, suggesting broad Indian consensus. Finally, numerous alchemical, tantric and medical texts are attributed to Nāgārjuna. There is, however, little reason to be confident of any of these attributions, and we will not address these texts here.

Most of Nāgārjuna's texts are written in elegant verse, with a very terse expository style. In two cases (*Śūnyatāsaptati* and *Vigrahavyāvartanī*) Nāgārjuna composed prose autocommentaries. The hymns are elegant devotional poetry. Nāgārjuna did compose two texts clearly addressed to a lay audience: *Ratnāvalī* and *Suhṛllekha*. Each of these is primarily concerned with moral themes and the cultivation of the spiritual path. But each grounds its ethical account in Madhyamaka metaphysics.

Nāgārjuna's philosophical context

Nāgārjuna wrote as Mahāyāna Buddhism was gaining momentum in India, and his work is foundational for what would become the Madhyamaka school. The Madhyamaka school finds its *sūtra* foundation principally in the Prajñāparamitā *sūtras* that appear around the beginning of the first millennium CE. These texts espouse doctrines that are in some ways revolutionary in the Buddhist context, and in some ways very continuous with earlier Buddhist theory (Veléz 2005). Fundamental Buddhist ideas such as the impermanence of all phenomena, the absence of a personal self, the absence of an intrinsic nature in ordinary phenomena and the dependently originated nature of all phenomena, familiar in pre-Mahāyāna (Śrāvakayāna) Buddhism, are also to be found in the Prajñāparamitā *sūtras*, and in Madhyamaka philosophical texts.

On the other hand, these fundamental doctrines are subtly, but importantly reinterpreted, and this reinterpretation is central to Nāgārjuna's philosophical outlook. The Śrāvakayāna Buddhist philosophical schools by this time had been articulated through the detailed metaphysics, epistemology and psychology of the *abhidharma* literature. The accounts presented in this literature are in general reductionist on the metaphysical and psychological side and foundationalist on the epistemological side. Conventional phenomena, such as persons and ordinary physical objects, are regarded as ultimately unreal, but as reducible to causally interdependent, momentary, atomic entities which do exist ultimately and which have intrinsic natures; knowledge is grounded in perceptual contact with these phenomena and in inference from that perceptual given. Impermanence is understood in terms of the constant succession of macroscopic phenomena, and the emptiness of self or intrinsic nature in terms of the ultimate composition of macroscopic phenomena by non-empty, ultimately real entities.

This picture is challenged in Madhyamaka texts by the doctrine that *all* phenomena are empty of self or intrinsic nature; *all* phenomena are impermanent; *all* phenomena are interdependent, and there are neither ontological nor epistemological foundations to be found. Nothing exists ultimately. The other Mahāyāna innovation is ethical. Whereas the ethical ideal in Śrāvakayāna Buddhism is the *ārhat*, or the being who achieves *nirvāṇa*—cessation of suffering—through the cultivation of the Buddhist eightfold path, in the Mahāyāna that ideal is replaced with that of the bodhisattva, who develops the altruistic aspiration to attain full awakening (buddhahood) for the sake of benefiting all sentient beings by bringing them all to liberation from suffering. The central value of this form of Buddhist moral theory is *karuṇā*, or a compassionate resolve to be of benefit to others.

Despite these doctrinal continuities, this emerging philosophical school was controversial, and the texts on which it sought to ground itself were not universally regarded as authentic. The systematic development of Madhyamaka philosophical theory was accomplished by Nāgārjuna. His philosophical corpus constitutes a response to *abhidharma* Buddhism, a defense and systematic articulation of the doctrines announced in the Prajñāparamitā *sūtras*, and an attempt to demonstrate that these metaphysical, epistemological and ethical views represent the correct development of Buddhist philosophy.

Outline of Nāgārjuna's philosophical views

Nāgārjuna defends a distinctive view of the nature of emptiness and of its relationship to dependent origination, encapsulated in his doctrine of the two truths, or two realities. Nāgārjuna argues that all phenomena are empty of *svabhāva*, a term we can translate in this context as *essence*, or *intrinsic nature*. To have *svabhāva* would be to exist independently; to have an inherent quality that makes a thing the thing that it is; to have an identity independent of language or conceptual imputation. Nāgārjuna characterizes *svabhāva* in all of these ways and takes them to be equivalent, capturing the idea that for any real entity, we can say what it is that determines its identity, that its identity conditions are internal to it, and that when we know it, our knowledge and language reflect its nature, rather than the other way around.

Nāgārjuna takes it that in our ordinary pre-reflective engagement with the world we take ourselves as well as other persons and objects to exist in this way; he also notes that much Buddhist and non-Buddhist metaphysics (particularly the Sarvāstivāda *abhidharma*), while it denies this status to macroscopic objects, posits a more fundamental reality of entities that exist in this way. Nāgārjuna argues that *nothing* exists in that way and that the very idea of *svabhāva* is incoherent. That is, things are *empty* of any such intrinsic nature. This is not to say that macroscopic entities do not exist at all; it is to say that actual existence is a merely conventional, nominal, relational, dependent existence. This conventional reality is not, Nāgārjuna argues, a second-class reality, but is rather the only kind of reality possible. This doctrine of emptiness is hence continuous with earlier Buddhist accounts of the emptiness of ordinary phenomena, but runs much deeper, both in terms of the account of that of which things are empty and in terms of the scope of the analysis.

To say that phenomena are empty of essence in this sense, according to Nāgārjuna, is to say that they are dependently originated (*pratītya-samutpāda*) or are merely dependent designations (*prajñaptir-upadāya*). In particular, he holds that wholes are ontologically dependent upon their parts, and that parts are reciprocally dependent for their identities on the wholes in which they figure; that events and objects depend for their existence on a variety of causes and conditions; and that the identities of the phenomena we encounter as events, enduring objects, classes, etc. are dependent upon our conceptual processes and interests. This multi-dimensional structure of interdependence guarantees that nothing has any independent existence or intrinsic nature that makes it the thing that it is. Interdependence and emptiness are thus, Nāgārjuna argues, the same thing, and they are universal characteristics of all phenomena.

This identity of dependent origination and emptiness underlies Nāgārjuna's distinctive account of the two truths, or realities (*satya*). Nāgārjuna argues that there are two truths, or ways the world is: a conventional truth (*saṃvṛti-satya* or *vyavahāra-satya*) and an ultimate truth (*paramārtha-satya*). The conventional truth comprises the world as we ordinarily experience it. The ultimate truth is the emptiness of all conventional phenomena. The perception of conventional truth is conditioned by confusion, in that we experience conventional phenomena as though they exist independently, with intrinsic natures. In this sense they are *deceptive*, for they are in fact empty of that independence and of those natures; this is the ultimate truth, which is non-deceptive. Conventional truth and ultimate truth are hence, from an epistemic perspective, according to Nāgārjuna, very different from one another.

Despite this difference, however, they are, from an ontological perspective, *identical*. For conventional phenomena are not, in virtue of being interdependent and essenceless, *nonexistent*. Their emptiness is not a separate reality that replaces them, but is their very mode of existence. Since they are dependently originated, they exist, and are empty. One important implication of this is that emptiness itself is dependent: rather than constituting a separate independent reality, the emptiness of any phenomenon, as a property of that phenomenon, is dependent for its existence on the existence of that which is empty. Just as the rectangularity of a table depends upon the table, so does its emptiness. Emptiness is thus, like every other phenomenon, empty. This doctrine of the identity of the two truths and of the emptiness of emptiness is perhaps Nāgārjuna's most original and important contribution to Buddhist and to world philosophy. (See Burton 1999; Garfield 1995, 2002; Siderits 1988; and Westerhoff 2009 for more detail.)

This ontology lies behind Nāgārjuna's metaphysical and epistemological anti-foundationalism. Because Nāgārjuna argues that all phenomena are empty and interdependent, there can be no ultimate ontology to which all others reduce. Any ontology one proposes will comprise only entities which themselves are interdependent and essenceless. Moreover, since epistemological foundationalism requires either that objects of knowledge (*prameya*) or instruments of knowledge (*pramāṇa*) be taken as the foundation of knowledge, and since these, Nāgārjuna argues, are themselves interdependent and empty of essence, depending on one another for their epistemic status, there can be no epistemological foundations, either. (See Siderits 1980; Garfield 2002.)

Nāgārjuna did not write much on ethics—only *Ratnāvalī* and *Suhṛllekha* (and perhaps *Bodhicittavivaraṇa*)—but enough that the outlines of his views are clear, and are clearly Mahāyāna in character. Nāgārjuna argues for the cultivation of care grounded in the realization of one's own emptiness and of universal interdependence and defends a welfare state in which the king is responsible for assuring adequate food, shelter, health care and comfort to citizens, and even to provide for the welfare of animals.

Nāgārjuna's philosophical method has drawn considerable philosophical and hermeneutical attention in India and Tibet (Tsongkhapa 2005), and more recently in the West (Hayes 1994; Garfield 2002; Westerhoff 2009). Most of his texts are developed primarily through the use of *reductio ad absurdum* reasoning (*prasaṅga*) in which an opponent's position (often an *abhidharma* Buddhist position, but sometimes non-Buddhist positions) is reduced to absurdity. Nāgārjuna rarely argues directly for a thesis of his own, and in fact importantly denies that he asserts any philosophical thesis (*pratijñā*), arguing that Madhyamaka consists in the rejection of all philosophical views (*dṛṣṭi*).

This method, and the assertion that he defends no view, has occasioned considerable debate. Some in India and in Tibet have denied that Nāgārjuna is committed to the *reductio* method as a matter of principle, and some commentaries (most notably those of Bhāvaviveka) reconstruct the *reductio* arguments as positive, direct arguments; others (most notably Candrakīrti) argue that this method is essential to Nāgārjuna's philosophical purport. Some (for instance Tsongkhapa) argue that the claim to positionlessness cannot be taken literally. Others (Candrakīrti or Phatshab) claim that it must be.

There is a straightforward way to take these claims seriously. Nāgārjuna is arguing against the enterprise of providing an account of the fundamental nature of reality, because he thinks that there simply *is no* fundamental nature of reality. He argues that emptiness is not the fundamental nature of things, but the *absence of any such nature*. This is why he refuses to assert any thesis about the nature of reality. His use of a *reductio* method is intended to show that *any* account of the nature of reality can be demonstrated to be absurd simply because such accounts always are incoherent.

Nāgārjuna's major philosophical works

Nāgārjuna's most influential work is *Mūlamadhyamakakārikā*. This work, divided (by Candrakīrti) into twenty-seven chapters, comprises over 400 sometimes cryptic, but always densely argued, verses. It addresses all major Buddhist ontological categories. In each case, Nāgārjuna argues that the relevant phenomena are empty of inherent existence or intrinsic nature, but nonetheless exist conventionally. The central chapter is the twenty-fourth, the examination of the four noble truths, in which Nāgārjuna articulates and defends his distinctive doctrine of the two truths.

Mūlamadhyamakakārikā is the subject of numerous Indian commentaries (as well as many Tibetan commentaries). The earliest of these, *Akutobhayā* (a text, as we noted, of uncertain authorship) is a terse gloss, expanding Nāgārjuna's verses into slightly more explicit arguments, but offering little general commentary on its purport. Much of *Akutobhayā* is reproduced in the earliest major Indian commentary, that of Buddhapālita (*c*. 500 CE), which offers an extensive interpretation of the text and account of Nāgārjuna's *reductio* method in early chapters, but which simply replicates *Akutobhayā* in the later chapters.

Bhāviveka (sixth century CE) responds to Buddhapālita in his *Prajñāpradīpa* (*Lamp of Wisdom*) and its sub-commentary *Tarkajvālā* (*Blaze of Argument*). Bhāviveka's are in general more detailed discussions of Nāgārjuna's arguments, and differ, as noted above, from Buddhapālita's analysis of the structure of those arguments. Candrakīrti (sixth to seventh century CE), in his commentary *Prasannapadā* (*Lucid Exposition*) defends Buddhapālita's view and thematizes this dispute over argument structure as a central philosophical issue within Madhyamaka. Candrakīrti's interpretation became the dominant reading of Nāgārjuna's view in Tibet. Avalokitavrata (*c*. eighth century CE) composed the last major Indian commentary on *Mūlamadhyamakakārikā*, a massive subcommentary on *Prajñāpradīpa*.

Vigrahavyāvartanī is a reply to objections raised to the arguments in *Mūlamadhyamakakārikā*. The opponent in this text is a Nyāya interlocutor who raises a number of objections, which cluster around two issues: first, Nāgārjuna is charged with undermining his own claim that all phenomena are empty on the grounds that his words and arguments would, if empty of intrinsic nature, fail to have any meaning; second, he is charged with undermining any claim to justification of his conclusions in virtue of having rejected the intrinsic reliability of the *pramāṇas* (epistemic instruments). Nāgārjuna responds by arguing that even if they are empty of intrinsic nature, words and arguments can perform semantic and pragmatic functions (and indeed, that were they not, they could not), and that it is the very interdependence of *pramāṇas* and *prameyas* (objects of knowledge) that makes epistemic activity, including justification, possible.

Yuktiṣaṣṭikā is a short text devoted to arguing against positive understandings of canonical Buddhist characterizations of phenomena. Nāgārjuna argues that ascriptions of interdependence, emptiness, impermanence, arising and ceasing should not be understood as indicating that phenomena possess properties inherently, but rather as negative assertions, implicating neither the inherent existence of the phenomena themselves, nor of the properties ascribed. *Śūnyatāsaptati* is a brief treatise on emptiness, emphasizing its consistency with dependent origination and the conventional reality of the world.

Ratnāvalī is an extensive text (500 verses), probably addressed to a Śātavāhana king in the lower Krishna valley, to whom Nāgārjuna may have been an advisor (Walser 2005). The text covers a number of topics, but consists primarily of advice to a lay leader regarding Buddhist life and the Buddhist administration of a kingdom, advocating a kind of welfare state. But the text also involves a great deal of advocacy for support of the Mahāyāna *sangha* and for the publication of Mahāyāna texts. *Ratnāvalī* is also important as an early account of the relationship between the Madhyamaka view of emptiness and the practice of Mahāyāna ethics and the bodhisattva path.

Vaidalyaprakaraṇa is a sustained attack on Nyāya which argues that neither the epistemology nor the theory of argument to which that school is committed are coherent. He follows the argument in *Vigrahavyāvartanī* closely in his attack on Nyāya epistemology, but breaks new ground in criticizing Nyāya argument forms and accounts of reasoning in detail.

Nāgārjuna's minor works

In addition to these well-known and influential works, a number of less-often-cited works are ascribed to him. Of these, perhaps the best known is *Suhṛlekha*. Like *Ratnāvalī*, it is addressed to a lay audience, and most specifically to a king, perhaps the same one to whom *Ratnāvalī* is addressed. But *Suhṛlekha* is more personal and more pastoral in character. Instead of developing broadly philosophical or policy themes, it provides advice on the abandonment of vice, on the cultivation of virtue, and in general on personal practice, incorporating a fair amount of admonition regarding the benefits of religious practice and rectitude and the dangers of a vicious life for future rebirths.

Two short texts—*Pratītyasamutpādahṛdayakārikā* and *Vyavahārasiddhi*—of the latter of which only fragments exist—are of contested attribution but, given their style and content, as well as regular canonical attribution, are quite likely the work of Nāgārjuna. The former argues that the traditional Buddhist formula of the twelve links of dependent origination is consistent with the doctrine of the emptiness of all phenomena, and the latter, at least from the evidence of the few surviving verses, argues that conventional reality exists only dependently, but nonetheless, exists. (See Lindtner 1982, 1986.)

The attribution of *Bodhicittavivaraṇa* to Nāgārjuna is more dubious. For one thing, despite being attributed to him by Tibetan biographers and by several minor Indian commentators, it is not mentioned by any of his principal Indian commentators. For another, it at least appears to be anachronistic in content, beginning with a sustained critique of the idealistic Cittamātra/Yogācāra school and its doctrine of three natures—regarded by most scholars as first articulated about a century after Nāgārjuna's death—and it then addresses the moral cultivation of a bodhisattva's compassion, a theme Nāgārjuna never develops elsewhere. If it is authentic, it is a very significant text indeed, demonstrating a much earlier appearance of Buddhist idealism than one would otherwise suspect, as well as an earlier systematic development of the bodhisattva ideal than is generally accepted.

There is sound reason to accept the *Sūtrasammuccaya* as authentic. For one thing, it is attested by Candrakīrti. For another, it makes good sense for Nāgārjuna, who seems to have been an active polemicist for the Mahāyāna, to have composed a compilation of sūtra quotations in order to grant an imprimatur to Mahāyāna *sūtras* that would have been of controversial authenticity in his time. This text is extant only in Tibetan, and provides important information regarding the *sūtras* that early Mahāyāna philosophers took to be important.

Most of the hymns attributed to Nāgārjuna are of little philosophical interest. The four collected in the *Catuḥstava* break no new philosophical ground, but repeat in devotional register many of the conclusions defended in his more systematic works. The *Dharmadhātustava*, on the other hand, is of considerable philosophical interest if it is authentic. This hymn attributes a number of positive properties to ultimate reality (Dharmadhātu), such as permanence, purity, etc. This text may pose interesting hermeneutical challenges, forcing us either to reject its authenticity, to read it in a way consistent with Nāgārjuna's more negative approach in his other texts, to treat its language as merely metaphorical in a devotional context or to attribute a change of view to Nāgārjuna prior to its composition.

Nāgārjuna's impact

Nāgārjuna's philosophical texts were enormously influential in Buddhist India, in Tibet and in East Asia. (But see Hayes 1994 for a contrary position.) As noted above, *Mūlamadhyamakakārikā* was the subject of numerous influential Indian commentaries. It is widely cited in a much larger Madhyamaka literature and is influential, if only as a foil, in Yogācāra. *Madhyanta-vibhāga* (*Discriminating the Middle from the Extremes*), for instance, attributed to Maitreya, and probably composed by Asaṅga, and its commentary by Vasubandhu reference Nāgārjuna's text obliquely, as does Vasubandhu's *Trisvabhāva-nirdeśa* (*Treatise on the Three Natures*). Nāgārjuna was also influential for the great Advaita Vedanta philosopher Śaṅkara—though whether he was a direct influence or a close *pūrvapakṣa* is a difficult hermeneutical question.

Nāgārjuna's disciple Āryadeva also composed a magisterial Madhyamaka text, *Catuḥśataka* (*Four Hundred Stanzas*) connecting Nāgārjuna's analysis of emptiness and its relation to conventional reality to Mahāyāna ethics, extending the analysis in *Ratnāvalī* (and possibly that of *Bodhicittavivaraṇa*). Candrakīrti's *Madhyamakāvatāra* (*Introduction to the Middle Way*) and its autocommentary owe a clear debt to Nāgārjuna. As late as the eighth and ninth centuries, such prominent Madhyamaka scholars as Śāntideva and Śāntarakṣita advanced arguments that clearly derived from *Mūlamadhyamakakārikā*.

Tibetan doxography ranks the school of philosophy deriving from Candrakīrti's interpretation of Nāgārjuna (*thal 'gyur pa/prāsaṅgika* madhyamaka / reductio*-wielding middle-way philosophy) as the most advanced Buddhist doctrine. As a consequence, Nāgārjuna's texts are accorded enormous prestige and are the subject of numerous commentaries.

Nāgārjuna's student and exegete Kumārajiva traveled to China, where he became an influential teacher and translator. In China a much-admired commentary on the *Aṣṭasāhasṛikā-Prajñāpāramitā-sūtra* (*The Perfection of Wisdom Sūtra in Eight Thousand*

Verses) probably composed by Kumārajiva is widely attributed to Nāgārjuna. The Tiantai school of Buddhism takes *Mūlamadhyamakakārikā* as foundational, and its doctrine of the three truths is grounded on a reading of verse XXIV:18 of that text. Nāgārjuna is also recognized as an Indian patriarch of Chan/Zen, for which his account of emptiness and its consistency with empirical reality is influential.

Recent and contemporary literature on Nāgārjuna

Most of Nāgārjuna's important philosophical texts are now available in reliable English translations. Several commentaries on his work, as well as many texts influenced by Nāgārjuna, have also been translated. As a consequence, and as a consequence of the increasing philosophical sophistication of the vast historical and philological literature on Madhyamaka, the past fifty years have seen increasing attention to Nāgārjuna's work in specifically philosophical (as opposed to philological) literature in the West. That attention has accelerated dramatically in the last two decades.

Western philosophers have developed connections between Nāgārjuna's thought and that of Kant (Murti 1960), Wittgenstein (Gudmunsen 1977; Garfield 1995, 2002), James (Kalupahana 1986) and others. Some (Robinson 1964; Hayes 1994) have criticized Nāgārjuna's arguments severely; others (Garfield 1995; Garfield and Priest 2003; Westerhoff 2009) defend his analysis. He has been read as a nihilist (Wood 1994), an idealist (Murti 1960), as a Pragmatist (Kalupahana 1986), a sceptic (Garfield 1995, 2002) and as an anti-realist (Siderits 1988). Tuck (1990) provides a survey of interpretative trends in Nāgārjuna scholarship over the twentieth century. Walser (2005) has recently contributed to our knowledge of Nāgārjuna's probable dates and location.

Selected bibliography of works by and about Nāgārjuna

Bhattacarya, K., Johnston, E. and Kundst, A. 1986. *The Dialectical Method of Nāgārjuna: Nāgārjuna's Vigrahavyāvārtanī*. New Delhi: Motilal Banarsidass.

Burton, D. 1999. *Emptiness Appraised*. London: Routledge.

Garfield, J. 1995. *Fundamental Wisdom of the Middle Way: Nāgārjuna's Mūlamadyamakakārikā*. New York: Oxford University Press.

Garfield, J. 2002. *Empty Words: Buddhist Philosophy and Cross-Cultural Interpretation*. New York: Oxford University Press.

Garfield, J. and Priest, G. 2003. "Nāgārjuna and the Limits of Thought." *Philosophy East and West* 53(1): 1–21.

Gudmunsen, C. 1977. *Wittgenstein and Buddhism*. London: Macmillan.

Hayes, R. 1994. "Nāgārjuna's Appeal." *Journal of Indian Philosophy* 22(4): 299–378.

Hopkins, J. 2007. *Nāgārjuna's Precious Garland: Buddhist Advice for Living and Liberation*. Ithaca, NY: Snow Lion Publications.

Huntington, C. 1986. "*Akutobhayā and Early Indian Madhyamaka*." PhD Dissertation, University of Michigan. Ann Arbor, MI: University Microfilms.

Kalupahana, D. 1986. *The Philosophy of the Middle Way: Mūlamadhyamakakārikā*. Albany: State University of New York Press.

Katsura, S. and Siderits, M. 2013. *Nāgārjuna's Middle Way: Mūlamadhyamakakārikā*. Boston: Wisdom Publishers.

Lindtner, C. 1982. *Nāgārjuniana*. New Delhi: Motilal Banarsidass.

Lindtner, C. 1986. *Master of Wisdom: Writings of the Buddhist Master Nāgārjuna*. Oakland, CA: Dharma Press.
Loizzo, J. 2007. *Nāgārjuna's Reason Sixty with Candrakīrti's* Reason Sixty Commentary. New York: Columbia University Press.
Murti, T. R. V. 1960. *The Central Philosophy of Buddhism*. London: Allen and Unwin.
Nagao, G. 1989. *The Foundational Standpoint of Mādhyamika Philosophy*. Albany: State University of New York Press.
Nāgārjuna. 2005. Letter to a Friend *with Commentary by Kangyur Rinpoche*. Padmakara Translation Group (trans.). Boston: Wisdom Publications.
Robinson, R. 1964. "Did Nāgārjuna Really Refute All Views?" *Philosophy East and West* 22(3): 325–331.
Seyfort-Ruegg, D. 1981. *The Literature of the Madhyamaka School of Philosophy in India*. Wiesbaden: Otto Harrasowitz.
Siderits, M. 1980. "The Madhyamaka Critique of Epistemology." *Journal of Indian Philosophy* 8(4): 307–335.
Siderits, M. 1988. "Nāgārjuna as an Anti-Realist." *Journal of Indian Philosophy 16*: 311–325.
Siderits, M. 2004. "Causation and Emptiness in Madhyamaka." *Journal of Indian Philosophy* 32(4): 393–419.
Siderits, M. and O'Brien, D. 1976. "Zeno and Nāgārjuna on Motion." *Philosophy East and West* 26(3): 281–299.
Tola, F. and Dragonetti, C. 1995. *Nāgārjuna's Refutation of Buddhist Logic*. New Delhi: Motilal Banarsidass.
Tsong Khapa. 2005. *Ocean of Reasoning: A Great Commentary on Nāgārjuna's* Mūlamadhyamakakārikā. N. Samten and J. Garfield (trans.). New York: Oxford University Press.
Tuck, A. 1990. *Comparative Philosophy and the Philosophy of Scholarship*. New York: Oxford University Press.
Velez, A. 2005. "Emptiness in the Pāli Canon and the Question of Nāgārjuna's Orthodoxy." *Philosophy East and West* 55(4): 507–528.
Walser, J. 2005. *Nāgārjuna in Context: Mahāyāna Buddhism and Early Indian Culture*. New York: Columbia University Press.
Westerhoff, J. 2008. "Nāgārjuna's Arguments on Motion Revisited." *Journal of Indian Philosophy* 36(4): 455–479.
Westerhoff, J. 2009. *Nāgārjuna's Madhyamaka*. New York: Oxford University Press.
Westerhoff, J. In press. *Nāgārjuna's Vigrahavyāvartanī*. New York: Oxford University Press.
Wood, T. 1994. *Nāgārjunian Disputations: A Philosophical Journey through an Indian Looking-Glass*. Honolulu: University of Hawai'i Press.

Chapter 32
NĀGĀRJUNA'S EARLY MADHYAMAKA: "DECONSTRUCTION" AND MODERATION

Douglas L. Berger

The self-understanding of this school of Buddhist philosophy, which became so profoundly influential to the development of Mahāyāna thought in India, Tibet and East Asia, can be gleaned from its name. Madhyamaka means "middlemost" or "central," and a member of the school, a Mādhyamika, denotes an "adherent to the middle." In one sense, this appellation echoes Buddha's advice to tread a path of moderation (*madhyama pratipad*) between the extremes of hedonistic indulgence and overly rigorous asceticism. But Nāgārjuna (c. 150–250 CE), the philosophical founder of Madhyamaka, asserted that true moderation could only be found in thought and practice by realizing that everything in the world comes about, passes away and is transformed through emptiness (*śūnyatā*). Other Indian Buddhists and Brāhmaṇical philosophers, despite their almost complete disagreement with one another, generally concurred Nāgārjuna's teaching was hardly a sign of moderation, but instead was a symptom of nihilism. Asaṅga, the fourth-century preceptor of Vijñānavāda Buddhism, believed Mādhyamikas to be so intellectually and spiritually dangerous that he counseled his own followers to avoid conversation with them entirely (*Bodhisattvabhūmi*, *Tattvārtha II*). The seminal seventh-century Buddhist logician Dharmakīrti warned that the Madhyamaka formulation of emptiness would make both practical action and enlightenment impossible (*Nyāyabindu* i.ii.4: 13–15:13). Vedic logicians and epistemologists, understanding the term *śūnya* in its primary sense as "null," "zero," "void" or "absent," charged that any philosophy declaring such nullity or voidness as its basis would undermine itself since, if everything is empty, so is the claim that all things are empty (Uddyotakara, *Nyāyavārṭika* 2,1:12). Nāgārjuna and his centuries of followers responded to such accusations with a stock-in-trade joke: the world is indeed brought about through emptiness, and since all of you who object to emptiness live and speak within that world, "you are like one who has mounted a horse and then forgets the horse" (*Mūlamadhyamakakārikā* (MMK) 24: 15). The key to understanding Madhyamaka as a school of Buddhism is seeing how its subtle teachings make a connection between emptiness and moderation in both thought and practice. How, according to Madhyamaka, does emptiness bring about a moderate view of the world? Why, on the Mādhyamika's convictions, does emptiness locate liberating religious practice where they believe it belongs, right in the midst of the world?

From its inception, the Buddhist tradition defined itself as a moderate path of thought and practice. In terms of conduct, Buddhist cultivation avoids "extremist" life-pursuits of dedication to sensual enjoyment (*kāmasukhalikānuyoga*) and dedication to ascetic self-mortification (*atthakilamathānuyoga*) (*Vinaya*. I, 10–17). The former ensues from a conviction that the physical body and personality are reduced to complete non-existence (*natthitā*) after death and so one must enjoy life while it lasts. The latter is motivated by faith in a permanently existing soul (*atthitā*) that transcends pain-stricken and finite physical life and which is to be completely liberated from rebirth (*Saṃutta Nikāya*, 2, 17, 8–30). In order to undermine these extreme beliefs the Buddha develops a method of analyzing four alternative views (*catuṣkoṭi*) regarding the nature of existents and the universe and formulates the right view (*sammādiṭṭhi*) of the dependently co-arisen (*paṭiccasamuppana*) nature of things. For the most part, the putative four alternative views supporting either the eternal or eliminative conceptions of personal existence are considered by early Buddhists to be among those kinds of human ponderings that cannot be made into coherent doctrine (*avyākatā*), and so, the Buddha denies that any of these worldviews can be advocated (*Saṃutta Nikāya*, 2, 19). The moderate position between these intellectual extremes, and thus the truth, was for the Buddha the view of dependent co-arising, which represents birth, death and conscious life as a twelve-limbed (*dvādasāṅga*) process beginning with persistent ignorance of the fundamentally transitory character of things that engenders dispositional attachment and obsessive clinging to the material or "eternal" world. Change in conduct is facilitated by a genuine understanding of change itself, an understanding revealing that, when the cognitive and dispositional orientations that cause human suffering are present, suffering will occur, while when these conditions are eliminated, suffering will also cease (*Majjima Nikāya* 1, 262–264). The removal of the conditions of suffering is precisely the aim of the conduct prescribed by the "eightfold path" (*attāṅgikamagga*) that rectifies insight, practice and meditation. Many of these features of the early Buddhist discourse of moderation, particularly focused on the view of dependent co-arising, are appropriated by Madhyamaka, as is the notion that convictions bear such a determining weight upon moral conduct. The Mādhyamikas, however, appropriate these features into a Mahāyāna commentarial context dramatically different from that of the Buddha, where new metaphysical tools were being analytically employed by Buddhist thinkers themselves, and in reaction to which the notions of *śūnyatā* and the *bodhisattva* were offered by the new school of Moderation as correctives.[1]

Nāgārjuna (*c.* 150–250 CE), Madhyamaka's preceptor, devoted his treatises to an articulation of Buddhist enlightenment which, in the atmosphere of bourgeoning philosophical developments of his day, needed refinement and revitalization.

Two primary culprits in distorting the nature and goals of awakening, in Nāgārjuna's estimation, were the Sarvāstivādins, a school then in early stages of commentary on the Abhidharma, and the Sautrāntikas, a school adjuring Abhidharma exegesis and attempting a hermeneutically independent philosophical explication of the Buddha's discourses. The latter group formulated the early Buddhist commitment to the notion of the impermanence (*anitya*) of all things in terms of "momentariness" (*kṣaṇikatva*) and "a-causal succession" (*asatkārya samantara*). Since no element of existence endures from one moment to the next, but rather perishes the very moment of its arising, no permanent or even enduring nature can be attributed to any phenomenon, which the Sautrāntikas apparently believed vindicated the Buddha's conception of change and rejection of "eternalism." The relevance of this vision of momentariness to enlightenment is that there is nothing essentially binding about one's karmic past and that liberation from such a past can occur through insight into the merely conceptually constructed nature of static being or essence and the radical contingency characteristic of each unique moment of actuality (*svalakṣaṇa*). Starkly opposed to this interpretation were the then relatively new camps of Vaibhāṣikas and Sarvāstivādins, who threw themselves into painstaking exegesis of the Mahāyāna Abhidharma. The principle objection of Sarvāstivādins to the Sautrāntika doctrine of momentariness was that, in undermining the very intelligibility of the causal connection of one moment of existence to the next moment, the Sautrāntikas rendered the Buddha's own doctrine of causality, dependent co-arising (*pratītyasamutpadā*), inexplicable. To address this breech, the Sarvāstivādins, in the guise of a number of slightly variant causal theories, maintained that the causal efficacy (*kāritra*) that accounts for the continuity (*śāśvata*) of phenomena from one moment to the next and their regular impact on one another derives from a core of autonomous substantiality (*svabhāva*). While the material and physical aspects of things (*bhāva*) undergo constant transformation, the capacity of substances to autonomously self-replicate determines what types of substances (*dharma*) are at hand, whether they be non-living organisms or dispositional habits of consciousness that, though at times dormant, can always be triggered and re-manifest in future behavior. Though sounding highly metaphysical, the notion of *svabhāva* is for the Sarvāstivādins fundamentally moral, for it explains how psychic seeds (*bīja*) of conduct, when pure, can produce acts autonomous of karma (*karma-svabhāvata*), and when impure can produce only conditionally limited acts (*pratyaya-samutannaṃ karma*). If a particular autonomous substance is either that of an element or a pure psychic seed, it is thought to exist in all three modes of time, past, present and future, so that its manifestation is always potential if not actual and can never be destroyed. Thus, purified psychic tendencies that facilitate enlightenment are always possible and are indestructible, making Buddhahood a kind of inherent and eternal feature of consciousness. Nāgārjuna, surveying these alternative theories of causality and their moral and soteriological relevance to Buddhist praxis, hermeneutically interprets them as new forms of the "extremes," "annihilationism" (*ucchedavāda*) in the case of the Sautrāntikas and "eternalism" (*śāśvatavāda*) in the case of the Sarvāstivādins (MMK 15:11, 18:10, 21: 14–15, 27:18, 29). He also revives and sharpens the early Buddhist analytical tool of the *catuṣkoṭi*, employing it as a means to refute these wayward theoretical models that led in his mind to morally dangerous representations of Buddhist awakening.

In his major treatise, the *Mūlamadhyamakakārikā*, Nāgārjuna attacks the Sarvāstivāda and Sautrāntika interpretations of causality and their implications for practice by testing these theories against the Abhidharma categorization of *dharma*-s. The notion of autonomous substantiality (*svabhāva*), according to Nāgārjuna, cannot theoretically explain the functioning of the sense-spheres (*āyatana*), aggregates (*skandha*) or elements (*dhātu*) or the manners of their classification (*vibhaṇga*), nor can they elucidate the weightier matters of the process of bondage and release (*bhandana-mokṣa*), the nature of enlightened existence (*tathāgata*), the noble truths (*āryasatya*) or *nirvāṇa*.[2] Whereas the major schools of Mahāyāna exegesis had insisted that some conception of *svabhāva* or *parabhāva* (heteronomy or extrinsic-causation, supposedly the view of the Sautrāntikas) had to be invoked in order to understand the Buddha's theory of dependent co-arising (*pratītyasamutpāda*) and its constitutive causes (*hetu*) and conditions (*pratyaya*), Nāgārjuna employs the *catuṣkoṭi* as a means of logically refuting these conceptions. If any *dharma* is thought to be autonomous (*svabhāva*), in that it causes and replicates itself through time, then no account of a cause–effect relationship is either possible or necessary, for, as the theory holds, the substance of the *dharma* was already in existence and had no need of being brought into being.[3] If the same *dharma* on the other hand is thought to have been brought about extrinsically (*parabhāva*), the complete difference of cause and effect would leave us with no way to comprehend how relation between them was possible.[4] Any *dharma* that could be brought about by both itself and another thing is inconceivable (*nopapadyate*), for this attributes contrary accounts of genesis to the same phenomenon.[5] Finally, it cannot be the case that things are not caused at all, for the Buddha taught that both suffering and release were effects of causes. These scholastic views (*dṛṣṭi*) that Nāgārjuna attacks are more in his mind than simply erroneous, but are conceptual fabrications (*prapañca*) and falsifications (*vikalpa*) which prompt the obsession-driven action (*karma-kleśa*) that furthers attachment to desire and rebirth (MMK 18:4–7). On Nāgārjuna's view, the Buddha had never propounded any theoretical formulations regarding the nature of *dharma*-s at all (MMK 25:24). On the contrary, the Buddha's teaching is meant precisely to rid human beings of both the "eternalist" and "nihilist" theoretical preoccupations that preclude any genuine understanding of what Buddhist practice entails (MMK 15:6). That teaching is consistently extolled as quelling conceptual fabrications, as reducing the entire edifice of reified ideas generated by any metaphysical system to so many magical phantasms as dreams are made of.[6]

In many places of the MMK, Nāgārjuna records, in the form of *pūrva-pakṣa*, the exasperated responses of Buddhist theoreticians to the Mādhyamika's insistence that the Buddha councils us to reject any theoretical understanding of causality. Wouldn't such a stance, they object, forfeit any right view of change, of the difference between acts that lead to pure and impure *karma*, of how the noble truths and the eightfold path facilitate enlightenment?[7] Nāgārjuna affirms that he is committed to faithful adherence to Buddhist practice and retorts that his own rigorous "deconstruction" of metaphysical categories has shown that they fail to explain the Buddha's central teaching of dependent co-arising. Conceptions such as *svabhāva* cannot even explain change in any generic sense, for such categories, when examined, make explanations of change incoherent and unnecessary (MMK 13:3–6). This being the case, the notion of *svabhāva* actually undermines the possibility of the liberating ethical and soteriological change that the four noble truths and eightfold path hold out (MMK 24:24–35). Change does not come about, Nāgārjuna insists, through either *svabhāva* as autonomous replication of phenomena or *parabhāva* as extrinsic causation, but instead through *niḥsvabhāva* or the lack of autonomous production, which he terms *śūnyatā* or "emptiness." Things on this construal do not change because they possess some intrinsic nature or substance that perpetuates their ontological status and particular causal efficacy, with for instance fire being only fire, water being only water and good and bad karmic seeds being fundamentally different. Instead, change can only occur if things are malleable, if their nature is not fixed, if they are mutually and relationally constitutive in an untrammeled and unobstructed way, if, that is, they are interdependent and not independent. Nāgārjuna's scholastic Buddhist opponents voice considerable alarm over the term *śūnyatā*, as for them it denotes privation, absence and nihilism; the word makes it seem as though Nāgārjuna is denying both causality and all the concrete phenomena that the process of causality produces. Nāgārjuna simply assures them that *śūnyatā* is nothing more than a synonym for dependent co-arising. "Whatever is dependently co-arisen, that is emptiness, in our view; this notion, once apprehended, is precisely the middle path. Any particular thing not dependently co-arisen is not acknowledged, and thus, any particular thing that is not empty is not acknowledged either" (MMK 24:18–19). In this regard, *śūnyatā* serves as a heuristic term, employed especially to remind Buddhists who are tempted to theorize about the nature of causality that the interdependence or mutual constitution of phenomena, the interdependence of suffering and attachment, the interdependence of liberation and ethical and meditative practice cannot be understood in terms of dualistically conceived pure and impure chains of causal processes. Even right and wrong action, on this account, are interdependent (*dharmādharma samutpannam*), for without wrong action, there will be no pain (*duḥkha*), with no pain there will be no understanding of pain, with no understanding of pain there will be no attempt to overcome it, and with no attempt to overcome pain there will be no meritorious action, Buddhist practice, or enlightenment.

The radical interdependence of suffering and enlightenment that Nāgārjuna sees as simply entailed by the Buddha's teaching of dependent co-arising appeared to other schools as fundamentally threatening Buddhism at its core. Is *nirvāṇa* not to be aimed for because it is complete release from the otherwise interminable round of suffering rebirths we know as *saṃsāra*? Are not the states of bondage and release, worldly ignorance and extinction absolutely different and wholly unrelated? Nāgārjuna utterly rejects such an understanding of Buddhism and, by invoking emptiness as interdependence, proclaims the indistinguishability of the two. "Nothing of *saṃsāra* is distinguished from *nirvāṇa*, nothing of *nirvāṇa* is distinguished from *saṃsāra*. The edge of *nirvāṇa* is also the edge of *saṃsāra*, between these two, not even the subtlest thing is acknowledged" (MMK 25:19–20). *Nirvāṇa* then is not some other state of being or non-being that can be set over, above, alongside or outside of *saṃsāra*, it does not represent some distinct realm of spiritual gain or relinquishing. *Nirvāṇa* is the very same realm as that of *saṃsāra*, since both are alternate results of belief and conduct within the world of dependent co-arising. Practice and its significance, the fruits of quelling attachments and enlightenment itself, are all found within and directed toward the world of our experience. "That which is the autonomous substance of the Enlightened One, that is the autonomous substance of the world. The non-autonomous substance of the Enlightened One is the non-autonomous substance of the world" (MMK 22:16). Buddhist teaching and praxis not only elevate the status of the world, but also make worldly convention or everyday business (*vyavahāra*) the very means of ultimate realization.

> The teaching of the Buddhas' doctrine is based upon two truths, the truth of worldly common activity and the paramount truth. Those who do not understand the distinction between the two truths do not understand the profound truth in the Buddha's teaching. Without being based in everyday business, the paramount is not taught, and not comprehending the paramount, *nirvāṇa* is not attained.
>
> (MMK 24:8–10)

Esoteric mystifications or convoluted philosophical systems are not the pedagogical keys to the kingdom of *nirvāṇa*, but instead, the conventions of the social world provide the guidance. In sum, the MMK in taking an overtly anti-metaphysical stance in opposition to Buddhist scholasticism, presents a picture of Buddhist thought wherein enlightenment takes place within the concrete, social, interrelated world, and that experience within that world is the very facilitator, under varying circumstances, of both suffering and liberation. Nāgārjuna's peculiar form of "deconstruction" leads to enlighteningly moderate attitude and conduct in the contingent world.

During the past fifteen years, a number of Western and Indian scholars have debated the merits of a Derridian or deconstructionist reading of Nāgārjuna's thought. The ground on this debate was broken by Robert Magliola. For Magliola, the "Middle Path" of Nāgārjuna does not traverse a "mean" between the concepts of existence and non-existence, but is a "slipping between and away from the binary categories" (1984, 87). Nāgārjuna's arguments against "self-causation" (*svabhāva*) are arguments against the "self-identity" of phenomena in the same vein as Derrida's attacks on the signifier–signified structure of language undermine the notion of a "pure signified" (107). The notion of self-causation is for Nāgārjuna nothing more than a *prajñapti* or "language construction," but because the *prajñapti* can be "cracked" or shown up as self-contradictory, it leads us to dependent co-arising and thus, in its very linguistic fabrication, also serves as a "guiding and conductal" word, very much in the manner of

Derrida's "trace" (105–106). This supposedly reveals a surprising but palpable correspondence between Derrida's *différance* and Nāgārjuna's *śūnyatā*, but the latter actually fares better, for since even emptiness declares itself to be empty, it at once places itself under erasure and reveals the differential character of language (118–120). David Loy concurred with the general assessment that Nāgārjuna's form of deconstruction went beyond that of Derrida, for the latter only criticizes the theory of identity and leaves "free-floating meaning" only within the "bad infinity" of the written text (1987, 60). Nāgārjuna, in deconstructing both identity and difference (*svabhāva* and *parabhāva*) destroys dualistic thinking utterly and leaves one open to a non-dualistic experience of the world (59). Harold Coward, however, saw two sorts of fundamentally opposed forms of deconstruction in the two philosophers. For Nāgārjuna, all language is ultimately *vikalpa* or utter falsification of reality, and so the realization of the nature of existence must take place beyond language, whereas for Derrida there is no realm of experience outside language or "outside the text," and so Nāgārjuna's preference for mystical silence over sheer linguistic fabrication would suggest to Derrida only another form of "negative" logocentrism (Coward 1990, 135–141). For B. K. Matilal, Madhyamaka and deconstruction bear some "family resemblances ... that are not entirely superficial" (1992, 348). The most pronounced of these resemblances include a staunch anti-metaphysical stance, the critique of the putative metaphysical presences of language existing simultaneously with the retention of inherited linguistic signs and meanings, and a critical acknowledgment of the contextuality and contingency even of one's own metaphysical critiques (346–351). B. S. Yadav saw in Nāgārjuna a form of "methodic deconstruction" that overturns both Brāhmaṇical and Buddhist ontologies of identity and difference in the name of the *bodhisattva*'s mission of acknowledging human equality and pursuing social enlightenment (1994: 117). The Mādhyamika critiques all epistemologists according to their own rules of logic and argument, uncovering the privilege placed on metaphysical identity and its underlying craving for elite social status on the part of Brāhmiṇical Logicians (Yadav 1992, 143; 1994, 116–117). In like manner, Nāgārjuna and Candrakīrti expose the Buddhist metaphysicians as creating a duality between the Buddha and *nirvāṇa* and the people and *saṃsāra* in ignorance of the facts that "there is no Buddha apart from the Buddhists," and that it is precisely the *bodhisattva*'s commitment to remain "in the middle" of the world, for "there is no curtain between *nirvāṇa* and *saṃsāra*, between *Tathāgata* and the people" (Yadav 1992, 160–163). In Yadav's view, the Madhyamaka deconstruction of ostensive reference in language was also a deconstruction of the essentialism that supports hierarchical elitism in both society and religious practice.[8]

The contemporary deconstructionist view of Nāgārjuna's thought has doubtlessly hit upon some strong general resonances between them. The strongest of these affinities seem to be their shared anti-metaphysical stances, their concessions that essentialist thought can only be uprooted in the analysis of its own categories and language and their respective warnings that neither the concepts of *śūnyatā* or *différance* should be re-inscribed within a metaphysical vocabulary, but instead should be put "under erasure." Indeed, the fact that the purveyors of metaphysical theories in both traditions charged Nāgārjuna and Derrida with outright nihilism serves as a good indicator of the kinship of their critical projects. The temptation to apprehend strong correspondences between deconstruction and early Madhyamaka is provoked by a certain understanding of Nāgārjuna's philosophy of language that is more attributable to his best-known commentator. All of the above scholars tended to see Nāgārjuna as holding that language constitutes one form or another of falsifying conceptual construction (*prajñapti* or *vikalpa*), in which signs refer only to their own meaning content within a system of conventional usages (*vyavahāra*), but never to things in the world. Clearly there are many examples in Nāgārjuna of certain *prajñapti* that are perniciously misleading, specifically metaphysical ideas of the autonomy of substances, the existence of an immutable self, the essentially fixed nature of *tathāgata* and so forth, and he even asserts that such ideas are rooted in cognitive (*citta-gocara*) and linguistic (*abhidhātavya*) fabrication (MMK 18:7). Such false concepts and theories (*prapañca*) lead to all the nefarious worldviews (*dṛṣṭi*) that the Buddha's teaching was meant to quell. But the Buddha's teaching, which effected the quelling of metaphysical fabrications, was precisely that of *pratītyasamutpāda*, which Nāgārjuna untiringly witnesses to as the true teaching (*saddharma*) of how things come to be, pass away and change in the world (MMK i, 17:20, 18:11, 27:30). The process of *pratītyasamutpāda*, it must be remembered, gives us an account of becoming, birth, aging and death, which are hardly mere linguistic signs within the differing and differentiating mechanics of language, but are actual interdependent events in the cycle of life, the right understanding of which is of the utmost importance in Buddhist praxis. As Nāgārjuna sees it, the terms *pratītyasamutpāda* and *śūnyatā*, far from conceptually and linguistically falsifying or failing to describe the way the world is, give us the right understanding (*prajñapti*) of life and in so doing infuse us with wisdom (*prajñā*).

If we are nonetheless to see Nāgārjuna as engaging in some form of philosophical deconstruction in his opposition to substantialist metaphysics and realist epistemology, his is a deconstruction that is thematized as wise moderation in both thought and practice. In terms of its analysis of change in the world, Nāgārjuna's Madhyamaka, in refuting substantialist, extrinsic or eliminative models of causality, opens a worldly space for liberating transformation. Human beings are not inherently fixed substances independent of environing conditions, nor are they extrinsically determined in ways over which they have no control, and least of all are their only alternative destinies either complete disassociation from the world or irredeemable entrapment in frustration and loss. Instead, human beings, in their births and deaths, failings and achievements, deteriorations and ennobling changes, are interdependent with one another and with the world. As Yadav has pointed out, in the Indian philosophical and practical context, Madhyamaka deconstruction locates the *bodhisattva*'s practice squarely in the midst of the world and charges her with the compassionate mission of ceaselessly coming to the aid of suffering beings, adjuring both "meta-language or linguistic hegemony" and "silence in a worldless emptiness" (Yadav 1992, 163). Nāgārjuna's Madhyamaka is not merely metaphysical counter-discourse invoked to decry a tradition's logocentric violence. That is only its first stroke. It goes on to elevate worldly language, over metaphysical language, into the facilitator of ultimate realization. Nor does Nāgārjuna leave the moral agent stretched or leaping to and fro between the ethical *aporias* of law and justice, reciprocity and infinite secret gifting, calculation and "impossibility," but instead propels her into the reciprocal trade of living worldly conduct (*vyavahāra*) with the imperative of "constant cultivation" (*bhāvanā-heya*).[9]

Notes

1 A controversy has persisted in the secondary literature as to whether Madhyamaka's founder Nāgārjuna was a Theravāda or Mahāyāna philosopher. The former alternative has been most staunchly maintained by Warder (1973, 13) and Kalupahana (1986, 5–9, 24–26), while the latter is embraced by Lindtner (1986, 331), Schroeder (2001, 91–98) and Walser (2005, 16–122).

2 Kalupahana has shown roughly how the MMK is structurally organized around these successive themes (1992, 160–169).

3 Instances of this argument can be found in MMK 4:2, 6:1, 8:2, 9:2–4, 10:2–4, 12:2, 20:1.

4 See MMK 4:3, 6:2, 8:3, 9:9, 10:5–6; 12:3–7, 20:4–6.

5 See MMK 4:4, 6:3, 12:9, 20:7.

6 See MMK i, 13:8, 17:33, 18:5, 22:15, 27:30.

7 These objections can be found in MMK 17:6–12, 24:1–6, 25:1–2.

8 The hermeneutic treatment of Madhyamaka thought found in Yadav's work aligns it not only theoretically with deconstruction but also as a social critique very strongly with modern Ambedkar Buddhism (Berger 2001, 282, 309–310).

9 MMK 17:13–17. For more on the comparison between Derrida's and Nāgārjuna's ethical thought, see Berger (2007).

References

Berger, D. L. 2001. "The Social Meaning of the Middle Way: B. S. Yadav and the Mādhyamika Critique of Indian Ontologies of Identity and Difference." *Journal of Dharma* 26(3): 282–310.

———. 2007. "Deconstruction, *Aporia* and Justice in Nāgārjuna's Empty Ethics." In Youru Wang (ed.). *Deconstruction and the Ethical in Asian Thought*, 40–59. London and New York: Routledge.

Coward, H. 1990. *Derrida and Indian Philosophy*. Albany: SUNY Press.

Cox, C. 1999. "Saṅghabhadra *Nyāyānusāra*." In K. H. Potter (ed.). *Encyclopedia of Indian Philosophy*, vol. 8 of 9, 650–716. Delhi: Motilal Banarasidass.

Garfield, J. L. (Trans.). 1995. *The Fundamental Wisdom of the Middle Way: Nāgārjuna's Mūlamadhyamakakārikā*. New York: Oxford University Press.

Kalapuhana, D. J. (Trans.). 1986. *Nāgārjuna: The Philosophy of the Middle Way*. Albany: SUNY Press.

———. 1992. *A History of Buddhist Thought: Continuities and Discontinuities*. Honolulu: University of Hawai'i Press.

Lindtner, Christian. 1986. *Master of Wisdom*. California: Dharma Publishing.

Loy, D. 1987. "The Culture of Deconstruction: A Mahāyāna Critique of Derrida." *Indian Philosophical Quarterly* 27(1): 59–80.

Magliola, R. 1984. *Derrida on the Mend*. West Lafayette, IN: Purdue University Press.

Matilal, Bimal K. 1992. "Is *Prasaṅga* a Form of Deconstruction?" *Journal of Indian Philosophy* 20(4): 345–362.

Schroeder, J. 2001. *Skillful Means: The Heart of Buddhist Compassion*. Honolulu: University of Hawai'i Press.

Tuck, A. P. 1990. *Comparative Philosophy and the Philosophy of Scholarship: On the Western Interpretation of Nāgārjuna*. New York: Oxford University Press.

Walser, J. 2005. *Nāgārjuna in Context: Mahāyāna Buddhism and Early Indian Culture*. New York: Columbia University Press.

Warder, A. K. 1971. "The Concept of a Concept." *Journal of Indian Philosophy* 1(2): 181–196.

———. 1973. "Is Nāgārjuna a Mahāyānist?" In Mervyn Sprung (ed.). *The Problem of Two Truths in Buddhism and Vedānta*, 78–88. Boston, MA: D. Reidel.
Williams, P. 1981. "On the Abhidharrma Ontology." *Journal of Indian Philosophy* 9(3): 227–257.
Yadav, B. S. 1992. "Methodic Deconstruction." In Shlomo Biderman and Ben-Ami Scharfstein (eds.). *Interpretation in Religion*, 129–168. Leiden: E. J. Brill.
———. 1994. "Vallabha's Positive Response to Buddhism." *Journal of Dharma* 18(2): 113–137.

Chapter 33

A SPECTRUM OF METAPHYSICAL POSITIONS CONCERNING THE EXISTENCE OR NON-EXISTENCE OF A SELF: NYĀYA, ŚAIVA SIDDHĀNTA, MĪMĀṂSĀ, JAINISM AND BUDDHISM[1]

Alex Watson

Introduction

What is the (essential/ultimate) nature of sentient beings such as people? The main traditions of classical Indian philosophy could be divided into four groups according to the answer they give to this metaphysical question. The first group, containing just one member, the Cārvākas, held that a person is just a body and the powers or properties of that body. They thus denied the possibility of the continuation of life after death. All other traditions claimed that people include a non-physical constituent, which is their core identity and which survives the death of the body. Do these immaterial entities remain permanently separate from each other or do they – at the time of liberation – lose their separate identities and merge into a greater whole? The latter answer was given by those in the second group: Advaita Vedāntins, Non-dualistic Śaivas and certain Pāñcarātrika Vaiṣṇavas. For them, individual souls/selves are identical with, or parts, emanations, evolutes, effects or contractions of, an Oversoul or Absolute Self, named by the respective traditions as Brahman, Śiva and Nārāyaṇa. The two remaining groups agree that the non-physical parts of people remain forever distinct from each other; they disagree over whether they should be characterized as souls/selves or not. For the Buddhists they should not; for those in the final fourth group – e.g. Nyāya, Vaiśeṣika, Mīmāṃsā, Sāṅkhya, Śaiva Siddhānta, Jainism – they should.

This chapter does not concern itself at all with the first two groups. It looks at some debates between the last two – between, on the one hand, the Buddhists and, on the other, those traditions that posited individual selves that remain permanently numerically distinct, there being no sense in which these selves are ultimately one. What precisely was the issue here? What was at stake in the question of whether that part of us that survives the death of the body should be termed a 'self' or not? Section 1 provides an answer to that question by identifying key points of dispute in the debate between Nyāya and Buddhism. Section 2 introduces the Śaiva Siddhānta view, honouring its self-representation as falling in the middle ground between Nyāya and Buddhism. Section 3 first argues that this self-representation is misleading, that Śaiva Siddhānta's position is just as extreme as Nyāya's, and then diagnoses this polarization of the debate as resulting from a shared presupposition. Section 4 identifies some better candidates for the middle ground – Bhāṭṭa Mīmāṃsā, Jainism, Personalist Buddhism (*pudgalavāda*), and 'Buddhism without momentariness' – and explicates their views by placing them on a spectrum.

1 Nyāya versus Buddhism

In this first section, then, we will observe three ways in which the self was conceived of by the Naiyāyikas, and in each case we will discern how the Buddhists denied such a conception.

Self as unitary essence

The Naiyāyikas conceived of the self as the unitary essence of a person. It is unitary in the sense that it is one thing over time: it endures without ceasing to exist and without its nature (*svabhāva*) changing in any way.

For the Buddhists we have no unchanging essence: we are something different in every moment. In this moment I am an association of particular mental and bodily states, and in the next moment I am a different association of mental and bodily states. By the time of the second moment, the first mental and bodily states have ceased to exist; and there is nothing that continues to exist from the first moment to the second.

This means that as a person moves across a room, it is inaccurate to speak of movement; rather than there being one thing that moves, there is a plurality of things arising in very quick succession, in neighbouring locations. It is like a film of a person projected on a screen, which actually consists of a plurality of separate frames, but each

Figure 33.1

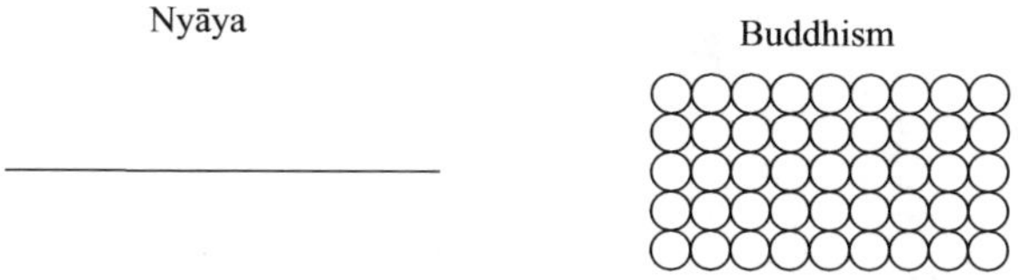

Figure 33.2

one follows the previous so rapidly, and resembles it so closely, that it produces the illusion of one continuous person.

This is the Buddhist doctrine of momentariness; it encourages us to see ourselves not as unitary and permanent, but plural and momentary. Figure 33.1 depicts the contrast between the Brāhmaṇical notion of an enduring, unchanging self (represented by a line) and the Buddhist idea that what we are in one moment is not what we are in next (illustrated by circles that are distinct but touch each other, as Buddhist moments are distinct but temporally contiguous).

Furthermore, even at one point of time, for Buddhism, we are not one thing but an association of five: a bodily state and four mental states (feelings [*vedanā*], ideation [*sañjñā*], impulses [*saṃskāra*] and consciousness [*vijñāna*]). See Figure 33.2.

Thus the Brāhmaṇical self, with its permanently unchanging essence, dissolves in Buddhism into a diachronic and synchronic plurality. Both sides in this debate, though, are dualists, in that for both there is a non-physical part of us that exists beyond the body and senses and is not brought to an end by death. Only the Cārvākas denied that. But the non-physical part was conceived of very differently: by one side as eternally unchanging and by the other as momentary (and as fourfold even in one moment).

Self as substance

The Naiyāyikas and Vaiśeṣikas distinguished substances (*dravyas*) from qualities (*guṇas*), the former being property-possessors (*dharmins*) and the latter properties (*dharmas*). A thing, such as a pot or a mango, is a property-possessor, and it has five qualities – taste, smell, colour, etc. – corresponding to our five senses.

The thing was regarded as a separate ontological entity from its qualities, as indicated by our use of language when we say, 'the smell of the mango', implying that the mango is something that exists over and above its smell. Nevertheless a quality is inextricably linked to a substance. It cannot exist without one. We do not find a colour

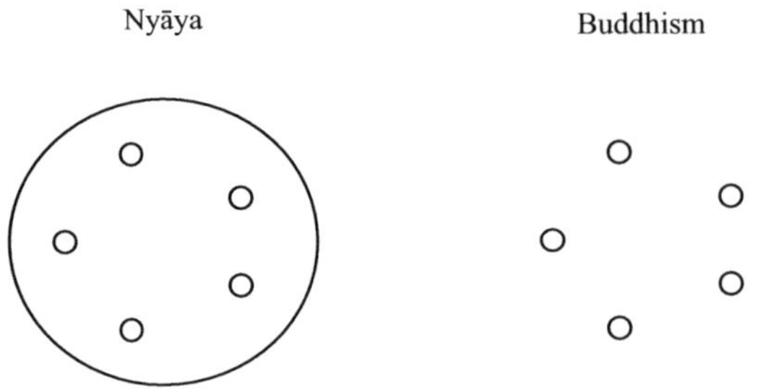

Figure 33.3

existing alone in mid-air. There must be some substantial object to which it belongs, some substrate (*āśraya*) that locates it.

The Naiyāyikas and Vaiśeṣikas use this principle to argue for the existence of the self. Just as colours or smells presuppose substances to which they belong, so consciousness presupposes a substance to which it belongs, that substance being the self.

The Buddhists denied the existence of a self conceived of as the substance to which consciousness belongs. This was part of a more general denial of the existence of substances over and above qualities. Whereas to a Naiyāyika a mango is one thing with five qualities, to a Buddhist it is five things occurring together, i.e. at the same time and in the same place. This is illustrated in Figure 33.3, taking the large circle to refer to a mango, and the small circles to refer to its smell, taste, colour, etc. Or the large circle can equally well represent a self, in which case the diagram illustrates that for Nyāya consciousness, etc. belong to a self, whereas for Buddhism consciousness and the other four constituents (*skandha*) of a person exist together, as part of a conglomeration, without belonging to anything else.

Self as agent

The Naiyāyikas and Vaiśeṣikas also conceived of the self as the agent of physical actions (*kartṛ*), and the agent/subject of cognitions (*jñātṛ*). (In Figure 33.4 the continuous line on the left to which all of the circles are attached represents the agent; the circles represent either physical actions or cognitions.) On the one hand it is that which, through the impulse of its will/effort (*prayatna*), initiates all of our physical actions. On the other it is the perceiver of our perceptions, the thinker of our thoughts, etc. The perception of a pot, say, lasts just for an instant but its perceiver outlives that perception and is the perceiver of the next and subsequent perceptions.

For Buddhists that which brings about a physical action is just that which causes it, which for them is the intention that occurred in the stream of consciousness in the moment preceding the action. The Vaiśeṣikas had compared the self as instigator of bodily movements to a puppeteer instigating the bodily movements of a puppet below. Such a notion of an agent standing above the sequence of mental and physical actions is precisely what is denied by the Buddhists. The intention that brings about my present action of touching the computer keyboard was itself caused by the previous

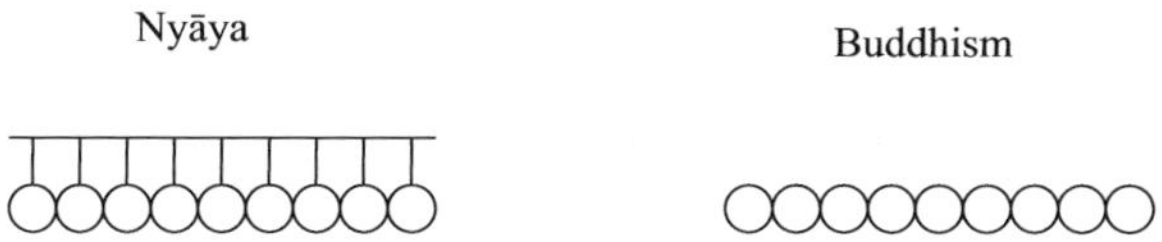

Figure 33.4

moment of consciousness, and so on. There is no part of a person standing, unconditioned, outside this chain of mental and physical events. So Buddhism, by bringing the agent down from its lofty position, dividing it up into discrete moments of intention and dispersing them into the psycho-physical stream, replaces a two-tier model with a one-tier model.

How did the Buddhists dispute the Naiyāyika and Vaiśeṣika notion of the self as the agent/subject of cognition? For Buddhism the agent of a cognition (*jñātṛ/grāhaka*) is simply the cognition itself (*jñāna/grahaṇa*). That which is conscious of a pot is consciousness at that particular moment. So if two consecutive cognitions occur to me, verbalizable as 'I see a pot' and 'I see a cloth', the two occurrences of 'I' have two different referents: two different instances of consciousness.

Each of the three Buddhist positions that we have just observed results from applying more general Buddhist principles to the specific case of the self. The denial of a permanent, unchanging self is a special case of the conception of the momentariness of everything. The denial of the self as a substance possessing qualities is a special case of the denial of substances over and above qualities. The denial of the self as autonomous agent is a special case of the general position that nothing stands outside the chains of causes and effects that make up the world.

2 Śaiva Siddhānta

Having observed the Naiyāyika and the Buddhist positions, we will now introduce Śaiva Siddhānta. As representative of Śaiva Siddhānta we will take Bhaṭṭa Rāmakaṇṭha (950–1000), who was the most influential and prolific of the early Saiddhāntika exegetes, that is to say those writers belonging to the phase of this tradition that came to an end in the twelfth century. From then on it survived only in the Tamil-speaking south, where it was transformed under the influence of Vedānta and devotionalism (*bhakti*). Rāmakaṇṭha was Kashmirian, as were most of the early exegetes of this tradition.

Rāmakaṇṭha does not think that Naiyāyika arguments are capable of establishing a self. He counters them by agreeing with Buddhist arguments against them. He agrees with Buddhism that there is no self as substance over and above consciousness, and no self as agent over and above consciousness. For him, as for Buddhism, consciousness does not require something other than itself in which to inhere. He concurs with Buddhism that the perceiver of our perceptions, the thinker of our thoughts, is just consciousness (*grāhaka/jñātṛ* = *jñāna*).

How then does he preserve the self? For him consciousness *is* the self. He equates the self and consciousness, or to put it another way, he characterizes consciousness as

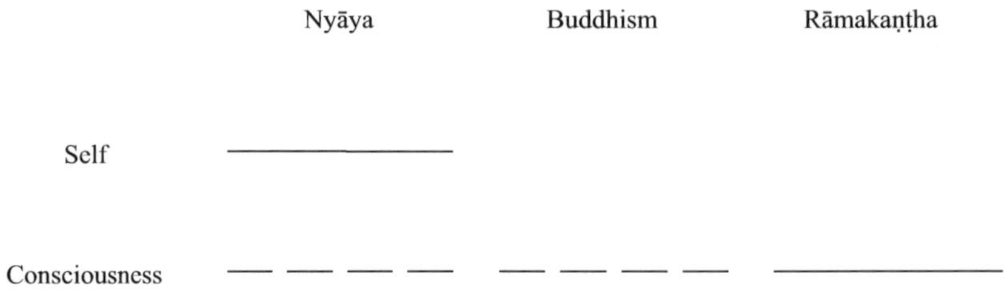

Figure 33.5

the nature (*svabhāva*), of the self.[2] This means that he holds consciousness to be permanent, not momentary, as it is for both Buddhism and Nyāya. Although consciousness for Nyāya belongs to a permanent self, it itself consists of discrete, momentary instances, as in Buddhism. The difference between the three views is represented in Figure 33.5.

For Nyāya, there is a self that is separate from consciousness. For Buddhism there is no self. For Rāmakaṇṭha, there is a self but it is just consciousness. Rāmakaṇṭha crosses out the line but joins up the dots into a line. He travels down the path of Buddhist argumentation quite a long way: he reduces the self to the stream of consciousness. But he then argues that the stream is unchanging.

So between Buddhism and Nyāya it was a debate about the existence or non-existence of an entity. Between Buddhism and Rāmakaṇṭha there is agreement about what exists; it is just a question of how to classify that: whether as something plural or unitary, changing or unchanging.

For Rāmakaṇṭha it is unitary and unchanging, but it is not a static entity like the self of the Naiyāyikas. It is dynamic, yet constant. Dynamic in that it is a process, the process of the shining forth of consciousness. Constant in that (1) the light of consciousness pours out always in the same form, and (2) there are no breaks in the process. Consciousness as envisaged by Rāmakaṇṭha, then, differs in two ways from consciousness as envisaged by Buddhism: it is differentiated neither qualitatively nor numerically. Consciousness for Buddhism, divided up as it is into dissimilar discrete entities, each one ceasing to exist before the next one comes into existence, resembles a light forever going on and off, and each time producing a different coloured light; consciousness for Rāmakaṇṭha resembles a light that is permanently on, forever sending out light of the same colour. This constant pouring forth of the illuminating light of consciousness is precisely what the self is, just as the sun is nothing more than a constant pouring forth of light.

3 Śaiva Siddhānta under scrutiny

Questioning Śaiva Siddhānta's location in the middle ground

We have seen, then, that there are ways in which Śaiva Siddhānta falls closer to Buddhism than Nyāya does. That is how Rāmakaṇṭha himself presents it. He sides with Buddhism against Nyāya, presenting the Naiyāyika position as one of ontological extravagance. In effect he says, 'We Śaivas, just like you Buddhists, recognize that a Naiyāyika self beyond consciousness is a fiction. We don't postulate such an unperceived entity. For us, as for you, consciousness does not require something other than itself in which to inhere. We accept no agent of consciousness separate from consciousness: for us as for you, the perceiver of our perceptions, the thinker of our thoughts, is just consciousness.'

But insofar as Śaiva Siddhānta too postulates a self that is completely unchanging and unmodifiable (*avikārya*), its view still occupies an extreme position. There is a sense, in fact, in which Śaiva Siddhānta's view is even more extreme than Nyāya's. Śaiva Siddhānta's self is arguably even more removed from change than Nyāya's, since individual cognitions inhere in the latter, whereas for Śaiva Siddhānta (as for Sāṅkhya) individual cognitions belong not to the self but to the *buddhi*, the faculty of intellect (responsible for conceptualization [*vikalpa*] and determining [*adhyavasāya*]).

I would now like to point to some problems with Śaiva Siddhānta's idea of an unchanging, unmodifiable self.

Critique of an unchanging self

A strong objection – and one that the Buddhists advanced – to the idea of an unchanging perceiver is that if it were unaffected by changes in its objects, it would not be able to register those changes, i.e. would not be able to perceive them. Śaiva Siddhānta (like Sāṅkhya) replies that the *buddhi* is modified. Since the *buddhi*, a faculty internal to the subject, registers object-changes, the subject can perceive them. But that just relocates the problem from the boundary between self and objects to the boundary between self and *buddhi*. How can the self, if it is unmodifiable, detect changes in the *buddhi*? Śaiva Siddhānta adduces the example of light: since it can illuminate different objects without being affected by them, surely consciousness can do the same. But light does not perceive the objects it illuminates, it enables them to be perceived by someone's consciousness. If that consciousness is in no way affected by the objects and the light, it remains mysterious how it could perceive them.

Śaiva Siddhānta maintains that the self is an agent; but how can the agent, that which brings about action, exist always in the same form? If it is unmodifiable, how could it produce a certain response at one time and a different response at a subsequent time?

Rāmakaṇṭha can respond that though the self does not change, the conditioning (*bhāvanā*) that operates on the mind does. This change in mental conditioning means that the self's habits can change. At one time it can be pulled in one direction, at another time in another. But this response is not compelling. If the self's choices are made not by it, but by forces external to it, then it is just a passive plaything that is manipulated and that offers no input into decision-making. If it is the self that chooses what to do, it is very difficult to see how it can be unmodified. The fact that it chooses one thing at one time and one thing at another implies a difference in it.

An analogy that Rāmakaṇṭha is fond of using to explain how something unchanging can be an agent is that of a magnet. The magnet, despite not moving, can cause movement in iron filings; so similarly a self, despite never being modified, can cause the body with which it is currently associated to move in various ways. But the analogy would only render plausible that an unmodifiable self could act in different ways at different times if the magnet were capable of making (identical) iron filings move in one way in one situation and in another way in another (identical) situation.

Diagnosis

Inasmuch as Śaiva Siddhānta postulates a self that is completely unmodifiable, it too can be placed close to Nyāya. At one end of the spectrum we have the Kṣaṇikavādins, the Buddhist proponents of momentariness, according to whom we are different in every single moment – not only qualitatively but also numerically. At the other end of the spectrum we can place Nyāya, Śaiva Siddhānta and Sāṅkhya, for whom what we are, essentially, is a self that is not only unitary over time, but also eternally unchanging. We thus have a polarized debate with each of two extremes attacking the other extreme, and no one adopting or attacking the middle ground. The view that we could be a self that changes – that has numerical identity but qualitative change – is mostly ignored.

Some will here object that that is precisely the Nyāya position. They will claim that a Naiyāyika self changes over time in the sense that it has changing cognitions, etc. inhering in it. But Naiyāyikas assert that the self and its cognitions are quite separate from each other. Any substance is a separate entity from its qualities, for Nyāya, in accordance with its doctrine of *guṇaguṇibheda*, the difference of qualities from that which possesses the qualities. This firm separation between the self and its qualities means that Nyāya ends up with the view that despite cognitions, etc. inhering in the self, changes in the former do not affect the nature of the latter.

I suggest that the explanation for this polarization of the debate – for the reluctance of these traditions to occupy the middle ground – lies in a shared assumption: the assumption that if an entity changes, it can no longer be the same thing, i.e. that at the level of the fundamental constituents of the world there can be no qualitative change without numerical change.

This is an explicitly stated presupposition of the Kṣaṇikavādins. It is what carries much of the weight in Dharmakīrti's inference of momentariness – leading to the postulation of consciousnesses that are numerically differentiated down to the level of every single moment. It can also be detected in Śaiva Siddhānta and Nyāya and is what explains their refusal to allow any change on the part of the self. For if it is accepted, then any change in the nature of a self will entail that that self ceases to exist and is succeeded by another. The concept 'self' would then no longer be applicable; the Buddhist position would have been lapsed into.

4 Between an unchanging self and momentariness

Bhāṭṭa Mīmāṃsā and Jainism

Does no one assert the existence of a self that is changing? Is the genuinely middle ground totally unoccupied? No, two traditions can be placed there: Bhāṭṭa Mīmāṃsā and Jainism.

The originator of the former, Kumārila, explicitly rejects the prevalent presupposition that qualitative change entails numerical change. He puts the following objection into the mouth of an opponent: surely if the self is transformed, it cannot be eternal (*Ślokavārttika*, *ātmavāda* 21). He responds that if non-eternal (*anitya*) means just being liable to transformation (*vikriyā*), he has no problem calling the self non-eternal. But the self is certainly not subject to destruction (*uccheda*, *nāśa*); for to be modified (and to be non-eternal in *that* sense) is not to cease to exist but rather just to 'assume another state' (*avasthāntaraprāpti*). Some aspects of the self are permanent and some (its states or qualities) are impermanent. Examples of the former are its consciousness (*caitanya*), its existence (*sattā*) and the particular substance (*dravya*) that comprises it; examples of the latter are its pleasures and pains. It is compared to a snake coiling into different positions, or a piece of gold that is remoulded from a dish to a necklace to an earring. The snake itself and the gold-atoms stand for its unchanging aspects; the different positions of the snake and the different shapes of the gold stand for its changing aspects.

Kumārila and those in his tradition refer to the self's pleasure, pain, etc. not just as its 'states' (*avasthā*), but also its 'qualities' (*guṇa*) or 'properties' (*dharma*). In that case how is this view different from that of the Naiyāyikas? In both cases we have an unchanging substance (*dravya*) with changing qualities/properties. It is different because Kumārila has a different take on the relation between substances and their qualities; he specifies the relation not as difference (*bheda*), but rather as both difference and non-difference (*bhedābheda*). This closer connection, or blurred boundary, between a substance and its qualities means that – unlike for the Naiyāyikas – modification of the latter *does* entail modification of the former. Kumārila has no problem accepting that the self is modified.

The same goes for Jainism. It distinguishes between the essence (*bhāva*, *jāti*) of the self and its modes (*paryāya*). But the two sides of this distinction are (unlike for the Naiyāyikas and like for Kumārila) not completely different/separate from each other; they are rather different aspects of the same thing. So one and the same self-substance is permanent and unchanging when viewed from one point of view, and impermanent and changing when viewed from another. Its permanence must be indexed to one aspect of it, namely its essence; if it were completely permanent (*sarvathā nityatve*), it could not be transformed, so the good conduct which causes someone to cease transmigrating would not be able to have any effect on it.

There is much similarity between the Bhāṭṭa and the Jaina views, as brought out by Uno (1999). But one dissimilarity is that for the Jainas the self, though immaterial, changes its size; it occupies the same dimensions as the body with which it is currently associated (*svadehaparimāṇa*). It is thus subject to contraction (*saṃharaṇa*) and expansion (*visarpaṇa*).

For both the Bhāṭṭas and the Jainas the self is one numerically identical thing that changes. Although these two traditions allow more change in the self than any of the other self-theorists, they only allow so much. In order to see what I mean by this, consider the example of the boat that over time has had all of its parts replaced. This would not serve as a valid analogy for a Jaina or Bhāṭṭa self, because the boat's numerical identity – if it is even considered numerically identical – consists not in it being the very same substance, composed of the same stuff, but in other factors such as continuity of structure and an uninterrupted spatio-temporal path. For Kumārila the stuff out of which the self is composed is eternal (that is the point of the gold analogy with its eternal gold atoms), whereas in the case of the boat there is nothing that continues to exist throughout the entire span of its life. Both the boat and a Bhāṭṭa/Jaina self are 'one thing that changes', but such a definition is not sufficient to capture the Bhāṭṭa or Jaina conception of self, for selfhood was taken by them to require a strong sense of numerical identity. Yes it can change, but to count as a self it must also be numerically identical in the strong sense of being the very same substance, composed of the same stuff, with no change whatsoever in its essence. With that we reach the limit of the self-theorists; any attempt to preserve numerical identity but in a weak sense – analogous to that of the boat – will count as a Buddhist view rather than a self-view.

We have reached the location on the spectrum we are delineating at which we pass from the self-views to the Buddhist views.

Two more Buddhist views

We have so far been using the expression 'the Buddhist view' to refer to that of momentariness-theorists (Kṣaṇikavādins) such as Vasubandhu, Dharmakīrti and their followers. That is because non-Buddhists, when they set about proving a self, took the momentariness-theorists to be representative of Buddhism. But two other Buddhist views will be mentioned here. The first view we meet after crossing the boundary into the Buddhist side of the spectrum is that of the Personalists (Pudgalavādins). They felt that the unqualified denial of a self on the part of their fellow Buddhists was not true to the Buddha's teaching, especially those places where he rejects both the view that there is a self and the view that there is not. They thus postulated a 'person' (*pudgala*) that cannot be said to be either the same as or different from the psycho-physical constituents (*skandha*).

If it were the same as the constituents, they reasoned, then it would be as momentary as them, and memory, rebirth and moral responsibility would be difficult to account for. If it were independent from them, then it would be as eternal and unconditioned as a Sāṅkhya or Naiyāyika self (*atman*), and hence all the problems that Buddhists see with such an entity ensue: it cannot enter into a mutual relationship with psycho-physical reality, it would seem to be already liberated and so makes the religious life redundant, etc. (Eltschinger and Ratie 2013, 84). The Personalists regarded their view as taking the proper middle way between the two extremes of eternalism and annihilationism.

They compared the relationship between the constituents and the person to that between a tree and its shadow, or fuel and the fire rising from that. As Eltschinger and Ratie (2013, 73–75) perceptively note, four aspects of the analogies seem to have been intended. (1) The shadow is neither the same as nor different from the tree, and the fire is neither the same as nor different from the fuel. (2) The shadow and the fire exist, but in a less substantial and determinate way than the tree and the fuel. (3) There is no shadow without the tree and no fire without the fuel. (4) The shadow and the fire are *caused by*, respectively, the tree and the fuel. The person, then, is a kind of epiphenomenon thrown up by the constituents; it cannot exist without them, but it is not reducible to them.

It is not difficult to distinguish this 'person' from the self of the Naiyāyikas, Śaiva Siddhāntins, etc.; but there is some overlap between it and the self of the Bhāṭṭas and Jainas. As the former is neither the same as nor different from the constituents, so the latter is neither the same as nor different from the self's qualities such as its pleasures, pains and cognitions. In what way, then, are the two concepts distinct? (1) A Bhāṭṭa or a Jaina self is not caused by its qualities. (2) It *can* exist without them – in the state of liberation and between incarnations. (3) It is not less substantial or determinate than its qualities. (4) It is a substance; the person is not. (5) It is eternal; the person is neither eternal nor momentary.

The 'person' of the Pudgalavādins thus falls between an enduring self-substance (as upheld by the Bhāṭṭas and Jainas) and the transient constituents (*skandha*). The next Buddhist view on the spectrum – let us call it 'Buddhism without momentariness' – is one that was not, to my knowledge, actually put forward by any Buddhists. It is a product of my reflection and a sense that there is conceptual space here for a 'Buddhistic' view that fits between the two properly Buddhist views dealt with in this chapter. It and the momentariness view of the Kṣaṇikavādins fall together, against the Personalists, in asserting that an individual consists in nothing more than the constituents. What separates the two of them is that for the former the constituents are temporally extended, for the latter they are momentary.

The 'Buddhist-without-momentariness' view is represented in Figure 33.6. The five rows represent the five kinds of constituent. If we take the top row as consciousness (*vijñāna-skandha*), each rectangle in that row denotes an instance of consciousness. All of these instances will be transient; some may last only for a moment, most for longer, but none forever. The same goes for the other four constituents. One kind of constituent, a feeling say, may or may not begin and end at the same time as another, an impulse or an instance of consciousness say. It is very unlikely that instances of all five constituents will stop and start at the same time. Thus this view avoids what some held to be a problematic feature of momentariness – that there are breaks in the process, that an individual is completely destroyed (in every moment) before arising again in the next, and that this seems equivalent to annihilationism. On this view there are no breaks in the process, no destruction of an individual, because at the point where one kind of constituent ceases, others will be existent. The overlapping of the constituents avoids annihilationism.

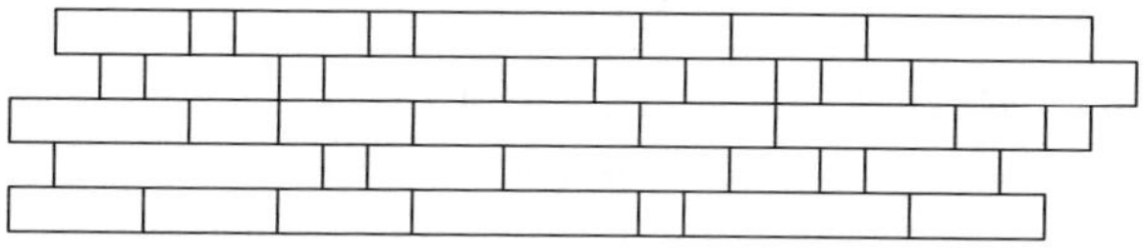

Figure 33.6

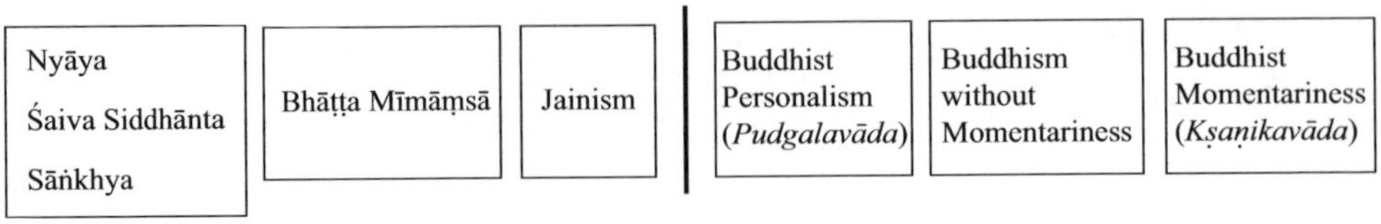

Figure 33.7

Conclusion

The chapter began by distinguishing four groups of classical Indian philosophical traditions. Having looked at several of the traditions that belong in the third and fourth groups – at the positions they take on the issue of selfhood and personal identity – we see that they can be arranged along a spectrum as shown in Figure 33.7.

Notes

1 This chapter is a shortened version of Watson (forthcoming); I thank Bloomsbury Publishing for allowing me to reuse material.

2 His view may remind some readers of either Sāṅkhya or Advaita Vedānta; for an analysis of the differences between his view and both of these, see Watson (2010).

References

Primary sources

Ślokavārttika: *Ślokavārttika of Śrī Kumārila Bhaṭṭa with the Commentary Nyāyaratnākara of Śrī Pārthasārathi Miśra*. Ed. Śāstrī, Dvārikādāsa. Prāchyabhārati Series 10. Varanasi: Chowkhamba Sanskrit Series Office, 1978.

Secondary sources

Eltschinger, V. and Ratie, I. 2013. *Self, No-Self, and Salvation: Dharmakīrti's Critique of the Notions of Self and Person*. Beiträge zur Kultur- und Geistesgeschichte Asiens 75. Sitzungsberichte (Österreichische Akademie der Wissenschaften, Philosophisch-Historische Klasse) 837. Vienna: Verlag der Österreichischen Akademie der Wissenschaften.

Uno, T. 1999. "Ontological Affinity between the Jainas and the Mīmāṃsakas", in Katsura, S. (ed.), *Dharmakīrti's Thought and Its Impact on Indian and Tibetan Philosophy. Proceedings of the Third International Dharmakīrti Conference, Hiroshima, November 4–6, 1997*. Österreichische Akademie der Wissenschaften, Philosophisch-Historische Klasse, Denkschriften 281. Vienna: Verlag der Österreichischen Akademie der Wissenschaften, 419–431.

Watson, A. 2010. "Rāmakaṇṭha's Concept of Unchanging Cognition (*nityajñāna*): Influence from Buddhism, Sāṃkhya, Vedānta", in J. Bronkhorst and K. Preisendanz (eds.), *From Vasubandhu to Caitanya. Studies in Indian Philosophy and Its Textual History. Papers of the 12th World Sanskrit Conference*. Volume 10.i. Delhi: Motilal Banarsidass, 79–120.

Watson, A. Forthcoming. "Self or No-Self? The Ātman Debate in Classical Indian Philosophy", in Joerg Tuske (ed.) *The Bloomsbury Research Handbook to Indian Epistemology and Metaphysics*. London: Bloomsbury Academic.

Chapter 34

SVĀTANTRIKA MADHYAMAKA METAPHYSICS: BHĀVAVIVEKA'S CONCEPTION OF REALITY

Sonam Thakchoe

Bhāvaviveka (*c.* 500–578 CE) is said to have founded the Svātantrika Madhyamaka movement in India. This philosophic movement gave rise to two subschools of thought within the Svātantrika: (1) Sautrāntika Svātantrika Madhyamaka and (2) Yogācāra Svātantrika Madhyamaka. The latter, the view held by Śāntarakṣita (*c.* 725-783 CE) and his student Kamalaśīla (*c.* 740–795 CE), following the Madhyamaka, affirms the ontological non-foundationalism, that all things are ultimately unreal. Although, following Yogācāra idealism, it claims, conventionally, only the inner domains are intrinsically real whereas the external objects are mere mental fictions. The former is the view held by Bhāvaviveka himself, and his student Jñānagarbha (eighth century CE). In three philosophical works, *Lamp of Wisdom* (*Prajñāpradīpamūlamadhyamakavṛtti*, *PPMV*), *Verses on the Heart of the Middle Way* (*Madhyamakahṛdayakārikā*, *MHK*), *Blazes of Reasoning: A Commentary on Verses of the Heart of the Middle Way* (*Tarkajvālā*, *TJ*), Bhāvaviveka, following the ontological realism of the Sautrāntika, asserts the intrinsic reality of both the external and the internal entities. Ultimately, following the Mādhyamika, he asserts intrinsic unreality of both the external and the internal entities.

The arguments Bhāvaviveka employs to affirm the conventional reality of the external objects are the same arguments he employs to reject the Yogācāra argument denying the reality of external objects.

The Yogācāra argues that a perceptual cognition apprehending an object blue-patch mistakenly apprehends the representation as the blue-patch, for it apprehends representation as a being distinct from the object like a perceptual cognition of the double moon. So Yogācāra's syllogistic argument takes the following form: a cognition of material form has no object, because it arises with the kind of image or representation like the cognition of material form in a dream. This follows, for Yogācāra, since the intentional objects are the only things we can claim to have cognition of, and since the intentional objects in the perceptual cognition of a blue-patch are, strictly speaking, mere mental representations, the images of a blue-patch created by the mind. What appear in the cognition are those representations, it therefore concludes that the external object are unreal.

Bhāvaviveka rejects this argument. If the Yogācāra "thinks that a cognition of material form is incorrect because it has the representation or the image of an object, the reason is mistaken, and the thesis fails" (*MHK* V.15 *dBu ma* Dza 20b). The reason is "mistaken" in the sense that it is "contradicted" (*viruddha*). This means a cognition of the material form cannot have any other nature than to have the representation of an object. Therefore the Yogācāra inference that "having the presentation of an object" excludes *correctness* of the cognition is contradicted (*viruddha*), because it proves the opposite of the nature of the subject. The Yogācāra thesis is that a cognition of material form is false. But how can this be false since perception (*pratyakṣa*), tradition (*āgama*) and common sense (*lokaprasiddha*) all prove the correctness of the cognition of the material form? For this reason, Yogācāra's inference is contradicted (*TJ* V.15, *dBu ma* Dza 204ab).

Yogācāra points out that consciousness arises even without an object such as material form, and therefore asserts that the consciousness of material form has no object because it arises with the representation, like the cognition of material form in dreams (*MHK* V.18 *dBu ma* Dza 20b) This Bhāvaviveka refutes as unsound argument, because "dream-consciousness and so forth have *dharmas* as their objects (*ālambana*)," hence the Yogācāra inference "lacks an example and it inappropriately denies the object (*viṣaya*)" (*MHK* V.19 *dBu ma* dza 20b). Yogācāra's syllogism is valid only if it has an example that is acceptable to Bhāvaviveka himself, since he is the other party to the argument. Bhāvaviveka rejects Yogācāra's claim that dreams are pure representations or images without corresponding objects, and that they illustrate the thesis that cognitions lack external object. He instead argues dream-consciousness has real objects (*ālambana*), and that they are intrinsically real conventional objects, because they are the repeated impressions of the objects that have been cognized previously, like memory (*TJ* V.19 *dBu ma* dza 205a).

Of the two schools of Svātantraka, we will focus on the central theses that are critical to the formation of the distinctive ontological character of the Sautrāntika Svātantrika Madhyamaka. The two theses are: (1) Conventionally all phenomena are intrinsically real, because they are established as intrinsic realities from the perspective of the non-analytical cognitions of the naïve ordinary beings. This is to say that Madhyamaka, according to Bhāvaviveka, accepts intrinsic reality of all things, both external and internal realities, at the level of conventional reality since it is intrinsic reality that constitutes what is conventionally real. (2) Ultimately all phenomena, with the exception to the emptiness which is ultimately real, are intrinsically unreal (*niḥsvabhāvataḥ*) or ultimately unreal because they are established as empty of any intrinsic reality from the perspective of analytical exalted cognition (i.e., ultimate cognition of *ārya*-beings). This is to say that Madhyamaka, according to Bhāvaviveka, rejects intrinsic reality at the ultimate level since ultimate reality constitutes that which is intrinsically unreal, therefore empty.

Conventional reality

We shall consider Bhāvaviveka's defence of the two claims by looking at two arguments: arguments for intrinsically real conventional truth; and arguments for intrinsically unreal ultimate truth. We begin with his account of conventional truth. In the *TJ*, Bhāvaviveka explains "conventionality" (*saṃvṛti*) as an incontrovertible linguistic convention (*lokavyvahāra*) consisting of every category of entities like forms; and this is the truth (*satya*) for it is the framework of everything that is epistemically warranted (*pramāṇa*) (*dBu ma* dza 56a). Such conventional truth on Bhāvaviveka's Svātantrika takes two forms:

(1) unique particulars (*svalakṣaṇa*) and
(2) universals (*sāmānyalakṣaṇa*).

The *TJ* III.8 explains: Phenomena have dual characteristics (*lakṣana*), differentiated on being a universal or a unique. (1) Unique particular (*svalakṣaṇa*) is thing's intrinsic nature (*svabhāvatā*), the domain of engagement which is definitively ascertained by "non-conceptual cognition" (*nirvikalpena jñānena*). (2) Universal (*sāmāṅyalakṣaṇa*) is the domain to be apprehended by an inferential cognition (*anumanavijñānena*) which is a "conceptual" (*Dbu ma* dza 55b).

Unique particulars (*svalakṣaṇa*) form the ontological structure of the conventional truth, unlike Sautrāntika and Sārvastivādins, who assert them as the ultimate truths. The Prāsaṅgika, by contrast, reject it entirely. Bhāvaviveka ascribes to the unique particular the ontological qualification of being "intrinsically real" (*svabhāvatā*), which explicitly affirms that he is committed to a form of conventional foundationalism of the unique particulars, at least at the level of conventional truth. And Bhāvaviveka wholeheartedly accepts the Pramāṇika's epistemology in which unique particular (*svalakṣaṇa*) is defined as intrinsically real (*svabhāvatā*), conventionally. Like the Pramāṇika, Bhāvaviveka also considers unique particulars as the domain of cognitive engagement certified by non-conceptual cognition (*nirvikalpena jñānena*), whereas the universal (*sāmāṅyalakṣaṇa*) is defined as the domain to be apprehended by an conceptual inferential cognition (*anumanavijñānena*).

Bhāvaviveka defines "unique particular" (*svalakṣaṇa*) in the *TJ* III.13 in terms of the five aggregates (*pañca skandha*) – form (*rūpa*), feeling or experience (*vedanā*), perceptual judgments (*saṃjñā*), mental dispositions (*saṃkāra*), and consciousness (*vijñāna*) (*Dbu ma* dza 56b). He also maintains unique particular as constituting conventional realities such as "being blue, yellow, long, short, form, sound, etc." (*Dbu ma* dza 56b–57a). The universals (*sāmānya-lakṣaṇa*), he explains, are "being impermanent (*anitya*), suffering (*dukḥa*), empty (*śūnya*), nonself (*nairātmya*), and the like" (*Dbu ma* dza 56b).

Unique particulars are intrinsically real although they are not *ultimately intrinsically real.* Bhāvaviveka's conclusion of his critique of the Sāṁkhya's theory of self-causation makes this point reasonably explicit.

> The statements: 'that is a self-existent' and 'that is a thing' are conventionalities. That which arises from them [i.e., conventionally self-produced] *ultimately* lacks intrinsic reality (*niḥsvabhāvataḥ*), for such a thing is [ultimately] neither produced from self, nor from another, nor from both nor [produced] causelessly.
>
> (*TJ* III.141 *Dbu ma* dza 93b)

When asked: "Is it not the case that the reality of things is just as they appear as being solid, liquid, heat, motion, etc.?" Bhāvaviveka replies: "That is the mode of conventional reality. Its reality exhausts in being merely dependent upon the *intrinsic nature* by excluding the other [i.e., excluding the ultimately real intrinsic nature]" (*TJ* III.152 *Dbu ma* dza 96a). Likewise in *MHK* III.171 an interlocutor raised an objection pointing out the fallacies entailing the denial of the ultimately intrinsic production: that it would entail (i) a denial of the realities that are the domains of the direct perception (*pratyakṣa*) and (ii) a denial of the realities given to the common-sense convention (*prasiddha*) (*Dbu ma* dza 10a). To this Bhāvaviveka replies as follows:

> Because productions such as a vase appear to accord [with how they appear to] the mind of the ordinary beings they are not negated. Hence the charges of the fallacies [of denying the objects of direct experience and the common-sense conventions] raised does not occur.
>
> (*MHK* III.172, *Dbu ma* dza 10a)

Commenting on the same point Bhāvaviveka offers, in the *TJ* III.172 (*Dbu ma* dza 99b–100a), two reasons to support why the fallacies do no occur. Both reasons are premised on the notion that conventionally things are intrinsically real, although they may be ultimately intrinsically unreal.

First, intrinsic arising of things such as a vase is not ultimately real, as such intrinsic arising does not ultimately withstand critical analyses, thus from the perspective of ultimately exalted cognition of the noble beings things are neither produced from self (*na-svataḥ*), nor from another (*na-parataḥ*), nor from both, nor from neither, i.e., causelessly (*ahetutaḥ*). Hence *MHK* III.240–241 concludes:

> *Ultimately* things neither arise from self nor from another, nor from both, nor arises causelessly. It neither 'is' nor 'is not'. Neither do they originate from the causes such as Īśvāra, Puruṣa, Pradhāna, atoms, etc. Therefore [ultimately] there is no thing whatsoever.
>
> (*Dbu ma* dza 12b)

Second, although the arising of things is, from the ultimate standpoint, empty of the conceptions of reality and unreality, even so, like illusions, mirages and the city of gāndharvas, from the perspective of naïve ordinary beings, the arising of things do appear to be intrinsically real. Since those things the mode of appearance of which is intrinsically real corresponds to the way in which the ordinary convention mistakenly assume them as being intrinsic realities. They are thus granted the status of conventional truths, which are the domains of direct experience and common-sense convention.

Another place where we find the same claim being defended is in his theory of causation – in particular in his refutation of the theory of causation from another. The denial of the theory of arising from another, according to Bhāvaviveka, does not contradict Madhyamaka thesis asserting that things arise from the collaborative communion of the objective condition (*ālambana pratyaya*), dominant condition (*adhipati pratyaya*), immediate condition (*samanantara pratyaya*), causal condition (*hetu pratyaya*) (*TJ* III.155 *Dbu ma* dza 96a). This is because, according Bhāvaviveka "The arising from other conditions is based merely on the conventional discourse. Thus it does not undermine the thesis. Such arising is not ultimate" (*MHK* III.155 *Dbu ma* dza 96b). Mādhyamika is not nihilistic on Bhāvaviveka's account because it accepts the conventional reality of all phenomenal processes as they appear intrinsically.

Bhāvaviveka argues that Mādhyamika has an intrinsically real conventional thesis, but it denies ultimately real thesis, and that they do not contradict each other. Here Bhāvaviveka supplies us with two arguments. First, the status of conventional truth such as the statement "conventionally, things are intrinsically real" is not undermined by the Mādhyamika thesis that says: "ultimately things are not intrinsically real." The conventional thesis reflects the standpoint of the convention of the ordinary beings whereas having no ultimate thesis reflects the standpoint of the convention of the exalted beings.

Bhāvaviveka adopts Pramāṇika's epistemological view according to which perceptual cognition is invariably non-conceptual, thus rejecting the possibility that perception can be conceptual – "Since perception is defined as being non-conceptual, it is not involved with conception and the recollective conception [i.e., memory]" (*TJ* III.271, *Dbu ma* dza 126a). Based on this theory, Bhāvaviveka, in his verse III.7 of *MHK*, classifies knowledge or cognition into two forms of knowledge (*mati*) according to dual objects of knowledge – conventional truth and ultimate truth – and knowledge that arises in dependence on the knowable. The knowledge of that which is conventionally real is regarded as a proper mundane cognition, and the knowledge of that which is ultimate reality is regarded as an exalted knowledge (*TJ*, *Dbu ma* dza 55a). On Bhāvaviveka's epistemology real conventionality is seen as the basis from which develops the ultimate knowledge, as he writes in *MHK* III.12–13: "Were it not the ladder of the real conventionalities, [even] for a competent to arrive at the grand mansion of the ultimate reality is an impossibility" (*Dbu ma* dza 4a).

In short, Bhāvaviveka's defence of the thesis that conventionally things are intrinsically real can be summed up in two arguments. First, as far as things are conventional realities they are also intrinsic or inherent realities, for being intrinsically real is the reason why things are designated as "conventional reality," since from the conventional standpoint – i.e., non-analytical cognitive engagements of the ordinary beings – things do appear to be inherently real. Therefore the term "intrinsic" (*svabhāvatā*), argues Bhāvaviveka, for instance "signifies that the *production is itself an intrinsic* nature of the [elements] such as the earth, hence production is intrinsic" (*Dbu ma* dza 59b). This means that being "intrinsic" is for Bhāvaviveka what defines *conventional reality* as a reality. Thus intrinsic reality is not an object to be negated and hence not be excluded from the categories of conventional truth. What is excluded is, however, *ultimately intrinsic reality* – hence Bhāvaviveka insists that "one should interpret that the [elements] such as the earth lack a production that is *ultimately intrinsic*" (*Dbu ma* dza 59b).

Bhāvaviveka's second argument states that as long as Madhyamaka accepts conventional truth it must also accept things as intrinsic in order to avoid the nihilism charge, for conventional reality is defined in terms of its being intrinsically real and unique particulars (*svalakṣaṇa*). Denying the intrinsic reality of things at the conventional level, would therefore entail the denial of their conventional existence, since it would entail the denial of the defining characteristics of the conventional reality. This follows, he argues, because "The Lord (*bhāgvan*) has taught the two truths. Based on this [explanatory schema] conventionally things are posited in terms of their intrinsic natures and [unique] particulars. It is only ultimately that [things are] posited as having no intrinsic nature" (*Dbu ma* dza 60a). For this reason also, according to Bhāvaviveka, an exclusion or negation of intrinsic reality of things would entail nihilism for it would entail the negation of what is conventionally real phenomena since conventionally all phenomena exist inherently as unique particulars, just as a production is inherent to becoming whatever things are conventionally. Things cannot exist conventionally without being intrinsically real.

Ultimate reality

Bhāvaviveka's second major thesis is that at the level of ultimate truth, all phenomena are intrinsically unreal, therefore Madhyamaka rejects ultimately intrinsic reality. Bhāvaviveka's advances several arguments to defend this thesis.

The first argument is the conditionality argument pertaining to the four elements, according to which all the four elements are ultimately empty of any intrinsic reality, for they all are conditioned by the causal factors appropriated for their becoming and their existence. As we read in *MHK* III.27: "[Ultimately] earth [element] (*pṛthivi*) is not inherently solid because it is an *element* (*bhūta*) like air (*vāyu*). The cohesiveness is not the function of the solidity because it is a conditioned like liquid (*āp*)" (*Dbu ma* dza 4b). That is, apart from water, heat, air, there is nothing that could be ultimately identified as "earth" for apart from being intrinsically composite. As *TJ* III. 27 explains, the ultimate identity of the earth element could not be demonstrated in its isolation. So also are the functions – solidity, liquidity, maturation, motion – attributed specifically to each element – respectively earth, water, fire, and air – ultimately unreal, since none is established as reality when subjected to the ultimate analysis. Thus ultimately intrinsic reality of the elements and their functional efficacy are not established ultimately (*Dbu ma* dza 61b).

The second argument comes from Bhāvaviveka's non-foundational atomic theory, which rejects the foundationalist ontology of the Hindus and the Buddhist Ābhidharmikas, according to which atoms are taken to be the foundational entities – either as substances (*dravyas*) or intrinsic realities (*svabhāva*) which are supposed to be self-natured, self-contained, stand as the foundations for all other ontological structures independent of any interpretative conventions. On Bhāvaviveka's ontology, all phenomena, including the atoms, are ultimately non-foundational, for ultimately there is nothing that can be taken as the foundational entity (*dravya*) or intrinsically real since the ultimate analysis reveals that all phenomena are composed of the atomic particles that are themselves composites. The *TJ* III.30 states that "the atomic particles of the four elements are inherently composite because," according to Bhāvaviveka, "each [atom] is composed of the eight substances (*dravyas*) – earth, water, fire, air, form, smell, taste, and tactility, none of which ever had mere characteristics and mere functions which could explain their individualities being intrinsically real and with [specific] functions" (*Dbu ma* dza 62a).

The so-called substantive reality or the foundational entity which is intrinsically real on the conventional level, in Bhāvaviveka's view, as he outlines in *MHK* III.32, are nevertheless ultimately non-intrinsic, non-substantial, and therefore non-foundational (*adravya*), because apart from being collective wholes, conceptually composed, none of the atoms withstands as the foundation or substance of other phenomena. Thus, like a forest, whatever is shown to be non-foundational cannot be apprehended as the foundational substance (*Dbu ma* dza 4b). The earth element for instance, as its commentary *TJ* III.32 explains, "is non-foundational" because, apart from the collective parts such as of the moisture, the *earth* so-called is not apprehended, and that which cannot be apprehended without apprehending its collective parts could not be the foundational substance. This is like a forest. The so-called forest, argues Bhāvaviveka, "could not be apprehended without apprehending specific trees like … acacia catechu (*khadīra*), palāśa tree. The name 'forest' is only appropriate to a collection [of trees]" (*Dbu ma* dza 63ab). Similarly the name "atom" applies only to a collective whole constituted by range of atomic properties such as solidity, moisture, heat, mobility, visibility, smell, taste, tactility, etc., without any foundational entity upon which they stand. Therefore phenomena such as form and seed, for instance, says Bhāvaviveka, are neither found to be identical to foundational entities nor different from them nor are the foundational entities present in the form and sprout, nor form and sprout present in the foundational entities.

In this way Bhāvaviveka applies the non-foundationalist ontological argument to establish a non-foundational epistemological account rejecting the epistemological foundationalism of Nyāya and Pramāṇikas. According to the latter protagonists, some cognitive faculties are ultimate truths acting as foundational, self-warranting, and thus stand as the foundation for all other epistemic processes. Bhāvaviveka disagrees. His argument runs as follows: because the elements such as the earth are non-foundational entities, the subjects – cognitions apprehending them – are also non-foundational on two counts: (1) they are causal phenomena and (2) they are subject to cessation (*MHK* III.33 *Dbu ma* Dza 4b). The former follows because the cognitions arise from the appropriate causal conditions even as the cognition of the forest depends upon apprehending individual trees as its object. The latter follows since the cognition ceases when the conditions supporting them cease to exist even as the cognition of the forest ceases to arise when the forest no longer exists.

It is clear, then, Bhāvaviveka's conception of truth/reality constitutes the theory that at the level of conventional truth all phenomena are intrinsically real and at the level of ultimate truth, all phenomena, with the exception of emptiness which is ultimately real, are intrinsically unreal. The arguments he advances in his works support this view.

References

Ames, L. William. 1993. "Bhāvaviveka's *Prajñāpradīpa*: A Translation of Chapter One: 'Examination of Causal Conditions' (Pratyaya)." *Journal of Indian Philosophy* 21: 209–259.

Avalokitavrata. 1998. *Prajñāpradīpaṭīkā* (Shes rab sgron ma rgya cher 'grel ba) (Dbu ma wa 1a–287a). Sde dge edition of the Bstan 'gyur. Dharmasala: Paljor Press.

Bhāvaviveka. 1998a. *Madhyamakaratnapradīpa (Dbu ma rin po che'i sgron ma)* (Sde dge bstan 'gyur, Dbu ma tsha 259b–289a). Sde dge edition of the Bstan 'gyur. Dharmasala: Paljor Press.

Bhāvaviveka. 1998b. *Madhyamakahṛdayakārikā (Dbu ma snying po'i tshig l'hur byas pa)* (Dbu ma dza 1a–40b). Sde dge edition of the Bstan 'gyur. Dharmasala: Paljor Press.

Bhāvaviveka. 1998c. *Madhyamakahṛdayavṛtti-tarkajvālā (Dbu ma snying po'i 'grel pa rtog ge 'bar ba)* (Dbu ma dza 40b–396b). Sde dge edition of the Bstan 'gyur. Dharmasala: Paljor Press.

Bhāvaviveka. 1998d. *Prajñāpradīpamūlamadhyamakavṛtti (Dbu ma rtsa ba'i 'grel ba shes rab sgron ma)* (Dbu ma tsha 45b–259b). Sde dge edition of the Bstan 'gyur. Dharmasala: Paljor Press.

Eckel, D. Malcolm. 2008. *Bhaviveka and His Buddhist Opponents*. Cambridge, MA: Harvard University Press.

Jñānagrabha. 1998. *Distinguishing the Two Truths (Satyadvayavibhaṅgakārikā SDVK* (Dbu ma sa 1b–3b). Sde dge edition of the Bstan 'gyur. Dharmasala: Paljor Press.

Lopez. S. D. 1987. *A Study of Svātantrika*. New York: Snow Lion Publications.

Ruegg, David Seyfort. 1990. "On the Authorship of Some Works Ascribed to Bhāvaviveka/Bhavya." In *Earliest Buddhism and Madhyamaka*. Ernst Steinkellner (ed.), 59–71. Vienna: Verlag der Österreichischen Akademie der Wissenschaften.

Chapter 35
THE TWO TRUTHS IN MADHYAMAKA: JÑĀNAGARBHA[1]

Sonam Thakchoe

In the late seventh and early eighth century Bhāvaviveka's conception of the two truths flourished in the work of three important figures often known as the "eastern trio": Jñānagarbha (?), Śāntarakṣita (*c.* 705–762 CE) and Kamalaśīla (*c.* 740–795 CE)

Jñānagarbha followed Bhāvaviveka's Sautrāntika-Svātantrika Madhyamaka line with only minor variations, whereas Śāntarakṣita and Kamalaśīla's deviations from that position give rise to the second Svātantrika sub-school, the Yogācāra-Svātantrika Madhyamaka. Whereas the Sautrāntika-Svātantrika synthesises the epistemological realism of the Sautrāntika with the Madhyamaka's non-foundational ontology, the Yogācāra-Svātantrika synthesises the epistemological idealism of the Yogācāra with Madhymaka ontology. In this chapter we specifically look at, albeit briefly, Jñānagarbha's theory of the two truths.

Jñānagarbha composed two primary works: *Distinguishing the Two Truths* (*Satyadvay avibhaṅgakārikā*, *SDVK*) and *Commentary on the Distinguishing the Two Truths* (*Satyadva yavibhaṅgavṛtti*, *SDVV*).[2] In these two works, and Śāntarakṣita's *Satyadvayavibhaṅgapañ jikā* (*SDVP*, *Subcommentary on Distinguishing the Two Truths*), Jñānagarbha argues that the two truths satisfy three criteria.

The first, according to *SDVK*, conventional reality is that which only appears to be real, while ultimate reality is the emptiness of that which appears:

> The Sage taught the two truths: conventional (*saṃvṛti*) and ultimate (*paramārtha*). That which corresponds to appearances (*yathādarśana*) is conventional [truth] whereas the other [i.e., ultimate truth] is the reverse.
>
> (*SDVK* 3 *dBu ma* Sa 1a)

Glossing this verse in his *SDVV*, Jñānagarbha argues that anything that appears, regardless of whether it appears to an ordinary or a noble (*ārya*) being, is conventionally real. Conventional reality is "conceived in accordance with the way in which things appear" (*SDVV* 3 *dBu ma* Sa 4a). But that surface reality, according to Śāntarakṣita's *Subcommentary*, has no basis in reason, and critical analysis quickly ascertains its ultimate unreality – emptiness (*SDVP* 2 *dBu ma* Sa 17b). Ultimate truth is simply the apprehension of that emptiness. It is in this sense ultimate reality is the reverse, or the opposite of conventional reality. Ultimate truth, the truth that can withstand critical analysis, is simply the truth that conventional appearance cannot.

The second criterion is that conventional truth is deceptive and contradictory, while ultimate truth is neither deceptive nor contradictory (*avisaṃvāda*). Conventional truth is deceptive and contradictory, because ultimately the way in which things appear does not correspond to the way they exist, for they do not appear at all to an enlightened cognition (*SDVK* 5 *dBu ma* Sa 1a). Jñānagarbha argues that were the appearance of things to correspond to its ultimate reality, then it would also have to correspond to the cognition which apprehends that reality – the cognition of an enlightened being.

In fact, according to Jñānagarbha, appearance is never the object of the cognition of such a being. Since an enlightened cognition "directly knows what exists and what does not exist, and if (it) does not see a thing, the nature of that thing should be carefully scrutinized" (*SDVK* 7 *dBu ma* Sa). It is for this reason, Jñānagarbha says, that the *sūtras* state that "to not see anything is to see reality itself" (*SDVV* 4 *dBu ma* Sa 4ab). The fact that appearance fails to arise as an object of enlightened cognition betrays its ultimate reality.

Ultimate truth, by contrast, is neither deceptive nor contradictory, Jñānagarbha says, it is so because it accords with reason:

> It is non-deceptive. Reason (*nyāya*) is an ultimate [truth], not a conventional [truth], because [conventional truth] deceives. Reason is real just as it appears.
> (*SDVK* 4 *dBu ma* Sa 1a)

Reasoning is not a conventional truth because reasoning cannot be deceived. Deception, we have repeatedly observed, is a function of unthinking, intuitive perception – precisely because such perception is divorced from reason (*SDVK* 4 *dBu ma* Sa 1a). Perception in accord with reason, on the other hand, ascertains the ultimate reality that the same perception divorced from it obscures. Reason that ascertains the reality as it is, for Jñānagarbha, is the very definition of ultimate truth:

> *That which is ultimately real* (*paramārtha-satya*) is the ultimate truth, for it is the reality verified by a rational cognition. Ultimate truth is the non-deceptive reason, for the reality ascertained through the power of reasoning cognition never deceives. Thus a cognition produced by means of the triple criterion[3] reasoning is the ultimate truth as it is [both] 'ultimate' as well as 'domain' (*artha*). The domain that reason ascertains is also an ultimate truth, just as a perception (*pratyakṣa*) [can be either a cognition or an object].
> (*SDVV* 4 *dBu ma* Sa 4a)

Let us turn now to Jñānagarbha's third criterion, which is that conventional truth cannot be analysed since it does not withstand deductive reasoning, while ultimate truth can be analysed since it does. To understand why Jñānagarbha holds the conventional to be unanalysable requires that we understand his distinction between the two types of conventional reality – *real* and *unreal* conventional truths. Jñānagarbha explains:

> [T]hough alike in the way in which it appears, conventional [truth] is subdivided into *real* (*tathya*) and *unreal* (*mithyā*) conventionalities on the basis of their causal efficiency (*arthakriyāsamartha*) or inefficiency.
>
> (*SDVK* 12, *dBu ma* Sa 1b)

The autocommentary explains that conventional realities are alike in their actuality (*vastutaḥ*) – that is, their lack of ultimately intrinsic reality (*niḥsvabhāvatā*) – and the manner in which they appear to mundane cognitions. Nonetheless, they may be distinguished (*vyavasthita*) according to their causal efficacy based on their appearance (*yathādarśana*). *Real* conventional truths (*tathyasaṃvṛtisatya*) are non-deceptive, because their causal function corresponds to their appearance. They fulfil the functions their appearances advertise. *Unreal* conventional truths (*mithyāsaṃvṛtisatya*), on the other hand, are deceptive because their causal function and appearance contradict. They fail to fulfil the functions of their advertised appearance. Whether they are real or unreal with regard to causally efficiency is a matter of common-sense agreement (*yathāprasiddha*).

Let us illustrate the division between real and unreal conventional truths. Water is a real conventional truth. It appears to be water, and efficiently functions as water. It is wet, transparent, liquid and satiates thirst. A mirage, on the other hand, is an unreal conventional truth. It is conventionally deceptive, for though it appears to be water, it lacks all of water's relevant causal functions (*SDVV* 12, *dBu ma* Sa 6b).

To qualify as a real conventional truth, or a "mere thing" (*vastu-mātra*) Jñānagarbha argues, requires satisfying four criteria, two prescriptive, two proscriptive:

(i) to not be conceptually imagined
(ii) to be dependently arisen (*SDVK* 8ab, *dBu ma* Sa 2a)
(iii) to be causally effective
(iv) to not be analysable (*SDVK* 21ab, *dBu ma* Sa 2b).

We will address each in turn.

To not be conceptually imagined

A real conventional truth cannot be an imaginary phenomenon. 'Imaginary phenomenon' (*kalpitārtha*) is an umbrella term for a conceptually constructed entity which violates the basic fundamentals of Madhyamaka philosophy. They include ultimately real elements (*bhūta*); the ultimately real arising, real cessation and real continuation proclaimed by the Indian philosophers such as the Ābhidharmikas; the ultimately real consciousness proclaimed by the Yogācārins; and the primal matter (*pradhāna*) proclaimed by the Sāṁkhya. For Jñānagarbha, all these imaginary objects fail to attain even conventional reality, much less ultimate reality. For something to be a real conventional truth (i.e., *mere thing*) thus requires that it not be such an imaginary object (*SDVV* 8 *dBu ma* Sa 5b).

Imaginary phenomena are described as "conceptually imagined" (*parikalpita*) because, for Jñānagarbha, any thing believed to possess ultimate reality *can* only be the figment of the philosophical (*siddhānta*) imagination (*SDVK* 8cd *dBu ma* Sa 2a). Ultimately real entities *do not appear* to us, and so they must be imagined. The very fact that there is disagreement between philosophical schools, Jñānagarbha says, is evidence of this fact. If such objects were directly perceived, there would be no disagreement between different philosophical schools, for neither party – the proponent and the opponent – could dispute that direct perception (*SDVV* 8c *dBu ma* Sa 5b; cf. *SDVP*8c *dBu ma* Sa 24a).

Thus, such phenomena imagined to exist ultimately fail both the ultimate standard of critical analysis, since critical analysis finds only the absence of ultimate reality, *and* the mundane standard of appearance, since they are philosophical posits which can be debated but never observed (*SDVV* 8c *dBu ma* Sa 5b). In this way, they are unreal conventions (*SDVV* 8d *dBu ma* Sa 5b).

To be dependently arisen

A real conventional truth is a dependently arisen phenomenon, which comes into existence on account of a constellation of causes and conditions (*SDVV* 8 *dBu ma* Sa 5b).

To be causally efficient

A real conventional truth, or mere "thing" (*vastu*) is, according to Jñānagarbha, causally efficient (*artha-kriyāsamartha*). It is able to effectively fulfil its advertised function, which is to say its behaviour is consistent with its appearance (*yathādarśana*) in the mundane cognitions of all ordinary beings.[4]

To be unanalysable

Finally, a conventional truth "cannot be subjected to critical analysis for its identity is derived from its appearance but, when analysed, it contradicts itself by turning out to be something else" (*SDVK* 21 *dBu ma* Sa 2b).

For Jñānagarbha, we have seen, conventional reality is simply a function of surface appearance. It is therefore inappropriate, he says, for us to subject conventional truth to critical analysis to search for substance below that surface. According to the *Subcommentary*, the specific critical analysis[5] at issue here examines deeper metaphysical questions such as for example: How many causes are required to produce one effect? Can many causes produce many effects? Can one cause produces many effects? Does one cause produce one effect? Is a cognition of conventional reality an effect produced by many causes or one cause (*SDVK* 14 *dBu ma* Sa 2ab)? These questions, according to Jñānagarbha, are quite unrelated to our ordinary practical concerns. Thus the answers to such questions are plainly irrelevant to conventional discourses. For this reason, Jñānagarbha argues, real conventional truth must remain unanalysed (*SDVP* 21ab *dBu ma* Sa 38a).

If a conventional truth is nevertheless subjected to analysis, its truth-status is quickly destabilised. Though it appears to be real, analysis exposes its ultimate unreality. Conventional truth may correspond to appearances, but not to reason. In the domain of appearances, conventional reality *is* real, but reason exposes the fraud of appearance, the ultimate emptiness of all conventionalities. It is for this reason, according to Jñānagarbha, that the Mādhyamika does not analyse conventional truth (*SDVV* 21cd, *dBu ma* Sa 10b).

We will conclude with two final points on Jñānagarbha's theory of the two truths: the conventionality of the conventional, and the conventionality of the ultimate.

Conventionality of the conventional

For Jñānagarbha there is no real ontological basis (*āśraya*) for any conventional truth. All conventional truths are mere designations (*prajñapti*):

> The [real] basis of designations (*prajñapti*) does not appear anywhere to anyone. Even trees and so forth do not depend on a real basis.
>
> (*SDVK* 23, *dBu ma* Sa 2b)

The example of a "tree" demonstrates how the search for an ontological basis to designation is interminable. The layman designates "tree" on the basis of its major components – trunk, branches, leaves and roots, etc. For the botanist, those components are crude markers designated on the strength of *their* components. A leaf, for instance, is designated on the basis of its epidermis, veins and mesophyll, each of which can be further technically divided. For the chemist, the botanist's designations are themselves crude, and even the most precise botanical designation can be reduced to its component atomic and sub-atomic particles. The physicist would be inclined to similarly reduce the chemist's designations, and so on.

Jñānagarbha take the analysis to the level of the atomic particles (*paramāṇu*) and determines that atomic particles are themselves baseless. Mādhyamikas, Jñānagarbha says, hold conventional truth to be only consistent with appearances and do not depend on any real basis, or cause (*SDVV* 23, *dBu ma* Sa 10b–11a). That conventional designations are thus without a real basis is precisely his point. Were they to have a real basis, they wouldn't be conventional at all – they would be ultimately real.

Since there is no real basis for conventionality, it must be a superimposition; it is superimposed by shared ignorance. Jñānagarbha argues that, etymologically, "*saṃvṛti* (conventionality) means either that by which or that *in* which reality is concealed."[6] In his commentary, Jñāngarbha explains that conventional truth is a type of cognitive error (*brānti*) which conceals reality – emptiness of intrinsic nature (*niḥsvabhāva*) – in plain sight (*SDVV* 15ab, *dBu ma* Sa 9a). In support, he cites the *Laṅkāvatāra Sūtra*, which says that things which arise conventionally (*saṃvṛtyā*) are ultimately empty of intrinsic nature (*niḥsvabhāva*), and so their source is a cognition which fails to grasp the emptiness of intrinsic nature, instead reifies the empty as existing intrinsically (*SDVV* 15, *dBu ma* Sa 9a).[7] Since there is no basis otherwise, were it not for erroneous cognition (*viparyāsa*), ordinary beings would not conceive of real entities at all. It is mistaken cognition which gives rise to the real entities about which we agree. In other words, consensus that comes from common-sense agreement (*yathāprasiddha*) is evidence not of a common correctness, but a common cognitive defect.

Conventionality of the ultimate

Jñāngarbha goes as far as to argue that even the so-called ultimate is also only a convention. He deploys two arguments in support of this claim. The first is that "ultimate statements" are self-defeating because they only make sense conventionally. For instance:

> [T]he meaning of the statement 'ultimately [things] do not arise' also does not arise from the ultimate standpoint of reason, and the same principle applies to all other statements.
>
> (*SDVK* 16, *dBu ma* Sa 2b)

Statements about the ultimate truth are empty of ultimate truth. They can be deconstructed just as easily and totally as everything else, including the things about which they make claims (arising, non-arising, and so on). Thus, "ultimate statements" are empty from the ultimate perspective of reason, and the same principle applies to the ultimate perspective. *Everything* is empty including the reason itself (*SDVV* 16, *dBu ma* Sa 9b).

Jñānagarbha's second argument stresses the identity of the conventional and the ultimate:

> [W]hatever is the reality of the conventional is itself considered [by the Buddha] as the meaning of the ultimate, for they are not distinct. Reason corresponds to the way of its appearance (*yathādarśana*).
>
> (SDVK 17, *dBu ma* Sa 2b)

It is for this reason, Jñānagarbha argues, that the Buddha said:

> O Subhūti, the mundane convention is not one thing and the ultimate another. Mundane conventional reality is identical in nature to the reality of the ultimate.
>
> (SDVK 19, *dBu ma* Sa 10a)

In other words, for Jñānagrabha, reason (the ultimate truth) corresponds to the way of its appearance (the conventional truth). Just as appearances "appear" strictly as conventional phenomena, so does reason *appear* and *function* strictly as a conventional phenomenon. It cannot appear and function any other way.

This follows because, according to Jñānagarbha, reason is syllogistic, and the components of the syllogism – the subject (*dharmin*), property (*dharma*), example (*dṛṣṭānta*), reason (*hetu*) of an inference (*anumāna*) and the property to be inferred (*anumeya*) – are things which *appear* to the minds of the parties to an argument (*SDVK* 18–19, *dBu ma* Sa 2b). Reason (*hetu*) cannot function in a vacuum. It is *applied* to things which appear. It is appearance, Jñānagarbha says, which establishes the components of the syllogism for both parties, and makes subsequent enquiries into their ultimacy possible (*SDVV* 19, *dBu ma* Sa 9b–10a). Here again, we see the ontological implications of the Svātantrika's methodological position.

It could be argued that Jñānagarbha's theory of the two truths offers a defence of Bhāvaviveka's metaphysics and it marks a decisive shift away from Candrakīrti's Prāsaṅgika Madhyamaka. Although neither Jñānagarbha nor the sub-commentator states Candrakīrti by his name, Jñānagarbha criticises Candrakīrti's position when he criticises:

> Some who are notorious for their bad arguments argue that because things do not arise in a real sense (*tattvataḥ*), they do not arise in conventional sense either, like the son of a barren woman and so on.
>
> (*SDVK* 25, *dBu ma* Sa 2b)

The position held by Candrakīrti is implausible, says Jñānagarbha's commentary, since it is refuted by common sense (*loka*) and direct perception, etc. (*SDVV* 25, *DBu ma Sa* 11ab).

Jñānagarbha's response is effective against the argument he attacks. Unfortunately, that argument is not Candrakīrti's. The autocommentary and the subcommentary make it clear that Jñānagarbha sees the Candrakīrti's categorical rejection of the four metaphysical causal theories as representing a wholesale rejection of causality. Candrakīrti says that is not the case. Like Bhāvaviveka's realistic Sautrāntika Svātantrika Madhyamaka, Jñānagarbha presents conventional truth in agreement with the epistemological realism of the Sautrāntika and ultimate truth in agreement with non-foundationalist ontology of the Madhyamaka.

Conclusion

As we have seen Jñānagarbha argues that the two truths satisfy three criteria. (1) Conventional truth is that which appears to be real, while ultimate truth is the emptiness of that which appears. (2) Conventional truth is deceptive and contradictory, while ultimate truth is neither deceptive nor contradictory (*avisaṁvāda*). (3) Conventional truth cannot be analysed since it does not withstand deductive reasoning, while ultimate truth can be analysed since it does.

Jñānagarbha's partial foundationalism is implicated in his conventional truth theory. Though alike in the way in which it appears, conventional truth is sub-divided, (from the Madhyamaka's own perspective, not from the mundane perspective like the Prāsaṅgika) into *real* (*tathya*) and *unreal* (*mithyā*) conventionalities based on the former being causally efficient (*arthakriyāsamartha*) and the latter being causally inefficient (*nārthakriyāsamartha*) (*SDVK* 12, *dBu ma* sa 1b). Real conventional truth, Jñānagarbha argues, satisfies four criteria, two prescriptive, two proscriptive: (1) not to be conceptually imagined (*kalpitārtha*), (2) to be dependently arisen (*SDVK* 8ab, dBu ma sa 2a), (3) to be causally effective (*arthakriyā*) and (4) not to be analysable (*SDVK* 21ab, *dBu ma* sa 2b).

Jñānagarbha's non-foundationalism thesis can partly be observed from the way in which he proposes the conventionality of the conventional, and the conventionality of the ultimate. The former is the case because there is no real basis (*āśraya* / *gzhi*) for any conventional truth. All conventional truths are mere designations (*prajñapti*). The latter is so because Jñāngarbha goes as far as to argue that even the so-called ultimate is also only a conventionality. Two reasons are given for this. The first is that "ultimate statements" are self-defeating because they only make sense conventionally. The second argument stresses the identity of the conventional and the ultimate. Whatever is the reality of the conventional is itself considered by the Buddha as the meaning of the ultimate, for they are not distinct.

Notes

1 My sincere thanks go to Joshua Quinn-Watson, who kindly improved the English in this chapter.

2 Eckel (1987) has a useful translation with a helpful introduction to this work in English.

3 Buddhist epistemologists, after Dharmakīrti have held that reason (*hetu* / *liṅga*) is valid when it satisfies triple criteria (*rūpa*): (a) the *pakṣadharmatā*, the fact that the reason qualifies the subject / thesis (*pakṣa* / *dharmin*); (b) the *anvayavyāpti*, or the reason's occurring in only "similar instances" (*sapakṣa*); and (c) the *vyatirekavyāpti*, the reason's complete absence from the "dissimilar instances" (*vipakṣa*). *Sapakṣa* are those items which are similar (*sa* = *samāna*) to the subject in possessing the property to be proved (*sādhyadharma*). *Sapakṣa* however cannot be identical with the subject, i.e., they cannot be the subject. That means sound is not a *sapakṣa* for proving sound's impermanence, but a vase is. *Sapakṣa* are all those items which have the *ṣādhyadharma*, except the subject. *Vipakṣa* are all those items which do not possess this latter property. *Sapakṣa* and *vipakṣa* are also known as "homologous example" (*sādhyadharmyaḍṛṣṭānta*) and the "heterologous example" (*vaidharmyaḍṛṣṭānta*) on the basis of which the *anvaya* and *vyatirekavyāpti* are established. *Sapakṣa* and *vipakṣa* can be characterised as follows (Tillemans 1999, 93). For all *x*: *x* is a *sapakṣa* for proving sound's impermanence if and only if *x* is impermanent. For all *x*: *x* is a *vipakṣa* for proving sound's impermanence if and only if *x* is not impermanent.

4 Śāntarakṣita's commentary explicitly makes mentions of those whose mind is fixated by the influence of any philosophical system. See *SDVP* 8, *dBu ma Sa* 23b.

5 The thesis that conventionally real phenomena must not be subjected to ultimate analysis is also found in the Śāntadeva's *Bodhicaryāvatārapañjikā* (*dBu ma* la 41b–288a), which states that mere causality (*idaṃpratyayatāmātraṃ*) satisfies only when it is not analysed (*avicāramanohara*), like a dream, magic or a reflection. Śāntarakṣita also hold this position in the *Madhyamakālaṃkāra* 63, *dBu ma* Sa 70a. For Kamalaśīla on this point see *Madhyamakālaṁkārapañjikā* 63, *dBu ma* Sa 11a.

6 Candrakīrti's *Prasannapadā* 24.8 uses a similar etymology where he first (i) defines *saṃvṛti* as ignorance (*avidyā*) which is equivalent to Jñānagarbha's in verse 15. Candrakīrti alternatively adds

two other definitions of *saṃvṛti*: (ii) mutual interdependence (*parasparasambhavana*) emphasising the causal dependency thesis and (iii) verbal conventions (*saṃketa / rda*). According to Franklin Egerton's *Buddhist Hybrid Sanskrit Dictionary* (New Haven: Yale University Press, 1953) Pāḷi and Sanskrit sources indicate that this third definition is prior to the other two. And according to Eckel (1987, 136), by Jñānagarbha's time *saṃvṛti* as ignorance or concealment of reality as its definition has taken priority.

7 *Saddharmalaṅkāvatāra Sūtra*, P. L. Vaidya (ed.), 1963, 135: *Bhāvā vidhanti saṃvṛtyā paramārthe na bhāvakāḥ / niḥsvabhāveṣu yā bhrāntis tat satyaṃ saṃvṛtir bhavet //*.

References

Dreyfus, Georges B. J. and McClintock, Sara L. 2003. *The Svātantrika-Prāsaṅgika Distinction: What Difference Does a Difference Make?* Boston: Wisdom Publications.

Eckel, Malcolm D. 1987. *Jñāngarbha's Commentary on the Distinction between the Two Truths: An Eighth-Century of Handbook of Madhyamaka Philosophy*. Albany: State University of New York Press.

Jñānagrabha. 1998a. *Distinguishing the Two Truths (Satyadvayavibhaṅgakārikā SDVK dBu ma Sa 1b–3b)*. Sde dge edition of the Bstan 'gyur. Dharmasala: Paljor Press.

Jñānagrabha. 1998b. *Commentary on the Distinguishing the Two Truths (Satyadvayavibhaṅgavṛtti [SDVV] dBu ma Sa 3b–15b)*. Sde dge edition of the Bstan 'gyur. Dharmasala: Paljor Press.

Śāntarakṣita. 1998. *Sub-Commentary on the Distinguishing the Two Truths (Satyadvayavibhaṅgapañjikā dBu ma Sa 15b–52b)*. Sde dge edition of the Bstan 'gyur. Dharmasala: Paljor Press.

Tillemans, Tom J. F. 1999. *Scripture, Logic, Language: Essays on Dharmakīrt and His Tibetan Successors*. Boston: Wisdom Publications.

Chapter 36
VAJRAYĀNA BUDDHISM

Joseph Loizzo, edited by Amy Rayner

Science and religion in Buddhism: background and context

With their literature encoded in symbolism and their practice veiled in secrecy, India's diverse Tantric traditions have provoked an array of speculative readings by modern Indian and Western scholars (Wallace 2002; Grey 2007). In this perspective, the Tantras appear not as a fossilized curiosity but as a living paradigm of contemplative science and civilization. In the Nālandā tradition, this spiritual science developed three cumulative paradigms, in which four main schools of therapeutic philosophy (*siddhānta*)—Analyst (*Vaibhāṣika*), Traditionist (*Sautrāntika*), Idealist (*Cittamātra*) and Centrist (*Mādhyamika*)—inform three vehicles (*triyāna*) of Buddhist practice, the Individual Vehicle (*Hinayāna/Theravāda*), Universal Vehicle (*Mahāyāna*), and Process Vehicle (*Tantrayāna*), also called the Poetic Vehicle (*Mantrayāna*) or Diamond Vehicle (*Vajrayāna*) (Loizzo 2009).

The basic science shared in common by all these philosophies and vehicles is the spiritual science framed in Shakyamuni's teaching of the four noble truths. To use a traditional metaphor, the first truth of suffering and the second truth of origin offer a diagnosis and etiology for the human condition, based on a philosophical investigation of everyday life and a scientific analysis of its evolution and development. Complementing them, the fourth and third truths describe a way of learning and healing meant to bring that condition to an unparalleled fruition: the optimal freedom, health, and happiness of a Buddha's enlightenment. In other words, the third truth of Nirvāṇa and the fourth truth of the path offer a prognosis and course of treatment for what ails ordinary humans (and other life forms including gods) based on Shakyamuni's own spiritual experience and on the transformative disciplines of contemplation and ethics he prescribed to those who sought to share his experience (Thurman 1995).

The Vajrayāna paradigm of contemplative science

As far back as the *Heart Scripture* (*Prajñāpāramitāhṛdayasūtra*), the quick path of Universalist practice called the Vajrayāna has also been known as the Poetic Vehicle. More than a reference to the role of *mantric* formulas in the imaginative creation of a sacred circle (*maṇḍala*) and its divine archetypes (*devatā*), this term describes the Tantric view of life as the product of linguistic construction. According to the Tantras, beings and worlds are seen to emerge when the space of emptiness is planted with poetic seeds (*bīja-mantra*). The use of the term *bīja* is instructive, since the context of its usage here is distinct from that of Idealist psychology. In the Tantras, these seeds are planted not in the disembodied ground of a subconscious mind, but rather in the embodied soil of creative, bliss-void (*sukha-śūnya*) states of mind, supported by the vital energy (*prāṇa*) of a nervous system with channels (*nāḍī*), complexes (*chakra*), and drops (*bindū*). While this nervous system was mapped by contemplation rather than gross anatomy, Tantric psychology and medicine see it as made of subtle matter (*sukṣma-rūpa*) and ascribe to it all the normal mind/body functions modern science ascribes to the nervous system.

The Buddhist Tantras serve primarily as a contemplative science meant to reproduce the enlightened cultural agency of Buddhahood. Informed by the refined aesthetics of classical Indian dramaturgy and poetics, Vajrayāna ritual is part of a sublimation practice (*rāga-dharma*) meant to purge the mind/body process of the compulsive self-state called the pride of ordinariness (*sadharana-mana*) and to evoke in its place the liberated self of selflessness (*anātamātma*) characterized by divine pride (*devamana*) or the dignity of Buddhahood (Thurman 1995).

As for its therapeutic philosophy, the esoteric Vajrayāna is often described as a fruitional or effectual vehicle (*phalayāna*) in contrast to the causal vehicle (*hetuyāna*) of the exoteric Mahāyāna. It approaches the path of philosophy from the standpoint of its fruit or consequence, namely, the enlightened experience of a spiritual master (*vajrācārya*). It does this by offering the disciple a master's-eye view of herself as a living Buddha within a Buddha's perfected natural, social, and cultural world (*maṇḍala*), as well as scripting his/her dialogue of enlightening speech (*mantra*) and repertoire of enlightening activities or gestures (*mūdra*). Creative imagery, poetic formulas, and performative gestures provide a working linguistic construction and imaginative simulation of enlightened perception that serves as an alternate system of reference by which the disciple can critique his or her compulsive misperception of self and world. Scientifically, the perfected world of the *maṇḍala* also serves as a map for the process of mind/body self-regulation that supports the process of guided self-transformation.

Although the spiritual path and fruit of Vajrayāna Buddhism are said to be congruent with the Mahāyāna tradition, its risks and benefits derive from its unique methodology. The accelerated change promised in this tradition is said to make it best suited to those whose concern for the world is so passionate that they find it intolerable to wait the three eons it takes to reach Buddhahood by ordinary means. Although the Vajrayāna commitment of one to sixteen lifetimes seems just as incredible to moderns, the hagiographies of its great adepts (*mahāsiddha*) recount success stories of just seven years, in range with Shakyamuni's six (Robinson 1979). What about Tantric methods allows them to yield not just Nirvana but the fruit of perfect, complete enlightenment (*samyaksaṃbuddhatva*) with such time compression?

By coordinating discursive learning with visual imagery, poetic recitation, and performative gestures, Vajrayāna practices can cultivate many faculties simultaneously that must be developed separately and then integrated in exoteric practice. When these symbolic tools are applied to the nervous system and conjoined with advanced breath control, they help induce altered states by accessing deeper layers of consciousness and neural function. Mastering these states gives the practitioner access to normally unconscious processes as well as state-specific faculties for influencing them, allowing her to expose and reform learned and instinctive habits of mind on their own level and providing the experiential basis for rapid maturation. Of course, these powerful methods are only psychologically safe and spiritually reliable if they are used in the human context of a congenial mentor–disciple bond, under the guidance of someone who has already mastered them.

One of the ways Vajrayāna Buddhism evolved to meet the needs of its increasingly diverse audience was to incorporate a wide range of Tantras of different types. They are, respectively: the action process (*krīya-tantra*); performance process (*cārya-tantra*); integral process (*yoga-tantra*); and optimal integral process (*anuttara-yogatantra*). In the action process, the mentor-archetype is encountered in awe, as a refuge above and beyond the practitioner's scope, and approached as a source of protection, aid, and blessing. In the performance process, the mentor-archetype is encountered in admiration, as one who represents the disciple's ideal potential, and is approached as a source of guidance, recognition, and inspiration. In the integral process, the mentor-archetype is experienced in communion, as a genius innate in the practitioner's being, and is known as a source of inner transformation and realization. In the optimal integral process, the mentor-archetype is joined in intimacy, as a senior partner in the work of communal self-transformation, and is embraced as a source of inspiration, correction, and validation.

The second descriptor used to characterize the four Tantras is emotional maturity and psychosexual intimacy. This differentiates the four levels using metaphors of romantic love to gauge the practitioner's capacity for sublimating passion. The action process is geared to those who can harness and transform the level of passion stirred by voyeuristic gazing; the performance process is for those who can harness the passion aroused by flirtation; the integral process is linked with the level of passion stirred by sensual embrace; and the optimal integral process, with the most primal passion stirred by full intercourse. This focus on sublimating passions is further reflected in the sub-categories of Father and Mother Tantras depending on whether they specialize in treating compulsive emotions or delusion. Exemplary of the latter class are *Hevajra* and *Chakrasaṃvara*, which specialize in sublimating instinctive delusion into the objective intuition of emptiness called the clear light (*prabhāsavara*). Father Tantras like *Guhyasamaja* or *Vajrabhairava* are further subdivided into those that specialize in sublimating addictive desire or compulsive anger into pure bliss-void intuition called the virtual body (*māyādeha*) (Chakravarti 1984, 4). While the later *Kālachakra* is often called "non-dual" because of its scientific synthesis of both classes, all optimal integral Tantras are said to be fully equipped to enable the adept to realize and integrate both the masculine and feminine, subjective and objective aspects of spiritual mastery (Loizzo 2009). In what follows, I will address the three phases of the optimal integral process: initiation (*abhiṣeka*); creation stage (*utpatti-krama*); and the perfection stage (*niṣpanna-krama*).

Once a student has chosen a mentor and archetype suited to her aims and needs, it is up to the mentor to assess the student's degree of preparedness and to prescribe a preliminary course of study and practice. In the Indo-Tibetan tradition, the psychospiritual prerequisites for initiation into the optimal integral process are three: renunciation; compassion; and a correct view of emptiness. A basic ability to renounce attachments is necessary to safely practice the art of sublimating passions. A strong altruistic resolve or compassionate intention to help is necessary to protect the practitioner from reinforcing self-centeredness and to build a motivation stable enough to overcome learned and innate blocks. And at least a clear intellectual understanding of emptiness is necessary to expose and correct the reifying habits and instincts that would otherwise block the therapeutic process. In addition, a series of common preliminaries is routinely prescribed. These typically involve the repetition of performative rituals of refuge, confession, prostration, mentor-bonding, and *maṇḍala* offering meant to speed the purification of obstacles and accumulation of merit that ensure success. These preliminary practices, usually performed in iterations of a hundred thousand each, serve to suppress the compulsive doubt, guilt, pride, envy, and greed that might otherwise taint initiation and early practice.

Entering the Vajrayāna: initiation

The initiation itself is a ritual enactment of the contract between the mentor-archetype and initiate that symbolically confers the mentor's blessing and permission to practice, while also binding both parties to a set of vows or virtuous precepts and commitments meant to ensure the safety and effectiveness of their collaboration. In one individual or group experience, typically lasting several days, the mentor-archetype introduces the initiate to the extraordinary universe of the Vajrayāna; imaginatively converting her misperception of self and world into the exalted vision of the archetype and *maṇḍala*; ritually consecrating her mind/body process as the holy terrain for the journey to complete spiritual mastery; symbolically mapping into that terrain the steps and stages of her spiritual individuation and integration, and fully prophesying and blessing the initiate's final attainment of perfect Buddhahood. The four initiations, vase (*kumbaka*), secret (*guhya*), intuitive-wisdom (*prajñā-jñāna*), and word (*vāc*), consecrate the practitioner's body, speech, mind, and intuition as the four bases of a *vajra* master's body, speech, mind, and intuition. Symbolically, they map the coarse, subtle, and extremely subtle levels of the mind and nervous system to be accessed and transformed, as well as their final integration into the translucent mind and virtual body of a *vajra* master.

One key interchange in the rite makes ethics as a component of Vajrayāna Buddhism explicit. At the threshold of the consecration, the initiate stands at the eastern gate of the palace seeking admission and knocks. From within, an agent of the mentor-archetype responds, "Who are you and what do you want?" The initiate then replies, "I am the fortunate one, and I want great bliss!" But the portal does not open yet. Instead, the divine gatekeeper questions the aspirant's true intent, "Why do you want it?" Here the one and only reply that will grant entry into the world of the Tantras insures the initiate's ethos of sublimation, to be spelled out later in the rite's vows: "To keep the commitments of the buddhas!" Of course, the initiation only sets the stage for a long apprenticeship in which the master and disciple must collaborate closely and consistently, guided by their vows as precepts and commitments, to ensure that their shared work comes to full fruition.

The creation stage: re-envisioning life as a culture medium for spiritual genius

The creation stage works to replace the practitioner's neurotic life narrative with a heroic vision of life that models the perceptual reconstruction of her ordinary self and world into the creative agency and community of a mentor-archetype. It does this by an imaginative conversion (*nayana**) of the dramatic nodes of an unenlightened life narrative—traumatic death, aimless afterlife, and compulsive rebirth—into the heroic modes of an enlightened, archetypal life: the embodiment of ultimate truth, sublime beauty and creative emanation (*dharma-*, *sambhoga-*, *nirmāṇa-kāya*). This conversion has two aims: to de-center the practitioner's mental life from the materialistic perspective (*satkāyadṛṣṭi*) which reifies and appropriates the human body and its environment as "I" and "mine," and to re-center that life around the divine pride of the emptiness intuition and the void appearance (*śūnya-bimba*) of the *maṇḍala*'s visual, auditory, and dramatic imagery. This process begins with rehearsing death through a sequence of dissolutions that primes the practitioner to de-reify and renounce all levels of the ordinary mind/body, preparing awareness to recognize and merge with its purified, primal source, the clear light of death. Out of this clear light, the subtle subjectivity and energy of the practitioner is resurrected in a heroic form conceived in the image of the mentor-archetype, revising the ordinary transition state (*anantabhava*) into an extraordinary embodiment of sublime beauty (*sambhoga-kāya*). This nascent form is then gradually developed into a full manifestation of enlightenment, revising ordinary life into an embodiment of creative emanation (*nirmāṇa-kāya*). The creation stage depicts the inner transformation of passion and intuition in the perfection stage, using alchemical imagery to symbolize the path to spiritual integration. Extending the iconography of the five Buddha clans, this imagery arrays five kinds of flesh and five bodily fluids in a skull cup crucible (*kapala*) where they melt and transform into the nectar of immortality (*amṛta*). This symbolizes the process of sublimation, in which the five systems and five compulsions of neurotic life, purified by blissful realization of emptiness, become the five euphoric energies and five ecstatic intuitions of a spiritual master.

While the tradition accepts the elaborate imagery of the creation stage as a mere fabrication, it is nonetheless viewed as an essential preliminary to the genuine spiritual experience of the perfection stage. In fact, in the divine pride and void appearance of this stage one can easily recognize the two holy intuitions (*āryajñāna*) that make up the Mahāyāna practice of transcendent insight (*vipaśyana*). In particular, the formless imagery which is the basis of divine pride is congruent with the holy spacious equipoise intuition (*akaśopama-samāhitajñāna*), while the formal imagery which is the basis of void appearance is congruent with the holy illusory aftermath intuition (*māyopama-pṛṣṭalabdhajñāna*). While in Mahāyāna practice, they are cultivated separately and later combined into the truth body and form body of Buddhahood, in the Vajrayāna they are cultivated simultaneously beginning with the conversions of the creation stage, and culminate in the poetic body (*mantra-kāya*) that serves as raw material for the perfection stage. This simultaneous practice is more efficient both because it cultivates the mental and physical aspects of enlightenment at once, but also because it fosters from the start the non-dual integration of de-reifying wisdom and de-objectifying compassion.

The imagery of the subtle creation stage corrects the misconception that the kind of spiritual agency cultivated in Vajrayāna Buddhism involves a withdrawal (*nivṛtti*) from the world, the body, and/or physical pleasures like sexuality. The iconography of the creation stage celebrates the aesthetic riches and sensual pleasures of life, placing its heroic archetypes in regal garb and palatial surroundings and, more importantly, in full sexual embrace with an intimate partner. The fact that the imagery of sexual union is used to symbolize the union of compassion and wisdom, blissful subjectivity and ecstatic objectivity, dispels any doubt that sensual passion is central to this contemplative process. The feminine archetype is specifically identified as the realization of the blissful emptiness of touch (*sparśavajra*). On the subtle creation stage, the central role of sexual imagery and arousal in this process is further revealed. This involves the contemplative art of sublimation, whose stages are defined in terms of three seals or partners (*mūdra*). Typically, the creation stage practice of sublimation involves meditation on an imaginary or ideal partner (*jñāna-mūdra*); ordinary perfection stage (1–2) practice, at least for lay practitioners, involves meditation with a real human or evolutionary partner (*karma-mūdra*); while great perfection stage (3–5) involves embracing the emptiness of all things as a universal partner (*mahāmūdra*).

Creation stage meditation on an ideal partner begins in earnest in the subtle creation stage, where it serves to arouse sexual bliss as a basis for contemplating the emptiness of touch in the so-called *vajra* offering. The explicitly sexual nature of this practice is clear in its five steps: (1) envisioning a seminal drop at the tip of the male partner's *vajra* or phallus, dwelling within the lotus or vagina (*bhaga*) of the female; (2) imagining sexual intercourse and drawing the orgasmic energy released back upward into the whole body to "satisfy" all the archetypes of the body *maṇḍala*; (3) inscribing a microcosmic *maṇḍala* complete with all thirty-two archetypes within the drop that has been released into the partner's womb; (4) withdrawing those archetypes, one by one, up the *vajra* through the central channel to the heart, from where they emanate, one by one, in all directions, benefiting all living beings then returning to the heart; and (5) converting those archetypes into seed mantras that circle the heart, then reciting them while envisioning that they radiate archetypes that travel out on exhalation, benefit beings, and coalesce back into the mantra circle at the heart on inspiration.

Despite the belief that Buddhism must be either world-negating or corrupt, the sublimation practice in the creation stage serves to sacralize the male and female body, physical bliss, and sexuality at the same time as it ethicizies them by harnessing bliss to inspire compassionate action in the world.

The perfection stage: embodying objectivity and spiritual integration

Like the creation stage, the perfection stage challenges widely held preconceptions about the nature of human development and spirituality. Unlike the creation stage, whose mastery of discursive and perceptual processing is mapped onto the coarse nervous system, the perfection stage and its work relates to the subtle and subtlest neural levels. These are mapped onto the central channel (*avadhūti*), constricted at six or more points called complexes (*chakras*) by the entanglement of two polar side channels. The two side channels embody a natural polarity of neural energy and chemistry that, along with the blissful energy and chemistry of the central channel, supports the functions of the subtle nervous system. Their impingement on the central channel graphically represents a neural disorder caused by the developmental effect of conflicting compulsions on the mind and nervous system. The subtle material structure of this disorder acts to block the natural flow of neural energy and the natural balance of neural chemistry, obstructing access to the core nervous system in which the instincts for these conflicting compulsions are rooted. By consciously fusing the polar energies of the side channels and directing them into the central channel, the practitioner gains full access to the deepest sources of blissful energy and chemistry, mapped onto the indestructible drop (*akṣara-bindū*) in the very center of the neural complex at the heart. Embedded within this extremely subtle, core level of the mind and nervous system, are the instincts of eighty natural constructions (*svabhāva-vikalpa*) that drive compulsive life. These instinctive patterns, such as sexual attraction, malevolence, and confusion, are grouped into three classes—thirty-three desire-oriented, forty anger-oriented and seven delusion-oriented—and mapped onto successively deeper layers of the subtlest mind. Since these anchor the innate and learned habits of compulsive life, progress on the perfection stage is defined by the gradual separation of perception, conception, and consciousness from those patterns, achieved by progressive mastery of the subtle and subtlest nervous system.

Gathering the energies from the side channels and inserting them into the central channel at any point along the neuraxis arouses warmth and stirs the flow of sexual neurochemistry, releasing a cascade of energy and drops that induces a progression of four euphoric states or blisses (*ānanda*). The four blisses become ecstasies when enhanced by contemplating their emptiness. They also induce an internal dissolution of mind/body processes of the same kind as naturally occurs unnoticed in the state transitions of sexual orgasm, the sleep cycle, or dying. Analyzed into eight stages, this begins with the fourfold dissolution of coarse into subtle mind/body processes and ends in a sequence of four lucid intuitions (*āloka-jñāna*) or voids (*śūnya*), reflecting the subtlest mind's progressive separation from the three classes of natural constructions. The release of desire-oriented instincts by luminence intuition (*pratibhāsa-jñāna*), of anger-oriented instincts by radiance intuition (*vṛddhiprāpta-jñāna*), and of delusion-oriented instincts by immanence intuition (*ālokasyopalabdhiśa-jñāna*) culminates in the realization of the perfect clarity or lucidity of the clear light intuition (*prabhāsvara-jñāna*). Based on this clarity, when subtle and coarse mind/body processes gradually reemerge in the reverse sequence, the practitioner cultivates a way of being in mind/body systems that is separated from the instincts and habits of compulsive life. Rather than a single sequence of events, the perfection stage involves a process of repeated dissolution and emergence through which the raw material of the human body/mind is gradually purified of its contaminating instincts and refined into the euphoric body and ecstatic mind of a master. The most direct path to this purification is by tapping and harnessing the primordial physiology of sex.

In Mother Tantras like *Hevajra*, the rush of inspiration is called psychic heat (*candalī*) and aroused with the help of an abdominal breath-holding art called pot-like (*kumbaka*) or pot-belly breathing. Optimal integral systems of both classes incorporated this art to prime and enhance the work of *vajra* recitation in gathering and applying blissful energies to unlock the heart. Although different systems start the recitation practice at different points along the central channel, the Ganden tradition is to start at the heart, where all systems finally culminate. When the coalescence of blissful energies at the heart finally touches the indestructible drop and the four blisses induce the dissolution process, the attainment of the lucid intuitions marks the endpoint of ecstatic speech—the separation of thought and speech from uninspired habit-energies—and begins the second stage leading to ecstatic mind.

While *vajra* recitation, with or without pot-belly breathing, continues on in some form through the second perfection stage, further progress towards full sublimation generally involves additional methods to deepen and enhance access to euphoric states. These take two main routes that may converge or diverge. One route involves enhancing *vajra* recitation with sublimation practice, recruiting more blissful energy from sexual arousal with the help of an imaginary partner or real partner. The other involves enhancing *vajra* recitation with the so-called immersion (*miśrana**) practice, recruiting the blissful energy induced by other natural state transitions including the sleep cycle and the death process. As for the first route, *vajra* recitation may be enhanced by envisioning a substantial drop of male and female sexual fluids commingling where the sexual organs touch in imaginary union. The energy of sexual arousal is then withdrawn *via* the central channel to the heart, permitting *vajra* recitation to absorb more of the body's ten energies into the indestructible drop, eliciting a more profound euphoria. Alternately, the internal condition of *vajra* recitation enhanced by a visualized sexual drop may be combined with the external condition of sublimated intercourse with a real partner. Such a partner must also be fully initiated and practicing at least at the level of the creation stage, and union may involve ritual dress and/or scripted dialogue. In either case, the sublimated intercourse involves control of the normal sexual response and withdrawal of orgasmic energy up to the heart. The alternate route involves deepening the combined effect of *vajra* recitation and sublimation practice with an imaginary partner by recruiting the normally unconscious euphoria of the dreamless sleep state or the clear light of death. This mapping of sublimation practice makes clear that the perfection stage treats sexuality not as an end in itself, but rather as one of two natural ways into the subtlest sources of blissful intuition within the human body/mind.

The final leg of the odyssey of complete spiritual mastery begins with reemergence from the approximate clear light of the ecstatic mind. At this point, the source consciousness and neural energy of the extremely subtle level have been accessed for the first time, and their union, supporting the mirage-like self-image of the practitioner's archetype, is called the virtual body (*māyā-deha*). Because the extremely subtle mind and energy body are still tainted by subtle residues of the eighty natural constructions, this new spiritual agency is the raw material to be refined on this stage, the so-called impure virtual body. Purification and cultivation progresses using the same arts practiced on the second stage, by refining the virtual body through repeated experience of dissolution and reemergence. As a result, sublimation practice finally fully releases the innate great bliss of the heart drop which naturally facilitates the non-constructed, non-dual realization of emptiness. Based on the subtle subjectivity of this orgasmic bliss, this stage yields the actual lucid intuitions: direct, perceptual realizations of the emptiness of the three kinds of instincts culminating in the actual or objective clear light. This is the translucent bliss-void intuition in which the mind is finally purged of the instincts for compulsive emotions or blocks to liberation (*kleśāvaraṇa*) (see Loizzo 2000, 147–197; Loizzo 2009, 333–336; Grey 2007).

Attaining the actual clear light is the doorway to the fourth perfection stage, called clear light or illumination. This stage begins with the emergence out of the clear light of a pure form of the virtual body purged of compulsive emotions and their subtlest instincts. On this penultimate stretch of the perfection stage, the practice involves repeatedly contemplating the objective reality of emptiness with the ecstatic subjectivity of the very subtlest body/mind. Called the universal seal, sublimation practice on this and the last stage shifts its focus from the external condition of a real partner to the objective condition of all things. In other words, the partner known by great bliss expands from the emptiness of a single mental image or real individual to embrace the universal emptiness of all persons and things. This residual dualism is removed at the end of this stage by immersing a more refined form of the pure virtual body into the actual clear light. The final sublimation practice of embracing universal emptiness as a partner gradually eliminates the subtlest instincts for reification that anchor the blocks to perfect objectivity or omniscience (*jñeyāvaraṇa*). This final purification yields the master's integration of translucent mind and virtual body that is the Vajrayāna form of perfect Buddhahood.

References

Chakravarti, C. (ed.). 1984. *Guhyasamajatantrapradīpodyotanaṭīkāsadkoṭivyākhyā*. Patna: Kashi Prasad Jayaswal Research Institute.

Grey, David. 2007. *The Cakrasamvara Tantra (The Discourse of Sri Heruka) by Śrīherukābhidhāna: A Study and Annotated Translation*. Treasury of the Buddhist Sciences. New York: AIBS/Columbia University Press.

Gyatso, Geshe Kelsang. 1994. *Tantric Grounds and Paths*. London: Tharpa Publications.

Loizzo, Joseph. 2000. "Meditation and Psychotherapy." In Philip R. Muskin (ed.). *Complementary Medicine and Psychiatry*, 147–197. Review of Psychiatry 19. Washington, DC: American Psychiatric Association Press.

———. 2009. "Kālacakra and the Nālandā Tradition." In E. A. Arnold, R. Thurman *et al.* (eds.). *As Long as Space Endures: Essays on the Kālacakra Tantra in Honor of His Holiness the Dalai Lama*, 333–336. Ithaca, NY: Snow Lion Press.

Robinson, R. 1979. *Buddha's Lions*. Berkeley: Dharma Publishing.

Thurman, Robert. 1995. *Essential Tibetan Buddhism*. New York: HarperCollins.

Wallace, Vesna. 2002. *The Inner Kālachakratantra*. Oxford: Oxford University Press.

IIc
PHILOSOPHICAL TRADITIONS

Chapter 37
HERMENEUTICS: HINDU, BUDDHIST, AND JAINA

Arthur Dudney

Scripture is a relatively unified concept throughout history: almost all societies have texts, either written or unwritten, that are believed to be divinely authored or inspired. Although transcendent and therefore not necessarily subject to the same rules as human writing, these texts nonetheless must be interpreted by humans. This interpretation has traditionally been the task of hermeneutics, although that term would not be coined until the seventeenth century.[1] In both India and in the West, the techniques developed to understand the divine Word came to be used for explaining the meaning of texts with acknowledged human authors. In many traditions, texts which were originally non-scriptural eventually came to be seen as scripture. This chapter will first consider how revelation has been conceived of in history, especially in the context of the doctrine of "authorless revelation" (*apauruṣeyatva*) in Hinduism. Second, this chapter will trace the ways in which scriptural interpretation allows a society to change the applied meaning of sacred texts without necessarily changing the revealed words themselves. It is this recognition that interpretation of a fixed text necessarily shifts over time that has led to hermeneutics as practised by modern Western philosophers and historians like Hans-Georg Gadamer and Reinhart Koselleck.[2] This chapter will provide a sketch of hermeneutics in the traditional Indian context, with the Abrahamic religions (Judaism, Christianity, and Islam) and modern historical hermeneutics as reference points.

In Hindu philosophy, "hermeneutics" commonly translates the Sanskrit term "*mīmāṃsā*," which was codified in Jaimini's *Mīmāṃsāsūtra* (*c.* 200 BCE) and elaborated by the commentators Śabara (after 200 CE), Kumārila Bhaṭṭa (*c.* 700 CE), and Prabhākara (*c.* 700 CE) (Clooney 1990, 221ff.). Indian traditions have historically been classified into two categories: the *āstika*, the so-called "orthodox" schools of Indian thought (including Mīmāṃsā), which accepted the authority of the Vedas, and the *nāstika*, "unorthodox" sects such as Cārvāka (so-called "materialist philosophy"), Jainism, and Buddhism, which denied the authority of the Vedas (Bilimoria 1989a,

21ff.). The concern of Mīmāṃsā within the *āstika* practices was ensuring the correct performance of the sacrifices prescribed by the Vedas. Ceremony thus constitutes the text and the text constitutes the proper role of the ceremony.[3]

One of the striking—and, to many modern people, dismaying—aspects of Mīmāṃsā is its specific brand of agnosticism (Bilimoria 2001). Hindu hermeneutics traditionally assumed the "authorlessness" (*apauruṣeyatva*) of the Vedas, which means that neither gods nor humans wrote them, and which is obviously contrary to our everyday experience of texts (Bilimoria 1989b). It is important to note that authorlessness is not the same as anonymity: the texts were literally thought to exist outside of time and space, even though they have attributed human "authors" within the text, who (like the Prophet Muhammad in the Islamic tradition) were believed by the tradition to have been the reciters of scripture rather than its composers.[4] Furthermore, speaking of Hindu "scripture" (the English word is derived from the Latin for "writing") is problematic because revealed texts are known in the tradition as "*śruti*" [literally: "what is heard"] as contrasted to the unrevealed "*smr̥ti*" ["what is remembered"].

In the Hindu tradition, unlike in some other traditions, revelation is understood as a gradual process that built up a corpus of textual knowledge rather than an event. According to the philosopher Bimal K. Matilal, "The Scriptures were regarded by tradition as embodying certain truths derived from the supposedly 'revealed' insights of the sages called 'seers' (= *r̥ṣi*). ... The Scriptures are in fact a body of statements" (1990, 4). The idea is glossed by Kumārila Bhaṭṭa, writing in the seventh century CE, in that "the Veda ... is an autonomous form of true knowledge as vouchsafed by its very form [*rūpād eva*]" and this is in contrast to the corrupt language [*asāduśabdabhūyṣṭa*] in which non-Brahmins write (Pollock 2005). The *Taittirīya-Brāhmaṇa* describes how the god Indra showed the sage Bharadvāja three mountain-like masses and saying, "These are the Vedas. Infinite indeed are the Vedas [*anantā vai vedāḥ*]" (3.10.11.4). Even when no actual text was extant to support a particular viewpoint, legal scholars have invoked the concept of a "lost Veda" whose practices the great and good (*śiṣṭas*) maintained even though the *śruti* text had been lost (Pollock 2005). For centuries, the *Atharvaveda* was not considered divine, but at some point its proponents argued that it was actually better than other Vedas and was thus certainly divine—this controversy led to scepticism over the status of all of the Vedas.[5] Sheldon Pollock concludes that it is not that history is unknown to the Sanskrit tradition (as Orientalists claimed) but rather that it is actively denied in favour of a model of ahistorical truth (1989).

Unlike Western philosophy, Indian philosophy has traditionally privileged the word itself as a means to knowledge (*śabdapramaṇa*), which removes some of the obstacles posed by an authorless text: If there is no author then there can be no unreliable narrator so the text is by definition authoritative (Bilimoria 1995, 158). The tradition has not been interested in justifying its belief in revelation but rather has focused on determining how language, both revealed and unrevealed, can be understood (Mohanty 2001, 8). The linguistic question has been taken up differently by different schools of thought: In *Mīmāṃāsūtra* 1.1.5, Jaimini argues that the relationship between word and meaning is "non-derived" or "uncreated" (*autpattika*), in contrast to *Vaiśeṣikasūtra* 7.2.24 which argues that the relationship between word and meaning is by convention (*samaya*)—former is the Mīmāṃsā position, latter is Nyāya and Vaiśeṣika (Bilimoria 1994).[6] This thread of philosophy combining language and knowledge lends itself to the following conclusion: "The relation between word and meaning is natural, inartificial and this is how the authority of the Veda is unquestionable" (Jha 2002, 7). Sanskrit became such a high prestige language that philosophers eventually put forward a theory that it was the only language which had the true power of signifying.[7] For the Pāṇinian commentator Bhartṛhari (c. fifth century CE), there can be no cognition without language and language holds the key to determining truth and falsehood. Hence grammar, which repairs improper usage, becomes a "door to salvation" [*dvāram apavargasya*] (Cardona 1976, 300; Coward and Raja 1990).

Consequently, the tradition has tended to view Sanskrit as an eternal language. The etymologist Yāska, for example, wrote around the middle of the first millennium bce that "Vedic stanzas are [still] meaningful because their words are identical with those of currently spoken Sanskrit" (*Nirukta* 1.16 cited in Deshpande 1993, 54). But even at this early stage in Sanskrit's development, he feels obliged to gloss Vedic expressions with contemporary usage (Laddu 1974, 9). Pāṇini goes a step further and makes a distinction between *chandas*, the Vedic dialect, and *bhāṣā*, contemporary usage, as well as pointing out regional variations (ibid.; cf. Pollock 2006, 46). To our historical way of thinking this description seems to damage Sanskrit's credibility as eternal, but as Madhav Deshpande argues, "Pāṇini's conception of Sanskrit is that of a panchronistic flatland. … It includes all known diachronic and synchronic facts of Sanskrit" (Deshpande 1993, 54–55). That is a fascinating interpretation because it suggests that Pāṇini recognized the raggedness at the edges of a language noted by post-structuralists (or to express it another way, the idea that "grammars leak"). Can we really say what is and is not Sanskrit without applying an arbitrary (i.e. extra-Vedic) standard? The commentator Śabara writes that words in scripture are to be understood as much as possible in their ordinary senses (Clooney 1990, 132).

Elsewhere in Indian thought, especially in *nāstika* interpretations, these views on Sanskrit as the language of salvation did not hold. Buddhist literature is full of references to Brahmin converts to Buddhism, who are criticized for being unwilling to give up their Sanskrit. In one early (perhaps fourth or third century BCE) manual, two Buddhist monks decide to translate the Buddha's words into Vedic Sanskrit verse and the Buddha rebukes them, saying that it is better to learn the Buddha's words in one's own language (Pollock 2006, 52ff., especially 54). Indeed, according to Janet Gyatso, the Buddhist perspective on language is that it "is flexible—and discardable. Ironically, what is seen as the ultimate meaninglessness of verbal expression makes it become, in certain Buddhist traditions, an ideal tool for teaching the ultimate truth, avowals of the inexpressibility of that truth notwithstanding" (1992, 189). Authority (*agama*) in Buddhism is subordinated to an adherent's reason (Thurman 1978, 20). Thus, the purpose of hermeneutics in Buddhism is the resolution of contradictions in what the Buddha said rather than the concerns about ritual inherent in Mīmāṃsā (ibid., 23).

Comparative hermeneutics (Judaism, Christianity, and Islam)

The Abrahamic religions have been strongly influenced by the neo-Platonic doctrine that interpretative truth is constantly revealed to us, which has some counterparts in Hinduism (as in the appeal to a "lost Veda" mentioned above), but ultimately interpretation in those traditions is more contingent on individual judgements than the precise ritualism of *mīmāṃsā*.

Christianity's check on scriptural misinterpretation is fundamentally neo-Platonic: In Saint Augustine's *De Doctrina Christiana* (426 CE), Plato's World of Forms has been replaced by God Himself, who "could give the gospel to man even without the help or agency of men" (IV.33).[8] Similarly in the Islamic tradition, the tenth-century grammarian Jābir and a group of anonymous letter writers calling themselves the I<u>kh</u>wān al-Ṣafā [Brethren of Purity] argued that the outward [*ẓāhir*] form of scripture is complemented with a hidden [*bāṭin*] meaning that is revealed to the faithful not through any act of interpretation but rather vouchsafed to the good-hearted.[9] Sri Aurobindo (1872–1950) observes the same process at work in Hinduism by arguing that the Vedas are filled with secret messages that are accessible only to initiates (Mohanty 1993, 129).

The Vedas appear to discuss historical circumstances and events, which has led in recent years to a rancorous debate over the nature of the historical content of the Vedas. The first historicist study of the Vedas came during the colonial period and is therefore thought to be tainted with racism and imperialism.[10] For pre-modern Hinduism, there was no problem in the apparent historicity of the Vedas, but today the question of history in scripture is prominent and vexed. Likewise, in Islam the idea that a sacred text can be moored to its temporal context is quite revolutionary in quranic hermeneutics [*ta'wīl*].[11] The Egyptian scholar Naṣr Ḥamıd Abū Zayd (1943–2010) was persecuted after he argued that quranic studies needed to be re-evaluated through "humanistic hermeneutics" (Abū Zayd 2004). Abū Zayd's comparatively modest proposal was to leave the Quran's theology intact while acknowledging the text's historicity. In other words, continuing to accept the orthodox view that the Quran was uncreated but approaching the text from the perspective that it was *meant* to be understood by those to whom it was revealed in their own societal context.[12] Following this reasoning, it is clear why the Quran should contain references to events and cultural practices of Arabia in the seventh century CE and not, for example, Paraguay in the 1930s.

Hermeneutics in colonial India

During the eighteenth century, British colonial officials were delighted to find that Sanskrit texts were perhaps older and therefore closer to the origin of mankind than anything known in the West. The textuality of Indian scriptures was critical for the British because interpreting those texts represented a means to put Indian culture into a frame of reference that was not alien to Europeans. The comparative project pressed ahead because it had a practical end: Warren Hastings, the Governor-General of Bengal from 1773 to 1785, strongly believed that British India should be ruled by Indian laws, and textual evidence for those laws needed to be discovered and codified in a form that could be useful to the colonial state. The task the British set for themselves was to peel away what they saw as folkloric accretions to scripture and return to the true, original meaning of the ancient texts. Never in recent history has hermeneutics on such a vast scale been so close to the seat of power, but the result was a hodgepodge because the British never reflected on their own role in *changing* the meanings of the texts they believed they were unproblematically interpreting.[13] Mīmāṃsā, whose coherence as a discipline had been in decline for centuries, did not enter in any meaningful way into colonial interpretations of Hindu scripture.[14]

Traditional Indian hermeneutics in modern times

What is the standing of hermeneutics in philosophical thought today? The study of Mīmāṃsā was revived in the mid-twentieth century by philosophers like J. N. Mohanty and Bimal K. Matilal because they thought it could be put into fruitful dialogue with recent developments in Western hermeneutics, like Martin Heidegger's reformulation of the field. Their work intentionally ignores the founding purpose of Mīmāṃsā (namely ensuring that ritual sacrifices were performed correctly) and separates the philosophy from the ritual system it underpinned. Thus philosophical hermeneutics no longer depends either on scriptural revelation or a special status for Sanskrit.

Mohanty, for example, rejects a special status for *śruti* outright because it privileges tradition over reason (Bilimoria 2000, 210). Because the purpose of philosophy is not to defend or clarify the scriptures, in a philosophical context we can understand *śruti* as the foundational texts of a tradition (Mohanty 1993, 7, cf. 10). Both Mīmāṃsā and Nyāya adherents through the centuries have claimed that only *śruti* could give guidance on *dharma*, but this distinction is now seen as irrelevant (Pollock 1997, 410). Likewise for Gadamer, because there is no difference between interpreting sacred texts and historical texts, there is only one hermeneutics that serves for both (2006, 178). Mohanty's thinking on *śruti* as tradition combines Edmund Husserl's phenomenology with the attention to the textures of a tradition in Gadamer (Bilimoria 1989b, 153). Mohanty engages with the traditional concept of "authorlessness" by taking it to mean simply "the concept of the primacy and autonomy of the eminent text over the subject intentions of the author" (Bilimoria 2000, 213). He observes that "the more we need to know the author to understand or interpret a text, the less fundamental it is" (Mohanty 1992, 156). This is in keeping with the work of Western philosophers like Michel Foucault, who emphasize the importance of discourse rather than authorial intent in producing textual meaning.

Theories that privilege Sanskrit have been replaced by those that take a more universal view to language, accepting the current consensus in linguistics that any language is capable of saying anything (Jha 2002). In addition, no language (whether Sanskrit or not), can be seen as self-interpreting, leading to the abandonment of a key tool of previous philosophers: According to Matilal, "*śabdapramāṇa* cannot any longer provide the theoretical basis for a satisfactory philosophy" (quoted in Bilimoria 2000, 202). Approaches substituted for this include Jacques Derrida's Deconstruction. For Derrida, language depends on a series of endlessly deferred meanings (a word is defined in relation to other words, each of which is defined in relation to other words *ad infinitum*).[15] Both Mīmāṃsā and Derrida's approach can lead to an endless self-referentiality, albeit by different paths (Bilimoria 1995, 149). For the American philosopher Richard Rorty, whose approach also radically questions the underpinnings of knowledge, hermeneutics is not a "successor subject" to epistemology but rather a testament to the impossibility of the task of epistemology and a reminder that knowledge is predicated on endless interpretative work (1980, 315).

In the post-colonial world, Mīmāṃsā seeks a balance between its rich tradition and new approaches that are not necessarily compatible with the whole of that tradition. Its engagement with Western philosophy is concerned in part with showing what is provincial about European philosophy despite claims of universality (e.g. Ellis 2009).

Notes

1 The term first arose in the seventeenth century when Protestants argued for the possibility of interpreting the Bible without the Church's intercession (Grafton 1997, 198).

2 Though the former refers to his project as "philosophical" hermeneutics and the latter as "historical" hermeneutics, Koselleck acknowledges the similarity between the methods (2004, xvi).

3 "Sacrifice was the principal institution and symbol of the Vedic tradition and knowledge" (Joshi 1991, 90; cf. Singh 2001, 91). The importance of hermeneutics in pre-modern India is underscored by the fact that while both Indian and pre-modern Western culture conceived of a set of three core disciplines having to do with language (known as the "*trivium*" in the Western world) and these shared grammar and logic, Western thought had rhetoric as the third component and Indian thought had hermeneutics (*mīmāṃsā*) instead (Pollock 2003, 46).

4 Kumārila Bhaṭṭa and others argue that the names of the composers mentioned in the text are fictitious (Bilimoria 1995, 140).

5 Similarly, Pollock has deconstructed the dichotomy of *śruti* and *smṛti* (commonly translated as "revelation" versus "tradition") to show that texts formerly understood as *smṛti* were sometimes declared *śruti* in order to solve problems in interpretation (Pollock 1997, 410). By declaring that later texts that have influenced one's reading of earlier texts were in fact part of the earlier texts (in the traditional understanding, *smṛti* was always derived from *śruti*), the hermeneutic circle neatly collapses into a hermeneutic line-segment, but of course this solution is not "historical" in the modern understanding of history.

6 Matilal 1990, 27. For Śabara and everyone after, *autpattika*, *apauruṣeya* and *nitya* were considered synonyms in this context (Bilimoria 1995, 143).

7 A good summary of Sanskrit as the identity language of upper caste Hindus (in comparison with ancient Greek ideas on the Greek language as a prerequisite for being civilized) appears at McEvilley 2002, 672–677.

8 The New Testament itself makes this claim at Matthew 10:19–20 (New Revised Standard Version): "For what you are to say will be given to you at that time; for it is not you who speak but the spirit of your Father speaking through you." Compare Jeremiah 1:6–9, where the prophet expresses doubt and is told "Now I have put my words into your mouth."

9 Versteegh 1993, 99. This doctrine was exceptionally influential in Islam since it becomes one of the core doctrines of the mystical tradition called Sufism. Furthermore, it is an exact parallel to the

medieval European idea of the *verbum cordis* [lit. "word of the heart"], which was a hidden, ineffable truth lodged in the believer's consciousness (Gadamer 2006, 420).

10 The truth or falsity of Aryan Migration Theory, or the idea that many Indians are described from western Asian populations that migrated into the Subcontinent in prehistory, is the main debate.

11 A term which appears in the Quran itself (Wild 2003, 428).

12 This could be seen as an extended implication of a famous passage in the Quran: "Indeed, We have sent it down as an Arabic Quran that you may understand" (Q 12:2).

13 Cohn 1996 is an excellent account of how administrative pressures shaped European knowledge gathering in India.

14 See McCrea 2008. Nor indeed did the Islamic hermeneutical tradition have much relevance for British studies of Islamic law. The failure of the British to create a workable legal system using indigenous texts is explored in Fisch 1983.

15 Derrida 1976, explained with clarity in Joseph *et al.* 2001, 188–202. For a detailed discussion of Derrida and Mīmāṃsā, see Bilimoria 1995, 147ff.

References

Abū Zayd, Nasr Hamid. 2004. *Rethinking the Qur'ân: Towards a Humanistic Hermeneutics*. Utrecht: Humanistics University Press.

Bilimoria, Purushottama. 1989a. "Hindu-Mīmāṃsā against Scriptural Evidence on God." *Sophia* 28(1): 20–31.

———. 1989b. "On the Idea of Authorless Revelation (*Apauruṣeya*)." In *Indian Philosophy of Religion*, Roy W. Perrett (ed.), 143–166. Dordrecht: Kluwer.

———. 1994. "Autpattika: The Originary Signifier–Signified Relation in Mīmāṃsā and Deconstructive Semiology." In *Studies in Mīmāṃsā: Dr Mandan Mishra Felicitation Volume*, R. R. Diwedhi (ed.), 187–203. Delhi: L.B.S. Rashtriya Sanskrit Vidyapitha.

———. 1995. "Authorless Voice, Tradition and Authority in the Mīmāṃsā: Reflections in Cross-Cultural Hermeneutics." *Nagoya Studies in India Culture and Buddhism* 16: 137–160.

———. 2000. "J. N. Mohanty's Critique of the Word as a Means of Knowing and 'Authorless Tradition'." In *The Empirical and the Transcendental: A Fusion of Horizons*, Bina Gupta (ed.), 199–218. Lanham, MD: Rowman & Littlefield.

———. 2001. "Hindu Doubts about God: Towards a Mīmāṃsā Deconstruction." In *Indian Philosophy: A Collection of Readings*, Roy W. Perrett (ed.), 87–106. New York and London: Garland Publishing.

Cardona, George. 1976. *Pāṇini: A Survey of Research*. The Hague: Mouton.

Clooney, Francis X. 1990. *Thinking Ritually: Rediscovering the Pūrva Mīmāṃsā of Jaimini*. Vienna: Institut für Indologie der Universität Wien.

Cohn, Bernard S. 1996. *Colonialism and its Forms of Knowledge*. Princeton: Princeton University Press.

Coward, Harold G. and Kunjunni Raja, K. eds. 1990. *The Philosophy of the Grammarians*. Princeton: Princeton University Press.

Derrida, Jacques. 1976. *Of Grammatology*. Trans., with Introduction, Gayatri Chakravorty Spivak. Baltimore, MD: Johns Hopkins University Press.

Deshpande, Madhav. 1993. *Sanskrit and Prakrit: Sociolinguistic Issues*. Delhi: Motilal Banarsidass.

Ellis, Thomas B. 2009. "On the Death of the Pilgrim: The Postcolonial Hermeneutics of Jarava Lal Mehta." In *Postcolonial Philosophy of Religion*, Purushottama Bilimoria and Andrew B Irvine (eds.), 105–120. Dordrecht and Berlin: Springer.

Fisch, Jörg. 1983. *Cheap Lives and Dear Limbs*. Wiesbaden: Franz Steiner.

Foucault, Michel. 1994. *The Order of Things*. New York: Vintage.

Gadamer, Hans-Georg. 2006. *Truth and Method*. Trans. Joel Weinsheimer and Donald G. Marshall. 2nd, rev. ed. New York: Continuum.

Grafton, Anthony. 1997. *Commerce with the Classics*. Ann Arbor: University of Michigan Press.

Gyatso, Janet. 1992. "Letter Magic: A Peircean Perspective on the Semiotics of Rdo Grub-chen's Dhāraṇī Memory." In *In the Mirror of Memory*, Janet Gyatso (ed.), 173–214. Albany: State University of New York Press.

Holdrege, Barbara A. 1996. *Veda and Torah: Transcending the Textuality of Scripture*. Albany: State University of New York Press.

Jha, Ujjwala. 2002. *Mīmāṃsā Philosophy of Language*. Delhi: Sri Satguru Publications.

Joseph, John E., Love, N., and Taylor, T. J. 2001. *Landmarks in Linguistic Thought II: The Western Tradition in the Twentieth Century*. London: Routledge.

Joshi, Kireet. 1991. *The Veda and Indian Culture*. New Delhi: Rashtriya Veda Vidya.

Koselleck, Reinhart. 2004. *Futures Past: On the Semantics of Historical Time*. Trans. Keith Tribe. New York: Columbia University Press.

Laddu, S. D. 1974. *Evolution of the Sanskrit Language from Pāṇini to Patañjali*. Poona: Centre of Advanced Study in Sanskrit.

McCrea, Lawrence. 2008. "Playing with the System: Fragmentation and Individualization in Late Pre-colonial Mīmāṃsa." *Journal of Indian Philosophy* 36: 575–585.

McEvilley, Thomas. 2002. *The Shape of Ancient Thought: Comparative Studies in Greek and Indian Philosophies*. New York: Allworth Press.

Matilal, Bimal Krishna. 1990. *The Word and the World: India's Contribution to the Study of Language*. Delhi: Oxford University Press.

Mohanty, J. N. 1992. *Reason and Tradition in Indian Thought*. Oxford: Clarendon Press.

———. 1993. *Essays on Indian Philosophy Traditional and Modern*. Ed., with Introduction, Purushottama Bilimoria. New Delhi: Oxford University Press.

———. 2001. *Explorations in Philosophy: Indian Philosophy*. New Delhi: Oxford University Press.

The Nighaṇṭu and the Nirukta of Yaska. 1920. Ed. Lakshman Sarup. Oxford: Oxford University Press.

Pollock, Sheldon. 1989. "Mīmāṃsā and the Problem of History in Traditional India." *Journal of the American Oriental Society* 9(4): 603–610.

———. 1997. "The 'Revelation' of 'Tradition': *Śruti*, *Smṛti* and the Sanskrit Discourse of Power." In *Lex et Litterae: Studies in Honour of Professor Oscar Botto*, Siegfried Lienhard and Irma Piovano (eds.), 395–417. Alessandria: Edizioni dell'Orso.

———. 2003. "Sanskrit Literary Cultures from the Inside Out." In *Literary Cultures in History: Reconstructions from South Asia*, Sheldon Pollock (ed.), 1–38. Berkeley: University of California Press.

———. 2005. "The Languages of Science in Early Modern India." In *Contributions of Indian and Cross-Cultural Studies: Volume in Commemoration of Wilhelm Halbfass*, Karin Preisendanz (ed.), 203–220. Vienna: Akademie der Wissenschaften.

———. 2006. *The Language of the Gods in the World of Men: Sanskrit, Culture, and Power in Premodern India*. Berkeley: University of California Press.

Reichenbach, Bruce. 2003. "The Hermeneutic Circle and Authoral Intention in Divine Revelation." *Sophia* 42(1): 47–59.

Rorty, Richard. 1980. *Philosophy and the Mirror of Nature*. Princeton: Princeton University Press.

Singh, Satya Prakash. 2001. *Vedic Symbolism*. New Delhi: Standard.

Thurman, Robert A. F. 1978. "Buddhist Hermeneutics." *Journal of the American Academy of Religion* 46(1): 19–39.

Versteegh, Kees. 1993. *Landmarks in Linguistics III: The Arabic Linguistic Tradition*. London: Routledge.

Wild, Stefan. 2003. "The Self-Referentiality of the Qur'ān: Sura 3:7 as an Exegetical Challenge." In *With Reverence for the Word: Medieval Scriptural Exegesis in Judaism, Christianity and Islam*, Jane Dammen McAuliffe, Barry D. Walfish, and Joseph W. Goering (eds.), 422–437. Oxford: Oxford University Press.

Chapter 38
BASIC JAINA EPISTEMOLOGY

Jayandra Soni

The Jaina contribution to philosophy in general, and to epistemology in particular, is often underestimated, if not completely ignored. Jaina thinkers drew from India's common pool of ideas (like the assumption of suffering as a characteristic feature of human existence, and the knowledge of reality as crucial for liberation and the possibility of liberation), and they couched these ideas in accordance with their own ontology, metaphysics, theory of knowledge, and ethics. Jainas have made significant contribution to the history and development of Indian philosophy as a whole. This chapter focuses on the basics of Jaina epistemology, its history, similarities and differences, demonstrating that the Jainas did not lag behind but kept up with the mainstream concerns in Indian philosophy.[1]

The presentation is based on the works of a selected number of thinkers: Kundakunda's (second or third century) *Pravacanasāra*, Umāsvāti's (perhaps fourth or fifth century CE) *Tattvārthasūtra*, and Māṇikyanandin's (ninth–tenth century) *Parīkṣāmukha*. These early thinkers have been chosen for their systematic clarity and are generally regarded as authoritative by the Jaina tradition. Other thinkers such as Siddhasena Divākara (fifth century), Akalaṃka (eighth century), and Vidyānandin (ninth century) have also made significant contributions, but their views will be referred to only in passing. Moreover, the later tradition, represented by such renowned thinkers as Hemacandra (eleventh century), Vādidevasūri (twelfth century), and the erudite polyhistor Yaśovijaya (seventeenth century), will not be discussed.

On the beginnings of Indian epistemology

A few words regarding the beginnings of Indian epistemology as a whole will demonstrate that the Jaina tradition was not isolated in the Indian tradition and that its views did not evolve in a vacuum.

The desire for knowledge, which basically reflects a philosophical inclination, is traceable throughout the history of Indian philosophy. It goes hand in hand with the emergence and history of debate among all the representatives of different schools of thought, and with it there is the necessity of dealing with epistemological categories. The significance of the Jaina contribution here is based on their predisposition to collect and copy all kinds of literature for the sake of knowing other views.

The emergence of philosophical debate in India contributed greatly to a sharpening of the philosophical tools and to the setting down of rules of debate that had to be adhered to strictly in the courts where the debates mostly took place. Caraka in the *Carakasaṃhitā* (CS 3.8) advises medical practitioners to debate with others because discussion increases the zeal for knowledge, clarifies knowledge, increases the power of speech, makes one famous, removes doubt, establishes the knowledge already gained, and can lead to new knowledge. In this very early period in the history of Indian debate it was also recognized that a discussion that forms the basis of a debate can be of different kinds, and Caraka distinguishes two kinds, one that is "friendly" and one that is "hostile."[2] In view of their extreme emphasis on nonviolence, the Jainas were probably exemplary debaters, well acquainted with their subject matter.

Caraka offers a list of forty-four items over which the physician should have a command before accepting an invitation to enter into a debate. Suffice it to mention a few terms from this list for the point made here:[3] perception, inference, comparison, the thesis, a statement of the proof for the thesis, the reason, the example, and the doubt. The list becomes more compact later, especially when the Nyāya school, whose favorite topic was epistemology, includes the list as a starting point for all the themes it deals with in its basic work. Sixteen terms are listed at the beginning of the *Nyāyasūtra*: (1) the instruments or means of knowledge, (2) the objects of knowledge, (3) doubt, (4) purpose, (5) example, (6) tenet, (7) members of the argument, (8) deliberation, (9) conclusion, (10) disputation, (11) debate, (12) wrangling, (13) fallacious reasons, (14) quibble, (15) false objections, and (16) reasons for defeat. Each school accepted a fixed number of instruments or means of cognition, each of which yields a particular kind of knowledge, and for the major schools of Indian philosophy the number ranges from one to six. So, for example, the materialist accepts only perception as the most important and reliable means of knowledge, the Buddhists and the Vaiśeṣika school accept inference as well, the Sāṃkhya school accepts verbal testimony or scriptural authority in addition to perception and inference, and so forth. There are certain implicit conditions on the basis of which the number of means of cognition were accepted by each school. At least four conditions need to be fulfilled: (a) the knowledge furnished by one means of cognition must be new and not attainable by any other means; (b) one means of cognition may aid another in making a particular knowledge possible, but the means of cognition in question should *not be reducible to another*—so, for example, when perception aids inference, as in inferring fire by seeing the smoke in the distance, the knowledge gained cannot be reduced to the knowledge obtained by perception alone; (c) the cognition obtained through one particular means of knowledge should not be contradicted by another means of knowledge; and (d) the accepted means of cognition should *appeal to reason*, and in the case of verbal testimony or scriptural authority, for example, knowledge concerning the revealed truth must appear probable and be made intelligible in terms of human experience, or otherwise such a means of cognition will fail in its purpose.[4]

Jaina thinkers did not lag behind in their concern with epistemological issues, and the relevant literature from the beginning of our era evinces this. What their basic theory of knowledge is will be seen with special reference to Kundakunda, Umāsvāti, and Māṇikyanandin.

Jaina epistemology

The Jaina tradition rests on one fundamental fact, namely that human beings are in a position to be omniscient and that this view is based on the teaching of omniscient beings who have taught the basic ideas after having become enlightened through a strict ascetic discipline. These beings are called "Jinas" or victors, who have conquered the passions that bind human beings to worldly life. Since such beings have seen through reality as such, their teaching is regarded as authoritative by the tradition, and Jaina thinkers throughout the ages have striven to reiterate their views in the hope of arriving at the same insight as the Jinas. The Jinas are regarded as Tīrthaṅkaras or "ford-makers" because their views are a bridge between the worldly and non-worldly banks of the stream of life. The tradition mentions twenty-four such teachers of humanity, the last two of whom were Pārśvanath and, 250 years later, Mahāvīra, who was a contemporary of the Buddha. The teachings of the Jinas are regarded as reliable and authoritative, and every basic idea concerning ontology, epistemology, and ethics is traced back to a tradition started by such beings.[5]

It must be noted that epistemological issues are in fact inalienably connected with the metaphysics and ontology of a particular school. What is the intrinsic nature of the things of the world that are open to human knowledge? How can one define the subject, the knower? What is the nature of the instruments of knowledge, such as sight and hearing? All these questions are basic to the concern with epistemology. It is also a well-known fact that, apart from the materialists, the Cārvākas (see earlier, Chapter 10), the teaching of each school is aimed at liberation (*mokṣa* or *nirvāṇa*), and each has its own view of the world, a knowledge of which forms part of the discipline that leads to the goal. Jainism made its own unique contribution to this mainstream development by also occupying itself with the basic issues concerning the nature of knowledge, how knowledge is derived, and in what way knowledge can be said to be reliable. For the Jainas the concern with epistemological issues served two main functions: it provided the basis for an intelligible discourse on matters of common, everyday experience, and, second, even if indirectly, it demarcated this area from what constitutes the knowledge of ultimate reality. Explaining how errors occur in human cognition was included in the epistemological theories, and it is not often noticed that epistemology dealt with theories of error as well. Indeed the success of a theory of valid cognition is commensurate with the success in which error in our cognition is also explained. In other words, granted that we can err in our cognition, a theory of cognition should also be able to explain the source of this occurrence, or at least be in a position to account for it. This point is implicit when, at the very beginning of his *Parīkṣāmukha* (*PM*), Māṇikyanandin says "the proper ascertainment of an object arises out of a valid means of knowledge (*pramāṇa*); the contrary of this happens when it is erroneous" (*PM* 1).[6]

In his *Pramāṇa-mīmāṃsā* (1.1.7), Hemacandra says that error "is a cognition that definitely takes a thing to be what it is not."

One superficial relation between Jaina ontology and Jaina epistemology is that just as there are only two fundamental ontological categories, the principles of sentience and non-sentience (*jīva* and *ajīva*, usually translated as soul and matter), there are only two basic means through which we can know things: in a direct way (*pratyakṣa*) or in an indirect way (*parokṣa*). For the Jainas sentience intrinsically possesses unlimited qualities of bliss and energy and, without the detrimental influence of matter, is omniscient. The association of the soul with the insentient principles hinders its capabilities, and therefore human beings possess limited knowledge. Unique to Jainism is the idea that direct knowledge in fact takes place through the soul.[7] On the basis of the twofold classification of a direct and indirect means of knowledge, an intricate theory of knowledge is built up concerning the fundamental principles or categories (*tattva*) (supplied below). The first systematic presentation of it in the classical *sūtra* style was given by Umāsvāti in his *Tattvārthasūtra* (*TS* 1.6–31), and his presentation is regarded as authoritative by all Jainas. Kundakunda's views, expressed in the Prakrit language, are also looked upon with great respect for his pioneering attempts.

The sentient principle is responsible for the fact that knowledge takes place at all. Hence, for the Jainas, knowledge takes place in the soul; when the soul is freed or isolated from the influence of matter, it has *kevalajñāna* (omniscient knowledge, which beings like the Jinas have attained). In the case of the concern with epistemology in the context of human knowledge, it is necessary in Jainism to understand clearly the context in which the following terms are used: *jñāna*, *pramāṇa*, and *naya*. Further, the theory of manifoldness (*anekāntavāda*, with its twofold aspects of *nayavāda* and *syādvāda*) also has to be seen in an epistemological context because it is concerned with how we know things. The theory of manifoldness, however, applies in a different context: it is concerned with particular standpoints (*naya*), like the common, the general, or the practical standpoint from which an object may be perceived, and the seven kinds of statements or predications that may be made about an object where it is said that, depending on the perspective (*syāt*), an object can be said to exist, not exist, and so forth.[8] What the theory of manifoldness does not do is discuss the means or instruments of knowledge in the Jaina tradition.

The word *jñāna*, translated as "knowledge," is used in the context of absolute knowledge, which can be had only by beings liberated from the detrimental effects of matter in the form of karma clinging to the soul. In other contexts it could be used in the sense of valid cognition, in contrast to erroneous cognition. In this case *jñāna* is synonymous with the *pramā* (also meaning "knowledge") of the thing to be known (*prameya*), obtained through a particular means or instrument of cognition (*pramāṇa*). A theory of knowledge (*prāmāṇyavāda*), therefore, deals with all three of these aspects, and the Jainas say that there are two general instruments of knowledge (the direct and the indirect ones), that the objects to be known are the seven basic categories of Jaina metaphysics (supplied below), and that knowledge takes place in the soul. In Jainism the basic twofold classification of knowledge derived through direct and indirect means is as unique as the classification of the different kinds of instruments of knowledge that come under the rubric of these two.

It seems that Kundakunda is the first independent thinker of the post-canonical period who dealt with epistemological issues. In this context his *Pravacanasāra* ("Essence of the Scripture") (*PrS*) is an insightful work, regarded as one of his philosophical masterpieces. The three sections of the work clearly show the issues he deals with: knowledge, the objects of knowledge, and conduct. It is interesting to see how he deals with some aspects of epistemology that have become part of the tradition, so that it can also be evident how the problem was thematized differently in the later period:[9]

> He who has manifested pure consciousness and is free from … karmic dust, has become self-sufficient; and fully comprehends the objects of knowledge.
>
> (*PrS* 1.15)

> The soul is co-extensive with knowledge; knowledge is said to be co-extensive with the object of knowledge; the object of knowledge comprises the physical and non-physical world; therefore knowledge is omnipresent.
>
> (*PrS* 1.23)

> The knower who is beyond sense-perception, necessarily knows and sees the world neither entering into nor entered into by the objects of knowledge, just as the eye sees the objects of sight.
>
> (*PrS* 1.29)

> He who knows is knowledge; the self does not become a knower with knowledge (as an extraneous instrument). The very self develops knowledge, and all the objects stand (reflected) in the knowledge.
>
> (*PrS* 1.35)

> Perception of things through a foreign agency is called *parokṣa*, indirect or mediate; whatever is perceived by the soul alone is *pratyakṣa*, direct or immediate.
>
> (*PrS* 1.58)

> The object of knowledge is made up of substances, which are said to be characterized by qualities, and with which, moreover, are (associated) the modifications; those who are deluded by modifications, are false believers.
>
> (*PrS* 2.1)[10]

> That is called a substance which is endowed with qualities and accompanied by modifications and which is coupled with origination, destruction and permanence without leaving its nature.
>
> (*PrS* 2.3)

> According to some modification or the other it is stated that a substance exists, does not exist, is indescribable, is both or otherwise.
>
> (*PrS* 2.23)

This random selection of the basic aspects of the problem in Kundakunda's own words has been supplied so as to demonstrate how the treatment of the theme changes with Umāsvāti. One of the basic differences is that Umāsvāti explicitly enumerates the different means of knowledge that are grouped under the rubrics of the direct (*pratyakṣa*) and the indirect (*parokṣa*). When the Jainas speak about a knowledge of objects they mean specifically a knowledge of the seven categories that comprise the metaphysics of the school. The seven categories are, as Umāsvāti mentions them in his *Tattvārthasūtra*: the sentient and insentient categories, the inflow (of matter into the soul; matter turns into karma particles, which obstruct the innate energy of the soul), bondage (caused by this inflow), stoppage (of further inflow), burning away (of the remaining particles of karma, through asceticism), and liberation (as a result of being isolated from the influence of matter) (*TS* 1.4).

In *TS* 1.6, Umāsvāti says that knowledge can be obtained through *pramāṇa* and *naya*, and he goes on to say (in *TS* 1.9–12) that knowledge is obtained through five kinds of *pramāṇa*, and of these the first two—sensory knowledge and scriptural knowledge—are indirect (*parokṣa*) means of knowledge, and the rest—clairvoyance, telepathy, and omniscience—are direct (*pratyakṣa*) means of knowledge. Not only is this list much more differentiated and explicit than Kundakunda's, but it also presents the characteristically Jaina view since then: sensory perception is defined as being indirect, whereas all other schools regard it as the only direct means of knowledge; what the Jainas regard as direct means of knowledge do not at all feature as valid means of knowledge in the other schools.[11]

In elaborating the Jaina view, Umāsvāti continues to say that synonyms for sensory knowledge are remembrance, recognition, 'induction,' and 'deduction,' all of which are caused by the senses and the mind (*TS* 1.13–14). Scriptural knowledge, which is based on sensory knowledge, is of two, several, or twelve kinds (*TS* 1.20), depending on which scriptural texts are regarded as authoritative. The range of sensory and scriptural knowledge extends to all the six substances (soul and the five insentient substances), but not in all their modes (*TS* 1.20). Divine and infernal beings possess clairvoyance or extra-sensory perception; if the karma that hinders this kind of knowledge is obliterated, or if its influence is neutralized, then animals and human beings, too, can have it (*TS* 1.21–22), and through it all entities that have form can be known (*TS* 1.27). Telepathy is of two kinds, distinguished on the basis of purity and infallibility (*TS* 1.23–24), and its range is infinitely greater than that of clairvoyance (*TS* 1.28). The scope of omniscience, on the other hand, extends to all substances in all their modes simultaneously (*TS* 1.29). Sensory knowledge, scriptural knowledge, and clairvoyance are explicitly referred to as instruments of knowledge that can also be erroneous (*TS* 1.31).

Māṇikyanandin begins his treatment of epistemology in his *Parīkṣāmukha* (*PM*) by saying that '*pramāṇa* is valid knowledge of itself and of things not proved before'

(*PM* 1.1),[12] and goes on to say that the validity of *pramāṇa* 'rises from itself or through another (*Pramāṇa*)' (*PM* 1.13). After referring to the basic kinds of knowledge as direct and indirect, in keeping with the tradition (*PM* 2.2), he says that direct knowledge is knowledge 'which is clear' (*PM* 2.3), with clearness meaning an "illumination without any other intermediate knowledge or illumination in details" (*PM* 2.4). Direct knowledge is then divided into two kinds: one that is current in everyday life and which is partially clear (*PM* 2.5), and the other, which is 'supreme,' not dependent on any sense organ, and is devoid of any kind of obstruction (*PM* 2.11). The indirect means of knowledge consists of memory, recognition, logic, inference, and scriptural testimony (*PM* 3.2). These are then defined, and the final three chapters of the work deal with universals and particulars, the results of inference, and, finally, the fallacies of inference.

One of the notable differences regarding the specific means of knowledge that are direct is given by Akalaṃka when dealing with sensory perception. It was seen above that for Umāsvāti direct perception (*pratyakṣa*), which takes place in the soul, occurs through clairvoyance, telepathy, and omniscience and that sensory knowledge and scriptural knowledge are indirect (*parokṣa*). According to Akalaṃka's classification, direct knowledge is basically of the two kinds that Māṇikyanandin takes over from him, namely the direct knowledge that takes place through the senses and that which takes place through memory, which is regarded as synonymous with remembrance, recognition, 'induction,' and 'deduction.' In another classification Akalaṃka identifies memory (and the other things regarded as synonyms of it) with sensory perception as direct knowledge and another kind of direct knowledge not derived through the senses, namely clairvoyance, telepathy, and omniscience. The differences are not merely a matter of classification. In view of the high regard and impact his views have in the Jaina tradition (inspiring masters such as Vidyānandin and Māṇikyanandin), a detailed study and further research of his works are still needed to assess their epistemological implications in the context of the Jaina view as a whole.[13]

In conclusion, the relation between epistemology and logic needs special mention here. These two areas are closely linked in the Indian tradition because logic in India primarily involved an investigation into the validity of inference, which, in turn, is regarded as a means of knowledge. The preoccupation with abstract, logical ideas related to inference was a favorite topic of the Nyāya school, and Jaina thinkers adopted its language and method, using natural language, not symbols, to present their abstract ideas. Siddhasena Divākara (fifth century) deals with the issues regarding the major, minor, and middle terms of an argument within a Jaina context in his *Nyāyāvatāra*. Here, too, the Jainas have kept up with the major issues within the Indian tradition.

Conclusion

The following points have hopefully emerged out of this short presentation of the basics of Jaina epistemology: (1) the Jaina tradition evinces insightful views that can be regarded as their contribution to the development of Indian philosophy as a whole, for example their own definition of what constitutes a valid means of cognition and their classification of the means or instruments of knowledge; (2) it is possible to speak of a history of epistemological ideas within Jainism itself, for example when one compares the views of the thinkers referred to above; and (3) a great deal of research is still required because not all significant works on epistemology are easily available, as in the case of Akalaṃka's works.

Notes

1 An earlier version of this chapter was published as an article in *Philosophy East and West*, 50(3), July 2000: 367–377 (University of Hawai'i Press) In its modified form it is used with permission from the editor, Roger T. Ames (dated August 5, 2012).

2 For a detailed description, also concerning the different kinds of assemblies that decide the outcome of a debate, see Dasgupta 1952, 378–388, and Frauwallner 1984, 66. Useful in this context also is G. Obherhammer, "Ein Beitrag zu den Vāda-Traditionen Indiens," in *Wiener Zeitschrift für die Kunde Süd- und Ostasiens* (Leiden: E. J. Brill) 7, 1963: 63–103.

3 For the complete list see Frauwallner 1984, 69–70.

4 According to Erich Frauwallner it was Vṛṣagaṇa (or Vārṣagaṇya, perhaps 300 CE), the renowned Sāṃkhya teacher, who was the first to investigate epistemological questions at the beginning of his work, the *Ṣaṣṭitantra* (available only in fragments), and thereby began a tradition followed by others. See his "Die Erkenntnislehre des klassischen Sāṃkhya-Systems," in *Erich Frauwallner Kleine Schriften* (Wiesbaden: Franz Steiner Verlag, 1982), 223–278. See also D. Seyfort Ruegg, "Note on Vārṣagaṇya and the *Yogācārabhūmi*," *Indo-Iranian Journal* (Hague: Mouton) 6, 1962: 137–140, and G. Oberhammer, "The Authorship of the Ṣaṣṭitantram," *Wiener Zeitschrift für die Kunde Süd- und Ostasiens* 4, 1960: 71–91.

5 The issue concerns the notion of *āpta*, one who can be regarded as an "authoritative person"; cf. Soni 1996.

6 I am using the edition mentioned in Māṇikyanandin 1940. The text is also embodied in the two main commentaries to the work: (1) the *Prameya-kamala-mārttaṇḍa* by Prabhācandra, ed. with introduction, indexes, etc. by Pt. Mahendra Kumar Shastri, 2nd ed. (Bombay: Nirnaya Sagar Press, 1941), and (2) the *Parīkṣāmukha-laghuvṛtti* (also called *Parīkṣāmukha-pañjikā* and *Prameya-ratna-mālā*) by Anantavīrya (eleventh century), ed. Satis Chandra Vidyabhusana (Calcutta: Asiatic Society of Bengal, 1909).

7 The point of direct knowledge taking place through the soul can be compared, e.g., with the function of *cic-chakti* in Śaiva Siddhānta. For the similarities and differences see 1996, 9–13.

8 For the philosophical significance of the Jaina theory of manifoldness, which is omitted here, see Soni 1997.

9 The translations are taken from Kundakunda's work given in Kundakunda 1984.

10 The reference here is to a fundamental issue in Jaina philosophy concerning substance, quality, and mode. For the philosophical context of this far-reaching problem see Soni 1991.

11 Umāsvāti says that knowledge can also be obtained through other means: by description, ownership, cause, resting place (or substratum), and division (*TS* 1.7); and by existence, number, place of abode, etc. (*TS* 1.8). These lists only broaden the scope of epistemology. I have chosen to deal only with those aspects that are clearly comparable with epistemology in the other schools.

12 The translations are from Māṇikyanandin's work given in Māṇikyanandin, 1940.

13 The first classification is contained in his *Pravacanapraveṣa* (a work that forms part of a trilogy called *Laghīyastraya*; the other two contained in this are *Pramāṇapraveṣa* and *Nayapraveṣa*). The second classification is contained in his *Nyayaviniścaya*. All these works have been published in a single volume: *Akalaṃka-grantha-trayam*, ed. Mahendra Kumar Śāstrī, Siṃghī Jaina Granthamala, no. 12 (Ahmedabad-Kolkata, 1931). The reference to these classifications is taken from K. K. Dixit, *Jaina Ontology*, 146. (Ahmedabad: L. D. Institute of Indology, 1971).

References

Bhattacharya, Hari Mohan. 1994. *Jaina Logic and Epistemology*. Calcutta and New Delhi: K. P. Bagchi and Co.

Dasgupta, Surendranath. 1952. *A History of Indian Philosophy*. Vol. 2. Cambridge: Cambridge University Press.

Frauwallner, Erich. 1984. *Erich Frauwallner: Nachgelassene Werke I: Aufsätze, Beiträge, Skizzen*. Vienna: Österreichische Akademie der Wissenschaften. (Translated from the German by J. Soni as *Erich Frauwallner's Posthumous Essays*. Delhi: Aditya Prakashan, 1994.)

Hemacandra (eleventh century). 1970. *Hemacandra's Pramāṇa-mīmāṃsā*. Text and translation with critical notes by Satkari Mookerjee. Varanasi: Tara Book Agency. Repr., 1986.

Kundakunda (second–third century). 1984. *Pravacanasāra (Pavayaṇasāra)*. 4th edition. Edited with commentaries and English translation of the text alone by A. N. Upadhye. Anand (Gujarat): Shrimad Rajachandra Ashrama.

Māṇikyanandin (ninth–tenth century). 1940. *Parīkṣāmukham* by Māṇikyanandī (with *Prameya-ratnamalā* by Anantavīrya). Edited with translation, introduction, notes, and an original commentary in English by Sarat Chandra Ghosal. Lucknow: Central Jaina Publishing House.

Padmarajiah, Y. J. 1963. *A Comparative Study of the Jaina Theories of Reality and Knowledge*. Delhi: Motilal Banarsidass. Repr., 1986.

Prasad, Jwala. 1939. *Indian Epistemology*. Lahore: Motilal Banarsidass.

Randle, H. N. 1930/1937. *Indian Logic in the Early Schools: A Study of the Nyāya-darśana in Its Relation to the Early Logic of Other Schools*. Oxford: Oxford University Press. Repr., Delhi: Munshiram Manoharlal.

Soni, Jayandra. 1991. "Dravya, Guṇa and Paryāya in Jaina Thought." *Journal of Indian Philosophy* 19: 75–88.

———. 1996. "The Notion of Āpta in Jaina Philosophy." The 1995 Roop Lal Jain Annual Lecture, Toronto, 25 November 1995. Toronto: University of Toronto, Centre for South Asia Studies.

———. 1997. "Philosophical Significance of the Jaina Theory of Manifoldness." In *Philosophie aus interkultureller Sicht = Philosophy from an Intercultural Perspective*, ed. N. Schneider *et al.*, pp. 277–287. Studien zur Interkulturellen Philosophie = Studies in Intercultural Philosophy 7, ed. H. Kimmerle and R. A. Mall. Amsterdam and Atlanta, GA: Rodopi.

———. 1998. "Jaina Philosophy, Issues in." In *Routledge Encyclopedia of Philosophy*, ed. Edward Craig. New York and London: Routledge.

Umāsvāti (fourth or fifth century). 1994. *Tattvārtha Sūtra: That Which Is: With the Combined Commentaries of Umāsvāti/Umāsvāmin, Pūjyapāda and Siddhasenagaṇi*. Translated with an introduction by Natmal Tatia. London: HarperCollins.

Chapter 39
ANEKĀNTAVĀDA, NAYAVĀDA, AND SYĀDVĀDA: THE HISTORY AND SIGNIFICANCE OF THE JAINA DOCTRINES OF RELATIVITY[1]

Jeffery D. Long

Introduction

A distinctive Jaina contribution to Indian philosophy with considerable relevance to today's world of inter-religious conflict is a complex of three teachings called the Jaina 'doctrines of relativity.' The first doctrine, *anekāntavāda*, teaches that reality is irreducibly complex, or *anekānta* (literally 'non-one-sided'). No entity can be reduced to a single characteristic or concept. To exist is to be multi-faceted. The second doctrine, *Nayavāda*, the doctrine of perspectives, is a logical implication of *anekāntavāda*: a claim about the nature of knowledge. Given the complexity of reality that *anekāntavāda* posits, an entity may be known from a variety of *nayas*, or perspectives, that correspond to its many facets. The third doctrine, *syādvāda*, the doctrine of conditional predication, asserts that the truth of a claim is dependent upon the perspective from which it is made. A claim can be true, in one sense or from one perspective (the technical meaning of the Sanskrit verb '*syāt*' in a Jaina context), false from another perspective, both true and false from another, have an inexpressible truth-value from yet another, and so on.

The gist of these doctrines is expressed in the famous story of the Blind Men and the Elephant.[2] Several blind men are brought before a king and asked to describe an elephant. An elephant is brought to them and they proceed to feel it with their hands. One, who grasps the elephant's trunk, claims that an elephant is like a snake. Another, grasping a leg, claims it is like a tree. Yet another grasps the tail and says it is like a rope; and another, feeling the elephant's side, claims it is like a wall. The blind men then proceed to argue amongst themselves about the true nature of the elephant. The moral of the story is that all of the blind men are partially correct – for an elephant does, indeed, possess all the qualities that the blind men attribute to it. Each is also partially incorrect, inasmuch as he denies the claims of the others. Only one who can see the whole elephant – an enlightened being, with a comprehensive view of reality – is in a position to say, unequivocally, what its true nature is. The rest of us are like the blind men. We can only speak with certainty from our limited perspectives, and remain open to the insights of others and what they can teach us about other aspects of reality from their points of view.

That the doctrines of relativity do *not* constitute a form of what is generally called *relativism*, the view either that there is ultimately no truth or that 'truth' is but a matter of convention, is evidenced from this story. There really is an elephant *there* and it really has particular characteristics. A sighted person can apprehend its full nature, in terms of which the claims of the blind men can be evaluated and placed in proper perspective, one is describing the trunk, one a leg, one the tail, etc. For a Jain, this ultimate truth is the truth taught by an omniscient Jina. This is why the term 'non-absolutism,' sometimes used to characterize these doctrines, can be deceptive; and yet many use this characterization (e.g. Mookerjee 1978). There *is* an absolute perspective in Jainism.

Of course, 'doctrines of relativity' may be just as deceptive, if this term is taken to mean *relativist* in the usual sense. The point is that, according to these Jaina doctrines, the truth-value of a claim is *relative to* an absolute perspective. The intended analogue is with Einstein's theories of relativity, which do not deny ontological realism, but affirm the relativity of points of view and frames of reference. The Jaina doctrines of relativity are deeply rooted in the ontological realism that characterizes the Jaina tradition.

The Jaina doctrines of relativity are thus closely related to the claim to omniscience made by Mahāvīra (or on his behalf) in the Jaina scriptures. In these texts, Mahāvīra is represented as answering profound metaphysical questions (considered 'unanswerable,' or *avyākata*, in the Buddhist tradition) with both a 'yes' and a 'no,' depending upon the perspective of the questioner. The *jīva*, or soul, is both eternal (in its intrinsic nature), and non-eternal (from the perspective of the karmic changes that it is constantly undergoing); the cosmos is both eternal (in the sense that it has no absolute beginning or end), and non-eternal (inasmuch as it passes through arising and descending cycles), and so on. Another rationale for these doctrines is to be found in the complex nature of the soul that is posited by Jainism, a nature extrapolated to apply to all entities. The soul has an unchanging, intrinsic nature; but it also experiences karmically conditioned states that arise and pass away. *Tattvārtha Sūtra* 5:29 states that, *utpādavyāyadhrauvyayukt aṃ sat*: 'Arising, passing away, and continuity characterize entities.' In other words, there is a sense in which all things come to be and perish, and a sense in which they endure.

In later Jaina texts, this understanding of reality is applied to the topic and endlessly debated among Buddhist and Brāhmaṇical schools of thought, asking if the nature of reality is either permanent or impermanent. Contrasting themselves with Buddhists, who uphold a doctrine of radical impermanence, and adherents of Brāhmaṇical systems, which uphold various doctrines of permanence, the Jains claim that entities are both permanent and impermanent, in different senses and from different perspectives. They thus present their view as a true 'Middle Path' between warring philosophies, claiming a metaphysical high ground that can integrate the perspectives of the others into their own.

Though the common use of the doctrines of relativity by pre-modern Jaina thinkers as described here shows the superiority of the Jaina perspective, the potential utility of these doctrines in resolving disputes among diverse philosophies has led to the popular view that these doctrines are an extension of the Jaina commitment to *ahiṃsā* or non-violence in thought, word, and deed to the realm of intellectual discourse.[3] Though historically dubious, this characterization of these doctrines renders them attractive as a way to address the issue of how to remain committed to a tradition while being open to the views of others: to be a good Jain while and *by* not attacking other traditions, but drawing attention to the ways in which they express truth. Modern Jains see the Jaina doctrines of relativity as a Jaina form of religious pluralism, and a major Jaina contribution to wider conversations about interfaith relations and the promotion of harmony among adherents of diverse worldviews. As we shall see, this way of using these doctrines is not without precedent in the pre-modern Jaina tradition.

Relativity in the Śvetāmbara *Āgamas*: Mahāvīra's inclusive middle path

How did the Jains develop the doctrines of relativity? Evidence for the approach that evolves into these doctrines is discernible in the earliest extant Jaina scriptures: those of the Śvetāmbara Jains. A common problem faced by the Buddha and Mahāvīra, according to the texts of their respective communities, was a set of *avyākata*, or unanswerable, questions that were sources of controversy among the various schools of thought in northern India around the middle of the first millennium before the Common Era. The Buddha, as portrayed in early Buddhist texts, often refused to answer these questions, viewing them as not conducive to spiritual liberation. When he did answer them, would clarify the assumptions that they involved. According to B. K. Matilal (1981, 19–29) the Jaina doctrines of relativity developed from a similar strategy on the part of Mahāvīra, as illustrated in this dialogue with his disciple, the monk Jamāli:

> [T]he Venerable Mahāvīra told the Bhikkhu Jamāli thus: … [T]he world is, Jamāli, eternal. It did not cease to exist at any time. It was, it is and it will be. It is constant, permanent, eternal, imperishable, indestructible, always existent.
>
> The world is, Jamāli, non-eternal. For it becomes progressive (in time-cycle) after being regressive. And it becomes regressive after becoming progressive.
>
> The soul is, Jamāli, eternal. For it did not cease to exist at any time. The soul is, Jamāli, non-eternal. For it becomes animal after being a hellish creature, becomes a man after becoming an animal and it becomes a god after being a man.
>
> (*Bhagavatı Sūtra* 9:386; trans. Matilal 1981, 19)

According to Jaina tradition, an enlightened being like Mahāvīra can perceive the complexity of reality from all perspectives, and answer metaphysical questions from all points of view. From the perspective of permanence the universe, Mahāvīra says, is eternal. From the perspective of change it is 'non-eternal.' (The 'progressive' and 'regressive' time-cycles of which Mahāvīra speaks here – the *utsarpiṇī* and *avasarpiṇī*, respectively – are periods of increasingly good and bad qualities in the cosmos, each of which characterizes half of a *kalpa*, or cosmic epoch. See P. S. Jaini 1979, 30–32.) Similarly, from the perspective of intrinsic qualities, the soul is eternal. 'It did not cease to exist any time.' From the perspective of its ever-changing, karmically determined experiences, its rebirths in many forms, it is non-eternal. The vision of the omniscient one encompasses all these perspectives.

Metaphysical foundations of relativity in Umāsvāti's *Tattvārtha Sūtra*

The *Tattvārtha Sūtra* bears the distinction of being authoritative for both major Jaina sects: Śvetāmbaras and Digambaras. It is attributed to Umāsvāti, who lived between the second and fifth centuries of the Common Era. The *Tattvārtha Sūtra* systematizes concepts found throughout Śvetāmbara and Digambara canonical literature, and has come to define the worldview shared by all practicing Jains. Most relevant to the Jaina philosophy of relativity are this text's systematizations of the concepts of existence and *naya*. Existence, as already mentioned, is characterized by 'Arising, passing away, and continuity' (*Tattvārtha Sūtra* 5:29). The importance of this formula for the Jaina tradition has to do with the character of the soul, or *jīva*, and the process of its liberation. This formula contrasts with those taught in various Brāhmaṇical traditions, which tend to affirm ontologies of substance, and in Buddhism, which affirms radical impermanence.

Jainism affirms the coexistence of permanence and impermanence, identity and difference, in the nature of the *jīva*; for the *jīva* is held to be, in one sense, permanent–eternally possessing infinite bliss, energy, perception and knowledge, but in yet another sense, impermanent, inasmuch as its karmic accretions are in a state of constant flux. The pluralistic character of reality that Jainism affirms – its claim that a variety of entities constitute the world and that these entities have a variety of aspects – gives rise to the variety of perspectives from which all issues can be addressed. Though it is not yet called this in the *Tattvārtha Sūtra*, this conception of reality is essentially *anekāntavāda*.

Nayas are philosophical perspectives from which a particular topic can be viewed and that determine the conclusions that can validly be reached about it. Umāsvāti's later commentators see the *nayas* as partial views collectively constitute a valid cognition, or *pramāṇa* (Tatia 1994, 8). Umāsvāti lists them as seven. However, several variants of this concept are expressed in Jaina thought, including one that lists *nayas* as two in number, and one that sees them as potentially infinite. Each of these approaches plays a role in Jaina thought on the relativity of perspectives.

Mundane and ultimate perspectives: Kundakunda's 'two truths'

The idea of *nayas* as two in number is associated with Kundakunda, who may have lived around the same time as Umāsvāt (Johnson 1995, 91–97). Kundakunda distinguishes between the *vyavahāranaya*, or 'mundane perspective,' and the *niścayanaya*: the 'ultimate' or 'certain perspective.' To understand the distinction between these two perspectives, recall the complex nature of the *jīva*. It has an unchanging aspect, with intrinsic qualities, like infinite bliss, energy, and consciousness, and a constantly changing aspect, including its embodiment in various forms and its experiences of emotive and cognitive states, release from which is the ultimate goal of the Jaina path.

Kundakunda takes the distinction between these aspects of the *jīva* as his point of departure. His mundane perspective is the less reliable of the two: the karmically determined perspective through which one sees reality as arising and passing away. It is the perspective of 'normal' persons, who have not yet realized the true nature of the soul. Such persons misunderstand the true nature of reality, mistaking extraneous, karmically determined activity for soul activity (*Samayasāra* 111–112; trans. J. L. Jaini 1930). The soul, however, does not actually *do* anything. All apparent action is due to the workings of karma.

The ultimate perspective perceives the soul in its intrinsic, unchanging nature: as blissful, energetic, perceptive, and omniscient. This, according to Kundakunda, is the perspective the Jaina aspirant strives to cultivate. The *vyavahāranaya* is deluded and must finally be superseded. The understanding of reality it yields is relative and uncertain. The *niścayanaya* reveals things as they truly are (*Samayasāra* 13). At first glance, Kundakunda's approach appears at odds with the system of *nayas* enumerated by Umāsvāti: partial and equally valid perspectives collectively constituting valid cognition. But Kundakunda's two *nayas* are starkly contrasted: one inadequate and relative, the other certain and absolute.

The Jaina doctrines of relativity, however, do presuppose an absolute perspective from which affirmations of relativity can be made. Close analysis of Kundakunda's two *nayas* reveals that they are not directly comparable to the *nayas* listed by Umāsvāti. The word *naya* is used by Kundakunda in another way. Kundakunda's *nayas* refer to the absolute and relative perspectives taken as totalities; but Umāsvāti's list refers to views available *within* the perspective of relativity. The differences between Kundakunda's version of *nayavāda* and that of Umāsvāti thus become a verbal issue. The compatibility of Kundakunda's and Umāsvāti's approaches can be illustrated schematically:

Kundakunda's position		**Umāsvāti's position**
niścayanaya	*corresponds to:*	*kevalajñāna/the absolute perspective of a Jina*
vyavahāranaya	*corresponds to:*	*The seven nayas taken collectively as a pramāṇa*

Kundakunda's view constitutes the strongest insistence found in Jaina philosophy on the importance of the affirmation of an absolute as foundational to the relativity of all perspectives – thus helping to refute the notion that Jainism represents a form of relativism in the contemporary sense – a view that the Jains call *anābhigrahika*, having no 'navel' or center.[4]

Relativity as the integration of contraries: Siddhasena and Samantabhadra

The fifth-century CE Jaina thinker, Siddhasena Divākara, like Umāsvāti, is claimed as an authority by Śvetāmbara and Digambara Jains (P. S. Jaini 1979, 83). His major contribution to the Jaina doctrines of relativity can be found in his *Sanmatitarka*, or 'Logic of the True Doctrine,' in which he divides Umāsvāti's seven *nayas* into two categories: those which affirm the substantiality of existence and those which affirm its impermanent, changing aspects. In this text, Siddhasena affirms that substantiality and modality, permanence and impermanence, identity and difference, are all necessary elements in an adequate account of reality. As one may recall, this understanding has its origins in Jaina beliefs about the nature of soul as having a permanent, intrinsic character while simultaneously undergoing a series of constantly changing states. With Siddhasena, this understanding of reality as characterized by a variety of seemingly contrary aspects becomes the matrix in terms of which Jaina thinkers assess all rival philosophical claims.

Two innovations introduced by Siddhasena are, first, to affirm that the number of *nayas* is potentially limitless. He uses his distinction between substance and change perspectives to define two poles between which views exist on a spectrum and are ranked in terms of their bent toward one or another side, with the Jaina position firmly in the middle. Second, he identifies the *nayas* on this spectrum with the positions of various schools of thought, setting the stage for what would become the standard Jaina criticism of alternative views as one-sided. He also defines the criterion by which the validity of the use of a *naya* should be assessed as the extent to which that usage is in conformity with Jaina doctrine – an approach to otherness known as *inclusivism* (*Sanmatitarka* 3:46–49). (On inclusivism, see Halbfass 1988, 403–418.)

Siddhasena's project is taken up and further elaborated by Samantabhadra, a fifth-century Digambara author. As K. K. Dixit writes:

> Samantabhadra had a clear consciousness of what constitutes the central contention of *Anekāntavāda*, viz. that a thing must be characterised by two mutually contradictory features at one and the same time. He also realised that the doctrine was applicable rather universally … that taking any thing and any feature at random it could be shown that this thing is characterised by this feature as also by the concerned contradictory feature.
>
> (Dixit 1971, 136)

This is what Samantabhadra does in his *Āptamīmāṃsā*, 'An Examination of the Authoritative Teacher.' He applies Siddhasena's concept of reality as involving contrary attributes to the resolution, through synthesis, of a variety of philosophical topics: being and non-being, permanence and impermanence, identity and difference, and so on. It is in this text that Samantabhadra introduces the sevenfold perspective, or *saptabhaṅginaya*, identified with the doctrine of conditional predication, or *syādvāda*, according to which a truth-claim has seven values, depending on the perspective from which it is asserted:

1 A claim is, in one sense, true.
2 A claim is, in another sense, false.
3 A claims is, in another sense, both true and false.
4 The truth of a claim is, in another sense, inexpressible.
5 A claim is, in another sense, both true and its truth is inexpressible.
6 A claim is, in another sense, both false and its truth inexpressible.
7 A claim is, in another sense, both true and false and its truth is inexpressible.

Haribhadra and the diversity of *yogas*

The eighth-century Śvetāmbara monk and scholar, Haribhadrasūri, continued the trend of evaluating rival schools of thought as teaching only partial truth in such works as his *Anekāntajayapaṭāka* ('Victory-Flag of Relativity'). His work as a whole, though, is noteworthy for emphasizing not the inferior, *partial* truth of diverse views, but the fact that they are true, seeking to interpret other views as charitably as possible.[5] 'Through his extensive writings, Haribhadra demonstrates his commitment to understand and respect the views of others, while maintaining his commitment to the core Jain beliefs' (Chapple 2003, 148). In his *Yogadṛṣṭisamuccaya*, or 'Collection of Views on Yoga,' Haribhadra argues that spiritual liberation is one, but is described differently by the great masters of various traditions in order to meet the needs of their disciples and the times in which they lived. The proper attitude, therefore, to hold toward all the great founders of the various paths to liberation, or *yogas*, is veneration and respect. Disputation with rival schools is to be avoided as non-conducive to the supreme and common goal of *mokṣa* or *nirvāṇa*.

Haribhadra's approach is striking both because it was fairly exceptional during his time, the classical period being marked by extensive polemic on the part of all schools, and because of the extent to which it suggests modern ideals of pluralism and tolerance:[6]

> The highest essence of going beyond *saṃsāra* is … *nirvāṇa*. The wisdom gained from discipline is singular in essence, though heard of in different ways. 'Eternal Śiva, Highest Brahman, Accomplished Soul, Suchness': With these words one refers to it, though the meaning is one in all the various forms.
> (*Yogadṛṣṭisamuccaya* 129–130; trans. Chapple 2003, 131)

This is similar to sentiments expressed by modern Hindu figures like Ramakrishna and Mahatma Gandhi, and Western religious pluralists influenced by them, such as John Hick: that truth is one, although known by many names and through many paths.[7]

Haribhadra identifies the ultimate goals of the various paths known to him – Hindu, Jaina, and Buddhist – as one. This is made possible by the fact that, despite the differences among these traditions, they describe the ultimate goal in ways that share certain traits: freedom from suffering, karma, rebirth, and so on (*Yogadṛṣṭisamuccaya*, verse 131; p. 132). Why do their teachings vary? This is due to the needs and capacities of their adherents (ibid., verse 134; p. 132). And if the founders of various traditions are enlightened beings, those who are not enlightened, but who rely on limited experience and reason, are not in a position to dispute their teachings (ibid., verses 141–147; pp. 134–135). Philosophical polemic is not a spiritually fruitful activity.

Though atypical, Haribhadra was not alone among pre-modern Jaina thinkers in his efforts to present other views as fairly as possible. Jains produced many doxographies, or compendia of the views of different traditions. The distinctive trait of these doxographies is their tendency to depict Jainism as one tradition among many, and to explain the views of other schools of thought with little or no polemical distortion (Folkert 1993, 341–409). This need not be seen as following from the Jaina philosophy of relativity; but it is certainly consistent with it.

Modern interpretations and contemporary relevance

In the modern period, prominent Jaina leaders like Śrīmad Rājacandra, Acharya Tulsi, Acharya Mahapragya, and Gurudev Chitrabhanu have promoted the more liberal interpretation of the doctrines of relativity as an authentic Jaina understanding, consistent with the ideal of nonviolence in thought, word, and deed. Relativity as an expression of religious pluralism has also attracted non-Jains, such as Mohandas K. Gandhi, who cites *anekāntavāda* and *syādvāda* as important influences upon his intellectual and spiritual development (Gandhi 1981, 30). The contemporary relevance of the Jaina doctrines of relativity lies with the way in which they embrace multiple perspectives while showing that pluralism follows logically from a specific view of reality. Pluralism is thus not only a pleasant, politically correct sentiment. It is a valid response to the real epistemic conundrum posed by the diversity of worldviews. In an era of intensified strife among adherents of various worldviews, religious and secular, the need for a 'deep religious pluralism' that takes difference seriously is clear (see Griffin 2005). The Jaina doctrines of relatively are a step in this direction.

Notes

1 Portions of this chapter are adapted with due permission from ch. 5 of Long 2009.

2 The earliest extant account of this story can be found the Pāli canonical literature of Theravāda Buddhism (*Udāna* 6.4:66–69).

3 A. B. Dhruva coined this term in 1933, and the idea behind it quickly came to be conventional wisdom among scholars of Jaina philosophy. See Cort 2000.

4 Dundas characterizes *anābhigrahika* as 'indiscriminate attachment to all views as being true' and 'a kind of misconceived relativism.' See Dundas 2004, 132.

5 A forthcoming work by Christopher Chapple suggests that there were actually two Haribhadras. Personal communication.

6 For discussion of the wide use of the Jaina doctrine of *anekāntavāda* and aligned *dharma/dhamma* principles in the promotion of toleration, see Bilimoria 2018.

7 It is also reminiscent of the ancient quotation from the *Ṛg Veda*, albeit one highly popular among modern religious pluralists, *Ekaṃ sat bahuḍha viprā vadanti*. 'Truth is one, but the wise speak of it in various ways' (*Ṛg Veda* 1.164:46c).

References

Bilimoria, P. 2018. "The Limits of Intolerance: A Comparative Reflection on India's Experiment with Tolerance." In Vicky Spencer (ed.) *Toleration in Comparative Perspective*. New York: Lexington Press, 219–245.

Chapple, Christopher Key. 2003. *Reconciling Yogas: Haribhadra's Collection of Views on Yoga*. Albany: State University of New York Press.

Cort, John. 2000. "'Intellectual *Ahiṃsā*' Revisited: Jain Tolerance and Intolerance of Others." *Philosophy East and West* 50(3): 324–347.

Dixit, Krishna Kumar. 1971. *Jaina Ontology*. Ahmedabad: LD Institute of Indology.

Dundas, Paul. 2004. "Beyond Anekāntavāda: A Jain Approach to Religious Tolerance." In Tara Sethia (ed.) *Ahiṃsā, Anekānta and Jainism*. Delhi: Motilal Banarsidass, 123–136.

Folkert, Kendall W. 1993. *Scripture and Community: Collected Essays on the Jains*. Atlanta, GA: Scholars Press.

Gandhi, Mohandas K. 1981. *Young India: 1919–1931*, vol. 8: 1926. Ahmedabad: Navajivan Publishing House.

Griffin, David Ray. 2005. *Deep Religious Pluralism*. Louisville, KY: Westminster John Knox Press.

Halbfass, Wilhelm. 1988. *India and Europe: An Essay in Understanding*. Albany: State University of New York Press.

Jaini, J. L. (Trans.). 1930. *Samayasāra (The Soul-Essence)*. Lucknow: The Central Jaina Publishing House.

Jaini, Padmanabh S. 1979. *The Jaina Path of Purification*. Delhi: Motilal Banarsidass.

Johnson, W. J. 1995. *Harmless Souls: Karmic Bondage and Religious Change in Early Jainism with Special Reference to Umāsvāti and Kundakunda*. Delhi: Motilal Banarsidass.

Long, Jeffery D. 2009. *Jainism: An Introduction*. London: I.B.Tauris.

Matilal, Bimal K. 1981. *The Central Philosophy of Jainism: Anekāntavāda*. Ahmedabad: LD Institute of Indology.

Mookerjee, Satkari. 1978. *The Jaina Philosophy of Non-Absolutism: A Critical Study of Anekāntavāda*. Delhi: Motilal Banarsidass.

Tatia, Nathmal. (Trans.). 1994. *That Which Is: Tattvārtha Sūtra*. San Francisco: HarperCollins.

Chapter 40
JAINA ETHICS AND MORAL PHILOSOPHY

Christopher Key Chapple

Moral philosophy in context

Moral philosophy concerns itself with decision-making. Knowing what is innately or culturally correct requires a process of acculturation as well as the cultivation of discernment. A moral person is shaped by many forces, including parental influence, the process of education which may or may not include religious instruction, and examples set by others.

The nature of human goodness or shortcomings thereof have been debated for centuries. In the Christian world, St. Paul and St. Augustine, and Martin Luther tended to emphasize the need for transcendent redemption in order to attain goodness. Pelagius and the early fathers of the Orthodox Church as well as the Buddha, Mahāvīra, and Mencius proclaimed that the original human state carries innate worthiness that with some encouragement can blossom into a state of human perfection. In this chapter we will investigate the Jaina position in regard to ethical behavior which, in this tradition, builds upon an essentially spiritualized ontology.

In the Jewish, Christian, and Islamic monotheistic prophetic traditions, the moral code dates back to the time of Moses. The first five books of the Bible, particularly Leviticus, set forth many rules to be observed, most famously the Ten Commandments. Both Christianity and Islam build upon these rules, with Jesus suggesting that they be practiced even more intensely, and Islam suggesting that these rules be applied for the uplift of all people. The Jewish and Islamic traditions even today may be characterized as emphasizing orthopraxy more than orthodoxy: what one does in the world carries more weight than what one thinks or believes. St. Paul, St. Augustine, and Martin Luther found justification through faith and found good works alone insufficient for redemption. Through petitionary prayer, the postulant requests assistance from the transcendent creator God to resist evil and find the inner strength to conform to the moral code.

The moral code within the monotheistic faiths requires obedience to God, beginning with the command that "You shall no other gods before me" (Exodus 20:3). From this beginning point, these faiths are most concerned with the relationship between the human realm and the transcendent. Though nature provides many metaphors for this relationship, concern for nature extends primarily to usage for agricultural purposes, with Leviticus suggesting best practices for the maturing of fruit trees (19:3) and allowing land to go fallow for purposes of rejuvenation periodically (25:1–7). Intimacy with land or other non-human beings for these traditions seems to have ended with the expulsion of Adam and Eve from the Garden (Genesis 3). Land and animals became utilities for the furtherance of human purposes, seen as soil and meat.

The Jaina approach to moral philosophy rests on premises radically different from those presented in the prophetic monotheisms and radically different from the views held by the sister faiths of Hinduism and Buddhism. Rather than assenting to the notion that the world was created by a benevolent presiding deity, Jainism holds that the world has always been present and will exist forevermore. Rather than following an externally imposed moral code, practitioners of the Jaina faith are taught the benefits of self-initiated virtuous action to be performed not for the sake of sheer obedience but for the purposes of self-improvement and purification. In contrast to Hinduism, Jainism does not advocate sacrificial activity such as the killing of animals to propitiate wrathful deities. Jainism does not posit an underlying unifying state of consciousness such as Brahman but insists upon the individual integrity of each and every soul, from beginningless time into an infinite future. Unlike Buddhism, Jainism posits the reality of a Self or Soul that holds the potential to attain its unique state of freedom. Buddhism teaches emptiness of self and other; Jainism teaches about a universe filled with innumerable living souls.

Jaina physics and metaphysics

The Jaina approach to the natural world is simultaneously respectful and cautious, and above all driven by moral concerns. First, according to Jaina ontology, the world is suffused with life forces (*jīva*) that merit protection. Hence, the lives contained in particles of earth, drops of water, rays of light, gusts of wind, as well as microorganisms, plants, and animals must be acknowledged and, to the greatest extent possible, not harmed. Each has entered its particular form due to the materiality of karma. One must exert caution because each harmful action causes the karma surrounding one's own soul to thicken and darken, obscuring the radiant consciousness of the soul and blocking its ascent to freedom. The Jaina universe thus conceived becomes a moral universe. In order to advance toward freedom, one must develop impeccable adherence to a moral code in order to purge all impedimentary karmas.

Physics and metaphysics, matter and spirit stand intertwined in the Jaina worldview. The tradition posits only four forces that do not possess life: matter or *pudgala* which can manifest as karma, time, space, and movement. Aside from these, all beings, including elemental realities and plants, possess consciousness, energy, and an innate state of bliss. The following passage from the *Ācārāṅga Sūtra*, the oldest extant Jaina text (c. 350 BCE), gives a sense of how the Jainas regard life to pervade all aspects of the natural world:

> As the nature of (human beings) is to be born and grow old, so is the nature of plants is to be born and grow old .... As (humans) fall sick when cut, also that (tree) falls sick when cut; as (the human) needs food, so that (plant) needs food; as the (human) will decay, so that (plant) will decay; as the human is not eternal, so that (plant) is not eternal .... As this is changing, so that is changing. One who injures plants does not comprehend and renounce sinful acts. The one who does not injure plants comprehends and renounces sinful acts. Knowing (those plants), a wise person would not act sinfully toward plants, nor cause others to act so, nor allow others to do so. The who knows the causes of sin relating to plants is called a reward-knowing sage.
>
> (*Ācārāṅga Sūtra* I:1.5.6–7, Jacobi 1968, 10–11)

This theory of plants accords with what Sir James Frazer observed in *The Golden Bough*. He wrote that for the early Austrians, "the tree feels the cut not less than a wounded man his hurt" (Frazer 1994, 113). David Haberman has written about the affection for trees felt in Varanasi, where he notes that the sentiment can be extended to "tree worship worldwide: trees have not only been commonly thought of as animate beings but also as powerful divine beings who when approached in a respectful manner offer in return life-enhancing benefits to human beings" (Haberman 2013, 57). In the Jaina context, the divinity of the tree would envision the future possibility that the tree, which is divine like all other souls, might take human birth and enter the path toward freedom from all karmic constraints.

In the coding of a pan-ethical universe, Jainism, particularly in the *Tattvārthasūtra* (fifth century CE) of Umāsvāti, each of the life forms stands within a hierarchy of ascent from elemental beings, microbes, and plants, said to possess the sense of touch; worms, which add the sense of taste; crawling bugs which add smell; flying insects which add sight; and the array of mammals, reptiles, fish, and amphibians who can also hear and think. Life constantly moves from one form to the next. A virtuous human may even take birth in a heavenly realm, while a person of dissipation may endure torture in one of the seven hells. The nature of one's next birth depends upon action performed in the immediate past body, implying that even microorganisms exert some degree of touch in terms of whom and why they make contact with other forms of life. The human birth stands supreme, being the only domain through which one can perform the necessary karmic purgations to attain freedom, a state at the edge of the universe untouched by the effects of karma.

Jaina vows as moral foundation

This coded universe carries a strong message: regardless of one's station in life, choice by each and every individual determines future circumstance. If one has earned the good fortune of human birth, a golden opportunity looms: to consciously and purposively commit oneself to the spiritual path of pursuing a life shaped by religiously inspired vows. These vows, applicable to both laypersons and monastics but in varying degrees of intensity, include a set of five greater vows (*mahāvrata*) and a set of twelve lesser vows (*anuvrata*). The *Ācārāṅga Sūtra* (AS) lists five forms of intensity for each of the five great vows, summarized as follows: In the observance of nonviolence (*ahiṃsā*), a monk (*nirgrantha*) must be "careful in his walk"; guard against any thought that "produces cutting or splitting or division and dissension, quarrels, faults, and pains, injures living beings, or kills creatures"; not engage in speech that is "sinful and blamable"; be "careful in lying down his utensils of begging" so as to not "hurt or displace or injure or kill all sorts of living beings," and must not "eat or drink without inspecting his food and drink" for the same reason (AS II:15.i.1–5, Jacobi 1968, 203–204).

The second vow, holding to truth (*satya*), requires the five following qualifications: speaking only after deliberation, not speaking from a place of anger, not speaking out of greed, not speaking due to fear, and not speaking for the purpose of ridicule. The third vow, not stealing (*asteya*), entails the pronouncement that "I shall neither take myself what is not given nor cause others to take it, nor consent to their taking it" (AS II.15.iii.). Because a monk's livelihood depends upon gathering alms, five further qualifications are given: thoughtfulness about where to ask for food, receipt of permission to do so from one's supervisory director, moving onto a new place after a fixed period of time in order to not become a burden, always asking permission to visit a new place, and consulting with other monks about the duration of stay.

The third vow involves restraint from sexual thought and activity. Acknowledging the range of ways in which sexual desire can manifest, the *Ācārāṅga Sūtra* proclaims: "I renounce all sexual pleasures, either with gods or humans or animals" (AS II.15.iv). The five clauses include to "not continually discuss topics relating to women," to "not regard and contemplate the lovely forms of women," to "not recall to mind the pleasures and amusements he formerly had with women," to "not eat and drink too much," and, to make certain that all options are covered, to "not occupy a bed or couch with women or animals or eunuchs" (AS II.15.iv).

The fifth vow, nonpossession (*aparigraha*), requires the monk or nun to renounce all attachments. The basic monastic vows restrict the postulant to a bare minimum of possessions, generally a change of robes, a begging bowl, and small satchel for carrying books for members of the Śvetāmbara order, and for male members of Digambara communities, no clothes, only a begging bowl and satchel. However, the *Ācārāṅga Sūtra* mandates that the senses must be controlled in each of five expressions. One must vow to "not be attached to, nor delighted with, nor desiring of, nor infatuated by, nor covetous of, nor disturbed by the agreeable or disagreeable sounds" (AS II.15.v). The text goes on to say that "If it is impossible not to hear sounds which reach the ear, the mendicant should avoid love or hate originated by them." The same is said of seeing, that if one "sees agreeable and disagreeable forms or colors, one should not be attached." This formula repeats for smelling, tasting, and touching.

The vow-based morality of the monks is somewhat lighter when reinterpreted for lay Jainas. For instance, Muni Kuśalcandravijay states, as summarized by John Cort, a layperson's adaptation of nonviolence would include "A layperson should not overwork either animals or people .... A layperson should not let people and animals in one's care go hungry" (Cort 2001, 27). Similarly, a Jaina business person is advised not to tell lies (*satya*), to not avoid taxes (*asteya*), to be faithful in marriage and avoid "ardent gazing or lewd gestures" (*brahmācārya*, ibid., 28), and to avoid attachment to one's wealth "limiting either the value of various types of possessions or all of one's possessions in total" (Cort 2001, 28). To these five basic vows the layperson adds three vows to restrict activity and four additional vows to undertake spiritual practices. The restrictions of activity include "restricting the geographical limits within which one travels," "restricting what one uses and consumes," and "restricting one's activities, particularly one's occupation" (ibid., 27). This last vow governs suitable professions, with the traditional occupations including merchant, artisan, publisher, jeweler, and so forth, all of which avoid direct harm to complex life forms.

The four spiritual vows include undertaking a daily forty-eight-minute meditation, periodic stricter restriction prohibiting travel, occasional days of temporary mendicancy, and making regular donations to monastic communities. All these activities are undertaken within the context of the three moral jewels of the Jaina faith: right outlook, right knowledge, and right action. The moral life begins with outlook and knowledge, from which proceeds moral action. Nine principal beliefs characterize the Jaina view of reality, summarized from the *Tattvārthasūtra* as follows:

1 multiple forms of life forces (*jīva*)
2 four non-living forces (*ajīva*): matter/karma, time, space, movement
3 influx of karma adhering to the life force (*āsrava*)
4 bondage of the soul by karma (*bandha*)
5 auspicious forms of karma (*puṇya*)
6 inauspicious forms of karma (*pāpa*)
7 stopping the influx (*saṃvara*) through adherence to vows
8 sloughing off karma (*nirjarā*)
9 liberation/freedom (*mokṣa/nirvāṇa/kevala*).

By analyzing activity in light of these categories, one applies knowledge leading to propitious action. The moral life, while essentially teleological, carries benefits in the realm of day to day living, as will be suggested in the examples provided below.

Moral conscience in Indian history

The influence of Jaina activists in the public sphere has been disproportionate to their numbers throughout Indian history. From earliest recorded times, they have campaigned (along with the Buddhists) against the violent Brāhmaṇical rituals that involve animal sacrifice, with some success. The Jainas became particularly influential during the period of approximately 700 to 1200 in two kingdoms, Karnataka in the south and Gujarat in the west. The Digambara community influenced legislation for a time in the south. King Kumarapala of Gujarat (ruled 1143–1175 CE) converted to Jainism under the tutelage of the great scholar and Śvetāmbara monk Hemacandra (1089–1172). Kumarapala enacted Jaina-friendly legislation and public work projects including temple construction. The Jainas were also somewhat influential at the Mughal court. In 1587, the Śvetāmbara Jaina teacher Hiravijaya Suri (1527–95 CE) so impressed Emperor Akbar that a decree was issued banning the slaughter of animals in the empire during the week-long Jaina celebration of Paryusan, a time of fasting and forgiveness and reconciliation held every September (Dundas 1992, 126). In the main, however, the Jaina community has been a small minority throughout the history of the subcontinent, currently number somewhere between 4 and 6 million, less than half of 1 percent of the population. Nonetheless, two twentieth-century Jaina figures made significant contributions to moral philosophy within public life in India: Acarya Tulsi (1914–1997) and L. M. Singhvi (1931–2007).

Acarya Tulsi

Acarya Tulsi was born into a large family in Ladnun, Rajasthan, during British colonial rule. He entered the Śvetāmbara Terapanthi order of Jaina monks at the age of 11 after meeting Acarya Kalugani, its eighth leader. This movement, established by Acarya Bhikshu in the eighteenth century, started as a more austere branch of the Sthānakavāsī Śvetāmbaras, renowned for their eschewal of all images that are generally used as part of worship. The year of separation came in 1759 when Bhikshu broke all formal ties, bringing six fellow monks with him to establish a new self-initiated order (Dundas 1992, 219). In many ways, this proved to be a Protestant movement, with Bhikshu decrying the notion that anyone can earn merit through donation. Only strict adherence to the rules of nonviolence can guarantee spiritual progress. From the onset, the Terapanthi pioneered education for Jaina nuns, who previously were not given the opportunity for study afforded to men.

Tulsi was elevated to leadership of the order at the age of 22 and presided for many decades over a dynamic period of growth. The numbers of monks, nuns, and lay followers increased within the Terapanthi community. A new order of Samanis was established, allowing women in particular to postpone their final vows. This has allowed the movement to be of service in particular to the growing number of diaspora Jainas. Samanis have established learning and meditation centers in London, Florida, New Jersey, and Texas. Acarya Tulsi established a learning institute on a hundred-acre campus in his home town of Ladnun in 1970, which achieved status as a deemed university in 1991.

Whereas Acarya Tulsi's successor Acarya Mahapragya focused on the development of a spiritual practice known as Preksha Meditation, Tulsi turned his attention in 1949 toward a campaign known as the Anuvrat Movement. He saw that newly independent India needed a moral compass for guidance and he distilled and reinterpreted the standard Jaina precepts for contemporary times. Though carrying no legislative weight, they remain a talking point for the process of making moral decisions and have influenced monastic and lay leaders within the Terapanthi community. The vows or virtuous precepts are eleven in number, with explanatory subdivisions:

1 I will not deliberately kill any innocent creature (includes suicide and feticide).
2 I will not attack anyone (non-support of aggression; advocacy of disarmament).

3 I will not take part in violent agitation or any destructive activity.
4 I believe in human unity (no discrimination allowed based on color, race, gender, caste).
5 I will practice unstinting tolerance (not engage in sectarian violence).
6 I will be honest in business and general behavior (commit no harm or deception).
7 I will practice continence and limit material possessions.
8 I will not apply unethical means in elections.
9 I will not encourage or practice evil social customs.
10 I will lead a life free from addiction (no alcohol, drugs, tobacco).
11 I will strive to minimize environmental pollution (no cutting of trees; no wastage of water).

Simplified versions were prepared over a number of years for students, teachers, business people, officers, employees, voters, and for those interested in spiritual practice. These *anuvrats* function similarly to the Quaker queries and the Jesuit Examen in that they prompt a reckoning with one's conscience in a systematic fashion. Though perhaps originally intended as a social movement with broad impact, they have served to sharpen attention within the Terapanthi community worldwide to the wider implications of Jaina moral teachings.

Some of the suggested precepts may seem timeless, such as the appeal against suicide, abortion, dishonest business dealings, and drug abuse. Others are timely and particular to India's emergence into modernity, including the vows of non-discrimination, religious tolerance, and promotion of ethical elections. The last one has proven to be quite prophetic, with India's staggering levels of environmental pollution. Years later, this final *anuvrat* was expanded into a larger document by L. M. Singhvi, as will be explored below.

Appeals for the development of moral conscience often prove to be an abstraction at best or a string of platitudes at worst. However, certain documents such as the Universal Declaration of Human Rights issued by the United Nations on December 10, 1948 became the cornerstone of United States foreign policy during the presidency of Jimmy Carter and helped prompt a discussion that still remains vital. The *anuvrat* declaration still plays an active role in shaping conversations within the Terapanthi community and has been particularly remembered at the many celebratory events associated with the birth centenary of Acarya Tulsi (2013–2014).

L. M. Singhvi

Member of a mixed Hindu–Jaina family, L. M. Singhvi rose to prominence in the fields of law and government. He served as High Commissioner (Ambassador) from India to Great Britain in the 1990s and as a member of India's Parliament for many years, in the Lok Sabha (Lower House of Representatives) from 1962 to 1967 and in the Rajya Sabha (Upper House; approx. Senate) from 1998 to 2004. He was tireless in his advocacy of Jaina causes. He presented the Jain Declaration on Nature to Prince Philip in 1990 on the occasion of Jainism's participation in the World Wildlife Fund Network on Conservation and Religion. It was reprinted in 2002 as the appendix to the book

Jainism and Ecology. The Declaration outlines the core principles of Jainism, reframing them as dialogue partners in the emerging discourse on religion and ecology.

The Declaration states that Jainism presents an ecological philosophy and consequently summarizes various aspects of its philosophy in light of its particular attention to nature. The first part discusses Jaina teachings on nonviolence, interdependence, recognition of multiple perspectives, emphasis on equanimity, and commitment to compassion, empathy, and charity. The second section provides a synopsis of Jaina biological categories as delineated earlier in this chapter. The third and final part highlights the Jain Code of Conduct as exemplary for bringing about environment justice. Key aspects include the restatement of the five Jaina vows as practical means for cultivating moral virtues (described earlier in this chapter), the history of Jaina kindness to animals, the Jaina advocacy of vegetarianism, the teachings on restraint and avoidance of waste, and finally, the value of charity in the tradition.

Decidedly more complex than Acarya Tulsi's eleven *anuvrats*, this Declaration demonstrates the philosophical commitment of the Jaina community not only to regard life but to advocate for sustaining and protecting life in all of its forms. By asserting the presence of conscious life within soil, rivers, fires, and wind as well as within the overly self-obsessed human realm, Jainism calls for an expansion of view, a broadening of horizon that can serve as an antidote to the damning anthropocentrism that has characterized most of human philosophical endeavor. When Singhvi writes about compassion and empathy, he intends not to limit one's scope to the merely human but to include all the animals and plants and the elements themselves.

Conclusion

This chapter began by contrasting the God-centered monotheistic faiths with the multivalent, multi-life Jaina perspective on the nature and purpose of the world. According to Jaina teachings, we live in a moral universe, governed by the laws of cause and effect. Moral agency requires paying attention and giving reverence to the natural world. Mahāvīra advocated the protection of trees, positing that any harm done to nature will immediate constrain and impede the soul. Adherents to the Jaina faith have produced a biological inquiry that reveals the inter-connectedness of all life forms. With this insight comes great moral obligation. Knowing that life depends upon other forms of life, the Jainas urge human beings to be careful and loving in all ways, and to never take more than what is absolutely needed, poignant lessons for today's world of over-consumption and rapacious use of resources. Through the moral voice of Jainism, all peoples can be reminded of the sanctity of life.

References

Chapple, Christopher Key. 1993. *Nonviolence to Animals, Earth, and Self in Asian Traditions*. Albany: State University of New York Press.

———. Ed. 2002/2004. *Jainism and Ecology: Nonviolence in the Web of Life*. Cambridge, MA: Harvard University Press; Delhi: Motilal Banarsidass.

Cort, John E. 2001. *Jains in the World: Religious Values and Ideology in India*. New York: Oxford University Press.

Dundas, Paul. 1992/2002. *The Jains*. London: Routledge.

Frazer, James George. 1994. *The Golden Bough: A History of Myth and Religion*. London: Chancellor Press. First published 1922.

Gandhi, S. L. Ed. 2000. *Acharya Tulsi: Fifty Years of Selfless Dedication*. Ladnun: Jain Vishva Bharati.

Haberman, David. 2013. *People Trees: Worship of Trees in Northern India*. New York: Oxford University Press.

Jacobi, Hermann. 1968. *Jaina Sutras in Two Parts. Part One: The Ākārāṅga Sūtra; The Kalpa Sūtra*. New York: Dover. First published 1884.

Jaini, Padmanabh S. 1979. *The Jaina Path of Purification*. Berkeley: University of California Press.

Mukhya Niyojika Sadhvi Vishrut Vibha. 2012. *Acharya Shree Tulsi: A Legend of Humanity*. New Delhi: Acharya Tulsi Janam Shatabdi Samaroh Samiti.

Tatia, Nathmal. Trans. 1994. *That Which Is Tattvārtha Sūtra, a Classic Jain Manual for Understanding the True Nature of Reality*. San Francisco: HarperCollins.

Chapter 41
TANTRA AND KASHMIRI ŚAIVISM

David Peter Lawrence

Introduction

The Pratyabhijñā school of nondual Kashmiri Śaivism, created by Utpaladeva (*c.* 900 – *c.* 950 CE) and Abhinavagupta (*c.* 950 – *c.* 1025 CE), was the most salient philosophical tradition to emerge from Hindu tantra. Issues important to scholars of broader Śaiva and tantric movements include the relations of religious conceptions of purity and transgression with power, divine gender and sexuality. The Pratyabhijñā, which is the chief focus of this chapter, is noteworthy for theorization on the relation of philosophical rationality and religion, the existence and nature of God, the epistemology and ontology of recognition, the semantics and syntax of agency and indexicals, philosophical psychology, and epistemic diversity.

Nondual Kashmiri Śaivism and the tantric quest for power

Asian and Western scholars have come to recognize that contemporary usages of the term "tantra" do not agree in extension with those of any premodern South Asian traditions. One relevant Sanskritic usage identifies as tantras a number of Hindu and Buddhist scriptures, and movements that adhere to those scriptures; however, it excludes other scriptures and movements with similar characteristics. Another widespread usage designates as tantra folk traditions of "sorcery." Since the nineteenth century a number of often highly sensationalized Western and Asian accounts have identified tantra on the basis of its real or imagined use of sexual rites.

Endeavoring to overcome confusions, scholars have converged towards using the term "tantra" to classify together religious movements on the basis of historical and thematic relations, regardless of their self-definitions. Probably the most distinctive feature of these movements, which began to flourish around the middle of the first millennium CE, is the pursuit of *power*, understood in Hindu traditions as in essence Śakti, the Goddess herself. Practitioners variously endeavor to identify with Śakti, to be ecstatically possessed by her, or to possess her. Practical manifestations of the realization of Śakti vary from limited magical proficiencies (*siddhis* or *vibhūtis*), through the sovereignty of kings, to the liberated saint's omnipotence of performing the divine cosmic acts.

Other features of tantra that may be understood as doctrinal and practical expressions of this quest for Śakti, include cosmogonic myths of the sexual union of Śakti with a male deity, associated with practices that recapitulate that union in contemplation or actual intercourse; circular diagrams (*maṇḍala*) and other theosophical symbolism of cosmogenesis and cosmocracy; empowered speech formulas (*mantra*); and syntheses of embodied enjoyment (*bhoga*) with spiritual practice (*yoga*) and liberation (*mokṣa*). Alexis Sanderson has illuminated the ways in which the tantric pursuit of powers transgresses upper-caste Hindu norms that delimit human agency for the sake of symbolic-ritual purity (*śuddhi*). Violating prescriptions regarding caste, sexuality, diet and death, many of the tantric rites were originally performed in cremation grounds.

What is called Kashmir Śaivism comprises a number of nondual tantric lineages, including varieties of Kaula, Krama, Trika, and Spanda. These must be distinguished from dualistic Śaivasiddhānta traditions that also flourished in medieval Kashmir. As may be surmised, a basic doctrinal position of the nondual Śaiva traditions is that the only reality is the God Śiva. These traditions appropriate the fundamental tantric principle of power, Śakti, within Śiva's metaphysical essence. Śiva is the *śaktimān*, the "possessor" of Śakti, including her within his androgynous nature as his integral power and consort. According to the predominant myth, Śiva divides himself from Śakti and then in sexual union emanates and controls the universe through her.

The basic pattern of nondual Śaiva practice, which also reflects the appropriation of Śāktism by Śaivism, is the *approach to Śiva through Śakti*. As the Śaiva scripture *Vijñānabhairava* proclaims, Śakti is Śiva's "door" or "face" (*mukha*). The adept pursues identification with the omnipotent Śiva by assuming his mythic agency, in a recapitulation of the emanation and control of the universe through Śakti. Thus in the usually patriarchal sexual ritual a man realizes himself as the possessor of Śakti immanent within his partner. More frequently, one realizes oneself as the possessor of Śakti through internalized contemplations of *maṇḍalas*, mantras, and theosophical and philosophical speculations.

Philosophical rationalization of tantric traditions

One of the crucial historical trends in early Kashmiri tantra was the traditions' efforts to assimilate to more established upper-caste Hindu orthopraxy. More radical practices were toned down and internalized, and the emphasis became more gnoseological and soteriological. A related development was the "rationalization" of nondual Śaivism through Sanskritic traditions of academic philosophical discourse. Nondual Śaivas began to consolidate their teachings in systematic manuals (*śāstras*) of doctrines and practices. Early milestones of this development were the ninth-century revelation to Vasugupta of the manual *Śiva Sūtra*, and the further systematization of its teachings by either Vasugupta or his disciple Kallaṭa in the *Spanda Kārikā*. These formed the foundation of the "Spanda system" of nondual Śaivism, known for its interpretation of Śakti as *spanda*, "cosmic pulsation."

The nondual Śaiva lineage called Trika ("Triadism," as adverting to triads of modalities of Śakti and cosmic levels) produced the first work of full-scale philosophical apologetics against rival schools of Hinduism and Buddhism. This was the *Śivadṛṣṭi*, "Cognition of Śiva," by Somānanda (c. 900 – c. 950 CE). Utpaladeva, a student of Somānanda, wrote a commentary on the *Śivadṛṣṭi*, the *Śivadṛṣṭivṛtti*. He additionally composed the foundational works of the Pratyabhijñā philosophy, which interpret and further the work of Somānanda with greater sophistication: the *Īśvarapratyabhijñākārikā*, "Verses on the Recognition of the Lord," and two commentaries on the *Verses*, the short *Īśvarapratyabhijñākārikāvṛtti*, and the more detailed *Īśvarapratyabhijñāvivṛti* (now fragmentary); and the subsidiary *Siddhitrayī*, "Three Proofs."

Abhinavagupta elaborated and augmented Utpaladeva's arguments in long commentaries, one directly on the *Verses*, the *Īśvarapratyabhijñāvimarśinī*; and the other on Utpaladeva's longer autocommentary, the *Īśvarapratyabhijñāvivṛtivimarśinī*. While those commentaries are of paramount importance, this thinker's greatest significance in the history of tantra is probably his effort, in his monumental *Tantrāloka* and numerous other works, to systematize and provide a critical philosophical structure to *non-philosophical* tantric theology. Abhinavagupta utilized Pratyabhijñā categories to interpret and organize the diverse aspects of Trika symbolism, doctrine, and practice, and synthesized under the rubric of this philosophically rationalized Trika an enormous range of symbolism and practice from Kaula, Krama, Spanda, and other Śaiva and Śākta traditions.

Abhinavagupta is also well known for his works on Sanskrit poetics, in which he interpreted aesthetic experience as homologous to, and practically approaching, the nondual Śaiva soteriological realization. The philosophical thought of Utpaladeva and Abhinavagupta came to have a great influence on tantric and devotional (*bhakti*) traditions throughout South Asia.

Purpose and methods of the Pratyabhijñā system

Belying Western dichotomies of religion (or mysticism) and reason, Utpaladeva and Abhinavagupta conceive the Pratyabhijñā simultaneously as a philosophical apologetics, structured according to Nyāya categories for publicly assessible discourse, and an internalized tantric ritual that may potentially lead "all humanity" to the soteriological *recognition* (*pratyabhijñā*) "I am Śiva." Even before actually describing their method, the Pratyabhijñā philosophers introduce considerations that dialectically *negate its efficacy*. As Śiva is a pure unity, there cannot ultimately be any dichotomy of the means (*upāya*) and the goal (*upeya*) of his recognition. The thinkers develop Upaniṣadic and Advaita Vedāntin conceptions of self-luminosity (*svaprakāśatva*) to explain his immediate, nondual evidence to himself. In the highest perspective, philosophy only removes the illusion that this is not the case. Furthermore, because Śiva is the sole, omnipotent cosmic actor, that removal through philosophy or any other means is ultimately accomplished by his grace.

Thus dialectically qualified, Utpaladeva and Abhinavagupta's chief *positive* description of the Pratyabhijñā method at one level follows the ritual pattern described above, that is, the "revealing of Śakti" (*śaktyāviṣkaraṇa*). However, they additionally frame Śakti as the *reason* of a classic Nyāya "inference for the sake of others" (*parārthānumāna*). According to the scholastic logic, the reason identifies a quality in the inferential subject, that is, "I," known to be invariably concomitant with the predicate, "Śiva." Thus I am Śiva because I have his quality, Śakti, the capacity of emanating and controlling the universe.

In technical discussions, Śakti is often divided into modalities that designate Śiva's emanatory power as operative in the particular spheres of explanation. The most encompassing of these are the Knowledge (*jñāna*) and Action (*kriyā*) Śaktis, invoked in fields roughly corresponding to epistemology and ontology.

Pratyabhijñā epistemology

The philosophers explain the realization they wish to convey as the *recognition*, "I am Śiva" in order to address debates on epistemology that were then current. The specific problems the writers address had been formulated by the Buddhist epistemology and logic school of Dignāga and Dharmakīrti, which contemporary interpreters have characterized as a species of phenomenalism akin to that of David Hume. According to this school, the foundation of knowledge is a series of momentary and discrete perceptual data (*svalakṣaṇa*). There are no grounds in those data for the recognitions of any enduring entities as identified by linguistic or conceptual interpretation (*vikalpa*). Over several centuries, the Buddhist logicians argued against many concepts that seemed commonsensical and were religiously significant to various Hindu schools, such as ideas of external objects, ordinary and ritual action, an enduring Self, God, and revelation.

The Pratyabhijñā philosophers' response to this problematic revolutionized earlier approaches, and may be characterized as a form of transcendental argumentation. Utpaladeva and Abhinavagupta interpret their central myth of Śiva's emanation and control of the universe through Śakti as itself an act of self-recognition (*ahampratyavamarśa*, *pratyabhijñā*). Furthermore, abjuring an agonistic stance Somānanda had taken toward Bhartṛhari, they equate Śiva's self-recognition (Śakti) with the principle of Supreme Speech (*parāvāk*), which they derive from the Grammarian; they thereby appropriate Bhartṛhari's explanation of creation as linguistic in nature. Thus the nondual Śaiva philosophers ascribe to recognition-Speech a primordial status, and affirm it *to constitute the very facts that the Buddhists say preclude it.* As ritual recapitulates myth, the Pratyabhijñā system endeavors to lead the student to participate in the recognition "I am Śiva," by demonstrating that all experiences and their contents are expressions of the recognition that "I am Śiva."

Utpaladeva's and Abhinavagupta's epistemology may best be illustrated by its approach to perceptual cognition. The Pratyabhijñā arguments on this subject may be divided into those centered around two sets of terms: *prakāśa*; and *vimarśa* and cognates such as *pratyavamarśa* and *parāmarśa*. Among the backgrounds to the concept of *prakāśa* are the aforementioned notion of self-luminosity and the Yogācāra Buddhist notion of self-consciousness (*svasaṃvedana*); it is an "illumination" or "bare subjective awareness" that validates each cognition, so that one knows that one knows. The thrust of the arguments about *prakāśa* is analogous to George Berkeley's thesis of idealism that *esse est percipi*. The Śaivas contend that, as no object is known without a universal validating awareness, this awareness actually constitutes all objects as its real but inseparable contents.

Vimarśa and its cognates have the significance of apprehension or judgment with a recognitive structure, as applying prepossessed linguistic interpretation to present items of experience, and may be glossed as "recognitive apprehension." Utpaladeva and Abhinavagupta's arguments centering on these terms develop earlier considerations of Bhartṛhari on the linguistic nature of experience. The philosophers refute the Buddhist contention that recognition is a contingent reaction to direct experience by claiming that it is integral or transcendental to all experience. Some considerations they adduce are: children must build upon a subtle, innate form of linguistic apprehension in their learning of conventional language; there must be a recognitive ordering of basic experiences of situations and movements in rapid behaviors; and a subtle application of language in all experiences is necessary for our ability to remember them.

The two phases of argument operate together. The idealistic *prakāśa* arguments make the recognition shown by the *vimarśa* arguments to be integral to all epistemic processes, *constitutive of them and their objects*. Moreover, according to the Śaivas, the recognition generating all things belongs to one subject. It must therefore be his self-recognition. As it is through the nondual subject's self-recognition that all phenomena are created, the Pratyabhijñā thinkers have ostensibly demonstrated their cosmogonic myth of Śiva's emanation through Śakti in terms of self-recognition. The student, by coming to see this self-recognition as the inner reality of all that is experienced, is led to full participation in it.

The author has previously compared the Pratyabhijñā theory of recognition with Western philosophical theologies of God's logos, "Word" or "reason." Aside from its Christian Trinitarian and incarnational aspects, the logos is an expression of God's subjectivity, often described as something like his self-recognition, through which he creates the universe. Whether described in terms of the Neoplatonic *nous*, the Aristotelian/Thomist divine intellect, Hegelian logic and phenomenology or theological appropriations of Heidegger, it thereby provides a ground for our interpretations of the world and the very underpinnings of our rationality.

Pratyabhijñā ontology: the grammar of omnipotence

Just as Utpaladeva and Abhinavagupta appropriate Bhartṛhari in equating self-recognition with Supreme Speech and thereby interpreting experience as linguistic in nature, they also follow Sanskrit grammatical and ritualistic traditions in interpreting being or existence (*sattā*), the generic referent of language, as *action* (*kriyā*). Following the account above, it is Śiva's mythic action through Śakti (self-recognition) that accounts ontologically for all things, and that is ritually reenacted by philosophical discourse.

Most illustrative of the Pratyabhijñā thinkers' approach to ontology is their explanation of Śiva's mythico-ritual action with a philosophical theory of *action syntax*. This pertains to the manner in which verbs expressing action relate to declined nouns referring to the concomitants of action (*kārakas*, described in the West in terms of grammatical cases). The author has previously compared Sanskrit speculations on this subject to Kenneth Burke's notion of a "grammar of motives," typifying divergent accounts of the generation of action, and characterized the distinctive Śaiva approach to it as a "mythico-ritual syntax of omnipotence."

Edwin Gerow and the author have separately argued that there is a tendency in many traditions of Hindu and Buddhist philosophy to denigrate the role of the agent (*kartṛ kāraka*) in the syntactic nexus. Among Hindu schools, this tendency appears to be strongest in Advaita Vedānta, while Buddhist philosophies negate the role of the agent in the syntax of dependent origination. This tendency seems to reflect not only the agent's bondage to karma in rebirth for Hindus and Buddhists but also its subordination to objective ritual behavior; pertaining to sacrifice, caste, life cycle, and so on in Brāhmaṇic orthopraxy.

Utpaladeva and Abhinavagupta develop a syntax of omnipotence by taking up and radicalizing earlier understandings of the positive, albeit delimited role of the agent, particularly from the Vyākaraṇa and Nyāya-Vaiśeṣika traditions. According to the Śaivas, all causal processes and things constituting the universe are synthesized and impelled by the agency of Śiva/the Self in his cosmic acts. The Self is *svatantra*, "self-determined," rather than *paratantra*, "other-determined," like all other things. The Śaivas ultimately reduce the entire action of existence to agency. As Abhinavagupta explains, "Being is the agency of the act of becoming, that is, the freedom characteristic of an agent regarding all actions."

This theory of universal syntactic agency is ritually axiomatic as well as mythical. Utpaladeva describes the Pratyabhijñā philosophy as leading to liberation through the contemplation of one's status as the agent of the universe. Abhinavagupta likewise explains that the aspirant's goal in ritual action is identification with Śiva as agent impelling all things indicated by other nouns, appropriately declined as nonagents, the ritual paraphernalia manipulated by the adept epitomizing all other cosmic entities.

Supplementing the Pratyabhijñā philosophy of action is theorization on the semantics and syntax of grammatical persons, gender, number, and verbal tenses. To briefly consider Abhinavagupta's approach to the first of these, the grammatical persons are the familiar triad – He/She/It/They (called in Sanskrit the "first person" and in English the "third person"), You (Sanskrit "middle person," English "second person"), and I/We (Sanskrit "final person," English "first person"). Abhinavagupta's treatment of grammatical persons is remarkable for ways in which it anticipates theorists such as Charles Peirce and Emile Benveniste on indexicals, although he has a very different view about the ultimate nature of the speech situation. Abhinavagupta acknowledges like contemporary thinkers that the three persons in ordinary discourse are defined by their mutual distinctions and are arbitrary in their reference. However, he also ranks them hierarchically. He affirms the privilege of I/We as indicating the enunciator of discourse, over the addressee You and the noninterlocutory "He/She/It," with an observation, anticipating Benveniste, about their degrees of extension. That is, You can include He/She/It/They and I/We can include You as well as He/She/It/They.

According to Abhinavagupta, the ranking of the three persons reflects the structure of emanation in a Trika Śaiva cosmological triad. That is, I as the enunciator of discourse corresponds to the omnipotent Self as Śiva, as the whole universe is ultimately My Supreme Speech. The addressee, You, is identified with Śakti according to the model of Śiva's self-revelatory dialogues with Śakti in the tantric scriptures. The noninterlocutory He/She/It represents the unenlightened human (*nara*) reduced to the condition of inert objects. The Self's foundational agency and act of Speech, with, as and through Śakti, constitutes all the limited circumstances of discourse, including all interlocutors and objects.

Abhinavagupta again prescribes a contemplation of return in which all forms of He/She/It are *personalized* as absorbed into You, Śakti. And I as cosmic discursive agent realize You to be my integral power and consort. The philosopher indicates in both his Pratyabhijñā and aesthetic writings that the same contemplative agenda should inform the hermeneutic *reception* of philosophy as well as poetry and drama. That is, I should identify with both what is stated in the philosophy and the universalized representations of the emotions of literary characters.

Philosophical psychology and ethics

Utpaladeva and Abhinavagupta articulate in their writings what may be described as a philosophical psychology. One of the principal terms they use to describe the higher, empowered identity recognized by the Śaiva practitioner is *pūrnāhaṃtā*, "perfect I-hood." For the Pratyabhijñā system and tantra informed by it, ordinary egoistic identity, described by such terms as "I-construction" (*ahaṃkāra*), "pride" or "self-conception" (*abhimāna*), "I-am-ness" (*asmitā*), and "I-hood" (*ahaṃtā*), is itself an immanent expression of God's identity. These traditions thus *do not advocate the surrender or sublation of such egoism, but rather its universalization or transfiguration into perfect I-hood.* Likewise in Abhinavagupta's interpretations of the sexual ritual as well as aesthetic experience, ordinary selfish pleasure must be transfigured into divine "self-enjoyment" (*svātmopabhoga*) or "self-relishing" (*svaviṣayāsvāda*).

Nondual Kashmir Śaivism correlates this psychological transformation with the realization of a new sense of one's body. Developing themes from earlier Brahmanism and tantra, the Śaivas equate the body of the God-realized saint with Śakti in all her cosmic manifestations. One empowered by the conviction that the universe is one's body is able even to move mountains as if by his or her own hands. A related model or metaphor used to account for the transformation of the adept's identity is reflection (*pratibimba*). Abhinavagupta interprets various means for identification with Śiva as contemplations that the emanated universe is a reflection of one's Śakti or self-recognition.

Such teachings have called to mind Western themes of *narcissism or self-love*. Sigmund Freud and later psychoanalysis have typically interpreted Indian and Western "mysticism," as well as "primitive magic," as pathological regressions to infantile narcissism. These interpretations invoke a problematic Orientalist dichotomy between modern Western "rationality" and Indian and premodern "mysticism." Also related are allegations of the self-absorbed, amoral, or immoral character of Asian mysticism.

To take a broader historical perspective on narcissism in particular, psychoanalysis continues a long legacy of Western moralistic interpretations of the self-love typified by the legendary character Narcissus, and the associated inability to love others. In addition, Western philosophy and theology since the Hellenistic period have frequently *ascribed a kind of self-love or narcissism to God*. Just as God recognizes himself through his creative logos, he also in a sense loves himself, creation likewise often being conceived as his reflection. Christians have often equated the human imitation of God in his self-love with original sin, while at the same time being inspired by this creative possibility in varieties of mysticism, Romanticism, and individualism. Heinz Kohut stands out among classic psychoanalytic theorists both for his greater sympathy toward religion, and for his formulation of an alternative psychoanalytic theory of mysticism as a healthy transformation of narcissistic energy, involving an empathic identification with all others, which he called "cosmic narcissism." The Indian psychoanalyst Sudhir Kakar has developed a related theory to describe creative and adaptive functions of such narcissism in the context of Indian family relationships.

The Śaiva philosophical psychology of the universalization of egoity suggests the possibility of a religious reinterpretation of the positive transformation of narcissism, as participation in, or assumption of, the self-satisfaction of a divine Self. Accordingly, the Śaivas articulate strong ethical concerns. Perhaps substantiating the linkage of cosmic narcissism with empathy, they affirm that the liberated person is occupied primarily with helping suffering creatures, and that it was with this motivation that they composed their philosophical works. Abhinavagupta also elaborates a long list of rules for Śaiva initiates, most of which are concerned with protecting and advancing the well-being of others.

Evolution and consciousness

A critical and constructive retrieval of Pratyabhijñā theories should be engaged with broad philosophical reflections on evolution and consciousness. The early twentieth-century Bengali thinker Sri Aurobindo endeavored to integrate what is basically a nondual tantric metaphysis with contemporary understandings of evolution and progress. An advancement of Aurobindo's agenda may perhaps be accomplished by a further appropriation of both the *śāstraic* inheritance in Kashmiri tantric philosophy and more up-to-date conceptions of evolution.

Over the last few decades, scholars such as Jesper Hoffmeyer and Terrence Deacon have developed Peircean philosophical approaches of pansemiotics and biosemiotics to deepen and broaden systems-theory analyses of the emergence of order within a thermodynamic context, and the consequent evolution of life and consciousness. Amidst the differences, these theories have some strong points of agreement with various theories of sacred speech, such as antecedent Western logos philosophies, Bhartṛhari, and the Pratyabhijñā, by identifying a subtly "linguistic" character of experience and experienced realities.

To mention a couple issues for engagement, for biosemiotics life as a whole, the life of species, and the life of individual organisms – as varieties of self-organizing systems – exercise forms of sign interpretation, or semiosis, in both their internal disposition and in their relations with broader informational and ecological contexts. As with Śaiva, Bhartṛharian, and related Indian theories, self-organizing life from the earliest and simplest systems through human consciousness has a kind of self-interpretative "narrative" character and thereby an incipient or actualized intentionality and agency. These new theories are largely naturalistic and agnostic about religion. Nevertheless, Hoffmeyer provides some support for Śaiva accounts of the recognition of universal first-person agency and egoity, in his contention that there is evidence in physical, cognitive, and cultural evolution of a teleology towards what he calls "semiotic freedom," that is, more semantically rich and practically efficacious interpretations of the world.

The neuroscientist Patrick McNamara has likewise shown that in varieties of "healthy" religious experience there is the amplification of what he describes as a higher executive function of the brain integrating all the others. As in the Śaiva accounts – and perhaps also reminiscent of C. G. Jung's notion of the Self archetype – religious experience involves a sort of decentering and reconfiguration around a higher sense of divine agency.

Approach to epistemic diversity

Medieval Kashmir was characterized by a remarkable ferment of cultural, religious, and philosophical diversity, and the Pratyabhijñā philosophers' reflections on epistemic divergence may be of great interest for current discussions. Anticipating contemporary hermeneutics, Utpaladeva and Abhinavagupta view perceptual and inferential claims (recognitive-linguistic apprehensions) as contingent upon traditions (*prasiddhi*, *āgama*). According to them, traditions likewise are diversified according to the various purposes and eligibilities of their adherents in different places and times. Cognitive claims are also affected by the emotional proclivities of those who make them. Nevertheless, as would be precluded by their overarching agendas, the Pratyabhijñā thinkers do not espouse a kind of relativism, but rather propound criteria for the evaluation of claims. As the Pratyabhijñā epistemology explains all experience and objects of experience to be idealistically generated by Śiva's self-recognition or Supreme Speech, there is no question of assessing correspondence with an independent objective reality. Each recognition must be tested as to *noncontradiction or coherence* (*abādha* or *sthairya*) in the realization of *practical values* (*arthakriyā*). The author has previously compared the Pratyabhijñā criteriology with that of David Tracy, who combines a hermeneutic conception of truth as disclosure (*aletheia*)/recognition with subsidiary tests derived from coherentism and pragmatism.

Philosophers relying on coherentism often posit a higher metaphysical condition in which coherence is fully realized. Abhinavagupta thus ranks cognitive claims according to their comparative "completeness" or "perfection" (*pūrṇatva*). He explains subordinated claims not as simply wrong but rather "imperfect" or "incomplete knowledge" (*apūrṇakhyāti*). For him, competing Hindu, Buddhist, and Jaina traditions all have *some truth* because their followers do achieve their goals, that is, various worldly objectives and sorts of spiritual liberation. However, the Śaiva liberation is perfect and includes the fruits of all other traditions. From this point of view, the Śaiva applications of the inference for the sake of others reveal facts once grasped only partially to be constituted in Śiva's self-recognition or Supreme Speech.

With unusual doxographical modesty, Abhinavagupta acknowledges that other traditions will inevitably view themselves as superior. We might say that epistemic hierarchization is entailed by the hermeneutic circle. The Śaiva hermeneutic and dialogical sensitivity, and rigorously nonobjectivist criteriology have endowed this mode of thought with a procedural openness and amenability to new and creative intellectual engagements.

References

Lawrence, David Peter. 1999. *Rediscovering God with Transcendental Argument: A Contemporary Interpretation of Monistic Kashmiri Śaiva Philosophy*. Albany: State University of New York Press.

———. 2008. *The Teachings of the Odd-Eyed One*. Albany: State University of New York Press.

———. 2011. "Kashmir Śaivism." In *Brill's Encyclopedia of Hinduism*, Knut A. Jacobsen (ed.). Leiden: E. J. Brill.

———. Forthcoming. "Pratyabhijñā Philosophy and the Evolution of Consciousness: Religious Metaphysics, Biosemiotics and Cognitive Science." In *Commemoration Volume for Hemendra Nath Chakravarty*, Bettina Sharada Bäumer and Hamsa Stainton (eds.). Delhi: Indira Gandhi National Centre for the Arts.

Nemec, John. 2011. *The Ubiquitous Śiva: Somānanda's Śivadṛṣṭi and his Tantric Interlocutors*. Oxford: Oxford University Press.

Ratié, Isabelle. 2011. *Le soi et l'autre: Identité, différence et altérité dans la philosophie de la Pratyabhijñā*. Leiden: Brill.

Sanderson, Alexis. 1985. "Purity and Power among the Brahmans of Kashmir." In *The Category of the Person*, Michael Carrithers, Steven Collins, and Steven Lukes (eds.), 190–216. Cambridge: Cambridge University Press.

Torella, Raffaele (ed. and trans.). 2002. *The Īśvarapratyabhijñākārikā of Utpaladeva with the Author's Vṛtti*. Corrected ed. Delhi: Motilal Banarsidass.

Urban, Hugh B. 2003. *Tantra: Sex, Secrecy, Politics, and Power in the Study of Religion*. Berkeley: University of California Press.

Chapter 42

LOOKING BEYOND THE DARŚANAS: TANTRIC KNOWLEDGE SYSTEMS AND INDIAN PHILOSOPHY

Jason Schwartz

The prospective student of Indic philosophy, enticed, perhaps, by the promise of the analytical clarity to be found in Nyāya reasoning, or intrigued by the manner in which the Vedāntic traditions implicate perception in the constitution of human experience, will often experience a moment of self-doubt when they set aside the representations of these systems by Western and Western-influenced scholars and engage with the text themselves. To put the matter rather bluntly, the foundational Sūtra texts of the Hindu Darśanas and their earliest commentaries contain much that confounds the normative expectations of the student of Western philosophy.

Despite a reputation for thoroughgoing ontological realism and hard-edged empiricism, Nyāya itself is exemplary of this larger trend. Its earliest texts commence by presenting the reader with byzantine taxonomies of substances, faculties, principles, and social practices. Even more jarringly, their analytical methods serve an explicitly soteriological aim. Thus, Nyāya Sūtra 1.1 informs us that from comprehending the actual nature (*tattvajñāna*) of the sixteen categories one obtains the highest good. Vātsyāyana (c. 500 CE), clarifies that knowing things as they really are (*tattvajñāna*), which is made possible through the analytical methods of the Nyāya system and its careful determination of what constitutes veridical knowledge, is no mere "academic" activity. When we understand things as they really are, our wrong notions and destructive tendencies—attachment to what is detrimental and aversion from the beneficial—cease, and with them our condemnation to transmigration. In other words, discursive knowledge in-and-of-itself resolves the problem of human suffering.

It is only through addressing our normative tendency to conflate discursive reasoning and the philosophical that we can make sense of what Tantric traditions contribute to the history of Indic thought. Succinctly, Tantric knowledge systems, and their predecessors, are founded on a deep skepticism toward the idea that discursive knowledge is intrinsically valuable. Furthermore, it is this stance that enables us to make sense of the marked anti-speculative orientation of many of the early Tantric scriptural sources and their aversion to analytical, as opposed to liturgically useful, formulations of doctrine.

If the Indic philosopher seeks to hone his mental faculties into a powerful analytical vehicle for parsing distinctions with ever increasing precision, the Tantric Sādhaka sets out to polish his intellect until it becomes a spotless mirror that can flawlessly replicate whatever enters into its field of vision. Through rigorously disciplining his body, sense faculties, and mental habits and inclinations, as well as restricting his activity to modalities that serve his particular stated aims, the Sādhaka is said to obtain direct apprehension of particular objects of perception, whether substances, entities, deities, or phenomenological states of being, which can then be translated into mastery over them.

For modern readers in the Western world, the identification of discursive knowledge with knowledge itself and its elevation as the highest aim of intellectual activity is seemingly self-evident. And yet, in the Western tradition, one can constructively compare the apprehension of the Sādhaka to formulations within the commentarial tradition on Aristotle's *De anima*, where the capacity for immediate mental viewing is treated as the highest human mental faculty. Founded on analogous processes of self-cultivation, for some philosophers, *nous* was understood as a receptive capacity, involving the apprehension of things-themselves, and not our mental representations of things, whereby the intellect takes on the form or nature of the object of perception. Its operation requires nothing less than unbroken and undivided attentiveness, which can be disrupted by the intrusion into awareness of one's own thought constructs or discursive reasoning. For instance, John Philoponus (490–570 CE) offers us a pithy account not only of the nature of the receptive faculty, but of how the Western philosopher goes about cultivating it:

> For just as sense perception, by coming into contact with what is white or with a particular shape, gets to know this in a way that is superior to demonstration (for it does not require a syllogistic proof that this particular object is white, rather it knows this by straightforward apprehension), likewise the intellect, too, gets to know the intelligible objects by straightforward apprehension in a way that is superior to demonstration. This activity of the intellect occurs only to those who have arrived at the extreme end of purification and knowledge, those who by means of the purifying virtues have got accustomed to activating the intellect without imagination and apart from sense perception. For the intellect is, somehow, the most perfect state of the soul.
>
> (Philoponus, 16)

As we shall see, a similar conceptual framework is absolutely inseparable from the practice of Tantric ritual. The practitioner visualizes himself becoming an empty vessel, directing his attention towards an intended object of perception, and uses the mind's receptive capacity to take on its essential features. Then, into the space where his subjectivity previously resided he installs a new and comprehensive network of signifiers, such as those that are constitutive of the deity being worshipped, anchored by a visualization. Of necessity, the Tantric practitioner becomes a consummate performer, engaging again and again in the construction, de-construction, and disaggregation of identities. As we shall see, it is through reflecting on these various practices that the later exegetes of the Tantric knowledge systems derive their sophisticated understandings of the socially and linguistically constructed nature of reality.

The philosophical roots of Tantric understanding

Kauṇḍinya's *Bhāṣya* on the *Pāśupata Sūtras* (c. 400 CE) offers us our sole glimpse of the apparently vibrant intellectual milieu, steeped in the idiom of the early Darśanas, that directly preceded the emergence of the Tantric knowledge systems. Perception (*pratyakṣa*), Kauṇḍinya tells us, is twofold, consisting of (1) that which derives from the senses and (2) self-awareness, which together form the necessary conditions for inferential reasoning (*Pāśupatasūtra*, 1.1.43). When our sense impressions are ordered in accordance with preexisting schematics such as dharma, adharma, time, place, and so forth, veridical knowledge (*pramāṇa*) concerning the precise logical relationships that exist between the different objects of our perception becomes possible. And yet, it is such transcendental categories as well as the network of causation itself (*hetujāla*) that bind the human soul. In fact, it is the boom and the buzz of sense impressions, involving an interfacing between human mental and perceptual faculties and external objects themselves, that degrade consciousness, interfering with its receptive capacity for apprehension. Thus for the practitioner to tame his mind and cease his suffering, he must gradually sever his connections with the whole conventional (*vyāvahārika*), disentangling from his constructed sense of self (*ātmabhāvaviśleṣaṇa*) (*Pāśupatasūtra*, 5.34.10).

According to Kauṇḍinya, classical Indian philosophy goes astray by attributing to each taxonomy unit specific fixed traits and propensities, thereby underestimating the mutability of objects and subjects. Informed by his epistemological account of how both direct sense impressions and the mental recollections and reformulation of these impressions are simultaneously informed by consciousness and inflect it, Kauṇḍinya surmises that even brief interactions create changes in the participating objects and subjects. The forging of sustained logical connections between disparate things results in an exchange of properties that, over time, reconstitutes the participants into new kinds of entities with new propensities and behaviors. This radically constructivist account of the objects of perception, in which human beings both create and are created by their environment, renders the notion patently absurd that any a priori insights can arise from the discursive recovery of the logical connections between the mutable objects that constitute our environment. On the other hand, such deliberate constitution of identity through habitual practice provides the practitioner with the keys to salvation: using mental focus to sideline his discursive thought in favor of direct apperception of the deity, the Pāśupata takes on the properties of his object apprehension to become, logically speaking, Rudra on earth.

The scriptural roots of Tantric philosophy

Tantric knowledge systems, in their discrete streams of revealed texts, formalize similar ideas into doctrinal stances, and then instantiate them into elements in a sequence of ritual practice. In place of advocating the gradual acclimation of the practitioner into a new mode of thinking and praxis, the tantras propose a rite of formal initiation (*dīkṣā*) that effects a permanent change in the initiate's ontological as well as social status, at once conferring Brahminhood and freeing the will from an externally imposed state of contraction. In more pragmatic terms, initiation provides one with access to a collection of ritual technologies for the ritual identification of the body with the components that make up the universe, followed by their systematic disaggregation and dissolution.

Contrarily, the same preparatory practice can also be used to gain mastery over the universe. The Tantric *sādhaka* does not set out to "understand" the various elements (*tattva*) that make up reality. Instead, he sets out to conquer them (*tattvajaya*) (see, for example, *YMV*, 148–150.). In much of Tantric discourse, virtually the entirety of human conceptualization and self-reflexivity, and the qualitative properties constitutive of experience, are treated as the direct mechanistic expression of subtle ontologies. In order to experience firsthand how the universe works, the Tantric *sādhaka* allows himself to be colonized by each of the elements in turn. By directing his receptive intellect towards an element like the earth and the architectonics that organize it for periods of months at a time, while depressing his nervous system through breath control and entering into a state resembling suspended animation, the practitioner gradually reaches a point where he locates his sense of self as having the same scope as the reality level. When this occurs, in logical terms he is more akin to the element than he is to his constructed self, and mastery over the plane has been obtained. Succinctly, such rites are understood to de-reify the objects of one's perception while at the same time making oneself into the object and not subject of perception, causing a rethinking of the relationship between self and other, subject and object (*YMV*, 293–306).

Language, reality, and the problem of identity in Trika and Kaula tantra

Though largely concerned with ritual praxis, the *Siddhayogeśvarīmata* (550 CE), the Trika's foundational scripture, offers us glimpses of a seemingly even more archaic worldview that stands behind the text within which human beings become absorbed in sense objects, not because of some innocent mechanistic process, but because they are compelled and possessed by a network of personified powers (*śaktijāla*) and their consorts, who "play in the body of men like children with clay bulls" (*Siddhayogeśvarīmata*, ch. 2). The doctrine of Siddhayogeśvarī is essentially an apotropaic practice whereby the practitioner prevents involuntary possession, i.e., normal awareness, by deliberately inducing the Goddess who both rules and constitutes the universe to permanently abide in his body in the form of the Sanskrit alphabet. The eight classes of letters of the Sanskrit language are in reality distillations of terrifying mother Goddesses, who command the countless horrid hosts of spirits that consolidate when we combine phonemes into a limitless variety of words and expressions. In this way, the foundation is laid for linking the hermeneutical process of working with and parsing language with the goals of soteriology.

If the Trika offers us what amounts to a linguistic turn within the Tantric knowledge systems, the originally unrelated traditions of the Kaulas, which are ultimately reabsorbed into the Trika and subsequent systems, enact a reorientation in the direction of phenomenology that forever alters the discourse. In place of the Heideggerian focus on Being, Kaula theology focuses on prelinguistic consciousness (*caitanya*): our capacity to cognize and experience both the external world and the contents of our own minds. No mere mechanical process, consciousness is indistinguishable from the Supreme Goddess who pervades all of reality. Cultivating the awareness that consciousness is equally distributed in a perfected form throughout everything in creation, and that this awareness in and of itself brings about the complete fulfillment of a human life is the core doctrinal stance of what the tradition calls Radical Non-Dualism (Parama Advaita).

For the *Kulasāra*, however, the primary cause of contracted human experience is the conceptualization of the world in terms of binaries—themselves essentially determinative thought constructs (*vikalpas*)—such as auspiciousness and inauspiciousness, merit and stain, *dharma* and *adharma* (e.g., *Kulasāra*, ch. 15). Whereas other traditions argue that the cultivation of the discriminatory awareness that helps one to distinguish the pure from the impure is integral to refining the mind as an instrument, the Kulasāra argues that true purity is nothing other than establishment in equanimity of perception, and that the real act of purifying the mind is eliminating its propensity to falsely conceptualize such binary pairs. Because this tendency operates on a precognitive level rooted in bodily experiences of attraction and aversion, nonduality must be viscerally experienced at the level of the nervous system, providing the rationale for transgressive rites involving the consumption of meat, wine, and ritual intercourse for which these traditions are best known (*Kulasāra*, ch. 14).

In the massive first chapter of the *Tantrasadbhāva* (eighth century), the epistemological and conceptual insights of the Kaula traditions are synthesized with the modes of practice of the Trika tantras as well as its preoccupation with the power of language. Succinctly, Tantric *yogins* fail in their practice, we are told, because of the modifications of the operation of their consciousness (*cittavṛttir apekṣayā*) (1.317). The text presents a standard account of the conquest of the ontological levels (*tattvajaya*) and then redescribes the hierarchy of reality levels as permeated by *mantric* phonemes. Taken as a totality, the entirety of the field of language and discourse forms the body of the God who consists of the heap of letters (*śabdarāśibhairava*). Lying behind him, accessible through meditations on increasingly subtle prelinguistic ontic states, dwells consciousness. Consciousness, the pervader, resides in the human body, in the same way that space fills a pot, or that a candle placed inside a vessel illumines (*prabhāsate*) the interior space. When the pot is shattered, the space inside merges into the vast expanse outside it, and the light shines forth in all directions (*Tantrasadbhāva*, 1.274–280). The *Tantrasadbhāva* teaches that the constructed self that resides within the human body is just like a pot, and that it has been crafted in accordance with the conduct and operations of the human mind through the medium of language. This constructed sense of self (*ātman*) cleverly protects itself from oblivion by making use of a linguistic feature inherent in most grammatically correct sentences: the grammatical subject. It then asserts that this sense of "I" and "mine" are actual extant things and crafts linguistically mediated conceptual constructions, such as gods or states of being it labels liberation, that operate as semblances of pre-linguistic entities and ontic realities. When the constructed sense of self is shattered—including such mentally constructed notions as God and Liberation—the self that is consciousness can shine forth everywhere restored to its unconditioned state. Thus, instead of worshipping a socially and linguistically constructed thing called a god, one should venerate one's own state (*svabhāva*) and become established in the direct experience of one's own form (*svarūpa*), which consists of nothing other than consciousness (*Tantrasadbhāva*, 1.283–1.303).

The contributions of the Trika exegetes of Kashmir

Although the Trika scriptural corpus forms the theological foundation of what is commonly called "Kashmir Śaivism," most of the core philosophical insights attributed to the Trika exegetes in reality pre-date them. What the Kashmiri exegetes, for all their considerable brilliance, introduce into this discourse are, on the one hand, new rhetorical formulations divorced from the intricacies of esoteric praxis, and, on the other, "properly philosophical" modes of argumentation that infuse the esoteric insights of these closed cultural systems into the rarefied idiom of the Sanskrit Knowledge systems. It is no accident, then that the earliest works of Kashmir Śaivism are presented in the form of Sūtras and Kārikās, thereby conforming to the formal conventions of the earlier Darśana systems.

The early ninth-century Śiva Sūtra of Vasugupta, generally treated as radically conceptually innovative work, in its original interpretive context serves as a précis of the main insights of the Trika system. In essence, the Śiva Sūtra begins the process of reorienting Tantric discourse to address the existential, as opposed to liturgical needs of individuals. Thus, we are told in rapid succession that what we call the self is in fact consciousness (*caitanya ātma*) (*Śiva Sūtra*, 1.1), what we think of as knowledge is in fact ontological bondage (*jñānaṃ bandhaḥ*) (*Śiva Sūtra*, 1.2). Bondage, in turn, is made possible by the aggregate of powers (*śaktis*), which is presided over by Mātṛkā, the phonemes of the Sanskrit language, which have as their true nature the eight mother goddesses. The subordination and sexual conquest of these dangerous powers by the supreme God is identified with the integration of various capacities (*śaktis*) by the practitioner into his own consciousness through the fusion and integration of perceptions (*saṃdhāna*). His conquest of the planes of reality, likewise, through acts of mentally concentrated apprehension—reversing the polarity between self and other, subject and object—disaggregates the human mind and dissolves *vikalpas* as a means of achieving unity with the fundamental underlying substrate, now identified with consciousness.

The *Spanda Kārikā* of Kallaṭa Bhaṭṭa, a disciple of Vasugupta, while expressing many analogous ideas, offers a more phenomenological account of the implications of Trika theology. Instead of focusing on consciousness, Kallaṭa is interested in the primordial vibration (*spanda*) that animates living things as well as the universe. The Lord, he tells us, is completely free and unobstructed and the *spanda* principle is operative in all ontic and mental states. When individuals have determinative cognitions about themselves, such as "I am happy, I am suffering, I am attached …" (*Spanda Kārikā*, 1.6), these *vikalpas* actually cause the epiphenomenal appearance of the retraction of the plentitude of being that makes up a person's real nature. In other words, linguistic statements operate not through increased specification of particulars, but through a logic of exclusion (*apoha*) that effects an apparent ontic retraction of human potential so that human beings come to conform to these statements. This process, as we might anticipate, is carried out by the mothers who use the power of language to ensnare and bind. The primordial vibration is utterly unaffected by this process, and for this reason a person can free himself from the snares of language and thought construction through focusing his attention at the gaps that exist between determinate cognitions, as well as centering his awareness on intense peak experiences of terror, joy, and heightened physical activity, where normal cognitions are obscured by pure sensation devoid of judgment or deliberation. As the text argues:

> Because the bound soul (*jīva*) consists of everything, for all states of being arise from within him, by means of having the awareness of that (being the case) he ascertains (*saṃvedana*) being identical with everything. For this reason, in regards to words, meanings, or thoughts, there is no state that exists that is not Śiva. It is the experient (*bhoktṛ*) himself, always and everywhere, who abides in the form of that which is to be experienced.
>
> (*Spanda Kārikā*, 2.3–4)

The school of recognition

Emerging out of a single preceptorial lineage in the tradition of the Trika, the school of recognition's (Pratyabhijñā Darśana) core precept is that a careful analysis of the epistemological processes that make possible any act of perception reveals the logical necessity of a perceiving agent, that, through the re-presenting and re-constitution of discrete perceptions within its own consciousness, generates meaning. This hermeneutical process makes it possible for human beings to understand the Supreme Lord, who is otherwise not a possible object of human cognition, just as the valid means of knowledge, the process of acquiring it, and the acquired knowledge itself are not independent entities, but merely our representation of moments in a sequential process that are ultimately inextricable from each other, so too are the apparent perceiving agent and object of perception simply relational elements internal to a single supreme cognizing agent. Thus, any kind of sustained delimited reflection on our perceptions of a particularized thing has the capacity to lead the perceiver to the awareness that the object of perception is identical with the subject of perception, who generates the world.

The *Īśvarapratyabhijñā kārikā* of Utpaladeva, the foundational text of this discourse, appropriates almost *in toto* the conceptual framework, terms of art, and modes of argumentation of the Buddhist Pramāṇa theorists, and strategically redeploys them in the service of the intellectual and theological values presented by the Trika tantras and the tradition of the Kaulas. Initially, the "Recognition of the Lord" makes use of Buddhist Pramāṇa theory to demolish the claims of ontological realists, like the Naiyāyikas and Vaiśeṣikas, who assert that external objects exist independent of perceiving agents and that the work of philosophy amounts to exercises in taxonimization informed by logical reasoning. Once the realists have been dispensed with, Utpaladeva then proceeds to locate within the arguments of Pramāṇa theorists themselves what he asserts are logically impeccable justifications for the stance that there is a single supreme perceiving agent who is the subject of all acts of perception and who objectifies the contents of his own consciousness, a process we perceive as the manifestation of a variegated empirical reality. Essentially, the object of knowledge that appears to our consciousness is nothing other than the flashing forth of consciousness itself in the form of the object. In other words, all cognitions work just like acts of yogic apprehension. Consciousness becomes a discrete cognition by divesting itself of content and assuming the likeness of the object of perception (*sarūpya*).

Given the scope of the present work, we will focus on just one small portion of Utpaladeva's argument with aim of shedding light on its constructive engagement with Buddhist logic and Trika Kaula metaphysics (*Īśvarapratyabhijñākārikā*, ch. 2) Utpaladeva begins his analysis by locating an apparent contradiction in the Pramāṇa theorist's understanding of the nature of memory and the logic of recognition. Essentially, cognitions, as the Pramāṇa theorists understand them, can be aware only of themselves and have no intrinsic logical connection to other cognitions. Memory, to say nothing of recognition, on the other hand, is intrinsically relational, in as much as it functions as a concept solely when there is the juxtaposition of two cognitions. His solution to this dilemma is to argue that there is a transcendental unity intrinsic to every act of memory, entirely untainted by conceptualizing elaboration, which is the true referent for the word "I," allowing for the juxtaposition within a single field of past and present cognitions. In place of the counterintuitive Buddhist account of an insentient intellect that passively takes on the form of apprehended objects, then, Utpaladeva demonstrates that his tradition's theological formulation of a conscious self has been logically inferred as forming the necessary precondition for the functioning of memory and recollection.

Now, according to the account of the Pramāṇa theorists, objects not only "appear" to consciousness as possible objects of perception, they at the same time register as unique and irreducible entities (*svalakṣaṇa*) with an array of specific properties. Utpaladeva makes sense of this feature of the philosophy of his rivals by establishing that the capacity of objects to appear to consciousness, which he represents as the illuminating light that reveals all things, itself has as its essential feature "reflective awareness" (*pratyavamarśaḥ*), which is nothing other than the preconceptualized registering within consciousness of the *svalakṣaṇa* of particular entities. In turn, it is these two features internal to Pramāṇa discourse, simplified in later Pratyabhijñā discourse as flashing forth (*prakāśa*) and reflexive awareness (*vimarśa*), that are constitutive of what we call consciousness.

Mining the rich resources of the Tantric scriptural traditions' linguistic turn, which we have explored earlier, Utpaladeva next informs his readers that consciousness, having as its essence reflexive awareness, is none other than a preconceptualized form of language, free from mental constructs. In other words, the abstract philosophical process underlying any act of human cognition is nothing other than the Śākta Goddess at the center of the Trika and Kaula tantras. By extension, the interfacing of that cognitive process with the perceiving agent is itself nothing other than the orgiastic union of the Lord Bhairava with his Śaktis. Cosmogonically speaking, the Supreme Lord "transforms himself into the reality that is the object of cognition." However, this representation of the generation of our cosmos as emanating from the godhead is simply different way of describing the normal features of any act of cognition, within which mental consciousness assumes the form of the objects of its perception, registers the object in consciousness, and then re-presents this constituted object to itself. Furthermore, the process we think of as human perception and cognition is nothing other than a mimetic replication of Supreme Lord's manifestation of the universe. This is possible because the agent that is acting, mediated through our discursive analytical capacities and receptive intellect, is nothing other than consciousness, the Supreme Goddess herself.

Utpaladeva next sets out to rehabilitate linguistically mediated understanding and discourse as modes of knowing, drawing again on Prāmaṇa theorists' novel account of the logic of linguistic signification. Essentially, words do not express meaning through specifying particular features, but rather through a logic of exclusion (*apoha*). Thus the intrinsic nature of a thing as denoted by a word has no positive content, but rather, all *vikalpas* are constituted in relation to an imagined opposite. What Utpaladeva demonstrates is the bare fact of an object of perception manifesting and becoming available to consciousness (*prakāśa*), by definition cannot be a thought construction (*vikalpa*). That is to say, we cannot cognize, or envision, the opposite of "being available to consciousness," because our cognitive processes and all possible objects of cognition have as their necessary precondition that they are available to our consciousness. While the eternal self, consisting of indivisible capacities of *prakāśa* and *vimārśa* cannot be negated, this is not the case with the conventional self, which engages the objects of the world of experience as well as its own capacities as if they were different from itself—in other words, constitutes its sense of self through a process of exclusion. The limited sense of self, then, is governed by the very process that enables us to identity something as a thought construction (*vikalpa*), representative of limited reality, which cannot serve as a valid source of direct knowledge. Utpaladeva has thus located the agenda inherited from his scriptural tradition in the conceptual framework of his Buddhist opponents.

Bibliography

Īśvarapratyabhijñākārikā of Utpaladeva with the Author's Vṛtti: Critical Edition and Annotated Translation. 2002. Raffaele Torella (trans.). Delhi: Motilal Banarsidass.

Kulasāra. n.d. Unpublished e-text. Provisionally ed. Somadeva Vasudeva.

Nyāyasūtras: With Vātsyāyana's Bhāṣya and Extracts from the Nyāyavārttika and the Tatpāryaṭīkā. 1984. Gangadhara Sastri Tailanga (ed.). Repr., Delhi: Sri Satguru Publications.

Pāśupatasūtra with Kauṇḍinya's Pañcārthabhāṣya. 1940. R. Anantakrishna Shastri (ed.). Travancore: Trivandrum Sanskrit Series.

Philoponus: On Aristotle on the Soul 1.1–2. 2005. Phillip J. van der Eijk (trans.). London: Bloomsbury Publishing.

Shiva Sūtra Vārttika by Bhāskara. 1916. Jagadisha Chandra Chatterji (ed.). Srinagar: Kashmir Series of Texts and Studies 4.

Siddhayogeśvarīmata = "The Doctrine of Magic Female Spirits: A Critical Edition of Selected Chapters of the *Siddhayogeśvarīmata(tantra)* with Annotated Translation and Analysis." 1999. Judit Torszok. Unpublished dissertation, Oxford University.

Spanda Kārikās with the Vṛitti by Kallaṭa. 1916. Jagadisha Chandra Chatterji (ed.). Srinagar: Kashmir Series of Texts and Studies 5.

Tantrasadbhāva. n.d. Unpublished e-text. Provisionally ed. Mark Dyckowski.

YMV = *The Yoga of the Mālinīvjayottaratantra: Critical Text, Translation and Notes.* 2004. Somadeva Vasudeva (ed. and trans.). Pondicherry: Institut Français de Pondichéry/École française d'Extrême-Orient.

Chapter 43
THE EPISTEMOLOGY OF CLASSICAL HINDU LAW[1]

Donald R. Davis, Jr.

Authoritative texts in Hinduism begin with the *śruti* (lit. "what is heard"), the collections of hymns, liturgical materials, ritual exegesis, and esoteric speculations dating from roughly 1500 BCE to 600 BCE. The most famous portions of the *śruti* are the Vedas (*saṃhitās*) and the Upaniṣads, representing the earliest and latest strata of the *śruti* literature, respectively. The sacred and foundational quality of these texts is beyond question[2] for they are said to be the repositories of eternal (*nitya*) and "beyond-human" (*apauruṣeya*) knowledge. When we speak of law, it is disconcerting that "strictly speaking the Vedas do not even include a single positive precept which could be used directly as a rule of conduct."[3] Practical law does not emanate directly from the injunctions of the *śruti*. Yet, all later Hindu legal texts, collectively known as Dharmaśāstra,[4] agree that the Vedas are the "root of *dharma*," or one's religious, legal, ethical, and social duties.[5] Given that the connection of religious and legal duties with the *śruti* is not direct, the connection should be imagined as one of inspiration. The *śruti* is held to be the spirit of the law in Hinduism.

The theological and jurisprudential tradition of Dharmaśāstra belongs to a second class of authoritative texts in Hinduism called *smṛti* (lit. "what is remembered"). The most famous Dharmaśāstra text is the well-known *Laws of Manu*, dated approximately to the first century CE.[6] However, other famous Hindu texts such as the manual of statecraft known as the *Arthaśāstra*,[7] the epics *Mahābhārata* and *Rāmāyaṇa*, and the sacred narratives of the Purāṇas also belong to the *smṛti* genre. All *smṛti* texts are authoritative, though some more than others and all less than *śruti*. In India, authority and sacredness are not like an on/off switches; they are ranked hierarchically. With respect to the authoritative texts on law, the measure of sacredness corresponds to the degree of epistemological authority (*prāmāṇya*) that a text has, i.e. the most sacred *śruti* texts constituted a direct and perfect means of knowing one's sacred duty while the derivative *smṛti* texts and the scholastic tradition that was built upon them provided a reliable, though less authoritative means of knowledge.[8] Theoretically, in cases of conflicting rules, the text with less authority in this sense must be dismissed. However, the kinds of rules found in the *śruti* differ to such a degree from those in the *smṛti* that conflict in practical terms was very limited.[9] The *dharmas*, or rules of religious and legal duty, in each genre had distinct and separate scopes. It is, therefore, the genre of *smṛti* that served as the foundation for Hindu jurisprudence and, much less directly and much less frequently, as a source of positive law. One must remember, however, that the authors of the *smṛti* texts understood the spirit of *dharma*, and thus of law, to come from the *śruti*.

A final category of texts must be considered here in order to complete the typology of sacred texts bearing an influence on law in the Hindu tradition. These are the commentaries and digests, the scholastic tradition that interpreted and elaborated on the *smṛti* texts. Commentaries (*bhāṣya*) take the form of linguistic exegesis, hypothetical examples, and theoretical disquisitions on a single Dharmaśāstra text. Digests (*nibandha*), by contrast, collect a variety of opinions from the *smṛti* texts and group them into topics, still interspersed with exegesis, example, and theory as before. The distinction between the two genres is not absolute and many commentaries incorporate myriad outside opinions in the manner of a digest. The authority of the commentaries and digests is in one sense derivative because it is based on the authority of *smṛti* texts themselves. At the same time, these scholastic works provide an essential interpretive framework for the *smṛti* genre and in many cases offer original insights on old problems. The most explicit jurisprudential discussions of Hindu law are to be found in the medieval commentaries of the Dharmaśāstra tradition.

We have noted already the qualitative difference between the subject matter of *śruti* and *smṛti*, especially the Dharmaśāstra, but more needs to be said about the origins of the latter. Whereas the injunctions of *śruti* (mostly concerned with ritual sacrifice) are held to be eternal and therefore without origin, the source of the *smṛti* rules is customary law (*ācāra*).[10] But the *smṛtis* are not *coutumières*, or mere collections of customs. Rather, "the Dharmaśāstra represents an expert tradition and, therefore, presents not a 'record' of custom but a jurisprudential, or in Indian terms, a śāstric *reflection* on custom. Custom is taken here to a second order of discourse."[11] If Dharmaśāstra is a second order of discourse, then the first order of discourse for *dharma* and law is customary law, in the form of well-known local standards and localized religious and legal systems. In other words, the first order of practical legal discourse in classical and medieval India was *ācāra*, not *dharma* and Dharmaśāstra.[12] The sacred quality of *ācāra*, and thus its authority, was preserved by certain checks that *theoretically* ensured that only the customary law of those educated in the Vedic tradition, i.e. knowledgeable of the *śruti* and *smṛti*, should be considered as valid. The practical authority of texts in India is largely dependent on the sanctity of the people who know and preserve them.[13] The close connection of person and text in India was significant in the realm of law as well for it means that the written law alone had but little authority without the force of a personal authority to corroborate and guarantee the text's value.

As before, in cases of conflict, the theoretical jurisprudence of Dharmaśāstra declares that no rule of *ācāra* can be accepted over a textual rule from *śruti* or *smṛti*—the hierarchy of the three sources is clear in theory.[14] In practice, however, just as the contents and concerns of the *smṛti* differ from those of the *śruti* to such an extent that a conflict of the two is unlikely or rare, so also should we understand that the scope (*viṣaya*) of *ācāra* differs to some extent as well. In fact, it seems likely that conflict between *ācāra* and the textual sources of *dharma* was more a hypothetical than a practical problem. Though *ācāra* is the principal source of rules of Dharmaśāstra, the scope of neither *ācāra* nor *dharma* is exhausted by the Dharmaśāstra. In practice, local law (*ācāra*) informed by the theoretical jurisprudence of Dharmaśāstra—and to a lesser extent its substantive and procedural rules—constituted the core of the Hindu law tradition in classical and medieval India.[15] Textual norms were accepted, rejected, and modified for use in the myriad regional and local legal systems of early India. Localized systems were influenced by the texts of the Dharmaśāstra tradition, not in the manner of a code but rather in the realms of legal education, legal reasoning, and jurisprudence.

In general, the explicit use of jurisprudential texts in practical Hindu law was very limited. Practical law, or positive law, did not depend upon appeals to written authority, whether sacred or not. One cannot leave the question so simply, however, because the positive law of classical and medieval India was circumscribed and imbued with a jurisprudence that emanated more or less directly from Dharmaśāstra. Authoritative texts in the Hindu tradition imparted a technique and a way of thinking about law that had myriad practical consequences. In this way, Hindu law does depend on texts, primarily Dharmaśāstra, and their epistemological hierarchy. To discern the role of authoritative texts in the practical law of classical and medieval India, one must recognize the limitations, or at least the ambiguities, of the English categories law, legal text, and sacred text. It would be nearer the mark to say that, in the Hindu tradition, Dharmaśāstra texts were used to educate Hindus in orthodox jurisprudence and that this jurisprudential knowledge and methodology was relied upon in many practical legal contexts. There was in early India a significant distance, both intellectual and institutional, between the production and learning of authoritative texts and the implementation of law on the ground. A mutual influence between the two nevertheless existed.

In this realm of jurisprudence, the connection between texts and law is to be found in the tradition of hermeneutics known as Mīmāṃsā. Mīmāṃsā texts are not "sacred" in any usual sense—they are not themselves part of a liturgy; they do not recount sacred mythological narratives; and they are not the central religious texts of any Hindu sect. However, it would be harder to argue that Mīmāṃsā as a system of hermeneutics was not central to the bearers and transmitters of Hindu theology.[16] In this extended sense, therefore, Mīmāṃsā and the form of legal reasoning it offers must be considered as part of the authoritative epistemological corpus of Hinduism, as well as the theoretical and practical jurisprudence of Hindu law.

Mīmāṃsā is a system of hermeneutics designed to facilitate correct interpretation and performance of the ritual injunctions of the Vedic texts, the *śruti*. Authors of Dharmaśāstra texts applied the same hermeneutical rules used for understanding religious texts for interpreting legal rules in their works.[17] Mīmāṃsā accepts certain presuppositions that established a distinctive religious and legal cosmology within which authors of the Hindu law tradition worked. The presuppositions include, for example: (1) the eternal and unauthored nature of the Vedas, (2) a denial of any creation or creator of the world, (3) the elevation of the ritual act above the gods, (4) the eternal connection of words and their meanings, and (5) the consonance of all authoritative injunctions of *dharma*. Two important consequences result. First, the morally disciplined and academically educated man (*śiṣṭa*) becomes the central figure in both the proper interpretation of religious and legal texts and in the extension or application of the spirit of those texts to contemporary situations. Second, a flexibility and realism with respect to legal questions obtains a theological justification in a rhetoric that generally censures variability, contradiction, and change but permits them nevertheless. The important point to remember in surveying the epistemology of classical Hindu law is that the hermeneutics of religion and law were precisely the same. Religious and legal texts were not distinguished in any way and the rules and categories of Mīmāṃsā established a framework for both the theoretical and practical solution of legal problems.

To summarize the epistemological function of texts, we should look to the use of texts in schools more than in courts. These texts cultivated in the educated classes a jurisprudence and legal outlook that shaped the intellectual and moral stance from which legal decisions and institutions developed in local contexts. Texts were not normally sources of positive law, but rather of jurisprudential training. A failure to recognize the nature and function of the texts on religion and law in the Hindu tradition, particularly the nature of Dharmaśāstra as both text and tradition, led to numerous misconceptions and misappropriations of the classical Hindu law tradition during and after the British colonial period in India.[18]

What we learn first from an examination of the epistemology of classical Hindu law is that texts and their rules have generally not been central to the positive law in any period of Indian history, either because their impact was in the realm of jurisprudence and legal education—i.e. at a considerable remove from the positive law—or because their use was an ornamental overlay on legal decisions arrived at by other means. However, one should not infer from this conclusion that texts, represented primarily by the Dharmaśāstra in this case, were not and are not taken seriously in Indian society and in Indian legal contexts. On the contrary, following Rajeev Dhavan, we can imagine that the legal worldview of Dharmaśāstra has always been a primary factor in the realm of civil society.[19] In this world beyond the state and the economy, Dharmaśāstra and its theological jurisprudence exerted and, to some extent, still exerts a tremendous hold on the moral imagination of Hindu society.[20]

With this brief review of Hindu legal epistemology in mind, we can now reflect on the philosophical implications of this hierarchy of legal authority and interpretation. Most striking to a modern reader is the absence of any epistemological presence of the state in the creation of law. John Austin's classic formulation of law as the command of a sovereign enforced by sanctions emphasizes the agentive role of a sovereign (king, legislature, etc.) in a way that is foreign to Hindu jurisprudence.[21] This is not to say that the king is helpless or disregarded in the Dharmaśāstra, but rather that his power to make law is circumscribed and not part of the theoretical sources of legal authority. Though overstated, Lingat's famous formulation of the Hindu king as an "administrator, not a legislator" captures the broad picture of both theory and practice.[22] The theoretical separation of the state from the substantive core of law makes Hindu law look more like other religious laws, such as Jewish, Islamic, or Canon law. Each of these defines and accepts a foundational textual corpus, and law theoretically emerges from the scholastic exegesis of those texts. Social changes and political realities also find a place in these systems but generally not at the level of basic legal epistemology. By comparison, Hindu law shows remarkable openness to the domain of customary law (*ācāra*), even as this area too is subject to an epistemological restriction to the customs of "good people," a criterion used, for instance, to exclude Buddhists and Jains.

More helpful is Hart's approach to law as the union of primary and secondary rules. Texts in the accepted epistemology of Hindu law make space for both the primary rules that impose duties and secondary rules that confer powers.[23] In the first place, the epistemology of law itself acts as the "rule of recognition," for any Hindu law must be a *dharma*, a duty recognized as falling within this epistemological scheme. As one would expect, various interpretive strategies developed to link practical laws with recognized *dharmas*. For example, the texts acknowledged the *dharmas* of localities and families (*deśadharma*, *kuladarma*) and labeled certain laws and institutions such as commercial regulations and "women's property" (*strīdhana*) as technical *dharmas* (*pāribhāṣika-dharma*).[24] Alternatively, with striking realism, some commentators flatly admitted that most secular laws did not originate in the Veda and yet were still authoritative as products of Vedic culture.[25]

Similarly, other secondary rules such as the "rule of change" and the "rule of adjudication" have correlates in Dharmaśāstra. Both temporal and geographic variability were permissible under specified conditions. Regionally specific practices (*durācāra*, *anācāra*), acts considered unworkable in our degenerate age (*kalivarjya*), and locally despised practices (*lokavidviṣṭa*) provide just some of the ways to permit legal variance and change. In judicial contexts, elaborate rules for formal trials with complex procedures are described, although almost no records of actual cases have survived. The standards for evidence, witness, and the qualification of judges form a central part of that procedural exposition. Alongside the formal adjudication of disputes, councils (*pariṣad*, *sabhā*) of Brahmins provided solutions, often in the form of responsa (*vyavasthā*), to personal and communal legal dilemmas as a way to avoid potential disputes.[26] In short, Hart's emphasis on law as an interlocking web of rules and rules about rules serves well to describe the epistemological basis of Hindu law and also, to some extent, the practical administration of law.

The element missing from Hart's scheme is the human agent who makes law happen. Legal agents, however, tend not to act independently, but institutionally.[27] In Hindu law, select students were trained extensively in Dharmaśāstra as part of institutional teacher–disciple lineages or in collective contexts such as the Hindu *maṭhas*. Corporate groups ranging from merchants and traders to religious renunciants to military groups acted as lawmaking and law-enforcing bodies for their members. Judges, assessors, and police were appointed by rulers to adjudicate disputes. Kings occasionally made new laws or guaranteed legal arrangements through their decrees. Brahmin councils served as local and regional repositories of wisdom and problem-solving for legal and religious affairs. Ideally, such institutional agents acted as "impersonal persons," people who embody and carry out the law in perfect reflection of the textual sources.[28] In practice, that did not matter, of course, as long as the secondary rules recognized these institutions as legally authoritative.

The interplay of rule and institution, of norm and agent runs through the epistemological foundations of Hindu law in a way that should draw our attention. The gap between positivist and realist views of law (to say nothing of natural law) stems from the difference between the philosophical centrality of rules in any jurisprudence and the inevitable intervention of practical exigencies beyond the rules in actual legal contexts. Hindu law's philosophical attention to *ācāra*, broadly customary law, forces us to consider the practical, institutional side of law in a theoretical way.[29] Customary law is so often defined in opposition to "real law" that it has become unusual to see the two domains put squarely in the same epistemological scheme. Especially when custom is seen as an unreflective, organic collection of static habits, its intersection with law is necessarily seen as problematic and antagonistic. Such a view is a modern product of the positivist focus on legislation, sovereignty, and sanction and flies in the face of most premodern concepts of law.[30] Like custom, *ācāra* "was a field of change and of contest, an arena in which opposing interests made conflicting claims."[31] None of this will feel foreign to an English legal historian for whom custom rests at the root of the Common Law.[32] With the triumph of utilitarianism and its offspring legal positivism, however, the dominance of commands and rules has come to erase the critical role of people and institutions in interpretation and administration of legal rules.

The epistemology of classical Hindu law teaches us to hold on to a formative role for textual rules as the body of *dharma* while also incorporating institutions of legal practice as its site of movement and dynamism. Modern legal solutions to real problems too often stop after the creation of rules intended to bring about a desired social outcome. The failure to consider how people are or will be empowered or hindered in their efforts to work within those rules contributes to increasing modern perceptions that government cannot improve social problems. It is, I would contend, the exclusive and all-consuming focus on rules and regulations in government, at the expense of the real people in institutions who have to bring those rules to life, that accounts for a big part of the mistrust of government institutions. There is no scope for the development of *ācāra* within this proliferating regime of rules; no "practices of the good" (*sadācāra*), only "best practices," which are but further rules; no creativity, only "audit cultures."[33] We are so obsessed with making sure that government workers follow the rules and report that they have done so and how, that we strangle their capacity to make rules function creatively and flexibly in response to real local needs. The prescription of classical Hindu law would be to pull back from explicit lawmaking and instead nurture the people tasked with the interpretation and administration of law by empowering them to use the law rather than simply obey it.

Notes

1 The bulk of this chapter was previously published in Davis, "Law and 'Law-Books'". Minor changes and a new concluding discussion have been added for the present volume.

2 *Mānava-Dharmaśāstra* 2.10 in Olivelle, *Manu's Code of Law*, 94.

3 Lingat, *Classical Law*, 8. Cf. Ludo Rocher, "Hindu Conceptions of Law."

4 See Olivelle, "Textual History," for an accessible overview of the texts of Dharmaśāstra.

5 *Mānava-Dharmaśāstra* 2.6 in Olivelle, *Manu's Code of Law*, 94.

6 The full details of the problems related to dating this and other ancient Sanskrit texts can be found in Olivelle, *Manu's Code of Law*, 19–25.

7 Olivelle, *King, Governance, and Law*. The tradition of Arthaśāstra was early on co-opted by the Dharmaśāstra tradition. The usual subject matter of Arthaśāstra, the *dharma* of rulers (*rājadharma*) was first incorporated into the *Mānava-Dharmaśāstra* (Olivelle, *Manu's Code of Law*, 46–50). The Arthaśāstra tradition introduced important innovations into the jurisprudence of Hinduism, most notably the 18 titles of law. In this chapter, the Arthaśāstra tradition will be implicit in its appropriated form in the discussions of Dharmaśāstra.

8 For a general study of authority in Hindu law, see Lubin, "Indic Conceptions."

9 Wezler, "*Dharma* in the Veda," 629.

10 Lariviere, "Dharmaśāstra," 611; Wezler, "*Dharma* in the Veda."

11 Olivelle, *Manu's Code of Law*, 62.

12 Davis, *Boundaries of Hindu Law*, 149–153.

13 Smith, *What is Scripture?*, 142–143.

14 Another source of *dharma*, *ātmatuṣṭi* "what pleases oneself," is listed in *Mānava-Dharmaśāstra* 2.6 and *Yājñavalkyasmṛti* 1.7, but this source of *dharma* never receives much elaboration or examination in the *dharma* texts.

15 Following this line of thought, I have attempted a description and tentative definition of Hindu law in practice in medieval Kerala in Davis, *Boundaries of Hindu Law*, 11–18. It is imperative to recognize here that not all legal cultures in classical and medieval India were Hindu, at least in the sense that I use the term, because only those that were influenced by the norms, jurisprudence, and institutions of Dharmaśāstra can reasonably be called Hindu. Many local legal systems in early India may not have been influenced by Dharmaśāstra in this way and only sustained historical research on India's legal history can determine the extent and nature of Hindu law in practice.

16 Olivelle, *Āśrama System*, 245 *et passim*.

17 For a thorough treatment of the use of Mīmāṃsā in Dharmaśāstra, see Kane, *History of Dharmaśāstra*, vol. 5, 1152ff.

18 Rosane Rocher, "Creation of Anglo-Hindu Law."

19 Dhavan, "Dharmasastra and Modern Indian Society."

20 Prasad, *Poetics of Conduct*.

21 Austin, *Province of Jurisprudence*, 133–134.

22 Lingat, *Classical Law*, 256.

23 Hart, *Concept of Law*, 81.

24 Davis, "Intermediate Realms," 99–100.

25 See the section on Medhātithi in Olivelle, *A Dharma Reader*.

26 Davis, "Responsa in Hindu Law."

27 See Raz, *Authority of Law*, 103–121, for a refinement of Hart's ideas that argues for the "institutional nature of law."

28 Davis, *Spirit of Hindu Law*, 55–56.

29 For a critique emphasizing the need for further study of "intermediate" social spaces as crucial to Hindu legal history, see Bilimoria, "Idea of Hindu Law."

30 Berman, "Integrative Jurisprudence."

31 Thompson, *Customs in Common*, 6.

32 Plucknett, *Concise History*, 307ff.

33 Strathern, *Audit Cultures*.

Bibliography

Austin, John. *The Province of Jurisprudence Determined.* Indianapolis: Hackett, 1998 [1832].

Berman, Harold J. "Toward an Integrative Jurisprudence: Politics, Morality, and History." *California Law Review* 76 (1988): 779–801.

Bilimoria, Purushottama. "The Idea of Hindu Law." *Journal of South Asia* 43 (2011): 103–130.

Davis, Jr. Donald R. "Intermediate Realms of Law: Corporate Groups and Rulers in Medieval India." *Journal of the Economic and Social History of the Orient* 48(1) (2005): 92–117.

Davis, Jr. Donald R. "Law and 'Law-Books' in the Hindu Tradition." *German Law Journal* 9(3) (2008): 309–325.

Davis, Jr. Donald R. "Responsa in Hindu Law: Consultation and Lawmaking in Medieval India." *Oxford Journal of Law and Religion* 3(1) (2014): 57–75.

Davis, Jr. Donald R. *The Boundaries of Hindu Law: Tradition, Custom, and Politics in Medieval Kerala.* Torino: CESMEO, 2004.

Davis, Jr. Donald R. *The Spirit of Hindu Law.* Cambridge: Cambridge University Press, 2010.

Dhavan, Rajeev. "Dharmasastra and Modern Indian Society: A Preliminary Exploration." *Journal of the Indian Law Institute* 34(4) (1992): 515–540.

Hart, H. L. A. *The Concept of Law.* 2nd ed. Oxford: Clarendon Press, 1994 [1961].

Kane, P. V. *History of Dharmaśāstra.* 5 vols. Poona: BORI, 1962–1975.

Lariviere, Richard W. "Dharmaśāstra, Custom, 'Real Law,' and 'Apocryphal' Smṛtis." *Journal of Indian Philosophy* 32 (2004): 611–627.

Lingat, Robert. *The Classical Law of India.* Trans. J. D. M. Derrett. Berkeley: University of California Press, 1973.

Lubin, Timothy. "Indic Conceptions of Authority." In *Hinduism and Law: An Introduction*, 137–153, ed. Timothy Lubin, Donald R. Davis, Jr., and Jayanth Krishnan. Cambridge: Cambridge University Press, 2010.

Michaels, Axel. "The Practice of Classical Hindu Law." In *Hinduism and Law: An Introduction*, 58–77, ed. Timothy Lubin, Donald R. Davis, Jr., and Jayanth Krishnan. Cambridge: Cambridge University Press, 2010.

Narayana Rao, Velcheru. "Purāṇa." In *The Hindu World*, ed. Sushil Mittal and Gene Thursby, 97–115. New York: Routledge, 2004.

Olivelle, Patrick. *The Āśrama System: History and Hermeneutics of a Religious Institution.* New York: Oxford University Press, 1993.

Olivelle, Patrick. "Dharmaśāstra: A Textual History." In *Hinduism and Law: An Introduction*, 28–57, ed. Timothy Lubin, Donald R. Davis, Jr., and Jayanth Krishnan. Cambridge: Cambridge University Press, 2010.

Olivelle, Patrick. *King, Governance, and Law in Ancient India: Kauṭilya's Arthaśāstra.* New York: Oxford University Press, 2013.

Olivelle, Patrick. *Manu's Code of Law: A Critical Edition and Translation of the Mānava-Dharmaśāstra.* New York: Oxford University Press, 2005.

Olivelle, Patrick. *A Dharma Reader: Classical Indian Law.* Historical Sourcebooks in Classical Indian Thought, ed. Sheldon I. Pollock. New York: Columbia University Press, 2016.

Plucknett, Theodore F. T. *A Concise History of the Common Law.* 5th ed. Boston: Little, Brown, 1956.

Prasad, Leela. *Poetics of Conduct: Oral Narrative and Moral Being in a South Indian Town.* New York: Columbia University Press, 2006.

Raz, Joseph. *The Authority of Law: Essays on Law and Morality.* 2nd ed. New York: Oxford University Press, 2009.

Rocher, Ludo. "Hindu Conceptions of Law." In *Studies in Hindu Law and Dharmaśāstra*, 39–58, ed. Donald R. Davis, Jr. New York: Anthem, 2012.

Rocher, Rosane. "The Creation of Anglo-Hindu Law." In *Hinduism and Law: An Introduction*, 78–88, ed. Timothy Lubin, Donald R. Davis, Jr., and Jayanth Krishnan. Cambridge: Cambridge University Press, 2010.

Smith, Wilfred Cantwell. *What is Scripture? A Comparative Approach*. Minneapolis: Fortress, 1993.

Strathern, Marilyn (ed.) *Audit Cultures: Anthropological Studies in Accountability, Ethics and the Academy*. New York: Routledge, 2000.

Thompson, E. P. *Customs in Common*. New York: Penguin, 1993 [1991].

Wezler, Albrecht. "*Dharma* in the Veda and the Dharmaśāstras." *Journal of Indian Philosophy* 32 (2004): 629–654.

Chapter 44
ABHINAVAGUPTA

Loriliai Biernacki

Abhinavagupta was a prolific Tantric philosopher who lived from approximately 950 to 1025 CE in Kashmir, India. He wrote in Sanskrit on a variety of topics, ranging from Tantric ritual to philosophy and cosmology to aesthetic theory, as well as poetry. While Abhinavagupta is especially well known today for his writing on Tantric philosophy and ritual, historically in India he was probably most known through the last thousand years for his work on aesthetic theory. His *Abhinavabhāratī*, a commentary on an early pioneering text, Bhārata's *Nāṭya Śāstra*, became a standard work and indispensable complement to this early second-century (CE) classic of aesthetic theory. Abhinavagupta in this context also added something new, by introducing an additional ninth category of aesthetic emotion, what is termed *rasa*, as *śānta rasa*, the mood of peace, to Bhārata's classical eight *rasas*. His innovation was influential, shaping aesthetic understanding through the following centuries. Another aesthetic treatise of Abhinavagupta's, the *Dhvanyālokalocana*, a commentary on Ānandavardhana's ninth-century aesthetic treatise, the *Dhvanyāloka*, circulated widely and garnered him a lasting reputation in aesthetic theory. In his masterful exposition of the inner workings of art, Abhinavagupta elaborated and refined Ānandavardhana's fairly radical conception that *dhvani*, or "suggestion"—rather than direct statement—is the "soul of poetry" (*Dhvanyālokalocana*, 1.1).[1] Abhinavagupta's eloquent advocacy of this position in his monumental *Dhvanyālokalocana* was so compelling that his theoretical understanding of how art functions eclipsed most other writing on aesthetic theory to gain widespread authority.

In fact, his name, "Abhinava," might be a title rather than a given name, as Abhinavagupta himself suggests, accorded to him by his teachers in light of his knowledge and devotion to the Hindu god Śiva.[2] There is a tradition as well, noted by K. C. Pandey (1963, 10), that Abhinavagupta was considered an incarnation of the cosmic serpent Śeṣa, who upholds the universe; Śeṣa as serpent is the bed where the god Viṣṇu takes rest in the cosmic ocean. This identification links Abhinavagupta to the great grammarian Patañjali, with the suggestion that Abhinavagupta, like Patañjali, was a master of language. Tradition also affords Abhinavagupta the status of enlightened teacher, *jīvanmukta*, one who has attained enlightenment while still in a physical body.

Abhinavagupta himself writes that he obtained insight from his teacher Śambhunātha, and he tells us that he writes his ritual masterpiece the *Tantrāloka* because he is given the authority and command to do so by his teacher: *gurunāthājñayā* (*Tantrāloka* 1.21; 1.19). Later commentators on his writings laud and expatiate upon his mystical and spiritual attainments. Yogarāja, who writes a commentary on Abhinavagupta's *Paramārthasāra*, tells us Abhinavagupta was established in the highest state of realization of the god Śiva.[3] Similarly, Jayaratha, the twelfth-century writer who commented on Abhinavagupta's *Tantrāloka*, tells us that Abhinavagupta had in fact personally experienced the signs of divine initiation that Abhinavagupta wrote about in the *Tantrāloka* (Rastogi 1987, 21) This divine initiation, *śaktipāta*, a "descent of energy" from on high, includes on the one hand mental characteristics such as unflinching faith in god and poetic skill, and on the other hand, some more elusive mystical attainments such as mastery of magical formulas, *mantras*, sudden, spontaneous knowledge of various subjects of study, and even control over various elements such as water and fire, along with control over the mind and the ego.[4] In general the "descent of energy" entailed a continuum of levels of intensity of divine initiation, from mild to intense and entailed a gradual accomplishment of inner and external attainments, which functioned for the tradition as key markers of a gnostic Tantric practice. Abhinavagupta himself does not lay claim to supernormal powers; however, he does allude to an innate spiritual mastery, even from his birth. In the playful *double entendre* verse at the opening of the *Parātrīśikāvivaraṇa* he insinuates his own special birth as '*yoginībhū*,' the child of two spiritual adepts who as an advanced soul about to take birth chooses parents who are spiritually advanced.[5] Moreover, he also tells us that he learned meditation (*dhyāna*) from his teacher Śambhunātha (*Tantrāloka* 5.43; see Rastogi 1987, 48), and elsewhere he tells us that he chose to forgo marrying and having a family, which in an Indian context tends to suggest a spiritual vocation.[6] One of his students, Madhurāja Yogin, gives us a visualization of Abhinavagupta, which may likely have been composed with actual details of Abhinavagupta in mind. In this portrait, Abhinavagupta has long hair tied with a garland of flowers and a long beard, and he wears the three lines of ash of a Śaivite on his forehead, along with *rudrākṣa* beads, a well-known insignia of devotees of Śiva and of ascetics more generally. Here he is also shown playing the vīna, a musical stringed instrument, and attended by his students and, in a delightfully suggestive Tantric fashion, with two women as well at his side holding lotuses and the aphrodisiac betel nut (Pandey 1963, 21–22). In this portrait Madhurāja Yogin also tells us that Abhinavagupta is singled out as a leader in the gathering of Śaivites, and extolled as a teacher of the *yoginīs*, female spiritual practitioners.[7]

Abhinavagupta was clearly a Śaivite, devoted especially to the god Śiva, and came from a family of eminent Śaivites, though we should keep in mind that Śaivite worship in this context also frequently entailed worship of goddesses as well. According to his description of his lineage in the *Tantrāloka*, his ancestor of approximately 200 years earlier, Atrigupta, migrated to Kashmir from the region of Antarvedi, in what is located now in the central part of Uttar Pradesh in North India. The king at the time of his migration, Lalitāditya, gave land and wealth for Atrigupta's move to Kashmir (Rastogi 1987, 28–30). Abhinavagupta's father and uncle and cousins were also Śaivites (Pandey 1963, 13). However, even though his primary religious affiliation was Śaivite, Abhinavagupta studied widely across religious traditions. He tells us in the *Tantrāloka* that his curiosity compelled him to move into other disciplines. He studied not only with teachers who taught the traditional Śaivite scriptural texts, the *Āgamas*, and not only with teachers of the Vedic texts and the Hindu logic traditions; he also studied with Hindus who followed the god Viṣṇu, and even more radically, he tells us he studied even with Buddhists and Jains as well.[8] An ecumenicist redolent of Ramakrishna in the modern period, Abhinavagupta's self-declared eclecticism no doubt helps us to rethink philosophical and theological boundaries in the medieval north in India.

We should also keep in mind that at least to some extent medieval Tantric practice incorporated transgressive practices; that Tantric practice finds its roots in antinomian cremation ground rites, which over time entailed also the use of illicit sexual practices as well. This embrace of illicit substances such as liquor and meat and transgressive sexual practices, known as the "left-handed practice" (*vāmācāra*), was not rejected by Abhinavagupta. Abhinavagupta's praise of his Kaula teacher Śambhunātha suggests his familiarity with left handed practices, and the twenty-ninth chapter of his opus on Tantric ritual, the *Tantrāloka*, explicitly addresses these secret, illicit practices. Abhinavagupta brought to this milieu a philosophical interpretation of practice. He sketched an overarching theoretical justification for a variety of practices, rooted in a nondualist philosophy. Alexis Sanderson has noted that a fundamental feature of Abhinavagupta's contribution to Tantric understanding was precisely a shift away from the more antinomian cremation ground practices towards less offensive, more socially acceptable practices (Sanderson 1988, 94). Abhinavagupta's writing resulted in a more respectable reputation for Tantra, a kind of sanitization of Tantric practice which stressed a fundamental shift in philosophical outlook entailed by the revelations of the Tantras.

Abhinavagupta's works

Abhinavagupta's writings have been mostly grouped into four categories: his writings on aesthetics, his writings on Tantra and Tantric ritual, his philosophical writings, and his poetry. Chronologically, this work falls into three major periods, his Tantric period, the period of his aesthetic writings, and his philosophical period, which will be addressed below (Pandey 1963, 41). His poetry likely continued throughout his life. At the end of this chapter is a list of writings attributed to Abhinavagupta, some of which are lost and some of which may not be his. Even while much of his writing has been preserved through the centuries, some has been unfortunately lost.[9] Some of these lost writings may have given us a much fuller picture of both Abhinavagupta's philosophical thought and the ideas circulating in his period, such as his commentary, the *Śivadṛṣ ṭyālocana*, on an important philosophical work, the *Śivadṛṣṭi* by his great-grand-teacher Somānanda. In this case particularly, much might have been gained by this lost text, since we see elsewhere in Abhinavagupta's work a fuller incorporation of ideas by the grammarian Bhartṛhari, while Somānanda himself strongly critiques the ideas of liberation and language propounded by the grammarian's school of thought, giving us a sense of the lively and interactive evolution of the school of monistic Śaivism in Kashmir to which Abhinavagupta belonged.

Tantric writings

His early writings on Tantric texts fundamentally focused on the three Tantric schools in which he was trained both doctrinally and in meditative practices, the Krama, the Trika, and the Kaula. The Krama involved a sequential worship of different forms of the goddess Kālī. Abhinavagupta's *Kramakeli*, which is now lost, appears to have been a commentary focused on a text of this school, the *Krama Stotra*. The Trika promoted a worship of the goddess Parā as an instantiation of divinity in a tripartite form of three goddesses, Parā (translatable as the "supreme"), Parāparā (a mix of "supreme and lower"), and Aparā (the "lower"). These three goddesses formed a core of Trika practice, "*trika*," meaning three. The Kaula, coming from *kula*, which means "clan," was a widely extensive tradition of Tantra, both chronologically and geographically, which emphasized an intensity of experience over ritual practice and historically incorporated illicit sexual practices. Abhinavagupta's teacher Śambhunātha taught Abhinavagupta the Kaula tradition and Abhinavagupta in several places holds his teachings in the highest regard (Rastogi 1987, 44–52).

In his writings related to his expositions of these Tantric teachings, Abhinavagupta propounded a monistic Śaiva interpretation of a number of popular current Tantric scriptural texts, including especially texts such as the *Mālinī Vijayottara Tantra*, also known as the *Śrīpūrva Śāstra*, which was understood to be divinely authored by the god Śiva and his consort the goddess in conversation. These writings commenting on scriptural texts include his *Mālinī Vijaya Vārtika* and his opus on the philosophical conception of the Trika and, by extension, the Krama practice, and Tantric yoga and ritual, the *Tantrāloka*, "Light on Tantra." This latter voluminous work covers thirty-seven chapters and close to 6,000 verses. If we add to Abhinavagupta's verses Jayaratha's twelfth-century commentary explaining the verses, it comes to twelve volumes and about 3,500 pages in its first publication in the twentieth century in the Kashmir Series of Texts and Studies. Abhinavagupta also wrote a number of shorter summations of this text, distilling its essence into several abridgements, including his *Tantrasāra* and his *Tantra Vaṭa Dhānikā*. In these and other works from his writings on Tantric scriptures, Abhinavagupta cohesively synthesizes an overarching nondualist framework with precise details of practice and doctrine. Alexis Sanderson has pointed out that while Abhinavagupta interprets this corpus of texts, particularly the *Mālinī Vijayottara Tantra*, in nondualist terms, the root scriptural texts can be easily also read from a dualist point of view (Sanderson 1988, 94).

Included in this grouping of Tantric writings, Abhinavagupta also wrote at least two commentaries on the *Parātrīśikā*, a very popular Trika scriptural text in tenth- and eleventh-century Kashmir.[10] In Abhinavagupta's works on the *Parātrīśikā*, he delineates a sophisticated understanding of divinity as perceptual phases of subjectivity and objectivity. His writing illustrates a keen psychological apprehension of how the mind tracks awareness, developed within the revelatory scheme of these three goddesses. This he implicates within a conceptual formulation of the three persons of grammar, the first person, "I," as the focal point of subjectivity, the third person, the "it," as the exemplification of the objective perceptual position, and the second person, the "you," as an intermixture of these two perceptual stances. In this context the subjectivity of the "I" is an instantiation of the goddess Parā, the objectivity of the "it" instantiates the goddess Aparā, and the "you" as Parāparā entails a mixture of objectivity and subjectivity. With this Abhinavagupta weaves a multi-layered psychological apprehension of self-awareness within a sophisticated analysis of how language functions psychologically—all of this mapped to a religious conceptualization of deity. Abhinavagupta offers in these texts also a subtle mapping of the phases of thought into speech, a particularly Tantric expression of deity evolving from pure awareness, *cid*, into embodied form. He delineates the four phases the goddess of speech, Parā Vāk, undergoes, from an initial all-encompassing indeterminate awareness, the *anuttara*, beyond which there is nothing higher. Succeeding this is her evolution to the next level of *Paśyantī*, the first stir of an idea in the mind, and from this to the phase of *Madhyamā*, where words begin to form mentally. Finally this *anuttara*, absolute consciousness evolves into *Vaikharī*, that very tangible level of speech that we associate with words that we hear through the physical sense of hearing with our ears.

Writings on aesthetics

In addition to the ground-breaking *Dhvanyālokalocana* and the *Abhinavabhāratī* mentioned earlier, Abhinavagupta's writings on aesthetics includes a commentary on poetics, the *Kāvyakautuka Vivaraṇa*, which was likely his first work on poetics, now lost (Pandey 1963, 38). He also wrote the *Ghaṭakarpara Kulaka Vivṛti*, a commentary on the aesthetic merit of a difficult poem, and a lost text on literary criticism, called the *Purūravovicāra*, on the well-known Sanskrit literary character Purūravas.

Philosophical writings

Abhinavagupta's philosophical writings primarily focus on the philosophical systems of the Trika and the Pratyabhijñā; however, he also ventured into other territories, with his commentary on that classic of texts, the *Bhagavad Gītā*, and a lost text on the sixteen categories of Nyāya philosophy, the *Kathāmukha Tilaka*. In particular, Abhinavagupta's writings on the Pratyabhijñā are extensive and have been extremely influential. The Pratyabhijñā, the "Recognition" school of thought, teaches that by a sudden act of "recognition," by becoming aware of one's true nature as the highest consciousness, one can attain a spontaneous enlightenment. Abhinavagupta wrote two especially authoritative commentaries on the Pratyabhijñā, both on the verses of his grand-teacher Utpaladeva's *Īśvara Pratyabhijñā Kārikā*: the *Īśvara Pratyabhijñā Vimarśinī* and the *Īśvara Pratyabhijñā Vivṛti Vimarśinī*. The root text, Utpaladeva's verses, contains eighty-eight verses and Utpaladeva himself wrote two commentaries for the verses. Utpaladeva's first, shorter commentary with the verses comes to thirty-six pages of Sanskrit. His second, longer commentary, the *Īśvara Pratyabhijñā Vivṛti*, appears to be irreparably lost. Abhinavagupta's commentaries on these are quite extensive, in particular his commentary on Utpaladeva's lost commentary, Abhinavagupta's *Īśvara Pratyabhijñā Vivṛti Vimarśinī* comes to 1,146 pages of Sanskrit in the version published for the first time in the Kashmir Series of Texts and Studies between 1938 and 1943. In these texts he lays out the philosophical system of the Pratyabhijñā in four sections covering the system's understanding of knowledge, of action, of cosmology, and of the means of enlightenment.

Abhinavagupta's philosophy is probably best characterized as a form of panentheism, an evolutionary panentheism that understands the divine to be both transcendent of the world and immanent within material reality. In his conceptual scheme the highest reality, designated by the term *Śiva* or *anuttara*, is a mass of pure consciousness and bliss, *cidānandaghana*. This highest consciousness unfolds through an evolutionary process into progressively denser forms of consciousness, all the way down to the insentient matter of the five elements, fire, water, earth, and so on. Dense matter, however, only appears insentient; it always retains, if only in latent form, its fundamental nature as the highest consciousness. A key philosophical principle which makes his vision fundamentally nondualist is that the essence of the highest reality, Śiva is present all through. As Abhinavagupta tells us in the opening verse of praise in the third section of his *Īśvara Pratyabhijñā Vivṛti Vimarśinī*:

> I bow to him who pierces through and pervades with his own essence this whole, from top to bottom, and makes this whole world to consist of *Śiva*, himself. I bow to the One who sprinkles the immortal nectar of his own self, rising to the highest abode.[11]

The divine unfolds itself into material forms, and yet maintains a presence all through material instantiation, *ota prota*, onomatopoeically from top to bottom. Precisely because there is always still this presence, there is also always still the possibility for recognizing this essential core of divinity, which is what the Pratyabhijñā teaches, this "recognition" as the means to enlightenment. It should be noted that Śiva, the highest reality which pervades through in Abhinavagupta's system, does not quite approximate our contemporary notions of deity as some external being. Rather, Abhinavagupta has two conceptions of Śiva, one as absolute deity, and in his philosophical system, the notion of Śiva as a principle, a *tattva*, more akin to an archetype than a deity. Abhinavagupta makes this clear in the *Īśvara Pratyabhijñā Vivṛti Vimarśinī*, where he makes a distinction between deities that reside in the *cakras*, the energetic stations in the body, Brahmā in the heart, and Viṣṇu in the throat and so on, and the *tattvas*, the principles of his cosmological system, where Śiva is the highest principle.[12]

The *tattva* system that Abhinavagupta presents is primarily a cosmology mapping the evolutionary progression of consciousness into material instantiation. The *tattva* system he uses derives originally from Sāṁkhya; however, the Pratyabhijñā school adds an additional eleven *tattvas* to Sāṁkhya's original twenty-five, making thirty-six.[13] The process of unfolding occurs through the *tattvas*. There is certainly in Abhinavagupta's model a notion of a great chain of being. The higher levels are characterized by a freedom and awareness absent in the lower levels. However, even with this, the lower levels still retain an innate sense of the essence which is awareness at the highest level. Speaking of the five powers of the highest Śiva, the powers to create, to maintain what one has created, to destroy, to obscure, and the power of grace, Abhinavagupta tells us that even the smallest beings, even an insect, retains the capacity for this fivefold activity that God has.[14]

Abhinavagupta's nondualism thus differs from the Advaita Vedantin system of the philosopher Śaṅkara precisely insofar as Śaṅkara's tends towards a transcendence of materiality; the material world for Śaṅkara is characterized as *Māyā*, illusion, best avoided. Abhinavagupta, on the other hand explicitly invokes *Māyā* as a creative power of the highest principle, in an explicit embrace of the materiality *Māyā* entails. We can see more similarities certainly with the nondualism of Bhartṛhari, the grammarian and author of *Vākyapadīya*, even though Abhinavagupta's predecessor, a seminal figure in the Pratyabhijñā, Somānanda, rejects affinities with the Grammarian school. What this means in terms of practical ramifications is that those things which *Māyā* entails have value for Abhinavagupta's nondualism. Positive attention is given to the body, in both its physical and subtle forms. The development of powers associated with the world of materiality, the magical *siddhis*, are not distractions on the path, but part of the path. Moreover, the body itself becomes a path, with a developed system of *cakras* and energetic flows, the *kuṇḍalinī*, as integral parts of the philosophical system. Two other key terms of Abhinavagupta's system should be noted: *prakāśa*, roughly "light," and *vimarśa*, "active self-awareness." These represent two complementary powers of consciousness, which function to generate subjectivity and objectivity. They operate within an integrated interplay of the capacity for both knowledge which moves towards the pole of transcendence, on the one hand, and activity, on the other, which moves towards the pole of material instantiation.

No doubt, one reason for Abhinavagupta's wide and sustained appeal as a philosopher is the sheer beauty and sophistication of his writing. A master at unpacking abstract philosophical concepts, he demonstrates a consummate elegance and refinement in expression. Moreover, we might say that a hallmark of his writing style is an unmatched capacity to illustrate multiple levels of discourse, integrating metaphorical, conceptual, and mundane spheres of experience. His writing displays an astute psychological comprehension that directly relates abstract concepts to comprehensible states of mind; his acute sensibility and delineation of the processes of mind makes his writing fresh and compelling even after ten centuries.

Notes

1 Citation taken from GRETIL, Göttingen Register of Electronic Texts in Indian Languages: http://fiindolo.sub.uni-goettingen.de/gretil/1_sanskr/5_poetry/1_alam/andhvy_u.htm.

2 Of his name he says it was proclaimed by his teachers "gurubhirākhyā" in *Tantrāloka* 1.20, taken from GRETIL, Göttingen Register of Electronic Texts in Indian Languages: http://fiindolo.sub.uni-goettingen.de/gretil/1_sanskr/6_sastra/3_phil/saiva/tantralu.htm. Also noted in Pandey (1963, 10) and Rastogi (1987, 19).

3 *Śivasya paraśreyaḥsvabhāvasya*. Sanskrit taken from commentary to verse 105, p. 198 in Muktabodha Indological Digital Library, *Paramārthasāra* by Abhinavagupta with the commentary of Yogarāja. Text copied from the Kashmir Series of Texts and Studies vol. 7, Shrinagar, 1916. Data entered by the staff of Muktabodha, text M00041.

4 Abhinavagupta writes of these various signs at *Tantrāloka* 13.214–15. I translate *tattva* here in terms of the classical *tattvas* of Abhinavagupta's system, which include the five elements, water, fire, etc., as well as other components of the world such as mind, ego, and which would include for Abhinavagupta's system even *kāla*, time.

5 In the *Parātriṃśikāvivaraṇa* 1.1; taken from GRETIL, Göttingen Register of Electronic Texts in Indian Languages: http://fiindolo.sub.uni-goettingen.de/gret_utf.htm#ParTri_VS. Also found in *Tantrāloka* 1.1.

6 Abhinavagupta, *Īśvara Pratyabhijñā Vivṛti Vimarśinī*, v. 3, 405, from Muktabodha Indological Digital Library, text M00022, input from Kashmir Series of Texts and Studies, vol. 65, Bombay, 1943, 405: "*dā rātmajaprabhṛtibandhukathāmanāptaḥ*."

7 "*deśikayoginīnām*," v. 7 in Madhurāja Yogin, "*Gurunāthaparāmarśaḥ*," included in Raghavan (1981, 4).

8 *Tantrāloka* 13.345b–346a: *ahamapyata evādhaḥśāstradṛṣṭikutūhalāt //tārkikaśrautabauddhārhadvaiṣṇavād īnnaseviṣi /*.

9 For instance, Raghavan (1981, 25) points out a lost text, the *Kathāmukhatilaka*, dealing with Nyāya philosophy and Pandey (1963, 35–41) gives titles of fourteen different works, including this one, that are now lost.

10 Titled the *Parātriṁśika* in the Kashmir Series of Texts and Studies, which Pandey and others have noted is misleading in that it suggests a text with thirty verses (Pandey 1963, 45). These two include the *Parātrīśika Laghu Vṛtti* and the longer *Parātrīśika Vivaraṇa*; Pandey (1963, 76) suggests a third may be the *Anuttara Tattva Vimarśinī Vṛtti*.

11 *Īśvara Pratyabhijñā Vivṛti Vimarśinī*, v. 3, p. 255: *otaprotaṁ sakalaṁ viddhvā? svarasena śivamayīkurute / . yo'nuttaradhāmnyudayansvayamamṛtaniṣecanaṁ tamasmi nataḥ //*.

12 *Īśvara Pratyabhijñā Vivṛti Vimarśinī*, pp. 305–309.

13 Abhinavagupta does also on occasion invoke a thirty-seventh *tattva*, *Bhairava*, as a way of incorporating a Kula notion of enlightened embodiment that supersedes the implication of simple transcendence that the thirty-sixth sometimes suggests, in much the same way that the fifth state, *turīyātitā*, offers an recovery of embodied awareness that the fourth state, *turīya*, transcends.

14 *Īśvara Pratyabhijñā Vivṛti Vimarśinī*, p. 261.

15 This list is taken from Pandey (1963, 27–28); the list includes texts that are not now extant, but that are known from references to these texts in other sources.

References

Abhinavagupta. 1943. *Īśvara Pratyabhijñā Vivṛti Vimarśinī*, v. 3, 405, from Muktabodha Indological Digital Library, text M00022, input from Kashmir Series of Texts and Studies, vol. 65. Shrinagar: Research Department Jammu and Kashmir State.

——— 1916. *Paramārthasāra* by Abhinavagupta with the commentary of Yogarāja; text from the Kashmir Series of Texts and Studies, vol. 7. Shrinagar: Research Department Jammu and Kashmir State. Muktabodha Indological Digital Library.

——— 1918. *Parātriṁśika* in the Kashmir Series of Texts and Studies, vol. 18. Shrinagar: Research Department Jammu and Kashmir State. Muktabodha Indological Digital Library. GRETIL, Göttingen Register of Electronic Texts in Indian Languages: http://fiindolo.sub.uni-goettingen.de/gret_utf.htm#ParTri_VS.

Pandey, K. C. 1963. *Abhinavagupta: An Historical and Philosophical Study*. Sanskrit Series 10. Varanasi: Chowkhamba Press.

Raghavan, V. 1981. *Abhinavagupta and his Works*. Varanasi: Chaukhamba Orientalia.

Rastogi, Navjivan. 1987. *Introduction to the Tantrāloka*. New Delhi: Motilal Banarsidass.

Sanderson, Alexis. 1988. "Śaivism and the Tantric Traditions." In Stewart Sutherland, Leslie Houlden, Peter Clarke, and Friedhelm Hardy (eds.). *The World's Religions*, 660–705. London: Routledge. Reprinted in *The World's Religions: The Religions of Asia*, edited by F. Hardy. London: Routledge and Kegan Paul (1990), pp. 128–172.

Torella, Raffaele. 2015. "Passions and Emotions in the Indian Philosophical-Religious Traditions." In P. Bilimoria and A. Wenta (eds.). *Emotions in Indian Thought-Systems*, 57–101. New Delhi: Routledge.

List of Abhinavagupta's writings

1 *Bodhapañcadaśikā*
2 *Mālinī Vijaya Vārtika*
3 *Parātriṁśikā Vivṛti* (aka: *Parātrīśikā Laghu Vṛtti*)
4 *Parātrīśikā Vivaraṇa* (aka: *Parātrīśikā*)
5 *Tantrāloka*
6 *Tantra Sāra*
7 *Tantravaṭadhānikā*
8 *Dhvanyālokalocana*
9 *Abhinavabhāratī*
10 *Bhagavad Gītārtha Saṅgraha*
11 *Paramārtha Sāra*
12 *Īśvara Pratyabhijñā Vivṛti Vimarśinī*
13 *Īśvara Pratyabhijñā Vimarśinī*
14 *Paryanta Pañcāśikā*
15 *Ghaṭakarpara Kulaka Vivṛti*
16 *Krama Stotra*
17 *Dehasthadevatā Cakra Stotra*
18 *Bhairava Stotra*
19 *Paramārtha Dvādaśikā*
20 *Paramārtha Carcā*
21 *Mahopadeśa Viṁśatika*
22 *Annutarāṣṭikā*
23 *Anubhavanivedana*
24 *Rahasya Pañcadaśikā*
25 *Tantroccaya*
26 *Purūravo Vicāra*
27 *Kramakeli*
28 *Śivadṛṣṭyālocana*
29 *Pūrva Pañcikā*
30 *Padārthapraveśa Nirṇaya Ṭīkā*
31 *Prakīrṇaka Vivaraṇa*
32 *Prakaraṇa Vivaraṇa*
33 *Kāvyakautuka Vivaraṇa*
34 *Kathāmukha Tilaka*
35 *Laghvī Prakriyā*
36 *Bhedavādavidāraṇa*
37 *Devīstotra Vivaraṇa*
38 *Tattvādhva Prakāśikā*
39 *Śivaśaktyavinābhava Stotra*
40 *Bimbapratibimba Vāda*
41 *Paramārtha Saṅgraha*
42 *Anuttaratattva Vimarśinī Vṛtti*[15]

Chapter 45
COGNITION AND LANGUAGE: BUDDHIST CRITICISM OF BHARTṚHARI'S THESIS[1]

Toshiya Unebe

Introduction

This chapter is primarily concerned with the fifth-century (*c.* 450–510 CE) Indian grammarian and philosopher Bhartṛhari. Bhartṛhari's thesis on the relation between cognition and language is frequently visited by various thinkers from other schools. We will examine arguments in a few Buddhist logico-epistemological compendia, in which certain authors criticized Bhartṛhari for neglecting non-conceptual (*avikalpa/nirvikalpa*) perception.

Bhartṛhari proclaims his thesis in the first book of his *magnum opus*, the *Vākyapadīya* (V) as follows:

> *na so 'sti pratyayo loke yaḥ śabdānugamād ṛte/*
> *anuviddham iva jñānaṁ sarvaṁ śabdena bhāsate//*
> (VP 1.131; VPwr, p. 49; VPI, p. 188)

> In the world there is no notion (*pratyaya*) without conforming to/accompaniment of language. All cognition (*jñāna*) appears as if penetrated by language.

As it reads, Bhartṛhari asserts that all cognition is closely related to language. The relationship between language and cognition intrigued ancient Indian scholars, and Bhartṛhari's theory generated arguments among them. Quoting this verse, many thinkers argue for and against his thesis.[2]

Criticism from the Buddhists

In the Buddhist logico-epistemological tradition after Diṅnāga (*c.* 480–510 CE) and Dharmakīrti (*c.* 600–660 CE), several scholars after the lifetime of Jitāri (*c.* 940–1000) wrote compendia to succinctly introduce their theories. In the following four compendia, VP 1.131 is quoted and criticized: (1) The *Bālāvatāratarka* of Jitāri (*c.* 940–1000 CE), (2) The *Tarkabhāṣā* of Mokṣākaragupta (eleventh to twelfth centuries CE.), (3) The *Tarkarahasya*, author unknown (presumably from the eleventh century CE. onward), (4) The *Tarkasopāna* of Vidyākaraśānti (twelfth century CE.). All four are considered to consist of three chapters: (1) *pratyakṣa* (perception), (2) *svārthānumāna* (inference for oneself), and (3) *parārthānumāna* (inference for others), reflecting the chapter organization of Dharmakīrti's *Pramāṇaviniścaya* and *Nyāyabindu*.

In the first section of the first chapter of these compendia, the Buddhists explain the general concept of *pramāṇa* (means of valid knowledge) and then classify it as perception and inference. In the second section, wherein they define and explain perception in detail, they quote Bhartṛhari's verses. In their view, the aforementioned VP 1.131 is representative of those who do not admit non-conceptual (*avikalpa/nirvikalpa*) perception prior to conceptual (*savikalpa*) cognition, which is related to language.

Dharmakīrti (PVin 1.4) defines perception as free from conception (*kalpanā*) and non-erroneous. For him, conception is a notion associated with speech. If all notions are associated with language as Bhartṛhari advocates, then a notion becomes the same as conception. Therefore, there would be no cognition that is free from conception, even direct perception would not be free from conception. Thus, Bhartṛhari's idea expressed in the aforementioned verse leads to a serious conflict with Dharmakīrti's definition. Consequently, the later Buddhists who composed the above-mentioned compendia needed to reject Bhartṛhari's idea and establish perception as a non-conceptual or language-free cognition.

I shall first examine the passage in the *Bālāvatāratarka* of Jitāri. In the section on the definition of perception (*pratyakṣalakṣaṇa*), after quoting the VP 1.131 and one more succeeding verse, he comments as follows:

> If [you say] all notions have a form followed by language, how can you deny the perception that is free from conception and is established as a bare experience (*anubhava*), since every act of cognition is associated with the visible presence of objects? A cow can be experienced at the same time that a horse is conceptualized [when both a horse and a cow are visibly present]. This (experience of a cow) constitutes a non-conceptual perception. The conception of a horse cannot entail the conception of a cow because the cow connected with its own name is not grasped by it. Therefore, the conception of a cow that is simultaneous with the conception of a horse is rejected.
>
> (BAT, pp. 80–82; cf. TSop, p. 279)

In this passage Jitāri regards a cognitive state called *anubhava* (a bare experience) as a non-conceptual or language-free perception. When both a horse and a cow are present in front of us, although we can perceive both, we cannot conceptualize them simultaneously. When we notice the horse, we cannot associate other things with any form of language, even if we simultaneously experience the cow and others. Thus, the bare experience of the cow is non-conceptual perception.

Jitāri's objection is simple: if those who oppose his position hold that all notions are connected to language, it becomes difficult to explain how we can perceive multiple objects at the same time; nevertheless we cannot simultaneously associate all objects in the range of our perception with language. When we cognize something, it is apparently connected to language. However, we cannot deny that we also see other objects at the same time. Only when we take notice of one of them, is it connected to language; while others remain as the objects of non-conceptual perception.

The author of the second compendium, *Tarkabhāṣā*, Mokṣākaragupta, also quotes VP 1.131 in the section on the definition of perception (TBh, pp. 13–14) and argues against it with essentially the same example as Jitāri's. Cognizing a jar we connect it to the word "jar." We perceive various other objects around the jar without connecting them to corresponding words. Because in theory two or more conceptions or cognitions associated with language cannot exist simultaneously, the objects around the jar continue to be objects of non-conceptual perception at the time of the cognition of the jar.

Although without detailed explanation, the unknown author of the *Tarkarahasya* appears to adopt a slightly stronger position. He only admits the language-free perception based on its object itself as constituting the first stage of perception, which simply perceives the form of objects such as a stone. The author (TR, p. 21) rejects a cognition associated with language, saying that it has only limited representation (*pratibhāsa*).

In this way, all authors consider perception to be free from language; the first two regard it as bare experience that occurs under the threshold of awareness. However, Bhartṛhari also distinguishes cognition that occurs under the threshold of awareness from cognition clearly associated with language as we will see in the next section. It appears the authors of Buddhist compendia miss the central point of the *Vṛtti* passage. Although chronologically speaking, it cannot be a rejoinder; Bhartṛhari's idea seems to invalidate the above criticism from the Buddhists.

Bhartṛhari on unaware cognition and its relation to language

In his *Vṛtti* on the verse above, Bhartṛhari illustrates the process of cognition that occurs when we are unaware of its occurrence and explains its relation to language. Following is a translation of the entire *Vṛtti* on the VP1.131 (VPI, pp. 188–190) divided into parts. In the first part, he exemplifies non-conceptual (*avikalpa*) cognition in the same manner as the Buddhists. However, unlike Buddhists, he finds language working therein.

> Even though cognition occurs with regard to cognizable things, when it is non-conceptual, no [cognition as the] consequence is made by it. It is similar to one's language impression (*śabdabhāvanā*) wherein forms are withdrawn. For example, even though a [non-conceptual] cognition arises from touching grass, clods and so on to the person that walks quickly, [only a certain state of the cognition is described as "cognized"].

When a person hurries, he or she is not aware of the grass, clods, and other elements that touch his or her feet. Even when making physical contact the consequence, namely, a cognition such as "I have touched the grass" does not arise at that time. However, a process of cognition of grass and clods occurs on some level at the time of contact. Bhartṛhari states such cognition is analogous to *śabdabhāvanā*, language impression that causes later recollection. It is our previous experience subliminally stored in mind as language we do not recognize its linguistic form nor any distinct image of the outer object corresponding to it, until we try to recollect it. Similarly, even in the case of the cognition we are unaware of, our present experiences are stored as language impression.

Just like the Buddhists, Bhartṛhari acknowledges the process of cognition that occurs while we are unaware of its occurrence, and calls it non-conceptual cognition. However, in his case, non-conceptual cognition is still connected to language. In contrast to the Buddhists, he regards language as working beneath the surface of our consciousness. According to Bhartṛhari, we do not "cognize" everything we perceive. Only certain experiences are "cognized," and the process is explained as follows:

> Only a certain state of the cognition is described as "cognized," namely, (1) in [the state of cognition] with the seeds of the language impression being in presence, (2) when the powers fixed to each object, which belong to object-revealing explicable and inexplicable words, are manifested, (3) a thing itself (*vastvātmā*) being figured and grasped by a cognition that is penetrated by language and following its power, (4) is followed by a notion that has a distinct form corresponding to representation (*pratyavabhāsa*).

This is how a state of cognition can be described as "cognized." (1) First, the *śabdabhāvanā-bīja*, the language impression stored as the cause (*bīja*: seed) of recollection is activated for collation of the present experience and the past one. (2) In such state of mind, the powers of words which reveal each corresponding object are manifested. (3) Then, an object is grasped by a cognition that is associated with language. The cognition follows the power of the words mentioned above. (4) In consequence, a notion with a clear image of the object is formed. It is the state of mind where this process works that can be described as "cognized."

When the power of the word corresponding to our present experience is manifested in such state of cognition wherein stored past experience has been activated, the object being experienced can occasion a notion with a clear image. In this case, we can state that we are cognizing the object. The rest of what we perceive enters the range of our cognition, although it leaves a language impression, or traces in the form of language.

Bhartṛhari adds one line in order to explain the role of the "language-seed" in our recollection.

> And it (the thing itself) becomes the cause of recollection when language-seeds manifest themselves upon another ground.

How can a person recall the blades of grass, clods, and other elements that his feet touched on the way, even though he was not aware that he had touched them? In daily life, we experience that we recollect many things, even things beyond our initial concern, after some triggering event.

Bhartṛhari acknowledges the non-conceptual form of cognition whose occurrence initially goes unnoticed. Such cognition yields the language impression beneath our surface consciousness. When we recall something, the impression, or language-seeds[3] need to be activated, and they constitute a cognition that is associated with language.

Subsequently, Bhartṛhari proceeds to explain another state of mind wherein the language-seeds are working, namely, sleeping:

> In the same way, according to some teachers, even one who is asleep has a stream of cognizing activities similar to the cognizing activities experienced by one who is awake. However, only the seeds of the language impression get a subtle activation at that time [of sleeping].

According to Bhartṛhari, scholars prior to him indicated one's cognizing processes are similar whether one is awake or asleep. The difference is a sleeping or dreaming person does not particularly need stimulation from the external world. In a dream, only the impression, or residual traces of our past deeds in the form of language—as seeds of cognition—are activated. Since the activity is very subtle, the person is often unaware of the dream, or even that there is a continuous stream of mental activity while sleeping.

Next, Bhartṛhari concludes his exploration of the relation between language and cognition that takes place in a state of unawareness:

> Therefore they call it the 'unaware' state (*asañcetitā avasthā*).[4] That very cognition [in the 'unaware' state], which has language as its origin as well as transformation, appears and disappears incessantly.

The subtle activity of language beneath the surface consciousness is also referred to as the "unaware" state (*asañcetitā avasthā*). The cognition that occurs in this "unaware" state continuously appears and disappears even in the mind of the person who is asleep.

It is clear that Bhartṛhari's scope is wider than that of the criticism from Buddhist authors of the compendia. Responding to the anticipated criticism, he would acknowledge that a person who focuses on a horse can experience the non-conceptual cognition of a cow and the one who focuses on a jar can experience the non-conceptual cognition of the ground as Jitāri and Mokṣākaragupta posit. Still, Bhartṛhari argues that subtle functions of language are active when cognition takes place. The experience of the cow is stored in the mind while the mind is unaware, in the form of language as a seed. Moreover, with the language-seed stored thus, the person can vividly remember the cow later. Therefore, for Bhartṛhari, the experience is inevitably associated with language.

The adversarial Buddhists should have put forward a theory that can supersede the theory of Bhartṛhari in this respect. However, they seem to have failed to do so. If their arguments with regard to non-conceptual cognition appear crude and stereotypical, one reason is that their arguments were confined to the framework of the *pramāṇavāda* from beginning to end and to their task which was to maintain their traditional views regarding what constituted valid means of acquiring knowledge.

Ambivalent attitude toward Bhartṛhari's theory

The validity of criticism from the Buddhists appears to be questionable. The Buddhists intended to establish non-conceptual perception according to their tradition. However, they may not have wanted to eliminate Bhartṛhari's theory completely, since they actually utilized Bhartṛhari's other theory in the same section of their compendia. This ambivalent attitude is worth examining.

Before criticizing Bhartṛhari's aforementioned verse in the section on the definition of perception of their compendia, both Jitāri and Mokṣākaragupta explain conception (*vikalpa*). To refute Kumārila (c. 600–650), who asserts that non-conceptual (*nirvikalpaka*) cognition is akin to cognition of those who cannot speak clearly, such as infants and the mute, they argue that the infants and the mute have conception in the form of an inner discourse as they are able to claim what they want and to abandon what they do not (TBh, p. 13; BAT, p. 78).

Although Jitāri and Mokṣākaragupta simply present this argument, this view is in fact based on Bhartṛhari's VP 1.129, which is located two verses prior to the verse examined in this chapter. Vidyākaraśānti in his *Tarkasopāna* quotes it and explicitly admits:

> For example, an infant moves onto mother's breast and so on after a halt of [sucking] its finger and so on. Thus it is said [in VP 1.129]: All [knowledge of] "what should be done,"[5] which even an infant who has a mental impression (*saṃskāra*) disposed in previous [life] understands, is in this world dependent upon language.
>
> (TSop, p. 278)

For Buddhists, to claim what we want and to abandon what we do not constitutes a worldly attachment that we must discard. As Vidyākaraśānti illustrates, even a new-born baby has such an attachment called *vikalpa* (conception). From the point of view of the Buddhists, this verse illustrates a negative nature of all human beings.

In contrast, Bhartṛhari takes the fact that babies begin to use vocal organs and pronounce speech sounds without explicit learning as an example in the next verse (VP 1.130), in order to positively show the function of innate language of new-born babies. Thus, Bhartṛhari's intention is different from that of Vidyākaraśānti; nevertheless, we can say it is appropriate to interpret this verse in the Buddhist context specified above.

Jitāri explains the difference between perception and conception as follows:

> In such an understanding of the object [namely in a conception], one cannot have a visible presence of the form of an object. The form of an object is indescribable by language. This is because, unlike the case of perception, there is no representation (*pratibhāsa*) in the knowledge based on language. It is said [in VP 2.422] that:
>
> In one way, one who is burnt knows burning through contact with a fire. In another way, through the word "burning," burning as its meaning is understood.
>
> (BAT, pp. 78–80)

The descriptive part of the passage is based on Dharmakīrti's *Prāmāṇaviniścaya* (PVin 1.15: p. 16). In order to support it, Jitāri quotes one verse, and this is also from the second book of Bhartṛhari's *Vākyapadīya*, which indicates the difference between the direct experience of fire and the understanding of the meaning of the word "fire." The connotation of the verse itself seems to be very suitable to the passage. Still, as we have examined in the previous section, it should be noted that Bhartṛhari thinks that an object is followed by a notion which has a clear representation (*pratyavabhāsa*) when grasped by a cognition penetrated by language. Therefore, his original idea is opposite to that expressed in the descriptive part.

Conclusion: Bhartṛhari and the Buddhists

Bhartṛhari's thought is rejected in one place and deployed as an authoritative source in another. There is no other non-Buddhist author like Bhartṛhari, whom Buddhists quote, reject, and use as often. How is the ambivalent attitude of the Buddhist authors justified?

One explanation is he is treated as just a grammarian by the Buddhists. The science of grammar is common to all scholars regardless of their theoretical preferences, as the Grammarians themselves thought. Maybe with regard to this shared view, Buddhist authors rather freely deployed Bhartṛhari's verses. Another explanation is that Bhartṛhari's theories can be interpreted as an inheritance from Buddhists and therefore, cannot be entirely abandoned.

Bhartṛhari assumes the seeds of language impression to explain unaware cognition and its recollection. However, he does not clearly explain where the seeds are stored. Could we consider Bhartṛhari's idea of the seed of language impression to be an echo of "the seed of the speech impregnation" (*abhilāpavāsanābīja*) of the Buddhist

Vijñānavādin?[6] It is in their elaborate theory of store-consciousness (*ālayavijñāna*) that the role of the seed of speech impregnation is explicated.

Since a more exhaustive examination of the relation between Bhartṛhari and the Vijñānavādin is outside the scope of the present chapter, we refer to only a few passages from the *Mahāyānasaṃgraha* of Asaṅga (*c*. 395–470) as evidence.

In the *Mahāyānasaṃgraha* (ch. 1.61.2: p. 23), Asaṅga explains that the seed of speech impregnation is one of the two natures of store-consciousness. He continues: "throughout time, it is this seed that occasions the discursive multiplicity (*prapañca*)" of the world experienced by ordinary people. Later (ch. 2.2.1–9: p. 25), Asaṅga refers to it as the cause of the notions (*vijñapti*) of (1) body (five sense organs), (2) the possessor of the body, (3) the enjoyer, (4) that which is known by the preceding three (the six sense objects), (5) one who knows the preceding (the six types of surface-level consciousness), (6) time, (7) number, (8) place, and (9) that which manifests as linguistic activity. Thus, the phenomenal world is experienced in such discursive form and the speech impregnation is described as its cause.

According to the Vijñānavādins, seeds are stored in store-consciousness, also called *sarvabījaka*, the consciousness that preserves all seeds (MS, ch. 1.21: p. 12). Bhartṛhari does not elaborate on the structure of human consciousness, he does refer to the cognition in the "unaware" state (*asañcetitā avasthā*) and the language therein functions as cause and effect. We may consider this to be a state of consciousness wherein language-seeds are stored, like the store-consciousness of the Vijñānavādins.

Further, Asaṅga, quoting a half-verse, shows that to teach the mutual causal relation between the things (*dharma*) we experience and speech impregnation is to explain one of the most basic doctrines of Buddhism, the dependent origination (*pratītyasamutpāda*): among them, an explanation of dependent origination is, for example, to teach: "*dharmas* result from speech impregnation and the latter from the former" (MS, ch. 2.32.1: p. 42). The idea expressed here, which Asaṅga relates several times,[7] seems to influence Bhartṛhari, who asserts cognition in the "unaware" state which has language as its origin and transformation, appears and disappears incessantly.

Bhartṛhari's theory of cognition and its relation to language is associated with Vijñānavādins' theory of store-consciousness to a significant extent. Their theory is a possible source for Bhartrhari. If Buddhists strongly argue against him, it can cut both ways. We may conclude that this is why they did not address Bhartṛhari's theory of *śabdabhāvanābīja*, the seed of language impression which is associated with even a non-conceptual cognition, or a cognition that takes place in a state of unawareness.

In conclusion, the criticism from the Buddhists against *Vākyapadīya* 1.131 trivializes the issue that the verse accompanying the *Vṛtti* addresses. Moreover, the Buddhist authors probably knew that Bhartṛhari had a wider scope. Nevertheless, they trimmed away the psychological and linguistic aspects of Bhartṛhari's theory to serve their purpose in the epistemological context. Their criticism is not so much a real polemic as it is a refutation of an imagined disputant, since their purpose at this point is to establish non-conceptual perception in the context of *pramāṇa-vāda*.[8]

Abbreviations

BAT Jitāri's *Bālāvatārararka*, ed. Kenjo Shirasaki, *Bulletin of Kobe Women's University Literature Department* 15(1) (1983): 63–135.

MS *La Somme du Grand Véhicule d'Asaṅga* (*Mahāyānasaṃgraha*), 2 vols., ed. Étienne Lamotte. Louvain: Université de Louvain, 1973.

PVin Dharmakīrti's *Pramāṇaviniścaya*, chs. 1 and 2, ed. Ernst Steinkellner, Sanskrit Texts from the Tibetan Autonomous Region 2. Beijing: China Tibetology Publishing House; Vienna: Austrian Academy of Sciences Press, 2007.

TBh *Tarkabhāṣā* of Acarya Moksakaragupta, ed. Losang Norbu Shastri, Bibliotheca Indo-Tibetica Series 54. Sarnath: Central Institute of Higher Tibetan Studies, 2004.

TR *Tarkarahasya*, ed. Hideomi Yaita, *Three Sanskrit Texts from the Buddhist Pramāṇa-Tradition*, Monograph Series of Naritasan Institute for Buddhist Studies 4. Chiba: Naritasan Shinshoji, 2005.

TSop Vidyākaraśānti's *Tarkasopāna*, ed. Giuseppe Tucci, *Minor Buddhist Texts*, part 1, Serie Orientale Roma 9. Rome: Istituto italiano per il Medio ed Estremo Oriente, 1956.

VP *Vākyapadīya* of Bhartṛhari, with the commentaries *Vṛtti* and the *Paddhati* of Vṛṣabhadeva, Kāṇḍa I, ed. K. A. Subramania Iyer, Deccan College Monograph Series 32. Poona: Deccan College, 1966.

VPI *The Vākyapadīya of Bhartṛhari with the Vṛtti:* English translation, ch. 1. Deccan College Building Centenary and Silver Jubilee Series 26. Poona: Deccan College, 1965.

VPwr Bhartṛhari's *Vākyapadīya*, ed. Wilhelm Rau, Abhandlungen für die Kunde des Morgenlandes 42.4. Wiesbaden: Franz Steiner, 1977.

Notes

1 This chapter is an abridged version of the author's "Cognition and Language: A Discussion of Vākyapadīya 1.131 with Regard to Criticism from the Buddhists," in Chikafumi Watanabe *et al.*, pp. 488–508. (The young author passed away mid-way through the editing process; hence the task was completed by the chief editor.) The editors on behalf of the author would like to express thanks to Dr. Chikafumi Watanabe for permitting this reproduction.

2 See Jan Houben, "Language and Thought in the Sanskrit Tradition," in *History of the Language Sciences: An International Handbook on the Evolution of the Study of Language from the Beginnings to the Present*, vol. 1, ed. S. Auroux *et al*. Berlin and New York: Walter de Gruyter, 2000, pp. 146–157.

3 Although Bhartṛhari uses the term *śruti-bīja* (language-seed) in only one more passage (VPI, 198), he seems to use the term with reference to the process of recollection or manifestation of the stored experience, in place of the term *śabdabhāvanā(-bīja)* which is more related to the stored state or the storing process.

4 Although no published text so far has this reading, I adopt it from Professor Aklujkar's unpublished edition of the VP with his kind concurrence. In *Paddhati* (p. 190, l. 10) we find a word "*asaṁcetite*". Moreover, *asañcetitāvasthā* is referred to in the *Vṛtti* on the next verse (VPI, p. 190). This term is used exclusively in this context on the "unaware" state of the consciousness in the *Vṛtti*.

5 See Toshiya Unebe, "Bhartṛhari on Text and Context," in *Indian Philosophy and Text Science*, ed. Toshihiro Wada. Delhi: Motilal Banarsidass, 2010, pp. 115–131.

6 See Hajime Nakamura's *A History of Early Vedānta Philosophy*, part 2, ed. Sengaku Mayeda. Delhi: Motilal Banarsidass, 2004, p. 613 (English translation of *Shoki no Vedanta tetsugaku*. Doctoral thesis, University of Tokyo, 1942).

7 MS 1.17 and 1.27 are referred to by Étienne Lamotte, *La Somme du Grand Véhicule d'Asaṅga (Mahāyānasaṁgraha)*, vol. 2. Louvain: Université de Louvain, 1973, p. 133.

8 If we examine the criticism from the Buddhists in the context of epistemology, the result has already been clearly shown by Ashok Aklujkar, "The Number of *Pramāṇas* According to Bhartṛhari," *Wiener Zeitschrift für die Kunde Südasiens* 33 (1989): §4.1. See also Bimal K. Matilal's response to this debate in the broader context of Indian philosophy in P. Bilimoria, "Bimal Matilal's Navya-Realism, Buddhist 'Lingo-Phobia' and Mental Things." In *Language and Mind*, vol. 2: *The Classical Indian Perspective*, ed. K. S. Prasad. New Delhi: Decent Books, 2008, pp. 17–34.

Other source

Saṃskṛta-sādhutā: Goodness of Sanskrit, Studies in Honour of Professor Ashok N. Aklujkar, ed. Chikafumi Watanabe, Michele Desmarais, and Yoshichika Honda. Delhi: DK Printworld, 2012.

Chapter 46
ALAMKĀRKAŚĀSTRA AS A PHILOSOPHICAL DISCIPLINE

David Mellins

Introduction

Alaṃkāraśāstra is the traditional science of analyzing Sanskrit poetry in classical India. Most actively practiced from the eighth to seventeenth centuries in South Asia, it inherited methodologies and categories from a pre-existing dramaturgical science, *Naṭyaśāstra*, and shares subjects with a parallel discipline, literary pedagogy (*kāvyaśikṣā*), which focused on the training of poets. While *alaṃkāraśāstra* was undoubtedly useful to aspiring Sanskrit poets, it was primarily concerned with educating poetic audiences, and was a critical component in the curriculum of philosophers and literati, and members of the Sanskrit speaking elite.

The earliest documented works of *alaṃkāraśāstra*, those of Daṇḍin and Bhāṃaha, concentrated on outlining technical functions in poetry, classifying proper literary genres, formats, structures and styles in poetry, identifying the literary excellences (*guṇa*) and demerits (*doṣa*), and most vital to the tradition, defining and illustrating the varieties of figures of speech (*alaṃkāra*) operative in the Sanskrit poetry of their eras.

As the tradition evolved, authors endeavored to identify underlying classes of literary tropes that served as the foundation for the figurative and suggestive diversity in Sanskrit poetry, and beginning with Vāmana (late eighth century), sought to identify and elucidate the animating essence (*ātma*) in poetry. Vāmana (ninth century) proposed this essence to be style (*rīti*), and, shortly thereafter, Ānandavardhana propounded a revolutionary view: that the soul of poetry is literary suggestion (*dhvani*), a unique operation of speech functioning in literature. His successor, Abhinavagupta, provided a slight modification, proposing the soul of poetry to be the literary suggestion of *rasa*, i.e., literary savor. The investigation of *dhvani* and *rasa* in copious varieties and subvarieties occasioned a detailed investigation of semantics, a cognitive geography of literary experience and a metaphysic of literary emotion, which required direct reference to the experiences of an educated literary audience.

The *Dhvanyāloka* and the *Locana* initiated the dominant paradigm for literary interpretation over the next several centuries, but not without eliciting several vehement contestations and counter theories. Mahimabhaṭṭa argued that "literary suggestion" was nothing other than a type of inference (*anumāna*), and Kuntaka stipulated the source of literary charm to be simply "indirect (crooked) language" (*vakrokti*). Other authors, notably Ruyyaka (eleventh century), persisted in analyzing poetry primarily through the purview of figures of speech.

Inevitably, rhetoricians such as Mammaṭa (twelfth century) sought to integrate the perspectives of both early and the mature period of poetics by presenting a continuum in methodology extending over the different phases of *alaṃkāraśāstra*. His *Kāvyaprakāśa* re-evaluates the figurative analysis characteristic of the early period in light of *rasa/dhvani* theory. Significantly, Mammaṭa proposes that aesthetic savor and figures of speech operate as two potentially independent sources of literary charm.

Treatises from the latter period of *alaṃkāraśāstra* (fourteenth to seventeenth centuries) have been underappreciated by scholars of the twenty-first century, who maligned these for a lack of innovation and for their attachment to "hairsplitting" distinctions (De: vol. 2, 247). More recently, however, scholars have begun to appreciate rhetoricians of this period for their application of logical and grammatical innovations to the study of poetry, and for adapting of *rasa/dhavni* theory for the purpose analyzing genres of devotional poetry composed in the middle of the second millennium.

Uncertain origins

The exact origins of *alaṃkārśāstra* are difficult to trace, particularly considering the comparatively late provenance of the earliest known and existing treatises: Bhāmaha's *Kāvyālaṃkāra* and Daṇḍin's *Kāvyadarśa*. Both texts were most likely composed in the early part of the eighth century, more than 500 years after the earliest known compositions of long formal and structured poems (*Mahākāvya*) and several centuries after the composition of the definitive treatise on dramaturgy, the *Naṭyaśāstra*. Bhāmaha mentions the views of an earlier *Ālaṇkārika* named Medhavin (240, 248), and his contemporary Daṇḍin acknowledges that predecessors had already laid down the principles for poetic composition (Daṇḍin, 1.10). Bharata's compendium on dramaturgy, the *Nāṭyaśāstra*, introduces many of the analytical categories later utilized in Sanskrit poetics: poetic excellences (*guṇa*), literary flaws (*doṣa*), figures of speech (*alaṃkāra*), regional style, and literary savor (*rasa*). Earlier works on logic (*nyāya*) and jurisprudence (*dharmaśāstra*) likewise analyze specific modes of diction and acknowledge the influence of region).

The elements of poetry

Form, structure, content of the poem

Both Bhāmaha and Daṇḍin went to considerable lengths to elucidate the proper formats, structures, styles, languages, subject matters, characters, settings, and plot developments for poetry. Bhāmaha states that poetry may be arranged in prose or verse and that it can be composed in the language of the elites (Sanskrit), the languages of commoners (Prākṛit), or a combination of the two, and that it can depict true stories of the gods and other classes of beings, invented stories, stories that have their bases in the arts, and those that have their basis in the sciences (*śāstras*). Bhāṃaha indicates five principle formats for poetry: (1) great poems (*mahākāvyas*), which are built of chapters, (2) dramas (*nāṭya*), (3) prose compositions (*ākhyāyikas*) based on elevated subjects, (4) stories (*kathā*), and (5) verse collections treating disparate subjects (*anibaddha*). Daṇḍin explains that the great poem (*mahākāvya*) should be based on historical events, i.e., episodes from the Indian epics, should relate to the four goals of life – virtue, pleasure, wealth and spiritual emancipation – should have a dignified hero, and should include descriptions of towns, oceans, mountains, season, the rising of the sun and moon, love sports in gardens and pools, accounts of drinking parties, romance, the separation and union of lovers, the birth of princes, diplomacies, and military expeditions and victories. Daṇḍin specifies the final verse of each chapter of a great poem should conclude with a different meter than that found in the main part of the chapter.

Four preliminaries

In general, the preliminaries for works in *alaṃkāraśāstra* are slightly different than the traditional preliminaries (*anubandhas*) of other sciences: (1) the qualified audience (*adhikāri*), (2) the subject matter (*viśaya*), (3) the purpose of the text (*prayojana*), and (4) the relationship (*sambandha*) of the text to the purpose. The specialized preliminaries in a work on poetics will be (1) a benedictory verse, (2) a statement of the purpose of poetry, (3) a succinct definition of poetry, and (4) an identification of the causes that produce a poet. Not infrequently, however, these preliminaries will indirectly convey the content of the more traditional preliminaries.

Unsurprisingly, most benedictory verses (*maṅgalācāraṇa*) from *alaṃkāraśāstra* works address some manifestation of the goddess of eloquence (Sarasvatī, Bhāratī, Vāc, Vākdevatā, Parā). Definitions of poetry are usually succinct but frequently intimate a specific approach to poetics. Bhāṃaha writes "poetry is sound and meaning united" (Bhāṃaha: 1.16). Daṇḍin states, "the body of speech is a series of words qualified by a desirable meaning" (Daṇḍin: 1.10). Vāmana succinctly attests, "poetry is recognized by figures of speech," (Vāmana: 1.1.1). Mammaṭa (twelfth century) specifies, "poetry is composed of faultless speech and sound, possesses poetic excellences, and sometimes lacks distinct figures of speech" (Mammaṭa: 4). Jagannātha Paṇḍitarāja simply states, "Poetry is speech productive of a delightful meaning" (Jagannātha: 4).

Typically, treatises on poetics fulfill the third scientific preliminary (*anubandha*), the purpose of the treatises (*prayojana*). However, while most scientific treatises (*śāstras*) directly state the purpose of their disciplines proper, *alaṃkāraśāstra* works generally state the purpose of poetry rather than poetics. Bhāṃaha provides the most widely practiced model:

> The composition of good poetry makes it possible for one to be righteous, wealthy, to fulfill one's desires and to achieve spiritual liberation.
>
> (Bhāṃaha: 1.2)

He does not specify whether the benefits pertain only to the poet himself or whether they extend to the poetic audience. Daṇḍin's stated purpose is broader and educational:

> Look in the mirror made of words (poetry), reflecting the fame of early kings. Even though they are no they are no longer with us, they have yet to perish.
>
> (Daṇḍin: 1.5–6)

The implication is that poetry enshrines history in an entertaining way. Mammaṭa (twelfth century) provides the most evocative statement of purpose:

> Poetry leads to fame, the ability to create wealth, knowledge of worldly affairs, the elimination of harm, and instantaneous, supreme bliss providing instruction like that of a beloved mistress.
>
> (Mammaṭa: 2)

The final preliminary, the cause of a poet, is motivated more by science than pedagogy. Almost all rhetoricians state that the cause of a poet is talent (*pratibhā*), when brought to fruition by careful study and practice. Vāmana and Mammaṭa write that poetry composed by someone without talent will be the subject of ridicule or scorn (Vāmana: 1.3.1; Mammaṭa: auto-comment to 3). Both Vāmana and Jagannātha Paṇḍitarāja posit talent as the fruition of latent seeds imbedded in the continuum of consciousness during previous lives. Jagannātha also states that the blessing of a holy person may plant the seeds of genius.

Corporeal analogies in Sanskrit poetics

Daṇḍin's definition of the "body of poetry" established a precedent for the use of corporeal analogies in poetic treatises. Early Sanskrit rhetoricians drew a distinction between the "body of speech," understood as its words and meanings or in the case of Daṇḍin words qualified by meanings and its ornaments, i.e., figures speech. Bhāmaha intimates (1.13):

> A woman's face, even when beautiful, does not shine without ornaments.

The analogy persisted, and with time became more nuanced and sophisticated. Ānandavardhana, the famed Kashmiri rhetorician from the ninth/tenth century, writes:

> For just as charm is a certain something in a women, a feast to the eyes of the discriminating, distinct from all the parts of the body after they have been examined, just so is this [suggested] meaning.
>
> (1.4; Ingalls: 78)

Abhinavagupta, commenting on this passage, extends the analogy:

> For charm is revealed by the configuration of the limbs, but is a special property different from [that of] any particular part. Charm does not consist in the mere faultlessness of the limbs or in their association with ornaments. For we find that discriminating critics will say of a woman, "She is not really beautiful," even though the parts of her body on being examined are found to exhibit no fault, such as dullness of the eye, and even though her limbs be ornamented with jewels. On the other hand, of a woman who is not such, they may exclaim that she is the very paragon of ambrosial charm.
>
> (comment to 1.4; Ingalls: 78–80)

The body, ornaments and soul of poetry: blemishes, excellences, ornaments, suggestion, and *rasa*

*Poetic blemish (*Doṣa*)*

Early rhetoricians were adamant that a poem should contain no faults. Daṇḍin (eighth century) compares a poem with a single blemish to a beautiful man with a spot of leprosy (1.7). There is a degree of consistency to the faults that are identified by different rhetoricians, even if their nomenclature varies. Many blemishes were identified by Bharata in the *Nāṭyaśāstra* (see Gerow 1977: 231), and are likewise described in treatises on jurisprudence (*arthaśāstra*), and logical disquisition (*nyāya*) (Raghavan: 210–212). While early rhetoricians depict faults as objective standards, they recognize a degree of relativity. Bhāṃaha and Daṇḍin provide examples where a flaw in one type of poetry becomes a virtue in another. In particular, both authors acknowledge that in different styles, the standards of blemish and excellence vary considerably (Raghavan: 221).

While Bhāṃaha and Daṇḍin to a limited degree classify poetic blemishes according to sound and meaning, Vāmana provides a fourfold classification: (1) word blemishes, (2) word meaning blemishes, (3) sentence blemishes, and (4) sentence meaning blemishes (2.1.1–2.2.24). He also explains how some faults pertain to specific figures of speech, in particular those of simile. Mammaṭa (67) provides the most comprehensive explanation regarding the destructive agency of poetic blemish:

> Blemish is that which damages the main purport. The purport may be an aesthetic savor, but it can also be a literal meaning associated with aesthetic savor. Blemish can also exist in the words and phonemes, etc., as these are what expedite the aesthetic savor as well as the literal meaning.

*The excellences (*guṇa*) of poetry*

Like the blemishes (*doṣa*), the excellences (*guṇa*) find their precedent in early treatises on logic (*nyāya*) and jurisprudence (*arthaśāstra*), but as Raghavan aptly point out, they also find a common ground in descriptions of excellences (*guṇa*) found in early examples found in the epic literature (*Mahābhārata* and *Rāmayaṇa*) and in poetry of Aśvaghoṣa (Raghavan: 244–250). Unlike, the blemishes, the excellences do not specifically relate to individual figures of speech, as they are consciously defined in contradistinction and are a distinct exegetical category. They do, however, directly accord with the different poetic styles (*rīti* – see below) and are described as inhering in specific excellences. Daṇḍin, rather simplistically argues that the ten excellences identified by Bharata in the *Nāṭyaśāstra* – phonetic cohesion (*śleṣa*), lucidity (*prasāda*), evenness (*samatā*), sweetness (*mādhurya*), tenderness (*sukumāratā*), directness (*arthavyakti*), nobility (*udāratvam*), force (*ojas*), illumination (*kānti*), and transference (*samādhi*) – are the life force (*prāṇa*) of the *vaidarbha* (the preferred) style and that the opposite properties are found in the *gaudi* style. Bhāmaha identifies a streamlined triad of excellences: sweetness, force and lucidity and moreover rejects, ultimately, the utility of style (*rīti*) in the analysis of poetry. Vāmana on the other hand, outlines two lists of ten excellences (*guṇa*), one pertaining to sound and the other to meaning, and purports these to inhere in the styles (*rīti*). Ānandavardhana and Mammaṭa resort to Bhāmaha's streamlined set of three excellences, but understand these to inhere directly in the *rasa*.

Even if we exclude Vāmana's bicameral presentation, the excellences (*guṇa*) are in certain cases understood acoustically and in others semantically. Sweetness is recognized by the absence of aspirated syllables, and long compounded expressions. Lucidity is the facility and clarity of comprehension and, according to Ānandavardhana, has its seat in erotic savor (*śṛṅgāra*). *Ojas* (force), in contrast, is marked by the presence of aspirated and conjunct consonants as well as long compounds, and, according to Ānandavardhana, has its seat in the savor of fury (*raudra*). Lucidity is understood to inhere equally in all aesthetic savors when these are understood with ease and universality.

Figures of speech (alaṃkāra)

Vāmana attests, "poetry is recognized by *alaṃkāra*." In the broadest semantic sense, the expression *alaṃkāra* signifies "cause of beauty." In its most popular conventional sense, *alaṃkāra* refers to ornaments such as necklaces and bracelets, and by extension, literary ornaments or figures of speech. Even in the earliest of rhetorical treatises, figures of speech were divided into two classes, those that pertain to sound (*śabdālaṃkāra*), such as alliteration (*anuprāsa*), and those that pertain to meaning (*arthālaṃkāra*), such as simile (*upamā*), metaphor (*rūpaka*), and verisimilitude (*svabhāvokti*).

For a number of centuries, figures of speech were the most prized feature in poetry and the sign of a poet's true talent and innovation. While Daṇḍin attributes the inherence of certain figures of sound, such as alliteration (*anuprāsa*) and twinning (*yamaka*), to individual styles, the figures of sense were analyzed as independent sources of charm in poetry. Indeed the primacy of this poetic element is seen in the Sanskrit designation for discipline of poetics: *alaṃkāraśāstra*. A more complicated and intriguing question concerns how the characterization and exemplification of figures leads to a cultivation of literary sensibility in connoisseurs of poetry.

The oeuvre of figures of speech grew steadily and swiftly throughout the history of *alaṃkāraśāstra*, beginning with Bharata's meager collection of four in his dramaturgical classic, Bhāṃaha's (eighth century) collection of forty-four, Ruyyaka's (twelfth century) eighty-four, and Jayadeva's (thirteenth century) 113 (see Gerow 1971: Introduction). This expansion was undoubtedly motivated by the figurative innovations of poets, which necessitated additions to the classificatory repertoire, as well as the professional dictates of rhetoricians who would be rewarded for discerning new systems of classification. Even in the era that favored analysis by way of literary suggestion (*dhvani*) and aesthetic savor (*rasa*), rhetoricians such as Ruyyaka, Jayadeva, and Appayadīkṣita continued to devise new systems for classifying figures of speech.

Ānandavardhana (ninth century) and Mammaṭa (twelfth century) subordinated the function of figures of speech to that of *rasa*, as Mammaṭa explains in the *Kāvyaprakāśa*:

> Sometimes figures of speech such as alliteration and simile come to the service of a dominant *rasa* just like necklaces and other jewelry, in [bestowing excellence] to the body, come to the service [of a woman's charm].
>
> (Mammaṭa: 67)

But Mammatā's auto-commentary clarifies that the word "sometimes" demonstrates that in certain cases figures of speech are beautiful on their own accord, i.e., they themselves provide the charm in a poem. A number of other rhetoricians, notably Ruyyaka, Jayadeva Pīyūṣavarṣa, and Appayadīkṣita, are more assertive in their view that figures of speech provide their own independent charm through relationships such as contrast (*vyatireka*), superimposition (*rūpaka*), concealment (*apahnuti*), exchange (*parivṛtti*), and a cause without effect (*viśeṣokti*), which characterize the figurative element in specific *alaṃkāras*.

Poetic styles (rīti)

The analysis of style (*rīti*) with regional associations finds a precedent in dramaturgy. Bharata had defined four styles (*vṛtti*): the articulate (*bhāratī*), the physical (*sāttvatī*), the expressive (*kaiśikī*), and the impetuous (*ārabhaṭī*) and four regionalities (*pravṛtti*): Northern/Northwest (*Pāñcālī*), Eastern (*Uḍhramāgadhī*), Southern (*Dākṣiṇātyā*), and Western (*Āvantī*) that orient the speech, singing, movementsm, and gestures of characters in a drama. In the context of poetics, rhetoricians have integrated *vṛtti* and *pravṛtti* in the form of literary style (*rīti*).

Bhāṃaha and Daṇḍin, most likely echoing a pre-existing convention, identify two literary varieties: *vaidarbha* and *gauḍīya* (1.30–135; 1.40–44). Vāmana adds a third style, *pāñcalī*, and Jayadeva a fourth, *lāṭīyā*. As a category of poetic exegesis, it received mixed reception ranging from Vāmana, who held it to be the "soul" (*ātma*) of poetry, to Bhāṃaha, who doubted both the efficacy and very legitimacy of regionally based styles. Nevertheless, throughout the history of *alaṃkāraśāstra*, it provided explanation as to why certain excellences (*guṇa*) were more constructive and likewise certain faults (*doṣa*) were more destructive in some types of poetry than in others.

Literary suggestion (dhvani/vyañjanā)

Most scholars, classical and modern alike, understand Ānandavardhana's theory of literary suggestion (*dhvani*) to be the most striking innovation in the history of *alaṃkāraśāstra*. At its time, the theory provoked great contestation in both literary and philosophical circles. Two issues were at stake, first whether such a thing as *dhvani/vyañjana* truly existed and second whether this constituted the fundamental source of literary charm, the soul of poetry.

Until Ānandavardhana, rhetoricians and philosophers alike accepted two operations of speech: direct designation/denotation (*abhidhā*) and metaphorical identification (*lakṣaṇā*). The first operation is self-evident in that it signifies a meaning that is bound to the word by force of convention (*saṃketa, śakti*). Metaphorical identification, while more complex, has a discernible process. Frequently a speaker or writer will use a word that points to a literal, but contradictory or seemingly illogical meaning, with the intention that the word signifies a secondary meaning. The metaphoric expression is used rather than the equivalent literal expression because it allows for the transfer of unstated qualities. The stock example in Indian philosophy is a "hamlet on the river Gaṅges." A listener, quite instinctively understands the hamlet to reside *on the bank* of the Ganges, but by force of the original metaphorical expression, unstated properties of the Ganges – holiness, coolness, etc. – are associated with the hamlet.

Suggestion on the other hand is not attributed to any such causal mechanism, and hence is associated with greater charm and surprise. In proposing his theory of suggestion, Ānandavardhana must appeal to the authority of literary connoisseurs, who are able to perceive charming meanings that cannot be traced to either denotation or indication. On this basis, Ānandavardhana apophatically infers the existence of a third operation of speech, which he terms *vyañjana*.

The bulk of the Ānandavardhana's *Dhvanyāloka* is devoted to exemplifying and classifying different varieties of literary suggestion. In so doing, he subsumes the function of the other elements of poetry – excellence (*guṇa*), style (*rīti*), and figures of speech (*alaṃkāra*). Literary suggestion has three basic varieties depending on whether the suggested meaning (*vyaṅgyārtha*) is a fact (*vastudhvani*), a figure of speech (*alaṃkāradhvani*), or an aesthetic savor (*rasadhvani*). There are two further classification: (1) *dhvani*, where the suggested meaning produces the sovereign charm in a poem, and (2) subordinate suggestion (*gunībhūtavyaṅgya*), where the charm of the suggested meaning is subordinate to that of some other source, e.g., a figure of speech. These two varieties in turn have their own subvarieties. As for *dhvani*, the two main divisions are (1) *avivakṣitavācya*, suggestion where the literal meaning is not at all intended, and (2) *vivakṣitāṇyaparavācya*, where the suggested meaning is intended, but subordinate to another meaning. Furthermore, where the literal meaning is not intended (*avivakṣitavācya*), it may be (1) immediately dismissed (*atyantatiraskṛta*), or (2) shifted in to another meaning (*arthāntarasaṃkramita*). In the case where the literal meaning is intended (*vivakṣitānyaparavācya*), the suggested meaning may arise (1) through a discernible sequence (*asaṃlakṣyakramavyaṅgya*), or (2) without a discernible sequence (*alakṣyakramvyaṅgya*). These distinctions have their basis in the semantic experience of an educated poetic audience (*sahṛdaya*) rather than formal and objective properties of the poem itself.

Aesthetic savor (rasa)

Although it is the most universal of aesthetic concepts in South Asia, and certainly the most popular, early rhetoricians were slow to recognize the full application of *rasa* in non-dramatic poetry. Prior to Ānandavardhana's *Dhvanyāloka*, rhetoricians restricted their discussions of *rasa* to definitions and illustrations of the figure of speech known as *rasavat* – "involving *rasa*" or "suitable for *rasa*." In his inventory of poetic elements, Bhāmaha states that a great poem (*mahākāvya*) "should be endowed with the individual *rasas*" (1.21), but does not specify the mode of expression, or the mechanics of this experience. Later in the *Kāvyālaṃkāra* he defines the figure of speech *rasavat* as "that wherein the *rasas* such as the erotic become manifest (Bhāmaha: 3.6)." Daṇḍin simply defines the figure *rasavat* as "beautiful on account of *rasa*" (2.275).

In Bharata's *Nāṭyaśāstra*, *rasa* is presented in eight varieties, arranged into four causally related pairs: the erotic (*śṛṅgāra*) is said to cause the comical (*hāsya*), the ferocious (*rāudra*) the pitiful (*karuṇa*), the repulsive (*bībhatsa*) the terrifying (*bhāyanaka*), and the steadfast (*vīra*) the wondrous (*adbhūta*). By some accounts, including Abhinavagupta's, a ninth *rasa*, the tranquil (*śānta*), should be admitted. It is not causally related to another *rasa*, but rather in Abhinavagupta's view, is regarded to be the source of all *rasas*.

The eight traditional varieties of *rasa* are associated with eight (four pairs of) 'standing' emotions (*sthāyibhāva*): desire (*rati*) and mirth (*hāsa*), anger (*krodha*) and grief (*śoka*), repulsion (*jugupsā*) and fear (*bhaya*), perseverance (*utsāha*) and amazement (*vismaya*). The varieties of *rasa* find their source in the emotional determinants (*vibhāva*) such as springtime, ornaments, gardens, and frolicking pools which convey the standing emotions such as desire (*rati*), the physical signs (*anubhāva*) such as the twitching of the mouth nose and cheeks and the grasping of one's sides which express standing emotions such as mirth (*hāsya*), and the transitory emotions (*vyabhicāribhāva*) such as excitement, stammering, and stupefaction which configure in the development of the standing emotions such as amazement.

In the ninth century, Vāmana states: "the aesthetic savors (*rasa*) shine in [the excellence (*guṇa*) known as] illumination (*kānti*) (3.2.14)," thus beginning a tradition of relating *rasa* to excellence (*guṇa*) rather than a figure of speech (*alaṃkāra*). This understanding would prevail in the works of later Kashmiri authors such as Ānandavardhana, Abhinavagupta and Mammaṭa In these works *rasa*, liberated from the province of figures of speech, assumes a more dynamic and independent role for *rasa* in poetry.

Ānandavardhana was the pioneer in recognizing the centrality of *rasa* as an aesthetic force in poetry. *Rasa* in his view, cannot be expressed literally, but must be revealed by the suggestive operation of speech (*vyañjana*). He further propounds that the excellences (*guṇa*) and figures of speech (*alaṃkāra*) produce charm through their service to *rasa* in poetry. In the tenth century, Abhinavagupta elucidated the psychological and metaphysical processes implicated in the experience *rasa*. His theory is based on a metaphysic of memory accepted by all but a minority of classical Indian philosophies: that activities and experiences in past and present lives leave emotional traces (*vāsana*) in the individual's inner consciousness, and that these traces are rekindled by future experiences. The suggestive operation in poetry, he argues, has a unique capacity to produce, through the rekindling of emotional traces, the blissful and detached contemplation of emotion known as *rasa*. Furthermore, the source of this bliss is said to be insight into one's true self (*ātma*), which is occasioned by the rekindling of emotional traces (Abhinavagupta, comment to 1.1; Ingalls: 70).

The frontier of logic in Sanskrit poetics

There are three modes by which one may appreciate the evolution of theories over the thousand years that *alaṃkāraśāstra* was actively practiced in South Asia. The first concerns the internal growth and modification of an intellectual tradition at it seeks to provide more cogent explanations and more precise categorizations of linguistic and aesthetic elements in poetry. The second mode concerns the evolution of rhetorical analysis occasioned by the changing face of poetry, as this adapts to evolving aesthetic expectations in South Asian cultures. The third mode of inquiry concerns development of rhetorical doctrines in response to the more comprehensive evolution of intellectual and philosophical doctrines.

We can, for instance, rather hermetically understand the addition of varieties of figures of speech throughout the history of *alaṃkāraśāstra* as an effort to refine and perfect a classificatory system. But we can also understand this refinement as an effort to keep pace with the figurative innovations of emerging generations of poets. Lastly, we might understand the dramatic increase in varieties of figures of speech in the second millennium as a response to epistemological innovations in the disciplines of logic and grammar, which in turn enhanced the precision and subtlety of rhetorical analysis.

The third mode of analysis is most appropriate for appreciating the innovations of Jagannātha Paṇḍitarāja, the seventeenth-century rhetorician and author of the *Rasagaṅgādhara*, who applied technologies of argumentation refined within the school of the New Logicians (*Navyanyāya*) over the course of the thirteen to seventeenth centuries. Utilizing the terminology and techniques of this school, Jagannātha was able to dispute a broad range of opinion of his rhetorical predecessors, in particular, those of Mammaṭa and Appayadīkṣita, providing razor-sharp delineations in support of his own views. One of Jagannātha's most insightful contributions to the history of poetics was his determination that figures of speech are the source of charm within the suggested meaning, thus integrating the views of rhetoricians such as Ruyyaka and

Kuntaka with more traditional presentation of *rasa/dhvani* theory. Jagannātha keenly demonstrates the enduring efforts of rhetoricians to preserve the relevance of literary studies in the increasingly technical and specialized environment of the Sanskrit intelligentsia in the latter half of the second millennium.

Bibliography

Abhinavagupta. *Locana*. Ed. Paṇḍit Paṭṭābhirāma Śāstri. Benares: Kashi Sanskrit Series, 1940.

Ānandavardhana. *Dhvanyāloka*. Ed. Paṇḍit Durgāprasād and Kāśināth Pāṇdurang Parab. Mumbai: Munishiram Monoharlal, 1998.

Bhāmaha. *Kāvyālaṃkāra*. Ed. Ramana Kumara Sharma. Delhi: Vidhyānidhi Prakāśan, 1994.

Bharata. *Nāṭyaśāstra*. 4 vols. Ed. K. A. Subramania Iyer. Pune: Deccan College Postgraduate and Research Institute, 1966.

Daṇḍin. *Kāvyādarśa*. Ed. Paṇḍit Rangacharya Raddi Shastri. Pune: Bhandarkar Oriental Research Institute, 1970.

De, Sushil Kumar. *History of Sanskrit Poetics*. 2 vols. Calcutta: Firma K. L. Mukhopadhyaya. 1960. 2nd rev. ed.

Gerow, Edwin. *A Glossary of Indian Figures of Speech*. Berlin: De Gruyter, 1971.

Gerow, Edwin. *Indian Poetics: A History of Indian Literature*. Wiesbaden: Otto Harrassowitz, 1977.

Ingalls, Daniel H. H., Jeffrey Moussaieff Masson, and M. V. Patwardhan (trans.). *The Dhvanyāloka of Ānandavardhana with the Locana of Abhinavagupta*. Cambridge, MA: Harvard University Press, 1990.

Jagannātha. *Rasagaṅgādhara*. Ed. Mathurā Nath Śāstrī. Delhi: Motilal Banarsidass, 1983.

Jayadeva. *Candrāloka of Shri Jayadeva with the Rākāgama Commentary of Gāgābhaṭṭa*. Ed. Ram Ananta Shastri Vetal. Benares: Chaukhamba Sanskrit Series Office, 1938.

Mammaṭācārya. *Kāvyaprakāśa of Mammaṭa*. Ed. Raghunath Damodar Karmakar. Pune: Bandarkar Oriental Society, 1950. 6th ed.

Raghavan, R. V. *Bhoja's Śṛṅgāraprakāśa*. Madras: Punarvasu, 1963. 3rd ed.

Ruyyaka. *Alaṃkārasarvasva*. Ed. Paṇḍit Durgaprasād and Kāśināth Pāṇḍuraṅg Parab. Delhi: Bhāratīya Vidyā Prakāśan, 1982.

Vāmana. *Kāvyālaṃkārasūtrāṇi*. Ed. Ratna Gopāl Bhaṭṭa. Benares: Vidya Vilas Press, 1908.

Chapter 47
INDIAN PHILOSOPHY OF MUSIC

William J. Jackson

Music worldwide is known as a powerful art, able to stir the martial heart, "soothe the savage breast," celebrate, help heal the body, and promote spiritual realization. What signs pointing to music's importance in Hindu culture in particular, can help us understand its status as a religio-cultural system with a philosophical underpinning? Which textual statements summarize Hindu views regarding the powers of music and sacred sound? What is the rationale whereby music offers the potential of spiritual realization?

For millennia Hindu society has repeatedly reconstituted its culture, often reiterating immemorial themes by way of *smārta* ("rememberer") brahmans, who are gatekeepers of orthodox tradition, maintaining the basic tenets of the Hindu lifeway, *vedānta* and the *sanātana dharma* system. For example, Bharata (*c.* first century BCE) wrote the *Nāṭyaśāstra*, a treatise on the performing arts which prevailed as authoritative, and philosopher and aesthetician Abhinavagupta (950–1020 CE) wrote a commentary on it, and on Ānandavardhana's *Dhvanyāloka*. Śārṇgadēva (d. 1247) was also a great compiler and systematizer of musical knowledge. He was the son of a Kashmiri brahman who migrated to South India. He wrote the *Saṅgītaratnākara* ("Ocean of Music") treatise "to propagate the principles of Sanātana Dharma," among other reasons. Śārṇgadēva's work, along with Bharata's *Nāṭyaśāstra*, was most influential in the evolution of the theory of the Karnataka and Hindustani music systems (Ramachandran 1936, 390).

In such traditions the past can be a cumulative presence influencing the present more deeply than current affairs. The work of cultural architects was often to renew enduring works of the past, articulating the honored tradition rather than originating a new view. Music, a progressive art, with exact rules and ongoing adaptiveness, needed to be summarized and updated repeatedly by knowledgeable musicologists, to reconcile authoritatively written theories of the past and actual practices of the day (Ramaswami Aiyar 1932, xv).

Music in Indian thought is important on at least three levels of existence: (1) *ātman*—the infinite Self as innermost reality; (2) the *cakra* system of energy centers in the body; (3) philosophical aspects of music in *bhakti*, as related to dharma and liberation.

Hindu theory of space and cosmogony

Ākāśa means "ethereal space" in Upaniṣadic thinking. Derived from the root *kāś*, "to shine pervasively," *ākāśa* is the luminous void, vibrant directionless space. In Indian traditions, *svara* means a recognizable sound in the musical scale ("the seven *svaras*") and sometimes was spoken of as having a luminous nature. While *dik* is directional space in the abstract, *ākāśa* is the primordial depth prior to divisions and utilizations. In Hindu thought, first there is absolute consciousness (*brahman*); then *ākāśa*, space, arises, then wind, fire, water, earth, herbs food, semen, and person, according to the *Saṅgītaratnākara* (Śārṇgadēva in Raja 1945, II.18–22). As an old Sanskrit saying puts it: "*Śabda niṣtham jagad*," which means, "The universe sprang from sound." Thus *ākāśa* is the subtlest of evolutants. It is space that is infinite and eternal, undivided and transcendent, the medium which makes sound possible. In subtlety it is surpassed only by subtler *brahman*, the all-pervasive consciousness basis of the universe, identical to *ātman*, knower of the field.

Ākāśa, "ether," is not just a medium for carrying vibrations; it allows sound to be the manifestation of beautiful order; which is music, mantra and raga. As Lewis Rowell puts it,

> sound is a quality inhering in the sub-stratum of *ākāśa* which pervades both the outer spaces of the world and inner spaces of the body. It is one, universal, eternal, causal (but not caused) space permeating both personal and transpersonal consciousness, manifested along the human pathway from inner to outer space. Its discharge in the form of vital breath (*prāṇa*) is both an act of worship and an affirmation of universal process.
>
> (Rowell 1992, 41)

The very nature of the universe is permeated by subtle vibrancy. The cosmos is of the nature of the person, who at core is *ātman*, and is composed of sheaths enlivened by *prāṇa* – that chanting is powerful in realizing the person's depth reality. The nesting of *prāṇa* in *ākāśa*, and *ākāśa* in *ātman*, gives structure for song to empower realization. Just as sight is thought to be the attribute of fire, sound is the primary attribute of *ākāśa*. The cosmos is "a humming field of continuous, subtle, audible sound, pulsating with vital energy and potential. *Ākāśa* provides the essential connections between ultimate reality, humanity, and the elemental components of the physical universe" (Rowell 1992, 49). The past, present, and future are woven across *ākāśa*, and *ākāśa* is woven across the imperishable *ātman* it is said in *Bṛhadāraṇyaka Upaniṣad*. *Ākāśa* is penultimately subtle, second only to *ātman*, the subtlest of all. "The Knower of the field abides in *ākāśa*" (*Saṅgītaratnākara* 1.II.18).

Vedic and other ancient narratives depict this dynamic in a variety of ways. The *anāhata nāda* ("unstruck sound") *Oṃ* is the primordial sound origin of the universe. And every aspect of *nāda* is manifested from Śiva the cosmic dancer whose rhythm pulses throughout the cosmos, a sacred symbol for ultimate consciousness. As early as the *Aitareya Upaniṣad* music is spoken of as a *sādhana* (praxis) leading to ultimate release from *samsāra*'s or the cyclic world's woes. Śārṇgadēva and others treat music as the easiest spiritual way to resonate with the subtlest and win the supreme release. Music's true intent is to ravish the outer layers of existence and reach the core of inherent bliss (Rangaramanuja Ayyanger 1978, Introduction).

Cakras: spiritual centers of the person

One of the enduring Hindu ways of envisioning the human situation was to conceptualize a seven-level system within the body. Yoga and tantra developed practices to reach the highest fulfillment possible. The view of embodied existence with several lotus-like centers along the spine became part of music theory. A major part of the treatise explains a yoga- and *tantra*-derived depiction of the body as a microcosm with six energy centers, *cakras*. Rising from the genital organs, extending up to the brain, distributed along the spinal center, the *cakras* are connected by two veins. From these two intertwining serpentine nerve-vines the *cakras* blossom like lotuses, a system in which energy deep in the body rises to the highest mind. "Two varieties of the subtle air and fire (*prāṇa* and *anala*) that sustain the human body" (Rangaramanuja Ayyanger 1978, 2–3) join together to awaken the compact spiral power of *Kuṇḍalīni* energy "coiled" in the root base, the bottommost of the six *cakras* or lotus-petalled nerve centers distributed along the spinal column. "Coiled" means compact potential inherent energy waiting to be released, capable of uncoiling and extending, like a snake springing forth and gliding. The *śakti* (energy) of this release is described as an experiential resonance, expressing the *prāṇava*'s vibration *Om*. In the intent focus of meditation the yogi hears this sound. The *cakra*-lotuses have a syllable associated with each petal, so, when the primeval sound (*anāhatadhvani*) moves them, each produces a sound. The spontaneous primordial "unstruck" sound is the *Prāṇava*, *Om*, essence of essences, source of the Vedas. The universe sprang from sound, and by returning to primal sound the person may merge with the sacred origin.

The *cakra* schema is concerned with finding the cosmic divine energy in the person, and ultimately transcending the cosmos (Eliade 1969, 245). In the *Kuṇḍalīni*-centered conception of the human being, one vein runs up the right side of the spine, *piṅgala*, symbolic of the masculine solar energy. The other, *ida*, runs up along the left side, a matching female lunar energy. The third vein, *suṣumnā*, runs between the two, and the joining of the two energy currents up through the middle vein amounts to realization. "Identified with Śabdabrahman, with OM, [the presence of] *Kuṇḍalīni* possesses all the attributes of all gods and all goddesses. Under the form of a snake, it dwells in the midpoint of the body (*dehamadhyaya*) of all creatures" (Eliade 1969, 245). The sound rises up the spine from the *mūlādhāra* at the base and the *cakras*, centers of energy, awaken – *svadhiṣṭh nama* (genitals), *maṇipūrakam* (navel), *anāhatam* (heart), *viśuddha* (throat), *ājñā* (between the eyebrows, site of the pineal gland), and the highest, at the top of the head, *sahasrāra*.

According to Śārṇgadēva, modifications of *vāyu* in this *cakra* system of the human body are the forces which produce the variety of human personalities and constitute the way to realize highest consciousness (II.59–167). One modification is *prāṇa*, another *apana*, and so on, each being a kind of energy that occupies and circulates in a region of the body. Śārṇgadēva visualizes the virtues and powers associated with the activated petals of the lotuses, the lower ones (such as the *ādhāra cakra*) producing heroic bliss, sexual passion, etc. (II.120 and124). "In the heart is the *anāhatam cakra*, the place for the worship of Śiva of the form of *prāṇava*" (II.126–127). Each lotus along the rising *nāḍis* has a certain number of petals (4-6-10-12-16-2) and the numbers signify fruits of the *ātman* abiding in them. The heart, throat, and mid-eyebrow *cakras* are crowned and transcended by a fourth at the top of the head: "In the *Brahmarandhra* there is the *cakra* with a thousand petals, which holds ambrosia. That develops the body with the currents of the showering of ambrosia" (II.139), in the fulfillment of life according to the *Saṅgītaratnākara*.

The system which Śārṇgadēva explicates is one of multi-potentiality – both positive and negative possibilities are present in each center, depending on the state of the individual petals of each *cakra* lotus. If the *ātman*, for example, is present in the Eastern eighth, eleventh, twelfth petals of the *anāhatam cakra* the person will be stimulated to develop musical abilities. However, the activation of the fourth, sixth, tenth petals, means music and related arts are destroyed (II.140–142). It is a system explaining the expression or the repression of spiritual advancement, depending on one's karmic results, by visualizing an inner structure. "The Self abiding in the *Brahmarandra*, as if immersed in ambrosia becomes satisfied and shall attain music, and other things to be accomplished, with great excellence. Abiding in the alternative remaining petals of these and in other *cakras*, the Self shall never attain accomplishment in music, etc." (II.144–145). Thus, the spiritual self, restricted or expanded depending on one's karma, empowers musical creativity, and there is also a counterforce which closes, impoverishing the same potential.

Thus the spiritual organs along the central axis of the human body are not entirely mental visualizations, since nerves meet there, but they clearly form an ideal to visualize: petals, with syllables written on them. Tones exist in an ascending order, and therefore in association with specific tones the *cakras* are made realizable. This vision of the body is part physical, part spiritual, with subtle solar and lunar paths in the body. Thus it is a paradigm which does not suffer from Cartesian dualism of body/mind. Instead it offers way to picture the whole person, solving the age-old conundrum.

Śārṇgadēva's third chapter begins:

> We worship the Nāda-Brahman, the divine sound which is the conscious spark of life in all beings (*caitanyam sarva bhūtānā*), which is manifest in the configuration of the cosmos, and which is the supreme bliss. Through the worship of Nāda the forms of Brahmā, Viṣṇu and Maheśvara are truly worshipped, because they personify the nature of that Nāda.
>
> (*Saṅgītaratnākara* III.1–2)

Thus at root, the gods and human beings are manifestations of divine sound, vital vibrancies. The quite exact and exacting system of *prāṇa*-and-*cakras* both is, and is not, the key to the life processes. It is, because it provides a basic meaning-structure. It is not, because it is not meant to be taken only literally, dogmatically, opaquely, but is meant as a transparent metaphor to envision the living situation, an experiential guide using symbolic language. Music is called a gentle, subtle way to charm the snake of divine energy through the centers, causing one to resonate with their inherent tones. *Kuṇḍalīni* is called a slender red flame humming with *anāhata nāda*, "eternal increate vibration of the godhead whose energy is the Word (*Vāc*)" (Padoux 1987, 403). On the symbolic divine level, in Hindu iconography Viṣṇu sleeps on a coiled serpent; on the human level, a coiled serpent sleeps in depths, the potentiality at the self's basis.

Viewed in this way the *cakras* are levels where ordinary people's consciousness may be active and may become stuck, the inner pitches at which material and spiritual life are possible. They are the six echelons or experiential levels of attention and expression in a system of progressive spirituality blooming. In this way the system describes not direct percepts (touch, sight, etc.) but concepts, a system of aspiration and hope, a vision of biospiritual tropism.

The *cakras* can be said to embody the levels of potency which make one a human being. The lower three are (1) security and survival, (2) sexuality and reproduction, (3) authority and fame. The upper three *cakras* raise the human above the animal level – (1) heart (love, faith and duty), (2) throat (knowledge), (3) mid-eyebrows (austerity, intuition, and realization). The seventh at the top embodies the full blossoming of cosmic consciousness. It is striking that in the *cakra* system the torso is most important, the vital spine of selfhood, and that this cerebrospinal system emerges first in the growth of the organism after conception; it generates electric current through delicate nerves. (Electricity is still a mystery of negative and positive forces, and we take for granted the constant discharge of subtle electrical pulses in the cerebellum.) Buried at the tail end of the system is the root treasury of energy. Blooming as the elaborate top vertebrae of the system, the head with its cerebral cortex is the site of amazing subtle electrical activity; the heart is roughly near the center of the torso.

The seven notes of the *Sāma Veda* are called "six plus one" because the gods live on the highest note of the *Sāma*; human beings live on the lower six. The *Atharva Veda* calls the seven-rayed Sun a macro-cosmic harp, corresponding to the human instrument of seven "breaths" (XV.15.2). In musical treatises the *vīna* (veena) is a divine instrument, its parts made up of Śiva, Pārvatī, etc. The human body is also called a *vīna*. The seven notes are *cakras*, etc. Such correlations are of the essence of mystical spirituality, which is the realization of connectivities, by tuning, truing, aligning. These Hindu symbols give interpretive schemes as well as programs for action.

Nādavidyā (or *nādayoga*) as a "vehicle of inner illumination and medium of aesthetic enjoyment" (Rangaramanuja Ayyangar 1978, vii) has often been highly praised from Upaniṣadic times onward. The philosopher Abhinavagupta brought out the link between aesthetic enjoyment and the religious experience of bliss. Characteristically, he taught that the etymology of the word *svara* (musical note) had to do with "that which restores one's true nature." In his view aesthetic emotions ultimately arise from the aesthetic emotion of tranquility (*śānta rasa*), which is also an experience of the absolute. In Indian thought, music is not only personal; it also figures in the work of vitalizing dharma in a society.

Philosophy of music in *bhakti* and *dharma* (social order)

Nādayoga represents an acoustic symbol system based on spiritual and musical experiences; it consists of observations of patterns realized by means of yogic practices. It concerns aspects of the Vedic concept *ṛta* – cosmic rhythm, order and rite, sacrifice and praise. Order plays an essential part on all levels of existence, including social. The roots of social order in ancient India involve the complementary interaction of Being and Nonbeing, Chant and Voice, Priest and King.

The *Jaiminīya Upaniṣad Brāhmaṇa* tells the story of the marriage between two worlds. A. K. Coomaraswamy translates the passage:

> In the beginning this was twofold Being and Nonbeing both. Of these two, Being is the Chant, the Intellect, Spiration. The Nonbeing is the Verse, the Voice, Expiration. She, the Verse, desired intercourse with (*mithunam*) him, the Chant. He asked her: "Who art thou?" She answered: "I am She" (*sāham asmi*). "Then, indeed, am I He" (*aham amo'smi*) he replied. What "She" (*sa*) is and what "He" (*ama*), that makes "Chant" (*sāman*), and this is the quiddity of the "Chant."
>
> (I. 53–55)

The ideal complementary roles of the kingly and priestly consist in this arrangement: What the priest envisions and conceives of, the king receives as program to institute. The brahman priest stands for the holy chant, singing the vision of the overarching *ṛta* pattern or musical harmony inherent in the nature of the cosmos. Coomaraswamy observes that in this ideal relationship the king follows in collaboration, accompanying the priest's work, going along in the vehicle already set in motion by inspiration. The king is dependent on the priest's vision and chant. "*The king brings forth (enacts) what the Priest knows.*" And "*the formation of a concept begotten by Manas or Brahmā on Vāc is a vital operation*" (Coomaraswamy 1942, 12–13). Revelation inspires organization in this old ideal. The sage encourages the warrior's personal self-mastery; social responsibility incarnates the priest's spirituality. At its best the relationships are mutually fulfilling – each requires the other.

A *Ṛg Veda* prayer reverently prays that musical offering be accepted by the divine: "May my song, from which oil trickles and that is filled with sweetness, be a fine-tasting meal for Indra" (Schneider 1989, 81). The term *bhakti* derives from the root *bhaj* – "to share, to share with, to participate in, (by so doing) to become one with." In this tradition devotional music is the meal which the surrendered soul and supreme being share. Already the *Upaniṣads*, with their repetitions and rhythms, had a music-like effect, bringing chanting and philosophy together. Later, *bhakti* composers carried this trend further, singing many songs with philosophical ideas.

Music's power is depicted in an old story about two *bhakti* saints. It is said that once when a kingdom's lamp of *dharma* was extinguished in the central temple only a holy musician could rekindle it with the power of song. Bhaktisara was an *aḷvār*, one of a group of twelve Tamil Vaiṣṇava saints. He wandered, practiced yoga, and became an exponent of Śaivism before he became a great Viṣṇu devotee. When the king asked Kanikannan, Bhaktisara's lifelong companion, to sing his royal glory. Kanikannan refused, saying "I only sing to the Lord." The king ordered Kanikannan to leave the kingdom. Bhaktisara prayed to Lord Viṣṇu: "Kanikannan is leaving here, and I who boldly sing Thy glory, follow him … Lord, please come with us." When this happened the townspeople also began leaving the city, and the state temple lost its light. No rains fell. Dharma was in disarray. The imperiled and regretful king, realizing his fault, repented, and sought refuge at the feet of Bhaktisara, begging him for forgiveness, and pleading with him to return to Kānçi (present-day Kanchi). To promote wellbeing in the kingdom the saint agreed. Arriving there, Bhaktisara prayed: "Lord, make your bed again in this temple, Kanikannan has returned. I have also." The two holy men sang, according to legend, and the temple again glowed with luster and the kingdom again grew prosperous (Sathianathan 1996, 150–152). This event, according to legends, occurred a thousand years ago. Other legends also depict holy musicians able to rekindle the extinguished light of neglected dharma with the mysterious power of *Dīpak raga* (Fyzee-Rahamin 1925, 88–89).

Vidyāraṇya, spiritual founder of the Vijayanagara empire, wrote a treatise on music, *Saṅgīta Sara* ("Essence of Music"), now lost. Two centuries later Haridāsa musician-saints like Purandaradāsa and Kanakadāsa used music in Kannada language songs to great effect. Annamācārya, a prolific Telugu-language singer-saint wrote thousands of devotional and philosophical songs. In the north, the Gosvamins of the Caitanya tradition, Brahmins who carried on the Nityānanda legacy, developed further Abhinavagupta's aesthetic-religious views, applying aesthetic experience categories to spiritual experience. Each generation has had its *rasikas*, following fine taste toward sapience. As the *Taittirīya Upaniṣad* taught, *raso vai saḥ*, meaning "The essence of the highest Self is transcendent bliss."

Musical vision's fluidity

In the Hindu vision, all things are bathed in a subtle plasma of their own unity, in waves of subtle cosmic sound. Thus the hearing of cosmic sound is a way to tune into the deepest reality. Music is placed so high in our esteem because it runs so deep in our experience; it is taken for granted as basic in the background because it is so integral to the whole. It is a subtle guide of the Hindu way, leader of the soul on its journeys.

Antonio de Nicolas writes appreciatively of "the Hindu theory of tuning by which *all possible perspectives* are kept open" (de Nicolas 1976, 285), and he sees wisdom in this choice:

> In India the *continuum* of pitch experienced was preserved under the hegemony of the ear, not number, in a way which rejected no possible "embodiment"

> (tuning, however defined) while declining to grant perspectival precedence to any one of them. In India *number* was apparently dethroned only after its lessons were thoroughly assimilated, some time before the Ṛg Vedic cosmological hymns were conceived, long *before* the *Gītā*.
>
> (de Nicolas 1976, 286)

In human history rigid exclusivist views have acted as a retardant epistemologically to dealing with reality on a sound basis.

Vaiṣṇava composer Annamācārya (d. 1503) sang in Telugu that the whole cosmos is God's ear, and that God's hearing is made up of all space; therefore, granting this omnipresent awareness and God's manifestation in every word and sound, none can justly complain that God doesn't listen to their prayers — the fault must lie within (Annamācārya 1980, #287). The Kannada composer Kanakadāsa (sixteenth century) sang in his song *Yeli nodi*:

> The gate to *karma* is the ear; / You can hear *mokṣasara* (the essence of liberation) through this ear. / This very ear is the axe of action; / in the inner ear you can perceive the eternal vibration / which is the root of existence. Wherever I turn I see Rāma. / Those who know this secret know/that in their own bodies they can see Rāma in devotion's inner space.

Tyāgarāja (1767–1847) wrote several Telugu songs on the theme of music's spiritual greatness, saying that with inspired devotional music we have a way to find ultimate reality's intrinsic depth, the order of the consciousness principle amidst the *kolāhala* – the chaotic roar of existence in the world. Amid the chaos, the lotus *cakras* in humans can fully open. These voices speak for an experiential philosophy which can be summed up as follows: Listen and know; make music and find being.

Music keeps growing on, nourishing other arts. Abhinavagupta's philosophy, Purandaradāsa *kirtanas* at the height of the Vijayanagara empire, and Tyāgarāja's *kṛtis*, have carried the ancient Indian philosophical vision of music into our age. Modern thinkers also affirm that in this disquieting world, music can still bring serene silence and fulfillment.

References

Annamācārya, Tallapaka. 1980. *Adhyātma Sankirtanalu*, vol. 2. Tirupati: TTD.

Bilimoria, P. and Wenta, A. 2015. "Emotions in Indian Thought-Systems: An Introduction." In *Emotions in Indian Thought-Systems*. P. Bilimoria and A. Wenta (eds.). New Delhi/London: Routledge.

Coomaraswamy, A. K. 1942. *Spiritual Authority and Temporal Power in the Indian Theory of Government*. New Haven, CT: American Oriental Society.

de Nicolas, Antonio T. 1976. *Avatāra: The Humanization of Philosophy through the Bhagavad Gītā*. New York: Nicolas Hays.

Eliade, Mircea. 1969. *Yoga: Freedom and Immortality*. Princeton, NJ: Princeton University Press.

Fyzee-Rahamin, Atiya Begum. 1925. *The Music of India*. London: Luzac & Co.

Gopi Krishna. 1971. *Kuṇḍalīni: The Evolutionary Energy in Man*. New York: Random House.

Padoux, André. 1987. "Kundalīni." In *Encyclopedia of Religion*, vol. 8. Mircea Eliade (ed.). New York: Macmillan.

Ramachandran, N. S. 1936. "The Evolution of the Theory of Music in the Vijayanagara Empire." In *Dr. S. Krishnaswami Aiyangar Commemoration Volume*. V. Rangacharya, C. S. Srinivasachari, and V. R. Ramachandra Dikshitar (eds.). Madras: G. S. Press.

Ramaswami Aiyar, M. S. (trans.). 1932. *Ramamatya's Svaramēlakalānidhi*, "Introduction." Annamalainagar: Annamalai University. Internet Archive, www.archive.org/stream/ramamaryassvaram014442mbp/ramamaryassvaram014442mbp_djvu.txt.

Rangaramanuja Ayyanger, R. 1978. *Saṅgītaratnākara of Nissanka Śārṇgadēva: A Study*. Bombay: Wilco Publishing House.

Rowell, Lewis. 1992. *Music and Musical Thought in Early India*. Chicago: University of Chicago Press.

Śārṅgadēva. 1945. *Saṅgītaratnākara*, vol. 2. C. Kunhan Raja (trans.). Madras: Adyar Library.

Sathianathan, S. 1996. *Contributions of Saints and Seers to Music of India*. New Delhi: Kanishka Publishers.

Schneider, Marius. 1989. "Acoustic Symbolism." In *Cosmic Music: Musical Keys to the Interpretation of Reality*. Joscelyn Godwin (ed.). Rochester, VT: Inner Traditions.

Tagore, Rabindranath. 1912. *Gitanjali (Song Offerings)*. London: The India Society.

Tagore, Rabindranath. 1922. *Creative Unity*. London: Macmillan.

III

ENGAGING AND ENCOUNTERS: MODERN AND POSTMODERN

Chapter 48
ISLAMIC MODERNISM IN INDIA

Muhammad Kamal

After the defeat of the Mughals in the second half of the nineteenth century, India came under the influence of modernity. Indian Muslims responded to this new historical situation in three different ways. Some of them had nostalgia for the glorious past, and thought of modernity as irreligious and antagonistic to Islam. For this group of Muslims, the revival of Islamic teaching and values became necessary and a way to regain the political hegemony of the past. Others sought to soften the anguish of defeat through spiritual redemption by taking refuge in the messianic movements and Sufi orders.

Some intellectual Muslims disapproved of these two responses. They felt a need for the intellectual re-orientation of Muslim society. They attempted to understand their new historic epoch rationally in order to demonstrate the compatibility of Islam with modernity. This direction in the development of Islamic thought had a twofold task: first, to deconstruct the aspects of religious dogma that remained an impediment to progress; second, to construct a new understanding of reality on a rationalistic discourse and the scientific cognition of the times, but in a way that did not stand in contradiction to Islam. This direction was undertaken by Muslim thinkers such as Sayyid Ahmad Khan (1817–1898), Jamal al-Din al-Afghani (1839–1897), Chiragh Ali (1844–1895), Shibli Nu'mani (1857–1914), Mawlana Hali (1837–1924), Ameer Ali (1849–1928), Muhammad Iqbal (1876–1938), Abul Kalam Azad (1888–1958), and others who created a reform movement known as Islamic modernism.

Islamic modernism originated in the Aligarh school; its architect was Sayyid Ahmad Khan. This Muslim thinker advocated the idea of reform in Islamic thought by returning to the essence of Islam and interpreting this essence in light of human reason. He rejected whatever was inconsistent with reason, took a position in which reason had precedence over other ways of acquiring knowledge, and placed faith in the secondary position. He shunned all ideas that were not in the domain of rationalistic discourse and its interpretation such as the supernatural, with the exception of God's existence (Khan 1966, 743). He urged Muslims to arm themselves with scientific knowledge of the modern world and seek the Western style of education. While a large number of

Muslims in India boycotted the British system of education and considered the natural sciences heretical, Sayyid Ahmad Khan established the Muhammadan Anglo-Oriental College in 1875, the only Islamic institution of learning offering courses on natural sciences and humanities to students at that time. Later, in 1921, this institution of learning was developed into the Muslim Aligarh University (Khan 1966). Sayyid Ahmad Khan tried to convince Muslims that since nature was the creation of God, attempting to explain nature scientifically did not contradict faith: 'In spite of all this I am fully convinced that the Work of God and the Word of God [Qur'an] can never be antagonistic to each other; we may, through the fault of our knowledge, sometimes make mistakes in understanding the meaning of the Word' (Khan 1966, 744). Chiragh Ali, another Muslim modernist and a patron of Sayyid Ahmad Khan, argued in an article in *Tahzib al-Akhlaq*, a periodical journal published by Sayyid Ahmad Khan, that the Qur'an makes several references to nature and the laws of nature, which could become a foundation for establishing a natural theology. On Western education and scientific knowledge Sayyid Ahmad Khan expressed his views clearly in a letter to Mawlawi Tassaduq, stating that 'If Muslims do not take to the system of education introduced by the British, they will not only remain a backward community but will sink lower and lower until there will be no hope of recovery left to them' (Khan 1966). Putting emphasis on the significance of scientific knowledge and the advancement of the modern world, he continued in the same letter,

> It is not only because the British are today our rulers, and we have to recognize this fact if we are to survive, that I am advocating the adoption of their system of education, but also because Europe has made such remarkable progress in science that it would be suicidal not to make an effort to acquire it.
>
> (Khan 1966, 745)

One of the intellectual ambitions of Islamic modernism is to solve the contradictions between reason and faith, religion and science. To achieve this, religion is reduced to a system of ethical values that distinguishes virtue from vice and to a set of propositions on the creation of the world and theodicy. Revelation is interpreted as a product of a faculty of reason manifested in some individuals such as the prophets, rather than a communicative knowledge from God to the prophets through an external mediation (Khan 1973, 114; Ahmad 1970, 41). On the ground of the rationalistic understanding of religion, the existence of miracles is also rejected because miracles contradict the laws of nature.

It is worth mentioning that Islamic modernism flourished under the influence of the Mu'tazilite theological school, Shah Wali Allah Dihlawi's reformist ideas, and the scientific advance of the West. Mu'tazilism was the first Islamic rationalist school, established in Basra and Baghdad in the eighth century; it placed faith under rationalistic scrutiny. Shah Wali Allah Dihlawi (1703–1763) was a pre-modernist reformer who blended opposing doctrines of Islamic thought and reconciled two major metaphysical doctrines of Sufism, namely the unity of being and the unity of experience. He held the view that on the ground of inductive reasoning, the evidence of revelation conformed to the axioms of reason (Al-Ghazali 2001, 6). Unlike the traditionalist *ulama*, he believed that the gate of individual reasoning (*ijtihad*) in interpreting religious creeds should remain open.

The focal point of Islamic modernism is the idea of reform in Islamic thought. This reform has three towers of strength: return to the 'essence' of Islam; a rationalistic interpretation of this essence; and its reconciliation with scientific knowledge. A return to the 'essence' of Islam is a move to get closer to the roots or ground on which this faith stands and without which it is unthinkable. It is proximity to the ground and at the same time remoteness from the non-ground or accretions that have concealed the 'essence' and not allowed it to manifest itself. The question which arises is what is the 'essence' of Islam? Muslim modernists believed that the Qur'an is the 'essence' of this religion. Proximity to the 'essence' is possible only by returning to the Qur'an. These thinkers also make a distinction between two aspects of the Qur'an, or between the permanent and temporary injunctions in the text. The former are considered binding while the latter are not (Khalifa 1961, 322). The permanent injunctions such as the unity of God, the divine attributes and their relationship to the essence of God, prophethood, revelation, creation *ex nihilo*, divine retribution, and so on are binding and mould the essential aspects of the faith; hence they should be acknowledged universally by believers. The temporary injunctions refer to certain social circumstances and rituals of the Arab society of the seventh century and are relevant to that time and society (Khan 1892, 4). They should not be seen as universally applicable. Their meanings are better understood in their historical context. After making this distinction between permanent and temporary injunctions, modernists endeavoured to develop a new hermeneutics for interpreting the Qur'an. Sayyid Ahmad Khan, for example, named fifteen permanent Qur'anic injunctions as the bedrock of this new hermeneutics. As a consequence of this return to the 'essence' of Islam, whatever had been produced in the formative process of Islamic thought or, more precisely, in historical Islam could be rejected because it was non-essential and nothing more than a system of corollaries inferred from the essential part of the faith.

Return to the 'essence' of faith has a historical significance without which reform remains unthinkable; it liberates faith from all the non-essential elements added to it by the *ulama* and commentators on legal matters. The engagement of the *ulama* with the non-essential aspects of Islam had produced a copious body of tradition and generated an inversion in the nearness–remoteness formula for understanding Islam. This led to remoteness from the essence and nearness to the non-essentials of the faith, which eventually made religious practices more ritualistic and too complicated to be followed by common believers. Ameer Ali openly accused the cluster of *ulama* and held them responsible for this inversion, as those religious scholars had played an important role in interpreting Islam for the political benefit of the establishment and for their own material gain (Ali 1922, 328).

The modernist approach to the temporary injunctions is grounded on understanding the historical situations (context) in which the injunctions are communicated. Since novelty rules over history, value systems are determined by socio-historical conditions and change. One needs to understand the meaning of the temporary

Qur'anic injunctions in terms of their modality in the past and their valid applicability to meet the social needs of today. In this way, these thinkers re-examined some temporary injunctions of the Qur'an dealing with issues such as polygamy, slavery, gender equality, human rights, and bank interest (*riba*). Sayyid Ahmad Khan, for example, in his interpretation of the Qur'anic verses on polygamy argued that polygamy was not permissible. His interpretation was based on three principles: natural law, social practice, and religious dogma (Ahmad 1970, 52). Mumtaz Ali, one of the disciples of Sayyid Ahmad Khan, campaigned for women's rights through education and published *Tahzib al-Niswan*, the first Islamic journal on women's rights in India and parallel to Sayyid Ahmad Khan's *Tahzib al-Akhlaq*. In arguing against slavery in Islam, Muslim modernists insisted on contradictions between the existence of this institution and the belief in free will. For them slavery and free will did not coexist because they were exclusive. It is not possible for a person to claim to be free and at the same time live in slavery or accept the existence of this institution. It is also not possible for a divine text to contain such a contradiction as it is believed to be free from contradictions. In examining the permanent injunctions of the Qur'an, these thinkers saw slavery as a historical phenomenon rather than a practice inherited from the essence of Islam (Ahmad 1970, 51). It is worth mentioning that the modernist approach to the Qur'an at the Aligarh school, despite its controversy, has influenced several Muslim intellectuals and activists dealing with human rights and feminism in the Middle East and Southeast Asia. Meanwhile it is hard to believe that it has shown the way to the creation of a hermeneutic method. Fazlur Rahman, an adherent of Islamic modernism stated that

> Muslims have not yet found an adequate method for interpreting the Qur'an and the *Sunnah* (or practice) of the Prophet to meet modern needs. Although almost all sections of the Muslim society are agreed in accepting at least the economically developmental forms of modernity and at the same time to preserve Islam, it has been difficult for them to devise a method whereby both are meaningfully integrated.
>
> (Rahman 1966, 118)

This criticism is based on the modernist individualistic approach to understanding and interpreting the Qur'anic verses, in which the verse is taken into consideration individually by isolating it from the rest. This finally creates a pluralistic approach and multiple meanings of a single verse, which is understood in isolation from the rest of the text by different individual readers and interpreters. The nearness–remoteness formula mentioned earlier has other logical consequences. Thinking of the Qur'an as the 'essence' means also withdrawing from all accretions, which are non-essential. Since these non-essentials belong to historical Islam they can be rejected. One of the problems faced by modernists is the rejection of the prophetic traditions; while they see the traditions as non-essential, to mainstream Muslims they make up the second foundation text after the Qur'an. The rejection of the prophetic traditions is, however, a logical consequence of the return to the 'essence'.

There are also other reasons for rejecting the traditions; the authenticity of the traditions was kept under scrutiny. For the modernist thinkers, it was not possible to examine whether the '*matn*' of each tradition (one of the two major aspects of a hadith, which contains the actual report) transmitted by the narrators was in the same phraseology articulated by the Prophet Muhammad during his time. In dealing with this problem, Chiragh Ali rejected all traditions that are abhorrent to human reason and in contradiction to the permanent injunctions of the Qur'an. Sayyid Ahmad Khan's view on the prophetic traditions was also built on the ground of doubt, as he saw their authenticity as exposed to fallibility. Mawlana Hali, who was a biographer and a disciple of Sayyid Ahmad Khan, did not reject the traditions completely, but classified them into those with a necessary connection with the permanent injunctions of the Qur'an and those in which the prophet deals with everyday affairs of the Arab-Muslim community. He considered the traditions of the second category to be non-binding (Siddiqi 1970, 40).

Another issue raised by Muslim modernist thinkers was predestination. This issue was a point of conflict and theological debate in medieval Islam between the rationalist and traditionalist Muslim theologians in Baghdad. The rationalist theologians, represented by the Mu'tazilite school, advocated the doctrine of free will and solved the contradiction between the notions of divine justice and predestination by reasoning. For them, the doctrine of predestination was in disagreement with the notion of divine justice as the latter presupposed free will. Muslim modernist thinkers categorically rejected the doctrine of predestination, but unlike the Mu'tazilites, not all of them promoted that of free will. Some of these thinkers were inspired by the dominant scientific knowledge of the nineteenth century and expressed their admiration for scientific determinism or an understanding of reality on the causal relationship between events in nature as well as history. Generally, their views on whether human beings are free or determined divided them into three groups: some of them adhered to scientific determinism; others rejected this ethical position and advocated a softer determinism that leaves room for human choice. The rest promoted the doctrine of free will.

The adherents of scientific determinism such as Sayyid Ahmad Khan, Mawlana Hali, and Shibli Nu'mani interpreted the universe on an onto-theological ground in the style of Aristotelian metaphysics, with the exception of the idea of creation *ex nihilo*. God is the creator and the First Cause of both the universe and human life, but due to the existence of a chain of cause and effect, God does not have direct contact with individual life. Events in nature and history take place in accordance with the laws of nature and are determined by natural causes. This interpretation has a twofold significance: first, the creator does not interfere in the life of individuals and historical events; second, whatever happens in history is not due to 'fate' or something predestined by the creator but is determined by natural causes.

Looking at the Qur'an, Sayyid Ahmad Khan believed that certain verses in the text stress the fact that the creator is the Prime Cause and all other causes exist only through the creator. These Qur'anic verses clearly explain events in human life in terms of causal relationships or scientific determinism. The Qur'an told human beings to investigate nature, and through this investigation the problem of predestination would be solved. Against the adherents of predestination, Mawlana Hali remarked:

> Even those who hold this belief [predestination] do not desist from making appropriate efforts in everyday life. They will repair their houses, put their valuables under lock and key and will not leave their houses open, if there is no inmate in it. But when they are faced with a difficult situation whose causes are a little bit complicated, they begin to talk of destiny and trust in God.
>
> (Khan 1973, 332)

Mawlana Hali argued against predestination but interpreted human history scientifically and saw the acceptance of the sequence of cause and effect among natural phenomena, the role of natural order and its governance by universal laws as fundamental for understanding religion.

Shibli Nu'mani insists that a scientific interpretation of nature, based on the law of causation, is not in contradiction to Islam. If everything in nature is dominated by God's direct interference, then why do Muslims enjoy victory at one time and suffer defeat at another? According to Nu'mani, the answer to this question is in our understanding of natural causes, which contribute to victory or defeat at different times. God does not have a direct relationship to these events. He/she should not be held responsible for them. These thinkers, as we see, rejected the doctrine of predestination or the view that God determines the choices and all outcomes of human actions. By doing this they also denied evil to God.

The second group of Muslim modernist thinkers does not agree completely with the views of the first group, because scientific determinism leaves no room for freedom of choice. Jamal al-Din al-Afghani developed his understanding of human freedom under the influence of the Ash'arite doctrine of acquisition (*al-kasb*) and scientific determinism. For the Ash'arites, a theological school of medieval Islam, human will is not original, but is derived from the will of God. For this reason they cannot agree with the view that holds human beings to be free. Since human beings are not the creators of their own power and will, they enjoy limited freedom. Al-Baqillani (*c.* 950–1013), an Ash'arite theologian, explained this type of soft determinism, stating that God creates all intentional activities in human life but their modes are produced by individuals themselves and they are held responsible for them. For example, the power to move our bodies is given by God, but walking or sitting is a human choice. Human beings are endowed with the ability to act, so not all events or states of affairs are produced by a transient causation. Unwilling to accept scientific determinism and abandon free will completely, Jamal al-Din al-Afghani also tried to endorse the middle position between predestination and free will and, like the Ash'arites, advocated a softer version of determinism. He speaks of freedom as the power of doing according to what one wills, but that power is derivative and limited.

Muhammad Iqbal and Ameer Ali are advocates of the doctrine of free will. As a modernist Muslim and the most outstanding poet-philosopher of the Indian subcontinent, Iqbal admitted the need for a new interpretation of Islamic thought in the face of new realities: 'the claim of the present generation of Muslim liberals to re-interpret the foundational legal principles, in the light of their own experience and the altered conditions of social life, is, in my opinion, perfectly justified' (Iqbal 1962, 180). Iqbal's early education introduced him to Hindu texts, particularly the *Bhagavad Gītā* (Bilimoria 2016). Iqbal went on to study philosophy in Cambridge and Munich and knew of the philosophical debates being pursued in the Occidental world. Being inspired by Nietzsche, Hegel, Bergson, Bradley and McTaggart he was familiar with the ideas of the *Übermensch*, the dynamics of consciousness, and creative evolution. Under the influence of these thinkers, particularly Nietzsche and Bergson, he made a distinction between rational knowledge and knowledge by religious experience (intuition) outside the domain of reason. Further, he interpreted consciousness as something which is not space-bound but is in constant change. He believed that Nietzsche's idea of the *Übermensch* should be given special attention as Muslim society was in need of such individuals (*Mard-e-mu'min*) for reconstructing higher morality and reflecting on the correlation between divinity and temporality (Iqbal 1962, 115). His relation to Nietzsche was also critical as he accused him of being a nihilist and negligent of the profession of faith or the acknowledgement of God's sovereignty. Iqbal tried to understand Nietzsche's *Übermensch* in religious terms, and his advocacy of human freedom was presupposed by the way Iqbal understood human consciousness as something substantially distinct from material reality; something that cannot be studied in a natural context and its relation to the laws of nature. According to Iqbal, the laws of nature are developed by consciousness for understanding material reality. They are not applied to consciousness. Consciousness is not bound by its own laws. There is no way to think that its own laws would bind consciousness and consciousness can be studied scientifically. Iqbal's interpretation of the myth of Adam's transgression and of Satan's seduction of Adam is the best example to prove that human beings are free and in constant struggle to achieve perfection, as the event gave the creator the possibility of using labour and strife to cultivate all possibilities in life. This myth can be understood only if human freedom is taken into consideration. Against the doctrine of predestination, Iqbal argues that future events are not determined by God, because they are mere possibilities that might come into existence with human and not God's initiation (Iqbal 1953, 80). Furthermore, he states that although the idea of destiny runs through the Qur'an, there are verses that deal with freedom of consciousness; for example it is written that human beings are free to choose their religion, and it is up to them whether they choose to do good or evil. For Iqbal, Islam does not deny human freedom; rather, it restores it by bringing human beings closer to God through a sense of their moral responsibilities, which is possible only on the ground of free will. As we see, Muslim modernist thinkers rejected the idea of predestination, which was advocated by traditionalist Muslims. They aimed to liberate the Muslim mind from the doom of predestination, but not all of them accepted free will. The majority however, in particular the members of the Aligarh school led by Sayyid Ahmad Khan, rejected predestination in favour of scientific determinism. Another important issue discussed by these thinkers was the relationship between religion and politics. With the exception of Jamal al-Din al-Afghani, who believed in pan-Islamism and fighting against Western colonialism, these thinkers were politically secular. They aimed at keeping faith in the subjective domain of human experience and were against the institutionalization of religion. For practical purposes Islam was reduced to a set of rituals and metaphysical injunctions appropriate to the private relationship between individuals and God. Unlike the Muslim traditionalists, the modernists did not treat Islam as the basis for understanding socio-economic policies in the public domain.

In the end, Islamic modernism as a reformist movement aimed at interpreting the dogmas of faith in the light of reasoning and at transcending the stagnant doctrinal body of literature produced by the medieval *ulama*. It set its sights on arming Muslim society with the scientific knowledge of the West and establishing Islamic compatibility with modernity. Today, the majority of Muslims seek scientific knowledge and technological advancement for practical reasons, but they have failed to recognize the significance and contributions of this reform movement. Unfortunately, instead of becoming a popular movement, Islamic modernism has remained in the circle of Muslim intellectuals and could not traverse the academic boundaries.

References

Ahmad, Aziz. 1970. *Islamic Modernism in India and Pakistan 1857–1964*. Oxford: Oxford University Press.

Al-Ghazali, M. 2001. *The Socio-Political Thought of Shah Wali Allah*. Islamabad: The International Institute of Islamic Thought.

Ali, Ameer. 1922. *Spirit of Islam*. London: Chatto & Windus.

Bilimoria, P. 2016. 'Muhammad Iqbāl and the Bhagavad Gītā'; 'Iqbal's "God" and the Gita's "Lord"' (two parts). *Sūtra Journal* (a curated journal on art, culture and dharma). May and July 2016. Minerva's Open Access Repository. www.sutrajournal.com/iqbals-god-and-the-gitas-lord-part-two-by-purushottama-bilimoria, accessed 1 July 2017.

Iqbal, Muhammad. 1953. *The Secrets of Selflessness*, trans. A. J. Arberry. London: John Murray.

———. 1962. *The Reconstruction of Religious Thought in Islam*. Lahore: K. Bazar.

Khalifa, A. 1961. *Islamic Ideology*. Lahore: Institute of Islamic Culture.

Khan, Sayyid Ahmad. 1892. *Al-tahrir fi usul al-tafsir*. Agra: Mufidiam Press.

———. 1966. 'Akhri Madamin', in *Sources on Indian Tradition*, ed. William Theodore de Bary. New York: Columbia University Press.

———. 1973. *Maqalati Sir Sayyid*, vol. 13, ed. Mohammas Isma'il Panipati. Lahore: Majlisi Taraqi Adab.

Rahman, Fazlur. 1966. 'The Impact of Modernity on Islam.' *Islamic Studies* 5(2): 112–128.

Siddiqi, Mazhaeruddin. 1970. 'Intellectual Basis of Muslim Modernity.' *Islamic Studies* 9(2): 149–171.

Chapter 49
GUR-SIKH *DHARAM*

Balbinder Singh Bhogal

The literature on the British colonization of India, the reform movements it instigated, and the anti- and postcolonial movements it inspired, is extensive. Yet texts focused on the Sikh tradition are relatively few. If the remit of this chapter is Sikh '*dharam*' (arguably Skt. *dharma*) and if by '*dharam*' we mean something like 'religion, tradition, culture', then the field narrows further still.[1] Two central works focus on Sikh *dharam*: Harjot Oberoi's 1994 *The Construction of Religious Boundaries* (CRB), and Arvind Mandair's more recent 2009 *Religion and the Specter of the West* (RSW). Although both chart the transformation of the Gur-Sikh way (*jugat*) or *dharam* into a 'monotheistic religion' of 'Sikhism' with its 'tenets or principles', it is only Mandair's postcolonial orientation that critically questions the European conceptualization of 'religion' as a general, indeed, universal category of control and containment employed to name and discipline various populations within its Empire (Bhogal 2010, 2012a).

For the following discussion I employ the term 'religion' in two distinct ways: first, as a possible site for resistance—to indicate a desire to recover and reclaim a heterogeneous Sikh '*dharam*', or premodern *sikhi* (an unsystematized way of listening, learning, and acting), from underneath the colonial and orientalist construction of a monolithic and 'monotheistic' 'Sikhism' (a systematized belief system) that belies a certain European form of 'religion-making' (Dressler and Mandair 2011). This latter modern Sikhism denotes my second way of using the term 'religion', to mark the historical reformation of *sikhi* through a European (Protestant Christian) gaze that is itself already over-determined by a conception of religion as *sui generis*; this gaze of Europe entrapped and continues to entrap *sikhi* within certain foreign, conceptual, and spatio-temporal frames (Bhogal 2010).

To highlight the displacement of (pre-colonial) *sikhi* by (colonial/modern) Sikhism, I employ a third term *sikhi(sm)* as a postcolonial strategy to foreground the legacy of powerful colonial inscriptions, to recall how colonial power continually affects the production of modern knowledge, and thus I hope to create a new space for *sikhi* or Sikh *dharam* in the modern/colonial present. The difference between an existential *sikhi* and a metaphysical Sikhism that a postcolonial *sikhi(sm)* pivots on, is the difference between representation (as capture) and translation (as open engagement). That is to say, the construction, 'Sikhism', operates within certain modes of representation according to an alien imperial/colonial and postcolonial power that orientalizes the other, but *sikhi* moves within practices of translation aligned to the sovereignty of the Guru Granth Sahib within concrete contexts of lived praxis. This crucial distinction implies that one must go beyond the dialectics and polemics of modernity-contra-tradition, secularism-contra-religion, and scientific reason-contra-emotional faith. I argue that a genealogical tracing of the terms 'religion' and 'Sikhism' to *dharam* and *sikhi* is needed to recover important suppressed and displaced differences. Put differently, Sikh *dharam* or *sikhi* needs to be recovered from under the prism of secular modernity's refashioning of it into a religion (Sikhism) as the historical past of today's postcolonial present, in order to enter a future with a horizon not yet colonized by the West's imagination. Indeed, the Guru Granth Sahib (GGS) repeatedly and consistently checks the hubris of any human's imagination when it comes to the 'real truth':

> Imperishable, incalculable, and unfathomable is the Lord;
> He is everywhere, inside and out.
>
> (GGS 456)

> As the One, as the Many (*ek-anek*) he completely fills and permeates all: Wherever I look, there He is. The marvelous image of Maya is so fascinating; how few understand this.
>
> (GGS 485)

Nevertheless, counter to the GGS's egalitarian and revolutionary notion that the center (of creative, fearless, and hateless being) is everywhere residing in all, revealing that all center–periphery distinctions are human-made and therefore arbitrary, Hegel located the center in Europe as the most evolved and superior, thus negating the East to an absolute spatio-temporal periphery:

> But Europe is absolutely the Center and the End (*das Zentrum und das Ende*) of the ancient world and of the West as such, Asia the absolute East.
>
> (Hegel, *Lectures on the Philosophy of History* 235, cited in Dussel 1993, 71)

Cutting across Europe's Hegelian schema, *sikhi* places the greatest authority and power of enunciation in the Guru's Word (*gur-shabad*). This Word can never be exclusively owned by any one individual (hence the Sikh Gurus, and the non-Sikh Bhagats and Sufi Sheikhs in the GGS), any one language (hence the various languages and dialects in the GGS), any one region or location (hence those included in the GGS come from various areas across north India, and the Word is located in the human guru, the textual guru, and in the community of the true, *sat-sangat*), any one caste (as the hymns of brahmins as well as lower-caste saints are included in the GGS), and does not depend upon any system of certification (as true living is open to the literate and illiterate). Thus this revolutionary access to the sovereignty and revelation of the Guru's Word (*gur-shabad*) is open to all—regardless of caste, gender, class, ethnicity, language, race, religion, place, and certification. But this radical openness and equality depends upon the recognition of the other as a gift—a gift beyond human estimations of good or bad.

From modernist Sikhism to postcolonial *sikhi(sm)*: recovering the details

> Of all 'religions' (*sarab dharam*), the best 'religion' (*saresat dharam*)—
> Is to chant Hari's Name (*hari ko naamu japi*) through pure conduct (*niramal karam*).
> Of all the rituals, the most sublime ritual—
> Is to erase the dirt of dualistic thinking (*duramati*) in the company of the holy (*sadhsangat*).
> Of all the efforts, the best effort—
> Is to always chant the Name in the heart (*hari ka nam japahu jia sada*).
>
> (GGS 266)

In the beginning, 'There was no *karam* no *dharam* nor the buzzing fly of *maia*'. Likewise there was no earth, sky, languages, air, no Brahmā, Vishnu, nor Mahesh (Śiva), no creation, no destruction, no coming and going, no celestial realms nor underworlds, only the One Supreme Being (*eko soi*) and His Infinite Will (*hukam*) who sat in utter darkness (*dhundhukara*) for countless eons in the profound meditation of His own being as essencelessness (*suṅn samādhi*) (GGS 1035). That unspeakable state of being wills to be, and in 'creating the Earth, He established it as the Temple of Dharam (*dharam-sala*)' (1033). *Dharam*, as the creation of that One through its Will, is often described as an impersonal principle of the realm established for humans to exist and practice living in harmony with, or personified as, Dharam Raja, who records each individual's deeds so that justice can be served. This system is understood as being perfect: 'priceless the unwritten law (*dharam*), priceless the Court of Justice (*Diban*)' (5); for through it the One Lord (Hari) administers perfect justice (*dharam niau*) (89). *Karam*, *dharam*, and *niau* therefore express different aspects of one process.

Given that this One stands apart from His creation (*veparvara*) as well as within it (*bhara puri*) to the extent that there is no other (*avar na duja*), human beings (unlike animals) possess the free will to do actions against the natural order of creation (*hukam* and *dharam*) via the fears, desires, and delusions of their self-conscious egos (*haumai*)—and thus incur *karam*—for justice means all have to reap just what they sow. Given this, then, there can be false '*karam* and *dharam*' as well as true actions and righteous living. Thus, all 'religions' and 'religious' rituals can become egotistical displays: '*karam dharam sabhi haumai phail*' (890). More simply, the same hymn states 'without the Name all is in vain'. This last quotation brings the uniqueness of Gur-Sikh understanding of *dharam*: 'One may perform any number of religious rituals and actions, but not know the Creator and Doer of all; He teaches, but does not practice what he preaches, he does not realize the essential reality of the Word' (380).

As the frequent coupling of *karam* with *dharam* indicates, *dharam* for Sikhs is about being true, not merely owning or knowing the truth, for higher than the truth is truthful living (62); this is the true praxis mentioned above. And not just simply doing an action, but a paradoxical doing without a doing, more accurately (though no less paradoxically) a doing without ego, then, action is said to be done with the Name, the Word, the Guru. And to be in the ego-less flow of true living (that is characterized by fearlessness, hatelessness, spontaneity, and ease) is not something that the ego can will, but falls into by the surprising grace of the True Guru: 'By His Grace (*parshad*) you remain in *dharam*' (270). Then, it follows that: 'all *karam*, *dharam* and deeds practiced are holy, for those who utter Hari's, Hari's, Ram's True Name' (648).

Being about action or merit, the Gurus were against hierarchical divisions based on caste, birth, and so on—the Name is the only social status of any reality—and all have equal access to it, though rare are those that connect with it and taste its 'sweetness and bliss' (154, 353). Though the One created the countless rituals and religions, that One also placed the glory of the Name above them all (1345).

Karam and *dharam* become false and the cause for bondage when done egotistically (*bandhan karam dharam hau kia*, 416). That is to say, the Sikh understanding of *dharam* shifts it onto an existential and quotidian ground (away from metaphysical musings of scriptures). This is because the 'whole of the *dharam* is within your body (*ihu sarir sabh dharam hai*) and within that is the light of the True One' (309). To access, activate, and taste that light one has a duty to walk on the path of *dharam* (*maragi dharam chalesahi*, 540) and practice righteous living (1279–1280)—in harmony with *hukam*. This walking goes astray via the vices: lust, anger, greed, intoxication with *maia*, jealousy, and so on, and regains a soteriological footing when innocence, contentment, compassion, *dharam*, truth are practiced (379). This is because the 'True Guru is the Field or Soil of Dharam (*satiguru dharati dharam hai*) in which one plants the seeds of one's actions—only the Gurmukhs are able to grow the ambrosial fruit' (302). This is because only they 'remain lovingly attuned to the Treasure of the Name night and day' (*anadhinu nami ratani liva lage*, 1332). Guru Nanak says, 'Without the Guru there is no gnosis, without *dharam* there is no meditation' (*gura bin gian dharam bin dhian*, 1412). And 'all *karam* and *dharam* lie in the meditation of the Name' (699).

Guru Nanak sings, 'the soul and body are composed of one chariot and one charioteer; in age after age they change' (470). In the *Satijug* they are contentment and *dharam* (righteousness), in the *Tretaijug* they are restraint (of senses) and power, in the *Dvapurjug* they are austerities and truth, and in the *Kalijug* they are fire (of desire) and falsehood. That is to say, each leg of the platform/earth of *dharam* is lost in each age, so that *dharam*'s (etymological) nature as support (from the root *dhr*) is progressively undermined, making our current *Kalijug* the most degenerate and unstable of ages. Thus, Guru Amar Das requests us to 'learn the *dharam* of this age: all understanding is obtained from the Perfect Guru' (230)—for 'each and every age has its own *dharam* (*jugi jugi apo apana dharam hai*)' (797). And furthermore, whereas 'celibacy, self-discipline and pilgrimages formed the *dharam* in past ages, in the current *Kalijug*, to sing the praises of Hari's Name is the *dharam* in this current *Kalijug*' (797).

Thus, for today, Guru Arjan sings, 'above all the countless religious rituals and good deeds (*karam dharam*) done is the right conduct of the Name (*nam achar*)' (405). From the Gur-Sikh point of view 'this is the truth of *karam*, dharma, and gnosis: to chant Hari's Name in the Company of the Holy (*sadhsang*)' (866). That having 'studied the *karam* and *dharam* of all the ages. Without the Name (*bin navai*), this mind is not awakened (*man na prabodhe*)' (913).

Now, as all paths are paradoxical, the Sikh *dharam* as the Way of Name (*nam-marga*) is no exception—that is, it is aporetically configured. Aporia is thus essential to the Sikh Way (*marga*), and indeed other Asian traditions. Compare the first lines of the opening verse of the Guru Granth Sahib, 'Truth cannot be thought, no matter how hard one thinks; silence cannot silence, even given the deepest unbroken meditation' (1, *Japji*, Guru Nanak), with the first lines of Lao Zi's Dao De Jing, 'The way that can be walked is not the eternal Way; The name that can be named is not the eternal Name'. Thus both Sikh and Daoist texts begin with, and dwell within, an impasse, an aporia, a perplexity and halting difficulty (Bhogal 2001). One cannot simply step over such a hurdle and translate the Way into 'religion', or a 'moral code' or a nameable path, without facing the essential untranslatability of the notion of a Way. It is this hermeneutic failure to keep the force of the impasse alive that we see in Hegel's encounter with the Indic Other. As noted above, Europe's (via Hegel's) shift to representation and stereotype (in the work of his concept of religion to capture and control the plurality on the ground) was irresistible, given the need to secure the power of enunciation and domination of the other. Nevertheless, one needs to ask: what if Sikh *dharam* as a *marga* remains actively untranslatable?

> Having created two sides (*dovai tarapha*), the One pervades both (*ik varatia*).
> Though the words of the Vedas (*beda bani*) became pervasive, within disputations arose.
> Worldly existence (*paravirati*) and liberation from worldly existence (*niravirati*)
> are the two sides—yet Dharam, the guide, dwells within both.
> (GGS 1280)

Gur-Sikh *dharam* exists, then, within a nondual frame where no one group, language, etc. can claim exclusive ownership of the Truth or the true Way—for Dharam, the guide, pervades both sides of any dispute. Though logic and reason are necessary to express the truth or discern its guiding voice, they are not sufficient. Hence the need for the Guru's Word (*gur-shabad*) to be sung rather than prosaically recounted. The affective mode of singing (and the emotional range of the thirty-one Indian classical ragas or musical melodies) is always a listening as much as a saying, and thereby reconnects both polarized groups and concepts. Duality is seen to be false for it denies the existence of a certain continuity between states and thus the possibility of maturation from ego-centeredness (*manmukh*) to Guru-centeredness (*gurmukh*). Hence the notion is not of them and us, good and evil, but of unripe (*kacha*) and ripe (*pakka*) in that every fruit starts bitter but may become sweet—given the presence of the particular conditions that allow it to naturally blossom. States exist but none are fixed, what matters is action (*praxis*) centered within a certain creative social-political structure and ethos (*polis*) created and maintained by a society of true actors (*sat-sangat*)—wherein the possibility of transfiguration or metamorphosis is open to all.

Before detailing the praxis of Sikh *dharam* (*sikhi*) any further, it is worth noting how the Sikh Gurus brought opposing groups and ideologies together, through a language that incorporated the rules of reason but also transcended logic to include contradictions, ambiguities, i.e., the aporias that love (*bhagati*) demands. God is therefore re-understood as a Timeless Form (*akal-murat*) that none can therefore exclusively name and possess, as being One and Many (*ek-anek*), existing within and without (*antar-bahar*), as directing both union with Him and separation from Him (*samjog-vijog*), as being All-Forms and Formless (*sargun-nirgun*), as being forever fresh and new (*nita-nava*) as well as being Immoveable, Permanent, and the only reliable Support (*nihacal, asthir, adhar*). 'The All is in the One and the One is in All' (*eka mahi sarab mahi eka*, GGS 907, *Ramkali Dakhani*, Guru Nanak). Out of the directives of loving devotion (*bhagati*), the Gurus conflated opposed vocabularies: the absolute is expressed through Tantric terms (*siva-sakti*), Abrahamic/Muslim terms (Allah, Rahim), Buddhist terms (*sunn, nirban*), as well as Hindu theistic names (Hari, Ram). Thus the Sikh Gurus' Ram-Rahim, a personal beloved God, is also, aporetically, an impersonal Nirvanic essencelessness. The Supreme Being-Becoming is both personal (God) and impersonal (One-Many), permanent and changing, visible and invisible, everywhere and nowhere. Logically, these abstractions become contradictions, but within the context of one's lived praxis within a 'community of the true ones'—they may become ambiguities of changing and illuminating meaning—indicating a maturation beyond black-and-white mentalities.

It is not surprising, then, that the polarized traditions of the 'other-worldly' ascetic and the 'this-worldly' householder are brought together (*jogi-bhogi*) into one praxis of the Sikh Gurus—whose yoga is therefore named the yoga of kings (*raj-jog*). The praxis of this royal or worldly yoga incorporates the traditional yogic mental absorption into the Fourth-State (*chauta-pad*; i.e., a transfigured and nondual consciousness beyond subject–object duality), alternatively expressed as Void consciousness (*sunn-samadh*)—where one's interdependent becoming is understood as an unearthly pure light (*man tu joti sarup he*). But this existential becoming is also expressed in the humble terms of a bride's simple and natural (*sahaj*) yearnings to meet her Beloved (*mili, samai*). Sikh *raj-jog*, then, is both the disciplined and meditative absorption of the yogi as it is the effortless and wholesome undertaking (*sahaj-jog*) of any householder. This natural way is one that requires the innocence and spontaneity of a child's intelligence (*bal-budh*), the fearlessness of a warrior (*nirbhau*), and the hatelessness/compassion (*nirvair*) of a saint. The Sikh ideal then is to become a warrior-saint (*sant-sipahi*)—who is neither necessarily passive and apolitical nor militaristic and violent but remains established unqualifiedly in an openness to *hukam* and its surprising way, with *haumai*'s predictability humbled. The devotee gains access to the rarefied states of mental and emotional calm but also enjoys a full life with all its attendant responsibilities and duties. In addition to the yogic grammar, the devotee's goal is as much to gain God's vision (*darshan*) and to be honored at God's Court (*daragah*, *darabar*) or be granted entry through his Door/Gate (*dar*, hence, *gur-dwara*). Since the Guru, Word, and Name (*guru*, *shabad*, *nam*) are within and without, they enact both the inner guide (*antarjami*) and the external Judge (Allah). Mediating both, however, is the notion that each moment has the possibility to become an event where what occurs is understood as a gift (*dat*) of the Giver (*datar*), should one's ego (*haumai*) be paused (*rahao*) so as to allow perception of God's Way/Will (*hukam*); action (*karam*) cannot therefore ever be separated from grace (*nadar*)—free will and determinism form a continuum expressing the aporias that shape the way of *sikhi*.

Though ultimately unnameable, the Sikh praxis of the Way (*jugat*, *bidh*, *marga*) involves living beyond the ego's (*haumai's*) desperate project to favor pleasure over pain (*sukh-dukh*), which can only lead to favoring vice over virtue (*pap-punn*). This allows a revolutionary mode of being/becoming to arise naturally—one that is attuned to God's/Nature's Law/Will/Way (*hukam*). This ambiguous 'I/not I' mode of existing beyond pleasure and pain is also immersed in an unchanging field of bliss (*anand*), that is, when the egoic mind is reconciled within the effortless mind (Bhogal 2012b). To instigate or encourage the ego's fall into the unconditional openness, bliss, and gnosis of the Way, Sikhs perform songful praise of the Guru's words (*gurbani-kirtan*); embark upon selfless service (*seva*), expressed in the institutionalization of social welfare in the form of a free community kitchen (*gur-ka-langar*); and share their earnings (*vand-chakana*) gleaned from hard and honest work (*kirat karna*). This, generally speaking, is what is involved in the injunction to meditate upon and remember God's Name (*nam-simaran*, *nam-japan*). The Sikh Gurus sought to create a community of those that had nothing necessarily in common except true conduct (*sach-acar*), the highest ideal in *sikhi*, above even Truth itself (GGS 62)—signifying that (an unnameable) praxis should always lead *theoria* (the formulation of the Way).[2]

Conclusion

Within the Sikh tradition, which constantly posits the ultimate as an interdependent being-with (*ek-anek*, *nirgun-sargun*, *asankh-apar*), where the multiplicity of Being is its oneness and that oneness does not come at the expense of the many, but by directly affirming and engaging its difference, there arises a new epistemological structure to understand comparison. This new comparative framing (that recognizes the other as both distinct and as an integral part of oneself) could potentially upset the epistemic hegemony of Euro-American modernity that posits Being as singular and homogenous, set apart from the diverse multitudes, as a single Master over many slaves. In this regard, one can see Gur-Sikh 'universals' that can contaminate the space dominated by the comparative imaginary of the West. Identifying a Sikh comparative imaginary that encompasses the call to see 'oneself as another' shows the primacy of relation—and thus transforms the relationship between colonizer and colonized not through inversion, or by making the latter the locus of intervention, but rather by re-theorizing the notion of how relation to the other is figured. Here a Sikh is a learner (literally) that never arrives at final knowledge (of the other) but connects to a mutually transforming self-other knowing-as-relating, viz., through a socio-political love (*bhagati*). This is where no single idiom, concept, or identity (for example a concept such as 'religion' or 'dharma', an identity such as 'the West' or 'India as Hindustan') can hold sway as universal to manage the multitude of belief and practice.[3]

As I have problematized the notion of 'religion' as carrier of Europe's desire and value, I would also like to note the other use of 'religion' as a possible site of resistance. For it should be clear that the aporetic point here is not to affirm religion as an identity marker, nor reject it for the same reason, but to re-invent multiple ways of orientating towards it. Can we not detect and differentiate different secularisms and/or religions that support an interdependent being-with-the-other from those that divide and conquer—one that respects and safeguards multiple centers of enunciation? Here one could see *sikhi(sm)* as a secularization given the scripture's existential, pragmatic, and in many ways Buddhistic focus (on death, suffering, and impermanence)—all of which oppose the ontotheological systematization that comes from reformist Sikhism of the Singh Sabha period—(as both CRB and RSW delineate). Thus the term 'religion' is not the problem but the mode of thinking (as representation) that it allows. The term 'religion' could also operate differently in a mode of thinking that is not led by concept but by feeling and action.

Through the voice of the other I gain my voice, not through mimicry but through the resonating difference of many strings on an instrument. The Sikh Gurus developed a new secular/sacred comparativism for they heard the voice of the other as a music. What is required today to allow socio-political and religio-cultural differences to 'sing together' the Gur-Sikh way? Perhaps only a political love (Sikh *dharam*)—responsive to the cries of the out-caste and lower-caste, the Damned — and a selfless will, composed by the discernment that at best it can only reach a humble knowing, yet cognizant that what is needed more than knowledge is the willing fall into unpredictable and compassionate liaisons—for justice and creativity demand nothing less.

> The True Name is my social status (*jat*) and honor (*pat*).
> Love of the Truth (*sat bhau*) is my *karam*, *dharam* and discipline.
>
> (GGS 353)

Notes

1 Sikh *dharam* is here used as a shorthand for Gur-Sikh *dharam*, as that *dharam* was revealed to the Sikhs by their Gurus.

2 For further elaboration of such ideas and terms see N. Singh 1990; G. Singh 1999; Shackle and Mandair 2005. Earlier works of writers like Professors Puran Singh (1881–1931) and Harinder Singh Mahboob (1937–2010) also touch upon such aporetic and nondual notions.

3 'Dharma' does *not* present a coherent alternative to the Western/Abrahamic notion of 'religion', for precisely the same reason that the Western construction of religion is not coherent; for just as the

world religions model has been historically over-determined by a Protestant discourse and its terms, so too is the recent Hindu-led 'Dharma Traditions' model over-determined by a Brahmanic discourse and its caste-imbued terms. Today Sikh *dharam*, along with Jaina *dharma* and Buddhist *dhamma*, are being co-opted by the Hindu-led model of Four *Dharma* Traditions, in a similar way that they had been by a Protestant discourse within the (Christian/secular) Western model of religion in the late nineteenth and early twentieth centuries.

References

Bhogal, Balbinder S. 2001. "On the Hermeneutics of Sikh Thought and Praxis." In *Sikh Religion, Culture and Ethnicity*. Ed. C. Shackle, G. Singh, and A. Mandair, 72–96. Richmond: Curzon.

———. 2010. "Decolonizations: Cleaving Gestures that Refuse the Alien Call for Identity Politics." *Religions of South Asia* 4(2): 135–164.

———. 2012a. "Sikh *Dharam* and Postcolonialism: Hegel, Religion and Zizek." *Australian Religion Studies Review* 25(2): 185–212.

———. 2012b. "The Animal Sublime: Rethinking the Sikh Mystical Body." *Journal of the American Academy of Religion* 80(4): 856–908.

Dressler, Markus, and Arvind-pal S. Mandair (eds.). 2011. *Secularism and Religion-Making*. New York: Oxford University Press.

Dussel, Enrique. 1993."Eurocentrism and Modernity." *Boundary 2* 20(3): 65–76.

Mandair, Arvind-Pal. 2009. *Religion and the Specter of the West: Sikhism, India, Postcoloniality, and the Politics of Translation*. New York: Columbia University Press.

Oberoi, Harjot. 1994. *The Construction of Religious Boundaries: Culture, Identity, and Diversity in the Sikh Tradition*. Chicago: University of Chicago Press.

Shackle, Christopher, and Arvind-Pal Mandair (eds.). 2005. *Teachings of the Sikh Gurus: Selections from the Sikh Scriptures*. London and New York: Routledge.

Singh, Gurbhagat. 1999. *Sikhism and Postmodern Thought*. Delhi: Ajanta Books.

Singh, Nirbhai. 1990. *Philosophy of Sikhism: Reality and its Manifestations*. New Delhi: Atlantic Publishers & Distributors.

Chapter 50
BUDDHIST ETHICS[1]

Damien Keown

Although newcomers to Buddhism are often struck by the variety and diversity of its schools and traditions, at the level of the moral teachings set forth for laity and monks there is arguably much common ground. In this respect it does not seem unreasonable to speak of a common moral core underlying the divergent customs, practices and philosophical teachings of the different schools. This core is composed of the principles and precepts, the values and virtues which were expounded by the Buddha in the fifth century BCE and which continue to guide the conduct of some 350 million Buddhists around the world today. A short introduction to these ethical teachings can be found in Keown (2005) and a more comprehensive one in Harvey (2000). For a philosophical overview see Gowans (2015).

Dharma

The ultimate foundation for Buddhist ethics is Dharma. Dharma has many meanings, but the underlying notion is of a universal law which governs both the physical and moral order of the universe. Dharma can best be translated as 'natural law', a term which captures both its main senses, namely as the principle of order and regularity seen in the behaviour of natural phenomena, and also the idea of a universal moral law whose requirements have been discovered by enlightened beings such as the Buddha (note that Buddha discovered Dharma, he did not invent it). Every aspect of life is regulated by Dharma; the physical laws which regulate the rising of the sun, the succession of the seasons, and the movement of the constellations. Dharma is neither caused by nor under the control of a supreme being, and the gods themselves are subject to its laws, as was the Buddha. In the moral order, Dharma is manifest in the law of karma, which, as we shall see below, governs the way moral deeds affect individuals in present and future lives. Living in accordance with Dharma and implementing its requirements is thought to lead to happiness, fulfilment, and salvation; neglecting or transgressing it is said to lead to endless suffering in the cycle of rebirth (*saṃsāra*).

In his First Sermon, the Buddha was said to have 'turned the wheel of the Dharma' and given doctrinal expression to the truth about how things are in reality. It was in this discourse that the Buddha set out the Four Noble Truths, the last of which is the Noble Eightfold Path which leads to *nirvāṇa*. The Path has three divisions—Morality

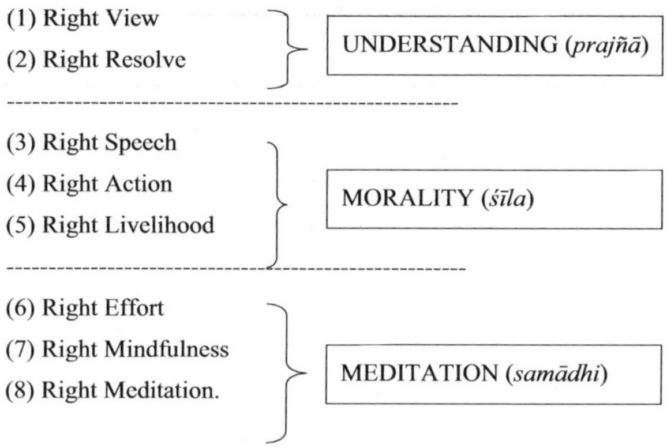

Figure 50.1 **The Eightfold Path and its three divisions**

(*śīla*), Meditation (*samādhi*), and Insight (*prajñā*)—from which it can be seen that morality is an integral component of the path to *nirvāṇa*.

Karma

The doctrine of karma is concerned with the ethical implications of Dharma, in particular those relating to the consequences of moral behaviour. Karma may be defined as a principle of moral retribution in terms of which good and bad deeds bring about pleasant and unpleasant consequences in the future as well as a transformation in the agent's present moral status. The remote effects of karmic choices are referred to as the 'maturation' (*vipāka*) or 'fruit' (*phala*) of the karmic act. Performing good and bad deeds is compared to planting seeds that will fruit at a later date. Good karma is often referred to as 'merit' (*puṇya*), and its opposite, bad karma, is known as *pāpa*. Some Buddhists go to extreme lengths to accumulate merit, for example by making large donations to the monastic community (*sangha*) or funding lavish construction projects such as the building of temples and shrines.

Belief in karma is common to many Indian religions and did not originate with the Buddha (O'Flaherty). The belief in reincarnation is also found outside of India (Obeyesekere 2002). Since it is one of the 'givens' of Indian thought, the Buddha rarely seeks to justify or defend the idea of karma explicitly. However, the notion permeates his teachings and frequent reference is made to it in the early discourses. There, the Buddha reserves a particular censure for those of his contemporaries—such as materialists, determinists, and others—who denied the belief that moral acts entailed future consequences (this was known as *akiryavāda* or 'the doctrine of non-retribution'). Six contemporary teachers were criticized by him, and the fullest exposition of their views is to be found in an early discourse entitled *The Fruits of the Religious Life* (*Sāmaññaphala Sutta*), the second discourse of the *Dīgha Nikāya* of the Pāli Canon. However, karma is not deterministic, and does not entail that everything that happens to a person is determined in advance. Instead many of the good and bad things that happen in life can simply be accidents. Karma does not determine precisely what will happen or how anyone will react to what happens (for a philosophical discussion see Reichenbach 1990). While a belief in karma and rebirth has been a central feature of traditional Buddhist teachings, Buddhist 'modernists' have proposed a 'secular' form of Buddhism in which ideas about karma and rebirth are not seen as an essential part of Buddhist doctrine and can be ignored by those who find them unscientific or otherwise problematic (see Batchelor 2016).

Precepts

In common with Indian tradition as a whole, Buddhism expresses its ethical requirements in the form of duties rather than rights. These duties are thought of as implicit requirements of Dharma. The most general moral duties are those found in the Five Precepts, such as the duty to refrain from evil acts such as killing and stealing. On becoming a Buddhist one formally 'takes' (or accepts) the precepts in a ritual context known as 'going for refuge', and the form of words used acknowledges the free and voluntary nature of the duty assumed.

The most widely known precepts in Buddhism are the Five Precepts, comparable in importance to the Ten Commandments of Christianity. The Five Precepts are undertaken as voluntary commitments in the ceremony of 'taking refuge' when a person becomes a Buddhist. They are as follows:

(1) I undertake the precept to refrain from harming living creatures.
(2) I undertake the precept to refrain from taking what has not been given.
(3) I undertake the precept to refrain from sexual immorality.
(4) I undertake the precept to refrain from speaking falsely.
(5) I undertake the precept to refrain from taking intoxicants.

Apart from the Five Precepts various other lists of precepts are found, such as the Eight Precepts (*aṣṭāṅga-śīla*) and the Ten Precepts (*daśa-śīla*). These are commonly adopted as additional commitments on the twice-monthly holy days (*poṣadha*), and supplement the first four of the Five Precepts with additional restrictions such as the time when meals may be taken. Another set of precepts similar to the Ten Precepts is the Ten Good Paths of Action (*daśa-kuśala-karmapatha*). Precepts like these which apply to the laity are comparatively few in number compared to those observed by monks and nuns, as explained below.

Vinaya

A term often found paired with Dharma is 'Vinaya'. This term denotes the code of rules governing monastic discipline. Particularly in early sources, the compound 'Dharma-Vinaya' ('doctrine and discipline') is used to denote the whole body of Buddhist teachings and practice. Originally, the Buddhist monastic order (*sangha*) existed as just another sect within a broad community of wanderering teachers and students known as *parivrājakas* or *śramaṇas*. From these simple beginnings evolved a complex code for the regulation of monastic life which eventually became formulated in the portion of the canon known as the Vinaya Piṭaka, or 'basket of discipline' (Holt 1981). The Vinaya Piṭaka also contains a large number of stories and biographical material relating to the Buddha, as well as a certain amount of historical matter regarding the Order (*sangha*). The purpose of the Vinaya is to regulate in detail life within the community of monks and nuns and also their relationship with the laity (Wijayaratana). In its final form the text is divided into three sections, the first of which contains the set of rules for monks and nuns known as the *Prātimokṣa*. The derivation of the term *prātimokṣa* is uncertain, perhaps 'that which should be made binding', or 'that which causes one to be released (from suffering)'. Different schools had their own versions of the *Vinaya* and the number of the rules varies in each. Those which have survived belong to the schools of the Theravāda, Mahāsaṃghika, Mahīśāsaka, Dharmaguptaka, Sarvāstivāda, and Mūla-sarvāstivāda, although only the Theravāda Vinaya survives complete in its original language. In the Theravāda Vinaya the rules for monks number 227. Across all schools the rules for monks vary from 218 to 263, and for nuns from 279 to 380. As noted, the rules are not all of an ethical nature and also deal with the behaviour of the members of the Order in respects of practical matters such as food, clothes, dwellings, furniture, etc. The rules are arranged in eight sections, in decreasing degree of punishment and therefore roughly corresponding to the degree of importance attached to their observance. The rules are recited once a fortnight on the days of the full moon and the new moon, and anyone who has infringed any of the rules is called upon to declare the transgression.

Virtues

Although the precepts, whether lay and monastic, are of great importance there is more to the Buddhist moral life than following rules. Rules must not only be followed, but followed for the right reasons and with the correct motivation. It is here that the role of the virtues becomes important, and Buddhist morality as a whole may be likened to a coin with two faces: on one side are the precepts and on the other the virtues. The precepts, in fact, may be thought of simply as a list of things which a virtuous person will never do.

Early sources emphasize the importance of cultivating correct dispositions and habits so that moral conduct becomes the natural and spontaneous manifestation of internalized and properly integrated beliefs and values, rather than simple conformity to external rules. The task of the virtues is to counteract negative dispositions called *kleśas* (what are known in the West as 'vices'). The lengthy lists of virtues and vices which appear in Buddhist commentarial literature are extrapolated from a key cluster of three virtues, the three 'cardinal virtues' of non-attachment (*arāga*), benevolence (*adveṣa*), and understanding (*amoha*). These are the opposites of the three 'roots of evil' (or 'three poisons') namely greed (*rāga*), hatred (*dveṣa*), and delusion (*moha*). Non-attachment means the absence of that selfish desire which taints behaviour by allocating a privileged status to one's own needs. Benevolence means an attitude of goodwill to all living creatures, and understanding means knowledge of Buddhist teachings such as the Four Noble Truths. While these are the three most basic Buddhist virtues, there are many others, some of the most important of which are discussed below.

Dāna

A key virtue for lay Buddhists in particular is *dāna*, which means 'giving' or generosity. The primary recipient of lay Buddhist generosity is the monastic community (*sangha*)—since monks and nuns possess nothing they are entirely dependent on the laity for support. The laity provides all the material needs of the *sangha*, everything from food, robes, and medicine to the land and buildings which constitute the monastic residence. In the *kaṭhina* ceremony, which takes place following the annual rains retreat in countries where Theravāda Buddhism is practised, cotton cloth is supplied to the monks by the laity for the purpose of making robes. The relationship is not just one-way, for in return monks provide Dharma teachings to the laity, and the gift of the Dharma is said to be the highest of all gifts. At all levels of society—between family members, friends, and even strangers—generosity is widely practised in Buddhist countries and seen as an indication of spiritual development. This is because the generous person, as well as being free from egocentric thoughts and sensitive to the needs of other, finds it easier to practise renunciation and cultivate an attitude of detachment. The story of Prince Vessantara, the popular hero of the *Vessantara Jātaka*, is well known in South East Asia. Vessantara gave away everything he owned, even down to his wife and children. Many Theravāda sources praise *dāna*, and Mahāyāna sources emphasize the extreme generosity of bodhisattvas who are disposed to give away even parts of their bodies, or their lives, in order to aid others. As we shall see below, *dāna* is also the first of the 'Six Perfections' (*pāramitā*) of a bodhisattva.

Ahiṃsā

Ahiṃsā is a fundamental Buddhist virtue. Literally it means 'non-harming' or 'non-violence', both of which are prohibited by the first precept, as we have seen. *Ahiṃsā* in addition encourages more positive dispositions such as compassion (*karuṇā*) and sympathy (*anukampā*) for living creatures. *Ahiṃsā* is a pre-Buddhist concept which came to prominence among the unorthodox renouncer (*śramaṇa*) movements such as Buddhism and Jainism. These groups rejected the Brahmanical practice of animal sacrifice and sometimes went to extreme lengths to avoid harming even tiny forms of life such as insects (see Ruegg 1980; Tahtinen 1976).

Compassion

Compassion (*karuṇā*) is a virtue which is of importance in all schools of Buddhism but which is particularly emphasized by the Mahāyāna (see below). In early Buddhism, *karuṇā* figures as the second of the four *Brahma-vihāras* or 'Divine Abidings'. These are states of mind cultivated especially through the practice of meditation. The four are loving-kindness (*maitrī*), compassion (*karuṇā*), sympathetic joy (*muditā*), and equanimity (*upekṣā*). The practice of the four *Brahma-vihāras* involves radiating outwards the positive qualities associated with each, directing them first towards oneself, then to one's family, the local community, and eventually to all beings in the universe. In

Mahāyāna iconography and art the symbolic embodiment of compassion is the great *bodhisattva* Avalokiteśvara, 'the one who looks down from on high'. He is portrayed as having a thousand arms extended in all directions to minister to those in need and is constantly appealed to by those in difficult circumstances. In the course of time in Buddhism there appeared a doctrine of salvation by faith according to which the mere invocation of the name of a Buddha was sufficient, given the extent of the Buddha's compassion, to ensure rebirth in a 'Pure Land' or heaven.

Mahāyāna morality

In the Mahāyāna, the bodhisattva who devotes himself or herself to the service of others becomes the new paradigm for religious practice, as opposed to the *arahant*, or saint in the early tradition, who is criticized for leading a cloistered life devoted to the self-interested pursuit of liberation. Schools which embraced the earlier ideal are henceforth referred to disparagingly as the Hīnayāna ('Small Vehicle'), or the Śrāvakayāna ('Vehicle of the Hearers', meaning those who were the Buddha's contemporaries). In the Mahāyāna great emphasis is placed on the twin values of compassion (*karuṇā*) and understanding (*prajñā*), and the *bodhisattva* practises six special virtues known as the 'Six Perfections' (*pāramitā*). These are Generosity (*dāna*), Morality (*śīla*), Patience (*kṣānti*), Perseverance (*vīrya*), Meditation (*samādhi*), and Understanding (*prajñā*). It can be seen that three of these (*śīla*, *samādhi*, and *prajñā*) coincide with the three divisions of the Eightfold Path of early Buddhism, demonstrating both continuity and change in the evolving moral tradition.

The Mahāyāna did not reject the ethical teachings of early Buddhism but subsumed them under an expanded framework of its own within which three levels were identified. The first level was known as 'Moral Discipline' (*saṃvara-śīla*) and consisted of the scrupulous observance of the moral precepts. The second level was known as the 'Cultivation of Virtue' (*kuśala-dharma-saṃgrāhaka-śīla*) and was concerned with the accumulation of the good qualities necessary for the attainment of nirvana. The third category was known as 'Altruistic Conduct' (*sattva-artha-kriyā-śīla*) and consisted of moral action directed to the needs of others. The Mahāyāna claimed that the early followers only observed the first two levels and that their moral practices were deficient in lacking concern for the wellbeing of others. The Mahāyāna is not a monolithic system and there is no one 'official' code of ethics for either laity or monks. The Vinayas of the early schools were not rejected and continued to be observed by monks and nuns alongside the new teachings recommended for bodhisattvas in Mahāyāna literature.

Skilful means (*upāya-kauśalya*)

An important innovation in Mahāyāna ethics was the doctrine of skilful means (*upāya-kauśalya*). This teaching was taken by some to mean that the clear and strict rules encountered in the early sources which prohibit certain sorts of acts could be interpreted more in the way of guidelines rather than as ultimately binding. In particular, bodhisattvas, the new moral heroes of the Mahāyāna, could claim increased latitude and flexibility based on their recognition of the importance of compassion. The pressure to bend or suspend the rules in the interests of compassion results in certain texts establishing new codes of conduct for bodhisattvas which sometimes allow the precepts to be broken. In some of these, such as the *Upāyakauśalya Sūtra* (*c*. first century BCE), even killing is apparently regarded as justifiable when committed by a bodhisattva who seeks to prevent someone committing a heinous crime and suffering karmic retribution in hell (Tatz 1994).

Tantra

In Tantric teachings, too, the precepts are sometimes set aside. Tantra, alternatively known as the Vajrayāna (Diamond Vehicle) or Mantrayāna (Vehicle of Mantras), is a form of Buddhism that developed in India in the sixth century CE and is characterized by antinomianism and the use of magical techniques which aim to speed the practitioner to enlightenment in a single lifetime. One of the basic techniques of Tantra is to transmute negative mental energies into positive ones using a form of mystical alchemy which is believed to transform the personality. By liberating energy trapped at an instinctual level in emotions such as fear and lust, it was thought that practitioners could do the psychological equivalent of splitting the atom and use the energy produced to propel themselves rapidly to enlightenment. In certain forms of Tantra such practices involved the deliberate and controlled reversal of moral norms and the breaking of taboos in order to help jolt the mind out of its conventional patterns of though into a supposedly higher state of consciousness. Examples of such activities include drinking alcohol and sexual intercourse, both serious breaches of the monastic rules. While some practitioners understood such teachings literally, however, others saw them as merely symbolic and simply useful subjects for meditation.

Buddhist ethics in the West

Despite an abundance of moral teachings of the kind described above, in common with other Indian traditions Buddhism down the centuries has shown little interest in ethics as an independent philosophical discipline. There are few treatises on the subject and it appears that ethics and politics (as also law and economics) were not subjects that Buddhist scholars felt drawn to pronounce on. Perhaps this is due to the different cultural histories of East and West. As is well known, the Greeks invented democracy, and the discipline of political science (which in the classical world included ethics as a subsidiary) arose to develop constitutions founded on principles such as justice. Since throughout its long history Buddhism has lived predominantly under non-democratic political systems, perhaps it is not surprising that we do not find ethics and politics featuring strongly in its intellectual curriculum. There are further reasons which might explain this discrepancy, such as that Buddhism is fundamentally a renouncer tradition which distanced itself from involvement in politics and the systems of religious law that govern social life (as exemplified in Hindu Dharmaśāstra or Sharia law in Islam).

It is only since Buddhism arrived in the West that a nascent discipline of Buddhist ethics has developed. Since ethics has always formed part of the Western philosophical canon scholars have naturally begun to analyse Buddhist teachings using Western ethical categories. But is it legitimate simply to compare Western ethics with Eastern ethics in a straightforward way, or are there cultural, historical, and conceptual differences which might distort or invalidate such a comparison? Problems of this kind have exercised the minds of scholars working in the field of comparative ethics in the last few decades, and as yet there is no agreed methodology for undertaking a comparative study. One school of thought maintains that Buddhist ethics bears a greater resemblance to virtue ethics than any other Western theory (Keown 2001). This is because Buddhism presents itself as a path of self-transformation which seeks the elimination of negative states (vices) and their replacement by positive or wholesome ones (virtues) such as understanding and compassion. But there are also differences, for example virtue ethics as developed in the West does not involve a belief in reincarnation or rebirth. Buddhism also has rules and precepts which give its teachings a deontological flavour, and the doctrine of karma teaches that there is a close relationship between good deeds and future happiness in a manner reminiscent of utilitarianism. The Mahāyāna doctrine of skilful means also has a utilitarian aspect since it seems to prioritize successful outcomes over respect for the precepts (for an interpretation of Buddhist ethics as consequentialist see Goodman 2009). An alternative view is that Buddhist ethics cannot be accommodated within any of the available Western theoretical models since it exhibits features of 'particularism' whereby situational factors take precedence in moral decision-making (Hallisey 1996).

More or less coinciding with the birth of Buddhist ethics was the appearance of a related movement known as 'socially engaged Buddhism'. While Buddhist ethics is concerned with the specifics of individual conduct, engaged Buddhism focuses on larger questions of public policy such as social justice, poverty, politics, and the environment (see King 2005). Clearly there is a connection, and it can be no coincidence that both these disciplines have arisen at roughly the same time as Buddhism encounters the West. Perhaps we can see Buddhist ethics and engaged Buddhism as corresponding to two major branches of Western thought—ethics and politics—which for one reason or another never attained an autonomous status in the canon of Buddhist learning.

Four styles of Buddhist ethics

One modern Buddhist writer on engaged Buddhism—Christopher Queen—has suggested that there are four different 'styles' of Buddhist ethics (2000, 11). The first is called 'The Ethics of Discipline', in which the conduct caused by mental impurities fuelled by the 'three poisons' of greed, hatred, and delusion are combated by observing the five precepts of the laity. Here the focus is on the individual refraining from certain acts. Then there is 'The Ethics of Virtue', in which the individual engages in such practices as the *Brahma-vihāras* already mentioned, namely loving-kindness, compassion, sympathetic joy, and equanimity. This marks a shift from observing strict rules to following a more internally enforced ethical framework. Third, there is 'The Ethics of

Altruism', in which service to others predominates. Finally, there is the comprehensive 'Ethics of Engagement', in which the three previous prescriptions for daily living are applied to the overall concern for a better society through the creation of new social institutions and relationships. Such an approach involves, as Queen maintains, awareness, identification of the self and the world, and a profound call to action. (It will be seen that this fourfold model builds on the threefold classification of Mahāyāna ethics described above.) With such an expanded concept of morality in mind, a number of engaged Buddhist activists have worked to extend the traditional principles of morality into a carefully developed plan of Buddhist social ethics.

Conclusion

We might summarize the key points of this survey by saying that Buddhist moral teachings are thought to be grounded in the cosmic law of Dharma rather than commandments handed down by God. Buddhism holds that the requirements of this law have been revealed by enlightened teachers and can be understood by anyone who develops the necessary understanding (*prajñā*). In leading a moral life a person becomes the embodiment of Dharma, and anyone who lives in this way and keeps the precepts can expect good karmic consequences such as happiness in this life and a good rebirth in the next. Buddhist moral teachings emphasize self-discipline (especially for those who have chosen the life of a monk or nun), generosity (*dāna*), non-violence (*ahiṃsā*), and compassion (*karuṇā*). Mahāyāna Buddhism places a special emphasis on service to others, which at times has led to a conflict between compassion and keeping the precepts. While the notion of skilful means and Tantric teachings have both had some influence on Buddhist ethics, however, the mainstream view has remained that the precepts express requirements of Dharma and should not be contravened. Questions of a more theoretical nature still outstanding include whether we can legitimately make use of Western concepts to understand the nature of Buddhist ethics, and if so how it is to be classified.

Note

1 This chapter has been adapted from Keown 2005, ch. 1, with due permission of the publisher.

References

Batchelor, Stephen. 2016. *After Buddhism: Rethinking the Dharma for a Secular Age*. New Haven, CT: Yale University Press.

Goodman, Charles. 2009. *Consequences of Compassion: An Interpretation and Defense of Buddhist Ethics*. Oxford and New York: Oxford University Press.

Gowans, Christopher W. 2015. *Buddhist Moral Philosophy: An Introduction*. New York: Routledge.

Hallisey, C. 1996. 'Ethical Particularism in Theravada Buddhism.' *Journal of Buddhist Ethics* 3: 32–43.

Harvey, Peter. 2000. *An Introduction to Buddhist Ethics: Foundations, Values and Issues*. Cambridge: Cambridge University Press.

Holt, John. 1981. *Discipline, the Canonical Buddhism of the Vinayapiṭaka*. Delhi: Motilal Banarsidass.

Keown, Damien. 2001. *The Nature of Buddhist Ethics*. Basingstoke: Palgrave Macmillan.

Keown, Damien. 2005. *Buddhist Ethics: A Very Short Introduction*. Oxford: Oxford University Press.

King, Sallie. B. 2005. *Being Benevolence: The Social Ethics of Engaged Buddhism*. Honolulu: University of Hawai'i Press.

Obeyesekere, Gananath. 2002. *Imagining Karma: Ethical Transformation in Amerindian, Buddhist, and Greek Rebirth*. Berkeley: University of California Press.

O'Flaherty, Wendy Doniger. 1980. *Karma and Rebirth in Classical Indian Traditions*. Berkeley: University of California Press.

Queen, Christopher S. 2000. *Engaged Buddhism in the West*. Boston, MA: Wisdom Publications.

Reichenbach, Bruce. R. 1990. *The Law of Karma. A Philosophical Study*. London: Macmillan.

Ruegg, David. S. 1980. 'Ahimsā and Vegetarianism in the History of Buddhism.' In *Buddhist Studies in Honour of Walpola Rahula*, ed. S. E. A. Balasooriya. London: Gordon Frazer.

Tahtinen, Unto. 1976. *Ahimsā: Non-Violence in Indian Tradition*. London: Rider.

Tatz, Mark. 1994. *The Skill in Means (Upāyakausalya) sūtra*. New Delhi: Motilal Banarsidass.

Wijayaratna, Mohan. 1991. *Buddhist Monastic Life: According to the Texts of the Theravada Tradition*. Cambridge: Cambridge University Press.

Chapter 51
PROCESS BUDDHISM: ETHICS AND SOCIAL ENGAGEMENT

Peter Paul Kakol, edited by Amy Rayner

Why Process Buddhism?

The relevance of the integration of Mādhyamika Buddhism and Process thought can ultimately be demonstrated pragmatically by its ethical and socio-political consequences. Process Buddhism is neither a form of idealism nor one of materialism, for a reality that is an open-ended process of dependent becoming cannot be characterized in terms of static concepts like 'matter' and 'idea'. The dependently becoming events or *dharmas* are psychophysical, as the words 'subject' and 'object' are relative designators that depend on whether we are talking about the interior or exterior perspective.

Process Buddhism seeks to transform both society (exterior) and culture (interior) by means of meditative thought, which is a direct psychophysical experience of reality. This is what Robert Thurman calls a 'cool revolution', which "transforms the outlook and behavior of many individuals and thereby slowly transforms a society" (Thurman 1998, 95). But this is not a solipsistic 'inner revolution' for there are no such things as atomic individuals. The point of deconstructive meditative thought is to realize this fact that there is no absolute self transcending this empirical 'social self', and thus that the future-self is the present self's other. Hence, self-interest is grounded in a disinterested altruism or other-interest . . . Process Buddhism thus makes possible the direct insight into reality as open-ended dependent becoming, which has become obscured "beneath the almost impenetrable layers of personal defilement and the tenacious superstructures of conventional belief with which human communities are always seeking to control behavior" (Jacobson 1983, 39). The Process Buddhist could thus say that "philosophers have only interpreted (*dṛṣṭi*) the world, in various ways; the point is to experience it directly (*darśana*)" (Hartshorne 1992, 149–151).

Process Buddhism attempts to replace the simplistic base–superstructure determinism with an understanding of social relations based on systems theory. In systems theory, society is a multi-level system where each level is at the same time a part of a larger whole and a whole made up of smaller parts. No whole is completely reducible to its parts as each level emerges creatively from lower levels. Thus there are top-down as well as bottom-up influences. This asymmetrical interdependence of bottom-up power and top-down information corroborates the Process Buddhist belief that society is changed by changing the way people think.

Process Buddhism is a liberating praxis which combines meditation and philosophy in a psychophysical direct experience of reality. This makes possible both a deconstruction of worldviews that reify abstractions and a reconstruction of a world-narrative that stresses the openness of dependent becoming.

A Process Buddhist ethics

What kind of ethical theory can we derive from the integration of Process thought and Mādhyamika Buddhism? Will it be superior to the ethical theories of either philosophy prior to integration? I argue that the mutual enrichment of both philosophies results in each gaining from the other a more rigorous development of aspects of their systems that have been undeveloped. Specifically, Process thought needs a more analytic and meditative approach towards creative emptiness, and Mādhyamika needs to take conventional truth more seriously and acknowledge that there is an ultimate actuality as well as an ultimate reality. The ethical implications of this theory of two ultimates is that there are two sources of compassion. First, there is the "emptiness that is compassion" (Nāgārjuna 1975, 76; Garfield 1995), as Nāgārjuna puts it, which results from the deconstruction of conceptual reifications that obscure the inter-related nature of things (Sebastian 2016, xi, 111). And second, there is the empty God who is, in Whitehead's words, "the fellow-sufferer who understands" (Whitehead 1978, 351), whose nature consists in a gradation of values. In this section I will try to show how the combination of both themes can result in a Process Buddhist ethics that is in many ways more adequate than the ethics of either philosophy taken separately.

Disinterested compassion

The basic ethical theme of both philosophies is compassion. In Process thought, reality is ultimately made up of nothing but sympathetic feeling-relations or prehensions; whereas the Mādhyamika teaching of the emptiness or openness of all phenomena means that there is ultimately nothing that is self-contained or selfish, rather everything is opened up and involved with everything else, thus making compassion possible. There are remarkable similarities between Śāntīdeva's and Charles Hartshorne's arguments that self-interest is in fact a special case of other-interest. Consider these excerpts from Śāntīdeva (1979, 109–110):

> What is so special about me?
> Why do I protect myself and not others?
> ...

> Being no (inherent) owner of suffering,
> There can be no distinction at all between (that of myself and others).

Compare this with the following from Hartshorne:

> We can love the other *as ourselves* because even the self as future is also another.... It is obvious that if rationality implies an interest in future consequences, and if the present self cannot benefit from any future good (since it is already all it ever can be), then a rational momentary self must in a generalized sense be unselfish. It must aim at a future good, although its own good is already complete.
> (Hartshorne 1959, 50; *author's* emphasis)

Both philosophers argue that there are no enduring selves that are 'owners' of suffering, only suffering-events that arise in dependence; so there can be no absolute distinction between self and other. But the relation between the self and the other cannot be established in terms of either identity or difference, which are symmetrical relations. For if self and other are identical (symmetrical dependence), the two become one and thus there is no relation; and if self and other are different (symmetrical independence), no relation can be established that does not itself require a relation and so on, in an infinite regress. Only an asymmetrical relation of identity–difference between the two can make sense: the self is in the future other whereas the future other is not in the self, except as a potentiality (hence there is an asymmetrical form of interdependence), which Levinas calls a 'trace' (Levinas 1969, 50). For Levinas, ethics is grounded in the 'for others', which has primacy over the 'for itself' (Levinas 1989, 230, 243–244). Since Levinas was influenced by the Process philosopher Henri Bergson, and in turn influenced the deconstructive post-structuralism of Derrida, there is much in his ethical theory that can be used to develop a Process Buddhist ethics that is both deconstructive and reconstructive. For Process Buddhist ethics can be understood as a disinterestedness which deconstructs all relations to others based on essence (interest), such as an enduring self or a group entity, and reconstructs relations with others based on compassion.

An ethic of the middle way

Process Buddhist ethics is thus an ethics of the middle way, as it is a middle between ethics based on self-interest and group-interest, mutual dependence and mutual independence, deontology and teleology, etc. Both Process philosophers and Mādhyamika Buddhists realize that every good is a middle way between two evils. On the one hand, we must avoid the violence of reducing the other to the same, which is to value the other only as something in me and not as other; and on the other hand, we have to avoid the violence of treating the other as something alien, and thus not human. We must pass beyond the dualistic moralism that takes up a pair of conceptual contrasts and labels one 'good' and the other 'evil' or 'bad', and replace it with the nonduality of middle-way ethics. This is not done by way of conjunction (both) or bi-negation (neither), but by the asymmetrical synthesis such that one term (becoming) is inclusive of the other (being). Of course, we *could* call the synthesis 'good' and non-synthesis else 'evil' or 'bad', but the 'duality' here is between inclusive nonduality and exclusive dualism. Nevertheless, we have an ethical choice here between dualism and the middle way.

The result of Process Buddhism is an ethics of responsibility based on the concept of the 'fitting'. H. Richard Niebuhr, whose ideas on responsibility I am closely following here, says:

> If we use value terms then the differences among the three approaches may be indicated by the terms, the *good*, the *right*, and the *fitting*; for teleology is concerned always with the highest good to which it subordinates the rights; consistent deontology is concerned with the right, no matter what may happen to our goods; but for the ethics of responsibility the *fitting* action, the one that fits into a total interaction as response and as anticipation of further response, is alone conducive to the good and alone is right.
>
> (Niebuhr 1963, 60–61)

Interestingly, Thurman is inspired by Niebuhr's ethics of responsibility in his development of a Buddhist ethic (Thurman 1981, 13). The notion of the 'fitting' has an obvious parallel in the Buddhist term *upāya*, 'skillful means'. Ultimately, this compassionate responsibility for others arises from the disinterested transcendence of both individuality and sociality. Compassion thus arises from a realization of the emptiness of all attempts to ground ethics in either subject (teleology) or object (deontology) instead of intersubjectivity (responsibility).

The need for a gradation of value

Although emptiness makes compassion possible, is it accurate to say that emptiness *is* compassion? Most mystical-meditative traditions – Buddhism included – do have an ethics and always warn novices that a mystical-meditative practice without ethical cultivation is highly dangerous. But an ethics requires a gradation of values that can guide creativity in the (fitting) direction—the direction that is conducive to both good and right actions. Such a hierarchy of values cannot transcend the universe since nothing escapes dependent becoming. Therefore it must be immanent, embodied in an everlasting psychophysical event-sequence which is all-inclusive and thus alone has the capacity to prehend the value hierarchy fully and exhaustively. Compassion must therefore be supplemented with wisdom, which guides it in the fitting direction.

Such a gradation of value is compatible with Mādhyamika, as insight into the ultimate truth can only be obtained by means of the hierarchies of conventional truth. The wise yogi, argues Candrakīrti, "does not reject the personal everyday world … outright, and so he does not reject outright actions and their moral consequences, the distinction between right and wrong, and so on" (Candrakīrti 1979, 232). As Guy Newland says of the conventional elements of the path, such as karma, ethics, and compassion: "They exist only conventionally, but *to exist conventionally is to exist*" (Newland

1992, 16). The emptiness of views means that they are relative or conditioned, which is not the same as saying that they are all 'equally false'. All it means is that there are no views that are absolutely true outside of context, which is not to deny that some views can be more true than others and can thus be organized into a hierarchy of relative truths. It is the same with ethical values. Thurman has shown that an ethical hierarchy exists in Mādhyamika Buddhism, where different levels of spiritual development demand different kinds of behavior. At the lowest level one must 'refrain from evil', after which comes 'do good', 'rely on dualism', 'rely on nondualism', and finally 'profound' (Thurman 1981, 28).

The argument for the equality of all phenomena due to their interdependence needs to be criticized in light of the Process Buddhist concept of 'asymmetrical interdependence'. Symmetrical interdependence only applies between abstractions (*a*-terms), whereas the relation between abstract and concrete (*r*-terms), as well as between concrete and concrete, takes the form of asymmetrical independence–dependence. Nevertheless, it was also argued that there is a kind of asymmetrical interdependence here too, for actual entities are inclusive of a potential future and of an actual past. This also means that abstractions such as bodies, structures, societies, etc., which condition subsequent concrete events and thus also condition the emergent forms that will serve as abstract conditions in their turn, include their future in the form of a vague potentiality; they are, in other words, the *sine qua non* of the more complex forms which they condition. This means that the more complex forms have a duty to preserve the existence of the total environment or ecosystem of simpler forms that condition their very existence. This extreme form of instrumental value, with its reverse hierarchy, needs to be combined with the equally extreme form of intrinsic value discussed above, via the concept of asymmetrical interdependence. Ken Wilber argues that it is necessary to see an interplay between intrinsic and extrinsic (or instrumental) values in this way, but he has not explicitly shown that they are asymmetrically interdependent, thus giving the impression that it is symmetrical.

In order to fully integrate the two kinds of value, we need to understand that intrinsic value is derivative from its intersubjective relations, rather than inhering (*svabhāva*-like) in separate and solipsistic subjects. Hence, inherent value can be measured by the extent to which an entity is internally related to other entities. Because ecosystems and even human societies are less complex than and lack the unity of a single human, we must supplement intrinsic value with instrumental value if we are to acknowledge the enormous duty we humans have towards preserving and promoting simpler life forms and ecosystems that are the very conditions of our existence.

A socially engaged Process Buddhism

We come now to a consideration of the social and political applications of Process Buddhism. I will begin with a discussion of the respective socio-political theories of Mādhyamika and Process thought. I will then show how these can be integrated in light of the Process Buddhist themes of asymmetrical interdependence and the two ultimates, as well as how post-structuralism—which was used in integrating the two philosophies—can indicate ways of putting Process Buddhism into practice. I will then discus how Process Buddhism can contribute to the liberal–communitarian debate.

Mādhyamika Buddhism and social engagement

Social engagement is a relatively recent concern on the part of Buddhists. For most of Buddhist history, Buddhists have tended to be concerned more with individual enlightenment and have not been interested in directly changing society—only indirectly via self-transformation. Now that Buddhism has come into contact with the Western Enlightenment's ideals of social revolution, it has begun to become interested in social enlightenment. This does not mean that social engagement was foreign to Buddhism and had to be imported from the West. Rather, as Kenneth Kraft puts it, "[q]ualities that were inhibited in pre-modern Asian settings ... can now be actualized through Buddhism's exposure to the West, where ethical sensitivity, social activism, and egalitarianism are emphasized" (Kraft 1988, xiii). The fact that these inhibited qualities were always implicit in Buddhism can be seen in their occasional blossoming-forth in history, a prime example being the third-century BCE Buddhist emperor Aśoka's rock edicts, which set forth a 'Buddhist politics' summarized by Thurman in five basic principles: transcendental individualism, nonviolence, educational evolutionism, social altruism, and universal democratism (Thurman 1998, 294–304). Thurman believes that since most of this text has to do with 'transcendent selflessness', it is clear that "the heart of Buddhist social activism is individualistic transcendentalism" (Thurman 1983, 35).

Robert Thurman, building on Nāgārjuna's socio-political ideas, has been at the forefront of developing a socially engaged Mādhyamika Buddhism, which he believes has many affinities with the Jeffersonian ideals of American liberalism. His 'politics of enlightenment' calls for an 'inner revolution'—he also calls it a 'cool revolution'—which transforms society by the transformation of the individual (via transcendence of the self). He sees this as a confirmation of liberal individualism and says that he affirms "the priority of the individual over the community in all areas" and that society's "highest collective interest is none other than the self-fulfillment of its individuals." He also sees the need for a strong and centralized executive leadership, a decentralized legislature in the form of electronic direct democracy, and the virtue of wealth accumulation by the virtuous and industrious so that it can be given away to the poor (ibid., 319–322).

Socio-political applications of asymmetrical interdependence

The socio-political application of a Process Buddhist concept of asymmetrical interdependence can be discerned from a consideration of the relationship between individual and society. Both the individual and society are abstractions from actual events which contain these abstractions as whole contains part. However, an individual has a dominant event-series—the mind—which provides a unity that is not present in a society. Thus, because the individual's mind is inclusive of its body, we can also speak of the event-series as the individual, in which case we can say that the individual is inclusive of society. Of course, the society includes its individuals, but this is an external relation and thus unlike the internal relation whereby the individual contains society. Thus there is an asymmetrical relation of inclusion, and since inclusion is a kind of dependence (the whole depends on its parts), we have an asymmetrical interdependence. Another reason why it is an asymmetrical relation is that it is not a one-to-one relation, but a one-to-many relation. Every individual in a society is dependent on society because its internal relation to society means that it would no longer be the same individual if removed from its society. But the society is independent of every individual in it because the removal of any one individual does not change the society—its form remains the same despite the presence of small fluctuations in its members. For the society is dependent on the totality of individuals and the latter are independent of society. This is because the society is not a transcendent thing over-and-above the individuals, but is immanent to them and thus reducible to the individuals. The fact that individuals are 'social selves' that are internally related to society means that society does exist; it's just that its mode of existence is one of immanence to the totality of individuals rather than something that transcends them. Thus, although society is independent of any given dependently becoming (internally related) individual, it too arises in dependence on the totality of individuals. Hence there is an asymmetrical interdependence between individual and society. In terms of the distinction that was made above between intrinsic and instrumental values, we can say that individuals have intrinsic value (deriving from their internal relatedness, not from any inherent nature) and society has instrumental value (which can sometimes override a small flock of intrinsic values.

Process Buddhism and the liberal–communitarian debate

The debate between liberalism and communitarianism can be resolved by the asymmetrical interdependence between individual and society. Process Buddhism's social understanding of the self has much affinity with communitarianism, which is based on the view that individuals are socially encumbered or embodied in their communities. This social embeddedness or 'internal relatedness' of individuals is contrasted with the atomic individualism or 'external relatedness' of liberalism.

The concept of the 'social self', which was fully worked out in the West by the sociologist and Process philosopher G. H. Mead, has been described as a "new model of the person as a bipolar social self arising through communicative interaction between individuality and sociality" (Odin 1996, 3). The social self's 'I' pole is a process which acts in the present and responds creatively to the socially determined 'Me' pole which is given by the past. Thus, the social self is a process which includes both individuality and sociality as abstract aspects. But Mead's social self was anticipated by Buddhist philosophers, who developed the idea that the self is a combination of impermanent mental events (*nāma*) and relatively stable form (*rūpa*), both of which are socially conditioned (*pratitya-samutpāda*). The reduction of the self to a spatio-temporal network of relational processes means that there is no simple self which has a fixed identity or essence; hence, ultimately there is no-self (*anātman*), only a social self (which is a node of inter-relations).

Process Buddhism avoids the extremes of liberal mutual independence and corporatist mutual dependence, affirming instead an asymmetrical interdependence between individual rights and the common good. So in a certain sense it is a middle way between liberalism and communitarianism.

The asymmetrical nature of the Process Buddhist concept of communitarianism outlined above leads to a form of liberal democracy which is different from the one popular in the West, where the liberal protection of individual and minority rights takes precedence over the democratic common good. Although rights transcend any given community, they are nevertheless immanent transcendentals abstracted from the universal community of dependent becomings. Each individual's freedom—which is its creative emptiness—is conventionally limited only by the freedom of others. Thus, freedom has primacy. Hence the Process Buddhist understanding of democracy is one that is inclusive rather than exclusive. For it includes the liberal concern with limits, but does not see them as limits; rather, rights make possible more freedom through the inclusion in the democratic process of all spheres of human life that are communal—local, national, global, political, social, cultural, religious, etc. For in the end rights come down to the protection of individuals from being hierarchically dominated along lines of class, gender, race, etc.

Inclusive democracy is not simply the practical consequence of Process Buddhist theory; rather the two—theory and practice—are united in Process Buddhist praxis, which uses democratic discourse (meditative thought) to awaken social insight into the nature of reality as an inclusive democracy of dependent becoming. This is why the Buddha modeled the Saṅgha on the *ganasaṅgha*, which was a type of political and territorial clan existent in the north of India at the time that was based on collective decision-making and communal ownership of assets, in contrast to the *jānapadas* of the laity, which were authoritarian and monarchical (Chakravarti 1992, 16). "When people have transformed their minds," says Thurman,

> they will naturally and coolly act to transform the society and eventually the polity. Śakyamuni turned politics on its head and proved that the best way to build a healthy society was from the bottom up – through the development of the individual – not from the top down.
>
> (Thurman 1998, 95)

However, such a transformation is not a solipsistic and private affair. For a self which becomes in dependence on other selves is always already a social self and thus can only transform itself in a social context. Hence, meditative thought must be seen in intersubjective rather than subjective terms, so it is thus really the same thing as democratic deliberation or 'multilogue'.

The 'dual allegiance' of Process Buddhism

The practical applications of Process Buddhism based on asymmetrical interdependence that I have been developing are in the realm of conventional truth. Thus, they are only provisional and cannot be taken as absolutes. So, how are we to reconcile these two different practical applications of Process Buddhism, participatory democracy and libertarian socialism?

In Process Buddhism, creativity is neither being nor becoming, but more like becoming than being; or: there is neither independence (*svabhāva*) nor dependence (*parabhāva*), and yet there is dependent becoming. It is the same in politics as in ethics: there is a need to say 'either/or', to have a hierarchy of value, even though ultimately—simultaneously—we must say 'neither/nor', that in creative emptiness there are no absolute hierarchies, that there is no 'top' and no 'bottom'. Hence, the need for a separation of powers between phenomenal and transcendental, conventional and ultimate, dependent becoming and creative emptiness, hierarchy and anarchy.

Conclusion

I have outlined the practical applications of the integration of Mādhyamika Buddhism and Process philosophy. I have argued that the integration can contribute to (1) Mādhyamika–Process dialogue and interreligious dialogue in general; (2) evaluative worldview analysis and a general theory of worldviews; (3) ethical theory (disinterested compassion, middle-way ethics, and gradation of value); and (4) socio-political theory (social engagement based on asymmetrical interdependence between individuals and society, the liberal–communitarian debate). But this discussion of Process Buddhism's practical applications is not merely intended to derive practice from theory, for these two are asymmetrically interdependent. The practical implications of the integration of these two systems—indeed of any systems—do not come after the integration, but are themselves a part of the praxis of integration. I have shown that Process Buddhism is a praxis that transcends individual and group interests by means of disinterested meditative thought which experiences reality directly as a creative emptiness in which knowing and acting are part of the same nondual process of creative synthesis, which is an experience that is always participatory and creative.

References

Candrakīrti. 1979. *Prasannapāda*, 495. In Mervyn Sprung (trans.), *Lucid Exposition of the Middle Way: The Essential Chapters from the 'Prasannapāda' of Candrakīrti*. Boulder, CO: Prajna Press.

Chakravarti, Uma. 1992. "Buddhism as a Discourse of Dissent? Class and Gender." *Pravada* 1(5): 12–18.

Garfield, Jay (trans.). 1995. *The Fundamental Wisdom of the Middle Way: Nāgārjuna's "Mūlamadhyamakakārikā."* Oxford: Oxford University Press.

Hartshorne, Charles. 1970. *Creative Synthesis and Philosophic Method*. London: SCM Press.

———. 1992. "Some Comments on Randall Morris' *Process Philosophy and Political Ideology*." *Process Studies* 21: 149–151.

Jacobson, Nolan Pliny. 1983. *Buddhism and the Contemporary World: Change and Self-Correction*. Carbondale and Edwardsville: Southern Illinois University Press.

Kakol, Peter Paul. 2009. *Emptiness and Becoming: Integrating Mādhyamika Buddhism and Process Philosophy*. Fore-word by P. Bilimoria; Introduction by Robert Neville. New Delhi: DKPrintworld.

Kraft, Kenneth. 1988. "Introduction." In Fred Eppsteiner (ed.), *The Path of Compassion: Writings on Socially Engaged Buddhism*. Berkeley, CA: Parallax Press.

Levinas, Emmanuel. 1969. *Totality and Infinity: An Essay on Exteriority*, trans. A. Lingis. Pittsburgh, PA: Duquesne University Press.

———. 1989. *The Levinas Reader*, ed. Sean Hand. Oxford: Blackwell.

Nāgārjuna. 1975. *Rājaparikatha-ratnamāla*. In Nāgārjuna and Kaysang Gyatso, *The Precious Garland and the Song of the Four Mindfulnesses*, trans. Jeffrey Hopkins and Lati Rinpoche with Anne Klein. London: George Allen and Unwin.

Newland, Guy. 1992. *The Two Truths in the Madhyamika Philosophy of the Ge-luk-ba Order of Tibetan Buddhism*. Ithaca, NY: Snow Lion Publications.

Niebuhr, H. Richard. 1963. *The Responsible Self: An Essay in Christian Moral Philosophy*. San Francisco, CA: Harper and Row.

Odin, Steve. 1996. *The Social Self in Zen and American Pragmatism*. Albany, NY: State University of New York Press.

Sebastian, C.D. 2016. *The Cloud of Nothingness The Negative Way in Nāgārjuna and John of the Cross*. New Delhi/Dordrecht: Springer.

Shantideva, Acharya. 1979. *A Guide to the Bodhisattva's Way of Life*, trans. Stephen Batchelor. Dharamsala: Library of Tibetan Works and Archives.

Thurman, Robert A. F. 1981. "The Emptiness that is Compassion: An Essay on Buddhist Ethics." *Religious Traditions* 4(2): 11–34.

———. 1983. "Guidelines for Buddhist Social Activism Based on Nāgārjuna *Jewel Garland of Royal Counsels*." *Eastern Buddhist* 16(Spring): 19–51.

———. 1998. *Inner Revolution: Life, Liberty, and the Pursuit of Real Happiness*. New York: Riverhead Books.

Whitehead, Alfred North. 1967. *Adventures of Ideas*. New York: Macmillan.

———. 1978. Process and Reality: An Essay in Cosmology. *The Gifford Lectures of 1927–1928* (corrected ed.), ed. D. R. Griffin and D. W. Sherburne. New York: Macmillan.

Chapter 52
INDIAN AND EUROPEAN PHILOSOPHY

Thomas B. Ellis

In all respects, the modern encounter between India and Europe betrays initial colonial interests and eventual, not to mention lingering, postcolonial concerns. From the socio-economic to the literary and philosophic, the negotiation of imbalanced relationship constitutes the nature of the exchange between India and Europe in the modern period (Breckenridge and van der Veer 1993). Despite philosophy's traditional scorn for matters material and practical, intellectual historians cannot but take into consideration the disparate, material realities in which Europeans and Indians engaged each other philosophically. It is for this reason that the preeminent historian of Indian philosophy, Wilhelm Halbfass, notes, "India has discovered the West and begun to respond to it in being sought out, explored, overrun and objectified by it .... This is a simple and familiar fact. Yet its fundamental significance for the hermeneutics of the encounter between India and the West is often forgotten" (1988, 172).[1] Pursuing a remedy for just such amnesia, I address in what follows the hermeneutics of the philosophical encounter between India and Europe in the colonial and postcolonial periods.

Accompanying first the establishment of their commercial interests in the eighteenth century and then their colonial administration in the nineteenth century, Europeans found in India a venerable history of intellectual accomplishments. Unlike some of Europe's other geo-political conquests of the period, India presented literate traditions rich in art, music, poetry, law, religion, and philosophy. For many Europeans, this exotic, yet cultured other proved rather titillating. Missionary, merchant, and administrative reports excited the European imagination back home, making of India a land of mystery and intrigue. Truly, India was the jewel in the crown.

As Europeans leisurely enjoyed the bounty of a cross-cultural encounter the material reality of which unfolded thousands of miles away, the conditions for the Indian reception of things European were quite different. India was host to a colonial presence. Offsetting the luxury with which Europeans could occasionally appropriate Indian materials, Indians suffered the company of an ineradicable other. As one party enjoyed the privilege of suspending the engagement at will, the other party saw its agency slowly ebb as a foreign presence became politically and materially entrenched. Such disparate material realities ineluctably affected the philosophical exchange. The twentieth-century Indian philosopher J. L. Mehta (1912–1988) aptly notes in this regard:

> The only difference in this two-sided, mutual participation is that from the Western end it is in the nature of supplementing the substance of their mainstream culture, an assimilation of the alien and subordinating it within a more widely based totality. From the non-Western, including Indian, the participation is an appropriation of the substance itself, not peripheral in the Western case.
>
> (1990, 230)

According to Mehta, European culture could absorb – ostensibly without discomfort or displacement – the Indian material, whereas India's appropriation of things European had substantively disruptive ramifications.

Considering these material realities, I propose that the modern, philosophical exchange between India and Europe has undergone three successive yet overlapping stages, that is, enthusiasm, chauvinism, and patience. For good or ill, there remain representatives of each stage in the contemporary moment. The stage of enthusiasm pertains to the belief that the other possesses something of great value that the self lacks. The stage of chauvinism pertains to the belief that the other lacks something of great value the self possesses. The stage of patience pertains to the recognition that what the other possesses may ultimately be beyond domestication and thus ultimately disruptive to the self. Though certain European philosophers may occasionally display the latter, it is the late twentieth-century Indian philosophers who best articulate and embody this position, that is, they show the greatest hermeneutical patience and as such may turn out to be the greatest philosophical patients.

India's history is anything but a tale of international isolation. In fact, the long history of Indian engagement with the foreign leads Halbfass to propose a "traditional Indian xenology," a xenology marked by indifference, disinterest, and occasional anathema (1988, 172). Indeed, it would appear that traditional Indian intellectuals seldom felt compelled to engage the other in intellectual debate, dialogue, or exchange. The "extra-Indian other" was an other unworthy. All of this was to change in the modern period.

India's intellectual encounter with Europe over the past couple of centuries betrays the extent to which Indian thinkers began to adjust their systems of self-understanding and representation in reaction to, and accommodation of European traditions, traditions particularly associated with rationalism, political liberalism, and the pursuit of empirical and metaphysical knowledge free of religious dogma and authority. Presumably for the first time, modern Indians found their traditions under a critical and persistent, not to mention occasionally disquieting, foreign gaze couched in material prosperity and promise. This combination eventually proved too provocative to ignore.

Upon introduction to the Indian intellectual traditions, European philosophers immediately faced the self-appointed task of defining what they had found. Indian intellectual traditions were, and often still are, seen as "spiritual" and "mystical" (King 1999).

For many, such characterization is evocative of either "violent antipathy or fervent enthusiasm"(Krishna 1991, 3), the two prominent Orientalist reactions to India (Inden 1986, 1990). For the European romantics of the eighteenth and nineteenth centuries who were reading with enthusiasm Anquetil Duperron's (1731–1805) *Oupenek'hat*, itself a translation of the seventeenth-century Dara Shukoh's Persian translation of select Upaniṣads titled *Sirr-i Akbar*, India's monistic idealism seemingly offset Europe's increasing commitment to materialism and mechanism (Clarke 1997, 61). From such a romantic perspective, India enjoyed an innocence long outgrown in Europe. Praising the "Indian child's" imagination and freedom of spirit, the romantics simultaneously criticized the "European adult" for its slavish commitment to reason and technology. European adulthood represented the impoverishment of a plentiful childhood preserved on the South Asian subcontinent. According to the fervently enthusiastic romantics, the passage of time proved deleterious to the spiritual pursuits of humanity.

While the romantics saw Indian philosophy as spiritual and mystical, inspired more by intuitive experience than reason, others employed this same designation to quite opposite ends. Where the romantics saw the deleterious impact of time, others saw progress. G. W. F. Hegel (1770–1831) (in)famously took this alternative approach. According to Hegel, philosophy could not remain detached from history. No longer the repository of timeless truths, philosophy had to countenance the development of thought through the centuries. Because Indian traditions were seen as spiritual and by extension ahistorical, they were deemed inferior to the historical consciousness of nineteenth-century Europe. That said, Hegel did not dismiss entirely India's traditions, "Idealism … is found in India, but only as an Idealism of imagination, without distinct conceptions …. Since, however, it is the abstract and absolute Thought itself that enters into these dreams as their material, we may say that Absolute Being is presented here as in the ecstatic state of a dreaming condition" (quoted in Inden 1990, 7). India represented for Hegel an integral period in world history that had been surpassed by the European present. Such chauvinism complemented the romantic's enthusiasm, the romantic is truly the despiser's loyal opponent (Inden 1986, 429).

While the romantic sought to recover a lost truth and the despiser sought to establish European triumphalism, A. Schopenhauer (1788–1860) sought to outdo both. Resonating with the romantic, Schopenhauer believed that Upaniṣadic monism resonated with his own transcendental idealism, thus distinguishing himself from his romantic colleagues who often sought in India truths not contained in the European present. Accordingly, and as a perennial philosopher at heart, he wrote, "in general, the sages of all times have always said the same thing" (quoted in Halbfass 1988, 111). Schopenhauer dismissed in this way both the romantic and Hegelian conceptions of time. Where the former saw return and recovery, the latter saw irreversible development. Schopenhauer, for his part, saw a constant in all periods of time, the metaphysical present is always present. Despite applauding them for their discovery of "perennial truths," Schopenhauer all the same criticized the Indian authors for their employment of "myths and meaningless words" (quoted in Halbfass 1988, 114). Like Hegel, Schopenhauer betrays in this regard the intellectual chauvinism of modern, European philosophy. Having lost its pristine origin to centuries of philosophical progress abroad or obfuscating religious mythology and practice at home, Indian philosophy was seemingly caught in an historical vacuum. Apparently, only a nineteenth-century European mind could restore to India its lost heritage, a sentiment to resurface in the twentieth century.

Finding their European counterparts engaged in a sustained disputation concerning the nature and value of India's spirituality, many eighteenth- and nineteenth-century Indian intellectuals adopted the dubious European definition of Indian philosophy as spiritual, overlooking thereby the various Indian traditions of materialism (e.g., Cārvāka), logic (e.g., Nyāya, Buddhist, and Jaina), and realism (e.g., Vaiśeṣika).[2] In much the same way as the European reception of matters Indian began with enthusiasm and shifted toward chauvinism, so too did the Indian reception of matters European. There is perhaps no better place to witness this shift than amid the Bengali elite.

Often considered the "Father of Modern India," Rammohun Roy (1772–1833) enthusiastically embraced the rational systems of European philosophy (Halbfass 1988, 206, 214; Mehta 1971, 491). As European romantics evinced enthusiasm for India's spiritual heritage, Roy evinced a certain enthusiasm for European reason. He undertook what could be considered an ambivalent reclamation of the Indian traditions: some elements of India's various traditions needed to be jettisoned in favor of those more immediately palatable to modern, European sensibilities. For instance, and in keeping with Schopenhauer, Roy privileged Upaniṣadic monism as opposed to the "idolatrous" *mūrti* worship of popular Hindu *pūjā*; he similarly denigrated the tantric traditions of Hinduism. For these and similar reasons, Roy's impact on the history of the modern encounter between India and Europe must not go unnoticed:

> The hermeneutic situation which is expressed in Rammohun Roy's 'multilingualism,' his cross-cultural horizon of self-understanding and appeal, his position between receptivity and self-assertion, 'Westernization' and 'Hindu revivalism,' forms the background and basic condition of modern Hindu thinking and self-understanding.
>
> (Halbfass 1988, 217)

While Rammohun Roy sought to employ European reason in his exposition of select Indian traditions, another member of the Bengali elite, Narendranatha Datta, or Vivekananda (1863–1902), eventually employed India's spirituality in much the same way that the European romantics did: India's spirituality was an antidote to and thus critique of Europe's materialism. Vivekananda redeployed in this way the romantic rhetoric regarding a material West and a spiritual East. What for Hegel had been a sign of intellectual stagnancy became for Vivekananda a badge of honor. Vivekananda, not to mention other Indian philosopher-nationalists, e.g., Mohandas K. Gandhi (1869–1948) and Aurobindo Ghose (1872–1950), conceded that Europe had achieved great success in the material realm but lagged far behind India's spiritual accomplishments. Accordingly, India could import Western material goods and sciences while exporting its spirituality. Vivekananda evinces in this way a certain "spiritual chauvinism": "Whenever there is a spiritual adjustment, it should come from the Orient .... When the Occident wants to learn about the spirit, about God, about the soul, about the meaning and the mystery of this universe, he must sit at the feet of the Orient to learn" (quoted in Halbfass 1988, 233). According to Vivekananda, and in direct opposition to Hegel, India's traditions could account for and contain the world's other religio-spiritual traditions: "Hindus are head and shoulders above all other nations in morality and spirituality" (quoted in Halbfass 1995, 325). Despite any political payoffs, Vivekananda, like Roy, was guilty of a hasty adoption of European definitions of Indian traditions. In this way, both Indian and European philosophers were guilty of a certain hermeneutic impatience and thus naiveté, a naiveté K. C. Bhattacharyya clearly denounced.

The preeminent academic philosopher of modern India, K. C. Bhattacharyya (1875–1949), described the nineteenth- and early twentieth-century Indian mind as a "shadow mind," contrasting this with what he called the "vernacular mind" (1954, 105). Shadow minds live off the luminescence of another, they are not active agents in the pursuit of matters intellectual. In this regard, Europe's "mind" was the active center of intellectual radiation – India's mind, a mere epiphenomenon. Uncritically adopting European philosophy as the yardstick by which to measure intellectual progress or arrest, Hindu intellectuals precipitately compromised their own philosophical traditions. According to Bhattacharyya, this betrayed a much more pernicious form of colonial rule than that of overt "political subjection":

> There is … a subtler domination exercised in the sphere of ideas by one culture on another, a domination all the more serious in the consequence, because it is not ordinarily felt …. Cultural subjection is ordinarily of an unconscious character and it implies slavery from the very start …. There is cultural subjection … when one's traditional cast of ideas and sentiments is superseded without comparison or competition by a new cast representing an alien culture which possesses one like a ghost.
>
> (1954, 103)

It is precisely the twentieth-century Hindu intellectual, according to Bhattacharyya, over whom the ghost of the colonial master continues to cast a shadow. He argued that only by the patient translation of European philosophies into Indian vernacular languages and philosophies could Indian intellectuals engage in a "Swaraj in Ideas," that is, a self-rule in ideas. While Bhattacharyya thus issued a certain call to philosophical nationalism, other Indian intellectuals of the twentieth century were a bit suspicious regarding the recuperation of India's vernacular mind, suggesting that it may be more of a romantic gesture than a viable option (Mehta 1990).

Hermeneutic issues dominated the cross-cultural, philosophical encounter in the twentieth century. For Europeans, however, hermeneutical difficulties apparently pertained only to understanding the other. For instance, Hans-Georg Gadamer (1900–2002) remarked, "Although … the research in Eastern philosophy has made further advances, we believe today that we are further removed from its philosophical understanding …. What can be considered established is only the negative insight that our own basic concepts, which were coined by the Greeks, alter the essence of what is foreign" (quoted in Halbfass 1988, 164). Others disagreed, the philosophical traditions of

India – not to mention China – were transparent enough to be judged as mere anthropological types subsumable under a European universal. Edmund Husserl (1859–1938), in particular, announced the inevitable "Europeanization of the Earth," suggesting that the natural and mathematical sciences, whose pedigree traces back to the early Greek philosophers (or so the triumphant [hi]story is told), would eventually enjoy a certain hegemony. For Husserl, India's vernacular mind ultimately amounted to a historical curiosity, destined only for the walls of the museum of philosophy. Whereas India and China will Europeanize themselves, "we, if we understand ourselves properly, will never, for example, Indianize ourselves" (Husserl 1970, 275). Maurice Merleau-Ponty (1908–1961) similarly thought, "Like everything built or instituted by man, India and China are immensely interesting. But like all institutions, they leave it to us to discern their true meaning .... China and India are not entirely aware of what they are saying" (quoted in Mehta 1985, 185). Though widespread, such intellectual chauvinism was not exhaustive. In fact, even Husserl's triumphalist statement itself suggests an alternative path of inquiry. Indeed, both Husserl and Merleau-Ponty concede that self-understanding is a necessary condition for true philosophy. Where Merleau-Ponty assigns a deficiency on this score to India and China, thereby presuming Europe's self-transparency, Husserl's oblique conditional raises the possibility that European philosophers may not in fact understand themselves properly. If this possibility were to realize itself, it would amount to a significant interrogation of European philosophical privilege, an interrogation eventually issuing from the pen of Martin Heidegger (1889–1976).

Heidegger is a pivotal figure in the cross-cultural, philosophical encounter in the twentieth century. He spent a career arguing that European philosophers did not in fact understand themselves properly. There was/is a subtle prejudice at the heart of European metaphysics that has largely gone unnoticed. The so-called "metaphysics of presence" informing the dominant Western tradition of ontotheology rests on the forgetting of the difference between Being and beings.[3] For J. L. Mehta, such opacity makes of the cross-cultural encounter

> an unthinking attempt at perpetuating Western 'philosophy' by translating Eastern thinking into the language of Western metaphysics, taken as the universally valid paradigm.... It hides an unthought opacity that stands in the way of adequately reaching out to the other, for it either prompts to an assimilation of the other or leads to a perpetuation of its otherness.
>
> (1985, 242)

According to W. V. Spanos, this "unthought opacity" so informs the colonial project that any postcolonial criticism failing to address this issue invariably falls short of the mark, "the Occidental interpretation of being – informs and is informed by, an imperial will to power. Any failure to recognize this 'ontological imperialism' renders postcolonial discourse and practice inadequate to its emancipatory task" (1996, 141).

Heidegger's philosophy establishes the irremediable incompletion of any one philosophical system, undermining thereby the philosophical justification of colonial projects. Insofar as all subjects are subject to historical limitations and contingencies, philosophical pretensions to superiority appear at best rather quaint. According to J. S. O'Leary, "Heidegger is the opposite of a Eurocentric imperialist, for his awareness of the historical contingency of Western ontology clears the path to a radical pluralism of what he calls the 'great beginnings'" (1997, 180). Mehta agrees, noting that Heidegger's work "is the necessary first step taken beyond Hegel, the breaking of the charmed circle of metaphysical thinking, an emergence into the open, where non-Western modes of thinking ... are no longer regarded as 'anthropological specimens', as Husserl called them" (1992, 86). Elsewhere he writes:

> For all non-Western civilizations, however decrepit or wounded, Heidegger's thinking brings hope ... by making them see that though in one sense ... they are inextricably involved in Western metaphysical history ... in another sense they are now free to think for themselves, in their own fashion.
>
> (Mehta 1990, 31)

Opposing the triumphalism inherent in pronouncements concerning the "Europeanization of the Earth," several Indian philosophers undertook in the waning decades of the twentieth century a reassessment of hermeneutic philosophy and by a certain extension a reassessment of the encounter between Indian and European philosophy. In particular, some saw in philosophical hermeneutics an imperial intention, that is, the very desire to understand the other may disguise a will-to-interpret that is tantamount to a will-to-power. Philosophical hermeneutics appears in this regard to be a bit impatient, or at least such is the takeaway message in Mehta's "postcolonial hermeneutics," R. Panikkar's (1918–2010) "diatopical hermeneutics," and finally J. N. Mohanty's (b. 1928) "philosophical agenda."

Mehta was suspicious of philosophical hermeneutics; in this, he was not alone (Taylor 1990, 142; King 1999, 95; Obeyesekere 1990, 274). Mehta described philosophical hermeneutics as a "mastery of the other ... as a weapon directed against the other" (1992, 183), stating elsewhere, "understanding (is) an instrument of the will-to-power ... to entrap and dominate other human groups" (1992, 271). This is not a wholly uncharitable reading of philosophical hermeneutics. Gadamer after all suggests that philosophical hermeneutics involves the conquest of the alien (1997, 387), the overcoming of the foreign (1976, 47). For philosophical, or better yet, colonial hermeneutics, the other is merely a moment in the self's becoming (Taylor 1990, 131). The other edifies the self. Contesting such hermeneutics, Mehta's postcolonial hermeneutics proposes that the other is a moment of the self's displacement. To be sure, while Gadamer speaks of edifications and supplementations, Mehta places his emphasis on ruptures and dislocations (Ellis 2013). The Indian encounter with the West was anything but edifying. For Mehta, the other is a moment of self-rupture and not self-expansion.

The rupture-of-self constitutive of Mehta's postcolonial hermeneutics likewise characterizes Panikkar's diatopical hermeneutics. Immediately interested in problematizing the very notion of a comparative philosophy, Panikkar argues that the cross-cultural, philosophical encounter will never allow itself the luxury of the comparative moment.

As philosophy itself pretends to the universal, it would appear that any neutral point from which to compare philosophies is wholly problematic. Indeed, there is no philosophically context-free point of departure, "any effort at comparing philosophies starts consciously or unconsciously from a concrete philosophical position" (Panikkar 1988, 127). Panikkar suggests in this regard that an imparative project replace the comparative one. Imparative philosophy proposes that "we may ... learn by being ready to undergo the different philosophical experiences of other people" (Panikkar 1988, 127–128). Associated with such imparative work is the recognition that everything is negotiable, including ontologies. Panikkar suggests that imparative philosophy employs in this regard a diatopical hermeneutics, that is, "the required method of interpretation when the distance to overcome ... is ... the distance between two (or more) cultures, which have independently developed different spaces (*topoi*) their own methods of philosophizing and ways of reaching intelligibility along with their proper categories" (Panikkar 1988, 130). As with Mehta's postcolonial hermeneutics, Panikkar's diatopical hermeneutics insists on the deconstructability of all traditions, "we need to be ready to contest our own conclusions" (Panikkar 1988, 135). From a colonialist's perspective this may seem confused, from a colonial subject's position, it is obvious. Mehta's postcolonial hermeneutics and Panikkar's diatopical hermeneutics anticipate Mohanty's philosophical agenda.

J. N. Mohanty (2001, 83–90) acknowledges four possible agendas in the cross-cultural, philosophical encounter. He first introduces the "Intellectualist's Agenda" aimed at using the other to help clarify a conceptual problem for the self. Second, he mentions the "Wisdom-Seeker's Agenda" as that approach most associated with Western romanticism, that is, the sense that India's traditions are spiritual as opposed to the West's materialism. Third, he recognizes the "Agenda of Supplementing," in which the other supplements the self's deficiencies, e.g., India uses the West to satisfy its material needs while the West turns to India for spiritual matters. Dissatisfied with all three, Mohanty endorses the "Philosophical Agenda," that is, "recognizing how a different tradition realizes a quite different possibility not envisaged in one's own" (Mohanty 2001, 87–89). Mohanty's philosophical agenda presents the true, dialogical option, "Indian philosophy can profitably learn from western philosophy, and vice versa, only if the two philosophical traditions open themselves to each other's differences, and, in the light of that recognition, if each examines itself" (2001, 86). In this regard, the recurring theme emerging at the end of the twentieth century reflects concerns regarding the self's capacity to see the other not merely as a dialectical opposite (e.g., the West's materialism versus the East's spirituality), but rather as a truly other other. To be other, the other must confound not only the self's prejudices but also the negation of the self's prejudices. As the French philosopher Jacques Derrida (1930–2004) was often wont to remark, the other explodes the self's calculus.[4] The other provides the means for true self-criticism, not aggrandizement.

The philosophical encounter between India and Europe in the modern period betrays a history of hermeneutic impatience. Intellectuals on both sides of the divide hastily assumed welcomed novelty, unrecognized correspondence, or pejorative conflict. With enthusiasm or chauvinism, all parties seemed too eager to applaud or dismiss their other. Today, there seems to be some recognition that hermeneutic patience is preferable. What is more, there is some agreement that the other-as-other has a dramatic, and possibly deconstructive, impact on the self's assurances. The future cross-cultural, philosophical encounter quite possibly begins in this way with what Michel Foucault once considered the impossibility of thinking that.[5] Postcolonial philosophers indeed recognize that the other affords the self the opportunity to revisit and rectify *its* prejudices, not those of the other. Perhaps for all the right reasons then (the wrong ones hopefully having been left by the wayside in the nineteenth and twentieth centuries), philosophical others, as true others, will always be mutually liberating.

Notes

1 I will, throughout this chapter, borrow generously from Wilhelm Halbfass's classic *India and Europe: An Essay in Understanding* (1988). For secondary perspectives on Halbfass's work, see Dallmayr (1996) and Franco and Preisendanz (1997).

2 For an excellent discussion of the dubious definition of Indian philosophy as spiritual see Krishna 1991.

3 See Heidegger 1969.

4 For an extended discussion of the other's disruptive force, see Derrida 1989.

5 Foucault 1970, xv.

References

Bhattacharyya, K. C. 1954. "Swaraj in Ideas." *Visvabharati Quarterly* 20: 103–114.

Bilimoria, P. 2010. "Hegel's Spectre on Indian Thought and its God-in-Nothingness." *Religions of South Asia* 4(2): 199–211.

Breckenridge, C. A., and P. van der Veer. 1993. *Orientalism and the Postcolonial Predicament: Perspectives on South Asia*. Philadelphia: University of Pennsylvania Press.

Clarke, J. J. 1997. *Oriental Enlightenment: The Encounter between Asian and Western Thought*. London: Routledge.

Dallmayr, Fred R. 1996. *Beyond Orientalism: Essays on Cross-Cultural Encounter*. Albany: State University of New York Press.

Derrida, J. 1989. "Psyche, Inventions of the Other." In *Reading de Man Reading*, ed. L. Waters and W. Godzich. Minneapolis: University of Minnesota Press.

Ellis, Thomas B. 2013. *On the Death of the Pilgrim: The Postcolonial Hermeneutics of Jarava Lal Mehta*. Dordrecht and New York: Springer.

Foucault, M. 1970. *The Order of Things: An Archeology of the Human Sciences*. New York: Vintage.

Franco, Eli, and Karin Preisendanz. 1997. *Beyond Orientalism: The Work of Wilhelm Halbfass and Its Impact on Indian and Cross-Cultural Studies*. Amsterdam: Rodopi.

Gadamer, Hans Georg. 1976. *Philosophical Hermeneutics*. Berkeley: University of California Press.

———. 1997. *Truth and Method*. Trans. J. Weinsheimer, D. G. Marshall. Second, rev. ed. New York: Continuum.

Halbfass, Wilhelm. 1988. *India and Europe: An Essay in Understanding*. Albany: State University of New York Press.

——— (ed.). 1995. *Philology and Confrontation: Paul Hacker on Traditional and Modern Vedānta*. Albany: State University of New York Press.

Heidegger, Martin. 1969. *Identity and Difference*, trans. J. Stambaugh. New York: Harper and Row.

Husserl, Edmund. 1970. *The Crisis of European Sciences and Transcendental Phenomenology: An Introduction to Phenomenological Philosophy*. Trans. D. Carr. Evanston, IL: Northwestern University Press.

Inden, Ronald B. 1986. "Orientalist Constructions of India." *Modern Asian Studies* 20(3): 401–446.

———. 1990. *Imagining India*. Oxford and Cambridge, MA: Basil Blackwell.
King, Richard. 1999a. *Indian Philosophy: An Introduction to Hindu and Buddhist Thought*. Washington, DC: Georgetown University Press.
———. 1999b. *Orientalism and Religion: Postcolonial Theory, India and 'the Mystic East'*. London and New York: Routledge.
Krishna, Daya. 1991. *Indian Philosophy: A Counter Perspective*. Delhi: Oxford University Press.
Larson, Gerald James, and Eliot Deutsch. 1988. *Interpreting across Boundaries: New Essays in Comparative Philosophy*. Princeton, NJ: Princeton University Press.
Mehta, J. L. 1971. "Commentary on Marc Galanter's 'Hinduism, Secularism, and the Indian Judiciary'." *Philosophy East and West* 21: 489–492.
———. 1985. *India and the West: The Problem of Understanding*. Chico, CA: Scholar's Press.
———. 1990. *Philosophy and Religion: Essays in Interpretation*. New Delhi: Indian Council of Philosophical Research.
———. 1992. *J. L. Mehta on Heidegger, Hermeneutics, and Indian Tradition*. Ed. W. J. Jackson. Leiden: E. J. Brill.
Mohanty, J. N. 2001. *Explorations in Philosophy: Indian Philosophy*. Ed. B. Gupta. New Delhi: Oxford University Press.
Obeyesekere, Gananath. 1990. *The Work of Culture: Symbolic Transformation in Psychoanalysis and Anthropology*. Chicago: University of Chicago Press.
O'Leary, Joseph S. 1997. "Heidegger and Indian Philosophy." In *Beyond Orientalism: The Work of Wilhelm Halbfass and its Impact on Indian and Cross-Cultural Studies*, ed. E. Franco and Karin Preisendanz. Amsterdam: Rodopi.
Panikkar, R. 1980. "Aporias in the Comparative Philosophy of Religion." *Man and World* 13: 357–383.
———. 1988. "What Is Comparative Philosophy Comparing?" In *Interpreting across Boundaries: New Essays in Comparative Philosophy*, ed. G. J. Larson and E. Deutsch. Princeton, NJ: Princeton University Press.
Rathore, Aakash Singh, and Rimina Mohapatra. 2017. *Hegel's India: A Reinterpretation, with Texts*. New Delhi: Oxford University Press.
Spanos, W. V. 1996. "Culture and Colonization: The Imperial Imperatives of the Centered Circle." *Boundary 2* 23(1): 135–175.
Taylor, Mark C. 1990. "Paralectics." In *Tears*. Albany: State University of New York Press.

Chapter 53
MODERN PHILOSOPHY IN INDIA

A. Raghuramaraju

One way to explicate the nature of modern philosophy in India is through a comparison with modern philosophy in the West. There are two types of claims available in modern Western philosophy. One is rejecting classical philosophy by rendering it as non-philosophical. Descartes followed this when he excludes, not merely rejects, classical philosophy including 'classical logic' as it is 'mixed up with' all sorts of things (Descartes 1985, 119–120). The other is rejecting something by treating it as philosophical. Rousseau uses this when he says in rejecting Aristotle's defence of inequality that, 'Aristotle was right; but he took the effect for the cause' (1952, 5). The predicament of modern philosophy in India oscillates between these two extremities.

With the advent of colonialism philosophy in India was dismissed as non-philosophical. That is, in relation to modern Western philosophy, the philosophical practices in India are not accepted as philosophy, for the same reason as classical Greek philosophy was not accepted by them as philosophy. This tendency prevailed during the early days of colonial rule in India. However, in addition to or in collaboration with Indologists, there have been several attempts to bring the philosophical activity in India under the umbrella of philosophy, which can be philosophically criticized and even rejected.

This is the task undertaken by several philosophers who did 'Indian philosophy in English', *à la* Nalini Bhushan and Jay Garfield (2011). These include Sarvepalli Radhakrishnan, Krishna Chandra Bhattacharyya, Jadunath Sinha, Ganganath Jha, M. Hiriyanna, S. N. Dasgupta, Debiprasad Chattopadhyaya, Bimal K. Matilal, J. N. Mohanty, to name a few. In this context we have to acknowledge the monumental translations of Jha, including, two volumes of *The Tattvasaṅgraha of Śāntarakṣita, with Commentary of Kamalaśīla*, *Pūrva Mimāṃsā Sūtras of Jaimini*, the four volumes of *Nyāya Sūṭra of Gauṭama*, *Khaṇḍanakhaṇḍakhāḍya of Śrī Harṣa* in two volumes and many other important translations. In this context one may also include: three import works on Gauḍapāda, *The Āgamaśāstra of Gauḍapāda* (ed. Vidhushekhara Bhattacharyya), *Gaudapāda Kārikā* (ed. Raghunath Damodar Karmarkar) and *Gauḍapāda: A Study in Early Advaita* by T. M. P. Mahadevan. Also important are: Anantalal Thakur's *Origin and the Development of Vaiśeṣika System*, N. S. Ramanuja Tatacharyya's work on

Gaṅgeśa and the only sceptic from India, Jayarāśi Bhaṭṭa's *Tattvopaplavasiṃha* (trans. Esther Solomon); Alam Khudmiri's (2001) work on contemporary thinkers, including Iqbal. These are some of the works that brings new dimensions into modern philosophy in India.

This task preoccupied the international journals such as *Philosophy East and West*, *Journal of Indian Philosophy*, *Asian Philosophy*, along with *Indian Philosophical Quarterly* and *Journal of Indian Council of Philosophical Research* from India. In addition to the universities in India and abroad there is sustained work done at the Indian Institute of Philosophy in Amalner by those such as R. D. Ranade, G. R. Malkani, Ras Vihari Das, Bharatan Kumarappa, D. D. Wadekar, T. R. V. Murti and Kalidas Bhattacharyya. Interestingly, this institute was started by a mill owner, Sri Pratap Seth.[1] Incidentally, Krishna Chandra Bhattacharyya's famous book *Subject as Freedom* was first published from this institute. *Philosophical Quarterly* too was first published from this institute before it was shifted to Poona University, where it is published as *Indian Philosophical Quarterly*. The University of Mysore, Vishwa Bharati University, Santiniketan and the Indian Academy of Philosophy, Calcutta, along with the Adyar Library and Research Centre, University of Madras University, of Mysore and Banaras Hindu University have published on Indian philosophy. Book series published by Chowkamba; Motilal Banarsidass; History of Science, Philosophy and Culture in Indian Civilization; the Indian Council of Philosophical Research also contributed substantially to the philosophical activity. Some aspects of the work in these places and by these philosophers is to do philosophy, both Indian and Western, to make comparisons between them and to write Indian philosophy in English that has been predominantly available in Sanskrit, Pali or other Bhāṣā languages of India.

This shift in medium has both positive and negative aspects. At the positive level it made philosophy available to large numbers of people. This is desirable given the prevailing state of philosophy at that time, where according to S. N. Dasgupta, even the 'best Pandits of our age follow the old traditional method, and are almost always profoundly ignorant of Buddhism and Jainism … and with few exceptions, they seldom publish anything which may be said to embody the results of their study and mature thinking' (1982, 220). M. P. Rege endorses this when he reports that traditional Indian philosophy 'gives the impression of moving in a closed circle …. The new argument is much likely to be a variation on an old argument. They could only produce improvements in style and not in substance' (1991, xxiii). On the contrary, at a negative level, this shift in the medium compromised on the nativity of these ideas. This made someone like Daya Krishna declare that Indian philosophy done in English is not Indian philosophy. When asked by Nalini Bhushan and Jay Garfield, he replied, and I quote:

> Anybody who is writing in English is not an Indian philosopher ….What the British produced was a strange species – a stranger in his own country. The Indian mind and sensibility and thinking [during the colonial period] was shaped by an alien civilization.
>
> (Bhushan and Garfield 2011, xiii)

In addition to this identity problem raised by Krishna, Indian philosophy in English becomes inaccessible to the early traditional scholars. So, there are both positive and negative claims and views regarding the shift in the medium of philosophizing.

However, those who did Indian philosophy in English claimed that Indian philosophy is also philosophy that can be criticized, extended and analysed. The anxiety and aspiration behind this second approach is best captured by S. Radhakrishnan, who in the preface to his *magnum opus*, *Indian Philosophy* discloses the reasons behind arriving at the present title of this book and the method that he adopted in presenting Indian philosophy in English. He writes:

> The naïve utterances of the Vedic poets, the wondrous suggestiveness of the Upaniṣads, the marvellous psychological analysis of the Buddhists, and the stupendous system of Śaṃkara, are quite as interesting and instructive from the cultural point of view as the systems of Plato and Aristotle, or Kant and Hegel, if only we study them in a true scientific frame of mind, without disrespect for the past or contempt for the alien. The special nomenclature of Indian philosophy which cannot be easily rendered into English accounts for the apparent strangeness of the intellectual landscape. If the outer difficulties are overcome, we feel the kindred throb of the human heart, which because human is neither Indian nor European. Even if Indian thought be not valuable from the cultural point of view, it is yet entitled to consideration, if on no other ground, at least by reason of its contrast to other thought systems and its great influence over the mental life of Asia.
>
> (2008, xi–xii)

This passage diligently reveals the nuances of the possible location and the approach that Indian philosophy in modern times can take. What is admirable about this passage is that along with making a case for Indian philosophy, it is bold in declaring its positive stand toward the past and the alien.

Further, modernity in the West succeeded in dismantling and disinheriting the social fabric on which its classical philosophy was based. However, when it turned to repeat the same on other, outside societies through colonialism it has succeeded only in disturbing them.[2] While there exists this significant difference between the Western and Indian experience, modern philosophy in India, in its preoccupation to get philosophical status, did not take into consideration modern philosophy's attitude towards its own classical philosophy in the West. That is, in its attempt to get philosophical status for Indian philosophy they contrasted it with Western philosophy without taking into consideration the internal dynamics within the West. In this context they failed to recognize modern philosophy's attitude in the West towards its own classical philosophy. With this background let me begin discussing the following five aspects of modern philosophy in India:

1 the presence of classical philosophy in modern philosophy in India;
2 those present in classical philosophy are, however, absent in the modern philosophy in India;

3 the incorporation of positive aspects from the modern West, such as egalitarianism, within modern philosophy in India;
4 novel modern ideas such as internal criticism that have no equivalents in the West; and
5 the terrain of academic philosophy and the nature of academic bureaucracy.

The presence of classical philosophy in modern philosophy in India

Let me identify some tangible continuity from classical Indian philosophy in modern philosophy in India. The importance of Vedas, Upaniṣads and Advaita on Indian society is acknowledged. Raimon Panikkar in his *magnum opus*, *Vedic Experience*, has attempted to contemporize Vedas. He says:

> What would you save from a blazing house? A precious, irreplaceable manuscript containing a message of salvation from mankind, or a little group of people menaced by the same fire? ... [I]f I am not ready to save the manuscript from the fire, that is, if I do not take my intellectual vocation seriously, putting it before everything else even at the risk of appearing inhuman, then I am also incapable of helping people in more concrete and proximate ways. Conversely, if I am not alert and ready to save people from a conflagration ... then I shall be unable to help in rescuing the manuscript.
>
> (1977, xxxv)

So the Vedas continue to have their influence in the modern times. Further, there have been several attempts to entice diverse schools of Indian philosophy into one school, namely, Advaita. Swami Vivekananda, Sri Aurobindo, Krishna Chandra Bhattacharyya and Radhakrishnan initiated and sustained this move (Bilimoria 2014). While the context of this equating is colonialism, imbricated in this act are two incompatible claims, namely, spiritualism on the one hand and parallel with modern science on the other. For instance, Vivekananda claims that

> The Vedas teach us that creation is without beginning or end. Science is said to have proved that the sum total of cosmic energy is always the same.
>
> (1994, vol. 1, 7)

And:

> [T]he religion of the Vedanta can satisfy the demands of the scientific world, by referring it to the highest generalisations and to the law of evolution. That the explanation of a thing comes from within itself is still more completely satisfied by Vedanta.
>
> (1994, vol. 1, 374)

Further, he claims:

> [T]he modern physical researches are tending more and more to demonstrate that what is real is but the finer; the gross is simply appearance ... we have seen that if any theory of religion can stand the test of modern reasoning, it is the Advaita, because it fulfils its two requirements.
>
> (1994, vol. 1, 376)

This argument, though in slightly sophisticated form, continues in the writings of Sri Aurobindo. This is one of the recurrent classical systems that figures prominently in modern philosophy in India.

The other important school of Indian thought whose impact continues is Sāṃkhya. B. R. Ambedkar considers Kapila, the founder of Sāṃkhya, as the most pre-eminent 'among the ancient philosophers of India' (2010, 207). Though Ambedkar outright rejects the Vedas, Brāhmaṇas and the Upaniṣads, he accepts, together with Buddhism, the importance of Sāṃkhya. Ambedkar says of Kapila that his 'philosophical approach was unique', and the 'tenets of his philosophy were of a startling nature', these qualities made him unique, so he stood 'in a class by himself'. Kapila insisted that 'Truth must be supported by proof.' He accepted only 'two means of proof' namely, 'perception' and 'inference'. While perception is defined as a 'mental apprehension of a present object', inference is 'threefold'. The three forms of inference are, writes Ambedkar, '(1) from cause to effect, as from the presence of clouds to rain; (2) from effect to cause, as from the swelling of the streams in the valleys to rain in the hills, and (3) by analogy, as when we infer from the fact that a man alters his place when he moves that the stars must also move, since they appear in different places' (2010, 207–208). The next tenet of Kapila's philosophy is related to 'causality – creation and its cause'. Resisting the obsession with knowing the creator of the universe, Kapila declared that 'a created thing really exists beforehand in its cause just as the clay serves to form a pot, or the threads go to form a piece of cloth' (2010, 208).

Further, Sāṃkhya continues to have its presence in the *Bhagavad Gītā*. Gita borrows the metaphysics from Sāṃkhya and morality from Yoga. To this extent Sāṃkhya and Yoga mediated or processed through Gita have an underlying presence in and impact on Indian society. In post-independent India, Nyāya in the Nyāya-Vaiśeṣika combination has staged a comeback prominently in the writings of Matilal, Daya Krishna. Interestingly the stage inhabited by these realist schools is in the academic realm. These philosophers, writing extensively, contested the claim that Advaita is the Indian philosophy. Simultaneously they, particularly Daya Krishna, pointed out the problems in accepting the *mokṣa*-centredness of Indian philosophy. Through this identification he alleged robs Indian philosophy of the status of philosophy (1996, 55–56). In this context there is a need to recognize the continuous, rigorous and numerous philosophical works on Indian logic published in journals and as books.

Buddhism, a forceful counter to the Brāhmaṇical traditions, has also become a rallying point for those protest and dissent movements in India against the hierarchical and high-caste social practices. In addition to the philosophical uniqueness available in Buddhism, this political aspect also becomes a prominent point of continued significance of this important school of Indian philosophy. The conversion of Ambedkar to Buddhism gave further and massive force to the historical legacy of Buddhism as a protest movement.

Yet another heterodox Indian philosophical system is Jainism. Its impact can be deciphered in an interesting form. Two important documents bear the name *Svarāj*, namely, *Hind Swaraj* (1989) by M. K. Gandhi and "Svarāj in Ideas" by Krishna Chandra Bhattacharyya (1984). Both these writers are influenced by Jainism. While the doctrine of *ahimsa* along with metaphysical doctrine of *anekāntavāda* influenced Gandhi, the latter had enormous impact on Bhattacharyya. This is evident when Gandhi admits that his position may be called *anekāntavāda* or *syādvāda*. However, he confesses that he may not be in a position to engage with the 'learned' scholars and to this extent this position is his 'own'. Notwithstanding this reluctance to engage with the learned scholars, let us look how similar is his position to Jainism. He says,

> It has been my experience that I am always true from my point of view, and am often wrong from the point of view of my honest critics. I know that we are both right from our respective points of view. And this knowledge saves me from attributing motives to my opponents or critics. The seven blind men who gave seven different descriptions of the elephant were all right from their respective points of view, and wrong from the point of view of one another, and right and wrong from the point of view of the man who knew the elephant. I am much like this doctrine of the manyness of reality.
>
> (Gandhi, CWMG, vol. 29, 1968, 411)

Bhattacharyya too inhabits the philosophy of Jainism, though not admitting it as explicitly as Gandhi did when, in his essay 'The Concept of Philosophy', he says: 'There is no question of philosophy progressing towards a single unanimously acceptable solution. All philosophy is symbolic and symbolism necessarily admits of alternatives' (2008, 477). This definition of philosophy has clear echoes of *anekānta vāda* of Jainism.

With the advent of materialism through the West there is a revival of interest in the classical Indian materialist school, Cārvāka. Debiprasad Chattopadhyaya declared that only this materialism is alive and the rest is dead in Indian philosophy. The neglect or rejection of the materialist school of philosophy, particularly the Cārvāka school, can be seen as an underlying reason for the lack of growth of natural sciences in India that substantially depend on the philosophy of materialism and empiricism. This may be the cause for India to become dependent on the West for borrowing their natural sciences, by those including Vivekananda and Aurobindo. Thus, modern philosophy in India is a strange mixture of both classical Indian philosophy and modern Western philosophy.

Those present in classical philosophy are, however, absent in modern philosophy in India

Having identified the continuities in modern philosophy in India let me now point out two major absences in modern times that were present in the classical period. First is the absence of philosophical debates in modern Indian philosophy. This absence has handicapped philosophical activity significantly during this period. An interesting feature of debate is that, in addition to deciding who wins or who loses thus providing evaluations of positions, it also forces both sides to keep their positions updated, clearly and sharply formulated. In the process the views will shed ambiguity, become sleek, strong, competitive and active. In addition, both parties in the debate become well versed in each other's positions in addition to their own position. This will solve the problem of complacency and lack of knowledge of the other schools. Given the knowledge of the ideas and systems by both sides they tend to become lively.

With the absence of debate philosophical activity merely produced more and more philosophical activity from the sub-continent. This thus has become a burden and a mere addition without lending itself to cumulative scholarship on any of the themes in a sustained manner. That is, the additional scholarship processed through criticism, debate and analysis takes it to advanced levels and more importantly the accrued clarity makes it lighter. In contrast, mere accumulation can and in fact has turned it into a burden.[3]

Now to come to the next absence in modern Indian philosophy; unlike in classical times, there have not been any new philosophical systems or a text from the subcontinent for several centuries. This is a serious absence as it has implications for the developments in other branches of study, such as human sciences, art and literature. Most of the developments in these areas both within India and outside have been largely dependent on philosophical break-throughs, whether Marxism, phenomenology, structuralism or existentialism.[4]

The incorporation of positive aspects from the modern West, such as egalitarianism, within modern philosophy in India

In addition to these absences there are two important presences that are available in modern philosophy in India. One, while modernity through colonialism has disturbed and even dislocated classical philosophy in India, it nevertheless drew the attention of Indian philosophy towards the need to be inclusive and inculcate egalitarianism. Even though not to the satisfaction of the liberals and radicals in India, there is an attempt by modern philosophers in India, starting from Vivekananda and Aurobindo, to bring the masses into the mainstream. There are those like Partha Chatterjee who credit Gandhi as a person who for the first time in Indian politics provided an 'ideological basis for indulging the *whole* people within the political nation' (1986, 110). Gandhi may have provided the ideological basis as well as attempted to bring the masses within the mainstream of political process.

But his predecessors like Vivekananda and Aurobindo made a claim to bring the masses into the mainstream of political discourse, thereby setting the theoretical background to these preparations. This surely is due to the exposure of Indians towards modernity from the West.

This political intervention brought along with it the ideals of modernity consisting of equality, liberty, freedom and individualism. Modernists in India embarked on critiquing classical Indian thought using these modern ideals. The major terms of this critique consist of stagnation of thought, hierarchy and elitism, lack of openness to new ideas,[5] absence of logical and rational rigour and proliferation of superstitions, keeping the large mass of the population outside the reach of knowledge acquisition, maintaining segregation, the worst form of which is the practice of untouchability, excessive obsession with spiritualism, neglect of the material world and mindless ritualism.

Novel modern ideas such as internal criticism that have no equivalents in the West

The other important presence is the idea of internal criticism. Unlike in the discourse of modernity where the past is disinherited and unlike romantics and anti-colonialists like Fanon, who attributes all the problems of the native to colonialism, these contemporary Indian philosophers while maintaining their critique of colonialism simultaneously embarked on pointing out the internal evils and problems within Indian society. In fact, their criticism of the other either immediately followed or even preceded their admission of the internal problems. For instance, see the following statement by Gandhi, 'I am against conversion whether it is known as *shuddhi* by Hindus, *tabligh* by Mussalmans or proselytizing by Christians' (Gandhi 1968, CWMG, vol. 38, 16). So this becomes one of the unique processes available in modern philosophy in India.[6] A close look at the temporal ordering reveals that internal criticism precedes criticizing others. This is also exhibited in other modern Indian thinkers including Vivekananda and Aurobindo.

The terrain of academic philosophy and the nature of academic bureaucracy

I have so far identified some presences and absences both positive and negative in modern philosophy in India. While these are present, however, they have not been presented systematically. So there is a need to identify them, systematically analyse them, rigorously evaluate them. The evaluation, and not mere promotion or mere dismissal, will give us a realistic picture of modern philosophy in India. However, most of the work in modern academic spaces has not paid enough attention in this aspect. The work done is largely confined to closed circles, and thus, unfortunately, becomes another instance similar to the scene pointed out by Rege with regard to Pandits; some interesting comparative philosophy, however, is hampered with structural problems. I have previously pointed out the temporal imbalance surrounding the comparative axis. Most of the comparison between Indian and Western philosophy is between modern Western philosophy compared with classical Indian philosophy. This temporary imbalance did not take this philosophical activity much further. This stock-taking should precede adding new knowledge. Otherwise modern philosophy in India will merely add without cumulating and progressing forward.[7]

In this context it may be useful to recall two types of philosophical activity. One type of philosophical activity is analysing available systems. There is yet another type of philosophical activity, namely building a system or preparing to build a new system. While the former tries to analyse various tools and arguments and evaluate them, the latter, like the process of building a new house, seeks to use various raw materials for this purpose. Philosophical activity in modern India is more akin to this second type. It made serious attempts and spent more time and resources in making adjustments to the new interventions, thereby displaying sensitivity to the context and did not remain a mute witness. The resources for the sensitivity to the context are internally available. For instance, Śaṃkara defended Veda and Upaniṣads against Buddhism. In opening himself in undertaking his critique he did allow himself to incorporate many shades or arguments from Buddhism. In fact it is this that makes many construe Śaṃkara's relation to Buddhism in diverse ways. There are some who allege that he was responsible for driving Buddhism out of India; there are others who allege that he 'secretly accepted' Buddhist doctrines and introduced as many of them as he could into the Vedanta. The extent of sensitivity to the contemporary context available in Śaṃkara can form the background to assess how modern philosophy in India has embarked on negotiating with both the classical and modern West. In this context we will have a better picture of assessing the contribution of modern philosophy in India, not only at the creative level, but also how it rewrote its classical heritage in the modern idiom and language, and the way in which it packaged these.

Notes

1 For the history of the Indian Institute of Philosophy, Amalner and a life sketch of its founder, see G. R. Malkani's *A Life-Sketch of Srimant Pratapseth and a Brief Account of the Advaitic System of Thought*, Amalner: Indian Institute of Philosophy, 1952. Also see a short piece titled, "Heritage", in the new series of the *Philosophical Quarterly*, 1(1), January 1995, by N. K. Thakare, the then Vice-Chancellor of North Maharashtra University, pp. i–iii.

2 See Raghuramaraju 2006.

3 See Raghuramaraju 2006.

4 See Raghuramaraju 2009.

5 See Dasgupta 1982.

6 For more on this see Raghuramaraju 2011.

7 Murti 1985 presents a good survey of the state of philosophy in India.

References

Ambedkar, B. R. 2010. *The Essential Writings of B. R. Ambedkar*, ed. Valerian Rodrigues. New Delhi: Oxford University Press.

Aurobindo, Sri. 1972. *The Social and Political Thought*, vol. 15. Pondicherry: Sri Aurobindo Birth Centenary Library.

Bhattacharyya, Krishna Chandra. 1984. "Svarāj in Ideas." *Indian Philosophical Quarterly* 11(4): 383–393.

———. 2008. "The Concept of Philosophy," in *Studies in Philosophy*, ed. Gopinath Bhattacharyya (3rd rev. and enlarged ed.), vol. 1/2, pp. 457–479. Delhi: Motilal Banarsidass.

Bhushan, Nalini and Jay Garfield, eds. 2011. *Indian Philosophy in English, from Renaissance to Independence*. New York: Oxford University Press.

Bilimoria, P. 2014. "*Śruti-prāmāṇya* (Scriptural Testimony) and the 'Imparative Philosophy' in Raimon Panikkar's Thinking." *Cirprit Review Symposium on the Dialogical Dialogue and Raimon Panikkar* (Mimesis and Cirprit Review, Intercultural Centre Dedicated to Raimon Panikkar, Milan, Italy). Issue 5, article no. 57, pp. 57–67. www.cirprit.raimonpanikaar.it/.

Chatterjee, Partha. 1986. *Nationalist Thought and the Colonial World: A Derivative Discourse?* Delhi: Oxford University Press.

Dasgupta, S. N. 1982. "Dogmas of Indian Philosophy," in *Philosophical Essays*, pp. 208–333. Delhi: Motilal Banarsidass.

Descartes, René. 1985. "Discourse on Method," in *The Philosophical Writings of Descartes*, vol. 1, pp. 111–151. Cambridge: Cambridge University Press.

Gandhi, M. K. 1968. *Collected Works of Mahatma Gandhi*, vols. 29 and 38. New Delhi: Government of India Publication Division.

Gangopadhyaya, Sunil. 1977. *Those Days: A Novel*, trans. Aruna Chakravarti. New Delhi: Penguin Books.

Khundmiri, Alam. 2001. *Secularism, Islam and Modernity: Selected Essays of Alam Khundmiri*, ed. with introduction by M. T. Ansari. New Delhi: Sage Publications.

Krishna, Daya. 1996. *Indian Philosophy: A Counter Perspective*. New Delhi: Oxford University Press.

Matilal, Bimal K. 1999. *The Character of Logic in India*, ed. Jonardon Ganeri and Heeraman Tiwari. New Delhi: Oxford University Press.

Murti, Satchidananda, K. 1985. *Philosophy in India: Traditions, Teaching and Research*. Delhi: Motilal Banarsidas.

Panikkar, Raimon. 1977. *The Vedic Experience: Mantramañjarī*. Pondicherry: All India Books.

Radhakrishnan, S. 2008. *Indian Philosophy*, vol. 1. New Delhi: Oxford University Press.

Raghuramaraju, A. 2006. *Debates in Indian Philosophy: Classical, Colonial and Contemporary*. New Delhi: Oxford University Press.

———. 2009. *Enduring Colonialism: Classical Presences and Modern Absences in Indian Philosophy*. New Delhi: Oxford University Press.

———. 2011. *Modernity in Indian Social Theory*. New Delhi: Oxford University Press.

Rege, M. P. 1991. "Introduction," in *Samvad: A Dialogue between Two Philosophical Traditions*, ed. Daya Krishna, M. P. Rege *et al*. New Delhi: Indian Council of Philosophical Research.

Rousseau, J. J. [1762] 1952. *The Social Contract and Discourse*, trans. with introduction by G. D. H. Cole. London: J. M. Dent & Sons.

Vivekananda, Swami. 1994. *The Complete Works of Swami Vivekananda*, vols. 1–8. Calcutta: Advaita Ashram.

Chapter 54
GANDHI'S TRUTH: DEBATING BILGRAMI[1]

Bindu Puri

Fifty years ago, Mohandas Karamchand Gandhi (fondly referred to as the father of the Indian nation) might not have found mention in a volume on the history of Indian philosophy. It would be fair to say that it is only in the last few decades that Mahatma Gandhi's (1869–1948) ideas have received increasing academic and, more specifically, philosophical attention. One of the most important recent references to Gandhi as a philosopher is in a book on *Gandhi and the Stoics* by the Oxford-based philosopher Richard Sorabji.[2] Sorabji has argued that Gandhi was a philosopher: "he was forever seeking a consistent rationale for all that he did, and, more than any philosophers I have encountered, he subjected his views to relentless criticism" (Sorabji 2012, 1). Akeel Bilgrami[3] is among the recent thinkers to bring Western analytical philosophical attention to Gandhi. His academic engagement with Gandhi's ideas makes for an interesting illustration of the thesis that Gandhi's ideas were not only of interest to philosophers but they constituted the stuff of moral and political philosophy itself. This chapter attempts to contribute to the philosophical recovery of moral and political arguments in Gandhi's writing and practice by paying serious attention to Bilgrami's arguments about Gandhi. In this context this chapter engages in a debate with some of the philosophical positions that Bilgrami attributes to Gandhi. In a fairly well-known set of essays (2006 and 2011), Akeel Bilgrami philosophically engages with Gandhi's understanding of truth and his position on the nature of moral judgment. This chapter interrogates Bilgrami's argument that Gandhi had a relativist, and purely experiential, understanding of truth and goes on to examine his interpretation of Gandhi's position on moral judgment, moral principles, moral criticism and truth.

Gandhi and the moral life

Gandhi's conception of the good human life involves three concepts: truth (*satya*), non-violence (*ahiṃsa*) and freedom (*swaraj*). As Akeel Bilgrami has argued, Gandhi's thought was highly integrated. This integrity is brought out by the interconnections between these three moral concepts. In Gandhi's understanding the moral life was a life spent in the pursuit of truth which could only be arrived at through non-violence (*ahiṃsā*). Just as he described truth and non-violence as "two sides of a coin" (Gandhi *FYM*, 12–3) Gandhi also thought of the relationship between truth and freedom in a somewhat circular way. An individual had to be free from an egoistic attachment to the self and to others for the sake of the self, in order to arrive at knowledge of how things *really were* in the world. As the individual came closer to truth she also became progressively free of ego-driven deceptions and thereby achieved freedom as self-rule (*swaraj*).

Gandhi had spoken of 'truth' in a dual sense. Firstly, as the *telos* or proper end of the moral life. In this context one can recall Gandhi's statement: "You will see the fine distinction between the two statements, viz. that God is truth and Truth is God. And I came to the conclusion after a continuous and relentless search after Truth which began nearly fifty years ago" (Gandhi *eCWMG*, vol. 54, 268). In this sense truth was the goal or *summum bonum* of individual moral life.

Gandhi also spoke of truth, in another sense, as one of the "cardinal ... virtues" (Gandhi *eCWMG*, vol. 33, 448) and thereby as an inherent part of the quest for the truth *qua* the good. Gandhi made this distinction explicitly:

> For me truth is the sovereign principle, which includes numerous other principles. This truth is not only truthfulness in word, but truthfulness in thought also, and not only the relative truth of our conception, but the Absolute Truth, the Eternal Principle that is God.
>
> (Gandhi *eCWMG*, vol. 44, 91)

It is at this point that it becomes philosophically interesting to take note of Bilgrami's reinterpretation of Gandhi's truth. Bilgrami (2011, 96) argues that Gandhi was not only a relativist about religious and moral truth but that there was an "unblushing relativism, indeed subjectivism" (ibid.) about Gandhi's "notion of truth (satya)" itself (ibid.) Furthermore he has argued that Gandhi was simply not interested in truth as a "*cognitive* notion" (ibid.) or how things really were in the world, but only in how an individual experienced them morally. According to Bilgrami, truth for Gandhi was "an exclusively and exhaustively moral and experiential notion" (ibid.). This reinterpretation is difficult to accept for two reasons.

First, far from being relativist about truth Gandhi appeared to believe that moral truths could be shared across religions and cultures. He described truth and *ahiṃsā* as "fundamental truths" (Gandhi *eCWMG*, vol. 38, 296), "fundamental rules of conduct" (Prabhu and Rao 2007, 74), "law(s) of our species" (Gandhi *eCWMG*, vol. 21, 134), "eternal principle" (Gandhi eCWMG, vol. 68, 260), "Universal Principle(s)" (Gandhi *eCWMG*, vol. 74, 129).

Second, Gandhi did not seem to be interested in truth as an exclusively moral value; he also seemed to be interested in how things *really were* in the world. It may be recalled that *satyāgraha* was a method of arriving at truth. Gandhi had argued that *satyāgrahis* have to be ready to suffer, even unto death, in order to arrive at the truthful solution of a conflict. This would make no sense if Gandhi believed that truth was relative to an individual's own moral experience. That Gandhi thought of truth as related to matters of fact also becomes clear by his refusal to distinguish between economic, political and moral truths, and his insistence on transforming reality in line with moral convictions. In this context, one may note the centrality of debate in Gandhi's mode of philosophy. Gandhi entered into three debates, with Vir Damodar Savarkar, Rabindranath Tagore and B. R. Ambedkar. He debated with Savarkar about Indian nationalism, with Tagore about freedom and education and with Ambedkar about caste and *varṇa*.[4] The Gandhian debates with these prominent national personalities make it clear that Gandhi believed that it was possible to arrive at truth. It is therefore difficult to sustain Bilgrami's philosophical reconstruction which unequivocally claims that Gandhi was a complete relativist about truth.

Bilgrami's Gandhi

Bilgrami's argument reconstructing Gandhi's truth as relative makes several related reinterpretations of Gandhi's position on moral principles, moral criticism and exemplarity. Bilgrami's argument starts with what he describes as a "spectacular misreading" (Bilgrami 2006, 252) of Gandhi's truth and its connection with non-violence. He quotes from Sumit Sarkar: "The search for truth was the goal of human life, and as no one could ever be sure of having attained the truth, use of violence to enforce one's own view of it was sinful" (Sarkar quoted ibid.). Bilgrami rightly concludes that such interpretations suggest that Gandhi was diffident about "his own convictions of the truth" (Bilgrami 2011, 97). This would seem to bring Gandhi's position fairly close to the argument made by Mill in favour of tolerance. In *On Liberty* Mill has argued that we often discover that much that we had thought true in the past turns out to be false. This implies that what we presently think true can also be found to be false. It follows that we should tolerate dissent from our present opinions just in case these opinions are found to be false (Mill 2006, 26).

Bilgrami points out that since Gandhi had spent his life in the quest for truth it seems difficult to accept that Gandhi should have thought of truth as "something we should seek, even if we cannot attain it" (Bilgrami 2006, 252). While Gandhi would approve of holding one's opinions with "modesty" (ibid.) he would not believe that one cannot arrive at truth or that one cannot know that one has arrived at truth.

One would perhaps be closer to an understanding of Gandhi's non-violence as a modesty in holding one's opinions, if one were to see that "its source is to be found in his conception of the very nature of moral response and moral judgment" (ibid., 253). According to Bilgrami Gandhian modesty should not be seen as a pervasive diffidence or lack of conviction about truth. On the other hand, Gandhi's interpretation of non-violence implies that: "It is equally important not to bear hostility to others or even to criticize them" (ibid.). This means that in Gandhi's understanding of moral judgments such judgments must not involve any criticism of others for "to think negatively and critically would be to give in to the spiritual flaws that underlie violence" (ibid.). Bilgrami goes on suggest that there is a distinction between resisting others and criticizing them. Gandhi argues that "resistance is not the same as criticism. It can be done with a 'pure heart'" (ibid., 254). However, he believes that criticism "reflects an impurity of heart, and is easily corrupted to breed hostility and, eventually, violence" (ibid.).

Bilgrami concludes that Gandhi "severed the assumed theoretical connection between moral judgment and moral criticism, the connection which, in our analytical terms, we would describe by saying that if one judges that 'x is good', then we are obliged to find morally wrong those who judge otherwise or fail to act on x" (ibid.). He argues that when Gandhi rejected the connection between moral judgment and moral criticism he denied a connection that had a long history in Western (primarily Kantian) philosophical thinking. A fairly important idea in such thinking was that moral judgments are universalizable. Universalizability, though weaker than universality, "still generates the critical power which Gandhi finds disquieting" (ibid., 255). This interpretation raises a challenge for Bilgrami's understanding of Gandhi. For, if going against a moral judgment does not entail the possibility that one can be criticized for going afoul, it would appear that choices of moral values might be significantly like those of taste. However, it is very clear that Gandhi did not think that one's moral thinking, like one's choices of tastes, was simply not relevant to others or was "closed off from others" (ibid., 256). In particular Gandhi "certainly did not want to sequester the relevance of one's religious and moral convictions to oneself" (Bilgrami 2011, 100). At this stage it becomes important to ask if it could be possible to "reconcile the rejection of universalizability and of a value's potential in being wielded in criticism with this yearning for the significance of one's choices to others?" (Bilgrami 2006, 256). Bilgrami argues that Gandhi makes such a philosophical reconciliation. "In Gandhi's writing there is an implicit but bold proposal: when one chooses for oneself, *one sets an example to everyone*" (ibid., 257). This replaces the standard Western Kantian reading which might go as follows: "*When I choose for myself, I generate a principle for everyone to follow*" (Bilgrami 2011, 100).

For Bilgrami the shift from a principled reading of a moral judgment to the idea of exemplarity makes the moral psychology of our response to differing others much weaker and entirely consistent with Gandhian *ahiṃsā*. Gandhi believed that, if others fall afoul, all we can do is feel "disappointed in others that they will not follow our example" (Bilgrami 2006, 258). Gandhi is able to sustain such a view of moral judgment simply because he believes that "truth *is* a moral notion, and it is *exclusively* a moral notion" (ibid., 260). Gandhi accepts the Jaina principle of *Anekāntavāda*[5] – a form of pluralism and *syādvāda* which is "a form of internalism about the truth, whereby the truth of a doctrine is judged entirely from within the point of view of the doctrine itself" (Bilgrami 2011, 96). Since truth is entirely experiential there is no problem in everyone following truth according to his/her individual insights. Moral judgments cannot be about principles for there are none. Everyone comes to his/her own understanding of moral value. However, one can reconcile this relativism with a belief in the relevance of our moral convictions to others simply by seeing ourselves as moral exemplars.

Bilgrami then moves on to criticize (what he has presented as) Gandhi's position on moral judgment, moral criticism and truth. Speaking of Gandhi's conception of truth Bilgrami argues (and correctly in my opinion, if this is how Gandhi really thinks of truth): "There is a palpable mistake in collapsing the cognitive value of truth into the moral value of truth telling, a mistake evident in the fact that somebody who *fails* to *tell* the truth can, in doing so, still value *truth*" (Bilgrami 2006, 263). The person who is an immoral liar wants to conceal the truth precisely because "he still values truth" (ibid.). On this view the only sort of person who does not value truth at all is the "bullshitter" (ibid., 264). "This is the person who merely sounds off on public occasions … simply because he is prepared to speak or write in the requisite jargon, *without any goal of getting things right* not even (like the liar) concealing the right things which he knows" (ibid.).

I will examine four points to ascertain whether Bilgrami has as a matter of fact correctly reconstructed the Gandhian position on morals and on truth, namely:

1. Whether Gandhi did indeed reject the connection between moral judgment and moral criticism.
2. That Gandhi thought about moral judgments as objective in the sense that they could be shared across traditions as they expressed "fundamental truths" (Gandhi *e*CWMG, vol. 38, 296). Gandhi believed that moral judgments involved moral convictions. I use the term 'conviction' in place of 'principle' though Gandhi himself often used the term "universal principle" (Gandhi, *e*CWMG, vol. 74, 129). It seems fair to assume that Gandhi was perhaps philosophically unacquainted with the history of association of that term with philosophical debates in Western moral philosophy.
3. That Gandhi did not think that moral judgments set examples for others and that the moral agent was an exemplar. This was because an important Gandhian insight into the moral life was that such a life should not be pervaded by an over-inflated sense of the self. Consequently, the idea of exemplarity would involve a moral egoism which could dismantle such a life.
4. Gandhi had an alternative understanding of truth as both experiential and cognitive.

Gandhi on moral criticism

Bilgrami has argued that *ahiṃsā* led Gandhi to reject moral criticism. Consequently, Gandhi did not believe that moral judgments involved principles. At a "deeper realm of violence … the very idea of principles and doctrines are subtly and *indirectly* implicated" (Bilgrami 2011, 98). Gandhi rejected universality, universalizability and finally moral principles. There has been a change in Bilgrami's position. While in earlier papers (Bilgrami 2006) he said that Gandhi was against moral criticism *per se* he later (Bilgrami 2011) argued that "Gandhi was not against criticism of institutions and policies and even of whole civilizational tendencies and himself made such criticism as, say, in *Hind Swaraj* where he is harshly critical of the modern west. But he tried throughout his life to avoid criticism of individuals" (ibid., 99).

There are philosophical difficulties with this interpretation of Gandhi. Though Gandhi argued at several places that *ahiṃsā* was a wider notion than physical nonviolence this *in itself* does not seem philosophically sufficient to establish that Gandhi rejected moral criticism and objective moral judgments. Yet this seems to be all the evidence that Bilgrami requires for his argument. First, it is important to note that the relevant Gandhian distinction is not that between the criticism of *individuals* and *institutions* but that between criticism of *positions* and *individuals*. While Gandhi argued that it was wrong to criticize individuals (for a man and his position/action are two different things) he accepted that the criticism of positions could be morally valuable. There are places where Gandhi makes this distinction:

> Man and his deed are two distinct things. Whereas a good deed should call forth approbation and wicked deed disapprobation, the doer of the deed, whether good or wicked, always deserves respect or pity as the case may be. 'Hate the sin and not the sinner'.
>
> (Gandhi *SWMG*, vol. 6, 171–172)

This distinction was significant for it made space for criticism in moral life. One could (on the Gandhian view) be critical of positions without being critical or violent towards individuals or institutions. There are two points to be made in this context. First, one must note that Gandhi not only criticized the positions taken by individuals or institutions but he also argued about the value of criticism in moral life. Second, it is possible to reconstruct a fairly straightforward argument which explains the value of criticism in Gandhi.

To substantiate these points one can recall Gandhi's comments about Subhas Chandra Bose:

> Though I did not accept Subhas Chandra Bose's belief in violence and his consequent action, I have not refrained from giving unstinted praise to his patriotism, resourcefulness and bravery.
>
> (Prabhu and Rao 2007, 151)

Gandhi also argued that moral criticism was valuable in individual life. During his debate with Tagore, Gandhi appreciated Tagore's criticism of his principles and movements, by describing Tagore as a sentinel who had issued a warning "against the approaching enemies called Bigotry, Lethargy, Intolerance, Ignorance, Inertia and other members of that brood" (Gandhi *eCWMG*, vol. 24, 413). It is possible to explain the moral value of criticism (for Gandhi) if one recalls that the chief difficulty in achieving Gandhian self-rule or moral excellence was caused by "pride and egoism" (Gandhi *eCWMG*, vol. 74, 383). It was in such a context that Gandhian *ahiṃsā* was conceived as the practise of "utter-most selflessness" (Gandhi *eCWMG*, vol. 36, 449–450) so that truth could be arrived at between conflicting parties. Criticism could be useful in moral progress because it performed the role of many "lighthouses" (Gandhi *eCWMG*, vol. 17, 379) which served "to give out warnings of dangers lying in the stormy paths of life" (ibid.). Given that an inflated ego can generate a moral blindness which leads to self-righteousness one can appreciate Gandhi's point that: "When it is relevant, truth has to be uttered, however unpleasant it may be" (Gandhi *eCWMG*, vol. 98, 47).

Gandhi on objective moral truths

The important question is whether Gandhi's acceptance of moral criticism reflected his belief in objective moral truths. On the face of it Gandhi's position on moral "principles" (Gandhi *SWMG*, vol. 6, 117) seems philosophically distant from Bilgrami's interpretation. On a seriously contrary note Gandhi was concerned with what he calls "moral principle(s)" (Gandhi *SWMG*, vol. 6, 117). It is important to note that though Gandhi refers to "fundamental Truths" (Gandhi *eCWMG*, vol. 38, 296) in individual moral life as "Universal Principle(s)" (Gandhi *eCWMG*, vol. 74, 129) the use of "principle" has to be seen in relation to the Gandhian context. I would suggest that Gandhi accepted objective moral convictions and was not a relativist about truth. However, Gandhi did not think that such moral convictions were strictly universalizable. This becomes apparent from two things. One, he himself discussed and admitted the possibilities of exceptions to the moral rule of *ahiṃsā* (Iyer 2009, 206–207). Two, he did not accept that moral convictions could be applied in an *a priori* manner independently of the actual experience of particular situations. Gandhi believed that, though moral convictions could be shared across individual experiences, yet one had an experiential relationship to one's moral convictions. One could become progressively at home in their practice and make "experiments" about their full implications for individual life. Consequently, for Gandhi, there could not be strictly universalizable moral rules whose application was *a priori* to the experience of actual situations.

It can be conclusively said that Gandhi accepted fundamental moral convictions which could significantly be shared by all human beings with the necessary rider of the context sensitivity of all moral rules. The fact is that all moral truths might admit of exceptions in certain human situations. Further it can even be argued that Gandhi believed that it is a part of the conception of a human moral conviction that it must admit of exceptions in order to count as 'moral'. For if a person who leads a good life believes in moral truths, the manner in which he holds on to them cannot be entirely self-assured. If there is so much self-assuredness it would indicate a moral self-righteousness/smugness which could seem inconsistent with human goodness. As Gandhi said himself: "It would be smooth sailing if one could determine the course of one's action only by one general principle whose application at a given moment was too obvious to need even a moment's reflection. But I cannot recall a single act which could be so easily determined" (Gandhi *eCWMG*, vol. 43, 14).

Gandhi: a self-styled exemplar?

I have argued above that the Gandhian principle of *ahiṃsā* is consistent with moral criticism and the belief in fundamental moral convictions. Gandhi accepted objective moral truths without being philosophically interested in their strict universalizability. The problem with Bilgrami's hypothesis about Gandhi and exemplarity is that it fails to take account of the self-righteousness involved in the idea of setting moral examples. Far from believing that his moral judgments were setting moral examples for others Gandhi was painfully aware of his own limitations and "Himalayan blunders" (Gandhi *SWMG*, vol. 6, 95) in moral matters: "Let no one say he is a follower of Gandhi. It is enough that I should be my own follower. I know what an inadequate follower I am of myself, for I cannot live up to the convictions I stand for" (*Harijan*, 2 March 1940; Gandhi 2005, 237).

Gandhi's truth: experiential and cognitive

Bilgrami has argued that Gandhi's understanding of *ahiṃsā* led him to "the separability of moral value and judgment from moral principle and moral criticism" (Bilgrami 2006, 261). Bilgrami realizes that this in turn might lead to the "worry" that as a result of such a separation "truth then drops out of the Gandhian picture in a way that seems un-Gandhian" (ibid.). He argues that as a matter of fact this worry is philosophically unfounded as far as Gandhi is concerned "since truth in the first place is not, for Gandhi, a notion independent of what his argument rests on, the nature of our own experience of moral value" (ibid.). What this means is that "truth for Gandhi is not a *cognitive* notion at all" (ibid.). Gandhi had no understanding of truth in the sense of getting things right about the world: "For him truth's relationship to virtue cannot consist at all in the supposed virtue of acquiring truths of this kind; it is instead entirely to be understood in how truth surfaces in our practical and moral relations" (ibid., 263).

Conclusion

All through this chapter I have been emphasizing that goodness for Gandhi consisted in a sort of moral realism and ability to step away from the self and see things as they really are. When Gandhi spoke of truth he understood it as a product of the relationship between the individual and matters of fact. He understood that relationship in terms of an individual's moral and practical relationships with herself, with 'others' and with reality. Gandhi was interested in getting things right about the world but he thought that the experience of truth as a moral value was significantly related to getting things right about the world. This is why he thought that moral considerations mattered to economic truths: "True economics never militates against the highest ethical standard, just as all true ethics to be worth its name must at the same time be also good economics" (Gandhi *eCWMG*, vol. 72, 258). Gandhi's divergence from the Enlightenment paradigm was simply that the Enlightenment had assumed that there could be a *purely* cognitive understanding of how things are without allowing for our moral and practical relations to matters of fact. Gandhi's notion of truth was constituted by how things really were, i.e. matters of fact, and by *our moral and practical relations* with those matters of fact.

Of course the fact that Gandhi believed in Absolute Truth, objective moral truths and possibilities of closure in debates about truth, only shows that Bilgrami might be mistaken about Gandhi being a relativist about truth. It does not make what Gandhi believes in any sense correct. But it does make that a plausible candidate for the truth and one deserving some serious scrutiny.

Notes

1 Part of the discussion here is an extension of my previous work, Puri (2015).
2 Richard R. K. Sorabji, CBE, FBA, American and Flemish Academies, Honorary Fellow, Wolfson College, Oxford.
3 Akeel Bilgrami is currently Sidney Morgenbesser Professor of Philosophy, Columbia University, New York. There were other philosophers in the 1980s and 1990s who worked intensely on Gandhi, notably Margaret Chatterjee, Ramchandra Gandhi, Glynn Richards, Bhikku Parekh, Nicholas Gier and Purushottama Bilimoria.
4 *Varṇa* is the ideal unit of a functionally divided Hindu society.
5 *Anekāntavāda* or the doctrine of the many-sided nature of reality is an important doctrine of Jaina philosophy. It refers to the principles of pluralism and multiplicity of viewpoints. According to this theory reality is perceived differently from diverse points of view. Though no single point of view is the complete truth, taken together, these viewpoints comprise the complete truth.

References

Bilgrami, Akeel. 2006. "Gandhi's Integrity: The Philosophy behind the Politics." In *Debating Gandhi: A Reader*, ed. Raghuramaraju, A., 248–266. New Delhi: Oxford University Press.

Bilgrami, Akeel. 2011. "Gandhi's Religion and Its Relation to His Politics." In *The Cambridge Companion to Gandhi*, ed. Brown, Judith M. and Parel, Anthony, 93–116. New Delhi: Cambridge University Press.

Bilimoria, P. 2015. 'A (Gandhian) Critique of Economic Reason: between tradition and postcoloniality'. In: *Value and Values: Economics and Justice in an Age of Global Interdependence*, eds. Roger T. Ames and Peter D. Hershock, pp. 309–333. Honolulu: University of Hawai'i Press.

Gandhi, M. K. 1933. *From Yeravda Mandir: Ashram Observance* (*FYM*), trans. V. G. Desai. Ahmedabad: Navajivan Publishing House. Accessible online at www.mkgandhi.org/ebks/yeravda.pdf (accessed 17 July 2016).

Gandhi, M. K. 1948. *Selections from Gandhi* (*SG*), ed. Bose, N. K. Ahmedabad: The Navajivan Trust.

Gandhi, M. K. 1968. *The Selected Works of Mahatma Gandhi* (*SWMG*), ed. Narayan, Shriman, vol. 6. Ahmedabad: Navajivan Trust.

Gandhi, M. K. 1999. *Collected Works of Mahatma Gandhi*, vols. 1–98, electronic edition (*eCWMG*), New Delhi: Ministry of Information and Broadcasting, Go. Accessible online at http://gandhiserve.org/e/cwmg/cwmg.htm (accessed 17 July 2016).

Gandhi, M. K. 2005. *Gandhi Selected Writings*, ed. Duncan, Ronald. New York: Dover Publications.

Iyer, Raghavan N. 2009. *The Moral and Political Thought of Mahatma Gandhi*. New Delhi: Oxford University Press.

Mill, J. S. 2006. *On Liberty and The Subjection of Women*. London: Penguin Classics.

Parekh, Bhikhu. 1989. *Gandhi's Political Philosophy: A Critical Examination*. London: Macmillan.

Prabhu, J. and Bilimoria, P. 2017. "Reflections on Moral Ideals and Modernity: Gandhi and Nonviolence." In *Indian Ethics Classical and Contemporary, Volume I.*, eds. P. Bilimoria, J. Prabhu and Renuka Sharma, pp. 329–337. London: Routledge.

Prabhu, R. K. and Rao, U. R. (eds.). 2007. *The Mind of Mahatma Gandhi*. Ahmedabad: Navajivan Publishing House.

Puri, Bindu. 2015. *The Tagore–Gandhi Debate on Matters of Truth and Untruth*. Sophia Studies in Cross-Cultural Philosophy of Traditions and Cultures 9. Dordrecht and New Delhi: Springer.

Sorabji, Richard. 2012. *Gandhi and the Stoics: Modern Experiments on Ancient Values*. Oxford: Oxford University Press.

Chapter 55
UNDERSTANDING INDIAN PHILOSOPHICAL TRADITIONS

Anna-Pya Sjödin

This chapter is a presentation of three important and influential ideas about how Indian philosophy and the Indian tradition of philosophy can be understood. Krishna Daya, Jitendranath Mohanty, and Wilhelm Halbfass have all reacted upon, and criticized, homogeneous and static conceptions of Indian philosophies and by articulating different ways of apprehending Indian philosophical traditions they have tried to come to terms with what they believe are limiting images. This chapter discusses their main ideas and then presents an extended way of apprehending tradition. I shall then present how the concept of *siddhānta* (the established) could be a way of understanding the ideas of what philosophy and philosophical tradition is in the philosophical school called Nyāya-Vaiṣeśika (King 1999; Halbfass 1991; Mohanty 1999).

Darśana and "philosophical tradition" in Sanskrit

Darśana, in its Sanskrit lexical form, means seeing, looking at or showing, in a philosophical context it conveys a point of view or perspective. This term became popular within the late eighth- to tenth-century philosophical compendiums in India. In this genre of texts, which could be called doxographical, the authors described the major tenets of what they sometimes called the *darśanas*. The term *darśana* was subsequently taken up and used within the field of Indian and comparative philosophy as a term for the so-called six classical orthodox Hindu schools of philosophy in India: Nyāya, Vaiśeṣika, Sāṃkhya, Yoga, Mīmāṃsā, and Vedānta. This use of the term *darśana* for Indian philosophy has been contested and discussed in later Indian philosophy and Indology. Halbfass, for example, has pointed out that the use of the term is somewhat restricted to the doxographical texts and moreover that it sometimes is extended to denote non-Hindu philosophies as well (King 1999, 43ff.; Halbfass 1991, 264, 273).

Mohanty's, Halbfass', and Krishna's discussion of *darśana* and philosophical tradition is centered within the relation between Indian and Western philosophy. That different conceptualizations of Western philosophy are important in these discussions, both explicitly and implicitly, is a very important fact to be aware of. None of these scholars writes in a vacuum; their ideas transpire from the complex web that constitutes the relationship, often unequal, between Indian and Western philosophy. Mohanty employs *darśana* in order to achieve a contrast between a Greek *philosophia* tradition and an Indian *darśana* tradition. Halbfass discusses it in the context of a debate over which Sanskrit term should be used for the term philosophy, and Krishna questions the very concept of schools of Indian philosophy within the idea of a philosophy proper.

Daya Krishna's styles of thought

Krishna's is perhaps the most radical and thought-provoking idea regarding tradition. He articulates and critiques three myths about Indian philosophy: the myth about spirituality, the myth about authority, and the myth about schools of thought. For him the questions on authority and schools of philosophy are bound together insofar as such an understanding of Indian philosophy implies an understanding of a finished system of thought carrying with it its own corrective framework. This is a thought that follows a kind of primordial and self-sufficient unfolding (i.e. Veda), which, in turn, determines any possible future thought and, most importantly according to Krishna, denies the possibility of newness. Krishna thus criticizes an idea of Indian philosophy in general as a system-bound, non-personal, and non-individual enterprise (Krishna 1991, 13). It is important to note here that Krishna's image of Indian philosophy could be understood in the light of, and as a reaction to the so- called partisanic/ethnic conceptions of Indian philosophy as spiritual and therefore more refined than its Western secular or de-spiritualized counterpart. Although such an issue might appear dated, Krishna (1991, 3–4, 16–17) apparently felt the need to continue to address it, and so does Mohanty, as we shall see in the next section.[1]

In order to understand Krishna's own ideas about Indian philosophy it is crucial to be aware of the fact that he explicitly strives to rescue Indian philosophy from its antiquarian state, as he puts it, and reinstate it as a living, evolving activity. His concern goes deeper than just to find and formulate a self-understanding belonging to the philosophers of the past. It seems that, for him, a different outlook would also change how we philosophically interact today with a Gaṅgeśa or a Nāgārjuna. And according to Krishna, this is exactly how he wants them – as individuals, as personal names for us to relate to.

> The dead, mummified picture of Indian philosophy will come alive only when it is seen to be a living stream of thinkers who have grappled with difficult problems that are, philosophically, as alive today as they were in the past. Indian philosophy will become contemporarily relevant only when it is conceived as philosophy proper.
>
> (Krishna 1991, 15)

In Krishna's thinking, it appears that philosophy's properness lies in its contemporaneity, which is achieved only when Indian philosophy is broken down into individual philosophers and what he calls styles of thought. These styles he articulates much in the same vein as European philosophers speak of neo-Kantianism, Platonism or Realism, a kind of fluid designation that an individual philosopher could very well be characterized by but never completely disappear behind or beneath. Krishna's aim is presented as the separation between a style of thought and an individual philosopher, so that his idea of tradition transpires neither as something that the individual philosopher is a representative of nor as something that corrects and steers the philosophical activity, but rather as a kind of toolbox for intellectual thought to utilize whenever and however the need arises. On the other hand he also articulates tradition as a collective abstraction, and it is this collective abstraction that develops and grows in time. This we should call style of thought rather than *darśana* or school (Krishna 1991, 13–15).

> Indian philosophy, therefore, is neither exclusively spiritual nor bound by unquestionable, infallible authority, nor constricted and congealed in the frozen moulds of the so-called 'schools' which are supposed to constitute the essence of Indian philosophy by those who have written on the subject.
>
> (Krishna 1991, 15)

Mohanty's *darśana*

Mohanty's main interest seems to lie in establishing a particular and specific space for Indian philosophy outside of, and in contrast to, its European counterpart. This he does in relation to, and against, Krishna's deconstruction of tradition. Mohanty is one of the few Indian philosophers who have taken seriously Krishna's analysis and acknowledged the problem with persisting ideas and images of the so-called spirituality of Indian philosophy and its alleged homogenized and static nature. Mohanty (1992) is by and large addressing the same issue of the binaries that have depicted the relation between Indian and European/American philosophy as Krishna takes up, that is, the images of static–dynamic, irrational–rational, and spiritual–scientific. He has, however, a radically different approach to the concept of schools and traditions within Indian philosophy than has Krishna, and in this he is clearly influenced by European hermeneutics. Although Mohanty also critiques a conception of Indian philosophy ordered in closed static systems of thought, he is hesitant in going as far as Krishna does; the Indian tradition still retains a knowable and articulatable essence for him. The *darśana*, that is, the tradition, according to Mohanty, is always supra-individual:

> In a *darśana*, the individual thinker, great or small, plays a subordinate role, he does not found a system but carries its explication forward. The *darśana* is a perception, which antecedates any individual thinker or expositor. Criticism, clarificatory-explicative as well as destructive, is either intrasystemic or intersystemic.
>
> (Mohanty 1992, 8)

Mohanty is here trying to emphasize a contrast between *philosophia* as generating truth and *darśana* as explicating truth already at hand, and this contrast seems to be the most central aspect in Mohanty's envisioning of *darśana*. The idea of *darśana* as authoritative should then perhaps not be understood in terms of a tradition being corrective or regulative of an individual philosopher's thinking but rather in terms of an ideological subsumption of the individual under the perception of the system. But, and this appears to be important for Mohanty, it is not a system in the sense of a closed grid into which one enters and is duly engulfed, as it were.

In order to articulate his understanding of tradition Mohanty turns to a Gadamerian point of view:

> Tradition is not a cluster of facts about texts and documents, but a horizon of interpretive possibilities opened up and instituted by the founding texts; but as the interpretive possibilities are actualized, new possibilities open up – possibilities that were not 'contained in' the original disclosure, but which are 'interpreted' to be carrying on 'anticipations' and 'pre-delineations' indicated in the texts.
>
> (Mohanty 1992, 53)

In his confutation of Krishna, Mohanty refers to the impossibility of attaining knowledge of any individual author's intentions and to the thick layers of interpretative history that need to be grasped before any understanding can be reached of a particular text. In this, Mohanty says, the individual author is completely peripheral and unimportant. Furthermore, he maintains that, in contrast to European philosophers, Indian philosophers always thought within a framework of a school and never understood themselves as founders or inventors (Mohanty 1992, 8–9, 54).

Halbfass on philosophy and newness

When Halbfass (1991) takes up the question of tradition, he does so in the context of both modern and historical ideas about a corresponding term for philosophy within the Indian philosophical discourse. In doing this, he discusses the idea of *darśana* as it is expressed in the above-mentioned doxographic literature, and it is in this discussion that his conceptualization of tradition, or rather Indian tradition, is visible.

Halbfass points to an important aspect of the doxographic genre by making a contrasting move, much in the same manner as Mohanty, drawing our attention to how the different *darśanas* are outlined in the texts. The schools are portrayed there as closed systems, in a kind of frozen state (in time) that does not point to possible development or progress (in time); all problems are, in a way, already solved and accounted for. The future is always and constantly absent; there is, in Halbfass' own expression, no thing that "has not yet been known" (Halbfass 1991, 361). According to Halbfass, this does not correspond very well to the idea of philosophy in the West, which, in its own self-understanding, is deeply connected to autonomy, critique, separation from soteriology, and perhaps most importantly, to ideas of development and progression. Halbfass readily admits that this reflects a certain prejudice in the understanding of Indian tradition, but he also states that it can function as knowledge-producing, if we remember that the above descriptions are not uniformly given, in either Western or Indian traditions (Halbfass 1991, 277).

The connection between the conceptualization of a non-individual tradition and a lack of awareness of historicity is also addressed by Halbfass when he poses the following questions:

> What possibilities does the non-historical self-understanding of classical Indian philosophy, with its apparent rejection of the ideas of progress and innovation, leave for the self-assessment of the individual thinker? What importance does it attach to the addition of new works to the old, whose validity is beyond dispute?
>
> (Halbfass 1991, 362)

Halbfass' answers are drawn on a textual basis, and he exemplifies his point with Jayanta Bhaṭṭa's classic *Nyāyamañjarī*. Jayanta explicitly engages in a discussion of the place of individual, or rather, of original thought, within the Nyāya school of philosophy. His is a tone of perfect humility; the role he takes upon himself is that of the expounder; there are no pretensions to write his own ideas or inventions. Halbfass connects this issue of originality, which in turn becomes the issue of the individual's role within tradition, to an idea of a cyclical time. For Halbfass there is a general case of, and particular deviations from, tradition. Much in the same manner as Mohanty, Halbfass speaks about a kind of subordination to tradition on behalf of the individual. Even though there is a certain openness in the Indian texts and thus room for explication and clarification of the given, tradition remains a truth already present, already laid bare in the past. This is how Halbfass links the two images, that of the anonymous philosopher/expounder and that of the timeless, eternal, non-progressing, and never-new philosophy (Halbfass 1991, 362–364).

The strategy of re-imagining philosophical tradition

What I am searching for in this chapter is a way to avoid a generalizing and essentializing idea of tradition within the context of understanding philosophy in classical India. In this and the following section I will clarify how it could be done and why it is important and needed for both comparative and Indian philosophy.

A re-imagining of tradition can function as a strategic practice when introducing philosophy from India in the academic context of philosophy in Europe. The three myths that Krishna articulates, and subsequently identifies as the background of an understanding of Indian philosophy as belonging solely to the past, in terms of being philosophy, are obviously also connected to the tendency to present an Indian tradition of philosophy as a homogeneous phenomenon. In connection to this I would like to point to the fact that Halbfass is writing Indian philosophy as a heterogeneous phenomenon. He is, it appears, elaborately fragmenting his recordings of different arguments and points of view. It is just that this does not seem to cause him to draw the obvious conclusion: that an Indian philosophy/Indian tradition as one single phenomenon is a fictional entity, something imagined. Despite the fact of a will to problematize or make visible a complexity, the outcome is still generalizing and, to a certain extent, not in concordance with the existing phenomena of a great number of texts and commentarial traditions. This generalizing tendency is visible in Mohanty as well, although he is explicitly searching for essences in a way that Halbfass is not.

The tendency to fall back on generalization and essentialization is devastating for how classical philosophy from India is conceptualized within a philosophical discourse, whether comparative or not. In this, I think Krishna has pointed towards something that needs to be reworked and re-imagined. As for the consequences, the need for generalizing comes out as a certain kind of sickness that attaches itself to all and every description of an Indian philosophy or an Indian tradition in the overview literature, the literature that is most often used in teaching and hence forms itself into a kind of lore, or myth, if we are to use Krishna's terminology, about the other. Still, we have to remember that European/American or Western philosophy is a constant looming backdrop in these discussions. It is indeed possible to understand many of Krishna's points of critique as imitating an already established, although objectionable, idea of how philosophy should be conducted – that is, in terms of Halbfass' articulated prejudices as connected to autonomy and critique, to separation from soteriology, and to ideas of development and progression.

Re-imagining tradition as "discoursing"

When individualizing tradition, the risk of dis-locating tradition outside of, or above, a writer of a text, is taken away. The imagining of tradition as removed from an acting individual thinker results in a process of hiding the changes visible in philosophy in India. But it also misrepresents the very act of doing philosophy, of continuously writing texts. Philosophy not connected to an activity comes out as an artifact, or object, a fact that encourages homogeneous or generalized conceptualizations. A solution to this problem is thus to dissolve the image of Indian tradition as one generalizable phenomenon and place it in relation to an individual philosopher. Thus accommodating philosophical tradition as not completely common or shared. This involves a movement away from tradition as a passive happening (impersonal) or tradition as a noun (reified) towards tradition as an act (discoursing). On the other hand, this image of tradition as discoursing does not fit, descriptively, all different kinds of philosophical writing within India; it is not to be understood as a universal conception of tradition at all. It is a particularized conception, possible in relation to certain Sanskrit texts written by certain philosophers and impossible in relation to other texts written by other philosophers.

This is a very important point to make because there are different conceptualizations of tradition within the extensive corpus of philosophical texts in Sanskrit that are in concordance with what Mohanty, Halbfass, and Krishna say about tradition. There are soteriologically centered texts as well as materialistic text fragments that deny the existence of a possible liberation, and skeptical texts that deny the possibility of knowing anything at all. There are exegetical traditions that do have root-texts considered to be un-authored just as there are texts where philosophers refer to other texts written by specific authors within the debate. There are philosophers who articulate tradition as explication of something that was already said, like Jayanta, and there are philosophers that describe their philosophy as new, like Gaṅgeśa. It is neither possible nor strategically meaningful to envision one single image of philosophical tradition encompassing what is expressed in all these different sources.

To clarify, then: the moving away from a universalized conceptualization of tradition and the subsequent re-imagining tradition is articulated in relation to three areas of interest. First of all it is understood as a strategic practice, breaking up myths or misconceptions about Indian philosophy in its meeting with Western/European philosophy. Second, this is needed philologically since the diversified phenomena of writing philosophy in classical India does not correspond to a universalizable idea of one, single, Indian philosophical tradition. The last point concerns a philosophical writing of hermeneutics in relation to and along with specific Indian philosophers, which in Krishna's words would be to do Indian philosophy as a living activity.

Imagining tradition along with Gautama, Vātsyāyana, Uddyotakara, and Vācaspati

With the preceding as a guiding principle I have chosen to do a reading of Gautama's *Nyāyasūtra*, which is a so-called root-text in the Nyāya commentarial tradition, together with Vātsyāyana, Uddyotakara, and Vācaspati, who all discuss the *sūtra* text in their commentaries (Halbfass 1991, 285). There is one section in the *Nyāyasūtra* where the concept of *siddhānta* (the established conviction) is defined and enumerated. The *sūtra* does not so much discuss the topic, but rather introduces a definition and a categorization/enumeration of what *siddhānta* entails. The discussion is left to the commentators.

Siddhānta as a concept could be thought of as that which has been established, or rather that which is a conviction about something. One might say that it is the point in thinking from where one begins, the conviction which is established, has already come into existence, it is in a way concluded (as a process of thinking at least), or it is conclusive. *Siddhānta* is further categorized into four groups: common philosophical discourse, specific philosophical discourse, implication, and finally presupposition (Jhā 1984, vol. 1, 34). What is important for the present discussion is the idea of philosophical discourse, tantra, meaning model or framework. Tantra (lit. model or framework) is mainly understood in the texts here as themes that have been discussed. One important point to make is that that the understanding of philosophy carries with it a sense that might best be understood as genre, or perhaps indeed as Krishna would like it, as style. Vātsyāyana explains philosophy by saying that it contains teachings or explanations that are collected/heaped together and that stand in relation to one another. These collections are then called knowledge discourse, meaning the discussion of means of knowledge present in the texts. This is called *pramāṇavāda* in Sanskrit, literally "the discussion of means of knowledge". According to Vācaspati, the other commentator, philosophy takes place within a specific kind of analysis, that is, the analysis, and use, of means of knowledge. Bringing in the idea of a knowledge discourse could be understood as a further specifying of this genre. In the *sūtra* and the commentaries the idea of philosophy thus appears to be one of the terms that are used for designating the activity of discussing what one would call philosophical questions in a modern academic context.

The four classifications in the text above function as established convictions, from, or out of which, philosophical thought expands. In the texts, however, there appears no definitive listing of what the discourse contains, that is, which viewpoint should be taken or not. There are of course examples – such as the presupposition that one sees with the eyes and smells with the nose – but the texts could in no way be read as authoritative in that sense, because they contain no information as to exactly what one should think or adhere to; there is no corrective impetus present, just the idea that one thinks in terms of convictions or presuppositions. What is present is an open-ended collection of examples. There are to some extent shared meanings and presuppositions as well as differing meanings and presuppositions within an ongoing discussion.

Even though there is no single universal and abstracted idea of what philosophy is – something that seems to bother European and American philosophers a lot (Halbfass 1991, 285–289) – there are indeed ideas about, and discussions of, how the philosophizing should be conducted, that is, as a method – or perhaps we could even call it a discursive practice. This discursive element consists in ideas about how one should reason. Most importantly, there is no consensus about this how amongst the commentators. In this way one could easily do away with a homogeneous conceptualization of this philosophical tradition (Nyāya-Vaiśeṣika) as authoritative or corrective, at least in the sense that the individual is subordinated to a specific and already articulated collection of ideas or doctrines.

Conclusions

An impersonalized idea of tradition is far removed from the texts in the above passage. They refer to one another by the words; the maker of this commentary says or the one who does the other commentary says. Although the *sūtra* text remains a text stating factual truths, as it were, it does not seem to create a situation of repetition or re-iteration in its commentaries. The philosophical tradition in these texts comes forth as a discourse-centered activity rather than a doctrine-centered substance. That is, the philosophical discourse as activity functions as a definition of philosophy as act-centered, and not substance-centered. Within an understanding of philosophy as activity the individual philosopher of course becomes pivotal in the sense of becoming the agent of the activity, and also simply by constituting the place out of which the activity is carried out.

It is, in conclusion, of utmost importance to speak of a double commitment in terms of strategy, double in the sense that it concerns images of both Indian and European/ American philosophies. If we retain an idea of philosophy as an already closed-up and once-and-for-all decided agenda (whether Indian or Western), this will continue to allow us to practice essentialized ideas of what philosophy is, or has been, and thus also to keep philosophy a closed-up discipline. To think philosophical tradition in terms of an ongoing, negotiating activity would give us space for a continuing and, most importantly, open philosophical enterprise. Only within such an idea of philosophical tradition could an Indian philosopher come alive just as a Plato or an Aristotle comes alive today.

Note

1 For other conceptualizations of Indian philosophy in relation to European and American philosophy, see for example Sprung 1978, 4–10; Halbfass 1991, 433; King 1999,16–17; Sjödin 2006, 22–25.

References

Bhushan, Nalini, Jay L. Garfield, and Daniel Raveh (eds.). 2011. *Contrary Thinking: Selected Essays of Daya Krishna*. New York: Oxford University Press.

Bilimoria, P. 2000. "J. N. Mohanty's Critique of Word as a Means of Knowing and 'Authorless Tradition'." In Bina Gupta (ed.) *The Empirical and the Transcendental: A Fusion of Horizons*, 199–218. New York: Rowman & Littlefield.

Halbfass, W. 1991. *India and Europe: An Essay in Philosophical Understanding*. Delhi: Motilal Banarsidass.

Jhā, G. 1984. *The Nyāyasūtras of Gautama, with the Bhāṣya of Vātsyāyana and the Vārttika of Uddyotakara*. Vols. 1–4. Delhi: Motilal Banarsidass [first published in *Indian Thought* 1912–1919].

King, R. 1999. *Indian Philosophy: An Introduction to Hindu and Buddhist Thought*. Edinburgh: Edinburgh University Press.

Krishna, Daya. 1965. "Three Conceptions of Indian Philosophy." *Philosophy East and West* 15(1): 37–51.

Krishna, Daya. 1991. *Indian Philosophy: A Counter Perspective*. New Delhi: Oxford University Press.

Krishna, Daya. 2007/2017. "The Myth of the Ethics of Puruṣārtha or Humanity's Life-Goals." In P. Bilimoria, J. Prabhu, and R. Sharma (eds.) *Indian Ethics*, vol. 1, 103–116. Aldershot: Ashgate; London and New York: Routledge.

Mohanty, J. N. 1992. *Reason and Tradition in Indian Thought: An Essay on the Nature of Indian Philosophical Thinking*. Oxford: Oxford University Press.

Mohanty, J. N. 1995. "Some Thoughts on Daya Krishna's 'Three Myths'." In P. Bilimoria (ed.) *J. N. Mohanty: Essays on Indian Philosophy. Edited with a Biographical Introduction*, 45–55. New Delhi: Oxford University Press.

Mohanty, J. N. 1999. *Classical Indian Philosophy*. Lanham, MD: Rowman & Littlefield.

Sjödin, A.-P. 2006. *The Happening of Tradition: Vallabha on Anumāna in Nyāyalīlāvatī*. South Asian Studies 1. Uppsala: Acta Universitatis Uppsaliensis.

Sprung, M. (ed.). 1978. *The Question of Being: East–West Perspectives*. University Park: Pennsylvania State University Press.

Chapter 56
G. R. MALKANI

Sharad Deshpande

Ghanshamdas Ratanmal Malkani (1892–1977) spent almost all his life at the Indian Institute of Philosophy at Amalner, a small town in the north-western region of the State of Bombay (now Mumbai), as its Director. He was the editor of the *Philosophical Quarterly* (Amalner, India), which for decades was the premier journal of philosophy in the pre-Independence era. Malkani was one of those modern Indian academic philosophers who were trying to give their own expositions of classical Advaita Vedānta which later came to be known as 'contemporary Vedānta' or the 'twentieth-century Vedānta'. These nomenclatures indicate the colonial context in which modern Indian philosophers were trying to reinvent the age-old tradition of Advaita Vedānta in the light of the idealistic metaphysics, particularly that of Kant and Hegel. In asserting that his presentation of Advaita Vedānta is not rooted in Sanskrit; Malkani, like many of his contemporaries, has freed it from the hegemonic classical texts, thereby making it accessible to English-educated modern Indians not by claiming erudition but by advocating a Vedāntic point of view by remaining faithful to its spirit. The simplicity with which he writes often overshadows the profundity of his thought. Malkani's thought remains unchanged, his views remain firm and he is convinced of their truth risking the charge of being dogmatic. What Malkani constantly tries to achieve throughout his writings is greater precision and clarity in expressing the basic non-dualist Vedāntic point of view to which he is committed throughout his life. Besides a large number of articles and monographs, his major publications include *Philosophy of the Self* (1939/1966), *A Study of Reality* (1927), *Vedāntic Epistemology* (1953), and *Metaphysics of Advaita Vedānta* (1961b). Although he read Śaṅkara's *Brahmasūtrabhāṣya* with a renowned pandit, he had little knowledge of Sanskrit and he never affiliated his thinking with any author of repute in the classical tradition of Advaita Vedānta. He presents himself as a free thinker claiming a particular interpretation of Advaita Vedānta which appeals him the most. Unlike many of his contemporaries, Malkani does not defend the Advaita point of view against any particular philosophical system of the West. Malkani explicates and defends only one thesis throughout, namely, the non-duality of *Brahman*. Therefore, a close textual reading of any one of his writings reveals his overall philosophical position as a firm Advaita Vedāntin.

Being a philosopher working under the colonial condition, Malkani, like every other modern Indian philosopher, had to negotiate with his own indigenous tradition of philosophical speculation and with those of the West to which he was exposed through the British educational system; particularly through his training at Cambridge. However, it is doubtful whether he or most of the modern Indian philosophers could claim either of these traditions as their own in the true sense of the term. These philosophers worked under the condition of double estrangement—from their own tradition, which was as alien as the other, which was not their own. On a positive note, in the colonial milieu the modern Indian philosophers' philosophizing was thus rooted in a cosmopolitan tradition which couldn't have been purely Indian or Western, and hence the activity of philosophizing that emerged during this period was bound to assume a different role that was, so to say, determined by the historical condition in which these philosophers were placed. This role assumes different forms in the writings of leading modern Indian philosophers. Some like Radhakrishnan and P. T. Raju followed the comparative method by putting Upaniṣadic philosophy and Advaita Vedānta alongside Western Idealism; others like K. C. Bhattacharyya followed the method of assimilation of Western ideas and ideals in terms of '*svarāj* in ideas', while philosophers like G. R. Malkani followed the method of a free rendering of both the Indian and the Western traditions of philosophy. The method of comparison and the method of assimilation presented problems of one kind, while the method of a free rendering presented problems of another kind. Within the bounds of methodological requirements, free rendering of texts involved a high risk of being inauthentic and unfaithful to the tradition of Vedānta. But Malkani takes this risk. His free rendering of Vedānta is not presented in the traditional form of commentary on *Brahmasūtrabhāṣya* or any other major or minor text that constitutes an integral part of the tradition of Vedānta, but rather takes recourse to a typically Western mode of self-contained essays in which philosophical problems are directly raised and answered.

The main feature of Malkani's exposition of Advaitic thought is his appropriation of Hegelian idealism as expounded by F. H. Bradley. But he was not alone in doing so. Like most of his contemporaries, he was working under the colonial context of self-assertion by way of presenting the indigenous philosophical world-view to the West. This world-view was rooted in a particular conception of philosophy which was held by most of the modern Indian philosophers. It was a restatement of the classical Indian view that philosophy is a science of self-realization and through it a path to liberation from suffering. Philosophy for Hegel is the science of the Absolute, which the modern Indian philosophers read and interpreted in terms of Śaṅkarācārya's doctrine of *Brahma-Vidyā* (the science of the ultimate reality, the Absolute). The comparison between Hegel and Śaṅkarācārya was based on the notion that both allegedly hold a similar philosophical theory about the nature of ultimate Reality which Hegel terms the Absolute and Śaṅkara *Brahman*. This assumption provided a common focus for self-assertion. Given their commitment to Advaita Vedānta and given the prevalent demand to present it to the West, Malkani and others needed a similar world-view which is rooted in the Western philosophical tradition and whose vocabulary is not only known but is also practiced in philosophical discourse in the West. This wider context, coupled with the reception of Hegel in the framework of the history of Western philosophy, also explains why the Hegelian doctrine of the Absolute, or what is popularly known as Hegelian Absolute Idealism, was thought to be as the most appropriate framework to present the philosophy of Advaita Vedānta to the West. Thus, the modern Indian philosophers focused on the central issue of the nature of Hegel's Absolute from the perspective of Vedānta. Malkani's *Metaphysics of Advaita Vedānta* (1961b) is representative of the general practice of translating Hegel's 'Absolute' as Śaṅkara's '*Brahman*' in so far as both these concepts stand for the ultimate reality. This discourse primarily involved discussing the relation between the one (single Absolute reality) and the many; which in Vedānta translates into the problem of the relationship between the *Brahman* (the absolute reality) and *Jagat* (the phenomenal world). It is within this framework that the relationship between the Absolute consciousness (i.e., *Brahman*) and the individual consciousness (i.e., *jīva*) becomes pertinent. Similarly, the problem of the relationship between truth and error is another central problem within the Vedāntic epistemology that deals with the mode in which erroneous perception is negated and the truth is arrived at. These controversies and the idiom of the Vedāntic discourse were thus mapped on the Hegelian framework that was appropriated via British Neo-Hegelianism. This was a typical adaptation of Hegel's concept of the Absolute taken in isolation from his overall perspective on the flow of history. Whether this appropriation leads to '*Hegelianization* of Advaita Vedānta or to the *Vedāntization* of Hegel—both in terms of their terminology and the structure and operation of concepts' (Deshpande 2015, 126)—remains an open question.

Though Malkani's main focus always remains logic, epistemology, metaphysics, and ontology from a Vedāntic point of view, he is not unaware of methodological issues of proof and explanation as they occur in philosophy. In some of his articles, such as 'Problem of Proof' (1926), 'Philosophical Explanation' (1932, 1948), and 'The Principle of Inexplicability in Philosophy' (1940), he discusses these issues as metaphysical issues and develops a problematic of proof and explanation in philosophy. The problem of explanation, i.e., the 'why', 'what', and 'how' of anything, addresses a twin questions, i.e., 'what things are in themselves or in their true nature' and 'how things come to be'. But as far as the self is concerned the twin questions rule out any explanation of the self which is self-existent unless we are clear as to what sort of explanation is still needed to explain the existence of self. There is thus an 'upper limit' to explanation where, to use Wittgenstein's remark, 'an explanation comes to an end.' But there is also a 'lower limit' to explanation which operates within the distinction between how a thing appears to us and its reality. But to admit this very distinction is to admit that an appearance is inexplicable in relation to reality. 'What demands to be explained is already rejected *in principle* as illusory and therefore inexplicable' (Malkani 1940, 55). Malkani's complex argument about the nature of explanation points out the paradox of explanation: 'a thing is fully explained when it is seen to be inherently and ultimately of the nature of inexplicable' (Malkani 1940, 55). Thus, for Malkani the problem of explanation does not even arise either in relation to the self (the Absolute or the *Brahman*) or in relation to the phenomenal world (the world of appearance). Anticipating the latter Wittgenstein, Malkani pronounces 'To resolve the question, we must show it to be ultimately illegitimate' (Malkani 1940, 56).

A selective reading of some of his writings in logic, epistemology, metaphysics, and ontology reveal the range of issues he addresses in his books and monographs. For instance, in discussing issues in logic and epistemology he takes up such core issues as intellect and intuition, the self in relation to knowledge, philosophical truth, validity and invalidity of knowledge, the authority of *Śrūti* (revelation), and *ajñāna* (ignorance). Likewise in discussing issues in metaphysics and ontology Malkani focuses on issues such as intuition of self, creation or illusion, reality and value, the nature of the Absolute, and the nature of consciousness and value which outline his philosophy of life. A reading of Malkani's writings on these issues gives an impression that he never changes his thoughts once they are formulated. His writings have evoked reactions of high appreciation as well as harsh criticism. On the one hand, Malkani is appreciated by the sympathizers with oriental metaphysics as a philosopher whose exposition of classical Vedānta is strictly rational and hence 'If it is true anywhere and at any time, it is true everywhere and always' (Burch 1970, 70). But on the other hand, he is critiqued as an ardent exponent of Radhakrishnan's 'spiritualist interpretation of the traditional or the classical Indian conception of philosophy', which, according to the critics of this interpretation, suppresses the critical, analytical, and empiricist trends in Indian philosophy and equates it with spiritualism and mysticism (Prasad 1982, 295). Although he did emphasize a form of reliabilism based on testimony of *śruti* or 'the revealed word', *sans* the spiritualist and esoteric elements, for an enlightened philosophical viewpoint (Bilimoria 2016, 505–506).

Thus Malkani's exposition of Advaita Vedānta is based on the dialectic of reason and faith. The employment of reason stresses the rational, argumentative, and critical side of Advaita Vedānta, while the faith stands for Vedānta as a *way* of life. While the faith is prescriptive, the rational, argumentative, and the critical side of Advaita Vedānta is concerned with refutation of rival views like dualism of *Puruṣa* and *Prakriti* and *anātma-vāda* and establishing the thesis of non-dual reality *Brahman*. However, like most of the Vedāntins Malkani too believes that the rational aspect of Vedānta culminates in faith, thus making Vedānta philosophy a part of Vedānta religion. The distinction between Advaita Vedānta as philosophy and Advaita Vedānta as religion, i.e., as a way of life, has always been a problem for those who emphasize the analytical and critical aspect of Advaita Vedānta. But for both the traditional Advaitin as well as for modern Indian philosophers like Malkani, the passage from reason to faith or revelation is not unnatural, since as a Vedāntin a Vedāntic philosopher accepts revelation of Veda-s and as a philosopher he accepts reason. This is similar to the problem of the relation between the two as conceived in Christianity and Malkani's approach is very much Augustinian. Malkani addresses this issue by posing two related questions, i.e., is intuition (or *Śrūti* or revelation) a distinct mode of knowledge as opposed to thought; and is there an intuition of ultimate reality? (Malkani 1930) He defines intuition as an immediate non-relational mode of knowledge. Given this definition, he is able to argue that intuitive knowledge has no content, where the content is understood in terms of subject–object distinction. But then he must address the immediate objection as to how intuition can be a specific mode of knowledge without content, since, 'to be a mode of knowledge is to be a particular way of knowing certain *content*' (Deshpande 1997, xxii). Malkani holds that intuition itself is reality and it knows nothing apart from itself. 'The contentless intuition is … a non-relational apprehension of the real' (Deshpande 1997, 8). Malkani's analysis of intuition thus replaces an epistemological notion of intuition by an ontological one as 'the very being … that knows itself' (Deshpande 1997, 8). This analysis leads to a related issue of the relationship between self and knowledge. Two questions become pertinent in this context, first, is the self a real substance or a formal unity needed to account for knowledge, and second, is knowledge identical with self or distinct from it? Malkani addresses both these issues from the familiar Vedāntic point of view which asserts the continuity of self through all and every state of consciousness and that knowledge is not an accidental but essential quality of self.

The above analysis of intuition is related to the problem of the intuition of self and Malkani discusses it at various places, as it is central to Vedānta metaphysics. The premise on which Malkani's analysis rests is that intuition of self 'cannot transgress the limit of 'I'-ness which is the ultimate ground' of the intuition of self (Deshpande 1997, xxvi). This limit is transcendental in the sense that in this intuition the being of the self is not distinct from its intuitiveness. This intuition is the basis of self-awareness which excludes any representation of self as objective. In other words, 'the self can never become the known' (Malkani 1928, 164). Since self is the transcendental condition of all experience and a ground of all reality, Malkani connects this analysis to the idea of the 'Absolute' which he elaborates in almost all his writings. Keeping in tune with the initial premise of Advaita, namely, the distinction between the subject and the object, or the self and the not-self (*yūṣmat* and *asmat*), Malkani maintains that this dualism is not tenable in the ultimate analysis. This dualism comes about due to reflective consciousness. But the reflective consciousness must be contained in a higher consciousness in which the said dualism disappears and knowledge coincides with reality. Malkani confirms the Vedāntic precept that 'to know *Brahman* is to become *Brahman*.' Implicit in this identity between 'to know' and 'to be' is the idea of self-evidence, and Malkani argues that the Absolute is the ultimate ground of self-evidence. 'It is the higher consciousness which is implicit in every stage of reflection and so real from the very start' (Malkani 1934, 202). But nevertheless the Absolute needs to be *realized*. Thus, Malkani considers various options such as intellectual, empirical, synthetic, mathematical intuitions and argues that none of these is adequate to the realization of the Absolute. Malkani uses the prevalent language consisting of terms like consciousness, content, and cognition. One of the chief preoccupations of Idealism, at least of that variety to which Malkani subscribes, has been to explicate the relation between consciousness and the content of consciousness. Malkani's argument is that consciousness is self-evident but its content is not. The content of consciousness implies consciousness but not vice versa. Consciousness is one single, indivisible whole which has no parts and thus the question of the relation of implication between the parts and the whole does not arise at all. '[W]hen content is said to imply consciousness, this implication is dependent upon an original division which it-self is illegitimate ... for consciousness in its true nature is never a presentation and can never be related to another presentation' (Malkani 1934, 210). Having asserted that consciousness as one single, indivisible whole, Malkani addresses the issue of identity and difference between consciousness and the content of consciousness. His analysis is in conformity with the standard Idealistic-Vedāntic position that consciousness alone is real and it is 'wrong to say that it has a necessary relation to the content, and is itself nothing without the relation' (Malkani 1934, 218). This means that the real consciousness or the pure subject is not relational either to some other content or to itself. This makes Malkani say that:

> If we realize this, consciousness is freed from its relatedness to content. It becomes the Absolute, the only free, real and self-contained being. The ideal we reach in this way is not the realization of ... some kind unity of subject *and* object but the realization of complete falsity of one of the terms and through it the freeing of the other of its apparent and misapprehended relatedness.
> (Malkani 1934, 218)

Malkani also reads the typical Vedāntic characterization of *Brahman*, the pure consciousness, as *ānanda* (bliss) into the Hegelian notion of Absolute which is open for critical engagement.

While reinventing the classical tradition of Advaita Vedānta, Malkani also actively participated in some of the debates of his times. One such debate is about doing 'pure' philosophy in the colonial and post-colonial context. Criticizing the fruitless attempts at a synthesis of two traditions he laments, saying 'we are alternately Hindu metaphysicians (*tattvajñānis*) and full-fledged European philosophers', the result being that 'we are not creative as philosophers' (Malkani 1955, 55). Malkani not only reflects on the issue of the difference between the Indian and the European methods of doing philosophy but also critically ponders over the difference between the goal and the ideal of Indian and Western philosophy. But the final answer that he gives to the questions posed by modern European thought is in terms of imbibing the spirit of Vedānta, which he could never give up.

References

Bilimoria, P. 2016. "Tapti Maitra: Advaita Metaphysics: A Contemporary Perspective. No. 18 of Contemporary Researches in Hindu Philosophy and Religion." *Journal of the Indian Council of Philosophical Research* 33(3): 503–514.

Burch, George. 1956. "Contemporary Vedānta Philosophy." *Review of Metaphysics* (10)1: 122–157.

———. 1970. "Oriental Metaphysics." In *The Future of Metaphysics*. Ed R. E. Wood, 64–76. Chicago: Quadrangle Books.

Deshpande, Sharad. (Ed.). 1997. *The Philosophy of G. R. Malkani*. New Delhi: Indian Council of Philosophical Research.

———. 2015. "G. R. Malkani: Reinventing Classical Advaita Vedānta." In *Philosophy in Colonial India*. Ed. Sharad Deshpande, 119–135. New Delhi: Springer.

Malkani, G. R. 1927. *A Study of Reality*. Amalner: Indian Institute of Philosophy.
———. 1928. "Intuition of Self." *Philosophical Quarterly* (Amalner, India) 4(3): 160–168.
———. 1930. "Intellect and Intuition." *Philosophical Quarterly* (Amalner, India) 5(4): 262–269.
———. 1932. "The Self in Relation to Knowledge." *Philosophical Quarterly* (Amalner, India) 7(4): 430–435.
———. 1934. "The Absolute." *Philosophical Quarterly* (Amalner, India) 10(3): 199–224.
———. 1939/1966. *Philosophy of the Self or A System of Idealism Based on Advaita Vedanta*. Repr. London: Johnson Reprint Company Ltd.
———. 1940. "The Principle of Inexplicability in Philosophy." *Philosophical Quarterly* (Amalner, India) 16(1): 49–60.
———. 1953. *Vedantic Epistemology*. Amalner: Indian Institute of Philosophy.
———. 1955. "Two Different Traditions of Pure Philosophy." *Philosophical Quarterly* (Amalner, India) 27(4): 55–61.
———. 1961a. "The Authority of *Śruti* or Revelation?" *Philosophical Quarterly* (Amalner, India) 33(1): 35–38.
———. 1961b. *Metaphysics of Advaita Vedānta*. Amalner: Indian Institute of Philosophy.
Prasad, Rajendra. 1982. "Tradition, Freedom and Philosophical Creativity." In *Indian Philosophy: Past and Future*. Ed. S. S. Rama Rao Pappu and R. Puligandla, 291–313. New Delhi: Motilal Banarasidass.

Chapter 57
POSTMODERN APPROACHES

Carl Olson

Postmodernism is a term that is difficult to define because it means different things to various philosophers. It can be viewed as an "assemblage of attitudes and discursive practices" (Schrag 1992, 14). This observation suggests that postmodernism is something plural instead of a unified philosophical position. From a historical perspective, it is closely associated with French philosophy of the twentieth century with such influential thinkers as Jacques Derrida, Maurice Blanchot, Gilles Deleuze, Felix Guattari, poet Edmund Jabès, Jacques Lacan, Julia Kristeva, Emmanuel Levinas, Jean-François Lyotard, Michel Foucault, and Americans Mark C. Taylor and Fredric Jameson.

The earlier French postmodern thinkers were inspired by Friedrich Nietzsche, whereas Martin Heidegger inspired postmodernists to oppose the Western metaphysical edifice by thinking "difference as difference" by which he means to think the unthought difference between Being and beings that involves thinking of the concealment of difference, a type of concealment that withdraws from its inception (Heidegger 1969, 50).

Among postmodern thinkers, there is a general agreement that they are reacting against the philosophical heritage of the Enlightenment especially its reliance on reason and concomitantly the representational mode of thinking that is characterized by a correspondence between appearance and reality. The representational mode of thinking is metaphorically expressed by imagining the mind to be like a mirror that reflects a conscious image. Richard Rorty clarifies this point: "Without the notion of the mind as mirror, the notion of knowledge as accuracy of representation would not have suggested itself" (Rorty 1979, 12). By rejecting the representational mode of thinking and its metaphysical support system, postmodernists are attempting to discover new paradigms that are devoid of any metaphysical position and coherence theory of truth.

In order to grasp postmodernism in greater detail, it is first necessary to briefly grasp what features of the Enlightenment it reacted against. Since reason and the representational mode of thinking are two features of Enlightenment philosophy against which postmodernists react, they will play a central role in this discussion. Finally, this chapter will discusses the ways that a couple of Indian thinkers have attempted to use some forms of postmodern thought to criticize the West from the stance of post-colonialism, such as Homi K. Bhabha and Gayatri Chakravorty Spivak.

Modernity and Enlightenment heritage

Similar to postmodernity, modernity is difficult to precisely define because scholars cannot come to a consensus about its nature. The etymological derivation of modernity is connected to the Latin term *modernus* meaning "now." Moreover, modernity presupposes self-consciously creating a distance from what preceded the present moment. Because modernity involves a perpetual critique of the past and many voices are involved in the unfolding assessment, it is probably more accurate to refer to a plural modernity instead of a single, unified modernity (Benavides 1998, 186–189).

From a historical perspective, modernity evolved in waves with the rise of a new humanism. The recognition of the power of human reason ushered in the second wave of modernity. The third wave represented an integration of earlier ideas into a more comprehensive notion of humanism. Dupré warns that the advent of modernity, which is represented by the rise of the Enlightenment, continued to be an ongoing project, and it never really became a full achievement (Dupré 2004, 4). This implies that postmodernism is the culmination of the project begun by Enlightenment thinkers.

In historical hindsight, the Enlightenment era manifested many cultural changes and acceptance of the importance of freedom, rationality, progress, individualism, and autonomy. By emphasizing rationalism, the human mind becomes the primary source of truth, in the process of eclipsing faith as the basis of truth. Moreover, Enlightenment thought ushered in a new sense of selfhood that was more self-conscious and reflective, and a shared optimism that truth could be identified by utilizing either a correspondence between an idea and reality or conceptually grasping a coherence among parts and the whole.

Postmodernism and its reaction to the Enlightenment

The difficulty of defining postmodernism is associated with the lack of a unified definition among adherents. And like the term "modernity," it is preferable to conceive of several versions of postmodernism. Some writers trace its origins to changes in architectural design, while other scholars trace it to certain philosophical attitudes. More precisely, Heidegger anticipates the term postmodernism: "Western history has now begun to enter into the completion of that period we call the modern, and which is defined by the fact that man becomes the measure and the centre of beings" (Heidegger 1982, 28). In addition to this type of comment, Heidegger presents a vision of the end of metaphysics in his latter works (Heidegger 1959, 83; Heidegger 1963, 91ff.).

Jean-François Lyotard thinks that the term postmodern is always implied in the term modern "because of the fact that modernity, modern temporality, comprises in itself an impulsion to exceed itself into a state other than itself" (Lyotard 1991, 25). In addition, the "post" of postmodernity suggests a matter of tone, style, experimentation, and multiplicity. Such an experiment means that postmodernity is not a new epoch, but it is rather a rewriting of modernity. Instead of knowledge of the past, rewriting is repetitive writing that makes modernity itself real. Therefore, Lyotard's type of experiment de-emphasizes the importance of grand theories, the end of all truth claims, and the cessation of all standards of valid argumentation. From Lyotard's perspective, postmodernism represents a crisis of narratives, which he thinks are the quintessential forms of knowledge. It is precisely this type of knowledge that refines our sensitivity to differences. But why is there a crisis? The reason for the crisis is related to knowledge that has been altered in such a way that it became a commodity to be produced in order to be sold to consumers much like forms of computer services. Consequently, knowledge ceases to be an end in itself and loses its use-value.

There is a general agreement among postmodern thinkers that the world envisioned by Enlightenment philosophers is too static, whereas postmodernists stress features such as becoming, contingency, and chance. Gilles Deleuze's philosophy is an excellent example of this type of attitude, emphasizing that becoming is contrary to imitation of conforming to a model because there is no firm starting point from which to venture and no goal at which one can eventually arrive (Deleuze and Parnet 1987, 2). On our journey, we encounter a world of flux within which there are no universal and timeless truths to be discovered because everything is relative and indeterminate; this suggests that our knowledge is always incomplete, fragmented, and historically and culturally conditioned. Within this world of flux, it is impossible to find any centre of society, culture, or history. This situation makes it impossible to secure a foundation for philosophy or any theory. Therefore, it is wise to be suspicious of any universal claims to validity made by reason.

The contingent nature of the world necessarily means that the postmodern era is characterized by discontinuity, irregularity, rupture, decentredness, and lack of hope for any type of utopia. Mark C. Taylor depicts postmodernism as a time of writing that he defines as a wandering, erring, marginal lifestyle in which a person can experiment with words and thoughts (Taylor 1984). Does this erring, wandering lifestyle lead anywhere? Fredric Jameson sees a destiny of decadence and futuristic fantastic forms adopted from misfits, eccentrics, and perverts (Jameson 1991, 382). This type of vision harkens back to Nietzsche's call for a period of frivolity, which represents a return to an artistic, erotic, and playful time.

Some postmodern thinkers use irony, humour, and play to convey their message. The philosophy of Derrida, for example, interweaves these elements in his notion of writing, which he thinks is nearly dead (Derrida 1981, 143). According to Derrida, writing is a *pharmakon*, a drug that is both a medicine and/or a poison, because it goes or leads astray; and thus it can either give or take away life. Because writing simply plays in an unreal semblance, it is an activity that possesses no positive or negative value or essence of its own. By supplanting memory, writing signifies forgetfulness. It is preferable to ironically comprehend writing as disseminating, or a scattering of seeds that can never be recovered nor inseminate anything. Therefore, writing means nothing, and to risk meaning nothing suggests entering into the spirit of play. To engage in play suggests entering into the play of *différance*, a neologism that represents a finite movement that precedes and structures all opposition. The movement of *différance* undermines presence, makes possible the difference between Being and beings, and represents the play of traces (Derrida 1973, 134). The play of traces makes no sense because a trace effaces itself as it presents itself, representing thus a presence-absence that dislocates, displaces, and refers beyond itself. A trace is actually a simulacrum of a presence that is effaced when it appears, changes place, or issues forth (Derrida 1973, 156).

Reason and representational thinking

The predominant thrust of postmodern criticism of Enlightenment thought focuses on reason and the representational mode of thinking that accompanies rational thought in a quest to devise new paradigms or a more open, free, and frivolous situation. Deleuze and Guattari advocate, for example, desire because of its ability to produce reality, affirm life, and serve as an anti-rational force. Kristeva's work on her notion of abjection undermines the order of Kantian rationality, and depicts the abject person as a marginal being who is suggestively external to the domain of rationality (Kristeva 1982). Wanting to investigate what is prior to reason, Derrida perceives an opacity embedded within rationality because the possibility of reason cannot be grasped intellectually in accordance with patterns of rational necessity. Derrida connects this problem with the supplementary nature of reason, which suggests the non-rational origin of reason (Derrida 1976, 259). Reason is further undermined in postmodern thought by its emphasis on heterogeneity, excess, relativity, and flaws in ontology and alterity of Western philosophy.

Numerous postmodern philosophers seek to break out of the representational mode of thought characteristic of rational ways of thinking. Deleuze and Guattari, for instance, challenge the representational mode of thinking by attempting to find something that is irreducible to the concepts of identity and representation by introducing a nomadological method of rhizomatics that they define as an anti-genealogy that is anti-memory (Deleuze and Guattari 1988, 21). Kristeva advocates carnivalesque play that exists only in and through relationships, is dialogical, played by disrupted people without individuality, marginal, rebellious, and anti-rational (Kristeva 1980a, 79).

In contrast to the rhizomatics of Deleuze and Guattari and the carnivalesque play of Kristeva, Derrida attempts to undermine the propriety of reason and its accompanying representational mode of thinking responsible for creating what Derrida calls onto-theology, which is identifiable with metaphysics. Although it does not produce anything, deconstruction reveals what is already present in a simultaneous process of smashing down and building up. What is already there is called logocentricism (that is, metaphysics of presence), which represents a subordination of writing to the spoken word. The fundamental error of logocentricism is the illusion that reality and its categories are directly present to the human mind. Deconstruction is exorbitant, which implies literally going outside the track while also being within the orbit. In order to exceed the track, one must cross it, which passes through the line that it traces and crosses it out, a kind of double-cross (Derrida 1987, 388–390). When deconstructing a text one re-traces the text to its limits and marks those limits, which is a kind of double reading, whereas whatever exceeds the text is the trace of *différance*.

The adoption of deconstruction by Indian thinkers

Rather than examining how classical and modern Indian philosophers would react to elements of the postmodern agenda, which I have attempted in other works (Olson 2002; Olson 2000; Olson 1999, 39–50; Olson 2013), I will concentrate on a couple of Indian thinkers who have used postmodern methods. In fact, it is Derrida's method of deconstruction that has been embraced by some Indian thinkers as a weapon to counter Western thought from within the context of post-colonialism. Homi K. Bhabha and Gayatri Chakravorty Spivak are two exceptions to the general trend of Indian thought, which tends to be opposed to the postmodern agenda, because they adopt the non-method of deconstruction to argue against Western rational hegemony. In Spivak's case, she includes Marxism and feminism in her critical arsenal, whereas Bhabha adds psychoanalysis, literary, and historical criticism to his embrace of deconstruction. The adoption by Spivak and Bhabha of the method of deconstruction is intended to overcome the representational mode of thinking that they perceive as a major factor in the way Indians and Western writers in particular have depicted subaltern people.

Before examining the positions of Spivak and Bhabha on the problematic nature of reason and representational thinking, it is useful to indicate their general points of agreement. Both thinkers focus on the margins of the present world because they image themselves living there. Human beings are at a transitional period "where space and time cross producing complex figures of difference and identity, past and present, inside and outside, inclusion and exclusion" (Bhabha 2002, 1). Within this type of situation, there is a feeling of being disorientated. This is evident during the period of transition because there is no past that we leave behind us, and there is no new horizon before us. This situation suggests wandering aimlessly and looking to the in-between spaces for answers. Mostly importantly, Bhabha and Spivak are concerned with the damage done by colonial discourse and reason, although Spivak asserts that her book is also a feminist text (Spivak 1999, xi). Moreover, both thinkers critique the Western notion of otherness as applied to people of India.

In her postmodern-jargon-laden book, Spivak considers in turn philosophy, literature, history, and culture. Since her positions on reason and representational thinking are fundamentally philosophical issues, although they have implications for the other major areas discussed, we will focus on her critique of philosophy. In order to get at the structures for the production of postcolonial reason, Spivak finds deconstruction useful. She observes that European philosophy remains untouched by the comparative impulse because it has been concerned with grand narratives, such as Kant's work, Hegel's itinerary of India, and Marx's socialist homeopathy. In contrast to these Germanic grand narratives, Spivak wants to counter them by exposing their foreclosure of the subject.

Borrowing the term "foreclosure" from Lacanian psychoanalysis, Spivak applies it to the native, who suffers expulsion after being named a man or a woman. In other words, to be foreclosed means to be crossed out and unable to enter into relationship with the

Westerner (Bilimoria, and Al-Kassim 2014, 235). This feature of the other is most evident in texts that assume normativity with European descent. At same time that the native is foreclosed, he/she is needed by European philosophers:

> In Kant he is needed as the example for the heteronomy of the determinant, to set off the autonomy of the reflexive judgment, which allows freedom for the rational will; in Hegel as evidence for the spirit's movement from the unconscious to consciousness; in Marx as that which bestows normativity upon the narrative of the modes of production.
>
> (Spivak 1999, 6)

The native is thus a convenient tool of the Western philosopher, and is never accepted as an equal subject, but is foreclosed and forgotten.

In order to make her case, Spivak specifically examines Kant's *The Critique of Judgment* with its connection between aesthetic judgment and theoretical reason. In Spivak's reading of Kant, reason is free and bound. What troubles Spivak is that "Kant does not give cognitive power to the subject of reason, and indeed he makes his own text susceptible to the system of determined yet sometimes wholesome illusions he seeks to expose" (Spivak 1999, 22–23). Spivak refers to this as a "tropological deconstruction" of the notion of freedom. Kant's notion of practical reason finds itself in a double bind: "It can work only by analogy, not through cognition or the ascription of 'proper signification.' Yet the faculty of desire is compelled to supplement every absence. This generates antinomies between 'physical and teleological … methods of explanation" (Spivak 1999, 25). Not only are there inherent problems with Kant's critique of judgment and how reason operates, Spivak wants to especially expose Kant's neglect of the native subject, who can never become the noumenonal subject for Kant because the native other is only a casual object of representational thought. Therefore, the native subject is excluded from Kant's world.

Instead of starting by criticizing Kant, Bhabha critically examines John Stuart Mill's essay "On Liberty" by reading the English thinker against the grain and indicating how he splits the subject of representation. Bhabha selects Mill because his work influenced colonial discourse, which Bhabha thinks is fixed within the ideological construction of otherness. Bhabha indicates the paradoxical nature of "Fixity, as a sign of cultural/historical/racial difference in the discourse of colonialism, is a paradoxical mode of representation: it connotes rigidity and an unchanging order as well as disorder, degeneracy, daemonic repetition" (Bhabha 2002, 66). As with Spivak, Bhabha wants to question the mode of the representation of otherness. The representational mode of thinking is "structurally similar to realism" (Bhabha 2002, 71). From this foundation of truth, colonial discourse typologizes the other as degenerate and racially inferior in order to justify conquest and exploitation (Bilimoria and Irvine 2009, 213, 230, 308).

The racism associated with the stereotype and grounded in representational thinking can be destroyed by enunciation, which renders the structure of meaning and reference ambivalent. According to Bhabha, enunciation works to displace the narrative created by Westerners of the native. Enunciation, which is a dialogic process, represents a disruptive temporality (Bhabha 2002, 37). Bhabha's notion of enunciation is not opposed to reason, but is a more preferable dialogic process that is apt to trace changes that cause cultural antagonisms. In short, enunciation subverts the rationale for hegemonic constructions and creates alternative possibilities for cultural dialogue.

Concluding critical remarks

As Derrida informs his readers, deconstruction is a parasitic non-method that is anti-dialectical and operates to subvert pre-existing structures. Nonetheless, Bhabha uses deconstruction to finally advocate his vision of a "vernacular cosmopolitanism" (Bhabha 2001, 39). Within this vision, the native other gains genuine political power from a complicit relationship between colonial and neocolonial discourses, a process that transforms the postcolonial subject into a historical person. Bhabha connects this vision with a subaltern secularism that is more inclusive than liberal secularism. Is not Bhabha replacing old "isms" with newer versions? If so, he violates the spirit of deconstruction by constructing another form of essentialism.

With respect to Spivak, her Marxism, feminism, and use of deconstruction would appear to be self-contradictory, even if she intends to hold them in tension with each other. Marxism and feminism are essentialistic constructs, which are the products of a representational mode of thinking, which is precisely what she is attempting to overcome. And despite the revolutionary rhetoric, Spivak is unconvincing when she claims to speak for the subaltern woman (Spivak 1985a Spivak 1985b, 120–130) if we take into consideration her middle-class status.

Finally, by using deconstruction for their political purposes, Bhabha and Spivak open themselves to charges of inconsistency by violating the spirit of Derrida's non-method. In the final analysis they travel a path that culminates with a radical scepticism that calls into question those notions deconstructed and their own positions. Thereby, they condemn themselves to the margins of culture.

References

Benavides, Gustavo. 1998. "Modernity." In *Critical Terms for Religious Studies*. Ed. Mark C. Taylor. Chicago: University of Chicago Press, pp. 186–204.

Bhabha, Homi. 2001. "Unsatisfied Notes on Vernacular Cosmopolitanism." In *Postcolonial Discourse: An Anthology*. Ed. Gregory Castle. Oxford: Blackwell, pp. 38–52.

———. 2002. *The Location of Culture*. London: Routledge.

Bilimoria, Purushottama and Dina Al-Kassim (eds). 2014. *Postcolonial Reason and Its Critique: Deliberations on Gayatri Chakravorty Spivak's Thoughts*. New Delhi: Oxford University Press.

Bilimoria, Purushottama and Andrew Irvine (eds.) 2009. *Postcolonial Philosophy of Religion*. Dordrecht and New York: Springer.

Deleuze, Gilles and Félix Guattari. 1988. *A Thousand Plateaus: Capitalism and Schizophrenia*. Trans. Brian Massumi. Minneapolis: University of Minnesota Press.

Deleuze, Gilles and Claire Parnet. 1987. *Dialogues*. Trans. Hugh Tomlinson and Barbara Habberjam. New York: Columbia University Press.

Derrida, Jacques. 1973. *Speech and Phenomena and Other Essays on Husserl's Theory of Signs*. Trans. B. Allison. Evanston, IL: Northwestern University Press.

———. 1976. *Of Grammatology*. Trans. Gayatri Chakravarty Spivak. Baltimore: Johns Hopkins University Press.
———. 1981. *Dissemination*. Trans. Barbara Johnson. Chicago: University of Chicago Press.
———. 1987. *Psyché: Inventions de l'autre*. Paris: Galilée.
Dupré, Louis. 2004. *The Enlightenment and the Intellectual Foundations of Modern Culture*. New Haven, CT: Yale University Press.
Heidegger, Martin. 1959. *Vorträge und Aufsätze*. Tübingen: Verlag Günther Neske Pfullingen.
———. 1963. *Holzwege*. Frankfurt: Vittorio Klostermann.
———. 1969. *Identity and Difference*. Trans. Joan Stambaugh. New York: Harper & Row.
———. 1982. *Nietzsche Volume IV: Nihilism*. Ed. David Farrel Krell and trans. Frank A. Capuzzi. San Francisco: Harper & Row.
Jameson, Fredric. 1991. *Postmodernism, or The Cultural Logic of Late Capitalism*. Durham, NC: Duke University Press.
Kristeva, Julia. 1980a. *Desire in Language: A Semiotic Approach to Literature and Art*. Trans. Thomas Gora, Alice Jardine, and Leon S. Roudiez. New York: Columbia University Press.
———. 1980b. "Postmodernism." *Bucknell Review* 25(11): 136–141.
———. 1982. *Powers of Horror: An Essay on Abjection*. Trans. Leon S. Roudiez. New York: Columbia University Press.
Lyotard, Jean-François. 1991. *The Inhuman: Reflections on Time*. Trans. Geoffrey Bennington and Rachel Bowlby. Cambridge: Polity Press.
Olson, Carl. 1999. "Rationality and Madness: The Postmodern Embrace of Dionysus and the Neo-Vedānta Response of Radhakrishnan." *Asian Philosophy* 9(1): 39–50.
———. 2000. *Zen and the Art of Postmodern Philosophy: Two Paths of Liberation from the Representational mode of Thinking*. Albany: State University of New York Press.
———. 2002. *Indian Philosophers and Postmodern Thinkers: Dialogues on the Margins of Culture*. New Delhi: Oxford University Press.
———. 2013. *The Allure of Decadent Thinking: Religious Studies and the Challenge of Postmodernism*. New York: Oxford University Press.
Rorty, Richard. 1979. *Philosophy and the Mirror of Nature*. Princeton: Princeton University Press.
Schrag, Calvin O. 1992. *The Resources of Rationality: A Response to the Postmodern Challenge*. Bloomington and Indianapolis: Indiana University Press.
Spivak, Gayatri Chakravorty. 1985a. "Can the Subaltern Speak? Speculation on Widow Sacrifice." *Wedge* 7(8): 120–130.
———. 1985b. "The Rani of Sirmur." In *Europe and Its Others*, 2 vols. Ed. Francis Barker *et al*. Colchester: University of Essex, vol. 1, pp. 128–151.
———. 1999. *A Critique of Postcolonial Reason: Toward a History of the Vanishing Present*. Cambridge, MA: Harvard University Press.
Taylor, Mark C. 1984. *Erring: A Postmodern A/theology*. Chicago: University of Chicago Press.

Chapter 58

PHILOSOPHY IN AN AGE OF POSTCOLONIALISM[1]

Joseph Prabhu

The nineteenth century was the great century of imperial power. Britain, France, the Netherlands, Belgium, Spain, Portugal, and Germany occupied or by various means controlled nine-tenths of the earth's surface and a quarter of its total population. For the first time, as Lenin remarked in 1916, "the world is completely divided up so that in future only redivision is possible." The momentous achievement of the twentieth century, however, was to attempt to make colonial rule largely a thing of the past. Starting with Indian independence in 1947, the colonized countries of Asia, Africa, and Latin America, which not accidentally came to be called countries of the so-called Third World, attained their political independence. As Nicholas Dirks says:

> Although that struggle has been successful, it has not only been drenched in violence but it has also led to the general recognition that the effects of imperialism have by no means disappeared with the demise of formal regimes of rule. Colonialism lives on in the massive disparities of wealth and control over capital between north and south, in the contradictory institutional legacies that inhabit political, juridical, educational, and economic systems and in differential manifestations of cultural entitlement and social capacity .... Even as the colonial past was written into every aspect of the early consolidation of Western metropolitan economic and political domination, it continues to be written into the new world order—in subnational ethnic violence, in national debates over immigration and identity, in the postimperial positioning of the United States after the end of the Cold War, in postnational developments around liberalization, globalization, and the late twentieth-century triumph of capitalism.
>
> (Dirks 2001, 303)

The entire world operates within the economic system primarily developed and controlled by the West in terms of political, economic, military, and cultural power that gives colonialism and its aftermath, postcolonialism, their continuing significance. Political liberation did not result in economic liberation and without economic liberation there can be no real political liberation in the full sense of the term for the countries of the Third World.

The term "postcolonialism" has been the subject of protracted debate for some time now. How does it differ in meaning and force from cognate terms like "imperialism," "neocolonialism," or "anti-colonialism?" What does the "post" of postcolonialism really signify? It is not necessary for my purpose to go into the details of these debates given that my interest and the interest of this chapter lie in tracing some of the implications of postcolonialism for philosophy. Postcolonialism is a dialectical concept that marks on the one hand the struggle against colonialism in all its different forms, political, economic, military, and cultural, in the quest for independence and sovereignty, and on the other hand the grim realities of existing in a new imperialistic context of economic and sometimes political domination. Robert Young (2001, 55) makes a useful suggestion when he distinguishes three different moments within this concept. First, the development of a postcolonial culture which radically revised the ethos and ideologies of the colonial state and sought to operate within the vastly transformed historical situation of political independence and autonomy. To cite just one example: there is considerable evidence to show how the British during the colonial period from 1857 to 1947 in India deployed conventional "divide and rule" tactics in playing Christians, Hindus, and Muslims off against each other. Since independence in 1947, Christians, Muslims, and some Hindus have been at pains to show that Islam and Christianity are not religions alien to the Indian ethos. The fact that this quest for a secular pluralism has been fraught with tensions, as demonstrated by the continuing religious conflict between these groups, is testimony to the fact that colonial legacies are not easily overcome. This is not to claim that the tensions between these faiths are entirely due to colonial influences, but there is little doubt that colonialism heightened and exacerbated them.

The second moment, which Young terms "postcoloniality," puts the emphasis on the economic, material, and cultural conditions that constitute the global system in which postcolonial nations are required to operate, one heavily weighted towards the interests of global capitalism and the G-8 powers. Postcoloniality can, however, still register the resistant pressures and agency of the postcolonial world within such conditions. This global system has in fact been dubbed imperial by Michael Hardt and Antonio Negri in their influential book *Empire*. I quote: "Along with the global market and global circuits of production there has emerged a global order, a new logic and structure of rule—in short, a new form of sovereignty. Empire is the sovereign power that governs the world" (Hart and Negri 2000, xi).

Finally, the third moment combines the anti-colonialist revisions of the first moment with the political critique of the conditions of postcoloniality embodied in the second. It attacks the status quo of hegemonic economic imperialism, but also signals an activist engagement with emancipatory political positions and new forms of political identity. In that sense, postcolonialism commemorates not the colonial but the attempted triumph over it. It combines critical history with a theorized account of contemporary culture, seen as a mode of resistance to the different forms in which colonialism may manifest (Young 2001, 57–66; Bilimoria 2012, 97–98).

Seen in this broad amplitude, postcolonialism can be credited with a long history. The founding father of European anti-colonialism was the Catholic bishop Bartolome de Las Casas, who in his book *A Short Account of the Destruction of the Indies* (1542), written only fifty years after Columbus's expedition to the New World, first questioned the moral and legal basis of the Spanish occupation of America. This chapter is focused more narrowly on postcolonial theory. Although the genealogy of postcolonial theory is historically complex and extensive, it was Edward Said's critique in *Orientalism* (1978) of the cultural politics of the production of knowledge about the Orient emanating from sites of colonial power in the West that effectively founded postcolonial studies as an academic discipline. Even though Said himself never claimed to have offered a theory of colonial discourse, confining his attention more narrowly to the phenomenon of Orientalism, it was his analysis of the European texts about the Orient in terms of the Foucauldian notion of "discourse," or an organized body of knowledge, that effectively served as the inauguration of contemporary postcolonial theory (Bilimoria 2012).

Since its putative founding in 1978, postcolonial theory has gone through a long and complex development in the work of such theorists as Homi Bhabha, Gayatri Spivak, Ranajit Guha, and the school of "subaltern studies," Partha Chatterjee, Walter Mignolo, Valentin Mudimbe, Anthony Appiah, and others. Rather than attempting to address their work in detail, which would be impossible in any case in this setting, it seems to me more profitable to assay a general characterization of the field. Postcolonial critique marks the stage where the political and cultural experience of the marginalized peripheries of the world ruled by the West could be developed into a more general theoretical position that could be set against Western political, intellectual, and academic hegemony. Postcolonial theory is designed to undo the ideological heritage of colonialism, not only in the decolonized countries but also in the West. What is attempted is nothing less than a decolonization of the Western mind, a deconstruction of the forms of thought, sensibility, and imagination that led to colonialism in the first place and perpetuate its continuation. This necessarily involves a decentering of the intellectual sovereignty and dominance of and a critique of Eurocentrism, that is, the assumption that the Western point of view is normative and thus is authorized to speak for the rest of the world (Bilimoria and Irvine 2009, 237–294).

To spell out the discursive and rhetorical strategies of colonial discourse in greater detail, I want as an illustrative example to examine some of Hegel's judgments about the non-Western world. This perhaps can best be done in this context by citing some of Hegel's actual comments on India and then providing an exegetical commentary.

Hegel's encounter with India

Perhaps the best way to encapsulate Hegel's critique of the Indian tradition is to provide two references from his work which, I think, give a succinct indication of his views.

> [F]or the most well developed form of Pantheism we may refer to the Indian religion. This full development is characterized by the fact that the absolute substance, the One itself, is conceived of as existing in the form of thought as distinct from the accidental world. This religion accounts for the relation of man and god, and being pantheist it does not isolate the One in pure objectivity which metaphysics … does. It is important to emphasize this peculiar subjectivization of substance. Conscious thought does not simply make this abstraction of substance, it is itself that abstraction, it is that One which exists by and for itself and which is this substance. This thought is known as a force which creates and sustains the world and changes its individual modes of existence. This thought is called 'brahman' and exists as the natural consciousness of the Brahmins and of others who achieve the complete extinction of the manifold contents of consciousness, of all emotions and sensual and intellectual interests and reduce everything to the complete simplicity and emptiness of substantial Oneness. In this way this thought, this abstraction of man in himself is conceived of a great force.
>
> … [T]his force unfolds itself wildly by transforming itself into its opposite. We are faced with uninhibited lunacy where the most ordinary presence is immediately raised to the rank of the divine and the one and only substance is conceived of in a finite form which may dissolve itself as quickly as it has been conceived of.
>
> (Hegel 1988, 270–272)

In this one passage we see the thrust of Hegel's criticisms of Indian philosophical theology.

1 In Hegel's terminology Indian thought remains "substantial" and has not advanced to the crucial stage of "subject," that of self-conscious subjectivity. Rather, there is a "peculiar subjectivization of substance," an abstract combination and mixing up of the two categories, rather than a dialectical mediation. As a result, the proper relation of the Infinite and the finite, God and man, has not been articulated. The Infinite has not posited the finite as its dialectical other, nor does the finite affect and play an essential role in the constitution of the Infinite.
2 Indian pantheism, therefore, is a wild, inherently unstable affair, continually swinging from the monism of the One to the polytheism of the many, from the abstraction of Brahman to the dissipation of this abstraction into its opposite "where the most ordinary presence is immediately raised to the rank of the divine."
3 India, says Hegel (1988, 271–272), is the land of dream and fantasy, and not of reason, incapable of the analytic distinctions and dialectical subtleties which have

been accomplished only by the "hard European intellect." India, for Hegel, exhibited the same tendencies in the spiritual development of mankind as a whole as the mental condition of a man dreaming, just before he awakes.

4 As a result, it is inappropriate here to talk of a rational freedom in history. The practical consequences of this lazy dreaming is the escapism inherent in Indian yogic and religious practice where practitioners "achieve the complete extinction of the manifest contents of consciousness" and take refuge in the "emptiness of substantial Oneness." With reference to political life, Hinduism is irredeemably a religion of unfreedom.

No single institution better typifies for Hegel the general serfdom of the Indian people than caste, whose differentiations are solely natural, based as they are on birth rather than merit or aptitude and hence, in Hegel's terminology, irredeemably "substantial." The special privileges of Brahmins, for example, inevitably produce a theocratic aristocracy, in which principles of purity or hierarchy prevail over other principles of political organization, be they kingship, the State, or constitutional rights. Once again, Hegel makes the point that Hindu social life fluctuates widely between an identity without difference and a difference without an identity.

If we submit these remarks of Hegel to a postcolonial critique there are four interrelated features of Hegel's Orientalist narrative which stand out: (1) Hegel's unquestioned and triumphalistic Eurocentrism; (2) his stance toward otherness and difference; (3) the temporal and spatial distancing of Asian cultures and their consignment to an archaic past; and (4) the particular relation of the knower to the known.

Hegel's Eurocentrism

What is fascinating in as rigorous a thinker as Hegel is to observe the way in which such Eurocentrism is both explained and legitimated. Logical system and historical development are perfectly fused in Hegel's thought. Philosophy, therefore, not only *has* a history, it *is* its own history, so that the sequence of philosophical systems in history mirrors advances in logic. Absolute spirit, both the *telos* and the ground of Hegel's system, is all-comprehending and in the process, self-comprehending, and this consummation is modern Europe's unique achievement (Hegel 1952, 12–13).

Hegel was by no means unique in this Eurocentrism, a posture adopted by most of the thinkers of his time, although he alone provides a logico-historical explanation and justification for such Eurocentrism (Halbfass 1988). That should not be surprising if one considers the balance of economic, political, and cultural power at the time. This Eurocentrism has at least two distinct through related aspects: first, the denial of rationality and self-determination to non-European peoples; and, second, an essentialist idea of human nature and what it means to be human which supports such a denial. The ascription of barbarism and primitiveness to Asian peoples is a form of historical social Darwinism culminating in white, European man, where all three predicates, though not explicitly spelt out, represent quite obviously an equation of *particular* notions of rationality, freedom, and culture with "humanity" and "human nature" as such. In fact, it redounds to Hegel's credit that he even studied India as extensively as he did, although one may validly question the objectivity and open-mindedness with which he conducted such study.

Hegel's stance toward otherness and difference

The irony of such Eurocentrism in Hegel's case is that he is reputed to be a philosopher of difference, whose dialectic is driven by the negativity posed by alterity. As many commentators from Kierkegaard and Adorno to Levinas and Derrida, more recently, have pointed out, however, the other as other with her own agency and self-understanding is not seen in her irreducible exteriority, but rather sublated and reabsorbed within the self-identity of Spirit. Consequently, as Levinas has expressed it succinctly, alterity has no singular *metaphysical* standing outside what is *ontologically* the same, it is simply a "moment" within the logic of "the Same":

> Hegelian phenomenology, whose self-consciousness is the distinguishing of what is not distinct, expresses the universality of the same identifying itself in the alterity of objects thought and despite the opposition of self to self.
>
> (Levinas 1969, 36)

This relentless *Identitaetslogik*, to use Adorno's term, the distinguishing of what is not ontologically really distinct, is clearly displayed in Hegel's treatment of India. On the one hand, from a historical and cultural standpoint, Hegel wants to make the spiritual distancing as great as possible:

> The European who goes from Persia to India observes, therefore, a prodigious contrast. Whereas in the former country he finds himself still somewhat at home … as soon as he crosses the Indus … he encounters the most repellent characteristics pervading every single feature of society.
>
> (Hegel 1956, 173)

On the other hand, however, these threatening differences are not allowed to stand and, from an ontological standpoint, are brought within a unitary and linear, evolutionary history of Absolute Spirit and consigned to a primitive stage of such a history, now altogether surpassed. The primitiveness is conveyed most powerfully by the image of childishness and dreaminess, which images in effect deny his Indian other full selfhood. Nor is much hope provided for change in the future because of the temporal and logical irreversibility of Spirit's march through history.

The temporal and spatial distancing

It is no accident that Hegel conjoins geographical and temporal distancing in his classification of "Hither" and "Farther" Asia. In his phenomenology of world religions (Hegel 1956, 173), Persian and Egyptian religions are placed in the category of

"Transition from Natural to Spiritual" religions, that is, as embodying some aspects of self-conscious subjectivity, whereas the religions of China and India are firmly placed in the category of the "Natural," dominated by notions of "substance" rather than "subject." And with this categorization goes a certain historical revisionism in that the Chinese and Indian civilizations are treated as the oldest ones in order to fit in with his particular narrative of world history (see Bilimoria 2010).

The particular relation of the knower to the known

What I wish to highlight here is what Foucault calls the "episteme," the mode of knowledge and its structuring by power relationships. This is not at all the same thing as the biases that a person or a culture has vis-à-vis another, which from a structural point of view would count as more epiphenomenal. In other words, depth-hermeneutical analysis here acquires a specifically epistemic focus.

Three points may perhaps be made here in summary fashion. First, in terms of social ontology, the relation of knowing subject and known "object" is not an equal or symmetrical one, even though, given that they are both subjects, intersubjective communicative understanding would seem to be normative. Hegel, as we have seen, denies subjectivity to Indians in their "natural vegetative state." The European knower is presented as rational, self-conscious, and objective, while Indians are portrayed as irrational, dreamy, and subjective. It follows, second, that the European's knowledge of Indians is superior to the Indians' own self-knowledge, which, to the extent that they have any, must be inadequate and unscientific because it is irredeemably subjective, immediate, and in so far as it lacks mediating principles, essentially empty or confused. Except for the religious classics that he read in translation, Hegel's reading about India and Indian philosophy in particular was confined solely to the commentaries written by Europeans. He does not seem to have read a single Indian philosopher even in translation. The same is true for Hegel's firsthand knowledge of Indian art, which in his extensive writings about it is confined to two actual instances of art. That did not stop him from waxing eloquent about its many deficiencies as a vehicle of Spirit. Finally, Hegel seriously believed that Indians were incapable of ever acquiring such knowledge for themselves. Rather, his discourse is confident of its power to represent India, to interpret and explain it not only to the West, but to Indians themselves. Hegel would have been in full agreement with Marx's statement expressed in a different context: "They cannot represent themselves; they must be represented" (Said 1978, 21).

Once the absolutistic, monological, and ethnocentric worldviews of Hegel and other orientalists of his ilk are challenged, a space is created for multiple agencies and voices. Pluralism is not, however, sheer plurality, the mere fact of differences and diversity, but rather the problem raised when these different voices debate and contest value judgments, truth-claims, and representations. Who gets to represent whom, under what conditions, and for what purposes? How are such representations structured methodologically, epistemically, and morally? What is the interrelationship between power relations and the production and reception of knowledge? What happens to the problematics of truth and validity, when considerations of power and rhetoric are introduced?

Philosophy in an age of postcolonialism

From a philosophical point of view, perhaps one of the most significant consequences of postcolonial theory is this epistemological awareness of the location from which the world is viewed and knowledge is produced, what Enrique Dussel and Eduardo Mendieta have called the "geopolitics of knowledge" (Dussel 2003).

Enrique Dussel (1996) has deconstructed the concept of "modernity" and shown what a difference such a deconstruction makes to our understanding and perception. He points out that thinkers as different as Charles Taylor, Stephen Toulmin, and Juergen Habermas in their accounts of modernity have presented it as an exclusively European occurrence centering on the key events of the Reformation, the Enlightenment, and the French Revolution, and, in Toulmin's case, the Renaissance. This Eurocentrism is most explicit in Max Weber (Weber 1958, 13) when he introduces the "problem of universal history" with the hypothetical question: To what combination of circumstances should the fact be attributed that in Western civilization, and in Western civilization only, cultural phenomena have appeared which (as we like to think) lie in a line of development having *universal* significance and value? According to this model, Europe had exceptional internal resources that allowed it to supersede through its superior rationality and organizational power all other cultures. What is forgotten in this account is the history of European world conquest and the wealth and power that Europe acquired through such conquests and the misery visited on the native peoples. The solipsism of Descartes' "*ego cogito*" is the mirror image and resonant expression of this inward-looking modern subjectivity, unwilling to acknowledge the oppression it caused to the subjected peoples of the New World (Dussel 1996, 2–80).

To this Eurocentric model of modernity, Dussel counterposes a planetary model, which conceptualizes modernity in global terms and incorporates the parallel histories of the conquered peoples. To quote Dussel:

> European modernity is not an independent, autopoietic, self-referential system, but is instead part of a world system, in fact, its center … the centrality of Europe in the world system is not the sole fruit of an internal superiority accumulated during the European Middle Ages over against other cultures. Instead, it is also the fundamental effect of the simple fact of the discovery, conquest, colonization, and subsumption of Amerindia. This simple fact will give Europe the determining comparative advantage over the Ottoman-Muslim world, India, and China. Modernity is the fruit of these events, not their cause.
>
> (Dussel 2003, 54–55)

That is Dussel's answer to Max Weber, who asks, "Why did not the scientific, the artistic, the political, or the economic development there (that is, in China and India) enter upon that path of rationalization which is peculiar to the Occident?" (Weber 1958, 25).

Postcoloniality, then, signifies those places and histories that resist the universalization of position and perspective, even as they highlight the power of the forces of universalization. In doing so, it complicates the question of universals and what might be regarded as legitimate rather than spurious universals, the representation as universal of what is obviously a quite particular and parochial view. It is not that a postcolonial position repudiates all talk of universality in favor of contextual pluralism, which taken to the extreme would make human communication very difficult if not impossible. It is rather that such universality should be seen as an achievement, attained in the face of contestation, rather than an *a priori* assumption or starting point.

One such site of contestation has been the debate over what counts as 'philosophy'. On the one hand, we have the widely accepted facts that India, China, and Greece are the three birthplaces of philosophy that have given rise to long-standing traditions of the discipline that, with both continuities and discontinuities, have unfolded to the present day. On the other hand, however, one encounters modern Western thinkers from Hegel, who has been discussed in this essay, to Husserl (1970) and Gadamer (1978, 45–53) in more recent times, who, like Hegel, privilege the West alone with having the normative concept of "true philosophy."

Here is Husserl again in a late work, *The Crisis of European Sciences and Transcendental Phenomenology*, written in the period from 1934 to his death in 1938:

> To bring latent reason to the understanding of its own possibilities and thus to bring to insight the possibility of metaphysics as a true possibility—this is the only way to put metaphysics or universal philosophy on the strenuous road to realization. It is the only way to decide whether the *telos* which was inborn in European humanity at the birth of Greek philosophy—that of humanity which seeks to exist, and is only possible, through philosophical reason, moving endlessly from latent to manifest reason and forever seeking its own norms through this, its truth and genuine human nature—whether this *telos*, then, is merely a factual, historical delusion, the accidental acquisition of merely one among many other civilizations and histories, or whether Greek humanity was not rather the first breakthrough to what is essential to humanity as such, its entelechy .... Only then could it be decided whether European humanity bears within itself an absolute idea, rather than being merely an empirical anthropological type like 'China' or 'India'; it could be decided whether the spectacle of the Europeanization of all other civilizations bears witness to that rule of an absolute meaning, one which is proper to the sense ... of the world.
> (Husserl 1970, 15–16)

Marginalization of non-Western philosophy is a feature of the academy in the former colonies, particularly in many Asian and African universities. Prestige in curricula, journals, and research opportunities still attaches to Western philosophy. Thus, in a discipline that is central to the self-understanding and self-respect of a people, one could argue that the postcolonial critique in any of the three senses delineated by Robert Young, as discussed earlier, is slow to emerge. Certainly, one would not be off the mark to suggest that the postcolonial critique in general is far more advanced in disciplines like history, literature, anthropology, or religious studies than it is in philosophy at present. The reasons for the dominance of modern Western philosophy and the marginalization of non-Western philosophy are complex and call for a longer and more nuanced account than is possible in this chapter. The privileging of a highly theoretical and self-reflective concept of reason, and the corresponding neglect not only of other possible notions of reason that serve other interests—practical, ethical, aesthetic, and spiritual—but also of other sources of knowledge like intuition, contemplation, emotion, and feeling has been called into question by both Western and non-Western thinkers, such as Heidegger, Wittgenstein, Rorty, Hilary Putnam, and Charles Taylor and by non-Western philosophers like Enrique Dussel, J. L. Mehta, Raimon Panikkar, and others.

Homi Bhabha says, "Postcolonialism operates through the dimensions of time or history and space, both geographical and the other, third space of cultural reconceptualization to bring about the reordering of social life through forms of knowledge reworked from their entanglement in longstanding, coercive power relations" (Bhabha 1994, 175). I have attempted in this chapter to point to some of these coercive power relations as they have been exercised discursively and epistemically by Hegel and by some thinkers who have followed him.

Note

1 A version of this chapter was published in a special issue on Religion and Postcolonialism, *Australian Religious Studies Review* 25(2) (2012): 123–138. (With permission of Equinox Press.) (See also Bilimoria 2012.)

References

Bhabha, Homi. 1994. *The Location of Culture*. London: Routledge.

Bilimoria, Purushottama. 2009. "What Is the 'Subaltern' of the Philosophy of Religion?" In *Postcolonial Philosophy of Religion*, ed. Purushottama Bilimoria and Andrew Irvine, 9–34. Dordrecht and New York: Springer.

———. 2010. "Hegel's Spectre on Indian Thought and Its God-in-Nothingness." *Religions of South Asia* 4(2): 199–211.

———. 2012. "Editorial Introduction: Religion and Postcolonialism." *Australian Religious Studies Review* 25(2): 97–101.

Dirks, Nicholas. 2001. *Castes of Mind*. Princeton, NJ: Princeton University Press

Dussel, Enrique. 1996. *The Underside of Modernity: Apel, Ricoeur, Rorty, Taylor, and the Philosophy of Liberation*, ed. and trans. E. Mendieta. Atlantic Highlands, NJ: Humanities Press.

———. 2003. *Beyond Philosophy: Ethics, History, Marxism, and Liberation Theology*. New York: Rowman & Littlefield.

Fabian, Johannes. 1983. *Time and the Other: How Anthropology Makes its Object*. New York: Columbia University Press.

Gadamer, Hans-Georg. 1978. "Plato and Heidegger." In *The Question of Being: East–West Perspectives*, ed. Mervyn Sprung, 45–53. University Park, PA and London: Pennsylvania State University Press.

Halbfass, Wilhelm. 1988. *India and Europe: An Essay in Understanding*. Albany, NY: State University of New York Press.
Hardt, Michael, and Antonio Negri. 2000. *Empire*. Cambridge, MA: Harvard University Press.
Hegel, G. W. F. 1952. *Hegel's Philosophy of Right*, trans. T. M. Knox. London: Oxford University Press.
———. 1956. *Philosophy of History*, trans. J. Sibree. New York: Dover Publications.
———. 1988. *Lectures on the Philosophy of Religion*, ed. and trans. Peter Hodgson. Berkeley, CA: University of California Press.
Husserl, Edmund. 1970. *The Crisis of European Sciences and Transcendental Philosophy*, trans. David Carr. Evanston, IL: Northwestern University Press.
Levinas, Emanuel. 1969. *Totality and Infinity: An Essay on Exteriority*, trans. Alphonso Lingis. Pittsburgh: Duquesne University Press.
Marx, Karl. 1965. *Pre-Capitalist Economic Formations*, trans. J. Cohen. New York: International Publishers.
Said, Edward. 1978. *Orientalism*. New York: Random House.
Weber, Max. 1958. *The Protestant Ethic and the Spirit of Capitalism*, trans. Talcott Parsons. New York: Charles Scribner's Sons.
Young, Robert. 2001. *Postcolonialism: An Historical Introduction*. Oxford: Blackwell.

GLOSSARY OF SANSKRIT TERMS

ābhāsavāda (appearance theory)
abhihitānvayavāda ("connection of what has been expressed" theory)
abhilāpa-vāsanā ("the impressions of speech")
abhilāpavāsanābīja ("the seed of the speech impregnation")
abhimāna ("pride" or "self-conception")
abhipraya (intention)
abhiṣeka (initiation phase of the optimal integral process)
abhyāsa (repetition of a statement)
ācāra (customary law/standards of good people)
acintya (inconceivable)
acit (non-conscious)
adarśana (fail to see clearly)
ādhāra (ontic ground)
adharma (demerit)
ādheya (dependent entity)
adhikāra (~~spiritual~~ eligibility, entitlement)
adhikaraṇasiddhānta (When proving one conclusion requires the proving (of) some other conclusion(s), and the original conclusion is the basis of the proof of the other conclusion(s), this is the term used for the original conclusion)
adhyāhāra (method of imagining words in a sentential context in absence of relevant word)
adravya (non-foundational)
adṛṣṭa (unseen force)
adṛṣṭa-niḥśreyasa (transcendental well-being)
adṛṣṭārtha (imperceptible entities or forces)
advaya (non-dual)
adveṣa (benevolence)
aguṇam (devoid of attributes)
ahaṃkāra (I-sense/'self-consciousness')
ahaṃ pratyaya (I-cognition)
ahaṃtā ("I-hood")
ahetutaḥ (causelessly)
aiśvarya ('lordship')
ajātivāda (no origination)
ajīva (non-living forces)
ājñā (between the eyebrows, site of the pineal gland)
ajñāna, mi ses pa (lack of cognition/nescience)[1]

akal-murat (timeless form)
ākāra (appearance/internal form)
ākāśa (ether/space)
ākasmikatāvāda (accidentalism)
akhaṇḍārtha (void of properties)
akhyātivāda (Mīmāṃsā theory of error)
ākhyāyikas (prose compositions)
Akṣaraṃ satyam (imperishable real)
ālambana (cognitive object/existent object/real objects)
ālambana pratyaya (objective condition)
Alaṃkāraśāstra (discipline of poetics/science of rhetoric applied to Sanskrit poetry)
ālayavijñāna ('store-house' consciousness/subliminal awareness/subliminal processes/ theory of store-consciousness)
āloka-jñāna (four lucid intuitions)
amitra (enemy)
amṛta ('not dying')
anabhilāpya (ineffable nature)
anādi-avidyā (beginningless global misconception)
anāhatadhvani (primeval sound)
anāhatam (heart)
ānanda (four euphoric states or blisses)
anavasthā (infinite regress)
aneka-dharma-upapatti (recognition of properties not common)
anekānta (literally 'non-one-sided')
anekānta-tva (non-one-sidedness of truth)
anekāntavāda (Jaina doctrine of the complexity of reality/theory of manifoldness)
anirvacanīya (that which cannot be spoken about/indescribable/indeterminable)
anityā (impermanence/non-eternal)
antar-bahar (existing within and without)
antaryāmin (inner moral guide)
anubhandha-s (four factors motivating study)
anubhava (a bare experience/experience)
anukampā (sympathy)
anumāna (rational inference)
anumanavijñānena / *anumiti* (inferential cognition[2])
anupalabdhi-avyavathātaḥ (irregularity of non-perception)
anupasaṃhārī-vyabhicāra (unsupported deviation fallacy)
anuprāsa (alliteration)
anutpattikadharmakṣānti ("certitude that dharmas are not produced")
anuttara (indeterminate awareness)
anuttara-yogatantra (optimal integral process)
anuvrata (twelve lesser Jaina vows)
anuvrats (systematic reckoning with one's conscience)
anuvṛtti (recurrence)

anvaya-vyatirekī (agreement in presence and absence)
anvayī (agreement in presence)
anvitābhidhānavāda ("expression through what has been connected" theory)
anyathā-siddha ('irrelevant')
anyonyābhāva (reciprocal negation)
anyonyāśraya (mutual dependence)
ap (water)
apahnuti (concealment)
apara (limited/narrow/narrowest universal)
apara sāmānya (limited class character)
aparatva (posteriority/proximity)
aparigraha (nonpossession vow)
aparokṣānubhūti
apauruṣeya ('beyond human/'non-human')
apauruṣeyatva ("authorlessness"/"authorless revelation")
apoha (logic of exclusion)
apramā (erroneous awareness/improper cognition)
āpta (an 'authority' on a subject)
Āptamīmāṃsā ('An Examination of the Authoritative Teacher')
apūrṇakhyāti ("incomplete knowledge")
apūrva (non-preceded)
arāga (non-attachment)
arahant (One who achieves *nirvāṇa*)
archē (ultimate principle of things)
artha (perceptible object/success/economic well-being and effort/wealth)
arthakriyā (practical values)
arthakriyāsāmarthya (causal efficacy)
arthālaṃkāra (figures of speech that pertain to meaning)
arthavāda (explication)
arthavyakti (clarity, directness)
ārya-aṣṭāṅga-mārga (eightfold noble path)
āryajñāna (two holy intuitions)
āryasatya (noble truths)
asādhāraṇa-vyabhicāra (uncommon deviation fallacy)
aśakti (incapacity)
asamavāyī-kāraṇa (similar-to-inherent cause)
asamprajñāta sāmadhi (deeper form of absorption)
asaṃskṛta (unconditioned)
āsana (yoga posture)
asañcetitā avasthā ('unaware' state)
asat ('unreal')
asatkārya samantara ("a-causal succession")
āsatti (continguity)
asiddha (unestablished fallacy)

asmitārūpa (absorption in sense of I-ness or awareness concerning self-knowledge faculty)
asmīti ("I am"/"I-am-ness")
āsrava (influx of karma adhering to the life force)
aśraya (locus/ontological basis)
āśrayāsiddha (unestablished locus fallacy)
aṣṭāṅga-śīla (Eight Precepts)
aṣṭāṅga-yoga ('eight-limbed' path)
asteya (vow not to steal/vow not to avoid taxes)
āstika ('orthodox')
asvabhāva ("no own-being")
atīndriya (super-sensuous nature)
ātman (sense of self/self/soul/one's true self)
atthitā (permanently existing soul)
atyantābhāva (absolute negation)
autpattika ('natural'/"non-derived"/"uncreated")
avacchedavāda (limitation theory)
avadhūti (central channel)
āvaraṇaśakti (power of concealing)
avasarpiṇī ('regressive' time-cycle)
avasthā (state)
avayava-avayavī (parts and the whole)
avibhāga ('non-separate')
avyabhicārī (non-erroneous or non-deviating)
avyākatā (coherent doctrine/'unanswerable')
avyakta (unmanifest ground)
avyapadeśyam (non-conceptual or non-verbal perceptions)
āyatana (sense-spheres)

bādha (absence of the probandum in the locus fallacy)
bādhārahitatva ('absence of falsification')
bandha (bondage of the soul by karma)
bandhu (connection)
bhagati (love)
bhāgvan (The Lord)
bhajāna-loka ('shared world')
bhakti (devotionalism/enthusiastic devotion)
bhandana-mokṣa (process of bondage and release)
bhāratī (articulate poetic style)
bhāṣya (basic commentary)
bhāva (material and physical aspects of things)
bhāvanā ('the causing to be'/conditioning)
bhavaṅga-citta (inactive states of mind during the break of two awarenesses)
bhāvas (personal dispositions or character traits)

bhaya (fear)
bhāyanaka (terrifying)
bheda (difference/separateness)
bhoga (embodied enjoyment)
bhrama (misleading)
bhūta (matter/ultimately real elements)
bhūtacaitanya (awareness of the body)
bhūtacatuṣṭaya (four matters)
bhūtānugraha (human beings)
bībhatsa (repulsive)
bīja (botanical seed/psychic seeds)
bīja-mantra (poetic seeds)
bodhi-pākṣika (thirty-seven wings of awakening)
bodhisattva ("one destined for awakening")
brānti (cognitive error)
bubhutsā (this desire to know)
buddha-vacana (word of the Buddha)
buddhi (discernment[3]/intentional consciousness/material intellect)
buddhīndriyas (the 'doors' through which sensory modes enter conscious experience)
buddhinirmāṇa (imagination)

caitanya (prelinguistic consciousness)
caitanya ātma (consciousness)
cakras (the energetic stations in the body/spiritual centers of the person)
candalī (psychic heat/rush of inspiration)
cārya-tantra (performance process)
catuṣkoṭi (early Buddhist analytical tool/four-cornered negation)
cetasika (mental concomitants)
chakras (complexes)
chala (quibble)
chauta-pad (Fourth-State)
cid (pure awareness)
cit (consciousness)
citta (mental capacity/reflection)
citta-gocara (cognitive)
citta-vīthi ("consciousness series")
cittavṛtti (movements of the mind)
cittavṛttinirodha (cessation of the changes of the awareness)

darabar/daragah (God's Court)
darśana-bhāga ('seeing-part')
darshan (God's vision)
Daśabhūmika-sūtra (*Sūtra on the Ten Grounds*)

daśa-kuśala-karmapatha (Ten Good Paths of Action)
daśa-śīla (Ten Precepts)
dat (gift)
datar (giver)
dehasya nāśo muktiḥ (destruction of the body)
de lasgzan du na[4] (differentiating factors)
deva (deity)
devatā (deities/divine archetypes/effervescent celestial beings)
dhamma (Buddha's discourses)
dharmabhāṇaka ("dharma preachers")
dharmakāya (ultimate Dharma-body)
dharmi-indriya-sannikarṣa (contact of the sense-organ with the possessor of property)
dharmi-jñāna (cognition of the possessor of the properties)
dharmins (property-possessors/substrata)
dhvani (literary suggestion/"suggestion")
dhyāna (insight)
dhyānam (meditative state)
dik (direction)
dīkṣā (rite of formal initiation)
dolotsava (festival of color)
dravyakāla (substantial time)
dravyatva (substancehood)
dṛṣṭi (scholastic views)
duḥkha (dissatisfaction or distress/pain)
dukkha ("unsatisfactory"/"unsatisfactoriness")[5]
durācāra (regionally specific practices)
dvādasanidāna (twelvefold formula)
dveṣa (aversion/hatred)

ekadravyam (inhering in one substance)
ek-anek (One and Many)
eko soi (One Supreme Being)
eukolia (contentedness)

gamana (going or moving in general)
gaudīya (literary variety)
grāhaka (grasping subject)
grāhya (grasped object)
guhya (secret initiation into Vajrayāna Buddhism)
guhyā ādeśā ('hidden instruction')
guṇa-guṇī (properties and the substance)
guṇatva (attributeness)
gurmukh (Guru-centeredness)

gur-shabad (Guru's Word)
guru-devatā (heroic role-model or mentor-archetype)
gurutva (weight)

hāsa (mirth)
hāsya (comical)
haumai (ego)
hetu (probans/reason/reason for a proposition/reasoning power)
hetujāla (network of causation)
hetu pratyaya (causal condition)
hetutāvacchedaka (limitor of the property of being the probans)
hetutva (causal dependence)
hetuyāna (causal vehicle)
hetvābhāsa (defective probans/pseudo-problems/pseudo reason)
hetvasiddha (unestablished probans fallacy)
heya (discarded)
hukam (God's Way/Will/His Infinite Will)

icchā (desire[6])
indriyādi (that which is given by the senses, etc.)
indriyārtha (objects of sensation)
indriyas (sense capacities/sense organs)
iṣṭa-devatā (patron deity)
Īśvara (divine teacher/god/lord)

jala (water)
jalatva (wateriness)
jalpa (type of debate where defeating the other party is the aim)
jāti (universal) 95
jātikṛtaṃ viśeṣaṃ (generic distinguishing property)
jātī-vyakti (universal and the individual)
jātīyatva (generic feature)
jīva (essential part of a living entity that survives death/life forces/soul)
jīvātman (individual self)
jñāna/grahaṇa (the cognition itself)
jñāna kānda (knowledge portion)
jñānaṃ bandhaḥ (ontological bondage)
jñāna-mūdra (imaginary or ideal partner)
jñānatva (the property of 'knowingness')
jña, puruṣa (the knower itself)
jñātṛ (subject of cognitions)
jñātṛ/grāhaka (agent of a cognition)
jñeyāvaraṇa (perfect objectivity or omniscience)
jugupsā (repulsion)

kacha (unripe)
kaiśikī (expressive poetic style)
kalivarjya (our degenerate age)
kalpa (cosmic epoch/endless cosmic cycles of creation and destruction)
kalpanā (mental constructions)
kalpanāpodhaṃ (devoid of conceptual construction)
kalpita (imagined)
kalpitārtha ('Imaginary phenomenon')
kāma (desire[7]/happiness/pleasure/sexual desire)
kānti (illumination[8])
karam (action)
kāritra (innovative efficiency theory)
karma kāṇḍa ('early' portions of Vedic texts)
karma-kleśa (obsession-driven action)
karma-mūdra (real human or evolutionary partner)
karman (action)
karma-svabhāvata (acts autonomous of karma)
karmopacaya (accumulated karmic potential)
kartṛ (agent of physical actions)
karuṇā (compassion)
kārya (one's duty)
kāryaikya (causal condition)
kathā (type of debate/stories)
kāyasampat (perfection of the body)
kevala (liberation/freedom)
kevalajñāna (omniscient knowledge)
khaṇa (crucial moment)
khyad par, viśeṣa (particular attributes or peculiarities)
kleśa[9] (afflictions/afflictive actions/state of affliction/negative dispositions)
kleśāvaraṇa (blocks to liberation)
kliṣṭa-manas (subliminal self-centeredness/subliminal self-grasping)
koṭidvaya (cognition touching two alternatives)
kratu (energy)
kriyā (action)
kriyā-kriyāvān (activity and the substance)
krīya-tantra (action process)
krodha (anger)
krtaḥ sargaḥ (doctrine of 'creative emergence')
kṛtya-anuṣṭhāna-jñāna (All-Accomplishing Wisdom)
kṣaṇa (the moment)
kṣaṇikatva ("momentariness")
kṣiti (earth[10])
kuladarma (*dharma* of families)
kumbaka (abdominal breath-holding art)

lakṣaṇā (secondary signification)
līlā (own delight)
loka (common sense/the 'world'/world of human beings)
lokaprasiddha (common sense)
lokasaṃvṛiti ('worldly conventions')
lokavidviṣṭa (locally despised practices)
lokavyvahāra (incontrovertible linguistic convention)
loke (desirable pursuit)

mādana mahotsava (festival of sex)
mādhurya (sweetness)
madhya (middle realm of existence)
madhyamā (the middle aspect of Word/where words begin to form mentally)
madhyama pratipad (path of moderation)
madhyastha (mediator)
mahābhūtas (the causes of the gross material world)
mahādarśana-jñāna (Mirror-Like Wisdom)
mahāmūdra (universal partner)
mahavākyas ("great sayings" of the Upaniṣads)
mahāvrata (five greater Jaina vows)
maitrī (loving-kindness)
manana (rational defense of the truths in the *Upaniṣads*)
manas (mental sense organ/mind)
maṇipūrakam (navel)
manmukh (ego-centeredness)
mano-vijñāna (mental cognitive awareness)
mantra-kāya (poetic body)
marga (Sikh Way)
māyā (illusion/illusory power)
māyādeha (virtual body)
mi ses pa, ajñāna (lack of cognition)[11]
mithyāsaṃvṛtisatya (*Unreal* conventional truths)
moha (delusion[12])
mokṣa (enlightenment)
muditā (sympathetic joy)
mūdra (enlightening activities or gestures)
mūlata ('basal'realm of existence)

nādavidyā/nādayoga ("vehicle of inner illumination and medium of aesthetic enjoyment")
nāḍī (channels)
naimittika dravatva (instrumental liquidity)
nairātmya (lack of essence)
nam-marga (Way of Name)

nāstika (heterodox / unorthodox)
na-svataḥ (produced from self)
natthitā (complete non-existence)
nāṭya (dramas)
Nāṭya Śāstra (dramaturgical science)
naya (partial character of understanding)
nayana (imaginative conversion)
nayavāda (Jaina doctrine of perspectives)
neti neti ("not this, not that"/Upaniṣadic *via negativa*)
neyārtha ("interpretable meaning"/interpretation)
nibandha (digests/subcommentarial additions)
nididhyāsana (meditation on the truths in the *Upaniṣads*)
nigamana (conclusion)
nigraha (defeat)
nihśreyasādhigamaḥ (transcendental)
niḥsvabhāva (emptiness of intrinsic nature)
niḥsvabhāvatā (independent substantial self-nature)
niḥsvabhāvataḥ (intrinsically unreal)
nimitta (sign)
nimitta-bhāga ('seen-part')
nimitta-kāraṇas (instrumental causal conditions)
nirākāra (formless/without form)
niravayava (a thing that is free from parts)
nirgrantha (monk)
nirguṇatvam (devoid of attributes)
nirīśvara ('without lord')
nirjarā (sloughing off karma)
nirmāṇacitta (created mind)
nirmocana (explicating)
nirvāhakaikya (common goal)
nirvikalpa (non-classificatory perception)
nirvikalpa-jñāna (non-discriminative wisdom)
nirvikalpaka (non-conceptual/unconceptualized)
nirviṣaya (without qualities)
nirviśeṣa-cinmātra (contentless awareness/undifferentiated pure consciousness)
niścaya (certitude)
niścayanaya ('ultimate' or 'certain perspective')
niṣkriyatvam (activities)
niṣpanna-krama (perfection stage)
nityā (eternal/fixed)
nivṛtti (detached from the world/renunciate disposition/withdrawal)
ṅiyāmaka (regulative preceding conditions)
nopapadyate (inconceivable)
nyāyābhāsas (invalid inferences)

ojas (force)
Oṃ (essence of essences, source of the Vedas/primordial sound origin of the universe)
ota prota (material instantiation)

padaccheda (splitting up euphonic textual combination and identifying the individual words)
padārtha-s (categorial features)
padārthokti (stating the meanings of the isolated terms identified by the first step)
pakka (ripe)
pakṣa (locus of inference/thesis)
pakṣatā (a special relational property of the locus)
pañca skandha (five aggregates)
pāpa (bad karma/inauspicious forms of karma)
para (wide/widest universal)
parabhāva (extrinsic-causation)
para guhya ('supreme secret')
parāmarśa (operation)
paramarṣi (prime seer/realized one)
paramārtha (highest perspective)
paramārtha satya (the highest truth/ultimate truth)
paramārthika avasthā (ultimate standpoint)
parārthānumāna ("inference for the sake of others")
parataḥ (truth is dependent on extraneous conditions)
parataḥ-prāmāṇya (extrinsic validity)
paratantra ("other-determined")
paratantra-svabhāva (dependent nature)
parāvāk (Supreme Speech), of Śiva
pare'kṣara ātmani ('the highest, undecaying self')
pāribhāṣikadharma (technical *dharmas*)
parikalpita ("conceptually imagined")
parikalpita-svabhāva (imagined nature)
parimāṇa (extension/magnitude)
pariṇāma (emanation/transformation)
pariniṣpannā-svabhāva (perfected nature)
parivrājakas (wandering teachers[13])
parivṛtti (exchange)
parokṣa ("mysterious")
parokṣa (indirect knowledge)
paśyantī (first stir of an idea in the mind/the seeing aspect of Word)
paṭiccasamuppāda (dependent co-arising)
phala ('fruit')
phalayāna (fruitional or effectual vehicle)
polis (ethos)

prabhāsvara-jñāna (realization of the perfect clarity or lucidity of the clear light intuition)
pradhāna (primal matter)
pradhvaṃsābhāva (consequent negation)
prāgabhāva (antecedent negation)
prajñā (conscious mode of being/dreamless sleep/supreme yogic insight/wisdom of the Buddha)
prajñā-jñāna (intuitive-wisdom initiation into Vajrayana Buddhism)
prajñapti (designations/"language construction")
prajñaptir-upadāya (dependent designations)
prajñapti-sat (conventional designations)
prakāra (dependent mode)
prakaraṇa (monographs)
pramā (knowledge/valid cognition)
pramāṇa-śāstra (closest equivalent of 'epistemology')
pramānasāstram (science of correct cognition)
prāmāṇya-saṃśaya (doubt of validity)
pramathā (subjective knowledge)
prameya-s (provable entities)
prāṇa (life force/vital energy)
prāṇava (spontaneous primordial "unstruck" sound)
prāṇa vāyu (vital air)
prāṇāyāma (breath control/moment of stillness within the movements of inhalation and exhalation)
prapañca (conceptual fabrications)
prapañca-sadbhāva (cosmos)
prapañca-śūnyatā (hypostatizing mental proliferation)
prasāda (lucidity)
prasāraṇa (expansion)
prasiddha (common-sense convention)
pratibhāsa (limited representation)
pratibhāsa-jñāna (release of desire-oriented instincts by luminence intuition)
pratibimba (reflection)
pratibimbavāda (reflection theory)
pratijñā (proposition/thesis)
pratipakṣa (anti-thesis)
pratisandhāna ('co-relation')
pratitantrasiddhānta (acceptance in a specific system only)
pratītyasamutpāda (dependent arising/dependent origination)
prativādī (counter-defender)
pratyakṣa (direct perception/sensory perception)
pratyavabhāsa (clear representation)
pratyavekṣaṇā-jñāna (Discerning Wisdom)
pratyaya-sarga (emergence of representations)

pravṛtti (poetic regionalities)
pravṛtti-sāmarthya (conduciveness to the successful inclination)
pravṛtti-vijñāna (manifest cognitive awareness)
prayatna (effort/will)
prayojana (purpose; treatises?)
pṛṣṭhalabdha-jñāna (pragmatic, subsequently attained wisdoms)
pṛthivī/pṛthvī (the earth element)
pṛthvītva (earthiness)
pudgala (person)
pudgalavāda (Personalist Buddhism)
puṇya (auspicious forms of karma/good karma/'merit')
pūrṇatva ("completeness" or "perfection")

rāga (desire[14]/greed)
rāga-dharma (sublimation practice)
rajas (energy/quality of motility and expansion/radiance)
rasadhvani (aesthetic savor)
rati[15] (desire)
rāudra (ferocious)
ṛta (natural order)
rūpa (colour)
rūpaka (metaphor/superimposition)

śabda (sound/Word)
śabdabhāvanā (language impression)
śabdabhāvanā-bīja (the language impression stored as the cause of recollection)
śabdālaṃkāra (figures of speech pertaining to sound)
śabdarāśibhairava (the body of the God consisting of letters)
śabdatva (soundness)
sadācāra ("practices of the good")
saddharma (true teaching)
sādhāraṇa ("shared aspect")
sadharana-mana (pride of ordinariness)
sādhāraṇa-vyabhicāra (common deviation fallacy)
sādhāraṇa-vyabhicārī-hetu (common deviating probans fallacy)
sādharmya (similarities)
sādhya (probandum)
sādhyāsiddha (unestablished probandum fallacy)
sahasrāra (at the top of the head)
sākṣin (witness consciousness)
śaktijāla (network of personified powers)
śaktiman (the "possessor" of Śakti)
śaktipāta (divine initiation)
śaktis (capacities/aggregate of powers)

śakti-viśeṣa ("special power")
śaktyāviṣkaraṇa ("revealing of Śakti")
sāmānyalakṣaṇa (general features/universals)
sāmarthya (desired goal / purpose)
sāmarthya-viśeṣa (special power)
samatā (evenness)
samatā-jñāna (Wisdom of Perfect Equality)
samavāyī-kāraṇa (inherent cause)
samaya (opportune time for occurrence)
sambandha (relation between the text and its subject-matter)
saṃbhoga-kāya, nirmāṇa-kāya (conventional Appearance and Visionary bodies)
saṃdhāna (perceptions)
saṃdhi (implicit intent)
saṃghāta (aggregation)
saṃgraha (surveys)
saṃharaṇa (contraction[16])
saṃjñā (recognition)
sammādiṭṭhi (right view)
saṃsāra (cycle of rebirth/reincarnation)
saṃsarga (relations)
saṃśaya (doubt)
samśayavāda (theory of skepticism)
saṃśaya-viparyaya-rāhitya (capacity of being devoid of doubt and error)
sāṃsiddhika dravatva (natural liquidity)
saṃskāra (impression/impulses)
saṃskāravaśāt ('momentum of impressions')
saṃskṛta-dharma (accommodating an element of duration within a moment)
saṃtāna (states of consciousness in a phenomenal stream)
saṃvara-śīla ('Moral Discipline')
saṃvṛti ("conventionality")
samvṛtti satya (conventional truth/empirical truth)
saṃyoga (conjunction)
sangha (monastic community)
sangha (Buddhist monastic order/monastic community)
sañjñā (ideation)
saṅkalpa (intentional focus)
saṅkhyā (number)
śānta (tranquil)
śānta rasa (mood of peace)
sant-sipahi (warrior-saint)
saptabhaṅginaya (sevenfold perspective)
sargun-nirgun (All-Forms and Formless)
śarīra-śarīrī-bhāva (the cosmos of souls and matter is the body of God)
sarvathā nityatve (completely permanent)

śāstras (sciences/systematic manuals)
śāśvata (continuity)
śāśvatavāda ("eternalism")
sat (original being)
satkāryavāda ('doctrine of pre-existent effect'/theory of causation)
satkāyadṛṣṭi (self-view/"view of self-existence")
sat-khyāti (the real)
satpratipakṣa (existence of counter-thesis fallacy)
sattā (supreme universal)
sattā sāmānya (oneness of being)
sattva (existence/purity/quality of being able to manifest)
sattva-artha-kriyā-śīla ('Altruistic Conduct')
sāttvatī (physical poetic style)
sāttvika (lucid)
satya (holding to truth/not to tell lies/realities/truth)
satya-saṃkalpa (ever-actualised)
savikalpaka (conceptual/conceptualized)
savikalpaka-pratyakṣa (conceptual perception)
śeṣa (ancillary)
seśvara ('with lord')
shing rta ("openers of the chariot ways")
siddhānta (therapeutic philosophy)
siddhi (excellence/proofs)
śīla (morality)
śiṣṭa (morally disciplined and academically educated man)
skandhas (constituents/five ever-changing aggregates of physical and non-physical aspects)
śleṣa (phonetic cohesion)
smārta (mainstream orthodox)
smṛti ("what is remembered")
smṛty-upasthāna (four stations of mindfulness)
sneha (viscidity/love/care)
śoka (grief)
sopādhi (conditioned[17])
spanda (cosmic pulsation/primordial vibration)
sparśa (touch)
śramaṇas (wandering teachers[18])
śrāvaka ("hearer")
śravaṇa (the hearing of the truths in the *Upaniṣads*)
śṛṅgāra (erotic)
śruti ("what is heard")
sthāyibhāva ('standing' emotions)
sthitisthāpaka saṃskāra (elasticity)
strīdhana ("women's property")

śuddhi (symbolic-ritual purity)
sukha (pleasure)
sukha-prāptiḥ (pleasure)
sukha-śūnya (bliss-void)
sukṣma-rūpa (subtle matter)
sukumāratā (tenderness)
summum bonum (highest good)
sunn-samadh (Void consciousness)
śūnya (empty/voids)
śūnyatā (doctrine of emptiness)
svabhāva (autonomous substantiality/ possessing essence/ /"own being"/"self-causation")
svabhāvatā (intrinsic/intrinsic nature)
svabhāvatva (intrinsic)
svabhāvokti (verisimilitude)
svalakṣaṇa (discrete perceptual data/unique particulars)
svalakṣaṇa-dhāraṇa ("carry their own mark")
svalakṣaṇas (objects of perception)
svaprakāśa (self-illuminating)
svaprakāśatva (self-luminosity)
svapuruṣadarśana (ultimate liberating state of self-knowledge)
svara (recognizable sound in the musical scale)
svarga kāmo yajeta ('the one who desires heaven must sacrifice')
svarūpa (fundamental form)
svarūpadarśana (embodied approach to self-awareness)
svarūpa-nirūpaṇa-dharma (essential property)
svarūpāsiddha (unestablished in the locus fallacy)
svasaṃvedana (Yogācāra Buddhist notion of self-consciousness)
svataḥ (truth is apprehended intrinsically)
svataḥ-prāmāṇya (intrinsic validity)
svatantra ("self-determined")
svātmopabhoga ("self-enjoyment")
svatovyāṛtta (self-differentiating)
svayaṃprakāśatva (luminous essence)
swaraj (freedom)
syādvāda (Jaina doctrine of conditional predication)
syāt (perspective) 391

tādṛk sahakāritva (co-functioning of particular states)
taijasa (dreaming sleep/the 'shining'/'shining' mode of being)
taijasa indriya (fiery object/fiery sense organ)
taijasa śarīra (fiery body)
tamas (inertia/opacity/quality of restriction and stability)
tāmasa (dull)
tanmātras (five modes of sensory content)

tarka (hypothetical argument/reductio ad absurdum)
tarka-apratiṣṭhānāt ("established [from] reasoning")
tathāgata (enlightened existence)
tathāgata-garbha (intrinsically pure awakened mind)
tathatā ("suchness")
tātparya (import)
tattva-abhyāsa ('the practice of that-ness')
tattvajaya (conquest of the ontological levels)
tattvajñāna (actual nature/right cognition)
"*tattvamasi*" (the import of the sentence)
tattvas (principles)
tejas (fire/light)
tejastva (fieriness)
telos (goal)

turīya (state of being beyond all mundane states of consciousness)
ucchedavāda ("annihilationism")
udāratvam (nobility)
upādāna-kāraṇa (material or substrative cause)
upadhis (limiting conditions)
upalabdhi (subjective apprehension)
upamā (simile)
upamāna ('analogy')
upanaya (application of the reason)
upanaya-vākya (application)
upekṣā (equanimity)
upeya (goal)
ūrdhva (upper realm of existence)
uṣṇa sparśa (fire heat/hot touch)
utkṣepaṇa (throwing upwards)
utpatti ('origin')
utpatti-krama (creation stage of the optimal integral process)
utsāha (perseverance)
utsarpiṇī ('progressive' time-cycle)

vaidarbha (literature variety/preferred)
vaijātya (heterogeneity)
vaikharī (the manifest aspect of Word/tangible level of speech)
vairāgya (power of detachment)
vaitathya (false)
vakrokti ("indirect (crooked) language")
vāmācāra ("left-handed practice")
vārttika (critical annotations/main subcommentary)
vāsanā (chemical perfume)

vastu ("thing")
vastu-mātra ("mere thing")
vāyavya indriya (airy sense organ)
vāyavya śarīra (airy body)
vāyavya viṣaya (airy objects)
vāyu (air)
vedanā (feelings)
vibhāga (disjunction)
vibhaṇga (classification)
vibhāva (emotional determinants)
vibhu (pervasive)
vicāra (absorption in the rational awareness concerning the subtle elements)
vidhi ("injunctions")
'*vidyācaraṇa*' (knowledge of *Veda*-s and good conduct)
vidyaivājñānahanāya (destruction of ignorance)
vijñāna (cognitive awareness)
vikalpa (concept//falsifications/idea/thought)
vikṣepaśakti (power of projecting)
vimarśa ("active self-awareness"/reflexive awareness/wavering judgment)
vipāka ('maturation')
viparyāsa (erroneous cognition)
viparyaya (delusion)
vipaśyana (transcendent insight)
vipratipatti (parties to a debate may have false awareness or ignorance regarding things that are the objects of debate or regarding the rules of argumentation)
vīra (steadfast)
viruddha ("contradicted"/opposed fallacy)
viruddhārthapratipādaka (deviant sentence expressing contrary meaning of another sentence)
visarpaṇa (expansion)
viṣayatā (relation of a cognition to its object)
viśeṣa-nityadravya (particularity and the eternal substances)
viśeṣatva (particularityness)
viśeṣokti (cause without effect)
vismaya (amazement)
viśuddha (throat)
viśva (universal mode of being/waking consciousness)
vitaṇḍā (type of debate where one party refutes the thesis of the other party, but never defends any thesis of its own)
vitarka (absorption in the awareness concerning the empirical objects)
vivarta (unreal manifestation)
viyoga (disconnected)
vohāra-mattako (conventional)
vṛddhiprāpta-jñāna (release of anger-oriented instincts by radiance intuition)

vyabhicāra (deviation fallacy)
vyabhicāribhāva (transitory emotions)
vyāghāta (contradictory/self-contradiction)
vyakta (manifest phenomena)
vyaktāvyaktajñavijñāna ("knowledge of the manifest, unmanifest, and the knower")
vyaṅgyārtha (suggested meaning)
vyāpaka-saṃśaya (doubt of the pervaded)
vyāpāra (operation)
vyāpti (general principle/invariable concomitance/rule)
vyāptijñāna (the cognition of invariable concomitance of the probans with the probandum)
vyāpya-saṃśaya (doubt of the pervaded)
vyāpyatvāsiddha (unestablished property of being the pervaded fallacy)
vyatirekī ('agreement in absence')
vyavahāra (everyday business/everyday usage)
vyavahāranaya ('mundane perspective')
vyavahāra-satya (conventional truth)
vyāvahārika avastha (relative standpoint)
vyavasāyātmaka (certain/well-ascertained/free from doubt/conceptual or determinate perceptions)
vyavasthā (law of individual retribution)
vyavasthita (distinguished)

yādṛacchikavāda (accidentalism)
yajamāna (body of the sponsor of the ritual)
yajña (sacrifice)
yathā-bhūtam ('truly are')
yathādarśana (appearance)
yathāprasiddha (common-sense agreement)
yathārtha (in accordance with the purpose that motivated)
yathārthya (such-as it actually is)
yoga-tantra (integral process)
yogyatā (semantic competence)
yukta-pramāṇa (synthetic inductive reasoning)

zāhir (outward) form of scripture

Notes

1 The first part of this entry is Sanskrit and the second part is Tibetan.
2 There are references to *anumanavijñānena*, to *anumiti*, and to inferential cognition with no Sanskrit term.
3 The Sanskrit term *viveka* is also referred to as discernment.
4 This is a Tibetan phrase.

5 This is a *Pāli* term.
6 The terms "*kāma*", "*prāthanā*", "*rāga*", and "*rati*" are also used for desire.
7 The Sanskrit terms "*icchā*", "*prāthanā*", "*rāga*" and "*rati*"are also referred to as meaning desire.
8 The Sanskrit term "*vidyā*" is also said to mean illumination.
9 Known in the West as 'vices' (page 508).
10 In addition to *kṣiti*, earth is also known as *pṛthivī* or *pṛthvī*.
11 The first part of this entry is Tibetan and the second is Sanskrit.
12 The Sanskrit term *viparyaya* is also referred to as delusion.
13 Also known as "*śramaṇas*".
14 The terms "*icchā*", "*kāma*", "*prāthanā*", and "*rati*" are also used for desire.
15 The terms "*icchā*", "*kāma*", "*prāthanā*", and "*rāga*" are also used for desire.
16 The Vaiśeṣikas use the term "*ākuñcana*" for contraction.
17 The term "*syād*" also means conditioned.
18 Also known as "*parivrājakas*".

INDEX

Bold = tables
Italics = figures
n = notes

abhāva (negation), in Vaiśeṣika 172–173
abhidharma 41, 56, 285–286, 287–289, 302–309; chronology 303; collections 304; definition of 302–303; ontological innovations 306–309; Sarvāstivāda 305–306; status of 304; Theravāda 304–305
Abhinavagupta 437–443; on aesthetics 441; evolutionary panentheism 442; philosophical writings 439, 441–443, 453–445; tantric writings 440–441
Abrahamic religions 373, 376, 399, 498, 570
academic philosophy 9, 529, 533; Sanskritic traditions 409–410
Acarya Tulsi 404–405
accidentalism (*yādṛacchikavāda*) 102
action syntax, theory of 413
activity (*karma*), in Vaiśeṣika 166–167
Adamantine Chariot, the Lord of the 268–270
Advaita (non-dualism) 7, 63; clarification methods 247–248, two schools 246–247
Advaita Extended Mind thesis 37n1
Advaita Vedānta 82–83; 233–240; *avidyā* (ignorance) problem 242–249; Bhāmatī 246–247; philosophical context of 234–236; Vivaran 246–247
Advaitic monism 253, 260
aesthetic savor (*rasa*) 456, 461, 462, 464–465
agency 66, 208–211, 256; cultural agency 360, 361; divine agency 53, 416; moral agency 406; spiritual agency 365, 368; universal syntactic agency, theory of 413
Ahiṃsā 500
air (*vāyu*), in Vaiśeṣika 160
Aitareya Upaniṣad 63, 468–469
Akbar, Emperor 12, 403–404
alaṃkāra (figures of speech) 461–462
Alexander the Great 11
Aligarh school 479
All-Accomplishing Wisdom (*kṛtya-anuṣṭhāna-jñāna*) 291
Allah (God as named in the Qur'an) 492, 493
aloneness (*kaivalya*) 68, 131, 138, 268; Yoga philosophy 273–274, 274–275, 277, 278
Analyst school of therapeutic philosophy (*Vaibhāṣika*) 91, 105, 323, 360
analytic philosophy 5, 89n7; and Buddhism 88
Ānandavardhana 437, 456, 459, 461, 462, 463–464, 464, 467
anātman[1] (no-self, or not-self, or "no abiding self") 82, 85–87, 126, 204, 205, 512
Annambhaṭṭa 10
"annihilationism" (*ucchedavāda*) 324
Anuvrat Movement 404
appearance theory (*ābhāsavāda*) 247
argumentation 64, 65, 214, 233, 465; analytical 55; Buddhist 335; coherent 65; in Indian philosophy 17–21; Jagannātha Paṇḍitarāja's 465; logical 215; Lyotard's 562; of Pramāṇa theorists 425; "properly philosophical" 423; Rāmānuja's 253; rational 59; rules of 20; syllogistic 102; theological 216; transcendental 411; Udayana 221n4; validity of 19; in western philosophy 9
Aristotle 4, 11, 84, 528; *De anima* 419; defence of inequality 526
Arjuna (Krishna's human friend) 62
asymmetrical interdependence, socio-political applications of 514, 510, 511, 513, 514
Atharvaveda (Vedic Saṃhitā) 122, 374
atomic temporality 53
atomism 51, 175, 306
atomistic view of consciousness and time 51
attribute (*guṇa*), in Vaiśeṣika 166–167
Austin, John 431
Avalokiteśvara 501
Avidyā 243–244

beings, hierarchy of 137
Benveniste, Emile 413
Berkeley, George 412
Bhagavad Gītā 60, 62, 64, 83, 128, 234, 251, 485, 530; Abhinavagupta's commentary on 441; Śaṅkara's commentary on 245–246
Bhagavad-Gītā philosophy 8
Bhāgavatapurāṇa 143, 144
Bhartṛhari 228–230; cognition and language, Buddhist criticism of 446–453; on unaware cognition and its relation to language 448–451
Bhartṛprapañca 226–228
Bhāsarvajña 177
Bhāṭṭa, Mīmāṃsā sub-school 149, 152, unchanging self and momentariness 338–340
Bhattacharyya, Krishna Chandra 8
Bhāvadeva 149
Bhāvaviveka: conception of reality 343–350; defence of conventional reality 345–348; ontology 349, 351; rejection of ultimately intrinsic reality 348–350

[1] The term "*anātman*" in Sanskrit is known as "*anattā*" in Pāli.

Bhedābheda (both difference and non-difference/ separateness and non-separateness) 339
Bhedābhedadavada (the doctrine of difference and non-difference) 231, 258
Bhedābheda school of thought 66
Bhedābheda Vedānta 225, 226
Bilgrami, Akeel 536; on Gandhi 536–543
biosemiotics 416
Blazes of Reasoning: A Commentary on Verses of the Heart of the Middle Way (*Tarkajvālā*) 343
bodhisattva path 297–298
Brahma-Mīmāṃsā ('The Exegesis of Brahman') 223
Brahman (Absolute Self/Oversoul/priest/sacred utterance/ultimate reality) 26, 113, 223, 332
Brāhmaṇas (class of Vedic texts) 113–114; and European indologists 114–115; philosophy 113–119; connections with Upaniṣads 118–119
Brahma Sūtra[2] 67, 128, 224–226, 234, 236
Brahma Sūtra Bhāṣya 67
Brahma-vihāras ('Divine Abidings') 500
Bṛhadāraṇyaka Upaniṣad 16
British empiricists 6
Buddha: awakening 40, 49, 54, 294, 295, 296, 297, 298, 299; causality doctrine 323, 324, 325, 328; compassion 56, 500–501; conception of change 323; dependent co-arising theory 322, 323, 324, 325, 326; Discourse Explaining the Thought 44, 45, 46; discourses/sermons 41, 43, 52, 302, 323; emptiness doctrine 44, 45; rejection of "eternalism" 323; First Sermon 496; "first wheel" 45; Great Instruction Discourse 41; Middle Way 283; path 53, 321; right view of the dependently co-arisen nature of things 322; "second wheel" 45; on the self 87–88; wisdom 291, 296, 298
Buddhahood 47, 294, 297, 299, 313, 323; Vajrayāna 361, 363, 365, 368
Buddhism: and analytic philosophy 88; a process philosophy 49; religion 60, 88, 360; science 360; the self 85–87
Buddhism, Madhyamaka 44, 312, 313, 315, 316, 317; Nāgārjuna's early 321–329; Svātantrika Madhyamaka metaphysics 343–350; truth (conventional and ultimate) 351–358
Buddhism, Personalist (*pudgalavāda*) 332, 340, 341
Buddhism, Process 49; asymmetrical interdependence 510; disinterested compassion 507–508; 'dual allegiance' of 513–514; ethics 507–510; gradation of value 507–509; liberal-communitarian debate 512–513; Mādhyamika 511; social engagement 511
Buddhism, Vajrayāna 360–368
Buddhist apologetics (*Milinda Pañha*) 11, 12, 17, 65
Buddhist ethics: compassion 500–501; dharma 496–497; generosity/giving 500; karma 497–498; Mahāyāna morality 501; non-violence 504; precepts 498; skilful means doctrine 501–502; styles 503–504; tantra 502; vinaya 498–499; virtues 499; Western 503
Buddhist hermeneutics 46–47
Buddhist impermanence 51
Buddhist interpretation theory 40
Buddhist monastic order (*sangha*) 317, 497, 498, 499
Buddhist noble path 54
Buddhist university, at Vikramaśīla 65
bureaucracy, academic 529, 533–534
Burke, Kenneth 413

Candrakīrti 44, 311, 312, 315, 316, 317, 318, 509
Caraka 28, 29, 382
Caraka-saṃhitā 28, 64, 382
'cardinal virtues' 499
Cartesian dualism 200
Cārvāka school materialism 99–107
causation: extrinsic 324, 325; law of 168, 484; moral 276; self- 326, 346; theory of 171, 181, 224, 257, 347
Centrist school of therapeutic philosophy (Mādhyamika) 360
cessation, of the ordinary mind (*nirodha*) 271–273, 274, 276, 278
cessation philosophy 142
Chakrabarti, Arindam 9, 96, 204
Chakrabarti, Kisor Kumar 200
Chāndogya Upaniṣad 62, 123, 124, 125, 126, 127, 132
character traits, in Sāṃkhya 136–137
chariot image (body–mind system) 264, 265
Christianity 373, 376, 399, 570; Ten Commandments 498
clairvoyance 386, 387
Classical Indian Philosophy of Mind: The Nyāya Dualist Tradition 200
classical Hindu law 428–433
classical Yoga philosophy *see* Yoga philosophy
cognitionhood 182
cognition (*jñāna*) 30–31; correct cognition, science of 27; erroneous 76, 152, 356, 384; inferential[3] 78, 185–186, 188–190, 345; improper 32, 34, 71, 73; and language (Buddhist criticism of Bhartṛhari thesis) 446–454; perceptual 92–94, 96; right 107; unaware, its relation to language 448–451; of Śiva 410; truth-making 100; unaware 448–451; uncertain 76; valid 71, 75, 77, 100
"Cognition of Śiva" (*Śivadṛṣṭi*) 410
cognitive awareness (*vijñāna*) 284
cognitive error (*brānti*) 244, 355
'Collection of Views on Yoga' (*Yogadṛṣṭisamucc aya*) 396
colour (*rūpa*) 132, 158, 159, 160, 161, 165, 333
Commentary on Distinguishing the Two Truths (*Satyadva yavibhaṅgavṛtti*) 351
Common Law 433
common-sense pluralistic realism 51
comparative hermeneutics (Abrahamic religions) 376
comparative philosophy 8–10
compassion (*karuṇā*) 68, 84, 106, 490; Bodhisattva 313; Buddhist ethics, disinterested 507–508, 514; Jaina teaching on 406; Mīmāṃsā 153; Process Buddhist ethics 507, 508, 509, 514; programme of (Buddha) 56–57; Sāṃkhya 133, 145; universal 363, 365; virtues in 496, 500, 501, 502, 503, 504; Yoga philosophy 276, 277

[2] The *Brahma Sūtra* is also known as the *Vedānta Sūtra*.
[3] There are references to *anumanavijñānena*, to *anumiti*, and to inferential cognition with no Sanskrit term.

conceptions of self, in Nyāya 126, 206, 211–212
conceptions of self-luminosity (*svaprakāśatva*) 410
conceptualism, versus non-conceptualism 10
conceptual perception (*savikalpaka-pratyakṣa*) 94–97, 255
conditionality argument 348
conditionality, general (*idappaccayatā*) 51, 57
conditional predication, Jaina doctrine of (*syādvāda*) 390, 396
conditions: regulative preceding 181
'Connectionism' (*Sannikarṣa-vāda*) 202
connectionism, embodied 195–202
consciousness: absolute 441, 468, 556; in Advaita Vedānta of Śaṅkara 233–240, 242–249; atomistic view of 51; cosmic 471; and evolution 415–416; higher state of 502; in Indian philosophy 418–427; individual 556; intentional acts of 51–52, 135, 136; mental 93, 426; nondual 492; Nyāya theory of 195–202; perception, contents of 91–97; perceptual 93, 94; prelinguistic 242, 338, 422; store-house 283; surface-level 453; in Tantric knowledge systems 418–427; temporal acts of 51–52; in Udayana 204–212; in Viśiṣtādvaita Vedānta 251–260; visual 93; in Yogācāra Buddhism 283–291 *see also* First-Order theory of consciousness; Higher-Order theory of consciousness
consciousness principle, of Sāṃkhya 142
'Consciousness School' (*Vijñāna-vādins*) 284
consciousness, theory of 195, 200, 453; Higher-Order 10
contemplative science 360, 360–363
contentment (*tuṣṭi*) 136, 139n3, 235, 490
conventional reality 205, 314, 316, 317, 318, 345–348, 351–356
conventional truth (*vyavahāra-satya*) 314, 345, 347, 348, 350, 352–355; process Buddhism 507, 509, 513
correct cognition, science of (*pramānaśāstram*) 27
"correspondence principle" 64
"cosmic narcissism" 415
cosmic ontology 136
cosmogony and space, Hindu theory of 468–469
cosmopolitan philosophy 8
Cratylus 11
creation stage, of optimal integral process (*utpatti-krama*) 362, 364–366, 372
creative emergence, doctrine of (*kṛtaḥ sargaḥ*) 133, *135*, 136–137
critical deference 6
critical thinking, role of doubt in development of 77
cross-cultural philosophy 8
'Cultivation of Virtue' (*kuśala-dharma-saṃgrāhaka-śīla*) 317, 501
cultural agency, in Vajrayāna Buddhism 361

Dāna 500
Daodejing 12
darśana: comparison with 'philosophy' 16; Mohanty on 545–546; in Sanskrit 545–546
Dasein (the being-there) 206, 277
Dasgupta, Surendranath (S. N.) 8, 15, 60, 143, 526
Daya, Krishna 12n8, 103, 527, 530, 546–547
De anima 419
debating procedures, in Indian philosophy 17–21
deconstruction 325, 326, 327, 328, 329, 507; adoption by Indian thinkers 565–567
deconstruction of time, in the Mādhyamika Nāgārjuna 56–57
De Doctrina Christiana 376
deduction 386, 387
Democritus 12
dependent arising (*pratītyasamutpāda*) 283–285
dependent co-arising (*paṭiccasamuppāda*): Madhyamaka 322, 323, 324, 325, 326; Process philosophy 49, 50–51, 53, 57; the self 85; time, phenomenology of 49, 50, 53, 57
Derrida, Jacques 326, 327, 378, 523, 574, 564, 574; deconstruction 326, 327, 378, 508, 565, 567
Descartes, René 4, 5, 6, 9, 200, 526, 576; dualism 197, 200, 201, 470; "*ego cogito*" 576
desire (*icchā*)[4] 163, 164, 165, 166
determinism, scientific 483
Devadatta 181
Devastating Discourse (*Vaidalyaprakaraṇa*) 74
devotionalism (*bhakti*) 145, 215, 251, 253, 257, 410, 472–473; philosophy of music in 472–473
Dhammapada 54, 63, 64
Dhammasaṅganī (Theravāda canonical text) 54, 302 *see also Aṭṭhasālinī*
dharam, Gur-Sikh (righteousness/unwritten law) 487–495
dharma (ethical action/merit/righteous acts/rules of religious and legal duty/teaching of the Buddha/universal law governing both the physical and moral order of the universe/virtue) 68; Abhidharma on the 306–309; Buddha's teachings 285–286; Buddhist ethics 496–497, 503–504; the Eight Thousand 299; in classical Hindu law 428–429; Madhyamaka 363; materialism (Indian) 104, 106, 107; in Nāgārjuna's early Madhyamaka 322–323; philosophy of music in 472–473; phenomenology of time and Process philosophy 50–51, 53–54, 55, 56; Sāṃkhya 136; the self 333
Dharmakīrti 94, 321, 338, 340, 411, 447, 452
Dharmaśāstras 61, 104, 133, 428, 429–430, 428–433, 457, 502–503
'Dharma-Vinaya' ('doctrine and discipline') 498
Dharmottara 6
dhvani (literary suggestion) 466, 471, 472–473
Dhvanyāloka 457, 463, 464
Dhvanyālokalocana 437, 441, 445
diachronically unitary subject 207–208
Diamond Vehicle of Buddhist practice (*Vajrayāna*) 360–361, 502
diatopical hermeneutics 522, 523
Digambaras 393, 395, 402, 403
Dignāga 8, 9, 33, 411
direct realism (or naïve realism) 35, 36, 91, 92, 96, 151, 254
discernible momentary events 285
discernment philosophy 142
Discourse Explaining the Thought (*Saṃdhinirmocana-sūtra*) 44, 45, 46

[4] The terms "*kāma*", "*prāthanā*", "*rāga*", and "*rati*" are also used for desire.

Discourse Spoken by Akṣayamati (*Akṣayamati-nirdeśa-sūtra*) 44
Discourse to the Kālamas (*Kālama-sutta*) 42, 43
"discoursing", re-imabining tradition as 550–551
disinterested compassion 507–508, 514
Distinguishing the Two Truths (*Satyadvayavibhaṅgakāri kā*) 351
Divākara, Siddhasena 381, 387, 395–396
'Divine Abidings' (*Brahma-vihāras*) 500
divine agency 53, 416
"divine pride" 361, 361, 364
doctrine, shifting attitudes toward 6–7
Doṣa (poetic blemish) 460
dramaturgical science (*Nāṭya Śāstra*) 456
dravya (substance) 95, 157–158, 167, 196, 205, 333, 339, 349; in Abhidharma 306, 307, 308; in Vaiśeṣika 157–165; in Viśiṣṭādvaita Vedānta 256, 257, 258
'dual allegiance' of Process Buddhism 513–514
dualism 134, 557; Abhinavagupta's non- 443; Advaita Vedānta non- 233, 234, 235, 236, 237, 240, 242; Cartesian 200, 470; exclusive 509; inclusive 509; Lockean 35; non- 63, 83, 129; Nyāya 197, 200; ontological 134, 243; property 201; qualified non- 251; radical non- 422; Sāṃkhya 134, 197; Sāṃkhya-Yoga-Vedānta 197; subject-object 238; substance 203; in the West 203
Dvaita Vedānta 128, 223

efficiency theory, innovative (*kāritra*) 55
egalitarianism 488, 511, 529, 532
eightfold noble path (*ārya-aṣṭāṅga-mārga*) 86, 268, 299, 313, 322, 324–325, 496, 497, 501
'eight-limbed' path (*aṣṭāṅga-yoga*) 275
Eight Precepts (*aṣṭāṅga-śīla*) 498
Eleatics, the 12
eliminative physicalism 201
embodied awareness 265–266
embodied connectionism (Nyāya philosophy of mind) 195–202
embodied self-awareness, philosopy of *see* Yoga philosophy, embodied self-awareness
embodiment, in classical Yoga philosophy *see* Yoga philosophy, embodiment
emergence of representations (*pratyaya-sarga*), in Sāṃkhya 134, 136
emptiness, doctrine/philosophy of (*śūnyatā*) 44, 45
Enlightenment, the 543
Epimenides 4
epistemé 71
epistemic diversity 408, 411–412
epistemology: abhidharma 302; Gettier problem 10; of classical Hindu law 428–433; Indian, beginnings of 381–383; Jaina 383–387; Mīmāṃsa 150; Nyāya 175–176, 178; Nyāya-Buddhist controversy 94–97; Pramāṇa 27–37, 180; Pramāṇika 345; Pratyabhijñā 405, 411–412; Yogācāra 291
erroneous cognition (*viparyāsa*) 76, 152, 356, 384
Essence of the Good Explanations (Legs bshad snying po) 43
"Essence of the Scripture" (Pravacanasāra) 385
ethics, Buddhist 496–504; *ahiṃsā* (non-violence) 500; compassion 500; dharma 496–497; generosity/giving 500; karma 497–498; Kashmiri Śaivism 408–409; Mahāyāna morality 501; precepts 498; Process Buddhist 507–510; skilful means, doctrine of 509; Tantra 408–409, 502; vinaya 498–499; virtues 499; Western 503–504
Ethics of Altruism/Discipline/EngagementVirtue 503–504
ethos (*polis*) 492
European indologists, and the Brāhmaṇas 115
European philosophy, encountering Indian philosophy *see* Indian philosophy, encountering European philosophy
event ontology 49
evolution: and consciousness 415–416; karmic theory of 288
excellence (*siddhi*) 136–137
existential temporal life 53
extended temporality 49, 53
extrinsic causation 324, 328
extrinsic validity theory (*prāmāṇyavāda*) 216–220; as foundationalism 217–220; infallible justification 218; in the Nyāyakusumāñjali 216

fallacies (*hetvābhāsa*) 5, 188–194; absence of the probandum in the locus 190–191; common deviating probans 190; common deviation 190–191; "contradicted"/opposed 344; deviation 190, 191–192; existence of counter-thesis 192–193; uncommon deviation 191; unestablished 188, 189–190; unestablished in the locus 189; unestablished locus 189; unestablished probandum 189; unestablished probans 189; unestablished property of being the pervaded fallacy 190; unsupported deviation 191–192
figures of speech (*alaṃkāra*) 461–462
"first council" 41
First Sermon, of the Buddha 496
Five Precepts, of Buddhism 498
"forest hypothesis" 295–296
forms of life 8, 54, 137, 401, 403, 406
foundationalism, extrinsic validity as 216–220, 315, 343, 345, 349, 358
foundationalist ontology 349
Foundational Verses on the Middle Way (*Mūlamadhyamaka-kārikā*) 230–231
Four Hundred Stanzas 318
Four Noble Truths 44, 86, 316, 325, 360, 496, 499
free will, doctrine of 483
Fruits of the Religious Life, The (*Sāmaññaphala Sutta*) 497
fusion philosophy 8

Gadādhara 177
Gadamer, Hans-Georg 46, 67, 373, 377, 520, 522, 548, 577
Gandhi, Mohandas Karamchand: Bilgrami on 538–540; as exemplar 542–543; on moral criticism 540–541; on the moral life 536–538; on objective moral truths 542; on truth 540
Gauḍapāda 66, 230–231, 244, 249, 526
Gautama 11, 86, 92, 93, 551–552; materialism (Indian) 107; Nyāya 175, 176, 196; skepticism (Indian) 72, 73, 77; Vaiśeṣika 164–165

general conditionality (*idappaccayatā*) 51
generosity (*dāna*) 500, 501, 504
Gettier, Edmund 5; problem 10
'giving' (*dāna*) 500, 501, 504
Gosvāmī, Rūpa 67
Grammarians, Sanskrit 7, 11, 95, 161, 168, 229, 452
"grammar of motives" 413
Great Commentary, The [on the *Jñānaprasthāna*]) 305
"Greater Vehicle" (Mahāyāna) 42
Great Instruction Discourse (Mahāpadesa-sutta) 41
guṇa: excellences in poetry 460–1; in Vaiśeṣika 165–166
Gur-Sikh dharam (righteousness/unwritten law) 487–495
Guru Arjan 491
Guru-centeredness (*gurmukh*) 491
Guru Nanak 490, 491
Guru's Word (*gur-shabad*) 488–489, 491
gymnosophists 12

Hadot, Pierre 8, 60, 69
Halbfass, Wilhelm 516, 517, 545, 546, 548–553
Haribhadra 16; and *yogas* 396–397
Hastings, Warren 376
Haṭha Yoga 269
heard word, the (*śruti)* 36
Heart Scripture (*Prajñāparāmitāhṛdayasūtra*) 360
Hegel, Georg Wilhelm Friedrich: on difference 574; eurocentrism 573–574; Indian tradition, critique of the 572; on otherness 574
Heidegger, Martin: Being 422, 561; Dasein 277; hermeneutics, Western 377; knowledge 578; postmodernism 562; philosophical privilege (European) 521; reason 578; self and person, distinction between 206; theological appropriations 412
Hellenistic skepticism 12
Hemacandra 381, 384, 403
hermeneutics ("*mīmāṃsā*") 373–378; Buddhist 40–47; colonial Indian 376–377; comparative (Abrahamic religions) 376; diatopical 522–523; Hindu 373–374; Mahāyāna 42–46; Mīmāṃsā 430–431; in the Pāli canon 41–42; postcolonial 522; for interpreting the Qur'an 481; traditional Indian 377–378
hermeneutic task, concerning meaning and interpretation 21–23
hierarchy of beings, in Sāṃkhya 137
Higher-Order theory of consciousness 10
Hindu law, epistemology of 428–433
Hindu theory of space and cosmogony 468–469
Hiriyana, Mysore 8, 29
human goodness 399, 542
human pursuits, theory of (*puruṣārtha*) 103, 104
human transformation 50
Hume, David 5, 9, 411
Husserl, Edmund 5, 206, 207, 521, 522, 577; on internal time-consciousness 52
Hymn on the Domain of Reality (*Dharmadhātustava* 312, 318
Hymn on the Ultimate 312
hypostatizing mental proliferation (*prapañca-śūnyatā*) 56
hypothetical argument (*tarka*)[5] 107

idealism 33, 560; Berkeley's 412; Buddhist 152, 323; Hegelian 565, 566; India's monastic 526; Process Buddhism 514; Western 566; Yogācāra 287, 288, 291, 344, 351
Idealist school of therapeutic philosophy (*Cittamātra*) 360
impermanence (*anityā*): Buddhist doctrine of 51: Gur-Sikh *dharam* 487; Jaina relativity 402, 403; Nāgārjuna 31, 323; phenomenology of time 49, 52, 54, 55; Process philosophy 50, 51, 54, 55; the self 82, 83; Yoga philosophy 266
impetuous poetic style (*ārabhaṭī*) 462
inactive states of mind during the break of two awarenesses (*bhavaṅga-citta*) 54
inclusivism 294; Jaina 392; social 255
incommensurability 4, 9, 11
independent substantial self-nature (*niḥsvabhāvatā*) 55
indexicals 413
Indian epistemology, beginnings of 383–388
Indian materialism 99–107
Indian philosophical traditions 554–559; darśana in Sanskrit 554; Halbfass on philosophy and newness 548–552; Daya Krishna thought 546–547; Mohanty's darśana 547–548
Indian philosophy, encountering European philosophy 516–524; academic bureaucracy 533; academic philosophy 533; continuity between classical and modern 529–533; discontinuity between classical and modern 533–534; incorporation of European thought 528; novel modern ideas with no European equivalent 533
Indian philosophy, the self in 81–88
Indian skepticism 71–78
indigenism 8–9
individual retribution, law of (*vyavasthā*) 432
individual self (*jīvātman*) 26; Avidya 243, 244, 245, 247; Nyāya 177, 179; early Vedānta 223, 226; Viśiṣtādvaita Vedānta 253, 256, 259; Yoga philosophy 263
Individual Vehicle of Buddhist practice (*Hinayāna/ Theravāda*) 360
indologists, European, and the Brāhmaṇas 115
induction 28, 62, 386, 387
infallible justification 218; ultimate criterion for 219
inferences 17, 28, 62; *anumāna* system of 11, 28; Cārvākas 99; inference, Nyaya on 184–194; invalid 186–187; rational 215, 216, 227, 228; *Sāṃkhya Karikā* 64; valid 186–187
inferential cognition (*anumanavijñānena/anumiti*)[6] 78, 185–188, 189–193, 345
"Inferior Vehicle" (Hīnayāna) 43, 293, 501

[5] The word "*tarka*" can also mean reductio ad absurdum.
[6] There are references to *anumanavijñānena*, to *anumiti*, and to inferential cognition with no Sanskrit term.

inherence[7] (*samavāya*): *Alaṃkāraśāstra* 461; materialism (Indian) 99; Nyāya 184; Pramāṇa epistemology 27; Vaiśeṣika categories 158, 163, 169, 172, 172–173
"injunctions" (*vidhi*) 23, 101, 113, 244, 264, 269, 493; of dharma 433; Qur'anic 481, 482, 483; of *śruti* 428, 429
instrumental causal conditions (*nimitta-kāraṇas*) 166, 185, 196
internal criticism 533, 536–537
internal time-consciousness, Husserl on 52
interpretation theory, Buddhist 40
intrinsic validity (*svataḥ-prāmāṇya*) 217
intuitive knowledge 15–16 *see also aparokṣānubhūti*; *prajñā*; *yogaja pratyakṣa*
invalid inferences 186–194
(ir)reality of external objects 289–290
Islam 373, 376, 399, 570
Islamic modernism in India 479–486; free will, doctrine of 483; predestination 483, 484, 485; religion and politics, relationship between 485; scientific determinism 485; scientific interpretation of nature 484; temporary Qur'anic injunctions 481–482
Islamic thought, reform of 480–481

Jagadīśa 177
Jaimini 11, 24, 148, 150, 235, 373, 374, 526
Jaina: epistemology 381–388; ethics 399–407; metaphysics 400–401; moral agency 406; moral conscience 403; moral philosophy 399–406; ontology 383, 400; perspectives, doctrine of 390–397; physics 400–401; vows 401–403
Jaina, relativity 397; conventional and ultimate truths 393–394; Haribhadra 396–397; metaphysical foundations of 393; modern interpretations 397; Samantabhadra 395–396; Siddhasena 395–396; Singhvi, L. M. 405–406; in the Śvetāmbara *Āgamas* 396–397; 'two truths', of Kundakunda 393–394; Tulsi, Acarya 404–406
Jainism 133, 214, 527, 531; epistemology 383, 384, 385, 387; ethics 399, 401, 405, 500; hermeneutics 373; moral philosophy 399, 400, 401, 404, 405, 406; relativity 390, 391, 392, 393, 394, 395; the self 332, 339; unchanging self and momentariness 338–339
Jātaka view of time 57
Jayadeva 462
Jayanta, Bhaṭṭa 92, 128, 177, 218
Jesus 62, 399
jīvanmukta (living enlightened, the) 276–277
jñāna 29–31
Jñānagarbha: causal efficiency 354; conventional truth 351–358; dependently arisen phenomena 354; imaginary phenomena 354; unanalyzable truth 354–355; ultimate truth 351–358
Judaism 373, 376
jurisprudence, treatises on (*Arthaśāstra*) 28, 103, 428, 434n7, 460

kaivalya (aloneness) 68, 131, 138, 268, 273; Yoga philosophy 268, 269, 271, 272
Kakar, Sudhir 415
Kālachakra 362
Kālama-sutta (Discourse to the Kālamas) 42, 43
Kallaṭa, Bhaṭṭa 409, 424
Kāma Sūtra 68
Kant, Immanuel: Gandhi's truth 539; Indian philosophy 4, 5, 9, 12, 528, 554, 565; Nāgārjuna 319; no-self view 208
Kapila 131, 131, 139, 143, 144, 146, 530
Kapilagītā (Vaiṣṇava theism) 143, 144, 146
karma (that which connects past lives to current life): Advaita Vedānta 233, 235, 239; Buddhism 49, 54; Buddhist ethics 496, 502, 503–504, 507; Jaina epistemology 381, 383; Jaina ethics and moral philosophy 399, 400, 401, 403; Jaina relativity 391, 394; Kashmiri Śaivism 408; Madhyamaka 321, 322; materialism (Indian) 99, 100; philosophy of music 472; Nyāya 175, 176; Process Buddhism 506; the self 81, 82, 84; Tantra 408; Upaniṣads 122, 123; Vaiśeṣika 166–167; Viśiṣṭādvaita Vedānta 251, 254; Yoga philosophy 276; Yogācāra Buddhism 284, 285, 287, 288, 290
Kashmiri Śaivism, non-dual 408–417
Kashmiri tantric philosophy 415, 420, 441
Kaṭha Upaniṣad 63, 127, 132, 143, 264
Kaula (one of three Tantric schools) 409, 410, 421, 422, 440; tantra 421–422, 425; theology 422
Kauṇḍinya 420, 421
Kauṭilya 28, 103
Kāvyaprakāśa 457, 462
Khapa, Tsong 43–44, 46
knowledge, testimony as (śabdapramāṇa) 36–37
knowledge, theory of (prāmāṇyavāda) 27, 32, 177, 179, 216, 217–218, 315, 386; Jaina epistemology 384, 386, 387, 388
Koran *see* Qur'an
Koranic injunctions 481–482
Krama (one of three Tantric schools) 409, 410, 440
Krishna 62
Krishna, Daya 103, 530, 546–547
Kumārila,Bhaṭṭa 6, 7, 9; cognition 451; language 451; Mīmāṃsa 149, 150, 151, 152, 155; the self 339, 340; extrinsic validity 217; *see also* Mīmāṃsaka
Kundakunda 381, 383, 384, 385, 386; 'two truths' 393–4

Laghu Bhāgavatāmṛta 67
Lamp of Wisdom (Prajñāpradīpa) 316, 343
language, and cognition (Buddhist criticism of Bhartṛhari thesis) 446–455
language, philosophy of 3, 4, 11, 175, 224, 328
Laws of Manu 428
legal agents 432
legal authority, from a philosophical perspective 431–433
Letter to a Friend (Ratnāvalī and Suhṛllekha) 311
Lévi, Sylvain 115
liberal-communitarian debate, and Process Buddhism 511, 512–514
liberation (kaivalya) 68, 131, 138, 268; Yoga philosophy 275, 276, 277, 278
liberation from cyclic existence (*saṃsāra*) 42

[7] The word "*samavāya*" can also mean necessary and sufficient conditions.

"Light on Tantra" (*Tantrāloka*) 440
limitation theory (*avacchedavāda*) 248
limiting conditions (*upadhis*) 227, 228, 266
literary suggestion (*dhvani/vyañjanā*) 456, 462, 463–464
living enlightened, the (*jīvanmukta*) 276–277
logical inference, as *pramāṇa* 28
'Logic of the True Doctrine' (*Sanmatitarka*) 395
Lokāyata school materialism 99–107
Lord of the Adamantine Chariot, the 268–270
Lotus Scripture of the True Doctrine (*Saddharma-puṇḍarīka-sūtra*) 46
Luther, Martin 399

McNamara, Patrick 416
Madhva 128, 129, 223
Madhyamaka (Middle Way School): causal efficiency 353–354; conventional truth 351–359; dependently arisen phenomena 353–354; imaginary phenomena 353–354; ontology 287, 351, 357; unanalysable truth 354–355; ultimate truth 351–359
Mādhyamika (Centrist school of therapeutic philosophy) 11; Buddhist hermeneutics 43–44, 49; Madhyamaka 321, 322, 324–325, 327–328, 343, 347, 355; Process Buddhism 507, 509–10, 511; Vajrayāna Buddhism 360; Vedānta 230; Yogācāra Buddhism 291
Mādhyamika Buddhism 506, 507, 510, 514; and social engagement 511
Mādhyamika Nāgārjuna, on deconstruction of time 56–57
Mahāyāna ("Greater Vehicle"/Universal Vehicle of Buddhist practice): authority of new sutras 298; bodhisattva path 296–298; bodhisattva tales 298–289; critiques 290–291; doctrine 299–300; early period 293–300; hermeneutics 42–6; morality 501; Śākyamuni Buddha 294; social aspects 294–296; transition to middle period 300
Maitreya 56, 290, 294, 298, 318
Maitrī Upaniṣad 104
Mālinī Vijayottara Tantra (*Śrīpūrva Śāstra*) 440
Malkani, G. R. 554–559
Mammaṭa 457, 458, 459, 460, 462, 465
maṇḍala (circular diagrams/perfected world/sacred circle) 361, 363, 409
Māṇḍūkya Upaniṣad 230
manifoldness, theory of (*anekāntavāda*) 384
Māṇikyanandin 381, 383, 386–7
mantras (enlightening speech/sacred verses) 264, 365, 409, 438
materialism, Lokāyata school 99–109
Mathurānātha 177
Matilal, Bimal Krishna 8, 69, 530; embodied connectionism 195; hermeneutics 373, 374, 375; Jaina relativity 390, 391, 392; Madhyamaka 327; materialism 107; methodology 16; Pramāṇa epistemology 30, 33, 34, 35, 36; skepticism 73, 74
meditation: Abhinavagupta 438; Buddhist ethics 497, 501, 502; Gur-Sikh *dharam* 491, 497; Jaina ethics and moral philosophy 403, 404; Madhyamaka 322; Mahāyāna 295; philosophy of music 469; Process Buddhism 507; the self 85; Tantric knowledge systems 422; Upaniṣads 129; Vajrayāna Buddhism 365; Vedānta 230, 236; Yogācāra Buddhism 286; Yoga philosophy 266, 267–269, 275
Meinheit (mineness) 206
Menander I *see* Milinda
Merleau-Ponty, Maurice 521
metaphilosophical question, the 7–8
"metaphysical generator" 66
metaphysical ultimacy 68
metaphysics 3, 54, 259, 531, 557, 559, 51, 562; Abhidharma 313; Aristotelian 483; Bhāvaviveka's 357; descriptive 62; European 52; of experience 136; idealistic 554; Jaina 386, 391, 392, 393, 400; Madhyamaka 312; multiplist 67; Nāgārjuna 313, 314; Nyāya 176; Pramāṇa epistemology 27; substantialist 328; Svātantrika Madhyamaka 343–350; Trika Kaula 425; Vaiśeṣika 155; Vedānta 233, 236, 237, 556, 557, 558; Western 522; Yoga philosophy 277, 278
methodology, in Indian philosophy 15–26
'Middle Path' 325, 326, 392–393
Middle Way School (Madhyamaka) 43
Mīmāṃsā (school of classical Indian philosophy) 88n1, 148–156, 430–431; atheist perspective 155; Bhāṭṭa sub-school 149; deontic issues 154–5; epistemological issues 150–152; as exegesis 150; and God 155; historical development of 148–150; legal interpretation 436–442; linguistic issues 152–154
Mīmāṃsā Sūtras 148–154
mind, elimination/negation of the 271–273
mind, philosophy of 3, 10, 49, 88, 195–203, 243
mind (*manas*), in Vaiśeṣika 164–165
Miśra, Paritoṣa 149
Miśra, Sucarita 149
Miśra, Vācaspati 8, 24, 551–552; Avidyā 246; extrinsic validity 218–219; Nyāya 178; perception 92; Sāṃkhya 137, 138; skepticism 78
modern philosophy in India 526–535
'Mokṣadharma' 64
Mokṣākaragupta 10, 448, 451, 454 *see also Tarkabhāṣā*
"momentariness" (*kṣaṇikatva*) 7, 51, 53, 55, 78, 93, 308, 323; the self 335, 336, 337, 338, 339–340, 341, 342
monism 82, 201, 253, 254, 260, 518, 519, 572
moral: agency, in Jaina teachings 406; conscience 403, 405; criticism, Gandhi on 536, 538, 539, 540, 540–541, 542; life, Gandhi on the 536–538; philosophy, Jaina 399–407
morality, Mahāyāna 501
motivating factors, to study a text (*anubhandha*-s) 23–24
Mozi 4
Mukherji, Anukul Chandra 8
musical vision, fluidity of 473
music, philosophy of 467–75; in *bhakti* 472–473; in *dharma* 472–473
mutual dependence (*anyonyāśraya*) 51, 72, 325, 508, 513

Nāgārjuna (founder of Madhyamaka school of Buddhist philosophy) 311–319; causality 323–325; commentators on 311; corpus 311–312, 313; as

deconstructionism 321–329; denial of doubt 73–75; enlightenment 321–327; influence of 318–319; life and times 311–312; literature on 319; early Madhyamaka 321–329; moderation 321–322; ontology 314, 315; philosophical context 312–313; philosophical views 313–315; philosophical works 315–317; suffering 325
Nāgasena 12, 65, 265
'naïve realism' (or 'direct realism') 35, 36, 91, 96, 151, 254
Naiyāyika 9, 10; on doubt 73; embodied connectionism 195, 197, 198, 200, 201, 202; materialism 107, 424; Mīmāṃsā 151, 152, 153; no-self view 208–211; perception 92, 95, 96, 97; the self 332, 333, 334, 335, 336, 337, 338, 339; skepticism 72, 73, 74, 75, 76; Vaiśeṣika 172; Vedānta 227, 255
Nārāyaṇa (Absolute Self/Oversoul) 332, 506
narrative philosophy 60, 68
nature, scientific interpretation of 484
necessary and sufficient conditions (*samavāya*[8]) 54
negation (*abhāva*), in Vaiśeṣika 172–173
'New Logic' (Navya-Nyāya) period 176, 177
'New Logicians' school (or 'new reason' school) 4, 32, 96, 97, 171, 177, 181, 465 *see also* Gaṅgeśa
Nietzsche, Friedrich 10, 485, 561, 563
nirodha (cessation, of the ordinary mind) 267, 271–273, 276
nirvāṇa (enlightenment/freedom/liberation) 50, 54, 82, 84, 85, 86, 313, 496–497, 501; Jaina 396, 403; early Mahāyāna 297, 299, 300; early Madhyamaka 325, 326, 327; Yogācāra Buddhism 285, 291
Noble Eightfold Path, to *nirvāṇa* 85, 496
noble truths (*āryasatya*) 44, 84, 316, 324, 325, 360, 496, 499
non-conceptualism 10
non-conceptual perception 93, 94–97, 255, 447, 448, 451
non-differentiated reality 255
Nondual Kashmiri Śaivism 408–409
non-foundational ontology 351, 357
non-reductive physicalism 201
nonviolence in thought, word, and deed to the realm of intellectual discourse (*ahiṃsā*) 392, 500, 511, 540
"no-self" (*anātman*) 51, 82, 85–87, 124, 236–237, 246–247, 512, 559; Nyāya critique of the no-self view 204–212; self versus no-self debate between Buddhism and the Brahmanical traditions 331–342
no-self theory, of Buddhism 85–87
Nussbaum, Martha 8
Nyāya (school of philosophy) 175–182
Nyāya-Buddhist controversy 94–97
Nyāya 88n1: agency 208–211; consciousness 199–200; diachronically unitary subject of cognitions 207–208; dualism, in comparison to Cartesian dualism 200–202; epistemology 177, 179, 180; fallacies 188–194; inference 184–188; inferential cognition 185–186; materialism 198–200; no-self view 204–12; ontology 177, 178, 180, 202; the self, tension between phenomenological and ontological conceptions of 211–212; the self and person, distinction between 204–207; theism 182
Nyāyakusumāñjali, extrinsic theory in 217–219

objective moral truths, Gandhi on 540, 542
omnipotence 253, 268, 269, 270, 409, 412–414
omniscience: Jaina 391, 393, 394; early Mahāyāna 297; Mīmāṃsā 152; Vajrayāna Buddhism 368; Viśiṣṭādvaita Vedānta 253; Yoga philosophy 268, 269, 270
'On Sentences and Words' (*Vākyapadīya*) 228
ontological: bondage 423; categories 27, 155, 384; dualism 134, 135, 243; imperialism 521; non-foundationalism 343, 349; realism 343, 391, 418, 425
ontology: Abhidharma 306–309; Bhāvaviveka 349, 356; cosmic 136; event 49; foundationalist 351; Jaina 383–384, 399; Madhyamaka 287, 351, 357; Nāgārjuna 314, 315; non-foundational 351, 357; Nyāya 175, 176, 178, 180, 202, 206, 212; pluralist 202; Pratyabhijñā 412–414; Ramanuja's 257; of recognition 408; Sāṃkhya 196; social 575; spiritualized 399; substance 49; 'three-level' 258; Western 521

Pāli Canon 43, 44, 47, 81, 87, 294, 497; hermeneutics in the 41–42
Pānini 25
pansemiotics 415
Paritoṣa Miśra 149
Pārthasārathi Miśra 149
particularity (viśeṣa), in Vaiśeṣika 171–172
Pāśupata Sūtras 420
Patañjali: Abhinavagupta 437; methodology 24, 25; Mīmāṃsā 149, 153; Sāṃkhya 131, 141, 143; Upaniṣads 127; Vedānta 228; Yoga philosophy 263, 264, 266, 267, 268, 269, 271, 272, 273, 274, 275, 276, 277, 278
Peirce, Charles 413
perception (*pratyakṣa*) 33–35, 91–97; conceptual 94–97, 258; definitions of 92–94; direct 177, 227, 255, 344, 385, 387; non-conceptual 94–97; as *pramāṇa* 28; sensory 178, 228, 255, 347, 385, 386, 387
Perfection of Wisdom in Eight Thousand Lines 296, 300
Perfection of Wisdom (Prajñā-pāramitā) 44, 296, 300, 312, 313
Perfection of Wisdom sūtras 44, 299, 318
perfection stage (*niṣpanna-krama*) 366
Personalist Buddhism (*pudgalavāda*) 332, 340, 341
person, and the self 207–209
phenomenalism 33, 91, 411
phenomenal separateness of self 204–213
phenomenology of time (in Buddhism) 49–57
philosophical: interventions 9–12; psychology 408, 414–415; religion 61–63; synthesis 8
philosophy: academic 9; analytic 5, 88, 89n7; of the Brāhmaṇas 113–119; cessation 142; comparative 8–10; comparison with *darśana* 16; cosmopolitan 8; cross-cultural 8; discernment 269, 277, 286, 399, 494; fusion 8; genealogical constraints 4–5; goals of 67–69; intertwining with religion in India

[8] The word "*samavāya*" can also mean inherence.

59–63; Jaina moral 406–7; Kashmiri tantric 423; of language 177, 178, 226, 333; the metaphilosophical question 7–8; of mind 3, 10, 49, 88, 195–202, 243; of music 467–474; narrative 60, 68; narrativisation of 60; postcolonialism 569–578; Pratyabhijñā 411, 412–413, 414, 415, 416, 442, 445; relation to religion in India 59, 60, 61, 62, 68; as spiritual practice 63–64; therapeutic 361, 363; Upaniṣad 129–130; Western bias of 4–5
Plato 4, 5, 12, 84, 376, 528, 547, 553
pluralist ontology 202
poetic: blemish (*Doṣa*) 460; regionalities 462
poetics, discipline of 456–466; aesthetic savor 464–465; corporeal analogies 49–60; evolution of theory 467–468; figures of speech 461–462; literary suggestion 463–464; origins of 457; as philosophical discipline 456–466; poetic blemish 460; poetic excellences 460–461; poetic styles 461–462; poetry 456; preliminaries 458–459
poetics, Sanskrit 413, 465; corporeal analogies in 459–160; logic in 465–466
Poetic Vehicle of Buddhist practice (*Mantrayāna*) 502
poetry: elements of 457; excellences of 463, 464, 465
point of arrest (*nirodha*) 267, 271–272, 277
postcolonial hermeneutics 522, 523
postcolonialism, philosophy in an age of 569–578; difference, Hegel on 574; the "episteme" 575–576; eurocentrism, Hegel's 573–574; Indian tradition, Hegel's critique of the 572–573; otherness, Hegel on 574; structuring of knowledge by power relationships 575–576
postmodernism 561–567; deconstruction of 565–567; enlightenment 564–565; modernity 563; reason 564 565; representational thinking 564–565
Prābhākara (sub-school of Mīmāṃsā) 149 *see also* Mīmāṃsaka
Prābhākara system 149
Prajāpati (creator god of Vedic ritual texts) 22, 116, 125
Prākṛit (the languages of commoners) 458
prakṛti (the material principle) 144, 267; severance from *puruṣa* 277–278
pramāṇa (epistemically warranted/knowledge/ means of valid cognition/means of knowing/ non-defective way of knowing/proof) 6; cognition 453; discourse 426; epistemology, origins and development of 27–37; extrinsic validity 217; Jaina epistemology 383, 384, 386, 387; Jaina relativity 393, 394; language 453; materialism 100, 107; methodology 21; Mīmāṃsā 150; Nyāya 177, 178, 179, 180; perception 91; philosophy 426; Prāmāṇya 31–33; program 180; skepticism (Indian) 72, 75; Svātantrika Madhyamaka metaphysics 343; Tantric knowledge systems 420; Upaniṣads 126, 128; Vedānta 255, 259; Yoga philosophy 263
pramāṇavāda (*pramāṇa* theory/the theory of the means or sources of knowledge) 4, 179, 425, 426; development of 27–29; origins of 27–29
Pramānika epistemology 345, 347, 349, 351
Prāmāṇya 31–33
Prāmāṇyavāda (theory of validity of knowledge) 216–217
Praśastapāda 163, 165, 166, 167, 172, 173
Praśna Upaniṣad 134
pratiprasava ('return to the source') 272–273
Pratyabhijñā 408; consciousness 423; Darśana 433–435; epistemology 411–412, 416–417; ethics 414–415; evolution 415–416; nondual Kashmiri Śaivism, school of 408, 408–409; ontology 412–414; philosophical psychology 414–415; purpose and methods 410–411; system 409–410
praxis (action) 277, 471; Buddhist 321; erotic 104; Process Buddhism 507, 513, 514; Sikh488, 490, 492, 493; Tantric philosophy 421, 423
precepts 363, 364, 404, 405, 498
predestination 483, 484, 485
pre-existent effect, doctrine of (*satkāryavāda*[9]) 137
primal impression 52, 56
primary rules (that impose duties) 432
Prince Vessantara 500
Process Buddhism 49–50; asymmetrical interdependence 511–12; disinterested compassion 507–508; 'dual allegiance' of 513–14; ethics 507, 508–509; gradation of value 509–510; liberal-communitarian debate 512–513; Mādhyamika 511; social engagement 510–511
Process Vehicle of Buddhist practice (*Tantrayāna*) 360
prophetic traditions, rejection of 482
protention 52, 56
psychology, philosophical 408, 414–415
Puruṣa (consciousness/consciousness principle/ (cosmic) Man/god/man/self: Brāhmaṇas 117, 118, 119; embodied connectionism 197; Malkani, G. R. 559; severance from *prakṛti* 277–278; Sāṃkhya 131, 132, 133, 134, 135, 137, 138, 143, 145, 146; Svātantrika Madhyamaka metaphysics 346; Upaniṣads 119; Vedānta 234, 243; Yoga philosophy 271, 272, 273, 274, 275, 276, 277, 278
Puruṣa Sūkta 235
Pūrva-Mīmāṃsā (Early Enquiry/Prior Exegesis) 148, 149; methodology 21, 22, 23, 25–26; Vedānta 225, 226, 236
Pyrrho 12
Pyrrhonian skepticism 71

'Questions of Milinda' (*Milinda pañha*) 11, 12, 17, 65
Quine, Willard Van Orman 5, 94
Qur'an 480, 481, 482, 483, 485; injunctions, temporary 481–482

Radhakrishnan, Sarvepall 16, 133, 526, 528, 529, 555, 557
Ramakantha, Bhaṭṭa 336
Rāmānuja, ontology 258
rasa (literary savor) 456, 457, 460–465
rational inference 216, 219, 227, 228
rational methodology, spread of 60
rational theology 215–216
Ratnakīrti 6, 16, 306
realism 431, 432, 519, 547, 566; Anglo-American 33; anti- 33; common-sense 256; direct 35, 36, 91,

[9] The term "*satkāryavāda*" can also refer to a theory of causation.

96, 151, 254; epistemological 351, 357; moral 543; naïve 35; Nyāya 176, 182; ontological 343, 391, 418; pluralistic 51; Vaiśeṣika 158
reality, conventional 345–348
reality, ultimate (*brahman*) 7, 67; Jaina epistemology 383; Madhyamaka 344; 348–350, 351, 353; Malkani, G. R. 554, 556, 568; methodology 26; Mīmāṃsā 150; philosophy of music 468, 473; Nāgārjuna 318; Process Buddhism 505; the self 84; Upaniṣads 124, 126; Vedānta 223, 225, 227, 229, 230, 235; Yogācāra Buddhism 291
reason: and religion 66–67; and representational thinking 564–565
reasoning as religious practice 60
rebirth, cycle of (*saṃsāra*) 83, 86, 88, 496, 501
recognition 198, 284, 386, 387, 406, 408, 411; Abhinavagupta teaching on 441, 442; ontology of 408; rule of 432; school of (Pratyabhijñā Darśana) 424–427, 441, 442, 443; in Nyāya critique of no-self view 207, 208, 211, 212; self- 411, 412, 414, 416, 417; soteriological 409; theory of 412
reductio ad absurdum (*tarka*[10]) 18, 44, 64, 78, 315, 316, 318
reductionism 195
reflection theory (*pratibimbavāda*) 247
reincarnation (*saṃsāra*) 83, 86, 497, 503
relativity: Jaina doctrines of 390–398; Samantabhadra and Siddhasena Divākara 395–396; in the Śvetāmbara Āgamas 392–393
reliable testimony, as *pramāṇa* 28
Religion and Philosophy of the Veda and Upanishads, The 115
religion in India: and philosophy 59–63, 67–69; and reason 66–67
Replies to Objections (*Vigrahavyāvartanī*) 311
representationalism 91, 93
representational thinking, and reason 564–565
retention 52, 56
'return to the source' (*pratiprasava*) 271–273
rhetoric, science of (as applied to Sanskrit poetry) 456, 457, 459, 461–466; aesthetic savor 464–465; corporeal analogies 459–460; evolution of theory 465–466; figures of speech 461–462; literary suggestion 463–464; origins of 457; as philosophical discipline 456–466; poetic blemish 460; poetic excellences 460–461; poetic styles 462–463; poetry 457; preliminaries 458–459
Rig Veda (Ṛgveda) 82, 264
rīti (poetic styles) 462–463
"Romantic Endeavor" 46
Rousseau, Jean-Jacques 526

Śabdapramāṇa (testimony as knowledge) 36–37, 374
Saint Augustine 9, 376, 399
Saint Paul 399
Śaiva Siddhānta 331, 332, 335–338, 339, 340, 341
Śaivism, Kashmiri 408–417; nondual 408–409
Śakti (self-recognition of Śiva) 409, 410, 411, 412, 414
Śākyamuni Buddha, the 294, 298
Śālikanātha Miśra 149
sāmānya (universal), in Vaiśeṣika 168–169
samavāya[11] (inherence): *Alaṃkāraśāstra* 462; materialism 100; Nyāya 185; Pramāṇa epistemology 35; Vaiśeṣika categories 157, 162, 168, 171, 171–172, 174
Sāmaveda (Vedic Saṃhitā) 113
Śambhunātha 438, 439, 440
Sāṃkhya 88n1, 131–139; character traits in 136–137; classical 133–138; creative emergence in 134–136; dualism in 134; in early sources 133–134; hierarchy of beings in 137; non-differentiated 142–143; ontology 196; origins of 131–133; pre-existent effect, doctrine of 137; representations in 134–136; post-Sāṃkhyakārikā 139–140; soteriology in 139; time 145–147; traditions 142–147
Sāṃkhya Karikā 64, 132, 135, 136, 138, 140; impact on Sāṃkhya 138–139
Sāṃkhyasūtra 139
Sāṃkhya-Yoga 9
Śaṅkara, prologue (non-dualism) 236–240
Sanskrit (the language of the elites) 458; Darśana in 545–546
Sanskrit poetics 409–410, 457–458; corporeal analogies in 459–460; logic in 465–466
Sartre, Jean-Paul 5, 7
Sarvāstivāda 53, 55–56; Abidharma 302, 302–309; Buddhist ethics 499; Nāgārjuna 313, 323
Sarvāstivāda literature, time in the 55–56
Sautrāntika (Traditionist school of therapeutic philosophy) 360
Sautrāntika literature, time in the 56
Sautrāntika representationalism 93
'sceptical religions' 59
scholastic theology 64–66
scholastic way of life 60
Schopenhauer, Arthur 12, 69, 518, 519
scientific determinism 483
secondary rules (that confer powers) 432–433
self (*ātman*) 265, 338; as agent 334–335; Bhāṭṭa Mīmāṃsā view of the 338–340; Buddhist no-self theory of the 85–88; 'Buddhist-without-momentariness' view of the 341; existence or non-existence of 331–342; in Indian philosophy 81–88; Jainism view of the 338–340; metaphysical positions regarding 331–332; and person 204–207; and personal identity 342; Personalist view of the 340–341; Pudgalavādin view of the 340–342; Śaiva Siddhānta on the 335–338; as substance 333–334; unchanging 337–338; as unitary essence 332–333; in the Upaniṣads 124–126; in Vaiśeṣika 163–164; Vedic accounts of 82–85
self-awareness, in classical Yoga philosophy 266–270
self-causation (*svabhāva*) 326, 346
'self-consciousness' (*ahaṃkāra*) 136, 195–196, 199, 201, 206, 266, 284; Yogācāra Buddhist self-consciousness) 411
self-recognition of Śiva (Śakti) 411, 412, 414, 416, 417
'Self-Sensation' (*Ātmapratyakṣa-vāda*) 202

[10] The word "*tarka*" can also mean hypothetical argument.
[11] The word "*samavāya*" can also mean necessary and sufficient conditions.

self-validity, theory of 151, 152
semantic competence (*yogyatā*) 21
"semiotic freedom" 416
sense capacities/organs (*indriyas*) 36, 127, *135*, 136, 158, 196, 265, 266
seven-level system, within the body 469
Seventy Verses on Emptiness (*Śūnyatāsaptati*) 311
Shah Jahan 12
shared cosmological concerns 59
Sharia law 502
Shukoh, Dārā 12, 518
Siddhasena Divākara 381, 387; relativity 395–396
Sikh Gurus 497, 500, 501, 502
Sikhism 495, 496; from modernist to postcolonial 497–501
Sikh Way (*marga*) 487, 491
Singhvi, L. M. 404, 405, 406
Śiromani, Raghunātha 6, 170, 177
Śiva (Absolute Self/Oversoul) 332, 506
Śiva Sūtra 409
'Six Perfections' 500, 501
Sixty Verses of Reasoning (*Yuktiṣaṣṭika*) 311
skepticism, Indian 71–78
skepticism, theory of (*samśayavāda*) 71
skilful means (*upāya-kausalya*) 501–502
Ślokavārttika 24, 149, 339
Someśvara, Bhaṭṭa 149
'Small Vehicle' (Hīnayāna) 43, 293, 501
social engagement, ethics and, in Process Buddhism 506–514
social ontology 575
Somānanda 410, 411, 439, 443
soteriological transformation 290–291
soteriology 421, 548, 550; Abhidharma 302; Advaita Vedānta 239; Bhartṛhari's 230, 236; Buddhist 42, 43, 54, 66; in Sāṃkhya 138; theistic 146; Yogācāra 291
space and cosmogony, Hindu theory of 468–469
Spanda Kārikā 409, 424
"Spanda system" 410
Spinoza, Baruch 84
spiritual agency, in Vajrayāna Buddhism 365, 368
spiritualized ontology 406
spiritual: mastery 361, 362, 363, 438; practice, philosophy as 63–64; *reasoning* 68
Śramaṇa movement (*Yogaśāstra*) 146
Sri Aurobindo 376, 415, 529
Śrīharṣa, Advaitin 10
Subcommentary on Distinguishing the Two Truths 351
substance (*dravya*) 95, 157–165, 170, 196, 201, 333, 339, 349; in Abhidharma 307, 308; in Vaiśeṣika 157–165; in Viśiṣṭādvaita Vedānta 256, 257, 258
substance ontology 49
Supreme Speech (*parāvāk*), of Śiva 411, 412, 414, 416
Sūtra Explaining the Thought 46
Sūtra on Lion's Roar of a Wheel-turning Monarch (*Cakkavatti-sīhanāda sutta*) 294
Sūtra on the Samādhi of Direct Encounter with the Buddhas of the Present (*Pratyutpanna-Buddha-saṃmukhāvasthitasamādhi-sūtra*) 300
Sūtra on the Ten Grounds (*Daśabhūmika-sūtra*) 300
sūtra-s (aphorisms/terse formulaic assertions) 5, 24
Sutta literature, time in the 53
svabhāvavāda, theory of 106
Svātantraka, central theses 344
Svātantrika Madhyamaka metaphysics 343–350; Bhāvaviveka's defence of conventional reality 345–348; Bhāvaviveka's rejection of ultimately intrinsic reality 348–350
Śvetāmbara *Āgamas*, relativity in the 392–393
"Swaraj in Ideas" (self-rule in ideas) 520
syllogistic argument, of Yogācāra 344
synthetic inductive reasoning (*yukta-pramāṇa*) 28
systematic reasoning 64–66
systems theory 416

Taittirīya Upaniṣad 473
tantra 408–417, 502
Tantrasadbhāva 422, 423
Tantravārttika (a commentary on the Mīmāṃsā *Sūtra*) 149
Tantra Vaṭa Dhānikā 440
Tantra Yoga 268, 440
tantric: philosophy, scriptural roots of 421; ritual 410, 419, 437, 439; theology 410; traditions, philosophic rationalization of 418; understanding, philosophical roots of 420–1; writings 440–441
tantric knowledge systems 418–422; Kaula tantra 421–422; recognition, school of (Pratyabhijñā Darśana) 424–427; Trika scriptural corpus 423–424; Trika tantra 422–423
Tarkabhāṣā 10, 447 *see also* Mokṣākaragupta
Tattvārtha Sūtra 493
telepathy 386, 387
temporal indexicals 50–51
temporality 50–51
temporal view of life 50
Ten Commandments 498
Ten Good Paths of Action (*daśa-kuśala-karmapatha*) 498
Ten Precepts (*daśa-śīla*) 498
testimony as knowledge (*śabdapramāṇa*) 36–37
theology: rational 215–216; tantric 410
theoria 277, 493
therapeutic philosophy (*Siddhānta*) 360, 361
Theravāda 47, 53, 82; *abhidhamma* 302, 304; Buddhism 500; Buddhist ethics 499; Buddhist hermeneutics 41, 42, 47; time 52–54
"Three Baskets" (*Tripiṭaka*) 24, 42, 61, 64, 302, 304
'three-level' ontology 258
Three Natures, the 283, 290–291, 317
"Three Proofs" (*Siddhitrayī*) 410
'Three Turnings of the Wheel of Doctrine' 287
three-wheels schema 45
time (*ākāśa*); atomistic view of 51; deconstruction of 56–57; in Jātaka 57; in Sāṃkhya 143–145; in Sarvāstivāda 55–56; in Sautrāntika 56; in *Sutta* 53; in Theravāda 53–55; in Vaiśeṣika 161–162; in Yogācāra 56
time-consciousness, internal, Husserl on 52
Traditionist school of therapeutic philosophy (*Sautrāntika*) 360
transcendental atemporality 49, 53

transcendent redemption 399
Trika (one of three Tantric schools/triadism) 409, 410, 414, 421–422, 439; Kaula metaphysics 425; medieval Kashmir 409, 423–424; philosophical system 441; recognition, school of 424–427; scriptural corpus 423–424, 441; tantras 421–422, 423, 424; theology 424
Trika tantra, identity in 421–422
truth, Gandhi on 536–543
truths: unreal conventional truths 353, 354
Tulsi, Acarya 397–404
Two Truths, the 287, 313, 351–357; of Kundakunda 393–394; Nāgārjuna's reformulation of 287, 311, 313, 314, 315, 316

Udayana *see* extrinsic validity, theory of (*prāmāṇyavāda*)
Uddyotakara 179, 204, 321, 551–552
Udyayana theistic monograph (Nyāyakusumāñjali) 214; extrinsic validity theory in 216–217
ultimately intrinsic reality 348–350, 353
ultimate reality (*brahman*) 7, 67; Jaina epistemology 383; Madhyamaka 345; 348–350, 352, 354; Malkani, G. R. 555, 556, 557; methodology 26; Mīmāṃsā 149; music, philosophy of 468, 474; Nāgārjuna 318; Process Buddhism 507; the self 84; Upaniṣads 124, 126; Vedānta 225, 227, 229, 232, 233, 238; Yogācāra Buddhism 296
Uṃveka, Bhaṭṭa 149
unaware cognition, its relation to language 448–451
'unaware' state (*asañcetitā avasthā*) 450, 453, 454n4
unchanging self (*ātman*) 126, 284, 333, 335; critique of an 337–338; between momentariness and the 338–340
Unexcelled Tantric practice 360
universal (*sāmānya*), in Vaiśeṣika 167–169
universal syntactic agency, theory of 413
universalism 13n11
Universal Vehicle of Buddhist practice (Mahāyāna) 360
Upaniṣads 122–130
Upaniṣads, connections with Brāhmaṇas 118–119; in Hindu darśanas before Vedānta 126–128; as philosophy 129–130; developing philosophy from ritual context 122–124; the self in the 124–126; from a Vedānta darśana perspective 128–129; part of the Vedas 122
upāya-kausalya (skilful means) 299, 501–502, 503
Utpaladeva 7, 408, 410–414, 416
Uttara-Mīmāṃsā[12] (Later Exegesis/Later Inquiry) 25, 148, 223

Vaiśeṣika school 88n1; ontological categories of the 157–173
Vaiṣṇava theism (*Kapilagītā*) 146
Vajrayāna Buddhism 360–368; contemplative science 360–363; creation stage 364–366; cultural agency in 361; initiation into 362–363; perfection stage 364–365; religion and science 360; spiritual agency in 365, 368
valid inferences 186–187
validity: extrinsic theory of (*prāmāṇyavāda*) 214–221; problem of 29; theory of self- 151–152
Vallabha 66
Vardhamāna 177, 219
Vasubandhu 56, 93, 285, 289–290, 305–306, 308, 318, 340
Vasugupta 409, 423, 424
Vasumitra 55
Vedānta[13] 88n1, 25–26, 236; Advaita 233–240; *avidyā* problem 242–249; early 223–231; Viśiṣṭādvaita 251–260
Vedānta school 32, 126, 128, 215, 233
Vedānta Sūtra[14] 128
Vedānta system (Uttara Mīmāṃsā) 148
Vedas 16–17; the Upaniṣad texts 122 *see also* Brāhmaṇas, Upaniṣads
Vedic ritual 6; Brāhmaṇas 113–114, 118; extrinsic validity 214, 216, 217, 218–219; Mīmāṃsā 152; Upaniṣads 125, 130; Yoga philosophy 264
Vedic sentences, explanation of 25
'Vehicle of the Hearers' (Śrāvakayāna) 501
Verses on the Heart of Dependent Origination (*Pratītyasamutpādahṛdayakārikā*) 311
Verses on the Heart of the Middle Way (*Madhyamakahṛd ayakārikā*) 343
"Verses on the Recognition of the Lord" (*Īśvarapratyabhijñākārikā*) 410
Vessantara Jātaka 500
Vijñānabhikṣu 139
Vijñāpti-mātra ((ir)reality of) 289–290
Vikramaśila, Buddhist university at 65
vinaya (code of rules governing monastic discipline) 41, 47, 294, 304, 322, 598–599
Vinaya Piṭaka ('basket of discipline') 499
virtues 499
viśeṣa (particularity), in Vaiśeṣika 170–171
Viśiṣṭādvaita ('integral unity of complex reality'/ qualified non-dualism) 251
Viśiṣṭādvaita Vedānta 251–260; causation, theory of 257; consciousness 255; direct realism (of Rāmānuja) 254; eternal soul 256; ontology (of Rāmānuja) 257; personal identity 256; transcendent reality (knowledge of) 259; truth about God 253; universe (reality of the) 251
Vivaraṇa (Advaita) school 246–247
Vivarta-vāda (theory that the world is an unreal manifestation of Brahman) 225, 229, 230, 231
vyañjanā (literary suggestion) 463–464, 465

water (*jala*), in Vaiśeṣika 159
Weber, Ralph 9, 576–577
Western ontology 522
Wisdom of Perfect Equality (*samatā-jñāna*) 291
Wittgenstein, Ludwig 8, 9, 319, 556–557, 578

[12] Uttara-Mīmāṃsā is also known as Vedānta.
[13] Vedānta is also known as Uttara-Mīmāṃsā.
[14] The *Vedānta Sūtra* is also known as the *Brahma Sūtra*.

xenology 517

Yājñavalkya 12, 103, 123, 125–126, 129
Yajurveda (Vedic Saṃhitā) 122
Yama, the Lord of Death 264
Yoga ('a state of meditative contemplation or absorption') 88n1
Yogācāra Buddhism (Yogic Practice School): Abhidharmic context 285–286, 287–289; dependent arising 283–285; external objects ((ir)reality of) 289–290; historical perspective 283; Mahāyāna critiques 286–287; soteriological transformation 290–291; Three Natures 290–291; Vijñapti-mātra 290
Yogācāra idealism 283, 289, 291, 343, 351
Yogācāra literature, time in the 56
Yogācāra syllogistic argument 344
Yoga philosophy 263–270; Adamantine Chariot, Lord of the 268–270; embodied self-awareness 263–264; embodiment 265–266; meditation 266–268; reassessment of 271–278; self 259–260; self-awareness 266–268; yogic meditation 264–265, 266–268; yogic perception 261
Yogaśāstra (Śramaṇa movement) 146
Yoga Sūtra 271, 277, 278
yogic meditation 264–265, 266–268
yogic perception 261
Yogic Practice School (Yogācāra) 43, 44